APA Handbook of

Research Methods
in Psychology

APA Handbooks in Psychology® Series

APA Addiction Syndrome Handbook—two volumes
    Howard J. Shaffer, Editor-in-Chief

APA Educational Psychology Handbook—three volumes
    Karen R. Harris, Steve Graham, and Tim Urdan, Editors-in-Chief

APA Handbook of Adolescent and Young Adult Development—one volume
    Lisa J. Crockett, Gustavo Carlo, and John E. Schulenberg, Editors

APA Handbook of Behavior Analysis—two volumes
    Gregory J. Madden, Editor-in-Chief

APA Handbook of Career Intervention—two volumes
    Paul J. Hartung, Mark L. Savickas, and W. Bruce Walsh, Editors-in-Chief

APA Handbook of Clinical Geropsychology—two volumes
    Peter A. Lichtenberg and Benjamin T. Mast, Editors-in-Chief

APA Handbook of Clinical Psychology—five volumes
    John C. Norcross, Gary R. VandenBos, and Donald K. Freedheim, Editors-in-Chief

APA Handbook of Community Psychology—two volumes
    Meg A. Bond, Irma Serrano-García, and Christopher B. Keys, Editors-in-Chief

APA Handbook of Comparative Psychology—two volumes
    Josep Call, Editor-in-Chief

APA Handbook of Consumer Psychology—one volume
    Lynn R. Kahle, Editor-in-Chief

APA Handbook of Contemporary Family Psychology—three volumes
    Barbara H. Fiese, Editor-in-Chief

APA Handbook of Counseling Psychology—two volumes
    Nadya A. Fouad, Editor-in-Chief

APA Handbook of Dementia—one volume
    Glenn E. Smith, Editor-in-Chief

APA Handbook of Ethics in Psychology—two volumes
    Samuel J. Knapp, Editor-in-Chief

APA Handbook of Forensic Neuropsychology—one volume
    Shane S. Bush, Editor-in-Chief

APA Handbook of Forensic Psychology—two volumes
    Brian L. Cutler and Patricia A. Zapf, Editors-in-Chief

APA Handbook of Giftedness and Talent—one volume
    Steven I. Pfeiffer, Editor-in-Chief

APA Handbook of Human Systems Integration—one volume
    Deborah A. Boehm-Davis, Francis T. Durso, and John D. Lee, Editors-in-Chief

APA Handbook of Industrial and Organizational Psychology—three volumes
    Sheldon Zedeck, Editor-in-Chief

APA Handbook of Intellectual and Developmental Disabilities—two volumes
    Laraine Masters Glidden, Editor-in-Chief

APA Handbook of Men and Masculinities—one volume
    Y. Joel Wong and Stephen R. Wester, Editors-in-Chief

APA Handbook of Multicultural Psychology—two volumes
    Frederick T. L. Leong, Editor-in-Chief

APA Handbooks in Psychology

APA Handbook of
Research Methods
in Psychology

SECOND EDITION

VOLUME 2

**Research Designs: Quantitative, Qualitative,
Neuropsychological, and Biological**

Harris Cooper, *Editor-in-Chief*

**Marc N. Coutanche, Linda M. McMullen, A. T. Panter,
David Rindskopf, and Kenneth J. Sher,** *Associate Editors*

🔱 **AMERICAN PSYCHOLOGICAL ASSOCIATION**

Published by
American Psychological Association
750 First Street, NE
Washington, DC 20002
https://www.apa.org

Order Department
https://www.apa.org/pubs/books
order@apa.org

Typeset in Berkeley by Circle Graphics, Inc., Reisterstown, MD

Printer: Sheridan Books, Chelsea, MI
Cover Designer: Mark Karis

Library of Congress Cataloging-in-Publication Data

Names: Cooper, Harris M., editor. | American Psychological Association, issuer.
Title: APA handbook of research methods in psychology / editor-in-Chief
    Harris Cooper; associate editors Marc N. Coutanche, Linda M. McMullen,
    A.T. Panter, David Rindskopf, and Kenneth J. Sher
Description: Second Edition. | Washington, DC : American Psychological
    Association, [2023-] | Series: APA handbooks in psychology | Revised
    edition of APA handbook of research methods in psychology, c2012. |
    Includes bibliographical references and index. | Contents: v. 1.
    Foundations, planning, measures, and psychometrics -- v. 2. Research designs:
    quantitative, qualitative, neuropsychological, and biological -- v. 3. Data
    analysis and research publication
Identifiers: LCCN 2022020492 (print) | LCCN 2022020493 (ebook) | ISBN
    9781433837135 (v. 1 ; hardcover) | ISBN 9781433841330 (v. 2 ; hardcover) |
    ISBN 9781433841354 (v. 3 ; hardcover) | ISBN 9781433841323 (v. 1 ; ebook) |
    ISBN 9781433841347 (v. 2 ; ebook) | ISBN 9781433841361 (v. 3 ; ebook)
Subjects: LCSH: Psychology--Research--Methodology--Handbooks, manuals, etc. |
    Psychology--Research--Handbooks, manuals, etc.
Classification: LCC BF76.5 .A73 2023 (print) | LCC BF76.5 (ebook) |
    DDC 150.72/1--dc23/eng/20220802
LC record available at https://lccn.loc.gov/2022020492
LC ebook record available at https://lccn.loc.gov/2022020493

https://doi.org/10.1037/0000319-000

Printed in the United States of America

10 9 8 7 6 5 4 3 2 1

Contents

Editorial Board

Contributors

Ananda B. Amstadter, PhD, Department of Psychiatry and the Virginia Institute for Psychiatric and Behavioral Genetics, Virginia Commonwealth University, Richmond, VA, United States

Michael T. Bardo, PhD, Department of Psychology, University of Kentucky, Lexington, KY, United States

Bradley J. Bartos, PhD, School of Government and Public Policy, University of Arizona, Tucson, AZ, United States

Rohit Batra, MSc, Department of Psychology, University of California, Davis, Davis, CA, United States

William Howard Beasley, PhD, Department of Pediatrics, University of Oklahoma Health Science Center, Oklahoma City, OK, United States

Dorret I. Boomsma, PhD, Department of Biological Psychology, Vrije Universiteit, Amsterdam, The Netherlands

Virginia Braun, PhD, School of Psychology, The University of Auckland, Auckland, New Zealand

Steven D. Brown, PhD, Department of Management, Nottingham Trent University, Nottingham, England

Daniel Bustamante, PhD candidate, Center for Life Sciences Education, Virginia Commonwealth University, Richmond, VA, United States

Christopher Cappelli, PhD, Department of Health and Human Sciences, Frank R. Seaver College of Science and Engineering, Loyola Marymount University, Los Angeles, CA, United States

Dianne L. Chambless, PhD, Department of Psychology, University of Pennsylvania, Philadelphia, PA, United States

JeeWon Cheong, PhD, Department of Health Education and Behavior, University of Florida, Gainesville, FL, United States

Larry Christensen, PhD, Department of Psychology, University of South Alabama, Mobile, AL, United States

Victoria Clarke, PhD, Department of Health and Social Sciences, University of the West of England, Bristol, England

Zachary K. Collier, PhD, College of Education and Human Development, University of Delaware, Newark, DE, United States

Adele Diederich, PhD, Department of Life Sciences and Chemistry, Jacobs University Bremen, Bremen, Germany

Urmitapa Dutta, PhD, Department of Psychology, University of Massachusetts, Lowell, MA, United States

Xitao Fan, PhD, Department of Educational Psychology, The Chinese University of Hong Kong, Shatin, NT, Hong Kong SAR, China

Elizabeth Fein, PhD, Department of Psychology, Duquesne University, Pittsburgh, PA, United States

Fred M. Feinberg, PhD, Stephen M. Ross School of Business and Department of Statistics, University of Michigan, Ann Arbor, MI, United States

Lesley K. Fellows, MDCM, DPhil, Department of Neurology and Neurosurgery, Faculty of Medicine and Health Sciences, McGill University, Montréal, QC, Canada

Jesica Siham Fernández, PhD, Department of Ethnic Studies, Santa Clara University, Santa Clara, CA, United States

Emilio Ferrer, PhD, Department of Psychology, University of California, Davis, Davis, CA, United States

John M. Ferron, PhD, Department of Educational and Psychological Studies, College of Education, University of South Florida, Tampa, FL, United States

Simon Fischer-Baum, PhD, Department of Psychological Sciences, Rice University, Houston, TX, United States

Daniel B. Fishman, PhD, Graduate School of Applied and Professional Psychology, Rutgers University, New Brunswick, NJ, United States

Anne Galletta, PhD, Department of Curriculum and Foundations, Cleveland State University, Cleveland, OH, United States

Joseph P. Gone, PhD, Department of Anthropology, Harvard University, Cambridge, MA; Department of Global Health and Social Medicine, Harvard Medical School, Boston, MA, United States

Richard Gonzalez, PhD, Departments of Psychology and Statistics, Institute for Social Research, University of Michigan, Ann Arbor, MI, United States

Nisha C. Gottfredson, PhD, Department of Health Behavior, Gillings School of Global Public Health, The University of North Carolina at Chapel Hill, Chapel Hill, NC, United States

Timothy C. Guetterman, PhD, Department of Family Medicine, University of Michigan, Ann Arbor, MI, United States

Gary T. Henry, PhD, College of Education and Human Development, University of Delaware, Newark, DE, United States

Karen Henwood, PhD, School of Social Sciences, Cardiff University, Cardiff, Wales

Terrell A. Hicks, MS, Department of Psychology, Virginia Commonwealth University, Richmond, VA, United States

Steven D. Hollon, PhD, Department of Psychology, Vanderbilt University, Nashville, TN, United States

Rick H. Hoyle, PhD, Department of Psychology and Neuroscience, Duke University, Durham, NC, United States

Floris Huider, PhD candidate, Department of Biological Psychology, Vrije Universiteit, Amsterdam, The Netherlands

Simran K. Johal, MA, Department of Psychology, University of California, Davis, Davis, CA, United States

R. Burke Johnson, PhD, Department of Counseling and Instructional Sciences, University of South Alabama, Mobile, AL, United States

Elaine Keane, PhD, School of Education, National University of Ireland, Galway, Ireland

Megan Kirby, PhD, Department of Child and Family Studies, University of South Florida, Tampa, FL, United States

Karestan C. Koenen, PhD, Harvard T.H. Chan School of Public Health, Boston, MA, United States

Andrea LaMarre, PhD, School of Psychology, Massey University, Auckland, New Zealand

Regina Day Langhout, PhD, Psychology Department, University of California, Santa Cruz, Santa Cruz, CA, United States

Lannie Ligthart, PhD, Department of Biological Psychology, Vrije Universiteit, Amsterdam, The Netherlands

Lodi Lipien, MSPH, Department of Educational and Psychological Studies, College of Education, University of South Florida, Tampa, FL, United States

Yanjun Liu, PhD, Department of Psychological Sciences, Vanderbilt University, Nashville, TN, United States

David P. MacKinnon, PhD, Department of Psychology, Arizona State University, Tempe, AZ, United States

Randi C. Martin, PhD, Department of Psychological Sciences, Rice University, Houston, TX, United States

Henry May, PhD, Center for Research in Education and Social Policy (CRESP), University of Delaware, Newark, DE, United States

Richard McCleary, PhD, School of Social Ecology, University of California, Irvine, Irvine, CA, United States

David McDowall, PhD, School of Criminal Justice, University at Albany, Albany, NY, United States

Andy McKinlay, PhD, School of Philosophy, Psychology, and Language Sciences, The University of Edinburgh, Edinburgh, Scotland

Chris McVittie, PhD, Division of Psychology, Sociology, and Education, Queen Margaret University, Edinburgh, Scotland

Yuri Milaneschi, PhD, Department of Psychiatry, Amsterdam UMC, Vrije Universiteit, Amsterdam, The Netherlands

Javier Monforte, PhD, Department of Sport and Exercise Sciences, Durham University, Durham, England

Nicole R. Nugent, PhD, Bradley Hasbro Children's Research Center and The Warren Alpert Medical School of Brown University, Providence, RI, United States

Patrick O'Keefe, PhD, Department of Neurology, Oregon Health and Science University, Portland, OR, United States

Brenda W. J. H. Penninx, PhD, Department of Psychiatry, Amsterdam UMC, Vrije Universiteit, Amsterdam, The Netherlands

Mary Ann Pentz, PhD, Institute for Health Promotion and Disease Prevention Research, Department of Preventive Medicine, Keck School of Medicine, University of Southern California, Los Angeles, CA, United States

Analay Perez, PhD candidate, Department of Educational Psychology, University of Nebraska–Lincoln, Lincoln, NE, United States

Corinne M. Pettigrew, PhD, Department of Neurology, Johns Hopkins University School of Medicine, Baltimore, MD, United States

Angela G. Pirlott, PhD, Department of Psychology, Saint Xavier University, Chicago, IL, United States

Rumi Kato Price, PhD, Department of Psychiatry, Washington University School of Medicine in St. Louis, St. Louis, MO, United States

Jon Prosser, PhD, Independent Scholar, Leeds, England

Maia S. Pujara, PhD, Department of Psychology, Sarah Lawrence College, Bronxville, NY, United States

Paula Reavey, PhD, Department of Psychology, London South Bank University, London, England

Charles S. Reichardt, PhD, Department of Psychology, University of Denver, Denver, CO, United States

Ulf-Dietrich Reips, PhD, Research Methods, Assessment, and iScience, Department of Psychology, University of Konstanz, Konstanz, Germany

Sarah Riley, PhD, School of Psychology, Massey University, Wellington, New Zealand

Joseph Lee Rodgers, PhD, Department of Psychology and Human Development, Vanderbilt University, Nashville, TN, United States

Fiona Shirani, PhD, School of Social Sciences, Cardiff University, Cardiff, Wales

Brett Smith, PhD, Department of Sport and Exercise Sciences, Durham University, Durham, England

Parker Smith, BS, Department of Psychology, University of Tübingen, Tübingen, Germany

Heather L. Smyth, PhD, Department of Biostatistics and Informatics, Colorado School of Public Health, University of Colorado, Anschutz Medical Campus, Aurora, CO, United States

Heidi H. Tastet, MD, Complete Care Clinic, Division of General Medicine, Department of Internal Medicine, Washington University School of Medicine in St. Louis, St. Louis, MO, United States

Paul ten Have, PhD, Department of Sociology and Anthropology, University of Amsterdam, Amsterdam, The Netherlands (retired)

Robert Thornberg, PhD, Department of Behavioral Sciences and Learning, Linköping University, Linköping, Sweden

Sally Thorne, PhD, RN, School of Nursing, University of British Columbia, Vancouver, BC, Canada

Roger Tourangeau, PhD, Westat, Rockville, MD, United States

James T. Townsend, PhD, Department of Psychological and Brain Sciences, Indiana University, Bloomington, IN, United States

Lisa A. Turner, PhD, Department of Psychology, University of South Alabama, Mobile, AL, United States

Avinash R. Vaidya, PhD, Department of Cognitive, Linguistic, and Psychological Sciences, Brown University, Providence, RI, United States

Trisha Van Zandt, PhD, Department of Psychology, The Ohio State University, Columbus, OH, United States

Frederick J. Wertz, PhD, Department of Psychology, Fordham University, New York, NY, United States

Malgorzata Wójcik, PhD, Department of Social and Organizational Behavior Psychology, SWPS University of Social Sciences and Humanities, Warsaw, Poland

Jonathan Yahalom, PhD, Department of Psychiatry, University of California, Los Angeles, Los Angeles, CA, United States

Ting Yan, PhD, Westat, Rockville, MD, United States

Brian T. Yates, PhD, Department of Psychology, American University, Washington, DC, United States

PART I

QUALITATIVE RESEARCH METHODS

OVERVIEW OF QUALITATIVE METHODS

CHAPTER 1

DEVELOPMENTS IN QUALITATIVE INQUIRY

Sarah Riley and Andrea LaMarre

At an airport cafe, two young, White men wait for their food. The server arrives carrying a salad plate in one hand and a meat pie in the other. The meat pie eater waves his fork in the direction of the salad, and sneers "Got the healthy option?" Sarah, overhearing their conversation thinks, "Well, that man's never ordering a salad again." In that moment, there is a lot for a psychologist to study, including what they said next, how they interpreted the conversation, or the wider discourses underpinning this "food talk." Deciding what to study and how to study it means thinking deeply about research, and, in this chapter, we provide some foundations for this thinking, starting with the big question: What can we know, and how can we know it?

APPROACHES TO QUALITATIVE RESEARCH: WHAT CAN WE KNOW, AND HOW CAN WE KNOW IT?

If *ontology* is the study of what is real, *epistemology* is the philosophy of what is knowable and the methods for knowing it. As a philosophical concept imported into our discipline, there are many opportunities for different interpretations along the way; resultantly, novice researchers often find the concept of epistemology threatening, while more experienced researchers disagree about

definitions and applications. With epistemology, as with everything we discuss in this chapter, there is variation, debate, and contestation. We start with epistemology, even at the risk of alienating our readers, because it is an orientation to knowledge, and, thus, implicitly or explicitly, epistemology underpins all research practice.

Epistemology also underpinned the development of three broad approaches in 20th century, qualitative psychology, which we term *positivist*, *phenomenological*, and *critically oriented*. We discuss here these approaches in relation to epistemology, their model of the person, and conceptualization of the researcher–participant relationship, highlighting their impact on how psychologists understand and deal with qualitative data.

POSITIVIST QUALITATIVE RESEARCH

Twentieth-century academic psychology sought methods for creating objective knowledge of the world. This was informed by objectivist epistemology, positivist and postpositivist philosophical thinking and underpinned by a realist ontology in which a real world existing independently of human perception and interpretation was imagined as available to be discovered. (See Crotty, 1998, for a detailed discussion of the distinctions between these terms, and Volume 1,

https://doi.org/10.1037/0000319-001
APA Handbook of Research Methods in Psychology, Second Edition: Vol. 2. Research Designs: Quantitative, Qualitative, Neuropsychological, and Biological, H. Cooper (Editor-in-Chief)

Chapter 1 by Willig, this handbook.) "Positivist psychology," as we will call it for simplicity, imagined the person as an autonomous individual, a separate being who interacted with the world. In this framework, the psychology researcher was a subject able to systematically study another as an object, generating objective, universal facts about humans. These facts could be combined in a progressive, linear trajectory towards the goals of prediction, control, and understanding cause and effect relations of individual thinking and behavior. These methods positioned the researcher–participant relationship as a problematic intervening variable.

Positivist psychology found little room for qualitative methods in its official narrative (although they were part of this history; Riley & Chamberlain, 2022). But the development of grounded theory in sociology opened up the possibility for imagining objective, systematic qualitative analysis (Glaser & Strauss, 1967/1999), which was taken up by researchers in psychology, particularly those in the United States (e.g., Boyatzis, 1998). This shifted the researcher–participant relationship from a problem to a tool (e.g., in the use of rapport to elicit rich data) but left unchallenged the goal of an objective researcher who worked to minimize bias as part of quality criteria associated more broadly with positivist psychological research, such as reliability and validity and the practices that mapped onto these, such as using interrater reliability in coding if analyzing our airport dinner talk. This positivist orientation treated language as reflecting reality as Terry et al. (2017) explained in their discussion of thematic analysis: Such work is "underpinned by the theoretical assumption that language reflects reality (either a singular universal reality, or the perspectival reality of a particular participant)" (p. 19).

Many qualitative researchers consider this realist framing of language to be oversimplified, preferring instead the phenomenological and critically oriented approaches that we discuss below. Realism, however, is increasingly visible in contemporary qualitative research across a range of countries, created partly by a broader "resurgence of positivism" (Brinkmann, 2015, p. 165) and partly as a consequence of more radical qualitative traditions being accepted by journals and research institutions (Riley et al., 2019). This is a somewhat ironic situation, given concerns that the increased presence of realist qualitative work might serve to bolster the idea that it is possible to do objective research in psychology, an idea radically challenged by those working in the epistemological traditions we describe below.

PHENOMENOLOGICAL QUALITATIVE RESEARCH

In contrast to positivist research questions around "what there is" and "what works," phenomenological research asks "what might become" when we try to understand experience (Brinkmann, 2015, p. 165). Central for phenomenological psychology was phenomenological philosopher Husserl's understanding of "intentionality," the idea that whenever we are conscious we are conscious of *something*, making the job of the researcher to better understand people's experiences of things "in their appearing" (Langdridge, 2007, p. 13). Here, distinctions between the subject and object become blurred in the understanding of people as interpretive beings producing their understanding of an object in an unfolding process of interpretation.

There are a variety of approaches informed by phenomenology, with significant debate as to what is or can be called *phenomenological psychology* (Langdridge, 2007; J. A. Smith, 2018; van Manen, 2017; also see Chapter 5 by Wertz, this volume). Simplified, phenomenological psychologists focus on trying to understand what is experienced and the way it is experienced, treating experience as not only a thing people encounter but also a process in which they are active. In psychology, phenomenology is linked with a critical realist epistemology; here, the real world exists, but it cannot be fully discovered because our experiences of it are always mediated (Shaw, 2019). The model of the person is of "a situated, meaning-making person" (Larkin, Eatough, & Osborn, 2011, p. 318), an individual engaging in a process of continuous interpretation as they make sense of the world and their experiences in it. These interpretations are structured by the person's sociohistoric context, life-events, and embodiment (e.g., Loaring et al., 2015). This model of the person is individualized, and their articulated thoughts originate from a coherent self who is the author of their own meaning making and interpretation of their experience.

In phenomenological psychology, the researcher–participant relationship is a meaning making collaboration between two interpretive beings, and methods that facilitate participants' deep reflections on their experiences, often in collaboration with the researcher, are favoured in order to produce "meaningful insight" (van Manen, 2017, p. 776). In relation to our vignette, for example, researchers might conduct individual in-depth interviews with each of the two men, aiming to understand and generate new insights in their lived experience of eating within the context of that meal experience; insights developed through the use of phenomenological ideas such as intentionality and "the sensuous, embodied relational engagements that shape, guide, and make possible both the accounts and the situations they describe" (Brown et al., 2011, p. 498–499). Such "phenomenological notions" are relatively absent in "interpretative phenomenological analysis" (IPA; J. A. Smith et al., 2009), a popular and highly structured research method developing themes from talk to better understand individual lived experience. Although phenomenological psychology does incorporate context (e.g., gender norms in the experience of mastectomy, Loaring et al., 2015), in contrast to the critical approaches that we turn to shortly, it remains individualistic and has limited engagement with power.

Critical and Contextual Orientations

In the second half of the 20th century, scholarship from a range of movements challenged the possibility of doing "objective" research. These included feminism, queer studies/theory, critical Black studies, liberationist psychology, Marxism, disabilities studies, community psychology, Indigenous psychology/ies, postmodernism and poststructuralist philosophies, as well as studies of scientific knowledge (e.g., Danziger, 1997; Goodley, 1999; Haraway, 1989; Henriques et al., 1984; hooks, 1989; L. T. Smith, 1999). Collectively, this diverse scholarship asked questions of whose voice was heard and to what effect, showing how research that appeared objective to those doing it actually reproduced researchers' subjective values and culturally located perspectives. These perspectives were often privileged frames of reference related to race, gender, sexuality, economic and social capital, able-bodiedness, and more. Critical scholarship also argued that emphasis on value neutrality either limited researchers' ethical and social change potential (Prilleltensky, 1994) or actively scaffolded social inequalities and marginalizations (Esposito & Perez, 2014, p. 423). Such critique meant "changing the subject" (Henriques et al., 1984) through a critical reflection on psychology, power, and its individualistic model of the person.

This individualism connected to 17th-century Enlightenment ideas conceptualizing the ideal human as autonomous, White, European, male, with a stable body imagined fully formed, in full health, and without dependency on others (Ahmed, 2017; Braidotti, 2013; Butler, 2020). Intersecting with colonial, racist, and sexist sense-making, this framework informed mainstream psychology's concept of an individualized, autonomous, universal, male-as-norm human, separate from, if interacting with, their social and material world. This construct is in sharp contrast with other cultural understandings of people as deeply interconnected, with porous boundaries between themselves, others, and their world (L. T. Smith, 1999).

In centering the individual, psychology was critiqued not just for reproducing Enlightenment "man" as a universal human but as a structuring force actively individualizing people's thinking about who they are. Subjectivity, here, aligned with neoliberal constructs of autonomous citizens able to respond dynamically to the needs of fluctuating market economies (Rose & Miller,

2008; Sugarman, 2015). Such critiques highlight the power of psychology to produce and normalize a limited understanding of human mind and behavior, treating a highly specific, individualized sociohistoric construction as a taken-for-granted universal (Henrich et al., 2010). As Danziger (1997) argued, "Psychological categories have a political dimension because they are not purely descriptive but also normative" (p. 4).

Critical and contextually oriented approaches to psychological research acknowledge that we are always "biased" because who we are and how we think about the world and our place in it impact the research we do. For example, although we chose our starting vignette as relatable for the diverse readership of this volume (we all eat, and eating is often gendered), as body image researchers we also knew that we could "work" this example easily. Further, using an example of two men talking orients to subdisciplinary concerns of which we are aware, in which qualitative methods can be devalued as "feminine," thereby reducing men's engagement with them (meaning that—dear male reader—we spoke directly to you to keep you with us). For critical orientations to psychological research, this is not so much a problem of bias, as an opportunity to reflect on what structures our understanding and associated practice.

Critical and contextually oriented approaches foreground the impossibility of psychological research delivering purely "objective knowledge," meaning we take context—of the researcher, the time, space, and place of the research and the participant, including the material and discursive sociohistorical, political, and economic contexts—into account. This orientation to context and a critical stance towards taken-for-granted knowledge connects with a relativist ontology (an independently existing world cannot be known or discovered) and a social constructionist epistemology (knowledge is socially constructed as culturally accepted truths about the world change across time and place). For those new to the topic, this is not to say that we can believe anything we want to, but that the concepts we draw on to understand an issue structure

our understanding with important effects on what we can say, think, feel, or do.

Unlike phenomenology, the unit of study in many critical and contextually oriented approaches is not the experiential account located in the individual but communication itself (Potter & Wetherell, 1987). This "decenters" the subject, representing a "turn to language." The outcome of such thinking is a model of the person as produced in and through their discursive milieu. In this discursive milieu, a range of actors circulate ideas about how the world works that people use to think with, opening up some possibilities for understanding and action, while closing down others (Riley et al., 2018, 2021). And because a person can dynamically draw on a range of different ideas for understanding an issue that circulate in a society at any one time, the self is theorized as more fluid, partial, fractured, and inconsistent (Alvesson & Sköldberg, 2017). This framework maps broadly onto what is sometimes called "poststructuralist psychology," itself informed by the work of philosopher and cultural historian Michel Foucault (Riley et al., 2021). The model of a person runs on a continuum from being a discourse user, actively using language to do interactional or identity work, to being "used by" discourse, where our deepest thoughts and feelings are understood to be structured by the linguistic concepts circulating within our discursive milieu (Foucault, 1980; Harré, 1980). Returning to our vignette, meat-pie man's sneering tone positions salad-man in a dispreferred identity, making him a discourse user, yet this linguistic action is "hearable" through discourses of consumption, health, and gender, only some of which, meat-pie man may be fully aware.

This orientation brought forth a focus on *language* as a site of analysis of meaning. But unlike phenomenological conceptualizing of language as a tool for interpretation, critical approaches saw language as a tool for "doing" psychology, providing the building blocks for what people can think and do—a productive power producing our experiences of the world (Gergen, 1985). Central to the idea of productive power is that it produces understandings that are socially constructed rather than objective descriptions of a natural world. These understandings can thus be evaluated in terms of their capacities for creating or challenging existing inequalities and privileges, a framing that legitimizes research concerns for social justice or change.

A range of discursive and narrative qualitative research methods have developed from such critical analysis, connected by a shared focus on language as the site for psychological study (e.g., Chapter 8 by McVittie and McKinlay, this volume). These methods also share an understanding that language should be studied in practice, so as to explore its function in situ— functions that might include identity claims, interpersonal interactional effects or other outcomes of interest to psychologists. These context-attuned and language-focused psychological approaches have their own procedures and quality criteria, but many share an understanding of the participant– researcher relationship as one of coconstruction, and for research decision making to be evaluated through the lens of power. For example, critical psychologists concerns about the use of rapport as a psychologically exploitative tool to extract personal information from participants, while others highlight the individualism of the semi-structured individual interview, a dominant method of data collection (Riley & Chamberlain, 2022).

A focus on power also highlights the importance of critically exploring positionality—that is, how we are variously and dynamically positioned in relation to our social locations and the associated affordances and vantage points these positions offer. A consideration of the contextualized features of research, including the researcher, becomes important for those orienting to the productive, constructive, and deconstructive force that is language, and the stories we tell about ourselves and our worlds. Reflexivity has thus become an important aspect of doing context-attuned and language-focused psychological research. Beyond just situating ourselves broadly in social location terms, reflexivity invites us to understand how we impact, and are impacted by, the research we do, as fellow human beings making meaning with participants (Rice et al., 2020). If research

is imbricated with the cultural values of the researchers, and if power structures psychological research, then reflexive praxis requires a deep and ongoing reflection on these.

Emphasizing positionality and reflexivity, and how we are always connected to what we study and how we study it, critical scholarship also challenges scientism—the idea that science is value-neutral and that we must always strive for objectivity. For critical psychology researchers, this emphasis on value neutrality obscures ethical imperatives and must be discarded if we wish to do justice to participants' accounts and promote social change through research (Prilleltensky, 1994). Sugarman (2015) suggested that researchers must "admit that psychology is ideologically laden" (p. 115); for Sugarman, this included contending with the ways in which psychology as a discipline perpetuates neoliberal values and practices.

Coming back to our vignette, we might develop our reflections above to consider how as White, highly educated women, our positionality might have an impact on the men if we interviewed them or how our own perspectives on the (often constraining) norms around "being healthy" might shape our lines of inquiry in the first place. We might invite, rather than deem problematic, multiple perspectives on or "reads of" the phenomenon at hand, exploring the knowledge generated from different vantage points, rather than trying to triangulate into a single "correct" understanding (Yardley, 2015).

Despite these radical departures from positivist psychology, elements of scientism carry over, for example, in quality criteria of a transparent, systematic process where the researcher outlines their method, decisions made, and rationale for those decisions in enough detail for a reader to evaluate them, and where part of this evaluation relates to evidencing a systematic approach to data coding and analysis (e.g., Sullivan et al., 2012; Yardley, 2015). However, as Brinkmann (2015) argued, we might benefit from recognizing that early positivist philosophy, with its focus on seeking methods to create knowledge outside of ideological dogma, contributed much to social sciences and qualitative research. From this perspective, we might see this scientism less of a problem than a recognition of shared values to knowledge generation, it also sets the scene for our upcoming discussion of postqualitative research that offers a more radical departure.

DEVELOPMENTS IN QUALITATIVE METHODS

Our previous description of qualitative research highlights the importance of developing skills in building research designs and relationships. Ideally, these skills would be underscored by a reflexive consideration of what the researcher wants to know, how they might go about knowing it, and how the researcher relates to their research interest(s) and participants. Focusing on meaning making, situating this in context, and considering the broader social impacts of the research we do entails a shift in thinking about how we go about doing research. We discuss, in the next section, such shifts in doing qualitative research: developments of existing methods and approaches, experimentations across epistemological silos, and radical paradigmatic shifts.

Extending Methods

We begin our exploration of recent developments in qualitative scholarship with a focus on *methods*—those pieces of doing qualitative research that offer exciting routes toward understanding people's meaning making in context. Many immediately jump to interviewing, but there is a range of methods to choose from and, even within interviews, a variety of options (see Volume 1, Chapter 15 by Madill, this handbook). In this section, we highlight online, visual, story-oriented, and participatory developments, all of which represent an extension and broadening of the field as qualitative psychologists develop existing methods from both within and outside of psychology.

Online methods. With some exceptions (e.g., https://thepsychologist.bps.org.uk/volume-28/august-2015/crossing-digital-realm), psychology was slow to engage with internet-based research,

mapping onto a cross-disciplinary concern that everyday digital technologies offered an underdeveloped methodological opportunity (Kaufmann & Peil, 2020, p. 231). The COVID-19 pandemic shifted this, making online methods vital for many qualitative researchers, increasing engagement and experimentation that should have lasting impact.

Online methods offer convenience and the potential for widening participation in research. For example, interviews via video conferencing software mean neither researcher or participant has to travel, which is especially valuable for research where participants are widely geographically distributed and for populations with limited mobility, including disabled people and young people without the ability to transport themselves easily. Online methods also open up opportunities for asynchronous engagement (such as contributing to an online discussion over a set time period) or real-time feedback from participants (for example, sharing experiences as they happen through text or image sent via software such as WhatsApp), experiences that can also be geographically mapped with mobile phone technology. This highlights another useful aspect of online tools—that researchers can use technologies already embedded in their participants' everyday lives. As Jowett et al. (2011) noted, however, some researchers question how well internet-mediated qualitative methods can generate meaning-rich data. Next, we show some of this complexity—and expected future developments.

A simple development has been to extend the traditional interview through its mediation with video conferencing software. Psychology in general was slow to adopt this approach, preferring in-person interviews for interactional or accessibility reasons (Janghorban et al., 2014; Rasche & Platt, 2014). Still, even before COVID-19, online interviewing was gaining traction, in part because researchers were describing new potentials that these modalities offered. For example, online interviewing capitalized on screen sharing functions, including presenting visual cues or sharing images or materials to enrich, rather than just replace in-person forms of interview research. These practices more easily connected the researcher to the participants' meaning making processes and contexts such as showing a wedding dress in bridal research (Broekhuizen & Evans, 2016).

Social and technological developments mean that, for many people, video conferencing is the norm. However, slow internet speeds and the need for at least a smartphone make these platforms inaccessible to some participants, particularly the most marginalized. Concerns about security also make some researchers hesitant to adopt these platforms as research tools.

Other researchers have turned to an older digital technology—text messaging—to significantly develop the qualitative interview. Asking and answering questions through text messaging can offer greater anonymity, comfort afforded by familiarity and convenience, and practical benefits (e.g., avoiding the need to transcribe, travel to interviews, and being more adaptive to varied schedules when done asynchronously); it might also work well with particular populations. For example, in her study with young people around mental-health, support-seeking behaviors in online spaces, Gibson (2022) argued that text-messaging interviews may enable more open communication between young people and adult researchers, particularly for sensitive issues.

Messaging also allows participants to share real-time, rather than retrospective, reflections with the researcher for immediate or later discussion. This benefit is enhanced by the multimedia affordances of contemporary digital messaging technologies. Kaufmann and Peil (2020), for example, used the technological affordances of WhatsApp, a mobile messaging platform that enables text, image, and video-based interaction with individuals and groups, to look at real-time experiences of media consumption. As distinctions between on and offline continues to blur, we expect it to be harder to *not* include an element of the online in qualitative research, especially for researchers interested in issues that are located in a particular time or place (which is most of us) or to which we have limited access. For example, in her study on the practices of "lads night out," Jacques (2019) invited her participants to post photos during nights out onto a private Snapchat story (which shares photographs with a chosen group of people for 24 hours), and used these photos in a subsequent interview to elicit discussion.

Disadvantages associated with text-messaging–based research include the potential for increased ambiguity or misunderstanding and, when asynchronous, a loss of the "in the moment" thought processes evoked through real-time communication, as well as some of the emotive character of the interactions (Jowett et al., 2011). Jowett et al. (2011) noted that this method can also yield less data over more time than face-to-face interviews. And, while power differentials may be different online, they still exist; rapport-building and insider/outsider status comes to bear on the research relationships built in text-messaging–based interviews.

Qualitative psychologists also explore how people are "doing" psychology in these mediated spaces. Blog research, for example, stretches back into the early 2000s with the advent of Web 2.0 (Hookway, 2008) and offers access to people's publicly shared descriptions and comments on experiences and opinions. Others explore communication in digital spaces, such as Riley et al.'s (2009) analysis of identity management in proanorexia and recovery internet forum discussions. More recently, Rúdólfsdóttir and Jóhannsdóttir (2018) conducted an analysis of #FreeTheNipple (Twitter-based protests against the trolling of a 17-year-old Icelandic girl who posted a topless photograph online) and showed the multiple and conflicting discourses operating in young women's engagement with social media, as well as "affective solidarity" (p. 135) within this digital space. In contrast, Evans and Riley (2022) analyzed 2,400 comments responding to an online news article about their research to examine the affective quality of "networked misogyny." These examples represent a recent shift in research on the entanglements of subjectivity, embodiment, and affect as mediated through digital technologies.

The affordances of social media in allowing people to represent or communicate through visual representations also offer opportunities for qualitative researchers. For example, using YouTube

(Braun & Carruthers, 2020) and Instagram (LaMarre & Rice, 2017), researchers examined how social media visualizes salient social ideas like "health" and "well-being." Social media analyses demonstrate how engaging with accounts not produced for the purposes of research allows exploration of meaning making in the contexts of people's being in the world. But doing this kind of research raises ethical questions: can those whose material or content is being explored reasonably expect that their words and images might be used in a research context? The Association of Internet Researchers has published guidelines around the use of internet data in research (https://aoir.org/ethics/). We invite researchers to become familiar with these guidelines and debates on the potential impact of this kind of work.

On a logistical level, there are also challenges in selecting data from the enormous amount of information available (Hookway, 2008). Search engine optimization tools are useful for selecting high-ranking blog posts (e.g., Kenny et al., 2020), but researchers may not always be looking for the most popular blog or social media posts and, thus, may need to use different strategies to narrow down the vast pool of internet content with which they are working.

Others (e.g., Camacho-Miñano et al., 2019; Lupton, 2019) have conducted social media analyses that simultaneously explored content online and people's engagement with online spaces. For example, Camacho-Miñano et al. (2019) explored girls' experiences of "fitspiration" cultures online, conducting focus groups with girls and inviting them to send along examples of content with which they engaged via Instagram.

Story completion.   Although it has a longer history (e.g., Kitzinger & Powell, 1995), story completion recently moved closer to the spotlight. In story completion research, participants are asked to write a story from a *story stem*, a short sentence or two given by the researcher. For example "David decided to start removing his hair . . ." is a story stem used for research on body hair meanings and practices (https://www.psych.auckland.ac.nz/en/about/story-completion.html).

Orienting somewhat differently to the process of meaning making, story completion "does not seek to uncover the truth behind respondents' experiences" (Gravett, 2019, p. 7) but invites participants to imagine outcomes for other people. These stories are understood as giving insight into "the sociocultural sense-making resources" available to respondents (Jennings et al., 2019, p. 77), as well as their creative solutions or alternative imagined possibilities. As such, story completion can be analyzed for dominant discourses, limits to existing meaning making, and resistant stories of how restrictive norms may be challenged (Clarke et al., 2019); it is, thus, particularly useful for researchers orienting critically to the role of discourses or stories in the world.

Visual and arts-based approaches.   Arts-based work has received resistance within psychology, as a discipline that has been long invested in being a "science" (Frith et al., 2005). Despite this resistance, qualitative researchers are enjoying the innovative possibilities afforded by visual methods, and this subfield has "reached a new level of maturity" (Reavey, 2021, p. xix) with several edited collections and special issues (e.g., Chamberlain et al., 2018; Frith et al., 2005; Reavey, 2021; also see Chapter 10 by Reavey et al., this volume). Here, we briefly comment on some arts-based and visual forms of inquiry that invite new ways of thinking about the researcher, the participant, and the process of meaning making in context.

Photovoice and photo-elicitation.   Photovoice and photo-elicitation are perhaps the most common forms of visual methods used in contemporary qualitative psychology; these ask participants to discuss taken or existing images, extending the semistructured interview or focus group through the use of visual stimuli to generate talk. Talk (and image) can then be analyzed within the approaches outlined in our earlier section (photo-elicitation) or from a participatory action research orientation (photovoice).

Photography has a long history in social science research, first as an elicitation aid and later as a cocreation approach with participants (Johnson, 2020). Formalized into a method in the 1990s (Wang & Burris, 1994), *photovoice* invites participants into the process of meaning making and can have policy-change aims (Catalani & Minkler, 2010). The SHOWeD approach (Shaffer, 1986) is typically used to guide photovoice explorations, asking participants to analyze photographs they have taken along the lines of what they see, what is happening, relevance to their lives, why the issue exists, and what can be done about it (Catalani & Minkler, 2010).

Photovoice and photo-elicitation are often enjoyable for participants as they record images from their lives to share with the researcher and often elicit rich and emotional talk, surfacing new meanings of an array of topics ranging from hospitalization experiences and narratives of recovery (Radley & Taylor, 2003), racial identity (Sackett & Dogan, 2019), body image (Trepal et al., 2020), bereavement experiences (Kim et al., 2021), and more. These and other similar studies evidence the complexity, ambiguity, and multi-layered nature of meaning in visual images, which rather than being a problem for qualitative psychologists, have provided opportunities to engage with the complexity of meaning making.

Body mapping. The use of alternative ways of exploring meaning with participants, including pushing beyond the voiced or written and towards the visual and embodied, means that while visual methods are not always employed in ways that align with a critical approach, they lend themselves to critical engagement. For example, body mapping work invites participants to create large body-shaped images representing their experiences; the method holds potential as a coproduction tool, inviting participants into the process of sharing their stories and making meaning of their stories and experiences. Some researchers propose that body mapping can be a decolonizing method (e.g., Gastaldo et al., 2018) that also helps "people to re-story their lives" (Boydell et al., 2020, p. 14). As such, it may align well with a social justice agenda in research.

Digital storytelling. Digital storytelling is a heterogeneous set of approaches and methods where researchers facilitate participants to create stories about an aspect of their lives using a combination of voiced and visual (still or moving) content. Digital storytelling finds its roots in humanities and education (Benmayor, 2008), and, in psychology, digital storytelling has been used as a teaching tool (e.g., Sheafer, 2017), intervention (e.g., Botfield et al., 2018; Ofoegbu et al., 2020; Rolbiecki et al., 2021) and research method (e.g., Vivienne, 2011). Digital storytelling positions the participant as active in the process of visualizing and narrating their stories as they wish (Brushwood-Rose, 2009; Gubrium et al., 2014). It is particularly valued amongst critical-oriented researchers as a route to thinking through substantive and theoretical issues. Making films with people interested in telling their stories invites researcher reflexivity and encourages a reimagining of what the process of gathering and analyzing "data" can look like (Rice et al., 2020). For example, Rice and Mündel (2018) reimagined digital storytelling as multimedia story making, noting how this approach enables "knowledge producing as well as understand[ing] it as a critical and processual praxis for generating multiperspectival knowledges about self, other, and world" (p. 214).

Digital storytelling is often connected to an action orientation to research with, for example, stories created by participants screened in contexts where they may invite those in positions of power over those who have created the films (e.g., health care providers, government officials; e.g., Laing et al., 2017; LaMarre & Rice, 2021; for examples of digital stories, see https://revisioncentre.ca/gallery). The change-making potential of these methods is exciting, as often the processes and products of arts-based research make inroads in policy, social, and medical arenas. However, just as qualitative methods are not inherently emancipatory and often serve to bolster the careers of researchers at least as much as they offer participants benefits (Limes-Taylor Henderson & Esposito, 2019), researchers employing arts-based methods likewise might be cautioned against overclaiming the emancipatory potential of their approaches (Johnston, 2016).

Collaborative, community-engaged and participatory research. The action oriented methods we have just described are part of a broader subfield of community-engaged and participatory approaches to research (see Chapter 15 by Dutta et al., this volume). These approaches have gained significant traction in psychology recently, representing a development in qualitative methods in psychology. But they are not *new*—they have long histories tied into traditions of doing research that invite a reconsidering of power dynamics involved in the process of knowing (e.g., Israel et al., 1998; Minkler & Wallerstein, 2008; Wallerstein & Duran, 2006). Indigenous scholars, especially, have long queried power dynamics and hierarchies in research and community interactions (e.g., L. T. Smith, 1999; also see Chapter 14 by Gone, this volume). Acknowledging these histories is key to enabling community-based approaches to work in intended ways of inviting power and knowing to be redistributed.

To make sense of this "development," or reuptake, we might return to our central questions about how approaches to research configure the person, the researcher, and the process of making meaning and generating knowledge. Engaging in truly collaborative work challenges existing systems and norms for doing research. These include ideas about whose knowledge matters, how this knowledge is produced, who it belongs to, and its role in making change.

At the heart of much collaborative and community-engaged research is the desire to engage in research that not only generates new knowledge but also provides some kind of useful knowledge or value to the communities involved in it (Israel et al., 1998; Wallerstein & Duran, 2006). This usually involves an extended period of collaborative learning as participants explore their experiences, identify shared challenges, and experiment with new responses to these challenges, with a view to initiating lasting change that might occur at personal, social, or political levels or some combination of these (Riley & Reason, 2015). Piran (2001), for example, conducted a cooperative inquiry, a small group-action research method, in a ballet school that culminated in new school practices protecting female dancers from harm.

The coupling of research with social change is acknowledged in traditions of public scholarship reaching back to the 1990s (e.g., Boyer, 1990) and 2000s (Burawoy, 2005), importantly including critical race public scholarship (Bhattacharyya & Murji, 2013). But this does not tell us the whole story. Huaman and Mataria (2019) highlighted the importance of attending to and acknowledging the ways in which Indigenous researchers have long invited a critical look at power as it flows through the research institution. They wrote that "the relevance of Indigenous research agendas to broader methodological teaching and practice is subdued by the dominance of universalizing terms de jure, the most recent of which is 'community-engaged scholarship'" (Huaman & Mataria, 2019, p. 281). Relatedly, L. T. Smith (1999) encouraged researchers to consider how the conduct of much research within settler-colonizer–led institutions and teams re-perpetuates harms against Indigenous participants.

Such scholarship puts the lie to the assumption that qualitative research practiced within dominant Western research paradigms is inherently empowering or emancipatory by virtue of engaging with participants' stories and voices. It highlights the danger in overstating claims of "giving voice" to communities, particularly when one does not identify as a member of those communities, and because, as researchers we often benefit from the knowledge shared (Limes-Taylor Henderson & Esposito, 2019). Thus, while collaborative, community-engaged and participatory research offer opportunities to redress power to a degree and offer up the potential of knowing and making change with participants, we cannot simply assume that they are emancipatory.

Given the marginalization of Indigenous academics and Indigenous ways of knowing globally and in the location from which we write (Aotearoa [New Zealand]), we would be remiss to ignore the ways in which "community engaged" and collaborative approaches are often written about in highly Westernized ways, palatable to those already holding power. As non-Indigenous scholars ourselves, we also do not claim expertise with Indigenous methodologies and frameworks, but invite readers to engage with, and learn from, the work of Indigenous scholars (e.g., Anderson & Cidro, 2019; Dion, 2009; Kidman, 2020; Kidman & Chu, 2017; McAllister et al., 2022; Naepi, 2019; Ruru & Nikora, 2021; L. T. Smith, 1999; TallBear, 2016).

Doing power-sensitive, community engaged, or collaborative research involves clearly and thoroughly thinking through ethics (Rice et al., 2018). Procedural ethics capture some essential aspects of ensuring data are kept securely and participants are given information about the research in which they are participating. But, a relational and reflexive stance on the conduct of research and/or whether the research should even be done in the first place is also needed. Involving people from the communities with which we seek to work early on in the process can help to mitigate the potential for doing research that nobody wanted done or that may even cause harm to the groups studied. There are examples of community engaged or collaborative research that involves people from the group "of interest" in meaningful ways throughout the crafting of a research question through to collecting data, analysis, and dissemination of findings, for instance in the coproduction literature (see Gordon & O'Brien, 2018, and Roper et al., 2018, for more on coproduction). However, people may have different levels of desired engagement with academic research for a number of reasons, ranging from not having the time or desire, to having experienced harm in academic and research contexts. In our desire to engage, we must consider academic power structures and processes. This is made all the more salient with discussions about open science, as requirements for open data enable a range of unknown actors access to participants' meaning making created in relationship with specific researchers. This potentially makes the most marginalized vulnerable to further marginalization (Siegel et al., 2021). These concerns apply across a range of approaches to qualitative research.

Experiments With Epistemological Silo-Busting

In the previous section we described research that extends and develops existing methods for data production, creating data that can be analyzed by researchers from any of the three approaches outlined in the section Approaches to Qualitative Research: What Can We Know and How Can We Know It?, although some may have a more obvious alignment, such as critical orientations and participatory approaches. In contrast, here, we describe epistemological experimentation that significantly "widens the envelope" in terms of what was thought possible.

In seeking to develop qualitative psychology, 20th-century psychologists engaged deeply with epistemological issues, seeking to create new foundations from which to do their work. While we can see this as a measure of conceptual integrity and rigour, one outcome was a relatively dogmatic framing of what was possible. The maturing of the field has opened up possibilities for epistemological experimentation (Riley et al., 2019; Riley & Chamberlain, 2022). One important example is experimentations with phenomenological-informed analysis and discourse analysis, where researchers reinterpret their experiential-focused analysis using analytics from social constructionism or poststructuralism, with view to understanding better the wider discursive conditions of possibility for that experience (e.g., Brown et al., 2011). Willig and Stainton Rogers (2017) described such work as "a welcome development . . . [addressing] the wider social context within which the individual's experience is produced" (p. 285). However, they noted that two epistemologically different methods cannot be brought together without careful consideration of the intersections between these methods. So far, solutions have included applying a more social constructionist approach to interpretative phenomenological analysis or treating phenomenologically informed and discursive methods as offering distinct lenses through which researchers might gain multiple insights to the topic of study.

Other epistemological experimentations include combining discourse analysis with critical realism to consider how the nondiscursive might structure the discourses people draw on to make sense of themselves. For example, Sims-Schouten et al. (2007) and Sims-Schouten and Riley (2019) considered material, policy, and discursive contexts as providing some of the conditions of possibility for, respectively, how mothers accounted for their use of child care and how mental health service users explained their need for these services. The focus of this work was on offering a method for identifying and mapping elements of "the real" that might impact on discourse, and, while the citations for this work suggests it resonates with a range of researchers, the authors recognized that focusing on method bypassed epistemological debates. Others have sought to challenge epistemology as the underlying foundation for qualitative psychological research. Hopner and Liu (2020, p. 179), for example, argue that a "relational ethics" that includes a focus on collaborative relationships based on sincerity, reciprocity, shared purpose, and agreement of what knowledge is produced and how it is to be acted upon, is as important as epistemology.

PARADIGMATIC SHIFTS

In contrast to extensions of and experimentations with existing methods and approaches, our third development represents a radical, paradigmatic shift that challenges previous understandings of the person, their context and epistemology. These postqualitative orientations represent a range of theories—new materialist and posthuman theories among them—that intersect with and diverge from the poststructuralist-informed critical approaches outlined earlier (Fullagar, 2017; St. Pierre, 2014). What they share is a blurring of ontological-epistemological divisions though the idea of a "process ontology," which, drawing on philosophers like Spinoza, Bergson, Deleuze and Guattari, and Barad, imagines the world in a dynamic, continuous "becoming" as a range of human and nonhuman elements interact and affect each other. This entangles the ontological and the epistemological, so that instead of determining what is knowable and how to know it,

researchers drawing on these approaches take an "onto-epistemological" perspective, understanding that the *thing* or phenomenon of study is made in part through the doing of research (Barad, 2007).

Conceptualizing knowledge as contextualized, relational, and processual means that any research outcome is a snapshot of a process, a process produced in part by the apparatus of the study. The implication is that we need to think carefully about how the doing of the research constantly shifts and changes the context and the phenomenon itself, which we can never fully know. This line of thought is not very far off from a perspective that has long infused traditions of qualitative inquiry, which invite us to consider whether any experience can truly be known or captured. It aligns with narrative research in an acknowledgment of how when we tell stories we are always engaged with an envisioned audience (e.g., Riessman & Quinney, 2005). It also aligns with discursive approaches in inviting a deep consideration of context.

Where discursive approaches represent a "turn to language," the new paradigm decenters language to consider a broader range of factors, including the human and the nonhuman, the felt or performed. These factors are understood as dynamically interacting, dynamics that are often discussed in terms of *affect* and *agency*, where agency is understood as the ability to impact another, such as how a bridge creates a conduit between islands. Research might focus, for example, on the sensory and affective dimensions of digital health technologies, understanding these technologies as having agency (Lupton, 2019). For example, how the vibration feature on an exercise app connected to a smartphone might create a pleasant feeling of achievement, motivating a person towards further physical activity. This approach attends to the specificity of online and technological spaces, so that a more-than-human approach foregrounds how digital spaces and technologies are active in the process of people's experiences and representation of themselves (Lupton, 2019).

Postqualitative approaches fully reject scientism, collapsing value-laden distinctions between systematic analysis of empirical and other forms of knowledge generation. This opens up the possibility for a methodological point of approach and style of doing research that deemphasizes the need to establish a particular style of proof and might lean toward, for instance, listening for silences (e.g., Bengtsson & Fynbo, 2018; Mazzei, 2013), making art (e.g., Fullagar & Small, 2019; Renold, 2018), making space for affect to matter (e.g., Ringrose & Renold, 2014), or poetry as a form of articulating research findings (e.g., Chadwick, 2018). Many of these studies represent interdisciplinary research or research not conducted within psychology, highlighting the significant potential for greater engagement for psychologists with these approaches. For example, we see significant potential in how postqualitative researchers draw on scholars like Barad (2007) and question "what matters" and "what is made to matter" in the research assemblage. Setchell et al. (2019), for example, showed how an upbeat positive atmosphere in a neuromuscular clinic made some things matter, such as positive emotions and test scores, while excluding others important for health care, including grief and loss.

Being and doing postqualitatively invites a curiosity toward how producing knowledge in different ways and asking different questions opens space for new embodied, affective knowledges. As Jackson and Mazzei (2012) argued, engaging with the postqualitative does not necessarily entail abandoning qualitative methods—and never coding again—but, rather, thinking through what and who else we might center and account for in our work and how. For example, Lupton (2020) wove more-than-human theory through analysis of stories generated in a story-completion study looking at health information seeking. The method looked similar to more traditional qualitative studies (a stem was created and shared via an online survey), but in analysis, Lupton focused on the connections between humans and non-humans within the stories, including affective forces of the nonhuman. In doing so, the analysis pushed toward an acknowledgment of not only the discourses that surround health information seeking practices but also the ways that feeling and emotion, as well as material engagement with people and things (e.g., places to exercise, relationships of care), shift access to this information.

When we start to move toward posthuman understandings, we must necessarily destabilize the assumption that humans and their thought processes are at the heart of phenomena. Returning to our opening vignette, instead of asking, "What is salad-man's experience of this interaction?" or "What discourses structure pie-man's talk?" a researcher can build in room for other pieces of the assemblage to come to matter. Questions become "What material, affective, and discursive flows come to matter as a part of this assemblage?" "What lines of flight (away from dominant understandings) are possible/impossible?" or "What capacities for action are enabled?" We might consider the interconnections of an assemblage that might include the cafeteria layout, anxieties about catching flights and associated stress hormones, the affective qualities of choosing food, discourses of health or masculinity, and so on. We might acknowledge how we can see only one part of this assemblage of factors at once, while acknowledging that what we cannot see still impacts what is going on. This approach is also likely to decenter the person, directing interest as much to the agency of the cafeteria menu as to the thought processes of pie-man and his need to sneer at a salad.

CONCLUSION

Contrasting our chapter with Pistrang and Barker's (2012) review of qualitative research in the first edition of this handbook, we see significant developments in the relatively short time period of a decade. The diversity we describe might point to the conclusion that psychologists using qualitative methods are connected by little more than a shared agreement that we can use data without converting them first into numbers for statistical analysis. But looking deeper, what comes across for us is a shared, generative passion for thinking about what we know and what we could know better. When better becomes less about accurate assessment than the ability to vision new possibilities that widen our capacities to support human flourishing. Our challenge now is to deepen our roots within our discipline so that the range of qualitative approaches are represented in psychology journals, while also connecting out to the experimentation happening within and across disciplinary boundaries.

References

Ahmed, S. (2017). *Living a feminist life*. Duke University Press.

Alvesson, M., & Sköldberg, K. (2017). *Reflexive methodology: New vistas for qualitative research*. SAGE.

Anderson, K., & Cidro, J. (2019). Decades of doing: Indigenous women academics reflect on the practices of community-based health research. *Journal of Empirical Research on Human Research Ethics*, 14(3), 222–233. https://doi.org/10.1177/1556264619835707

Barad, K. (2007). *Meeting the universe halfway: Quantum physics and the entanglement of matter and meaning*. Duke University Press. https://doi.org/10.2307/j.ctv12101zq

Bengtsson, T. T., & Fynbo, L. (2018). Analysing the significance of silence in qualitative interviewing: Questioning and shifting power relations. *Qualitative Research*, 18(1), 19–35. https://doi.org/10.1177/1468794117694220

Benmayor, R. (2008). Digital storytelling as a signature pedagogy for the New Humanities. *Arts and Humanities in Higher Education*, 7(2), 188–204. https://doi.org/10.1177/1474022208088648

Bhattacharyya, G., & Murji, K. (2013). Introduction: Race critical public scholarship. *Ethnic and Racial Studies*, 36(9), 1359–1373. https://doi.org/10.1080/01419870.2013.791399

Botfield, J. R., Newman, C. E., Lenette, C., Albury, K., & Zwi, A. B. (2018). Using digital storytelling to promote the sexual health and well-being of migrant and refugee young people: A scoping review. *Health Education Journal*, 77(7), 735–748. https://doi.org/10.1177/0017896917745568

Boyatzis, R. E. (1998). *Transforming qualitative information: Thematic analysis and code development*. SAGE Publications.

Boydell, K. M., Collings, S., Dew, A., Senior, K., & Smith, L. (2020). Applying body mapping to research with marginalised and vulnerable groups. In K. M. Boydell, A. Dew, S. Collings, K. Senior, & L. Smith (Eds.), *Applying body mapping in research:*

An arts-based method (pp. 6–17). Routledge. https://doi.org/10.4324/9780429340260-1

Boyer, E. L. (1990). *Scholarship reconsidered: Priorities of the professoriate*. The Carnegie Foundation for the Advancement of Teaching.

Braidotti, R. (2013). *The posthuman*. Polity.

Braun, V., & Carruthers, S. (2020). Working at self and wellness: A critical analysis of vegan vlogs. In D. Lupton & Z. Feldman (Eds.), *Digital food cultures* (pp. 82–96). Routledge. https://doi.org/10.4324/9780429402135-8

Braun, V., Clarke, V., Frith, H., Hayfield, N., Malson, H., Moller, N., & Shah-Beckley, I. (2019). Qualitative story completion: Possibilities and potential pitfalls. *Qualitative Research in Psychology*, 16(1), 136–155. https://doi.org/10.1080/14780887.2018.1536395

Brinkmann, S. (2015). Perils and potentials in qualitative psychology. *Integrative Psychological & Behavioral Science*, 49(2), 162–173. https://doi.org/10.1007/s12124-014-9293-z

Broekhuizen, F., & Evans, A. (2016). Pain, pleasure and bridal beauty: Mapping postfeminist bridal perfection. *Journal of Gender Studies*, 25(3), 335–348. https://doi.org/10.1080/09589236.2014.959478

Brown, S. D., Cromby, J., Harper, D. J., Johnson, K., & Reavey, P. (2011). Researching "experience": Embodiment, methodology, process. *Theory & Psychology*, 21(4), 493–515. https://doi.org/10.1177/0959354310377543

Brushwood Rose, C. (2009). The (im)possibilities of self representation: Exploring the limits of storytelling in the digital stories of women and girls. *Changing English*, 16(2), 211–220. https://doi.org/10.1080/13586840902863194

Burawoy, M. (2005). 2004 American Sociological Association Presidential address: For public sociology. *The British Journal of Sociology*, 56(2), 259–294.

Butler, J. (2020). *The force of nonviolence: An ethico-political bind*. Verso.

Camacho-Miñano, M. J., MacIsaac, S., & Rich, E. (2019). Postfeminist biopedagogies of Instagram: Young women learning about bodies, health and fitness. *Sport Education and Society*, 24(6), 651–664. https://doi.org/10.1080/13573322.2019.1613975

Catalani, C., & Minkler, M. (2010). Photovoice: A review of the literature in health and public health. *Health Education & Behavior*, 37(3), 424–451. https://doi.org/10.1177/1090198109342084

Chadwick, R. (2018). *Bodies that birth: Vitalizing birth politics*. Routledge. https://doi.org/10.4324/9781315648910

Chamberlain, K., McGuigan, K., Anstiss, D., & Marshall, K. (2018). A change of view: Arts-based research and psychology. *Qualitative Research in Psychology, 15*(2–3), 131–139. https://doi.org/10.1080/14780887.2018.1456590

Clarke, V., Braun, V., Frith, H., & Moller, N. (2019). Editorial introduction to the special issue: Using story completion methods in qualitative research. *Qualitative Research in Psychology, 16*(1), 1–20. https://doi.org/10.1080/14780887.2018.1536378

Crotty, M. (1998). *The foundations of social research: Meaning and perspective in the research process.* Allen & Unwin.

Danziger, K. (1997). *Naming the mind: How psychology found its language.* SAGE. https://doi.org/10.4135/9781446221815

Dion, S. (2009). *Braiding histories: Learning from Aboriginal peoples' experiences and perspectives.* UBC Press.

Esposito, L., & Perez, F. M. (2014). Neoliberalism and the commodification of mental health. *Humanity & Society, 38*(4), 414–442. https://doi.org/10.1177/0160597614544958

Evans, A., & Riley, S. (2022). The righteous outrage of post-truth anti-feminism: An analysis of TubeCrush and feminist research in and of public space. *European Journal of Cultural Studies, 25*(1), 25–42. https://doi.org/10.1177/1367549420951574

Foucault, M. (1980). *Power/knowledge: Selected interviews and other writings, 1972–1977.* Pantheon.

Frith, H., Riley, S., Archer, L., & Gleeson, K. (2005). Editorial: Imag(in)ing visual methodologies. *Qualitative Research in Psychology, 2*(3), 187–198. https://doi.org/10.1191/1478088705qp037ed

Fullagar, S. (2017). Post-qualitative inquiry and the new materialist turn: Implications for sport, health and physical culture research. *Qualitative Research in Sport, Exercise and Health, 9*(2), 247–257. https://doi.org/10.1080/2159676X.2016.1273896

Fullagar, S., & Small, I. (2019). Writing recovery from depression through a creative research assemblage. In D. C. Parry, C. W. Johnson, & S. Fullagar (Eds.), *Digital dilemmas* (pp. 121–141). Springer.

Gastaldo, D., Rivas-Quarneti, N., & Magalhães, L. (2018). Body-map storytelling as a health research methodology: Blurred lines creating clear pictures. *Forum Qualitative Social Research, 19*(2), 1–26. https://doi.org/10.17169/fqs-19.2.2858

Gergen, K. J. (1985). The social constructionist movement in modern psychology. *American Psychologist, 40*(3), 266–275. https://doi.org/10.1037/0003-066X.40.3.266

Gibson, K. (2022). Bridging the digital divide: Reflections on using WhatsApp instant messenger interviews in youth research. *Qualitative Research in Psychology, 19*(3), 611–631. https://doi.org/10.1080/14780887.2020.1751902

Glaser, B. G., & Strauss, A. L. (1967/1999). *Discovery of grounded theory: Strategies for qualitative research.* Routledge. https://doi.org/10.4324/9780203793206

Goodley, D. (1999). Disability research and the "researcher template": Reflections on grounded subjectivity in ethnographic research. *Qualitative Inquiry, 5*(1), 24–46. https://doi.org/10.1177/107780049900500102

Gordon, S., & O'Brien, A. J. (2018). Co-production: Power, problems and possibilities. *International Journal of Mental Health Nursing, 27*(4), 1201–1203. https://doi.org/10.1111/inm.12504

Gravett, K. (2019). Story completion: Storying as a method of meaning-making and discursive discovery. *International Journal of Qualitative Methods, 18*, 1–8. https://doi.org/10.1177/1609406919893155

Gubrium, A. C., Hill, A. L., & Flicker, S. (2014). A situated practice of ethics for participatory visual and digital methods in public health research and practice: A focus on digital storytelling. *American Journal of Public Health, 104*(9), 1606–1614. https://doi.org/10.2105/AJPH.2013.301310

Haraway, D. (1989). *Primate visions: Gender, race, and nature in the world of modern science.* Routledge.

Harré, R. (1980). *Social being: A theory for social psychology.* Rowman & Littlefield.

Henrich, J., Heine, S. J., & Norenzayan, A. (2010). The weirdest people in the world? *Behavioral and Brain Sciences, 33*(2–3), 61–83. https://doi.org/10.1017/S0140525X0999152X

Henriques, J., Hollway, W., Urwin, C., Venn, C., & Walkerdine, V. (1984). *Changing the subject: Psychology, social regulation, and subjectivity.* Psychology Press.

hooks, b. (1989). *Talking back: Thinking feminist, thinking Black.* Between-the-Lines.

Hookway, N. (2008). "Entering the blogosphere": Some strategies for using blogs in social science research. *Qualitative Research, 8*(1), 91–113. https://doi.org/10.1177/1468794107085298

Hopner, V., & Liu, J. H. (2020). Relational ethics and epistemology: The case for complementary first principles in psychology. *Theory & Psychology, 31*(2), 179–198. https://doi.org/10.1177/0959354320974103

Huaman, E. S., & Mataira, P. (2019). Beyond community engagement: Centering research through Indigenous epistemologies and peoplehood. *Alternative,*

15(3), 281–286. https://doi.org/10.1177/1177180119871705

Israel, B. A., Schulz, A. J., Parker, E. A., & Becker, A. B. (1998). Review of community-based research: Assessing partnership approaches to improve public health. *Annual Review of Public Health, 19*(1), 173–202. https://doi.org/10.1146/annurev.publhealth.19.1.173

Jackson, A. Y., & Mazzei, L. A. (2012). *Thinking with theory in qualitative research: Viewing data across multiple perspectives*. Routledge.

Jacques, E. (2019, July 15–17). *How is masculinity practised on a lads' night out? A poststructuralist informed ethnographic analysis of gendered drinking in British towns and cities* [Paper presentation]. International Society of Critical Health Psychology 11th Biennial Conference, Bratislava, Slovakia.

Janghorban, R., Latifnejad Roudsari, R., & Taghipour, A. (2014). Skype interviewing: The new generation of online synchronous interview in qualitative research. *International Journal of Qualitative Studies on Health and Well-being, 9*(1), 24152. https://doi.org/10.3402/qhw.v9.24152

Jennings, E., Braun, V., & Clarke, V. (2019). Breaking gendered boundaries? Exploring constructions of counter-normative body hair practices in Aotearoa/New Zealand using story completion. *Qualitative Research in Psychology, 16*(1), 74–95. https://doi.org/10.1080/14780887.2018.1536386

Johnson, K. (2020). Visualising mental health with an LGBT community group: Method, process, (affect) theory. In P. Reavey (Ed.), *A handbook of visual methods in psychology: Using and interpreting images in qualitative research* (2nd ed., pp. 259–276). Routledge. https://doi.org/10.4324/9781351032063-1915

Johnston, G. (2016). Champions for social change: Photovoice ethics in practice and 'false hopes' for policy and social change. *Global Public Health: An International Journal for Research, Policy and Practice, 11*(5–6), 799–811. https://doi.org/10.1080/17441692.2016.1170176

Jowett, A., Peel, E., & Shaw, R. (2011). Online interviewing in psychology: Reflections on the process. *Qualitative Research in Psychology, 8*(4), 354–369. https://doi.org/10.1080/14780887.2010.500352

Kaufmann, K., & Peil, C. (2020). The mobile instant messaging interview (MIMI): Using WhatsApp to enhance self-reporting and explore media usage in situ. *Mobile Media & Communication, 8*(2), 229–246. https://doi.org/10.1177/2050157919852392

Kenny, T., Boyle, S. L., & Lewis, S. P. (2020). #recovery: Understanding recovery from the lens of recovery-focused blogs posted by individuals with lived experience. *International Journal of Eating Disorders, 53*(8), 1234–1243. https://doi.org/10.1002/eat.23221

Kidman, J. (2020). Whither decolonisation? Indigenous scholars and the problem of inclusion in the neoliberal university. *Journal of Sociology, 56*(2), 247–262. https://doi.org/10.1177/1440783319835958

Kidman, J., & Chu, C. (2017). Scholar outsiders in the neoliberal university: Transgressive academic labour in the whitestream. *New Zealand Journal of Educational Studies, 52*(1), 7–19. https://doi.org/10.1007/s40841-017-0079-y

Kim, M. A., Yi, J., Sang, J., & Jung, D. (2021). A photovoice study on the bereavement experience of mothers after the death of a child. *Death Studies, 45*(5), 390–404. https://doi.org/10.1080/07481187.2019.1648333

Kitzinger, C., & Powell, D. (1995). Engendering infidelity: Essentialist and social constructionist readings of a story completion task. *Feminism & Psychology, 5*(3), 345–372. https://doi.org/10.1177/0959353595053004

Laing, C. M., Moules, N. J., Estefan, A., & Lang, M. (2017). "Stories take your role away from you": Understanding the impact on health care professionals of viewing digital stories of pediatric and adolescent/young adult oncology patients. *Journal of Pediatric Oncology Nursing, 34*(4), 261–271. https://doi.org/10.1177/1043454217697023

LaMarre, A., & Rice, C. (2017). Hashtag recovery: #Eating disorder recovery on Instagram. *Social Sciences, 6*(3), 68. https://doi.org/10.3390/socsci6030068

LaMarre, A., & Rice, C. (2021). Healthcare providers' engagement with eating disorder recovery narratives: Opening to complexity and diversity. *Medical Humanities, 47*(1), 78–86. https://doi.org/10.1136/medhum-2019-011723

Langdridge, D. (2007). *Phenomenological psychology: Theory, research and method*. Pearson Education.

Larkin, M., Eatough, V., & Osborn, M. (2011). Interpretative phenomenological analysis and embodied, active, situated cognition. *Theory & Psychology, 21*(3), 318–337. https://doi.org/10.1177/0959354310377544

Limes-Taylor Henderson, K., & Esposito, J. (2019). Using others in the nicest way possible: On colonial and academic practice(s), and an ethic of humility. *Qualitative Inquiry, 25*(9–10), 876–889. https://doi.org/10.1177/1077800417743528

Loaring, J. M., Larkin, M., Shaw, R., & Flowers, P. (2015). Renegotiating sexual intimacy in the context of altered embodiment: The experiences of women with breast cancer and their male partners following mastectomy and reconstruction. *Health Psychology, 34*(4), 426–436. https://doi.org/10.1037/hea0000195

Lupton, D. (2019). Toward a more-than-human analysis of digital health: Inspirations from feminist new materialism. *Qualitative Health Research, 29*(14), 1998–2009. https://doi.org/10.1177/1049732319833368

Lupton, D. (2020). *The story completion method and more-than-human theory: Finding and using health information.* SAGE Research Methods Cases. https://doi.org/10.4135/9781529715194

Mazzei, L. A. (2013). A voice without organs: Interviewing in posthumanist research. *International Journal of Qualitative Studies in Education, 26*(6), 732–740. https://doi.org/10.1080/09518398.2013.788761

McAllister, T. G., Naepi, S., Wilson, E., Hikuroa, D., & Walker, L. A. (2022). Under-represented and overlooked: Māori and Pasifika scientists in Aotearoa New Zealand's universities and crown-research institutes. *Journal of the Royal Society of New Zealand, 52*(1), 38–53. https://doi.org/10.1080/03036758.2020.1796103

Minkler, M., & Wallerstein, N. (2008). *Community based participatory research for health: Process to outcomes* (2nd ed.). Jossey Bass.

Naepi, S. E. (2019). Why isn't my professor Pasifika? A snapshot of the academic workforce in New Zealand universities. *MAI Journal: A New Zealand Journal of Indigenous Scholarship, 8*(2), 219–234. https://doi.org/10.20507/MAIJournal.2019.8.2.9

Ofoegbu, T. O., Asogwa, U. D., Ogbonna, C. S., Aloh, H. E., Eseadi, C., Eskay, M., Nji, G. C., Ngwoke, O. R., Agboti, C. I., Nnachi, R. A., Nnachi, O. C., & Otu, M. S. (2020). Effect of digital storytelling intervention on burnout thoughts of adolescent: Athletes with disabilities. *Medicine, 99*(30), e21164. https://doi.org/10.1097/MD.0000000000021164

Piran, N. (2001). Re-inhabiting the body from the inside out: Girls transform the school environment. In D. L. Tolman (Ed.), *From subjects to subjectivities: A handbook of interpretive and participatory methods* (pp. 218–238). NYU Press.

Pistrang, N., & Barker, C. (2012). Varieties of qualitative research: A pragmatic approach to selecting methods. In H. Cooper, P. Camic, D. Long, A. T. Panter, D. Rindskopf, & K. Sher (Eds.), *APA handbook of research methods in psychology: Vol. 2. Research designs: Quantitative, qualitative, neuropsychological, and biological* (pp. 5–18). American Psychological Association. https://doi.org/10.1037/13620-001

Potter, J., & Wetherell, M. (1987). *Discourse analysis: Beyond attitudes and behaviour.* SAGE.

Prilleltensky, I. (1994). Psychology and social ethics. *American Psychologist, 49*(11), 966–967. https://doi.org/10.1037/0003-066X.49.11.966

Radley, A., & Taylor, D. (2003). Remembering one's stay in hospital: A study in photography, recovery and forgetting. *Health, 7*(2), 129–159. https://doi.org/10.1177/1363459303007002872

Rasche, A., & Platt, C. A. (2014). *Online interviewing: investigating female undergraduates' perceptions of pornography.* Sage Research Cases.

Reavey, P. (2021). *A handbook of visual methods in psychology: Using and interpreting images in qualitative research* (2nd ed.). Routledge.

Renold, E. (2018). 'Feel what I feel': Making da(r)ta with teen girls for creative activisms on how sexual violence matters. *Journal of Gender Studies, 27*(1), 37–55. https://doi.org/10.1080/09589236.2017.1296352

Rice, C., LaMarre, A., Douglas, P., & Changfoot, N. (2020). Making spaces: Multimedia storytelling as reflexive, creative praxis. *Qualitative Research in Psychology, 17*(2), 222–239. https://doi.org/10.1080/14780887.2018.1442694

Rice, C., LaMarre, A., & Mykitiuk, R. (2018). Cripping the ethics of disability arts research. In C. MacLeod, J. Marx, P. Mnyaka, & G. Treharne (Eds.), *Palgrave handbook of ethics in critical research* (pp. 257–272). Palgrave. https://doi.org/10.1007/978-3-319-74721-7_17

Rice, C., & Mündel, I. (2018). Story-making as methodology: Disrupting dominant stories through multimedia storytelling. *Canadian Review of Sociology/Revue canadienne de sociologie, 55*(2), 211–231. https://doi.org/10.1111/cars.12190

Riessman, C. K., & Quinney, L. (2005). Narrative in social work. *Qualitative Social Work: Research and Practice, 4*(4), 391–412. https://doi.org/10.1177/1473325005058643

Riley, S., Brooks, J., Goodman, S., Cahill, S., Branney, P., Treharne, G., & Sullivan, C. (2019). Celebrations amongst challenges: Considering the past, present and future of the Qualitative Methods in Psychology (QMiP) Section of the British Psychological Society. *Qualitative Research in Psychology, 16*(3), 464–482. https://doi.org/10.1080/14780887.2019.1605275

Riley, S., & Chamberlain, K. (2022). Designing qualitative research in psychology. In U. Flick (Ed.), *SAGE handbook of qualitative research design.* SAGE. https://doi.org/10.4135/9781529770278.n68

Riley, S., Evans, A., & Robson, M. (2018). *Postfeminism and health.* Routledge. https://doi.org/10.4324/9781315648613

Riley, S., & Reason, P. (2015). Co-operative inquiry: An action research practice. In J. Smith (Ed.), *Qualitative psychology: A practical guide to methods* (3rd ed., pp. 168–198). SAGE.

Riley, S., Robson, M., & Evans, A. (2021). Foucauldian-informed discourse analysis. In M. Bamberg, C. Demuth, & M. Watzlawik (Eds.), *Cambridge handbook on identity*. Cambridge University Press.

Riley, S., Rodham, K., & Gavin, J. (2009). Doing weight: Pro-ana and recovery identities in cyberspace. *Journal of Community & Applied Social Psychology*, *19*(5), 348–359. https://doi.org/10.1002/casp.1022

Ringrose, J., & Renold, E. (2014). "F**k rape!": Exploring affective intensities in a feminist research assemblage. *Qualitative Inquiry*, *20*(6), 772–780. https://doi.org/10.1177/1077800414530261

Rolbiecki, A. J., Washington, K., Bitsicas, K., Teti, M., Temple, D., & Lero, C. (2021). Digital storytelling: Narrating meaning in bereavement. *Death Studies*. Advance online publication. https://doi.org/10.1080/07481187.2021.1900452

Roper, C., Grey, F., & Cadogan, E. (2018). *Co-production: Putting principles into practice in mental health contexts*. https://healthsciences.unimelb.edu.au/__data/assets/pdf_file/0007/3392215/Coproduction_putting-principles-into-practice.pdf

Rose, N., & Miller, P. (2008). *Governing the present*. Polity Press.

Rúdólfsdóttir, A., & Jóhannsdóttir, Á. (2018). Fuck patriarchy! An analysis of digital mainstream media discussion of the #freethenipple activities in Iceland in March 2015. *Feminism & Psychology*, *28*(1), 133–151. https://doi.org/10.1177/0959353517715876

Ruru, J., & Nikora, L. W. (2021). *Ngā Kete Mātauranga: Maori scholars at the research interface*. Foyles.

Sackett, C. R., & Dogan, J. N. (2019). An exploration of Black teens' experiences of their own racial identity through photovoice: Implications for counsellors. *Journal of Multicultural Counseling and Development*, *47*(3), 172–189. https://doi.org/10.1002/jmcd.12140

Setchell, J., Abrams, T., McAdam, L. C., & Gibson, B. E. (2019). Cheer* in health care practice: What it excludes and why it matters. *Qualitative Health Research*, *29*(13), 1890–1903. https://doi.org/10.1177/1049732319838235

Shaffer, R. (1986). *Beyond the dispensary*. The African Medical and Research Foundation.

Shaw, R. (2019). Interpretative phenomenological analysis. In M. Forrester & C. Sullivan (Eds.), *Doing qualitative research in psychology: A practical guide* (2nd ed., pp. 185–208). SAGE.

Sheafer, V. (2017). Using digital storytelling to teach psychology: A preliminary investigation. *Psychology Learning & Teaching*, *16*(1), 133–143. https://doi.org/10.1177/1475725716685537

Siegel, J. A., Calogero, R. M., Eaton, A. A., & Roberts, T. A. (2021). Identifying gaps and building bridges between feminist psychology and open science. *Psychology of Women Quarterly*, *45*(4), 407–411. https://doi.org/10.1177/03616843211044494

Sims-Schouten, W., & Riley, S. (2019). Presenting critical realist discourse analysis as a tool for making sense of service users' accounts of their mental health problems. *Qualitative Health Research*, *29*(7), 1016–1028. https://doi.org/10.1177/1049732318818824

Sims-Schouten, W., Willig, C., & Riley, S. (2007). Critical realism in discourse analysis: A presentation of a systematic method of analysis using women's talk of motherhood, childcare and female employment as an example. *Theory & Psychology*, *17*(1), 101–124. https://doi.org/10.1177/0959354307073153

Smith, J. A. (2018). "Yes it is phenomenological": A reply to Max Van Manen's critique of interpretative phenomenological analysis. *Qualitative Health Research*, *28*(12), 1955–1958. https://doi.org/10.1177/1049732318799577

Smith, J. A., Flowers, P., & Larkin, M. (2009). *Interpretative phenomenological analysis: Theory, method and research*. SAGE.

Smith, L. T. (1999). *Decolonizing methodologies: Research and indigenous peoples*. Zed Books.

St. Pierre, E. A. (2014). A brief and personal history of post qualitative research: Toward "post inquiry." *Journal of Curriculum Theorizing*, *30*(2), 2–19.

Sugarman, J. (2015). Neoliberalism and psychological ethics. *Journal of Theoretical and Philosophical Psychology*, *35*(2), 103–116. https://doi.org/10.1037/a0038960

Sullivan, C., Gibson, S., & Riley, S. (2012). *Doing your qualitative psychology project*. SAGE.

TallBear, K. (2016). Dear Indigenous Studies, it's not me, it's you. Why I left and what needs to change. In A. Moreton-Robinson (Ed.), *Critical Indigenous studies: Engagements in First World locations* (pp. 69–82). University of Arizona Press.

Terry, G., Hayfield, N., Clarke, V., & Braun, V. (2017). Thematic analysis. In C. Willig & W. S. Rogers, (Eds.), *The SAGE handbook of qualitative research in psychology* (pp. 17–36). SAGE. https://doi.org/10.4135/9781526405555.n2

Trepal, H., Cannon, Y., & Garcia, J. (2020). Using photovoice to promote body image resilience in college women. *Journal of College Counseling, 23*(1), 44–56. https://doi.org/10.1002/jocc.12148

van Manen, M. (2017). But is it phenomenology? *Qualitative Health Research, 27*(6), 775–779. https://doi.org/10.1177/1049732317699570

Vivienne, S. (2011). Trans digital storytelling: Everyday activism, mutable identity and the problem of visibility. *Gay & Lesbian Issues and Psychology Review, 7*(1), 43–54.

Wallerstein, N. B., & Duran, B. (2006). Using community-based participatory research to address health disparities. *Health Promotion Practice, 7*(3), 312–323. https://doi.org/10.1177/1524839906289376

Wang, C., & Burris, M. A. (1994). Empowerment through photo novella: Portraits of participation. *Health Education & Behavior, 21*(2), 171–186.

Willig, C., & Stainton Rogers, W. (2017). *The SAGE handbook of qualitative research in psychology.* SAGE.

Yardley, L. (2015). Demonstrating validity in qualitative psychology. In J. A. Smith (Ed.), *Qualitative psychology: A practical guide to research methods* (3rd ed., pp. 257–272). SAGE.

CHAPTER 2

METASYNTHESIS OF QUALITATIVE RESEARCH

Sally Thorne

Scholars in the social and behavioral sciences and in the applied practice disciplines, such as health care, that draw upon such sciences, have long been intrigued by the question of what can be done to integrate and interpret bodies of qualitative material so as to answer increasingly in-depth questions about various human experiential phenomena. They were concerned that, as the methodology of qualitative metasynthesis has evolved, it has been considered analogous to quantitative meta-analysis in some respects, but, given the diversity and complexity of the qualitative enterprise, this approach to synthesis has encountered a number of new dimensions and directions of its own. The aim of this chapter is to help the reader interpret an array of methodological options within the overall domain of "meta" studies of qualitatively derived products. This includes a critical reflection on trends within the enterprise, some of which have become a disservice to the genre and to the prior studies themselves. As prospective researchers consider the kinds of questions they might ask using qualitative metasynthesis methods and the nature of the bodies of qualitative research about which they might ask those questions, it is important that they appreciate the necessity of a coherent alignment between the processes of meta work and the kinds of logical conclusions one can reasonably draw from it.

In this chapter, therefore, readers will find ample guidance to make informed decisions about when and where metasynthesis can be appropriate, what methods might best apply to any given research question, and what kinds of conclusions they can meaningfully draw from the style of metasynthesis study they design.

ORIGINS OF THE APPROACH

The collection of approaches we now think of as *qualitative metasynthesis* arose within the social sciences as an attempt to bring together ideas that had been developed on the basis of diverse theoretical and disciplinary perspectives into more coherent and comprehensive "grand theories." As Glaser and Strauss wrote in 1971, qualitative studies were at risk for remaining "little islands of knowledge" (p. 181) unless a means could be found to link them to one another. Drawing on the idea of *metasociology* (Furfey, 1953), which was an attempt to focus the underpinnings, approaches, and outcomes central to social research, Ritzer (1991) coined the term *metatheorizing* to refer to the study of social theorizing itself, and within this context, Zhao (1991) introduced *metastudy* as a systematic, cross-comparative, and interpretive approach to analysis of the existing body of sociological knowledge on a specific topic.

https://doi.org/10.1037/0000319-002
APA Handbook of Research Methods in Psychology, Second Edition: Vol. 2. Research Designs: Quantitative, Qualitative, Neuropsychological, and Biological, H. Cooper (Editor-in-Chief)

Taking the idea beyond sociology, educators Noblit and Hare (1988) developed *metaethnography* as way of identifying current understandings within a field of study and raising issues for consideration and further research.

Over the next decade, in what Sandelowski and Barroso (2007) referred to as "the urge to synthesize" (p. 1), scholars in the applied health disciplines enthusiastically took up the general challenge of strengthening the impact of the growing but undervalued body of qualitative research reports in parallel with the advances that were being made using quantitative meta-analysis as a foundation for evidence-based practice and policy (Barbour & Barbour, 2003; Estabrooks et al., 1994; Jensen & Allen, 1996; McCormick et al., 2003; Paterson et al., 2001; Sandelowski et al., 1997; Schreiber et al., 1997; Sherwood, 1999; Thorne et al., 2004). It must be remembered that quantitative meta-analysis was being hailed at that time as among the most significant methodological advancements of the 20th century, increasing the precision and power of research and allowing it to answer questions not anticipated within primary studies (Sandelowski & Barroso, 2007). Proponents of these new qualitative metasynthesis approaches, concerned that the evidence-based movement was progressing without the benefit of insights that are qualitatively derived, sought a similar kind of impact for qualitative products. Within this evolving methodological space, authors articulated variants on the theme, often using distinctive terminology to signify a particular slant on what they thought they were doing and why (Dixon-Woods et al., 2007). Some of the earlier forms of qualitative metasynthesis included *qualitative data aggregation* (Estabrooks et al., 1994), *qualitative meta-analysis* (Schreiber et al., 1997), and *qualitative systematic review* (Popay et al., 1998).

Over time, an array of specialized approaches, such as *grounded formal theory* (Kearney, 2001), or *metanarrative* (Greenhalgh, 2004; Greenhalgh et al., 2005), became specific to a particular methodological orientation, while others, such as *metasummary* (Sandelowski & Barroso, 2003b), *metainterpretation* (Weed, 2005), and *metastudy*

(Paterson et al., 2001), were oriented around a particular synthesis technique. And despite its name, metaethnography became a technique for use across methodological orientations (Britten et al., 2002). Their collective hope was that metasynthesis, in all of its various forms and nomenclatures, could become a way to create overarching or synoptic claims on the basis of a sequence of analytic and synthetic strategies applied to bodies of extant qualitative studies (Finfgeld, 2003).

WHAT IT IS AND IS NOT

It is important at the outset to distinguish qualitative metasynthesis from a number of other intellectual processes that have grown up during a similar era across various disciplines. The kinds of products that can legitimately be considered qualitative metasynthesis represent a form of original research, taking as its database a specific set of previously published qualitative research reports and producing findings that extend beyond what could have been known on the basis of a less formal reading of the extant literature. This contrasts it with the conventional literature review—a tradition across all knowledge-producing disciplines as scholars locate their work within a review of what is already known within their field of study. In the cultural convention of that form of literature review, the scholar describes each of the previous key studies on the topic and explains their contributions and, most importantly, the limitations that justify a new study.

More recently, and particularly within critical social theorizing and other interpretive traditions, we see a critical and/or integrative form of narrative literature review in which the focus of reflection is on variations of approach, angle of vision, or perspectival distinctions rather than methodological flaws. These kinds of reviews critically reflect on a body of work, exposing the theoretical assumptions on which previous studies have been developed, illuminating the political or ideological nature of previous inquiries, or raising questions with regard to the underlying aims of previous investigators. As a result, they typically strive for conclusions about the body of work that attempt to shift the reader's perspective of its relevance and positionality (Greenhalgh et al., 2018).

Metasynthesis must also be distinguished from qualitative secondary analysis, a tradition in which extant data sets—either one or many, one's own or those of multiple scholars—is tapped for additional insights that may have eluded the original qualitative researcher (Hinds et al.,1997; Thorne, 1994). Each of these processes may well reflect some of the same aspirations to take that which has been previously studied to a higher level of conceptualization and development but should be understood as quite different from the more formal inquiry approach that the idea of qualitative metasynthesis implies.

A further consideration is that qualitative metasynthesis is a form of systematic review that has evolved during a time in which reviews that are considered "systematic" have taken on a life of their own. Building on the original inspiration of Archie Cochrane (1972), the Cochrane Collaboration and Library was established as a global research synthesis organization in 1993 (Chalmers, 1993) and over time developed distinctive methods sections, including, in 2006, the Cochrane Qualitative Methods Group (CQMG; Chandler & Hopewell, 2013). The CQMG has dedicated enormous effort to the project of including in systematic reviews the evidence that derives from research using qualitative methods. Its motivation has been the standardization of reviews of qualitative research findings, such that the products can be legitimately and effectively integrated into the body of evidence that informs health care interventions (Noyes et al., 2020). Although CQMG guidelines have become the gold standard for qualitative evidence development in many sectors, there is also considerable concern within the disciplines that draw upon qualitative inquiry that this direction has depreciated and coopted that which qualitative methods can contribute to knowledge (Sandelowski & Barroso, 2007). In its extreme form, which some would argue the Cochrane approach exemplifies, the form of knowledge that qualitative researchers seek to generate is weakened, assimilated, and

even erased by being "brought into conformity with the very practices they were meant to subvert" (Sandelowski & Barroso, 2007, p. 5). Or, as Sandelowski et al. (1997) expressed it, just as it goes against the nature of poetry to attempt to summarize even one poem, it seems both epistemologically and ethically inappropriate to try to summarize the findings from one or more qualitative studies (p. 366).

Thus, qualitative metasynthesis is a form of literature review that explores as its primary data set a body of prior reports from qualitative investigations on a topic, approaching the process in a structured, transparent, and auditable manner that seeks to build upon what has been previously interpreted or concluded to advance a field of knowledge. It exists within a larger research world that presumes reviews conducted systematically are preferable in answering certain kinds of questions than those that are done in a more narrative form. It has evolved over a time in which the tensions between simplifying its technique and respecting the complexity of the ideas in which it operates have led to lively debate and disagreement. Thus, rather than presenting a "how to" in the most simplistic form, this chapter draws readers into the challenges so that they can decide for themselves how best to approach "dialoguing with texts" (Zimmer, 2006, p. 311).

CONCERNS AND CONTROVERSIES IN THE QUALITATIVE METASYNTHESIS DOMAIN

The field of qualitative metasynthesis is clearly fraught with controversies and debates having to do with the nature and purpose of the enterprise as well as the appropriate manner in which to do it. Here we address the primary issues of contention as they appear in the methodological literature.

Objectivity Versus Subjectivity

The defining characteristic of a systematic review in the Cochrane sense of the term is the use of predetermined and highly structured protocols for searching, screening, appraising, selecting, and summarizing study findings in answer to a narrowly focused research question (Eden et al., 2011; Higgins & Green, 2011). What the researcher seeks to do in this kind of review is to identify all possibly relevant primary studies and then apply clearly justified exclusion criteria to delimit the subset eligible to be included in the final analysis and synthesis. Often, hundreds or even thousands of possible sources are reduced to a fraction of the whole and a fraction characterized by their similarity (of samples, methods, approaches, and reporting forms). From that, claims are made that appear to represent the full body of research but in the worst case scenario capture only that which seemed common across the subset that were captured by the tight webbing of the design (Greenhalgh et al., 2018).

While this depiction may sound harsh, it does reflect an appreciation for what systematic review is meant to accomplish in the quantitative research world. In the quantitative synthesis context, including findings from studies whose methodology is flawed, tapping a significantly different sample population or using a slightly altered intervention could yield dangerously misleading findings. So when we ask a question such as "What is the best approach to a particular clinical problem?" we really do require that kind of rigor and precision in our systematic review methodology.

In the qualitative world, we are rarely asking the kinds of questions that lend themselves to the development of definitive truth claims. Rather, we are working in the world of human experiential subjectivities, trying to understand things like worldviews and perspectives, ways of interpreting, and individual impacts of multiple and intersecting social forces. Our questions are more around what we can learn from in-depth exploration of how people think, behave, or reason things when confronted with somewhat similar kinds of circumstances. Our methods are rarely oriented toward uncovering incontrovertible truths, but more likely to be surfacing possibilities for how we might think about various human or social phenomena in ways that help solve some of our problems in understanding or addressing them. Our aim is not, therefore, a narrowing of our

thinking but rather an expansion of interpretive options toward some theoretical or applied goal.

If we conceive of qualitative research products as windows into objective reality, then a tightly protocol-driven systematic review process might make sense. But because the scholars that designed and conducted the vast majority of what exists in the qualitative research literature did not see that as their aim, did not design their studies to develop truth claims, and did not present their findings as objective facts, then using them in that manner in a synthesis study seems highly inappropriate. It seems important, then, to tease out the idea of being systematic in a comprehensive review process from the rigid and restrictive conventions we have come to associate with such reviews. A qualitative or narrative review can be methodical, deliberative, and critically interpretive in working through the process of determining what insights might reside in an extensive body of qualitative reports, regardless of their varieties and diversities. Despite every attempt to be procedurally objective, all reviews are ultimately a form of "disciplined subjectivity" in that they are inherently situated, partial, and a product of their moment in time (Sandelowski, 2008).

Interpretation Versus Aggregation

Dating back to the metatheorizing sociology of Ritzer (1991) and Zhao (1991) as well as the applied theorizing tradition of Noblit and Hare (1988), the early days of qualitative metasynthesis envisioned an inherently critical and reflective process of cross-interrogating the ideas contained within a body of studies, such that the unpacking of the impact of method, theory, and the peculiarities of data sets became the terrain within which journeys into more comprehensive understandings might be realized. This sort of work involved a highly complex set of processes associated with interpreting (across disciplines and methodologies) what each primary researcher was doing and thinking and how the findings from each study came to take shape in the manner they did. Much of the qualitative metasynthesis literature of that era explained in detail why even the most apparently straightforward of steps, such as locating the findings within a written study report, let alone classifying, interpreting, and integrating them, were in fact considerably more complex than one might have anticipated (Sandelowski & Barroso, 2007). As scholars wrestled with various methodological options to strengthen the comprehensiveness of the process and work out technique, they often recommended that this kind of work was best done in the hands of experienced, interdisciplinary teams, within which a wide range of formal and disciplinary cultural knowledge could be brought to bear in deep interpretation of the origins, intellectual underpinnings, and procedural ingredients in each primary study (Thorne et al., 2004). As disciplinary traditions were so various in what they considered essential ingredients of a research report, what they meant when they used methodologic terminology, and what form and format was considered appropriate for a fulsome written report, it was assumed that depth of experience was essential to navigating the language signifiers and the theoretical traditions at which they hinted. It was further assumed that this kind of knowledge of the ingredients would be essential to the quality of the claims that arose in the final synthesis product (Thorne, 2019).

Over time, however, a number of concurrent forces acted to shift the center of gravity in the world of qualitative metasynthesis from that vision of an approach characterized by that level of complexity and intensity and toward one that was considerably more rapid-fire and streamlined. Certainly the possibility of bringing qualitatively derived insights into the evidence-based practice context was a driver in many of the applied disciplines. In addition, there was tremendous allure to an approach to investigation that allowed one to work with qualitative material while bypassing the exhaustive, expensive, and time-consuming effort inherent in producing original qualitative databases. Finally, as the idea of systematic review gained hold across many disciplines, pitched as a superior way of socializing new scholars into the literature of their fields and potentially more publishable than conventional narrative reviews, the more contained and manageable form of qualitative metasynthesis came to dominate the field.

The rapid explosion in scholarship that considers itself to represent qualitative metasynthesis products can be broadly estimated by a simple Google Scholar search. From 10 new publications for the calendar year 1995, it grew to "38 in 2000, 245 in 2005, 985 in 2010, and 3,250 in 2015" (Thorne, 2017, p. 4). As of the year 2021, the count has risen to 11,500. For the most part, these reviews follow a tightly focused and rigidly structured process along the lines set out by the aforementioned Cochrane Collaboration or by the Joanna Briggs Institute (JBI), a network of collaborating entities for the purpose of training systematic reviewers and articulating best practice information guides for systematic review (Lockwood et al., 2017).

Using the Cochrane/JBI model, the vast majority of the qualitative metasynthesis products that now appear in the literature can be characterized as aggregative rather than interpretive (Greenhalgh, 2012; Ioannidis, 2016). As Bergdahl (2019) provocatively characterized it, much of this body of work is "turning rich descriptions into thin reductions" (p. 1). In her view, meta-aggregation falls short of being a sound method in that it is incompatible with the philosophy underling qualitative research methodologies. She, therefore, argued that its products ought not to be described as *qualitative metasynthesis* and suggested that term be reserved for studies that reinterpret, compare, and translate disparate qualitative findings into a new conceptual apparatus. In a response to Bergdahl's critique, Lockwood et al. (2019) acknowledged that the diversity of qualitative synthesis methods should be encouraged, given the "broad range of knowledge needs associated with scholarship and theory generation, as well as policy and practice" (p. 1). They reaffirmed their position that, although it differs from the more interpretive approach, the more pragmatist approach that works best for qualitative evidence synthesis is well justified as a proper scientific method.

Thus, there is evident tension within the literature as to what the point of qualitative metasynthesis is in the first place and, depending on how you situate yourself in relation to that question, how it ought to be conducted. One set of methodologists positions it securely within the evidence-based approach, prioritizing methodological rules as the primary quality indicator. Some such studies can add value to the literature, such as when additional meta-analysis confirms whether a clinically significant effect is or is not also statistically significant (Egger et al., 2008). But there are also times in which the characterization of being a "systematic review" creates the impression that a qualitative data aggregation can justifiably claim a more privileged position within the knowledge hierarchy than it actually deserves (Alper & Haynes, 2016). At the opposite end of the spectrum are those who consider qualitative metasynthesis to be an entirely interpretive and inductive knowledge product (Malterud, 2019). Proponents of this approach will be far less concerned about rule-following, or reliance on the validity of the results that a study came from, and more attentive to the auditable line of reasoning that mindful researchers display in demonstrating how they came to the interpretive conclusions that were made possible on the basis of deep cross-comparative inquiry (Sandelowski, 2008; Thorne, 2019).

THE CONDUCT OF QUALITATIVE METASYNTHESIS

Having read to this point, you will easily recognize that there can be no singular methodological approach to inquiry processes that aim to do such different things. Thus, the conduct of a qualitative metasynthesis study requires a series of choices along the way. If you are new to the process, the instinct is to search out the most straightforward guide, and follow it meticulously. I have already pointed you in the direction of where such guides exist. However, you do run the risk of your study being relegated to the heap of qualitative metasynthesis reports that are routinely rejected by top journals in your field on the basis that they offer nothing further to an understanding of the literature than a reasonably informed scholar could have gained from an afternoon reading any collection of recent publications in the field. In other words, if hundreds

of intriguing studies have been conducted on your topic, and you have selected only 10 of the most similar and reported only their most common results, scholars with any knowledge of the field (i.e., your journal peer reviewers) will have difficulty seeing the value in the exercise beyond demonstrating that you can read and follow a manual. As Malterud (2019) put it, "qualitative metasynthesis is supposed to have an interpretive ambition beyond renarration" (2019, p. 16).

In the following discussion, I invite you into thinking about qualitative metasynthesis as a potentially useful form of inquiry, something that can illuminate hidden insights in a body of literature, critically comment on what has gone on between the lines of text and in the interspaces between the studies, and a final written product that adds value to the way something is interpreted, worked with, or theorized within your discipline and beyond. I firmly believe that a well-done qualitative metasynthesis can become a gem that stands out in the literature, representing a truly meaningful new contribution, and one that can shift perception and direction in the field. Over a period of 14 years serving as associate editor for metasynthesis for the popular journal *Qualitative Health Research*, I reviewed hundreds of "meta" submissions and had a privileged window into the evolution of reviewer perceptions as to their worth. Increasingly, those that truly had something new to say were capable of doing so on the basis of idiosyncratic methodological decisions they explained to their readers along the way, not simply relying on a protocol. And by engaging their readers in the twists and turns that always characterize a good detective story, showing that they clearly understood their craft, they aligned what they thought they had to contribute with the path they had taken to get us there.

Posing a Question

The first step in any research is posing a question. Although that sounds straightforward, it is anything but. You will likely have a general idea of the issue you are concerned with or the body of knowledge within which you want to propose a metasynthesis, but in this kind of work, it is expected that you will fine tune and clarify the precise focus along the way.

To begin the process of deciding for what you are looking, you need to familiarize yourself with the literature. The paradox is that you do need an understanding of what is out there before you can know whether the specific question you ask makes sense, given the existing body of published qualitative research on your topic. As Malterud (2019) explained, you are aiming to develop a research question that is "both flexible and determined" (p. 22), meaning that it is not only sufficiently flexible to allow you to approach most of the research literature within the area you want to explore but also specific enough for your ultimate synthesis project to contribute something beyond a "catalogue of what is already known" (p. 23). As you become increasingly well informed by what the body of literature does and does not contain, you can work on refining your question so that it will guide you through that jungle of existing research toward meaningful decisions on what to include and what to do with it. In this manner, the research question for this kind of study, much like the question you develop for any qualitative investigation, is best considered "more like a compass than an anchor" (Eakin & Mykhalovskiy, 2003, p. 190).

Setting Your Aperture

As you work on refining your question informed by what you are finding in your searches through the literature, you will want to be mindful of how comprehensive or focused you intend to be in your metasynthesis or, said differently, how much light you will let in on the subject at hand. As is the case with any qualitative study, there are validity threats associated with going too big or too small. When samples are overly large, they preclude the intensive kind of analysis that can yield meaningful findings and force your attention toward the more quantifiable or superficial aspects of a body of studies. When they are overly small, whatever useful insights you uncover about them may not reflect anything useful about the field.

One consideration in determining your focus is whether you are seeking to synthesize qualitative

findings of a similar nature or to explore what can be learned from a diversity of qualitative methods and approaches. In the early days of qualitative metasynthesis, some researchers assumed it would make better sense to narrow the focus to phenomenological studies, or grounded theory studies, for example. However, since methodological cultures are incredibly diverse across scholarly communities and disciplines, it is unwise to consider that all studies that purport to a particular methodological tradition actually look alike, or that those who claim different methodologies are all that different. For the most part, you will find it difficult enough to discern which studies reflect sufficiently inductively derived findings to count as qualitative that you don't want to add to the challenge by having to enforce exclusionary rules on definitions of method that irritate your readers and likely delimit your findings to the point that you are reporting on too few studies of too similar a nature to have anything to offer to the wider field.

You may also need to consider the disciplinary perspective of the body of studies you are seeking to review. Here again, there is no right answer, but it is important to reflect on how you might justify your decision. If you stick to your own discipline's body of work, then you are orienting your findings toward what your discipline thinks about a phenomenon, not what that phenomenon might look like more broadly. Your decision here determines which databases you search, which journals you look to, and how you interpret what you find. And while it sounds straightforward to expect to know the disciplinary angle of vision from which the individual studies are directed, of course it is not. Journals differ in terms of what they reveal about authors, and many research teams are interdisciplinary.

Language is certainly another consideration. If you are not fluent in multiple languages, you need to limit your scope. While digital translation of an abstract can help you determine whether a study looks interesting, such systems are not sufficiently sophisticated to allow you to catch the nuances of a qualitative research report in a language you don't understand. You also need to make the decision as to whether you are looking to synthesize that which is only published in peer review venues, or whether you are open to exploring the "gray" or "fugitive" literature produced outside of the traditional academic and publishing channels. Dissertations and theses, which can easily escape notice, can be an excellent source of insight into the inner workings of a study; however, they may be difficult to access and may complicate the challenge associated with comparing and contrasting research products that appear in such various lengths and depths.

Beyond these considerations, you should consider any number of possibilities for setting boundaries on your focus and delimiting your search. For example, in relation to your phenomenon of interest, do you want to delimit or leave open the timeframe? Going back as far as is recorded can provide a marvelous perspective on changes in thinking within a field of study, while staying within a window of recent studies can give you a snapshot in time. The answer may lie in your sense of whether you need to be concerned more with what a field of study looks like today or whether you are intrigued as to why it has become that way. You also need to consider what Sandelowski (2012) called the "permeable boundaries" of the kinds of phenomena that we tend to study qualitatively. The more you immerse yourself in critical reflection on the qualitative literature in your field, the more relevant options you are likely discover. If you bound yourself tightly within a particular manifestation of a phenomenon without considering the occasions in which it might have arisen coexistent with other phenomena in the literature, you may miss out on the marvelous complexity that is what inspires the qualitative enterprise in the first place.

As Brinkmann et al. (2014) observed, "qualitative research does not represent a monolithic, once-and-for-all, agreed-upon approach to research but is a vibrant and contested field with many contradictions and different perspectives" (p. 17). While there are no straightforward answers to these questions as to what you do and do not include in your ultimate synthesis, thinking them through and making note of your decisions (at least for now) help focus your sense of what you are intending and how you set the boundaries for your project. They will help you think through how much variation you can welcome (or tolerate) within the set of primary studies you ultimately include. And be prepared for the possibility that you may need to change your mind about one or more of these decisions as your insight about the nature of what is there in the literature and what is there to be learned through metasynthesis becomes increasingly astute through the process.

Search and Retrieval

Once you have a preliminary set of decisions with respect to your question and focus, you are ready to create a search strategy. You may find the PICO (population-intervention-comparison-outcome), which is popular in the systematic review literature, to be a useful starting point (Higgins & Green, 2011). However, as the purpose of your project is to synthesize knowledge about human phenomena rather than to calculate effects, it may not be particularly useful in qualitative metasynthesis (Booth, 2016). Another approach, known as SPIDER (sample, phenomenon of interest, design, evaluation, research type), may be more applicable to the synthesis of qualitative studies (Cooke et al., 2012). And while it may ultimately be helpful to report that you used one of these approaches, they serve more as a general guide than a comprehensive list, as your sense of appropriate delineations for your study evolves.

In general, you are aiming to use search terms that are precise, and in logical sequence, and to use them intelligently. Keyword listings such as can be found in major literature databases such as PubMed can help you determine the terms that have gained official status and are, therefore, most likely to be relevant. However, never forget that keyword usage has evolved over time, and the original authors will have been operating on the basis of what they knew then. Because of that, be aware that indexing is often insufficient and faulty and highly dependent on a researcher's grasp on the available options. If your topic is not one for which a standard lexicon is predictable, you may want to try "wisely chosen significant expressions from the text of an article" to search for similar text in other sources (Malterud, 2019, p. 30).

For this kind of research, you will likely want to draw on the skills of an experienced research librarian to assist you with operators (e.g., AND, OR, NOT) and using terms with plural forms and different truncations or closing forms (e.g., «emotion$»). You may want to choose filters for such features as publication year or methodology. However, don't assume that filters always mean what you think they will mean. For example, while more recent studies may appear to have better methodological quality than will earlier studies, historic results may not have been as fettered by the standardizing conventions that have stripped many qualitative products of their richness and texture. As has been alluded to earlier, the historical lines within a body of research can also reveal the footprints of dialogues between various researchers that have worked within the field at different points and for different reasons over time (Thorne, 2017).

As you develop your search strategy, you will typically find that it needs multiple refinements, as you see what a particular search yields and as you become increasingly familiar with how to think about what you are trying to study. You need to be conscious of trying not to search out too much or too little—what Sandelowski (2012) described as balancing the optimal level of *specificity* with the optimal level of *sensitivity*. Given the number of decision points along the way, it is essential to document your search strategy so that you can recreate your logic when some aspect of it arises later on (such as in the manuscript review process when you try to publish). Readers do expect a search strategy to be comprehensive and reproducible (Booth, 2016; Tong et al., 2012). However, for this kind of work, it is important to remember that there is no perfect way to do this. Given the number and nature of the decisions and justifications you need to make along the way, regardless of whether your protocol is tight or more exploratory, metasynthesis is not the sort of work that you would expect another scholar to precisely duplicate, even with an almost identical research question. As you variously

narrow or expand your focus in this process, your decision trail, therefore, becomes an essential part of your internal audit and helps you explain what was included and excluded and why as your process continues.

Beyond what can be accomplished using electronic database searches, you inevitably need to expand your search using more manual processes. Among the processes used by most researchers doing qualitative metasynthesis work are mining the references listed in the literature you find on your selected topic for sources you may have missed—steps known as *footnote chasing* or *backward chaining* (Cooper, 2010). You may also need to do *forward chaining* to find other works that contain the citation to your article to see if any constitute related works. Hand searching through the most likely journals in your field may also surface studies that slipped through the net of your search engine. This is also the case for material published in anthologies, as it may not have been indexed in a manner that makes them as accessible as those in scholarly journals. Finally, you may want to consider author searching as a way of tracking down additional publications that may have come from the work of the same individual or team.

Although more will be said when we delve into data management, it is important to understand that a search will identify exponentially more "hits" than you will ultimately make use of in the metasynthesis data analysis and interpretation to come. The *data extraction* process is one of winnowing down a large volume of potentially relevant pieces of scholarship into those that serve your ultimate criteria. Some of the initial screening will be conducted through the database search strategy, but from there much more must be done by human decision making, first through a review of titles, then abstracts, then full manuscripts or documents. This becomes a series of exclusion processes, sorting out which of the many pieces of material are not useful, appropriate, or relevant to your ultimate collection. You may find duplicate reports of the same study and somewhat related studies that may or may not fit. While some studies may be clearly unrelated to your focus of interest, many others may be partially related, albeit not quite what you expected. In such cases, you may find you need to read them in full to be able to confidently conclude whether they should be excluded or whether there might be a critically important "gem" hidden within. While classic systematic review relies on a tightly controlled protocol, decisions around qualitative study reports are rarely so straightforward. You may have to adjust along the way, and document your evolving criteria and decision points. Often it is wise to have more than one researcher review along the way, as a "conformity check" helps you see if there is a resemblance when two interpretations of a set of criteria are compared and revealed. When discrepancies surface, as they often do, it is ideal to have dialogue among your team members to help determine a consensus and articulate a logic by which you came to it.

The Place of Quality Criteria

Among the more contentious of the decisions you need to make along the way is when and how to deal with quality criteria of the primary qualitative studies on your topic. It seems self-evident that you will want to exclude weak or problematic studies, and indeed the exclusion of "flawed" studies, in a process that is independent of their findings, is a hallmark of integrity for synthesis work in the quantitative world (Greenhalgh, 1997). To address this, various authors and groups have sought to develop and enforce consistent reporting standards for qualitative as well as quantitative studies. Therefore, when authors submit to certain journals, they are typically asked to confirm, via various checklists, their compliance with various aspects that are believed to be common across most qualitative research processes. Among the most frequently encountered are Consolidated Criteria for Reporting Qualitative Research (COREQ; Tong et al., 2007) and Critical Appraisal Skills Programme (CASP; 2013); however, as Santiago-Delefosse et al. (2016) learned when they attempted to evaluate 58 of such existing guidelines across four major health science fields (medicine and epidemiology, nursing and health education, social sciences and public

health, psychology/psychiatry research methods and organization), although they were able to name 12 consensual criteria, there was limited consensus on the way in which many of them were defined across fields of study. Therefore, it is clear that there is considerable variation in how different disciplines that may be contributing to the growing body of qualitative health research literature explain, enact, and report on the attributes that are most likely to be considered in a quality assessment.

Adding a further complication, in the domain of qualitative research literature, the quality of what was actually done is typically inferred from the quality of reporting (Carroll et al., 2012), and, therefore, exclusion on the basis of what appear to be quality criteria can reflect an artifact of journal style constraints, disciplinary methodological reporting preferences, or other factors that are not terribly relevant to whether a study was well conducted and is worth including. Compounding this is the reality that the uptake of checklists as reporting standards has been gradual and is not universal; therefore, it will have affected newer research and that which is published in journals relying on such systems. It is easy to see how an unconscious bias against that which is differently reported could lead to an overly delimited body of material for qualitative metasynthesis.

Given these complexities of reporting standards as a proxy for quality criteria, researchers engaged in a qualitative metasynthesis project encounter something of a dilemma in terms of how they think about and enact a quality appraisal on the body of studies that have passed the test of relevancy. As Malterud (2019) pointed out, we need to remember that high scores on checklists do not guarantee that the article presents rich and sustainable results, and similarly, low scores may mean that the study was conducted in a time, place, or discipline for which the expectations of the current reporting world did not apply. Perhaps the most obvious element would be the reporting standard for evidence of ethical review; the fact that some national systems do not provide review for nonintervention studies in no way implies that the studies done by scholars in those countries are unethical. Although it may seem the path of least resistance to eliminate any studies that rank particularly low on the assessment scale, many researchers doing qualitative metasynthesis work have discovered that their findings may be highly relevant to the ultimate synthesis interpretations, and eliminating them would detract from the ultimate product. Thus, while the checklists appear to be a reasonable window into the conduct of qualitative research for the purpose of quality appraisal, it is also apparent that they "over-simplify and standardize the complex and non-formulaic nature of qualitative inquiry" (Eakin & Mykhalovskiy, 2003, p. 187). More importantly, these authors say, "the guidelines' concern with procedural correctness restricts the reader's field of vision on the research process and diverts attention away from the analytic content of the research" (p. 192).

Once the distinction between reporting and quality measures in this kind of research is understood, the business of quality assessment requires careful thought and judgment. What is called for is a critical assessment of the actual conduct of the study, to the extent that it can be discerned and interpreted from the written report (Dixon-Woods et al., 2004) and the degree to which the interpretations and propositions arising from the research "are (or are not) produced and rendered convincing by the research practices used" (Eakin & Mykhalovskiy, 2003, p. 192). This, of course, makes it "quintessentially qualitative" form of assessment.

What the researcher doing the metasynthesis really needs to know about the studies under consideration has to do with the integrity of their accounts, the skill with which the author has demonstrated such characteristics as the authenticity of the subjective meanings they report, and their responsiveness to social context (Popay et al., 1998). Thus, what is called for is something of a compound judgment, or a determination of whether a study has sufficient "information power" to be justifiably included (Malterud, 2019). For this reason, and in recognition of these paradoxes, many authors are now

reporting that they conducted appraisals according to a specific checklist but failed to exclude any studies on the basis of their score. It seems a reasonable compromise to be able to respond to the inevitable reviewer inquiry on the basis of current trends but to retain an integrity to the nature and purpose of this kind of scholarship.

Data Management

As you begin to winnow down the possible body of studies to the set you ultimately include in your analysis, you need to create tracking and display systems to help you work with them. Among the most characteristic elements of a synthesis, including a qualitative meta-synthesis is a flowsheet that reports on some of the background steps in your selection process. PRISMA (preferred items for systematic review and meta-analyses; Moher et al., 2009) is the most popular version. Some journals publish the PRISMA flowsheet as a table within a study; others include it as supplementary information. But it is important to remember that it only records the numeric indicators of the decision trail, not the reasoning that went into the decisions.

Just as you need to think about sorting and coding to manage a qualitative data set, you need to establish a display mechanism within which you can visualize key features of the set of studies you have decided warrant inclusion in your collection. Most authors find it helpful to develop a table that systematizes the hallmarks of each primary study included. These may include the basic features that have relevance to your tracking and ultimately to your analysis and synthesis, such as first author name, year, country, title, design data collection, context, and relevant study population characteristics (Malterud, 2019). This table helps to serve in much the same manner that your overview of demographic data might serve you in a primary qualitative study.

The year of publication becomes especially important when your purpose is a critical reflection on how the body of current research came to be. It helps you reflect on who has read what, and where the cross-fertilization of thinking may or may not have occurred in explaining some of the variations across what is currently being reported. Some researchers reporting on qualitative meta-synthesis projects make what I consider to be a logical error in their reporting, adding up the study populations of all of the studies included, and reporting as if you have a study population of that size. This kind of reporting may well exaggerate the effect of study size differences, as larger studies may quickly gloss over individual differences while smaller ones tap each study participant in considerable depth. Sample size is certainly among the factors about which you want to think critically when you reflect on what it is that can be learned from the findings of a study as reported, but it is never the case that larger samples necessarily mean more comprehensive, coherent, or even plausible findings in a qualitative product. Many authors writing about qualitative metasynthesis encourage you to categorize your studies by method. It is important to remember, however, that your authors do not necessarily "speak the same language" in terms of how they characterize their work (Creswell, 2013; Sandelowski & Barroso, 2007). As you familiarize yourself with the variations within the body of work you are investigating, you may find a suitable way to consistently group them, but don't try too hard to squeeze them into a schema that feels like a force fit as the effort may not be worth any potential benefit (Sandelowski & Barroso, 2003a). In many of the aspects in which you need to be analyzing and interpreting them, you may be better off thinking of them as individuals, and if you do ultimately conclude that they are best considered in groupings, they are more likely to be by virtue of the nature of the findings than by their methods.

Beyond the more technical features of the studies in your synthesis collection, you may also want to develop a mechanism for data (i.e., findings) extraction. This allows you to display in some form the key findings that you want to be able to capture in your ongoing analysis process, so that your mind can work with what you need. Although it is always the case that the full meaning of an excerpt or an idea is best under-stood in the context of the study from which it

came, you need to be able to cross reference and compare and require some mechanism by which to track the major features and their origins, taking care always to try to capture meaning, rather than strip it out. As is the case with coding in primary qualitative research, being too quick to slap a meaning term onto a piece of data (or an idea arising from a set of findings) can make it difficult to keep your mind open to new and emerging possibilities for it. Thus, your scheme for tracking what is relevant about the data (indexing, sorting, and displaying) should be set up in a manner that stimulates your inductive analytic juices as you move forward with seeing what the body of studies might reveal.

A final note about finding the findings. Although it might seem self-evident that these would be located in the section of a published report entitled "results" or "findings," you need to assess critically the full report more broadly to be sure (Sandelowski & Barroso, 2002). Although you will be trying to focus your thinking on the results of the study, what is reported here may at times be almost indistinguishable from the preconceptions with which the author went into the study. In some instances, authors build reference to other authors into their report of findings, making it difficult to know whether the inductively derived insight prompted the look to the literature or the other way around (Malterud, 2019; Sandelowski, 2008). And while you may be trying to distinguish between results and the author's commentary about them (interpretations and reflections for example), sometimes these are the place where what constitutes truly interesting findings actually come to light.

Analysis Versus Synthesis

Once you have your data set searched, selected, appraised, and managed, you are ready to begin analysis proper. As Malterud (2019) observed, the basic seven-step process that Noblit and Hare (1988) first reported in relation to meta-ethnography seems to generally characterize much of what is done in most varieties of qualitative metasynthesis. It also parallels the kind of general principles most often associated with rigorous qualitative analysis, so is indicative of the typical manner in which inductive findings are coaxed out of a set of data. However, thinking through and trying to articulate how you intend to approach your analysis is a wise move, so that you don't fall prey to some of the classic analytic hazards along the way, such as being overly attracted to the "bright and shiny objects" in the data set or drawing inappropriate inferences on the basis of the frequency with which certain ideas are mentioned (Thorne & Darbyshire, 2005). In addition, you want to always keep in mind that you are not observing the phenomenon in question directly, but rather, as Sandelowski and Barroso (2007) expressed it, human experience "thrice removed" (p. xvi).

By this point in the process, you likely have a better sense of what you have and what you might be able to do with it than you had at the outset of your study. As your thinking about the project becomes more refined and informed by the steps you have taken to get here, you should be able to come to a more reasoned determination of whether your primary focus ought to be analysis or synthesis. As with most research, the better approach is to take things apart before you can decide whether putting them back together again adds value to the ultimate report. And although most researchers embarking on a qualitative metasynthesis imagine their end product to be a complete and wholly integrated new synthesis, that is rarely as straightforward as it might seem. If you focus your attention on synthesis too early, you generally end up searching for like entities and then simply adding them up—creating the "meta-aggregations" I referenced earlier. In order to allow yourself to move beyond those kinds of (sometimes irrelevant and meaningless) reports, a thorough and in-depth analytic process will serve you well.

The ideal approach to analysis is to be reflective critically and look at your data set from every imaginable angle. Ask yourself questions about how each original report has fit into a sequence of evolving knowledge. Consider why studies have been done in some communities (e.g., nations, disciplines) and not others. Reflect on what theoretical and/or methodological scaffolding the various authors may have brought into their studies that allowed for illumination of some features of the phenomenon while also potentially obscuring others.

Often, when you engage in this kind of deeply reflective analysis of a body of studies, you find you learn a great deal about the data set but possibly also find yourself less and less confident about what a credible synthetic conclusion might be (Paterson et al., 2001). So although it may seem odd to have to get to this stage of a process before you can feel truly comfortable with knowing what it is you are doing with your research, that tends to be how it feels when you are allowing the process to remain sufficiently open to have done it well. A qualitative metasynthesis is much more than simply a summary and renarration of what has previously been reported (Malterud, 2019). It is supposed to lead us toward something different, and become more than the sum of its parts (Riese et al., 2014). So, if there is no particularly meaningful synthesis you can generate on the basis of the set of studies you arrived at, don't stretch it to claim that there is. Such claims are not credible to your informed readership and do not serve you well in the arena of ongoing critical scrutiny. Instead, stick with the "deconstruction" at which you can arrive after interrogating and cross-interrogating your body of material. Figure out (hypothesize, and follow along with a course of detective work) why certain patterns within it have emerged, and even speculate about what the circuitous history of the qualitative knowledge development in this field may have contributed to the insights we collectively hold about it today. From my experience in the qualitative metasynthesis world, there are always stories to be told if you ask enough questions—but not always the ones that you thought you would end up telling. Because the topics within which we do qualitative inquiry are so inherently interesting, and the terrain of qualitative methodology is itself so complex and various, if your conclusions are not about the human phenomena you thought you were studying, they will be equally useful about the study of it.

Writing It Up

There are innumerable available approaches to writing up your qualitative metasynthesis report, and itemizing them goes well beyond the scope of this chapter. However, you will find a helpful explanation in Sandelowski and Barroso's (2007) *Handbook for Synthesizing Qualitative Research*. The manner of your write-up is dependent both on what you intended to accomplish and what actually happened in the course of your analysis and synthesis. Just as an excellent piece of qualitative research writing is never formulaic in its presentation, you must decide whether your best approach should be more empirical/analytical or critical/discursive and work from there. Sandelowski (2008) recommended that you think of your metasynthesis process and your writeup of its findings as "a highly disciplined and yet still inherently subjective interaction between resisting readers and resistant texts" (p. 109). Resisting readers are your ultimate reviewers who need to be convinced by your arguments, and the resistant texts are the studies themselves, products of another researcher's attempts to use writing to convey what are often complex and fluid ideas and interpretations. From Sandelowski's perspective, this allows for "a more mindful, or reflexive, understanding of the reading and writing practices that define systematic review" (p. 109). We are not, after all, generating factual claims and new truths but rather engaging in dissecting how a scholarly community has come to know what it thinks it knows.

It is a practical reality that few scholarly journals allow publication of a full reference list that includes hundreds of sources, and fewer still are comfortable with text that is peppered with extensive lists citing each source of a particular aspect you want to discuss in your written report. Within this space, the "right way" to report on a qualitative metasynthesis is still under development. You may wish to consider the use of tables, supplementary information, and summaries of bodies of literature rather than itemized reports in order to convey your findings within the normal publication word limits of the journals in your field. Alternatively, you may be able to make the full listings available to readers with a special interest in your topic. That material is, after all, your database, and increasingly we are being asked to make databases transparent. If your study is of a size and scope that it looks like it may run into barriers with publication in the journals you think it most deserves to appear in, you may want to search recent editions for similar kinds of reports to explore how they managed it, or send an inquiry to the journal editor.

A FINAL WORD ABOUT QUALITY CRITERIA FOR THE METASYNTHESIS PRODUCT

As discussed at the outset of this chapter, there has been a rapid proliferation of publications claiming themselves to be qualitative metasynthesis reports that add nothing of particular substance or nuance to the available literature in their fields. I am heartened to see that reviewers are increasingly pointing that out and rejecting submissions that seem to have been conducted as a learning exercise in lieu of a more fulsome critical review of the literature. Further, I believe that the mystique associated with naming the product as being derived from metasynthesis terminology will be lifted as an increasingly sophisticated generation of readers learns to see a quick and dirty search, exclusion, and aggregation exercise as the technical operation it entails and not as a robust contribution to scholarship. Thoughtful scholars always see the difference.

Toward that end, I have proposed a set of questions that might be useful in the process of quality appraisal of the written reports of qualitative metasynthesis products (Thorne, 2017, p. 10):

- Are the exclusion processes justified by the explicit aims of the review?
- Have the mechanisms for data display demonstrably furthered the analytic capacity?
- Is there evidence of critical reflection on the role played by method, theoretical framework, disciplinary orientation, and local conditions in shaping the studies under consideration?
- Does the interpretation of the body of available studies reflect an understanding of the

influence of chronological sequence and advances in thought within the field over time?

- Does the synthesis tell us something about the collection of studies that we could not have known without a rigorous and systematic process of cross-interrogation?

CONCLUSION

Carefully conceptualized and crafted qualitative studies can spark the imagination, fill gaps in extant knowledge, humanize our understandings of psychosocial, behavioral, and health phenomena, and challenge the complacency that a discipline can arrive at when it has become too confident in its command of its science. Similarly, thoughtfully conceptualized and implemented qualitative metasynthesis can uncover hidden intersectional, political, and ideological influences on the body of qualitative work within a field of study and push our collective thinking to new places in what we believe we know and what we have yet to learn. In this way, qualitative metasynthesis can lift us beyond the inherent limitations of original qualitative studies, bounded as they are by time, space, and context, and afford us an aerial perspective from which we might glimpse and critically reflect upon the voices and standpoints that have shaped the way we know our world.

References

Alper, B. S., & Haynes, R. B. (2016). EBHC pyramid 5.0 for accessing preappraised evidence and guidance. *Evidence-Based Medicine, 21*(4), 123–125. https://doi.org/10.1136/ebmed-2016-110447

Barbour, R. S., & Barbour, M. (2003). Evaluating and synthesizing qualitative research: The need to develop a distinctive approach. *Journal of Evaluation in Clinical Practice, 9,* 179–186. https://doi.org/10.1046/j.1365-2753.2003.003 71.x

Bergdahl, E. (2019). Is meta-synthesis turning rich descriptions into thin reductions? A criticism of meta-aggregation as a form of qualitative synthesis. *Nursing Inquiry, 26*(1), e12273. https://doi.org/10.1111/nin.12273

Booth, A. (2016). Searching for qualitative research for inclusion in systematic reviews: A structured methodological review. *Systematic Reviews, 5*(1), 74. https://doi.org/10.1186/s13643-016-0249-x

Brinkmann, S., Jacobsen, M. H., & Kristiansen, S. (2014). Historical overview of qualitative research in the social sciences. In P. Leavy (Ed.), *The Oxford handbook of qualitative research* (pp. 17–42). Oxford University Press.

Britten, N., Campbell, R., Pope, C., Donovan, J., Morgan, M., & Pill, R. (2002). Using meta ethnography to synthesise qualitative research: A worked example. *Journal of Health Services Research & Policy, 7*(4), 209–215. https://doi.org/10.1258/135581902320432732

Carroll, C., Booth, A., & Lloyd-Jones, M. (2012). Should we exclude inadequately reported studies from qualitative systematic reviews? An evaluation of sensitivity analyses in two case study reviews. *Qualitative Health Research, 22*(10), 1425–1434. https://doi.org/10.1177/1049732312452937

Chalmers, I. (1993). The Cochrane collaboration: Preparing, maintaining, and disseminating systematic reviews of the effects of health care. *Annals of the New York Academy of Sciences, 703*(1), 156–165. https://doi.org/10.1111/j.1749-6632.1993.tb26345.x

Chandler, J., & Hopewell, S. (2013). Cochrane methods—Twenty years experience in developing systematic review methods. *Systematic Reviews, 2*(1), 76. https://doi.org/10.1186/2046-4053-2-76

Cochrane, A. L. (1972). *Effectiveness and efficiency: Random reflections on health services.* Nuffield Trust.

Cochrane, A. L. (1989). *Effectiveness and efficiency: Random reflections on health services.* The Royal Society of Medicine Press. (Original work published 1972)

Cooke, A., Smith, D., & Booth, A. (2012). Beyond PICO: The SPIDER tool for qualitative evidence synthesis. *Qualitative Health Research, 22*(10), 1435–1443. https://doi.org/10.1177/1049732312452938

Cooper, H. (2010). *Research synthesis and meta-analysis: A step-by-step approach* (4th ed.). SAGE.

Creswell, J. W. (2013). *Qualitative inquiry and research design: Choosing among five approaches* (3rd ed.). SAGE.

Critical Appraisal Skills Programme [CASP]. (2013). *CASP qualitative research checklist: 10 questions to help you make sense of qualitative research.* https://casp-uk.net/wp-content/uploads/2018/01/CASP-Qualitative-Checklist-2018.pdf

Dixon-Woods, M., Booth, A., & Sutton, A. J. (2007). Synthesizing qualitative research: A review of published reports. *Qualitative Research, 7*(3), 375–422. https://doi.org/10.1177/1468794107078517

Dixon-Woods, M., Shaw, R. L., Agarwal, S., & Smith, J. A. (2004). The problem of appraising qualitative research. *Quality & Safety in Health*

Care, 13(3), 223–225. https://doi.org/10.1136/qshc.2003.008714

Eakin, J. M., & Mykhalovskiy, E. (2003). Reframing the evaluation of qualitative health research: Reflections on a review of appraisal guidelines in the health sciences. Journal of Evaluation in Clinical Practice, 9(2), 187–194. https://doi.org/10.1046/j.1365-2753.2003.00392.x

Eden, J., Levit, L., Berg, A., & Morton, S. (2011). Finding what works in health care: Standards for systematic reviews. National Academies Press.

Egger, M., Smith, G. D., & Altman, D. (2008). Systematic reviews in health care: Meta-analysis in context. Wiley.

Estabrooks, C., Field, P., & Morse, J. (1994). Aggregating qualitative findings: An approach to theory development. Qualitative Health Research, 4(4), 503–511. https://doi.org/10.1177/104973239400400410

Finfgeld, D. L. (2003). Metasynthesis: The state of the art—so far. Qualitative Health Research, 13(7), 893–904. https://doi.org/10.1177/1049732303253462

Furfey, P. H. (1953). The scope and method of sociology: A meta-sociological treatise. Cooper Square.

Glaser, B. G., & Strauss, A. L. (1971). Status passage. Routledge.

Greenhalgh, T. (1997). Papers that summarise other papers (systematic reviews and meta-analyses). BMJ (Clinical Research Ed.), 315(7109), 672–675. https://doi.org/10.1136/bmj.315.7109.672

Greenhalgh, T. (2004). Meta-narrative mapping: A new approach to the systematic review of complex evidence. In B. Hurwitz, T. Greenhalgh, & V. Skultans (Eds.), Narrative research in health and illness (pp. 349–381). Blackwell. https://doi.org/10.1002/9780470755167.ch21

Greenhalgh, T. (2012). Outside the box: Why are Cochrane reviews so boring? The British Journal of General Practice, 62(600), 371. https://doi.org/10.3399/bjgp12X652418

Greenhalgh, T., Robert, G., Macfarlane, F., Bate, P., Kyriakidou, O., & Peacock, R. (2005). Storylines of research in diffusion of innovation: A meta-narrative approach to systematic review. Social Science & Medicine, 61(2), 417–430. https://doi.org/10.1016/j.socscimed.2004.12.001

Greenhalgh, T., Thorne, S., & Malterud, K. (2018). Time to challenge the spurious hierarchy of systematic over narrative reviews? European Journal of Clinical Investigation, 48(6), e12931. https://doi.org/10.1111/eci.12931

Higgins, J. P., & Green, S. (2011). Cochrane handbook for systematic reviews of interventions (Vol. 4). John Wiley & Sons.

Hinds, P. S., Vogel, R. J., & Clarke-Steffen, L. (1997). The possibilities and pitfalls of doing a secondary analysis of a qualitative data set. Qualitative Health Research, 7(3), 408–424. https://doi.org/10.1177/104973239700700306

Ioannidis, J. P. (2016). The mass production of redundant, misleading, and conflicted systematic reviews and meta-analyses. The Milbank Quarterly, 94(3), 485–514. https://doi.org/10.1111/1468-0009.12210

Jensen, L., & Allen, M. (1996). Metasynthesis of qualitative findings. Qualitative Health Research, 6(4), 553–560. https://doi.org/10.1177/104973239600600407

Kearney, M. H. (2001). New directions in grounded formal theory. In R. Schreiber & P. N. Stern (Eds.), Using grounded theory in nursing (pp. 227–246). Springer.

Lockwood, C., Porrit, K., Munn, Z., Rittenmeyer, L., Salmond, S., Bjerrum, M., Loveday, H., Carrier, J., & Stannard, D. (2017). Systematic reviews of qualitative evidence. In E. Aromataris & Z. Munn (Eds.), JBI manual for evidence synthesis. Joanna Briggs Institute. https://synthesismanual.jbi.global. https://doi.org/10.46658/JBIMES-20-03

Lockwood, C., Porrit, K., Munn, Z., Rittenmeyer, L., Salmond, S., Bjerrum, M., Loveday, H., Carrier, J., & Stannard, D. (2019). Systematic reviews of qualitative evidence. In E. Aromataris & Z. Munn (Eds.), Joanna Briggs Institute reviewer's manual. The Joanna Briggs Institute. Available from https://reviewersmanual.joannabriggs.org/

Malterud, K. (2019). Qualitative metasynthesis: A research method for medicine and health sciences. Routledge. https://doi.org/10.4324/9780429026348

McCormick, J., Rodney, P., & Varcoe, C. (2003). Reinterpretations across studies: An approach to meta-analysis. Qualitative Health Research, 13(7), 933–944. https://doi.org/10.1177/1049732303253480

Moher, D., Liberati, A., Tetzlaff, J., Altman, D. G., & the PRISMA Group. (2009). Preferred reporting items for systematic reviews and meta-analyses: The PRISMA statement. PLOS Medicine, 6(7), e1000097. https://doi.org/10.1371/journal.pmed.1000097

Noblit, G., & Hare, R. (1988). Meta-ethnography: Synthesizing qualitative studies. Sage. https://doi.org/10.4135/9781412985000

Noyes, J., Booth, A., Cargo, M., Flemming, K., Harden, A., Harris, J., Garside, R., Hannes, K., Pantoja, T., & Thomas, J. (2020). Qualitative evidence. In J. P. T. Higgins, J. Thomas, J. Chandler, M. Cumpston, T. Li, M. J. Page, & V. A. Welch (Eds.), Cochrane handbook for systematic reviews of interventions, version 6.1. Cochrane.

Paterson, B. L., Thorne, S., Canam, C., & Jillings, C. (2001). *Meta-study of qualitative health research.* Sage. https://doi.org/10.4135/9781412985017

Popay, J., Rogers, A., & Williams, G. (1998). Rationale and standards for the systematic review of qualitative literature in health services research. *Qualitative Health Research, 8*(3), 341–351. https://doi.org/10.1177/104973239800800305

Riese, H., Carlsen, B., & Glenton, C. (2014). Qualitative research synthesis: How the whole can be greater than the sum of its parts. *Anthropology in Action: Journal for Applied Anthropology in Policy and Practice, 21*(2), 23–30. https://doi.org/10.3167/aia.2014.210204

Ritzer, G. (1991). *Metatheorizing in sociology.* Lexington Books.

Sandelowski, M. (2008). Reading, writing and systematic review. *Journal of Advanced Nursing, 64*(1), 104–110. https://doi.org/10.1111/j.1365-2648.2008.04813.x

Sandelowski, M. (2012). Metasynthesis of qualitative research. In H. Cooper, P. M. Camic, D. L. Long, A. T. Panter, D. Rindskopf, & K. J. Sher (Eds.), *APA handbook of research methods in psychology, Vol. 2. Research designs: Quantitative, qualitative, neuropsychological, and biological* (pp. 19–36). American Psychological Association. https://doi.org/10.1037/13620-002

Sandelowski, M., & Barroso, J. (2002). Finding the findings in qualitative studies. *Journal of Nursing Scholarship, 34*(3), 213–219. https://doi.org/10.1111/j.1547-5069.2002.00213.x

Sandelowski, M., & Barroso, J. (2003a). Classifying the findings in qualitative studies. *Qualitative Health Research, 13*(7), 905–923. https://doi.org/10.1177/1049732303253488

Sandelowski, M., & Barroso, J. (2003b). Creating metasummaries of qualitative findings. *Nursing Research, 52*(4), 226–233. https://doi.org/10.1097/00006199-200307000-00004

Sandelowski, M., & Barroso, J. (2007). *Handbook for synthesizing qualitative research.* Springer.

Sandelowski, M., Docherty, S., & Emden, C. (1997). Focus on qualitative methods. Qualitative metasynthesis: Issues and techniques. *Research in Nursing & Health, 20*(4), 365–371. https://doi.org/10.1002/(SICI)1098-240X(199708)20:4<365::AID-NUR9>3.0.CO;2-E

Santiago-Delefosse, M., Gavin, A., Bruchez, C., Roux, P., & Stephen, S. L. (2016). Quality of qualitative research in the health sciences: Analysis of the common criteria present in 58 assessment guidelines by expert users. *Social Science & Medicine, 148*, 142–151. https://doi.org/10.1016/j.socscimed.2015.11.007

Schreiber, R., Crooks, D., & Stern, P. N. (1997). Qualitative meta-analysis. In J. M. Morse (Ed.), *Completing a qualitative project: Details and dialogue* (pp. 311–326). SAGE.

Sherwood, G. (1999). Metasynthesis: Merging qualitative studies to develop nursing knowledge. *International Journal for Human Caring, 3*(1), 37–42. https://doi.org/10.20467/1091-5710.3.1.37

Thorne, S. (1994). Secondary analysis in qualitative research: Issues and implications. In J. M. Morse (Ed.), *Critical issues in qualitative research methods* (pp. 263–279). SAGE.

Thorne, S. (2017). Metasynthetic madness: What kind of monster have we created? *Qualitative Health Research, 27*(1), 3–12. https://doi.org/10.1177/1049732316679370

Thorne, S. (2019). On the evolving world of what constitutes qualitative synthesis. *Qualitative Health Research, 29*(1), 3–6. https://doi.org/10.1177/1049732318813903

Thorne, S., & Darbyshire, P. (2005). Land mines in the field: A modest proposal for improving the craft of qualitative health research. *Qualitative Health Research, 15*(8), 1105–1113. https://doi.org/10.1177/1049732305278502

Thorne, S., Jensen, L., Kearney, M. H., Noblit, G., & Sandelowski, M. (2004). Qualitative metasynthesis: Reflections on methodological orientation and ideological agenda. *Qualitative Health Research, 14*(10), 1342–1365. https://doi.org/10.1177/1049732304269888

Tong, A., Flemming, K., McInnes, E., Oliver, S., & Craig, J. (2012). Enhancing transparency in reporting the synthesis of qualitative research: ENTREQ. *BMC Medical Research Methodology, 12*(1), 181. https://doi.org/10.1186/1471-2288-12-181

Tong, A., Sainsbury, P., & Craig, J. (2007). Consolidated criteria for reporting qualitative research (COREQ): A 32-item checklist for interviews and focus groups. *International Journal for Quality in Health Care, 19*(6), 349–357. https://doi.org/10.1093/intqhc/mzm042

Weed, M. (2005). "Meta interpretation": A method for the interpretive synthesis of qualitative research. *Forum Qualitative Sozialforschung/Forum: Qualitative. Social Research, 6*(1), 37.

Zhao, S. (1991). Metatheory, metamethod, meta-data-analysis: What, why and how? *Sociological Perspectives, 34*(3), 377–390. https://doi.org/10.2307/1389517

Zimmer, L. (2006). Qualitative metasynthesis: A question of dialoguing with texts. *Journal of Advanced Nursing, 53*(3), 311–318. https://doi.org/10.1111/j.1365-2648.2006.03721.x

THEMATIC APPROACHES

CHAPTER 3

GROUNDED THEORY AND PSYCHOLOGICAL RESEARCH

Robert Thornberg, Elaine Keane, and Malgorzata Wójcik

Grounded theory (GT) is a qualitative, explorative, systematic, and data-driven research approach designed to generate a middle-range theory on the studied phenomenon. In contrast to *grand theories* that make universal claims across time and space, *middle-range theories* (Merton, 1968) have "limited scope and refer to certain societies, cultures or specific social cultures" (Kelle, 2019, p. 82). In the GT tradition, a middle-range theory means that the constructed theory is delimited to a social phenomenon such as, for example, everyday coping with social anxiety, negotiating social roles in particular workplaces, bystander intervention in school bullying, problem-solving processes in certain small groups, living with anorexia nervosa, and managing student misbehavior in classrooms.

GT is particularly helpful for examining individual, social psychological, organizational and wider social processes, interaction patterns, and participants' actions, interpretations, and understandings (Charmaz, 2006, 2014; Thornberg & Charmaz, 2012, 2014; Thornberg & Keane, 2022). By being explorative and data-driven, this method is usually described in the literature as an inductive method (e.g., Glaser, 1978; Glaser & Strauss, 1967). *Induction* here means that the researcher examines empirical and individual

cases or instances to interpret patterns and make general statements, which are grounded in data but always considered as hypothetical and provisional. GT is, however, driven not only by induction but also abduction, which is acknowledged by a growing number of GT researchers as a significant logic of inquiry (Bryant, 2017; Charmaz, 2014; Clarke et al., 2018; Flick, 2018; Reichertz, 2019; Thornberg, 2012; Thornberg & Keane, 2022).

Abduction refers to a selective and creative process in which the researchers carefully examine which hypothesis explains a particular case or part of data better than any other. It is akin to working as a detective in a search for patterns and best possible understandings and explanations (Bryant, 2009; Carson, 2009; Eco & Sebeok, 1988; Lipton, 2007; Thornberg, 2022; Truzzi, 1976). The logic of inquiry in GT can, therefore, be considered as an interplay between induction and abduction, in which the grounded theorist moves back and forth between both during the whole research process (Charmaz et al., 2018; Thornberg & Charmaz, 2012, 2014; for further reading on induction and abduction, see Kennedy & Thornberg, 2018; Thornberg, 2022).

GT research is also an *iterative* process, which means that data collection and analysis take place

https://doi.org/10.1037/0000319-003
APA Handbook of Research Methods in Psychology, Second Edition: Vol. 2. Research Designs: Quantitative, Qualitative, Neuropsychological, and Biological, H. Cooper (Editor-in-Chief)

in parallel and inform each other. The researcher moves back and forth between gathering and analyzing data. By being a *systematic* method, GT offers a set of rigorous yet flexible guidelines to collect and analyze data. Bryant (2017) argued that systematic should not be confused with recipe-like, mechanical operations but should be understood as "an approach to research that is most certainly not ad hoc, but on the contrary is guided by well-founded activities that have been clearly articulated in the form of a set of heuristics or rules-of-thumb" (p. 90). This, in turn, calls for an active, *sensitive,* and *reflexive* researcher. Grounded theorists need to be open-minded, curious, empathic and sensitive toward the field and the participants.

In this chapter, we first trace the development of GT and its versions. From a constructivist GT perspective, we then examine the role of the literature review. Moving on to data collection, we emphasize the central role of theoretical sampling in GT and consider the various stages of coding and the function of memo-writing throughout the research process. We end by considering criteria for quality in GT studies.

THE DEVELOPMENT OF GROUNDED THEORY

GT was originally developed by sociologists Barney Glaser and Anselm Strauss in the 1960s (Glaser & Strauss, 1967) while conducting a field study on dying in hospitals (Glaser & Strauss, 1965a, 1968). They created their approach in a time when quantitative research and theorizing from the "armchair" rather than from data-dominated sociology and qualitative research had become increasingly marginalized. Glaser and Strauss, therefore, needed to justify their qualitative and theory-generating approach. While some shorter descriptions of GT had appeared in 1965 as a journal article (Glaser & Strauss, 1965b) and in an appendix of their book *Awareness of Dying* (Glaser & Strauss, 1965a), Glaser and Strauss' (1967) groundbreaking presentation of their research approach was their highly cited book *Discovery of Grounded Theory.*

According to this first textbook in GT, Glaser and Strauss intended to (a) provide explicit, systematic strategies for analyzing qualitative data; (b) counter criticisms of qualitative research as anecdotal, impressionistic, and unsystematic; (c) oppose the dominance of quantitative research in sociology; (d) demonstrate the significance of qualitative research for theory construction; and (e) question the arbitrary division of labor between theorists and researchers (Thornberg & Charmaz, 2012). Although their book is considered as the original textbook on GT, and indeed as the main presentation of the original GT, *Discovery of Grounded Theory* is actually more a manifesto arguing for and positioning Glaser and Strauss' new research approach rather than a practical handbook on how to design, plan, conduct, and report GT studies (Bryant, 2017, 2021). This created a need for a more detailed, elaborated, and hands-on statement about *how* to do GT research.

Glaser published his first textbook in the 1970s (Glaser, 1978) and has since published several books in which he put forward new concepts and procedures (e.g., Glaser, 1998, 2001, 2003, 2005, 2007, 2011). The three most important books in Glaserian GT are *Theoretical Sensitivity* (Glaser, 1978), *Doing Grounded Theory* (Glaser, 1998), and *The Grounded Theory Perspective III: Theoretical Coding* (Glaser, 2005; for a recent textbook on Glaserian GT, often termed *classic GT* by its advocates, see Holton & Walsh, 2017). Glaserian GT emphasized an objective, detached, and unbiased researcher position, induction instead of deduction and preconception (as in the original GT), and the emergence and discovery of concepts and theory by using Glaser's particular prescription of GT methods. Strauss, in turn, first presented his version of GT in the 1980s, in his book *Qualitative Analysis for Social Scientists* (Strauss, 1987) and then developed it further, together with Juliet Corbin, in two editions of their book *Basics of Qualitative Research* (Strauss & Corbin, 1990, 1998). Straussian GT involves more technical procedures, using a particular coding approach to sort data and codes into a matrix of causal, intervening and contextual conditions, actions/interactions, and consequences. In addition to induction, Straussian GT also draws on deduction and the idea of testing and confirming the emerging GT and its concepts with further data gathering. Thus, by the 1990s, two distinct versions of GT were evident: Glaserian GT and Straussian GT. After Strauss' death in 1996, Corbin continued to write about and further elaborate on Straussian GT, publishing two further editions of their book, in which their approach is presented as being less technical and more flexible (Corbin & Strauss, 2008, 2015). Corbin's contribution to this version should, therefore, be recognized, even though the term *Straussian GT* is widespread.

The earlier versions of GT have been criticized for incorporating a taken-for-granted vocabulary and research discourse of positivism, an impossible pure inductivism, a naïve realist view of data, and an objectivist researcher position (Bryant, 2017; Charmaz, 2014; Clarke, 2019; Clarke et al., 2018; Thornberg, 2012; for further reading on epistemology, see Volume 1, Chapter 1 this handbook, by Willig). There is, in fact, a common criticism of the original and Glaserian GT approaches in the literature regarding their reliance upon induction and the original ideal of an objective and neutral researcher who collects and analyses data without preconception (Alvesson & Kärreman, 2011; Thomas & James, 2006). Straussian GT rejects a tabula rasa research ideal and assumes that grounded theorists are guided by literature and move back and forth between induction and deduction. However, GT continued to develop into new versions beyond the original, Glaserian and Straussian GT approaches, particularly as a result of epistemological debates, the emergence of the constructivist or interpretative turn, the "crises of representation," and postmodernism in qualitative inquiry towards the end of the last century (Birks & Mills, 2015; Bryant & Charmaz, 2007; Clarke, 2019; Morse et al., 2009).

The sociologist Kathy Charmaz (1995, 2000, 2005, 2006, 2009, 2014) developed a third version of GT called *constructivist GT* that builds on the original, Glaserian and Straussian GTs but aims to overcome their epistemological shortcomings. It represents a major shift "from the mythical approach of discovery to the more reflexive approach of construction" (Flick, 2018, p. 11). Constructivist GT assumes that neither data nor theories are discovered but that researchers construct them as a result of their interactions with their participants and interpretations and analyses of their coconstructed data, which are always influenced by researchers' perspectives and situated in particular sociocultural contexts (Charmaz, 2006, 2009, 2014; Charmaz et al., 2018; Keane, 2015; Thornberg & Charmaz, 2012, 2014; Thornberg & Keane, 2022). From a constructivist GT perspective, researchers must understand and reflect upon how their own experiences, perspectives, values, and training, situated in particular historical, social, and cultural contexts, inform their work. Researcher positionality impacts researchers' starting points and influences data collection, interactions with participants, analysis, and writing (Charmaz, 2014, 2017; Charmaz et al., 2018; Keane, 2015, 2021; Thornberg & Keane, 2022). This version explicitly emphasizes abduction as a logic of inquiry and acknowledges pragmatism, symbolic interactionism and constructivism as its epistemological roots (Charmaz, 2009, 2014; Charmaz et al., 2018).

Charmaz (2014) stated that *symbolic interactionism*, rooted in the work of George H. Mead, Charles H. Cooley, Dorothy and William I. Thomas, Herbert Blumer, Anselm Strauss and others, is "a dynamic theoretical perspective that views human actions as constructing self, situation, and society" (p. 262) where interpretation and action affect each other in a continuous and reciprocal process. Language and symbols play a significant role in (re)constructing and sharing meanings and actions. Social groups and societies exist and have to be seen in terms of action (Blumer, 1969). According to Blumer (1969), who coined the term *symbolic interactionism*, this theoretical perspective is built upon three premises: (a) human beings act toward things (including other people, activities, practices, institutions, and situations) on the basis of the meanings that things have for them; (b) meanings are derived from, or arise out of, the social interaction human beings have with each other; and

(c) these meanings are handled in, and modified through, an interpretative process used by the person in dealing with things they encounter. Symbolic interactionism focuses on social life, action and interaction, and on how people understand and make meaning of these social processes. Blumer (1969) emphasized the importance of qualitative, exploratory research on social life where "a research scholar can form a close and comprehensive acquaintance with a sphere of social life" (p. 40) to increase the familiarity. Simultaneously, exploratory research is the means of developing and sharpening the inquiry so that the researcher's problem, "directions of inquiry, data, analytical relations, and interpretations arise out of, and remain grounded in, the empirical life under study" (Blumer, 1969, p. 40). This requires an open and sensitive involvement in the empirical world, and an iterative and flexible research procedure. Symbolic interactionism is indeed a flexible and open theoretical framework. It is "a perspective, not an explanatory theory that specifies variables and predicts outcomes" (Charmaz, 2014 p. 262; also see Charmaz et al., 2019, pp. 19–21). It offers flexible thinking tools (or what Blumer, 1969, called *sensitizing concepts*) when studying social and social psychological processes, individual and collective actions, and people's shared (and nonshared) understandings and interpretations of social actions, interactions, and practice. Therefore, symbolic interactionism helps researchers to remain open and sensitive to participants' social world, interactions, interpretations, and meanings rather than being concerned with deriving and testing prestudy hypotheses (for further readings on symbolic interactionism, see Charmaz et al., 2019; Charon, 2010; Hewitt & Shulman, 2011).

Both constructivist GT and symbolic interactionism derive from the pragmatist tradition primarily developed at the University of Chicago during the early 20th century (the so-called Chicago School), which includes pragmatist thinkers such as John Dewey, William James, Charles S. Peirce, and George H. Mead. *Pragmatism* is a philosophy of action interested in understanding human inquiry aimed at resolving problems people face in their transactions with their environment. According to Thayer-Bacon (2001, 2003), social science research that is informed by pragmatism emphasizes pluralism, an acceptance of fallibilism (that knowledge is always provisional, partial, and interpreted), and an understanding of knowledge as culturally embedded and in continual need of adjustment and readjustment and construction and reconstruction (also see Thornberg, 2022). This is related to Dewey's (1938) theory of inquiry as a social, transactional, and continuing process and truth as *warranted assertability*. Even though Dewey's position

> does assert that knowledge is a construction, it is not a construction of the human mind, but a construction that is located in the organism–environment transaction itself. What is constructed—over and over again—is the dynamic balance of organism and environment, which manifests itself both in specific changes in the environment and specific changes in the patterns of action of the organism. (Biesta & Burbules, 2003, p. 11)

Thus, knowledge is simultaneously a construction and based on reality (for further readings on pragmatism, see Biesta & Burbules, 2003; Hickman et al., 2009). Constructivist GT explores and constructs theories on the interpretative realities of participants in social settings. Constructivist GT assumes an "obdurate reality" (cf. Blumer, 1969) while also assuming multiple realities and multiple perspectives on these realities as they are subject to redefinition and are somewhat indeterminate (Bryant & Charmaz, 2007; Charmaz, 1995, 2009; for a review of differences among Glaserian GT, Straussian GT, and constructivist GT, see Thornberg, 2017).

A fourth version of GT termed *situational analysis* (SA) has been developed by the sociologist Adele E. Clarke as an extension of Straussian GT and constructivist GT, in which she has sought to push GT more fully around the "postmodern turn"

(Clarke, 2003, 2005) or the "interpretative turn" in a broad sense (Clarke et al., 2018). This means that SA draws upon postmodernism, poststructuralism, and posthumanism, in addition to pragmatism and symbolic interactionism (for a further reading on poststructuralism and postmodernism in research, see Peters & Burbules, 2004; and for a further reading on posthumanism in research, see Snaza & Weaver, 2015). Like constructivist GT, SA rejects a naïve inductivism and considers knowledge as situated, partial, provisional, and socially constructed. SA adds the method of *mapping* to describe and analyze complex, ecological, and relational situations (situations, social worlds/arenas, and positionings), as well as discursive analysis and a focus on human and nonhuman elements in the situation (Clarke, 2003, 2005; Clarke et al., 2018).

More recently explicated versions of GT include multi-GT (Freeman, 2018; Goldkuhl & Cronholm, 2010; Goldkuhl et al., 2020), discursive GT (Fairhurst & Putnam, 2019; Johnson, 2014; McCreaddie & Payne, 2010), and critical realist GT (Belfrage & Hauf, 2017; Bunt, 2018; Oliver, 2012). Numerous textbooks and manuals provide guidelines for conducting GT research (e.g., Birks & Mills, 2015; Bryant, 2017; Charmaz, 2014; Corbin & Strauss, 2015; Dey, 1999; Flick, 2018; Holton & Walsh, 2017; Stern & Porr, 2011; Tarozzi, 2020). Drawing on Wittgenstein's concept of *family resemblances*, Bryant (2017) stated that GT can be considered as a family of methods with similarities or resemblances based on core features, as well as differences and tensions between its "family members." This chapter focuses in particular upon the constructivist version of GT.

LITERATURE REVIEW IN GROUNDED THEORY

Dey (1993) argued that "there is a difference between an open mind and an empty head. To analyze data, we need to use accumulated knowledge, not dispense with it. The issue is not whether to use existing knowledge, but how" (p. 63). According to Thornberg and Dunne

(2019), there are at least three phases in conducting a literature review when doing GT research: initial, ongoing, and final literature review. The first phase is an *initial literature review* that takes place prior to and during the early stage of the research process. While the original GT (Glaser & Strauss, 1967) and Glaserian GT (e.g., Glaser, 1998, 2013) require researchers to delay the literature review until the analysis is nearly completed in order to remain open to discovery and to avoid biases and "contamination," Straussian GT (Corbin & Strauss, 2015; Strauss & Corbin, 1990, 1998), constructivist GT (Charmaz, 2014; Charmaz et al., 2018; Thornberg, 2012; Thornberg & Charmaz, 2014; Thornberg & Keane, 2022), and SA (Clarke et al., 2018) strongly advise researchers to do an initial review prior to data gathering. These grounded theorists emphasize that doing an initial literature review helps researchers to familiarize themselves with previous theories and empirical studies on the research problem and phenomenon of interest, and to gain knowledge of how the phenomenon has been examined to date, including possible gaps or contradictions in the literature. Doing an initial literature review also assists grounded theorists to further elaborate (or revise) their open-ended research problem particularly in terms of establishing a defensible rationale for the study, necessary when writing research proposals and ethical applications (Thornberg & Dunne, 2019).

The second phase is an *ongoing literature review* that occurs throughout the iterative research process of gathering and analyzing data, as it enhances researchers' sensitivity to nuances in their data (Strauss & Corbin, 1990, 1998) and assists them in remaining critical and in engaging in abductive reasoning (Thornberg, 2012). During data gathering and analysis, grounded theorists might seek to identify previous studies, theoretical concepts, and possible understandings that relate to their own emerging and constructed codes, categories, and theorizing. The ongoing literature review assists researchers in making comparisons and reviewing their data, codes, and tentative findings from different angles. It helps them to avoid "reinventing the wheel" and producing a trivial "product." At the same time, in order to remain open and sensitive to the participants and the data, researchers need to *take a theoretical agnostic and pluralistic stance*, and, thus, treat pre-existing theories and research findings as fallible, as partial and provisional interpretations, not as "truths" to be confirmed in the study (Thornberg, 2012). They have to remain noncommitted to the literature and aware of its limitations (Martin, 2006; for further reading on the rationale for doing initial and ongoing literature reviews in GT studies, see Dunne, 2011; Thornberg, 2012; Thornberg & Dunne, 2019). The third and *final literature review* takes place towards the end of the study. At this point, the grounded theorist seeks to contextualize and situate their own findings (i.e., their constructed grounded theory) in relation to the relevant literature as reference points against which to compare, contrast, and discuss their findings.

DATA COLLECTION IN GROUNDED THEORY

In terms of data collection, GT has its origins in the field research tradition (Glaser & Strauss, 1965a, 1968), which allows great flexibility in choosing data collection methods, such as ethnographic observations, informal conversations, interviews, focus groups, and document analysis. GT data collection, therefore, is not confined to a particular method; instead, the researcher chooses methods that best align with the research aim and the ongoing analysis of the data. Thus, a single GT study might be based on qualitative interviews, ethnographic field work, or a combination of methods. A constructivist position stresses that, although data gathering methods are just tools, the choice of methods has consequences: "*How* you collect data affects *which* phenomena you will see, *how, where,* and *when* you will view them, and *what* sense you will make of them" (Charmaz, 2014, p. 26). Reflexivity, flexibility, focus, and openness for further adapting, adding, or combining methods are, therefore, crucial in the research process (Charmaz et al., 2018; Thornberg & Charmaz, 2014). During the iterative GT research process, the emerging analysis may

suggest the need to use a different data collection method. This may happen, in particular, during and as a result of theoretical sampling (see the next section), which helps the GT researcher to discern gaps within and between provisional conceptual categories and suggests ways forward for the research project, in terms of what type of data is subsequently needed to explicate the emerging analysis.

INITIAL AND THEORETICAL SAMPLING

At the outset of a study, the grounded theorist conducts initial sampling to select fields and/or participants for data collection guided by the research problem. In GT, this may be a form of *convenience sampling*, which means that the researchers recruit fields and participants that are convenient and available for the study (Bryant, 2017; Flick, 2018). Convenience sampling may be followed by *snowball sampling,* meaning that participants that have already been recruited suggest others who might be of interest (Bryant, 2017).

A more sophisticated initial sampling approach is that of *purposeful sampling*, meaning that researchers choose fields and/or participants with a certain purpose in mind, seeking participants who can best answer their research question(s). Purposeful sampling is considered as a more appropriate initial sampling approach in GT (Birks & Mills, 2015; Bryant, 2017). For example, based on local knowledge or statistical data, a researcher who wishes to study disruptive behavior in a school may recruit one known to have problems with disruptive behaviors. Alternatively, purposeful sampling could be accomplished by selecting a school with a lot of behavioral problems and a school with few behavioral problems in order to be able to make comparisons from the beginning to explore similarities and differences between the different schools and their social processes with regard to the topic of the study. Such an approach is related to a kind of purposeful sampling called *open sampling* in which the grounded theorist seeks to maximize variations in experiences and descriptions by recruiting and including participants from contrasting milieux and backgrounds (Hallberg, 2006).

Continuing with the example above, imagine that the researcher starts with purposefully sampling and subsequently conducts field observations in a set of classrooms. Following analysis of their field notes, they may decide to conduct interviews with teachers. In GT, the process of data analysis evokes insights, hunches, "aha!" experiences or questions and subsequent reflections, which can lead the researcher to change the data collection method or add a new one.

At first, purposeful sampling guides further data collection in this iterative research process. Once researchers have begun to develop one or more tentative categories, the iterative process between data collection and analysis turns to gathering data to illuminate the categories, fill out their properties and define their implications and interrelations. This process is called *theoretical sampling,* "seeking and collecting pertinent data to elaborate and refine categories in your emerging theory" (Charmaz, 2014, p. 192), including defining variation within a category and specifying how categories may interrelate. Initial purposeful sampling and subsequent theoretical sampling in an iterative process of data collection and analysis prevents researchers from becoming unfocused and overwhelmed and helps them to focus on checking and refining their constructed codes and categories (Charmaz et al., 2018).

CODING

In GT, coding begins as soon as initial data are gathered and continues throughout the research process. Coding is about "naming segments of data with a label that simultaneously categorizes, summarizes, and accounts for each piece of data" (Charmaz, 2006, p. 43). Through coding, grounded theorists create codes and categories grounded in the data by scrutinizing and interacting with the data. A *code* is a label that the grounded theorist constructs to depict what is happening in a piece of data (Charmaz, 2014). Codes capture patterns or themes and can vary in levels of abstraction. A *category* in turn is a higher level code that is

more abstract (Corbin & Strauss, 2015) and has been given a conceptual definition (Charmaz, 2014).

While coding, researchers ask analytical questions and employ the *constant comparison method,* which means that they compare data with data, data with codes, codes with codes, etc., to identify similarities and differences (Glaser & Strauss, 1967). Constant comparison and memo-writing (which we consider later in this chapter) are crucial when coding (Belgrave & Seide, 2019). Bryant (2017) argued that constant comparison "lies at the heart of the iterative approach between data gathering and analysis" (p. 93), and grounded theorists engage in this method throughout the research process. According to Glaser (2011), the aim of constant comparison is to discover patterns in data to code. Corbin and Strauss (2015) argued that it helps the grounded theorist to develop concepts from data: "Data that appear to be conceptually similar are grouped together under a conceptual label" (p. 94). Charmaz (2014) stated that constant comparison is used to construct analytical distinctions and to make comparisons at each level of the analysis. According to constructivist GT, coding includes at least two phases, initial coding and focused coding (Charmaz, 2006, 2014). Coding, however, is not a linear process; due to the iterative research process, and in order to be sensitive to the field and the participants, grounded theorists move back and forth between coding phases, even though they conduct more initial coding at the start and more focused coding at the end of the study.

Initial Coding

In the *initial coding* phase, grounded theorists engage intensely with and remain close to their data, reading word by word, line by line, and paragraph by paragraph. They code line by line, with one line of data sometimes producing several codes. They ask analytic questions of their data such as "What are these data a study of?" "What category does this incident indicate?" "What is actually happening in the data?" "What is the participant's main concern(s)?" "What process(es) is at issue here?" "How can I define it?" "What do the data suggest? Pronounce? Leave unsaid?" "What is the participant taking for granted?" "What is the participant doing here?" (cf. Charmaz, 2006, 2014; Glaser, 1978, 1998).

In order to facilitate a focus on process and action in their coding, grounded theorists usually use *gerunds* (verbal nouns) when constructing code names (Charmaz, 2006; Glaser, 1978), such as "avoiding attention," "missing out on opportunities," and "feeling like an outsider." Initial codes are provisional and open to revision and refinement. Researchers keep them "short, simple, precise and active" (Charmaz et al., 2018, p. 425). Their aim is to define in summary form—critically and analytically—what is happening in the data. A core concern is that researchers' *codes fit the data*; grounded theorists stick very closely to their data during initial coding. An example of initial coding is presented in Table 3.1 from Wójcik's GT research on school bullying (Wójcik, 2018; Wójcik & Mondry, 2020; Wójcik et al., 2022). The excerpt is from an interview with a 21-year-old woman, Marta, who had been victimized for nine years during elementary school.

The initial codes remain close to the data and that Wójcik uses gerunds and, therefore, portrays a strong sense of action and process. An aim of initial coding is to capture and summarize critically and analytically what is happening in the data. Sometimes grounded theorists may need to revisit initial codes to provide more detail. Constant comparison and memo-writing during initial coding lead to the reviewing, comparing, sorting, and clustering of initial codes, which in turn results in revising some codes and combining or merging other codes that are identical or similar into new, more elaborated and comprehensive codes.

Focused Coding

By reading and rereading, comparing, further developing, and sorting initial codes, researchers identify the most significant and/or frequent codes and through *focused coding*, they bring them forward and use them to sift through large amounts of data (Charmaz, 2006, 2014). While some initial codes may be selected and brought forward as they stand, without any reformulation, new codes may also be constructed at this stage to capture a cluster of initial codes in a more elaborated, comprehensive and conceptual fashion (Charmaz et al., 2018). Thus, in focused coding, the researchers use codes identified as *focused codes* to sift through large amounts of data, as focused codes guide subsequent data collection and analysis (Charmaz, 2000, 2006, 2014).

In Wójcik's research on school bullying, an in-depth review of initial codes, using the constant comparative method of comparing and sorting codes, resulted in the identification and production of focused codes that captured larger segments of data. The example in Table 3.2 illustrates focused coding from the same interview excerpt with Marta that was considered in Table 3.1. As can be seen in Table 3.2, focused codes capture, summarize, and synthesize larger amounts of data.

As can be seen in the example above, focused codes capture and synthesize the main concerns and processes in Marta's statements. These codes were subsequently further developed as part of major categories, explicated through the process of memo-writing. Focused coding means giving these categories provisional conceptual definitions, which can be revised through further data gathering, coding, constant comparisons, and memo-writing (Charmaz, 2006, 2014). Grounded theorists engage in memo-writing (see upcoming section) throughout the research process, and it is especially important during coding phases and when constructing provisional categories. Keane (2021) argued that memo-writing is an essentially *generative* enterprise in that the analysis is further produced through writing about the constructed codes.

In addition to initial and focused coding, grounded theorists might also take advantage of Glaser's (1978, 1998, 2005) *theoretical coding* to analyze how categories and codes constructed from data might relate to each other as hypotheses to be integrated into a grounded theory. To do that, researchers inspect, choose, and use *theoretical codes* as analytical tools and lenses from a range of bodies of knowledge and theories. Theoretical codes consist of ideas, terms, abstract logics, and perspectives that help researchers to organize

TABLE 3.1

Example of Initial Coding

Initial coding	Interview data
	Int: Tell me about this time at school.
Thinking what is normal at school	Marta: I must have been 12 at that time. Everything was ok, normal days at school with
Being teased for the first time about appearance	couple of friends, sport activities, homework . . . Just normal. And one day, don't remember when exactly those three girls started to laugh at me and tease me.
	Int: What were they saying?
Ignoring first attack, thinking it is normal at school, not telling anyone	Marta: Couple of things. But at the beginning it was my appearance. Girls were laughing at my hair, but I didn't think much of it at the beginning. People laugh at each other at school. It is normal. So, I remember thinking "Well, it is ok, they will stop soon." I didn't even say anything, just ignored.
	Int: Did you mention to anyone that they were laughing at you?
Being seen as easy victim	Marta: I thought there was no need. I didn't, so they might have seen me as an easy,
More deviant features	helpless victim. Next, they hitched on my sneakers, which according
Getting irritated	to them were cheesy, and next, as I remember, my t-shirt or something. I got irritated
Blaming bullies	but still didn't worry much. I thought they were just so immature.
	Int: What do you mean "irritated"?
Realizing being different from others in class	Marta: Well, annoyed, I didn't like it. I noticed more and more that my t-shirts and sneakers and clothes were not as nice or trendy as other girls in my class. I think they were better off than me. I started to see it clearly.
	Int: You mentioned that you had a couple of friends. What did they do when girls were laughing at you?
Getting support from friends; trying to change to stop bullying (trying to fit better)	Marta: They told me to ignore stupid bullies. And I tried to. But I remember that I took my money, that I was saving for holidays, and bought a hoodie just to shut them up. Then I asked my mom to buy me new sneakers, which she did.
	Int: Did it shut them up?
Intensification of bullying; more deviant features; realizing the cumulation of negative label	Marta: No, it got worse day by day. Everyday something more. From laughing at my hair, it went to saying that I had no idea about fashion and no taste. And to ridiculing my mom as she was a cashier and other moms were doctors and managers. And then to the fact that I had no dad, but others also had just their moms. So, they were saying that I was from a poor, broken, uneducated family, and, therefore, couldn't hang out with them.
	Int: Why do you think they said that?
Doubting oneself, getting low self-confidence, starting to agree with bullies	Marta: They were kind of right.
	Int: What do you mean?
	Marta: I had awful hair, my mom was a cashier, and my family was broken. I think that even my friends started to look at me that way as they kind of distanced from me?
	Int: What do you mean "distanced"?
Being left by friends	Marta: Kind of didn't seek my company. Stopped texting me that often. That kind of thing. And also, they didn't defend me when I was attacked.
	Int: What did you do when you were attacked?
Avoiding school; feeling lonely and isolated	Marta: Nothing. Tried not to be with my class. I was very sad and unhappy, hated school and wanted to stay home. And my classmates . . . literally nobody cared. I kind of
Getting lower self-confidence; blaming oneself	wasn't the one to hang out with them. So, there was nothing I could have done to change it.

TABLE 3.2

Example of Focused Coding

Focused coding	Interview data
	Int: Tell me about this time at school.
Initial attacking	Marta: I must have been 12 at that time. Everything was ok, sport activities, homework . . .
Normalizing bullying	Just normal. And one day, don't remember when exactly those three girls started to laugh at me and tease me.
	Int: What were they saying?
Coping (ignoring)	Marta: Couple of things. But at the beginning it was my appearance. Girls were laughing at my hair, but I didn't think much of it at the beginning. People laugh at each other at school. It is normal. So, I remember thinking "Well, it is ok, they will stop soon." I didn't even say anything just ignored.
	Int: Did you mention to anyone that they were laughing at you?
Cumulating negative features	Marta: I thought there was no need. I didn't, so they might have seen me as an easy, helpless
Externally attributing bullying	victim. Next, they hitched on my sneakers, which according to them were cheesy and next, as I remember, my t-shirt or something. I got irritated but still didn't worry much. I thought they were just so immature.
	Int: What do you mean "irritated"?
Identity/self-confidence shifting	Marta: Well, annoyed, I didn't like it. I noticed more and more that my t-shirts and sneakers and clothes were not as nice or trendy as other girls in my class. I think they were better off than me. I started to see it clearly.
	Int: You mentioned that you had a couple of friends. What did they do when girls were laughing at you?
Coping (adjusting)	Marta: And I tried to. But I remember that I took my money, that I was saving for holidays, and bought a hoodie just to shut them up. Then I asked my mom to buy me new sneakers, which she did.
	Int: Did it shut them up?
Initial stage of bullying	Marta: No, it got worse day by day. Everyday something more. From laughing at my hair, it went to saying that I had no idea about fashion and no taste. And to ridiculing my mom as she was a cashier and other moms were doctors and managers. And then to the fact that I had no dad, but others also had just their moms. So, they were saying that I was from a poor, broken, uneducated family and, therefore, couldn't hang out with them.
	Int: Why do you think they said that?
Cumulating negative labels	Marta: They were kind of right.
	Int: What do you mean?
Internally attributing	Marta: I had awful hair, my mom was a cashier, and my family was broken. I think that even my
Identity/self-confidence shifting	friends started to look at me that way as they kind of distanced from me?
	Int: What do you mean "distanced"?
Full blown bullying stage	Marta: Kind of didn't seek my company. Stopped texting me that often. That kind of thing. And also, they didn't defend me when I was attacked.
	Int: What did you do when you were attacked?
Coping (remaining passive)	Marta: Nothing. Tried not to be with my class. I was very sad and unhappy, hated school and
Identity/self-confidence shifting	wanted to stay home. And my classmates . . . literally nobody cared. I kind of wasn't the one to hang out with them. So, there was nothing I could have done to change it.

and integrate their analysis into a coherent grounded theory. They suggest possible relationships between categories, "give integrative scope, broad pictures and a new perspective" (Glaser, 1978, p. 72) and can help the researcher to construct an analytic story that has coherence (Charmaz, 2006).

Glaser (1998, 2005) advised scholars to study numerous theories across various disciplines in order to identify, figure out, and learn a large number of theoretical codes embedded in theories, and to see how such codes are used. Examples of theoretical codes are causes, contexts, consequences, conditions, phases, dimensions, types, classes, strategies, goals, identity, basic social process, basic social psychological process, turning point, norms, values, shared beliefs, opposite pairs, and mutual influence (Glaser, 1978, pp. 72–82; Glaser, 1998, pp. 170–175; Glaser, 2005, pp. 21–30). Theoretical coding may be embedded more implicitly in focused coding or be conducted in a more explicit fashion in parallel and in interaction with focused coding as an iterative process (Charmaz, 2014; Charmaz et al., 2018; Thornberg & Charmaz, 2014). Keane (2021) argued that memo-writing together with diagramming constitute very useful vehicles for theoretical coding, allowing the researcher to think through the use and "fit" of theoretical codes in their emerging analysis. Implicitly or explicitly conducted, theoretical coding is a clear example of abductive reasoning in GT because researchers have to choose (or invent) and use theoretical codes *that fit the data*, that have earned their way into the analysis, and that best "conceptualize how the substantive codes may relate to each other as hypotheses to be integrated into a theory" (Glaser, 1978, p. 72).

MEMO-WRITING

While grounded theorists are gathering and coding data, they also raise new questions and come up with ideas about their codes and categories and how they might be related to each other. They write them down to remember them. According to Glaser (1978), *memos* are "the theorizing write-up of ideas about codes and their relationships as they strike the analyst while coding" (p. 83). Researchers step back and ask, "What is going on here?" and "How can I make sense of this?" (Thornberg & Charmaz, 2012, 2014). Thus, *memo-writing* refers to writing analytical, conceptual, or theoretical notes. It means "putting things down on paper, which makes codes, categories, thoughts, reflections and ideas manageable and stimulates further theorizing" (Thornberg & Charmaz, 2014, p. 163). It is about creating an intellectual workplace to make sense of data, codes, categories, and analysis, and to document the researcher's meaning making, thinking process,

and theorizing from data. Abduction as a logic of inquiry is essential in memo-writing.

According to Pidgeon and Henwood (1996), memos can include things like working definitions of codes and categories, comparisons between data and between codes and categories, hunches and questions to be checked out and further investigated, identified gaps or vagueness in categories, fresh ideas and newly created concepts, comparisons between categories and a number of theoretical codes, examinations of possible links between categories by using theoretical codes, and comparisons with and links to relevant literature.

While researchers write memos throughout the research process, the general character and length change over time. Early memos are usually shorter and less conceptualized. Early memos may be "preparatory" in nature and "story the data" (Keane, 2021). They may include brief notes, analytical questions, and hunches to follow up. Exhibit 3.1 illustrates an early memo from Wójcik's research.

EXHIBIT 3.1

Early Memo Example

Bullying Roads

Many initial codes indicate that participants see their bullying victimization as a journey from being fine or OK to being very unhappy, sad, isolated, and unable to do anything about it. There seem to be two parallel, interrelated "roads" with certain stops or milestones. One road is "travelled" by classmates. Their behavior and how it changes step by step. Second road is "travelled" by victim and it consists of responses to what is going on in the class (also step by step). It seems like action and reaction, which is obvious, but from transcripts I see that it goes much deeper than victim's behavior. It is seen in codes:

> Being teased for the first time about appearance; Ignoring first attack, thinking it is normal at school; Getting support from friends; Blaming bullies; Realizing being different from others in class; Trying to change to stop bullying (trying to fit better); Blaming oneself; Starting to agree with bullies; Getting lower self-confidence; Avoiding what I need to see now is how those changes in victims are inflicted. Are they triggered by some behaviors or situations? What is the reason for changing attribution from external to internal (focus code attribution)? Are those changes divided into phases/stages? What are the consequences of changes in attribution (focus code identity/self-confidence shift)?

As can be seen in Exhibit 3.1, Wójcik took an active, open, and critical stance by formulating analytical questions about the path of bullying victimization that she had identified in the interview data and indicated in initial codes. All the questions in the memo can be related to the basic question in initial coding: "What is happening or actually going on here?" (Thornberg & Charmaz, 2014). By asking such questions in the memo, she formulated hunches and strategies for further data collection and coding. For instance, the analytical questions she formulated in the memo led her to add new questions to her interview guide for subsequent data collection. She also then coded these new data with the analytic questions in mind. Memo-writing helped Wójcik to make sense of her data, to investigate, compare, and sort her initial codes, and to identify recurrent patterns for further investigation. The memo above, along with other memos, helped her to shift from initial coding to focused coding.

Later, memos become longer and more comprehensive, and look more like completed analyses. These later-stage memos are more conceptual in nature, with the researcher asking analytic questions of the data, often employing theoretical codes as prompts, and diagramming as an aid, and writing on a more abstract level (Keane, 2021). In Exhibit 3.2, we see a memo that Wójcik wrote during the later part of the study. The title of the memo starts with the provisional name of the main category considered in the memo, "victimization journey." The next part of the memo title indicates how it is related to another main category "causal attribution." The subtitle of the memo captures the basic process of the victimization journey, which is about a change in causal attribution— how the former victims of bullying in the study made sense of and explained why they were bullied and how these attributions changed over time.

During focused coding, researchers write memos to raise focused codes into tentative conceptual categories. They compare categories with data, codes, subcategories, and other categories. A part of theoretical coding is *memo sorting*, which is about further comparing, sorting, and integrating memos in a search for possible or

---

EXHIBIT 3.2

Example of Memo in the Later Stages of the Research Process

Victimization Journey—Causal Attribution: From External to Internal Behavioral to Internal Characterological

After *first realization of one's own victimization* (on the edge of the first attack and initial stage of bullying), they attributed the bullying to the fact that bullies were "mentally disturbed, stupid, bored, didn't know what they were doing" or to the fact that they (victims) were different. But at that stage they thought that the difference was positive, "I was smarter; I had achievements; It was that I was calm and reasonable; We [Alex and his family] went on holiday and had nice clothes, unlike many others at my school. So, I guess, I stood out."

With time, more and more attacks, and with more students joining the bullies (or becoming indifferent), they began to see their own actions as accountable for the bullying and started to suspect that they might be at some fault. Thus, causal attribution gravitated toward *internal attribution.* During initial stage of bullying, victims blamed their behavior: clothes, getting good notes, laughing in a funny way, talking too much or being too quiet. In full blown stage of bullying (friend left – no more support) they altered the way they reasoned about their situation even further. They had already employed *behavioral self-blame* after the initial stage but gradually (in the absence of any kind of disconfirming evidence) it evolved into *characterological self-blame* (e.g., being socially awkward; having Arab blood or darker skin, fat, weird, coming from a poorer family; having impediment of speech), which are nonmodifiable sources of attribution. This attributional stage is connected to substantial changes in coping strategies.

---

plausible relationships between categories in order to integrate the constructed categories into a coherent grounded theory of the studied phenomenon. In other words, memo-writing and memo sorting are keys to constructing a GT and writing drafts of papers. A GT can look very different depending on what version of GT version has been employed. The "finished" GT is also influenced by the nature of the research problem, the data, as well as by the researcher's approach and style. For example, Thornberg et al. (2013) interviewed former victims of school bullying and their analysis resulted in a "finished" GT with a core category representing a basic process of victimizing in school bullying. This process consisted of four phases: initial attacks, double victimizing, bullying exit, and aftereffects of bullying. Some of the phases included different subprocesses; for example, double victimizing involved both external and internal victimizing, with the latter consisting of a sense of not fitting in, distrusting others, self-protecting, self-doubting, self-blaming, and resignation). A "finished" GT can portray a social process by presenting a set of categories that represent and define conditional or contextual factors through subprocesses, and further describe how these categories are related to or influence each other and the main social process (Thornberg, 2014, 2015; Wójcik & Mondry, 2020). While Keane (2009) employed constructivist GT, in her "finished" GT, her analysis suggested the relevance of a core category exemplifying a basic social process through which the participants' main concern ("making the most" of higher education) was "resolved." This core category was "strategizing," constituting five subcategories (differential prioritizing, negotiating the transition, distancing to self-protect, figuring out and enacting academic practice, and memorizing; cf. Keane, 2011a, 2011b, 2012, 2015). Each of the subcategories had a number of properties. Each subcategory was theorized internally to explicate the relationships between properties. Additionally, relationships between subcategories, and between subcategories and the core category, were examined and defined as part of the overall explication and statement of the grounded theory. In line with constructivist GT, Keane's (2009) theoretical emphasis was on abstract and conceptual understandings, rather than explanations (cf. Charmaz, 2014).

QUALITY IN GROUNDED THEORY

A common quality criterion is that a GT study should produce a middle-range theory of the studied phenomenon that fits and is well grounded in data. Criticisms have been levelled at studies claiming to have used a GT approach but which have produced descriptive narratives instead of conceptualized theories (Becker, 1993; Glaser, 2003; Suddaby, 2006; Wilson & Hutchinson, 1996). However, two issues can be raised here. First, while a qualitative study that claims to have

adopted a full GT approach must have a theory as its outcome, we argue that GT can be viewed as a package or toolkit consisting of rigorous and powerful procedures that can be employed in qualitative research more broadly. For example, depending on the research aim and questions, researchers might choose to use one or more elements of GT in a study that is not aimed at producing a middle-range theory. What is vitally important here, however, is that the researcher understands what they are doing and why, the resulting limitations, and, above all, that they are fully aware that they are *not doing a full GT study* but are simply borrowing GT methods, techniques, or thinking tools for their purpose. For example, in one study, Thornberg (2008) used GT methods (i.e., coding, constant comparison, memo-writing, and theoretical sampling) to construct a category system of school rules based on his field work in two schools, while in other studies, Thornberg used GT more completely to construct grounded theories (e.g., Thornberg, 2010, 2014, 2015, 2018; Thornberg et al., 2013; Thornberg et al., 2018). Similarly, Keane employed specific GT coding procedures in more general qualitative (or mixed-methods) studies (cf. Keane, 2017, 2016; Keane et al., 2020), while also producing full grounded theories studies (e.g., Keane, 2011a, 2011b, 2012, 2015).

Second, due to differences in paradigms, ontological, epistemological, and methodological assumptions across various disciplines and traditions as well as within the discipline of psychology, there is no straightforward, unambiguous, and universally agreed upon definition of what theory actually means. As a concept, theory can be defined and understood in various ways, which in turn, makes it more difficult to determine whether the outcome of a GT study constitutes a theory (or not). This multiplicity of understandings of theory can also be observed in the varying ways in which scholars have problematized theory in GT (Charmaz, 2014; Clarke et al., 2018; Layder, 1982; Thomas & James, 2006).

In the original GT, "theory" refers to conceptual categories (or concepts) and their conceptual properties and hypothetical relations among the categories and their properties (Glaser & Strauss, 1967). The relations are hypothetical in that they are considered to be provisional and modifiable in the light of new data collection and analysis. In both Glaserian GT and Straussian GT, the constructed theory is thought of as having a core category, which is identified as the most significant and frequent category in the data. Other categories are integrated around the core category (Corbin & Strauss, 2015; Glaser, 1998, 2013; Strauss & Corbin, 1990). In Glaserian GT, the outcome is a theory that explains how participants continually resolve their main concern (Glaser, 1998, 2013), while in Straussian GT, context and process in terms of conditions, actions and interactions, and consequences are expected components in the theory, which "offers a theoretical explanation about the why and how something happens" (Corbin & Strauss, 2015, p. 15).

Charmaz (2014), in turn, argued that constructivist GT gives *abstract understanding* greater priority than *abstract explanation*; in line with the interpretative qualitative research tradition, constructivist GT aims to "understand meanings and actions and how people construct them" (p. 231). Thus, when evaluating whether a study has produced a theory, readers need to consider that theories come with different functions, shapes, and forms and that study authors may not necessarily share the same ontological, epistemological, and methodological assumptions and scientific ideals as the reader.

Considering its emphasis on data and "groundedness," researchers who are conducting GT need to ensure high quality in terms of rigor, trustworthiness, and credibility at all stages of the research process, including during data collection (Charmaz & Thornberg, 2021; Strauss & Corbin, 1998). The principle of "garbage in, garbage out" is very much applicable to GT as in many other research approaches (Charmaz & Thornberg, 2021).

> Trustworthiness, rigor, and credibility . . . in gathering data matter even if you reject an objectivist and naïve-realist researcher position

and acknowledge that data are co-constructed. If a researcher assumes that data are co-constructed by the researcher and the participant, they must attend to their input and remain open and sensitive to the field and its participants. Thus, constructivism is no excuse for poor, sloppy, and haphazard data collection. (Thornberg, 2022, p. 253)

Researchers, therefore, should make efforts to learn everything they can about their data collection methods, as well as about the GT version they adopt in their study (particularly how coding, memo-writing, and analysis can guide further data collection through first purposeful sampling and then theoretical sampling). Moreover, Charmaz and Thornberg (2021) included in their checklists and guidelines for quality in constructivist GT an emphasis on researchers gathering *rich* data: "For psychologists, rich data usually means learning and collecting the stories of people who have had or are having a specific experience" but also "an openness to the empirical world and a willingness to try to understand the experiences of people who may be different from you" (p. 322). Adopting a curious, open, empathic, and nonjudgmental approach toward participants is crucial when gathering and coconstructing data.

Charmaz and Thornberg (2021) also underlined the importance of collecting *sufficient* data. This is guided by theoretical sampling aimed at achieving *theoretical saturation*, which refers to "the point at which gathering more data about a theoretical category reveals no new properties nor yields any further theoretical insights about the emerging grounded theory" (Charmaz, 2014, p. 345). This means that "theoretical completeness" has been reached (Glaser, 1998). Theoretical sampling, collecting sufficient and rich data, and theoretical saturation help the grounded theorist to avoid a lack of "groundedness," incomplete findings, and "premature closure" (Wilson & Hutchinson, 1996. However, considering the pragmatist perspective on inquiry and knowledge as being provisional, fallible, and constantly open to revision, whether one has achieved theoretical saturation is a judgment that always can be questioned. Such a decision cannot be made in a mechanical fashion; instead, it is based on the researcher's interpretation (Dey, 2007). In fact, Glaser and Strauss (1967) themselves argued that even when a GT study is completed and published, "the published word is not the final one, but only a pause in the never-ending process of generating theory" (p. 40). For example, collecting new data in other settings or contexts might lead to modifications of categories and the overall grounded theory. Researchers, therefore, have to be reflexive and self-critical about theoretical saturation (Charmaz, 2014). Indeed, Dey (1999) suggested that grounded theorists should replace the term *theoretical saturation* with *theoretical sufficiency*, which refers to "the stage at which categories seem to cope adequately with new data without requiring continual extensions and modifications" (p. 117). The guiding principle is "good enough" rather than being exhaustive. At the same time, Dey emphasized that even reaching "theoretical sufficiency" means that the researcher has to make an interpretive judgement about when it has been reached and, we emphasize that this decision is also a provisional and fallible judgement.

We recommend that researchers pay attention to general criteria and guidelines for judging quality in qualitative research (cf. Corbin & Strauss, 2015, pp. 341–368), even though GT has its own set of criteria due to its unique features (Charmaz & Thornberg, 2021). However, as Charmaz and Thornberg (2021) highlighted, criteria for evaluating quality in GT research can vary depending on which GT version is of concern. For instance, Glaser (1998) suggested four criteria:

(a) *Workability:* Does the theory work to explain relevant behavior that has been studied?
(b) *Relevance:* Does the theory have relevance for those in the studied field?
(c) *Fit:* Does the theory fit the studied field, and does the theory and its categories fit the data?
(d) *Modifiability:* Is the theory readily modifiable as new data emerge?

Charmaz (2006, 2014) proposed four other main criteria for constructivist GT studies (although there are some overlaps):

(a) *Credibility* refers to having achieved intimate familiarity with the setting or empirical world under study, sufficient data to merit the claims, systematic comparisons within data, a wide range of data covered by the categories, strong logical links between data, arguments and analysis, and enough excerpts from data to allow readers to assess the claims in the findings.
(b) *Originality* is achieved when the findings (i.e., the constructed grounded theory and its categories) offer new insights, a new conceptual rendering of the data, have social and theoretical significance, and challenge, extend, or refine the current literature and the practices.
(c) *Resonance* refers to whether the theory and its categories portray the fullness of the studied phenomenon, reveal taken-for-granted meanings, and make sense to the participants and others who share their circumstances.
(d) *Usefulness* relates to what degree the theory and its categories can be used by people in their everyday worlds, to what extent the theory suggests any generic processes (and their tacit implications), sparks further research in other fields, and contributes to knowledge and making a better world.

CONCLUSION

In this chapter, we have provided an overview of the development and core features of GT methodology. As we have shown, GT is an iterative, systematic methodology aimed at producing middle-range theories grounded in and fitting the data. In constructivist GT, researchers acknowledge that their theories are *coconstructed* with their participants and are conscious of the role and impact of researcher positionality and the wider sociocultural context. GT offers significant possibilities for qualitative psychological research in its capacity to explore and generate meaningful, grounded conceptual analyses that prioritize and foreground participants' concerns as well as meanings and voices on intra- and interpersonal, group, social psychological, organizational, and wider social processes.

References

Alvesson, M., & Kärreman, D. (2011). *Qualitative research and theory development: Mystery as method.* SAGE.

Becker, P. H. (1993). Common pitfalls in published grounded theory research. *Qualitative Health Research, 3*(2), 254–260. https://doi.org/10.1177/104973239300300207

Belfrage, C., & Hauf, F. (2017). The gentle art of retroduction: Critical realism, cultural political economy and critical grounded theory. *Organization Studies, 38*(2), 251–271. https://doi.org/10.1177/0170840616663239

Belgrave, L. L., & Seide, K. (2019). Coding for grounded theory. In A. Bryant & K. Charmaz (Eds.), *The SAGE handbook of current developments in grounded theory* (pp. 167–185). SAGE.

Biesta, G. J. J., & Burbules, N. C. (2003). *Pragmatism and educational research.* Rowman & Littlefield.

Birks, M., & Mills, J. (2015). *Grounded theory: A practical guide* (2nd ed.). SAGE.

Blumer, H. (1969). *Symbolic interactionism.* University of California Press.

Bryant, A. (2009). Grounded theory and pragmatism: The curious case of Anselm Strauss. *Forum Qualitative Social Research, 10*(3), Article 2. https://doi.org/10.17169/fqs-10.3.1358

Bryant, A. (2017). *Grounded theory and grounded theorizing: Pragmatism in research practice.* Oxford University Press. https://doi.org/10.1093/acprof:oso/9780199922604.001.0001

Bryant, A. (2021). Continual permutations of misunderstanding: The curious incidents of the grounded theory method. *Qualitative Inquiry, 27*(3–4), 397–411. https://doi.org/10.1177/1077800420920663

Bryant, A., & Charmaz, K. (2007). Grounded theory in historical perspective: An epistemological account. In A. Bryant & K. Charmaz (Eds.), *The Sage handbook of grounded theory* (pp. 31–57). SAGE.

Bunt, S. (2018). Critical realism and grounded theory: Analysing the adoption outcomes for disabled children using the retroduction framework. *Qualitative Social Work: Research and Practice, 17*(2), 176–194. https://doi.org/10.1177/1473325016664572

Carson, D. (2009). The abduction of Sherlock Holmes. *International Journal of Police Science & Management, 11*(2), 193–202. https://doi.org/10.1350/ijps.2009.11.2.123

Charmaz, K. (1995). Between positivism and postmodernism: Implications for methods. *Studies in Symbolic Interaction, 17*, 43–72.

Charmaz, K. (2000). Constructivist and objectivist grounded theory. In N. K. Denzin & Y. S. Lincoln (Eds.), *The SAGE handbook of qualitative research* (2nd ed., pp. 509–535). SAGE.

Charmaz, K. (2005). Grounded theory in the 21st century: Applications for advancing social justice studies. In N. K. Denzin & Y. S. Lincoln (Eds.), *The SAGE handbook of qualitative research* (3rd ed., pp. 507–535). SAGE.

Charmaz, K. (2006). *Constructing grounded theory: A practical guide through qualitative analysis.* SAGE.

Charmaz, K. (2009). Shifting the grounds: Constructivist grounded theory methods. In J. M. Morse, P. N. Stern, J. Corbin, B. Bowers, K. Charmaz, & A. E. Clarke (Eds.), *Developing grounded theory: The second generation* (pp. 127–154). Left Coast Press.

Charmaz, K. (2014). *Constructing grounded theory* (2nd ed.). SAGE.

Charmaz, K. (2017). The power of constructivist grounded theory for critical inquiry. *Qualitative Inquiry, 23*(1), 34–45. https://doi.org/10.1177/1077800416657105

Charmaz, K., Harris, S. R., & Irvine, L. (2019). *The social self and everyday life: Understanding the world through symbolic interactionism.* Wiley Blackwell.

Charmaz, K., & Thornberg, R. (2021). The pursuit of quality on grounded theory. *Qualitative Research in Psychology, 18*(3), 305–327. https://doi.org/10.1080/14780887.2020.1780357

Charmaz, K., Thornberg, R., & Keane, E. (2018). Evolving grounded theory and social justice inquiry. In N. K. Denzin & Y. S. Lincoln (Eds.), *The SAGE handbook of qualitative research* (5th ed., pp. 411–443). SAGE.

Charon, J. M. (2010). *Symbolic interactionism: An introduction, an interpretation, an integration* (10th ed.). Pearson.

Clarke, A. E. (2003). Situational analysis: Grounded theory mapping after the postmodern turn. *Symbolic Interaction, 26*(4), 553–576. https://doi.org/10.1525/si.2003.26.4.553

Clarke, A. E. (2005). *Situational analysis: Grounded theory after the postmodern turn.* SAGE. https://doi.org/10.4135/9781412985833

Clarke, A. E. (2019). Situating grounded theory and situational analysis in interpretative qualitative inquiry. In A. Bryant & K. Charmaz (Eds.), *The SAGE handbook of current developments in grounded theory* (pp. 3–47). SAGE.

Clarke, A. E., Friese, C., & Washburn, R. (2018). *Situational analysis: Grounded theory after the interpretative turn* (2nd ed.). SAGE.

Corbin, J., & Strauss, A. (2008). *Basics of qualitative research* (3rd ed.). SAGE.

Corbin, J., & Strauss, A. (2015). *Basics of qualitative research* (4th ed.). SAGE.

Dewey, J. (1938). *Logic: The theory of inquiry.* Henry Holt and Company.

Dey, I. (1993). *Qualitative data analysis.* Routledge.

Dey, I. (1999). *Grounding grounded theory: Guidelines for qualitative inquiry.* Academic Press.

Dey, I. (2007). Grounding categories. In A. Bryant & K. Charmaz (Eds.), *The Sage handbook of grounded theory* (pp. 167–189). SAGE. https://doi.org/10.4135/9781848607941.n8

Dunne, C. (2011). The place of literature review in grounded theory research. *International Journal of Social Research Methodology, 14*(2), 111–124. https://doi.org/10.1080/13645579.2010.494930

Eco, U., & Sebeok, T. A. (Eds.). (1988). *The sign of three: Dupin, Holmes, Peirce.* Indiana University Press.

Fairhurst, G. T., & Putnam, L. L. (2019). An integrative methodology for organizational oppositions: Aligning grounded theory and discourse analysis. *Organizational Research Methods, 22*(4), 917–940. https://doi.org/10.1177/1094428118776771

Flick, U. (2018). *Doing grounded theory.* SAGE.

Freeman, S. (2018). Utilizing multi-grounded theory in a dissertation: Reflections and insights. *Qualitative Report, 23*(5), 1160–1175.

Glaser, B. G. (1978). *Theoretical sensitivity.* Sociology Press.

Glaser, B. G. (1998). *Doing grounded theory: Issues and discussions.* Sociology Press.

Glaser, B. G. (2001). *The grounded theory perspective I: Conceptualization contrasted with description.* Sociology Press.

Glaser, B. G. (2003). *The grounded theory perspective II: Description's remodeling of grounded theory methodology.* Sociology Press.

Glaser, B. G. (2005). *The grounded theory perspective III: Theoretical coding.* Sociology Press.

Glaser, B. G. (2007). *Doing formal grounded theory: A proposal.* Sociology Press.

Glaser, B. G. (2011). *Getting out of the data: Grounded theory conceptualization.* Sociology Press.

Glaser, B. G. (2013). *No preconceptions: The grounded theory dictum.* Sociology Press.

Glaser, B. G., & Strauss, A. L. (1965a). *Awareness of dying.* Aldine.

Glaser, B. G., & Strauss, A. L. (1965b). Discovery of substantive theory: A basic strategy underlying qualitative research. *American Behavioral Scientist, 8*(6), 5–12. https://doi.org/10.1177/000276426500800602

Glaser, B. G., & Strauss, A. L. (1967). *The discovery of grounded theory.* Aldine.

Glaser, B. G., & Strauss, A. L. (1968). *Time for dying.* Aldine. https://doi.org/10.1097/00000446-196812000-00048

Goldkuhl, G., & Cronholm, S. (2010). Adding theoretical grounding to grounded theory: Toward multi-grounded theory. *International Journal of Qualitative Methods, 9*(2), 187–205. https://doi.org/10.1177/160940691000900205

Goldkuhl, G., Cronholm, S., & Lind, M. (2020). Multi-grounded action research. *Information Systems and e-Business Management, 18*(2), 121–156. https://doi.org/10.1007/s10257-020-00469-1

Hallberg, L. R.-M. (2006). The "core category" of grounded theory: Making constant comparisons. *International Journal of Qualitative Studies on Health and Well-being, 1*(3), 141–148. https://doi.org/10.1080/17482620600858399

Hewitt, J. P., & Shulman, D. (2011). *Self and society: A symbolic interactionist social psychology* (11th ed.). Pearson.

Hickman, L. A., Neubert, S., & Reich, K. (Eds.). (2009). *John Dewey between pragmatism & constructivism.* Fordham University Press. https://doi.org/10.5422/fso/9780823230181.001.0001

Holton, J. A., & Walsh, I. (2017). *Classic grounded theory: Applications with qualitative & quantitative data.* SAGE. https://doi.org/10.4135/9781071802762

Johnson, L. (2014). Adapting and combining constructivist grounded theory and discourse analysis: A practical guide for research. *International Journal of Multiple Research Approaches, 8*(1), 100–116. https://doi.org/10.5172/mra.2014.8.1.100

Keane, E. (2009). *'Widening participation' and 'traditional-entry' students at an Irish university: Strategising to 'make the most' of higher education* [Unpublished PhD dissertation]. National University of Ireland.

Keane, E. (2011a). Dependence-deconstruction: Widening participation and traditional-entry students transitioning from school to higher education in Ireland. *Teaching in Higher Education*, *16*(6), 707–718. https://doi.org/10.1080/13562517.2011.570437

Keane, E. (2011b). Distancing to self-protect: The perpetuation of inequality in higher education through socio-relational dis/engagement. *British Journal of Sociology of Education*, *32*(3), 449–466. https://doi.org/10.1080/01425692.2011.559343

Keane, E. (2012). Differential prioritising: Orientations to higher education and widening participation. *International Journal of Educational Research*, *53*, 150–159. https://doi.org/10.1016/j.ijer.2012.03.005

Keane, E. (2015). Considering the practical implementation of constructivist grounded theory in a study of widening participation in Irish higher education. *International Journal of Social Research Methodology*, *18*(4), 415–431. https://doi.org/10.1080/13645579.2014.923622

Keane, E. (2016). Considering the 'impact' of widening participation: The employment experiences of access graduates from an Irish university. *Widening Participation and Lifelong Learning: The Journal of the Institute for Access Studies and the European Access Network*, *18*(2), 130–153. https://doi.org/10.5456/WPLL.18.2.130

Keane, E. (2017). Being altruistically motivated: The postgraduate and career motivational orientations of access students at an Irish university. *Cambridge Journal of Education*, *47*(4), 567–583. https://doi.org/10.1080/0305764X.2016.1221886

Keane, E. (2021). Critical analytic memoing. In C. Vanover, P. Mihas, & J. Saldaña (Eds.), *Analyzing and interpreting qualitative data: After the interview* (pp. 259–274). SAGE.

Keane, E., Heinz, M., & Lynch, A. (2020). Identity matters? 'Working class' student teachers in Ireland, the desire to be a relatable and inclusive teacher, and sharing the classed self. *International Journal of Inclusive Education*, 1–17. Advance online publication. https://doi.org/10.1080/13603116.2020.1853255

Kelle, U. (2019). The status of theories and models in grounded theory. In A. Bryant & K. Charmaz (Eds.), *The SAGE handbook of current developments in grounded theory* (pp. 68–88). SAGE.

Kennedy, B. L., & Thornberg, R. (2018). Induction, deduction, abduction. In U. Flick (Ed.), *The SAGE handbook of qualitative data collection* (pp. 49–64). SAGE.

Layder, D. (1982). Grounded theory: A constructive critique. *Journal for the Theory of Social Behaviour*, *12*(1), 103–122. https://doi.org/10.1111/j.1468-5914.1982.tb00441.x

Lipton, P. (2007). Alien abduction: Inference to the best explanation and the management of testimony. *Episteme*, *4*(3), 238–251. https://doi.org/10.3366/E1742360007000068

Martin, V. B. (2006). The relationship between an emerging grounded theory and the existing literature: Four phases for consideration. *The Grounded Theory Review*, *5*(2/3), 47–50.

McCreaddie, M., & Payne, S. (2010). Evolving Grounded Theory Methodology: Towards a discursive approach. *International Journal of Nursing Studies*, *47*(6), 781–793. https://doi.org/10.1016/j.ijnurstu.2009.11.006

Merton, R. (1968). *Social theory and social structure*. Free Press.

Morse, J. M., Stern, P. N., Corbin, J., Bowers, B., Charmaz, K., & Clarke, A. E. (Eds.). (2009). *Developing grounded theory: The second generation*. Left Coast Press.

Oliver, C. (2012). Critical realist grounded theory: A new approach for social work research. *British Journal of Social Work*, *42*(2), 371–387. https://doi.org/10.1093/bjsw/bcr064

Peters, M. A., & Burbules, N. C. (2004). *Poststructuralism and educational research*. Rowman & Littlefield.

Pidgeon, N., & Henwood, K. (1996). Grounded theory: Practical implementation. In J. T. E. Richardson (Ed.), *Handbook of qualitative research methods for psychology and the social sciences* (pp. 86–101). The British Psychological Society.

Reichertz, J. (2019). Abduction: The logic of discovery of grounded theory—An updated review. In A. Bryant & K. Charmaz (Eds.), *The SAGE handbook of current developments in grounded theory* (2nd ed., pp. 259–281). SAGE.

Snaza, N., & Weaver, J. A. (Eds.). (2015). *Posthumanism and educational research*. Routledge.

Stern, P. N., & Porr, C. J. (2011). *Essentials of accessible grounded theory*. Left Coast Press.

Strauss, A., & Corbin, J. (1990). *Basics of qualitative research*. SAGE.

Strauss, A., & Corbin, J. (1998). *Basics of qualitative research: Grounded theory procedures and techniques* (2nd ed.). Sage.

Strauss, A. L. (1987). *Qualitative analysis for social scientists*. Cambridge University Press. https://doi.org/10.1017/CBO9780511557842

Suddaby, R. (2006). From the editors: What grounded theory is not. *Academy of Management Journal*, *49*(4), 633–642. https://doi.org/10.5465/amj.2006.22083020

Tarozzi, M. (2020). *What is grounded theory?* Bloomsbury. https://doi.org/10.5040/9781350085275

Thayer-Bacon, B. J. (2001). An examination and redescription of epistemology. In J. L. Kincheloe & D. K. Well (Eds.), *Standards and schooling in the United States: An encyclopedia* (pp. 397–418). ABC-CLIO.

Thayer-Bacon, B. J. (2003). Pragmatism and feminism as qualified relativism. *Studies in Philosophy and Education, 22*(6), 417–438. https://doi.org/10.1023/A:1025735417682

Thomas, G., & James, D. (2006). Reinventing grounded theory: Some questions about theory, ground and discovery. *British Educational Research Journal, 32*(6), 767–795. https://doi.org/10.1080/01411920600989412

Thornberg, R. (2008). A categorization of school rules. *Educational Studies, 34*(1), 25–33. https://doi.org/10.1080/03055690701785244

Thornberg, R. (2010). A student in distress: Moral frames and bystander behavior in school. *The Elementary School Journal, 110*(4), 585–608. https://doi.org/10.1086/651197

Thornberg, R. (2012). Informed grounded theory. *Scandinavian Journal of Educational Research, 56*(3), 243–259. https://doi.org/10.1080/00313831.2011.581686

Thornberg, R. (2014). Consultation barriers between teachers and external consultants: A grounded theory of change resistance in school consultation. *Journal of Educational & Psychological Consultation, 24*(3), 183–210. https://doi.org/10.1080/10474412.2013.846188

Thornberg, R. (2015). School bullying as a collective action: Stigma processes and identity struggling. *Children & Society, 29*(4), 310–320. https://doi.org/10.1111/chso.12058

Thornberg, R. (2017). Grounded theory. In D. Wyse, N. Selwyn, E. Smith, & L. E. Suter (Eds.), *The BERA/SAGE handbook of educational research* (Vol. 1, pp. 355–375). Sage. https://doi.org/10.4135/9781473983953.n18

Thornberg, R. (2018). School rules and fitting into the peer landscape: A grounded theory field study. *British Journal of Sociology of Education, 39*(1), 144–158. https://doi.org/10.1080/01425692.2017.1330680

Thornberg, R. (2022). Abduction as a guiding principle in qualitative research design. In U. Flick (Ed.), *The SAGE handbook of qualitative research design* (pp. 243–256). SAGE. https://doi.org/10.4135/9781529770278.n16

Thornberg, R., & Charmaz, K. (2012). Grounded theory. In S. D. Lapan, M. T. Quartaroli, & F. J. Reimer (Eds.), *Qualitative research: An introduction to methods and designs* (pp. 41–67). John Wiley/Jossey-Bass.

Thornberg, R., & Charmaz, K. (2014). Grounded theory and theoretical coding. In U. Flick (Ed.), *The SAGE handbook of qualitative analysis* (pp. 153–169). SAGE. https://doi.org/10.4135/9781446282243.n11

Thornberg, R., & Dunne, C. (2019). Literature review in grounded theory. In A. Bryant & K. Charmaz (Eds.), *The SAGE handbook of current developments in grounded theory* (2nd ed., pp. 206–221). SAGE.

Thornberg, R., Halldin, K., Bolmsjö, N., & Petersson, A. (2013). Victimising of school bullying: A grounded theory. *Research Papers in Education, 28*(3), 309–329. https://doi.org/10.1080/02671522.2011.641999

Thornberg, R., & Keane, E. (2022). Designing grounded theory studies. In U. Flick (Ed.), *The SAGE handbook of qualitative research design* (pp. 452–466). SAGE. https://doi.org/10.4135/9781529770278.n28

Thornberg, R., Landgren, L., & Wiman, E. (2018). 'It depends': A qualitative study on how adolescent students explain bystander intervention and non-intervention in bullying situations. *School Psychology International, 39*(4), 400–415. https://doi.org/10.1177/0143034318779225

Truzzi, M. (1976). Selective attention: Sherlock Holmes: Applied social psychologist. In W. B. Sanders (Ed.), *The sociologist as detective* (2nd ed., pp. 50–86). Praeger.

Wilson, H. S., & Hutchinson, S. A. (1996). Methodologic mistakes in grounded theory. *Nursing Research, 45*(2), 122–124. https://doi.org/10.1097/00006199-199603000-00012

Wójcik, M. (2018). The parallel culture of bullying in Polish secondary schools: A grounded theory study. *Journal of Adolescence, 69*(1), 72–79. https://doi.org/10.1016/j.adolescence.2018.09.005

Wójcik, M., & Mondry, M. (2020). "The game of bullying": Shared beliefs and behavioral labels in bullying among middle schoolers. *Group Dynamics, 24*(4), 276–293. https://doi.org/10.1037/gdn0000125

Wójcik, M., Thornberg, R., Flak, W., & Leśniewski, J. (2022). Downward spiral of bullying: Victimization timeline from former victims' perspective. *Journal of Interpersonal Violence, 37*(13/14), NP10985–NP11008. https://doi.org/10.1177/0886260521990835

CHAPTER 4

THEMATIC ANALYSIS

Virginia Braun and Victoria Clarke

For several decades, thematic analysis (TA) was a widely used yet poorly defined method of qualitative data analysis. Procedures for TA started to be published in the 1990s (e.g., Boyatzis, 1998; Hayes, 1997; Miles & Huberman, 1994; Ritchie & Spencer, 1994) and often came from outside of psychology or were never widely taken up within the discipline. Instead, qualitative researchers tended to use either the method without any guiding reference or techniques from another approach (e.g., grounded theory) to rationalize what essentially was TA. Braun and Clarke (2006) developed TA for psychology in a "systematic" and "sophisticated" way (Howitt & Cramer, 2008, p. 341). TA has since become widely recognized as a unique and valuable method in its own right, alongside other qualitative approaches like grounded theory, narrative analysis, or discourse analysis.

In this chapter, we first outline the basics of what TA is, including, crucially, the fact that TA is best thought of as a family of *methods* rather than a *method*, singular. We introduce our typology of TA, which encompasses three clusters of approaches we classify as coding reliability, reflexive, and codebook. The main part of the chapter then demonstrates how to do TA, using the reflexive approach we have developed (see also Braun & Clarke, 2022b; Terry & Hayfield, 2021;

https://www.thematicanalysis.net). We use a worked example with data from one of our own research projects—an interview-based study of lesbian, gay, bisexual, and transgender (LGBT) students' experiences of university life—to illustrate the different phases and processes of reflexive TA. We conclude by discussing how to conduct reflexive TA well and how to avoid doing it poorly.

WHAT IS THEMATIC ANALYSIS?

Thematic analysis is a family of methods for systematically developing and offering insight into patterns of meaning (themes) across a data set. Through focusing on meaning *across* a data set, TA methods allow the researcher to develop and make sense of collective or shared meanings and experiences. Identifying unique and idiosyncratic meanings and experiences found only within a single data item is not the focus of TA (that said, TA has been used in case-study research).

What is common, however, is not necessarily in and of itself meaningful or important. The patterns of meaning that TA allows the researcher to develop need to be important in addressing a question, even if, as in some qualitative research, the specific question that is being addressed only becomes apparent through the analysis. Numerous

https://doi.org/10.1037/0000319-004
APA Handbook of Research Methods in Psychology, Second Edition: Vol. 2. Research Designs: Quantitative, Qualitative, Neuropsychological, and Biological, H. Cooper (Editor-in-Chief)

patterns could be developed across any data set—the purpose of analysis is to develop those relevant to addressing *a particular* research question. For instance, in researching white-collar workers' experiences of sociality at work, a researcher might interview people about their work environment and start with questions about their typical workday. If most or all reported that they started work at around 9:00 a.m., this would be a pattern in the data, but it would not necessarily be a meaningful or important one. If many reported that they aimed to arrive at work earlier than needed so that they could chat with colleagues, this could be a meaningful pattern.

WHY THEMATIC ANALYSIS?

TA offers an excellent approach for exploring and interpreting patterned meaning across a data set. TA methods are flexible enough to allow the researcher to focus on the data in numerous different ways. With TA methods you can legitimately focus on analyzing meaning across the entire data set, or you can examine one particular aspect of a phenomenon in depth. You can report the obvious or semantic meanings in the data, or you can interrogate the latent meanings, the assumptions and ideas that lie behind what is explicitly stated (see Braun & Clarke, 2006, 2022b). The many forms TA methods can take means that they suit a wide variety of research questions and research topics (see Braun & Clarke, 2022a).

For people new to qualitative research, TA provides an accessible entry into a way of doing research that otherwise can seem vague, mystifying, conceptually challenging, and overly complex. It offers a way into qualitative research that teaches the mechanics of analyzing qualitative data systematically, which can then be linked to broader theoretical or conceptual issues. For much qualitative research, the relationship is reversed. For example, to do discourse analysis (DA), the researcher needs to first be familiar with complex theoretical perspectives on language (see Chapter 8, this volume), which invert the commonsense view of language as a mirroring reality—instead, language is theorized as *creating* reality. Knowing the theory that informs the DA methodology is essential because it guides what the researcher notices about the data, how they analyze the data, and the claims that they make. In contrast, TA is closer to a *method*, a theoretically flexible tool or technique, rather than being a *methodology*, a theoretically informed and delimited framework for conducting qualitative research. We see this as a strength because it ensures the accessibility of the approach, as well as its flexibility.

TA methods offer a way of separating qualitative research out from these broader concerns (e.g., around metatheoretical and philosophical assumptions, research values, and conceptualizations of language), where appropriate, and making qualitative research results available to a wider audience. TA can also be used comparatively easily within participatory research projects—such as participatory action research (see Chapter 15, this volume) or memory work (Delgado-Infante & Ofreneo, 2014)—in which many involved in the analysis are not trained researchers.

THE THEMATIC ANALYSIS FAMILY: SIMILARITIES AND DIFFERENCES

An important first step for researchers using TA is to decide *which* approach to TA they will use. Scores of different approaches have appeared since the 1990s—some in psychology (e.g., Joffe, 2012; King & Brooks, 2017) and some in other social science disciplines (e.g., Guest et al., 2012). We have organized these approaches into three main types, which we call coding *reliability*, *reflexive*, and *codebook* (see Braun & Clarke, 2019, 2021a, 2021b). All of these versions of TA have elements in common—including processes of coding and theme development—and all differ, both in terms of specific procedures and the conceptualization of key elements such as the theme, and in terms of underlying research values. A useful way of making sense of the differences, and why they matter, is Kidder and Fine's (1987) small q versus Big Q qualitative distinction. Small q qualitative conceptualizes qualitative research as providing researchers with tools and techniques for collecting and analyzing qualitative data, whereas Big Q qualitative offers both tools and techniques and underlying research values or paradigms. In practice, small q qualitative typically involves the use of qualitative techniques combined with (post)positivist research values, those that underpin quantitative research, and emphasizes reliability and replicability of measurement and striving for objective knowledge; here, researcher subjectivity—the constellation of a researcher's social positionings, experiences, values, and assumptions—is a potential threat that must be contained. Big Q qualitative research values can vary, but there is usually an emphasis on the partial and situated nature of knowledge, with researcher subjectivity understood as a resource for research, rather than a threat to be contained (see Braun & Clarke, 2013, 2022b).

Coding reliability TA has the hallmarks of small q qualitative as it typically combines qualitative techniques of data analysis (coding and theme development) and the reporting of the output of this analysis (e.g., themes illustrated by extracts of qualitative data) with (post)positivist research values. These values are evident through the orienting of coding techniques to securing the reliability and accuracy of data coding. Coding reliability approaches (e.g., Boyatzis, 1998; Guest et al., 2012; Joffe, 2012) typically start with theme development following some data familiarization or with the themes already conceptualized prior to data analysis (e.g., the data collection questions are used as the themes). So although themes are the output of analysis, they are also an input into the analysis that delimits the scope and focus of the analysis.

This brings us to a vital issue: the conceptualization of themes in TA. One might expect TA researchers to agree on what a theme is, but they do not! There are two main conceptualizations of themes evident across the TA family: themes as topic summaries and themes as shared meaning. In the former rendering, themes summarize data content in relation to a particular topic, that is, what is shared is the topic, but there is not just one "take" or key message about that topic. Rather, what is reported is everything or the key things that participants said in relation to that topic. In the latter rendering, what unites the theme is a central concept or idea (the central organizing concept). What is shared is meaning rather than topic; themes may cut across several topics. The themes we report below provide an example of shared meaning themes.

Returning to coding reliability TA, themes are typically conceptualized as topic summaries. Coding is conceptualized as a process of finding evidence for themes or of allocating data to the relevant predetermined topic. Coding typically involves a coding frame or codebook, which may be determined in advance or generated following familiarization with some or all of the data content. This means codes are fixed at the start of the coding process. Two or more researchers apply the coding frame to the data. Ideally these coders work separately; some TA researchers even argue that at least some of the coders should be ignorant of the research question and/or have no prior knowledge of the research area, to avoid contamination of the coding process. The level of agreement between coders—the reliability of coding—is assessed with statistical tests. Any areas where coders may have differed are resolved through reaching consensus between coders (for empirical examples that illustrate various facets of coding reliability TA, see Bond et al., 2008; Reaney et al., 2018).

Reflexive TA can be thought of as the distant cousin of coding reliability TA, as the similarities between these two approaches—on close inspection—are relatively limited. Both involve processes of coding and theme development and distinguishing between semantic and latent coding and between inductive and deductive orientations. (An inductive analysis is grounded in the data; reflexive TA emphasizes the impossibility of "pure" induction as researchers always bring things such as their research values to the data analysis process. Conceptualizations of deductive vary; for reflexive TA, this means using existing theory and concepts to inform data interpretation.) But the family resemblance largely ends there, as reflexive TA combines qualitative approaches to coding and theme development with qualitative research values that embrace researcher subjectivity and emphasize the provisionality of knowledge (see Braun & Clarke, 2006, 2022b; Hayes, 1997). In reflexive TA, following data familiarization, analysis begins with coding. There is no coding frame or codebook that guides this. Instead, coding is an organic process. Codes are developed as the researcher works through their data; as their insight deepens, codes can evolve to reflect this—through being renamed, combined with other codes, split into two or more codes, or having boundaries redrawn. If there are multiple coders—and this is not typical or desired—differences are explored to enrich analytic insight, not reach consensus. There is no codebook; finishing the coding process by turning the final coding into a codebook, then recoding the data, makes no conceptual sense. The finalized coding is always provisional, retaining the potential for new insights and new coding.

Themes are conceptualized as patterns of shared meaning underpinned by a central organizing concept. They are developed from codes, and the coded data, through the analytic process. They are solely an analytic output. Their scope and potential would be virtually impossible to develop prior to coding—were it even desirable (it is not!). The researcher is active in coding and theme development—their subjectivity is a resource for analysis, and inevitably and inescapably shapes the processes and outcomes of coding and theme development. This is why we adopted the term *reflexive TA* to describe our approach (see Braun & Clarke, 2019; Braun et al., 2022)—reflexive qualitative research acknowledges the role of the researcher in knowledge construction (Finlay & Gough, 2003). For quality practice, the onus is on the researcher to be reflexive throughout their research journey, ideally keeping a research journal, and reflecting on how their social positioning, research values, design choices, and research practices are shaping, and potentially delimiting, their knowledge production.

Codebook approaches to TA—such as template (King & Brooks, 2017), framework (Ritchie & Spencer, 1994), and matrix analysis (Miles &

Huberman, 1994)—combine elements of these distant cousins, coding reliability and reflexive TA. To introduce another analogy, imagine different TA approaches as placed on a continuum, with coding reliability TA at one end and reflexive TA at the other. Codebook TA sits somewhere in between. In common with coding reliability TA, codebook approaches typically involve early theme development, the conceptualization of themes as topic summaries, and the use of a codebook and a structured approach to coding. But the qualitative values also evident in reflexive TA tend to predominate. This means the "accuracy" or "reliability" of coding is not of preeminent concern. A key reason to use codebook approaches appears pragmatic: These approaches have typically been developed for applied research—where there are often predetermined information needs, tight deadlines for producing outputs, and large teams of researchers including qualitative novices. The codebook is used to map or chart the developing analysis, and this is argued to facilitate team-working, efficiency, and rapid delivery of outputs (for examples of codebook TA in the form of framework and template analysis, see Leal et al., 2015; Matthews et al., 2018).

Understanding the sometimes profound differences in procedure and underlying research values associated with these different types of TA is vital for quality practice, yet the diversity within TA is often poorly understood. This is evidenced by researchers claiming to combine, for example, Boyatzis's (1998) coding reliability approach with our reflexive approach (see Braun & Clarke, 2021a; Braun et al., 2022).

FLEXIBILITY AND CHOICES IN REFLEXIVE THEMATIC ANALYSIS

One of the main reasons TA methods are so flexible is that they can be conducted in a number of different ways. Any researcher doing TA—and reflexive TA especially—needs actively to make a series of choices as to what approach to TA they are using and then how exactly they are using it (Braun & Clarke, 2006, 2021a, 2022a). Reflexive TA has the ability to straddle three main continua along which Big Q qualitative research approaches can be located: inductive versus deductive or theory-driven data coding and analysis, an experiential versus critical orientation to data, and a contextualist versus constructionist theoretical perspective. Where the researcher locates their research on each of these continua carries a particular set of assumptions, and this delimits what can and cannot be said in relation to the data, as well as how data can and should be interpreted (for a detailed discussion of these positions, see Volume 1, Chapter 1, this handbook).

An inductive approach to data coding and analysis is a bottom-up approach and is driven by the data; but the data are interpreted by an active, subjective researcher, so we do not mean "pure" induction. What we mean is that the codes and themes are derived by the researcher from the data content, so that what is mapped by the researcher during analysis closely matches the content of the data. In contrast, a deductive approach to data coding and analysis is a top-down approach, where the researcher brings to the data a series of concepts, ideas, or topics that they use to code and interpret the data. What this means is that the codes and themes derive both from the data and the concepts and ideas the researcher brings to the data—here, what is mapped by the researcher during analysis does not necessarily closely link to semantic data content.

In reality, researchers often use a combination of both approaches. Being purely inductive is impossible, as we always bring something to the data when we analyze them. And we rarely completely ignore the semantic content of the data when we code for a particular theoretical construct—at the very least, we have to know whether it is worth coding the data for that construct. One tends to predominate, however, and a commitment to an inductive or deductive approach also signals an overall orientation that prioritizes either participant- or data-based meaning or researcher- or theory-based meaning. For this reason, inductive TA often is experiential in its orientation and contextualist in its theoretical framework, assuming a knowable world and "giving voice" to experiences and meanings

of that world, as reported in the data. Deductive TA is often critical in its orientation and constructionist in its theoretical framework, examining how the world is put together (i.e., constructed) and the ideas and assumptions that inform the data gathered. These correspondences are not given, however, or necessary. Consistency and coherence of the overall framework and approach to TA, and the analysis, are what is important.

Braun and colleagues' analysis of gay and bisexual men's experiences of sexual coercion provides a good example of a more inductive, experiential form of TA, in which different forms or modes of sexual coercion were identified from men's reported diverse experiences (Braun et al., 2009). Clarke and Kitzinger's (2004) analysis of representations of lesbian and gay parents on television talk shows is a good example of more deductive, critical, constructionist TA. Their study drew on the concept of *heteronormativity* to examine how participants in liberal talk-show debates routinely invoked discursive strategies of *normalization*, emphasizing lesbian- and gay-headed families' conformity to norms of White, middle-class heterosexuality, as a response to homophobic and heterosexist accounts of lesbian and gay parenting and its impact on children.

Like any form of analysis, TA can be done well, and it can be done poorly. Essential for doing good TA are a clear understanding of the researcher's positioning in relation to these possible options, a rationale for making the choices they do, and the consistent application of those choices throughout the analysis (further criteria are discussed later in the chapter). We now lay out how you actually do reflexive TA.

REFLEXIVE THEMATIC ANALYSIS: A WORKED EXAMPLE

We illustrate how to do reflexive TA using an interview study of LGBT-identified students' experiences of university life in New Zealand and Britain; our worked example uses data from four gay male British students. The students were all studying social science subjects but varied on race/ethnicity (one British Asian; three White, one born in mainland Europe), social class (working or middle class), and age (one middle-aged student). The scope of university life was broadly conceived in the interviews, which lasted around an hour. Participants were asked about their expectations of university life, whether they were out (open) about their sexuality at university, their experiences of the classroom and the curriculum, their views on LGBT lecturers coming out in the classroom, and whether LGBT issues were included when relevant. Experiences and perceptions of the wider campus environment and of student housing, interactions with other students, friendship networks and social life, and the best and worst things about university life as a LGBT student were also covered.

The interviews were audio recorded and then transcribed orthographically, reproducing all spoken words and sounds, including hesitations, false starts, cutoffs in speech (indicated by a dash; e.g., thin-), the interviewer's "guggles" (e.g., mm-hm, ah-ha), laughter, long pauses (indicated by (pause)), and strong emphasis (indicated by underscore). Commas signal a continuing intonation, broadly commensurate with a grammatical comma in written language; inverted commas are used to indicate reported speech; three periods in a row (. . .) signal editing of the transcript—usually for brevity (for transcription notation suitable for reflexive TA, see Braun & Clarke, 2013, 2022b).

This topic, research question, and data collection method all suited reflexive TA. The research question was experiential and exploratory, so our worked example illustrates a primarily experiential form of TA, within a contextualist framework, which assumes that truth can be accessed through language, but that accounts and experiences are socially mediated (Madill et al., 2000). It illustrates a combination of inductive *and* deductive TA: inductive as we mainly code from the data, on the basis of participants' experiences (meaning our analytic lens does not completely override their stories); deductive as we draw on theoretical constructs like compulsory heterosexuality (Rich, 1980), heteronormativity (Warner, 1991), and the hidden curriculum of heteronormativity (Epstein et al., 2003) to render visible issues that participants did not explicitly articulate. This means that the data are broadly interpreted within feminist and queer theoretical frameworks.

A SIX-PHASE APPROACH TO REFLEXIVE THEMATIC ANALYSIS

The six phases in our approach to reflexive TA represent an approach *to* TA and to *learning to do* TA. More experienced analysts will (a) likely have deeper insights into their data during familiarization, (b) find the process of coding quicker and easier and be able to code at a more conceptual level early on, and (c) more quickly and confidently develop themes that need less reviewing and refining, especially if working with a smaller data set. Writing is also likely to take a more embedded or central place throughout analysis as experience builds. The point we wish to emphasize is that certain skills of analysis develop only through practice. Even experienced researchers, however, will draw and redraw lots of thematic maps when developing themes and will engage in extensive review processes when working with larger data sets. A thematic map is a visual tool to map out the facets of your developing analysis and to identify themes, any subthemes, and interconnections between these (see Braun & Clarke, 2006, 2022b).

Phase 1. Data Familiarization

Common to all forms of qualitative analysis, this phase involves immersing yourself in the data by reading and rereading textual data items (e.g., transcripts of interviews, responses to qualitative surveys) and listening to or watching recordings if you have them. We recommend listening to or watching recordings at least once as well as reading the transcripts, especially if you did not collect the data or transcribe them. Making notes on the data as you read—or listen or watch—is part of this phase. Use whatever format works for you to highlight items potentially of interest (e.g., annotating transcripts, writing comments in a notebook or using the comment function in

Microsoft Word). Note-making helps you start to read the data as data. Reading data *as data* means not simply absorbing the surface meaning of the words, as you might read a novel or news article, but reading the words actively, analytically, and critically and starting to think about what the data mean. This involves asking questions like: How does this participant make sense of their experiences? What assumptions do they make in interpreting their experience? What kind of world is revealed through their accounts? We illustrate this with a brief example from Andreas's interview.

> *Andreas: let's say I'm in a in a seminar and somebody a a man says to me "oh look at her" (Int: mm) I'm not going "oh actually I'm gay" (Int: mm [laughter]) I'll just go like "oh yeah" (Int: mhm) you know I won't fall into the other one and say "oh yeah" (Int: yep) "she looks really brilliant."*

Our initial observations included (a) Andreas reports a common experience of presumed heterosexuality, (b) coming out is not an obvious option, (c) social norms dictate a certain response, (d) the presumption of heterosexuality appears dilemmatic, and (e) he colludes in the presumption but minimally (to avoid social awkwardness). Looking a bit more deeply, we speculated that (a) Andreas values honesty and being true to yourself, but (b) he recognizes a sociopolitical context in which that is constrained, and (c) he walks a tightrope trying to balance his values and the expectations of the context. Reading Andreas's account as data reveals the richness that can be found in even brief extracts of text. We did deliberately pick a particularly rich extract; however, not all extracts will be as vivid as this one, and you may have little or nothing to say about some parts of your data.

The aim of this phase is to become intimately familiar with the content of your data set and to begin to notice things that might be relevant to your research question. You need to read through your entire data set at least once—if not twice, or more—until you feel you know the data content

intimately. Make notes on the entire data set as well as on individual data items. Note-making at this point is observational and casual rather than systematic and inclusive. You are not coding the data yet, so do not agonize over it. Notes would typically be a stream of consciousness rather than polished prose. Such notes are written only to and for you to help you with the process of analysis—think of them as memory aids and triggers for coding and analysis. At most, they may be shared among research team members.

Phase 2. Data Coding

Phase 2 begins the systematic analysis of the data through coding. Codes are the building blocks of analysis: If your analysis is a brick-built house with a tile roof, your themes are the walls and roof, and your codes are the individual bricks and tiles. Codes capture a single facet; themes contain multiple facets. Codes identify and provide a label for a feature of the data that is potentially relevant to the research question (Exhibit 4.1 shows an example of coded data). Codes are succinct and work as shorthand for something you, the analyst, understands; they do not have to be fully worked-up explanations—those come later.

Coding can be done at the semantic or the latent level of meaning. Codes can provide a pithy summary of a portion of data—such descriptive or semantic codes typically stay close to content of the data and to the participants' meanings and use of language. An example of this is "fear/anxiety about people's reactions to his sexuality" in Exhibit 4.1. Codes can also go beyond the participants' meanings and provide a conceptual "take" on the data content. Such conceptual or latent codes develop meanings that lie beneath the semantic surface of the data. An example of this is the "coming out imperative"; this code offers a conceptual interpretation to make sense of what Andreas is saying (see Exhibit 4.1). What is important for all codes is that they are relevant to addressing your research question. Codes are almost always a mix of the descriptive and conceptual. A novice coder will likely (initially) generate more descriptive codes; as noted, conceptual approaches to coding

---

EXHIBIT 4.1

Example of Coded Transcript (Andreas)

Transcript	Codes
Andreas: . . . I sometimes try to erm not conceal it that's not the right word but erm let's say I'm in a in a seminar and somebody- a a man says to me "oh look at her"	Not hiding (but not shouting) Heterosexual assumption Hidden curriculum of heteronormativity
VC: mm	
Andreas: I'm not going "oh actually I'm gay" (Int: mm [laughter]) I'll just go like "oh yeah" (VC: mhm) you know I won't fall into the other one and say "oh yeah" (VC: yep) "she looks really brilliant"	Coming out is difficult (and not socially normative) Dilemmas created by the heterosexual assumption Managing the heterosexual assumption by minimal agreement
VC: yep	
Andreas: but I sorta then and after them you hate myself for it because I I don't know how this person would react because that person might then either not talk to me anymore or erm might sort of yeah (VC: yep) or next time we met not not sit next to me or that sort of thing	Coming out imperative Being a "happy, healthy" gay man It's important to be honest and authentic Fear/anxiety about people's reaction to his homosexuality Heterosexism is a constant possibility Heterosexism = exclusion
VC: yep	
Andreas: so I think these this back to this question are you out yes but I think wherever you go you always have to start Afresh	Heterosexual assumption
VC: yep	
Andreas: this sort of li-lifelong process of being courageous in a way or not	Coming out is difficult (and not socially normative)

Note. VC is the interviewer Victoria Clarke.

---

develop with experience. This does not mean that conceptual codes are better—they are just harder to develop sometimes. Coding is something at which we get better with practice.

Reflexive TA is not prescriptive about how you segment the data as you code them (e.g., you do not have to produce a code for every line of transcript). You can code in larger or smaller chunks; some chunks may not be coded at all. Coding requires another thorough read of every data item. Every time you identify something that is potentially relevant to the research question, code it. We say "potentially" because at this early phase of analysis, you do not know what might be relevant: Inclusivity should be your motto. It is much easier to discard codes than go back to the entire data set and recode data, although some recoding is part of the coding process.

Once you identify an extract of data to code, you need to write down the code and mark the text associated with it. You can code a portion of data with more than one code (as Exhibit 4.1 shows). Some people code by writing on hard-copy data, clearly identifying the code name, and highlighting the portion of text associated with it. Other techniques include using computer software to manage coding (see Volume 1, Chapter 13, this handbook), using the comment function in Microsoft Word, annotating hard copy data with lots of different colored sticky notes, or cutting and pasting text into a new electronic file (ensure that you record where all excerpts came from). An advantage of some of these techniques—such as software and the more low-tech cutting and pasting—is that you collate your coded data as you code. There is no right or wrong way to manage the practical process of coding. Work out what suits you best. What is important is that coding is inclusive, thorough, and systematic.

After you generate your first code, keep reading the data until you identify the next potentially relevant excerpt: You then have to decide whether you can apply the code you have already used or whether a new code is needed to evoke that piece of data. You repeat this process throughout each data item and the entire data set. As your coding progresses, you can also tweak and rework existing codes to better fit your evolving take on the data. For example, our code "modifying behavior, speech, and practices to avoid heterosexism" was initially titled "modifying behavior to avoid heterosexism." Because students also reported modifying speech and things like dress or self-presentation to avoid "trouble," we expanded this code beyond behavior to make it better fit what participants said. It is a good idea to revisit the material you coded at the start because your codes will have likely developed during coding: Some recoding of earlier coded data may be necessary.

This phase of the process ends when your data are fully coded and the data relevant to each code have been collated. Depending on your topic, data set, and precision in coding, you will have generated any number of codes—there is no maximum. What you want are enough codes to parse out the diversity and evoke the patterning of meanings within the data, and most codes should appear across more than one data item.

Phase 3. Generating Initial Themes

In this phase, your analysis starts to take shape as you shift from codes to themes. Some qualitative researchers make reference to "themes emerging from the data," as if their data set were a pile of crocodile eggs and analysis involved watching the eggs until each baby crocodile (theme) emerged, perfectly formed, from within. In reflexive TA, developing themes is an active process, meaning we generate or construct themes rather than discover them. In other TA—coding reliability and codebook—approaches, researchers are more like archaeologists digging around, searching for the themes that are assumed to lie hidden within

the data, preexisting the process of analysis. But reflexive TA researchers are more like sculptors, making choices about how to shape and craft their piece of stone (the "raw" data) into a work of art (the analysis). Like a piece of stone, the data set provides the material base for analysis and limits the possible end product, but many different variations could be created when analyzing the data.

This phase involves reviewing the coded data to identify areas of similarity and overlap between codes: can you identify any broad pattern or concept around which codes cluster? The basic process of generating themes involves collapsing or clustering codes that seem to share some unifying feature together, so that they reflect a coherent and meaningful pattern in the data. In our data, we noticed codes clustering around heterosexism and homophobia. Examining these in more detail, we identified that the codes either focused on experiences of the fear and uncertainty created by heterosexism and homophobia, or responses to, and ways of managing, heterosexism and homophobia. We then constructed one theme using all the codes relating to the participants' experiences of fear and uncertainty in the hetero-normative environment of the university (e.g., "incident of (naming) homophobia/heterosexism"; "tensions in relating to straight men") and another using the codes relating to the participants' management of (actual and feared) heterosexism (e.g., "monitoring/assessing people and the environment for the possibility of heterosexism"; "modifying speech, behavior, and practices to avoid heterosexism") (Exhibit 4.2).

A lot of codes also clustered around the issue of negotiating sexual identity but did not form one obvious theme. In this case, after exploring lots of different ways to combine these codes into themes and drawing lots of thematic maps, we generated two themes: one around coming out and being out ("I'm not hiding, but I'm not throwing it in people's faces": Being out [but not too out] at university), and one around different versions of being a gay man ("Mincing queens versus ordinary guys who just happen to be gay"). These provided the best mapping of the identity data in relation to our broad research question around LGBT students' experiences of university life. A number of codes cut across both themes, such as the notion of "good gays" (who conform to the norms of compulsory heterosexuality as much as possible by being "straight-acting" and "straight-looking"; Taulke-Johnson, 2008) and "bad gays" (who are "politically active and culturally assertive"; Epstein et al., 2000, p. 19). This example is not a case of undesirable overlap between themes; it illustrates that certain concepts or issues may cut across themes and provide a unifying framework for telling a coherent story about what is going on in the data, overall. Another important element of this phase is starting to explore the relationship between themes and to consider how themes will work together in telling an overall story about the data. Good themes are distinctive and, to some extent, stand alone, but they also need to work together as a whole. In your analysis, one central concept may draw together or underpin all or most of your themes—for our example, this would be heteronormativity. In some cases, we would (ultimately) develop an overarching theme that captured or accounted for this broad connecting concept or meaning.

During this phase, there will be codes that do not clearly fit anywhere, but do not discard or forget these; they may end up as part of revised or new themes for the finalized analysis. That said, not everything will end up being included or reported in your analysis. Being able to let go of coded material and indeed provisional themes if they do not fit within your overall analysis is an important part of qualitative analysis. Remember, your job in analyzing the data, and reporting them, is to tell a particular story about the data, that addresses your research question. It is not to represent everything that was said in the data.

How many themes are enough or too many? Unfortunately, there is no magic formula that states that if you have X amount of data, and you are writing a report of Y length, you should have Z number of themes. The more data you have, the more codes and, thus, themes, you will likely generate; if you are writing a longer report, you will have space to discuss more themes. For our

data set, we generated six themes; for brevity, only two are summarized in Exhibit 4.2 and only four are discussed in this chapter. In an 8,000- to 10,000-word article, we typically report no more than two to six themes.

With a larger number of themes, your analysis can lose coherence. What is essential is that your themes are presented in sufficient depth and detail to convey the richness and complexity of your data—you are unlikely to achieve that if you report more than six themes in a 10,000-word report. Your themes will likely be "thin." If you are trying to provide a meaningful overview of your data, one to two themes are likely insufficient; however, two themes may be sufficient for an in-depth analysis of part of the data set.

You should end this phase with a thematic map or table outlining your candidate themes, and you should collate all the data extracts relevant to each theme, so you are ready to begin the process of reviewing and further developing your themes.

Phase 4. Reviewing and Developing Themes

This phase is about both quality checking and analytic development. It involves a recursive process whereby your developing themes are reviewed in relation to the coded data and entire data set and your analysis developed accordingly. This phase is particularly important for novice researchers and for those working with very large data sets, where it is simply not possible to hold your entire data set in your head. The first stage is to consider your themes against the collated extracts of data and to explore whether each theme works in relation to the data. If it does not, you might need to discard some codes or relocate them under another theme; alternatively, you may redraw the boundaries of the theme, so that it more meaningfully captures the relevant data. If these tweaks do not work, you might need to discard your theme altogether and start again—you should not force your analysis into coherence. Key questions to ask are as follows:

- Is this a (multifaceted) theme—or is it just a (single facet) code?

- If it is a theme, what is the quality of this theme (does it tell me something useful about the data set and my research question)?
- What are the boundaries of this theme (what does it include and exclude)?
- Are there enough (meaningful) data to support this theme (is the theme *thin* or *thick*)?
- Are the data too diverse and wide ranging, without a clear central organizing concept unifying them (does the theme lack coherence)?

You may end up collapsing a number of potential themes together or splitting a big broad theme into a number of more specific or coherent themes.

Once you have a distinctive and coherent set of themes that work in relation to the coded data extracts, you should undertake the second phase in the review and development process—evaluating your candidate themes in relation to the entire data set. This involves one final reread of all your data to determine whether your themes meaningfully capture patterning across the entire data set or an aspect thereof. What you are aiming for is a set of themes that evoke the most important and relevant elements of the data, and the overall tone of the data, in relation to your research question.

If your thematic map and set of themes do this, good. You can move to the next phase. If not, further refining and reviewing will be necessary to adequately capture the data. A mismatch will most likely occur if selective or inadequate coding has taken place, or if coding evolved substantially over the coding process, and earlier items in the data set were not recoded for consistency. Revision at this point might involve creating additional themes or tweaking or discarding existing themes.

Phase 5. Refining, Defining, and Naming Themes

This phase involves a more fine-grained analytic development and refinement of your themes. This phase centers on the deep analytic work involved in TA, the crucial shaping up of analysis into its final detail. As analysis now necessarily involves writing, the separation between Phase 5 and Phase 6 is often slightly blurry.

Defining your themes is an important part of the reflexive TA process, as it helps clarify whether you can clearly state what is unique and specific about each theme—whether you can sum up the "essence" of each theme in a few sentences is a good test of this (see Exhibit 4.2). A good

---

EXHIBIT 4.2

Definitions and Labels for Two Example Themes

Theme 1. "There's always that level of uncertainty": Compulsory heterosexuality at university. Maps the participants' experiences of (infrequent) homophobia and (constant) heterosexism and highlights tensions experienced in relating to (straight) others, particularly people who were felt to be common sources of heterosexism and overt homophobia (i.e., straight men; members of religious and some ethnically and racially minoritized groups), and feelings, or fear, of exclusion and not belonging. Heterosexism meant participants negotiated their sexual identities in an uncertain environment and experienced constant (but minimized) fear of people's reactions to their sexuality. They had expected university students to be liberal and open-minded and were surprised and disappointed they weren't. But they felt this applied if you were "straight-acting," indicating university is a safe space only if you are a "good gay." Participants experienced difficulty coming out at university but also internalized and took responsibility for these difficulties rather than viewing coming out as something that is difficult because of compulsory heterosexuality. Although participants expressed some anger about experiences of overt homophobia, some homophobic and heterosexist "banter" (e.g., antigay humor) was acceptable if from friends—an indication that friends were comfortable with their sexuality—but wasn't acceptable if from strangers. The heterosexual assumption and compulsory heterosexuality were typically framed as to-be-expected parts of normal life.

Theme 2. "I don't go out asking for trouble": Managing heterosexism. Outlines the ways the participants modified their speech, behavior, and practices to avoid heterosexism and homophobia and continually monitored people and the environment for evidence of potential heterosexism or homophobia. They constantly weighed whether it was safe to come or be out with a particular person or in a particular space. The participants typically assumed responsibility for managing heterosexism (they don't "ask" for trouble) and accepted this as a normal part of life. They seemed to lack a sense of entitlement to live free from heterosexism and a political and conceptual language with which to interpret their experiences of heterosexism and homophobia.

TA will have themes that (a) do not try to do too much, as themes should ideally have a singular focus; (b) are related but do not overlap, so they are not repetitive—although they may build on previous themes; and (c) directly address your research question. The two example themes in Exhibit 4.2 both have a clear focus, scope, and purpose. In our final analysis, each of the six themes in turn builds on and develops the previous theme(s), and together the themes provide a coherent overall story about the data. In some cases, you may want to have subthemes within a theme. Subthemes are useful where there are specific or notable ways the central organizing concept of a theme is manifest in the data set, and you want to highlight this for analytic clarity or emphasis. We recommend the judicious use of subthemes; too many can produce a thin, fragmented analysis.

This phase involves selecting extracts to present and analyze and then setting out the story of each theme with or around these extracts. What makes good data to quote and analyze? Ideally, each extract would provide a vivid, compelling example that clearly illustrates or evidences the analytic points you are making. It is good to draw on extracts from across your data items to show the coverage of the theme, rather than drawing on only one data item (this can be frustrating when one source articulates it all perfectly—the analysis in Exhibit 4.3 quotes Asha because he expressed that part of the theme particularly well).

The extracts you select to quote and analyze provide the structure for the analysis—the narrative informing the reader of your interpretation of the data and their meaning. Data do not speak for themselves—you must not simply paraphrase the content of the data. In analyzing the data, you tell a story of the data. Your analytic narrative needs to tell the reader *what* about the data were interesting and *why*. Sometimes, you will use data extracts to illustrate claims you are making about the data set. Sometimes, you make specific analytic comments about a particular extract. Your analytic narrative might use data extracts in just one of these ways, or

might combine both. Throughout the analysis section of your report, you would typically have at least as much narrative surrounding your data as extracts.

Data must be interpreted and connected to your research questions and to the scholarly fields within which your work is situated. Some qualitative research includes this as a separate discussion section; other research incorporates discussion of the literature into the analysis, creating a Results and Discussion section. Both styles work with TA. An integrated approach works well when strong connections exist with existing research and when the analysis is more theoretical or interpretative. This approach can also avoid repetition between results and discussion sections.

Exhibit 4.3 shows part of the analysis of our theme "managing heterosexism." It starts with a general summary of the theme's core issue, and then expands on this by providing specific examples of different aspects of the theme, illustrated using brief extracts. Once sufficient detail has been provided to show the scope of the theme, the longer extract offers rich and evocative detail of what this actually meant for one participant. Analysis of that extract begins by highlighting some data features that provide the basis for our interpretation around a broader practice of minimization and individualization—a pattern across the data set. There is an interweaving of detailed and specific analysis of what happens in a particular data extract, and more summative analysis that illustrates the broader content of the data set in relation to the theme. This reflects our combination of two broad styles of reflexive TA: (a) *descriptive*, in which data tend to be used in illustrative ways; and (b) *conceptual and interpretative*, in which extracts tend to be analyzed in more detail, often for the latent meanings on which they draw. Both offer important analyses of data and serve different purposes, but they can usefully be combined, as we show. The latter can be a more difficult form of analysis to grasp because it moves from surface or obvious meanings to latent or implicit meanings; it can take experience to learn to notice these in data.

EXHIBIT 4.3

Report of Theme 2: *"I Don't Go Out Asking for Trouble": Managing Heterosexism* [excerpt]

In common with others (e.g., Taulke-Johnson & Rivers, 1999), our participants described monitoring and assessing people and the environment for evidence of potential heterosexism, weighing up whether it would be safe to come and be out. They decided *not to* come out when people made overtly antigay comments. Asha, for instance, took the comment "one thing I just can't understand is gay people" as strong evidence of a potential negative response to his coming out and chose not to. They made decisions *to* come out when people discussed gay-related issues in a broadly positive way, mentioned gay friends, or expressed "gay-friendly" sentiments (e.g., "want[ing] to be the ultimate personal fag hag," Asha).

This monitoring was sometimes a relatively passive process ("I just picked up tell-tale signs about it," Asha); at other times, participants actively "test[ed] the waters" (David) and "tr[ied] and manipulate the conversation to head in that direction and see how to respond to it" (Asha). Asha described this rather evocatively:

Asha: *just basically erm er, does he have a gay friend? Yes or no, is he alright with a gay friend? Yes or no. This person is alright to go out with—you know to come out with and basically if the answers are different the questions are different and the outcomes would be different . . . you're just trying to you know answer all the questions to see what the outcome is and it's kinda a bit of a headache*
VC: *It sounds exhausting and stressful*
Asha: *It is, very much so but it's kinda something that I have in the back of my mind . . . I find out you know which box they tick, which box they don't tick, and if they tick the right ones or if they tick the wrong ones I know what action to take from there . . .*
VC: *Yep yep, god that sounds very hard*
Asha: *Well the thing is it's almost kinda-I wouldn't, I don't know it's something that just happens in the background you know— I hardly notice it*
VC: *Yeah, like this processing that going on and kinda churning away*
Asha: *Yeah all these things that you just happens that you're not even completely aware of but it's building up and you know you look back at it you see all these point, and you say to my—you say to yourself right "I'm gonna tell this person I'm gay" "I'm gonna" you know and yeah*

After initially agreeing with the interviewer, VC's, assessment that this is an "exhausting stressful process" ("It is, very much so"), Asha described it as a more subconscious process, something he "hardly notice[d]." When VC *again* suggested it sounded "very hard," he offered no agreement. Despite his detailed and vivid account, Asha appeared invested in framing this as a mundane rather than negative and, therefore, "hard" process. This "minimizing the negative" approach was common: The participants consistently framed phenomena that could be read as evidence of heteronormativity and instances of prejudice (Taulke-Johnson, 2008) as to-be-expected parts of normal life.

Asha earlier vividly described this process in a way that suggested it *was* negative yet implicitly located the problem within his own psychology rather than the environment:

Asha: *constantly monitoring, keeping an eye out, keeping an ear out just you know, the little checklist this worst case—or not a worst case scenario, but you're having a list in your mind of all the possible things that can go wrong and you—you're always going over that list of all the things that could go wrong I've kinda built—well personally for me it builds on my paranoia.*

In describing himself as *paranoid*, Asha suggests his response, rather than a heterosexist context, is at fault. All the participants interpreted difficulties they experienced in navigating a heterosexist world in this way. John, for example, associated his difficulties with coming out with his personality (he got embarrassed and *feared* getting and looking embarrassed) rather than with the inherent difficulties that can exist around coming out in heterosexist contexts (see Flowers & Buston, 2001; Markowe, 2002). In internalizing their response to heteronormative contexts thus, responsibility for change is located *within the* participants, making it a personal rather than a political issue.

The degree to which students implicitly accepted responsibility for *managing* heterosexism to avoid "trouble" (David) by constantly modifying their speech, behavior, and other practices was the most striking feature of how they navigated the university climate. They had a strong sense that behaving or speaking in certain ways (being a "bad gay"; Taulke-Johnson, 2008) invited "trouble" and placed the onus on themselves to avoid it and protect themselves: "you have to sort of be very careful how you sort of came across to people" (David). The participants censored their speech and behavior ("tell . . . half of the truth," Andreas); avoided coming out or making "overt" displays of homosexuality, such as by showing affection to a same-sex partner, being too camp and acting like "a mincing queen" (John), or wearing "obviously gay" clothing; and avoided certain people ("groups of lads," John) and areas. Campus and city were seen as safe "as long as you took the measures—you know as long as you're sensible about it you don't go throwing it in people's faces you don't go down to you know places like [predominantly working class and ethnically diverse city suburb]" (Asha). [**analysis continues**]

Note. VC is the interviewer Victoria Clarke.

Even when we present a lot of short extracts of data, however, seemingly reporting quite closely what participants said, the analysis always moves beyond the data. It does not just report words—it interprets them and organizes them within a larger overarching conceptual framework. Regardless of what form of reflexive TA is done, analysis uses data to make a point. Analysis needs to be driven by the question "So what?" What is relevant or useful here to addressing my question? This process of telling an analytic narrative around your data extracts needs to take place for all your themes. Each theme also needs to be developed not only in its own right but also in relation to your research question and in relation to the other themes. Conclusions should be drawn from across the whole analysis.

The other aspect of this phase is working out what to call each theme. Naming might seem trivial, but this short title can and should signal a lot. A good name for a theme is informative, concise, and catchy. The name "Mincing queens versus ordinary guys who just happen to be gay" is memorable and signals both the focus of the theme—different ways of being gay—and something about the content of the analysis— that participants navigate between two different versions of being a gay man. "Mincing queens" is also a direct quotation from the data. Using quotations in titles (see also Exhibit 4.2) can provide an immediate and vivid sense of what a theme is about while staying close to participants' language and concepts. One of the risks of poorly named themes—including one-word theme names—is creating the impression you are report- ing topic summaries rather than fully realized shared meaning themes.

Phase 6. Producing the Report

Although the final phase of analysis is the production of a report such as a journal article or a dissertation, you do not complete Phases 1 through 5 and then write up your analysis in reflexive TA. Writing and analysis are thoroughly interwoven in (Big Q) qualitative research— from informal writing of notes or memos and

journaling to the more formal processes of analysis and report writing. This phase formalizes and finalizes your analysis and writing. The purpose of your report is to provide a compelling story about your data based on your analysis. The story should be convincing and clear yet complex and embedded in a scholarly field. In general, qualitative research is best reported using a first- person active tense, but check the requirements for your report.

The order in which you present your themes is important: Themes should connect logically and meaningfully and, if relevant, should build on previous themes to tell a coherent story about the data. We decided to use "'There's always that level of uncertainty': Compulsory heterosexuality at university," which documents the participants' experiences of homophobia and heterosexism, as our first theme because these experiences, particularly the constant possibility, and fear, of heterosexism, shaped almost every aspect of the students' university life and would be referenced throughout the rest of the analysis. From there, it made sense to discuss the partici- pants' experiences of managing heterosexism. We decided the two identity themes (a) "I'm not hiding, but I'm not throwing it in people's faces": Being out (but not too out) at university and (b) "Mincing queens versus ordinary guys who just happen to be gay," were the logical next step because the theme of coming out and being out closely related to the participants' fear of heterosexism and the ways in which they sought to avoid heterosexism. The second identity theme—which discussed different conceptualizations of gay identity and the participants' desire to be perceived as ordinary guys who just happen to be gay—had a less immediately obvious connection to the first two themes but linked well to the first identity theme. With reflexive TA, you are not aiming to map a structure of responses and connections in the data set; the developed themes should provide a compelling response to your research question, individually and collectively. Your "write-up" should highlight relevant connections and continuities between themes, but marking these is not the primary purpose of reflexive TA, and we recommend against overly complex thematic structures, as they risk losing analytic depth and insight.

DOING REFLEXIVE THEMATIC ANALYSIS WELL

Our guidelines lay out the process for producing a good reflexive TA that is thorough, plausible, and sophisticated. But like any analysis, TA can be done well, and it can be done poorly (see Braun & Clarke, 2021a). Common errors include providing data extracts with little or no analysis that tells us how they are relevant to addressing the research question or simply paraphrasing or summarizing data (see Braun & Clarke, 2006, 2022b). Using data collection questions as themes is another common error and risks the resulting analysis reporting topic summaries rather than fully realized themes—themes are better identified across the content of what participants say rather than via the questions they have been asked. Something like "incidents of homophobia" would be a weak—topic summary—theme because it would involve describing different things participants reported in response to an interview question on the topic. "'There's always that level of uncertainty': Compulsory heterosexuality at university" is a much stronger theme because it captures something more complex about how the participants' constant fear of homophobia and heterosexism shaped their university lives. It also incorporates data from across the whole interviews not just responses to specific questions about homophobia and heterosexism.

On a different level, an analysis can be weak or unconvincing if themes are not coherent or try to do too much. Analysis can also suffer from lack of evidence. You need to provide examples of, and analyze, enough data excerpts to convince the reader that this pattern you claim really was evident—consider the balance of data and analysis in Exhibit 4.3. A TA does have to relate to patterns found across your data set. This does not mean every data item has to evidence each

theme, but it has to be more than idiosyncratic. TA can also suffer because of mismatches between the data and analysis or between the form of TA done and the theoretical position of the report and from confusing topic summaries and shared meaning themes. Finally, problems arise from "mashing up" reflexive TA with other approaches to TA that differ profoundly in procedures, conceptualization of key constructs, and in what constitutes meaningful knowledge production (for more discussion of these and for checklists for doing good-quality TA, see Braun & Clarke, 2006, 2021a). In developing and revising your analysis, make sure data-based claims are justified and that the claims fit within your overall theoretical position (e.g., whether you are using an experiential or critical form of TA). Your task in convincingly telling your analytic story is a combination of "showing"—what is in the data—and "telling"—telling the reader what sense you make of the data set, to convince them that is what sense they should make of it, too.

References

Bond, L. A., Holmes, T. R., Byrne, C., Babchuck, L., & Kirton-Robbins, S. (2008). Movers and shakers: How and why women become and remain engaged in community leadership. *Psychology of Women Quarterly, 32*(1), 48–64. https://doi.org/10.1111/j.1471-6402.2007.00406.x

Boyatzis, R. E. (1998). *Transforming qualitative information: Thematic analysis and code development.* Sage Publications.

Braun, V., & Clarke, V. (2006). Using thematic analysis in psychology. *Qualitative Research in Psychology, 3*(2), 77–101. https://doi.org/10.1191/1478088706qp063oa

Braun, V., & Clarke, V. (2013). *Successful qualitative research: A practical guide for beginners.* Sage.

Braun, V., & Clarke, V. (2019). Reflecting on reflexive thematic analysis. *Qualitative Research in Sport, Exercise and Health, 11*(4), 589–597. https://doi.org/10.1080/2159676X.2019.1628806

Braun, V., & Clarke, V. (2021a). One size fits all? What counts as quality practice in (reflexive) thematic analysis? *Qualitative Research in Psychology, 18*(3), 328–352. https://doi.org/10.1080/14780887.2020.1769238

Braun, V., & Clarke, V. (2021b). To saturate or not to saturate? Questioning data saturation as a useful concept for thematic analysis and sample-size rationales. *Qualitative Research in Sport, Exercise and Health, 13*(2), 201–216. https://doi.org/10.1080/2159676X.2019.1704846

Braun, V., & Clarke, V. (2022a). Conceptual and design thinking for thematic analysis. *Qualitative Psychology, 9*(1), 3–26. https://doi.org/10.1037/qup0000196

Braun, V., & Clarke, V. (2022b). *Thematic analysis: A practical guide.* Sage.

Braun, V., Clarke, V., & Hayfield, N. (2022). "A starting point for your journey, not a map": Nikki Hayfield in conversation with Virginia Braun and Victoria Clarke about thematic analysis. *Qualitative Research in Psychology. 19*(2), 424–445. https://doi.org/10.1080/14780887.2019.1670765

Braun, V., Terry, G., Gavey, N., & Fenaughty, J. (2009). 'Risk' and sexual coercion among gay and bisexual men in Aotearoa/New Zealand—Key informant accounts. *Culture, Health & Sexuality, 11*(2), 111–124. https://doi.org/10.1080/13691050802398208

Clarke, V., & Kitzinger, C. (2004). Lesbian and gay parents on talk shows: Resistance or collusion in heterosexism. *Qualitative Research in Psychology, 1*(3), 195–217. https://doi.org/10.1191/1478088704qp0140a

Delgado-Infante, M. L., & Ofreneo, M. A. P. (2014). Maintaining a "good girl" position: Young Filipina women constructing sexual agency in first sex within Catholicism. *Feminism & Psychology, 24*(3), 390–407. https://doi.org/10.1177/0959353514530715

Epstein, D., Johnson, R., & Steinberg, D. L. (2000). Twice told tales: Transformation, recuperation and emergence in the age of consent debates 1998. *Sexualities, 3*(1), 5–30. https://doi.org/10.1177/136346000003001001

Epstein, D., O'Flynn, S., & Telford, D. (2003). *Silenced sexualities in schools and universities.* Trentham Books.

Finlay, L., & Gough, B. (Eds.). (2003). *Reflexivity: A practical guide for researchers in health and social sciences.* Blackwell Science. https://doi.org/10.1002/9780470776094

Flowers, P., & Buston, K. (2001). "I was terrified of being different": Exploring gay men's accounts of growing-up in a heterosexist society. *Journal of Adolescence, 24*(1), 51–65. https://doi.org/10.1006/jado.2000.0362

Guest, G., MacQueen, K. M., & Namey, E. E. (2012). *Applied thematic analysis.* Sage. https://doi.org/10.4135/9781483384436

Hayes, N. (1997). Theory-led thematic analysis: Social identification in small companies. In N. Hayes (Ed.), *Doing qualitative analysis in psychology* (pp. 93–114). Psychology Press.

Howitt, D., & Cramer, D. (2008). *Introduction to research methods in psychology* (2nd ed.). Prentice Hall.

Joffe, H. (2012). Thematic analysis. In D. Harper & A. R. Thompson (Eds.), *Qualitative methods in mental health and psychotherapy: A guide for students and practitioners* (pp. 209–223). Wiley.

Kidder, L. H., & Fine, M. (1987). Qualitative and quantitative methods: When stories converge. In M. M. Mark & L. Shotland (Eds.), *New directions in program evaluation* (pp. 57–75). Jossey-Bass. https://doi.org/10.1002/ev.1459

King, N., & Brooks, J. (2017). Thematic analysis in organisational research. In C. Cassell, A. L. Cunliffe, & G. Grandy (Eds.), *The Sage handbook of qualitative business and management research methods* (pp. 219–236). Sage.

Leal, I., Engebretson, J., Cohen, L., Rodriguez, A., Wangyal, T., Lopez, G., & Chaoul, A. (2015). Experiences of paradox: A qualitative analysis of living with cancer using a framework approach. *Psycho-Oncology, 24*(2), 138–146. https://doi.org/10.1002/pon.3578

Madill, A., Jordan, A., & Shirley, C. (2000). Objectivity and reliability in qualitative analysis: Realist, contextualist and radical constructionist epistemologies. *British Journal of Psychology, 91*(1), 1–20. https://doi.org/10.1348/000712600161646

Markowe, L. A. (2002). Coming out as lesbian. In A. Coyle & C. Kitzinger (Eds.), *Lesbian and gay psychology: New perspectives* (pp. 63–80). BPS Blackwell.

Matthews, H., Turner, A., Williamson, I., & Clyne, W. (2018). 'It's a silver lining': A template analysis of satisfaction and quality of life following post-mastectomy breast reconstruction. *British Journal of Health Psychology, 23*(2), 455–475. https://doi.org/10.1111/bjhp.12299

Miles, M. B., & Huberman, A. M. (1994). *Qualitative data analysis: An expanded sourcebook* (2nd ed.). Sage.

Reaney, M., Chmiel, N., & Churchill, S. (2018). Foot care, 'spousal' support and type 2 diabetes: An exploratory qualitative study. *Psychology & Health, 33*(9), 1191–1207. https://doi.org/10.1080/08870446.2018.1481215

Rich, A. (1980). Compulsory heterosexuality and lesbian existence. *Signs: Journal of Women in Culture and Society, 5*(4), 631–660. https://doi.org/10.1086/493756

Ritchie, J., & Spencer, L. (1994). Qualitative data analysis for applied policy research. In A. Bryman & R. G. Burgess (Eds.), *Analyzing qualitative data* (pp. 173–194). Taylor & Francis. https://doi.org/10.4324/9780203413081_chapter_9

Taulke-Johnson, R. (2008). Moving beyond homophobia, harassment and intolerance: Gay male university students' alternative narratives. *Discourse, 29*(1), 121–133. https://doi.org/10.1080/01596300701802813

Taulke-Johnson, R., & Rivers, I. (1999). Providing a safe environment for lesbian, gay and bisexual students living in university accommodation. *Youth & Policy, 64*, 74–89.

Terry, G., & Hayfield, N. (2021). *Essentials of thematic analysis*. American Psychological Association. https://doi.org/10.1037/0000238-000

Warner, M. (1991). Introduction: Fear of a queer planet. *Social Text, 29*(1991), 3–17.

CHAPTER 5

PHENOMENOLOGICAL METHODOLOGY, METHODS, AND PROCEDURES FOR RESEARCH IN PSYCHOLOGY

Frederick J. Wertz

We shall find in ourselves, and nowhere else, the unity and true meaning of phenomenology. It is less a question of counting up quotations than of determining and expressing in concrete form this phenomenology for ourselves that has given a number of present-day readers the impression of recognizing what they had been waiting for. Phenomenology is only accessible through a phenomenological method. Let us, therefore, try to bring together the celebrated phenomenological themes as they have grown together spontaneously in life. Perhaps we shall then understand why phenomenology has for so long remained in an initial stage, as a problem to be solved, and a hope to be realized.

—Merleau-Ponty (1945/1962, p. viii)

Among qualitative research traditions, phenomenology is by far the oldest, largest, and most challenging to communicate in a single writing. Formally entering American psychology only in the 1960s, phenomenology has generated a wealth of original resources for psychologists that have been operative throughout psychology's history, though informally and unevenly practiced. Phenomenology offers psychological researchers of all traditions much of value, ranging from philosophical foundations to methodological principles (norms), essential methods, and a large family of well-articulated procedures for conducting research. The ubiquity of phenomenology— its significant overlap with all other qualitative methods and its essential place among quantitative methods—is elaborated below. Phenomenology is an immensely rich, self-sufficient approach to research as well as being integral, even when only implicit, within other research traditions. Phenomenology is not a closed or univocal approach but a multipronged, living tradition with tensions, controversies, lively self-criticism, and continuing innovations that continue to develop. It is multidisciplinary and multinational.[1]

---

[1] The *multidisciplinary* span of phenomenology includes archaeology, architecture, art history, cognitive science, communicology, counseling, cultural anthropology, dance, ecology, economics, education, English, ethnic studies, ethnology, ethnomethodology, film studies, French, gender studies, geography, hermeneutics, history, linguistics, law, literature, medical anthropology, medicine, musicology, neuroscience, nursing, philosophy, political science, psychiatry, psychology, psychopathology, religious education, religious studies, social work, sociology, sport, and theology. The *multinational* span includes Argentina, Australia, Austria, Belarus, Belgium, Brazil, Bulgaria, Canada, Chile, China, Colombia, Croatia, Czech Republic, Denmark, Finland, France, Germany, Greece, Hong Kong, Hungary, Iceland, India, Indonesia, Iran, Ireland, Israel, Italy, Japan, Korea, Latvia, Lebanon, Lithuania, Malta, Mexico, Netherlands. New Zealand, Norway, Peru, Poland, Portugal, Romania, Russia, Serbia, Slovenia, South Africa, Spain, Switzerland, Taiwan, Tunisia, Turkey, United Kingdom, United States of America, and Venezuela (Embree, 2010).

I would like to thank the following for their kind and generous help with this manuscript: Lee Bach, Diane Blau, Scott Churchill, Larry Davidson, Sarah Kamens, Linda McMullen, Lisa Osbeck, Tone Roald, and Mary Watkins.

https://doi.org/10.1037/0000319-005
APA Handbook of Research Methods in Psychology, Second Edition: Vol. 2. Research Designs: Quantitative, Qualitative, Neuropsychological, and Biological, H. Cooper (Editor-in-Chief)

Phenomenology has creatively evolved in the hands of new generations of researchers who, with their own unique personal and communal sensibilities and talents, address novel topics and problems across the full spectrum of humanities and scientific disciplines including psychology. This chapter aims to clarify the phenomenological method and how it has been employed in various traditions of psychological research, with attention to its historical context and original concepts. To that end, the underlying unity of contributions rather than internal criticisms among these traditions is emphasized.

When I began to study psychology 50 years ago, I was sadly disappointed by the discipline's remoteness from its phenomena—the experience and conduct of humans and other animals. Psychology failed to sufficiently address such everyday life engagements as perception, problem solving, and empathy; enigmatic complexities as crime, political activism, and emigration; human comedies and tragedies as humor and sickness; and burning social and historical problems as poverty, racism, and war. It struck me that psychology's remoteness, deafening silences, sterility, and irrelevance resulted from the narrowness and inadequacies of its research methods. Fortunately, I encountered works of William James, Sigmund Freud, Jean Piaget, Karen Horney, Abraham Maslow, James Gibson, Herbert Simon, John C. Flanagan, Edith Stein, and countless others whose research and contributions were more faithful to, and however imperfect, revelatory of real-world psychological life. However, their research methods were given little and often no attention in textbooks and classes. In the context of well-institutionalized quantitative methods and methodological norms, qualitative research methods were judged to be inferior, denied importance, accorded little if any formal standing, and considered prescientific or even pseudoscientific. Their primary value was considered to be the suggestion of hypotheses that require verification by more truly scientific methods, even though a large literature has long contested this limited contribution.

I was fortunate to discover an approach to science older than the institution of psychology itself, one that insightfully delineated the problems of psychology and resolved them with an approach to science developed across the full spectrum of disciplines through the 20th century: phenomenology. Because this approach is eminently scientific, rigorous, self-critical, methodical, and systematic, and because it places special emphasis on the problems of investigating consciousness, phenomenology offers psychology the capacity to better achieve its goal of investigating human experience. Phenomenological philosophy has critically elucidated the nature and history of science with epistemology, ontology, and ethics that inform research methodology; has identified methods that are essential for the achievement of psychology's goals; and has expanded procedural resources to investigate mental life. Although not widely acknowledged even today, phenomenology has been taken up by psychological researchers in many different ways, establishing a treasure trove of generative procedures.

I have spent the last 5 decades learning about the contributions of phenomenology to psychology, and I continue to be humbled by the flow of new publications. One of the most important and promising developments over the last half century has been the emergence, codification, legitimization, and institutionalization of qualitative methods that produce psychological knowledge. On the one hand, phenomenological psychology offers distinct research procedures that can produce wide ranging knowledge in its own right, and, on the other hand, phenomenology articulates methodology and methods that are required in both qualitative and quantitative psychology. Because these methods bring rigor to the study of mental life, they are fundamental for the achievement of psychology's scientific, professional, and social goals. Researchers of all orientations can benefit from understanding phenomenological psychology.

PHENOMENOLOGY

The word *phenomenology* has various meanings in different contexts. It is important to understand these usages given their occasional obscurity, nuances, overlap, controversies, and commonality. Kockelmans (1967, p. 24) documented the use of the word in philosophical writings as early as 1785, though a well-defined technical meaning originated with Hegel.[2] The term is used in medicine, especially psychiatry, to refer to the empirical description of patients' signs and symptoms. This context includes ideographic case studies and nomothetic, statistical analyses of populations (Spitzer & Uehlein, 1992). Such descriptions play a crucial role in taxonomic systems and entail significant detail, which decreases for diagnostic entities with neurological etiology and increases when etiology is unknown or possibly psychosocial. Such psychiatric research emphasizes patients' first-person experience and includes behavior and expressivity without any inference or theory. The *Diagnostic and Statistical Manual of Mental Disorders* (*DSM*) series of manuals, "phenomenological" in the limited sense indicated above, is the basis of diagnosis, research, and treatment.

Carl Rogers's personality theory and person-centered approach, which have had wide application in psychotherapy, industry, education, government, and health care, are regularly considered phenomenological in textbooks and the broader literature (see Douglas et al., 2016). Though Rogers (1961) did not use the term regularly, he frequently used the phrase the *phenomenal field* to denote first-person experience as the very center of the psychological life of all persons, including patients, therapists, students, workers, politicians, and scientists. The open, detailed understanding of the first person frame of reference was of the utmost importance to Rogers, and extensive concrete descriptions were the methodical cornerstone of his practice, theorizing, and research.

Phenomenology as a scientific method has been most extensively developed by the philosopher Edmund Husserl as required for any study of experience. Husserl (1901/1970) called his early work "descriptive psychology," and he wrote extensively about phenomenology as a research method necessary for genuine psychology and

human sciences (Husserl, 1977). This descriptive method, open-ended and historically evolving, eschews dogma, prejudice, and inference. It is employed to freshly conceptualize topics apart from prior theory and has varied procedurally according to individual investigators, topics, problems, and purposes. As a broad, complex movement, phenomenology has been considered realist, transcendental, existential, hermeneutic, narrative, ethical, and critical. In all its variations, the phenomenological method has been appropriated and continues to develop today in psychology and across the human sciences.

Phenomenology has been recognized in other disparate contexts, some historically prior to modern science, others never before called or recognized as phenomenological, and even others usually contrasted with phenomenology. For instance, Johann Wolfgang von Goethe (1749–1832), who never used the term *phenomenology*, has regularly been identified by historians of psychology as phenomenological on account of his meticulous and faithful descriptions of experience and his work on color perception (Boring, 1929). Hennigfeld (2015) compellingly documented Goethe's phenomenology, with reference to Husserl's method and later applications, not only in his general thinking and psychology of perception and cognition but also in his philosophy, poetry, and even natural science! Spiegelberg (1981) identified "proto-phenomenology" in the research of Newton, Einstein, and others. Feest (2021) found phenomenological method in experimental psychology, for instance Titchener's psychophysical experimentation, and claimed that the method was also employed, but with superior rigor, in experiments by Gestalt psychologists. Contemporary historians have found many overlooked applications of phenomenology throughout multiple schools of psychology (Benetka & Joerchal, 2016). I have documented phenomenological procedures as essential, though neither named nor acknowledged, in psychological research methods employed by

---

[2]Kockelmans (1967) begins his book with the statement "Anyone familiar with the situation knows that as soon as he uses the term 'phenomenology,' he enters a sphere of ambiguity" (p. 24).

nonpsychologists (e.g., the obstetrician Leboyer's investigation of fetal experience; Wertz, 1981) as well as in psychological traditions considered theoretically antithetical to phenomenology, such as psychoanalysis (Wertz, 1986; Wertz & Olbert, 2016), and methodologically antithetical, such as testing and mathematical modeling (Wertz, 2019). New recognitions of phenomenology are often critical inasmuch as they identify limits and flaws in extant implementations of the method. Such shortcomings may be attributed to a lack of formal education, training, and understanding.

The common core meaning of the word *phenomenology* is far from trivial across all these contexts: The unprejudiced, nonimposing methodical clarification and elucidation of experience as concretely lived through by persons. The ubiquity of this method in psychology is understandable inasmuch as this central subject matter requires faithful conceptualization and description as a basis for all inquiry, qualitative and quantitative, empirical and theoretical. All psychology must in this important way be phenomenological or at least phenomenologically based to some extent, whether self-conscious, rigorous, and systematic or informal, haphazard, poor, and even erroneous. In its core meaning, phenomenology contrasts with methods that focus on the material world apart from experience, especially physical reductionistic methods, as well as all methods that entail causal inference, speculation, ungrounded belief, personal opinion, social judgment, and theory. Always rich with illustrative examples, phenomenology *shows* rather than proves or argues (Hennigfeld, 2015). Phenomenology is not to be identified primarily with particular *results* of research, whether empirical or theoretical; rather, it is fundamentally a kind of *method* that may entail diverse procedures in its observations (in the broadest sense), analyses, and descriptions. Research results vary with new topics, questions, data, and procedures

by researchers employing it's fundamentally open, flexibly adaptive, and dynamically changing method through history.

PHENOMENOLOGICAL METHODOLOGY: PHILOSOPHICAL FOUNDATIONS OF HUMAN SCIENCE

Phenomenology has been traced back to Greek and Asian antiquity, identified throughout the West, and even found in indigenous cultures (Wertz, 2017). Its methodology, developed in the modern science by Edmund Husserl (1859–1938), has important precursors in Wilhelm Dilthey (1833–1911) and Husserl's teacher, Franz Brentano (1838–1917). Commonly, these three thinkers demonstrated that the scientific investigation of mental life requires a methodology different from that of the sciences of physical nature.

Dilthey (1894) asserted that because material nature exists outside of and apart from mental life and is composed of independent parts, knowledge of "nature" must proceed by inference (e.g., of causal relations) and explanatory models (e.g., to interrelate its separate parts). In contrast, "mental life" is immediately lived through, a seamless unity of meaningfully interrelated and interdependent moments[3] conceptualizable without inference. Natural sciences (*Naturwissenschaften*) proceed by inferential explanation, whereas human sciences (*Geisteswissenshaften*) proceed first and primarily by descriptive understanding. Dilthey understood that psychological life flows, streams, and develops through various processes (perceiving, remembering, anticipating, thinking, feeling, acting) that are interrelated in meaning. Experience includes an embodied "I" efficaciously and practically engaging in the value-laden, social and collective world. Impactfully shaping that world through involvements with others, the person reforms and develops as a participant in world history. The multifaceted, teleological, temporal, and social sphere of meaning

---

[3]The term *moments* contrasts with *parts* in phenomenological parlance and has multiple references, not exclusively temporal. Whereas parts are independent and separable from the wholes they compose, moments are interdependent, contextually interrelated, holistically organized, and, therefore, inseparable.

must be the central focus of psychology. Unlike the physical world, which is independent of the scientist's experience and composed of objects external to each other, psychological life is lived through by the scientist and must be grasped and understood in its meaningful organizations. Practices of abstracting, measuring, and functionally analyzing variables in isolation must be informed by prior description and analytic understanding.

Brentano (1973) emphasized the universal *intentionality* of consciousness—its directedness toward meaningful objects. This subtle and profound insight is as elusive as it is obvious: I perceive a tree, love my spouse, remember my childhood home, anticipate commencement, imagine a unicorn, read a sentence, paint a swirl, protest racism, and think 2 + 2 = 4. Consciousness in each case is *of objects*, in various ways presents something beyond itself. Whereas material things rest entirely within themselves, experience transcends itself, illuminates something else. A nonsubstantial process, experience involves acts best described with gerunds—perceiv*ing*, remember*ing*, imagin*ing*, think*ing*, behav*ing* that relate to objects, whether such objects exist as in perceiving, do not exist as in imagining, are past as in remembering, or are ideal as in counting. The study of consciousness, therefore, requires attention to the ways objects, situations, and the world meaningfully present themselves.

Husserl, a mathematician and philosopher, greatly admired the achievements and contributions of modern science. He attributed much success to the brilliant application of quantitative reason to material nature, which was appropriately stripped of its subjective meanings in practices of measurement, statistics, and mathematical theory. *Naturalism* is the philosophy that universalizes the perspective of natural sciences theoretically (e.g., reduction to the physical) and methodologically (e.g., hypothesis testing, operational definition of variables, quantitative reasoning) across all sciences, including those of mental life. Naturalism reduces psychological processes to material nature (e.g., the nervous system) and/or understands them similarly (e.g., by means of experimentation and causal explanation). Husserl,

like Dilthey and Brentano, recognized consciousness is fundamentally different from the material world and developed phenomenological methodology and methods as a necessary alternative to naturalism.

Husserl viewed naturalism as rooted in an even more pervasive and habitual stance in prescientific life. He called the primary orientation of persons in everyday life the *natural attitude*—the concern with objects in their independence from consciousness. Straightforward interest in objects is necessary and habitual in both practical life and natural science, for instance, as a gardener identifies what first appeared as a leaf to be an injured bird and as scientists conceptualize the earth as revolving around the sun. The natural attitude is an unreflective interest in the nature of things independent of the myriad ways they are experienced. Logically, the study of consciousness, and human sciences generally, require methods tailored to the very subjectively relative ways things appear—their experiential meanings, values, and purposes. Phenomenology, as a method to study consciousness, does not involve doubt or disbelief of natural science or any denial of realities independent of consciousness. However, it does require the adoption of a different attitude, vocational focus, and methods suited to the study of experience, which is methodically excluded from natural science and usually inaccessible in the natural attitude. Phenomenological methodology, for knowledge of the vast, complex, and intricate phenomena of experience, is necessarily neither naturalistic nor restricted to the natural attitude.

Knowledge of experience requires a reflective explication of intentional processes that are blended, interdependent, and temporally flowing in meaningful structural wholes. Husserl carried out analyses of perception, imagination, logical thinking, embodied movement, empathy, scientific theorizing, and many other conscious processes. One of Husserl's insights was that consciousness, as an intentional process, is not a thing like objects in the world. It does not exist as an isolated entity in the world, in individual minds, but is *for* the world—a world constituting process that is intrinsically embodied, social, cultural, and historical. Mental life is shared and concerns the uses, values, meanings, and purposes of objects and situations. Husserl wrote over 40,000 unpublished pages of meticulous analyses that anticipated the work of many subsequent researchers in the phenomenological movement (Welton, 2001). Objects, situations, and the world, which Husserl called the *lifeworld* (*Lebenswelt*), is nothing apart from personal engagements—the playground of the child, the solar system for the astronomer, the film for the cinematographer. The methodology (logic of method) of human science requires reflection on and analysis of intentionality, existence (being-in-the-world)—how situations present themselves experientially, the world as given in temporal, personal, social, cultural living. No mental process can be accurately understood as static, self-enclosed, or in isolation; each is a moment in a larger streaming through worldly situations, whose meaningful organization must be holistically and contextually described just as it is given through living experience. Phenomenological methodology is based on and justified by these characteristics of the very being of its subject matter, just as natural science methodology (e.g., hypothesis testing and mathematical modeling) is based on the requirements and demands of material objects.

Husserl's philosophical anthropology emphasizes the essential dependency of psychological processes on a functioning physical body. Though persons, as conscious beings, are structurally whole and not reducible to their physicality, they are situated in the causal nexus of reality and are affected by their surroundings. Persons may be considered objects, even as physical objects whose causal relations with surroundings can be functionally analyzed by natural science. Human beings, however, are not merely and exclusively material or objects of any kind. Persons, as structural wholes including embodiment, are centers of experiences and action toward the world. Phenomenology provides psychology and the human sciences with methods for investigating the specifically *personal*, which includes and requires procedures capable of knowing experience purely (in its own right), even when it is integrated with research that relates experience to physical phenomena and objective surroundings, such as psychophysics and experimental psychology.

The Phenomenological Method

Phenomenology is, above all, methods for investigating lived experience.[4] Husserl's (1913, 1954) most important contribution was the rigorous specification of methods required for genuine knowledge of subjectivity. These methods are employed seamlessly, even simultaneously, by the expert. The *phenomenological attitude* (technically the *epoché* and *reduction*), a wondering thrall, faithfully discloses lived experience in concrete examples of the phenomena under investigation. *Intentional, existential analysis* reflects on lived experience in all its details, including implicit and hidden dimensions, and explicates its processes and meaningful presentations of objects and situations. *Eidetic analysis* methodically moves from individual examples of the phenomena under investigation to grasp and conceptualize their *essential* (common, general) structures by imaginatively varying their features and distinguishing invariance from the incidental facts of examples. *Description* in natural language faithfully elucidates insights into experiential phenomena, including those that are non-, pre-, and extra-linguistic. Knowledge claims are supported and illustrated with *evidence* in concrete examples.

The Phenomenological Attitude and Reduction

The phenomenological attitude, composed of the phenomenological *epoché*(s) and *reduction*,

---

[4]The expression *lived experience* (*Erlebnis*, German), originally coined and used by phenomenologists, refers not to experience as it is construed in mentalistic philosophical or psychological theory, but to what we live through concretely and relationally in the world. Lived experience includes not only such first person processes as perceiving, remembering, and imagining but such social engagements as empathy and love as well as such embodied comportments as playing, learning and other kinds of conduct—what psychology has called *behavior*. As employed in this chapter, the terms *experience*, *mental life*, *consciousness*, and *psychological* are not intended with any particular conceptual commitment but rather to be problematized and conceptualized freshly. They may be readily replaced or elucidated by such synonymous terms as *existence*, *being-in-the-world*, *engagement*, and *participation*, which help overcome *mentalistic* and *subjectivistic* connotations.

makes research of experience possible. The phenomenological epoché is a free act, a voluntary practice that can be implemented more and more perfectly and can become habitual in the scientific investigation. "Epoché" means abstention, and the phenomenological epoché refers specifically to suspensions of (a) natural science and (b) the natural attitude (Husserl, 1954). These abstentions allow one to turn from received knowledge and the independent reality (or unreality) to the ways situations are given or presented for consciousness. Attention is then free to focus on objects-as-experienced, as-intended, as-meant. The investigative field is thereby "reduced" to experience for the purpose of investigation. This *phenomeno-logical reduction* methodically functions to delineate the field of experience for inquiry, which reflectively turns from the "objects intended" to the "intentional object"—the object-as-intended, for the purpose of studying existence-as-experienced. This method is different from "introspection" in that it is object-relational, focuses on the way objects beyond consciousness are experienced rather than on an interior mind. The phenomeno-logical field is the intentional "correlation" between experiencing and what is experienced, precisely as experienced/meant. The phenomenological researcher is concerned with the fence experienced-as-climbable-to-the-child, not its weight bearing capacity or chemical composition independent of experience. The phenomenologist focuses on the world-as-experienced by means of reflection (with one's own experience) or empathy (on another's experience). The phenomenological reduction brings to the fore the fence's affordance for climbing, perhaps as a *short cut to arrive at school on time*. The phenomenologist is interested in the child's world, in what situations mean to the child rather than in the reality of objects in and of themselves, apart from experience. Without the phenomenological epoché and reduction, the genuine investigation of experience is impossible. Ubiquitous in psychology to the extent that it

focuses on meaning, this attitude is nothing more or less than the distinctive focus of attention on experience for the scientific investigation, even when it is not explicitly acknowledged.

The Analysis of Intentionality and Personal Existence

Phenomenology employs a qualitative method technically called *intentional analysis*, or *existential analysis* because it investigates pure experience,[5] existence-as-lived. This method takes up examples of one's own experience through reflection and others' experience through empathy. It examines the related processes of experiencing (technically called *noesis*, e.g., perceiving, remembering, imagining) and the experienced (*noema*, e.g., the perceived, remembered, imagined). For instance, in analyzing the experience of three-dimensional material objects, the phenomenologist analyzes the temporal process of seeing, touching, bodily orbiting, and handling objects as they present their color, hardness, distance, shape, beauty, uses, unseen sides, and relatedness to surrounding situations as given in a holistic synthesis of identification. At any given moment of such a synthesis, some aspects of the object are actually perceived ("thematically given") and other hidden aspects are also given ("horizontally" or virtually given) through retention (previously perceived). Intentional analysis reveals the holistic structure of experience that includes both actual and potential aspects as well as temporality—past, present, and future—in its meaningful constitution of objects. Particular experiences may include other experiences, as recollection may recall prior perceptions, images, thoughts, and anticipations. Personal existence is a whole, including the stream of experience beginning from birth (if not concep-tion) and directed toward an open future present in protention (the implicit sense of what is coming) and possibly anticipation (the explicit conscious-ness of future). Recollection is capable of bringing the retained past to actual givenness, but only

---

[5]*Pure* here refers to the exclusive focus (by means of the phenomenological reduction) on intentional processes and meanings present in expe-rience, in contrast to the psychophysical and causal relations of mental life with the surrounding world that are studied using the quantitative and mixed methods of psychology.

partially, for the past—including many meanings implicitly lived in the present—has trailed off into obscurity. Analyses of intentionality and the larger personal existence in psychological life require careful reflection/empathy and sensitive knowledge which, however faithful and evidence-based, is never complete, for the temporal and contextual structure of experience can never be fully known.

Analysis of Essential (Eidetic) Structures

The scientific character of phenomenological knowledge requires a method Husserl called the *eidetic analysis* (the eidetic "reduction"), which is rooted in the *intuition of essences* (*Wesensschau*). This method entails the grasp and understanding what is the essential in the phenomena under investigation—what is invariant in the structure of concrete examples of the subject matter. "Essence" as Husserl understands it, concerns "what is." For Husserl (1913; Wertz, 2010), essences are not detached from the world but are one with and are grasped in existence itself. As such, essence is an existential notion rather than implying idealism (Platonism) and demands fidelity to whatever quality or qualities are concretely given in "the matters themselves" under investigation. There is no presumption that essences are clear and distinct, static and unchangeable, context-free, mutually exclusive, transparently known, or culturally universal. While formal essences such as those known in mathematics (numbers, equations, geometrical forms) are exact, context-independent, and mutually exclusive, the morphological essences of other phenomena, including experience, are inexact, context-dependent, changing, given in partial profiles, and may be vague or ineffable. Essences concern what and how things are, as given for consciousness and lived prior to being conceptually known. We are conscious of, live through, are familiar with, and are often practically competent in relation to phenomena before and without knowing what they are in a conceptually rigorous way. We encounter "anger," "love," "intelligence," and "personality" prior to knowing what they are, their essences. Knowledge requires

conceptualization (beyond mere practical familiarity) that is faithful to phenomena as they are given prior to being known. Husserl called the process of knowing essences *eidetic analysis*. Eidetic findings may vary greatly in clarity, rigor, fidelity, adequacy, and certainty. Morphological essences such as those of experience and the person can be known only inadequately, that is, in a partial manner that precludes any final certainty, and their description in ordinary language can always be improved. Merleau-Ponty (1945) wrote, "Husserl's essences are destined to bring back all the living relationships of experience, as the fisherman's net draws from the depths of the ocean quivering fish and seaweed" (p. xv).

Description, the Expression of Phenomenological Knowledge

Phenomenological method is above all *descriptive*. Descriptions, which report reflective findings, are written in ordinary prose. The primary criterion for the validity of knowledge claims is their *fidelity to experience*. Words are not used merely to name themes or categories but to disclose the subject matter as fully and concretely as possible, in all its detail and depth. Phenomenological knowledge is illustrated with individual examples of the lived experiences under investigation in which evidence of general (eidetic) structures is provided. Describing experience is not the same as living through experience; the purpose of description is to establish knowledge, to disclose experiential reality as accurately as possible. Description paradoxically involves both distance and intimacy, not unlike the relationship of a lover and loved one. Openness, closeness, connection, respect, and care, if not affection and admiration, animate phenomenological description. Because one can never do full justice to experiential phenomena, which remain beyond descriptive knowledge, elaborate description with multiple statements is required. Expressions may be drawn directly from others' descriptions of individual examples, which contain all general features, or from the investigator's vocabulary. Language must often be used creatively and new terms may be invented when extant language is inadequate. If language is drawn from received sources, one clarifies the meaning of terms not from theory but in direct relation to the phenomena under investigation, for only concrete examples reveal the meaning and reference of terms with compelling evidence. The phenomenological literature is replete with language that has been carefully developed to describe the subtleties and complexities of experience with high fidelity, but the investigator must show how expressions apply specifically to the phenomenon under investigation. Phenomenological description has a strong ring of truth that is both familiar and fresh, if not shocking, in its resonance with experiences that have been lived but never before known or expressed. Phenomenological description does *not* express opinions, hunches, hypotheses, and external value judgments of the experiences under investigation. Speculative statements that go beyond evidence exhibited in examples, when necessary to fulfill the goals of research, must be both compatible with and grounded in the careful phenomenological analysis of concrete examples.

The particular language used in phenomenological description depends on the intended audience—whether scholarly, professional, or lay. Audiences vary tremendously not only in their linguistic competencies and preferences but in their relationships with the phenomenon and their purposes in appropriating knowledge. Supportive diagrams and/or tables can be useful as supplements in order to summarize and differentiate the phenomenon's constituents or types and their organization. Depending on the audience as well as the investigator's style and goals of the research, phenomenological description can range widely from being cut and dry to being poetic. Describing lived experience is difficult because of the prelinguistic nature of and structural complexities inherent in experience. Therefore, extended discourse using a rich and diverse vocabulary and prose is necessary to describe the flow through time, multiple facets, and implicit dimensions of the subject matter. When entire experiences or aspects of experience are numinous or ineffable in their very essence, as Otto (1958) found with "the holy" and Fink (1995) found with "the world," ordinary language may not be adequate; indirect language such as metaphors, analogies, and ideograms may be necessary. Phenomenologists offer descriptions self-critically and reflexively, given their inevitable perspectivity, limits, evocative function, and relative distance from phenomena, which remain beyond even our best descriptive knowledge.

PHENOMENOLOGICAL RESEARCH PROCEDURES IN PSYCHOLOGY: VARIETY AND CORE PRINCIPLES

In contrast to philosophy, psychology is an empirical science. As a human science, psychology must often remain in the natural (not naturalistic) attitude[6] as it seeks knowledge of realities like human development and psychopathology, including empirical regularities related to gender, ethnicity, and culture as well as the acting person's complex relationships with objective (physical, biological, social, spiritual) surroundings that philosophy does not provide. Person-centered psychology, which highlights the unique characteristics of the person as a center of experience and action, requires the integration of phenomenological method with other methods in order to address issues outside of philosophy. Husserl (1954) clarified the relationship between the two disciplines in what he called the *paradox of subjectivity* (Wertz, 2016). The paradox results from there being two seemingly incompatible perspectives through which consciousness can be given and known. From one—the transcendental,[7] perspective (developed in philosophy), subjectivity

---

[6]The *naturalistic attitude* is that of natural science, which approaches experiential phenomena as physical phenomena, for instance, isolating measurable variables, testing theories, and hypotheses and inferring causal explanations based on quantitative analysis. The *natural attitude*, in contrast, is that of everyday life—it concerns the ordinary attention of consciousness to independent objects rather than attention to the consciousness constituting and positing those objects.

[7]Because the term *transcendental* is mystifying, often misunderstood, and unfamiliar in psychology. I introduce it here with caution but include it because of its importance in phenomenology. For clarification by philosophers, see Heinämaa et al. (2016) and by psychologists, see Wertz (2016) and Davidson (2021).

(sometimes called "*for* the world") is not an object (*in* the world) but rather the very process of transcendence that constitutes meaningful objects and the world. From the other—the natural or personalistic perspective (distinctive of psychology), subjectivity is human (*in* the world)—an entity among other entities in space and time. Transcendental and human subjectivity are identical in an important sense and distinct, parallel and intertwined in another. Partially overlapping, knowledge of transcendental subjectivity and of human subjectivity can contribute to each other. Philosophy has provided psychology with knowledge of many kinds and aspects of experience—perception, image-consciousness, empathy, and temporality to name but a few. However, philosophy cannot be expected to address all the phenomena and problems of psychology, such as moral development, adult sequelae of childhood trauma, kinds of psychopathology such as schizophrenia, and psychotherapeutic change, not to mention all the empirical facts concerning those phenomena. Although psychology begins in, often works within, and elaborates the implications of its knowledge in the natural attitude, research must also include the original utilization of the phenomenological method to offer genuine knowledge of experience, which is not merely another object in the world but involves meaningful constitution—the transcendental (Wertz, 2016).

Phenomenological research has been practiced with considerable variation and nuance on a wide variety of psychological topics (Cloonan, 1995; Halling & Nill, 1995; Wertz, 2006). Explicit procedures and norms for valid data, analysis, and findings did not develop until the 1960s, when Amedeo Giorgi undertook the project of delineating practices that would satisfy the dual criteria of science and fidelity to psychological phenomena.

AMEDEO GIORGI: "DESCRIPTIVE"

Giorgi's contributions over more than 50 years are monumental in providing a correct understanding of phenomenological philosophy and articulating the potential of phenomenological method to provide a foundation for psychology (Giorgi, 1970; Wertz & Aanstoos, 1999). For Giorgi, science is methodical, systematic, self-critical, general, and intersubjective. He spent the 1960s searching for explicit phenomenological research procedures appropriate for the full spectrum of psychological subject matter. Not finding them, he developed their first formal specification. In 1970, Giorgi founded the *Journal of Phenomenological Psychology*, began offering formal courses in research methods, and soon published procedures for conducting research. Prior to 1980, Giorgi and the Duquesne Circle led the emergence of qualitative methods in psychology (Rennie et al., 2000). Giorgi (1975, 1985, 2009) has published numerous articles on methodology, procedural steps, and standards. All are explicitly guided by the fundamental principles of phenomenology: Collecting concrete examples of what is investigated, adopting the phenomenological attitude, focusing on meaningful intentional relationships, grasping invariant patterns through empirical and imaginative variation, and describing general structures of experience.

The procedures delineated by Giorgi emphasize rigor and afford depth by means of obtaining good descriptions, which reveal the research phenomenon, and the careful use of phenomenological method. Giorgi's extensive writings on method apply to the entire spectrum of psychological phenomena. Dissertations directed by Giorgi are known for creatively tailoring specific procedures to the research phenomenon and goals. Giorgi and his students have collected many kinds of descriptions, for instance, descriptions from writing; interview; focus groups; naturalistic, clinical, and laboratory observations; and archives. Descriptions must reveal the research phenomenon as concretely lived. Giorgi has not placed strict requirements or constraints on the number of participants or examples of the phenomenon collected, although he has indicated that at least three may be required for variance sufficient to grasp generality (invariance). Giorgi's steps for protocol analysis utilize the fundamental principles of phenomenology adapted to psychology. Four basic sequential procedures have remained consistent since the 1970s:

1. reading the entire description to understand the experiences as a whole
2. demarcating spontaneous shifts in meaning, "meaning units," in the described experience that reveal the phenomenon under investigation
3. reflecting psychologically on each meaning unit in context in order to grasp what it reveals about the phenomenon under investigation and to answer the research questions
4. synthesizing insights in order to describe the general (including typical) psychological structure(s) of the experience

These procedures ensure that knowledge of psychological life and the answers to research questions are grounded in a close analysis of concrete lived experience in order to achieve fidelity to psychological subject matter. All collected data are accounted for; all knowledge claims can be traced back to data; and findings are presented with multiple examples in which evidence is provided for general structures, which are distinguished from their incidental empirical variations, in order to meet scientific criteria. These procedures enable the most profound psychological insights of which the researcher is capable and require a holistic integration of insights in knowledge of multiple constituents of complex phenomena. They are relevant and applicable to virtually all subject matter when adapted to research interests, data, and the personal styles and sensibilities of researchers. These steps do not constrain a researcher from adopting or innovating additional complementary procedures based on the emerging contours of the phenomenon, the research questions and goals, or inclinations of the researcher. Giorgi (1975) himself used the procedure of *naming themes* demarcated in meaning units as some other researchers have subsequently featured in their procedures. Giorgi (1975) also integrated the psychological insights (Step 3) in each protocol analysis in descriptions of *situated psychological structures* prior to the synthesis of general psychological structures of Step 4. Although neither themes nor individual structures are included in Giorgi's (2009) most recent articulations, many researchers, including myself (Wertz, 1985; Wertz et al., 2011), have fruitful used these procedures.

Giorgi's elegant, fundamental procedures may be considered necessary in any rigorous phenomenological psychological research. Nevertheless, each investigator must appropriate and shape them in the context of their preferred style and particular research aims. Many publications over the last 50 years demonstrate the practice of Giorgi's basic four procedural steps, even by researchers unfamiliar with Giorgi's work. This is understandable for, as Giorgi has argued, these procedures follow from the very demands of science and psychological phenomena. Some researchers have not explicitly carried out the demarcation of "meaning units" (Step 2) because they found it tedious and unfruitful. However, differentiating meaning shifts in complex descriptions, in one way or another even if highly implicit, would seem to be necessary in any methodical and careful treatment of experiential data.

Psychological reflection (Step 3) is the most important and the most elusive procedure, not only in Giorgi's framework but in qualitative research generally. In a study of the experience of being criminally victimized, I explicated, elaborated, and exemplified the constituents of the phenomenological attitude and the analytic operations in employed of Giorgi's steps (Wertz, 1983a, 1985). This study has served as a model because it comprehensively delineates and illustrates the operations of protocol analysis, including the phenomenological reduction, identification of recurrent patterns, implicit meanings, part-whole relations, imaginative variation, eidetic insight, generalization through comparison, and the formulation of psychological structures. These operations of analytic reflection have been found to be operative broadly across the existential-phenomenological literature (Wertz, 1983b) and psychoanalysis (Wertz, 1986). Many of these same procedures have been identified in other contemporary qualitative research traditions (Wertz et al., 2011) and can be found in the work of Moustakas (1994), van Manen (1990), Smith (Smith & Osborn, 2015), and Churchill (2022).

The stepwise order of Giorgi's procedures may be viewed as a constraint and not practiced in a rigid way. Researchers often go back and forth among Giorgi's four steps rather than enacting them in an irreversible, linear sequence. The results of each step in these procedures may be modified or revised as one engages more and more deeply with the data. Nevertheless, there is a necessary logic to the sequence: In principle each step presupposes and builds on prior step(s). Though not to be practiced mechanically or rigidly, they must be adapted to the demands of data, researchers' personal styles, and goals of the research. Giorgi's procedures have been used to research such traditional topics as perception (Wertz, 1982) and cognition (Aanstoos, 1985). Watkins and Shulman (2008) have documented the use of phenomenological procedures in research aiming to liberate oppressed peoples. Davidson's (Davidson et al., 2017) body of work on recovery among persons diagnosed with schizophrenia provides many examples of the employment of these procedures. His participatory action, community-based team research has recently involved teaching phenomenological methods to persons with schizophrenia who are in recovery. They have presented their findings not only in peer reviewed journals but in neighborhood theatrical performances. Another creative use of Giorgi's procedures is Deligio's (2020) analysis of archival materials and interviews in decolonial, liberation research on restoration after state violence among African Americans wrongly convicted of crimes and incarcerated.

PROCEDURAL GUIDES AND RESOURCES

The phenomenological movement offers a treasure trove of resources that have guided researchers in psychology: Realistic, genetic (i.e., concerning temporal genesis), transcendental, existential, hermeneutic, narrative, critical, ethical, and constructive (Wertz, 2016). Psychologists have modified existing methods, including Giorgi's, and established various procedures over the last half century, all rooted in phenomenological methodology and employing the phenomenological method. Even if controversial, all these procedures have been inspired by phenomenology.[8] Early on, Paul Colaizzi (1973) developed and compared individual reflection on the part of the investigator with the analysis of empirically collected data, including alternative kinds of findings afforded by various procedures. Halling (Halling & Leifer, 1991) developed dialogal procedures for doing research in teams. Englander (2020) developed methods of interviewing and participant observation as well as empathy training. The possibilities for developing new complementary procedures are infinite, limited only by the scholarly understanding, ingenuity, and vision of individuals and research communities. Lively mutual critique among phenomenological psychological methodologists continues to bring problematic issues and controversies to light and to suggest resolutions.

I briefly sampled guides by Moustakas (1994), Smith (Smith et al., 2009), van Manen (1990), and Churchill (2022). Each appropriated phenomenological methods and included expositions of procedures for projects from top to bottom, including philosophical background, key concepts, research goals and design, participants, data collection, analysis, and reporting. Each framework is evolving and will no doubt be modified in the future. These guides are overlapping, and each articulates procedures that may be implicitly practiced in the others. While each offers some distinctive features, they are largely compatible. Therefore, researchers can legitimately and fruitfully borrow, combine, and modify procedures from multiple sources for their own phenomena, goals, styles, and preferences.

"Transcendental"

Clark Moustakas (1994), pioneer of humanistic psychology, developed a set of procedures based on fundamental methodological principles,

---

[8]Binswanger, an early innovator in phenomenological psychiatry, characterized his contribution as "a creative misinterpretation of Heidegger," and yet his work was nevertheless defended as legitimate and fruitful by the philosopher Jacob Needleman (Needleman, 1975, viii). Even misunderstandings of phenomenology can make valuable contributions to psychology!

far-ranging scholarship, and broadly shared values. Familiar with the research literature, Moustakas was especially influenced by Husserl and an unpublished manuscript now available by Ernest Keen (1975/2003). Moustakas's work reflects his examination of primary and secondary literature in phenomenology, technical terms, concepts, and insights relevant to research. Moustakas was greatly concerned with the achievement of closeness to the qualities of lived experience. He coined new terms such as *horizonalization*, which creatively drew on Husserl's concept of *horizon*, instituting a procedure in which the investigator maintains open attention on all statements in a participant's data. He focused on what Keen called the *textures* of experience and crafted *textural* analysis and description of both "individual" and "composite" (across participant) themes. Moustakas instituted a "structural" procedure, which uses seven universal themes drawn from existential literature as lenses in analyses: temporality, spatiality, bodyhood, materiality, causality, relations with others, and relations with self. Moustakas's analytic process culminates in *textural structural synthesis*, which integrates research findings from the textural and structural analyses previously conducted. Moustakas illustrates some of these procedures in examples from the phenomenological psychological research literature, suggesting their prior informal practice. A wonderful example of research using these procedures is MacAdams's (2021) study of the experience of a significant partner's chronic pain. MacAdams, herself a "silent sufferer" of chronic pain, put her expectations aside prior to each interview by writing them on index cards and then destroying the cards.[9] She delineated seven textural themes of the "unseen warriors'" experience: increased burden and responsibility, tolerance of uncertainty, powerlessness and help-lessness, a shrinking world, loneliness, mitigating distress through self-care and social support, and personal growth and meaning making.

"Interpretative"

Jonathan Smith and colleagues (Smith et al., 2009; Smith & Osborn, 2015) developed interpretative phenomenological analysis (IPA), which has gained considerable appeal. IPA has been widely employed in the UK and increasingly in North America. IPA was originally developed in health psychology and has since been extended to other applied areas such as counseling, social, and educational psychology. It distinctively focuses on circumscribed and extended highly significant experiences (e.g., decision making in candidates for genetic testing, living with an ileostomy, and chronic, benign lower back pain) that involve reflections, new anticipations, important decisions, and changes in persons' lives rather than on the full range of psychological subject matter, including prereflective experiences. Given its focus on reflective experience, IPA involves a "double-hermeneutic" that involves "sense-making" on the part of both participants and researchers. IPA is informed by the phenomenological philosophies of Husserl, Heidegger, Merleau-Ponty, and Sartre, as well as the hermeneutic tradition of Schleiermacher, Heidegger, and Gadamer, and ideography. IPA has a close theoretical affinity with cognitive psychology, sharing its focus on thinking. IPA tends to be idiographic, using case studies and small homogenous samples that may eventually and need not immediately lead to general knowledge. The fundamental question is, "What is this experience *like*?" Data are usually collected in semistructured interviews. Beyond single-case studies, research may include samples of three to 10, and may involve more than one interview with a single participant. This evolving tradition offers procedures for sampling and conducting interviews as well as detailed accounts of various iterative and inductive data analytic strategies, including open reading, line-by-line note taking, theme identification, hermeneutic circling between parts and wholes, structural interrelation of

---

[9]The phenomenological attitude, with its intense focus on experience being investigated, can be sufficient to suspend the researchers' expectations and prior experiences. However, some researchers employ prior reflection on and documentation of their preconceptions to clear the way for a fresh, open presence to the phenomena. MacAdams (2021), who had salient experiences of her husband/partner responding to her own chronic pain, reported that the latter strategy facilitated her collecting data on experiences different from her own.

themes, linguistic deconstruction, abstracting superordinate themes, identification of functions, and discerning frequent patterns within and across cases. IPA is procedurally nonprescriptive. For instance, explicit demarcation of meaning units in transcripts is not required. Procedural innovations and a flexible, nonlinear order of analytic operations are encouraged. Participants have sometimes been engaged as coresearchers. Explicit procedures for writing research reports have been offered with attention to the construction of diagrams and tables that summarize findings.

"Hermeneutic"

Although he is not a psychologist, Max van Manen's (1990) work has been a rich, fruitful resource for psychology and other human science disciplines, especially those involved in practice areas. Drawing broadly on phenomenological philosophy, especially the hermeneutic phenomenology of Heidegger and semiotics (language orientation), van Manen uses his familiarity with Dutch phenomenology in research that seeks deep insight into lived experience. Van Manen's inclusion of the process of reflective writing as a research procedure is especially sophisticated and edifying. For van Manen, descriptive/interpretive science mandates poetic, incantative, evocative, primal language in order to rigorously achieve objective validity. The focus on praxis also entails an emphasis on practice-sensitive language. Rather than merely attempting to set aside presuppositions, van Manen advocates making them explicit lest they unreflectively creep into the analysis. His procedures include the researcher's analysis of their own personal experience and etymologies of words in order to explicate prelinguistic meanings. Van Manen provided valuable guidelines for writing protocols that illuminate concrete examples as well as for interviewing; literature, biography, journals and various personal documents; art (music, painting, theater, dance, cinema); and the philosophical and psychological literature, which contain valuable descriptions of lived experience. Van Manen emphasized the development of thematic analyses that go beyond superficial categorical labeling of incidentals.

He also documented the value of conversation and group collaboration as well as solitary analyses by the researcher. Universal existential themes such as death and otherness as well as structures of temporality, spatiality, corporeality, and social relationality are suggested as hermeneutic lenses. For van Manen, writing is not merely a final stage of research in formal reporting but is integral throughout every phase of the research. Sensitive writing includes listening to the ineffable, the unspeakable. Writing is a naturally decontextualizing (eidetic) grasp of essence drawn directly from concrete examples in which meaning is originally seen. Writing is presented as a stepwise process that develops greater elucidation of nuance, multiple levels, connections among moments, increasing depth, ambiguity, and realization of inherent mystery. Van Manen advocated strong, rich, profound texts that not only provide knowledge but prepare the reader for action that is intimate, ethical, and wise. He offered many alternative ways of presenting findings: thematic, analytic, exemplifying, exegetic, existential, and newly invented forms. A wonderful example of research inspired by van Manen is Struthers's (2001) innovative indigenous research on Native American women's practices of healing.

"Existential-Phenomenological"

Scott Churchill's (2022) recent volume on phenomenological research methods provided a broad overview and practical step-by-step guide through the research process based on his many years of teaching, supervising, and conducting research. This resource offers a didactic in the philosophy of science, empathy as an investigative posture in general and in interview dialogue, Sartre's appropriation of phenomenological method, Heidegger's treatment of temporality, the existential analysis of human choice, and often overlooked contributions of the Duquesne University tradition including those of Colaizzi, Von Eckartsberg, and Fischer. This resource offers some unique procedural uses of philosophy, such as Schutz's distinction of "because of" and "in order to" motives and existential ontological insights of Heidegger and Sartre, in analyzing psychological data. Churchill articulated important procedures implicit in other sources, such as the researcher writing first person protocols (following Colaizzi) and differentiating the research phenomenon (and problem) from the situations that are analyzed in order to produce insights and knowledge regarding the former.

AN ILLUSTRATION: HETEROGENEITY IN THE SCHIZOPHRENIA DIAGNOSIS

Sarah Kamens's (in press) research serves well to illustrate the phenomenological method in psychology because it employed the method rigorously, explicitly utilized the aforementioned procedures, and highlights the basic contribution of construct clarification. Indeed, "schizophrenia" is the quintessentially enigmatic psychological term/concept. Empirical research, theorizing, and practice have been perennially riddled with problems due to the lack of adequate clarification of that to which the term schizophrenia refers. Kamens studied the lived experiences of persons diagnosed with schizophrenia-spectrum disorders. Her specific focus concerned the "heterogeneity problem," that is, the difficulties and controversies in psychiatric taxonomy due to the wide range of experiences considered to be symptoms of schizophrenia and used in diagnosis. Persons can meet the criteria for schizophrenia (at least two among delusions, hallucinations, disorganized speech, disorganized or catatonic behavior, and negative symptoms such as flat affect, avolition, and alogia with reduced functioning for more than 6 months) with a tremendous variety of specific symptoms. Two persons can be given this diagnosis with no symptoms whatsoever in common. This heterogeneity and frequent comorbidity have led to suspicions that the diagnostic category may not represent a natural kind, may comprise complex syndromes, may include multiple disorder entities, or may involve unrelated sets of symptoms. Some have viewed this problem as responsible for the lack of univocal etiological research, which requires a valid taxonomy. The heterogeneity problem has also been related to cultural variations, including contrasting prevalence rates across

cultures and culture-bound phenomena such as the *Jerusalem syndrome*, in which tourists visiting Israel-Palestine develop the delusion that they are historical religious figures on special religious missions. Some have suggested that cultural variations may involve different diagnostic entities and etiologies. Redefinition, new diagnostic models and renaming schizophrenia are under consideration but lack an empirically grounded, conceptually valid account of *what schizophrenia is*—its essence(s). Kamens investigated heterogeneity using phenomenological inquiry into the experiences of diagnosed persons.

Adopting the phenomenological attitude, Kamens (in press) did not assume the independent reality of "schizophrenia," which she placed in quotation marks. Nor did she assume the validity of any psychiatric diagnostic system, etiological theory, interpretive model, or prior research. She considered her personal view of this controversy irrelevant for the investigation and set it aside. Testing no hypothesis and without assuming that the lived experiences of those diagnosed constitute one, several, or any coherent psychological structures, she also abstained from any judgments of participant experiences' veridicality, which was also irrelevant to her interest. Her investigation focused only on the lived experiences themselves— how her participants experienced situations and the world in the course of their experiencing. Her aim was to investigate the essential meaning, structure(s), and heterogeneity of these experiences.

Kamens (in press) recruited 21 culturally diverse, hospitalized, psychiatrically diagnosed patients (six females, 13 males, one transgender participant, one biologically male with unknown gender identification, age range 23–61 years old). She also enlisted four pilot-comparison participants (two females, two males, age range 24–32 years old) who were not psychiatrically diagnosed with a psychotic disorder at the time of the interview, which elicited their life narratives. Based on strict inclusion criteria, three hospitalized patients failed to meet diagnostic criteria and served with the four pilot participants in comparisons with the 18 validly diagnosed patients. Kamens selected demographically diverse patients with positive and negative symptom profiles, idiosyncratic symptoms, and culturally related syndromes based on gold standard instruments. Participants included African Americans; a Latinx individual; persons born in Israel and the United States; immigrants from Morocco, France, Trinidad, China, and the Philippines; various faiths including Islam, Judaism, and Christian; speakers of several languages; and one person with Jerusalem syndrome.

Kamens (in press) gathered numerous kinds of data, utilizing in depth interviews (2–4 hours per participant) as well as an open-ended life prompt as well as select items from the Examination of Anomalous Self-Experience (EASE) interview; the Examination of Anomalous World-Experience (EAWE); and the Positive and Negative Syndrome Scale (PANSS) to assess positive, negative, and mixed symptom profiles. The interview solicited a narrative including significant life events and descriptions of background identity, present context, affiliation groups, recent history, everyday life, and present/past mental health treatment. Selected items from the EASE and EAWE were used to collect detailed descriptions of anomalous experiences, self-representations, relations with others, and the world. Prioritizing open-ended description in the participant's own words, data collection began with the life narrative, then employed more specific probes from the EASE and EAWE, and ended with diagnostic assessment in order to preclude the latter influencing the former. Arabic and Hebrew translators assisted with non-English speakers. Data were audio-recorded and transcribed in English as needed. Standard and the pentagonal models—two quantitative methods for analyzing heterogeneity using PANSS data–and two subtyping methods indicated widely varying symptoms among participants, including a large range of total scores and symptom severity, several positive syndromes, several negative syndromes, several mixed syndromes, and several with neither syndrome.

Giorgi's procedures were used to analyze all descriptions of experience, including participants' responses to EASE and EAWE questions. Following Husserl's (1970, p. 168) call "to the things themselves (*zu den Sachen selbst*)," Kamens employed the phenomenological reduction to set aside assumptions and expectations arising from the scientific literature, naturalism, and the natural attitude—in order to focus exclusively on the lived experiences described by her participants. She openly read each description; demarcated meaning units; recorded her psychological reflections on each as it revealed her phenomenon and answered her research questions; and synthesized the reflections in individual and general psychological structures to reveal the interconnections, similarities, and differences among experiences. Her intentional and existential analyses explicated psychological structures of the participants' world experience and meanings. She used free imaginative variation and empirical descriptions from other sources including nonfiction, clinical observations, and the phenomenological literature on schizophrenia in order to differentiate essential, invariant structures from incidental factual variations among all these examples. Kamens compared her individual structures in order to discern more general essential structures, continuing to use imaginative and empirical variations in order to grasp invariances at various levels of generality. Her analyses were conducted with a team including research assistants whose insights were integrated into the analyses.

The unexpected findings identified one general structure in all examples of phenomena present in the data of those participants rigorously diagnosed with schizophrenia using the above tools. Kamens's description of the general structure included three distinct manifestations or moments (described below), each with numerous constituents and typical variations. Cultural commonalities and variance as well as ideographic variations were detailed. The general psychological structure entailed a unique mode of being-in-the-world with two facets—characteristic meanings that ran through all examples: (a) profound vulnerability, a lack of safety in an inhospitable world and (b) being socially alienated, invalidated, and unacknowledged with a profound sense of not belonging in human communities. Although some participants did not live through this general psychological structure pervasively or chronically, for others it was always present and persisted indefinitely. For all, this psychological structure was existential—a primordial meaning horizon of their specific experiences. Naming this structure as a whole was difficult because it is meontic (Fink, 1995)—difficult to describe. After many considerations, Kamens invented and adopted the idiom *urhomelessness* to holistically name its radical quality, fundamental presence even in short-lived factical (incidental) variations. This structure was found in the experiences of all 18 participants who met diagnostic criteria for schizophrenia. Although none of the comparison participants (who failed to meet criteria, including those misdiagnosed) experienced the full urhomelessness structure, some lived through nondistressing anomalous experiences or fleeting, partial aspects during specific contexts of their lives such as when they were children, partially awake, not sober, or going through difficult life stressors or transitions. Another difficult descriptive task in this research was to name the three qualitatively distinct manifestations, considered moments of urhomelessness. Kamens adopted the descriptive terms (a) *nomadic*, (b) *settled*, and (c) *destitute* to describe distinct yet blended, overlapping, and structurally interrelated moments that may be central and thematic or horizonal (i.e., an implicit possibility). Each manifestation, highly variable in its empirical duration, is both a style of living through and a strategy for meeting the crisis of urhomelessness. Kamens found all three manifestations to be essential in the unitary structure of this phenomenon though each was dramatically present in some instances and highly implicit, only a vague potentiality, in others.

The basic structure of urhomelessness contrasts with experiences entailing social acknowledgment, sharing, and belonging in a world-horizon of safety experienced even in severe interpersonal loss, personal failure, and social isolation. Some participants like Charles[10] could not remember any time in their lives when they felt safe and welcomed. Others described their world becoming increasingly uninhabitable (violent, alienating, invalidating, or "unreal") as they passively endured suffering, and some described actively "jumping ship" when the social world became unbearable. Kamens presented vignettes describing individual examples, for instance, Crystal's experience of strangers on the street as remote family members from whom she kept distant, whereas her mother, father, and, eventually, the police were experienced as hostile agents attempting to poison her food. Strange voices narrated her humiliation and heartbreak as she was transported by police to the hospital, where she sought refuge in stone-cold motionlessness. When political violence was flaring on the streets outside, Haseeb sat at home and felt increasingly disconnected not only from school but also from his family, and his world became increasingly empty. To his horror, he could see *jinn* (Arabic for "demons") outside of his windows. He eventually began to believe he could hear the prayers of those dying in the streets where he wandered to escape the jinn. As Haseeb began to feel responsible for wars and peace in Israel-Palestine and the broader Middle East, he increasingly identified as a blessed medium between the supplicants he heard and God. The three moments—nomadic, settled, and destitute—are paradoxical strategies that both mitigate suffering and deepen the person's radical sense of danger, risk, and social disconnection. Some participants seemed to predominantly experience one of the three, some shifted between them, and some simultaneously lived through multiple manifestations, showing that all are essential possibilities of the general structure of urhomelessness.

Nomadism involves the being-mode of wandering, feeling dislodged, and diasporic in efforts to achieve safety or to explore the vastness of surroundings. Charles took himself out of his body and traveled through other extra-terrestrial worlds. Wandering may be embodied or imaginal as a person explores unknown streets, parks, shelters, hospitals, and city jails or inhabits otherworldly mystical, divine realms, speaking with

---

[10]All participant names are pseudonyms.

dead ancestors and gods while transforming into the animality of a monkey or the omniscient, all-powerful creator of the universe. Even as this nomadic mode seeks and finds a kind of consolation, it deepens and intensifies alienation and nonrecognition by others. Kamens described in great detail passive and active wandering, dialectics of unfamiliarity and familiarity as well as of proximity and alienation, hypothetical and interpretive wandering, temporary sheltering, relations with others, styles of communication, dysphoria and euphoria, prolonged and temporary subkinds, and other typical variants.

Settling involves the imaginative adoption of urhomeness, inhabiting a "settlement" that secures safety and self-recognition including a meaningful role in the world where one is otherwise not socially available, recognized, and validated. Imaginative settling secures stability and yet exiles the person from others, deepening their painful disconnection and alienation. Often settling emerges in a dramatic revelation, a dawning discovery, an "a-ha" experience of an ultimate, unquestionable, fixed meaning-configuration in the world that is believed with unquestionable conviction contrary to apparent counter-evidence. One is an elite member of a secret society of revolutionaries, the princess of a royal family, a famous television star, or a magical being with superpowers. Settling, which provides continuity through time and across different situations can afford an answer to the restless and fleeting explorations of nomadism even when fraught with dangers of persecution, poisoning, and demise at the hands of inimical others. Infinite variants have an essential meaning of unshakable certainty around which a coherent of life events can constellate. Settlement may be constructed of mundane and unworldly elements that take on novel and revolutionary meanings. Although the person often knows that others reject the veridicality of these meanings, one may imagine that they secretly know and are engaged in the settlement, which one participant called "the system," in which he, as "Chief" or "Head," was under its threats. Yuval prayed passionately day and night at a holy site without food or sleep and in terrible weather, hearing the voice

of God and striving for extraordinary righteousness thanks to divine endurance, even as he was repeatedly dragged by authorities to the hospital. Prominent typical constituents of settling include "the unveiling," "initial relief and clarity," "adoration and worship," and "fixing the world." Typical variations involved utopic and/or malicious as well as outlandish and/or ordinary meanings. The settlement expands beyond mundane time, looms beyond factical events of life, and may temporarily include nomadic wandering or being destitute, which it may motivate (note the integral interrelations of the three moments in a single general structure). Kamens presented extensive analysis of the elaborate language and symbolic systems and relations with others in settling. She was often considered "a believer" by participants in response to her unusual attentiveness and lack of commonly expressed disbelief and condemnation on the part of others. Kamens described the doubt, inherent precariousness, and ultimate failure of settling to achieve basic belonging and recognition.

In *being-destitute*, the world becomes radically uninhabitable (dangerous, torturous, rejecting, and nightmarish) and the person, relinquishing any attempt to traverse or achieve security in the world, accepts utter hopelessness and the impossibility of belonging and recognition. Previous nomadic exploration and settling are relatively modified with no expectation of relief, considered to be futile whereas being destitute provides a refuge by eliminating the disappointment of any striving, even in its more extreme vulnerability and alienation. Persons distance themselves from the world, disconnect, and, in extreme variants, reside "nowhere" as "nobody" in a wasteland that may continue to threaten invasion. A fortitude may be found in the endurance of inexorable suffering, intolerable distress, and destruction. The person paradoxically inhabits uninhabitable places, strives for relief in sheer emptiness, intimate utopia in the most distant fantasy, peace in silence, or comfort in the embrace of dark death. To others, including Kamens during interviews, persons being-destitute appear frozen, stiff, mute, and unresponsive; they speak laconically if at all. Some participants who were no longer experiencing urhomelessness attempted with difficulty to retrospectively describe their shut-off life in detail. Kamens characterized destitution as the most austere and devastating manifestation or moment of urhomelessness and provided many idiographic examples, including such essential meaning constituents as the inhospitality of the world, radical alienation in relations with others, passive wandering, and becoming shelter. She also found typical and sometimes vacillating variants such as *evacuation*, in which the person exits worldly existence, and *hibernation*, in which one finds sheltering protection in a no-person's land of barren, empty solitude. Further, she delineated voluntary and involuntary as well as active and passive modes, and extreme destitution in concrete detail with examples.

Kamens viewed as extremely important her finding of the possibility of being at home in the world as essential, virtually present, within the structure of urhomelessness, even in its most extreme privative variants of being destitute. Participants not only traversed various moments of urhomelessness, but some also cycled into *urhomeness*. Some thereby gained or regained a sense of belonging and recognition in their social world. Urhomeness was present in urhomelessness in numerous ways: as a fleeting actuality, as a goal strived for in reaching out to others for help, as a desirable possibility, and as a distant horizon.

My present focus on Kamens's research remains on method. I lack the space to follow her extensive analysis of cultural heterogeneity or the implications of this study for reconceptualizing schizophrenia, psychiatric taxonomy, cultural psychology, theories and research on schizophrenia, interdisciplinary scholarship, or therapy. To reiterate, Kamens set aside all prior research on schizophrenia as well as her personal assumptions and hunches in order to attend to the lived experiences of persons diagnosed with schizophrenic-spectrum disorders. Her descriptions contain no assumptions about brain disease or any etiological theories. Kamens did not presuppose the existence of schizophrenia as a natural kind, the validity of diagnostic criteria, or any taxonomic system.

She did not coperform belief in or in any way judge the veridicality of what her participants experienced but instead reflectively turned to their modes of experiencing and the meanings of their situations. Kamens's research illustrates intentional, existential, and eidetic analysis, for she explicates the correlative structures of the modes of experiencing and world-as-meant at virtually every turn. Kamens performed no empirical analyses such as frequency tabulations of the three manifestations or statistical correlations with participants' demographics, which were suggested for future quantitative research. Themes were not reported as empirical facts but rather as essential manifestations of holistic structures. In her report, Kamens presented the empirical facts and variance of her participants' experiences as illustrative exemplifications of essential, invariant psychological structures.

Kamens employed the systematic rigor of Giorgi's procedures, from the open reading of all data to the articulation of invariant psychological structures at many levels of generality, ranging from the overall structure of urhomelessness, with its two essential aspects, to the three typical manifestations and lower level subtypical structures, such as mundane versus imaginative nomadic wandering. All data were accounted for, and Kamens's reflections were documented with evidence from meaning units to findings.

Although Kamens did not follow the works of Moustakas, Smith, van Manen, or Churchill, her research demonstrates virtually every procedure they articulated. For instance, Kamens did not use the term *textural* for her analysis or thematic descriptions, but her work vividly reveals what Moustakas called *texture* and enumerates *textural themes*, offering the reader intimate proximity to and understanding of recurrent phenomenal regularities. Kamens's analysis and descriptions explicitly reflect Moustakas's universal structures, such as "relations with self," and the "textural-structural synthesis," even though she did not follow his procedural steps or use his terms. Kamens focused on the kind of "important," "life transformative" experiences for which Smith crafted the procedures of

IPA, and she focused extensively on participants' "reflective sense making" as they came to terms with life events related to their diagnosis. She identified and interrelated numerous themes, for instance the overlapping mutual implications and movement among the three manifestations of urhomelessness. She continually employed the "hermeneutic circle," moving back and forth from parts to whole and repeatedly brought her fore-understanding (familiarity, for instance from clinical experience, in contrast to preconceptions) to bear on her participants' experiences, whose fresh presence afforded new insights that transformed her understanding. Kamens' work also exemplified IPA's *double hermeneutic*, in which her interpretations and those of her participants formed a methodical unity. She presented tables delineating the constituents of the general psychological structure very much like those suggested for IPA. Virtually all the directives of van Manen can be found in Kamens' work, notably her hermeneutic sensitivities to participants' language and her use of metaphoric, poetic discourse in such terms as *urhomelessness, nomadism, settlement,* and *destitution* that evoke elusive and ineffable nonverbal, prereflective experiences. Kamens utilized such existential themes as suggested by Churchill as *temporality, choice,* and *in-order-to motivation* in her analysis. Overall, this example of psychological research vividly illustrates, in unitary practice, the full spectrum of procedures codified by the available resources for phenomenological psychology.

PHENOMENOLOGY ESSENTIAL FOR PSYCHOLOGY: IMPLICATIONS AND CHALLENGE

Phenomenology is ubiquitous in psychology because it is essential, inasmuch as the science requires a knowledge and understanding of the qualitative structures and types of its subject matter (Wertz, 2021). Valid theoretical constructs have their origin in the conceptual grasp of concrete examples of psychological life explicated in general descriptive language. Taxonomic systems codify genera, species, and subspecies and their common constituents, and casebooks for their use provide detailed empirical variants of the types. The validity of measurement requires operational procedures for determining the magnitude and/or frequency of the essential components of phenomena. Experiments can and in some cases do empirically realize the invariant structures of phenomena and then employ measures of psychologically significant factual sequelae. However, these crucially important phenomenological practices may be performed informally, haphazardly, inadequately, or even incorrectly. In order to be scientific in the full sense, they require a method that is epistemologically, ontologically, and ethically grounded, systematic, one that is self-critical, accountable, corrected over time, and institutionalized in education and literature. It should therefore not surprise us that the implicit and informal practice of phenomenological method has been demonstrated through the history of psychology—in experimental psychology, in psychoanalysis, in cognitive psychology, in the spectrum of other qualitative methods (Wertz, 2014; Wertz & Olbert, 2016; Wertz et al., 2011). However, without inclusion in education and formal training, the method has been employed unevenly—brilliantly at best but sometimes partially, superficially, or even erroneously at worst. In the current milieu of methodological pluralism, a new generation of psychology students has begun to employ phenomenology in advanced education and training (Wertz, 2019; Wertz et al., 2017). Although this method has not been widely institutionalized in psychology, it is still developing and its ongoing contributions are as important as ever.

Phenomenology does not provide knowledge of empirical facts, except inasmuch as they exemplify essential structures at various levels of generality. Although empirically based, purely phenomenological psychological research does not aggregate empirical data concerning gender, culture, specific populations, and contexts. The factual investigation of psychological life, based on phenomenological clarification and description, requires other methods, both qualitative and quantitative. Those who understand the central, scientific importance of qualitative research uneasily face the proliferation of "methods" in our contemporary pluralism. Research practices have often developed in silos by individuals and communities motivated to present their practices as unique, distinctive, complete in themselves, and different from if not superior to other methods. This chapter avoids polemic, remains silent on trumped up controversies, and focuses on unifying methodological principles, explicit norms, widely shared essential methods, and procedures for human science that are available to researchers across diverse traditions that are by no means incommensurate. This is a small step toward the sorely needed unified methodology, foundational methods, and rich heterogeneity of procedural strategies for psychological research. Phenomenology is to be appropriated flexibly, adaptively, and innovatively, synthesized with other traditions carefully, in accordance with the demands of each research phenomenon, project goals, and the investigator's abilities and preferences. The current disciplinary challenge is to integrate deeply principled methodology, essential methods, unifying values, and appropriate procedures throughout psychological science.

References

Aanstoos, C. M. (1985). The structure of thinking in chess. In A. Giorgi (Ed.), *Phenomenology and psychological research* (pp. 86–117). Duquesne University Press.

Benetka, G., & Joerchel, A.C. (2016). Psychology as a phenomenological science. In A. Valsiner, G. Marsico, N. Chaudhary, T. Sato, & V. Dazzani (Eds.), *Psychology as a science of human being* (pp. 17–32). Springer International Publishing.

Boring, E. G. (1929). *A history of experimental psychology* (Vol. D). Appleton-Century Company.

Brentano, F. (1973). *Psychology from an empirical standpoint*. Routledge. (Original work published 1874)

Churchill, S.D. (2022). *Essentials of existential phenomenological research*. American Psychological Association. https://doi.org/10.1037/0000257-000

Cloonan, T. F. (1995). The early history of phenomenological psychological research methods in America. *Journal of Phenomenological Psychology*, *26*(1), 46–126. https://doi.org/10.1163/156916295X00033

Colaizzi, P. F. (1973). *Reflection and research in psychology: A study of learning*. Kendall Hunt Publishing Co.

Davidson, L. (2021). *Overcoming psychologism: Husserl and the transcendental reform in psychology*. Springer. https://doi.org/10.1007/978-3-030-59932-4

Davidson, L., Nellamy, C., Flanagan, E., Guy, K., & O'Connell, M. (2017). A participatory approach to person centered research: Maximizing opportunities for recovery. In B. McCormack, S. van Dulmen, H. Eide, K. Skovdahl, & T. Eide (Eds.), *Person-centered healthcare research* (pp. 69–83). John Wiley & Sons Ltd. https://doi.org/10.1002/9781119099635.ch6

Deligio, E. (2020). *Coming home: Restoration after state violence* [Doctoral dissertation, Pacifica Graduate Institute]. ProQuest Dissertation Publishing.

Dilthey, W. (1978). *Descriptive psychology and historical understanding* (R. M. Zaner & K. L. Heiges, Trans.). Martinus Nijhoff. (Original work published 1894)

Douglas, B., Woolfe, R., Strawbridge, S., Kasket, E., & Galbraith, V. (2016). *The handbook of counselling psychology* (4th ed.). SAGE. https://doi.org/10.4135/9781529714968

Embree, L. (2010). Interdisciplinarity within phenomenology. *The Indo-Pacific Journal of Phenomenology*, *10*(1), 1–7. https://doi.org/10.2989/IPJP.2010.10.1.2.1074

Englander, M. (2020). Phenomenological psychological interviewing. *The Humanistic Psychologist*, *48*(1), 54–73. https://doi.org/10.1037/hum0000144

Feest, U. (2021). Gestalt psychology, frontloading phenomenology, and psychophysics. *Synthese*. *198*(4), 2153–2173. https://doi.org/10.1007/s11229-019-02211-y

Fink, E. (1995). *Sixth Cartesian meditation: The idea of a transcendental theory of method*. Indiana University Press.

Giorgi, A. (1970). *Psychology as a human science: A phenomenologically based approach*. Harper and Row.

Giorgi, A. (1975). An application of phenomenological method in psychology. In A. Giorgi, C. Fischer, & E. Murray (Eds.), *Duquesne studies in phenomenological psychology* (Vol. 2, pp. 82–103). Duquesne University Press. https://doi.org/10.5840/dspp197529

Giorgi, A. (Ed.). (1985). *Phenomenology and psychological research*. Duquesne University Press.

Giorgi, A. (2009). *The descriptive phenomenological method in psychology: A modified Husserlian approach*. Duquesne University Press.

Halling, S., & Leifer, M. (1991). The theory and practice of dialogal research. *Journal of Phenomenological*

Psychology, 22(1), 1–15. https://doi.org/10.1163/156916291X00019

Halling, S., & Nill, J. D. (1995). A brief history of existential-phenomenological psychiatry and psychotherapy. *Journal of Phenomenological Psychology, 26*(1), 1–45. https://doi.org/10.1163/156916295X00024

Heinämaa, S., Hartimo, M., & Miettinen, T. (Eds.). (2016). *Phenomenology and the transcendental*. Routledge.

Hennigfeld, I. (2015). Goethe's phenomenological way of thinking and the Urphänomen. *Goethe Yearbook, 22*(1), 143–167. https://doi.org/10.1353/gyr.2015.0036

Husserl, E. (1962). *Ideas: General introduction to pure phenomenology* (W. R. B. Gibson, Trans.). Collier Books. (Original work published 1913)

Husserl, E. (1954). *The crisis of European sciences and transcendental phenomenology* (D. Carr, Trans.). Northwestern University Press.

Husserl, E. (1970). *Logical investigations*. Humanities Press. (Original work published 1900)

Husserl, E. (1977). *Phenomenological psychology: Lectures, summer semester, 1925* (J. Scanlon, Trans.). Martinus Nijhoff. (Original work published 1925) https://doi.org/10.1007/978-94-010-1083-2

Kamens, S. R. (in press). *Reconceptualizing schizophrenia: The phenomenology of urhomelessness*. Routledge.

Keen, E. (2003) Doing psychology phenomenologically: Methodological considerations. *The Humanistic Psychologist, 31*(4), 5–33. (Original work published 1975) https://doi.org/10.1080/08873267.2003.9986932

Kockelmans, J. J. (Ed.). (1967). *Phenomenology*. Doubleday.

MacAdams, E. I. (2021). *Silent sufferers and unseen warriors: The significant other's chronic experience of pain* [Doctoral dissertation, Michigan School of Psychology]. ProQuest Dissertations Publishing.

Merleau-Ponty, M. (1962). *Phenomenology of perception* (C. Smith, Trans.). Routledge & Kegan Paul. (Original work published 1945)

Moustakas, C. (1994). *Phenomenological research methods*. SAGE.

Needleman, J. (1975). Preface. In J. Needleman (Ed., Trans.), *Being-in-the-world: Selected papers of Ludwig Binswanger* (pp. vii–ix). Condor.

Otto, R. (1958). *The idea of the holy* (J. W. Harvey, Trans.). Oxford University Press. (Original work published 1923)

Rennie, D., Watson, K. D., & Monteiro, A. (2002). The rise of qualitative research in psychology. *Canadian Psychology, 43*(3), 179–189. https://doi.org/10.1037/h0086914

Rogers, C. R. (1961). *On becoming a person*. Houghton Mifflin Company.

Smith, J. A., Flowers, P., & Larkin, M. (2009). *Interpretive phenomenological analysis: Theory, method, and practice*. SAGE.

Smith, J. A., & Osborn, M. (2015). Interpretative phenomenological analysis. In J. A. Smith (Ed.), *Qualitative psychology: A practical guide to research methods* (pp. 51–80). SAGE.

Spiegelberg, H. (1981). *The phenomenological movement: A historical introduction*. Springer. https://doi.org/10.1007/978-94-017-3270-3

Spitzer, M., & Uehlein, M. A. (1992). Phenomenology and psychiatry. In M. Spitzer, F. A. Uehlein, M. A. Schwartz, & C. Mundt (Eds.), *Phenomenology, language, and schizophrenia* (pp. 35–45). Springer-Verlag. https://doi.org/10.1007/978-1-4613-9329-0_3

Struthers, R. (2001). Conducting sacred research: An indigenous experience. *Wicazo Sa Review, 16*(1), 125–133. https://doi.org/10.1353/wic.2001.0014

van Manen, M. (1990). *Researching lived experience: Human science for an action sensitive pedagogy*. State University of New York Press.

Watkins, M., & Schulman, H. (2008). *Toward psychologies of liberation*. Palgrave Macmillan. https://doi.org/10.1057/9780230227736

Welton, D. (2001). *The other Husserl: The horizons of transcendental phenomenology*. Indiana University Press.

Wertz, F. J. (1981). The birth of the infant: A developmental perspective. *Journal of Phenomenological Psychology, 12*(2), 205–220. https://doi.org/10.1163/156916281X00245

Wertz, F. J. (1982). The findings and value of a descriptive approach to everyday perceptual process. *Journal of Phenomenological Psychology, 13*(2), 169–195. https://doi.org/10.1163/156916282X00055

Wertz, F. J. (1983a). From everyday to psychological description: Analyzing the moments of a qualitative data analysis. *Journal of Phenomenological Psychology, 14*(1), 197–241. https://doi.org/10.1163/156916283X00108

Wertz, F. J. (1983b). Some components of descriptive psychological reflection. *Human Studies, 6*(1), 35–51. https://doi.org/10.1007/BF02127753

Wertz, F. J. (1985). Method and findings in a phenomenological psychological investigation of a complex life-event: Being criminally victimized. In A. Giorgi (Ed.), *Phenomenology and psychological research* (pp. 155–216). Duquesne University Press.

Wertz, F. J. (1986). Common methodological fundaments of the analytic procedures in phenomenological and psychoanalytic research. *Psychoanalysis and Contemporary Thought, 9*(4), 563–603.

Wertz, F. J. (2006). Phenomenological currents in 20th century psychology. In H. Dreyfus & M. A. Wrathall (Eds.), *Companion to existential-phenomenological philosophy* (pp. 394–411). Blackwell Publishing Inc. https://doi.org/10.1002/9780470996508.ch27

Wertz, F. J. (2010). The method of eidetic analysis for psychology. In T. F. Cloonan & C. Thiboutot (Eds.), *The redirection of psychology: Essays in honor of Amedeo P. Giorgi* (pp. 261–278). Interdisciplinary Circle of Phenomenological Research.

Wertz, F. J. (2014). Qualitative inquiry in the history of psychology. *Qualitative Psychology, 1*(1), 4–16. https://doi.org/10.1037/qup0000007

Wertz, F. J. (2016). Outline of the relationship among transcendental phenomenology, phenomeno-logical psychology, and the sciences of persons. *Schutzian Research: A Yearbook in Lifeworldly Phenomenology and Qualitative Social Sciences, 8*, 139–162.

Wertz, F. J. (2017, May 24–25). *Phenomenology and indigenous methodologies: Potential allies in the science of subjectivities* [Paper presentation]. Annual Conference of the Society for Quali-tative Inquiry in Psychology, New York, NY, United States.

Wertz, F. J. (2019). Qualitative methods as fundamental tools: Autonomy and integration in mixed-methods research. In B. Schiff (Ed.), *Situating qualitative methods in psychological science* (pp. 43–60).

Routledge/Taylor & Francis Publishing. https://doi.org/10.4324/9781351136426-4

Wertz, F. J. (2021). Objectivity and eidetic generality in psychology: The value of explicating fundamental methods. *Qualitative Psychology, 8*(1), 125–140. https://doi.org/10.1037/qup0000190

Wertz, F. J., & Aanstoos, C. (1999). Amedeo Giorgi and the project of human science. In D. Moss (Ed.), *Humanistic and transpersonal psychology* (pp. 287–300). Greenwood Publishing.

Wertz, F. J., Charmaz, K., McMullen, L. M., Josselson, R., Anderson, R., & McSpadden, E. (2011). *Five ways of doing qualitative analysis: Phenomenological psychology, grounded theory, discourse analysis, narrative research, and intuitive inquiry.* Guilford Press.

Wertz, F. J., Desai, M. U., Maynard, E., Morrissey, M. K., Rotter, B., & Skoufalos, N. C. (2017). Research methods for person-centered healthcare science: Fordham studies of transcendence and suffering. In M. Englander (Ed.), *Phenomenology and the social foundations of psychiatry* (pp. 95–120). Bloomsbury Publishing.

Wertz, F. J., & Olbert, C. (2016). The convergence of Freud's psychoanalysis and Husserl's phenomenol-ogy on a research approach for human sciences. In C. Fischer, L. Laubscher, & R. Brooke (Eds.), *The qualitative vision in psychology: Invitation to a human science approach* (pp. 249–269). Duquesne University Press.

NARRATIVE AND LANGUAGE-BASED APPROACHES

CHAPTER 6

NARRATIVE ANALYSIS

Javier Monforte and Brett Smith

We all have stories. These may not be objective representations of reality, but they are all we have. We depend on them. We need them to understand our existence, to be who we are, to change, and to navigate the world around us. We think in story form, and we make sense of our experiences via the stories we tell ourselves and others. As Gergen (2001) summarized, stories are the "vehicle through which the reality of life is made manifest" (p. 248). Stories, therefore, matter. They are a vital resource to understand and live life.

Psychologists have been paying attention to stories for decades. In 1986, Sarbin coined the term *narrative psychology*, arguing that stories are useful to understand human conduct. From then on, researchers in psychology have become increasingly interested in narrative forms of inquiry (Bruner, 2002; McAdams, 2001; Murray, 2003; Polkinghorne, 1988; Smith & Sparkes, 2006). This is not to say that psychology has undergone a narrative revolution or turned to narrative. As Schiff (2017) argued, making such claims would be going too far, as the field of psychology as a whole has not yet turned to narrative. It would be safer to say instead that the irruption and growth of narrative methods in the last decades has shifted the trajectories of some scholars and students educated in conventional psychology. Liz Partington is a case in point.

My background as a psychology student meant that I had been trained in the traditional positivistic paradigm of scientific inquiry. . . . Although I enjoyed scientific inquiry I always felt slightly uncomfortable with it and was left feeling frustrated by the results. My research did not seem to get to the real issues; it did not embrace or accept the complexity of the human condition. I was introduced to narrative at the postgraduate level and at first my positivistic training rebelled against it. I wasn't convinced that this was proper research, however, as I sat down to try to conceptualise my MSc thesis I began to realise that narrative was the way forward for me. It captured my interest in a way that other approaches did not. (Smith, 2010, p. 89)

As the above quotation shows, the idea of turning to narrative can be charming for psychology students and researchers. This charm might contribute to its proliferation, which in principle is positive. However, the turn to narrative is merely tokenistic if it does not come hand in hand with a labour of hard reading. We should not then engage with narrative methods if we are

https://doi.org/10.1037/0000319-006
APA Handbook of Research Methods in Psychology, Second Edition: Vol. 2. Research Designs: Quantitative, Qualitative, Neuropsychological, and Biological, H. Cooper (Editor-in-Chief)

not willing to labour over the texts that created them. In other words, every person who feels appealed by and to narrative ought to engage in deep readings of the various dimensions that compose narrative scholarship.

One of these key dimensions is analysis. Researchers need to know and understand narrative analysis with a certain depth and accuracy. What is or what can be narrative analysis? Why have researchers used it to go after psychological knowledge? Which forms of narrative analysis are available? How can we assess the quality of a narrative analysis? When we ignore such questions there is a risk of producing superficial, stagnant, and incoherent narrative research that is easier to condemn—even for inappropriate reasons. Accordingly, this chapter offers initial guidance about how to enter narrative analysis in a responsible, rigorous, and fruitful manner.

The chapter is devoted not only to researchers, students, and practitioners with good predisposition to narrative analysis but also to those who may be, a priori, unfriendly to it. Our intention is not to convince the doubters to do narrative. Instead, we want to help them in becoming connoisseurs of this form of analysis. Being a connoisseur of narrative analysis does not mean one must like it; it means to judge narrative studies appropriately and appreciate them, even when narrative research is an object of doubt and criticism. This appreciative form of scholarship is crucial to build a rich scholarly community. Seen in this light, the present chapter concerns, to a lesser or greater extent, every single psychologist.

CONCEPTUAL BACKDROP: STORIES, NARRATIVES, AND NARRATIVE INQUIRY

Before introducing narrative analysis, it is necessary to define (at least) three concepts: *story*, *narrative*, and *narrative inquiry*. It is difficult to give a single and clear-cut definition of such concepts, since multiple and often conflicting definitions exist within the specialized literature. Here, there is scope for only a schematic overview. To be both consistent and offer the best of our knowledge, we draw extensively on the theoretical work of

Arthur Frank, a narrative scholar that we recognize as the most important influence in our understanding of narrative.

Stories

A *story* is a tale that an individual or group embedded in a social world tells and performs. Like chronicles, public policy statements, laws, instructions, or technical reports, stories are one genre within which a discourse is expressed (Frank, 2016). *Discourse* refers to a relatively consistent set of socially constructed ideas that people use to navigate the social world and to make sense of their experiences (Potter & Edwards, 2001). According to Frank (2010), two key aspects distinguish stories from other forms of discourse. One is *sequence* and *consequence*. In stories, things happen like the ticking of a clock: each tick creates an expectation for the corresponding tock to follow. One thing happens in consequence to another. The other key aspect is imagination. Stories are like a portal through which we see imaginative possibilities about how things are now, how they were in the past, and how they might be in the future. As Frank (2010) pointed out, even if a narration has sequence and consequence it is not much of a story if it does not elicit a sufficient degree of imagination.

Importantly, stories rest on context. This means that their capacities and values depend on who shares them, when, where, and how. Stories can do good or bad, but not on their own; they are symbiotic with people who tell them and with situations in which telling happens. As Frank (2010) noted, the responsibility falls on people to recognize which stories cause trouble in which situations and to navigate that trouble. Some psychological struggles are related with being trapped in a story that causes trouble. One example, as Boden and Eatough (2020) showed, is guilt. Individuals remain psychologically stuck when they keep returning to the story that causes them guilt feelings. Whilst not easy, a way of moving on from the guilt experience is telling an alternative, fitting story that feels right and adequately contains the lived experience. Hence the importance of knowing different stories and knowing how to make them our own. Frank (2013), however, cautioned that a person who is saturated with so many stories and points of view would struggle to hold one point of view that can be recognized as their own. In this sense, stories are like water. We need them to live, we are made of them, and we can drown in them.

Narratives

According to Frank (2010), we use the term *story* when referring to actual tales people tell and *narrative* when discussing general dimensions or properties that comprise specific stories. One single narrative has a recognizable plot and character structure that informs multiple stories and marks a similarity between them. Narratives, therefore, can be described as generalized types of stories. As Frank (2013) put it, a narrative is "the most general storyline that can be recognized underlying the plot and tensions of particular stories" (p. 75). While stories are unique and individual, people compose their stories by adapting and combining the narratives that cultures make available.

To elucidate, Frank (2013) proposed restitution as one illness narrative that people use to organize and tell their illness stories. The restitution narrative holds a basic structure of "yesterday I was healthy, today I'm sick, tomorrow I'll be healthy again" (p. 77). This narrative is adopted by many ill (and disabled) people irrespective of the intricate details that characterize their own personal story. Whether it is cancer, injury, or an eating disorder, restitution is often the template on which to map personal stories of illness. As Papathomas (2016) stressed, this speaks to the difference between narrative and story: we can have two different stories (e.g., cancer and eating disorders) guided by the same narrative (restitution). Interestingly, we can also find the restitution narrative in stories that do not talk about illness whatsoever. The work of Monforte et al. (2018) showed this through the case of Patrick, a man living with cancer and spinal cord injury. Typically, the restitution narrative is conveyed by and learned from those who have traversed the territory of illness (Sparkes, 2009). However,

instead of drawing on some illness story, Patrick took an ancient war tale called "Anabasis" (written in the year 370 BCE by Xenophon) as relevant to his illness experience. He positioned his own story in relation to Anabasis, in turn building a restitution story. This was possible because the narrative structure of Anabasis and restitution are allegorical. Like restitution, Anabasis is about a "fight to make a comeback" (Smith & Sparkes, 2004). It tells a journey back from loss to recovery. In adapting Anabasis to his situation, Patrick crafted a self-story structured by restitution. The point that this example illuminates with intensity is that looking at narratives allows us to understand the relation of a story to a prior story, even when such stories take place within vastly different contexts.

Narrative Inquiry

Narrative inquiry is the careful study and interpretation of stories and narratives as they unfold over time. As a tradition, narrative inquiry associates with psychological humanities, which are different from psychological science in that the former moves from disciplinarity to transdisciplinarity, from empirical to reflexive work, and from hypothesis-testing to asking questions about human subjectivity (Teo, 2017). In terms of its philosophical assumptions, narrative inquiry is largely (yet not always) underpinned and informed by interpretivism: a relativist ontology and a constructionist epistemology. This means that narrative researchers accept there is a physical reality but believe that humans socially construct knowledge and our realties in multiple and subjective ways (see Volume 1, Chapter 1 by Willig, this handbook).

Narrative researchers are deeply committed to the truth; however, they suggest that truth is enacted and dynamic, that "stories *become true* as they are told" (Frank, 2010, p. 41). Hence, narrative researchers do not claim to capture and produce "the truth" or "the reality" of a phenomenon. Instead, they focus on exploring which kind of truths a participant is telling, which are not necessarily verifiable or objective, though they may be one or both of these (Andrews, 2020).

What is meant here is captured in Bakhtin's (1984) understanding of truth: "Truth is not born, nor is it to found, inside the head of an individual person. It is born between people, collectively searching for truth, in the process of their dialogic interaction" (p. 10). In keeping with this notion of truth-seeking, narrative researchers recognize the "unfinalizability" of people (Frank, 2010). In practice, this means that their research does not claim to speak the last word about who the participants are or might become. Because people can and do change, this recognition is both ethical and an empirically faithful account of human life. Indeed, narrative inquiry bears within it the promise of fashioning a kind of scholarship that seeks to practice a deep fidelity to the possibilities of change, resistance, and living life differently. The point is that transforming the stories people live by is a way of transforming people's lives and society as well.

WHAT "IS" NARRATIVE ANALYSIS?

After presenting some of the concepts that constitute the basis of narrative analysis, we now turn to the fundamental question of what narrative analysis is. As an umbrella term, *narrative analysis* can be described as a psychosocial approach that takes storytelling as its object of enquiry. According to Riessman (2008), it is "a family of methods for interpreting texts (e.g., oral, written, and visual) that have in common a storied form" (p. 11). It is an approach that seeks to describe and interpret the ways in which people perceive reality, make sense of their worlds, and perform social actions (Griffin & Phoenix, 2016). This is a useful understanding from which to start. It captures the distinguishing feature of a narrative analysis and its centre of gravity, that is, a focus on stories. To add some nuance to this definition effort, narrative scholars have discussed the subtle divergences (Smith, 2016) and overlaps (McGannon & Smith, 2015) between narrative analysis and some other kinds of qualitative analysis, including interpretative phenomenological analysis (IPA) and discursive analysis. Suffice to say here is that, unlike many other

qualitative research perspectives, narrative research offers no overall rules about suitable materials or modes of analysis or the best level at which to study stories (Andrews et al., 2013). Clear accounts of how to analyze data as found, for instance, in grounded theory and in IPA are also rare in narrative analysis.

Adding to the challenge of understanding narrative analysis is that there is a huge variety in what constitutes narrative analysis (Holstein & Gubrium, 2012). For example, some narrative researchers emphasize during data analysis the *whats* of narratives, that is, the content, characters, and themes. Others focus more on the *hows* of narrative production. To organize these divergent views into a summary representation, we present a typology of narrative analysis (Figure 6.1). Illuminated by the typology are two contrasting standpoints on narrative analysis. These are known as the *story analyst* and *storyteller*.

On the one hand, a *story analyst* places narratives under analysis to produce an analytical account *of* narratives (Bochner & Riggs, 2014). *Narrative-under-analysis* refers to the practice of using one or more specific types of narrative analysis to scrutinize, think about, and interpret theoretically certain elements of a story. The research conducted then is *on* stories, where stories are fundamental data for systematic, rigorous, principled narrative analysis. The researcher, when operating as a story analyst, collects stories for data, turns these stories into stories to be formally analyzed, extrapolates theoretical propositions and categories from them, and then represents the findings of the analytical process (Smith, 2016).

For story analysts, the findings are often then represented using the conventions of the realist tal—the most common genre of representation in qualitative research (Sparkes & Smith, 2014). According to Sparkes and Smith, this genre has three key characteristics. Firstly, the researcher/author is almost completely absent from most segments of the finished text. There is no use of the first person and no reflections upon the author's role in constructing the report. This is termed *experiential authority*. Secondly,

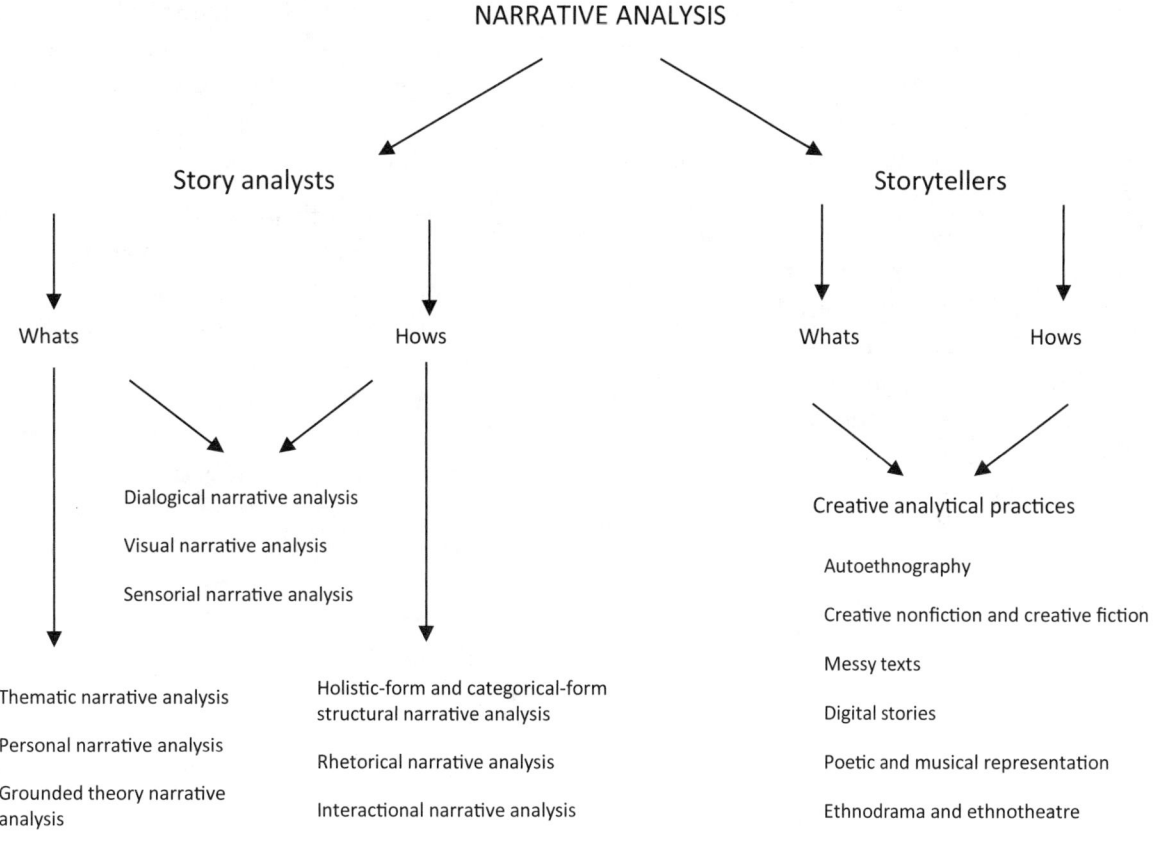

FIGURE 6.1.   A typology of narrative analysis.

the researcher/author presents extensive and closely edited storied data to reveal what is known as the participant's point of view. Thirdly, illustrated through empirical data, the researcher/author tells a theoretical account of the story to provide an explanation of it. This is known as *interpretive omnipotence*. What the researcher as author then ends up with is an abstract tale of narratives rather than a story itself. Examples of the types of narrative analysis that a researcher might use when operating as a story analyst are the following:

■ *Thematic narrative analysis.* With a focus on the *whats* of stories, the purpose is to identify central narrative themes (i.e., a pattern that runs through a story or set of stories) and relationships among these within stories (Riessman, 2008).

■ *Holistic-form structural narrative analysis.* With a focus on the *hows* of stories and, more concretely, on their formal plot and organization, the purpose is to tease out the distinct structures that hold it together with a view to identifying a particular narrative type (Lieblich et al., 1998).

■ *Categorical-form narrative analysis.* With a focus on the *hows* of stories, this narrative analysis focuses on defined linguistic characteristics of the story (e.g., adverbs, intensifiers, repetitions) that offer emphasis and style in retelling the story (Lieblich et al., 1998).

■ *Personal narrative analysis.* With a focus on the *whats* of stories, the purpose is to examine the internalized and evolving life stories of individuals (McAdams, 2013).

■ *Grounded theory narrative analysis.* With a focus largely on the *whats* of stories, the purpose is to develop categories and produce a theory grounded in data while being sensitive to narratives by looking at the ways narrativity can be integrated conceptually and used systematically for shaping the way in which coding, category development, and the representation of results in study proceed (Ruppel & Mey, 2015).

- *Rhetorical narrative analysis.* With a focus on the *hows* of stories, the purpose is to identify the oppositions (e.g., good and bad therapy) and enthymemes (e.g., incomplete or probable arguments) that make up stories (Feldman et al., 2004).
- *Interactional narrative analysis.* With a focus on the *hows* of stories and borrowing ideas and techniques from conversation analysis (Potter & Edwards, 2013), the purpose is to examine the interactional activity through which stories are constructed (Bamberg, 2012; Gubrium & Holstein, 2009).
- *Dialogical narrative analysis.* With an interest in the *whats* and *hows* of stories, the purpose is to examine what is told in the story, how it is told, and what happens as a result of telling that story—its effects (see below).
- *Visual narrative analysis.* With a focus on the *whats* or *hows*, the purpose is to examine how and when visual material was made and who created it; what is included (and excluded) in the image itself, how component parts are arranged, and use of color and technologies; and, ideally, people's responses to an image (see Riessman, 2008).
- *Sensorial narrative analysis.* With a focus on moving between the *whats* and *hows*, the purpose is to examine what senses are used and how for making sense of human life and social actions (Sparkes & Smith, 2012).

In contrast to a story analyst, when operating as a storyteller analysis is the story and the research is communicated as a story. Thus, when operating as a storyteller, the end product of your research would read more "like a story" than a traditional research report like a realist tale. To say that analysis is the story is to emphasize that, rather than putting a story under analysis and doing research on narratives, the story in its own right is analytical and theoretical. Stories help us understand aspects of our lives. Hence, "narrative analysis assumes that a good story is itself analytical and theoretical. When people tell their stories, they employ analytic techniques to interpret their worlds. Stories are themselves analytic" (Ellis, 2004, pp. 195–196).

According to the aforementioned arguments, for psychologists who operate as storytellers there is a move from explaining toward a goal of he(art)ful engagement and thinking with stories. There are indeed several moves:

> from abstract theorising toward a goal of evocation; from transferring information and toward communication; from categorical thought and abstracted theory and toward embracing the values of emotionality and performing theory; from assuming the stance of disinterested spectator and toward assuming the posture of a feeling and vulnerable observer; from closing down interpretations and toward laying open and encouraging multiple interpretations; from the gaze of the distanced observer toward the embrace of intimate involvement; and away from a head, cut off from the living body toward feeling, hearing, tasting, breathing, smelling, and emotionally witnessing an embodied life. (Smith & Sparkes, 2009, p. 282)

To show rather than explicitly tell readers what stories mean, storytellers produce written, oral, theatrical performances, and/or, for example, visual *creative analytic practices*. As described by Richardson (2000), this is an umbrella term for different kinds of writing, visual, oral, and, for example, ethnodramatic practices that are both creative and analytic. Here textual, verbal, ethnodramatic, or visual representation cannot be divorced from analysis, and each should be thought as analytic in its own right. When written, for instance, as Richardson noted, they display "the writing process and the writing product as deeply intertwined; both are privileged. The product cannot be separated from the producer or the mode of production or the method of knowing" (p. 930). Examples of the types of creative analytical practices that a researcher might use when operating as a storyteller follow:

- *Autoethnography.* The focus is on creating stories about the researcher's lived experience, relating the personal to the cultural (Ellis & Adams, 2014).

- *Creative nonfiction.* The focus is on creating a story that is grounded in research findings and composed using the techniques of fiction (Sparkes, 2002).
- *Creative fiction.* This is different from the creative nonfiction genre in that it includes things that never happened, giving the narrative imagination free rein (Sparkes, 2002).
- *Messy texts.* The focus is on showing and telling a story in a manner that is characterized by a continuous movement throughout among description, interpretation, and voice (Griffin & Phoenix, 2014).
- *Digital stories.* The focus is on using the internet (e.g., Facebook or blogs) to construct and communicate a digital story (Cunsolo Willox et al., 2013).
- *Poetic representation.* The focus is on transforming data into a poem-like composition (Richardson, 2000).
- *Ethnodrama.* The focus is on producing a written play script based on stories collected and interpreted (Mura, 2020).
- *Ethnotheatre.* The focus is on turning a written play script into an actual theatrical production. The play becomes another layer of analysis (Mura, 2020).
- *Musical performance.* The focus is on using music as way of analyzing data and communicating findings (Sparkes & Smith, 2014).

Story analyst and storyteller are different standpoints, but neither one is better than the other. Researchers may, for certain purposes, choose to operate as one or the other. Or they might move from one standpoint to another within a project, utilizing both rather than pledging allegiance to one standpoint only (e.g., storyteller) and seeing the other (e.g., story analyst) as a family enemy. Examples of researchers moving back and forth between standpoints, operating in some instances as story analyst and then at other times as storyteller to thicken understandings of a specific topic, can be found in the work of Smith et al. (2013) on spinal cord injury rehabilitation and Owton

and Sparkes (2017) on sexual abuse and the grooming process. Next, we back up to consider how narrative analysis can be put into practice from each of the two presented standpoints.

HOW NARRATIVE ANALYSIS MIGHT PROCEED?

As highlighted, there are multiple types of narrative analysis that fall under the umbrella of a story analyst and a storyteller. For space and affinity reasons, we narrow the focus on how to practice two analyses that belong to different standpoints but have in common their emphasis on the reflexive interplay between the *whats* and *hows* of storytelling. These are *dialogical narrative analysis*, and *creative nonfiction*.

Dialogical Narrative Analysis

Dialogical narrative analysis (DNA) examines how a story is put together in terms of the narrative resources that are artfully used. It also "studies the mirroring between what is told in the story—the story's content—and what happens as a result of telling that story—its effects" (Frank, 2010, pp. 71–72). Thus, in a DNA, stories are examined not simply for what is said or the narrative resources used to help structure storytelling. It extends analytic interest to what stories do both for and to people.

Unlike other methods, DNA does not prescribe a step-by-step approach in which the analyst must follow a set list of stringent procedures. Instead, it functions as a heuristic guide—a guide to interpretation. Drawing on Frank (2010, 2012) and articulated in Smith and Monforte (2020), what follows is a guide for doing a DNA. It represents an attempt to help aspiring narrative analysts to steer a way through the analytic process. This guide consists of various analytic strategies. These are mostly presented as a set of questions that are grounded in the theoretical assumptions outlined earlier and that orient a DNA. The rationale for approaching analysis as a method of questioning is based on several observations. For Frank (2010) "Some methods are more useful for the questions they offer than for any procedures they prescribe" (p. 72). Questions do more than act as a guide for how to move along in the analytic process. Approaching data with a set of carefully considered questions in mind and examining the data with the aid of these questions can help to get thought moving. It can spur imagination and inspiration that, in turn, can lead to insight and understanding.

The analytic process. The contour of the guide for doing a DNA can be viewed as cyclical and iterative as opposed to linear and fixed. The researcher engages in the process of moving forward through each strategy outlined in the guide but can move back and forth between each, circling backward and forward sometimes, even jumping between strategies as well as appreciating that some have different utility with respect to different stories. That said, we might begin by "getting the story." This might be done as follows.

- *Deciding what is a story and/or narrative.* Many definitions of a story and narrative exist, but to analyze stories a researcher needs to decide what is a story and if they see it as different from a narrative. These were differentiated earlier in this chapter, but to help decide what is a story a researcher can also use their experiences: Often we know a story when we hear one.

- *Collect big and/or small stories.* It may be stating the obvious, but to analyze stories a researcher needs stories! While interviews are commonly used to collect stories, autobiographies, letters, diaries, vignettes, the media (e.g., newspapers), ethnographic fieldwork notes, the internet (e.g., blogs), visual material (e.g., photographs), and conversations in everyday life can all be good sources of stories—big stories, small stories and everything in between. Big stories are long stories that entail a considerable amount of reflection on an experience or event, a significant part of a life, or the whole of it. In contrast, small stories are fleeting conversations told during interaction about mundane things and everyday occurrences (Griffin & Phoenix, 2016).

- *Transcribe data.* If collecting stories from interviews, for instance, you should transcribe the data verbatim as soon as possible after collecting them. Transcription is much more than a technical exercise. It is a constructive process in which analytical thoughts can emerge and "percolate." Thus, not only should a researcher carefully decide on what to include and how to present the transcribed data, they should also think of transcription as part of the analytic process. You should jot down notes as you transcribe. For instance, ask yourself what types of stories might be emerging, which ones seem crucial, and how particular stories unfold.

- *Writing.* Write continuously throughout the research project. Writing is not a "mopping activity," something to be done just at the end of the research to communicate the results. Writing is a form of analysis, because analysis happens in the process of writing (Sparkes & Smith, 2014). As you jot down notes, write memos, edit your report, and so on through the entire research process, you can progressively discover ideas, what counts, and how stories "hang together." Think of writing as an iterative and inductive process of hearing stories speak to the research aims, representing those stories and theoretical thoughts in writing, revising your selection of stories and theory as you develop your arguments, and revising the writing as those stories and theory require (Frank, 2012).

But, of course, writing has to start somewhere. To get analysis moving, to open it up, the following strategies are offered.

Getting to grips with stories.
- *Indwelling.* Like familiarization or immersion within other types of analysis, indwelling involves reading the data (for example, an interview transcript) several times while, if possible, listening to any recording and jotting down initial impressions. But, according to Maykut and Morehouse (1994), it also "means to live within . . . understanding the person's point of view from an empathetic

rather than a sympathetic position" (p. 25). As part of this, rather than thinking of the person as a vessel from which to extract information, the researcher orients themselves to the participant as someone who is a storyteller and who shares a story with another person or other people.

- *Identify stories.* Identify the story or stories in the actual data (e.g., in the transcript). To help with this, look out for new beginnings in talk where there are marked shifts in content. The researcher might also try to look for where each line might be seen to begin and end. Once a collection of lines is established, a story may come into view. Another strategy is to look for classic elements of story structure in the text: Is there an orientation or setting introduced? Is there a complicating action and a resolution? Is there a coda (a summary or concluding event) that returns to the present? To help with this, look for phrases like "It all started with . . ." because these can signal an opening to a story, and declarations such as "So that's why I left" because these can highlight the end of the story. Finally, try to get a feel for stories being developed across the interview/transcript as a whole.

- *Identify narrative themes and thematic relationships.* The focus here is on "what" is said, that is, the content of the story. A narrative theme is a pattern that runs through a story or set of stories. To search for and identify themes in a manner that keeps the story or stories intact, look for patterns within the stories by closely reading the text. To help with identifying patterns, the researcher can ask, "What is the common theme(s) or thread(s) in each story?" "What occurs repeatedly within the whole story?" As you systematically work through the text, identify theme materials by highlighting key sentences in different colors, underlining key phrases in the text, and/or circling key words. In addition, in the margins of the transcript, field notes, or other data source, write extended phrases (in four or five words) that summarize the manifest (apparent) and latent (underlying) meanings of the data.

Do not think of this process as a typical sort of coding that, in other qualitative approaches, usually involves coding line by line and summarizing data in a code of one, two, or three words. This can result in overcoding that can break the text down too much for a narrative analysis to work; the researcher is left with a set of codes, not a story. Thus, rather than overcode by coding the data line by line, think of the process as "theme-ing" the data.

- *Identify the structure.* The focus here is on how the story is put together. To help with identifying the structure, consider (a) the direction(s) of the story (e.g., decline and then progress) and depict this in a graph; (b) the use of terms that point to structure (e.g., when the participant refers to experiencing a "crossroads"); (c) the participant's reflections on specific phases or chapters in their life (e.g., "It was then that I realized I had to fight to recover from my illness"); (d) the use of evaluative comments (e.g., "My life has gone downhill since I retired from the Army"); (e) tone and changes in tone within the story (e.g., pessimistic and later optimistic); and (f) the objectives or "wants" of the characters involved (e.g., after spinal cord injury a person wants to walk again); the conflicts or obstacles they face as they try to achieve their objectives (e.g., doctors say that medicine has not yet found a cure for spinal injury); tactics or strategies they employ to reach their objectives (e.g., going to the gym to keep muscles healthy for when a cure does come); their attitudes towards others and towards given circumstances (e.g., optimistic about walking); the particular emotions they experience throughout (e.g., sadness and a sense of loss); and/or their "subtexts" or underlying and unspoken thoughts (e.g., scared about a cure not happening).

Opening up analytical dialogue further. Following Frank (2010, 2012) and Sparkes and Smith (2012), when reading the data, thinking with them, and travelling with the stories in their everyday lives, a researcher might next ask the following questions. Some questions can open up what was unnoticed about the story; the usefulness of others will arise from thinking about why they do not apply to a story. Each set of questions and each response to them will not always be applicable for inclusion in the final research report, but asking each question can enhance understandings of the story. In addition, when asking each question, a researcher can think with the story as a whole. It can also be useful to write a paragraph or two in response to each question or group of questions, revising and editing as needed.

- *Resource questions.* What narrative resources (e.g., plot, metaphors) does the storyteller draw upon to shape their experiences? What resources shape how their story is told? Not everyone can simply access any narrative resource they wish, and people cannot simply tell any story they choose about their lives and expect to be believed. Who, then, has access to which resources? Who is under what constraints in the resources they use? To understand the resources being used, it might be useful also to ask what other resources might lead to different stories. What might be preventing those alternative resources from being mobilized? How does the story reiterate, borrow, or counter these narratives?
- *Circulation questions.* Understanding who your participants tell their stories to in every-day life can reveal useful insights into who those stories are intended for and how they may have been constructed with that intended audience in mind. Who, then, tells which stories to whom? Who would immediately understand that story and who would not understand it? Are there some people to whom the storyteller would not tell that story, and why not?
- *Connection questions.* The stories we tell to others can appeal to or repel those others. To whom does a person's story connect them? Who is placed outside this connection? How might groups be formed through sharing a common understanding of a certain story? Whom does the story render external or "other" to the group? Who is excluded from the "we"

who share the story? Who does the storyteller speak against? Who does the storyteller want to hear the story, and who might they be afraid to hear it?
- *Identity questions.* What stories give people a sense of who they are? How do these stories do this? How do people tell stories to explore who they might become, and if not, why?
- *Body questions.* Stories are told not only about our bodies but using—and out of—our bodies. We often get a sense or a feeling within our bodies of what stories are good, virtuous, and worth listening to or acting on and which are bad, loathsome, or best ignored. What stories do the participant and the researcher hold close to their hearts? How do these stories enable and constrain the ways we understand participants' experiences? What stories evoke fear in our bodies? What is our body telling us about the story, the storyteller, and what it means to live well? How does your body respond to the story and what might that tell you about the story that was told? For an example in action, see Sparkes and Smith (2012).
- *Function questions.* As an actor or form of action, what does each story do for and on the person? That is, how might the story a person tells be useful to them, help them live a good life, and do things "for" them, and how might it lead them down dangerous roads and do things "on" them? What does this story do for and on other people? How does a story shape a person's conduct, affecting what they do, and do not do?

Pulling the analysis together. This can be done in numerous ways. For example, a researcher might choose to move from a story analyst to a storyteller. Drawing upon a creative analytical practice like creative nonfiction, they might synthesize the results of a DNA in and as a story. The researcher might also produce a traditional realist tale in which the story—and its effects—are described systematically and explained to the reader. Here a researcher might blend the results generated from the strategies around a set of interacting and interplaying themes that capture the content of stories and their functional dynamics or they might begin with a particular analytic interest and then organize the stories around it. Alternatively, there can be a focus on pulling the results together to build a typology of narratives. This analytical move of identifying different types of narratives that people draw on to construct their stories is summarized as follows:

- *Build a typology.* This can be done by reading through each result from the phases and then bringing these together—clustering them—into a set of narratives that constitute various "ideal types" (i.e., clearly defined narratives that are different from other ideal types and express something unique about participants' experiences). A story identified as belonging to a particular ideal type should capture not only content and/or structure but also functions—what it can do. To help with this process the researcher can (a) translate the stories into images and then imagine these impacting on people and consider the consequences; (b) create time to think about the story, tell the story slowly to themselves, wait and listen to it, and reflect some more without rushing the thinking process along; and (c) structure their writing around each type, revising and editing along the way to help "discover" further the types of narratives used. After identifying the types of stories people tell, name each in a way that captures the essence of each narrative, for example, a "quest" narrative that speaks of life as an adventure or a "chaos" narrative that speaks of life as an endless series of destructive events or a meaningless and empty vacuum. It can be useful after this to revisit the data to ensure the typology being built is grounded in the stories collected. The researcher may then need to revise the typology and names of the narratives.
- *Represent the results.* Structure the report around the typology (e.g., see the paper by Smith and Sparkes, 2004, which is structured around a typology of three ideal types). The report can take the form of a realist tale, but, given the

commitment to "unfinalizability," any ending of a DNA as represented in a realist tale is necessarily provisional. This does not mean that the results or end report are tentative. Rather, while all reports need to close for practical reasons, participants in most studies are still alive and, rather than giving their last word, can tell new stories in which they may become someone different (Frank, 2010).

Some useful examples of DNA in action are Caddick (2016), Frank (2010, Chapter 5), Monforte et al. (2018), Smith (2013), and Sparkes (2015).

Creative Nonfiction

As articulated in Smith, McGannon, and Williams (2015), the following are some guiding tips for how to help craft a creative nonfiction. When we speak about what a creative nonfiction might look like, these tips should not be seen as a set of prescriptive techniques or recipe. Rather, we hope that some of the tips are useful for thinking about how to transform data into a story.

- *Epistemological and ontological awareness.* Throughout writing, be attentive to how, as a researcher, one's epistemology and ontology inform the story. Also consider the world views of the people in the story and how these are inseparable from culture and the social world.
- *A purpose.* A creative nonfiction needs to have and communicate an important point. This helps enable stories to succeed not only as artful literary pieces but also as human science research. Make sure the purpose is clear to readers.
- *Analysis and theory.* Some researchers opt first to operate as story analyst by conducting a formal analysis of the data (e.g., a narrative thematic analysis) and interpreting the results theoretically. The results of the analysis, along with theoretical interpretations of these, are then gathered together and used to help assemble the story in terms of what the content of the story is about (e.g., what characters say, enact, and don't say), and how the story

unfolds in relation to people (e.g., how people say things in interaction with other people). Researchers may also add findings from other research to their story. This can help create a more complex picture and show tensions, contradictions, and connections between research. Collating all analytic results and theories in a table can sometimes be useful. It condenses points to be made, is easily accessible, and can help jog the memory about ideas to be included when crafting the story. No matter what, it is important that the story is crafted from and delivers a thick and rich analysis.

- *Verisimilitude*. Seek truthfulness, not "The Truth." The story needs to demonstrate how true to an experience a narrative can be and with that, the evocation of emotion and feeling from the reader(s). This might include trying to create an account that feels close to the participant's own telling, attempting to be faithful to the experiences and emotions described, the meanings they inscribed, and their own styles of speech.
- *Think with your body*. Draw on your senses, listen to the many voices you've heard in your heart and head, feel these stories pulsating through your body, and tell them as if they were your own while respecting the fact you can never truly know the other.
- *Select and develop characters*. Consider how many characters are needed to tell the story, who the characters are and become, how they drive the story along, what stories each tells, and how they interact with each other. Make characters complex too, not simply all good or all bad. Consider intersectionality, that is, the intersection of identities grounded in gender, sex, ethnicity, religion, disability and ability, and so on.
- *Use dialogue*. Show what has happened, the point of the story, emotions, and so on through conversations where appropriate.
- *Embodiment*. Evoke a sense of the character's body in motion and being still. Show bodies being emotionally expressive (or not) and

enacting on, within, and against stories. Let the characters act out the story in relation to other people and reveal things about themselves to others through these actions.

- *Write evocatively and engagingly*. As well as showing through dialogue, use different senses (e.g., smell, sound, taste) to evoke emotions, create suspension, and engage the readers viscerally as well as cognitively. It can also be useful to use flashback, metaphor, and dramatic evocation.
- *Develop a plot*. A plot can't always contain tension, as everyday life is not like that. But a story needs to have some dramatic tension. It needs to connect points across time, be cohesive, and have a consequence(s). A story needs a beginning, middle, and end (not the final word) but not always told in that order. To help drive the plot along also consider the characters, what obstacles along the story they face, what they care about, and how they might change, even if only very subtly.
- *Scene setting*. Think about where (e.g., places) and when (e.g., morning breakfast) to locate people and their conversations (including internal dialogues with phantom others). Ask yourself about the back stages and front stages people behave in as well as how many scenes readers are willing to move in and out of.
- *Selectivity*. No one can tell the whole story of a research topic. Select what needs to be told in that paper, to meet a certain purpose (e.g., to answer your research question), and to communicate an important point for a particular audience.
- *Edit*. Revise your work numerous times—editing, revising, editing more, and revising again—over a period of time (often this is over many months). Make every word count. Don't make the story too long.

Some useful examples of this creative analytical practice in action are in Smith et al. (2013), Smith, Tomasone, et al. (2015), and Owton and Sparkes (2015). Also, Orr et al. (2020) offered an accessible discussion of the process of developing a creative nonfiction.

QUALITY AND RIGOR IN NARRATIVE ANALYSIS

How can we tell a good narrative analysis from the not so good? How might the quality and rigor of narrative inquiry in psychology be judged? Having a response to these questions is vital if we are to make fair, appropriate, and informed judgments about narrative analysis. To offer an appropriate response, we should follow an initial premise. That is, any research method needs to be evaluated in terms of the logic that is inherent to it. According to Burke (2016), we can differentiate two basic logics: the *criteriologist* and the *relativist*.

The criteriologist logic parallels the dominant positivist views of what constitutes rigor in quantitative research and advocates the need of adopting universal, fixed, and established criteria to determine whether a narrative study is of value, regardless of its purpose (Burke, 2016). Such a criteriological view that seeks to judge all narrative inquiry against preestablished notions creates problems when put in front of a more unusual form of inquiry and genre of representation, such as autoethnography and creative nonfiction. If we apply the criteriologist logic, only one conclusion is possible from the start regarding these works, and that is they are "bad" research. Indeed, we may even judge them not to be worthy of the name *research* at all (Sparkes & Smith, 2009). For this reason, the criteriologist logic is antithetical to narrative analysis. This problem is especially visible in relation to the storyteller standpoint, although it applies to most kinds of interpretivist research. In view of that, it would be more sensible to adopt a relativist approach to judge a qualitative study using narrative analysis.

The label *relativist* should not be misunderstood with the idea that quality and rigor are of relative importance in narrative research. This is not the case, not even in the case of arts-based, experimental research. As Richardson and St. Pierre (2005) stated, creative analytical practices need to be "held to high and difficult standards: mere novelty does not suffice" (p. 960). So, relativism does not mean that "anything goes"; it means

that anything that goes depends. A researcher adopting a relativist logic is willing to describe what one might do but is not prepared to mandate what one must do across all contexts and on all occasions prior to any piece of research being conducted (Sparkes & Smith, 2009). Researchers do not determine criteria in advance of any particular piece of inquiry. The term *criteria* is, thus, not seen as meaning an absolute or preordained standard against which to make judgment, as this position is laden with foundational implications. The process of judging research is viewed as a craft skill, whereby the relativist must make informed decisions and ongoing judgements about which criteria reflect the inherent properties of a particular study as it develops over time. As Burke (2016) noted, these judgements are based on a time-and-place-contingent list of characteristics. For example, Sparkes (2020) compiled various lists of criteria for judging the quality of autoethnographic texts. Meanwhile, Smith, McGannon, and Williams (2015) offered some possible starting points on how supervisors, researchers, reviewers, and editors might pass judgment on creative nonfiction stories. These authors provided a list that illustrates what an ongoing list of criteria might look like:

- *Substantive contribution and worthiness*. Does research contribute empirically, methodologically, theoretically, and/or practically to our understanding of social life, and how? Is the topic of the research relevant, timely, significant, and interesting? Has the work provided me new knowledge, fresh insights, or a deeper understanding? Did the work provide me with things I didn't know before?
- *Focus*. Is there a purpose or point to the research? Is there a sense of focus throughout or does the story go too far off track?
- *Aesthetic merit*. Does this research succeed aesthetically? Do the stories open up the text and invite interpretive responses? Is the text artistically shaped, satisfying, complex, and not boring? Do they "work"?
- *Expression of a reality*. Does this text embody a fleshed out, embodied sense of lived experience?

Does it seem "true"—a credible account of a psychological, cultural, social, individual, or communal sense of the "real"?

- *Evocation and illumination.* Does the work emotionally and/or intellectually illuminate a terrain, a process, individual, group, and/or theory? Does the researcher begin to feel meanings within the story being told?
- *Engagement.* Does the research keep me emotionally and intellectually interested? Do I want to carry on reading half way through?
- *Incitement to action.* Does the research move me intellectually and emotionally? Does it generate new questions? Does it move people to act? How well does the work create a plausible and visceral lifeworld and charged emotional atmosphere as an incitement to act within and outside the context of the work? What might I do with this research?
- *Meaningful coherence.* Does the study achieve what it purports to be about; use methods and procedures that fit its stated goals; and meaningfully interconnect literature, research questions/foci, findings, and interpretations with each other?

One should not think of this list as an enclosed and precisely specified list that must be applied to all narrative work. To do that would be to miss the point of thinking of criteria as list-like. Lists are always open-ended and ever subject to constant reinterpretation so that items can be added to the list or taken away. While there is utility in commonality, there is also liability in that one can get locked into criteria in ways that constrain innovation and dampen the imagination. Criteria, then, as Sparkes and Smith (2009) concluded, should be viewed as lists of characterizing traits that are open to reinterpretation as times, conditions, and purposes change.

A NEW NARRATIVE: NARRATIVE ANALYSIS AFTER NEW MATERIALISM

Robinson (2007) argued that "of all subjects, psychology has most to learn from sources external to itself" (p. 197). Accordingly, psychology has forged interdisciplinary connections with a number of intellectual projects from the social sciences and the humanities (Held, 2021). One intellectual project that is just beginning to connect with psychology is *new materialism* (Coole & Frost, 2010). We are interested to sit with new materialism because it intersects and seeks to retain critical insights of social constructionism and narrative inquiry but suggests, at the same time, that narrative analysis draws on problematic conventions. The argument follows that such conventions lead researchers to overemphasize human knowing, meaning, and methods and in turn to neglect ontology, material entities, and theory (Monforte & Smith, 2021). To be sure, we do not intend to suggest that the task now should be for narrative researchers to become new materialists. Rather, we invite narrative psychologists to reinterpret their concepts and practices after the new materialist provocation. Doing so affords some opportunities to rethink narrative analysis and, without giving it up, to "do something different *from the beginning*" (St. Pierre, 2021, p. 7, original emphasis). But where might new materialist ideas enter into deliberations about narrative analysis? How might ideas from new materialism modify how we think about narrative analysis and how we frame our narrative research? For the purpose of illustration, we identify three aspects through which new materialism can make interesting changes in narrative analysis: materiality, pluralism, and fiction.

Materiality

Narrative analysis might contribute to a glorification of meaning at the expense of materiality. Memorably, Barad (2007) suggested that narrative has been granted too much power. For her, overemphasizing "narrative matters" has reduced the space for materiality to the point where "the only thing that doesn't seem to matter anymore is matter" (p. 132). This observation, however, should not simply be taken to mean that narrative psychologists have not acknowledged the importance of material bodies and the material world. In fact, it is difficult to find occasions where narrative researchers have explicitly denied the existence of an extranarrative realm. Rather, the problem is the treatment of material things as relatively passive, as "neutral bearers of meanings" or "symbols of underlying social mechanisms" (Aagaard & Matthiesen, 2016, p. 35). As Alaimo and Hekman (2008) clarified,

> Even though many social constructionist theories grant the existence of material reality, that reality is often posited as a realm entirely separate from that of language, discourse, and culture. This presumption of separation has meant, in practice, that feminist theory and cultural studies have focused almost entirely on the textual, linguistic, and discursive. (p. 3)

As an interpretivist approach that reacts to postpositivism, narrative inquiry has become a paired opposite to forms of analysis linked to cognitive approaches in psychology. Importantly, new materialism is said to cut across the backbone of cognitive and interpretivist traditions as it shows that *both* start from a distinctive pole, that is, they are consistently predicated on dualist structures. New materialism traverses such dualist structures by conceptualizing discourse (including stories) and materiality (including material things and bodies) as coconstitutive instead of predetermined (Figure 6.2).

New materialist is a monist (as opposed to dualist) tradition; however, it is not necessarily new or different from any other monist tradition. As Dolphijn and van der Tuin (2012) explained, new materialism "does not add something to thought (a series of ideas that wasn't there, that was left out by others)" (p. 13). Rather, it "traverses and thereby rewrites thinking *as a whole*, leaving nothing untouched, redirecting every possible idea according to its new sense of orientation." It "works through" intellectual traditions; it "says 'yes, *and*' to all of them, traversing them all" (p. 89). It changes the way we understand and treat stories.

Echoing Law (2000), in new materialism *"there is no important difference between stories and materials"* (p. 2, original emphasis). Law (2019) himself noted that this "materialsemiotic" proposition might be seen as a "scandal." Analytically, it is indeed counterintuitive for the psychological researcher. This is because they are "accustomed

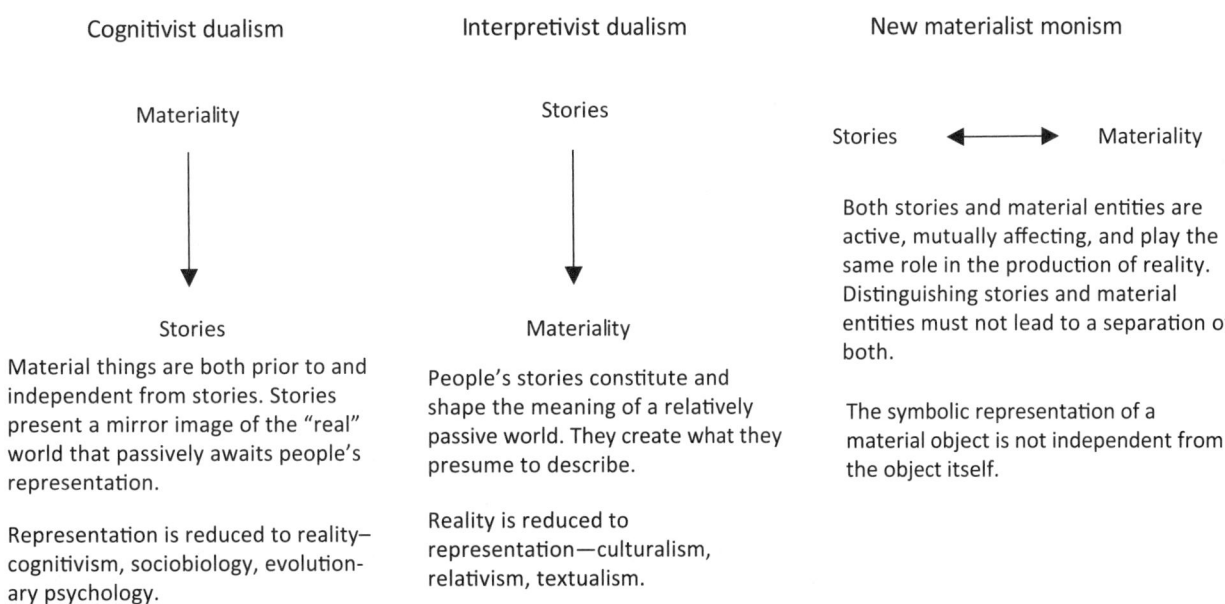

Cognitivist dualism

Materiality

Stories

Material things are both prior to and independent from stories. Stories present a mirror image of the "real" world that passively awaits people's representation.

Representation is reduced to reality—cognitivism, sociobiology, evolutionary psychology.

Interpretivist dualism

Stories

Materiality

People's stories constitute and shape the meaning of a relatively passive world. They create what they presume to describe.

Reality is reduced to representation—culturalism, relativism, textualism.

New materialist monism

Stories ⟷ Materiality

Both stories and material entities are active, mutually affecting, and play the same role in the production of reality. Distinguishing stories and material entities must not lead to a separation of both.

The symbolic representation of a material object is not independent from the object itself.

FIGURE 6.2. Inspired by Feely (2016) and Zembylas (2017), the figure shows in simplified terms the way in which new materialism views stories, material things, and the relation between both, as well as how such view contrasts with dualist perspectives.

to academic analyses which, implicitly or explicitly, privilege one order of analysis, and read an entire system through that particular order" (Feely, 2016, p. 874). While for the sociobiologist it is the gene, for the narrative researcher it is the story. In contrast, by engaging with new materialism, narrative researchers would refuse to privilege and grant final causality to a particular order. Instead, they think through complex networks or assemblages made of stories and other elements that come together over time and produce a whole. In these assemblages, what matters is not the elements that compose them but rather their relations, as it is through such relations that the elements come to exist (Feely, 2016; Law, 2019).

In line with this relational philosophy, Monforte et al. (2020) argued that narratives could be recast as assemblages of material and semiotic forces, which are mutually affecting. For example, the restitution narrative that we have mentioned in this chapter could be reimagined as an open-ended assemblage of stories, interactions, medical and rehabilitation procedures, bodies, objects, buildings, and fluids, which work together as a whole to shape the process of recovery from illness. In this terms, it is most appropriate to analyze narrative data through engaging, for example, with the stages of *assemblage analysis* highlighted by Feely (2020). Here, the analytic emphasis is not put in how people construct reality symbolically through stories, but rather in how stories produce reality materially in tandem with, and as, material resources.

Pluralism

Narrative inquiry and new materialism have different philosophical assumptions. Despite some overlaps (e.g., Rosiek & Snyder, 2020), the narrative approach and new materialism are incommensurable. According to Kuhn (1962), if two paradigms are incommensurable, we cannot compare them with one another because there is no common language into which both can be translated. Incommensurability also means that paradigms are not compatible with each other and, therefore, should not be combined. Kuhn would have argued that the term *story* actually means something different from narrative and new

materialism, as the philosophical assumptions in which each embed the term are different. This implies that narrative and new materialism are in effect speaking different languages, which complicates any attempt to use them together.

Without neglecting the lessons learned from Kuhn, some researchers have sought dialogue across "different languages." One way such dialogue can occur is through engaging with the idea of ontological and analytical pluralism (Frost & Nolas, 2011). This idea refers to the never unproblematic use of different views of reality and forms of analysis within the same study. Acknowledging the risks and tensions that pluralism entails, Smith and Monforte (2020) showed how a variant of narrative analysis (*dialogical narrative analysis*) and a new materialist form of analysis (*assemblage analysis*) can coalesce via a form of pluralism advanced by new materialist scholars. Such a kind of pluralism can be identified with the concept of diffraction (e.g., Barad, 2007; Haraway, 1997). Smith and Monforte found in the words of Geerts and van der Tuin (2016) an accessible definition of this concept:

> Rather than employing a hierarchical methodology that would put different texts, theories, and strands of thought against one another, diffractively engaging with texts and intellectual traditions means that they are dialogically read "through one another" to engender creative and unexpected outcomes (Barad, 2007, p. 30) while acknowledging and respecting the contextual and theoretical differences between the readings in question. This methodology, thus, stays true to Haraway's idea of diffraction: Rather than flat-out rejecting what has been theorized before, the foundations of the old, so to say, are being reused to think anew.

Through diffraction, narrative dialogism and new materialism became two in one body, generating what Anzaldúa (1987, p. 194, quoted by Barad, 2014) called "the coming together of opposite qualities within." Despite that new materialism principles served to reimagine the principles of narrative dialogism, previous narrative foundations were not completely abandoned. Following Clark and Thorpe (2020), Smith and Monforte (2020) did not take up diffractive reading to move on from or counter narrative analysis but rather to work the limits of theory-method to prompt new connections, relations, and transformations. Such transformations allowed them to see beyond narrative. And yet, without the narrative approach, they could have not reimagined and extended previous narrative knowledge. Diffraction, in this sense, reveals an interesting paradox: Thinking with narrative helps thinking beyond narrative and transcending its own boundaries.

Fiction

From a storyteller standpoint, some researchers have experimented with creative fiction, using the imagination (instead of conventional empirical materials) to discover and embody truth (Richardson, 2000). Caveats have been offered that help make responsible use of fiction in and for research (Best, 2021; Richardson & St. Pierre, 2005; Sparkes, 2002). Despite this, psychology seems to offer little or no serious role for fictional literature. Some think that using fiction in psychology research would be another "scandal," one that trivializes the power of reality (Law, 2019). Against the tide, however, a few psychologists have argued for its value. For example, Moghaddam (2004) argued that literature can be a source of psychological data and theory, helping psychologists gain a better understanding of long-term psychological processes and change. Further, Brinkmann (2009) argued that "literature can be considered as qualitative research in itself" given that "we can learn as much from fiction novelists about contemporary human lives, experiences, and sufferings as we can from traditional forms of empirical qualitative research" (also Lehmann & Brinkmann, 2020). These arguments are quite rare, though. As Sparkes (2002) pointed out, for many disciplines (including psychology) fiction remains a no-no, a mode of expression that is simply off limits in academic discourse.

In new materialism, however, postures like the aforementioned are not exceptional. As Skiveren (2020, p. 2) noted, "fiction is not a mark of disqualification in the field of new materialism." In particular, scholars in this field do draw on literary works to grasp phenomena that are "true" and that, in principle, reside beyond the limits of intelligibility. In other words, fiction is used as "an epistemological tool for envisioning that which cannot (yet) be perceived as 'true'" (p. 3). As Knausgaard (2018) clarified,

> this truth is the novel's truth. The novel [but also the short story and other fictional forms] is a place where that which cannot be thought elsewhere can be thought and where the reality we find ourselves in, which sometimes runs counter to the reality we talk about, can be manifest in images.

In addition to illuminating what there is (the actual), fiction might allow us to imagine what might become (the virtual). This is particularly interesting for new materialist scholars, as for them "'what there is' *is* just a process of becoming" (Brinkmann, 2017, p. 116). For new materialist scholars, then, one epistemological value of engaging with fiction is to explore alternative possibilities for society, communities, organizations, and individuals—to expand narrative resources. In Benjamin's (2016) words, fictions that observe the future "are not meant to convince others of what is, but to expand our own visions of what is possible" (p. 2). Haraway's (2016) work provided an example in practice. Instead of summing up the findings of her research on the acceleration of human population, she closed her book with the Camille Stories, a set of speculative fabulations that encourage the reader to imagine life on Earth five generations into the future. For Skiveren (2020, p. 10), the Camille stories are tentative prophecies, tools for the imagination to envision a future. The quality of these futuristic fictionalizations, then, cannot be evaluated in terms of likelihood or probability, insofar as the aim of these stories is not to predict but to direct. When Haraway makes stuff up, it is in order to carve out perceptions of a sustainable world that had, until then, seemed unimaginable.

In keeping with the welcoming attitude of new materialism towards fiction, both storytellers and story analysts can benefit from engaging with the truth of fiction to understand and provide understanding of the psychological processes they study. Moreover, they can harness the potential of fiction to produce imaginative and effective psychology work. For example, in working with participants, researchers might use a technique that has regained attention in psychology: story completion. This entails participants writing stories about hypothetical scenarios created by the researcher, through responding to a stem consisting of at least one complete sentence that represents the beginning of a story (Clarke et al., 2019). Again, story completion might be used not only to study multiple topics but also for political and therapeutic ends. As Smith (2019) suggested, maybe it could modestly contribute to individual and social change by enabling people to imagine difference, expand the stories they have available to make meaning, and contemplate a world that could be. This "possibility of renewal and change," Andrews (2014) noted, "is one of the greatest gifts of our narrative imagination" (p. 115).

CONCLUSION

This chapter has offered a concise overview of narrative analysis in psychology. We hope that readers are now a little more confident about their knowledge of narrative analysis. At the same time, we invite them to consider the chapter as an initial, general, and embarrassingly incomplete resource, which ought to be complemented by further resources. Many are already available that will help readers enrich their understandings and ask themselves deeper questions. Some have been quoted here. As such, we encourage readers to keep reading once this very sentence ends, to find in the reference list some more exciting stories about stories . . . and more.

References

Aagaard, J., & Matthiesen, N. (2016). Methods of materiality: Participant observation and qualitative research in psychology. *Qualitative Research in Psychology, 13*(1), 33–46. https://doi.org/10.1080/14780887.2015.1090510

Alaimo, S., & Hekman, S. (2008). *Material feminisms.* Indiana University Press.

Andrews, M. (2014). *Narrative imagination and everyday life.* Oxford University Press. https://doi.org/10.1093/acprof:oso/9780199812394.001.0001

Andrews, M. (2020). Quality indicators in narrative research. *Qualitative Research in Psychology. 18*(3), 353–368. https://doi.org/10.1080/14780887.2020.1769241

Andrews, M., Squire, C., & Tamboukou, M. (Eds.). (2013). *Doing narrative research.* SAGE. https://doi.org/10.4135/9781526402271

Anzaldúa, G. (1987). Borderlands/la frontera. aunt lute books.

Bakhtin, M. (1984). *Problems of Dostoevsky's poetics.* University of Minnesota Press. https://doi.org/10.5749/j.ctt22727z1

Bamberg, M. (2012). Narrative analysis. In H. Cooper (Ed.), *APA handbook of research methods in psychology: Vol. 2. Quantitative, qualitative, neuropsychological, and biological* (pp. 85–102). American Psychological Association. https://doi.org/10.1037/13620-006

Barad, K. (2007). *Meeting the universe halfway: Quantum physics and the entanglement of matter and meaning.* Duke University Press. https://doi.org/10.2307/j.ctv12101zq

Barad, K. (2014). Diffracting diffraction: Cutting together-apart. *Parallax, 20*(3), 168–187. https://doi.org/10.1080/13534645.2014.927623

Benjamin, R. (2016). Racial fictions, biological facts: Expanding the sociological imagination through speculative methods. *Catalyst: Feminism, Theory, Technoscience, 2*(2), 1–28.

Best, J. (2021). To teach and delight: The varieties of learning from fiction. *Review of General Psychology, 25*(1), 27–43. https://doi.org/10.1177/1089268020977173

Bochner, A. P., & Riggs, N. A. (2014). Practicing narrative inquiry. In P. Leavy (Ed.), *The Oxford handbook of qualitative research* (pp. 195–222). Oxford University Press.

Boden, Z. V., & Eatough, V. (2020). Parallel returns: Feelings, temporality and narrative in the experience of guilt. *Qualitative Research in Psychology, 17*(1), 36–52. https://doi.org/10.1080/14780887.2019.1569188

Brinkmann, S. (2009). Literature as qualitative inquiry the novelist as researcher. *Qualitative Inquiry, 15*(8), 1376–1394. https://doi.org/10.1177/1077800409332030

Brinkmann, S. (2017). Humanism after posthumanism: Or qualitative psychology after the 'posts.'

Qualitative Research in Psychology, 14(2), 109–130. https://doi.org/10.1080/14780887.2017.1282568

Bruner, J. (2002). *Making stories: Law, literature, life.* Harvard University Press.

Burke, S. (2016). Rethinking 'validity' and 'trustworthiness' in qualitative inquiry: How might we judge the quality of qualitative research in sport and exercise sciences? In B. Smith & A. C. Sparkes (Eds.), *Routledge handbook of qualitative research in sport and exercise* (pp. 330–339). Routledge.

Caddick, N. (2016). Doing narrative analysis. In E. Lyons & A. Coyle (Eds.), *Analysing qualitative data in psychology* (2nd ed., pp. 222–239). SAGE.

Clark, M. I., & Thorpe, H. (2020). Towards diffractive ways of knowing women's moving bodies: A Baradian experiment with the Fitbit-motherhood entanglement. *Sociology of Sport Journal, 37*(1), 12–26. https://doi.org/10.1123/ssj.2018-0173

Clarke, V., Braun, V., Frith, H., & Moller, N. (2019). Editorial introduction to the special issue: Using story completion methods in qualitative research. *Qualitative Research in Psychology, 16*(1), 1–20. https://doi.org/10.1080/14780887.2018.1536378

Coole, D., & Frost, S. (2010). Introducing the new materialisms. In D. Coole & S. Frost (Eds.), *New materialisms: Ontology, agency, and politics* (pp. 1–43). Duke University Press. https://doi.org/10.1215/9780822392996-001

Cunsolo Willox, A., Harper, S. L., Edge, V. L., 'My Word': Storytelling and Digital Media Lab, & Rigolet Inuit Community Government. (2013). Storytelling in a digital age: Digital storytelling as an emerging narrative method for preserving and promoting indigenous oral wisdom. *Qualitative Research, 13*(2), 127–147. https://doi.org/10.1177/1468794112446105

Dolphijn, R., & van der Tuin, I. (2012). *New materialism: Interviews and cartographies.* Open Humanities Press. https://doi.org/10.3998/ohp.11515701.0001.001

Ellis, C. (2004). *The ethnographic I.* Altamira Press.

Ellis, C., & Adams, T. E. (2014). The purposes, practices, and principles of autoethnographic research. In P. Leavy (Ed.), *Oxford library of psychology. The Oxford handbook of qualitative research* (pp. 254–276). Oxford University Press.

Feely, M. (2016). Disability studies after the ontological turn: A return to the material world and material bodies without a return to essentialism. *Disability & Society, 31*(7), 863–883. https://doi.org/10.1080/09687599.2016.1208603

Feely, M. (2020). Assemblage analysis: An experimental new-materialist method for analyzing narrative data. *Qualitative Research, 20*(2), 174–193. https://doi.org/10.1177/1468794119830641

Feldman, M., Sköldberg, K., Brown, R., & Horner, D. (2004). Making sense of stories: A rhetorical approach to narrative analysis. *Journal of Public Administration: Research and Theory, 14*(2), 147–170. https://doi.org/10.1093/jopart/muh010

Frank, A. W. (2010). *Letting stories breathe: A socio-narratology.* University of Chicago Press. https://doi.org/10.7208/chicago/9780226260143.001.0001

Frank, A. W. (2012). Practicing dialogical narrative analysis. In J. Holstein & J. Gubrium (Eds.), *Varieties of narrative analysis* (pp. 33–52). SAGE.

Frank, A. W. (2013). *The wounded storyteller: Body, illness, and ethics.* University of Chicago Press.

Frank, A. W. (2016). From sick role to narrative subject: An analytic memoir. *Health, 20*(1), 9–21. https://doi.org/10.1177/1363459315615395

Frost, N. A., & Nolas, S. M. (2011). Exploring and expanding on pluralism in qualitative research in psychology [Editorial]. *Qualitative Research in Psychology, 8*(2), 115–119. https://doi.org/10.1080/14780887.2011.572728

Geerts, E., & van der Tuin, I. (2016, July 27). *Diffraction and reading diffractively.* New Materialism. https://newmaterialism.eu/almanac/d/diffraction.html

Gergen, K. (2001). Self narration in social life. In M. Wetherell, S. Taylor, & S. J. Yates (Eds.), *Discourse theory and practice* (pp. 247–259). SAGE.

Griffin, M., & Phoenix, C. (2014). Learning to run from narrative foreclosure: One woman's story of aging and physical activity. *Journal of Aging and Physical Activity, 22*(3), 393–404. https://doi.org/10.1123/JAPA.2012-0300

Griffin, M., & Phoenix, C. (2016). Becoming a runner: Big, middle and small stories about physical activity participation in later life. *Sport Education and Society, 21*(1), 11–27. https://doi.org/10.1080/13573322.2015.1066770

Gubrium, J. F., & Holstein, J. A. (2009). *Analyzing narrative reality.* SAGE. https://doi.org/10.4135/9781452234854

Haraway, D. (1997). *Modest_witness@second_millennium. femaleman©_meets_oncomouse™: Feminism and technoscience.* Routledge.

Haraway, D. (2016). *Staying with the trouble.* Duke University Press.

Held, B. S. (2021). Taking the humanities seriously. *Review of General Psychology. 25*(2), 119–133. https://doi.org/10.1177/1089268020975024

Holstein, J. F., & Gubrium, J. A. (2012). Introduction. In J. Holstein & J. Gubrium (Eds.), *Varieties of narrative analysis* (pp. 1–11). SAGE. https://doi.org/10.4135/9781506335117.n1

Knausgaard, K. O. (2018). *The end: My struggle. Book 6.* Vintage Publishing.

Kuhn, T. (1962). *The structure of scientific revolutions.* University of Chicago Press.

Law, J. (2000). On the subject of the object: Narrative, technology, and interpellation. *Configurations, 8*(1), 1–29. https://doi.org/10.1353/con.2000.0003

Law, J. (2019, January 30). *Material semiotics.* Heterogeneities. http://www.heterogeneities.net/publications/Law2019MaterialSemiotics.pdf

Lehmann, O. V., & Brinkmann, S. (2020). Revisiting "the art of being fragile": Why cultural psychology needs literature and poetry. *Culture and Psychology, 26*(3), 417–433. https://doi.org/10.1177/1354067X19862183

Lieblich, A., Tuval-Mashiach, R., & Zilber, T. (1998). *Narrative research: Reading, analysis and interpretation.* SAGE. https://doi.org/10.4135/9781412985253

Maykut, P., & Morehouse, R. (1994). *Beginning qualitative researchers: A philosophical and practical guide.* Falmer.

McAdams, D. (2001). The psychology of life stories. *Review of General Psychology, 5*(2), 100–122. https://doi.org/10.1037/1089-2680.5.2.100

McAdams, D. (2013). *The redemptive self* (2nd ed.). Oxford University Press.

McGannon, K. R., & Smith, B. (2015). Centralizing culture in cultural sport psychology research: The potential of narrative inquiry and discursive psychology. *Psychology of Sport and Exercise, 17,* 79–87. https://doi.org/10.1016/j.psychsport.2014.07.010

Moghaddam, F. M. (2004). From 'psychology in literature' to 'psychology is literature': An exploration of boundaries and relationships. *Theory & Psychology, 14*(4), 505–525. https://doi.org/10.1177/0959354304044922

Monforte, J., Pérez-Samaniego, V., & Devís-Devís, J. (2018). The Anabasis of Patrick: Travelling an allegorical narrative map of illness and disability. *Psychology of Sport and Exercise, 37,* 235–243. https://doi.org/10.1016/j.psychsport.2017.10.005

Monforte, J., Pérez-Samaniego, V., & Smith, B. (2020). Traveling material↔semiotic environments of disability, rehabilitation, and physical activity. *Qualitative Health Research, 30*(8), 1249–1261. https://doi.org/10.1177/1049732318820520

Monforte, J., & Smith, B. (2021). Introducing postqualitative inquiry to sport and exercise psychology. *International Review of Sport and Exercise Psychology,* 1–20. Advance online publication. https://doi.org/10.1080/1750984X.2021.1881805

Mura, P. (2020). Ethnodrama and ethnotheatre in tourism. *Current Issues in Tourism, 23*(24), 3042–3053. https://doi.org/10.1080/13683500.2020.1746746

Murray, M. (2003). Narrative psychology. In J. Smith (Ed.), *Qualitative psychology* (pp. 95–112). SAGE.

Orr, K., Smith, B., Arbour-Nicitopoulos, K. P., & Wright, F. V. (2020). The café talk: A discussion of the process of developing a creative non-fiction. *Qualitative Research in Sport, Exercise and Health.* Advance online publication. https://doi.org/10.1080/2159676X.2020.1834443

Owton, H., & Sparkes, A. C. (2017). Sexual abuse and the grooming process in sport: Learning from Bella's story. *Sport, Education and Society, 22*(6), 732–743. https://doi.org/10.1080/13573322.2015.1063484

Papathomas, A. (2016). Narrative inquiry: From cardinal to marginal . . . and back? In B. Smith & A. C. Sparkes (Eds.), *International handbook of qualitative methods in sport and exercise* (pp. 37–48). Routledge.

Polkinghorne, D. (1988). *Narrative knowing and the human sciences.* State University of New York Press.

Potter, J., & Edwards, D. (2001). Discursive social psychology. In W. P. Robinson & H. Giles (Eds.), *The new handbook of language and social psychology* (pp. 103–118). John Wiley.

Potter, J., & Edwards, D. (2013). Conversation analysis and psychology. In J. Sidnell & T. Stivers (Eds.), *The handbook of conversation analysis* (pp. 702–725). Blackwell.

Richardson, L. (2000). Writing: A method of inquiry. In N. Denzin & Y. Lincoln (Eds.), *Handbook of qualitative research* (2nd ed., pp. 923–948). SAGE.

Richardson, L., & St. Pierre, E. (2005). Writing: A method of inquiry. In N. Denzin & Y. Lincoln (Eds.), *Handbook of qualitative research* (3rd ed., pp. 959–978). SAGE.

Riessman, C. K. (2008). *Narrative methods for the human sciences.* SAGE.

Robinson, D. N. (2007). Theoretical psychology: What is it and who needs it? *Theory & Psychology, 17*(2), 187–198. https://doi.org/10.1177/0959354307075042

Rosiek, J. L., & Snyder, J. (2020). Narrative inquiry and new materialism: Stories as (not necessarily benign) agents. *Qualitative Inquiry, 26*(10), 1151–1162. https://doi.org/10.1177/1077800418784326

Ruppel, P. S., & Mey, G. (2015). Grounded theory methodology—Narrativity revisited. *Integrative Psychological & Behavioral Science, 49*(2), 174–186. https://doi.org/10.1007/s12124-015-9301-y

Sarbin, T. (1986). *Narrative psychology: The storied nature of human conduct*. Praeger.

Schiff, B. (2017). *A new narrative for psychology*. Oxford University Press. https://doi.org/10.1093/oso/9780199332182.001.0001

Skiveren, T. (2020). Fictionality in new materialism: (Re)Inventing matter. *Theory, Culture & Society*. *39*(3), 187–202. https://doi.org/10.1177/0263276420967408

Smith, B. (2010). Narrative inquiry: Ongoing conversations and questions for sport and exercise psychology research. *International Review of Sport and Exercise Psychology*, *3*(1), 87–107. https://doi.org/10.1080/17509840903390937

Smith, B. (2013). Disability, sport and men's narratives of health: A qualitative study. *Health Psychology*, *32*(1), 110–119. https://doi.org/10.1037/a0029187

Smith, B. (2016). Narrative analysis. In E. Lyons & A. Coyle (Eds.), *Analyzing qualitative data in psychology* (2nd ed., pp. 202–221). SAGE.

Smith, B. (2019). Some modest thoughts on story completion methods in qualitative research. *Qualitative Research in Psychology*, *16*(1), 156–159. https://doi.org/10.1080/14780887.2018.1536396

Smith, B., McGannon, K. R., & Williams, T. (2015). Ethnographic creative non-fiction: Exploring the what's, why's and how's. In L. Purdy & G. Molner (Eds.), *Ethnographies in sport and exercise* (pp. 59–73). Routledge.

Smith, B., & Monforte, J. (2020). Stories, new materialism and pluralism: Understanding, practising and pushing the boundaries of narrative analysis. *Methods in Psychology*, *2*(3), 100016. https://doi.org/10.1016/j.metip.2020.100016

Smith, B., Papathomas, A., Martin Ginis, K. A., & Latimer-Cheung, A. E. (2013). Understanding physical activity in spinal cord injury rehabilitation: Translating and communicating research through stories. *Disability and Rehabilitation*, *35*(24), 2046–2055. https://doi.org/10.3109/09638288.2013.805821

Smith, B., & Sparkes, A. (2004). Men, sport, and spinal cord injury: An analysis of metaphors and narrative types. *Disability & Society*, *19*(6), 613–626. https://doi.org/10.1080/0968759042000252533

Smith, B., & Sparkes, A. C. (2006). Narrative inquiry in psychology: Exploring the tensions within. *Qualitative Research in Psychology*, *3*(3), 169–192. https://doi.org/10.1191/1478088706qrp068oa

Smith, B., & Sparkes, A. C. (2009). Narrative analysis and sport and exercise psychology: Understanding lives in diverse ways. *Psychology of Sport and Exercise, 10*(2), 279–288. https://doi.org/10.1016/j.psychsport.2008.07.012

Smith, B., Tomasone, J. R., Latimer-Cheung, A. E., & Martin Ginis, K. A. (2015). Narrative as a knowledge translation tool for facilitating impact: Translating physical activity knowledge to disabled people and health professionals. *Health Psychology*, *34*(4), 303–313. https://doi.org/10.1037/hea0000113

Sparkes, A. C. (2002). Fictional representations: On difference, choice, and risk. *Sociology of Sport Journal*, *19*(1), 1–24. https://doi.org/10.1123/ssj.19.1.1

Sparkes, A. C. (2009). *Sporting heroes, autobiography and illness narratives: A brief comparison of Bob Champion and Lance Armstrong*. University of Huddersfield.

Sparkes, A. C. (2015). When bodies need stories. Dialogical narrative analysis in action. In M. O'Neill, B. Roberts, & A. C. Sparkes (Eds.), *Advances in biographical methods* (pp. 30–42). Routledge.

Sparkes, A. C. (2020). Autoethnography: Accept, revise, reject? An evaluative self reflects. *Qualitative Research in Sport, Exercise and Health*, *12*(2), 289–302. https://doi.org/10.1080/2159676X.2020.1732453

Sparkes, A. C., & Smith, B. (2009). Judging the quality of qualitative inquiry: Criteriology and relativism in action. *Psychology of Sport and Exercise*, *10*(5), 491–497. https://doi.org/10.1016/j.psychsport.2009.02.006

Sparkes, A. C., & Smith, B. (2012). Embodied research methodologies and seeking senses in sport and physical culture: A fleshing out of problems and possibilities. In K. Young & M. Atkinson (Eds.), *Qualitative research on sport and physical culture* (pp. 167–190). Emerald Press. https://doi.org/10.1108/S1476-2854(2012)0000006011

Sparkes, A. C., & Smith, B. (2014). *Qualitative research methods in sport, exercise and health: From process to product*. Routledge.

St. Pierre, E. A. (2021). Post qualitative inquiry, the refusal of method, and the risk of the new. *Qualitative Inquiry*, *27*(1), 3–9. https://doi.org/10.1177/1077800419863005

Teo, T. (2017). From psychological science to the psychological humanities: Building a general theory of subjectivity. *Review of General Psychology*, *21*(4), 281–291. https://doi.org/10.1037/gpr0000132

Zembylas, M. (2017). The contribution of the ontological turn in education: Some methodological and political implications. *Educational Philosophy and Theory*, *49*(14), 1401–1414. https://doi.org/10.1080/00131857.2017.1309636

CHAPTER 7

ETHNOMETHODOLOGY AND CONVERSATION ANALYSIS

Paul ten Have

Ethnomethodology (EM) and conversation analysis (CA) are the somewhat confusing names of two related research traditions that were developed in the 1960s in the United States by Harold Garfinkel and by Harvey Sacks (with his coworkers Emanuel Schegloff and Gail Jefferson), respectively. The contexts for their initiatives were the theoretical and methodological debates in sociology that were current at the time. Since then, EM and CA have become more or less established paradigms that have attracted researchers from a range of disciplines around the world. As a first characterization, one can note their interest in the detailed ways in which members of society collaboratively constitute the situations in which they find themselves and the (inter)actions that take place in those situations. The general sociological issue of social order is reconsidered as a local achievement of members in situations, and the research objective is to explicate *how* this is done in an accountable way. CA can be seen as a specialized form of EM, originally focusing on verbal interaction and later also considering nonvocal aspects. It has developed a rather specific, relatively conventionalized research style using audio or video recordings and detailed transcripts as basic data. Other forms of EM use a much wider range of data types, such as ethnographic observations, while the approach is closely fitted to the chosen topic and the properties of the research site.

THE EMERGENCE OF THE ETHNOMETHODOLOGICAL PROGRAM

To summarize a rather complex net of influences and inspirations, it can be said that Harold Garfinkel's initiative started with his critical confrontation with the theories of his dissertation supervisor, Talcott Parsons at Harvard, from a phenomenological perspective informed by the work of Schutz, Gurwitsch, and Husserl (Garfinkel, 1967; Heritage, 1984b; Rawls in Garfinkel, 2002). When he was involved with a study of jury deliberations and listened to the tapes of those discussions, he was struck by the carefulness of the jury members' commonsense reasoning: their serious "lay methodology." So, in line with anthropological disciplines like ethnomedicine and ethnobotany, he coined the term *ethnomethodology* for the study of the methods that ordinary members of society use and take for granted. As a professor in sociology at the University of California, Los Angeles, he undertook a series of empirical studies to further develop EM as a research program. Some of these studies used a procedure of breaching commonsense background expectancies as demonstrations of their importance in everyday sense making. It turned out that such breaches were often experienced as upsetting and that they led to instant efforts to normalize the situation (Garfinkel, 1967, pp. 35–75).

These background expectancies are part of an immense collection of taken-for-granted, "seen but

This chapter is reprinted from the first edition. References to other chapters in the handbook have been updated.
The author thanks Paul Camic, Harrie Mazeland, and Jonathan Potter for their remarks on earlier versions of this chapter.

https://doi.org/10.1037/0000319-007
APA Handbook of Research Methods in Psychology, Second Edition: Vol. 2. Research Designs: Quantitative, Qualitative, Neuropsychological, and Biological, H. Cooper (Editor-in-Chief)

unnoticed," and silently presupposed capacities and understandings that can be taken as foundational for both ordinary and specialized forms of social life. Imagine trying to make a dish by following a recipe from a cookbook without understanding what the terms used meant, how to handle a knife to cut the vegetables, how to boil water, and so on. It is this level of presupposed, ordinarily unnoticed but essential capacities and understandings that is of interest to ethnomethodologists. Of course, they do not limit their attention to things like following a recipe. They have, indeed, studied this level of unnoticed phenomena for a very wide range of activities.

A critical point in all this is that the level of concrete capacities and understandings is not only ignored in instructions such as recipes but also in all sorts of plans; reports; and scientific analyses of various sorts, including, of course, sociology. In that discipline, social life is generally investigated in terms of pregiven concepts or preelaborated theories, on the basis of data gathered in terms of pregiven categories and methods. In fact, Talcott Parsons was a champion of this approach of first elaborating an extensive, rationally organized category system, *before* doing any empirical work. In contrast to this external top-down approach, Garfinkel maintained that members of society should not be treated as "dopes" whose task it was to act according to some theories but rather as actually capable of "doing social life," which can be investigated "from within actual settings" (Garfinkel, 1967, p. 68).

To explicate the specifics of his approach, Garfinkel developed a complex writing style, which tends to be rather incomprehensible to the uninitiated, and which, in combination with the breaching procedures, led quite often to strongly negative reactions from other sociologists. I discuss a key excerpt from the preface to *Studies in Ethnomethodology* (Garfinkel, 1967) to present Garfinkel's general ideas and to familiarize readers with his style and basic concepts.

> Ethnomethodological studies analyze everyday activities as members' methods for making those same activities visibly-rational-and-reportable-for-all-practical-purposes, i.e., "accountable," as organizations of commonplace everyday activities. The reflexivity of that phenomenon is a singular feature of practical actions, of practical circumstances, of common sense knowledge of social structures, and of practical sociological reasoning. By permitting us to locate and examine their occurrence the reflexivity of that phenomenon establishes their study. (Garfinkel, 1967, vii)

The first sentence tells us that EM studies focus on the fact that members in their ordinary actions in various ways make the sense and purpose of those actions recognizable for other members. Accountability refers to the moral obligation among members to produce their actions in ways that are recognizably reasonable in the situation in which they are done. By using reflexivity, Garfinkel stresses the self-explicating and self-referencing aspect of practical actions. What is made clear in the doing of an action is its *local* and *situated* meaning, what anthropologists might characterize as *emic* in contrast to *etic*. The frequent use of words like *everyday*, *practical*, and *common sense* further stresses the EM focus on the achieved ordinariness of actions. It is the local sense displays rather than some theorized general sense of actions that is of interest to ethnomethodologists. The last sentence in the excerpt formulates the methodological basis of EM studies. To conduct EM studies, the ethnomethodologist has to immerse himself or herself in the situation of interest, mentally if not physically. One has to acquire "membership knowledge" to become what Garfinkel has elsewhere called "vulgarly competent" in the setting (Garfinkel & Wieder, 1992).

In later work, Garfinkel elaborated the ethnomethodological program in various ways, but most often in terms of the contrast between EM and the established sociological approach characterized as *constructive* or *formal analysis*. The general theme of these elaborations is that in EM studies the phenomena that established approaches study in terms of predefined concepts of social order are *respecified* as members' methods for creating a locally account-able order. In their search for analytic generalities, mainstream sociologists ignore or gloss over the specific, locally required concrete details of actions, which are the phenomena of interest for ethno-methodologists (cf. Garfinkel, 2002).

Ethnomethodology's Methods

As the phenomena of interest for an ethnomethodol-ogist occur on a level of seen but unnoticed or used but taken for granted, a first practical problem for EM is how to make those phenomena noticeable. Garfinkel's own efforts, as reported in his *Studies in Ethnomethodology* (Garfinkel, 1967), were quite strongly oriented to this problem of noticeability, or rather as an effort to demonstrate the existence and relevance of phenomena of this type. His so-called breaching experiments were part of a pedagogy, a strategy to convince his students and colleagues that he was after something relevant, not just for sociol-ogy but for everyday life. By breaching expectancies, or having them breached by his students, such as asking for the meaning of ordinary expressions, he did two things. He made noticeable their relevance and moral quality in the production of everyday situations, and he provoked extra sense-making activities to repair the experienced disturbances. The people exposed to the breaches showed they were puzzled and shocked, but they immediately made efforts to normalize the situation, by taking it as a joke or finding some other motive or explana-tion for the breach. In addition to these provocative interventions, Garfinkel also studied what might be called *natural breaches*, such as the efforts by a biological male to pass as a natural female.

Later ethnomethodologists turned to other means to study the details of situated practices, most often intense ethnography supplemented with audio-visual recordings of in situ activities (cf. Chapter 9, this volume). This serves two purposes. On the one hand, it allows researchers to acquire a certain measure of membership knowledge by immersing themselves in the social life of the setting under study. In this way, they gain access to relevant local understandings and even some competence to act as a member. And on the other hand, the ethnographic fieldwork (and especially the audiovisual recordings)

gives them access to the fine details of the verbal and visible activities in ordinary settings of the specific form of life.

In their *Invitation to Ethnomethodology*, Francis and Hester (2004) formulated the process of EM research in the following summary way:

> Doing ethnomethodology involves taking three methodological steps: 1. Notice something that is observably-the-case about some talk, activity or setting. 2. Pose the question "How is it that this observable feature has been produced such that it is recognizable for what it is?" 3. Consider, analyse and describe the methods used in the production and recognition of the observable feature. (pp. 25–26)

And they added,

> In other words, then, ethnomethodology starts out with what might be called the "common-sense appearance of the social world" and then seeks to describe how they will have been produced "from within" such that they do indeed have the appearances they have. (p. 26)

Some Examples of Ethnomethodological Study

Scanning any list of ethnomethodological studies, one may be struck by the enormous variety of topics, or rather of settings and activity types studied. There are, for instance, studies of the ways in which both staff and inmates used a so-called convict code to explain situations in a halfway house for former drug users (Wieder, 1974), of laboratory practices focusing on the identification of artifacts (Lynch, 1985), of the art of piano improvisation (Sudnow, 1978), of the interactions of users with a complex copy machine (Suchman, 1987, 2007), or of the reasoning practices of Tibetan monks (Liberman, 2004).

These examples can be invoked to illustrate several of the methodological aspects of EM research. Wieder (1974) has done intensive ethnography, which Lynch (1985) and Liberman (2004) have also used, together with recordings. Sudnow (1978) has studied his own actions. Wieder, in his report, referred to a tradition of ethnography in which a local subculture, such as the convict code, is invoked to explain the actions of a local gang of people. In contrast to this tradition, he described the ways in which such a subculture is actually used by its members to account for the situation in which they have to act as they do, as a "folk sociology." Here access was mainly gained by his experience in the setting, by seeing and hearing the inmates and staff members telling the code, and also in accounting for their actions in dealing with him.

In the study by Suchman (1987, 2007), a special setup was created in which two subjects were asked to carry out some tasks at the copier, with one having to read out the instructions and the displays, while the other had to handle the practical actions at the machine. In this way, she gained access to the users' situated reasoning, which she could confront with the preplanned reasoning implemented in the machine, as part of an artificial intelligence project. In her analysis she contrasted the plans implemented in the machine with the observed situated actions. She stressed the inability of such plans to foresee the local circumstances and ad hoc practical reasonings that guide the actual actions of the users at the machine in situ.

In whatever way access to the phenomena of interest is acquired, the researcher will have to produce a record in one way or another, as ethnographic notes, audio or visual recordings, or transcriptions thereof, as an aid to the process of *noticing* in the sense of the quote from Francis and Hester (2004). These records constitute the material the researcher works on, fixing what has happened, in a way objectifying these happenings to help make them "anthropologically strange" rather than just to be taken for granted (Garfinkel, 1967, p. 9). Almost always, EM research reports contain quotes, longer fragments or pictures from such records, inviting the readers to check what is reported with the data as rendered in such quotes and excerpts. So recordings serve a double purpose: as research materials to explore and as demonstrations to support the arguments.

The studies by Lynch (1985, 1993), Sudnow (1978), and Liberman (2004) illustrated the fact that to do an ethnomethodological study of some specialized activity, the researcher has to have or acquire a sufficient level of competence in doing that activity (Garfinkel & Wieder, 1992; Lynch, 1993, pp. 265–308). This is a special case of the more general, noted requirement that an ethnomethodologist has to have the relevant membership knowledge to understand, in the sense used earlier, members' practical activities (ten Have, 2002). So Lynch had to have some competence in reading images produced by the electronic microscope, Sudnow had to be able to play the piano, and Liberman had to learn the Tibetan language as well as acquire a basic understanding of Tibetan Buddhist philosophy. The practical issue, of course, is how far the researcher should go in this matter.

A persistent theme in both the programmatic statements of EM as well as most if not all ethnomethodological studies is the discrepancy between, on the one hand, general statements and ideas about practical activities, like plans, instructions, protocols, and formal accounts, and on the other, the activities to which they refer in their actual, particular, and methodic detail. This theme has surfaced in the discussions of Wieder's and Suchman's studies, but is also discernible in the others mentioned. As Heap (1990, pp. 42–43) has noted, ethnomethodological studies can bring different kinds of "news": In a "critical news approach," the researcher claims that things are *not* as they appear or are presented, whereas in a "positive news approach," the message is that something *is* organized in a particular way, which is of interest in itself. I return to these issues in a later section on applied studies.

A MAJOR OFFSHOOT: CONVERSATION ANALYSIS

Garfinkel's (1967) explorations quite soon became a source of inspiration for a number of other sociologists of younger generations. A prominent one was Sacks, who came to focus on spontaneous talk, that is, conversation. Both Sacks and his close colleague Schegloff had studied with Goffman, who was already famous for his studies of interaction, although in a different framework than the one Sacks came to develop. At first, Sacks explored various aspects of verbal interaction, including the use of categorization of persons, in what later became known as *membership categorization analysis* (MCA; see the section A Minor Offshoot), but gradually he concentrated on the actual organization of talking together, in collaboration with Schegloff and later Jefferson. This became what is now known as CA. Since their publication of a paper on the organization of turn-taking in 1974, CA became a recognizable paradigm in the Kuhnian sense, a research tradition with its own approach to data and analysis, with a prominent exemplar, and a growing set of people working along the lines set out by the originators.

The relations between EM and CA can be characterized as ambivalent (cf. Clayman & Maynard, 1995). Like EM, CA also studies the ways in which members of society organize their dealings with each other with an eye on the local circumstances in which they find themselves and with a stress on the local achievement of a social order. But whereas EM tended more and more to stress the local specificity of these methods, CA would often formulate those in more general terms, as is clearly the case in the paper on turn-taking. Furthermore, whereas ethnomethodologists have studied many aspects of an immense variety of situations, CA concentrated, at least originally, on the organization of talking together in itself, whatever the situation. Later, many conversation analysts turned to studying how the specifics of talk related to aspects of the situation in which it occurred, quite often an institutional setting. Although the expression CA is well established, at the initiative of Schegloff (1987), CA's object is now mostly termed *talk-in-interaction*. And although CA originally was conducted almost exclusively on the basis of audio recordings, video is now in general use. In a way, this seems to have brought EM and CA closer together again, as current studies of multimodal activities often combine inspirations from both EM and CA, as I illustrate later in this chapter.

The specificity of CA's analytic perspective can be characterized in terms of a restricted set of organizations, including most prominently those of turn-taking and sequence. The basic idea of turn-taking

organization is that a turn-at-talking consists of one or more units, such as sentences or single words like *yes*, called *turn-constructional units* (TCUs). When one such unit comes to a possible end, the turn might go to another participant; this moment is called a *transition-relevance place* (TRP). Then the current speaker may select another to take over, or another may self-select to speak, or the current speaker may continue, either immediately or a bit later (see Sacks, Schegloff, & Jefferson, 1974, for details and illustrations).

The organization of sequences, more or less coherent sets of subsequent turns, is rather more complicated, as can be seen in a recent book-length overview by Schegloff (2007b). The core idea is that a sequence can minimally consist of a pair of turns, one acting as an initiative such as a question, to be followed immediately by a response such as an answer. The technical term for such a two-part sequence is *adjacency pair* (Schegloff & Sacks, 1973, pp. 295–296), and other examples besides question–answer are *invitation–acceptance/decline, greeting–greeting*, and so forth. In sequences consisting of more than two parts, the core of such sequences quite often consists of one basic adjacency pair to which other parts are added in a *sequence expansion*. The first speaker may, for instance, react to the second part with a *third-turn response*, such as a thanks or an evaluation of the response. The core sequence may also be prepared in some way by a so-called *presequence*, such as, "May I ask you a question?" Another possibility is that the response to the first part of the pair is delayed, for instance, by an inquiry like "Now or tomorrow?" which starts an *inserted sequence*. And, of course, the core sequence may be followed up in many ways by *postexpansions*.

A few more technical terms deserve to be explicated, if only to show the kinds of complexities of sequences considered in CA. First-pair parts like invitations, requests, proposals, or accusations have possible second-pair parts that can be divided into two *alternate types*, such as acceptance or declination. The ways in which responses of these two types are designed tend to differ: Some are relatively short and produced promptly, whereas others may be much more elaborated, delayed in various ways, and accounted for in often a rather complex manner.

The first type has been called a *preferred* response and the latter *dispreferred*. Accepting an invitation tends to be done using the first, preferred format, whereas a declination will be done in the second, dispreferred way. This is one example of what more generally is called *preference organization,* which can be observed in many other sequential environments as well. It should be stressed that preference here does not refer to any psychological entity, such as the willingness or not to accept an invitation, but just to the conventional formatting of turns. It has been suggested that these various forms of preference have to do with an underlying very general *preference for progressivity*, that is, to get on or to move forward in any interactive activity (Schegloff, 1979; Stivers & Robinson, 2006).

Insertion sequences are quite often initiated to clarify the meaning and purpose of a first-pair part. In that case it can also be called a *repair sequence.* Repair can be initiated any time a speaker decides to do something about a preceding utterance, the so-called *trouble source,* which is in some way problematic. And, of course, a repair can be initiated and done by the speaker of that trouble source, which is called *self-initiated self-repair.* That is in fact the preferred way of doing repair (Schegloff, Jefferson, & Sacks, 1977), compared with *other-initiated self-repair* or *other-repair.* Here also, the preference for progressivity can be seen at work; self-repair, especially when done quickly, is the least disturbing to the flow of the conversation of these alternatives.

Whereas the original concepts of CA, like the ones noted thus far, have been mainly developed on the basis of audio recordings, it has become clear by analyzing videos that visual impressions also may impact heavily on the social organization of face-to-face interactions. Goodwin (1981), who initiated the use of video for CA study, has shown, for instance, that speakers may adapt their utterances-in-course in response to visual displays of attention, agreement, disagreement, puzzlement, and so forth.

Doing CA: Recordings and Transcriptions

EM tends to use two kinds of data-gathering methods: intensive ethnography or recordings. For CA the use of recordings is absolutely required, whereas ethnography may be used as an adjunct way of gathering background data. It is only through the observation of the details of interaction that CA can be convincingly done. As in EM generally, CA prefers naturally occurring situations, that is, situations in which the impact of the researcher is minimal or absent. This, of course, is an important contrast with other types of social and behavioral sciences, but it fits EM's and CA's situationalist interests and their generally observational approach.

The most important aspect of working with recordings is that it allows repeated inspection, listening, or viewing, as the case may be. The results of this observational process are laid down in a transcript, in which the words spoken are rendered in a way that suggests *how* this was done, partly with a specialized use of typographical symbols. Jefferson has developed a set of conventions for this job, which is now in general use (cf. Jefferson, 2004). The example in Extract 7.1 may illustrate some of the complexities involved.

The extract is introduced, within double brackets, with a description of the interactional context, to assist the reader in understanding the episode. In the actual transcript a number of special symbols are used to render the specific, hearable details of the speech production. Underlining indicates stress; square brackets ([]) are used to indicate those parts that were spoken in overlap; when one utterance follows another very quickly, this is indicated by an equal sign (=); and a marked prolongation of a sound is indicated by the colons (:). Punctuation marks are used to indicate intonation: a question mark indicates a rising tone, a comma indicates a nonfinal flat tone, and a dot indicates a downward falling tone. The dot-preceded .hhh, finally, renders an inbreath. In interaction the shaping of an utterance and the timing of one in relation to others is essential, therefore such details have to be noted as exactly as possible.

CA as a Data-Driven Approach

It has often been noted that CA uses a *data-driven* approach. This means that at first the researcher takes an attitude that has been characterized as *unmotivated looking,* that is, without a prespecified

---

Extract 7.1.   Coworkers on the Phone

(Coworkers Maggie and Sorrell went to a wedding reception where Maggie had some sort of momentary blackout and felt ill. Next morning she phones Sorrell at work to say that she will not be coming to work, is going to the doctor)

1	Maggie:	.hh because I (.) you know I told Mother what"d ha:ppened yesterday
2		there at the party,
3	Sorrell:	[°Yeah.°]
4	Maggie:	[a::] n d uh, .hhhhh (0.2) uh you know she asked me if it was
5		because I'd had too much to dri:nk and I said no=
6	Sorrell:	=[No ::::::.]
7	Maggie:	=[because at the t]i:me I'd only ha:d,h you know that drink "n
8		a ha:lf when we were going through the receiving line.
9	Sorrell:	Ri:ght.

Note. From "Is 'No' an Acknowledgment Token? Comparing American and British Uses of (+)/(–) Tokens," by G. Jefferson, 2002, *Journal of Pragmatics, 34*(10–11), p. 1346 (https://doi.org/10.1016/S0378-2166(02) 00067-X). Copyright 2002 by Elsevier. Reprinted with permission.

---

problem or question in mind. This does not deny the fact that one has a broadly focused interest in CA in the *how* of interactional organization. Furthermore, now that there is a well-defined and elaborate tradition, the CA is structured by an extensive conceptual apparatus, which would be silly to ignore (see the section A Major Offshoot). So although much is already known about the organization of interactive talk, the interest in much current CA work is still to discover previously unnoticed phenomena. At the same time, one would also want to extend and refine what is known or to apply CA to new substantive areas. The news that CA can offer to existing non-CA knowledge is often that the latter is too simple in the sense that it ignores or glosses over the *actual* details of interactive talk or that it starts from and is limited by current cultural, mostly individualistic and mentalistic, preconceptions. Like EM more generally, it demonstrates in detail that persons act in more intersubjectively responsible ways than is recognized in most other approaches in the human sciences (Button, 1991).

In a typical CA approach (see ten Have, 2007, for a more extensive treatment), the researcher starts with inspecting some recordings or transcripts looking for episodes that seem somehow interesting, maybe puzzling or especially apt. That episode

should be analyzed in depth using CA's conceptual repertoire. As argued elsewhere (ten Have, 2007), such an analysis essentially takes two steps, which I call *understanding* and the *analysis* proper. Listening to the recording and reading the transcript, the analyst first tries to understand what the interactants are doing organizationally when they speak as they do. They may, for instance, be requesting information, offering to tell a story, changing the topic, and so forth. Such understandings will be based, at first, on the researcher's own membership knowledge, as, one might say, a *cultural colleague* of the speakers. Second, however, the analyst will check the sequential context and especially the uptake of the utterances in question in subsequent talk, immediately following or later in the conversation, for instance, by granting a request. Understanding the actions, although not the purpose of the research, is a necessary requirement for the next step, the analysis proper, which is to formulate the procedures used to accomplish the actions as understood. Because CA's interest is organizational and procedural, the ultimate object of CA research is what Schegloff (1992) has called the *procedural infrastructure of interaction*, and, in particular, the practices of talking in conversation. This means that conversational practices are not analyzed in terms of individual properties or institutional expectations, but as situated collaborative accomplishments.

Such an analysis results in an analytic formulation of a device, a typical sequence, or whatever may be reported as such in a single-case study. Most of the time, however, the researcher will go on to inspect other cases, which may be relevantly compared with the first one. This may lead to a confirmation, a reformulation, a specification, or a differentiation into types. The researcher may formulate conditions for, and effects of, the device or sequence, in general, its functions. This more extended type of research is often called a *collection study*. The idea is that the analysis of a first case can be used as a starting point for a more systematic exploration of an emerging analytic theme. The researcher searches an available data set of newly collected data for instances that seem to be similar to the candidate phenomenon, the first formulation of the theme as well as data that seem to point in a different direction, the so-called *deviant case analysis*. In short, the researcher builds a collection of relevant cases in search of patterns that elucidate some procedural issues. This may seem to suggest a kind of principled independence of a single research project from existing knowledge, but this is not the case for all of CA reports. An investigation may take off from an issue internal to the CA tradition, or even from some problem or idea external to it, but all the same each and every piece of data should be first analyzed in its own terms.

This stress on analyzing each instance in its own terms is, of course, at odds with a general preference for quantification, which is dominant in the social sciences at large. Whether quantification makes sense in CA has been debated by some of its major practitioners, notably Schegloff (1993) and Heritage (1999). The general upshot seems to a need for caution and a limitation of sensible quantification to some of the most easily differentiable aspects, such as the choice of a word in an identical position or a clearly defined (yes–no) outcome (cf. examples in Heritage, 1999, and an experiment reported in Heritage, Robinson, Elliott, Beckett, & Wilkes, 2007; see also the discussions in Chapter 8 of this volume contrasting discursive psychology with mainstream methods).

Later Developments in CA

A particular aspect of the development of CA is that during the first 15 years of its existence, its basic approach and its core concepts had been developed by a very small number of people, mainly Sacks, Schegloff, and Jefferson (1974). So everything coming after that could be seen as extensions, additions, or applications, in one or another direction. The CA as it emerged in the 1960s and 1970s might be characterized as *CA-in-general*, or *pure CA*, in the sense that it took as its core task to study talk-in-interaction as such, without taking into account its particular setting or interactional genre. In their turn-taking paper, Sacks et al. had already hinted at the possibility to compare conversation to other kinds of speech-exchange systems (1974, pp. 729–731). Some years later, CA researchers began to take up the implied challenge and started to study interactional talk in a variety of settings, such as law courts, medical consultations, new interviews, and many others. Such studies can be characterized as *applied CA* and I will discuss some examples in a later section. But at the same time, pure CA continued to be elaborated, by the originators, like Schegloff and Jefferson, and by others who started doing CA later, many of whom had a background in functional or interactional linguistics (cf. Ford, Fox, & Thompson, 2002; Ochs, Schegloff, & Thompson, 1996). One of the interests that this strand of CA has added to the earlier ones is the issue of *linguistic resources* that speakers have at their disposal as members of a speech community. By comparing findings on the basis of the study of English-speaking interactants with data on conversations in Finnish or Japanese, it became clear that the devices actually used partly depend on what particular linguistic systems allow or facilitate (cf. Hayashi, 2005; Sidnell, 2009; Sorjonen, 2001; Tanaka, 1999). The English system, for instance, facilitates the early projection of the action an utterance will be doing, whereas in Japanese the verbs that embody the action tend to be produced in sentence final positions. So Japanese speakers can still change the action in their talk at a relatively late moment, but they may also at times use an early placeholder word if they need to inform their recipients on what they are up to (Hayashi, 2005).

A MINOR OFFSHOOT: MEMBERSHIP CATEGORIZATION ANALYSIS

As noted, apart from the approach that later became known as CA, Sacks also for some time worked on a rather different enterprise that is currently called MCA. He noted that a large part of the knowledge that people use and rely on in their interactions is organized in terms of categories of people, either in general terms (as in *children*) or in reference to a particular person (as in *my husband*). These insights and their elaborate explication was at first part of his doctoral research on calls to a suicide prevention center (cf. Sacks, 1972b; also a number of lectures in Sacks, 1992) in which callers explained their life situation and their feeling that they had "no one to turn to." What Sacks noted, among other things, was that people use person-categories as part of *sets* of categories, which he called *membership categorization devices* (MCDs; Sacks, 1972a, 1972b). For instance, within the MCD *sex*, people use two basic categories, female and male, whereas the MCD *age* does not have a fixed number of categories because their use depends on situational considerations. Sometimes two categories suffice, *old* and *young*, but often more subtle differentiations are called for.

Categories are not just named or implied, they also carry a number of different associated properties, later called *category predicates*, like the one that Sacks used a lot: *category-bound activities*. So, for instance, he noted that the activity *crying* may be considered bound to the category *baby*, and the activity *picking up (a child)* is typical of the category *mother* (Sacks, 1972a). Other kinds of predicates might involve properties like rights and responsibilities, specialized knowledge, and competencies. Sacks (1972b) also made an effort to explicate "rules of application," such as an *economy rule* (one category is often sufficient) and a *consistency rule* (once a category from a specific MCD is used, other categories from that device tend to be used also). Although many different categories may be *correct*, there are most often only a few that are also *relevant* in the situation at hand.

It is remarkable, as can be seen by reading Sacks's (1992) *Lectures on Conversation* in chronological order, that his interest in these matters became less

prominent after about 1967, being more strongly focused on issues of turn-taking and sequence. He did, however, publish some of these mid-1960s explorations of categorization much later (Sacks, 1972a, 1972b), so apparently he did not disavow them. In his introduction to the first volume of Sacks's (1992) *Lectures*, Schegloff commented on this shift as mainly a methodological one. Although the work on membership categorization tended to stress the recognizability of expressions such as category terms, for any member of the culture, Sacks later sought to substantiate such claims in terms of the demonstrable understanding by the participants, as visible in their uptake.

Although MCA more or less disappeared from the CA enterprise, it was later taken up again by more ethnomethodologically inclined authors, including Hester and Eglin (1997), Jayyusi (1984), and Watson (1997). In the introduction to a volume collecting some of these later MCA studies, Hester and Eglin (1997, pp. 11–22) commented on an ambiguity in Sacks's observations on membership categorization. Some of his formulations suggest a decontextualized model of membership categories and collections of categories as preexisting any occasion of use, whereas at other times, he stresses the occasionality of any actual usage. Hester and Eglin (1997, p. 21) stressed that for EM "membership categorization is an *activity* carried out in particular local circumstances." It should be seen as "in situ achievements of members' practical actions and practical reasoning." In recent years MCA continues to be used and debated (cf. Carlin, 2010; Schegloff, 2007a, 2007c).

Currently, MCA is often used to analyze written texts (Watson, 2009), but the underlying theme of MCA, namely, the social organization of knowledge, emerges regularly in CA proper, for instance, in a series of papers by Heritage (1984a) on the use of *Oh* as a marker of a change of knowledge of the speaker and more recently on what he has called *epistemics*, or more particularly *epistemic rights* and *epistemic authority* (Heritage, 2005; Heritage & Raymond, 2005; Raymond & Heritage, 2006). As he wrote, "Interactants not only keep score on who knows what, they also keep rather close watch over the relevant rights that each may have to know particular facts" (Heritage, 2005, p. 196), and that they do can be shown in the details of their actions and reactions, when analyzed in sequential terms. In my view, then, terms like EM, CA, and MCA denote variants of one big enterprise to study the local organization of human action or even of human sociality.

APPLIED STUDIES

As used in this section, the notion of *application* can refer both to projects in which the insights and methods of EM and CA are applied to specific substantive themes or areas and ones in which EM and CA insights are used to criticize or educate specific practices, although the first is much more frequent than the second. The basic idea is that the detailed attention that EM and CA give to everyday practices can be used to extend or correct available, often quantitative, knowledge about such practices. Established knowledge about some practice is often too general to cover the details of such practices in the situations in which they occur. Therefore such knowledge, as available in theories, plans, or reports, is quite often not able to effectively predict or understand the relative success or failure of practical projects. This theme was already discernible in Suchman's work (1987, 2007), as the instructions provided by an "intelligent" copier were misunderstood by the users, while the machine also misunderstood some of the users' actions, together leading to various type of practical troubles.

In the past 3 decades an increasing number of studies in EM and CA have been of an applied character. For reasons of space only a few themes can be developed at some length, and only a small number of topical areas are mentioned in this chapter. Most applied CA studies deal with interactions between institutional agents and their clients of some sort, such as patients, defendants, interviewees, and so on. In line with the remarks by Sacks et al. (1974) about the comparison of speech-exchange systems, these studies quite often (especially in the 1980s) used a comparison between the institutional interaction studied with informal conversation as an implicit or explicit frame of reference. Early studies of doctor–patient interaction, for instance, noted

the restrictions on turn-taking opportunities and turn-type selection to which patients seemed to be subjected (cf. Frankel, 1984, 1990; West, 1984). They also made it clear that such encounters tended to be organized in a restricted number of phases, such as history taking, examination, diagnosis, and treatment. What was discernible then, and confirmed later (cf. Beach, 2001; Heritage & Maynard, 2006; Stivers, 2007), was that the speaking opportunities for patients depend very much on the phase of the encounter. One can note a shift, in these later studies, from a somewhat moral noting of restrictions to a more diversified description of the uses by patients of their speaking opportunities, and the ways in which physicians do react to (or anticipate) patients' moves. In other words, whereas at first it was the asymmetry that was noted, it was later seen that the asymmetry-prone context of medical interaction also allowed for half-hidden negotiations, especially about treatment options. Application in the second, practical sense also seems to be on the rise in recent years, as CA-based insights and studies are used in medical education and professional training (Maynard & Heritage, 2005; Stein, Frankel, & Krupat, 2005).

When CA emerged in the 1960s, some psychotherapists were already recording their sessions with patients. Sacks, for instance, used some recordings, in his case of group therapy with teenagers, to explore conversation (cf. Sacks, 1992). That these interactions were not just conversations but rather therapy sessions was largely ignored in his comments. Later, the tendency was to use data from ordinary interactions. It was only since about the turn of the century that CA researchers turned to psychotherapy as a topic for the application of CA. Since then, a substantial number of papers and a book (Peräkylä, Antaki, Vehviläinen, & Leudar, 2008) have been published. Of course, therapists use quite a varied set of the verbal practices that, for them, constitute therapy. The challenge for CA is to explicate these practices in greater detail than has been done before and to point out and describe features of interaction that are part of psychotherapy but that psychotherapeutic theories have not recognized or discussed (Peräkylä et al., 2008). A major difference between CA research and previous studies of psychotherapy lies in CA's stress on sequence organization: how one utterance relates to previous and subsequent utterances in detail.

A major characteristic of psychotherapy sessions, in contrast to physician–patient encounters, is their lack of an overall structural organization in phases. Therefore, CA studies in this field tend to focus on local sequential relations, for instance, the ways in which a therapist's comments relate to previous utterances by the patient, or the ways in which a patient reacts to such a recipient action. In psychotherapy, recipient actions are among the major means at the therapist's disposal to influence the patient is a more or less subtle manner. Peräkylä et al. (2008) distinguished different types of such actions. A therapist may (a) propose a different, probably more focused term for one used by the patient, (b) extend a patient's sentence as a display of understanding, (c) reformulate what was just said, or (d) offer a different interpretation than the one suggested by the patient. In so doing, the therapists may be seen as "stretching the boundaries of ownership of knowledge" (Peräkylä et al., 2008, pp. 192–193), suggesting that they know the patient better than the individual. Such reworkings are mostly selective and thus reshape what was said by the other party. Therapists' questioning initiatives and patients' responses to therapist sayings are also discussed. CA studies of psychotherapy offer a detailed sociological account of therapeutic processes rather than a psychological one. CA foregrounds the collaborative and negotiative character of such interactions. What therapists do is a specialized use of quite ordinary conversational means.

From the mid-1990s onward, there have been quite a number of CA-based studies of interaction in which at least one of the participants is communicatively impaired in one way or another. In Goodwin's edited book *Conversation and Brain Damage* (2003), he collected work by the major contributors to this area, focusing on aphasia. The core message that is stressed in all of these contributions is that whatever communicative success is achieved in the encounters under study has to be seen as a collaborative achievement. It depends on the use of quite ordinary conversational methods, adapted to the particularities of the impairment in the case at hand, in which both the aphasics and their interlocutors have to be creative. In this way, the book's essays have a polemical subtheme in relation to conventional psycholinguistic and neurological approaches, which are oriented to individual failings rather than collective communicative successes.

A number of contributions deal explicitly with the contrast between ordinary, real-life interactions with an aphasic and formal tests. In the latter type of situations, an aphasic may be asked, for instance, to tell a story on the basis of a set of cartoon drawings, or to answer standardized questions, at the request of a tester who has only a professional interest in the performance displayed in those tellings or answers. This situation is contrasted with naturally occurring situations in which an aphasic wants to tell the story of a personal experience to a close relative, for instance, or participate in the arrangement of eating out with a family group. In such situations it is the achievement of shared understanding that matters and not the objective assessment of the linguistic quality of an individual performance.

The concept of aphasia covers a range of impairments, and the patients whose speech is exemplified and analyzed in the various chapters suffer from a variety of types of linguistic insufficiencies, including quite prominently the inability to find the right word in time. In such cases, the speakers often use general terms instead of a more specific ones, requiring a more specific interpretation or (implicit or explicit) guess made on the basis of shared knowledge or situational cues. This also accounts for the fact that mutual understanding is best achieved in active collaboration with intimates.

Although these three types of applied studies mostly applied CA concepts and methods and based their findings in most cases just on audio or video recordings, a different type of applied studies emerged in the late 1980s that, in addition to video recordings, also used ethnographic fieldwork. I have mentioned the early work of Suchman (1987) on users' work on an advanced copier, which she carried out as part of a research job in an industrial firm. She continued her studies there focusing on specialized work activities involving complex technological support devices like computers and various communication technologies. Later, other researchers were able to start similar projects, so now one can speak of a tradition of "workplace studies." Apart from Suchman, important contributions have been made by Button, Heath, and Whalen (cf. collections edited by Button, 1993; Heath & Luff, 2000; Luff, Hindmarsh, & Heath, 2000). Heath has led a particularly successful Work, Interaction and Technology Research Group at King's College in London, which has studied a wide range of settings, including control rooms for the London Underground system, museums, and art galleries as well as journalists working in a news agency.

In these studies, the use of video is crucial because the activities often take place in a group setting involving team members and the extensive use of various technological artifacts. Analyzing such activities requires, on the one hand, visual access to the local environment to study bodily actions and nonvocal exchanges in situ, and, on the other, a deeper, locally specialized understanding of the activities under study than is generally used for agent–client interactions. Some participant observation—as well as studying relevant documents and interviewing experts—is used to acquire the necessary background to really understand what is going on. To mention one example, Nevile (2004), from Australia, collected the core data for his studies of talk-in-interaction in the airline cockpit by video-recording the activities of flight crews on scheduled flights by commercial airlines. But before he even approached the airlines to ask for their cooperation, he prepared his research by extensively reading whatever he could find about the operation of commercial airlines, training and operations manuals, official accident reports, and so on. He also watched available information videos showing pilots at work, visited conferences, and talked to research psychologists working with flight crews and accident investigators.

In such workplace studies, the concepts, findings, and methods of CA are applied as part of a wider undertaking that is broadly inspired by EM. I mention a few general insights that can be gained from these studies. First, such specialized (team)work requires an experience-based practical knowledge that goes far beyond what can be acquired through formal instruction in a nonwork setting. Second, effective

teamwork not only requires the individual worker's understanding of the task at hand but also an understanding *at a glance* of what others are doing. A lot of actual coordination of activities occurs in an implicit fashion, often by seeing in peripheral vision or by overhearing talk and adapting one's own activities accordingly. So, for instance, the worker in a London Underground control room who is tasked with making announcements to the traveling public knows from observing and overhearing his colleagues at work on some crisis situation what to announce, to whom, and when without getting a request to do so (see Heath & Luff, 2000). Third, formal accounts of work activities cannot make this hidden work and the competencies involved in it visible to outsiders, including the overseeing management (cf. Whalen & Vinkhuyzen, 2000).

To illustrate how CA can figure in this more encompassing endeavor, let me refer shortly to some of Nevile's (2004) findings when studying airline cockpits. In the first part of his book, he analyzed the use of personal pronouns: *I, you,* and *we.* Some of these uses are officially prescribed in the relevant manuals, and others are voluntary and impromptu, chosen on the spot. They function, in any case, as designators of local and momentary cockpit identities, with associated tasks and responsibilities. In the second part of the book, Nevile, by discussing a range of concrete examples, examined how pilots coordinate their talk and nontalk activities as they perform the routine tasks necessary to fly their plane. Such coordination is essential to maintain a shared understanding of where they are in the flight and what has to be done then and there, as pilots have to perform their tasks with split-second precision and strictly in sequence, one after the other. In doing this work, talk is just one of the resources that participants use and orient to; others include gaze direction, gesture, and placement and movement of parts of the body, such as head, arms, hands, legs, and eyebrows. In the third and final part of his book, Nevile widened his perspective on talk *in* the cockpit to investigate how it is coordinated with talk to participants *outside* the cockpit, such as air traffic controllers and cabin crew members. Again, the issue is that the two pilots have to attain and demonstrate a shared understanding of the local consequences of the outside talk, which they can do by internal talk or nonvocal but visible activities. Investigation of such fine-tuned activities requires finely detailed transcriptions of talk with descriptions of the associated activities.

To give an impression of how this is done, I quote one of Nevile's examples in Extract 7.2, which in the original text is accompanied by a picture of the pointing finger that is mentioned.

The arrows indicate the moment in the talk at which the nonvocal activities start or stop. Workplace studies are a rather demanding kind of study, but they are also extremely rewarding and necessary because they reflect the subtle but too often ignored complexity of specialized work.

There are many other types of applied studies using EM, CA, or MCA. In all these it has been proven that it is useful to explicate the ways in which (inter)action and communication depend on the local application of *infrastructural* practices. The stress on restrictions that are operative in institutional settings, which was stressed in early applied CA, can now be broadened in saying that task-oriented interactions basically depend on *general* interactional capacities, which in the setting at hand get a specialized application.

CONCLUSION

Within the limits of the space available, I have offered a summary characterization of EM and its offshoots CA and MCA. Contrary to most of the human sciences and Western culture at large, EM does not take off from the individual and his or her mind. Instead, ethnomethodologists observe human action as inherently social and situated. Therefore they largely abstain from precategorized and researcher-provoked ways of collecting data but rather use intense ethnography and audio or video recordings. In so doing, they can reveal news about human life that was previously unavailable.

Extract 7.2.   In the Cockpit

C = Captain
PNF = Pilot not flying
FO = First officer
PF = Pilot flying

```
1               (50.3)
2    C/PNF:     one thousand to altitude.
                ↑————↑
2a   C/PNF:     ((moves right hand up from lap, then left to right, at chest height, with index finger
                extended))
                         ↑———↑
2b   C/PNF:                 ((holds right hand still, just to the right of own chest, index finger points to
                            FO/PF's side of main instrument panel))
                                 ↑
2c   C/PNF:                                    ((moves right hand down and left, back to right leg))
3               (3.2) = (0 > 1.4 > 2.4 > 3.2)
                         ↑———↑
4                        ((sound of altitude alert buzzer))
5    FO/PF      >alert (.) for level (.) two fi::ve zero
6               (27.5)
```

Note. From *Beyond the Black Box: Talk-in-Interaction in the Airline Cockpit* (p. 131), by M. Nevile, 2004, Ashgate. Copyright 2004 by Maurice Nevile. Reprinted with permission.

Quite often this can lead to what has been called a respecification of previously developed concepts in the human sciences, including sociology and psychology, as *members' situated practices* (Button, 1991; Garfinkel, 2002). This kind of work as applied to psychological concepts has been taken up by discursive psychology, which is discussed in Chapter 8 of this volume. That chapter also provides an exemplary sketch of the different stages of a research project, including an analysis of some interactional episodes that clearly demonstrate the impact of sequentiality in human interaction.

References

Beach, W. A. (Ed.). (2001). Introduction: Diagnosing "lay diagnosis." *Text & Talk, 21*(1-2), 13–18. https://doi.org/10.1515/text.1.21.1-2.13

Button, G. (Ed.). (1991). *Ethnomethodology and the human sciences.* Cambridge University Press.

Button, G. (Ed.). (1993). *Technology in working order: Studies of work, interaction and technology.* Routledge.

Carlin, A. P. (2010). Discussion note: Reading "A tutorial on membership categorization" by Emanuel Schegloff. *Journal of Pragmatics, 42*(1), 257–261. https://doi.org/10.1016/j.pragma.2009.06.007

Clayman, S. E., & Maynard, D. W. (1995). Ethnomethodology and conversation analysis. In P. ten Have & G. Psathas (Eds.), *Situated order: Studies in the social organization of talk and embodied activities* (pp. 1–30). University Press of America.

Ford, C. E., Fox, B. A., & Thompson, S. A. (Eds.). (2002). *The language of turn and sequence.* Oxford University Press.

Francis, D., & Hester, S. (2004). *An invitation to ethno-methodology: Language, society and interaction.* Sage.

Frankel, R. M. (1984). From sentence to sequence: Understanding the medical encounter through micro-interactional analysis. *Discourse Processes, 7*(2), 135–170. https://doi.org/10.1080/01638538409544587

Frankel, R. M. (1990). Talking in interviews: A dispreference for patient-initiated questions in physician–patient encounters. In G. Psathas (Ed.), *Interactional competence* (pp. 231–262). University Press of America.

Garfinkel, H. (1967). *Studies in ethnomethodology.* Prentice-Hall.

Garfinkel, H. (2002). *Ethnomethodology's program: Working out Durkheim's aphorism.* Rowman & Littlefield.

Garfinkel, H., & Wieder, D. L. (1992). Two incommensurable, asymmetrically alternate technologies of social analysis. In G. Watson & R. M. Seiler (Eds.), *Text in context: Studies in ethnomethodology* (pp. 175–206). Sage.

Goodwin, C. (1981). *Conversational organization: Interaction between speakers and hearers.* Academic Press.

Goodwin, C. (Ed.). (2003). *Conversation and brain damage.* Oxford University Press.

Hayashi, M. (2005). Referential problems and turn construction: An exploration of an intersection between grammar and interaction. *Text: Interdisciplinary Journal for the Study of Discourse, 25*(4), 437–468. https://doi.org/10.1515/text.2005.25.4.437

Heap, J. L. (1990). Applied ethnomethodology: Looking for the local rationality of reading activities. *Human Studies, 13*, 39–72. https://doi.org/10.1007/BF00143040

Heath, C., & Luff, P. (2000). *Technology in action.* Cambridge University Press. https://doi.org/10.1017/CBO9780511489839

Heritage, J. (1984a). A change-of-state token and aspects of its sequential placement. In J. M. Atkinson & J. Heritage (Eds.), *Structures of social action: Studies in conversation analysis* (pp. 299–345). Cambridge University Press.

Heritage, J. (1984b). *Garfinkel and ethnomethodology.* Polity Press.

Heritage, J. (1999). Conversation analysis at century's end: Practices of talk-in-interaction, their distributions and their outcomes. *Research on Language and Social Interaction, 32*(1-2), 69–76. https://doi.org/10.1080/08351813.1999.9683609

Heritage, J. (2005). Cognition in discourse. In H. te Molder & J. Potter (Eds.), *Conversation and cognition* (pp. 184–202). Cambridge University Press. https://doi.org/10.1017/CBO9780511489990.009

Heritage, J., & Maynard, D. W. (Eds.). (2006). *Communication in medical care: Interaction between primary care physicians and patients.* Cambridge University Press. https://doi.org/10.1017/CBO9780511607172

Heritage, J., & Raymond, G. (2005). The terms of agreement: Indexing epistemic authority and subordination in talk-in-interaction. *Social Psychology Quarterly, 68*(1), 15–38. https://doi.org/10.1177/019027250506800103

Heritage, J., Robinson, J. D., Elliott, M. N., Beckett, M., & Wilkes, M. (2007). Reducing patients' unmet concerns in primary care: The difference one word can make. *Journal of General Internal Medicine, 22,* 1429–1433. https://doi.org/10.1007/s11606-007-0279-0

Hester, S., & Eglin, P. (Eds.). (1997). *Culture in action: Studies in membership categorization analysis.* University Press of America.

Jayyusi, L. (1984). *Categorization and the moral order.* Routledge & Kegan Paul.

Jefferson, G. (2002). Is "no" an acknowledgment token? Comparing American and British uses of (+)/(–) tokens. *Journal of Pragmatics, 34*(10–11), 1345–1383. https://doi.org/10.1016/S0378-2166(02)00067-X

Jefferson, G. (2004). Glossary of transcript symbols with an introduction. In G. H. Lerner (Ed.), *Conversation analysis: Studies from the first generation* (pp. 13–31). Benjamins.

Liberman, K. (2004). *Dialectical practice in Tibetan philosophical culture: An ethnomethodological inquiry into formal reasoning.* Rowman & Littlefield.

Luff, P., Hindmarsh, J., & Heath, C. (Eds.). (2000). *Workplace studies: Recovering work practice and informing systems design.* Cambridge University Press. https://doi.org/10.1017/CBO9780511628122

Lynch, M. (1985). *Art and artifact in laboratory science: A study of shop work and shop talk.* Routledge & Kegan Paul.

Lynch, M. (1993). *Scientific practice and ordinary action: Ethnomethodology and social studies of science.* Cambridge University Press.

Maynard, D. W., & Heritage, J. (2005). Conversation analysis, doctor–patient interaction and medical communication. *Medical Education, 39*(4), 428–435. https://doi.org/10.1111/j.1365-2929.2005.02111.x

Nevile, M. (2004). *Beyond the black box: Talk-in-interaction in the airline cockpit.* Ashgate.

Ochs, E., Schegloff, E. A., & Thompson, S. A. (Eds.). (1996). *Interaction and grammar.* Cambridge University Press. https://doi.org/10.1017/CBO9780511620874

Peräkylä, A., Antaki, C., Vehviläinen, S., & Leudar, I. (Eds.). (2008). *Conversation analysis and psychotherapy.* Cambridge University Press.

Raymond, G., & Heritage, J. (2006). The epistemics of social relationships: Owning grandchildren. *Language in Society, 35*(5), 677–705. https://doi.org/10.1017/S0047404506060325

Sacks, H. (1972a). On the analyzability of stories by children. In J. J. Gumperz & D. Hymes (Eds.), *Directions in sociolinguistics: The ethnography of communication* (pp. 325–345). Rinehart & Winston.

Sacks, H. (1972b). An initial investigation of the usability of conversational data for doing sociology. In D. Sudnow (Ed.), *Studies in social interaction* (pp. 31–74). Free Press.

Sacks, H. (1992). *Lectures on conversation* (Vols. 1–2). Basil Blackwell.

Sacks, H., Schegloff, E. A., & Jefferson, G. (1974). A simplest systematics for the organization of turn-taking for conversation. *Language, 50*(4, Pt. 1), 696–735. https://doi.org/10.2307/412243

Schegloff, E. A. (1979). The relevance of repair to syntax-for-conversation. In T. Givon (Ed.), *Syntax and semantics 12: Discourse and syntax* (pp. 261–286). Academic Press.

Schegloff, E. A. (1987). Analyzing single episodes of interaction: An exercise in conversation analysis. *Social Psychology Quarterly, 50*(2), 101–114. https://doi.org/10.2307/2786745

Schegloff, E. A. (1992). Repair after next turn: The last structurally provided defense of intersubjectivity in conversation. *American Journal of Sociology, 97*(5), 1295–1345. https://doi.org/10.1086/229903

Schegloff, E. A. (1993). Reflections on quantification in the study of conversation. *Research on Language and Social Interaction, 26*(1), 99–128. https://doi.org/10.1207/s15327973rlsi2601_5

Schegloff, E. A. (2007a). Categories in action: Person-reference and membership categorization. *Discourse Studies, 9*(4), 433–461. https://doi.org/10.1177/1461445607079162

Schegloff, E. A. (2007b). *Sequence organization in interaction: A primer in conversation analysis* (Vol. 1). Cambridge University Press. https://doi.org/10.1017/CBO9780511791208

Schegloff, E. A. (2007c). A tutorial on membership categorization. *Journal of Pragmatics, 39*(3), 462–482. https://doi.org/10.1016/j.pragma.2006.07.007

Schegloff, E. A., Jefferson, G., & Sacks, H. (1977). The preference for self-correction in the organization of repair in conversation. *Language, 53*(2), 361–382. https://doi.org/10.2307/413107

Schegloff, E. A., & Sacks, H. (1973). Opening up closings. *Semiotica, 8*(4), 289–327. https://doi.org/10.1515/semi.1973.8.4.289

Sidnell, J. (Ed.). (2009). *Conversation analysis: Comparative perspectives.* Cambridge University Press. https://doi.org/10.1017/CBO9780511635670

Sorjonen, M.-L. (2001). *Responding in conversation: A study of response particles in Finnish.* Benjamins.

Stein, T., Frankel, R. M., & Krupat, E. (2005). Enhancing clinician communication skills in a large healthcare organization: A longitudinal case study. *Patient Education and Counseling, 58*(1), 4–12. https://doi.org/10.1016/j.pec.2005.01.014

Stivers, T. (2007). *Prescribing under pressure: Parent–physician conversations and antibiotics.* Oxford University Press.

Stivers, T., & Robinson, J. D. (2006). A preference for progressivity in interaction. *Language in Society, 35*(3), 367–392. https://doi.org/10.1017/S0047404506060179

Suchman, L. (1987). *Plans and situated action: The problem of human–machine communication.* Cambridge University Press.

Suchman, L. A. (2007). *Human–machine reconfigurations: Plans and situated actions* (2nd ed.). Cambridge University Press.

Sudnow, D. (1978). *Ways of the hand: The organization of improvised conduct.* Routledge & Kegan Paul.

Tanaka, H. (1999). *Turn-taking in Japanese conversation: A study in grammar and interaction.* Benjamins.

ten Have, P. (2002, September). The notion of member is the heart of the matter: On the role of membership knowledge in ethnomethodological inquiry. *Forum: Qualitative Social Research, 3*(3). https://doi.org/10.17169/fqs-3.3.834

ten Have, P. (2007). *Doing conversation analysis: A practical guide* (2nd ed.). Sage.

Watson, R. (1997). Some general reflections on "categorization" and "sequence" in the analysis of conversation. In S. Hester & P. Eglin (Eds.), *Culture in action: Studies in membership categorization analysis* (pp. 49–76). University Press of America.

Watson, R. (2009). *Analysing practical and professional texts: A naturalistic approach.* Ashgate.

West, C. (1984). *Routine complications: Trouble with talk between doctors and patients.* Indiana University Press.

Whalen, J., & Vinkhuyzen, E. (2000). Expert systems in (inter)action: Diagnosing document machine problems over the telephone. In P. Luff, J. Hindmarsh, & C. Heath (Eds.), *Workplace studies: Recovering work practice and informing systems design* (pp. 92–140). Cambridge University Press.

Wieder, D. L. (1974). *Language and social reality: The case of telling the convict code.* Mouton.

CHAPTER 8

DISCOURSE ANALYSIS AND DISCURSIVE PSYCHOLOGY

Chris McVittie and Andy McKinlay

Discourse analysis is the study of discourse in its many forms, verbal, written, and mediated through a diversity of means of communication. We spend much of our everyday lives engaging in and with discourse in one form or another. When we talk to other people, we discuss who we are, who they are, and the actions and the events that go on in the world around us. We also respond to the talk of those others, commenting on, accepting, challenging, or otherwise dealing with what they in turn say to us. Much of our lives also involves less direct contact with others, such as reading news media, watching or listening to broadcast media transmissions, communicating via text messaging or social media networks, and so on.

The social interactions across this diversity of settings provide a focus of study for many researchers, both within psychology and beyond. Where discourse analysis differs from other approaches in looking at these interactions is that its central interest lies in the study of discourse in itself within all realms of social life. For, as we communicate with others, we do not (merely) report what is going on elsewhere, either in terms of our internal thoughts or feelings, or what is happening externally, in terms of neutral descriptions of social phenomena. Instead, we are constructing versions of ourselves, of other

people, of social actions, and events. For discursive psychologists, interest lies in the detailed examination of how individuals in discourse deploy and negotiate the concerns that are central to psychology, including cognitions, emotions, identities, and social groups. Through this focus, discursive research provides an understanding of core psychological topics that does not rely on claims about internal mental process, states, or how individuals respond to an external and distinct social world.

DISCOURSE ANALYSIS

Discourse analysis, in its broadest sense, can be taken to refer to any approach that takes the study of discourse to be the primary focus of interest. The term *discourse analysis*, however, has been used by many different writers to refer to approaches that examine discourse from very different perspectives. Each of these approaches has its own standpoint as to how discourse should most usefully be understood. For example, approaches such as critical discourse analysis (Fairclough, 2013; van Dijk, 2008; Wodak & Meyer, 2015) and Foucauldian discourse analysis (Parker, 2013, 2014) combine an interest in discourse with an emphasis on explicating broader social practices that give rise to that discourse.

https://doi.org/10.1037/0000319-008
APA Handbook of Research Methods in Psychology, Second Edition: Vol. 2. Research Designs: Quantitative, Qualitative, Neuropsychological, and Biological, H. Cooper (Editor-in-Chief)

Reviews of these approaches, and other approaches to the study of discourse, can be found elsewhere (e.g., McKinlay & McVittie, 2008) and are beyond the scope of this chapter. Our focus here is different, foregrounding the study of how people use discourse in interaction and treating what they say as the primary topic for investigation.

The systematic study of discourse in interaction was first introduced to psychology in the landmark text of Jonathan Potter and Margaret Wetherell (1987) *Discourse and Social Psychology: Beyond Attitudes and Behaviour*. In developing this approach to discourse analysis, Potter and Wetherell drew together previous theoretical strands from various fields, including speech act theory (Austin, 1962), ethnomethodology (Garfinkel, 1967), and the sociology of scientific knowledge (Gilbert & Mulkay, 1984), setting out the case for what a discursive approach offered to social psychology. Central to their argument was a focus on discourse as discourse: Instead of treating discourse as a resource for accessing what is occurring elsewhere, Potter and Wetherell argued for a turn to discourse as the primary topic of study.

To set out their argument, Potter and Wetherell (1987) offered the example of attitudes. Within other approaches, quantitative and qualitative, the attitudes that individuals express are usually treated as reflections of stable and enduring dispositions held towards the targets of those attitudes. These dispositions might be regarded as indicators of cognitive representations, or as subjective understandings, but, in either case, they are taken to be consistent for the individual. As Potter and Wetherell noted, however, the attitudes that an individual can and will express towards any attitudinal object inevitably vary from one setting to another. This inherent variability casts doubt on the value of seeking to understand attitudes as stable and consistent on the one hand and as internal to the individual on the other. Instead, then, of being indicators of internal dispositions, attitudes can more usefully be understood as the positions that people express in the immediate discursive context.

Discourse analysis, therefore, seeks to investigate what individuals are doing through discourse. Key to this process is a focus on how participants themselves make sense of their interactions. In this, discourse analysis draws on the central tenet of ethnomethodology (Garfinkel, 1967) that people in everyday life make sense of and display their understandings of social life as they live it. The task for the analyst is to render explicit these everyday understandings, not to treat them as self-evident or to impose some other form of order on them. Consistent with this focus, Potter and Wetherell (1987) identified three central properties of discourse:

1. Discourse is always *action oriented*. When people use discourse, they are doing so not merely to describe or communicate aspects of life; rather, they use discourse to do things, to accomplish particular interactional outcomes. Potential outcomes can include a wide and diverse range of possibilities, including, for example, accounting for or justifying one's own activities, criticizing or blaming others, arguing for specific consequences, or achieving agreement with another.

2. Discourse is *constructed and constructive*. The discourse that we use draws upon shared and recognized components, including lexical terms and grammatical organization. In using discourse, speakers are mobilizing these readily available linguistic resources. As speakers deploy them, however, they are constructing particular versions of social phenomena. Individuals, actions, and events are open to being described in all sorts of ways. There is, for instance, the oft-quoted example that the same person might be described either as a freedom-fighter or a terrorist, according to the perspective of the person offering the description. For all aspects of everyday life, there is no single or "true" description that reflects an underlying reality; people produce versions of social phenomena according to the demands of the local context.

3. Discourse is *situated*. In everyday life, we interact with others in a broad range of

different contexts, perhaps in family settings, meetings with friends or work colleagues, communications on social media, to take just a few possibilities. The versions of social life that we construct vary from one context to another, as do the actions that these versions make relevant. More than this, how we describe things varies from one interactional encounter to another, and even within a single interaction. Language is inevitably variable; there is no single consistent version that may be found across all settings. Analyzing discourse, then, requires attention to the context in which the discourse is found and situated.

The three properties of discourse are not independent of each other. A version of events is designed to accomplish a specific action in a local context. Discourse analysis requires the analyst to attend to all these properties in producing an account of what is occurring. However, this left the question of how these insights could be applied in practice. Potter and Wetherell (1987) argued for examination of "interpretative repertoires" or "recurrently used systems of terms used for characterizing and evaluating actions, events, and other phenomena. A repertoire . . . is constituted through a limited range of terms used in particular stylistic and grammatical constructions" (p. 149). For Potter and Wetherell, then, emphasis lay on identification of broad forms of talk and how they functioned in local contexts.

As the approach developed, however, subsequent writers revised this focus, arguing first for increased attention to be paid to what individuals construct in their talk and second for closer examination of the organization of the local settings in which individuals interact. Through these developments in the detailed study of discourse in interaction, discourse analysis was overtaken by discursive psychology.

DISCURSIVE PSYCHOLOGY

Discursive psychology retains a focus on the three properties of language in use identified in discourse analysis: the action orientation of discourse, its constructed and constructive qualities, and its situatedness. Where discursive psychology differs, however, is in how it attends to these, especially the latter two properties. Firstly, discursive psychology has a primary focus on how individuals in discourse construct and deploy versions of a wide range of psychological phenomena. Second, attention has come to focus not just on how specific forms of discourse are found in local contexts but also on the detailed organization of these local settings. We consider these developments below.

Construction of Psychological Phenomena

In arguing for the study of discourse, Potter and Wetherell (1987) demonstrated how a discursive perspective could throw new light on understanding attitudes and behavior. Respecifying these concepts showed how attitudes could be approached as discursive constructions instead of internal psychological dispositions. One development of the discursive psychology approach has been similar reworking of many, if not all, of psychology's interests. For example, in an early formulation of discursive psychology, Edwards and Potter (1992) showed that memory could be investigated as a participants' interactional concern instead of a cognitive state or process. An ability or failure to recall specific events, and the versions of events that are recalled, can be seen as practices that are designed to attend discursively to the matter immediately at hand and not as reflections of inner states. Similarly, Edwards (1997) showed that perceptions, emotions, and memories are equally amenable to discursive reworking.

As discursive psychology has developed further, the attention of researchers has turned from a focus on mental processes and states to the broad range of topics found within psychology. Indeed, discursive research has made a substantial contribution to study of all topics across social psychology (McKinlay & McVittie, 2008). Topics such as intergroup relations, prejudice, relationships, and health are as open to discursive inquiry as are descriptions of mental states and processes.

One topic that has proved especially fruitful for discursive work is that of identities, where discursive research has shown how individuals claim, resist, or rework forms of identity to accomplish certain outcomes in their immediate settings (McKinlay & McVittie, 2011).

As an example of how discursive psychology has become central to the study of psychological topics, consider Extract 8.1 below. This extract comes from a study of talk from interviews broadcast on an evangelical television program (Xanthopoulou, 2010). The interviews were organized around the topic of *defectiveness*, with participants being invited to discuss how they had failed to live up to the standards appropriate to an allegiance to God. Below we see one interviewee, Jessie, describing how she ceased to sing in a church choir to pursue a personal musical career.

The talk in the extract has been transcribed using the conventions of the transcription notation system developed by Jefferson (2004); therefore, there are many symbols that appear strange to those unfamiliar with that system. We return to issues of transcription below, but, for now, let us examine some key elements of the talk of particular interest to the discursive psychologist.

In Extract 8.1, Jessie refers at several points to her inner psychological world. We see that Jessie's account is framed in terms of personal experience and feelings, in that she refers at line 25 to an experience of being "really challenged" and concludes this description at line 41 by saying that she "felt" challenged. She refers at lines 33 to 34 to the cognitive process of having to make a "dec↑ision." Jessie also describes her inner motivations involved in this decision, whether "playing it safe" or looking to "↑push [her]self forward." But, as we see throughout the extract, this construction of Jessie's inner world is only part of the picture. These descriptions are bound up with possible actions, either to "keep singing in the church" or to "get a band together and start rec[o:rding]." And Jessie links her descriptions of these actions to her motivations and decision-making, invoking cognitions and dispositions as the bases for choosing one course of action over the other.

Jessie's description, thus, is permeated with references to inner mental processes and states.

Extract 8.1

25. Jessie: ((looking down)) God really challenged me
26. (.) >and I had wr↑itten< (.) a whole album worth of
27. so:ngs (0.4) e:rm (.) ↑non Christian songs but just
28. kinda like out of my own experience and they were
29. just s↑itting in (0.2) in a- (.) a b:oo:k (0.4)
30. a:nd ↑God really said to me J↑essie? you've been
31. that wicked lazy ((pointing with hands)) servant
32. (0.3) who: is just playing it safe ↓a:nd I'm: I'm
33. not having it (.) ↑so I guess right then I had a
34. dec↑ision (0.3) whether (0.2) to: (0.2) ↑stay
35. c↑omfortable and keep singing in the church (0.2)
36. and you know doing the ou and a:r (.) o:r (0.2)
37. ↑push myself forward (.) as a singer song wri:ter
38. (.) and get a band together and start rec[o:rding]
39. Host: [°mm::°]
40. Jessie: (0.4) a:nd (.) I di:d ((nodding))(0.2) ↓because
41. (0.2) I felt the lord had challenged me

(Xanthopoulou, 2010, p. 686, original formatting)

And Jessie attributes the basis for these thoughts, feelings, and motivations to what she had been challenged to do by a higher entity in the form of "God" or "the lord." Thus, the inner states and decisions are reported not as a matter of choice but as one of obedience: Jessie is obeying the will of "God." This identity that emerges from her description is especially salient in a context where the issue of "defectiveness" is a live concern for Jessie and others. Instead of being identified as someone who is "defective" in making choices that promoted individual ambition over church allegiance, Jessie identifies herself as someone who is following the course that she was instructed to take by a higher authority.

Now, there is of course no means of assessing the veracity of Jessie's claims; we cannot access Jessie's inner thoughts, motivations, or feelings or perceptions of her experiences. But we do not need to do so. Instead, we can examine her descriptions for what they accomplish in this setting. Discursive psychology allows us to look at the detail of what is happening and, thereby, to derive an understanding of how Jessie is constructing her inner world and how she identifies herself, without any attempt to uncover an inner psychology. Through such analysis of talk, we can see how central concerns of psychology, including inner states and individuals' identities, are worked into the moment-to-moment of discourse.

Detail of Local Settings

Discourse analysis, as proposed by Potter and Wetherell (1987), comprises the identification of interpretative repertoires, or recurring forms of talk, and investigation of the occasions of their use as participants deployed these repertoires in local settings. There is, however, a tension in such an approach. An emphasis on analyzing broad forms of talk does not sit easily with a focus on local contexts as the sites of language use or with a focus on the variability of discourse according to the requirements of the local context. For such reasons, discursive psychology has turned to closer inspection of the settings in which participants are involved, especially how the settings are organized and structured. In this, discursive psychology took up central features of another

approach developed to study the use of language in immediate interaction but which had from its beginnings studied the structures of that interaction: conversation analysis.

Conversation analysis (Sacks, 1992; Sacks et al., 1974) prioritizes close study of the fine details of talk-in-interaction. Analysts are concerned not just with the lexical terms used but also with the sequential organization of talk and the turns found within conversational exchanges. For example, in everyday talk a question from one party commonly is followed by an answer from another, and other forms of turn similarly lead to particular forms of response, in what are termed *adjacency pairs*. Conversation analysis also draws attention to other features of talk, such as *footing* (Goffman, 1981) where the way in which a speaker aligns with or attributes the view being expressed in an utterance to another displays either commitment to or distance from what is being expressed. Other features, such as conversational pauses and the conversational "repair" of turns that might be treated as problematic, are also common elements of everyday conversation.

Perhaps, however, the overriding concern of conversation analysis is its emphasis on the study of participants' understandings of the talk at hand. This mirrors ethnomethodology's concern with how participants' themselves make sense of everyday life. A central principle of conversation analysis is that analysis should focus on what is demonstrably relevant for those involved. Thus, the way in which a recipient of talk frames his or her turn indicates how he or she is treating the turn that has gone before. For example, are they offering an answer that suggests that the prior turn is being treated as a question? Are they providing an account demonstrating that such a response was made relevant by what preceded it, or otherwise? This provides for a *next turn proof* procedure, whereby conversation analysts can ground their analytic claims in how a subsequent speaker orients to what was said previously.

One consequence of this focus on the organization of talk has been increased attention to the rhetorical aspects of talk. Given that there are always available multiple versions of social phenomena, one task for a speaker is to persuade recipients of the talk that the version on offer is one that should be accepted. In this, conversation analytic writers have identified a range of discursive devices that speakers deploy in presenting their arguments to others. One common device takes the form of an *extreme case formulation* (Edwards, 2000; Pomerantz, 1986) in which speakers present an extreme case in support of a claim that they are making. Statements such as "it was the worst thing that ever happened" are not designed to be treated as literally accurate but rather to convince others of the speaker's commitment to the argument that is being advanced. Other devices, such as disclaimers ("I have no axe to grind, but . . ."), hedging ("This is just my view, but . . ."), and lists ("I put blood, sweat, and tears into . . ."), also demonstrate the commitment or lack of commitment of a speaker to a description that is being produced or how a recipient of talk is orienting to a preceding turn. Interactional features such as hesitations, qualifiers, and pauses can demonstrate that what is being said is being treated as (potentially) problematic and that the speaker is not wholly aligning with what is on offer. Further details of devices that commonly occur in discourse are given by Wiggins (2017).

It should of course be borne in mind that the central concerns of conversation analysis are not the same as those of discursive psychology. Nonetheless, the analytic tools and approach of conversation analysis have had considerable influence as discursive psychology has developed. Close attention to the sequential organization of the immediate setting, along with a focus on the key properties of discourse, can usefully inform the discursive psychologist's examination of how participants negotiate psychological concerns in interaction.

CONDUCTING A DISCURSIVE STUDY

The central features of discursive psychology mark it out as an approach to studying psychology that is very different from other forms of qualitative analysis. The emphases on (a) the action orientation of discourse, (b) the constructed and constructive nature of discourse, and (c) the situatedness of talk, as central properties of discourse are reflected in all stages in the conduct of a discursive study, as outlined here.

Step 1. Designing a Study

In conducting a discursive study, it is important from the earliest stages to be aware of what such a study will address and to set up the study in appropriate terms. These considerations immediately bear upon the selection of a topic and the questions that can relevantly be asked.

Research topics. Topics that are readily amenable to investigation through discursive research tend to fall into two groups. First, discursive researchers have previously investigated a broad range of psychological topics, bringing discursive insights to these. Work conducted to date, however, is by no means the full story. The discursive study of prejudice is one example of this continuing process of investigation. Since the 1980s, researchers have been examining how people in their talk can be seen to express negative views towards minority groups in ways that are designed to distance them from accusations of prejudice. The oft-quoted phrase "I am not a racist but . . ." (van Dijk, 1984) is an example of this form of talk, combining an explicit denial that the speaker is prejudiced towards the group in question with a statement that expresses negative or discriminatory views towards that group. The study of prejudice, however, continues to attract considerable interest from discursive psychologists, who look at how speakers attempt to negotiate issues of prejudice in relation to different groups, in various forms, and in an ever-expanding range of media. There is also a wealth of possibilities for researchers to build upon previous work to develop new insights into how discourse functions in different contexts, the forms of identities that individuals deploy, the arguments for and against ongoing social phenomena, as well as the discursive forms and structures that individuals use in mobilizing descriptions. All of these, and indeed other options, offer a wide-ranging set of potential topics for the discursive researcher.

A second group of topics derives from work that previously had been conducted from other perspectives but which has received little if any attention from discursive psychology. For example, prior to the work of Edwards and Potter (Edwards, 1997; Edwards & Potter, 1992), topics such as *cognitions* or *emotions* had been largely taken to be objects of study for cognitive psychologists but of rather less interest to discursive researchers. Yet, the study of topics such as these became central to the early development of discursive psychology. Another example of this focus can be seen in studies that have examined the interactional management of *confabulations*, productions of false memories that are presented without any intention to deceive. Usually, confabulations stemming from brain injury have been regarded as falling within the domain of neuropsychology where the emphasis lies on establishing the extent of the injury that has been sustained and the consequent deficits for the individual concerned. However, discursive research into how individuals produce confabulations in their interactions with others has shown that this approach can reveal much about the local contexts in which individuals produce such confabulations and the role of those with whom they are interacting in the production (McVittie & McKinlay, 2018; McVittie et al., 2014). Confabulations, from this perspective, come to be understood at least in part as interactional outcomes rather than as individual deficits. Topics, then, that have been investigated primarily through other approaches and methods are also open to discursive inquiry.

Research aims or questions. In view of the central focus that discursive research places on the action orientation of discourse, the research aims or questions that you find in a discursive study differ from those found in other forms of qualitative research. It would not be appropriate to devise a research question of the form "what are people's views of *x*," or "what do individuals think about *y*." Such questions adopt a stance towards the research topic that what is being investigated are consistent mental representations that participants hold of a readily discernible element of social life. As we have seen, a discursive approach eschews the acceptance of both consistent mental representations and the assumption that social phenomena can be readily described in neutral straightforward terms. Where the emphasis is on discourse as action, this opens up for inquiry a rather different set of possibilities. First, the focus is on action, not static views, leading to a question of what people are doing through discourse. Second, in line with the emphasis on discourse as construction, the focus is on the version or versions of social life that individuals are presenting at any time.

Taking these considerations together, then, research questions appropriate for a discursive study tend to be of the form "how do individuals construct *x*," "what identities do individuals negotiate in relation to *y*," or "how do individuals contest *z*." In each, the emphasis is on action and the constructive role of discourse. Consider the following examples of research aims or questions found in various recent discursive studies:

1. The research questions are (therefore): (a) What is talk about refugee integration used to do, and (b) How is it used to legitimize the acceptance and rejection of refugees? (Goodman & Kirkwood, 2019)
2. The aim of the current study is to extend existing work on thinking by examining how people make use of thinking as a rhetorical device in the practical accomplishment of subjectivity. (Horowitz & Kilby, 2019)
3. The current study examines how eating practices and diet talk are constructed and made sense of in interviews with mostly older men who are categorized as obese. (Seymour-Smith et al., 2020)
4. This article explores how the relationship between support for Brexit and prejudice is discursively constructed in lay talk; how these constructions are grounded in a complex web of ideological traditions; and how they are negotiated and managed in the context of focus group discussions about the EU referendum. (Andreouli et al., 2020)

These examples prove a useful illustration of the sorts of statements of research aims or research questions commonly found in discursive studies. In looking at these, we can see that these statements refer to actions that are to be studied, with action-oriented verbs such as "legitimize," "make use of," "made sense of," and "negotiated and managed." The sense is of active processes occurring within talk.

We can also note the references to the constructive role of discourse, including "what is talk . . . used to do," "practical accomplishment," "how eating practices and diet talk are constructed," and "how the relationship . . . is discursively constructed." Each statement is directed to the examination of how people use discourse not (merely) to describe phenomena but to develop versions of social practices and actors.

Finally, we see in the latter two statements references to the site of discourse that is to be examined, "interviews" in the third statement and "lay talk" in the fourth statement. While the first two statements do not make any such site explicit, the locus of the study is reported elsewhere.

In these ways, the statements of research aims or questions in each study set out clearly the central elements of the discursive approach and make it immediately relevant to the topic. A research aim that does not reflect one or more of these in some form, or one that is based on a more static or realist approach to studying social life, is not readily commensurate with a discursive study. It is important in conducting a discursive psychology study to be clear about both the approach itself and the understanding of social life that it makes available.

One further point marks out the research aims or questions found in discursive psychology studies as different from those found in other forms of qualitative research. The usual advice given to those embarking on research studies is to begin the process by devising an appropriate aim or question that thereafter directs the research process, guiding the data to be collected, and so on. This is not necessarily the case in discursive psychology work. Given discursive psychology's emphasis on examining discourse from the participants' perspective, it cannot be assumed that what people say inevitably relates to the initial considerations of the researcher. People can and do make sense of topics in their own ways and the discourse that they produce might relate less directly than anticipated to the research goals. Moreover, close examination of data collected in conducting the research might suggest that what is most important for the participants is not what was initially expected, and this can open up different possibilities for the focus of the research. The research aims, therefore, need not be specified at the outset of the study but can emerge in the course of the work.

Step 2. Data Collection

The methods of data collection commonly found in other qualitative approaches, such as interviewing, conducting focus groups, recordings of visual diaries, and so on, also offer possibilities for discursive work. For discursive research, however, the possibilities for data collection go far beyond these familiar methods: potential data are everywhere. The ubiquity of discourse throughout all areas of life makes available almost unlimited possibilities for discursive research. People use language in face-to-face settings, when meeting others informally, interacting in more formal settings such as medical consultations or counselling sessions. Print media publish discursive accounts of events, people, and actions. Television and radio broadcast programs on an ever-increasing diversity of topics. Social media sites, such as discussion forums, online support groups, and others, offer endless sources of potential data. Subject to practical and ethical considerations, all such sources can provide data that are suitable for discursive research.

Uses of different forms of data for research purposes give rise to different ethical considerations. Collection of research data through interviews, focus groups, or other participant-focused methods raises ethical issues similar to those for the collection of research data more generally. Thus, a discursive study should be conducted in accordance with the requirements of the relevant code of ethics, whether the American

Psychological Association (2017) *Ethical Principles of Psychologists and Code of Conduct*, the British Psychological Society's (2018) *Code of Ethics and Conduct*, or otherwise. Studies that seek to use other forms of data carry their own ethical issues. For example, where a study seeks to collect data from a setting provided by a specific organization, then the agreement and consent of that organization should be obtained in addition to compliance with other ethical principles. The use of public documents or records, or collection of data from other publicly available sources such as media reports and programs, often requires little more than formal institutional approval for the research, there being in effect no participants from whom informed consent to the research study might be obtained.

Step 3. Transcription

Given discursive psychology's interest both in what is said and how it is said, one requirement for conducting a discursive project is that the researcher has a full record of the data that are to be examined. Features of spoken discourse, including speech particles, intonation of words and phrases, pauses between utterances, and other elements of spoken discourse provide material for examining the detail of what is going in an interaction. Of course, such detail is not always present in discourse: written materials such as newspaper reports or official documents do not have such features, nor do tweets on Twitter or postings to other forms of social media (unless included for specific aims, e.g., Lange, 2008). And, in some instances, the written records of proceedings can be more relevant for research purposes than the proceedings themselves. For example, the reports of UK Parliamentary proceedings provided in Hansard (The Official Report of the Proceedings of the House of Commons) become the permanently available public records of these events (Sambaraju et al., 2017).

Where, however, researchers have access to recordings of the interactions that are to be examined, the recordings should be transcribed to a level that includes all features that are potentially relevant for the analysis to follow.

Often, transcription of recorded interaction is carried out using the notation system developed by Jefferson (2004). This system provides symbols for detailed transcription not just of words spoken but also of speech particles, length of pauses between utterances, and how speech is delivered (speed, intonation, and pitch) among other elements.

Transcribing data to include all such features is of course a somewhat time-intensive task, involving repeated listening and relistening to recordings and subsequent recording of all elements on the page. For such reasons, many researchers initially transcribe data to a first-pass level, aiming to record as much as possible of the talk but without necessarily including details of how the talk was delivered. They return to the data after the selection of extracts to produce a fuller transcription of the data that are to be used in their study. It should also be borne in mind that Jefferson transcription notation was developed for use in conversation analytic research not discursive psychology. Thus, a common practice is to transcribe data to a "Jefferson-lite" level (Potter & Hepburn, 2005), including utterances, some elements of stress and intonation, and untimed pauses but omitting other elements of the full notation system. This level of transcription is sufficient for many discursive psychology studies and leaves open the option of fuller transcription later if required for analysis.

Of course, when working with data that are already presented solely in written form, transcription is not a relevant consideration. Data in the form of documentary evidence or written proceedings offer a record that is open to analysis and, indeed, ordinarily it is that very record that is the subject of interest. However, care should be taken to ensure that the record provides full context of the words to be examined and those to whom they have been attributed. Many online sources exist solely or primarily in written form. Thus, data from sources such as online discussion forums, or Twitter, are available to be reproduced without further transcription by the researcher. Where, however, online sources such as transcripts of news interviews are to be used, then the researcher should aim to access also the online recordings of the interviews themselves in order that a fuller transcript can be produced than is commonly provided by news organizations.

Step 4. Selecting Data for Analysis

For the newcomer, embarking on discourse analysis can be a daunting task. There is no ready formula to be applied, and analysis does not usually proceed in an orderly linear fashion. Instead, analysis can be more usefully understood as an iterative process in which initial analysis leads the researcher to revisit the data set which in turn informs further analysis. These recursions between data and analysis continue until there is little more that can usefully be included in the analysis.

The first stage of analysis involves the researcher becoming totally familiar with the data. This involves careful reading and rereading of the data, or transcripts, as appropriate. Where transcripts are being used, familiarity comes also from alternating between reading the written transcripts and listening to the verbal recordings, allowing for a developing understanding of what was said and how. This process of developing familiarity provides an initial sense of recurring patterns in the data. At this point, it is useful for a researcher to record by way of memo or notes what these patterns appear to be, as they will inform further stages of the analysis.

There is no definitive list of the patterns than can provide a focus at this point. These, however, should be guided by, first, the research aim or question (however loosely framed at this stage) and, second, the central features of the discursive psychology approach. Thus, initial observations might refer to specific instances of one of the following:

1. The actions that the participants are involved in, such as justifying their own actions, criticizing or blaming others, or arguing for certain outcomes
2. Constructions of specific psychological phenomena, such as identities, social groups, or cognitions, in the data

3. Organization of discursive structures in the data, such as comparisons or contrasts, adjacency pairs, collaborations, or disagreements among coparticipants

These examples are not exhaustive but rather indicative of the patterns that can be used to inform initial analysis. After identification of recurring elements, the next stage is to select out from the data set passages of discourse in which these elements are found. This process of selection should be conducted inclusively, with all passages of potential relevance being taken forward for further consideration. In doing this, it is important in each case to include in each passage sufficient material to make sense of the context in which the topic of interest occurred, for example, the turn that immediately preceded the talk that is to be examined, and/or the following turn in which a reader can see the coparticipant's uptake of what has been said. A passage, therefore, might well include a substantial stretch of talk involving several interactional turns.

Step 5. Analysis

After the selection of data that are to be analyzed in detail, the next stage of analysis involves close examination of how the discourse works in situ. Again, here, it is important to bear in mind the three key concerns of discursive psychology, namely, action orientation, the construction of psychological matters, and the situatedness of the discourse. If initial analysis has identified and been guided by the recurrence of action A in the data, then the next step is to look in detail at how this action is accomplished. For example, an action of justifying one's own behavior often involves certain constructions of events or circumstances surrounding that behavior. Conversely, analysis that begins by focusing on the constructions of certain phenomena should examine the actions that are accomplished by these constructions. If, for instance, an individual claims one form of identity, then the question becomes one of what use that identity is being put to or what action it is designed to bring off.

There is also the question of how participants' talk is organized in the interaction. If an initial observation is that a certain type of question is commonly followed by a certain form of answer, then there are the issues of how these are framed, what constructions they involve, and what actions result from these sequences. Analysis of context should also involve close attention to the turns that surround the talk in question. How does a turn relate to the preceding one, and what does it indicate about how the speaker is treating the prior speaker's utterance? If a speaker attempts to accomplish an action, or presents a version of events, how are these taken up by the next speaker? Does that person indicate agreement with what is on offer, seek to challenge what has been said, introduce a new topic, or otherwise? In this respect, attention to the discursive devices that participants are using can be useful in highlighting how the participants are treating the immediate talk. This focus not only provides further detail for analysis but can also inform further stages in that analysis: If the participants are treating a claim as problematic, then the construction of the claim merits further detailed attention. This, in turn, can lead to a return to the data set to examine whether other instances display similar features.

To illustrate how this analytic process works, let us turn to Extract 8.2. This extract comes from a study we conducted to examine how UK nationals constructed and identified Polish people working in the United Kingdom. The study was conducted in the period prior to the United Kingdom's 2016 referendum on the issue of UK membership in the European Union (EU). At that time, EU citizens had free movement between member states (the United Kingdom included), and Polish nationals comprised the largest group of immigrants into the United

---

Extract 8.2

```
 1   Ted em (1.0) just like (.) seen a couple programs on them (.) they're stealing
 2   our ↑jobs
 3   Vicki Like on TV?
 4   Ted Yeah
 5   Vicki OK
 6   Ted But eh (w's) it wasn't like on channel four it was like proper channel one
 7   so=
 8   =[(Laughter)
 9   Jenny [look out= ((joking voice))
10   Ted =I'm easily [seen there ((joking voice))
11   [(Laughter)=
12   Jenny =got more (↑tickets?) ((joking voice))
13   Jim This is true
14   Ted Aye >I know I know< ehh
15   Jim ( )
16   Ted If they're if they're bringing something new (.) 'n like they're offering
17   spe- like something new but like (.) that helps us but if they're just
18   coming in (.) and like putting British people >out of work< which they
19   are 'cos they're more skilled and (.) they work for ↓less (.) then I don't
20   agree with it
```

(McVittie & McKinlay, 2019, p. 23, Extract 3)

Kingdom. Previous research had found that UK nationals often described Polish people as hard-working, in contrast to other groups of immigrants. The aim of the study was to see how UK nationals constructed Polish people at a time when a large part of public sentiment was running against the presence of EU nationals in the United Kingdom. We collected data from focus groups, each comprising UK nationals from a variety of backgrounds and employment histories.

Our initial readings indicated that a recurring pattern in the data was that participants, although asked to discuss wide-ranging topics, frequently constructed Polish people in relation to their working activities. These constructions identified Polish workers as hard-working but, at the same time, as being unwelcome in the United Kingdom. Extract 8.2 comes from a discussion among five participants responding to a question about their views of Polish immigration into the United Kingdom.

This extract was selected on the basis that, as in other parts of the data, the discussions involved specific constructions of Polish workers. What is clearly apparent here is that the sequence involves an identification of Polish workers as people who engage in illegitimate activities. At lines 1 to 2, Ted describes them as people who are "stealing our ↑jobs." The action is, thus, one of blaming or criticizing. To understand further how this action was being performed, our attention turned to other features of the extract, particularly the grounds on which the criticism was being made. Above, Ted in making this criticism offers a warrant as to how he has acquired the knowledge on which this criticism is based, namely that he has "seen a couple programs on them." The substantive basis for the criticism, however, is made out in terms of Ted constructing a specific version of Polish workers and their activities. Thus, we see at lines 16 to 19 how Ted builds up a picture of Polish workers as people who do not offer any contribution to the UK economy but rather who put British people "out of work." Perhaps ironically, this version of Polish workers relies on a description that might elsewhere be treated as reflecting

positive attributes, that "they're more skilled and (.) they work for ↓less" at line 19. Here, this construction is deployed to warrant Ted's initial criticism.

In grounding his criticism in a particular version of Polish workers themselves, Ted draws upon a form of talk seen in other studies of prejudice. For example, writers have shown how speakers of different nationalities produce criticisms of Romanies by attributing the behaviors to features inherent in Romany character (Rowe & Goodman, 2014; Tileaga, 2005). Constructing the identities of those being blamed in this way is designed to allow those who are doing the criticizing to distance themselves from being the source of that criticism. Here Ted's claim is designed similarly to distance himself from having a predetermined negative disposition towards Polish workers; instead, the negative evaluation arises due to knowledge that he has gained about the work practices of Polish workers themselves.

At this point, we have analyzed the action that is in play and the constructions of identities on which this action proceeds. But this is not yet a full analysis. Let us consider how this construction is treated in the discussion among group members. Ted's initial criticism is met with minimal response from Vicky in the turns that follow. At lines 3 to 8 there is some discussion as to whether the source for Ted's claim should be treated as authoritative. This stage of the discussion ends with Ted credentialing his source as being a "proper" one and discounting an alternative source, a move that is met with laughter from other group members. Later in the discussion at line 13, following some intervening talk, Jim indicates agreement with Ted's claim, stating "this is true." This agreement leads Ted to develop his construction of Polish workers at lines 16 to 20. The consequential outcome of Ted's continued description is, however, indeterminate, as the discussion turns to other topics immediately thereafter.

At various parts across the data set, we found the participants constructing Polish people in ways similar to that seen in Extract 8.3. We also found, however, instances that appeared to be deviant cases in that they differed in their

Extract 8.3

1   Kirk You see speaking from a person- speaking from a personal experience (.)
2   I've found that em (.) I've had (.) just recently we had one >member of
3   staff< who was ↑born and ↑bred in Britain and they were
4   completely unreliable they didn't want to work they were so::o lazy jes
5   couldn't care ↑less and we've just recently hired someone who (.) came
6   to Britain when she was about (.) thirteen (.) twelve (1) and (.) she has
7   >very good< education she's at university and she works >part time< and
8   she works all the hours that she can get because she wants ↓money and
9   she works she does work ↑hard and she's always eager to learn
10   something ↑new (.) and do something and I've [found
11   Kenny [but (.) what you were
12   prior talking about was talking about like people on the benefits system
13   (.) would it not be ↑better to get someone out workin' (.) rather than just
14   claiming loads of benefits?

(McVittie & McKinlay, 2019, p. 25, Extract 4)

constructions of Polish workers and activities. These cases necessitated further examination; without further analysis it would be problematic to suggest that the findings demonstrated general discrimination. One such deviant case is seen in Extract 8.3.

This sequence is also marked by a construction of Polish workers. Here, however, in contrast to the previous extract, the identification of Polish workers initially appears highly positive. At lines 1 to 10, Kirk develops a construction of one Polish worker in very favorable terms. This is built up through a contrast between the work-related attributes of two members of staff within his personal experience. Of these, the first was "↑born and ↑bred in Britain" and is described in extremely negative terms, whereas the second is someone who "came to Britain" at a later age who is described in an extremely favorable manner. We can note the use of discursive devices, especially extreme case formulations, that are designed to heighten the rhetorical effect of his description. Here, these extreme case formulations rhetorically emphasize Kirk's descriptions of the negative attributes of the British worker on the one hand and the

positive qualities of the worker who came to Britain on the other.

As with all constructions, this is oriented to an action outcome. This is projected by Kirk's talk at lines 1 to 10, where the employment of non-British workers is likely to be favored. Before Kirk can reach this point, however, he is cut off by Kenny's intervening turn at line 11. Not only does this prevent Kirk from making his argument, it also introduces a quite different construction at line 12 in the form of "people on the benefit system." This might at first glance appear general and nonspecific to any nationality. On closer inspection, however, this group cannot include the Polish worker that Kirk has previously been describing so favorably. A category of those claiming benefits necessarily excludes those who are in employment. Thus, without any reference to Polish workers, favorable or unfavorable, Kenny can argue against their inclusion in UK employment. This construction, thus, enacts a form of *safe prejudice*, one that is designed to be difficult to challenge.

There is, of course, more that could be said about the detail of these two extracts. Here, however, we have shown how UK nationals can seek to justify discrimination against Polish workers. Analysis of both sequences that appear immediately relevant and those that initially seem to be deviant cases demonstrates how participants ascribe identities to Polish workers and the actions that are associated with these constructions. The analysis has also considered how these descriptions are produced and how others who are copresent respond to them in the local settings. Attention to these properties of the talk demonstrates the principles of discursive psychology in action.

Step 6. Disseminating Your Research

Although many discursive researchers, like researchers working within other approaches, are looking at new and innovative ways of disseminating research findings, discursive research usually is disseminated through the familiar routes of conference presentations, journal articles, and book chapters. Many of the considerations relating to publishing research generally apply equally to findings from discursive work. There is one issue that merits specific and careful attention in planning to disseminate discursive findings, that of who is to be the audience or readership of the output. As noted above, discursive studies often seek either (a) to build upon previous discursive research or (b) to apply a discursive approach to a topic on which there has previously been little if any discursive work. Each of these possibilities brings its own considerations as to how discursive findings should most usefully be presented.

There are now numerous journals that publish findings from discursive studies. A list of many of these can be found at http://www.discurs.org/en/resources/journals. Where findings are to be presented to an audience that is already familiar with a discursive approach, it is usually unnecessary to discuss in detail all the elements of the approach. The audience or readership can be treated as having this knowledge, and attention should be focused on the originality of the findings for those who study discourse. If the findings are pointing to previously unidentified discursive devices, linguistic structures, or other features

of discourse, then the primary focus should be on reviewing previous literature on that topic to demonstrate the novelty of what is being presented. A discursive readership is likely to be rather less interested in being told about aspects of a study that has less relevance for them, such as intricacies of cognitive processing or symptomology of illness. If the study has used a context involving these for the collection of data, then such elements are more window-dressing than substance for the presentation of findings.

Conversely, when findings are presented to a journal that is not primarily directed at discursive work, then the article should be framed in terms of the scope of the journal as outlined. Many journals have a readership that are reasonably familiar with discursive research, albeit that discourse is not the primary focus of the journal. Social psychology journals frequently publish discursive work, and it is unnecessary to spell out fully what is involved in the discursive approach. One should realize, however, that the main interests of readers lie in social psychology and not discourse. An article should be framed in terms of key social psychological concerns and demonstrate what discursive findings can bring to these, not vice versa. Other journals, however, have a readership that is unfamiliar with the discursive psychology approach, and the researcher must demonstrate the relevance of such an approach to them. For example, a readership that is primarily focused on the details of memory processing is unlikely to be immediately interested in the deployment of discursive devices. Here, the discursive researcher must make a case for the advantages of studying discourse in such instances. Before submitting to a journal in fields not associated with discursive work, it is a good idea to look at previous issues of the target journal. Questions that might usefully be asked are along the lines of, has this journal previously published such work, has it published qualitative studies at all, are there any published studies there that the findings could (however obtusely) be tied to and that could be included in an introduction as a basis for the current study, and so on. For instance, a journal publishing research on memory might have published studies on the construction of memory in social settings or similar. This allows for an argument to the effect that the topic is important and that discursive research can contribute to showing how construction is accomplished or similar. The most important point to get across here is that discursive research has something to offer to the topic that might be of interest to the readership.

Step 7. Quality in Discursive Psychology Research

The question of what constitutes quality in discursive research, or "How do I know when I'm doing it right?" (Wiggins, 2017, p. 135) is a tricky one. In recent times, various writers have proposed criteria for the evaluation of qualitative research in general, discursive research included. By contrast, other writers have offered criteria specifically for the evaluation of discursive research, many arguing in doing so that more general criteria have limited relevance for this form of research. And, to complicate matters further, the criteria proposed in each case differ from writer to writer, sometimes in substance and often in emphasis. There is no settled consensus as to the criteria to be applied in evaluating discursive research. We do not propose here to rehearse the arguments on both sides. Instead, let us examine recent work from each and consider briefly how it might apply to discursive research.

A recent set of guidelines for evaluating all forms of qualitative research is provided by Levitt and colleagues (Levitt et al., 2017). Their *Recommendations for Designing and Reviewing Qualitative Research in Psychology* is designed to offer a framework for the evaluation of any research falling within the realm of qualitative psychology. These authors proposed that qualitative research can be evaluated against a central principle of *methodological integrity*. This central concept incorporates two elements: (a) fidelity to the subject matter and (b) utility in achieving research goals. Based on examples that we do not detail here, the authors suggest that in the design and review of a qualitative study, these two features can demonstrate the methodological integrity of a study, which in turn establish that the work is trustworthy and that readers and others can have confidence in the research and its findings.

One advantage of such an overarching framework for the evaluation of qualitative research is that, if established, it provides a common point of reference across the qualitative research community. Researchers and those reviewing and accessing research are not required to be overly familiar with perhaps minor differences among a range of approaches, and the framework, thus, might operate to the benefit of all forms of qualitative research, discursive work included. The potential downside, however, is the potential applicability (or nonapplicability) of such a framework. Such a framework for broad evaluation is possible only through some level of abstraction from specific forms of research; the question arises as to whether it glosses over potentially key differences among qualitative approaches and how usefully it reflects the nuances of evaluation that are relevant to discursive work (Gergen 2014; Reicher, 2000).

By contrast, McMullen (2021) offered a set of five criteria designed specifically to apply to evaluation of discursive research. These can be summarized as follows:

1. *Documentation.* Referred to by other writers as *transparency* (e.g., Wiggins, 2017), this involves the researcher keeping a record of the decisions that have been made in the course of designing and conducting the research. These details should be reported to readers of the research outcomes in order that they can assess the procedures that have been followed.
2. *Demonstration.* It is accepted practice in discursive research to include in any report extracts of data on which the analysis proceeds. By doing this, the researcher demonstrates how the analysis is linked to and derives from the data that were collected. Providing a reader with the raw data, as well as analysis of those data, allows readers to assess for themselves the analysis that is being offered.
3. *Plausibility.* This is closely linked to demonstration. Clearly for the analysis to be accepted, it should be a plausible account of what is occurring in the data. One key aspect of this in discursive research is the use of participants'

orientations and the next turn proof procedure. If the report shows that participants themselves are treating matters at hand in the manner indicated by the analysis, then a reader can have greater confidence that the analysis does not rest solely on a particular interpretation by the researcher.

4. *Coherence.* It should be self-evident that the analysis should aim to be coherent in presenting a clear account of what is happening across the data. Here, the use of deviant cases is an important consideration. If an analysis not only makes sense of obvious examples of what is being examined but also accounts for instances that do not immediately fit that pattern, then this suggests that the analysis presents a coherent and complete account.

5. *Fruitfulness.* An aim of discursive research is to produce outcomes that are worthwhile and that contribute to knowledge. Often discursive work, as well as producing new insights, can point to the benefits of adopting a different approach to the topic being studied or open up new avenues for investigation.

As is immediately obvious, the criteria set out above are rather more detailed than the more generic criteria offered by Levitt et al. (2017). This is unsurprising in that they have been designed to be specific to discursive research. However, this does not mean that they should be viewed as incompatible with the more general principle of methodological integrity. Rather, perhaps, they spell out in greater detail how such considerations are addressed in the specific instance of discursive research.

CURRENT ISSUES IN DISCURSIVE PSYCHOLOGY

Let us now return to two points that have provided the focus for ongoing debates among discursive researchers. Both debates center on the use, or nonuse, of particular forms of data in discursive studies. The first issue involves the ethics in the use of certain data; the second issue, the value of collecting particular data in discursive psychology research.

Ethics and Online Research

We noted previously that online sources provide a rich range of opportunities for collecting data for discursive studies. At the same time, however, the ethical issue of whether all such data should be treated as readily available for research purposes is by no means settled. People engage with a diversity of online sites, but this is done for purposes of interacting with other users. It is less clear if people are aware that the contributions that they make on these sites are available for inspection and subsequent use for research purposes.

One view is that contributions are in the public domain, that indeed is a central element of the internet. And, especially in relation to online sites that do not require registration or other steps to be taken to gain access, the contributions that people make are immediately accessible to any internet user. It is difficult to imagine a more public location. On this argument, the contributions fall to be treated as public in the same manner as observations carried out in any other public spaces, and it is accordingly reasonable to use them in research studies in the same way as data from public media such as television broadcasts, newspaper reports, and so on.

The opposite view is that when people contribute to internet sites and discussions, they do so to interact with others in these settings. While they might reasonably expect other internet users to access what they said, this access is expected to be for purposes of response, comment, or similar. People, online or elsewhere, do not expect that their words will be taken up by a researcher for a purpose that is entirely different from that intended. Thus, for a researcher (discursive or other) to use such material, they should have regard for these participants' expectations and use such data only where explicit consent can be obtained or where it is in the public interest for the material to be treated as immediately available.

On these points, the ethics guidance provided to psychology researchers is unclear. The American Psychological Association and the British Psychological Society in their respective guidelines to psychologists for conducting research with internet-based data (American Psychological Association

Board of Scientific Affairs Advisory Group on Conducting Research on the Internet, 2002; British Psychological Society, 2017) highlight the difficulties involved in attempting to specify what is to be considered public or private, and the risks to internet users if their anonymity or confidentiality is breached. Beyond this, much is left to the individual researcher to consider.

In practice, many discursive researchers treat as private any data that originate on a site that requires an individual to register with it and/or to log in to gain access. By contrast, data that can readily be located by anyone with internet access are considered to be in effect in the public domain. This, however, leaves questions of anonymity and confidentiality, especially where topics under discussion might reasonably be regarded as sensitive (Jowett, 2015; Roberts, 2015).

One example of how online discussions of sensitive topics might be approached comes from a study by Wiggins and colleagues (2016). Extract 8.4 is from this study of how users of an online suicide discussion forum sought to construct their identities and how users provided support to each other.

It is difficult to imagine a more sensitive topic than that being discussed in Extract 8.4. As Wiggins et al. (2016) noted, many of the postings to the forum are taken up with descriptions such as this one, with references to the particularly difficult feelings and thoughts of the contributor. The authors examined the ways in which contributors build and manage identities

as people who are genuinely suicidal and seeking help. We do not need to recount these details here, but, for purposes of considering ethical issues in the use of data such as these, there are several points of note. First the discussion forum from which the data were collected was accessible by anyone and did not require a password. Second, while the data are reproduced to allow for demonstration of how the analysis was generated, details of the individual have been relatively anonymized with the contributor being designated as "member." Finally, the use of these data and the analysis offer insights into a topic that would otherwise be difficult to study; it is, for example, unlikely that a researcher could collect similar data from a face-to-face setting. In these ways, the authors sought to address the risks for users of the forum and to produce research that might inform how support could be provided to people who report suicidal feelings.

Researcher-Generated Data and Naturally Occurring Data

The use of research interviews as a method of data collection has a long history across the social sciences, to the point that interviewing is often treated as a "default option" in qualitative research (Hepworth & McVittie, 2016, p. 65). Interviews offer advantages over other forms of data collection in allowing the researcher to guide discussion towards the research topic in an organized and familiar form of interaction.

The use of research interviews in discursive research has, however, come under scrutiny over

---

Extract 8.4

1. 12.03 am. Day 1
2. Member 13. Join date: Sept 2012. Posts: 212. 1/3 in thread
3. Stress and depression got to me so bad that I'm starting to think about suicide
4. in a different way than I did before . . . Suddenly it just doesn't seem like a
5. bad way to go after all. All my fears about the afterlife, eternity in hell,
6. family, people who'd miss me, things I might be missing on just don't
7. seem to matter anymore.
8. I just feel stuck, with no way out.

(Wiggins et al., 2016, p. 1245, Extract 3)

recent years. Various writers have argued that the very features that make interviews attractive as a means of data collection at the same time reduce its value for conducting discursive psychology work. For example, it has been argued there is a risk that an interview will be "flooded" with the researcher's agenda (Potter & Hepburn, 2005). A related but separate criticism is that in research encounters, "the stakes are low" for participants (Stokoe, 2010). Taken together, these criticisms provide the argument that in effect research interviews are unlike other encounters in every-day life, in that it is primarily the researcher who directs the encounter and who has an interest in it happening at all. On this view, participants, notwithstanding that they have given informed consent to participate, really have little interest in the outcomes, and whatever they say will have little relevance to other aspects of their lives. For such reasons, Potter and Hepburn (2005) argued that discursive researchers should forego the use of "researcher-generated" data, including those collected in research interviews, and instead look to collect "naturally occurring" data from settings that have not been organized solely for research purposes.

On the opposing side, writers have argued that such concerns are unfounded and that interviews provide data suitable for discursive psychology as long as sufficient attention is given to the interview context (e.g., Griffin, 2007). Indeed, Potter and Wetherell (1987) argued for the use of research interviews, provided that such interviews were not treated merely as data-gathering exercises but as conversational encounters with analytic attention being given to the turns of the interviewer as well as those of the interviewee.

To consider the arguments for and against the use of research interviews, let us look at Extract 8.5, which is taken from a study conducted

---

Extract 8.5

7   R9 so I mean (.) a lot of things ↑happened when I since I came here

8   INT okay

9   R9 yeah >for instance< you know I was attacked twice

10 INT °oh really°

11 R9 I came he::re (.) in (.) Glasgow having all my teeth

12 INT really

13 R9 and as you see now all this part ((points to gap in teeth)) (.) is fully gone

14 INT °yeah°

15 R9 and (.) now I was attacked twice

16 INT geez=

17 R9 =in the ↑city

18 INT god

19 R9 and I did nothing to nobody

20 INT geez=

21 R9=and even I don't know (.) them those people who are (.) did >did this to me<

22 INT god

23 R9 and they just came me I'm (0.7) I mean four-three guys

24 INT geez=

25 R9 =giving me punches y- you know b- you know (.) and that was you know I mean

26 (.) I said I mean (.) these guys you know they're animals even the eh- I even I (.)

27 even (1.0) they were not even an- m- animals but they're more than animals

(Kirkwood et al., 2013, pp. 755–756, Extract 4)

---

with asylum-seekers and refugees living in Scotland. This extract comes from an interview conducted with a male refugee who had lived in the United Kingdom for seven years.

We can immediately note three features from this exchange in which the interviewee, R9, describes his experiences of living in Glasgow. First, the majority of the talk comes from R9. The interviewer's turns are minimal, mostly comprising a single word that acknowledges the prior turn of the interviewee. Second, what R9 describes are experiences that were for him very difficult, in that he is reporting being the victim of serious assault that has resulted in permanent physical damage. And third, as the exchange progresses the interviewer's turns change from being relatively noncommittal ("okay," "really") to expressions that indicate a strong response to what is being described ("geez," "god"). These changes lead to the interviewee providing further detail of his experiences and offering a characterization of his attackers.

Taking these features together, it is difficult to argue that this sequence is "flooded" with the interviewer's agenda: The interviewee produces most of the talk in reporting his experiences. Equally, what R9 is reporting suggests that for him the "stakes" are anything but low, in that he has been subjected to physical violence. Moreover, it is the shape of the interaction that allows R9 to describe what is for him a significant part of his experiences of living in the United Kingdom.

Exchanges such as seen in Extract 8.5 demonstrate the difficulties involved in any attempt to draw an a priori distinction between data that are "researcher-generated" on the one hand, and data that are "naturally occurring" on the other. There are more useful ways to determine the value of using data that come from research interviews and similar settings.

A first way to approach these data, consistent with the principles of the discursive psychology approach, is to examine what is going on as a participants' concern. From this perspective, we can ask how the participants orient to the interaction at hand: does close analysis demonstrate that the participants treat the encounter as one

in which they have little stake, or, conversely, do they treat it as one that is important for them? Here, the next turn proof procedure is all the more important in considering how participants respond to the turns of the interviewer.

A second way to approach discursive psychology research based on "researcher-generated" data is to apply the same criteria for evaluation relevant to all such work, especially that of fruitfulness. Rather than discounting the value of an interview-based study from the outset, we might instead look at its contribution to knowledge and at its potential to offer new insights into what otherwise would be unknown.

CONCLUDING COMMENT

Discursive psychology is an approach that is very different from other approaches to psychology, quantitative and qualitative. It requires close examination of the details of social life and invites reconsideration of topics of interest to psychologists. In this chapter, we have looked at the steps involved in conducting discursive psychology research, and at a range of findings from discursive psychology studies. These findings, and those from other discursive work, offer rich understandings of elements of life. More than this, discursive psychology is an approach that evolves as life changes, providing ways for us to examine discourse across all sites, from our daily face-to-face encounters with others to communications on more recently established forms of social media. Doing discursive psychology, then, is not a matter of simply following routinized procedures to discover what these can tell us about topics of possible interest. It is rather an approach that is designed to take seriously life as it is lived and to offer us insights into our own lives and the social worlds that we inhabit.

References

American Psychological Association. (2017). *Ethical principles of psychologists and code of conduct* (2002, Amended June 1, 2010 and January 1, 2017). Retrieved from http://www.apa.org/ethics/code/index.aspx

American Psychological Association Board of Scientific Affairs Advisory Group on Conducting Research on the Internet. (2002). *Psychological research online: Opportunities and challenges.* https://www.apa.org/science/leadership/bsa/internet/internet-report

Andreouli, E., Greenland, K., & Figgou, L. (2020). Lay discourses about Brexit and prejudice: "Ideological creativity" and its limits in Brexit debates. *European Journal of Social Psychology, 50*(2), 309–322. https://doi.org/10.1002/ejsp.2625

Austin, J. (1962). *How to do things with words.* Oxford University Press.

British Psychological Society. (2017). *Ethics guidelines for internet-mediated research.* https://www.bps.org.uk/guideline/ethics-guidelines-internet-mediated-research

British Psychological Society. (2018). *Code of ethics and conduct.* British Psychological Society. https://www.bps.org.uk/news-and-policy/bps-code-ethics-and-conduct

Edwards, D. (1997). *Discourse and cognition.* SAGE. https://doi.org/10.4135/9781446221785

Edwards, D. (2000). Extreme case formulations: Softeners, investment, and doing nonliteral. *Research on Language and Social Interaction, 33*(4), 347–373. https://doi.org/10.1207/S15327973RLSI3304_01

Edwards, D., & Potter, J. (1992). *Discursive psychology.* SAGE.

Fairclough, N. (2013). *Critical discourse analysis: The critical study of language.* Routledge. https://doi.org/10.4324/9781315834368

Garfinkel, H. (1967). *Studies in ethnomethodology.* Prentice-Hall.

Gergen, K. J. (2014). Pursuing excellence in qualitative inquiry. *Qualitative Psychology, 1*(1), 49–60. https://doi.org/10.1037/qup0000002

Gilbert, G. N., & Mulkay, M. (1984). *Opening Pandora's box: A sociological analysis of scientists' discourse.* Cambridge University Press.

Goffman, E. (1981). *Forms of talk.* Blackwell.

Goodman, S., & Kirkwood, S. (2019). Political and media discourses about integrating refugees in the UK. *European Journal of Social Psychology, 49*(7), 1456–1470. https://doi.org/10.1002/ejsp.2595

Griffin, C. (2007). Being dead and being there: Research interviews, sharing hand cream and the preference for analysing 'naturally occurring data.' *Discourse Studies, 9*(2), 246–269. https://doi.org/10.1177/1461445607075340

Hepworth, J., & McVittie, C. (2016). The research interview in adult mental health: Problems and possibilities for discourse studies. In M. O'Reilly & J. Lester (Eds.), *The Palgrave handbook of adult mental health* (pp. 64–81). Palgrave Macmillan. https://doi.org/10.1057/9781137496850_4

Horowitz, A. D., & Kilby, L. (2019). Thinking out loud: A discourse analysis of 'thinking' during talk radio interactions. *Text & Talk, 39*(6), 699–724. https://doi.org/10.1515/text-2019-0235

Jefferson, G. (2004). Glossary of transcript symbols with an introduction. In G. H. Lerner (Ed.), *Conversation analysis: Studies from the first generation* (pp. 13–31). Benjamins. https://doi.org/10.1075/pbns.125.02jef

Jowett, A. (2015). A case for using online discussion forums in critical psychological research. *Qualitative Research in Psychology, 12*(3), 287–297. https://doi.org/10.1080/14780887.2015.1008906

Kirkwood, S., McKinlay, A., & McVittie, C. (2013). 'They're more than animals': Refugees' accounts of racially motivated violence. *British Journal of Social Psychology, 52*(4), 747–762. https://doi.org/10.1111/bjso.12007

Lange, P. G. (2008). An implicature for um: Signaling relative expertise. *Discourse Studies, 10*(2), 191–204. https://doi.org/10.1177/1461445607087008

Levitt, H. M., Motulsky, S. L., Wertz, F. J., Morrow, S. L., & Ponterotto, J. G. (2017). Recommendations for designing and reviewing qualitative research in psychology: Promoting methodological integrity. *Qualitative Psychology, 4*(1), 2–22. https://doi.org/10.1037/qup0000082

McKinlay, A., & McVittie, C. (2008). *Social psychology and discourse.* John Wiley & Sons. https://doi.org/10.1002/9781444303094

McKinlay, A., & McVittie, C. (2011). *Identities in context: Individuals and discourse in action.* John Wiley & Sons. https://doi.org/10.1002/9781444397222

McMullen, L. M. (2021). *Essentials of discursive psychology.* American Psychological Association. https://doi.org/10.1037/0000220-000

McVittie, C., & McKinlay, A. (2018). Collaborative processes in neuropsychological interviews. In M. Meade, A. Barnier, P. van Bergen, C. Harris, & J. Sutton (Eds.), *Collaborative remembering: Theories, research, and applications* (pp. 216–230). Oxford University Press.

McVittie, C., & McKinlay, A. (2019). 'Would it not be better to get someone out workin?': 'Safe prejudice' against Polish workers. *European Journal of Social Psychology, 49*(1), 19–30. https://doi.org/10.1002/ejsp.2382

McVittie, C., McKinlay, A., Della Sala, S., & MacPherson, S. E. (2014). The dog that didn't growl: The interactional negotiation of momentary confabulations.

Memory, 22(7), 824–838. https://doi.org/10.1080/09658211.2013.838629

Parker, I. (2013). Discourse analysis: Dimensions of critique in psychology. *Qualitative Research in Psychology, 10*(3), 223–239. https://doi.org/10.1080/14780887.2012.741509

Parker, I. (2014). *Discourse dynamics (psychology revivals): Critical analysis for social and individual psychology*. Routledge. https://doi.org/10.4324/9781315888590

Pomerantz, A. (1986). Extreme case formulations: A way of legitimizing claims. *Human Studies, 9*(2), 219–229. https://doi.org/10.1007/BF00148128

Potter, J., & Hepburn, A. (2005). Qualitative interviews in psychology: Problems and possibilities. *Qualitative Research in Psychology, 2*(4), 281–307. https://doi.org/10.1191/1478088705qp045oa

Potter, J., & Wetherell, M. (1987). *Discourse and social psychology: Beyond attitudes and behaviour*. SAGE.

Reicher, S. (2000). Against methodolatry: Some comments on Elliott, Fischer, and Rennie. *British Journal of Clinical Psychology, 39*(1), 1–6. https://doi.org/10.1348/014466500163031

Roberts, L. D. (2015). Ethical issues in conducting qualitative research in online communities. *Qualitative Research in Psychology, 12*(3), 314–325. https://doi.org/10.1080/14780887.2015.1008909

Rowe, L., & Goodman, S. (2014). A stinking filthy race of people inbred with criminality: A discourse analysis of prejudicial talk about Gypsies in discussion forums. *Romani Studies, 24*(1), 25–42. https://doi.org/10.3828/rs.2014.2

Sacks, H. (1992). *Lectures on conversation*. Blackwell.

Sacks, H., Schegloff, A. E., & Jefferson, G. (1974). A simplest systematics for the organization of turn-taking for conversation. *Language, 50*(4), 696–735. https://doi.org/10.1353/lan.1974.0010

Sambaraju, R., McVittie, C., Goodall, K., & McKinlay, A. (2017). "Just an excuse people are just using these days": Attending to and managing inter-actional concerns in talk on exclusion of immigrants. *Journal of Language and Social Psychology, 36*(6), 654–674. https://doi.org/10.1177/0261927X17706939

Seymour-Smith, S., Gough, B., Matthews, C. R., & Rutherford, Z. (2020). Food assessment: A discursive analysis of diet talk in interviews with older men who are obese. *Psychology & Health, 35*(8), 946–967. https://doi.org/10.1080/08870446.2019.1701673

Stokoe, E. (2010). 'I'm not gonna hit a lady': Conversation analysis, membership categorization and men's denials of violence towards women. *Discourse & Society, 21*(1), 59–82. https://doi.org/10.1177/0957926509345072

Tileaga, C. (2005). Accounting for extreme prejudice and legitimating blame in talk about the Romanies. *Discourse & Society, 16*(5), 603–624. https://doi.org/10.1177/0957926505054938

van Dijk, T. A. (1984). *Prejudice in discourse*. Benjamins.

van Dijk, T. A. (2008). Critical discourse analysis and nominalization: Problem or pseudo-problem? *Discourse & Society, 19*(6), 821–828. https://doi.org/10.1177/0957926508095897

Wiggins, S. (2017). *Discursive psychology: Theory, method, and applications*. SAGE. https://doi.org/10.4135/9781473983335

Wiggins, S., McQuade, R., & Rasmussen, S. (2016). Stepping back from crisis points: The provision and acknowledgment of support in an online suicide discussion forum. *Qualitative Health Research, 26*(9), 1240–1251. https://doi.org/10.1177/1049732316633130

Wodak, R., & Meyer, M. (Eds.). (2015). *Methods of critical discourse studies*. SAGE.

Xanthopoulou, P. (2010). The production of 'defectiveness' as a linguistic resource in broadcast evangelical discourse: A discursive psychology approach. *Discourse & Society, 21*(6), 675–691. https://doi.org/10.1177/0957926510381221

MULTILAYERED APPROACHES

CHAPTER 9

ETHNOGRAPHY IN PSYCHOLOGICAL RESEARCH

Elizabeth Fein and Jonathan Yahalom

WHAT IS ETHNOGRAPHY?

Our psychological lives are profoundly intertwined with our surrounding worlds. Similar child-rearing techniques produce very different outcomes, depending on the broader values of the community within which they are used (Chao, 1994; Chapin, 2014). Psychotherapies that encourage cathartic displays of feeling can be healing in societies privileging emotional self-expression but damaging in societies that prioritize emotional composure (Christopher et al., 2014). Even our vulnerability to optical illusions is influenced by the kinds of spaces we've lived in throughout our lives (Henrich et al., 2010). *Ethnography* is a research sensibility and method that attends to these processes: to the ways that the structures, materials, expectations, and beliefs around us inevitably shape our ways of being in the world.

The word "ethnography" derives from the Greek words *ethnos* (meaning people, nation, class, caste, or tribe) and *graphia* (meaning to write). Contemporary use of the term *ethnography* involves the immersion of the researcher into the everyday, natural, ordinary environments of other people—however people might be distinguished according to nationality, culture, age, profession, experience, disability, etc.—in order to better understand

and convey something about the perspectives of insiders within that world. The term is used for both a common set of research practices—field work, participant observation, interviews that range from casual conversations to in-depth explorations, note-taking, and write-up—and their outcome: an "ethnography of" a particular place, topic, and/or phenomenon. The word can be used to describe both a method and a methodology, a set of techniques and an overall sensibility about how scientific knowledge is embedded within particular ways of life. For psychologists, ethnography allows us to build an evidence base that appreciates how human experience is contingent on time and place, past and future, and larger social horizons.

Attention to the social context and meaning of psychological phenomena is fundamental to psychology as a scientific practice (Gone, 2011), an observation that dates back to the foundations of the field. Wilhelm Wundt (1916/2018) defended studying "folk [or cultural] psychology" after observing that instrumentation he used in his pioneering work in experimental psychology was limited when addressing questions about meaning, language, and social values. William James (1912/1976) defended a "radical empiricism" that called upon researchers to prioritize human

The authors would like to thank both Thomas S. Weisner and Linda McMullen for comments on an earlier draft of this manuscript.

https://doi.org/10.1037/0000319-009

APA Handbook of Research Methods in Psychology, Second Edition: Vol. 2. Research Designs: Quantitative, Qualitative, Neuropsychological, and Biological, H. Cooper (Editor-in-Chief)

experience in itself and to stop treating psychological constructs as naturally existing. Alexander Luria (1976) found in Uzbekistan that even something as fundamental as perception is shaped by social conditions. And Lev Vygotsky (1978) argued that all human mental functioning is mediated through cultural tools and artifacts; from this perspective, "society is the bearer of the cultural heritage without which the development of mind is impossible" (Cole & Wertsch, 1996, p. 253).

Today, researchers recognize that what we know of mental illness and its treatment is inherently steeped in social factors, a perspective recognized in the *DSM-5*, which states that "all forms of distress are locally shaped—including DSM disorders" (American Psychiatric Association, 2013, p. 758). There is increasing awareness that psychology research must move beyond taken-for-granted assumptions about cognition, perception, reasoning, and the self arising out of the WEIRD (Western, educated, industrial, rich, and democratic) contexts within which much previous research has been conducted (Henrich et al., 2010), especially as transnational migration and globalization destabilize the presumption of fixed relationships between space, nations, cultures, and identities (Bhatia, 2007). These historical trends are consistent with viewing psychology as a human science, avoiding reductionist depictions of experience, meaning, and values by accounting for life as inextricably situated in the broader world (Brooke, 2016; Burston & Frie, 2006; Fischer, 1977; Giorgi, 2014; Laubscher, 2016).

Many psychologists may not be familiar with ethnography because its traditional disciplinary home is in anthropology and sociology. Psychologists have also noted that time constraints, lack of training in ethnographic methods, and the discipline's general adherence to experimental and statistical methods that foreground the individual and the universal over cultural and contextual specificity all contribute to ethnography's underutilization for addressing psychological topics (Bartholomew & Brown, 2019). Nevertheless, ethnography provides critical access to many of psychology's most pressing questions about

culture, development, and social life—dimensions of human experience that are fundamentally embedded in broader worlds.

WHY DO ETHNOGRAPHY?

Scholars might conduct ethnographic research for a number of reasons: out of an interest in the kinds of psychological phenomena that can only be understood in their cultural contexts—as, for example, Patricia Greenfield (2004) and Barbara Rogoff (2011) did in their decades studying Mayan women in southern Mexico and Guatemala to understand cognitive and socialization processes involved in transmitting knowledge across generations, or as Gaskins et al. (1992) did in their approach to children's play and its impact on development in specific social settings. Or they may be seeking to develop psychological concepts that are closer to those that are lived and local, as Catherine Lutz (1988) did when she studied the particular words for emotions—and the particular emotions those words describe—on the Micronesian atoll of Ifaluk. Perhaps they want to understand how "people's participation in cultural practices is essential to the scientific study of learning" (Lee et al., 2020, p. xvii), given that "psychological development . . . reflects the incorporation and embodiment—literally, 'taking into the body'—of blueprints for psychological experience deposited over historical time in the structure of everyday cultural worlds" (Adams & Kurtiş, 2018, p. 162).

Ethnography can help us get a better sense of the relationship between what people say and what they do, as Hartmann et al. (2018) did when they observed the relationship between "culture talk" and cultural practice (i.e., the difference between explicitly articulated understandings of culture and the tacit, value-laden assumptions that shape everyday practice) in a Native American behavioral health clinic (see also Gone & Alcántara, 2010). As Gobo and Marciniak (2016) pointed out, ethnography provides opportunity for "observing actions and behaviours instead of opinions and attitudes only" (p. 113). When we are able to do so, the consequences are not only theoretical . . . but also practical, because a closer view of the routines and practices of social actors facilitates the crafting of remedies and solutions to social problems. In other words, it is easier to outline proposed social, political, or organizational changes after having directly observed partici- pants' actual social actions. (p. 113)

Thus, another reason to do ethnography is because it helps us to get something done, to make some kind of difference in the world: to bear witness, shape policy, or seek justice. When incor- porated into intervention research, ethnography can provide evidence about why the predicted impacts did and did not occur, what participa- tion in the intervention meant to participants, and how to design and implement changes for better policy and practice (Duncan et al., 2007). Ethnography can be transformative, informing action towards social and political change in a way that is responsive to the particular conditions and priorities of those most directly affected. When McGranahan (2014) asked anthropologist Kirin Narayan the question "Why ethnography?" Narayan responded,

> For the discipline of paying attention; for becoming more responsibly aware of inequalities; for better understanding of the social forces causing suffering and how people might somehow find hope; and most generally, for being perpetually pulled beyond the limits of one's own taken-for-granted world. (p. 33)

Ethnography can also be personally trans- formative, leading the researcher to cultivate their own adaptivity and responsiveness in confronta- tion and/or collaboration with unfamiliar social lifeways. Such confrontations with other ways of doing, thinking and knowing can shake up fixed disciplinary assumptions or practices in a con- structive and generative way. Ethnography also allows us to communicate these new insights,

as Adler and Adler (1987) pointed out, with a vividness available to few other scholarly techniques: ". . . no surprise, then, that the books that students overwhelmingly remember, that touch closest to their emotional chords, are usually ethnographies" (p. 17).

RESEARCH DESIGN IN ETHNOGRAPHY

Research design in ethnography requires careful planning alongside an openness to the unexpected. The ethnographer needs to select and hone a research question or topic; locate a situation through which to investigate that question or topic; and arrange, in collaboration with the people who are in that situation, how they will participate in it. In what follows, we discuss each of these steps. While we have organized this chapter in a roughly chronological way—starting by formulating a research question, moving on to choosing a site and situating oneself there, then gathering the data, analyzing the data, and finally writing them up—the actual process of doing ethnography is often somewhat less linear and more reflexive and iterative. Ethnographers may refine their research question while in the field; the writing process really begins with the taking of notes during data collection; the researcher may alternate between data collection and analysis, and the two may not feel like distinctly separate phases, as the ethnographer's growing sense of what's going on in the field shapes their attention to what is taking place around and through them.

Developing a Question

Ethnographic projects often begin with a question: a specific curiosity informed both by what the researcher knows (or thinks they know) and by what they do not already know and want to understand better. Elizabeth's research project (Fein, 2020) with youth on the autism spectrum, for example, was inspired by debates in the autism community about whether autism should be considered a disease to be eradicated or a minority identity to be protected. These alternatives were often presented as radically incompatible, funda- mentally irreconcilable. Yet the young people on the spectrum that she encountered in her clinical practice grew up steeped in both of these understandings and seemed to be drawing on both in their understandings of autism—so how did they do that? Jonathan's (Yahalom, 2019) ethnography on caregiving in Oaxaca, Mexico, started with his observation that in the United States Alzheimer's disease was often a solitary experience that threatened the core of personhood, as defined by values centered on cognition, autonomy, and self-determination. How might a similar set of mental changes be experienced elsewhere, like Oaxaca—a more collectivistic setting known for its social cohesion?

Ethnographic research often starts with a moment of informed perplexity—what Miller and her colleagues (2003) called an "interpretive puzzle." For Miller, it was the question of why middle-class parents in Chicago avoid telling stories about their children's transgressions when parents in other settings, like Taiwan, consider this a valuable tool in child socialization (Miller et al., 2003). For Luhrmann (2012), it is the "puzzle of belief": How do we sustain religious faith in entities whose existence we cannot confirm with our senses? Or perhaps the researcher wants to use ethnography to question popular assumptions about the meanings and manifestations of behavior. For example, Alper (2018) contested depictions of "screen time" as passive consumption by observing (and playing, twirling, spinning, and jumping with) youth with disabilities as they engage actively with a wide range of digital technologies—a process that involved showing up with her whole body in an "inclusive sensory ethnography."

Regardless of their motivation, the most useful ethnographic research questions are both flexible and focused. Such questions allow the researcher to adapt to the unexpected discoveries that can be the greatest gift and challenge of field work, while also protecting them from being overwhelmed by floods of data as they learn to focus their attention on what is most relevant. If Elizabeth had gone into the field merely thinking, "I want to understand how young people on the spectrum talk and think about autism," she would have

been unsure what to record, attend to, and analyze. Centering her project on how youth use two models of autism that she had previously identified through analyzing popular discourse—autism as disease and autism as identity—helped focus her observations around the terms and concepts that constitute those models. Surprisingly, partway into her field work, Elizabeth began to notice that her young informants were providing rich, vivid accounts of embodied differences that were both disease-like and identity-like—yet they were doing so not when talking about autism but when imaginatively depicting themselves as the demon-possessed antiheroes of fantasy literature during their informal creative play. Listening for these particular themes, and their coexistences, helped her find them somewhere unexpected.

The ethnographer engages in a careful balancing act when developing a research question: preparing for the field by studying previous related research; identifying what might be misperceived, missing, or overlooked from current understandings; and reflecting on one's own biases. Developing a research question is enhanced by the degree to which one is informed by previous studies and aware of implicit social dynamics. While the ethnographer's expectations are likely to be revised in the course of doing research, they also provide a preliminary roadmap.

Delineating a Site

Choosing a research site—a particular situation through which to attend to the phenomenon in question, in some situation-specific manifestation—is one of the most consequential decisions an ethnographer faces. And yet, for all its importance, the nature of "what is the field" is far from obvious (Gupta & Ferguson, 1997). People often lead multicultural lives, belonging to communities that traverse traditional geographic, ethnic, and linguistic boundaries. For example, upon starting his field work in Oaxaca, Jonathan learned that Oaxacans experienced what Stephen (2007) terms *transborder life*—speaking Zapotec at home but Spanish to outsiders, crossing the U.S.–Mexico border for business, and maintaining local traditions while living abroad. Indeed, to his surprise, Jonathan was able to converse about his own U.S. background and hometown streets with relative ease after learning that a large contingency of Oaxacans had migrated to a town near where he grew up. The way in which Jonathan's research participants traversed cultural, linguistic, economic, and geographic boundaries exemplifies the multicultural nature of many contemporary ethnographies (e.g., Duncan, 2018; Holmes, 2013; Tsing, 2015).

Contemporary ethnographers commonly observe that local culture is often woven within global trends (Wilk, 2006) and that there are multiple and seemingly exclusive factors that comprise an individual's everyday lived experience (Holstein & Gubrium, 2000). Hence, in conducting ethnography, there exists an implicit awareness of the "arbitrariness of boundary making" when deciding what, whom, or where to study (Connor, 2001) and that the ethnographer might instead be "concerned with articulation of the global and local, [that is to say] how globalizing processes exist in the context of realities of particular societies" (Inda & Rosaldo, 2002, p. 7). For this reason, contemporary ethnography can also be—indeed, often becomes—multisited, taking place in different locations, across different modes of communication (including online interaction), among nominally different groups of people, settings, and ways of life. Ethnographers may follow or "trace" the topic of their research extemporaneously, wherever it manifests, across different locations, among different people, and through various traditionally defined boundaries (Packer, 2017; Wacquant, 2011). Elizabeth's current research project, at the time of this writing, is on autism in the furry community, an international subculture drawn together by appreciation for anthropomorphic animals. The work takes place not only at conventions and other social events where furries come together but also on the internet and social media apps like Telegram, through art commissions, and within other such geographically dispersed symbolic exchanges; the movement between these different kinds of social spaces opens up new possibilities for sociability (Magnifico et al., 2018).

Digital technologies are transforming shared social spaces and with them, ethnographic theory and practice. "Ethnography *in, of,* and *through* the virtual" (Hine, 2000, p. 65) requires us to rethink our ideas about space, place, location, and embodiment; the nature of phenomena under study; and the methods through which we work. New technologies shape our experiences of self and relationship (Gergen, 1991). Digital spaces are themselves varied in their nature and in the connections between them: studying "virtual worlds" designed to be immersive will call for different ethnographic approaches than studying participation in loosely linked systems of apps and digital platforms (Góralska, 2020).

Place matters, of course. Geography continues to have an impact on lifeworlds: Ecologies and their multispecies coexistences are shaped by contours of land and water; federal, state, national, and international policies constrain and facilitate opportunity; the way built structures are arranged shapes the way in which people engage with and within them (Adams, 2016; Fullilove, 1996; Simms, 2008; Snyder, 2020). But community can be constituted in many ways—through geography, perhaps, but also through affinity, as with furries, or with players drawn to a particular online game world (Gee, 2004), or through communities of practice characterized by "situated learning," such as the tailors and butchers described by Lave and Wenger (1991), or through "processes involving configurations of relations among different actors or institutions" involved in mutual dependence, struggle or conflict, as in the "relational ethnographies" proposed by Desmond (2014, p. 547), or through contested and even invisible claims to kinship, as Leite (2017) described in her study of Marrano ("hidden Jews") in Portugal. Meanwhile, individual participants are likely to occupy an intersectional array of identities, positions, and places, as (for example) Jenkins and Csordas (2020) observed in their study of the varied experiences of adolescents receiving psychiatric treatment in the American Southwest.

So the ethnographer has some nonobvious questions to ask themselves, along the lines of: Where is the thing happening? What is the situation through which the process of interest is taking place, and how is it situated? Figuring this out can require some immersion in and of itself. At one of her first furry get-togethers, Elizabeth had to be told repeatedly by one of her furry interlocutors to join the social media platform Telegram before she actually finally did it, at which point a whole new dimension of the social world opened up to her. For the ethnographer, doing research that is defined by culture and place, these considerations constitute much of the research process.

Arranging Access

Negotiating access to a community for research purposes is among the more delicate opening stages of the long-lasting and often complicated relationships that make up ethnographic practice. Prior to commencing field work, and after identifying what participants and settings the ethnographer wants to study, the ethnographer begins to develop relationships and introduce themselves to the community of interest. Depending on the setting, making initial contact can occur remotely, although the ethnographer can benefit from physically visiting the field as well. Initial access can take the form of emailing or calling possible participants, working through existing social connections, or reaching out to previous researchers who have already established themselves in the field. Arranging ethnographic field work also often involves obtaining official permission from institutions that may constitute part of the field site, such as schools, clinics, churches, or other organizations. Although this stage might be considered preparatory, in reality it is already a part of field work—even remote contact with participants gives the ethnographer a preliminary, firsthand perspective of the social dynamics inherent to the field.

There is no single approach to establishing contact, but it is advantageous for the ethnographer to initiate contact in a manner that is congruent with local social practices. When, for example, Jonathan was still in Pittsburgh, he initially emailed Oaxacan community centers, only to find they were not responsive. He later came to understand

that community members were uncomfortable collaborating with foreigners about an intimate family topic like Alzheimer's. Eventually, Jonathan was introduced to a local resident who expressed interest in his research. They developed a correspondence and later formed a working relationship that became central to his project. Within a community that would have otherwise viewed him with reservation, Jonathan was introduced as a friend of a trusted neighbor, and this gradually allowed other individuals to develop trust in him as well.

Common challenges to maintaining access often involve logistics (e.g., maintaining physical presence), language (e.g., understanding linguistic differences, including differences between professional and lay language), and social norms (e.g., stigma, discomfort talking, and discomfort being observed). For this reason, the ethnographer must maintain awareness of their own position in relation to cultural norms and how others perceive them. When Jonathan arrived in Oaxaca intent on studying Alzheimer's, he was told that not a single case existed in the community. He later came to appreciate that Alzheimer's was highly stigmatized in the community, as it was understood to be caused by family negligence and the abandonment of cultural traditions. He readapted his focus to this social reality, inquiring instead about families who cared for forgetful elders.

The ethnographer strives to observe the ordinary routines and practices that constitute a given way of life—to be in sync with the social rhythms of participants—and to develop insight into the implicit thoughts, emotions, and experiences that underlie experience. However, people also change what they say or do when they know they are being observed (Suchman & Jordan, 1990). Indeed, as Packer (2017) noted, the ethnographer is not an inconspicuous observer of everyday life but, at best, strives to achieve "obtrusive access"—their very presence as researcher is disruptive, a departure from ordinary affairs. Over time, though, the researcher's presence can become routinized, accepted, and even woven into the fold of everyday lived experience. Hence, the ethnographer at once strives to collect data that are as congruent as possible with everyday life, while remaining aware of how conducting research might alter the phenomena under study.

Access concerns not only how data are logistically acquired but also a larger epistemological stance about the type of data the ethnographer is collecting. Instead of being concerned that data are sampled to represent a given population (as would be the case for researchers who conduct studies by random sampling), the ethnographer also deliberately makes choices about whom to study, knowing that the data they collect is specific to people engaged in specific activities. As Miller et al. (2003) wrote on this point, "Each ethnographer will come to an understanding that is inevitably partial. The rigor of this approach lies partly in delineating that partiality, which itself contains clues as to how local meanings are constructed" (p. 226). Rigor can also be found through triangulating multiple sources of data and multiple perspectives from local allies, family members, and people throughout the community. In her study, Elizabeth listened closely to people on the autism spectrum, their families, and the professionals who worked with them in order to get a sense of how their perspectives on the topic differed and converged. The decision about whom and what to study can be informed by the ethnographer's research question, through identifying which participants, social settings, and behaviors are most relevant to that topic of interest.

CONDUCTING THE RESEARCH

What does an ethnographer actually do when doing research? And how long does an ethnographer remain in the field? There are varying answers to these questions. For some research topics, a "focused" or "mini" ethnography might make sense and occur within a few weeks or months (Simonds et al., 2012; Weinstein & Ventres, 2000); for other topics, especially those invested in varying nuances of social life, a more sustained year or multiyear commitment to the field is justified.

In what follows, we focus on three components of ethnographic data collection: participant obser-

vation, field note writing, and interviews. Though we focus this section on these areas, numerous other techniques can contribute to the fidelity and utility of an ethnographic project (Levitt et al., 2017). As Weisner (2012), Hay (2016), and Small (2011) argued, ethnographic research can be strengthened through the integration of mixed methods hailing from both traditions that have been called *quantitative* and those called *qualitative*, foregrounding their common questions and goals. Surveys and questionnaires, assessment tools, and structured activities such as sorting techniques can be constructively synthesized with interview narratives, observations, and arts-based methods. Multiple sources of data can be brought together with a variety of intentions, such as to confirm findings or to make them more robust, to expand those findings into new domains, or to elucidate some of their underlying mechanisms of action. Creswell and Clark (2017) provided a series of step-by-step roadmaps for thinking through the process of triangulating various sorts and sources of data (see also Webb et al., 1981).

Participant Observation

Participant observation is usually considered to be the cornerstone of ethnographic research, the standard practice through which the bulk of ethnographic data gathering takes place. The ethnographer immerses themselves in the daily life of a community (however that community is defined), hanging out among members in the spaces where that life takes place. Through participant observation, the researcher seeks to gain a sense of the actions and activities, rituals and routines, and daily practices that constitute that life and their meanings for participants. To the extent possible, the ethnographer takes part in these activities, learning through experience and sometimes through mentorship what insiders to the community already know, and adding to that knowledge their own unique perspective as a sensitive and theoretically informed guest. Sometimes the ethnographer sits on the sidelines observing these activities; other times the ethnographer is in the thick of it, doing their best to do (that is, participate in) the way of life they want to understand. In either case, the researcher is a part of the field that they are learning from and about and is contributing to the scene by being present within it.

Here are some things that Elizabeth has done under the umbrella of participant observation: attended classes at a junior high school; played a mad scientist in a futuristic, live-action role-playing game; helped to lead an "exploring the city" social group for young adults on the autism spectrum; sat around the waiting room of a research lab; filled out paperwork; attended support groups; presented at a conference for autism researchers; participated in a collective reading aloud of the phone book; danced in costume at a rave party; met with a lawyer; drank beer at a makeshift outdoor bar; had blood drawn; and attended a workshop on writing erotic fiction. Here are some things that Jonathan has done under the umbrella of participant observation: shared meals with families as they kept a watchful eye on their elders; visited markets and ran errands for families; studied Zapotec in language class; danced at an event celebrating Oaxacan elders; attended community lectures about healthy aging; witnessed hospital intake processes; visited local healers; engaged locals about the local news; attended a local psychiatry conference on aging; and raised a cup of mezcal to cheer life and health at religious, family, and wedding parties. What all these diverse activities have in common is that they allowed us to gain a better understanding of how the participants in our respective communities enact, experience, and negotiate the meanings of their lives.

Writing Field Notes

What differentiates ethnography from everyday hanging out? One of the key steps to move from experience to ethnographic data is the careful documentation of that experience through the writing of field notes. Writing is an intrinsic element of the ethnographic process, and it begins in the field, as the ethnographer keeps written records of their experiences, observations, and emergent sense-making. Keeping detailed notes is a key component of maintaining rigor, fidelity, and

veridicality in ethnographic data collection. As psychologists know, our memory is a fickle place. Moments that feel so intense and significant as to be unforgettable fade from memory with astonishing speed, their details blurring together and our minds filling in the blanks with our own assumptions and expectations. Careful, thorough, and attentive note-taking keeps us honest and aware of our own constructive and reconstructive work as we strive to represent and report our experiences in the field. Writing up events as they occur (rather than trying to reconstruct them far after the fact) allows the researcher to capture their own unfolding understanding of events, benefitting from the insights that come with encountering the previously unfamiliar. Field notes are integral to the data set that the ethnographer weaves into the analysis, as much or more so than the interview data. The researcher should allow several hours per day to this part of the process—sometimes a difficult commitment to honor when it involves stepping away from the fascinating doings of one's field site.

The most comprehensive guide to field note writing is Emerson et al.'s (2011) *Writing Ethnographic Field Notes* (see also Sanjek, 1990). They divide the process of writing field notes into three phases: quickly scribbling "jottings" in the field, turning those jottings into filled-out written accounts "at the desk," and then transforming those field notes into "scenes on the page" for publication. As they observe, taking notes in public is one of the clearest performances of the ethnographer's role. Visible note-taking immediately differentiates the ethnographer from others as someone who is there not only to participate but also to observe and document in writing. It can produce a range of situation-specific consequences, ranging from awkwardness, embarrassment, and fear on the part of research participants to a deeper understanding and fuller support of the ethnographer's role and purpose. Furthermore, the very act of writing itself has different meanings in different communities. The ethnographer needs to be sensitive to the ways in which note-taking is perceived by members of the community in which they work. There are some places, like a classroom, where it's easy to write notes all day. There are other situations, like when cooking or doing other hands-on activities, where it's harder. At such moments, Elizabeth's technique is to keep a running mental list of single reminder words or brief phrases (*keyhole; too abstract; who's a derp; wolverine*) that she repeats in her mind until she can write them down in a quick list on the small pad she carries in her pocket—perhaps during a brief visit to a private place such as a bathroom or empty hallway. Those lists then serve as prompts to elaborate at the end of the day—she likes to stop at a diner on the way home and write notes over dinner, then return home to finish them up.

When inscribing the day's events in a longer set of field notes, the researcher writes them down in as much detail as possible as soon as possible—the same day if at all possible, before sleeping, before processing the day's events with a friend or partner. The most useful field notes foreground description over evaluation: "Jennifer got angry in a really inappropriate way" will be less helpful in the long run than a description of what in Jennifer's behavior suggested she was angry and what responses this behavior provoked from community members. That being said, the ethnographer's own appraisal of Jennifer's expression of anger is useful data as well. Many ethnographers hold deliberate spaces within their notes to track their own feelings, reactions, and emerging assessment of phenomena in the field. When psychological anthropologist Jean Briggs (1970) was living with and learning from an Inuit community, her first indication that she had grievously violated social norms against expressing anger came when she noticed herself feeling cold, sad, and under the weather. Only with time did she realize that she was being ostracized by community members, and with that realization came a new understanding of the subtlety and power of their emotional expression. Attention to the ethnographer's own positions, actions and behaviors, their "activities, circumstances, and emotional responses" (Emerson et al., 2011, p. 15) constitute an important part of ethnographic documentation.

Interviewing

Ethnographic studies often also involve interviews with members of the community being studied. These interviews may be very structured, with the same or similar sets of questions and follow-up probes being asked of all participants. They may be semistructured, with a list of topics guiding the interview while also giving space for the conversation to travel in unexpected directions. Or they may be quite open-ended, allowing the interviewee to take up the topic of the interview however they see fit—or to suggest topics that matter to them. Participants may be interviewed multiple times over the course of a given project. Formal interviews might mix with informal conversations and other interactions.

Interviews can serve many different purposes. They can help the ethnographer to gather information about a setting and its parameters and everyday practices, to assess the reasoning, motivations, beliefs, desires, and intentions of participants, and to infer the implicit cultural models and the mental tools people are using to make sense of their surroundings. In their work on "person-centered interviewing," Levy and Hollan (1998) observed the ways that these interviews engage the interviewee as both an informant, "that is, as a knowledgeable person who can tell the anthropologist-interviewer about culture and behavior in a particular locale" and also as a respondent, by which they mean "as an object of systematic study and observation in him- or herself" (pp. 335–336). Ethnographic interviewing can also provide key information regarding which beliefs and practices are shared as part of cultural models and schemas, and which are more idiosyncratic to individuals or subgroups in a community.

Whatever their purpose, interviews are rarely a transparent transmission of the internal state of an interviewee; they are complex communicative events that are powerfully shaped by the developing relationship between the ethnographer and the interview coparticipant(s). In addition to ensuring that interviews align with the research question, interview techniques should also align as closely as possible to participants' cultural norms around interaction, mentorship, and information sharing (Briggs, 1986). The ethnographer must not only strategize about whom to interview but also make important decisions about conducting individual versus group interviews and single occurrence versus longitudinal interviews, the setting where interviews take place, and language. Prior to arriving to Oaxaca, Jonathan anticipated conducting individual interviews with dementia caregivers in Spanish. Yet upon engaging with locals, he recognized that his research plan did not align with Oaxacan social life: People did not feel comfortable talking about intimate family life to a person outside the community, they were more familiar speaking in Zapotec than Spanish, and they understood themselves in the context of their membership to the larger household. Jonathan adapted to these circumstances by conducting focus group interviews with entire households (rather than individual interviews), by having those interviews be guided by a local research assistant (rather than conducting them himself), and by inviting participants to speak in Zapotec. Interview strategies are ideally developed prior to field work, based on previous review of relevant research, and subsequently adapted to the realities encountered firsthand, but they may also require revision based on the realities the ethnographer encounters.

Embracing the Unexpected

At least implicitly, the ethnographic approach to conducting research understands data much like Michel Foucault (1972) characterized "discourse"—what is interesting for the ethnographer exceeds the explicit things said or observed and includes the broader social practices, implicit power relations, and forms of subjectivity that constitute human experience. This approach to data invites the ethnographer to benefit from embracing the unexpected hurdles, surprises, and blunders that so often arise during field work.

Ethnographic lore is full of stories of ethnographers who arrive at a site only to discover that the site, as they envisioned it, has become inaccessible: it has closed, or changed, or the imagined phenomenon-site relationship is actually completely different from what they expected. The practice has gone out of style and nobody does it anymore; the belief cannot be discussed with outsiders; the religion has been eradicated by evangelical missionaries. For her dissertation research, Elizabeth had planned a year-long comparison of two treatment sites taking different approaches to autism, had made arrangements with each to conduct the field work, and had moved halfway across the country to do so. Each of them closed down (for reasons unrelated to the project!) within a month of her arrival. Having formed some strong relationships during that first month with some people who were then willing to help her out, she wound up arranging a multisite ethnography that brought her to a variety of classrooms, support groups, research laboratories, and clinics. In doing so, she gained a fuller picture of the confusing journeys youth on the spectrum and their families go through as they seek both help and a sense of belonging.

In contrast to viewing these experiences as something to minimize or overcome during research, we encourage researchers to embrace a type of "methodological agility" wherein methods accommodate to the contingencies of a given field site (Yahalom, 2020). This approach posits that unexpected setbacks to research can be advantages in themselves; they serve as invitations to strengthen design rigor by directly addressing, embracing, and understanding the broader structures that contextualize the data the ethnographer seeks to acquire. Further, remaining agile helps redefine research categories to become more congruent with local realities. Of course, there is a limit to agility, and some external constraints and research setbacks can simply be losses. Agencies can refuse access, key community members might decline to participate, or the institutional review board of an ethnographer's institution could reject a research proposal. While this fact is true of most research, ethnography renders the parameters of research more explicit by attending to the way data are situated in broader social dynamics.

While immersed in the field, the ethnographer continuously encounters additional information on local culture—that is to say, data that might not have been anticipated but nevertheless come to be valuable. During one of the first weeks of his year of field work, Jonathan stumbled upon a local newspaper with a front-page headline that announced, "20 ALZHEIMER'S CASES HAVE BEEN DETECTED." He was struck by the way Alzheimer's was here portrayed as an epidemic, in language that was similar to news stories about the Ebola virus. The story put into focus the way Alzheimer's was perceived locally as something new and alarming, a threat facing the Oaxacan community. There are many such things the ethnographer encounters in the course of data collection that are not solely based on interviews and field notes: the collection of a pamphlet, the texture of a piece of fabric, a child's drawing. The researcher is likely to collect a number of such cultural artifacts while in the field. They might also make detailed maps of the community: where do people live, work, and socialize? How are shared and private spaces arranged? How are different virtual spaces linked together, and how visible and accessible are these links? They may take field recordings, capturing the ambient sound in a space or a musical performance. They may take photographs, or encourage their participants to take photographs on topics of interest to the ethnographer or participants. Any of these materials can also be worked into interviews on these topics. Ethnographers may make drawings, both formal and informal—anthropologist Michael Taussig (2011) has written an entire book about the role of the drawings he made in his own field notes. As such, an ethnographic data corpus is often far more than a series of texts, requiring agility, thoughtfulness, and creativity from the researcher in both data collection and analysis.

PRODUCING RESULTS

Data Analysis

Alongside and after acquiring this mass of stuff—field notes, interview recordings and transcripts, photos, maps, surveys, field recordings, drawings, artifacts, perhaps a few scars—comes the task of making sense of it all. Ethnographic projects require a discrete, dedicated phase of working through the data, and the ethnographer should allow ample time for this phase of work in their research plan. Ethnographic data, and qualitative methods research more generally, now also have the advantage of a number of software tools to organize what often becomes a hefty data set. Moreover, computer software makes it possible to collaborate more efficiently and transparently with larger research teams (Deutsch & Tolan, 2018).

Compared to the vivid depictions of field work and the careful articulation of a research question that can be found in many ethnographic texts, the work of data analysis can seem somewhat murky and mysterious. There is little consensus around a single best approach to ethnographic data analysis; the techniques chosen by the researcher are guided instead by their own epistemological commitments. A researcher working within a constructivist grounded theory tradition should take a different approach from a researcher steeped in Foucauldian discourse analysis. However, in our opinion, there are a few guiding principles that all ethnographers would do well to keep in mind during this phase.

The first is to make these commitments as explicit and intentional as possible within one's own research design. In this, as in all phases of the research process, researchers should work toward what the American Psychological Association's Task Force on Resources for Qualitative Research Publication refers to as *methodological integrity*:

> Integrity is established when research designs and procedures (e.g., auto-ethnography, discursive analysis) support the research goals (i.e., the research problems/questions); respect the researcher's approaches to inquiry (i.e., research traditions sometimes described as world views, paradigms, or philosophical/epistemological assumptions); and are tailored for fundamental characteristics of the subject matter and the investigators. (Levitt et al., 2017, pp. 9–10)

From the very inception of the project, researchers should have a plan in mind for how they will work with the data they collect, including a plan for how to integrate data from multiple sources. Therefore, it is helpful for the ethnographer to familiarize themselves with a range of methodologies in order to design an approach that best fits the data and research question.

Secondly, this plan can, and in many cases should, include ample flexibility for adjustment in response to discoveries that take place both during and after field work. As Richard Shweder (1997) articulated,

> Ethnography is about discovery . . . It is about entering the field without totally predefining the domain of interest and without presuming that you already know what is universal, because most of the time those presumptive universals are generated out of one's own perspective-dependent, context-dependent, and hence local world. (p. 154)

Hence, when conducting data analysis, the ethnographer benefits from suspending or bracketing their own understanding of things, and attempts to glean understanding through, or "abduct" from, the data (Timmermans & Tavory, 2012). As Quinn (2005) observed, this quality of naturalistic research makes it difficult if not impossible to precisely specify analysis methods in advance, and researchers are often in a position to develop their own methods based on the particular requirements of the material they encounter; this makes it all the more important to think carefully and critically about the rationales that guide methodological decisions throughout the process.

Lastly, the plan should involve the opportunity for deep and iterative immersion into the data—multiple passes through interview transcripts and field notes, strategies for reconsidering prior conclusions in light of new perspectives, opportunities to become familiar with the full contents of what is likely to be a dauntingly rich and varied data set. For Elizabeth, for whom a

2-year period of field work left her with four large binders of field notes, over 100 lengthy interview transcripts, and numerous artifacts including newsletters from various organizations, copies of medical records, and drawings and comics created by participants, the first step was to create a numbered catalogue of each item. While this was somewhat helpful when she needed to find things later, its main benefit was to help her familiarize herself more deeply with what she had.

Ethnographic Writing

Toward the end of analysis, and after gaining a sense of findings, the ethnographer begins to formally organize and draft study results. The presentation of research findings can take many forms, both within and beyond written texts. While it remains commonplace to write a textual account of research findings, contemporary ethnographers have also begun to challenge conventional understanding of the nature of text, producing ethnographies in the forms of graphic novels (Hamdy & Nye, 2017; McMullin, 2016), film (Barnard & Borges, 2016; Lemelson & Tucker, 2017), and other creative forms.

Ethnographic writing is both a product of the social sciences that produces unique, valid, veridical, and scientific understanding, as well as a self-reflexive narrative about the development of that understanding. In one sense, the ethnographer is aware that no written account is complete in itself—that with more time in the field, additional experiences with a given group, and further research on history, language, and culture, the ethnographer would acquire greater (and perhaps different) understanding. That is why ethnographic writing is often told through narrating the story of research, reflecting on how findings are contingent (rooted in particular encounters with specific people, in distinct places), and conveying that those findings could have been different had the story of research been different. And yet, in another sense, ethnography is more than narrative. It systematically documents, analyzes, and builds upon our understandings of the nuanced facets of human experience. It expands previous empirical knowledge, and engages with the broader scientific community. That is why ethnography is not experimental, but it is scientific—at its core, it is a systematic study of structure, behavior, and experience through sustained observation, inquiry and analysis. The best of ethnographic writing holds these tensions in place, producing text that is characterized by both reflexive humility and empirically minded rigor.

Perhaps the most defining feature of writing ethnography involves what Geertz (1973) famously popularized as *thick description*. This term refers to the ethnographer's goal of writing to provide a qualitatively nuanced (or *thick*) perspective of social life, combining observations drawn in the field (e.g., about behaviors) with deeper dimensions of lived experience (e.g., the meaning people imbue to things, the emotions they feel, and the strategies involved in decision making). With thick description, the ethnographer attempts to make sense of what is underneath the surface by attending to implicit power relations, subtle social practices, and other forms of subjectivity that constitute everyday life. This approach to writing avoids being reductionistic—that is to say, it does not reify or simplify inherently complex experience. Instead, in the words of Clifford (1988), ethnographic writing "struggle[s] self-consciously to avoid portraying abstract, ahistorical 'others'" (p. 23). One way to do that is by highlighting the agency behind decision making and what Kleinman (1997) described as being "at stake" in people's everyday lives. For example, the observation that Alzheimer's carries social stigma in Oaxaca is a thinner description than the observation that Jonathan made later in his field work that Alzheimer's is seen as the consequence of family neglect—and that neglect has particular meaning in a setting marked by social change due to poverty and migration. What was at stake about recognizing Alzheimer's was Oaxacans' acknowledging that their community is beginning to change.

Writing about other people is inherently complicated, and the ethnographer encounters questions about representation: how to describe people in a manner that is informative, honest, sensitive, and ethical. Any form of research on another cultural group risks engaging in what Said (1978) famously called the "politics of othering" (see also Abu-Lughod, 1991). The ethnographer faces many questions in writing about other people. Do I write with my participants in mind as a potential audience? Will I return to this community with my research findings— and if so, how, and when in the process? Am I concerned that what I observe of their experience is agreeable to them? What might other readers, outside the community, be led to do with the information I provide? There is no single way to answer these questions, but it is generally a best practice to remain ethically minded and maintain a strategy that avoids harm and maintains respect for the people one studies.

The ethnographer often faces difficult decisions about what to include for the purposes of advancing scientific understanding and what to omit out of concern for the privacy, well-being, and safety of others. Removing, altering, or creating composite character details is common practice in ethnographic writing; when authors describe their process of doing so, it contributes to the integrity and usefulness of their final product.

In addition to writing with thick description that highlights people's agency, the ethnographer also strives to represent people with respect and dignity. This means not only writing to describe the details of someone's lived experience but to do so with respect for their values and appreciation for how those values arose in the context of their lives. Equally important, the ethnographer writes in a manner that strives to bear witness and do justice to participants' everyday experience— chronicling with compassion the struggles, aspirations, losses, and stagnation that people experience. Behar (1996) asked of the central dilemma of writing on human tragedy, "If you can't stop the horror, shouldn't you at least document it?" (p. 2). Many ethnographers hold rhetorical questions like this to heart, viewing writing itself as a critical element of social justice and advancing awareness of potentially overlooked dimensions of human experience that can invite action for needed change (see also Case et al., 2014; Weis & Fine, 2012).

Concerns about writing for the purposes of social justice also evoke the history of ethnography itself. Early ethnographic projects of the late 19th and early 20th century made claims to objectivity and transparent representation that occluded the ways in which these observations often distorted the lives of the people involved, supporting scientific racism and projects of colonial domination and exploitation. The latter half of the 20th century brought an increased focus on reflexivity,[1] interpretation, and the possibility of a more collaborative research ethic, characterized by the co-construction of knowledge, the importance of humility on the part of the researcher, and a recognition of the political potentialities of ethnographic findings. Efforts to "decolonize ethnography" (Bejarano et al., 2019) led to understanding research participants as "epistemic agents and interlocutors, rather than informants" (Nev Jones, quoted in Aftab, 2020): community partners who contribute theory and interpretation as well as data, whose practical and political interests shape the form and format of research products, and who could be involved and credited as coauthors. Ethnographers write with awareness of these historical trends and attempt to move toward a more equitable and honest way to represent the subject of their research.

A FEW FINAL THOUGHTS

This chapter has introduced some of the major issues and questions to consider for a psychology researcher thinking of embarking upon an ethnographic project. For those who want to learn more, there are many useful methods guides available: Hammersley and Atkinson's (2019) *Ethnography: Principles in Practice* and Angrosino's (2007) *Doing Ethnographic and Observational Research* for a general introduction to ethnographic techniques; Packer's (2017) *The Science of Qualitative Research* as a guide to further considering the epistemological and practical questions of ethnographic research; Creswell and Clark's (2017) *Designing and Conducting Mixed Methods Research* on integrating qualitative and quantitative data into a thoughtful research design; Briggs' (1986) *Learning How to Ask: A Sociolinguistic Appraisal of the Role of the Interview in Social Science Research* and the volume *Finding Culture in Talk: A Collection of Methods* edited by Quinn (2005) for approaches to conducting and analyzing interviews in their cultural contexts; *The Routledge Companion to Digital Ethnography* (Hjorth et al., 2017) and *Ethnography and Virtual Worlds: A Handbook of Method* (Boellstorff et al., 2012) for those seeking guidance on conducting ethnographies that engage with virtual or digital spaces. Perhaps most importantly, we recommend that ethnographers read a lot of really good ethnographies, certainly including but also extending beyond their field site, drawing from across the many disciplines in which ethnography is actively used including anthropology, sociology, and psychology. In our own training and development as researchers, the ethnographic books and articles that most moved and inspired us have been important guides and accompaniments through the worlds we have explored.

A theme we have emphasized throughout this chapter is that psychological phenomena exist in a coconstitutive relationship with their contextual and relational surroundings. The decision to conduct ethnography and the decisions that go into its design are no exception. The very possibility of doing ethnographic research is itself constrained and supported by institutional policies (Bartholemew & Brown, 2019), as well as by the personal relationships of the ethnographer—particularly the spouses, children, and other family members and loved ones whose presence (or keenly felt absence) may accompany the ethnographer into the field (Yates-Doerr, 2020).

---

[1]We are using the term *reflexivity* here in the sense defined by Walsh (2003): a process of "turning back upon oneself or upon the subject of study" to take a "second look" (p. 51) at the otherwise taken-for-granted parameters of that research, including the attitudes and expectations of the researcher, the relationship between the researcher and their participants, the theoretical commitments undergirding methodological choices, and the cultural and historical milieu of the work.

Ethnography is a research method that attends to the intersection of psychology and social life. From an ethnographic perspective, any piece of psychological knowledge is incomplete without recourse to the way in which broader communal practices, economic and political structures, shared values, histories, aspirations, and other dimensions of life constitute human experience. As such, ethnography is consistent with many trends within the contemporary field of psychology. Indeed, to quote the first of the American Psychological Association's (2017) *Multicultural Guidelines*,

> Psychologists seek to recognize and understand that identity and self-definition are fluid and complex and that the interaction between the two is dynamic. To this end, psychologists appreciate that intersectionality is shaped by the multiplicity of the individual's social contexts. (p. 6)

Ethnography is a primary way to pursue the multicultural goals of psychology, and we believe it will continue to enhance the scope, rigor, and sophistication of psychological inquiry.

References

Abu-Lughod, L. (1991). Writing against culture. In R. Fox (Ed.), *Recapturing anthropology: Working in the present*. School of American Research Press.

Adams, G., & Kurtiş, T. (2018). Context in person, person in context: A cultural psychology approach to social-personality psychology. In K. Deaux & M. Snyder (Eds.), *The Oxford handbook of personality and social psychology* (pp. 161–188). Oxford University Press.

Adams, W. W. (2016). Ecopsychology by way of phenomenology. In C. T. Fischer, L. Laubscher, & R. Brooke (Eds.), *The qualitative vision for psychology: An invitation to a human science approach* (pp. 221–243). Duquesne University Press.

Adler, P. A., & Adler, P. (1987). *Membership roles in field research*. Sage. https://doi.org/10.4135/9781412984973

Aftab, A. (2020, October 8). Phenomenology, power, polarization, and the discourse on psychosis: Nev Jones, PhD. *Psychiatric Times*. https://www.psychiatrictimes.com/view/phenomenology-power-polarization-psychosis

Alper, M. (2018). Inclusive sensory ethnography: Studying new media and neurodiversity in everyday life. *New Media & Society, 20*(10), 3560–3579. https://doi.org/10.1177/1461444818755394

American Psychiatric Association. (2013). *Diagnostic and statistical manual of mental disorders* (5th ed.).

American Psychological Association. (2017). *Multicultural guidelines: An ecological approach to context, identity, and intersectionality*. https://www.apa.org/about/policy/multicultural-guidelines

Angrosino, M. (2007). *Doing ethnographic and observational research*. SAGE. https://doi.org/10.4135/9781849208932

Barnard, S., & Borges, S. (Directors). (2016). *Maxamba* [Film]. Maxamba Film.

Bartholomew, T. T., & Brown, J. R. (2019). Entering the ethnographic mind: A grounded theory of using ethnography in psychological research. *Qualitative Research in Psychology, 19*(2), 316–345. https://doi.org/10.1080/14780887.2019.1604927

Behar, R. (1996). *The vulnerable observer: Anthropology that breaks your heart*. Beacon Press.

Bejarano, C. A., Juárez, L. L., García, M. A. M., & Goldstein, D. M. (2019). *Decolonizing ethnography: Undocumented immigrants and new directions in social science*. Duke University Press. https://doi.org/10.2307/j.ctv11smmv5

Bhatia, S. (2007). Rethinking culture and identity in psychology: Towards a transnational cultural psychology. *Journal of Theoretical and Philosophical Psychology, 27–28*(2–1), 301–321. https://doi.org/10.1037/h0091298

Boellstorff, T., Nardi, B., Pearce, C., & Taylor, T. L. (2012). *Ethnography and virtual worlds: A handbook of method*. Princeton University Press. https://doi.org/10.2307/j.cttq9s20

Briggs, C. L. (1986). *Learning how to ask: A sociolinguistic appraisal of the role of the interview in social science research*. Cambridge University Press. https://doi.org/10.1017/CBO9781139165990

Briggs, J. L. (1970). *Never in anger: Portrait of an Eskimo family*. Harvard University Press.

Brooke, R. (2016). Some common themes of psychology as a human science. In C. Fischer, L. Laubscher, & R. Brooke (Eds.), *The qualitative vision for psychology: Invitation to a human science approach* (pp. 17–30). Duquesne University Press.

Burston, D., & Frie, R. (2006). *Psychotherapy as a human science*. Duquesne University Press.

Case, A. D., Todd, N. R., & Kral, M. J. (2014). Ethnography in community psychology: Promises and tensions. *American Journal of Community Psychology, 54*(1-2), 60–71. https://doi.org/10.1007/s10464-014-9648-0

Chao, R. K. (1994). Beyond parental control and authoritarian parenting style: Understanding Chinese parenting through the cultural notion of training. *Child Development, 65*(4), 1111–1119. https://doi.org/10.2307/1131308

Chapin, B. L. (2014). *Childhood in a Sri Lankan village: Shaping hierarchy and desire.* Rutgers University Press.

Christopher, J. C., Wendt, D. C., Marecek, J., & Goodman, D. M. (2014). Critical cultural awareness: Contributions to a globalizing psychology. *American Psychologist, 69*(7), 645–655. https://doi.org/10.1037/a0036851

Clifford, J. (1988). *The predicament of culture.* Harvard University Press.

Cole, M., & Wertsch, J. V. (1996). Beyond the individual-social antinomy in discussions of Piaget and Vygotsky. *Human Development, 39*(5), 250–256. https://doi.org/10.1159/000278475

Connor, L. (2001). Healing powers in contemporary Asia. In L. Connor & G. Samuel (Eds.), *Healing powers and modernity: Traditional medicine, shamanism, and science in Asian societies* (pp. 3–21). Greenwood Publishing Group.

Creswell, J. W., & Clark, V. L. P. (2017). *Designing and conducting mixed methods research.* SAGE.

Desmond, M. (2014). Relational ethnography. *Theory and Society, 43*(5), 547–579. https://doi.org/10.1007/s11186-014-9232-5

Deutsch, N. L., & Tolan, P. (2018). Qualitative methods. In M. Bornstein (Ed.), *The SAGE encyclopedia of lifespan human development* (pp. 1793–1796). SAGE.

Duncan, G. J., Huston, A. C., & Weisner, T. S. (2007). *Higher ground: New hope for the working poor and their children.* Russell Sage Foundation.

Duncan, W. L. (2018). *Transforming therapy: Mental health practice and cultural change in Mexico.* Vanderbilt University Press. https://doi.org/10.2307/j.ctv167560w

Emerson, R. M., Fretz, R. I., & Shaw, L. L. (2011). *Writing ethnographic fieldnotes.* University of Chicago Press. https://doi.org/10.7208/chicago/9780226206868.001.0001

Fein, E. (2020). *Living on the spectrum: Autism and youth in community.* NYU Press. https://doi.org/10.18574/nyu/9781479864355.001.0001

Fischer, C. T. (1977). Historical relations of psychology as an object-science and a subject-science: Toward psychology as a human science. *Journal of the History of the Behavioral Sciences, 13*(4), 369–378. https://doi.org/10.1002/1520-6696(197710)13:4<369::AID-JHBS2300130409>3.0.CO;2-Z

Foucault, M. (1972). *The archaeology of knowledge.* Tavistock Publications.

Fullilove, M. T. (1996). Psychiatric implications of displacement: Contributions from the psychology of place. *The American Journal of Psychiatry, 153*(12), 1516–1523. https://doi.org/10.1176/ajp.153.12.1516

Gaskins, S., Miller, P. J., & Corsaro, W. A. (1992). Theoretical and methodological perspectives in the interpretive study of children. *New Directions for Child and Adolescent Development, 1992*(58), 5–23. https://doi.org/10.1002/cd.23219925803

Gee, J. P. (2004). *Situated language and learning: A critique of traditional schooling.* Routledge.

Geertz, C. (1973). *The interpretation of cultures: Selected essays.* Basic Books.

Gergen, K. J. (1991). *The saturated self: Dilemmas of identity in contemporary life.* Basic Books.

Gobo, G., & Marciniak, L. (2016). What is ethnography? In D. Silverman (Ed.), *Qualitative research* (pp. 103–120). SAGE.

Gone, J. P. (2011). Is psychological science a-cultural? *Cultural Diversity & Ethnic Minority Psychology, 17*(3), 234–242. https://doi.org/10.1037/a0023805

Gone, J. P., & Alcántara, C. (2010). The ethnographically contextualized case study method: Exploring ambitious achievement in an American Indian community. *Cultural Diversity & Ethnic Minority Psychology, 16*(2), 159–168. https://doi.org/10.1037/a0013873

Góralska, M. (2020). Anthropology from home: Advice on digital ethnography for the pandemic times. *Anthropology in Action: Newsletter of the British Association for Social Anthropology in Policy and Practice (BASAPP), 27*(1), 46–52. https://doi.org/10.3167/aia.2020.270105

Greenfield, P. M. (2004). *Weaving generations together: Evolving creativity in the Maya of Chiapas.* School for Advanced Research.

Giorgi, A. (2014). Phenomenological philosophy as the basis for a human scientific psychology. *The Humanistic Psychologist, 42*(3), 233.

Gupta, A., & Ferguson, J. (Eds.). (1997). *Anthropological locations: Boundaries and grounds of a field science.* University California Press.

Gubrium, J. F., & Holstein, J. A. (2000). *Aging and everyday life.* Blackwell.

Hamdy, S., & Nye, C. (2017). *Lissa: A story about medical promise, friendship, and revolution.* University of Toronto Press.

Hammersley, M., & Atkinson, P. (2019). *Ethnography: Principles in practice*. Routledge.

Hartmann, W. E., St Arnault, D. M., & Gone, J. P. (2018). A return to "the clinic" for community psychology: Lessons from a clinical ethnography in urban American Indian behavioral health. *American Journal of Community Psychology, 61*(1–2), 62–75. https://doi.org/10.1002/ajcp.12212

Hay, C. (Ed.). (2016). *Methods that matter: Integrating mixed methods for more effective social science research*. University of Chicago Press. https://doi.org/10.7208/chicago/9780226328836.001.0001

Henrich, J., Heine, S. J., & Norenzayan, A. (2010). The weirdest people in the world? *Behavioral and Brain Sciences, 33*(2–3), 61–83. https://doi.org/10.1017/S0140525X0999152X

Hine, C. (2000). *Virtual ethnography*. SAGE. https://doi.org/10.4135/9780857020277

Hjorth, L., Horst, H., Galloway, A., & Bell, G. (Eds.). (2017). *The Routledge companion to digital ethnography*. Taylor & Francis. https://doi.org/10.4324/9781315673974

Holmes, S. (2013). *Fresh fruit, broken bodies: Migrant farmworkers in the United States*. University of California Press.

Holstein, J. A., & Gubrium, J. F. (2000). *The self we live by: Narrative identity in a postmodern world*. Oxford University Press.

Inda, J. X., & Rosaldo, R. (Eds.). (2002). *The anthropology of globalization: A reader*. Blackwell Press.

James, W. (1976). *Essays in radical empiricism*. Harvard University Press. (Original work published 1912)

Jenkins, J. H., & Csordas, T. J. (2020). *Troubled in the land of enchantment: Adolescent experience of psychiatric treatment*. University of California Press.

Kleinman, A. (1997). *Writing at the margin: Discourse between anthropology and medicine*. University of California Press. https://doi.org/10.1525/california/9780520209657.001.0001

Laubscher, L. (2016). Introduction: Invitation to psychology as a human science. In C. Fischer, L. Laubscher, & R. Brooke (Eds.), *The qualitative vision for psychology: Invitation to a human science approach* (pp. 1–16). Duquesne University Press.

Lave, J., & Wenger, E. (1991). *Situated learning: Legitimate peripheral participation*. Cambridge University Press. https://doi.org/10.1017/CBO9780511815355

Lee, C. D., Nasir, N. S., Pea, R., & de Royston, M. (2020). Introduction. Reconceptualizing learning: A critical task for knowledge-building and teaching. In N. S. Nasir, C. D. Lee, R. Pea, & M. M. de Royston (Eds.), *Handbook of the cultural foundations of learning* (pp. xvii–xxxv). Routledge. https://doi.org/10.4324/9780203774977-0

Leite, N. (2017). *Unorthodox kin: Portuguese Marranos and the global search for belonging*. University of California Press. https://doi.org/10.1525/california/9780520285040.001.0001

Lemelson, R., & Tucker, A. (2017). *Afflictions: Steps toward a visual psychological anthropology*. Palgrave. https://doi.org/10.1007/978-3-319-59984-7

Levitt, H. M., Motulsky, S. L., Wertz, F. J., Morrow, S. L., & Ponterotto, J. G. (2017). Recommendations for designing and reviewing qualitative research in psychology: Promoting methodological integrity. *Qualitative Psychology, 4*(1), 2–22. https://doi.org/10.1037/qup0000082

Levy, R. I., & Hollan, D. W. (1998). Person-centered interviewing and observation. In R. Bernard (Ed.), *Handbook of methods in cultural anthropology* (pp. 333–364). AltaMira Press.

Luhrmann, T. M. (2012). *When God talks back: Understanding the American evangelical relationship with God*. Knopf.

Luria, A. R. (1976). *Cognitive development: Its cultural and social foundations* (M. Lopez-Morillas, Trans.). Harvard University Press.

Lutz, C. A. (1988). *Unnatural emotions: Everyday sentiments on a Micronesian atoll and their challenge to Western theory*. University of Chicago Press.

Magnifico, A. M., Lammers, J. C., & Fields, D. A. (2018). Affinity spaces, literacies and classrooms: Tensions and opportunities. *Literacy, 52*(3), 145–152. https://doi.org/10.1111/lit.12133

McGranahan, C. (2014). What is ethnography? Teaching ethnographic sensibilities without fieldwork. *Teaching Anthropology, 4*(1), 23–36.

McMullin, J. (2016). Cancer and the comics: Graphic narratives and biolegitimate lives. *Medical Anthropology Quarterly, 30*(2), 149–167. https://doi.org/10.1111/maq.12172

Miller, P. J., Hengst, J. A., & Wang, S. (2003). Ethnographic methods: Applications from developmental cultural psychology. In P. M. Camic, J. E. Rhodes, & L. Yardley (Eds.), *Qualitative research in psychology: Expanding perspectives in methodology and design* (pp. 219–242). American Psychological Association. https://doi.org/10.1037/10595-012

Packer, M. J. (2017). *The science of qualitative research* (2nd ed.). Cambridge University Press. https://doi.org/10.1017/9781108264907

Quinn, N. (2005). How to reconstruct schemas people share, from what they say. In N. Quinn (Ed.), *Finding culture in talk: A collection of methods* (pp. 35–81). Palgrave Macmillan. https://doi.org/10.1007/978-1-137-05871-3_2

Rogoff, B. (2011). *Developing destinies: A Mayan midwife and town*. Oxford University Press. https://doi.org/10.1093/acprof:oso/9780195319903.001.0001

Said, E. (1978). *Orientalism*. Vintage.

Sanjek, R. (1990). A vocabulary for fieldnotes. In R. Sanjek (Ed.), *Fieldnotes: The makings of anthropology* (pp. 92–121). Cornell University Press. https://doi.org/10.7591/9781501711954

Shweder, R. A. (1997). The surprise of ethnography. *Ethos, 25*(2), 152–163. https://doi.org/10.1525/eth.1997.25.2.152

Simms, E. M. (2008). *The child in the world: Embodiment, time, and language in early childhood*. Wayne State University Press.

Simonds, L. M., Camic, P. M., & Causey, A. (2012). Using focused ethnography in psychological research. In H. Cooper (Ed.), *APA handbook of research methods in psychology: Vol. 2. Research designs: Quantitative, qualitative, neuropsychological, and biological* (pp. 157–170). American Psychological Association. https://doi.org/10.1037/13620-010

Small, M. L. (2011). How to conduct a mixed methods study: Recent trends in a rapidly growing literature. *Annual Review of Sociology, 37*(1), 57–86. https://doi.org/10.1146/annurev.soc.012809.102657

Snyder, G. (2020). *The practice of the wild: Essays*. Counterpoint.

Stephen, L. (2007). *Transborder lives: Indigenous Oaxacans in Mexico, California, and Oregon*. Duke University Press.

Suchman, L., & Jordan, B. (1990). Interactional troubles in face-to-face survey interviews. *Journal of the American Statistical Association, 85*(409), 232–241. https://doi.org/10.2307/2289550

Taussig, M. (2011). *I swear I saw this: Drawings in fieldwork notebooks, namely my own*. University of Chicago Press. https://doi.org/10.7208/chicago/9780226789842.001.0001

Timmermans, S., & Tavory, I. (2012). Theory construction in qualitative research: From grounded theory to abductive analysis. *Sociological Theory, 30*(3), 167–186. https://doi.org/10.1177/0735275112457914

Tsing, A. L. (2015). *The mushroom at the end of the world: On the possibility of life in capitalist ruins*. Princeton University Press.

Vygotsky, L. (1978). Interaction between learning and development. In M. Gauvain & M. Cole (Eds.), *Readings on the development of children* (4th ed., pp. 34–41). Worth Publishers.

Wacquant, L. (2011). Habitus as topic and tool: Reflections on becoming a prizefighter. *Qualitative Research in Psychology, 8*(1), 81–92. https://doi.org/10.1080/14780887.2010.544176

Walsh, R. (2003). The methods of reflexivity. *The Humanistic Psychologist, 31*(4), 51–66. https://doi.org/10.1080/08873267.2003.9986934

Webb, E., Campbell, D., Schwartz, R., Sechrest, L., & Grove, J. (1981). *Nonreactive measures in the social sciences* (2nd ed.). Houghton Mifflin.

Weinstein, J., & Ventres, W. (2000). Mini-ethnography: Meaningful exploration made easy. *Family Medicine, 32*(9), 600–602.

Weis, L., & Fine, M. (2012). Critical bifocality and circuits of privilege: Expanding critical ethnographic theory and design. *Harvard Educational Review, 82*(2), 173–201. https://doi.org/10.17763/haer.82.2.v1jx34n441532242

Weisner, T. S. (2012). Mixed methods should be a valued practice in anthropology. *Anthropology News, 53*(5), 3–4.

Wilk, R. (2006). *Home cooking in the global village: Caribbean food from buccaneers to ecotourists*. Bloomsbury Academic. https://doi.org/10.5040/9781350047686

Wundt, W. (2018). *Elements of folk-psychology: Outlines of a psychological history of the development of mankind* (E. L. Schaub, Trans.). Macmillan Company. (Original work published 1916)

Yahalom, J. (2019). *Caring for the people of the clouds: Aging and dementia in Oaxaca*. University of Oklahoma Press.

Yahalom, J. (2020). Toward a methodology of chance: On obstacles to research and their advantages. *Qualitative Psychology, 7*(2), 153–168. https://doi.org/10.1037/qup0000172

Yates-Doerr, E. (2020). Reworking the social determinants of health: Responding to material-semiotic indeterminacy in public health interventions. *Medical Anthropology Quarterly, 34*(3), 378–397. https://doi.org/10.1111/maq.12586

CHAPTER 10

VISUAL RESEARCH IN PSYCHOLOGY

Paula Reavey, Jon Prosser, and Steven D. Brown

The aim of this chapter is to review and make clear the variety of ways in which psychologists might use visual images to answer research questions. Visual research has been developed mainly by qualitative researchers as a means to study human experiences and to engage participants more fully in the research process. In contemporary culture more generally, visual images have become important mediators for expressing feelings and communicating with one another using emerging technologies (e.g., mobile phones; social networking sites, such as Instagram, Pinterest, or TikTok; app-based dating; online gaming). It should, therefore, come as no surprise that psychologists have seized the opportunity to study the impact of visual technologies and media on the way we experience our worlds. This chapter aims to discuss the range of possibilities for researching the visual and the implications for the ways in which we study human experience more generally.

In order to address these aims, we have structured the chapter as follows. First, we outline exactly what we mean by visual research as it has developed in psychological research methods (the section What Is Visual Research?). Second, we provide a brief history of how visual techniques have previously been used to study psychological phenomena (Psychology and the Visual: A Brief History). We then explain how qualitative researchers have initiated the use of visual approaches to study experience via a broader range of modalities (the means by which we communicate—written, spoken, visual, touch, and sound). This has entailed a shift from a monomodal position (where language alone is studied) to a multimodal one (where language and images are studied together) (Moving from the Mono- to the Multimodal in Qualitative Research). We then, in the section A Review of Five Psychological Topics and Visual Research, introduce five main ways in which qualitative researchers have used visual techniques to study experience: (a) a review of how qualitative researchers have sought to bring emotions or affect to the foreground of research, (b) an exploration of the role of the environmental setting in making sense of experience, (c) an examination of the role of the body and appearance in making sense of self and identity, (d) the study of social memory, and (e) the use of the visual as a medium to study communication and interaction. After this section, we concentrate on how visual research methods can alter the context of the research setting by increasing a sense of collaboration between researcher and participant (Increasing Collaboration Between Researcher and Participant). Following this,

https://doi.org/10.1037/0000319-010
APA Handbook of Research Methods in Psychology, Second Edition: Vol. 2. Research Designs: Quantitative, Qualitative, Neuropsychological, and Biological, H. Cooper (Editor-in-Chief)

we set out a number of ways in which qualitative researchers have analyzed visual material, almost always alongside verbal data, generated through interviews, focus groups, diaries, or observations (Analyzing Visual Data). Finally, we provide some guidance on the ethical issues that inevitably arise for visual research in the section Ethics and the Visual before moving on to the Conclusion.

WHAT IS VISUAL RESEARCH?

Visual research focuses on what can be seen. How humans *see* is part nature, part nurture. It is governed by perception, which, like other sensory modes, is mediated by physiology, culture, and history. Visual researchers use the term *visible* when referring to images as part of a naturally occurring physiological phenomenon, with a disregard for meaning or significance (i.e., literally what can be seen). *Visual*, on the other hand, refers to the process whereby meanings and significance are attributed to an object in and of itself. The phrases *to visualize* and *visualization* refer to a perceiver's sense-making capacities, which are epistemologically grounded and include concept formation, analytical processes, and modes of representation (Wagner, 2006).

There are two basic approaches to undertaking qualitative visual research. The first is where researchers create or manufacture visual artefacts during the research process (Banks, 2001; Pink, 2007). The second has its origins in *the visual turn* (Mirzoeff, 2009), where researchers explore visual artifacts in terms of their mode, production, interpretation, and application (Emmison and Smith, 2000; Rose, 2007). Increasingly, researchers combine these approaches to enhance analytic insights (Stanczak, 2007).

Empirically orientated visual researchers frame their work theoretically or pragmatically to meet their needs, which may be shaped by research questions, disciplinary norms, or analytical frameworks. The visual anthropologist Banks (2007) organized his field work into three basic strands. The first is concerned with documentation and researcher-created imagery that may include photographs, moving images, sketches, and

concept maps. These are collected and stored along with the usual handwritten field notes and voice recordings. Visual researchers may then analyze these visual data using concept maps or flow diagrams and represent their findings using particular images, graphs, or diagrams. Throughout this process the researcher is pivotal to the creation of the images. The second strand involves the collection and study of images produced, consumed, or used by the participants or respondents of the research. Here the emphasis is on understanding the participant's engagement with differing types of media, their mode of production, along with the context in which visual data are set, as they are important in determining the meaning participants ascribe to imagery. Bank's third strand is a combination of the first two and is currently the preferred approach. Here researchers collect visual data (e.g., video of complex interpersonal inter-action) and combine this information with participants' insights and meaning making of the imagery they employ or adapt. The mix of researcher and researched insights represents an epistemological shift towards a more collabora-tive mode, often referred to as the *postmodern turn*, because there are multiple ways in which to interpret visual data and carry out visual research.

A complementary question to "What is visual research?" is "Why is visual research currently so popular?" A simple answer is because there has been a general awakening to the significance and ubiquity of imagery in contemporary lives:

> All around us are screens on computers, game consoles, iPods, handheld devices and televisions . . . where the internet was once held to be the revival of text, there are already over 100 million video clips on YouTube, more than 3 billion photos on the file-sharing Flickr, and over 4 billion on the social networking site Facebook. (Mirzoeff, 2009, p. 2)

The term *visual culture* is now commonly used to reflect a combination of visuality (generalized insights into the visual in everyday spaces, not merely as entities or visual texts) and meaning making through taken-for-granted practices of engaging with images. The visual is pervasive in public, work, education, and private space: we have no choice but to look. Qualitative psychologists no longer act as though they were sightless and increasingly embrace the challenge to understand the behavior of individuals and groups within a society dominated by visual culture.

A visual approach has also gained prominence among sensory research methods. It is argued that because visual culture is the dominant modality of sensory engagement, visual research methods are of primary importance. It has also been argued that, anatomically, modern humans appeared about 200,000 years ago and it was their highly developed visual and sensory acuity rather than language skills (which appeared much later) that were central to their survival. The possibility that the ability to interpret and represent visually are innate and central to the human psyche is echoed in Harper's (2002) statement, "The parts of the brain that process visual information are evolutionarily older than the parts that process verbal information" (p. 13). Of course, older does not here mean superior, but it does suggest that visual capacity is deeply ingrained. Evolutionary psychologists, drawing on Darwinism, argue that multiple generations of people (including researchers) have innate and unchangeable visually orientated natures (Buss, 2005). Despite a continual evolution marked by instinctual deprivation, humans have never lost the primacy of the visual as a means to understanding the world around them. The upsurge in interest in visuality by psychologists reflects a deeply rooted need to see closer and higher and to make visible what is hidden.

PSYCHOLOGY AND THE VISUAL: A BRIEF HISTORY

As a discipline, psychology has a long-standing concern with the visual and with technologies of visualization. This goes way beyond the specialized subdiscipline of the psychology of perception; it is, instead, part of the conceptual roots of the discipline as a whole (see Reavey, 2021, for a more comprehensive discussion of this history). The emerging visual technology of photography was a central part of how the nascent discipline of psychology established its scientific credibility in the late 19th century, through the visual recording of scientific observations. For example, in *The Expression of the Emotions in Man and Animals*, Charles Darwin (1872/1999) made comparisons across photographs and illustrations of children and animals as the evidential base for his theory of universal emotional expressions. This approach greatly influenced the growth of comparative psychology in the late 19th century (Richards, 2002). Moreover, photographs and minute observations of his son William Erasmus Darwin, which Darwin and his wife collected as a "developmental diary" from his birth, are arguably the template from which developmental psychology established itself (Fitzpatrick & Bringmann, 1997).

The use of visual records to differentiate species and meticulously categorize plants and animals into various types and subtypes became the hallmark of 19th-century natural science. It marked the systematization of observation, indicating accuracy, evidential recording, and careful attention to detail. What is measurable, therefore, is assumed to be what is observable. In the case of psychology, the fledgling discipline sought to separate itself from philosophy, and the myriad metaphysical difficulties that appeared to prohibit a "science of mind," by emulating the natural sciences such as functional physiology as far as possible (Richards, 2002). Recent successes at that time in physiology had arisen from mapping functional connections between anatomy and behavior. This same logic was applied to what Gustav Fechner (1860/1966) called "an exact theory of the functional relationships between body and soul and between the bodily, mental, somatic and physiological world" (cited in Meischner-Metge & Meischner, 1997, p. 102).

Photography also greatly influenced the development of psychopathology and clinical psychology. Visual categorization of different personality types and the categorization of the "mad," "subnormal," or "criminal" were performed by assembling photographic arrays in which purported mental differences could be made legible to the "trained eye" (Jackson, 1995). Photographs were also commonly used to lend visual credibility to diagnostic categories of mental defects or "feeblemindedness." Through careful visual recording, the spaces between a person's eyes, the size of a forehead, or the body posture of an asylum inmate could provide direct evidence for an observable and, thus, categorical difference in the person under study. The multiple exposure technique used by Marey, in which a series of images are exposed on the same photographic plate, was also used by Francis Galton (Draaisma, 2000). Galton argued that his "compound photographs" of criminals and of "consumptives" taken one-by-one onto the same photographic plate showed their common features, because individual, or noncommon, features would be effectively washed out during the process. The technique was, Galton claimed, a sort of "pictorial statistics" where norms of human development and diversity could be visually represented. This idea fed into popular notions of normality and abnormality around mental health that gained currency in the late 19th and early 20th centuries (Porter, 2003). Visual techniques such as the Rorschach ink blot tests—surely one of the most recognizable representations of psychology—and the thematic apperception test (Cramer, 1996) were and still are used to provide insight into a person's personality type and their unconscious motivational state or are used to detect signs of 'mental ill-health.'

Social psychology has throughout its history used film and photography as a means of documenting research and shoring up the "face validity" of its claims. The images of participants in Stanley Milgram's (2005) infamous studies on obedience in the early 1960s appear to leave little room for doubting the validity of his claims. Close analyses of the statistical evidence and the ecological validity of the experimental set-up, regarding the tendency for "ordinary" people to follow orders that can lead to the harming of others, is somewhat overshadowed by these powerful images. Similarly, the video recordings taken by Philip Zimbardo and colleagues of the Stanford Prison Experiment have been promoted as a powerful testimony to the ease with which people take on the aggressive or passive behavior in their respective roles as prisoner or guard. This material was captured using the sort of "hidden camera" techniques that have become the mainstay of reality-TV shows such as *Candid Camera* or, more recently, *Big Brother* (where people are filmed and "observed" and a team of psychologists provided an analysis of subsequent changes in behavior and/or mental state). Interestingly Zimbardo himself has claimed that Alan Funt, creator of the first reality-TV show, *Candid Camera,* was "one of the most creative, intuitive social psychologists on the planet" (Zimbardo et al., 2000, p. 197). Kurt Lewin also used hidden camera techniques to make a series of films that focused on the spaces of child development, the best known being the 1935 film *The Child and the World*, which he discussed with the great Soviet filmmaker Sergei Eisenstein (Van Elteren, 1992; Van Elteren & Luck, 1990).

To summarize, an historical analysis of the role of visual within psychology can reveal its instrumental effects in providing the context for "the psychological" to become observable and, therefore, measurable and more "scientific." In using visual images as evidence, and in employing visual technologies to increase the accuracy and, thus, the status of psychological observations, the discipline of psychology has also made its findings more publicly accessible. Despite these noteworthy uses of visual images throughout psychology, there has been very little in the way of methodologies attempting to accommodate the visual in making sense of how people experience the world. This is especially difficult to understand regarding qualitative methodologies that claim to focus on meaning making in everyday experience (see Chapter 1, this volume).

MOVING FROM MONO- TO MULTIMODAL IN QUALITATIVE RESEARCH

Qualitative research is now well established in certain subdisciplines of psychology (e.g., critical, community, social, clinical, educational). In contrast to searching for generalizable laws, qualitative researchers focus on how individuals experience and make meaning (Stainton Rogers & Willig, 2017; Willig, 2008). It is the participant rather than the researcher who occupies the center of meaning generation within the research process. In recent years, several publications have emerged that meticulously chart the best way to collect, store, and analyze qualitative data in systematic and logical fashion. However, not until the publication of Donald Ratcliff's chapter on video methods in the American Psychological Association's first handbook on qualitative methods (Ratcliff, 2003) did any major handbook include chapters on visual approaches. Furthermore, the first ever publication of a psychology-based volume of visual methods (Reavey, 2011) did not arrive until comparatively recently.

The majority of qualitative research still continues to use solely verbal data, in the form of semistructured and unstructured interview data, natural conversations, focus groups discussions, diaries, or written reports. A common focus is either the broad sense making patterns contained in transcripts, or the minute details of the way in which the language is structured and performed in social interactions. This reliance on the spoken or written word as a source of data has been referred to as a *monomodal approach* (Reavey, 2021). Many visual researchers (e.g., Pink, 2007; Radley, 2009) have outlined the limitations of examining human narratives and experiences using language alone and have pointed to a number of neglected areas that might benefit from a *multimodal* approach; that is, an approach that attends to extradiscursive modalities such as visual stimuli. If qualitative researchers wish to make sense of experience, they must surely acknowledge that a variety of modalities—verbal, visual, sound, touch—make up a person's experience of the world.

The Potential for Multimodal Approaches

In the decade that has passed since the appearance of the first volume on visual methods in psychology (Reavey, 2011), there has been a steady stream of publications in health, social, clinical, and cultural psychology. Topics range from the body and embodiment (Del Busso, 2009; Gillies et al., 2005), health and illness (Radley, 2009; Radley & Taylor, 2003a, 2003b), disability (McGrath et al., 2020), drug use and couple intimacy (Anderson et al., 2019), memory (Brookfield et al., 2008; Fawns, 2021; Kuhn, 2007; Middleton & Brown, 2005; Middleton & Edwards, 1990; Radley 1990; Reavey, 2010), identity and appearance (Gleeson & Frith, 2006), space and the environment (McGrath, 2012; Reavey et al., 2019), and mental health difficulties (Boden & Larkin, 2021; Reavey et al., 2019; Silver & Reavey, 2010). This multimodal work has often combined visual (photography, drawing, and painting) and verbal/written (interview, focus group discussions, and diaries) data to create a richer picture of the topic under study. Photographs are perhaps the most popular visual medium to be used in psychology. A variety of visual-photographic techniques are deployed in such research to elicit or trigger discussion in an interview or focus group (here referred to as *photo-elicitation*). Photographic images generated by participants within the context of the research can also be used within interviews (here referred to as *photo-production*[1]). Regardless of the specific technique, visual researchers in psychology share an acknowledgment that (a) individuals experience the world not only through narrative, but through spatial settings and embodiment,

---

[1]Sometimes authors refer to *photo-elicitation* to describe both approaches. We have, however, separated the two terms to distinguish between two very different approaches.

and that (b) individuals are already using multi-modal forms of expression and communication when (re)presenting their experiences in everyday life. As people become more proficient in using new communication technologies to convey ideas and feelings and engage in new forms of social interaction, relationality, and subjectivity, it is ever more vital that researchers in psychology engage with these everyday forms of communication and representation.

Images can act as a means to disrupt well-rehearsed narrative accounts of a topic within an interview and help surface the affective qualities of an experience (Brookfield et al., 2008; Gillies et al., 2005; Reavey, 2008; Silver & Reavey, 2010). A photograph from the past, for example, can enable the individual to imagine or feel the emotion from that time, such that the past can enter into the present moment and facilitate the creation of a new narrative or more complex account (especially if the reemergence of the past collides with narratives of the present). This is not to say that the visual somehow "fools" the person or, contrastingly, compels them to uncover some hitherto "unsaid truth" about the past. This is probably best character-ized as a process whereby the image allows for a more complex and layered account, immersed in emotional resonance, where setting, envi-ronment, or world (the actual place) of the experience is brought into sharper view. John Collier (1957), who developed photo-elicitation in anthropology and sociology, noted that the visual interviews tend to be more focussed, detailed, and precise in comparison with non-visual interviews:

> The material obtained with photo-graphs was precise and at times even encyclopedic; the control interviews were less structured, rambling, and freer in association. Statements in the photointerviews were in direct response to the graphic probes and different in character as the content of the pictures differed. (p. 856)

A REVIEW OF FIVE PSYCHOLOGICAL TOPICS USING VISUAL RESEARCH

Emotions

A noteworthy feature of using images is their ability to help articulate the unspeakable or to evoke emotions that could be displaced or over-looked in a spoken interview. Charity campaigns often use powerful visual cues, such as starving children, to incite an emotional reaction and encourage people to dig deep into their pockets. Without such cues, it is difficult to see how many charities would survive, as they require potential donators to witness—or to see with their own eyes—the difficulties their recipients endure. In visual research, images can be used to incite emotion, especially in situations where partici-pants may need reminding of how they once felt, because they have chosen to move on from, or have actively forgotten an experience that has been difficult (see Frith, 2021, for an example of how those who have recovered from breast cancer actively "forget" aspects of their illness). However, individuals may also use images to engage deliberately with feelings. A video of a wedding, or a child's first steps, may be played in order to activate difficult to reach memories and emotions. It is no surprise that photographic and video footage is an integral feature of modern households in industrialized societies, as the impetus and even compulsion to remember how things feel is intrinsic to our sense of well-being (Middleton & Brown, 2005).

Visual researchers in psychology have embraced the power of the visual to incite emotion and bring it to the conversational fore in an interview or focus group. A powerful example of this can be found in Radley and Taylor's (2003a, 2003b) *photo-production* study of hospital patients' recovery on a hospital ward. The study involved participants taking pictures of the hospital spaces in which they were recovering, followed by an interview one month after they had been discharged. According to Radley and Taylor, the photographs served as a useful way to jointly steer the interview discussion, with the image itself inviting participants to explain emotive aspects of their experience and ground the accounts in the environment itself.

A photo-elicitation study (using participants' domestic photographs) by Kunimoto (2004), with Japanese-Canadians interned during the Second World War, revealed different kinds of memories and emotions through the use of images to the ones initially spoken about in a previous interview. Kunimoto, for example, noted how the photographs introduced accounts that were far more emotional, specific, and rich and contrasted significantly with the "dry" accounts offered prior to the introduction of the image.

Silver and Reavey (2010) used drawing and photo-elicitation to explore issues of selfhood and appearance over time (from childhood to adulthood), with participants diagnosed with body dysmorphic disorder (BDD). What Silver and Reavey found particularly interesting was the way in which participants engaged with their photos, which covered the period from childhood through to the present day. They found that participants were able to move away from accounting for their BDD solely in terms of their current lives and brought an intensely emotional account of their childhood self that they were then able to connect with their present preoccupation with facial disfigurement (Silver & Reavey, 2010). This emotional connection between past and present in the clinical literature on BDD had been absent up until this point. Silver and Reavey argued that visual methods were key to affording an examination of the emotional connection between past and present, due to participants having a "ready to hand" visible portrait of the self physically and emotionally changing over time.

Space and Objects

Almost all qualitative methods use purely verbal methods to ask participants to recall and reflect on experiences, which can lead to participant accounts that are overwhelmingly organized in terms of time sequences only (Goodwin, 2008).

A number of studies incorporating visual methods have, on the other hand, succeeded in disrupting such narratives, encouraging participants to reflect also on the social and material contexts (spaces and places) from which their experiences emerge (Bowes-Catton et al., 2021; Brown & Reavey, 2015; Hodgetts et al., 2021; Hodgetts, Chamberlain, & Radley, 2007; Majumdar, 2011; McGrath, 2012). Objects also form part of the setting and can be used by individuals to anchor or to bring alive a discussion or to reminisce. In a photo-production study on homelessness by Hodgetts and colleagues (2021), for example, one of the participants had taken photos of a cardboard sign he used to write amusing messages that successfully captured the attention of passers-by (Figure 10.1).

In certain subdisciplines of psychology, such as cognitive science, extended cognition paradigms, and in social and cultural psychology, photographs of objects and spaces are commonly used to emphasize that what we feel, remember, and think, and how we act cannot be separated out from the world (and the objects and spaces that occupy that world) in which such experiences emerge (Stenner, 2017). It is much easier to start with a familiar object when recollecting, for example, than it is to begin with a sometimes unmanageable and entangled set of memories. If we can take a visual record at the time at which we experience something or can gather together existing visual images of an event (e.g., our existing personal photographs) we can bring the space and setting of the experience explicitly into an interview, focus group, or diary (Reavey et al., 2019).

In a photo-production diary study by Del Busso (2009, 2021) on young women's experiences of embodiment,[2] participants were asked to take pictures of objects or spaces that reflected experiences of embodied pleasure (e.g., eating, having sex, exercise) and places in which these occurred (Figure 10.2). The data comprised people's verbal accounts alongside the photographs and the

---

[2]By *embodiment*, we mean how it feels to be in one's body—the physical and emotional sensation.

FIGURE 10.1.   Homeless man with ninja sign. Adapted from *Visual Methods in Psychology: Using and Interpreting Images in Qualitative Research* (p. 310), by P. Reavey (Ed.), 2011, Routledge. Copyright 2011 by D. Hodgetts. Adapted with permission.

analytical approach taken was hermeneutic phenomenological analysis (Langdridge, 2007; see Langdridge, 2021, for an account of the use of visual methods within phenomenology).

In a follow-up interview, participants used the photos and written diaries to organize the discussion. The data reveals how the manner in which it became clear that the manner in which participants experienced embodied pleasure was integral to the setting in which those experiences occurred. In other words, it was not only what they experienced but also where that was important.

FIGURE 10.2.   Ann's photograph of the woods. From *Being in Motion: Femininity, Movement, and Space in Young Women's Narratives of Their Embodied Experiences in Everyday Life* (p. 154), by L. Del Busso, 2009 (Unpublished doctoral dissertation), London South Bank University. Copyright 2009 by L. Del Busso. Reprinted with permission.

Embodiment and Appearance

The role of our outward appearance and the felt sensation of our bodies in making sense of emotions, identity, and selfhood have become increasingly noted in social psychological accounts of experience (Brown et al., 2008; Frost, 2005; Gillies et al., 2004, 2005; Howarth, 2011). How we feel in our bodies, how we see ourselves, and how others see us has become acknowledged as key ways in which we make sense of who we are and how we experience the world (Stam, 1998). Many researchers in this field have long documented difficulties in accessing people's embodied experiences and appearances using language-based methodologies alone (Brown et al., 2008). One obvious problem facing researchers studying appearance and embodiment is the difficulty with which participants recall information relating to their bodies, especially if they are having to recall events or changes over significant periods of time. Frith and Harcourt (2007) conducted a photo-production study using interview methodology and photographs produced by patients over a period of time. They found that gradual changes in appearance sometimes went unnoticed by patients until they were able to look at a series of photographs in the interview discussion. For example, on looking at the photographs, some patients who had undergone treatment for breast cancer, noticed they looked older or had put on weight—something they had not picked up before viewing the visual material. As one participant remarked:

> One of the things that I've been aware of is the fact that over a period of a couple of months I put on quite a lot of weight when I was having my chemo, and I can see from the start of the chemo to the end, that I actually found quite upsetting. I feel I look so much older and looking at those photographs and when I see photographs of myself just a couple of months before, or even after I'd had the operation before I lost my hair, I feel like I've aged a lot. . . . I mean I always had lines on my forehead

but I used to, my fringe used to cover them, do you know what I mean, in a sense I used to hide a bit behind my longer hair and now I can't. (Frith & Harcourt, 2007, p. 1345)

In a study attempting to research embodied experiences, where the researchers also acted as participants, Gillies et al. (2005) found that language-based methodologies alone were insufficient in securing data that met their research aims. Not only did their previous language-based work (e.g., Gillies et al., 2004) tend to reproduce the traditional separation of "mind" and "body," but the participant–researchers were unable to escape cultural and stereotypical accounts of their bodies and sensations. In order to overcome these past difficulties, the research group used painting as a means to circumvent. The group painted pictures of their experiences (feelings, thoughts, and sensations) invoked by the trigger term *ageing* by attending to the physical and emotional sensations that arose without thinking or trying to justify their picture. Furthermore, there were no rules associated with painting, which could be as literal or abstract as they wished (Figure 10.3).

Painting the pictures was followed by a series of focus-group discussions about the paintings, which were transcribed and analyzed thematically (Gillies et al., 2005; Reavey & Johnson, 2008). The group found that, on the whole, the visual data afforded a less culturally stereotypical and less dualistic (where mind and body were split) representation of the embodied experience of aging. The paintings also evoked more in-depth descriptions of physical sensations and of emotions and dramatically disrupted the narrative of aging that the group members had previously drawn on. In part, this was due to the paintings starting from a more personal account of what each painting was about, the feelings it evoked, and/or the experience or event on which it was based.

Remembering

Much qualitative research (and cognitive research; Conway, 1997) conducted in the area of

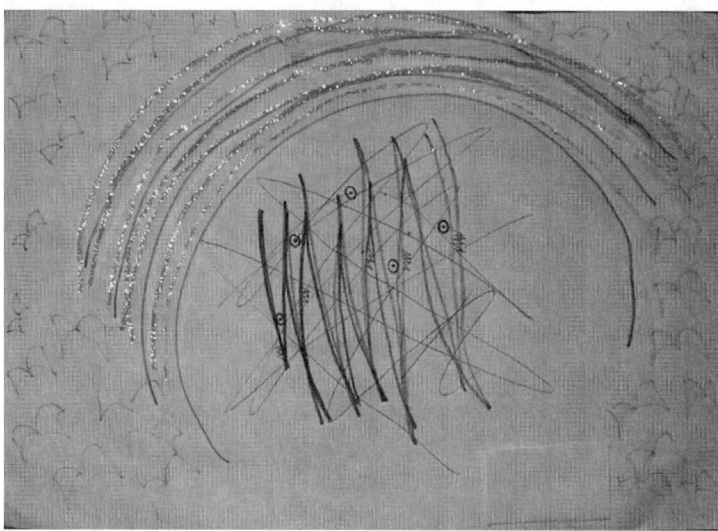

FIGURE 10.3.   A painting of an experience of aging.

memory has highlighted how individuals recon-struct the past to fit with their present concerns (Brown & Reavey, 2015; Conway, 1997; Fawns, 2021; Middleton & Brown, 2005). Who we are in the present (our present self) helps organize and structure our recollections of the past (our memory). As a result of this *reconstructive turn* in studies of memory, many qualitative researchers use detailed verbal transcripts as a way to examine the various ways in which individuals make sense of and interpret the past in relation to the present (Haaken & Reavey, 2009).

Despite the richness of verbal interview data, however, a number of researchers have high-lighted how remembering in everyday life is often facilitated by visual images—personal videos, photographs, or wider cultural images (e.g., of the traditional and "ideal" nuclear family). Looking through a photo album or watching a home video of ourselves as children, or seeing our own children as they grow up, are key means through which we are able to keep the past alive. Such activities can also serve as useful memory prompts, since we inevitably forget the specific details of certain events, particular phases in life and/or any feelings associated with them. However, it is also worth noting which photo-graphs participants actively choose to forget and leave out of a research study: participants'

discussions of *absent images* can be just as inter-esting and illuminating as the images they decide to use or focus upon (Frith, 2021; Radley & Taylor, 2003b).

Visual researchers in psychology have made use of the visual to allow participants the opportunity to recollect using familiar images. For example, adoptive parents who participated in a photo-elicitation study conducted by Brookfield and colleagues (2008) were asked to bring photographs of their adopted children's past families and/or any items and belongings that dated prior to the adoption (e.g., teddies given to them by their biological parents) to a focus group discussion. The verbal discussions of the photographs and objects were analyzed, using a discourse analytic approach. In the United Kingdom, adoptive parents are strongly encouraged to keep any verbal and visual records of their adopted children's previous families in order to be able to create a coherent story about the past. These so called *life-story books* are used to establish a version of the past for the child that they can understand and "live with." Adoptive parent participants were entirely familiar with this technique of using images to talk about their children in their everyday lives. However, the process by which family photographs are managed and integrated into the process of remembering is far from straightforward and involves possible tensions between different individuals' versions of the past, as well as dilemmas associated with how to speak around images that evoke difficult feelings (Reavey et al., 2022). Visual images help form part of how we piece together the relevancy of the past in relation to our present concerns, as well as acting as aids to recollection. This is a complex and multilayered activity and goes far beyond treating visual images as simple "reminders" or "evidence" of past events or experiences.

Communication and Interaction

The study of communication in the context of social interaction has grown significantly in the last 3 decades. Social psychologists, in particular, have examined more closely what people are doing when they speak to one another (blaming, justifying, withdrawing), rather than merely what they are saying (Stokoe, 2018). Rather than regarding language simply as a window onto the mind's activities, language is treated as actively producing psychological states in the context of interactional exchanges (e.g., conversations). In recent years, discursive psychologists who analyze various forms of discourse (e.g., conversations, counselling sessions, help-line calls, internet dialogue) have become increasingly interested in nonverbal data (e.g., expression, eye contact, gesture, gaze) and the role this plays in mediating the discursive exchange (Goodwin, 1994, 2000; Lomax, 2021; Speer & Green, 2007). A defiant look or a roll of the eyes, for example, can successfully disrupt a conversational exchange and potentially change the meaning and course of (inter)action. Increasingly sophisticated video technology has facilitated this shift towards examining "seen phenomena" (e.g., gaze, facial expression, eye movement, gesture) to advance research practice in this area. Goodwin has also examined a number of ways in which professionals (including archeologists and police officers) are taught to read visual information in particular ways, resulting in a professional gaze that structures their interactions greatly and has an impact on decision making (Goodwin, 1994, 2000, 2008).

INCREASING COLLABORATION BETWEEN RESEARCHER AND PARTICIPANT

All qualitative researchers go through a process of establishing rapport with participants, but a participatory approach is far more radical. According to this perspective, participants in a research study should be treated as collaborators, capable of providing expert testimony in their own lives and offering unique and specific insights.

Throughout the evolution of visual studies, researchers have acted as instigator, designer, collector, interpreter, and producer within the empirical process. After 1960, attention broadened to include external narratives and combine researcher and participant insights. One of the earliest documented examples of this genre in qualitative visual research was Chalfen and colleagues' (2017) "Through Navajo Eyes" project conducted in the mid-1960s. The aim of this study was to investigate the Whorf–Sapir hypothesis (language is a guide to social reality) by providing the Navajo participants with film cameras and instruction in using and editing films they were asked to make of their customs and traditions. This approach was an alternative to maintaining a distinct separation between "outsider" researcher and subjects by providing participants with the means to visually depict their own culture to gain an emic or "experience near" perspective.

This 'collaborative' approach has given rise to a research tradition that involves researchers seeking out ways of *giving voice* to participants, engaging them more closely in the research process. Technical or academic language is the preserve of professional researchers and can be disempowering to many participants. This is particularly the case where language skills are limited or in which images and their mode of production are more central to participants' everyday culture. Participants may feel more confident in creating drawings, photographs, and videos to articulate their experiences rather than using words alone. Here creative enthusiasm and aesthetic capacity—expressed through techniques involving visualization, mobile technology, doodling, graffiti, sketching, dreaming, blogging, and video and digital photography—can be harnessed to elicit otherwise seldom heard perspectives.

Qualitative visual methods tend to emphasize research 'with' rather than 'about' or 'on' participants. Experienced researchers think very carefully before exploring the meaning of images or objects with the interviewee. Whilst photo-elicitation is commonly used as an "ice-breaker," what is of especial value is the capacity of the photograph or video to act as a "third party" between researcher and researched (particularly when the power differential is considerable). Radley and Taylor provided sound exemplars of image-elicitation from a social psychologist's perspective within a broad framework of health research (Radley, 2009; Radley & Taylor, 2003a). Although some evidence exists of its effectiveness in decreasing the power differential (Warren, 2005; Packard, 2008), the method is not researcher-proof and the greatest danger to the democratization of the research process remains when researchers arrive at an interview with too many preconceptions relating to focus, process, or direction.

Participants feel less pressured when discussing sensitive topics through intermediary artifacts (Thomson, 2008). Speaking directly about a topic on which they feel vulnerable may be too much of a risk, but working through a difficult experience or topic using a material go-between (e.g., a doll, toy, line drawings, mobile phone images, or memorabilia) can provide the means to express difficult memories and powerful emotions (Reavey, 2021).

Arts-based approaches are especially participant-friendly and invoke beyond-text sensations and meaning making. Art-based research is defined by McNiff (2008) as

> the systematic use of artistic process, the actual making of artistic expressions in all of the different forms of the arts, as a primary way of understanding and examining experience by both researchers and the people that they involve in their studies. (p. 29)

The *Handbook of the Arts in Qualitative Research* (Knowles & Cole, 2008) promotes the notion that art should be regarded as a participatory-sensitive form of knowledge and not merely an ornamental product of human experience. In that book, Higgs's (2008) chapter, "Psychology: Knowing the Self Through the Arts," provides an example of a burgeoning and important link between psychology, arts-based research, and participatory qualitative visual research. This work is part of a distinctive movement that uses creative approaches to improve the quality and trustworthiness of data and findings by drawing on participants' resourcefulness and ingenuity. Gauntlett uses what he terms *creative research methods*, which involve asking participants to produce items with collage, by drawing, or making a video in order to help represent themselves and their thinking. In his book *Creative Explorations: New Approaches to Identities and Audiences* (2007), Gauntlett explained how adopting the methodological middle-ground between method-sparse postmodern/cultural studies thinking and method-limiting word-dominated approaches can result in fresh and insightful data and findings about people's experiences. In his recent work, participants are invited to spend time playfully and creatively making something meta-phorical or symbolic about their lives and then reflecting on their creation (www.artlab.org.uk). His approach is far removed from psychotherapists and art therapists of a past era, who asked their participants to construct or create something, only to then refer to a diagnostic manual in order to lay claim to expert insight into what a patient's artwork "actually" meant. Gauntlett (2007) believes that

> . . . pictures or objects enable us to present information, ideas or feelings simultaneously, without the material being forced into an order or a hierarchy. Language may be needed to *explain* the visual, but the image remains primary and shows the relationships between parts most effectively. (p. 15)

His critique of orthodox verbal interviews rests on the perspective that interviewers have unreasonable expectations of interviewees and curtail their freedoms as a consequence. He proposes that individuals do not usually retain ready-made lists of "what I think" about topics such as identity. However, a caveat to arts-based participatory visual methods, is that the process of creating artwork entails a sensual experience, and analysts need to take account of a participant's enthusiasm to create an artistic rendition of events rather than communicate personal insights.

Changes in research practice often reflect broader changes in technology and vice versa. Tools and techniques for seeing more and differently are key factors in step changes in visual research including participatory approaches. Advanced such as the telescope, microscope, X-ray, ultrasound, MRI scanner, photography, and computers reflect our innate capacity to "see," "store," "organize," and "represent" knowledge. Current participatory visual research and method owes much to Sasson's invention of the digital camera in 1975 and subsequently to the everyday uses of digital photography enabled by mobile phones. Qualitative visual researchers in psychology are aware of the speed at which technology is changing what and how they study. For example, improvements in intensive care have led to an increase in the number of patients who survive severe brain injury. Some of these patients go on to have a good recovery, but others awaken from the acute comatose state and do not show any signs of awareness. Those who yield no evidence of purposeful sensory response are given a diagnosis of a vegetative state. Monti et al. (2010) reported a study giving credibility to the possibility that some patients classified as vegetative are actually conscious, and a few may be able to communicate and actively participate in research on their lived experiences. They used functional magnetic resonance imaging to scan 54 patients' brains to record any activity generated in the patients' brains following verbal prompts and questions from the doctors. They found signs of awareness in five patients who demonstrated the ability to generate

willful, neuroanatomically specific responses during two established mental-imagery tasks, one of whom was able to answer basic yes-or-no questions by activating different parts of the brain. The results show how much we still have to learn about visual evidence, sensory consciousness, and participatory methods and further illustrate the power of applied technology to question assumptions of what is possible in participatory research.

ANALYTICAL APPROACHES

In this section, we provide a brief overview (see Reavey & Brown, 2021, for an extended discussion) of the kinds of analyses used by qualitative researchers to examine visual data, including

(a) the study of images only
(b) the study of images produced by participants, alongside their verbal description and interpretation of them
(c) when the image is used only as a trigger to elicit discussion, which then does not go on to form part of the analysis
(d) the co-study of visual and verbal data as they occur in real time, such as the study of nonverbal and verbal communication in a video recording of an interaction

The Study of Images Only

In cultural studies and sociology, it is not unusual to find research based on analyses of visual images only, especially in the semiotic tradition. Often the aim of such research is to study how cultural and social phenomena are represented through visual images, asking questions such as what and how certain values are communicated through them (van Leeuwen, 2008). This is not to say that images have a transparent or fixed meaning, as they must always be understood in relation to shifting cultural contexts (Hall, 1997). In psychology, there is a greater reluctance to study images by themselves, as psychologists tend to be more interested in not just what or how images communicate, but how people mobilize, interpret, and use them in everyday life. As Goodwin (2008) noted, "The focus of analysis is not . . . representations or vision per se, but instead the part played by visual phenomena in the production of meaningful action" (p. 157). However, there are examples of psychologists analyzing images to study social psychological phenomena. Gleeson, a social psychologist interested in learning disabilities, for example, has studied the range of identities available to individuals with disabilities by analyzing portraits of disability produced by UK charities. Her *Polytextual Thematic Analysis* of these images involves 11 clear stages of data analysis (see Gleeson, 2021, for specific details). The general principle is to identify themes relevant to the main research question and involves (a) identifying themes across a whole data set of images; (b) describing the features of each theme and providing a justification for why an image can be categorized under this theme; (c) viewing the description of all themes in relation to one another, highlighting any similarities and differences; and (d) seeing if any themes cluster together to provide a "higher order" theme that connects them. Results are written up and presented verbally, but it is recommended that the images are central to the presentation, to illustrate and provide face validity to the emerging themes.

The Study of Images Produced by Participants, Alongside Their Verbal Description and Interpretation of Them

Researchers who invite participants to produce their own photographs or artworks see the images produced as central to the analytical process. The images are not relegated to the status of a trigger for further discussion; they are analyzed with the participant as key analytic objects. Radley and Taylor (2003b), for instance, invited participants to take 12 photographs of their hospital environment during a period of recovery from surgery or illness. The participants were then interviewed immediately after taking the photographs and one month later, with the photographs forming the central part of the interview procedure.

In the interview, participants were asked to talk about and explain five aspects of the photography, including

1. what the picture showed
2. what the focus of the image was
3. their response to the objects and places in the photograph
4. the most significant image that captured the experience of their hospital stay
5. reflections on the choice of images, the act of taking pictures, and whether they had taken the pictures they would have liked to (i.e., potential limitations) (Reavey & Johnson, 2017, p. 310).

The ways in which participants responded to images at the moment of production, as well as the subsequent descriptions and memories emerging from the captured images were argued to be indicative of feelings or tendencies towards their world (Radley & Taylor, 2003a). The final images, therefore, represent patients' prior engagements with the objects and spaces captured, their act of selecting significant features of the space, and a comment on their experiences of their hospital stay. This approach calls for a continued reflexive process by participants, who are invited to comment on all aspects of the production of images, as well as the associated meanings discussed in relation to the final photographic image. During this process, the researchers observed that many of the images in themselves are not interesting or aesthetically pleasing. What was of interest, however, were the associated meanings contained within them, which were often highly complex and even profound.

The Image Is Used Only as a Trigger to Elicit Discussion and Does Not Form Part of the Final Analysis

Ready-made images, whether domestic or mass-produced, have been used in a number of qualitative research projects to elicit discussion and/or encourage debate within interviews and focus groups. The images used can be photographs, film, cartoons, graffiti, advertising billboards, and art in general (including objects) (Harper, 2002; Reavey, 2021). Individuals may find it easier to talk about aspects of identity and the self or body image via images relating to those topics. Pictures of differently shaped bodies, for example, can make it easier for participants to start with wider cultural themes before focusing down on their own particular experiences. Starting with the general can put participants at ease and enable them to make comparisons between themselves and others. In psychological studies of memory, for example, the use of family photographs may be used to access the joint process of remembering among family members (Middleton & Brown, 2005).

The Study of Visual and Verbal Data as They Occur in Real Time

It has already been noted that a growing number of researchers (e.g., discursive psychologists) are using visual phenomena such as video recordings to study processes of communication, cognition, and interaction as they occur in real time. Rather than asking participants to reflect on an image to produce data, their experiences are studied as they occur. Video data can then capture what is being said, gestures, gazes, and the spatial environment wherein the actions unfold (Hodgetts et al., 2007; Pini & Walkerdine, 2021). The researcher may also use additional materials deployed within an interaction, such as the use of graphs, charts, and tables to study how professionals communicate ideas and facts to one another (Goodwin, 1994). In terms of visual phenomena, the researcher may be interested in identifying a number of activities that then form part of the whole interaction (Goodwin, 2008):

1. gaze
2. body posture/movement
3. gesture
4. setting, including background objects or objects handled by participants

The analysis of video data begins with some form of transcription, as it does for verbal qualitative data. It is, therefore, vital that the researcher is able to transcribe adequately visual phenomena in conjunction with the verbal data. Academic

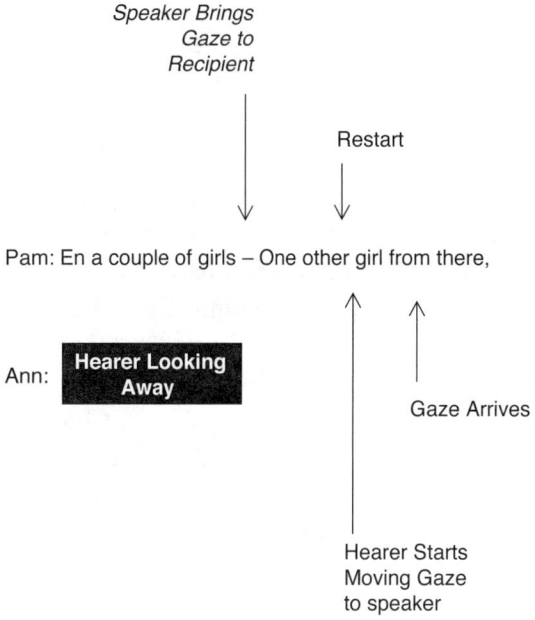

FIGURE 10.4. Gaze between speakers and hearers: transcript of Pam and Ann. Adapted from *Handbook of Visual Analysis* (p. 158), by T. van Leeuwen and C. Jewitt (Eds.), 2008, Sage. Copyright 2008 by Sage. Adapted with permission.

journals still do not yet accommodate alternative modes of presentation, so transcripts are often the only way to provide concrete examples from a data set. Goodwin (2008), for example, has used a range of transcription symbols (e.g., a hand to signal pointing) and diagrams (Figure 10.4) to denote gaze, body movement, and gesture to indicate how an interaction unfolds.

In research presentations, which are much less constrained by academic convention, the researcher should consider accompanying the presentation of data from transcripts with the video material itself to illustrate better the analytic points. Not only does this increase the ecological validity of the approach and analysis, it also makes for a more engaging presentation.

ETHICS AND THE VISUAL

Conducting research ethically is viewed as both the cornerstone of good practice and a professional necessity. Following a surge of interest in research ethics globally, there is an expectation that visual researchers act reflexively and critically in order to protect respondents and participants. Making sound ethical decisions during research projects in order to fulfil this expectation depends on researchers' personal moral frameworks, disciplinary or paradigm alliance, compliance with legal requirements, and an acceptance of regulations governing research ethics frameworks from funding bodies, professional body guidelines, and institutional ethical committees.

Approaches to ethics within psychology are typically closely aligned to medical research ethics (Alderson, 2004; Israel & Hay, 2006). Consideration of these is important in helping to guide researchers in thinking through the ethical challenges that confront them. An *ethics of care* approach, for example, is based on compassion and a desire to act in ways that benefit the individual or group who are the focus of research, rather than following universalist principles or absolute norms and rules that may govern ethical decision making. Qualitative visual researchers seek to implement collaboration in their research relationships, which often bear some commonality with an ethics of care approach (e.g., Banks, 2001; Harper, 1998; Pink, 2007; Rose, 2007).

The most common principles that underpin ethical approaches and codes of practice have been referred to as mutual respect, noncoercion and nonmanipulation, and support for democratic values and institutions. Similar themes are raised by Papademas (2004):

> Respect for person and the moral requirement to respect autonomy and the requirement to protect those with diminished autonomy; Beneficence and complementary requirement to do no harm and to maximise possible benefits and minimise possible harms; Justice and the fair distribution of the benefits and burdens of research. (p. 122)

Wiles et al. (2008, p. 8) provided a useful list of key practical issues following the principles outlined by Papademas:

- Researchers should strive to protect the rights, privacy, dignity, and well-being of those that they study.

- Research should (as far as possible) be based on voluntary informed consent.
- Personal information should be treated confidentially and participants anonymized unless they choose to be identified.
- Research participants should be informed of the extent to which anonymity and confidentiality can be assured in publication and dissemination and of the potential reuse of data.

Visual Ethics and the Law

There is an unspoken assumption that psychologists using visual methods comply with national and international law. Cultural and community pluralism added to technical legal language makes this area difficult for researchers using imagery. While laws provide a basic framework and minimum standards, they do not necessarily equate with what the research community would consider to constitute acceptable ethical or moral practices. Indeed, for many the law represents a minimalist requirement for visual researchers' ethics and much more is to be expected.

There are generic laws that apply to citizens and researchers and effectively span national laws. The general rule, for example, in the United States and the United Kingdom is that anyone may take photographs in public places or places where they have permission to take photographs. Problems may occur in determining what constitutes a public and semipublic space, such as shopping centers, schools, or railway stations, but we assume that usually researchers seek prior permission from owner or managers. New laws may cause researchers to interpret their relevance to the research environment. The UK Data Protection Act 1998, for example, may affect photography. An image of an individual may be considered personal data for the purpose of the Act, requiring consent to be obtained that is impractical when recording people's behavior in busy public spaces. Most researchers consider the spirit of the law is not contravened if consent is not obtained in these circumstances.

Copyright is an aspect of the law that few psychologists using visual methods take into account. For copyright purposes, images come under *artistic works* and include paintings, cartoons, sketches, graphs, diagrams, sketches, photographs, and moving images such as films. Copyright of artistic works is an automatic right given to creators of original material that allows them to control copying, adaptation, issuance of copies to the public, performance, and broadcasting. Researchers wishing to retain control of images they have created (and own the copyright) or to use images made by others (who own the copyright) by, for example, publishing them, should be aware of laws that safeguard copyright. Often visual researchers ask participants to assign copyright to them at the onset of a study if they intend to ask respondents to create artistic works such as web pages, drawings, and photographs as part of the data collection process. Intellectual property rights such as data protection and copyright are convoluted and are continually modified to meet changing circumstances. The rights are analogous throughout Western countries, and, although images are normally covered by the particular copyright law of the country in which they are made, copyright owners are automatically protected in many other countries as most are signatories to the Berne Convention for the Protection of Literary and Artistic Works, which provides reciprocal protection.

Banks (2007) reminded us that visual researchers should be vigilant with regard two important issues: "The first is legal: are they producing, reproducing or altering an image that someone else might claim to own? The second is moral, by what right (legally enforceable or otherwise) are they producing, reproducing or altering an image?" (p. 89).

Banks (2007, p. 88) suggested an intellectual rather than legal-ethical resolution to ethical decision making and proposes that the best way to avoid problems is to develop an awareness of context: the researcher should know enough about the society or community through their research, both in the library and in the field, to anticipate what the likely response will be.

Contemporary societies comprise a mix of religions and ethnicity, and visual researchers should be aware of the significance of this. It is important, for example, that visual researchers seeking to photograph women of Islamic faith negotiate consent prior to taking a photograph and, if married, this may involve seeking the husband's approval before agreeing (a point that researchers themselves may find highly problematic). Sharia law is concerned with day-to-day aspects of Islamic life, including social issues, family, dress and behavioral codes, but it is not explicit on the topic of photography. There are multiple interpretations of Sharia law, and different countries and communities have different understandings of the use of photography, which must be examined beforehand.

Critical Issues

In this section, we consider two issues relevant in conducting ethical research that pose particular challenges for visual researchers: informed consent and anonymity along with confidentiality.

Obtaining informed consent entails gaining agreement or permission not only to take or produce visual images but also to reproduce or display those images to different audiences and in different contexts. In providing informed consent, participants are expected to not be deceived or coerced into taking part in research, are informed of the purpose of the research and the research process, and to understand the uses to which the research will be put (Wiles et al., 2007). In ethnographic research, detailed discussion of the research, its purpose, and plans for dissemination, might all be part of the consent procedure (Rose, 2017). On other occasions, for example, if an image is required for illustration purposes, then a simple request to take a photograph with accompanying explanation as to the purpose may be sufficient (Banks, 2001). The process requires careful consideration, and there are a number of epistemological as well as ethical benefits of obtaining informed consent to collect and use visual images (Banks, 2007; Pink, 2007). Chief among these is the argument that obtaining consent is a requisite of obtaining good quality data. Visual data alone may provide limited understandings of the meanings and experiences that are recorded within those data, and it is through discussion with participants that researchers can pick up and reflect the realities and experiences of participants (Banks, 2001; Harper, 1998). The public display, publishing, or wider dissemination of visual data without the consent of individuals pictured has been described as ethically questionable (Pink, 2007; Prosser & Schwartz, 1998). Gaining consent is also important for maintaining rapport and a relationship of trust between researchers and individuals in the field and to avoid a detrimental impact on the success of ongoing or subsequent research (Prosser, 2000). Like other visual researchers, Chaplin (2004, p. 45) is clear in her advice to "always ask permission before photographing someone, and always get written permission before publishing the photograph." However, while this is good ethical practice, obtaining informed consent is not always straightforward. Obtaining consent for photographing children, for example, requires careful deliberation. Parental consent is needed if a child is not viewed as having the capacity to consent (Masson, 2004). In some circumstances, both the parents and the children must be asked for their consent to photograph or video regardless of the child's capacity to consent. The notion of a person's capacity to give consent is a judgment that relates to vulnerable members of a society, for example, the young, older people, and those with disabilities and even mental health difficulties (Reavey et al., 2019).

Another challenging dilemma relating to what it is that participants are consenting to. There are differences between consenting to take part in visual research and consenting for an image to be published in a book. For example, consent may be required not only to produce a photograph or film footage but also for the specific formats and contexts in which the image is displayed such as books, conference papers, exhibitions, or for general illustrative purposes (Pink, 2007; Prosser & Loxley, 2008). While participants might give consent to having their photograph taken, they may not be consenting to subsequent display of those images. The question of what it is that participants are consenting to becomes more complex if visual data are archived, resulting in unknown further

reuses of data. It is increasingly common for visual researchers to seek blanket consent to use the images collected as part of a project, to be used in any way they (the researcher) deem fit, which does not in their view endanger the participant.

Visual data present particular challenges for the anonymity and confidentiality of individuals, particularly when photography is employed (Brown et al., 2021). The benefits of collaborative research, where participants are encouraged to take part in the production, analysis, and dissemination of visual research, are well documented (Banks, 2001; Pink, 2007). The close relationships established between researchers and participants in certain instances enable discussion of the implications of showing images and films to be undertaken. However, some participants who engage in the research process because they see benefits in terms of voice and agency, may question the need to be anonymized—indeed, they may object if they are not "seen" (Wiles et al., 2008). If one of the aims of participatory visual research is to empower and give voice to seldom heard groups and individuals, but those individuals and groups are anonymized against their wishes, this raises important questions about power relationships in research and control of the research (Hodgetts et al., 2021).

Given that visual data reveal important information that text or word-based methods may not uncover, attempting to disguise visual data can remove the very point of including the data in the first place. Hence, visual researchers tend to favour gaining consent from participants to display their images unchanged. An alternative is partial anonymization where decisions are made about what to anonymize in an image as, for example, clothing, jewelry, tattoos, and the environments where individuals are photographed can all potentially breech confidentiality. Barrett (2004), on the other hand, took a minimalist approach in her photographic essay of a needle exchange facility in an American city by only showing photographs of hands or people with backs turned. Similarly, Brown and colleagues asked patient participants in a secure forensic mental health facility not to take pictures of either staff or other patients (Brown et al., 2021). Clark et al. (2010) illustrated how overanonymizing data can also be a danger with a photograph showing a distinctive feature of a building, a car number plate, and an adult and a child all anonymized, rendering the image almost meaningless. Researchers adopt a range of techniques when anonymizing participants and respondents. These may include using actors and reenacting events, using software packages that render photographs in the form of a cartoon style graphic, or various forms of pixilation for the blurring of faces (Wiles et al., 2008). However, it has been argued that pixelating images can dehumanise the individuals in them, and because of its widespread use on television, can invoke associations with criminality (Banks, 2001).

Maintaining internal confidentiality (between members of a specific group) can cause anonymity problems from media other than photographic rendition. Clark et al. (2010) located various ways in which family members and the creator could be identified by members of a school or neighborhood community (Figure 10.5). They pointed out that

> the author's name, although hidden by a black pen, can be guessed by the size of the first and second name, and be seen when the paper on which the original is made, is held up to the light and the drawing shows all the information required to identify a family of four, of mixed race, comprising two adults and two children of each gender and a mother with one leg. (p. 87)

The digitization of data and the growth of the internet to display, store, and exchange visual data have created further ethical challenges (Pauwels, 2006). It is no longer possible to make firm assurances to participants that visual data will be used appropriately once they are disseminated in the academic domain and, therefore, potentially made public. Once in the public realm, participants and researchers have no control over how images might be interpreted by audiences or the different purposes for which

FIGURE 10.5.   Example of participant's drawing. From "Ethical Issues in Image-Based Research," by A. Clark, J. Prosser, and R. Wiles, 2010, *Arts and Health*, 2(1), p. 407, Routledge. Copyright 2010 by Routledge of the Taylor & Francis Group. Reprinted with permission.

they may be used by others. This means particular care should be taken to ensure participants understand the implications of consenting to the displaying of images used in research, given that they may by placed online. The flipside is that visual researchers may themselves access and use visual data from the internet in their own research. Lee (2000) suggested that images appropriated in this way should still "fall within the scope of existing guidelines on ethical research practice in respect of informed consent, privacy and confidentiality and the need to protect research participants from harm" (p. 135). While empirical visual researchers may support this position (Godel, 2007; Pauwels, 2006), those adopting a critical or sociosemiotic analysis of "found" visual data are less enamoured with the prospect of seeking approval of copyright owners for those depicted, given logistical considerations, and because some consider the posting of images on public sites to be an acceptable form of consent for the further use of those images.

Visual psychologists may feel hesitant and unprepared to field the ethical probes of nonvisual methodologists. Evidence of the relationship between visual researchers and institutional ethics committees is rare and often anecdotal. Pauwels (2008) recounted how

> [a] recent conference session on ethics in visual research and in particular on the role of ethics review committees (International Visual Sociology Association Annual Conference, New York, August 2007) revealed the urgent need to address these (ethical) issues and also the willingness of most parties involved to improve the situation. Many participants testified about Institutional Review Boards, which worked strictly by the book and were ignorant of the specific demands of visual research, and thus in good faith provided obstacles to innovative and well thought through research. But there were also examples of review boards

that did include people experienced in visual research, and which succeeded in making headway. (p. 256)

This is indicative rather than substantive data, but nevertheless it suggests that there are important issues to be explored by consulting members of ethics review boards and applicants to those boards. Visual psychologists, like their qualitative cousins in sociology and anthropology, are uneasy with the difficulties posed by acquiescing to various regulatory mechanisms and nervous at the complexity of applied moral decision making. Although negotiating informed consent and applying appropriate strategies of anonymity and confidentiality make for ethical complexity, this should not be taken to mean the endeavour should be avoided.

CONCLUSION

Psychology has a long and complex historical relationship with the visual. While a qualitatively driven visual dimension has not featured as prominently in psychology as it has in other social science disciplines, a distinctive and robust body of work has now emerged that bodes well for the future (Reavey, 2021). There are many excellent ways of undertaking visual research and applying visual methods within psychology and what is described in this chapter does not exhaust all possibilities. Our advice is to ignore, or at the very least treat with caution, any visual researchers who claim theirs is the "only," "proper," or "best" way, without a robust clear rationale. We recognized that in attempting to provide a resource useful to a cross section of psychologists and applied researchers, we would necessarily sacrifice depth for breadth.

Over the last decade the landscape of qualitative visual research has changed. Qualitative psychologists have taken up the challenge to understand the experiences of individuals and groups within a society, dominated by visual culture, by adopting visual methodologies. The richness of possibilities that once constrained visual studies in psychology appears to be dissipating fast, and now visual researchers are gaining ground in higher impact journals and in competitive funding bids. The visual and other sensory approaches have opened up possibilities for understanding individual embodied and emotional experiences. The most significant challenge facing visual researchers today lies in developing the capacity to be sufficiently flexible, creative, and critical in order to provide solutions to problems facing humanity. As one would expect given the rate and nature of change, this has brought diversity and methodological problems such as visual analysis and complex ethical considerations. There is, however, every reason to be positive. A methodologically framed, qualitatively driven, visually oriented, mixed-method, interdisciplinary approach to examining overarching and substantive psychological themes and research questions continues to grow. Visual centric qualitatively driven research is widely practised across a range of disciplines, and it is timely and appropriate to continue to apply these approaches to the study of all forms of psychology. In the decade following the first edition of Reavey's (2011) edited collection on visual methods in psychology and the first version of this chapter (Reavey & Prosser, 2012), the legitimacy of visual research in psychology has increased significantly, with funding awarded to visual researchers and publications of visual work in high-quality medical and psychology journals. We believe that the rising demand from funding bodies and government for researchers to work more collaboratively with stakeholders will inevitably increase the need for image-based methodologies, as it is what people are already doing in their everyday lives to make sense of themselves, other people, and the world; something researchers in psychology cannot afford to ignore.

References

Alderson, P. (2004). Ethics. In S. Fraser, V. Lewis, S. Ding, M. Kellett, & C. Robinson (Eds.), *Doing research with children and young people* (pp. 97–112). SAGE.

Anderson, K., Reavey, P., & Boden, Z. (2019). 'Never drop without your significant other, cause that way lies ruin': The boundary work of couples who use MDMA together. *International Journal on Drug Policy*, *71*, 10–18. https://doi.org/10.1016/j.drugpo.2019.05.004

Banks, M. (2001). *Visual methods in social research*. SAGE. https://doi.org/10.4135/9780857020284

Banks, M. (2007). *Using visual data in qualitative research*. SAGE. https://doi.org/10.4135/9780857020260

Barrett, D. (2004). Photo-documenting the needle exchange: Methods and ethics. *Visual Studies*, *19*(2), 145–149. https://doi.org/10.1080/1472586042000301647

Boden, Z., & Larkin, M. (2021). Moving from social networks to visual metaphors with the relational mapping interview: An example in early psychosis. In P. Reavey (Ed.), *A handbook of visual methods in psychology: Using and interpreting images in qualitative research* (2nd ed., pp. 358–375). Routledge.

Bowes-Catton, H., Barker, M., & Richards, C. (2021). 'I didn't know that I could feel this relaxed in my body': Using visual methods to research bisexual people's embodied experiences of identity and space. In P. Reavey (Ed.), *A handbook of visual methods in psychology: Using and interpreting images in qualitative research* (2nd ed., pp. 409–427). Routledge.

Brookfield, H., Brown, S. D., & Reavey, P. (2008). Vicarious and post-memory practices in adopting families: The re-production of the past through photography and narrative. *Journal of Community & Applied Social Psychology*, *18*(5), 474–491. https://doi.org/10.1002/casp.960

Brown, S. D., Kanyeredzi, A., McGrath, L., Reavey, P., & Tucker, I. (2021). Reflections on a photo-production study: Practical, analytic and epistemic issues. In P. Reavey (Ed.), *A handbook of visual methods in psychology: Using and interpreting images in qualitative research* (2nd. ed., pp. 113–132). Routledge.

Brown, S. D., & Reavey, P. (2015). *Vital memory & affect: Living with a difficult past*. Routledge. https://doi.org/10.4324/9781315713939

Brown, S. D., Reavey, P., Cromby, J., Harper, D., & Johnson, K. (2008). On psychology and embodiment: Some methodological experiments. In J. Latimer & M. Schillmeier (Eds.), *Un/knowing bodies (sociological review monographs)*. Blackwell. https://doi.org/10.1111/j.1467-954X.2009.00823.x

Buss, D. (2005). *The evolutionary psychology handbook*. John Wiley.

Chalfen, R., Worth, S., & Adair, J. (2017). *Through Navajo eyes: An exploration in film communication and anthropology* (Revised 2nd ed.). University of New Mexico Press.

Chaplin, E. (2004). My visual diary. In C. Knowles & P. Sweetman (Eds.), *Picturing the social landscape: Visual methods and the sociological imagination* (pp. 34–48). Routledge.

Clark, A., Prosser, J., & Wiles, R. (2010). Ethical issues in image-based research. *Arts & Health: An International Journal for Research, Policy & Practice, 2*(1), 81–93.

Collier, J., Jr. (1957). Photography in anthropology: A report on two experiments. *American Anthropologist, 59*(5), 843–859. https://doi.org/10.1525/aa.1957.59.5.02a00100

Conway, M. (Ed.). (1997). *Cognitive models of memory*. Psychology Press.

Cramer, P. (1996). *Storytelling, narrative and the thematic apperception test*. Guilford Press.

Darwin, C. (1999). *The expression of the emotions in man and animals: Definitive edition*. Fontana Press. (Original work published 1872) https://doi.org/10.1037/10001-000

Del Busso, L. (2009). *Being in motion: Femininity, movement and space in young women's narratives of their embodied experiences in everyday life* [Unpublished doctoral dissertation]. London South Bank University.

Del Busso, L. (2021). Capturing embodied experience: The use of photographs in research on young women's embodied experiences in everyday life. In P. Reavey (Ed.), *A handbook of visual methods in psychology: Using and interpreting images in qualitative research* (2nd ed., pp. 70–82). Routledge.

Draaisma, D. (2000). *Metaphors of memory: A history of ideas about the mind*. Cambridge University Press.

Emmison, M., & Smith, P. (2000). *Researching the visual: Images, objects, contexts and interactions in social and cultural inquiry*. SAGE.

Fawns, T. (2021). The photo-elicitation interview as a multimodal site for reflexivity. In P. Reavey (Ed.), *A handbook of visual methods in psychology: Using and interpreting images in qualitative research* (2nd ed., pp. 487–501). Routledge.

Fechner, G. T. (1966). *Elements of psychophysics*. Holt, Rinehart & Winston. (Original work published 1860)

Fitzpatrick, J. F., & Bringmann, W. G. (1997). Charles Darwin and psychology. In W. G. Bringmann, H. E. Lück, R. Miller, & C. E. Early (Eds.), *A pictorial history of psychology* (pp. 51–52). Quintessence Books.

Frith, H. (2021). Narrating biographical disruption and repair: Exploring the place of absent images in women's experiences of cancer and chemotherapy. In P. Reavey (Ed.), *A handbook of visual methods in psychology: Using and interpreting images in qualitative research* (2nd ed., pp. 83–96). Routledge.

Frith, H., & Harcourt, D. (2007). Using photographs to capture women's experiences of chemotherapy: Reflecting on the method. *Qualitative Health Research, 17*(10), 1340–1350. https://doi.org/10.1177/1049732307308949

Frost, L. (2005). Theorizing the young woman in the body. *Body & Society, 11*(1), 63–85. https://doi.org/10.1177/1357034X05049851

Gauntlett, D. (2007). *Creative explorations: New approaches to identities and audiences*. Routledge. https://doi.org/10.4324/9780203961407

Gillies, V., Harden, A., Johnson, K., Reavey, P., Strange, V., & Willig, C. (2004). Women's collective constructions of embodied practices through memory work: Cartesian dualism in memories of sweating and pain. *British Journal of Social Psychology, 43*(1), 99–112. https://doi.org/10.1348/014466604322916006

Gillies, V., Harden, A., Johnson, K., Reavey, P., Strange, V., & Willig, C. (2005). Painting pictures of embodied experience: The use of nonverbal data production for the study of embodiment. *Qualitative Research in Psychology, 2*(3), 199–212. https://doi.org/10.1191/1478088705qp038oa

Gleeson, K. (2021). Polytextual thematic analysis for visual data—Pinning down the analytic. In P. Reavey (Ed.), *A handbook of visual methods in psychology: Using and interpreting images in qualitative research* (2nd ed., pp. 536–554). Routledge.

Gleeson, K., & Frith, H. (2006). (De)constructing body image. *Journal of Health Psychology, 11*(1), 79–90. https://doi.org/10.1177/1359105306058851

Godel, M. (2007). Images of stillbirth: Memory, meaning and memorial. *Visual Studies, 22*(3), 253–269. https://doi.org/10.1080/14725860701657159

Goodwin, C. (1994). Professional vision. *American Anthropologist, 96*(3), 606–633. https://doi.org/10.1525/aa.1994.96.3.02a00100

Goodwin, C. (2000). Action and embodiment within situated human interaction. *Journal of Pragmatics, 32*(10), 1489–1522. https://doi.org/10.1016/S0378-2166(99)00096-X

Goodwin, C. (2008). Practices of seeing visual analysis: An ethnomethodological approach. In T. van Leeuwen & C. Jewitt (Eds.), *Handbook of visual analysis* (pp. 157–183). SAGE.

Haaken, J., & Reavey, P. (Eds.). (2009). *Memory matters: Contexts of understanding sexual abuse recollections* (pp. 24–42). Routledge. https://doi.org/10.4324/9780203873632

Hall, S. (1997). Introduction. In S. Hall (Ed.), *Representation: Cultural representations and signifying practices* (pp. 13–35). SAGE.

Harper, D. (1998). An argument for visual sociology. In J. Prosser (Ed.), *Image-based research: A sourcebook for qualitative researchers* (pp. 24–42). Falmer Press.

Harper, D. (2002). Talking about pictures: A case for photo elicitation. *Visual Studies, 17*(1), 13–26. https://doi.org/10.1080/14725860220137345

Higgs, G. E. (2008). Psychology: Knowing the self through the arts. In J. G. Knowles & A. L. Cole (Eds.), *Handbook of the arts in qualitative research* (pp. 545–557). SAGE.

Hodgetts, D., Chamberlain, K., & Groot, S. (2021). Reflections on the visual in community research and action. In P. Reavey (Ed.), *A handbook of visual methods in psychology: Using and interpreting images in qualitative research* (2nd ed., pp. 519–535). Routledge.

Hodgetts, D., Chamberlain, K., & Radley, A. (2007). Considering photographs never taken during photo-production project. *Qualitative Research in Psychology, 4*(4), 263–280. https://doi.org/10.1080/14780880701583181

Hodgetts, D., Radley, A., Chamberlain, K., & Hodgetts, A. (2007). Health inequalities and homelessness: Considering material, spatial and relational dimensions. *Journal of Health Psychology, 12*(5), 709–725. https://doi.org/10.1177/1359105307080593

Howarth, C. (2011). Towards a visual social psychology of identity and representation: Photographing the self, weaving the family in a multicultural British community. In P. Reavey (Ed.), *Visual methods in psychology: Using and interpreting images in qualitative research* (pp. 241–255). Routledge.

Israel, M., & Hay, I. (2006). *Research ethics for social scientists: Between ethical conduct and regulatory compliance.* SAGE. https://doi.org/10.4135/9781849209779

Jackson, M. (1995). Images of deviance: Visual representations of mental defectives in early twentieth-century. *British Journal for the History of Science, 28*(3), 319–337. https://doi.org/10.1017/S0007087400033185

Knowles, J. G., & Cole, A. L. (Eds.). (2008). *Handbook of the arts in qualitative research.* SAGE.

Kuhn, A. (2007). Photography and cultural memory: A methodological exploration. *Visual Studies,* 22(3), 283–292. https://doi.org/10.1080/14725860701657175

Kunimoto, N. (2004). Intimate archives: Japanese-Canadian family photography, 1939–1949. *Art History, 27*(1), 129–155. https://doi.org/10.1111/j.0141-6790.2004.02701005.x

Langdridge, D. (2007). *Phenomenological psychology: Theory, research and method.* Pearson Prentice Hall.

Langdridge, D., Gabb, J., & Lawson, J. (2021). Working with group-level data in phenomenological research: A modified visual matrix method. In P. Reavey (Ed.), *A handbook of visual methods in psychology: Using and interpreting images in qualitative research* (2nd ed., pp. 301–322). Routledge.

Lee, R. (2000). *Unobtrusive methods in social research.* Open University Press.

Lomax, H. (2021). Visual identities: Choreographies of gaze, body movement and speech in video-based mother-midwife interactions. In P. Reavey (Ed.), *A handbook of visual methods in psychology: Using and interpreting images in qualitative research* (2nd ed., pp. 202–220). Routledge.

Majumdar, A. (2011). Using photographs of places, spaces and objects to explore South Asian Women's experience of close relationships and marriage. In P. Reavey (Ed.), *Visual methods in psychology: Using and interpreting images in qualitative research* (pp. 69–85). Routledge.

Masson, J. (2004). The legal context. In S. Fraser, V. Lewis, S. Ding, M. Kellett, & C. Robinson (Eds.), *Doing research with children and young people* (pp. 43–58). SAGE.

McGrath, L. (2012). *Heterotopias of mental health care: The role of space in experiences of distress, madness and mental health service use* [Unpublished doctoral dissertation]. London South Bank University.

McGrath, L., Mullarkey, S., & Reavey, P. (2020). Building visual worlds: Using maps in qualitative psychological research on affect and emotion. *Qualitative Research in Psychology: Feelings, Affect and Emotions in Qualitative Psychology, 17*(1), 75–97. https://doi.org/10.1080/14780887.2019.1577517

McNiff, S. (2008). Art-based research. In J. G. Knowles & A. L. Cole (Eds.), *Handbook of the arts in qualitative research* (pp. 29–41). SAGE.

Meischner-Metge, A., & Meischner, W. (1997). Fechner and Lotze. In W. G. Bringmann, H. E. Lück, R. Miller, & C. E. Early (Eds.), *A pictorial history of psychology* (pp. 101–106). Quintessence Books.

Middleton, D., & Brown, S. D. (2005). *The social psychology of experience: Studies in remembering and forgetting.* SAGE.

Middleton, D., & Edwards, D. (Eds.). (1990). *Collective remembering*. SAGE.

Milgram, S. (2005). *Obedience to authority: An experimental view*. Pinter and Martin.

Mirzoeff, N. (2009). *An introduction to visual culture* (2nd ed.). Routledge.

Monti, M. M., Vanhaudenhuyse, A., Coleman, M. R., Boly, M., Pickard, J. D., Tshibanda, L., Owen, A. M., & Laureys, S. (2010). Willful modulation of brain activity in disorders of consciousness. *The New England Journal of Medicine*, 362(7), 579–589. https://doi.org/10.1056/NEJMoa0905370

Packard, J. (2008). 'I'm gonna show you what it's really like out there': The power and limitation of participatory research methods. *Visual Studies*, 23(1), 63–77. https://doi.org/10.1080/14725860801908544

Papademas, D. (2004). Editor's introduction: Ethics in visual research. *Visual Studies*, 19(2), 122–126. https://doi.org/10.1080/1472586042000301610

Pauwels, L. (2006). Discussion: Ethical issues in online (visual) research. *Visual Anthropology*, 19(3–4), 365–369. https://doi.org/10.1080/08949460600656691

Pauwels, L. (2008). A private practice going public? Social functions and sociological research opportunities of web-based family photography. *Visual Studies*, 23(1), 34–49. https://doi.org/10.1080/14725860801908528

Pini, M., & Walkerdine, V. (2021). Girls on film: Video diaries as 'autoethnographies.' In P. Reavey (Ed.), *A handbook of visual methods in psychology: Using and interpreting images in qualitative research* (2nd ed., pp. 187–201). Routledge.

Pink, S. (2007). *Doing visual ethnography* (2nd ed.). SAGE. https://doi.org/10.4135/9780857025029

Porter, R. (2003). *Madness: A brief history*. Oxford University Press.

Prosser, J. (2000). The moral maze of image ethics. In H. Simons & R. Usher (Eds.), *Situated ethics in education research* (pp. 116–132). Routledge.

Prosser, J., & Loxley, A. (2008). *Introducing visual methods*. National Centre for Research Methods Review Paper 010. http://eprints.ncrm.ac.uk/420/1/MethodsReviewPaperNCRM-010.pdf

Prosser, J., & Schwartz, D. (1998). Photographs within the sociological research process. In J. Prosser (Ed.), *Image-based research: A sourcebook for qualitative researchers* (pp. 115–130). Falmer Press.

Radley, A. (1990). Artefacts, memory and a sense of the past. In D. Middleton & D. Edwards (Eds.), *Collective remembering* (pp. 46–59). SAGE.

Radley, A. (2009). *Works of illness: Narrative, picturing and the social response to serious disease*. InkMen Press.

Radley, A., & Taylor, D. (2003a). Images of recovery: A photo-elicitation study on the hospital ward. *Qualitative Health Research*, 13(1), 77–99. https://doi.org/10.1177/1049732302239412

Radley, A., & Taylor, D. (2003b). Remembering one's stay in hospital: A study in photography, recovery and forgetting. *Health: An Interdisciplinary Journal for the Social Study of Health, Illness and Medicine*, 7(2), 129–159. https://doi.org/10.1177/1363459303007002872

Ratcliff, D. (2003). Video methods in qualitative research. In P. M. Camic, J. E. Rhodes, & L. Yardley (Eds.), *Qualitative research in psychology: Expanding perspectives in methodology and design* (pp. 113–129). American Psychological Association. https://doi.org/10.1037/10595-007

Reavey, P. (2008). *Back to experience: Material subjectivities and the visual* [Keynote address]. Visual Psychologies Conference, University of Leicester, UK.

Reavey, P. (2010). Spatial markings: Memory and child sexual abuse. *Memory Studies*, 3(4), 314–329. https://doi.org/10.1177/1750698010370035

Reavey, P. (2011). The return to experience: Psychology and the visual. In P. Reavey (Ed.), *Visual methods in psychology: Using and interpreting images in qualitative research* (pp. 1–14). Routledge.

Reavey, P. (Ed.). (2021). *A handbook of visual methods in psychology: Using and interpreting images in qualitative research* (2nd ed.). Routledge.

Reavey, P., & Brown, S. D. (2021). Analysing visual data. In E. Lyons & A. Coyle (Eds.), *Analysing qualitative data in psychology* (3rd ed., pp. 100–121). SAGE.

Reavey, P., Brown, S. D., Kanyeredzi, A., McGrath, L., & Tucker, I. (2019). Agents and spectres: Life-space on a medium secure forensic psychiatric unit. *Social Science & Medicine*, 220, 273–282. https://doi.org/10.1016/j.socscimed.2018.11.012

Reavey, P., Brown, S. D., Ravenhill, J., Boden, Z., & Ciarlo, D. (2022). Choreographies of sexual safety and liminality: Forensic mental health and the limits of recovery. *SSM—Mental Health*, 2, 100090. https://doi.org/10.1016/j.ssmmh.2022.100090

Reavey, P., & Johnson, K. (2008). Visual approaches: Using and interpreting images. In W. Stainton Rogers & C. Willig (Eds.), *The SAGE handbook of qualitative research* (pp. 296–315). SAGE.

Reavey, P., & Johnson, K. (2017). Visual approaches revisited: Using and interpreting images. In W. Stainton Rogers & C. Willig (Eds.), *SAGE handbook of qualitative research* (2nd ed., pp. 296–314).

Open University Press. https://doi.org/10.4135/9781526405555.n21

Reavey, P., & Prosser, J. (2012). Visual research in psychology. In H. Cooper (Ed.), *APA handbook of research methods in psychology: Vol. 2. Research designs: Quantitative, qualitative, neuropsychological, and biological* (pp. 185–207). American Psychological Association. https://doi.org/10.1037/13620-012

Richards, G. (2002). *Putting psychology in its place: A critical historical overview* (2nd ed.). Routledge.

Rose, G. (2007). *Visual methodologies* (2nd ed.). SAGE.

Rose, G. (2017). *Visual methodologies* (4th ed.). SAGE.

Silver, J., & Reavey, P. (2010). "He's a good-looking chap aint he?": Narrative and visualisations of self in body dysmorphic disorder. *Social Science & Medicine, 70*(10), 1641–1647. https://doi.org/10.1016/j.socscimed.2009.11.042

Speer, S. A., & Green, R. (2007). On passing: The interactional organization of appearance attributions in the psychiatric assessment of transsexual patients. In V. Clarke & E. Peel (Eds.), *Out in psychology: Lesbian, gay, bisexual, trans and queer perspectives* (pp. 335–368). Wiley & Sons. https://doi.org/10.1002/9780470713099.ch16

Stainton Rogers, W., & Willig, C. (Eds.). (2017). *The SAGE handbook of qualitative methods in psychology.* SAGE.

Stam, H. (Ed.). (1998). *The body and psychology.* SAGE. https://doi.org/10.4135/9781446279175

Stanczak, G. (Ed.). (2007). *Visual research methods: Image, society and representation.* SAGE.

Stenner, P. (2017). *Liminality and experience: A transdisciplinary approach to the psychosocial (studies in the psychosocial).* Palgrave Macmillan.

Stokoe, E. (2018). *Talk the science of conversation.* Robinson.

Thomson, P. (Ed.). (2008). *Doing visual research with children and young people.* Routledge.

Van Elteren, M. (1992). Kurt Lewin as filmmaker and methodologist. *Canadian Psychology, 33*(3), 599–608. https://doi.org/10.1037/h0078734

Van Elteren, M., & Luck, H. (1990). Lewin's films and their role in field theory. In S. A. Wheelan, E. A. Pepitone, & V. Abt (Eds.), *Advances in field theory* (pp. 38–61). SAGE.

van Leeuwen, T. (2008). Semiotics and iconography. In T. van Leeuwen & C. Jewitt (Eds.), *Handbook of visual analysis* (pp. 92–119). SAGE.

Wagner, J. (2006). Visible materials, visualised theory and images of social research. *Visual Studies, 21*(1), 55–69. https://doi.org/10.1080/14725860600613238

Warren, S. (2005). Photography and voice in critical qualitative management research. *Accounting, Auditing & Accountability Journal, 18*(6), 861–882. https://doi.org/10.1108/09513570510627748

Wiles, R., Crow, G., Charles, V., & Heath, S. (2007). Informed consent in the research process: Following rules or striking balances? *Sociological Research Online, 12*(2), 99–110. https://doi.org/10.5153/sro.1208

Wiles, R., Prosser, J., Bagnoli, A., Clark, A., Davies, K., Holland, S., & Renold, E. (2008). *Visual ethics: Ethical issues in visual research.* National Centre for Research Methods: Methods Review Paper 011. https://eprints.ncrm.ac.uk/id/eprint/421/

Willig, C. (2008). *Introducing qualitative methods in psychology: Adventures in theory and method.* Open University Press.

Zimbardo, P., Maslach, C., & Haney, C. (2000). Reflections on the Stanford Prison Experiment: Genesis, transformations, consequences. In T. Blass (Ed.), *Obedience to authority: Current perspectives on the Milgram paradigm* (pp. 193–238). Lawrence Erlbaum.

CHAPTER 11

RESEARCHING THE TEMPORAL

Karen Henwood and Fiona Shirani

This chapter showcases methodologically innovative work in the psychological and social sciences that is qualitative and longitudinal in research approach and where questions about time and temporal experience are of significant interest. It considers the case for conducting qualitative enquiries longitudinally and for putting concern for the significance of time and temporality in people's lives at the heart of empirical, interpretive studies (Neale & Flowerdew, 2003). Time is useful to social researchers as a *vehicle of study* because it provides a means of designing studies around key moments, transitions, trajectories, and periods of elapsed time of longer duration so that significant change is more likely to have occurred. It can also be treated as a topic of study where how people think about and relate to time, the ways in which life changes are experienced in and through time, and how such personal life experiences can be made sense of in cultural terms (Salmon, 1985) are all scrutinized to generate substantive insights. Time is a multidimensional construct and, for this reason, needs to be approached not just biographically but generationally and historically (Neale, 2007).

There is a long-standing commitment in the United Kingdom and in the United States, as well as in other countries, to investing in large-scale quantitative longitudinal (or panel) studies in which the same group of people is interviewed repeatedly with standardized questions. However, qualitative longitudinal research has also seen a recent rise in popularity, with rapid update over the first 2 decades of the 21st century as part of a broader temporal turn in social research (Neale, 2019; Thomson & McLeod, 2015). Qualitative longitudinal research "explores dynamic processes through an in-depth qualitative lens. This gives insights into how people narrate, understand and shape their unfolding lives and the evolving world of which they are a part" (Neale, 2019, p. 1). Longitudinal methodologies have variously been described as embodying the notion of time (Neale & Flowerdew, 2003), centring time and change (Holland, 2007), and recognizing that participants' thoughts, actions, emotions, attitudes, and beliefs are all dynamic through time (Saldaña, 2003). This dynamic, temporal focus makes it well-suited for exploring processes of change, rather than simply outcomes (Thomson, 2007).

In an attempt to sharpen and clarify understanding that there are different forms taken by longitudinal studies, Elliott et al. (2008) addressed both the shared and distinctive contributions of quantitative and qualitative approaches to long-term study. They portray longitudinal study generically as the means of generating

https://doi.org/10.1037/0000319-011
APA Handbook of Research Methods in Psychology, Second Edition: Vol. 2. Research Designs: Quantitative, Qualitative, Neuropsychological, and Biological, H. Cooper (Editor-in-Chief)

"unique insights into process, change and continuity in time in phenomena ranging from individuals, families and institutions to societies" (p. 228), while also pointing firmly to the way that each of the two established traditions of longitudinal study produces "different types of data, privileging particular forms of understanding and pursuing different logics of inquiry" (p. 228). Other researchers have explicitly advocated the merits of qualitative longitudinal study within predominantly quantitative research communities. For example, social policy researchers have pointed to the need for attentiveness to the ways in which the same experiences are recounted differently at different time points, in order to study people's experiences and perceptions before, during, and after an intervention (Corden & Millar, 2007; Lewis, 2007). Qualitative longitudinal research addressing the complexity of transitions and how they are differently experienced by the people involved has also been portrayed as a complementary method to the narrative study of lives (Miller, 2000).

This chapter is written in the spirit of pursuing what lies behind the different logic of the qualitative inquiry tradition, while accepting that there is also value in integrating quantitative and qualitative studies in ways that may be qualitatively or quantitatively led (Mason, 2006). The chapter starts with coverage of some of the key ideas and arguments providing the theoretical and methodological background to temporal study before proceeding to illustrate these discussions by drawing upon a qualitative longitudinal inquiry into the dynamics of men's identities, relationships, and personal lives. Known as the *men-as-fathers study*, it was part of the Timescapes network,[1] the first major large-scale qualitative longitudinal study in the United Kingdom. The network was designed to scale up the reach and impact of qualitative longitudinal studies in a number of ways. We highlight some of the core methodo-logical and analytical issues addressed in the men-as-fathers study relating to its use of qualitative longitudinal methodology (QLL) and commitment to researching the temporal more generally. We also highlight the way in which our temporal research has evolved over the decade since the original publication of this chapter in the first edition (Henwood & Shirani, 2012), with specific focus on efforts to expand temporal horizons through discussion of anticipated futures.

INTELLECTUAL BACKGROUND

Some of the key theoretical and methodological issues at stake in temporal research are encapsulated in the turn to biographical or life course methods (e.g., Chamberlayne et al., 2000; Heinz & Krüger, 2001; Rosenthal, 2004). According to Chamberlayne et al. (2000), the burgeoning of life course methods across the social sciences has to do with their capacity to offer an antidote to commonly adopted research approaches (positivism, determinism, and social constructionism) that divorce researchers from understanding the lived realities of people's lives. These authors advocate paying attention to the meanings people attach to the events they encounter in their daily lives and giving them prominence as the basis for their actions.[2] Collecting life stories, often in the form of oral histories, and understanding them in ways that see interconnections between personal meanings with wider patterns of sociohistorical change is a particularly emphasized feature of life course study (Thompson, 1975) and one that corresponds closely with more qualitative, cultural, and psychological perspectives on the narrative study of lives (Andrews et al., 2000; Squire, 2008).

Family studies are another field of inquiry that has built the case for developing principles and practices of temporal inquiry. Such inquiries generate knowledge about family formation and function in the context of wider societal

---

[1] https://timescapes-archive.leeds.ac.uk/timescapes/

[2] In this way, life-course research recapitulates two of the most long-established principles in qualitative inquiry: (a) studying ordinary meanings in ways that make them interesting and relevant objects of study (Charmaz, 2006; Charmaz & Henwood 2008) and (b) taking seriously participants' *meaning frames* (also known as the *actors' perspective*) as the basis for understanding why they do what they do (Henwood, 2008; Henwood et al., 2008).

organization and change and include the study of personal lives. As with life-course research, there is a conviction that social theorizing at a macroscopic level fails to address the complex patterns of people's lives on the ground, and a particular concern is that theories overstate the extent of changes over continuities in people's relationships in (post)modern times[3] (Smart, 2007). Out of this field, methodological initiatives have developed to counter researchers' preoccupation with theoretical abstractions and lack of engagement with the vitality and bedrock of people's lives. Timescapes, a major qualitative longitudinal study of identities and relationships across the life course, was one of these, and its particular concern was with providing an alternative to family researchers' static, atemporal focus so that is possible to study the *dynamics* of personal lives. Qualitative longitudinal study is adopted as a means of walking alongside people through time as their lives unfold (Neale, 2007; Neale & Flowerdew, 2003). This leads to a focus on continuities and changes occurring in daily life—called *microtemporal processes*—that are unlikely to follow single or linear trajectories, as the phenomena under study are in-the-making and so may, themselves, be changing. This is where a definitive contrast is set up between qualitative and quantitative longitudinal study given that the latter measures discrete variables, at specific moments in time, on a linear metric so that their intrinsic (and, hence, unchanging) qualities can be reliably counted and validly compared.

By drawing on the work of the temporal theorist Barbara Adam (1990), the Timescapes program further underpinned its conceptualization of what she has called the *extraordinary temporal dimensions* of everyday life. Clock, or quantitative time, is determined by calendars and timetables; it is a dominant form of time, often central to

adult life, and operates according to the logic of commodities and markets (it is not to be wasted, it rushes past us, and it can run out). But, equally important, are the other times that are intricate, multiple, and join us to our worlds of lived, everyday experience—our "lifeworlds"[4]—in many and varied ways: as normative times (e.g., socially approved timings and sequences); synchronisation and timeliness; expectancy and anticipation; prioritization, pace, and duration; personal time; and task times (each with their own boundaries). These times are produced at moments in everyday living, providing us with experiential modes that extend beyond the visible present. For example, they can affirm the durability of what we hold deeply significant; create a sense of security; alter or change; bridge or create distance between who we think we are at different times; and, through imagination, bring the future into the present (Salmon, 1985). As the temporal processes that engage us most in our lifeworlds may be invisible to research participants and researchers alike, making them visible requires an awareness of temporal process and movement of time that is not available to us in the realm of the everyday. The name of the QLL network "Timescapes" derives from the concept in Adam's work referring to the multiple vantage points for looking in and across time that bring our lives and worlds into view.

Time is central to QLL research most notably through the prospective–retrospective plane of time, which orients to the past, present, and future. Neale (2019) argued that this plane of time is foundational in discerning the dynamic unfolding of lives and the way we orient ourselves to time. Reflexivity is central as participants are asked to reflect back or project forward in time (McLeod, 2003). This reflexivity means recognition that past and future both influence how the participant experiences the present (Brannen & Nilsen, 2007;

---

[3]*Postmodernity* refers to the condition of societies that have undergone a fundamental shift to a mode of organization characterized by technological advancement, information technology, and a culture sceptical of absolute truth claims and sometimes to where economies are underpinned by consumption rather than industrial production.

[4]*Lifeworlds* is a term used in the philosophy of social science to refer to directly apprehended experiences of the world and the contextual ways in which such experiences become meaningful as part of everyday life. Meaningful experiences of the lifeworld arise from practical engagements between people and the worlds they inhabit and involve sense-making within sociocultural contexts. Knowledge of lifeworlds, therefore, is not created through formal theory testing or scientific modes of interpretation (Hughes, 1990).

Corden & Millar, 2007) through repercussions of past decisions or preparations for future trajectories. Understanding the intersection of biographical, historical, and generational time through a detailed view of individual lives is made possible through QLL and can help to elucidate wider social processes. Thus, in QLL, time is both vehicle and topic. A particular strength of QLL research is the way in which it can shed light on the processual, on "how" something happens over time (Thomson, 2007). Interviews over time can indicate how change occurs at the individual, household, and broader structural level (Miller, 2019). This makes it particularly suitable for exploring dynamic processes of change.

ILLUSTRATIVE STUDY

This chapter focuses on work from the men-as-fathers project in order to illustrate an innovative methodological approach, combining an interest in subjective experiences of everyday life, continuity and change, and time and temporal process. The study began in 1999, lay dormant for a period, and was then reactivated 8 years later in 2008. Both phases researched how men's identities come to be formed in a relational and contextual way. Our investigative approach involved asking how men who become fathers experience and make sense of this major life transition over the short and longer term. It also addressed how their personal sense and identity making is embedded within a broader set of sociopolitical contestations and cultural possibilities over what the lives of men who are fathers, and their significant others, should and can be (Edley & Wetherell, 1999; Wetherell & Edley, 1999). Expectations that fathers should be emotionally and practically involved with their children have been described as representing a moral discourse of contemporary fatherhood (Ives, 2015; see also Dermott & Miller, 2015, for comprehensive discussion of contemporary fathering practices).

In describing the context of contemporary lives and times in which our study participants became fathers, a salient issue is the way that individuals appear to be living out their lives in

rapidly changing times, involving a fundamental questioning of the identities and relationships that are necessary now, and will be in the future, to sustain human sociality and personal life (Henwood et al., 2002; Hollway & Featherstone, 1997). Over time, we have come to see particular value in asking questions about whether such changes have implications for how people move through life-course transitions, their timing, people's temporal experiences more generally, and their orientations to past, present, and future (Shirani & Henwood, 2011b). In this chapter, we are concerned primarily with the varied lines of exploration we conducted into a key subjectively and culturally meaningful issue, *paternal involvement*. Paternal involvement is a contemporary signifier of good fatherhood, and interrogating men's ways of relating to it can help inform sociopolitical and scientific understanding of the practices and meanings of fatherhood and masculinity today (Dermott & Miller, 2015; Doucet, 2007; Henwood & Procter, 2003; Ives, 2015). It can also elucidate men's experiences of intensive parenting culture (Shirani et al., 2012). Prior to presenting analytic insights from our research, we first detail methodological development of our QLL interview study and our use of supplementary methods and data, including our use of visual data (Henwood et al., 2008).

The first analysis we describe deploys the well-honed techniques of qualitative thematic analysis (see Chapter 4, this volume), developed in ways appropriate to meeting the challenges and potentials of QLL study. Other well-established forms of qualitative analysis can be conducted within QLL research, some of which we have drawn upon in our own work—especially discursive and narrative (e.g., Coltart & Henwood, 2012). However, thematic analysis has particular importance as a means of generating substantive categories for more in-depth qualitative analysis, as has been elucidated extensively by research conducted in the grounded theory tradition (e.g., Henwood, 2006; Pidgeon & Henwood, 2004). As a highly skilled practice, a thematic approach is of considerable value as a means of judiciously underpinning both in-depth engagement with, and the construction and comparison of, carefully crafted case data (Shirani & Henwood, 2011a).[5] By focusing on themes of involvement and redundancy identified in the data through thematic analysis across multiple waves of interviews, we describe the process of developing a case analysis, which utilizes the temporal data so integral to QLL research. Subsequently, we go on to describe a second style of analysis that pursues a more specialised, psychosocial inquiry concerning how men identify themselves as modern fathers in ways that may be imagined as much as real in order to deal with some of the elusive complexities of the dynamics of identities and relationships in and through time (Finn & Henwood, 2009). Before proceeding to present these, we first address some methodological concerns relating to our QLL interview study and our use of supplementary methods and data including our use of visual data (Henwood et al., 2008).

QLL Design, Interviewing, and Ethics

Longitudinal study has the unique potential of allowing for forward planning in data collection, including in the long term, making it possible to follow through an interest in topics through times of change. In qualitative longitudinal interview studies it is also possible to take advantage of initially unforeseen opportunities and serendipity; the flexible approach to devising actual questions and interviewing style means that adaptations can be made to meet the needs of research situations as they are encountered at moments in time (Farrall, 2006; Saldaña, 2003). Further, QLL provides more scope for methodological innovation and experimentation than other forms of qualitative research, given its extended time-scales and inherent flexibility (Holland et al., 2006; Shirani et al., 2016).

When the first phase of the study was undertaken in 1999 to 2000 (in East Anglia, England), we followed the design that is often preferred in studies of parenting transitions: three waves of interviews: the first before the birth of the child, the second after a suitable period of time has elapsed after the birth for basic routines around care of the child to be established, and a third later on in the first year (Hollway, 2010; Miller, 2011, 2019; Thomson et al., 2011). Subsequently, we again used this pattern with our second sample of first-time fathers in 2008 to 2009. On this occasion, the third interview was convened around the time of the child's first birthday to incorporate issues to do with the celebration of a significant family event into the interviewing strategy.

Our own experience of using three, sequentially organized interviews as our core study design was that it enabled us to track participants at a level of intensity (Thomson, 2010) that was not overburdening or overly intrusive. However, we were aware of having to weigh up practical and ethical issues that edged us to pursue less intensive modes of data collection with our interest in maximizing opportunities to generate rich, qualitative data that are replete with personal and social meanings regarding the men's subjective responses and the circumstances of their fathering. A QLL design also presents unique ethical challenges. For example, asking participants to revisit their earlier responses, particularly previously anticipated futures, can present ethical challenges if lives have not unfolded as envisaged (Miller, 2019). We dealt with these tensions by making reference to guidance on relational research ethics that is appropriate for research of this kind (Mauthner et al., 2002), and especially to the need for careful attentiveness to situational demands (Edwards & Mauthner, 2002).

Having a second phase to our research provided us with an opportunity to revisit our data collection strategy and adapt it to take into account what had transpired in the intervening 8 years. Although we had not anticipated doing this in the earliest phase of the study, we were able to serendipitously increase our

---

[5]For almost 3 decades, there has been extensive intellectual engagement with thematic analysis of substantive meanings within the grounded theory qualitative research tradition within psychology (Charmaz & Henwood, 2008; Henwood & Pidgeon, 1992), highlighting ways of working with data that are emergent and dynamic in and through time.

aspirations to include studying men and fathers across the life course and make researching the temporal a more explicit strategy for studying personal and social change in our study. It is often assumed in QLL studies that interviewer continuity is especially advantageous for enabling regularity of contact, intensity of involvement in the research encounter, and the generation of insight through making comparisons over longer time frames (McLeod & Thomson, 2009; Thomson & Holland, 2003). In particular, maintaining relationships between researcher and the researched and between members of a research team over extended time periods is deemed to be a key part of QLL method for researching the long view. In our study, different interviewers were involved as membership of the research team changed. Yet, we found that different team members brought complementary interests and specialist commitments with them, expanding the possibilities of study (Shirani, 2010).

In 2008, when we undertook our second main data collection phase, we decided to repeat the initial intensive study design, carrying out three waves of interviews over a period of transition with a second cohort of first-time fathers, this time in Wales. The aim was to further mine the possibilities inherent in intensive QLL design that involves a high frequency of data collection and enables rapid alterations in the pace of daily life to be studied, along with experiences of irreversible change over a specified time period. At the same time, as change can take time to occur, our second phase featured a set of interviews with our original participants from the East of England 8 years after their first child was born, by which time their lives had moved on a variety of ways. This design combination of intensive (frequently over a short time period) and extensive (after a significant period of time has elapsed) is fit for generating insights about dynamic processes, for example, through making comparisons of diachronic and synchronic cross sections of data. Through looking at data synchronically (that is across a wave of data collected at a single time point) patterns can be identified, and these can be studied further by making diachronic comparisons

(across data collected at different time intervals) for how they continue and/or change and involve movement though different time periods (Henderson et al., 2012; Holland et al., 2006; Neale, 2007, 2019).

Our study has adopted an in-depth, qualitative interviewing strategy (see Volume 1, Chapter 15, this handbook) with the aim of eliciting interviewees' experiences and expectations around fathering and any changes over time, together with the implications of fathering for other spheres of life, including relationships with significant others. Interviewees were encouraged to indicate how they construed fatherhood in relation to salient social models, whether such models had changed over time and how they positioned themselves and other people in relation to them. Participants were asked about their aspirations and hopes for family life and the future. Utilizing the possibilities inherent in reinterviewing in QLL study, some key issues raised in earlier interviews were reintroduced by the researcher or followed up in later ones. In this way, interviewees' responses could be traced through, including how they reflected upon earlier remarks. Going back into lives and experiences and reminding the participant of an earlier version of themselves, can enrich theorizing of temporal subjectivity (Miller, 2019).

During the second phase of the study, the kinds of strategies that worked best for generating temporal data were worked on and temporal questioning became a more prominent feature. Where appropriate, interviewees were asked to talk about issues from the perspectives of past, present, and future. Questions were asked directly about key milestones in their lives so far and the timing of significant events. The implications of such issues were asked about more indirectly, in ways that took account of where interviewees were now in their own life course. In an attempt to directly elicit temporal data, interviewees were asked about the meaning of the word "time" with mixed results: While some interviewees engaged with the questions at length, others found it too abstract and philosophical to engage with easily. How men looked back on previous moments and thought about the future, in the short and long term, was addressed, for example, by asking them to reflect upon or envisage fathering their children at different ages. How they reacted to their own parents becoming grandparents and to themselves moving generational position within their families, provided other windows on how they engaged with temporal questions—here about biographical and generational time.

Supplementary Methods and Data

To assist in the collection of temporal data, prior to interviews participants were asked to complete a timeline of significant events in their lives in order to generate some initial data on the past. They were also asked, "Where do you see yourself in 10 years' time?" to generate insights related to imagined futures. For the most part, the timeline proved useful as a prompt to facilitate discussion. In temporal terms, it was possible using this technique to ask interviewees about futures they had envisaged in the past on a range of occasions where they were situated differently within an ever shifting present. The timeline also served as a device in later interviews for participants to rework the past from the perspective of the present or comment on its continuing relevance.

One of the prime developers of QLL methodology, Johnny Saldaña (2003), advocated including visual methods within QLL studies, as "visual images, whether still or in motion, provide some of the richest and most tangible data for accessing change through time" (p. 25; see also Chapter 10, this volume). Visual images, and especially photographs, can be uniquely informative about time and place because their particular properties (e.g., facial expressions, gestures, clothes) evoke an era, linking people to historical epochs of which they have no experience. On other occasions, where people do see themselves in an image or describe themselves as being unlike the person in the image (i.e., disidentifying with

the person they see depicted in it), this can help them talk about their own personal lives and engage with larger social realities. Photo-elicitation techniques offer a way for the researcher to enable people to speak of thoughts, hopes, and fears that may otherwise be difficult and of things that have not actually happened but that operate as part of their imaginary worlds (Barthes, 1981; Henwood et al., 2020; Smart 2007).

Our approach to using visual images in the men-as-fathers project was experimental. While following the early example of visual methods as an aid in interpretive qualitative research (Beloff, 1997), we drew more extensively on subsequent developments in visual psychology (Reavey, 2010) and tried a number of different ways of generating and presenting photographic images. We found that, while each has its own merits, there are reasons to critique each one for its usefulness for our specific study and beyond, as we now go on to briefly illustrate (for more lengthy discussion, see Henwood et al., 2020).

One of our study techniques has been to present interviewees with a sequence of images depicting how social representations of fatherhood have altered through historical time.[6] It was developed as an alternative to a collage technique in which multiple images from magazines and the internet were presented to interviewees at once, and interviewees chose to talk about the ones they most wished to emulate or avoid. Although this made it a useful technique, it failed to elicit extended narratives about each of the images in terms of ideas they potentially encoded about change in time. Therefore, we needed a different methodological tool that would enable interviewees to engage with each presented image.

With the technique of presenting a sequence of images depicting sociocultural change in ideas of fatherhood and masculinity over time, interviewees were invited to comment on each individual image before being presented with the

[6]The sequence started with a black-and-white image of Victorian vintage depicting a distant, formal father figure, while the final image was a contemporary depiction of father and child face-to-face and in mutual gaze to represent the latest idea of a relational (Dermott, 2008) father. In between were images from the 1950s and 1980s. At each subsequent point in the sequence, fathers appeared in less gender-role-bound activities and poses. The famous Athena "man and baby" image was included to depict a cultural turning point in depictions of fatherhood and masculinity.

next. In addition, because each image appeared in succession, the sequence presented a representation of changes in fatherhood over time.[7] The technique proved valuable as it enabled men to make temporal comparisons more easily than they were otherwise able to do. One result of this was that it showed how our participants could reconfigure their thoughts about fatherhood and rerepresent themselves in relation to the flow of the images. It proved possible for the interviewees, when speaking in this way, to articulate their shifting and coexisting identifications with ideas of masculinity encoded in more traditional and modern representations of fatherhood and elicited some sense from them of their experiences of how masculine identities may be changing and, crucially, not changing in and through time (Henwood et al., 2008).

In visual methodology (Rose, 2001), limitations are imposed by using researcher-generated images because their framing of responses in cultural terms may or may not have relevance in the context of someone's lived life. In the second phase of our study, where we conducted a long-term follow up with our English sample, participants were asked to select favorite photographs from their own family pictures. They were initially asked why they had chosen the pictures, which led on to discussion about family life. For example, one participant described liking the picture representing his happy, smiling children as it was removed from his experience of day-to-day family life, which was often overshadowed by family disagreements. This method offered some temporal data as participants discussed family resemblances between them and their child, which often prompted them to reflect back on their own childhood experiences. Fathers in the Welsh sample were asked to discuss personal photographs from the first year of their child's life, with detailed questioning around temporal experiences. Participants were asked questions such as, "Did you think about what the child would be like before s/he was born?" and "Do you have

any thoughts on what the child will be like as s/he gets older?" in an attempt to temporally extend their talk about fatherhood. It proved challenging for these men to reflect on past or future in relation to the images, instead they preferred to focus on the present joys of fatherhood. The success of using personal photographs to elicit temporal data appeared to be dependent on the age and sex of the child, working best with older sons as the men could more easily pick up on resemblances and recall their own childhood memories with this age group than with babies.

This method also has its limits in that not all fathers regularly took photographs or were able to engage in tasks involving reading images in such imaginative ways. Of those who could provide an abundance of images, some related quite restricted cultural scripts about them devoid of personal meaning. Nonetheless, some of the participant generated images did prove to be extraordinarily rich in personal and cultural meanings associated with different dimensions of time and the ways in which they interpenetrate one another. For example, one man chose an image taken at a family wedding of his child sitting on a war memorial with people passing by. In light of his recent house move and a time of significant change, the image represented to him the significance of life constantly changing as indicated by the close juxtaposition of the memorial (depicting the end of life), his child (at the beginning of life), and passersby (only there for a fleeting moment).

Inclusion of visual methods has strengthened our methodological project of studying the personal and cultural processes of men and fathers' identities-in-the-making. Our visual strategies added possibilities for developing a more fine-grained understanding of how masculine and paternal identities are worked up and worked out in relation to time in everyday life. Our experience is that such methods are useful because they enable people to make temporal comparisons more easily than they would otherwise be able to

---

[7]The technique could also be described as involving a narratively organized set of images, presented in visual mode, of time and change in fatherhood ideals.

do and to show their awareness and consideration of diverse temporalities (generational, historical, and biographical). As a result, they are able to talk about issues that are less visible when spoken about outside a questioning framework designed to highlight matters of time and change. More generally, lessons have been learned about when and why deploying visual, especially visual narrative, photo-elicitation methods is likely to be fruitful.

QLL and Data Analysis

Initially, our approach to data analysis involved carefully reading men's accounts and interpreting their significance for understanding how men's lives and aspects of paternal subjectivity are and are not changing in the context of sociopolitical transformations in gender relationships and family life. A much-discussed issue is whether the emergence of a model of new fatherhood can be taken to indicate that new forms of masculinity are being produced and reproduced in the context of changing expectations of fatherhood. Accordingly, our earliest line of data analysis (Henwood & Procter, 2003) addressed this issue, centering on the common theme of *paternal involvement* that we identified as featuring throughout the data. Our analysis went on to point to the tensions this aspiration generated in their personal lives and opened up different ways to frame the meanings of paternal involvement. We present two examples of our efforts to conduct data analysis in this vein.

Analysis: Example 1.   Our first example analysis looks explicitly at continuities and changes in

the men's accounts by comparing them across the different waves of QLL/temporal data. Coming to the data for the first time, the analyst could see that the theme of paternal involvement that had emerged from the data and been analyzed in the initially published analysis (Henwood & Procter, 2003) unfolded and changed over time as a set of relationships developed with two further linked, emergent themes of—in the participants' own terms—exclusion (from involvement) and redundancy (from a fathering role).

Some of the men who had strongly invested in the ideal of full involvement in their child's life before the birth expressed very different sentiments 8 years later. They looked forward to a time when they would no longer be so responsible for their child. Furthermore, other interviewees who had earlier acknowledged the ideal of involvement but retained a stronger practical and emotional investment in more traditional models of fathers as breadwinners raised the issues of responsibility and dependency as problematic much earlier than those investing in involvement (Shirani & Henwood, 2011a).

Working up a full analysis of the data involved carefully inspecting the initially established pattern. To this end we tabulated each interviewee's articulation of the three interlinked themes—involvement, exclusion, and redundancy. This was our first attempt at representing our interviewee's data sequentially or narratively in case-study format. This is demonstrated in Table 11.1 with data from one participant.

TABLE 11.1

Representing Key Themes

Personal name	Before birth	Feeding	Round 2	Round 3	Round 4
Simon	Some exclusion from embodied experience of pregnancy, not really happening to him; does not mind at this stage	Breast	Helpless during labor although more involved as it was a home birth; feels powerless at not being able to feed baby and this is more frustrating than anticipated	Is a marginal part of the threesome that partner's attention has been diverted	Balances periods of high involvement with time away travelling to self; happy with this balance although difficult for relationship with partner

The tabulation clearly documented changes in talk about involvement and exclusion/redundancy and contained a very brief summary of how these issues were discussed in each interview and contributory circumstances (e.g., child being breastfed). This made it possible to see change and continuity in the accounts over time and highlighted those cases in which the issues were discussed in most depth. At the same time, it conveys how there were times when what was being narrated was more contradictory, ambiguous, and less clear cut. Following the themes of inclusion and redundancy—identified in our initial thematic analysis—over time, these initial tabulations enabled us to identify productive cases for more detailed longitudinal analysis. We discussed these case analyses to identify commonalities and contrasts between the men's accounts.

Case-study construction and analysis is strongly advocated as a way of handling longitudinal and temporal data to capture lived experiences of transition, time, and change. Thomson (2007) offered a range of specific ideas about how to enrich and thicken the construction of case-study data to gain insight into the subjective experience of social change and to study how processes of wider sociocultural change are played out through the trajectories of people's lives as both narrated and as lived. A summary of the main points involved in her QLL case-study method are (a) narratively/temporally represent accounts of linkages between emergent themes, (b) embed linkages in contextual details of lives and worlds, (c) bring complexity of subjective experiences to the fore, and (d) carefully select cases and bring them into dialogue to highlight the dynamics of continuities and change over time and identify insights with wider relevance across the sample in ways that further strengthen the developing analysis. These ideas have helped us to conduct our analysis so that it was possible to bring out the significance of the three interlinked themes—involvement, exclusion, and redundancy. An overview focusing on patterns of continuity and change for four cases analyzed in this way is given in Figure 11.1.

As a result of following these steps in our published case study analysis (Shirani & Henwood, 2011a), we were able to show important commonalities and differences within the data regarding fathers' greater involvement over time. This illustrated how often the paternal involvement ideal does not play out in men's lives in ways that follow their anticipated trajectories due to alterations in their lived experiences, emergent concerns about dependency, and changing work and family circumstances. These men adopted a temporal strategy of deferment to the future; at each interview they were looking forward to a life-course stage that they felt would be preferable to their current situation. Thomson (2009; see also Østergaard & Thomson, 2020) noted that longitudinal research brings with it the promise of capturing and interrogating action in the form of continuity, change and maturation—when things happen they can be considered in relation to what has happened before and what takes place subsequently. Our analysis showed the shifting views of participants in relation to life experiences as their anticipated futures became present and past experience over the course of our study.

Exhibit 11.1 gives a summary account of our analytical work

Analysis: Example 2. This analysis in its published form (Finn & Henwood, 2009) takes as data the connections and disconnections men in the study made with their own fathers and explores what we have called the men's fluctuating "identificatory imaginings" as involved fathers. The analysis points to the fluctuations in men's accounts across the interviews where they invest in ways of doing fatherhood and being a man that are similar or different to their own fathers and men of their generation. It shows how, to understand such biographical and generational imaginings, they need to be seen as dynamically mediated by cultural discourses (of the modern father), the men's social conditions (making it more or less difficult for them to spend time in the home), and processes of intergenerational transmission (as they involve flows of meaning and affect).

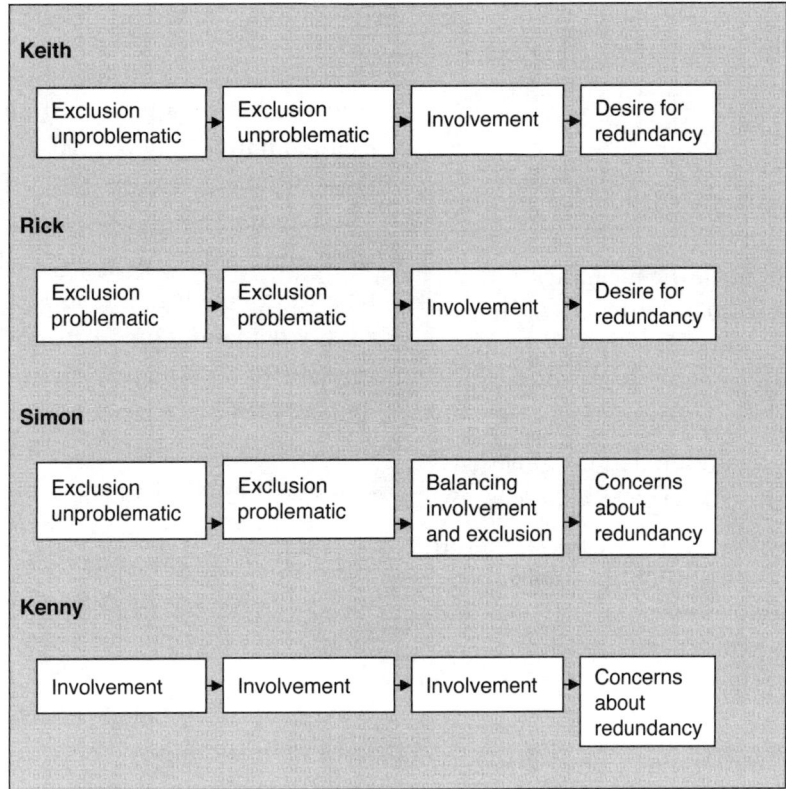

FIGURE 11.1. Representing changes/continuities over time.

This form of analysis was not only informed by a Timescapes agenda but also shaped in specific disciplinary ways by a psychosocial research perspective (Frosh et al., 2020; Hollway, 2006; Walkerdine, 2010). In our own study, its dual focused agenda is marked out in three main ways: (a) investigating the specific ways in which our participants come to live out cultural ideals of fatherhood and paternal involvement socially and psychically, (b) bringing into view the dynamics of masculine and paternal subjectivity, and (c) asking questions about the significance of shifting cultural ideas about what it means to be a man and a father in contemporary times. Continuing with the psychosocial aspects of our work analytically and theoretically enabled us to open up further ways of investigating intergenerational transmissions between fathers and their own fathers (and mothers) by building into the earlier analysis concern for intangible identity positionings relating to class-inflected experiences and dynamics (Coltart & Henwood, 2012).

EXHIBIT 11.1

Relevance Without Responsibility—Qualitative Longitudinal Methodology Analysis Process

Comparative analysis: noticing how paternal involvement— an emergent theme from the data—unfolded and changed over time as a set of relationships developed with exclusion and redundancy

Initial tabulation of linked themes (careful inspection of the pattern): (a) to see change and continuity in accounts over time and (b) to gather cases in which issues were discussed in the most depth

Qualitative longitudinal case construction and presentation

REFLECTIONS FROM THE MEN-AS-FATHERS PROJECT

In this chapter, we have discussed programmatic statements that have been made in favor of taking a qualitative longitudinal and temporal approach to researching identities and relationships in

225

changing lives and times. We have also shown how these statements have translated into the methodological and analytical work of our own, specific inquiries into men and fathers' identities and relationships through the life course. Our inquiries have been conducted amidst a growing awareness of the importance of possible sociocultural transformations in the meanings and practices of fatherhood and of the heterogeneity and plurality of masculine identities and subjectivities. They were taken forward as part of a unique experiment—the Timescapes study—aimed at scaling up the undoubted insights that can be generated from carefully crafted qualitative and case study research focused on understanding the personal, social, and cultural meanings that are at the center of people's everyday activities and life changes—their identities, relationships, and lives-in-the-making (Henwood et al., 2012).

A major excitement—but also a challenge—became apparent to us in the men-as-fathers project: the sense of how many possibilities are being opened up for inquiring into the dynamics of identities and relationships in and through time. Taking up the Timescapes way of dealing with this challenge (Adam, 2008; Neale, 2007), we adopted a QLL design capable of generating microtemporal data that are both qualitative (i.e., they articulate people's everyday subjective experiences and understandings of contextual/sociocultural meanings) and biographical, dynamic, or temporal (rather than fixed in particular moments in time). This way of working brought into view the times and textures of people's everyday lives, making it possible to investigate dynamic ways of experiencing, negotiating, and working out the significance and meanings of relationships, identities, and lives in and through time (Neale & Flowerdew, 2003). Hence, adopting this approach represents one way in which we set ourselves up to study the ways in which everyday experiences, ideas, understandings, and issues of masculinity and fathering are implicated in the dynamic processes of men's identity and subjectivity formation.

TAKING FORWARD TEMPORAL RESEARCH

Following the conclusion of the men-as-fathers study in 2011, we have continued to develop our qualitative longitudinal work across several projects; energy biographies, FLEXIS, and ABC.[8] These projects move our research into different substantive fields: environmentally (un)sustainable transitions, energy systems change, and reducing energy demand. Our contribution has been to focus predominantly on understanding the dynamics of everyday energy use and the significance they hold for efforts by policy makers and practitioners seeking to promote systemic, sociotechnical change (Henwood, 2019; Shirani et al., 2020). At the same time, we have continued to explore the significance of relationships and linked lives through both case study and broader thematic analysis (Butler et al., 2014; Shirani et al., 2021). This follows calls for family researchers to be more attentive to environmental issues (Jamieson, 2016) and for energy researchers to heed the significance of family life, transitions, and personal relationships (Burningham, 2017).

In Energy Biographies we sought to make the temporal more explicit. Again utilizing a three-interview design, but this time over a more intensive 1-year period, each interview had a different temporal focus: past, present, and future. Unlike many QLL studies, Energy Biographies was not designed around a specific life-course transition, and participants were drawn from different age groups and life stages as well as a range of geographical areas. This enabled us to elucidate the significance of more mundane changes for people's everyday lives and energy use (Shirani et al., 2017). Moreover, it brought to light different kinds of relational entanglements involving extended temporal horizons, identificatory shifts, and generational forms of subjectivity as part of our enquiries into wider "stories of change" (Henwood et al., 2016). These developments underscore the importance of other qualitative longitudinal researchers' efforts to address the challenges of intergenerational study

---

[8]https://www.energybiographies.org/; https://www.flexis.wales/; https://abc-rp.com/

by elucidating the significance of emotive experiences, psychosocial investments, and affective intensities and flows (Walkerdine et al., 2002). How to design qualitative longitudinal studies with these considerations in mind has potential relevance for the development of policy and ethical studies of responses to contemporary environmental crises and means of addressing societal grand challenges coming in their wake (Dal Gobbo, 2020; Pidgeon et al., 2021).

While the visual approaches we invoked for Timescapes had helped elicit discussion about fathering in the past and present, talk about the future was more challenging. Given expectations about the significant changes to lifestyles that will be required if we are to meet decarbonization targets (Ofgem, 2020), exploring anticipated futures was of particular importance in Energy Biographies, and, in designing the study, we sought ways to extend temporal horizons further into the future. One successful way of doing this was through the creation of a visual narrative. Over the course of several weeks, all Energy Biographies participants were sent a SMS message on the same days and times asking them to take a photograph that represented what they were currently doing and return this to the research team. Once all images had been received, the researchers compiled a timeline of the 10 images for each participant, which was then used as a prompt for discussion in the following interview. Participants were asked to reflect on the images as a representation of their current lives, then asked to think about how things might have looked differently one year earlier, then one and, finally, 15 years into the future. We found that having a tangible reference point enabled participants to talk more expansively about imagined futures. For example, one participant drew on an image of driving to discuss how technological infrastructure might change in the future to enable different kinds of car use, as well as how his own family structure and needs would alter as family members aged (see Shirani et al., 2016, for further discussion of this approach).

In asking participants to talk about the future, it is important to be attentive to ethical issues,

for example, considering how participants are differently positioned in relation to the future. While young people may be used to routine discussion of their future educational and employment plans, asking older people about the longer term future can raise issues around finitude, although this does not mean they are unwilling to discuss the future (Bornat, 2014). Previous life events may also have an impact upon individual ability or willingness to imagine the future, as experience of unexpected transitions may highlight a sense of uncertainty, meaning participants are reluctant to plan for the future (Shirani & Henwood, 2011b). We have found that the multimodal approaches we have utilized appear to make some aspects of the future easier to discuss, particularly for participants who had previously found adopting a future perspective challenging (Shirani et al., 2016). The advantage of qualitative longitudinal research is that it provides greater space and flexibility for incorporating a range of approaches to encourage greater temporal reflexivity. Within these spaces it is possible to build in potentials to promote reflectiveness about what is otherwise difficult to say about routines of ordinary life when these are brought into question by extraordinary narratives and efforts to transform everyday practice (Henwood, 2022; Henwood et al., 2018; Groves et al., 2016c, 2017).

CONCLUSION

When researching people's lives temporally, it is not enough simply to track them as they make their way through significant moments, episodes, and transitions that are part of the life course. It is also necessary to inquire how they live out their lives within historical periods or epochs and as members of particular generations or cohorts. In our Timescapes study, we considered men and fathers' identities as being constituted not just biographically but in the context of change in (post)modern times. This does not mean setting up a singular, linear model of progressive change with categories such as pre- and postmodern necessarily preceding sequentially from one to the other. Rather, we sought to bring out the (all-too-often invisible) multidimensionalities and multidirectionalities, pluralities, and complexities of time and change associated with shifts towards (and away from) modernity as they are experienced and created by people (Salmon, 1985) and in order to explore their dynamic involvement in the unfolding of varied life forms and social processes (Adam, 2008).

Embedded in our approach to QLL study is an interest in being able to pursue questions of continuity and change within the multiple conditions and flows of time. We specifically wish to avoid the implication that any one modality alone (such as the discursive vs. other experiential/ phenomenological/sensory modes) is constitutive of subjectivities (Henwood et al., 2008). In developing our interest in the conditions and flows of time, we have used visual methods alongside the pursuit of a psychosocial qualitative longitudinal/temporal research perspective (Finn & Henwood, 2009; Henwood & Finn, 2010). As our research has developed, we have studied how processes of continuity and change may involve movements into liminal, psychosocial transition spaces where imagined lives disconnect from taken-for-granted practices (Groves et al., 2016a, 2016b). However, in this chapter, we have illustrated our methodological and analytical practices by drawing on our work within the Timescapes consortium. Our efforts in this research involved studying participants' fine-grained alignments with, or distancings from, their own fathers' personal and generational ways of doing masculinity and fathering. This allowed us to open up to inquiry the resultant tensions and adaptations that are apparent in study participants' aspirations or desires as men and as fathers, the ways in which men reflect on these from various vantage points in time, and how their meaning and significance alter in the processes of reworking and reflection.

Continuing our QLL work beyond Timescapes into new projects, we have sought ways to extend participants' temporal horizons and expand discussion of anticipated futures—both personal and wider social. Careful development

of supplementary methodological techniques has been key to this. Such extended timescales raise new ethical issues for temporally focused researchers. Yet, as Neale (2019) argued, researching lives through time makes us sensitive to ethical issues and responsibilities in ways that are impossible to grasp through single-visit studies.

One insufficiently vocalized ethical issue arises in research that uses qualitative and temporal research strategies to understand people's personal lives in times of change when inquiries become intertwined with interlinked social transformation agendas. How we live out our lives with others and undertake forms of identity-(re)making in such times may involve considerable uncertainty about what is actually required of us as we undertake significant and possibly irreversible change. For example, expectations that changes to everyday life are required in order to meet decarbonization goals or to address climate change may be divorced from day-to-day life experiences where climate change is sometimes viewed as a temporally and spatially distant problem that can be difficult to keep in view in the context of the immediate pressures of everyday life (Shirani et al., 2013). In addition, the potential for benefits and challenges of social transformation to be experienced unevenly raises important ethical questions about the perpetuation of disadvantage and how to ensure no-one is "left behind" (Welsh Government Smart Living Initiative, 2019). When undertaking inquiries into social transformation and other kinds of change process, researchers must not shy away from considering psychosocial challenges posed to societies experiencing intractable social problems (Hochschild, 2016) while recognizing diverse, interpretive claims to legitimacy in extraordinary times of change (Henwood, 2022; Henwood et al., 2016). By working temporally, QLL research has the potential to offer a unique perspective on these important ethical issues.

References

Adam, B. (1990). *Time and social theory*. Polity.

Adam, B. (2008). The Timescapes challenge: Engagement with the invisible temporal. In B. Adam,

J. Hockey, P. Thompson, & R. Edwards (Eds.), *Researching lives through time: Time, generation and life stories*. Timescapes Working Paper Series (Vol. 1, pp. 7–12), University of Leeds.

Andrews, M., Day Sclater, S., Squire, C., & Treacher, A. (Eds.). (2000). *Lines of narrative: Psychosocial approaches*. Routledge.

Barthes, R. (1981). *Camera lucida: Reflections on photography*. Hill and Wang.

Beloff, H. (1997). Making and unmaking identities: A psychologist looks at artwork. In N. Hayes (Ed.), *Doing qualitative analysis in psychology* (pp. 55–68). Psychology Press.

Bornat, J. (2014). Researching the future with older people: Experiences with the oldest generation. In J. Bornat & R. L. Jones (Eds.), *Imagining futures: Methodological issues for research into ageing*. Centre for Ageing and Biographical Studies at the Open University and the Centre for Policy on Ageing.

Brannen, J., & Nilsen, A. (2007). Young people, time horizons and planning: A response to Anderson et al. *Sociology, 41*(1), 153–160. https://doi.org/10.1177/0038038507072288

Burningham, K. (2017). Energy use: The significance of relationships. *Nature Energy, 2*(12), 914–915. https://doi.org/10.1038/s41560-017-0056-1

Butler, C., Parkhill, K. A., Shirani, F., Henwood, K., & Pidgeon, N. (2014). Examining the dynamics of energy demand through a biographical lens. *Nature and Culture, 9*(2), 164–182. https://doi.org/10.3167/nc.2014.090204

Chamberlayne, P., Bornat, J., & Wengraf, T. (Eds.). (2000). *The turn to biographical methods in social science: Comparative issues and examples*. Routledge.

Charmaz, K. (2006). *Constructing grounded theory*. SAGE.

Charmaz, K., & Henwood, K. L. (2008). Grounded theory. In C. Willig & W. Stainton-Rogers (Eds.), *Handbook of qualitative research in psychology* (pp. 240–260). SAGE.

Coltart, C., & Henwood, K. (2012). On paternal subjectivity: A qualitative longitudinal and psychosocial case analysis of men's classed positions and transitions to first-time fatherhood. In K. Henwood, B. Neale, & J. Holland (Eds.), Advancing methods and resources for qualitative longitudinal research: The timescapes initiative [Special issue]. *Qualitative Research 12*(1), 35–52. https://doi.org/10.1177/1468794111426224

Corden, A., & Millar, J. (2007). Time and change: A review of the qualitative longitudinal research literature for social policy. *Social Policy and Society, 6*(4), 583–592. https://doi.org/10.1017/S1474746407003910

Dal Gobbo, A. (2020). Everyday life ecologies: Crisis, transitions and the aesthetics of desire. *Environmental Values, 29*(4), 397–416. https://doi.org/10.3197/096327120X15868540131297

Dermott, E. (2008). *Intimate fatherhood*. Routledge.

Dermott, E., & Miller, T. (2015). More than the sum of its parts? Contemporary fatherhood policy, practice and discourse. *Families, Relationships and Societies, 4*(2), 183–195. https://doi.org/10.1332/204674315X14212269138324

Doucet, A. (2007). *Do men mother?* University of Toronto Press.

Edley, N., & Wetherell, M. (1999). Imagined futures: Young men's talk about fatherhood and domestic life. *British Journal of Social Psychology, 38*(2), 181–194. https://doi.org/10.1348/014466699164112

Edwards, R., & Mauthner, M. (2002). Ethics and feminist research: Theory and practice. In M. Mauthner, M. Birch, J. Jessop, & T. Miller (Eds.), *Ethics in qualitative research* (pp. 14–28). SAGE.

Elliott, J., Holland, J., & Thomson, R. (2008). Longitudinal and panel studies. In P. Alasuutari, L. Bickman, & J. Brannen (Eds.), *The SAGE handbook of social research methods* (pp. 228–248). SAGE. https://doi.org/10.4135/9781446212165

Farrall, S. (2006). What is qualitative longitudinal research? [Papers in Social Research Methods. Qualitative Series No. 11]. London School of Economics and Political Science Methodology Institute.

Finn, M., & Henwood, K. (2009). Exploring masculinities within men's identificatory imaginings of first-time fatherhood. *British Journal of Social Psychology, 48*(3), 547–562. https://doi.org/10.1348/014466608X386099

Frosh, S., Vyrgioti, M., & Walsh, J. (Eds.). (2020). *The Palgrave handbook of psychosocial studies*. Palgrave Macmillan.

Groves, C., Henwood, K., Shirani, F., Butler, C., Parkhill, K., & Pidgeon, N. (2016a). Energy biographies: Narrative genres, lifecourse transitions and practice change. *Science, Technology & Human Values, 41*(3), 484–508. https://doi.org/10.1177/0162243915609116

Groves, C., Henwood, K., Shirani, F., Butler, C., Parkhill, K., & Pidgeon, N. (2016b). The grit in the oyster: Using energy biographies to question socio-technical imaginaries of 'smartness.' *Journal of Responsible Innovation, 3*(1), 4–25. https://doi.org/10.1080/23299460.2016.1178897

Groves, C., Henwood, K., Shirani, F., Butler, C., Parkhill, K., & Pidgeon, N. (2016c). Invested in unsustainability? On the psychosocial patterning of engagement in practices. *Environmental*

Values, 25(3), 309–328. https://doi.org/10.3197/096327116X14598445991466

Groves, C., Henwood, K., Shirani, F., Thomas, G., & Pidgeon, N. (2017). Why mundane energy use matters: Energy biographies, attachment and identity. *Energy Research & Social Science, 30*, 71–81. https://doi.org/10.1016/j.erss.2017.06.016

Heinz, W. R., & Krüger, H. (2001). The life course: Innovations and challenges for social research. *Current Sociology, 49*(2), 29–45. https://doi.org/10.1177/0011392101049002004

Henderson, S., Holland, J., McGrellis, S., Sharpe, S., & Thomson, R. (2012). Storying qualitative longitudinal research: Sequence, voice and motif. *Qualitative Research, 12*(1), 16–34. https://doi.org/10.1177/1468794111426232

Henwood, K. (2019). Investigating risk: Methodological insights from interpretive social science and sustainable energy transitions research. In A. Olofsson & J. Zinn (Eds.), *Researching risk and uncertainty: Methodologies, methods and research strategies* (pp. 129–152). Palgrave Macmillan.

Henwood, K., & Finn, M. (2010) Researching masculine and paternal subjects in times of change: Insights from a qualitative longitudinal (QLL) and psychosocial case study. In R. Thomson (Ed.), *Intensity and insight: Qualitative longitudinal methods as a route to the psycho-social* (pp. 34–45). Timescapes Working Paper Series No. 3. University of Leeds.

Henwood, K., Finn, M., & Shirani, F. (2008). Use of visual methods to explore parental identities in historical time and social change: Reflections from the 'men-as-fathers' project. *Qualitative Research, 9*, 112–115.

Henwood, K., Groves, C., & Shirani, F. (2016). Relationality, entangled practices, and psychosocial exploration of intergenerational dynamics in sustainable energy studies. *Families, Relationships and Societies, 5*(3), 393–410. https://doi.org/10.1332/204674316X147584383416945

Henwood, K., & Procter, J. (2003). The 'good father': Reading men's accounts of paternal involvement during the transition to first-time fatherhood. *British Journal of Social Psychology, 42*(3), 337–355. https://doi.org/10.1348/014466603322438198

Henwood, K., & Shirani, F. (2012). Researching the temporal. In H. Cooper, P. M. Camic, D. L. Long, A. T. Panter, D. Rindskopf, & K. J. Sher (Eds.), *APA handbook of research methods in psychology, Vol. 2. Research designs: Quantitative, qualitative, neuropsychological, and biological.* American Psychological Association. https://doi.org/10.1037/13620-013

Henwood, K., Shirani, F., & Finn, M. (2020). So you think we've moved, changed, the representation got more what? Methodological and analytical reflections on visual (photo-elicitation) methods used in the men-as-fathers study. In P. Reavey (Ed.), *A handbook of visual methods in psychology* (2nd ed., pp. 555–571). Routledge.

Henwood, K., Shirani, F., & Groves, C. (2018). Using photographs in interviews: When we lack the words to say what practice means. In U. Flick (Ed.), *The SAGE handbook of qualitative data collection* (pp. 599–614). SAGE.

Henwood, K. L. (2006). Grounded theory in mental health and related research. In M. Slade & S. Priebe (Eds.), *Choosing methods in mental health research* (pp. 68–84). Brunner Routledge.

Henwood, K. L. (2008). Qualitative research, reflexivity and living with risk: Valuing and practicing epistemic reflexivity and centring marginality. *Qualitative Research in Psychology, 5*(1), 45–55. https://doi.org/10.1080/14780880701863575

Henwood, K. L. (2022). Interpretive risk ethnography as a means of understanding risk problems: Encounters with the ordinary-extraordinary and what comes after? In B. Switek, A. Abramson, & H. Swee (Eds.), *Extraordinary risks, ordinary lives* (pp. 297–327). Palgrave Macmillan. https://doi.org/10.1007/978-3-030-83962-8_12

Henwood, K. L., Gill, R., & Mclean, C. (2002). The changing man. *The Psychologist, 15*(4), 182–186.

Henwood, K. L., Neale, B., & Holland, J. (Eds.). (2012). Advancing methods and resources for qualitative longitudinal research: The Timescapes initiative [Special issue]. *Qualitative Research, 12*(1).

Henwood, K. L., Pidgeon, N., Sarre, S., Simmons, P., & Smith, N. (2008). Risk, framing and everyday life: Epistemological and methodological reflections from three socio-cultural projects. *Health Risk & Society, 10*(5), 421–438. https://doi.org/10.1080/13698570802381451

Henwood, K. L., & Pidgeon, N. F. (1992). Qualitative research and psychological theorizing. *British Journal of Psychology, 83*(1), 97–111. https://doi.org/10.1111/j.2044-8295.1992.tb02426.x

Hochschild, A. R. (2016). *Strangers in our own land: Anger and mourning on the American right.* The New Press.

Holland, J. (2007). *Qualitative longitudinal research: Exploring ways of researching lives through time.* Real Life Methods Node of the ESRC National Centre for Research Methods. Workshop held at London South Bank University.

Holland, J., Thompson, R., & Henderson, S. (2006). *Qualitative longitudinal research: A discussion paper.* Families and Social Capital ESRC Research Group, London South Bank University.

Hollway, W. (2006). *The capacity to care: Gender and ethical subjectivity.* Routledge.

Hollway, W. (2010). Preserving vital signs: The use of psychoanalytically informed interviewing and observation in psycho-social longitudinal research. In Thomson, R. (Ed.), *Intensity and insight: Qualitative longitudinal methods as a route to the psycho-social. Timescapes Working Paper Series No. 3* (pp. 19–33). University of Leeds.

Hollway, W., & Featherstone, B. (Eds.). (1997). *Mothering and ambivalence.* Routledge.

Hughes, J. (1990). *The philosophy of social research* (2nd ed.). Longman.

Ives, J. (2015). Theorising the 'deliberative father': Compromise, progress and striving to do fatherhood well. *Families, Relationships and Societies, 4*(2), 281–294. https://doi.org/10.1332/204674314X14184029517584

Jamieson, L. (2016). Families, relationships and 'environment': (Un)sustainability, climate change and biodiversity loss. *Families, Relationships and Societies, 5*(3), 335–355. https://doi.org/10.1332/204674316X14758387773007

Lewis, J. (2007). Analysing qualitative longitudinal research in evaluations. *Social Policy and Society, 6*(4), 545–556. https://doi.org/10.1017/S1474746407003880

Mason, J. (2006). Mixing methods in a qualitatively-driven way. *Qualitative Research, 6*(1), 9–25. https://doi.org/10.1177/1468794106058866

Mauthner, M., Birch, M., Jessop, J., & Miller, T. (2002). *Ethics in qualitative research.* SAGE. https://doi.org/10.4135/9781849209090

McLeod, J. (2003). Why we interview now—reflexivity and perspective in a longitudinal study. *International Journal of Social Research Methodology, 6*(3), 201–211. https://doi.org/10.1080/1364557032000091806

McLeod, J., & Thomson, R. (2009). *Researching social change.* SAGE. https://doi.org/10.4135/9780857029010

Miller, T. (2000). Narrative construction and childbirth. *Qualitative Health Research, 10*(3), 309–323. https://doi.org/10.1177/104973200129118462

Miller, T. (2011). *Making sense of fatherhood: Gender, caring and work.* Cambridge University Press.

Miller, T. (2019). Qualitative longitudinal research: Researching fatherhood and fathers' experiences. In E. Dermott & C. Gatrell (Eds.), *Fathers, families and relationships: Researching everyday lives* (pp. 31–46). Policy Press.

Neale, B. (2007). *Timescapes: Changing relationships and identities through the lifecourse* (RES 347 25 0003) [grant]. Timescapes Consortium, University of Leeds. https://timescapes-archive.leeds.ac.uk/wp-content/uploads/sites/47/2020/07/TIMESCAPES_Blueprint.pdf

Neale, B. (2019). *What is qualitative longitudinal research?* Bloomsbury.

Neale, B., & Flowerdew, J. (2003). Time, texture and childhood: The contours of longitudinal qualitative research. *International Journal of Social Research Methodology, 6*(3), 189–199. https://doi.org/10.1080/1364557032000091798

Ofgem. (2020). *Ofgem decarbonisation programme action plan.* https://www.ofgem.gov.uk/system/files/docs/2020/02/ofg1190_decarbonisation_action_plan_revised.pdf

Østergaard, J., & Thomson, R. (2020). Thinking through cases: Articulating variable and narrative logics on a longitudinal analysis of drug use and school drop out. *International Journal of Social Research Methodology, 23*(4), 423–436. https://doi.org/10.1080/13645579.2020.1719616

Pidgeon, N., Groves, C., Thomas, G., Shirani, F., Cherry, C., & Henwood, K. (2021). 'A little self-sufficient town close to the beach': Local energy system transformation through the lens of place and public things. In J. Webb, M. Tingey, & F. Wade (Eds.), *Research handbook of energy and society* (pp. 299–316). Edward Elgar.

Pidgeon, N., & Henwood, K. (2004). Grounded theory. In M. Hardy & A. Bryman (Eds.), *Handbook of data analysis* (pp. 625–648). SAGE.

Reavey, P. (Ed.). (2010). *Visual psychologies: Using and interpreting images in qualitative research.* Routledge.

Rose, G. (2001). *Visual methodologies.* SAGE.

Rosenthal, G. (2004). Biographical research. In C. Seale, G. Gobo, J. F. Gubrium, & D. Silverman (Eds.), *Qualitative research practice* (pp. 48–64). SAGE. https://doi.org/10.4135/9781848608191.d7

Saldaña, J. (2003). *Longitudinal qualitative research: Analyzing change through time.* AltaMira.

Salmon, P. (1985). *Living in time: A new look at personal development.* J.M. Dent & Son.

Shirani, F. (2010). Researcher change and continuity in a qualitative longitudinal study. In F. Shirani & S. Weller (Eds.), *Timescapes working paper series No.2. Conducting qualitative longitudinal research: Fieldwork experiences* (pp. 49–59). University of Leeds.

Shirani, F., Groves, C., Henwood, K., Pidgeon, N., & Roberts, E. (2020). 'I'm the smart meter': Perceptions and experiences of smart technology amongst vulnerable consumers. *Energy Policy*, *144*(5), 111637. https://doi.org/10.1016/j.enpol.2020.111637

Shirani, F., Groves, C., Henwood, K., Roberts, E., Thomas, G., Cherry, C., & Pidgeon, N. (2021). 'Who cares about valley people?' Lived experiences of energy vulnerability in the South Wales valleys. *Journal of Poverty and Social Justice*, *29*(1), 103–120. https://doi.org/10.1332/175982720X16074511160827

Shirani, F., Groves, C., Parkhill, K., Butler, C., Henwood, K., & Pidgeon, N. (2017). Critical moments? Life transitions and energy biographies. *Geoforum*, *86*, 86–92. https://doi.org/10.1016/j.geoforum.2017.09.006

Shirani, F., & Henwood, K. (2011a). Continuity and change in a qualitative longitudinal study of fatherhood: Relevance without responsibility. *International Journal of Social Research Methodology*, *14*(1), 17–29. https://doi.org/10.1080/13645571003690876

Shirani, F., & Henwood, K. (2011b). Taking one day at a time: Temporal experiences in the context of unexpected life course transitions. *Time & Society*, *20*(1), 49–68. https://doi.org/10.1177/0961463X10374906

Shirani, F., Henwood, K., & Coltart, C. (2012). Meeting the challenges of intensive parenting culture: Gender, risk management and the moral parent. *Sociology*, *46*(1), 25–40. https://doi.org/10.1177/0038038511416169

Shirani, F., Parkhill, K., Butler, C., Groves, C., Pidgeon, N., & Henwood, K. (2016). Asking about the future: Methodological insights from energy biographies. *International Journal of Social Research Methodology*, *19*(4), 429–444. https://doi.org/10.1080/13645579.2015.1029208

Shirani, F., Butler, C., Henwood, K., Parkhill, K., & Pidgeon, N. (2013). Disconnected futures: Exploring notions of ethical responsibility in energy practices. *Local Environment: The International Journal of Justice and Sustainability*, *18*(4), 455–468.

Smart, C. (2007). *Personal life: New directions in sociological thinking*. Polity.

Squire, C. (2008). Approaches to narrative research. *ESRC National Centre for Research Methods Review Paper*. NCRM 009.

Thompson, P. (1975). *The Edwardians: The remaking of British society*. Weidenfeld and Nicolson.

Thomson, R. (2007). The qualitative longitudinal case history: Practical, methodological and ethical reflections. *Social Policy and Society*, *6*(4), 571–582. https://doi.org/10.1017/S1474746407003909

Thomson, R. (2009). *Unfolding lives: Youth, gender and change*. Policy Press. https://doi.org/10.2307/j.ctt9qgqhf

Thomson, R. (2010). Creating family case histories: Subjects, selves and family dynamics. In Thomson, R. (Ed.), *Intensity and insight: Qualitative longitudinal methods as a route to the psychosocial. Timescapes Working Paper Series No. 3* (pp. 6–18). University of Leeds.

Thomson, R., & Holland, J. (2003). Hindsight, foresight and insight: The challenges of longitudinal qualitative research. *International Journal of Social Research Methodology*, *6*(3), 233–244. https://doi.org/10.1080/1364557032000091833

Thomson, R., Kehily, M. J., Hadfield, L., & Sharpe, S. (2011). *Making modern mothers*. Policy Press. https://doi.org/10.2307/j.ctt1t898c8

Thomson, R., & McLeod, J. (2015). New frontiers in qualitative longitudinal research: An agenda for research. *International Journal of Social Research Methodology*, *18*(3), 243–250. https://doi.org/10.1080/13645579.2015.1017900

Walkerdine, V. (2010). Communal beingness and affect: An exploration of trauma in an ex-industrial community. *Body & Society*, *16*(1), 91–116. https://doi.org/10.1177/1357034X09354127

Walkerdine, V., Lucey, H., & Melody, J. (2002). Subjectivity and qualitative method. In T. May (Ed.), *Qualitative research in action* (pp. 179–196). SAGE.

Welsh Government Smart Living Initiative. (2019). *Annual review of progress and learnings*. AD Research and Analysis With the Centre for Sustainable Energy for the Decarbonisation and Energy Division, Welsh Government.

Wetherell, M., & Edley, N. (1999). Negotiating hegemonic masculinity: Imaginary positions and psycho-discursive practices. *Feminism & Psychology*, *9*(3), 335–356. https://doi.org/10.1177/0959353599009003012

WORKING ACROSS EPISTEMOLOGIES, METHODOLOGIES, AND METHODS

CHAPTER 12

MIXED METHODS RESEARCH IN PSYCHOLOGY

Timothy C. Guetterman and Analay Perez

This chapter covers the foundations of rigorous mixed methods research. We first provide a definition of mixed methods research and its applications, followed by an overview of major mixed methods designs. The designs offer a starting point for discussing rationales for mixed methods and conceptualizing the integration of quantitative and qualitative research as *mixed methods analysis*, which is a defining characteristic and focus of the chapter. We discuss how mixed methods designs intersect with major quantitative and qualitative designs for a more comprehensive understanding of research questions. The chapter concludes with a brief summary of key points and how to assess quality in mixed methods research.

MIXED METHODS RESEARCH IN PSYCHOLOGY

Mixed methods research involves the collection, analysis, and, most importantly, the integration of quantitative and qualitative research. Mixed methods research has been growing in popularity (Coyle et al., 2018), perhaps as more researchers recognize the value of mixing methods for a more complete understanding of aims or research questions. While quantitative methods can identify trends, group differences, and relationships among variables, qualitative methods allow researchers to explore nuances and complexity through direct interviews and observations with participants. For example, Watkins et al. (2017) conducted a mixed methods investigation of the association between nonspousal family support and mental health among older African American men who regularly attend church. The authors explained that the issue had not been investigated using both quantitative and qualitative methods in a single study. They began by developing an understanding of African American men's experiences of helpful support using rapid qualitative analysis techniques. The researchers then mapped qualitative findings to items in the National Survey of American Life to examine six family support variables (help, communication, closeness, feeling loved, listening, and expression of concern or interest) through a latent variable of "nonspousal family support" and a mental health latent variable they identified as *psychological distress*. The qualitative phase allowed them to identify these characteristics of support, specifically, the family support variables that were helpful to African American men, and the subsequent quantitative structural analysis tested this conceptual model and found that nonspousal family support is associated with less distress. Throughout this chapter, we share examples across psychology subdisciplines of how mixed methods research has been used.

https://doi.org/10.1037/0000319-012
APA Handbook of Research Methods in Psychology, Second Edition: Vol. 2. Research Designs: Quantitative, Qualitative, Neuropsychological, and Biological, H. Cooper (Editor-in-Chief)

The purpose of this chapter is to provide an introduction to mixed methods research in psychology. We begin with defining mixed methods and cover major research designs. The designs provide a way to conceptualize when and how to integrate quantitative and qualitative data, methods, or results. Because integration unlocks the true potential of mixed methods for addressing different types of research questions, this chapter focuses on how to think about and conduct substantive integration.

DEFINING MIXED METHODS RESEARCH

Five characteristics define mixed methods research: (a) collection and analysis of quantitative and qualitative data; (b) use of rigorous methods; (c) selection of a mixed methods design; (d) application of theoretical frameworks or philosophical paradigms; and (e) the integration of quantitative and qualitative data, methods, or results (Creswell & Plano Clark, 2018). Each of these characteristics is an important consideration in mixed methods research. Beginning with the *collection and analysis of quantitative and qualitative data*, quantitative data in mixed methods studies consist of commonly used types such as psychological assessments or tests, surveys, biological measures, and structured observations. Qualitative data often take the form of interviews, focus groups, open-ended text, and observational field notes, among others. In a mixed methods study, both the quantitative and qualitative *strands* (a term for the individual components) follow *rigorous methods* independently. Often, there is interaction where the two strands of research inform one another, but clear and rigorous methods, such as defining data collection instruments, interview protocols, and using appropriate methods of analysis, are necessary. Researchers examining published mixed methods research have identified that the qualitative strand has the most quality concerns in comparison with the quantitative strand (Bryman, 2006; Morse, 2002; Guetterman & Fetters, 2018; Guetterman et al., 2019; O'Cathain et al., 2008) and, thus, is more likely to be subjugated to the quantitative methods. One of the major

controversial issues stems from the transferability of quantitative quality criteria such as validity and reliability to qualitative research and making generalizations in the same manner as quantitative research. Although we should aim towards generalization in qualitative research as well, we should also be mindful of employing alternative types of generalizations, such as naturalistic, statistical, analytical (Flyvbjerg, 2006), and the researcher- and reader-generalization (Roald et al., 2021). Qualitative research is systematic and involves the typical research process of developing questions, collecting and analyzing data systematically, and reporting results to address research questions. In high-quality mixed methods research, each strand needs to be substantive.

Next, *mixed methods designs* provide a map of the research procedures to guide the entire process of research. Though some criticize mixed methods designs as being too prescriptive (Creamer, 2018), the designs are not intended to be rigid. Rather, they are meant to help researchers by providing a starting point "as a guiding framework to help inform design choices" (Creswell & Plano Clark, 2018, p. 59), and by enabling them to consider a range of options, anticipate challenges and limitations, and plan for integration. Major designs include the convergent design with the intent of integrating data or results to relate or compare, the explanatory sequential design with the intent of beginning with a quantitative phase followed by a qualitative phase to explain or expand on the initial quantitative results, and the exploratory sequential design with the intent of beginning with a qualitative exploration and using findings to inform a quantitative phase (e.g., instrument, survey, experiment, intervention) of research (Creswell & Plano Clark, 2018). However, researchers can also intersect mixed methods designs with other designs, such as randomized controlled trials (see Chapter 13, this volume) or qualitative grounded theory.

An additional characteristic of mixed methods is that mixed methods researchers apply *theoretical frameworks and philosophical paradigms* as a lens to guide mixed methods studies. Theories, such as social learning theory, the health belief model, the theory of planned behavior, and numerous other examples, have been helpful in guiding what sorts of data to collect and as an interpretive lens to make sense of results. Philosophical paradigms, including constructivism, postpositivism, social justice orientation, participatory paradigms, pragmatism, dialectical pluralism, critical realism, and others (see Volume 1, Chapter 1, this handbook), also provide a lens to think about all aspects of the research (Shannon-Baker, 2016). For example, when using a participatory paradigm such as community-based participatory research, the community is involved at all aspects of the research process.

The final and most important characteristic, *integration,* is the defining feature of mixed methods research and is discussed in detail later in this chapter. Integration refers to intentionally combining quantitative and qualitative research so that the two become interdependent (Bazeley, 2018). Integration has a synergistic effect beyond what is possible if the two strands are kept separate. Through this synergy, integration generates new inferences, samples, data collection methods, or follow-up studies.

To assist with reading mixed methods research studies and writing proposals and manuscripts, Table 12.1 provides definitions of common terms used in mixed methods research.

MIXED METHODS RESEARCH DESIGNS

Several ways of conceptualizing mixed methods designs have been developed in the field (Creswell & Plano Clark, 2018; Johnson & Christensen, 2020; Leech & Onwuegbuzie, 2009; Morse & Niehaus, 2009; Teddlie & Tashakkori, 2009). A mixed methods study involves seven major design dimensions, some of which include purpose, theoretical drive, timing, and integration, as well as several secondary dimensions related to the quality of the study, combination of sampling methods, and the degree to which the research participants, the researchers on the research team, and the methods will be similar and different

TABLE 12.1

Terminology in Mixed Methods Research

Term	Definition
Mixed methods design	A set of quantitative, qualitative, and integrative research procedures to guide the entire process of research.
Theoretical framework	Broadly refers to theories, conceptual models, and frameworks that guide a mixed methods study.
Philosophical paradigm	A set of worldview beliefs that guide mixed methods research. Examples include constructivism, postpositivism, social justice orientation, participatory paradigms, pragmatism, dialectical pluralism, and critical realism.
Strand	A quantitative or qualitative component or phase in a mixed methods study.
Integration	The intentional combination of quantitative and qualitative research, results, or data so that they become interdependent.
Intersecting	The addition of design elements in which one or more core mixed methods designs are combined with another design, approach, or framework.

(Schoonenboom & Johnson, 2017). Creswell and Plano Clark's (2018) approach has been known to include several "commonly used designs" (Schoonenboom & Johnson, 2017, p. 117) because the intent of their set of designs is to serve as both a parsimonious and practical tool among researchers across various fields. The three core mixed methods designs described by Creswell and Plano Clark are convergent, explanatory sequential, and exploratory sequential. As discussed later in this section, core designs can also intersect with other research approaches.

Mixed methods designs are not meant to be prescriptive; instead they should aid researchers in conceptualizing and designing their study beginning with the research questions leading to data collection and integration. Moreover, some flexibility and revision of the design is common in mixed methods research. We have included a procedural diagram for each of the mixed methods designs using studies from various subdisciplines in psychology. These procedural diagrams outline the steps of the study, including the procedures and products of each stage (e.g., data collection, analysis, integration). In addition, Morse's (2003) notation is presented in the diagrams with capital QUAN or QUAL reflecting the methodology that was prioritized in the study.

Convergent Design

The convergent design (also known as concurrent, simultaneous, or parallel design) is implemented when the researcher aims to collect and analyze data from each strand separately (i.e., quantitative and qualitative) and then merges the results to obtain a more comprehensive understanding of the research phenomenon (Creswell & Plano Clark, 2018). By merging the quantitative and qualitative strands, this design capitalizes on offsetting the strengths and weaknesses of each individual strand. The procedures for the quantitative and qualitative strands of a convergent design can occur either within a short time interval or simultaneously. The process includes collecting data for both strands concurrently but separate from each other, analyzing each independent strand, and merging them by either comparing the results from each strand or transforming the data to explore convergence, divergence, or expansion of metainferences. The integration of the quantitative and qualitative results leads to metainferences of the full mixed methods study.

In the field of educational psychology, Schmidt and colleagues (2019) used a convergent design to understand how middle school teachers communicated the importance of science in their classrooms and, in response, assessed the students' perceptions. Teacher interviews and classroom observations were collected to understand how teachers expressed the relative importance of science in their classrooms as well as student surveys assessing their perceived science utility. These data were merged by quantitizing the qualitative data (e.g., converting words to numbers) and teacher profiles were developed based on the interviews, observations, and student surveys to account for differences among teachers. Similarly,

in the area of educational psychology, Usher et al. (2019) used a convergent design to explore the experiences of rural Appalachian students and the experiences that contribute to their math and science self-efficacy. A quantitative survey assessed predicted relationships between levels of self-efficacy at Year 1 and the following school year, and open-ended questions were used to understand life events that contributed to their feelings of self-efficacy. A procedural diagram (Figure 12.1) is used to illustrate the research design by Usher et al.

Explanatory Sequential Design

In an explanatory design, the data collection and analysis of the quantitative phases occur first, followed by the qualitative data collection and analyses, to better understand the quantitative results. The explanatory design can be particularly effective for further investigating significant (or nonsignificant) results, potential outliers in the dataset, surprising results, or for following up with groups to obtain a richer understanding of the quantitative results (Bradley et al., 2009; Creswell & Plano Clark, 2018; Morgan, 2014; Morse, 1991). The first phase in conducting an explanatory design involves collecting and analyzing quantitative data. Researchers then identify quantitative results that warrant additional exploration through qualitative data collection and analyses and plan a subsequent qualitative phase. The qualitative phase then proceeds with data collection and analysis for the purpose of expanding on the initial results to add detail, describe variation, or add context. The final step includes integrating results from both strands and evaluating how the qualitative results helped to further understanding of the quantitative results.

A study by Matthews and López (2019) in educational psychology examined the application of *asset-based pedagogy* (ABP), which refers to teachers' instructional choices grounded in students' ethnic and cultural backgrounds, in the classroom and curriculum. An explanatory design was used to quantitatively examine the moderated and mediated effects of several variables such as teacher beliefs, ABPs, and students' math

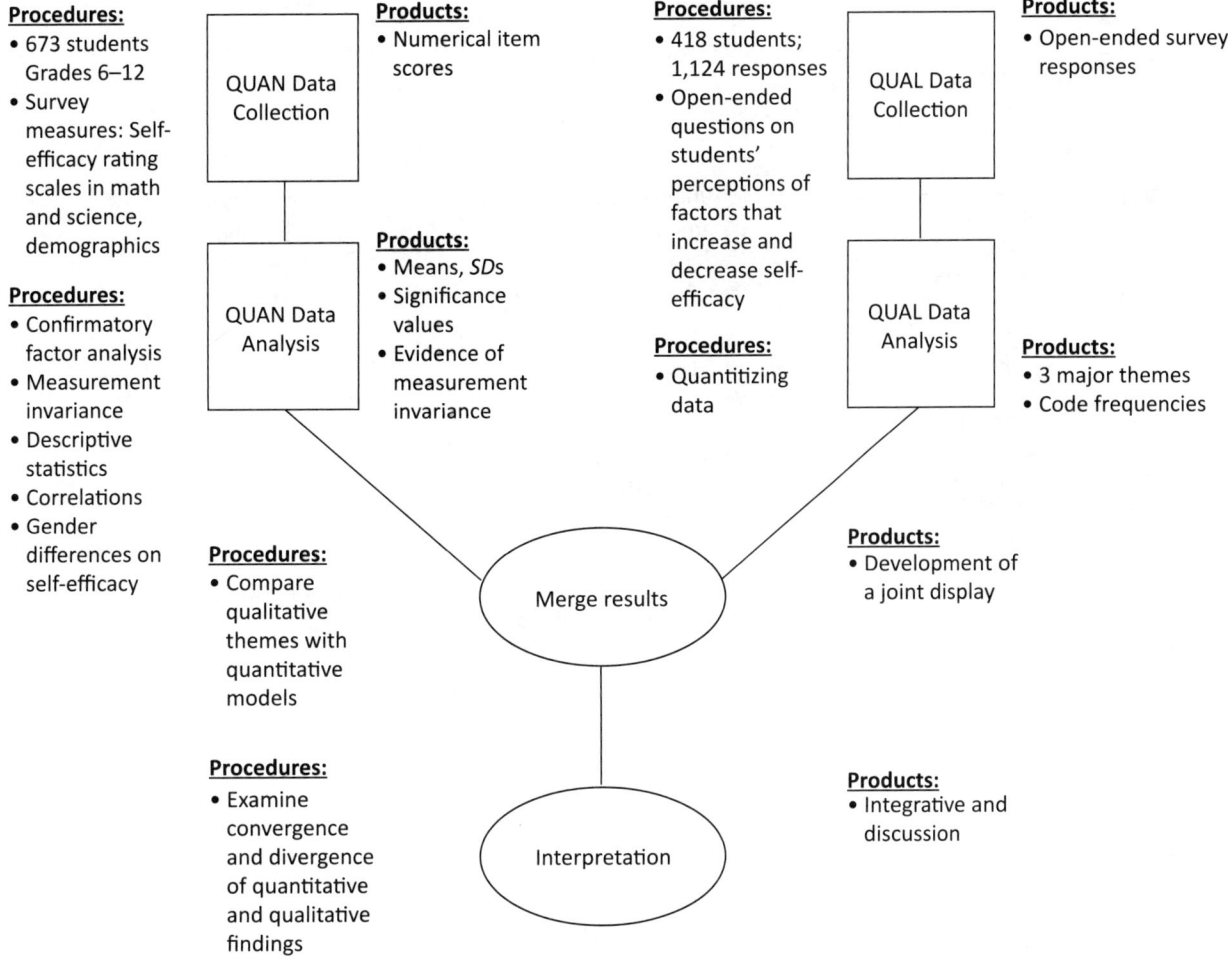

Procedures:
• 673 students Grades 6–12
• Survey measures: Self-efficacy rating scales in math and science, demographics

QUAN Data Collection

Products:
• Numerical item scores

Procedures:
• Confirmatory factor analysis
• Measurement invariance
• Descriptive statistics
• Correlations
• Gender differences on self-efficacy

QUAN Data Analysis

Products:
• Means, *SD*s
• Significance values
• Evidence of measurement invariance

Procedures:
• 418 students; 1,124 responses
• Open-ended questions on students' perceptions of factors that increase and decrease self-efficacy

QUAL Data Collection

Products:
• Open-ended survey responses

Procedures:
• Quantitizing data

QUAL Data Analysis

Products:
• 3 major themes
• Code frequencies

Procedures:
• Compare qualitative themes with quantitative models

Merge results

Products:
• Development of a joint display

Procedures:
• Examine convergence and divergence of quantitative and qualitative findings

Interpretation

Products:
• Integrative and discussion

FIGURE 12.1.   Convergent design example. Adapted from *Designing and Conducting Mixed Methods Research* (3rd ed., p. 76), by J. W. Creswell and V. L. Plano Clark, 2018, SAGE. Copyright 2018 by SAGE. Adapted with permission. Study example from Usher et al. (2019).

achievement scores. Follow-up interviews using a subset of the teacher sample were used to explore how teachers integrate cultural components and language practice in the classroom. Qualitative findings both confirmed and expanded on the quantitative results. Similarly, Matteucci and Farrell (2019) conducted an explanatory sequential design to investigate the roles of school psychologists in a district of northern Italy. Quantitative survey measures were initially used to assess the availability of school psychology services and ways they were delivered in the schools. Surveys were administered to principals or teachers across all schools in the district.

Follow-up semistructured interviews with seven stakeholders of school psychology services including principals, parents, teachers, and school psychologists were conducted to understand better each school's needs, challenges, and perceptions of psychology. Figure 12.2 demonstrates a procedural diagram for Matteucci and Farrell's study.

Exploratory Sequential Design

The exploratory design is similar to the explanatory design except the sequence of the strands is flipped such that the qualitative data collection and analyses are initially conducted followed

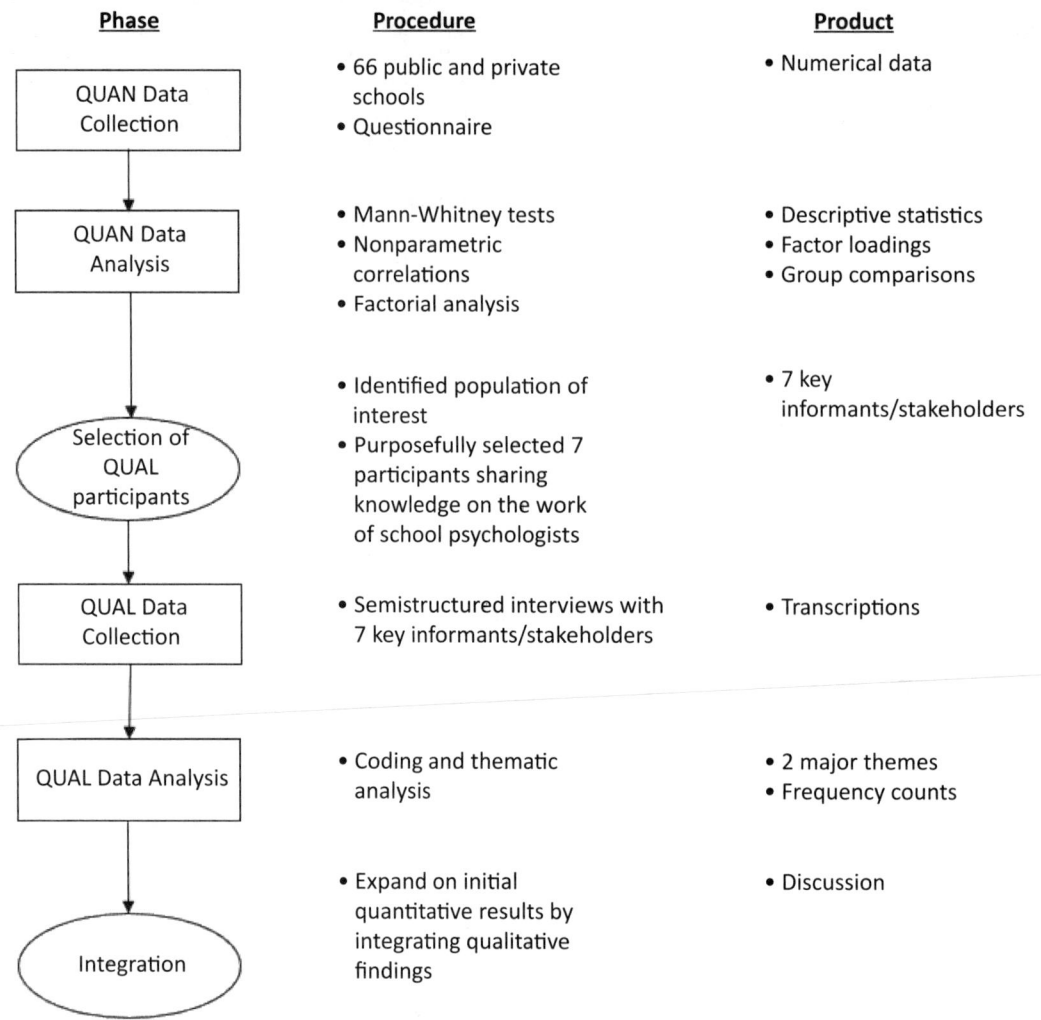

Phase

QUAN Data Collection

QUAN Data Analysis

Selection of QUAL participants

QUAL Data Collection

QUAL Data Analysis

Integration

Procedure

- 66 public and private schools
- Questionnaire

- Mann-Whitney tests
- Nonparametric correlations
- Factorial analysis

- Identified population of interest
- Purposefully selected 7 participants sharing knowledge on the work of school psychologists

- Semistructured interviews with 7 key informants/stakeholders

- Coding and thematic analysis

- Expand on initial quantitative results by integrating qualitative findings

Product

- Numerical data

- Descriptive statistics
- Factor loadings
- Group comparisons

- 7 key informants/stakeholders

- Transcriptions

- 2 major themes
- Frequency counts

- Discussion

FIGURE 12.2.   Explanatory sequential design example. Adapted from *Designing and Conducting Mixed Methods Research* (3rd ed., p. 85), by J. W. Creswell and V. L. Plano Clark, 2018, SAGE. Copyright 2018 by SAGE. Adapted with permission. Study example from Matteucci and Farrell (2019).

by quantitative data collection and analyses with the purpose of expanding on the qualitative findings. The purpose of the exploratory design is to use the initial qualitative findings and themes for further testing and analysis, to identify variables, develop an instrument, or explore the efficacy of an intervention. The steps for conducting an exploratory design include first collecting and analyzing qualitative data and then using results systematically to build or adapt an instrument, intervention, or variables. Beginning with a qualitative strand can help to ensure that whatever is developed is contextually and culturally

sensitive. In the subsequent quantitative phase, researchers administer the instrument, implement an intervention, or measure variables and collect and analyze data using quantitative methodology. Findings from both strands are integrated to develop metainferences that are grounded in participants' views.

Glover et al. (2020) proposed an exploratory sequential design with the intent of obtaining diverse perspectives from participants on brain donation research in the area of lifespan developmental and aging psychology. Focus groups were used to identify variables for the development of an instrument that assessed possible factors that influence brain donation decision making among older minorities. In the subdiscipline of clinical psychology, O'Keeffe et al. (2019) used an exploratory design to explore reasons why adolescents drop out of therapy for treatment of depression using three distinct types of interventions: (a) brief psychosocial intervention, (b) cognitive-behavioral therapy, and (c) short-term psychoanalytic psychotherapy. The initial qualitative strand included interviews of adolescents and therapists to understand reasons for dropout. From the qualitative analyses, three types of dropout classifications were identified and consequently used to test for group differences on multiple psychological outcomes. Figure 12.3 depicts a procedural diagram for

O'Keeffe et al. to demonstrate the procedures and products of the study. Overall, these core mixed methods designs provide researchers with guidance on the mixed methods design process and support researchers when implementing methods of integration to develop high-quality metainferences.

Alternative Mixed Methods Design

Overall, core mixed methods designs are used to help researchers select a design most pertinent to their research questions and to inform the researcher about critical mixed methods design components such as the timing of data collection and analysis of each strand, integration, and generation of metainferences. Nonetheless, when a core design does not fit with one's research

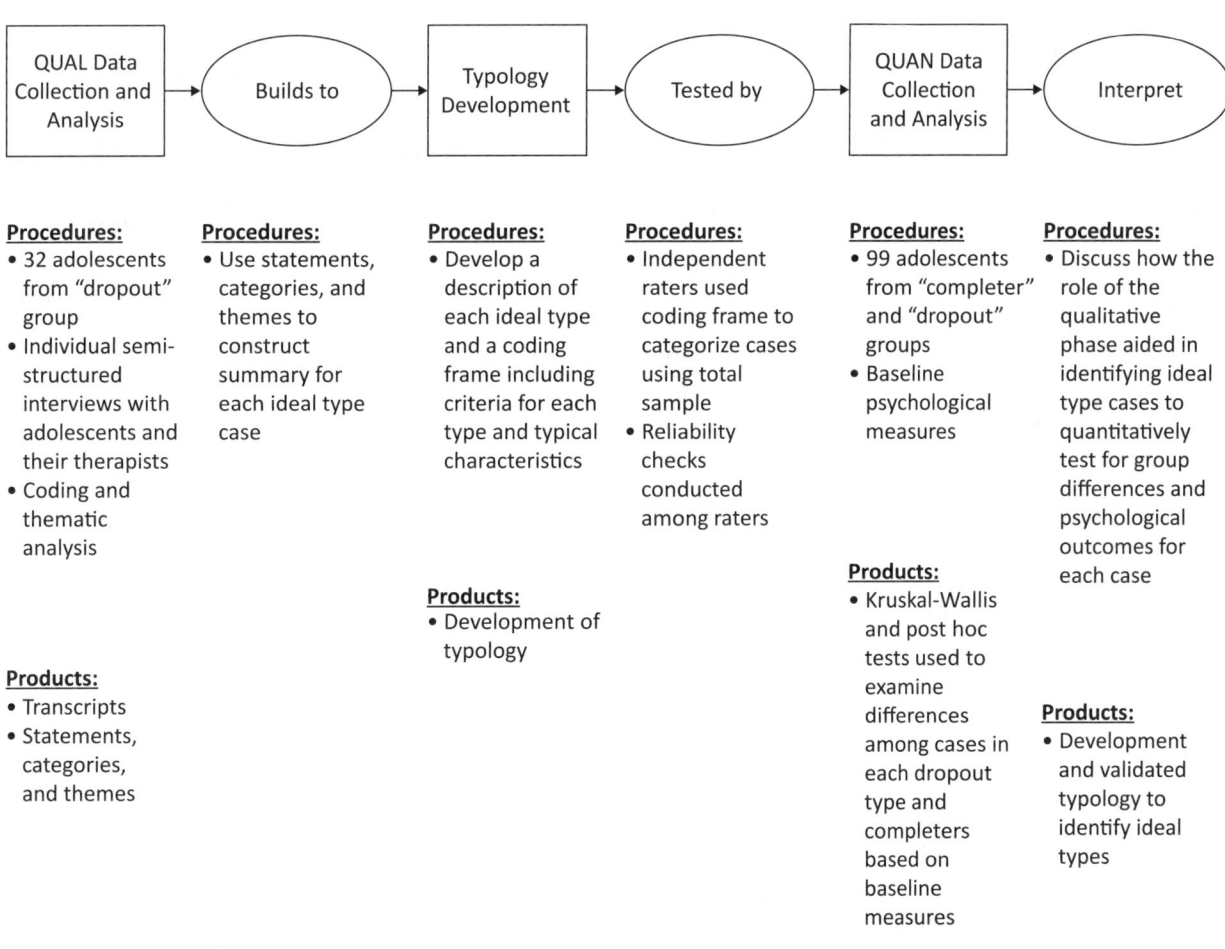

FIGURE 12.3. Exploratory sequential design example. Adapted from *Designing and Conducting Mixed Methods Research* (3rd ed., p. 94), by J. W. Creswell and V. L. Plano Clark, 2018, SAGE. Copyright 2018 by SAGE. Adapted with permission. Study example from O'Keeffe et al. (2019).

questions, researchers may consider alternative mixed methods designs. Another type of design is the conversion mixed methods design that involves transforming data from one strand (i.e., quantitative or qualitative) and then analyzing data using methods of the other strand through thematic or statistical analyses. The hybrid design is another mixed methods design that incorporates three or more strands and two or more mixed methods core designs (Tashakkori et al., 2021). More recently, the sequence-sources matrix has been advanced as a design typology comprising four mixed methods designs, parallel, sequential, conversion, and hybrid, that allow researchers to incorporate a combination of mixed methods designs given the research questions, sampling, data collection, and sequencing of strands (Tashakkori et al., 2021). Researchers using the sequence-sources matrix should consider the following when choosing an appropriate design: the initiation of a mixed methods study, quantitative and qualitative data sources, and the sequence of each strand (Tashakkori et al., 2021). The initiation of a mixed methods design refers to whether the mixed methods study was preplanned or emergent. The use of data sources for each strand is intended to reinforce sample specifications for the quantitative and qualitative strands. This includes whether data sources were collected from the same sample for both strands, a subsample, multiple samples, or multilevel samples. The sequence of the strands (i.e., parallel, sequential, conversion, or hybrid design) should be identified to make adequate use of the sequence-sources matrix. Overall, researchers should consider four guiding questions when using this typology: (a) Is a mixed methods design most appropriate to answer the research questions?; (b) What type(s) of mixed methods designs are most relevant to answer the research questions?; (c) What are the most appropriate data sources for each strand?; and (d) When does integration occur? (Tashakkori et al., 2021). This typology allows researchers to incorporate a family of designs for their mixed methods study to answer adequately the research questions.

INTERSECTING MIXED METHODS DESIGNS WITH OTHER DESIGNS

Building on the core designs are complex mixed methods research designs. The aims or research questions should drive the choice of design, and in many cases a core design is the appropriate choice. However, some research calls for intersecting other designs or frameworks in addition to the core mixed methods designs. Also called *complex designs* (Creswell & Plano Clark, 2018) or *advanced applications of mixed methods designs* (Plano Clark & Ivankova, 2016), the concept of intersection refers to adding design elements in which one or more core mixed methods designs are combined with another design, approach, or framework. Plano Clark and Ivankova (2016) noted that intersection can occur in several ways:

- intersecting mixed methods with another research design (e.g., quantitative experiment, qualitative interpretative phenomenological analysis, qualitative case study)
- intersecting mixed methods with a novel methodological approach (e.g., social network analysis, community-based participatory research, program evaluation)
- intersecting mixed methods with a theoretical framework (e.g., positive psychology, critical disability theory)

We now focus on three common ways of intersecting mixed methods: mixed methods randomized controlled trials (RCTs), mixed methods transformative designs, and mixed methods–grounded theory designs.

Mixed Methods Randomized Controlled Trials

Mixed methods can be applied to intervention research, including developing and testing interventions. To intersect mixed methods with an RCT, one or more of the mixed methods designs is used to enhance the trial. The integration of quantitative and qualitative research often occurs at several time points. Using an exploratory sequential core design, a qualitative strand before the trial could be used to develop features of the intervention, improve acceptability or accessibility, develop outcome measures, or inform recruitment strategies. In addition, a convergent core design could be used in which the qualitative strand of research during the trial is used to understand participant experiences with the intervention or processes. For example, investigators might identify individuals who had better versus worse outcomes in the intervention and then plan a qualitative phase to understand the differential experiences of individuals. Finally, by intersecting an explanatory sequential design, the results of the RCT could lead to planning a follow-up qualitative phase to understand better outcomes or mechanisms. A concern unique to mixed methods RCTs is the potential for qualitative data collection to introduce bias. For some behavioral interventions, participating in qualitative interviews could further reinforce intervention concepts and produce effects similar to the intervention itself (Le et al., 2021).

Researchers in a variety of psychology sub-disciplines have intersected mixed methods with RCTs, and we now provide two examples of mixed methods RCTs to illustrate the value of the design. Peterson et al. (2013) began with a qualitative phase consisting of interviews to explore values related to behavioral change and used those results to inform an intervention to increase physical activity and medication adherence for individuals with chronic disease. Specifically, they used qualitative results to develop culturally relevant informational workbooks, to refine the interview, and to refine recruitment, such as focusing recruitment for individuals early in the recovery phase. They then tested the intervention in subsequent pilot and RCT phases with measures to assess primary outcomes of physical activity and antihypertensive medication adherence. In another example, Le et al. (2021) used a mixed methods observational trial to evaluate a cognitive behavioral therapy intervention to prevent perinatal depression among Latinas. Their core design was explanatory sequential, evaluating depressive symptoms, and psychopathology as primary outcomes in the trial and then conducting follow-up qualitative interviews with intervention completers and noncompleters. The quantitative results indicated both completers and noncompleters benefited, and the qualitative phase added the understanding that, while both groups had similar experiences, differences in learning and application of cognitive behavioral concepts were evident. The mixed methods results helped to elucidate the need to consider risk factors to maximize outcomes and the need for case management and referral for mental health and domestic violence services.

Mixed Methods Transformative Designs for Social Justice

Mixed methods research can also be intersected with a transformative worldview that promotes social justice. The transformative worldview is best defined by the overarching purpose, which is to use research to address issues of inequity and marginalization by challenging the status quo and calling for action. When intersecting a transformative worldview with mixed methods, the researcher attends to "power issues, social justice, and cultural complexity throughout the research process" (Mertens, 2007, p. 213). These nuanced issues are an ideal fit for mixed methods because of its ability to develop a deeper understanding of complexity. Transformative methods research encompasses approaches and designs, such as community-engaged research, community-based participatory research, and action research. Often, there is a participatory element in which participants or community members are involved in the research as equal partners, informing the research focus, data collection, analysis, interpretation, and, most importantly, dissemination to the community. As with other intersections, any of the core designs can be used with transformative mixed methods research. Similarly, integrating these designs depends on the core mixed methods design being used. Most important is keeping the transformative goal as a focus of all aspects of research. For example, if a researcher is using critical race theory to understand the role of race in mental health outcome inequity, then race needs to be central to all quantitative, qualitative, and mixed methods research questions.

In the field of educational psychology, Kumar et al. (2019) intersected a transformative worldview with an exploratory sequential design to investigate learning environments in multicultural schools that are culturally responsive and inclusive. The first phase involved focus groups with students in culturally diverse middle schools to explore and describe culturally inclusive and responsive curricular learning environments. In the subsequent phase, they used the qualitative findings to develop and test an instrument to measure inclusivity and cultural responsiveness. The authors stated that their study "sheds light on the experiences of students who lack visibility, and often experience cultural insensitivity and prejudice from teachers and peers" (Kumar et al., 2019, p. 101).

Mixed Methods–Grounded Theory

Another option is to intersect a mixed methods design with a qualitative research design, a variety of which now exist and are differentiated by both their intent and their procedures. Choosing to intersect a qualitative design has both conceptual and practical implications. Conceptually, the qualitative design is a major focus, as the researcher is thinking about what the qualitative component brings to the mixed methods study. For example, the intent of a *case study* is to develop an in-depth and comprehensive understanding of a case, while a *grounded theory study* is suited for developing a theory, model, or framework (see Chapter 3, this volume). In a mixed methods study, the researcher considers the intent of the qualitative strand. If the intent is to develop a detailed understanding of a case, such as an intervention or program, then perhaps case study is the design to intersect. If the intent is to develop a theory of a process, such as how individuals are psychologically affected by an event or the mechanisms of action of an intervention, then grounded theory might be a good fit. Practically, the choice of qualitative design also brings decisions about specific research procedures

and methods. For instance, case study methods involve the use of multiple data sources, and the combination of quantitative and qualitative data makes it a natural fit for mixed methods research. Grounded theory methods include procedures of theoretical sampling, memoing, and assessing theoretical saturation that we discuss later. When selecting a qualitative design to intersect, we recommend being mindful of both the intent and the procedures needed for rigorous research. Mixed methods intersection can occur with any traditional qualitative design, such as case study (see Chapter 13, this volume; Guetterman & Fetters, 2018), grounded theory (Guetterman et al., 2019; Shim et al., 2020), and phenomenology (Mayoh & Onwuegbuzie, 2015). Here, we elaborate on intersecting a mixed methods research with a grounded theory design to provide an in-depth exploration of one of these options.

Mixed methods–grounded theory designs have elements of mixed methods (e.g., the integration of quantitative and qualitative research) and grounded theory (e.g., the goal of developing a theory, model, or framework). Mixed methods–grounded theory is well-suited to aims that call for both developing and testing theory within a single study (Guetterman et al., 2019; Howell Smith et al., 2019). Alternatively, mixed methods–grounded theory is useful when collecting, analyzing, and integrating quantitative and qualitative data for developing the theory, as in conducting interviews and gathering survey data iteratively to develop a grounded theory. As previously advocated in best practices for this design (Guetterman et al., 2019), features of mixed methods–grounded theory include collecting, analyzing, and integrating quantitative and qualitative data; theoretical sampling to support analytic development of theoretical concepts; coding data using grounded theory techniques, using constant comparison of data collected to develop categories, concepts, and theory; memoing to document reflections and analytical ideas; and assessing theoretical saturation to determine when sampling and recruitment can cease. Most importantly, mixed methods–grounded theory culminates in presenting a theory, model, or framework. Mixed methods–grounded theory can employ any of the core designs, and integration is often aimed at developing or refining the theory. This design can be applied to understanding mechanisms of psychological interventions, developing culturally sensitive models of psychological processes, understanding behavioral change, and any situation in which developing theory would be useful.

Focusing on organizational behavior, Taheri et al. (2019) examined factors related to the process of employee well-being in public organizations. They used mixed methods–grounded theory with an exploratory sequential core design that began with a grounded theory phase consisting of interviews with employees at 15 organizations, grounded theory coding, and the development of a theoretical model of employees' subjective well-being. The model's categories included contextual and intervening conditions, causal factors, strategies, and consequences at the personal and organizational levels. The first way in which they integrated was by using these findings to develop hypotheses to test through a questionnaire derived from those categories. In the subsequent quantitative phase, they analyzed the data to assess a measurement and structural model to determine whether the initial, qualitative, grounded theory model generalized. The authors noted the research approach provided "better insights into understanding incentives behind life satisfaction and positive affect than just the use of either the qualitative or quantitative method alone" (Taheri et al., 2019, p. 449).

WHEN TO USE MIXED METHODS RESEARCH: RATIONALES FOR INTEGRATING

There exist several mixed methods rationales to justify why using a mixed methods design allows for a more complete understanding of the research phenomenon (Bryman, 2006; Collins et al., 2006; Greene et al., 1989; Morgan, 2014; Plano Clark & Ivankova, 2016; Reichardt & Cook, 1979; Teddlie & Tashakkori, 2009). Providing a clear rationale

allows researchers and reviewers to understand why a mixed methods design was most appropriate. Greene and colleagues (1989) developed five common mixed methods rationales: triangulation, complementarity, development, initiation, and expansion. *Triangulation* refers to corroborating results from the quantitative and qualitative strands to increase the validity of the findings (Greene et al., 1989). A mixed methods study in social psychology by Wesely (2010), exploring motivation, employed a mixed methods design because each strand alone was unable to capture the complexities of language learning motivation in early adolescents. The authors stated, "A mixed methods study of motivation has the potential to be particularly informative in addressing a problem where both qualitative and quantitative approaches have produced inconsistent or contradictory findings" (p. 299).

Complementarity is another mixed methods rationale that argues for a greater understanding of the phenomenon by using both quantitative and qualitative methods to obtain convergent and divergent results from different aspects of a study (Greene et al., 1989). Roques and colleagues (2020) conducted a mixed methods study in the subdiscipline of clinical psychology to examine traumatic experiences among bullied adolescents and indicated "we believe that combining quantitative and qualitative approaches may make it possible to benefit from the richness of the qualitative method while maintaining the rigor of the quantitative method" (p. 4), and they further explained that the complementary results enhanced their understanding of how the findings were related. *Development* refers to using the results of one strand to inform or guide the sampling or measurement of the other strand (Greene et al., 1989). In the area of industrial and organizational psychology, an exploratory sequential design was employed by Ladge et al. (2018) examining maternal confidence and workplace support and the contributing factors in a mother's desire to stay within the organization. The initial qualitative strand included interviews of mothers' experiences, which aided in the development of a survey used to quantify relationships and examine the extent to which these findings were generalizable (Ladge et al., 2018). *Initiation* refers to exploring divergent findings and can result in new interpretations and perspectives of the research phenomenon, whereas *expansion* refers to increasing the magnitude of the study by incorporating a quantitative and qualitative strand (Greene et al., 1989).

Bryman (2006) also proposed a mixed methods rationale typology comprising 16 different rationales, including some of the common types (i.e., *explanation*, triangulation) as well as variants of Greene's et al. (1989) typology such as *unexpected results, instrument development,* and *sampling*. A notable addition to mixed methods rationales is *offsetting the strengths and weaknesses*, which refers to obtaining more rigorous inferences from both strands in cases where the quantitative strand might have been stronger and, therefore, can offset the weaknesses of the qualitative strand or vice versa (Bryman, 2006; Plano Clark & Ivankova, 2016). In educational psychology, Matteucci and Farrell (2019) conducted a mixed methods study to explore the role of school psychologists in an Italian district. Specifically, the quantitative strand provided an overarching understanding of school psychologists in practice, while the qualitative strand further explained and "deepened those statistical results by exploring the main stakeholders' views in more depth" (Matteucci & Farrell, 2019, p. 242). Therefore, the weaknesses of the quantitative strand were strengthened by the in-depth interviews of the qualitative strand.

Although these are some commonly used mixed methods rationales, there are several others that can also be particularly relevant to several subdisciplines in psychology. For instance, the *social justice rationale* is focused on the researchers' values, and highlights the need to conduct both quantitative and qualitative studies to include various individuals from the community such as community members and stakeholders or to elucidate the conditions or injustices of community members (Caracelli & Greene, 1997; Plano Clark & Ivankova, 2016). From the field of legal psychology, Campbell et al.'s (2017) rationale for

conducting a mixed methods study was embedded within a social justice framework as they assert

> Methodologically, this focal question was well-suited for a mixed methods research design, given the sparse literature on the issue of untested SAKs [sexual assault kits] and the need for both a contextually nuanced understanding of rape kit testing and also the press for data that could inform public policy. (p. 456)

Collins et al. (2006) also developed four mixed methods rationales particularly within the context of special education comprising *participant enrichment, instrument fidelity, treatment integrity,* and *significance enhancement*. These rationales have a stronger relationship with key design features of a study such as participant selection, the appropriateness of using or developing an instrument, the assessment of treatment fidelity, and strengthening the interpretation of findings by incorporating the quantitative and qualitative strands (Collins et al., 2006). Overall, we have highlighted several mixed methods rationales to justify the need for advancing research using a mixed methods design. Importantly, researchers should have a sound basis and clearly articulate their purpose(s) in using mixed methods research in journals, grant applications, and theses and dissertations.

How to Ensure Integration

Integration is the defining feature of mixed methods and arguably the most important, yet achieving integration remains a challenge (Fetters & Freshwater, 2015; Fetters & Molina-Azorin, 2017). As a reminder, *integration* is the intentional combination of quantitative and qualitative research such that the two become interdependent and synergistic (Bazeley, 2018). Integration in mixed methods research studies occurs at many levels: philosophical, design, methods, and representation levels (Fetters et al., 2013). At a *philosophical level*, integration occurs as researchers blend often differing philosophical worldviews. The field of mixed methods research has moved past the paradigm wars and embraced the concept of dialectical pluralism as a meta-paradigm that takes into consideration varying paradigmatic and philosophical stances (Johnson, 2012). This metaparadigmatic approach, originally advanced by Greene (2007), maximizes the viewpoints of each member on the research team, while also bringing these differences together resulting in a "package of values" (Johnson, 2017, p. 166). Integration also happens at the *design level* as researchers use mixed methods designs to guide the methods of collection, analysis, and points of integration of quantitative and qualitative research. Closely related is integration at the *methods level*, through which researchers merge quantitative and qualitative data or results, connect from one form of research to sampling for the other, or build from the results of one form of research to data collection of the other. Finally, researchers integrate at the *representation level* by writing about how they integrated and reported integrated results both in prose and through visual displays (Guetterman, Creswell, et al., 2015).

To ensure integration, we recommend that the aims or research questions become the guiding principle for thinking about integration. Consider whether the objective of mixing methods is to compare quantitative and qualitative results, to examine quantitative results relative to qualitative results (e.g., how do themes differ for those with quantitatively higher vs. lower scores), to explain results with a follow-up qualitative phase, or to develop contextualized instruments or interventions. We focus on three ways to ensure integration: (a) planning for integration through careful attention to data collection and analysis, (b) selecting a strategy for mixed methods integration, and (c) articulating integration through writing and visual representations.

Plan for Integration by Identifying Data Sources

Returning to the characteristics of mixed methods research, one way to ensure integration is to plan for integration by identifying both quantitative and qualitative data sources and using rigorous data collection and analysis methods. Simply, both quantitative and qualitative data (e.g., assessment scores and interviews) are needed in order to integrate. Tashakkori and colleagues (2021) identified two mixed methods data collection strategies: within-method mixed method data collection (also known as *intramethod* or *within-method mixing*) and between-methods mixed methods data collection (also known as *intermethod* or *between methods mixing*). *Within-method mixed methods data collection* refers to using the same data collection method for both the quantitative and qualitative strands, and mixing typically occurs within one method of data collection. *Between-methods mixed methods data collection*, however, uses several methods of data collection, such as qualitative interviews and quantitative surveys. Hence, mixing in the between-methods mixed methods data collection typically occurs between two or more methods of data collection (Tashakkori et al., 2021). Particularly relevant in convergent designs, a step researchers can take when planning a mixed methods study is to match data sources to ensure parallel concepts in the quantitative and qualitative data (Fetters, 2020). Using a convergent design, Bacchus et al. (2018) matched semistructured interviews with survey data to understand domestic violence and abuse among gay and bisexual men, which illustrates a between-method mixed methods data collection. The matching does not have to be one-to-one (e.g., several items on a scale might match to a single interview question). Most important is to be thoughtful and strategic, guided by the aims or research questions of the study. Alternatively, sometimes there is no existing measure of a particular phenomenon or qualitative methods are needed to expand understanding in a more nuanced way. For example, researchers sought to understand the future work and family plans of adolescents at risk for educational and developmental issues (Cinamon & Rich, 2014). Using quantitative questionnaires, Cinamon and Rich (2014) gathered questionnaire data about work-family conflict and facilitation, and they collected interviews to expand their understanding of the related, yet slightly different, concept of personal perceptions of future work and family plans.

Planning to collect data about related ideas positions researchers better for integrative analysis.

A potential exception to collecting both forms of data is gathering a single data set that is analyzed using mixed methods analysis rather than forcing two dichotomous forms of data (Bazeley, 2018). This design is a type of within-method mixed method data collection. Examples of these inherently mixed methods data sources include video analysis, social network analysis, and natural language processing. For example, a large social media data set could be analyzed using natural language processing, which is a computational process for identifying clusters of meaning in text phrases. Augmenting the quantitative natural language processing analysis with traditional qualitative coding and analysis and integrating the results can lead to more comprehensive, complex results (Guetterman et al., 2018). However, most mixed methods studies will have distinct quantitative and qualitative data sources.

Strategies for Mixed Methods Integration

In addition to considering data sources, mixed methods researchers identify one, or often more, strategies for conducting integration. The synergy of integration means that integration produces something new. Integration could generate new insights, called *metainferences*, new follow-up studies or samples, or new forms of data collection. Integration can also generate new variables, intervention features, or recruitment strategies. Three common strategies for integration are merging, connecting, and building (Creswell & Plano Clark, 2018; Fetters et al., 2013).

Merging can involve comparing or relating quantitative and qualitative results to generate metainferences. Thus, a preliminary step in merging is to analyze both forms of data. By comparing results, researchers might relate statistical test results to themes or categories. For example, White et al. (2019) studied the relationship of racial identity with science identity, self-efficacy, and achievement. They merged results by comparing key quantitative descriptive statistics and significant correlations to qualitative themes from interviews and determined the extent of agreement

or dissonance, essentially to corroborate results. Another way of merging involves relating themes to statistics. Relating is similar to a crosstabulation. One option is to examine a statistical profile of each theme, and another option is to examine themes for quantitative variables (e.g., thematic comparison of those with higher vs. lower depression scores). A variant of merging is data transformation. The most common data transformation is converting qualitative codes to counts and frequencies (i.e., quantizing), conducting statistical modeling of the counts, and merging the statistical model with the qualitative findings. The culmination of merging is developing metainferences—the new insights that emerge from the mixed methods analysis.

Connecting is the use of results of one strand of research to plan the sampling of the other strand (Fetters et al., 2013). Research questions and aims that call for explaining quantitative results with a qualitative follow-up are ideally suited for connecting. Studying grit in successful working adults, Clark and Plano Clark (2019) selected individuals in the top quartile of grit and career success for follow-up interviews. Although connecting is common in explanatory sequential mixed methods studies, it could also be used in convergent designs to identify a purposeful qualitative subsample from a larger quantitative sample.

Building is the use of the results of one strand of research to plan the data collection of the other (Fetters et al., 2013). Building is amenable to both exploratory sequential and explanatory sequential designs. One application of building is to use results from an initial qualitative phase to systematically develop or adapt an instrument. Qualitative codes can inform variables to measure, qualitative themes can inform scales or major sections on the instrument, and quotes can assist with item writing using language of participants. For example, Kumar et al. (2019) used themes and quotes from qualitative focus group interviews to write 19 items to measure culturally responsive and inclusive education. Another application of building is in explanatory sequential mixed methods, as researchers use quantitative results to develop interview or focus group protocols.

When selecting an appropriate strategy, we recommend first considering research questions or aims and the research design. Researchers often employ more than one strategy for integration, which is perfectly appropriate. Although merging, connecting, and building are common integration strategies, there are numerous additional strategies to consider (see Bazeley, 2018; Fetters, 2020), including developing your own unique approach.

How to Represent and Write About Integration

The onus to describe integration is on the author. Perhaps the most daunting challenge of integration is representing and writing about integrated results. Too often, mixed methods studies are published with little integration as quantitative and qualitative results are presented in their own subsections. Attending to both a description of integration methods, as discussed in the previous section, and a clear report of integrated results is necessary for a strong mixed methods research manuscript. Table 12.2 provides definitions of common integration terms that may be helpful in writing about integration.

Reporting integrated results can involve a narrative writing of results or the use of joint displays in the results section of a manuscript. Narrative reporting is traditional and consists of weaving quantitative and qualitative results and the reporting of metainferences. Joint displays have emerged as one approach to represent integration in mixed methods research. Joint displays are a visual means of facilitating and representing integration through tables, matrices, or figures (Guetterman, Fetters, et al., 2015). Joint displays can be used with any strategy of integration. To depict merging, Clark and Stubbeman (2021) produced a side-by-side joint display organized by research question(s) that included a column for quantitative results, salient qualitative results, and metainferences (labeled "interpretation"). To show building, Kumar et al. (2019) included a joint display that mapped themes and quotes to specific items on their instrument to measure culturally responsive and inclusive curricular education. Recent innovative joint displays include figures (e.g., a path model or grounded theory model), images (e.g., photographs), or other graphics (e.g., boxplots or bar graphs). The creation of joint displays is often a form of integrative analysis itself as researchers juxtapose related quantitative and qualitative results along with metainferences that emerge. A joint display can be an excellent starting point for reporting integrated results when accompanied by a narrative reporting of results.

TABLE 12.2

Integration Concepts

Concept	Definition
Metainferences	New insights that emerge from integrative analysis
Matching	Alignment of related data sources to ensure parallel concepts in the quantitative and qualitative data
Merging	Comparing or relating quantitative and qualitative results to generate metainferences
Connecting	The results of one strand of research are used to plan the sampling of the other form of research
Building	The results of one strand of research are used to plan the data collection of the other
Weaving	Narrative reporting of integrative results
Joint displays	Visual means of facilitating and representing integration through tables, matrices, or figures

ASSESSING QUALITY IN MIXED METHODS RESEARCH

Evaluating the quality of a mixed methods research study requires the researcher to assess the validity and trustworthiness of the quantitative and qualitative strands, respectively, as well as the full mixed methods study. To assess the quantitative strand, there are four distinct validity types: internal, external, construct, and statistical conclusion (Shadish et al., 2002). *Internal* validity is the degree to which an inference is made about the causal relationship between two variables, and *external* validity examines whether results can be generalized across different populations, settings, treatments, and times. *Construct* validity investigates whether the construct has been accurately and appropriately operationalized and measured, and *statistical conclusion* refers to the extent to which an inferred relationship between two variables (i.e., independent and dependent) exists and estimates the magnitude of that relationship.

To assess the trustworthiness of the qualitative strand, several concepts or procedures have been developed including Lincoln and Guba's (1985) widely used criteria of *credibility, transferability, dependability,* and *confirmability*. Respectively, the quantitative equivalents of the concepts are internal validity, external validity, reliability, and objectivity. Creswell and Miller (2000) also developed nine types of trustworthiness assessment divided into three categories: researcher's lens, participant's lens, and reader's or reviewer's lens. Although the researcher should incorporate several of these strategies to add to the integrity of the study (Creswell & Poth, 2018), we recommend that researchers address at least two validation strategies to account for different perspectives.

Given the importance of integration in mixed methods research, it is critical that the methods of the quantitative and qualitative strands are sound and credible to develop high-quality metainferences of the mixed methods study. Metainferences are mixed methods inferences developed from the integration of quantitative and qualitative inferences. Some researchers argue that quality assessment of a mixed methods study is both a process and an outcome and should be conducted throughout the study including the research purpose, design, and inferences (Onwuegbuzie & Johnson, 2006; Tashakkori et al., 2021). One of the first conceptualizations of quality stems from Teddlie and Tashakkori's (2003) call for an integrative framework for inference quality in mixed methods research. This work has been instrumental in furthering discussions of quality in mixed methods research and has led to the development of various quality frameworks.

Several quality frameworks have been advanced in mixed method research (i.e., legitimation typology [Onwuegbuzie & Johnson, 2006], validation framework [Dellinger & Leech, 2007], comprehensive framework for assessing quality of mixed methods research [O'Cathain, 2010], and critical appraisal framework for quality in mixed method studies in health sciences [Curry & Nunez-Smith, 2015]). The *legitimation typology* by Onwuegbuzie and Johnson (2006), with a more recent iteration by Johnson and Christensen (2020), details 11 types of legitimation of a mixed methods study. These legitimation types can be thought of as potential threats to quality; however, researchers should mainly address the quality types most pertinent to their study with the aim of developing high-quality metainferences. The comprehensive framework for assessing quality in mixed method research developed by O'Cathain (2010) is another quality framework comprising eight quality domains addressing different stages of the research process including planning to the interpretation phase and the study's utility (Plano Clark & Ivankova, 2016). In general, these quality frameworks may be particularly helpful to novice mixed methods researchers due to their all-encompassing criteria and can be used across various subdisciplines of psychology.

The purpose of introducing quality frameworks is to increase their use and the overall rigor of mixed methods studies. To date, the field of mixed methods has not reached an agreed upon set of standards and terminology for assessing quality. Therefore, it is often referred to in the literature as either quality, legitimation, inference quality, or validity among several other terms (Fàbregues & Molina-Azorín, 2017). We recommend that researchers view quality types as evidence of quality and assess the types most pertinent to their mixed methods study to increase the evidence of quality for the full mixed methods study and generate high-quality metainferences. Assessing the quality of a mixed methods study is not only crucial to mixed methods researchers but also can be used by reviewers of grant applications and journals in evaluating the quality of the full mixed methods study (Curry & Nunez-Smith, 2015). We have proposed a quality framework for psychology covering the major quality tenets across various frameworks with the overarching aim of developing high-quality metainferences as illustrated in Table 12.3.

TABLE 12.3

Quality Framework in Psychological Research

Component	Characteristics	Example
Mixed methods rationale	Explicit mention of a mixed methods rationale Demonstrate appropriateness of a mixed methods design above and beyond a single methodology (i.e., QUAN or QUAL)	Glover et al. (2020) proposed a mixed methods study to gain a better understanding of older adults' brain donation decision-making and develop a culturally based instrument to assess this construct.
Mixed methods design	Discuss the mixed methods design (if applicable) (e.g., convergent, sequential mixed methods design) or key aspects of the mixed methods design	Roysircar et al. (2019) used an exploratory sequential design to develop a conceptual model of Haitian mothers' coping mechanisms and beliefs using qualitative interviews and then quantitatively tested children's levels of traumatic adjustment based on the conceptual model.
Mixed methods objectives and questions	Extent to which the research aims, objectives, and research questions are clearly stated and relate to the mixed methods design and inclusion of integrated mixed methods research questions	Youngs and Piggot-Irvine (2012) outlined three research questions and discussed why a mixed methods approach was most suitable for their research questions.
Paradigm(s)	Address paradigmatic/philosophical stance	Implementing a transnational feminist approach, Roysircar and colleagues (2019) used a community-level approach to better understand mothers' coping mechanisms in relation to their children's traumatic adjustments within the Haitian community.
Sampling	Describe the sampling scheme and size of each strand and the full mixed methods study	Al Hariri (2018) used a sample of 20 foster care experts for the qualitative strand and expanded the sample to 450 teenage girls for the quantitative strand to develop a multidimensional model of factors attributed to adolescent girls' elopement.
Methods	Adequate descriptions of methods used for each strand (e.g., questionnaires, interviews, focus groups)	O'Keeffe et al. (2019) included six different measures to assess a variety of psychological factors (i.e., depression, anxiety, antisocial behavior) for the quantitative strand and followed up with individual qualitative interviews of adolescents and their therapists.
Individual quality	Assess the validity and the trustworthiness of each strand ■ QUAN: Report reliability and validity estimates of psychological measure, ensuring the construct is appropriately and adequately assessed ■ QUAL: Use validation strategies to assess the trustworthiness of the data	Neto et al. (2015) provided evidence of construct validity and reported validity and reliability estimates of the Beck Depression Inventory. Authors engaged in peer debriefing audits for the qualitative strand.
Analysis	Provide in-depth details on analysis of each individual strand (i.e., QUAN or QUAL) Include rationale and methods to ensure quality of transformed data	Sheehy-Skeffington and Obradović (2020) used thematic analysis to analyze the qualitative data and regression and moderated mediation analyses of survey data for the quantitative strand.
Mixed methods integration	Evaluate whether integration resulted in data convergence, divergence, and/or expansion Inclusion of a joint display	Wesely (2010) analyzed quantitative and qualitative findings separately and focused on the literature in its respective field to evaluate how findings could be refined and combined. Then, they explored how findings converged and diverged in the study.
Utility	Address how metainferences contribute to the study's field, mixed methods community, and ways stakeholders benefit from the study	Serrat et al. (2017) used a mixed methods design to contribute to the literature on the different facets of generativity among older adults.

Note. Data from Greene (2007); Johnson and Christensen (2020); O'Cathain (2010); and Teddlie and Tashakkori (2003).

STEPS IN CONDUCTING A MIXED METHODS RESEARCH STUDY

To illustrate the steps in conducting a mixed methods study, we have used a study from the subdiscipline of clinical psychology by Bacchus et al. (2018) to outline each of these procedures (Table 12.4). The steps are meant to guide researchers when conducting a rigorous mixed methods study as well as in identifying rigorous mixed methods studies to include in systematic reviews, for example.

CONCLUSION

Advancements in mixed methods research within the past few decades shed light on the utility of this methodology across disciplines. Recent developments in the field include the use of hierarchical linear modeling in mixed methods research (e.g., Bash et al., 2021), alternative conceptualizations to integration (e.g., Lynam et al., 2020; Knappertsbusch, 2020), longitudinal data analysis using qualitative approaches in a mixed methods design (Waller et al., 2021), and the use of mixed methods research for program and policy evaluation (Palinkas et al., 2019). These developments reflect the methodological maturity of mixed methods research. Nonetheless, several topics are ripe for continued exploration, such as methods for integrating multiple theories and philosophical worldviews and methods for consolidating or expanding on discordance. Discordance refers to inconsistent or contradictory findings between the quantitative and qualitative strands. A challenge for those new to mixed methods is the terminology and lack of consensus on the use of terms (Riazi & Candlin, 2014) and staying true to the nature of dialectical pluralism that calls for respectfully engaging with differences (Hesse-Biber & Johnson, 2013). As mixed methods research continues to develop and grow, we anticipate these areas will be enhanced and will evoke further methodological discussions.

Within the discipline of psychology, researchers might use mixed methods to gain a deeper understanding of phenomena and interventions, to explain quantitative results with a qualitative phase that can uncover nuances and complexity, and to explore qualitatively first in order to develop instruments or identify variables for measurement. The goal of this chapter is to provide an introduction to mixed methods research, which involves the collection, analysis, and thoughtful integration of quantitative and qualitative research. Although we have shared

TABLE 12.4

Steps in Conducting a Mixed Methods Research

Step	Examples
Mixed methods research question or aim	A mixed methods design was implemented to demonstrate the use of a case series mixed methods display and provide a more complete understanding of domestic violence and abuse of gay and bisexual men.
Philosophies/ theories	A pragmatist approach acknowledging the strengths of quantitative and qualitative methodologies guided the mixed methods design.
Design	A convergent design was conducted by collecting quantitative and qualitative data concurrently, while analyzing them independently and integrating results.
Data collection and analysis	Survey and semistructured interviews were collected. Quantitative analyses such as descriptive statistics and logistic regressions were conducted. Deductive and inductive coding methods were used to analyze the qualitative data.
Integrating quantitative and qualitative data	Integration occurred at various stages including the methods as well as interpretation and reporting with the aim of connecting quantitative and qualitative results.
Using joint displays	A joint display including survey and semistructured interviews data was provided to illustrate the development of metainferences.
Assessing quality	The validity and trustworthiness of each strand were assessed using appropriate methods for each.
Value added by mixed methods	A mixed methods design capitalized on the use of a case series mixed methods display to integrate quantitative and qualitative data, resulting in metainferences that would not have been identified from one single methodology.

Note. Data from Bacchus et al. (2018).

and expanded on several topics that define mixed methods research, we encourage outside-the-box thinking in order to address research questions and aims. Mixed methods research is an evolving methodology steeped in continual innovation and refinement of methods. This chapter has situated the value of mixed methods for psychology research, and we invite you to share your methodological innovations.

References

Al Hariri, A. (2018). A multidimensional model of adolescent girls' elopement and related factors in Saudi Arabia. *Children and Youth Services Review*, *94*(1), 148–154. https://doi.org/10.1016/j.childyouth.2018.09.039

Bacchus, L. J., Buller, A. M., Ferrari, G., Brzank, P., & Feder, G. (2018). "It's always good to ask": A mixed methods study on the perceived role of sexual health practitioners asking gay and bisexual men about experiences of domestic violence and abuse. *Journal of Mixed Methods Research*, *12*(2), 221–243. https://doi.org/10.1177/1558689816651808

Bash, K. L., Howell Smith, M. C., & Trantham, P. S. (2021). A systematic methodological review of hierarchical linear modeling in mixed methods research. *Journal of Mixed Methods Research*, *15*(2), 190–211. https://doi.org/10.1177/1558689820937882

Bazeley, P. (2018). *Integrating analyses in mixed methods research*. SAGE.

Bradley, E. H., Curry, L. A., Ramanadhan, S., Rowe, L., Nembhard, I. M., & Krumholz, H. M. (2009). Research in action: Using positive deviance to improve quality of health care. *Implementation Science*, *4*(1), 25. https://doi.org/10.1186/1748-5908-4-25

Bryman, A. (2006). Integrating quantitative and qualitative research: How is it done? *Qualitative Research*, *6*(1), 97–113. https://doi.org/10.1177/1468794106058877

Campbell, R., Fehler-Cabral, G., Bybee, D., & Shaw, J. (2017). Forgotten evidence: A mixed methods study of why sexual assault kits (SAKs) are not submitted for DNA forensic testing. *Law and Human Behavior*, *41*(5), 454–467. https://doi.org/10.1037/lhb0000252

Caracelli, V. J., & Greene, J. C. (1997). Crafting mixed-method evaluation designs. In J. C. Greene & V. J. Caracelli (Eds.), Advances in mixed-methods evaluation: The challenges and benefits of integrating diverse paradigms. *New Directions for Evaluation* (Vol. 74, pp. 19–32). Jossey-Bass.

Cinamon, R. G., & Rich, Y. (2014). Work and family plans among at-risk Israeli adolescents: A mixed-methods study. *Journal of Career Development*, *41*(3), 163–184. https://doi.org/10.1177/0894845313507748

Clark, R. S., & Plano Clark, V. L. (2019). Grit within the context of career success: A mixed methods study. *International Journal of Applied Positive Psychology*, *4*(3), 91–111. https://doi.org/10.1007/s41042-019-00020-9

Clark, R. S., & Stubbeman, B. L. (2021). "I had hope. I loved this city once": A mixed methods study of hope within the context of poverty. *Journal of Community Psychology*, *49*(5), 1044–1062. https://doi.org/10.1002/jcop.22502

Collins, K. M., Onwuegbuzie, A. J., & Sutton, I. L. (2006). A model incorporating the rationale and purpose for conducting mixed methods research in special education and beyond. *Learning Disabilities: A Contemporary Journal*, *4*(1), 67–100.

Coyle, C. E., Schulman-Green, D., Feder, S., Toraman, S., Prust, M. L., Plano Clark, V. L., & Curry, L. (2018). Federal funding for mixed methods research in the health sciences in the United States: Recent trends. *Journal of Mixed Methods Research*, *12*(3), 305–324. https://doi.org/10.1177/1558689816662578

Creamer, E. G. (2018). Striving for methodological integrity in mixed methods research: The difference between mixed methods and mixed-up methods. *Journal of Engineering Education*, *107*(4), 526–530. https://doi.org/10.1002/jee.20240

Creswell, J. W., & Miller, D. L. (2000). Determining validity in qualitative inquiry. *Theory Into Practice*, *39*(3), 124–130. https://doi.org/10.1207/s15430421tip3903_2

Creswell, J. W., & Plano Clark, V. L. (2018). *Designing and conducting mixed methods research* (3rd ed.). SAGE.

Creswell, J. W., & Poth, C. N. (2018). *Qualitative inquiry and research design: Choosing among five approaches* (4th ed.). SAGE.

Curry, L., & Nunez-Smith, M. (2015). *Mixed methods in health sciences research: A practical primer*. SAGE. https://doi.org/10.4135/9781483390659

Dellinger, A. B., & Leech, N. L. (2007). Toward a unified validation framework in mixed methods research. *Journal of Mixed Methods Research*, *1*(4), 309–332. https://doi.org/10.1177/1558689807306147

Fàbregues, S., & Molina-Azorín, J. F. (2017). Addressing quality in mixed methods research: A review and recommendations for a future agenda. *Quality & Quantity: International Journal of Methodology*, *51*(6), 2847–2863. https://doi.org/10.1007/s11135-016-0449-4

Fetters, M. D. (2020). *The mixed methods research workbook: Activities for designing, implementing, and publishing projects.* SAGE.

Fetters, M. D., Curry, L. A., & Creswell, J. W. (2013). Achieving integration in mixed methods designs-principles and practices. *Health Services Research, 48*(6 Pt. 2), 2134–2156. https://doi.org/10.1111/1475-6773.12117

Fetters, M. D., & Freshwater, D. (2015). The 1 + 1 = 3 integration challenge. *Journal of Mixed Methods Research, 9*(2), 115–117. https://doi.org/10.1177/1558689815581222

Fetters, M. D., & Molina-Azorin, J. F. (2017). The *Journal of Mixed Methods Research* starts a new decade: The mixed methods research integration trilogy and its dimensions. *Journal of Mixed Methods Research, 11*(3), 291–307. https://doi.org/10.1177/1558689817714066

Flyvbjerg, B. (2006). Five misunderstandings about case-study research. *Qualitative Inquiry, 12*(2), 219–245. https://doi.org/10.1177/1077800405284363

Glover, C. M., Shah, R. C., Bennett, D. A., Wilson, R. S., & Barnes, L. L. (2020). The Health Equity Through Aging Research and Discussion (HEARD) study: A proposed two phase sequential mixed-methods research design to understand barriers and facilitators of brain donation among diverse older adults: Brain donation decision making among diverse older adults. *Experimental Aging Research, 46*(4), 311–322. https://doi.org/10.1080/0361073X.2020.1747266

Greene, J. C. (2007). *Mixed methods in social inquiry.* Jossey-Bass.

Greene, J. C., Caracelli, V. J., & Graham, W. F. (1989). Toward a conceptual framework for mixed-method evaluation designs. *Educational Evaluation and Policy Analysis, 11*(3), 255–274. https://doi.org/10.3102/01623737011003255

Guetterman, T. C., Babchuk, W. A., Howell Smith, M. C., & Stevens, J. (2019). Contemporary approaches to mixed methods–grounded theory research: A field-based analysis. *Journal of Mixed Methods Research, 13*(2), 179–195. https://doi.org/10.1177/1558689817710877

Guetterman, T. C., Chang, T., DeJonckheere, M., Basu, T., Scruggs, E., & Vydiswaran, V. G. V. (2018). Augmenting qualitative text analysis with natural language processing: Methodological study. *Journal of Medical Internet Research, 20*(6), e231. https://doi.org/10.2196/jmir.9702

Guetterman, T. C., Creswell, J. W., & Kuckartz, U. (2015). Using joint displays and MAXQDA software to represent the results of mixed methods research. In M. McCrudden, G. Schraw, & C. Buckendahl (Eds.), *Use of visual displays in research and testing: Coding, interpreting, and reporting data* (pp. 145–176). Information Age Publishing.

Guetterman, T. C., & Fetters, M. D. (2018). Two methodological approaches to the integration of mixed methods and case study designs: A systematic review. *American Behavioral Scientist, 62*(7), 900–918. https://doi.org/10.1177/0002764218772641

Guetterman, T. C., Fetters, M. D., & Creswell, J. W. (2015). Integrating quantitative and qualitative results in health science mixed methods research through joint displays. *Annals of Family Medicine, 13*(6), 554–561. https://doi.org/10.1370/afm.1865

Hesse-Biber, S., & Johnson, R. B. (2013). Coming at things differently: Future directions of possible engagement with mixed methods research. *Journal of Mixed Methods Research, 7*(2), 103–109. https://doi.org/10.1177/1558689813483987

Howell Smith, M. C., Babchuk, W. A., Stevens, J., Garrett, A. L., Wang, S. C., & Guetterman, T. C. (2019). Modeling the use of mixed methods–grounded theory: Developing scales for a new measurement model. *Journal of Mixed Methods Research.* Advance online publication. https://doi.org/10.1177/1558689819872599

Johnson, R. B. (2012). Dialectical pluralism and mixed research. *American Behavioral Scientist, 56*(6), 751–754. https://doi.org/10.1177/0002764212442494

Johnson, R. B. (2017). Dialectical pluralism: A meta-paradigm whose time has come. *Journal of Mixed Methods Research, 11*(2), 156–173. https://doi.org/10.1177/1558689815607692

Johnson, R. B., & Christensen, L. B. (2020). *Educational research: Quantitative, qualitative, and mixed approaches* (7th ed.). SAGE.

Knappertsbusch, F. (2020). "Fractal heuristics" for mixed methods research: Applying Abbott's "fractal distinctions" as a conceptual metaphor for method integration. *Journal of Mixed Methods Research, 14*(4), 456–472. https://doi.org/10.1177/1558689819893573

Kumar, R., Karabenick, S. A., Warnke, J. H., Hany, S., & Seay, N. (2019). Culturally inclusive and responsive curricular learning environments (circles): An exploratory sequential mixed-methods approach. *Contemporary Educational Psychology, 57*, 87–105. https://doi.org/10.1016/j.cedpsych.2018.10.005

Ladge, J. J., Humberd, B. K., & Eddleston, K. A. (2018). Retaining professionally employed new mothers: The importance of maternal confidence and workplace support to their intent to stay. *Human Resource Management, 57*(4), 883–900. https://doi.org/10.1002/hrm.21889

Le, H.-N., Perry, D. F., Villamil Grest, C., Genovez, M., Lieberman, K., Ortiz-Hernandez, S., & Serafini, C. (2021). A mixed methods evaluation of an intervention to prevent perinatal depression among Latina immigrants. *Journal of Reproductive and Infant Psychology*, *39*(4), 382–394. https://doi.org/10.1080/02646838.2020.1733504

Leech, N. L., & Onwuegbuzie, A. J. (2009). A typology of mixed methods research designs. *Quality & Quantity: International Journal of Methodology*, *43*(2), 265–275. https://doi.org/10.1007/s11135-007-9105-3

Lincoln, Y. S., & Guba, E. G. (1985). *Naturalistic inquiry*. SAGE.

Lynam, T., Damayanti, R., Rialine Titaley, C., Suharno, N., Bradley, M., & Krentel, A. (2020). Reframing integration for mixed methods research. *Journal of Mixed Methods Research*, *14*(3), 336–357. https://doi.org/10.1177/1558689819879352

Matteucci, M. C., & Farrell, P. T. (2019). School psychologists in the Italian education system: A mixed-methods study of a district in northern Italy. *International Journal of School & Educational Psychology*, *7*(4), 240–252. https://doi.org/10.1080/21683603.2018.1443858

Matthews, J. S., & López, F. (2019). Speaking their language: The role of cultural content integration and heritage language for academic achievement among Latino children. *Contemporary Educational Psychology*, *57*, 72–86.

Mayoh, J., & Onwuegbuzie, A. J. (2015). Toward a conceptualization of mixed methods phenomenological research. *Journal of Mixed Methods Research*, *9*(1), 91–107. https://doi.org/10.1177/1558689813505358

Mertens, D. M. (2007). Transformative paradigm: Mixed methods and social justice. *Journal of Mixed Methods Research*, *1*(3), 212–225. https://doi.org/10.1177/1558689807302811

Morgan, D. L. (2014). *Integrating qualitative and quantitative methods: A pragmatic approach*. SAGE. https://doi.org/10.4135/9781544304533

Morse, J. M. (1991). Approaches to qualitative-quantitative methodological triangulation. *Nursing Research*, *40*(2), 120–123. https://doi.org/10.1097/00006199-199103000-00014

Morse, J. M. (2002). Qualitative tokenism. *Qualitative Health Research*, *12*(6), 729–730. https://doi.org/10.1177/104973230201200601

Morse, J. M. (2003). Principles of mixed methods and multimethod research design. In A. Tashakkori & C. Teddlie (Eds.), *Handbook of mixed methods in social and behavioral research* (pp. 189–208). SAGE.

Morse, J. M., & Niehaus, L. (2009). *Mixed method design: Principles and procedures*. Left Coast Press.

Neto, D. D., Baptista, T. M., & Dent-Brown, K. (2015). Development and validation of a system of assimilation indices: A mixed method approach to understand change in psychotherapy. *British Journal of Clinical Psychology*, *54*(2), 147–162. https://doi.org/10.1111/bjc.12066

O'Cathain, A. (2010). Assessing the quality of mixed methods research: Toward a comprehensive framework. In A. Tashakkori & C. Teddlie (Eds.), *SAGE handbook of mixed methods in social and behavioral research* (2nd ed., pp. 531–556). SAGE. https://doi.org/10.4135/9781506335193.n21

O'Keeffe, S., Martin, P., Target, M., & Midgley, N. (2019). 'I just stopped going': A mixed methods investigation into types of therapy dropout in adolescents with depression. *Frontiers in Psychology*, *10*, 75. https://doi.org/10.3389/fpsyg.2019.00075

O'Cathain, A., Murphy, E., & Nicholl, J. (2008). The quality of mixed methods studies in health services research. *Journal of Health Services Research & Policy*, *13*(2), 92–98. https://doi.org/10.1258/jhsrp.2007.007074

Onwuegbuzie, A. J., & Johnson, R. B. (2006). The validity issue in mixed research. *Research in the Schools*, *13*(1), 48–63.

Palinkas, L. A., Mendon, S. J., & Hamilton, A. B. (2019). Innovations in mixed methods evaluations. *Annual Review of Public Health*, *40*(1), 423–442. https://doi.org/10.1146/annurev-publhealth-040218-044215

Peterson, J. C., Czajkowski, S., Charlson, M. E., Link, A. R., Wells, M. T., Isen, A. M., Mancuso, C. A., Allegrante, J. P., Boutin-Foster, C., Ogedegbe, G., & Jobe, J. B. (2013). Translating basic behavioral and social science research to clinical application: The EVOLVE mixed methods approach. *Journal of Consulting and Clinical Psychology*, *81*(2), 217–230. https://doi.org/10.1037/a0029909

Plano Clark, V. L., & Ivankova, N. V. (2016). *Mixed methods research: A guide to the field*. SAGE. https://doi.org/10.4135/9781483398341

Reichardt, C. S., & Cook, T. D. (Eds.). (1979). *Qualitative and quantitative methods in evaluation research*. SAGE.

Riazi, A., & Candlin, C. (2014). Mixed-methods research in language teaching and learning: Opportunities, issues and challenges. *Language Teaching*, *47*(2), 135–173. https://doi.org/10.1017/S0261444813000505

Roald, T., Køppe, S., Bechmann Jensen, T., Moeskjær Hansen, J., & Levin, K. (2021). Why do we always generalize in qualitative research? *Qualitative Psychology*, *8*(1), 69–81. https://doi.org/10.1037/qup0000138

Roques, M., Laimou, D., Camps, F. D., Mazoyer, A. V., & Husseini, M. E. (2020). Using a mixed-methods approach to analyze traumatic experiences and factors of vulnerability among adolescent victims of bullying. *Frontiers in Psychiatry, 10*, 890. https://doi.org/10.3389/fpsyt.2019.00890

Roysircar, G., Thompson, A., & Geisinger, K. F. (2019). Trauma coping of mothers and children among poor people in Haiti: Mixed methods study of community-level research. *American Psychologist, 74*(9), 1189–1206. https://doi.org/10.1037/amp0000542

Schmidt, J. A., Kafkas, S. S., Maier, K. S., Shumow, L., & Kackar-Cam, H. Z. (2019). Why are we learning this? Using mixed methods to understand teachers' relevance statements and how they shape middle school students' perceptions of science utility. *Contemporary Educational Psychology, 57*, 9–31. https://doi.org/10.1016/j.cedpsych.2018.08.005

Schoonenboom, J., & Johnson, R. B. (2017). How to construct a mixed methods research design. *KZfSS Kölner Zeitschrift für Soziologie und Sozialpsychologie, 69*(Suppl. 2), 107–131. https://doi.org/10.1007/s11577-017-0454-1

Serrat, R., Villar, F., Warburton, J., & Petriwskyj, A. (2017). Generativity and political participation in old age: A mixed method study of Spanish elders involved in political organisations. *Journal of Adult Development, 24*(3), 163–176. https://doi.org/10.1007/s10804-016-9255-4

Shadish, W. R., Cook, T. D., & Campbell, D. T. (2002). *Experimental and quasi-experimental designs for generalized causal inference.* Houghton Mifflin.

Shannon-Baker, P. (2016). Making paradigms meaningful in mixed methods research. *Journal of Mixed Methods Research, 10*(4), 319–334. https://doi.org/10.1177/1558689815575861

Sharif Matthews, J., & López, F. (2019). Speaking their language: The role of cultural content integration and heritage language for academic achievement among Latino children. *Contemporary Educational Psychology, 57*, 72–86. https://doi.org/10.1016/j.cedpsych.2018.01.005

Sheehy-Skeffington, J., & Obradović, S. (2020). Power, identity, and belonging: A mixed methods study of the processes shaping perceptions of EU integration in a prospective member state. *European Journal of Social Psychology, 50*(7), 1425–1442. https://doi.org/10.1002/ejsp.2691

Shim, M., Johnson, R. B., Gasson, S., Goodill, S., Jermyn, R., & Bract, J. (2020). A mixed methods-grounded theory design for producing more refined theoretical models. *Journal of Mixed Methods Research, 15*(1), 61–86. https://doi.org/10.1177/1558689820932311

Taheri, F., Jami Pour, M., & Asarian, M. (2019). An exploratory study of subjective well-being in organizations–A mixed method research approach. *Journal of Human Behavior in the Social Environment, 29*(4), 435–454. https://doi.org/10.1080/10911359.2018.1547671

Tashakkori, A., Johnson, R. B., & Teddlie, C. (2021). *Foundations of mixed methods research: Integrating quantitative and qualitative approaches in the social and behavioral sciences.* SAGE.

Teddlie, C., & Tashakkori, A. (2003). Major issues and controversies in the use of mixed methods in the social and behavioral sciences. In A. Tashakkori & C. Teddlie (Eds.), *Handbook of mixed methods in the social & behavioral research* (pp. 3–50). SAGE.

Teddlie, C., & Tashakkori, A. (2009). *Foundations of mixed methods research: Integrating quantitative and qualitative approaches in the social and behavioral sciences.* SAGE.

Usher, E. L., Ford, C. J., Li, C. R., & Weidner, B. L. (2019). Sources of math and science self efficacy in rural Appalachia: A convergent mixed methods study. *Contemporary Educational Psychology, 57*, 32–53. https://doi.org/10.1016/j.cedpsych.2018.10.003

Waller, M. R., Nepomnyaschy, L., Miller, D. P., & Mingo, M. (2021). Using a narrative approach to analyze longitudinal mixed methods data. *Journal of Mixed Methods Research, 15*(2), 261–283. https://doi.org/10.1177/1558689820953237

Watkins, D. C., Wharton, T., Mitchell, J. A., Matusko, N., & Kales, H. (2017). Perceptions and receptivity of non-spousal family support: A mixed methods study of psychological distress among older, church-going African American men. *Journal of Mixed Methods Research, 11*(4), 487–509. https://doi.org/10.1177/1558689815622707

Wesely, P. M. (2010). Language learning motivation in early adolescents: Using mixed methods research to explore contradiction. *Journal of Mixed Methods Research, 4*(4), 295–312. https://doi.org/10.1177/1558689810375816

White, A. M., DeCuir-Gunby, J. T., & Kim, S. (2019). A mixed methods exploration of the relationships between the racial identity, science identity, science self-efficacy, and science achievement of African American students at HBCUs. *Contemporary Educational Psychology, 57*, 54–71. https://doi.org/10.1016/j.cedpsych.2018.11.006

Youngs, H., & Piggot-Irvine, E. (2012). The application of a multiphase triangulation approach to mixed methods: The research of an aspiring school principal development program. *Journal of Mixed Methods Research, 6*(3), 184–198. https://doi.org/10.1177/1558689811420696

THE "CASES WITHIN TRIALS" (CWT) METHOD: AN EXAMPLE OF A MIXED METHODS RESEARCH DESIGN

Daniel B. Fishman

This chapter describes a method called *case studies within controlled trials*, or the *cases within trials* (CWT) method for short. This method consists of three phases. First a randomized controlled trial (RCT) is conducted, the goal of which is to determine the relative efficacy of an applied psychological intervention, such as psychotherapy, the promotion of socioemotional learning in schools, feedback systems to improve organizational performance, or rehabilitation for prison inmates. In the second phase, systematic and intensive case studies are conducted on representative clients who achieve good-outcome, limited-outcome, or poor-outcome results in response to the experimental condition of the RCT. The third phase consists of a synthesis of knowledge gained from the first two phases. This design is, thus, a mixed methods approach: The RCT provides group-based, exclusively quantitative knowledge of the differential impact between types of interventions, while in a complementary way the case studies provide individual-based, primarily qualitative knowledge of differential impact within a particular intervention.

As context to presenting the details of the CWT method, consideration is given to the general nature of quantitative, RCT designs versus the mixed qualitative and quantitative, case study designs in psychological research. In addition, for a further understanding of the CWT method, the postpositivist, pragmatic epistemology underlying theoretical knowledge generated by the CWT method will be described. Specifically, because (a) the CWT method is designed for evaluating and interpreting applied psychological interventions, and because (b) the ultimate goal of these interventions is to create positive change, theoretical knowledge generated by the CWT method is viewed and judged first and foremost as a conceptual tool for creating positive problem solving, not necessarily as a reflection of objective reality.

THE CLASSIC EXPERIMENTAL DESIGN VERSUS THE SYSTEMATIC CASE STUDY DESIGN AS A PATH TO LEGITIMATE SCIENTIFIC KNOWLEDGE IN PSYCHOLOGY

Examine any introductory psychology textbook or most high-impact mainstream journals in scientific psychology, and it is clear that the widely acknowledged gold standard method of psychological research is the controlled experiment studying groups of participants using quantitative measures (hereinafter called the *classic design*).

I thank Arthur C. Bohart, Tracy D. Eells, Gregg Henriques, John McLeod, Ronald B. Miller, Louis Sass, William B. Stiles, and Jamie Walkup for comments on drafts of this chapter.

https://doi.org/10.1037/0000319-013
APA Handbook of Research Methods in Psychology, Second Edition: Vol. 2. Research Designs: Quantitative, Qualitative, Neuropsychological, and Biological, H. Cooper (Editor-in-Chief)

The dominance of the classic design is also reflected in the fact that virtually every undergraduate psychology major and every psychology graduate student takes a course in group designs and statistics but not in qualitative designs or the case study method (hereinafter called the *case design*; Norcross et al., 2016).

The classic design takes place within the context of the hypothetico-deductive model. That is, the researcher starts off with a particular psychological theory, which posits general laws about relationships among the theory's constructs, which in turn can be designated as independent and dependent variables. From the theory, the researcher can deductively derive a hypothesis that a particular independent variable (or set of variables) should be associated with a particular dependent variable (or set of variables) and can then test this hypothesis by using operational definitions of the theory's constructs to observe whether or not the results of the experiment conform to the hypothesis.

In line with the above, the classic design advantages data (a) that are experimental and not naturalistic, so as to control for the effect of any variables other than the independent and dependent variables identified by a research study's hypothesis; (b) that are quantitative and not qualitative, so as to reduce subjectivity of measurement and enhance precision; and (c) that are group-based to tap into laws of human behavior and experience that have a high degree of generality across large populations of people, in line with scientific psychology's Newtonian tradition (see upcoming paragraphs).

These three priorities—for experimentation, for quantification, and for group results—and the aforementioned rationales for them—fundamentally derive from a natural science paradigm established in the late 1600s by Isaac Newton, whose findings are represented in laws like $f = ma$, as described by Leahey (1995),

> The success of Newtonian style in physics was made possible by the fact that the physical universe can be described or modeled as a collection of spatiotemporal identical objects subject to spatiotemporal [quantitative] universal laws. However, so great was Newton's hold on subsequent thought that the basis of Newton's success— the nature of physical reality— became a presupposition of the social sciences. . . . [This has led to] what Michael Scriven calls "the Newtonian fantasy" . . . that underlying overt behavior, thought, or phenomenology there lies a theoretical structure which awaits discovery, and will yield precision and power. (p. 13)

These three priorities—for experimentation, for quantification, and for group results—are opposite to the priorities of the main type of psychological research design described in this chapter, the generic case design and one of its specific variants, the *pragmatic case study*, which is the case study design employed in CWT studies. That is, in the case design, the basic unit of analysis is typically the individual person who is studied in an uncontrolled, naturalistic context and in a manner that emphasizes qualitative data.

Because the case design directly opposes the Newtonian-based epistemological priorities of the dominant classic design in research psychology, one must consider whether there is a logical justification for placing the case design at the same level of epistemological legitimacy regarding the truthfulness of its knowledge as the classic design. I address this question in the next section both in terms of the history of scientific psychology per se and in terms of the philosophy of science that underlies scientific psychology and provides an epistemological justification for the knowledge it produces.

The Ascendance of the Newtonian Model: Wundt and Logical Positivism

As a field of study, psychology can be traced back at least to the Greek philosophers (e.g., Plato and Aristotle) who wrote about areas like "sensation, perception, learning, memory, emotion, imagination, and reasoning" (Goldenson, 1984, p. 60).

However, according to many historians, it was in 1879, when Wilhelm Wundt established his psychological laboratory, which resulted in psychology making its "declaration of independence" from the discipline of philosophy (Harper, 1950). Instead, in the spirit of Newton mentioned earlier, Wundt's laboratory was designed to align psychology with the Enlightenment-inspired natural science disciplines such as physics, chemistry, and biology.

What made Wundt's laboratory distinctive was not what it addressed, like sensation and perception, which Aristotle had written about, but how these topics were studied, that is, by using methods that associated psychology with the objective, empirical laboratory experiments of the natural sciences rather than with the subjective, "armchair speculations" of philosophy. Specifically, Wundt's laboratory focused on psychophysiology, that is, the primarily quantitative measurement of the relationship between the physical and the psychological worlds, such as optical illusions, and reaction time to different, objectively measured physical stimuli under different physical conditions (Fishman, 2017, p. 239; see also Benjamin, 2014).

In the words of Leahey (1991), Wundt's laboratory marks the beginning of psychology as a separate discipline because "he brought the empirical methods of physiology to the questions of philosophy and also created a new identifiable role—that of psychologist, separate from the roles of philosopher, physiologist, or physician" (p. 182).

Wundt's laboratory had an immediate international impact, stimulating, by 1900, the establishment of 42 such laboratories in the United States (Benjamin, 2014, p. 80), and this success basically baked the Newtonian model into psychology's early identity.

After Wundt set the model for scientific psychology as laboratory experiments that focus on directly observable and quantifiable behaviors, there ensued a dialectic over the years concerning the extent to which (a) scientific psychology could only study directly observable behaviors that were free of subjective influences versus (b) scientific psychology could also study phenomena that were investigated systematically and carefully but which involve subjective elements associated with consciousness, language, and culture.

For an early example of that dialectic, in the late 1800s and the early 1900s, two highly contrasting models were competing for legitimacy and influence in scientific psychology. On one hand, Edward Titchener was interested in finding the structure of the underlying components of consciousness, parallel to chemistry's periodic table of the elements (Benjamin, 2014, p. 85). However, while Titchener set up a laboratory like Wundt's that emphasized experimental control, the basic data in Titchener's research involved introspective reports of conscious experience, which violated the Newtonian focus on the behavior of physical objects.

Many of Titchener's opponents championed behaviorism as a way to avoid the unscientific aspects of consciousness. Following Watson's (1913) Behavioral Manifesto, behaviorism only studied behavior directly associated with muscular movements in three-dimensional space, and, thus, behaviorism was drawn to studying behavior in animals where subjective elements like language and consciousness could be avoided and genetically determined variation could be controlled through experimentally controlled breeding.

Behaviorism won the battle and came to dominate much of the field of scientific psychology until the late 1950s. In addition to its publicly appealing appearance to be "real science" like physics and chemistry, behaviorism's dominance was undergirded by a simultaneous development in the Anglo American philosophy of science called *logical positivism* (Ayer, 1936, 1966), which can be dated to Vienna in the early 1920s and which resonated with Newton and the earlier British empiricist philosophers like Hume.

The logical positivists proposed that

> there are only two kinds of knowledge: the truths of logic and the "positive," value-neutral facts of sense experience (empiricism), which are determined by good experimental science in the tradition of the physical sciences.

They believed that such science could discover truth that was objective and thus independent of human subjectivity, and that such truth could be expressed in general, quantifiable laws, like Newton's $f = ma$, or Einstein's $e = mc^2$. (Fishman, 2017, p. 240)

Challenges to the Newtonian Model: The Cognitive Revolution and Postpositivism

The next stage in the dialectic over limiting psychology to overt behavior versus including the study of conscious experience came in the late 1950s. At this time behaviorism's exclusive control of much of mainstream scientific psychology was challenged by the *cognitive revolution* (Baars, 1986). Once accepted, the cognitive revolution gave legitimacy to psychological phenomena that went beyond what could be perceived by the senses and that required inner experience, which could only be communicated to others through words and language. This led to words rather than only numbers being accepted as legitimate data for psychological science research, in what could be called the *qualitative revolution*. One indicator of this latter movement's methodological acceptance into the field of scientific psychology was its formal recognition in 2011 by the American Psychological Association as the Society for Qualitative Inquiry in Psychology section (https://www.sqip.org/) of the newly renamed Division 5, Quantitative and Qualitative Methods (Gergen et al., 2015).

The legitimacy of the cognitive and qualitative revolutions was crucially bolstered by a change that was taking place starting in the late 1950s and early 1960s, as logical positivism was being challenged by an alternative philosophy of science—called *postpositivism*—influenced by both social constructionism and pragmatism and resonating with continental hermeneutic philosophy (Fishman, 1999, p. 106).

A major figure in the postpositivist movement was Ludwig Wittgenstein. In his 1922 book, *Tractatus*, he conceives of an objective world composed of directly and objectively observable "things" that are reflected in basic, knowable "atomic" fact statements, and, thus, this work became a classic philosophical rationale for positivism. However, in his later years (from the 1930s until his death in 1951), Wittgenstein (1953) passionately rejected his earlier position and developed the *linguistic analysis* approach summarized in his famous, posthumous *Philosophical Investigations*. In fact, the latter book is explicitly designed as an attack upon the atomic-facts and language-as-naming model of language that he had set forth in the *Tractatus*. In contrast, Wittgenstein adopted a view of language as a structure in which we are completely embedded. Our view of the world is then dependent upon language, and the meaning of that language is based on meanings shared by a particular language community.

Other postpositivist philosophers of science—Karl Popper, Thomas Kuhn, Willard Quine, and Paul Feyerabend—reinforced Wittgenstein's critique of the basic assumption of logical positivism that objective physical reality is knowable. These philosophers emphasized the limitations if not the impossibility of objective, scientific knowledge because of our embeddedness in the logical, cultural, cognitive, and linguistic preconditions of that knowledge—preconditions that change according to historical and cultural context. For Popper, these preconditions include the deductive theoretical principles that we simply have to assume without being able to prove them; for Kuhn, these preconditions are scientific paradigms; for Quine and Feyerabend, they are webs of belief; and for Wittgenstein, they are language games (and their built-in rules). "We can never step out of these preconditions and see the world objectively; for our ability to 'see' is contingent upon these preconditions being in place" (Fishman, 1999, p. 88).

The idea of reality as objectively unknowable in any direct sense and the associated challenges to the classic design's hegemony in psychology was supported by other, overlapping and intermixing movements coming to the fore in the 1960s and beyond (Fishman, 1999; Gergen et al., 2015). Some of these include (a) humanistic psychology, which in important ways links psychology to the humanities rather than just to the natural sciences; (b) general systems theory, which questioned the idea that there were simple, mechanistic laws underlying human behavior, parallel to Newton's gravity; (c) hermeneutic philosophy, which emphasized the necessity to interpret sense experience in a variety of ways with a variety of meanings rather than to take that experience in directly; (d) postmodern philosophy, which challenges the idea that there is a single, rational, true way to organize a culture; and (e) social constructionism, which posits that "instead of being [empirically] 'discovered,' the social reality of any group or 'language community' is constructed through the communal interchange of the group's members" (Fishman, 1999, p. 62), and, thus, it can and does change over time and place. For example, regarding social constructionism, by the mid-1980s, social constructionism could be found in mainstream, high-profile psychological journals, such as the *American Psychologist*:

> All the world's a stage, but the script is not *As You Like It*, it is *Rashomon*. Each of us has our own reality of which we try to persuade others. Facts do not have an independent existence. Rather, facts guide the selection of observations and the invention of reality. . . . [In short], we do not discover scientific facts; we invent them. Their usefulness to us depends both on shared perceptions of the "facts" (consensual validation) and on whether they work for various purposes, some practical and some theoretical (Scarr, 1985, p. 499; in a similar vein, see Krasner & Houts, 1984; and Gergen, 1985).

Pragmatism and Pragmatic Relativism

Pragmatism is a philosophical approach that was developed in part in the late 19th and early 20th centuries by William James and John Dewey, two philosopher–psychologists who were each a president of the American Psychological

Association. Pragmatism's ideas complement those of the postpositivists and the related other thinkers mentioned earlier, in that philosophical pragmatism is grounded in a social constructionist theory of knowledge. In James's (1890) view, the world that exists independently of our minds is an unlimited complex of change and novelty, order and disorder. Fishman (1999) explained James' view:

> To understand and cope with the world, we take on different conceptual perspectives, as we might put on different pairs of glasses, with each providing us a different perspective on the world. The pragmatic "truth" of a particular perspective does not lie in its correspondence to "objective reality," since that reality is continuously in flux. Rather, the pragmatic truth of a particular perspective lies in the usefulness of the perspective in helping us to cope and solve particular problems and achieve particular goals in today's world. (p. 130)

How are these problems and goals to be selected, defined, articulated, and addressed? The social constructionist epistemology associated with pragmatism specifies that human problems and goals are not intrinsic in the natural world. Rather, these problems and goals represent the purposes, intentions, desires, interests, and values of individuals and groups, which typically contain differences and conflicts (Pitkin & Shumer, 1982). In dictatorial societies, these conflicts are dealt with in a top-down fashion by a small group of autocrats militarily enforcing the decisions they make, while in democratic societies there is a political and moral consensus that these problems and goals should be pursued through dialogue and negotiation among relevant individuals, groups, and communities who are stakeholders in the particular problems and goals involved.

While the positivist's search to discover general "laws of nature" is thus doomed, the process of natural science inquiry—which encourages disciplined openness to new experiences and empirical data—is one of the best techniques for deriving pragmatically useful knowledge [in a democratic society]. (Fishman, 1999, p. 130)

The pragmatic philosophy of James and Dewey fell out of favor after the Newtonian-based rise in the psychology of behaviorism, grounded as it was in animal-based learning, the classic design's hypothetico-deductive method, and logical positivism.

However, with the rise of postpositivism and the related movements previously mentioned, like social constructionism, a group of neopragmatist philosophers—such as Richard Bernstein (1983), Steven Toulmin (1990), and Richard Rorty (1979)—became prominent. Rorty's (1982) idea of "pragmatic relativism" is particularly important here. While denying transhistorical and cross-cultural "foundational" standards, Rorty pointed out that the pragmatist does not buy into "anything goes relativism," where there are no standards of truth and morality. Rather, he posited "pragmatic relativism," which bases claims of truth on standards and procedures that have been already established and agreed-upon for determining truth and morality in particular contexts. Examples are

> the procedures and standards used
> to elect government officials demo-
> cratically, to settle civil and criminal
> disputes in our court system, to
> conduct academic scholarship in our
> universities, to carry out investigative
> journalism, and to describe social
> behavior "objectively" in quantitative
> surveys like the U.S. Census, using
> the statistical methods derived from
> natural science. (Fishman, 1999,
> p. 131)

In the spirit of Newton, logical positivism assumes that it is possible to discover objective

knowledge about nature—be it physical or psychological—and that the ideal nature of this knowledge is in the form of general laws expressed in quantitative terms. In contrast, pragmatism embraces theory but judges its value not in terms of its having a particular form but rather in a theory's capacity to solve human problems and/or to correlate and predict functionally among observable events.

Thus the pragmatist views theories not as a mirror of nature (Rorty, 1979) but as conceptual tools (Stiles, 2009) with which to navigate life's challenges and possibilities for human beings. A striking example of this is Rorty's (1982) reconceptualization of the type of knowledge developed by Galileo and his followers like Newton, who

> discovered, and subsequent
> centuries have amply confirmed,
> that you get much better predictions
> by thinking of things as masses of
> particles blindly bumping against
> each other than by thinking of them
> as Aristotle thought of them—
> animistically, teleologically, and
> anthropomorphically. They also
> discovered that you get a better handle
> on the universe by thinking of it as
> infinite and cold and comfortless than
> by thinking of it as finite, homey,
> planned, and relevant to human
> concerns. . . .
>   These [types of] discoveries are
> the basis of modern technological
> civilization. But they do not . . .
> tell us anything about the language
> which nature itself uses, . . . [about]
> the Book of Nature. (p. 191)

For a parallel in psychology, one can view the results of rigorously conducted psycho-therapy RCTs as valuable in developing prag-matically successful technologies for addressing mental and emotional disorders but not *as* evidence that the theory behind the RCT mirrors objective reality.

THE CASES WITHIN TRIALS METHOD: GENERAL CONSIDERATIONS ABOUT EMPLOYING BOTH RANDOMIZED CONTROLLED TRIALS AND CASE STUDY DATA

This section provides an overview of the logic of the CWT method, including such considerations as the relationship of qualitative and quantitative data, the logical commonality between RCTs and case studies, and the distinction between description and theoretical interpretation.

The Complementary Strengths and Weaknesses of Qualitative and Quantitative Data

As mentioned in the first paragraphs of this chapter, the CWT method brings together in an integrated manner both (a) quantitative knowledge from an RCT and (b) systematic, qualitatively intensive case studies that are conducted on representative clients who achieve good-outcome, limited-outcome, or poor-outcome results in response to the experimental condition of the RCT. As such, the CWT method is a member of the mixed methods movement. This is a new epistemological paradigm in medicine, education, and the social sciences that offers a variety of different procedures and rationales for how quantitative and qualitative data can be integrated (e.g., Chapter 12, this volume).

Within the context of the postpositivist and social constructionist epistemological paradigm set forth above, the mixed methods model begins with an analysis that (a) quantitative and qualitative data each have not only their own strengths but also their own weaknesses in terms of knowledge that has pragmatic validity in describing and impacting upon the world, that (b) these strengths and weaknesses are in fact complementary, and, thus, that (c) putting together both types of data provides a more valid overall picture of the phenomenon being studied. So, for example,

numerical, quantitative data have the advantages of (a) stable meanings across time; (b) the ability to achieve quality control via established psychometric procedures; (c) the capacity to efficiently reduce large amounts of complex differences among the multiple individual cases included in group research designs; (d) the ability to obtain an objective, normative context for comparing individual clients; and (e) the capacity to create top-down deductive laws. (Fishman, 2013, p. 406; also see Stiles, 2006)

On the other hand,

the capacity of numbers to achieve reliability among different observers and their ability to reduce large and complex bodies of information is offset by their disadvantages in oversimplifying information, discarding much that is valuable. It is just this type of "lost" information that words and qualitative description excel at: (a) creating thick descriptions that include the detail, complexity, context, subjectivity, and multifaceted nature of human knowledge; (b) capturing the narrative, storytelling structures of human knowledge; and (c) having the capacity to ground generalizations in particular instances, so that the generalizations are derived from concrete reality, from the bottom up. (Fishman, 2013, p. 406)

Aside from the pragmatic capacity of past observable data and associated theory to be effective in problem solving, there are other complementary virtues associated with quantitative data versus qualitative data. From a societal and political point of view, the public associates quantitative data with the physical and biological sciences, with their attendant very positive connections to (a) experimental studies, complex statistics, and highly specialized language that the public can view as connected to profound "rocket-science" and "brain-surgery" knowledge; and (b) powerful and positive technologies like television, computers, electric cars, and COVID-19 vaccines. Both of these connections lend impressive societal credibility and status to psychology if it embraces quantitative data. On the other hand, as described in the next section, qualitative case studies are associated with best professional psychological practice; practitioners typically find qualitative case studies more engaging and helpful in their work (Stewart & Chambless, 2007); and the public resonates with narrative stories to which it can relate, as seen in newspaper and other media reports of societal, political, and economic issues.

RCTs and Case Studies Answer Different Questions

In applied psychology, the complementary nature of qualitative and quantitative methods can be seen in how they are positioned to answer different research questions. This is reflected in the typical structure of one version of the classic design, an RCT for a psychotherapy study, as shown in Table 13.1. The table illustrates this structure with a study comparing an experimental condition

of cognitive-behavioral treatment for a problem such as depression and a control condition of a "waiting list" control. In terms of the classic design, in this RCT the independent variable is a cognitive-behavior treatment manual for depression, which varies between present (in the experimental condition) and absent (in the control condition), and the dependent variable is one or more measures indicating therapeutic success (a high score versus a low score on decrease in depression).

Examining Table 13.1, we can see that

> the advantage of the quantitative group data is that it can answer a question like: Is the experimental condition *on average* more effective than the non-treatment control condition? Specifically, as shown in the table, since 60% of the clients in the experimental condition were successful compared to 20% in the no-treatment control condition, the answer to the question is that the experimental condition was *on average* more effective than the control condition. (Fishman, 2013, p. 407)

On the other hand,

> the advantage of the qualitative case study data is that they can answer questions like: Why did some particular individual clients in the experimental condition—like subjects E01 and E02—have successful therapy outcomes, while other subjects in the experimental condition—like E13 and E14—did not? Were there different reasons for success between E01 and E02? and Did patients E13 and E14 have different reasons for their therapeutic failures? Qualitative case studies can also provide informed— although not necessarily definitive— answers to these questions and similar questions about the differences between patients in the control condition, like subjects C21 and C22,

---

TABLE 13.1

Typical Outcome Structure of a Randomized Clinical Trial for a Problem Such as Depression

Experimental condition, e.g., CBT treatment for depression	E01, E02, E03, E04, E05, E06, E07, E08, E09, E10, E11, E12, *E13, E14, E15, E16, E17, E18, E19, E20* **(60% successful)**
Control condition, e.g., "waiting list" control	C21, C22, C23, C24, *C25, C26, C27, C28, C29, C30, C31, C32, C33, C34, C35, C36, C37, C38, C39, C40* **(20% successful)**

Note. Items in underlined italics indicate unsuccessful resolution of depression and items in plain text but larger font indicate successful resolution of depression. From "The Pragmatic Case Study Method for Creating Rigorous and Systematic, Practitioner-Friendly Research," by D. B. Fishman, 2013, *Pragmatic Case Studies in Psychotherapy*, 9(4), p. 416 (https://doi.org/10.14713/pcsp.v9i4.1833). Copyright 2013 by D. B. Fishman. Reprinted with permission.

who had successful outcomes compared with subjects C25 and C26, who had unsuccessful outcomes. (Fishman, 2013, p. 406)

In sum, quantitative group data are of value in describing general relationships across groups of participants involving a few variables—in line with Isaac Newton's and Wilhelm Wundt's previously reviewed paradigms—while qualitative case data are of value in thickly described processes within individual cases, processes that can vary in complex patterns between and among individual patients.

The Logical Commonality Between Randomized Controlled Trials and Case Studies: Ensuring Rigor in Both via the Nomological Network

While the RCT component and the case study component of the CWT method are different, both involve the same underlying structure when conducted properly, that is, the structure of the interplay between the level of observation and the level of theory. Thus, in spite of the fact that the observation-based data are different in substance—quantitative versus qualitative,

experimental versus naturalistic, and group-based versus individual-person-based—the logical relationships between observation and theory are the same.

This structure is captured in Cronbach and Meehl's (1955) classic model of the nomological network, shown in Figure 13.1 with the following components: (a) observations of psychological phenomena, represented by rectangles; (b) theoretical constructs or concepts to help understand, predict, and effect change in the psychological phenomena, represented by ovals; (c) interconnections among the observables, represented by the curved arrows below the observational rectangles; (d) interconnections among the theoretical construct ovals, represented by curved arrows among them; and (e) for at least for some of the constructs, deductive connections between the constructs and the observables, represented by straight down arrows between them. (The latter connections are defined in terms of operational definitions, to maintain a tight logic between the meaning of the constructs and the observables.)

In Figure 13.1 there are three logical relationships between the level of observation and the

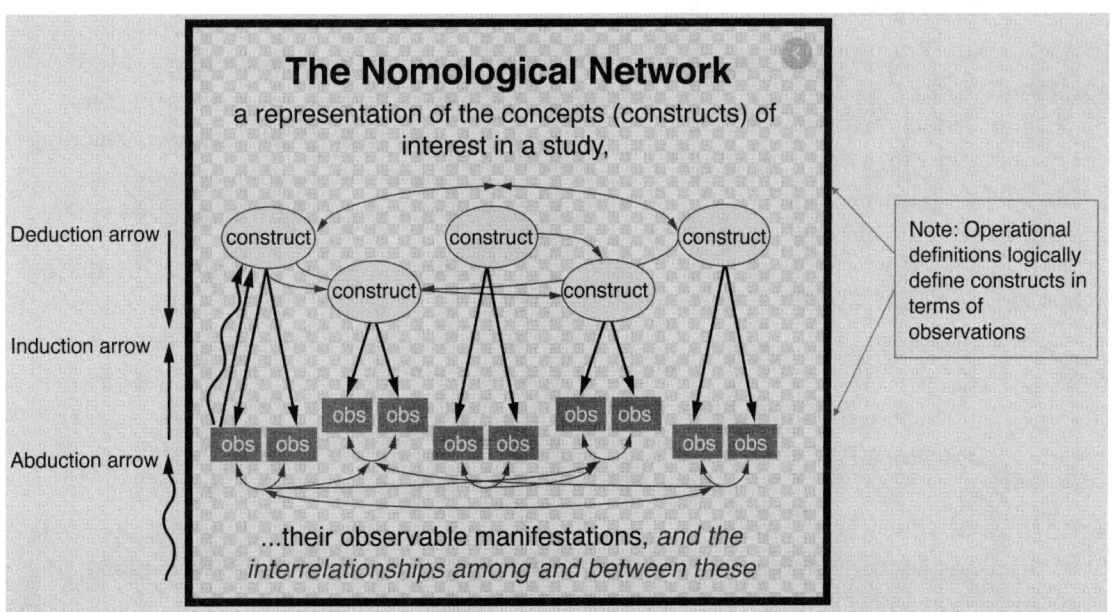

FIGURE 13.1. The nomological network. Adapted from *The Research Methods Knowledge Base* (3rd ed., p. 67), by W. M. K. Trochim and J. P. Donnelly, 2007, Thomson Publishing. Copyright 2007 by William Trochim. Adapted with permission.

level of theory, represented by three types of arrows; and again, these relationships are the same within RCTs and within case studies. The one mentioned above involves *deduction*, going from the general level of theory to the specific level of observation. Such a conclusion is intrinsically true because the specific is logically contained in the general.

Two additional types of relationships—induction and abduction—involve logically going from the specific level of observation to the general level of theory. *Induction* involves "applying observations to theory" (Stiles, 2009), such that we generally think that the observations we make are able to justify some expectations or predictions about similar-seeming types of observations we have not yet made, as well as general claims that go beyond the observed (Kolodner, 1992). *Abduction* involves "creating, refining, and elaborating theory" (Stiles, 2009), by developing a tenet such that, if the new tenet were the case, then the observation would be expected. For example,

> You happen to know that Tim and Harry have recently had a terrible row that ended their friendship. Now someone tells you that she just saw Tim and Harry jogging together. The best explanation . . . [from these premises] that you can think of is that they made up. You conclude that they are friends again. . . .
>
> [Unlike deduction this conclusion does] not follow logically from the premises. . . . [However], what according to a considerable number of philosophers may . . . warrant this conclusion, is precisely the fact that Tim and Harry's being friends again would, if true, *best explain* the fact that they have just been seen jogging together. (Douven, 2017)

Methodological Quality Control

In light of the above on the nomological network, to provide maximum rigor and transparency in conducting a CWT study, it is important for the researcher to spell out as explicitly as feasible, across both the RCT component and the case study component, (a) the empirical observations that are the basic data of the study; (b) the theory behind the study; and (c) the specific connections between (a) and (b) and whether those connections are deductive, inductive, or abductive. In addition, (d) the theory must be clear and coherent; (e) the observations must be clear and coherent and shown to be reliable, that is, intersubjectively agreed upon; (f) the interconnections between the theory and the observations must be clear, coherent, and logical; and (g) the role of the researcher in the research process must be transparent so that the researcher's perspective can be taken into account in interpreting the results. Regarding the latter, in a classic design like an RCT, the researcher is considered to have possible bias unless this is explicitly controlled for in different ways, such as by double-blind studies. In the case study design, as in other qualitative research, researcher bias is addressed by requiring researchers to "own" their perspective, that is,

> Authors [of qualitative studies] specify their theoretical orientations and personal anticipations . . . [and] recognize their values, interests and assumptions and the role that these play in the understanding . . . [in order for the reader to] interpret the researchers' data and understanding of them, and to consider possible alternatives. (Elliott et al., 1999, p. 221)

A range of methods for meeting these standards of quality for a variety of designs and for both qualitative and quantitative data are spelled and discussed in the other chapters of this handbook.

The Nature of Observed Data

To place the above description of the nomological net in the context of the postpositivist, pragmatic epistemology outlined previously, it is necessary first to clarify more precisely the notion of *observation*, how it differs from *theory* and a *theoretical interpretation*, such as the case formulation in a case study.

For an observing person to report a sense-based observation, such as watching a man run, there are a number of processes: (1) the stimuli from the man impinging on the person's open eye; (2) the information then being processed neurologically by the person's perceptual system; (3) the person being aware of that perceptual processing through conscious awareness; (4) the person having a history of previous experience for being able to understand the present experience of visual information as a man running; and (5) the person having learned language and the ability to use that language to describe the sensory experience as "I see a man running." Thus for sense impressions to be meaningful, accurate, and communicated, they have to go through a variety of interpretive, experiential filters, based on both present and past experience, including the learning of language (Neisser, 1967).

Building on this, Stiles (2009) pointed out that not only sensory-based observations but also theoretical concepts are experience-based.

> Scientific theories are descriptions of aspects of the world, such as how psychotherapy works, stated in words or numbers or diagrams or other signs. Scientific research provides quality control on theory by comparing these theoretical descriptions with observations. The theory is a good one if people's experiences of the theoretical descriptions (i.e., the meanings of the descriptions to them) correspond with their experiences of observing the objects and events in the world (or, conversely, if the descriptions of the events match the theories). I . . . [call] this the *experiential correspondence* theory of truth. . . . The job of researchers, then, is to gather and describe appropriate observations, to see how well they match the theory. (p. 10)

Description Versus Theoretical Interpretation

The nomological net makes clear the important distinction between the level of

> observation and the level of theoretical interpretation through constructs. Within the postpositivist, pragmatic perspective laid out above, the validity of a theory is its ability to positively impact on the world of the observed. That is, what happens at the level of observation is the ultimate goal of psychological interventions. In line with this, it is important not to let theories control the process of observation. In the words of Sherlock Holmes in the story, "A Scandal in Bohemia": "It is a capital mistake to theorize before one has data. Insensibly one begins to twist facts to suit theories, instead of theories to suit facts." (Conan Doyle, 2009/1892, p. 4)

Yet, as just summarized, observation involving even the description of direct sensory experience involves both interpretation and language, which itself adds subjective elements to any description. Thus, it doesn't seem possible to differentiate in an absolute way reports of psychological phenomena that consist of a "purely objective" description from those that involve a significant degree of interpretation.

However, we can make important, relative distinctions between description and interpretation to make sure that our ultimate outcome focus is on the level of observation. Two markers of difference between description and interpretation are particularly important. First, description is associated with ordinary, common, unspecialized language and theoretical interpretation, with technical, theory-specific and theory-embedded, specialized language. Second, for description but not for interpretation, reliability among multiple observers independently reviewing the same information should be able to be reached at a relatively high level among adults without technical background.

THE CASES WITHIN TRIALS METHOD: SPECIFIC CONSIDERATIONS

We now turn to the nuts and bolts of how the CWT method works. This includes exploring both the nature of the individual pragmatic case study component of the method along with how case studies can be employed for general knowledge via (a) inductive and abductive reasoning as described above and as listed in the nomological net outlined in Figure 13.1 and (b) case-based reasoning. In addition, the section below provides an outline of how the CWT method combines both an RCT and successful and unsuccessful case studies drawn from the RCT.

The Nature of the Pragmatic Case Study Component of the Cases Within Trials Method

As described in the previous section (see also Figure 13.1), the logical relationships between observation and theory are the same in RCT studies as in case studies. In each, there are three epistemological needs that are met by theory. Specifically, theory is the basis for (a) selecting what observations to make, (b) determining how to make these observations, and (c) ascribing larger meaning to the observations that go beyond just describing the observations themselves. In the context of the pragmatic epistemology outlined earlier, this larger meaning should in part have payoff for being able to meet human problem-solving goals as reflected in desired changes over time in what is observed.

From the viewpoint of epistemological quality, just like the RCT design, the case study design should be clear and useful in meeting the goal of spelling out the interaction of theory and observation. The case study model that was chosen for the CWT model—the pragmatic case study (Fishman, 2005, 2013; McLeod 2010)—was selected in part because it meets this goal.

The pragmatic case study is based on *disciplined inquiry*, a model of best professional practice developed by Peterson (1991). Peterson in turn based his approach on the empirical work of Schön (1983), who showed how successful, expert

professionals—in different fields like psychotherapy, engineering, architecture, management, and town planning—function. The focus on best practice is particularly important because of the pragmatic epistemology underlying the CWT model. Specifically, if the aim of knowledge from pragmatic case studies is to create and enhance strategies and tools for solving human problems, then it is necessary to base the relevant case study structure on a best-practice model, that is, a model that has been empirically associated with the best outcomes.

In the next section, I first spell out the structure of a pragmatic case study in Figure 13.2, outlining how an applied psychologist—like a psychotherapist—functions within such a model. (In Figure 13.2, I have adapted the model to psychotherapy specifically, but it is relevant for all other applied psychology interventions by replacing "F. Course of Therapy" with "F. Action," and "G. Therapy Monitoring" with "G. Monitoring Evaluation.") Then I describe how this structure shown in Figure 13.2 allows the researcher to determine the ways in which theory and observations are highly interconnected throughout the conduct of a case intervention.

The pragmatic case method from the perspective of the therapist. Specifically, as shown in Figure 13.2, the therapist starts by focusing on the client and their presenting problems and goals (component A). In this context, the therapist identifies a guiding conception (component B) for addressing the problems and goals. The guiding conception incorporates relevant clinical experience and research support (component C), including past cases the practitioner has seen or heard about, for example, through supervision or reading. Next the therapist conducts a comprehensive assessment (component D) including history, personality, living situation, symptoms and other problems, diagnosis, and strengths. Then, application of the guiding conception and previous experience to the assessment data creates an individualized formulation and treatment plan (component E). This plan is implemented during the course of therapy (component F).

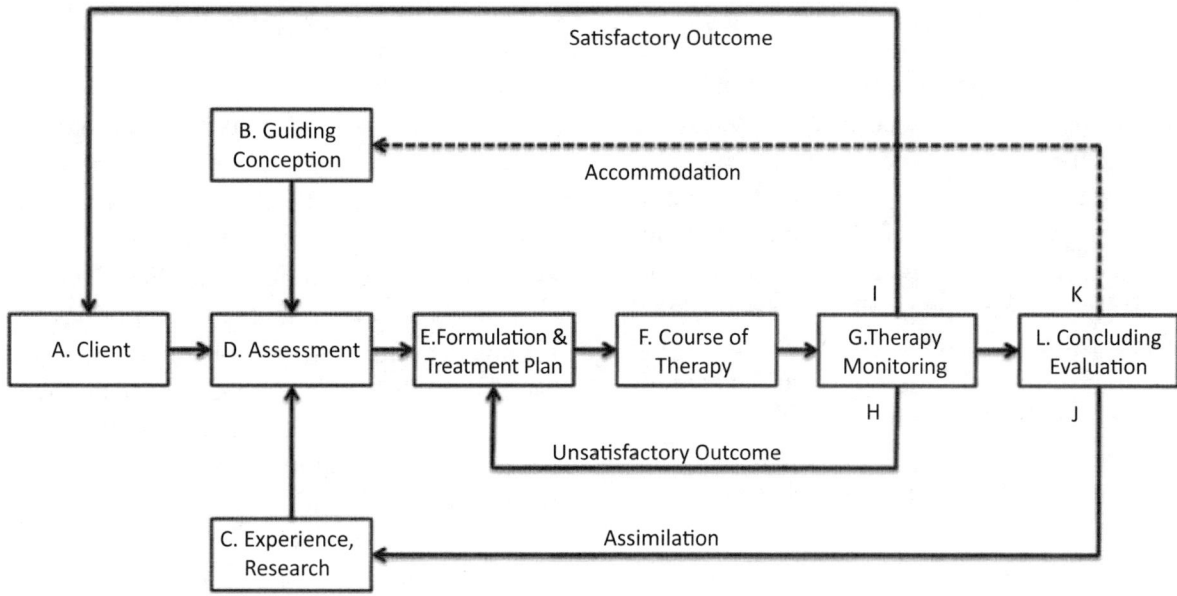

FIGURE 13.2. Professional activity as disciplined inquiry. From "The Pragmatic Case Study Method for Creating Rigorous and Systematic, Practitioner-Friendly Research," by D. B. Fishman, 2013, *Pragmatic Case Studies in Psychotherapy*, 9(4), p. 425 (https://doi.org/10.14713/pcsp.v9i4.1833). Adapted from "Connection and Disconnection of Research and Practice in the Education of Professional Psychologists," by D. R. Peterson, 1991, *American Psychologist*, 46(4), 422–429 (https://doi.org/10.1037/0003-066X.46.4.422).

Therapy monitoring (component G) is then consistently applied to the clinical process, creating the feedback loops. If the therapy is not advancing well, possible changes in the formulation and treatment plan are considered (component H); and if the case is advancing well and meeting the needs of the client, arrangements for termination in consultation with the client might be made (component I).

If the therapy monitoring results indicate that the client has been successful and/or the therapist and client are in agreement that additional treatment will not be productive, therapy is terminated and a concluding evaluation (component L) is carried out. This can yield feedback either for confirming—via assimilation—the original guiding conception (arrow J) or for revising that theory through accommodation (component K).

The pragmatic case study from the perspective of the researcher: The interplay of theory and observation in the nomological net of disciplined inquiry.   The disciplined inquiry model in Figure 13.2 directly reflects the nomological network in Figure 13.1. Specifically, there are

four ways in which the researcher can identify the interplay of theory and observation in a disciplined-inquiry-based case study. First, the guiding conception (B) involves a general theory for connecting to and understanding a client's observed presenting problems and goals, which are captured in the assessment data (D).

Second, the result of applying the guiding conception (B) to the observed assessment (D) data is a case formulation of and related treatment plan (E) for the client and the client's problems and goals. This case formulation is, thus, a type of mini-version of the guiding conception, a version that is tailored to explain the particular client's situation.

Third, the therapy monitoring (G) phase consists of observations during the therapy with a focus on how well the course of therapy (F) is going. These observations can then be compared with what was theoretically predicted by the formulation and treatment plan (E). If these observations are consistent with the formulation and treatment plan, this is confirmatory evidence of their pragmatic validity and a reason for the therapist to continue their use as the therapy proceeds. If these observations are not consistent with the formulation and treatment plan, then this is disconfirmatory evidence of their pragmatic validity and a reason for the therapist to revise them as a guide as therapy proceeds. This process follows the logic of Lewin's (1946) model of action research, in which there is a continuing spiral so that theory leads to action, and then observational feedback from the action leads to confirmation or revision of the original theory, which then guides further action leading to new observational feedback, and so forth.

Fourth, observations in the concluding evaluation (L) phase are compared with the predictions made by the guiding conception (B). If those actual observations are consistent with the predicted observations derived from the guiding conception (see the assimilation arrow [J]), then this is confirmatory evidence of the validity of the guiding conception. If those actual observations are inconsistent (see the accommodation arrow [K]), then this is disconfirming evidence of the validity of the guiding conception calling for its revision in some way.

In sum, the structure and detailed documentation of the various parts of the pragmatic case study allow the researcher to trace the patterns of interconnection between theory and observation, with the goal of developing and improving the validity of applied psychology theories.

Disciplined inquiry as best professional practice via case-based reasoning. As mentioned in the previous section, Peterson's (1991) disciplined inquiry model was in part derived from Schön's (1983) empirically developed model of best practice across a variety of professions. Called *reflective practice*, Schön's model distinguishes between novice and expert practitioners (Dreyfus & Dreyfus, 1986; Flyvbjerg, 2006). Novices follow the rules and procedures they were taught in their training in a cookbook type of manner. In contrast, experts rework these procedures to meet the unique nature of a particular applied situation. Thus, there is a type of dialogue between (a) the expert's repertoire of cognitive, emotional, and behavioral understanding, in part based

on their relevant past experience and (b) their responsiveness to the environmental cues in the case at hand.

The relevant past experience of the expert practitioner consists of context-dependent knowledge from each case with which the practitioner has worked. Over time, part of the practitioner's developing expertise comes from their remembered database of cases and is then applied to new practice situations. In drawing on relevant past cases in the database for guidance on the target case, both similarities and differences of the database cases are important in applying them to the target case.

The finding of a solution in a present target case by matching it to past solutions drawn from a database of relevant past cases is an example of case-based reasoning (Kolodner, 1992). In the words of the well-known social science methodologist, academic, and program planner, Brent Flyvbjerg (2006) "Common to all experts . . . is that they operate on the basis of intimate knowledge of several thousand concrete cases in their areas of expertise. Context-dependent knowledge and experience are at the very heart of expert activity" (p. 222).

In terms of the nomological net in Figure 13.1 and just discussed, case-based reasoning can be seen as involving matching a pattern of characteristics of an immediately observed target situation in the present with past cases that are in effect at the theoretical level. The past cases can be viewed as hypothetical models that have the capacity to guide understanding and action for change and problem-solving regarding the target case. Also in terms of the nomological net in Figure 13.1, case-based reasoning is an example of generalizing from the specific to the general either by emphasizing the similarities of the present target case to actual past cases, a process of induction, or by being inspired by past cases to refine or develop new theory, a process of abduction.

Case-based reasoning in pragmatic case study research. Deeply informed case-based reasoning is required not only for best practice in psychotherapy but also for best practice in research with pragmatic case studies. Specifically, in some qualitative research the project involves the relatively straightforward coding of small qualitative units to convert them into quantitative variables, and then quantitative analysis is performed; and, in this type of research, expertise in the complexities of the qualitative data is less required.

In contrast, in other qualitative research, like pragmatic case studies, there is a need to analyze contextually based holistic patterns in rich, "thick" qualitative and narrative material as such—for example, material that involves the complexities and subtleties of the role and personhood of the therapist; the nature of the therapy relationship; and the interaction of a client's personality with their problems and with their responses to the therapy. One important key to analyzing such patterns is the use of case-based reasoning for comparing a present case situation with previous ones the researcher has experienced and analyzed. In a related way, as therapists employ case-based reasoning, the pragmatic case study researcher needs to be adept in case-based reasoning to understand therapists' thought processes.

In sum, case-based knowledge of relevant psychotherapy processes (or other applied psychology interventions) is important for both best-practice practitioners and best-practice researchers who participate in CWT projects. For this reason, therapists in the cases analyzed within a CWT project often participate in the research write-up and interpretation of those cases (e.g., see the CWT projects in Fishman et al., 2017, Chapters 3, 4, and 6).

Outline of the Method

Table 13.2 outlines the structure of the CWT model as represented by the headings in the final research report. While the structure of the model below is illustrated for psychotherapy RCT studies, as mentioned above the structure can applied to RCT studies involving any other applied psychological intervention, such as socioemotional learning in school, work performance, athletic performance, or rehabilitation from prison.

I. The RCT Study

As shown in Table 13.2, first the RCT study is conducted and reported employing the usual headings employed in a classic design study: introduction, methods, results, and discussion. In conducting the RCT, a manual of the psychotherapy intervention (the independent variable in the classic design) is set forth and its administration is checked for fidelity, by videotaping all the therapy sessions and then reviewing them for manual adherence.

With this done, logically any changes in the clients can be attributed to the independent variable—that is, to the experimental condition (employing the therapy manual) versus the control condition (not employing the therapy manual). (Note that some RCT designs call for more than two comparison groups; for ease of presentation to highlight the basic logic of an RCT study, only two conditions are presented here.)

Another crucial dimension of an RCT therapy study that reflects the classic model is the use of quantitative data to operationalize theoretical variables. Specifically, the psychological problems being addressed in the therapy are operationalized in terms of standardized measures of problems like depression, anxiety, interpersonal difficulties, and thought disorder.

II. The Case Studies

1. *Selecting the Clients.* At the end of the RCT, the researcher has, thus, accumulated the videotapes of all of the therapy client participants, together with complete quantitative measures of the clients' outcome. The researcher can then employ these quantitative results to select out from the experimental condition representative clients with a positive therapy outcome, those with a negative therapy outcome, and—optionally—those with a mixed therapy outcome. If there are special design and/or theoretical reasons why the relevant clients aren't just randomly selected based on positive-outcome and negative-outcome criteria alone (e.g., if some clients have more complete videotaped data and/or a particularly good or poor outcome), this is explained (see item II.1 in Table 13.2).

TABLE 13.2

Headings in a Full Report of Implementation of the Cases Within Trials Method

Component of disciplined inquiry (see Figure 13.2)	Headings in the final research report
	I. The RCT STUDY
	1. Introduction
	2. Method
	3. Results
	4. Discussion
	II. THE CASE STUDIES
A	1. The Nature and Rationale for Specific Cases Selected for the Case Studies
B, C	2. The Clients
	3. Guiding Conception: Overview of Intervention
	4a-6a. Therapy with a Positive-Outcome Client
D-a	4a. Assessment of Client's Problems, Goals, Strengths, and History
E-a	5a. Client's Formulation
F-a	6a. Client's Course of Therapy
	4b-6b. Therapy with a Negative-Outcome Client
D-b	4b. Assessment of Client's Problems, Goals, Strengths, and History
E-b	5b. Client's Formulation
F-b	6b. Client's Course of Therapy
	4c-6c. *Optional*: Therapy with a Mixed-Outcome Client
D-c	4c. Assessment of Client's Problems, Goals, Strengths, and History
E-c	5c. Client's Formulation
F-c	6c. Client's Course of Therapy
G,H,I	7. Therapy Monitoring and Use of Feedback Information
J,K,L	8. Concluding Evaluation of the Therapy's Process and Outcome
	III. SYNTHESIS OF FINDINGS FROM THE RCT AND CASE STUDY APPROACHES
	IV. OPTIONAL. COMMENTARY BY ONE OR MORE OUTSIDE EXPERTS

Note. Adapted from "*Case Studies Within Psychotherapy Trials: Integrating Qualitative and Quantitative Methods*" (pp. 29–31), by D. B. Fishman, S. B. Messer, D. J. A. Edwards, and F. M. Dattilio, 2017, Oxford University Press (https://doi.org/10.1093/med:psych/9780199344635. 001.0001). Copyright 2017 by Oxford University Press. Adapted with permission.

Once the clients with whom pragmatic case studies are to be conducted are chosen, their therapies are recreated via the videotapes of the original therapy process. This therapy process is qualitatively described in rich detail and analyzed to determine the patterns and reasons—for example, the moderators and mediators—for why one or more clients with a positive outcome obtained such an outcome in comparison with one or more clients who obtained a negative outcome. Ideally in such a comparison, not only have the positive-outcome and negative-outcome clients received the same experimental manualized therapy but also that therapy has been conducted by the same therapist—so that there is experimental control for variables that are associated with (a) the therapy model and the therapy interventions (as contained in the therapy manual) and (b) the therapist as a practitioner of the therapy model in addition to the therapist as a person.

2–8. The Case Studies Proper. As shown in Table 13.2, headings II. 2–8 in the final research report follow the structure of a pragmatic case study as outlined in the disciplined inquiry model shown in Figure 13.2. Having a common structure allows the researcher the opportunity to make comparisons among case studies. As mentioned above, the structure also allows the researcher to identify particular points of contact and reciprocal connection between observations and theory in the case study. In addition, organizing the case studies by the disciplined inquiry approach builds a model of best professional practice into the research, helping the researcher to create knowledge with pragmatic value.

In section 8, the case study is analyzed in a mixed methods manner. Thus the standardized, quantitative information about the client from the RCT study—both before and after therapy, and sometimes during to capture therapy process—is employed to complement the qualitative data about the case. In the quantitative analysis of case study, frequently a statistic like the reliable change index (Jacobson & Truax, 1991) is used to determine if quantitative changes during the therapy are statistically significant.

III. Synthesis of Findings From the RCT and Case Study Approaches

This section focuses on how knowledge from the RCT and knowledge from the case studies converge, diverge, and/or generate new components in the guiding conceptual theory. This knowledge generation takes place from a wide variety of perspectives, for example, from the perspective of (a) the guiding theory and related interventions that flow from the manualized psychotherapy model; (b) moderators and mediators of change; (c) the client's background, life situation, personality characteristics, and presenting problems; (d) the therapist's background, skills, and personality; and (e) the nature and quality of the therapeutic relationship established between the therapist and client and the related detailed process interactions between them.

The knowledge in an RCT report, such as a psychotherapy RCT, is intentionally "thin" and concise, focusing upon a brief description of the treatment manual employed, the demographics and presenting problems of the clients, the demographics of the therapists, and the standardized quantitative measures used.

In contrast, the knowledge of the case study is "thick" and expansive, including the contextual details and personhood of the clients and the therapists; and the nature of therapy as it actually evolves moment to moment and session to session. In other words, unlike the RCT article, the case study is designed to provide an in-depth sense of the "lived experience" of the clients and therapists, including both during the therapy and in retrospect via qualitative follow-up interviews. Thus, the decontextualized knowledge from the quantitative findings of the RCT is contrasted with and complemented by the contextualized, qualitative findings of the case studies.

As just mentioned, sometimes the quantitative and qualitative information converge to provide confirmation of the theory that is operationalized in the RCT's therapy manual. When this happens, the case studies provide a lived experience sense of the therapy that professionals and lay people alike can respond to at the level of a vivid documentary to better understand the therapeutic process at a concrete level.

When the two types of information diverge, the researcher is challenged to make conceptual sense of this divergence. Examples of such divergence are presented below in the upcoming example of the motivational interviewing (Miller & Rollnick, 2002) therapy for depression among adult Latinos. (The particular version of motivational interviewing involved, which I'll soon describe, is called "motivational enhancement therapy for antidepressants" or "META," for short.) This example illustrates how case studies propose ways to explain why the therapeutic model operationalized in the therapy manual did not work as predicted, and the ways in which that theory could be changed to better account for the RCT and case-study findings. As explained in the next section, the unpredicted results in the META study and the processes in the case studies led to explaining the empirical results of the RCT with a theory that differed from the original META RCT theory not only in substance but also in type. Specifically, the original META theory had a few variables and was linear and mechanistic (i.e., it was Newtonian). In contrast, the new logic model that was generated was multidimensional and systemic, with numerous instances of non-linear, mutually reciprocal causation, including virtuous and vicious circles of causation, that is, feedback loops that enhanced improvement or deterioration in functioning, respectively.

Mining the Value of a Pragmatic Case Study

As mentioned previously, there are two ways to create generalized knowledge from a group of case studies: by case-based reasoning or by a combination of induction and abduction. Each of these is discussed the next section.

Case-based reasoning. Once completed, a pragmatic case study like the one outlined in Figure 13.2 can be productively used in at least two general ways. One involves placing a completed case study in the framework of case-based reasoning as described above. This involves providing a practitioner guidance for action in a present target case by systematically comparing this case with a similar completed case with successful components.

Because each case takes place in a particular, at times idiosyncratic, context, the more completed cases there are that are relevant to a particular target case, the greater their value. This is because generally, the greater the variety of contexts sampled by relevant completed case studies, the greater the chance of a particularly relevant match to the target case. Also, seeing how a therapeutic or other applied psychology process occurs in a variety of instances aids in inductively generalizing to principles of action.

William Stiles's "Theory-Building Case Study." A second way to productively use completed pragmatic case studies is to analyze them using William Stiles's (2009) "theory-building case study" model.

Stiles's (2009) model closely parallels the same nomological network logic as does the hypothetico-deductive classic design. Specifically, in comparing the classic design and the case design, Stiles pointed out that in the classic design

an investigator extracts or derives one statement (or a few statements) from a theory and attempts to compare this statement with a large number of observations [across a group of participants]. If the observed events tend to match the derived statement then people's confidence in the statement is substantially increased, and this, in turn, yields a small increment of confidence in the theory as a whole.

In a case study [i.e., in the case design], instead of trying to assign a firm confidence level to a particular derived statement, an investigator simultaneously compares a large number of observations based on a particular individual with a correspondingly large number of theoretically based statements. Each statement that describes some aspect of the case in theoretical terms represents a comparison of the theory with an observation. . . . For a variety of familiar reasons (selective sampling, low power, potential investigator biases, etc.), the increase (or decrease) in confidence in any one theoretical statement may be very small. . . . Nevertheless, because many statements are examined, the increase (or decrease) in confidence in the theory may be comparable to that stemming from a statistical hypothesis-testing [i.e., a classic design] study. A few systematically analyzed cases that match a theory in precise or unexpected detail may give people considerable confidence in the theory as a whole, even though each component assertion may remain tentative and uncertain when considered separately. (Stiles, 2009, p. A-7)

As an example of his theory-building case study, Stiles and his colleagues (Honos-Webb et al., 1998) described two cases, "Lisa," who had a successful outcome, and "George," who had an unsuccessful outcome. Both cases were drawn from a manualized treatment called *process-experiential psychotherapy*, which consisted of a version of manualized, Rogerian, client-centered treatment.

Honos-Webb et al. (1998), employed the process transcripts of the therapy from these cases to test hypotheses drawn from a theory of psychotherapy outcome called the *assimilation model*. This model proposes that during successful therapy, a client goes through "a sequence of cognitive/affective levels through which a problematic experience is assimilated into [the client's] . . . schema during successful psychotherapy" (p. 264). These levels are operationalized by an *assimilation of problematic experiences scale* (APES), which ranges from the problem experience to

0 = warded off
1 = unwanted thoughts occur
2 = vague awareness/emergence
3 = problem statement
4 = understanding/insight
5 = application/working through
6 = problem solution
7 = mastery (p. 265)

The hypotheses tested were variations of this basic question: By looking in detail at the client's statements and externally reflected affect in the therapy transcripts, was there evidence that more movement from a lower level to a higher level on the APES scale was found in Lisa's successful case than in George's unsuccessful case? The answer to this question was yes, confirming the assimilation theory. For example, in Lisa's case, "interrelated themes could be tracked from vague awareness (APES level 2) to understanding/insight (level 4), with elements of application/working through (level 5) identified in one theme" (p. 282).

In contrast, in George's case,

> All three of George's themes that we tracked began as unwanted thoughts (APES level 1), but they appeared to become blocked at two different APES levels. His desire to run away from his wife (theme 1), progressed to around APES level 3, as George formulated

a statement of the problem but then failed to gain new understanding. The other two themes reached only the vague awareness level (APES level 2), as George acknowledged the indescribable pain of "what it is not to have a mother's love" (Session 18 . . .) and stated, but later retracted, his ambivalent, rageful longings for affection from his father. (Honos-Webb et al., 1998, p. 282)

THE CASES WITHIN TRIALS METHOD: AN EXAMPLE—MOTIVATIONAL ENHANCEMENT THERAPY FOR INCREASING ANTIDEPRESSANT MEDICATION ADHERENCE AND DECREASING CLINICAL DEPRESSION AMONG ADULT LATINOS

In the book *Case Studies Within Psychotherapy Trials: Integrating Qualitative and Quantitative Methods* (Fishman et al., 2017), my coauthors and I described the CWT method in detail and presented four project examples that follow the structure shown in Table 13.2. For illustration, one of these (Interian et al., 2017) is presented here.

The RCT for this project (Interian et al., 2013) addressed the problem of high rates of depression among Latinos. The therapy consisted of employing a Latino-culture–adapted, manualized version of the theoretical model of motivational interviewing (Miller & Rollnick, 2002), the earlier-mentioned motivational enhancement therapy for antidepressants or META, for short. Motivational interviewing is built on a foundation of Carl Rogers's (e.g., Rogers & Dymond, 1954) client-centered therapy, with an emphasis upon developing a warm, accepting, empathetic relationship with the client. This relationship is then employed to help the client voice the different sides of their ambivalence about positive change and subsequently feel the dissonance between their current and desired behavior and their goals, beliefs, or values. Hearing themselves defend the positive direction of the ambivalence helps the client to become more committed to it, and this new commitment is reinforced by the therapist.

In the RCT, 50 Latino patients with a *DSM-IV* diagnosis of major depression or dysthymia who were receiving treatment at a community mental health center were randomized to receive only usual care (UC) or usual care plus three sessions of META designed to increase their adherence with taking antidepressant medication. After the RCT was completed, three clients were selected for case studies—Lupe, Maria, and Ana, who were representative of clients who had a positive outcome, a negative outcome, and a mixed outcome, respectively.

At the end of the intervention, after adjusting for covariates, the RCT results confirmed the original hypothesis that the META intervention would significantly increase medication adherence overall (although in line with Table 13.1, there were still some clients in the experimental condition who had negative outcomes, and some clients in the control condition who had positive outcomes). However, the results did not confirm the related hypothesis that the increase in medication adherence would significantly decrease depression. In addition, there was an unexpected positive finding that the three sessions of META, while a small amount of intervention by psychotherapy standards, did by itself produce a significant decrease in depression.

How were the case study results integrated with the RCT findings? In other words, how could the case study findings explain the unexpected result that the three META sessions in themselves were therapeutically effective for the clients' depression? An analysis of the case studies revealed that there were a large variety of factors and forces stimulated in the clients by the META sessions that helped to explain the unexpected findings. Three of these are presented to illustrate the distinctive types of knowledge that emerge from systematic case studies. First, using abduction, the researchers developed a revised guiding conception in the form of a *logic model* (Yin, 2014) that would encompass and conceptualize both the original hypothesis of the project—to increase medication adherence and the impact of medication on depression—and the findings that the META intervention had therapeutic results in and of itself.

Second, an independent expert reviewer, reading over the detailed META session transcripts, discovered in the detailed narrative descriptions therapeutic ingredients unknown from the manual only. Third, the researchers examined how the logic model, in terms of virtuous cycles versus vicious cycles, helped to explain Lupe's positive outcome and Maria's negative outcome.

Reconceptualizing the Guiding Conception

The reconceptualized guiding conception is presented in Figure 13.3. It is an expansion of the individualized, cognitive-behavioral case formulation approach of Persons (2008), which is a model that fits into Component E of the disciplined inquiry approach (see Figure 13.2) and that is consistent in terms of the other components of disciplined inquiry.

Specifically, as shown in Figure 13.3, the Persons model has four components. First, the client's *History* (Box 1) results (Arrow A) in the client developing different underlying, dynamic, causal dispositions, and processes (Boxes 2–5). Persons calls these underlying *mechanisms* of positive and negative change in behavior and experience at the levels of biochemistry, psychology, interpersonal relationships, and culture. Arrows among the Boxes 2–5 mechanisms indicate the reciprocally causal interactions among them.

The client's history also creates (Arrow B) potential precipitating events that can activate these mechanisms. At a particular point in time, an actual *Precipitating Event* (Box 6) in fact activates (Arrow C) one or more of the negative mechanisms, leading to (Arrows D–G) *Depressive Symptoms* and other *Problems* (Box 7).

At the same time, there are positive processes and components in a client's life that provide protective factors against the development and/or intensity of symptoms and problems. These are captured in a client's *Strengths* (Box 8) that emerge (Arrow H) from an individual's history. In addition, a client's history (Box 1) helps to create (Arrow I) their present *Social Support System* (Box 11), which adds to (Arrow J) their strengths (Box 8).

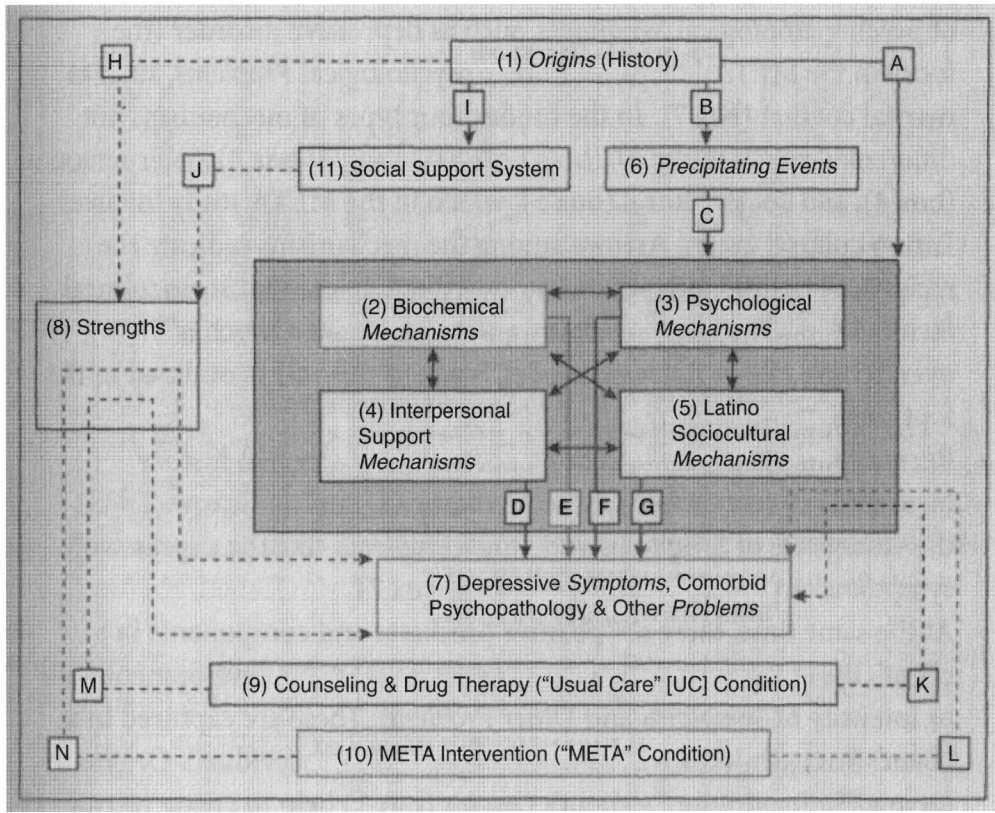

FIGURE 13.3. Logic model for the motivational enhancement therapy for antidepressants study. From *Case Studies Within Psychotherapy Trials: Integrating Qualitative and Quantitative Methods* (p. 267), by D. B. Fishman, S. B. Messer, D. J. A. Edwards, and F. M. Dattilio, 2017, Oxford University Press (https://doi.org/10.1093/med:psych/9780199344635.001.0001). Copyright 2017 by Oxford University Press. Reprinted with permission.

Finally, the "usual care" *Counseling* in the RCT's control condition (Box 9) and the *META Intervention* (Box 10) are both aimed at reducing the client's difficulties in two ways: by directly impacting on the *Mechanisms* causing those difficulties (Arrows K and L), and by building up and drawing upon (Arrows M and N) the client's strengths (Box 8).

The Figure 13.3 model can identify a variety of possible causal processes by which the addition of the three META sessions to a client's treatment could reduce a client's depression, such as: (a) having an impact on the biological mechanisms (Box 2) maintaining the depression, for example, by the prescription of antidepressant medication; (b) by having an impact on psychological mechanisms (Box 3) maintaining the depression, for example, by positive cognitive restructuring to help the client combat their tendency to externalize successes and instead to internalize them; (c) by having an impact on interpersonal support mechanisms (Box 4) maintaining the depression, for example, by reducing a client's reluctance to confide in others or to ask for help; (d) by having an impact on Latino cultural mechanisms (Box 5), for example by helping a client to connect with cultural sources of inspirational strength, such as Latino cultural values like *trabajando dura* (working hard) and *luchar* or *luchando* (surviving difficult times; to enhance the therapeutic relationship and the connection to these values, the META sessions were conducted in Spanish to the primarily Spanish-speaking clients); (e) by building on the client's strengths (Box 8), for example, by tapping into a client's readiness for change;

and (f) by reconnecting a client with their support system (Box 11).

The logic model in Figure 13.3 is in contrast with the classic design–based theory that initially generated the RCT, which as mentioned had relatively few variables and was linear. A detailed reading of the META intervention process in the cases of Lupe and Maria helped to generate the very different type of logic model presented in Figure 13.3.

Discovering Therapeutic Ingredients Not Knowable From Reading the Manual or RCT Report Only

John Norcross (2017), an outside psychotherapy expert, reviewed the qualitative, narrative detail of the three case studies that are presented in the Case Studies section of Interian et al.'s (2017, pp. 264–307) chapter in Fishman et al.'s (2017) book, *Case Studies Within Psychotherapy Trials*. In reading this detail, Norcross was able to go beyond the standard description in the RCT article that simply stated that the META clinicians were "a licensed clinical psychologist and three psychology doctoral students" (Interian et al., 2013). What Norcross could see coming through the case study narratives was that the META treatment was "led by passionate, bilingual clinical psychologists and doctoral students specifically trained and continually supervised in META" as compared with "treatment as usual provided by the typically overburdened, underfunded staff at a CMHC" (p. 317). In other words, what Norcross was able to see in the case descriptions—but was not in the RCT report—was the particular enthusiasm, commitment, time availability, and relationship skills of the META therapist team that were part of its therapeutic effectiveness, in addition to their just following the META treatment manual.

Second, Norcross found that the Latino cultural adaptation of the META manual was distinctive and powerfully connected to the META clients, with a particular focus on religious imagery, again going beyond just following a standard motivational interviewing manual. While there was a description of the cultural adaptation of the META manual in the RCT report (Interian et al., 2013), which

did provide examples from the META manual of certain Spanish sayings that were to be employed, it was only when Norcross read the detailed case descriptions that he saw the impact of these sayings on the process:

> Reading segments from the session transcripts . . . [indicated that what was taking place was] a religious adaptation of secular META. Many of the sayings allude to faith and God as sources of motivation; for example, the *dichos* 'A quien madruga, Dios le ayuda' ('God helps he who rises to the occasion'), and 'Dios aprieta pero no ahorca' ('God squeezes but does not choke'). (Norcross, 2017, p. 319)

Finding Contrasts in Therapeutic Process Between the Positive-Outcome and Negative-Outcome Cases

Table 13.3 presents three categories of important details about the treatment of Lupe and Maria, the positive-outcome and negative-outcome clients, respectively. The first two categories summarize each client's presenting demographic and clinical background and outcome. In the context of this information, Table 13.3 describes a crucial difference in the impact of the META sessions on Lupe versus Maria in terms of stimulating a virtuous circle of events for Lupe, in contrast to a vicious circle of events for Maria. Such a cycle is a function of a series of factors and how they interact, including (a) how the client initially responds to the opportunity to express her emotions with an empathetic therapist— with Lupe feeling "relief in being able to 'unload' her emotional distress" versus Maria focusing on the trauma of being rejected by her husband and feeling more depressed; and (b) subsequent events, such as Lupe feeling more closely connected to her social support system and building on that to feel less depression and increased motivation to work towards her positive goals versus Maria's husband's rejection undoing part of her support system, which increased her depression and decreased her motivation to work on positive goals.

TABLE 13.3

Finding Contrasts in Therapeutic Process Between the Positive-Outcome Case
and the Negative-Outcome Case

Lupe, positive-outcome case	Maria, negative-outcome case
Presenting background. At the time of the study, Lupe was a 46-year-old, married, monolingual, Spanish-speaking, Ecuadorian woman with two children, ages 13 and 23. Lupe's first experience of depression occurred during her adolescent years but was left untreated. Her depression emerged for the second time 20 years later, at the age of 35, after immigrating to the United States from Ecuador. At the intake phase of the study, Lupe met the *DSM-IV* diagnostic criteria for a major depressive episode with subthreshold psychotic features (i.e., hearing her name being called, hearing doors open, hearing people talk when nobody was present; p. 265). Aside from mental health problems, Lupe reported a history of medical problems including gastric pain, obesity, constipation, asthma, chest pain, liver problems, headaches, and arthritis. For these medical problems, Lupe took an additional four medications on a daily basis (p. 280).	**Presenting background.** At the time of the study, Maria was a 30-year-old, monolingual Spanish-speaking, Venezuelan woman. She had immigrated to the United States 2 and a half months prior to becoming a participant in the study. After learning that her husband had been having an extra-marital affair and that he fathered a child with another woman, she fell into a depressive episode. Maria met the *DSM-IV* criteria for a major depressive disorder, recurrent with psychotic features (p. 266). The psychotic features consisted of auditory hallucinations (voices telling her to kill herself) and visual hallucinations (black spots that appeared when she was sad and having suicidal ideation). She stated that she received special messages or premonitions from God telling her why her husband was not calling her and that he was being unfaithful (p. 286). Maria noted that these psychotic symptoms had only been present for the last 2 months in the context of her depression (p. 286).
Outcome on the Beck Depression Inventory. Beginning of treatment: 43, severe depression. End of treatment: 3, minimal or no depression.	**Outcome on the Depression Inventory.** Beginning of treatment: 48, severe depression. End of treatment: 33, severe depression.
Cycle of change. Lupe's case shows "a 'virtuous circle' in which (a) she felt relief in being able to 'unload' her emotional distress and concerns to an empathetic and sympathetic therapist, leading her (b) to feel that 'others [her social support system] cared about her,' in turn (c) motivating her to come to her next appointment, during which she clarified her misconceptions about medication, so as to (d) view the medication as helpful in overcoming her depression (in spite of it leading to weight gain) and in meeting her positive personal and life goals, which in turn (e) fueled her motivation to continue taking her medication and activating her to work on her goals, which in turn (f) elicited a positive response from her family, which in turn (g) further motivated her to continue with her medication plan and to work on her [positive] goals." (Fishman et al., 2017, p. 308)	**Cycle of change.** Maria's case shows "a 'vicious circle' . . . illustrated by (a) her recent experience of a traumatic rejection by her husband, resulting in (b) her now lacking a strong social support system, and (c) in fact, having a social support system that stigmatized her depression, all of which (d) decreased her motivation to take her medication and work on her life goals, which in turn led to (e) an increase in her depression, leading to (f) the need for hospitalization between her second and third META session, which precipitated (g) a further rejection by her social support system of her severe depressive experience, with all of the above leading to (h) a reduction in her motivation for complying with her antidepressant medication." (Fishman et al., 2017, p. 308)

Adapted from "*Case Studies Within Psychotherapy Trials: Integrating Qualitative and Quantitative Methods*" (pp. 343–346), by D. B. Fishman, S. B. Messer, D. J. A. Edwards, and F. M. Dattilio, 2017, Oxford University Press (https://doi.org/10.1093/med:psych/9780199344635.001.0001). Copyright 2017 by Oxford University Press. Adapted with permission.

Table 13.3 describes how part of the virtuous circle for Lupe was to increase her motivation to take the medication, while part of the vicious circle for Maria was to decrease her motivation to take the medication. However, while the medication might have had a positive impact on Lupe and its lack a negative impact on Maria, the pattern of results indicates that degree of medication adherence is just one possible link in a virtuous or vicious circle of interconnected causes. Thus, for particular patients like Lupe and Maria, such adherence seems not a "deep" cause of change, but rather more an effect of a pattern of other changes. This conclusion is supported by the finding in the RCT that across all the clients, medication adherence by itself was not significantly associated with a decrease in depression.

RESOURCES FOR THE CASES WITHIN TRIALS METHOD

Procedures for completing a rigorous pragmatic case study can be found in Fishman (2013). Examples of pragmatic case studies that met peer-reviewed standards for publication can be found in the journal *Pragmatic Case Studies in Psychotherapy* (https://pcsp.nationalregister.org/). Pragmatic case studies in this journal that were representatively drawn from RCTs can be found in articles by Burckell and McMain (2011), Ciuca et al. (2017), Durland (2020), Frankl et al. (2020), Goldman et al. (2011), Schultz et al. (2017), and Watson et al. (2011). For more details on the CWT method, including the META project and three other detailed examples that each follow the full outline in Table 13.2, see Fishman et al. (2017).

The Fishman et al. (2017) case studies that follow the outline in Table 13.2 can be seen as a "proof of concept" of the CWT method. Note that in an RCT like the one previously described in the META case study, all 50 cases could provide useful information if analyzed as pragmatic case studies. This is because there are positive-outcome, mixed-outcome, and negative-outcome cases in the control and experimental conditions in the typical RCT, and systematic case analyses of these can yield insights into both qualitative patterns within subgroups and individual differences within subgroups.

SUMMARY: GUIDING PRINCIPLES FOR CONDUCTING AND DRAWING CONCLUSIONS FROM A CASES WITHIN TRIALS STUDY

1. *Pragmatic equivalence of the two types of knowledge.* Within the postpositivist, pragmatic framework of the CWT method, case study knowledge and RCT knowledge from a CWT study are equivalent in potential validity and should be analyzed in equal depth in terms of drawing theoretical conclusions from the overall study.
   a. *Validity* is defined as the pragmatic capacity to understand and help solve sociopsychological problems like mental and emotional distress, underachievement in school and at work, gun violence, and neighborhood conflict.
   b. In line with "validity," theoretical knowledge generated by the CWT method is viewed and judged first and foremost as a conceptual tool for creating positive problem-solving, not necessarily as a reflection of objective reality.
   c. Also in line with "validity," disagreement between RCT knowledge and case knowledge is an occasion to revise the original theory underlying the RCT design. In this process, sometimes the case-study knowledge suggests ways to alter the RCT theory not only in particular substance but also in type, for example, from a linear, mechanistic theory to a nonlinear, systems-based theory.

2. *The additive value of the two types of knowledge.* The particular strength of the CWT method is to combine two complementary, additive sources of knowledge, from an RCT design and a case-study design, each of which answers different questions. The former aids in assessing the overall quantitative capacity of a manualized intervention to help solve problems, while the latter's qualitative knowledge provides the lived experience of the participants and a contextualized picture of the actual process of the intervention.

3. *The logical commonality of the two types of knowledge.* Via the framework of the nomological network, RCT and case-study knowledge have logical commonality in terms of the relationship between observation and theory, as mediated by the processes of deduction, induction, and abduction.

4. In a postpositivist world, all sensory-based impressions are mediated through subjective

experience, just as the description of inner experience is (Stiles, 2009). Thus, absolutely objective knowledge is not possible. However, the relative distinction between the description of observations and the theoretical interpretation of them makes a crucial pragmatic difference in the development of valid theories (see item 1 in this list) to help solve problems, as our ultimate outcome focus is at the level of observing to what degree problems are in fact solved.

5. *The pragmatic case study and best practice.* This type of case study was chosen in part for the CWT method because this type of case study is based on an empirically validated model of best practice (Schön, 1983; Dreyfus & Dreyfus, 1986; Flyvbjerg, 2006).

6. *Ways to mine the knowledge in case studies.*
   a. Via case-based reasoning, a completed case study can help to guide a practitioner in productively addressing a current, similar type of case.
   b. Via Stiles's (2009) theory-building case-study model, case studies can be used to test theoretical hypotheses using logical elements from the hypothetico-deductive method

In summation, the CWT method is designed to capture the best features of RCTs and of systematic case studies in which each offsets the limitations of the other, capturing group trends in intervention effectiveness together with the individual experiences and outcomes of clients. Thus, systematic, detailed case studies make the findings from RCTs relevant and useful for practitioners while pointing out directions for building and refining intervention theories, including enriching our understanding of mechanisms of positive change.

References

Ayer, A. J. (1936). *Language, truth, and logic.* Dover Publications.

Ayer, A. J. (Ed.). (1966). *Logical positivism.* Free Press.

Baars, B. J. (1986). *The cognitive revolution in psychology.* Guilford Press.

Benjamin, L. T. (2014). *A brief history of modern psychology* (2nd ed.). Wiley.

Bernstein, R. J. (1983). *Beyond objectivism and relativism: Science, hermeneutics, and praxis.* University of Pennsylvania Press.

Burckell, L. A., & McMain, S. (2011). Contrasting clients in dialectical behavior therapy for borderline personality disorder: "Marie" and "Dean," two cases with different alliance trajectories & outcomes. *Pragmatic Case Studies in Psychotherapy, 7*(2), 246–267. https://doi.org/10.14713/pcsp.v7i2.1090

Ciuca, A. M., Berger, T., & Miclea, M. (2017). Maria and Andrea: Comparing positive and negative outcome cases in an online, clinician-guided, self-help intervention for panic disorder. *Pragmatic Case Studies in Psychotherapy, 13*(3), 173–216. https://doi.org/10.14713/pcsp.v13i3.2011

Conan Doyle, A. (2009/1892). *The adventures of Sherlock Holmes.* Dover Publications.

Cronbach, L. J., & Meehl, P. E. (1955). Construct validity in psychological tests. *Psychological Bulletin, 52*(4), 281–302. https://doi.org/10.1037/h0040957

Douven, I. (2017). Abduction. In E. N. Zalta (Ed.), *The Stanford encyclopedia of philosophy* (Summer 2017 ed.). Stanford University. https://plato.stanford.edu/archives/sum2017/entries/abduction/

Dreyfus, H. L., & Dreyfus, S. E. (1986). *Mind over machine.* Free Press.

Durland, L. (2020). Telephone-based, clinician-guided self-help cognitive behavioral therapy for depression in Parkinson's disease (dPD): The responder cases of "Alice" and "Carl," and the nonresponder cases of "Ethan" and "Gary." *Pragmatic Case Studies in Psychotherapy, 16*(1), 1–103. https://doi.org/10.14713/pcsp.v16i1.2068

Elliott, R., Fischer, C. T., & Rennie, D. L. (1999). Evolving guidelines for the publication of qualitative research studies in psychology and related fields. *British Journal of Clinical Psychology, 38,* 215–229.

Fishman, D. B. (1999). *The case for pragmatic psychology.* NYU Press.

Fishman, D. B. (2005). Editor's introduction to PCSP—from single case to database: A new method for enhancing psychotherapy practice. *Pragmatic Case Studies in Psychotherapy 1*(1), 1–50. https://doi.org/10.14713/pcsp.v1i1.855

Fishman, D. B. (2013). The pragmatic case study method for creating rigorous and systematic, practitioner-friendly research. *Pragmatic Case Studies in Psychotherapy, 9*(4), 403–425. https://doi.org/10.14713/pcsp.v9i4.1833

Fishman, D. B. (2017). The pragmatic case study in psychotherapy: A mixed methods approach informed by psychology's striving for methodological quality. *Clinical Social Work Journal, 45*(3), 238–252. https://doi.org/10.1007/s10615-016-0612-3

Fishman, D. B., Messer, S. B., Edwards, D. J. A., & Dattilio, F. M. (Eds.). (2017). *Case studies within psychotherapy trials: Integrating qualitative and quantitative methods.* Oxford University Press. https://doi.org/10.1093/med:psych/9780199344635.001.0001

Flyvbjerg, B. (2006). Five misunderstandings about case-study research. *Qualitative Inquiry, 12*(2), 219–245. https://doi.org/10.1177/1077800405284363

Frankl, M., Wennberg, P., Berggraf, L., & Philips, B. (2020). Affect phobia therapy for mild to moderate alcohol use disorder: The cases of "Carey," "Michelle," and "Mary." *Pragmatic Case Studies in Psychotherapy 15*(3), 214–257. https://doi.org/10.14713/pcsp.v15i3.2057

Gergen, K. J. (1985). The social constructionist movement in modern psychology. *American Psychologist, 40*(3), 266–275. https://doi.org/10.1037/0003-066X.40.3.266

Gergen, K. J., Josselson, R., & Freeman, M. (2015). The promises of qualitative inquiry. *American Psychologist, 70*(1), 1–9. https://doi.org/10.1037/a0038597

Goldenson, R. M. (Ed.). (1984). Aristotle. *Longman dictionary of psychology and psychiatry* (p. 60). Longman.

Goldman, R. N., Watson, J. C., & Greenberg, L. S. (2011). Application of the "individual-case-comparison" method to cases in emotion-focused therapy: "Eloise," a case of good outcome. *Pragmatic Case Studies in Psychotherapy, 7*(2), 305–338. https://doi.org/10.14713/pcsp.v7i2.1093

Harper, R. S. (1950). The first psychological laboratory. *Isis, 41*(2), 158–161. https://www.jstor.org/stable/227184

Honos-Webb, L., Stiles, W., Greenberg, L., & Goldman, R. (1998). Assimilation analysis of process-experiential psychotherapy: A comparison of two cases. *Psychotherapy Research, 8*(3), 264–286.

Interian, A., Lewis-Fernández, R., Gara, M. A., & Escobar, J. I. (2013). A randomized-controlled trial of an intervention to improve antidepressant adherence among Latinos with depression. *Depression and Anxiety, 30*(7), 688–696. https://doi.org/10.1002/da.22052

Interian, A., Prawda, A., Fishman, D. B., & Buerger, W. (2017). Motivational enhancement therapy for increasing antidepressant medication adherence and decreasing clinical depression among adult Latinos. In D. B. Fishman, S. B. Messer, D. J. A. Edwards, & F. M. Dattilio (Eds.), *Case studies within psychotherapy trials: Integrating qualitative and quantitative methods* (pp. 256–315). Oxford University Press.

Jacobson, N. S., & Truax, P. (1991). Clinical significance: A statistical approach to defining meaningful change in psychotherapy research. *Journal of Consulting and Clinical Psychology, 59*(1), 12–19. https://doi.org/10.1037/0022-006X.59.1.12

James, W. (1890). *Principles of psychology* (Vols. 1–2). Henry Holt.

Kolodner, J. L. (1992). An introduction to case-based reasoning. *Artificial Intelligence Review, 6*(1), 3–34. https://doi.org/10.1007/BF00155578

Krasner, L., & Houts, A. C. (1984). A study of the "value" systems of behavioral scientists. *American Psychologist, 39*(8), 840–850. https://doi.org/10.1037/0003-066X.39.8.840

Leahey, T. H. (1991). *A history of modern psychology.* Prentice Hall.

Leahey, T. H. (1995). Waiting for Newton. *Journal of Mind and Behavior, 16*(1), 9–19.

Lewin, K. (1946). Action research and minority problems. *Journal of Social Issues, 2*(4), 34–46. https://doi.org/10.1111/j.1540-4560.1946.tb02295.x

McLeod, J. (2010). *Case study research in counseling and psychotherapy.* SAGE. https://doi.org/10.4135/9781446287897

Miller, W. R., & Rollnick, S. (2002). *Motivational interviewing: Preparing people for change.* Guilford Press.

Neisser, U. (1967). *Cognitive psychology.* Appleton-Century-Crofts.

Norcross, J. C. (2017). Best of both worlds. In D. B. Fishman, S. B. Messer, D. J. A. Edwards, & F. M. Dattilio (Eds.), *Case studies within psychotherapy trials: Integrating qualitative and quantitative methods* (pp. 316–324). Oxford University Press.

Norcross, J. C., Hailstorks, R., Aiken, L. S., Pfund, R. A., Stamm, K. E., & Christidis, P. (2016). Undergraduate study in psychology: Curriculum and assessment. *American Psychologist, 71*(2), 89–101. https://doi.org/10.1037/a0040095

Persons, J. B. (2008). *The case formulation approach to cognitive-behavior therapy.* Guilford Press.

Peterson, D. R. (1991). Connection and disconnection of research and practice in the education of professional psychologists. *American Psychologist, 46*(4), 422–429. https://doi.org/10.1037/0003-066X.46.4.422

Pitkin, H. F., & Shumer, S. M. (1982). On participation. *Democracy, 2,* 43–54.

Rogers, C. R., & Dymond, R. F. (Eds.). (1954). *Psychotherapy and personality change.* University of Chicago Press.

Rorty, R. (1979). *Philosophy and the mirror of nature.* Princeton University Press.

Rorty, R. (1982). *Consequences of pragmatism.* University of Minnesota Press.

Scarr, S. (1985). Construing psychology: Making facts and fables for our times. *American Psychologist, 40*(5), 499–512. https://doi.org/10.1037/0003-066X.40.5.499

Schön, D. A. (1983). *The reflective practitioner: How professionals think in action.* Basic Books.

Schulz, A., Vincent, A., & Berger, T. (2017). Daydreamer and night owl: Comparing positive and negative outcome cases in an online, clinician-guided, self-help intervention for social anxiety disorder. *Pragmatic Case Studies in Psychotherapy, 13*(3), 217–252. https://doi.org/10.14713/pcsp.v13i3.2012

Stewart, R. E., & Chambless, D. L. (2007). Does psychotherapy research inform treatment decisions in private practice? *Journal of Clinical Psychology, 63*(3), 267–281. https://doi.org/10.1002/jclp.20347

Stiles, W. B. (2006). Numbers can be enriching. *New Ideas in Psychology, 24*(3), 252–262. https://doi.org/10.1016/j.newideapsych.2006.10.003

Stiles, W. B. (2009). Logical operations in theory-building case studies. *Pragmatic Case Studies in Psychotherapy, 5*(3), 9–22. https://doi.org/10.14713/pcsp.v5i3.973

Toulmin, S. (1990). *Cosmopolis: The hidden agenda of modernity.* University of Chicago Press.

Trochim, W. M. K., & Donnelly, J. P. (2007). *The research methods knowledge base* (3rd ed.). Thomson Publishing.

Watson, J. B. (1913). Psychology as the behaviorist views it. *Psychological Review, 20*(2), 158–177. https://doi.org/10.1037/h0074428

Watson, J. S., Goldman, R. N., & Greenberg, L. S. (2011). Contrasting two clients in emotion-focused therapy for depression 1: The case of "Tom," "Trapped in the tunnel." *Pragmatic Case Studies in Psychotherapy, 7*(2), 268–304. https://doi.org/10.14713/pcsp.v7i2.1093

Wittgenstein, L. (1953). *Philosophical investigations* (G. E. M. Anscombe, Trans.). Macmillan.

Yin, R. K. (2014). *Case study research: Design and methods* (5th ed.). SAGE.

CHAPTER 14

RESEARCHING WITH AMERICAN INDIAN AND ALASKA NATIVE COMMUNITIES: PURSUING PARTNERSHIPS FOR PSYCHOLOGICAL INQUIRY IN SERVICE TO INDIGENOUS FUTURITY

Joseph P. Gone

American Indians and Alaska Natives (AIANs) are the remnant descendants of hundreds of exceedingly diverse Indigenous North American peoples whose fates changed dramatically with the arrival of European explorers to the "new world." In time, European and Euro American colonization reduced the Indigenous population of the United States to fewer than 250,000 individuals at the close of the 19th century (Thornton, 1987). Today, many Americans lay claim to distant Indigenous ancestry, but AIAN identities persist most strikingly among the roughly 3.5 million members of more than 570 federally recognized Tribal Nations. These communities occupy a distinctive political status owing to international treaties initially struck with European powers and subsequently shaped by U.S. federal law and policy. Operating as "domestic dependent nations," tribal governments continue to exercise (curtailed) powers of political sovereignty on behalf of their citizens even as they struggle to recover from the ravages of historical dispossession, subjugation, discrimination, and marginality (Pevar, 2012). Owing to their provisional postcolonial status

(depending on the national mood), AIAN communities represent the proverbial "canaries in the coalmine" when it comes to the formulation, cultivation, production, and application of academic knowledge. That is, even though other ethnoracial constituencies in the United States have advanced legitimate historical grievances against research and researchers, AIANs represent the consummate challenge for ethical academic inquiry due to the vexed intersection of our unique collective rights and our long history of brutal colonization. In sum, if research in AIAN communities can be accomplished through ethical, relevant, and useful means, then substantial progress will have been made in addressing similar imperatives of research for other historically marginalized communities as well.

There can be little doubt that ethical and relevant research is desperately needed by AIAN communities. Saddled with centuries of ignorant, misguided, exploitative, and hostile intrusion by outsiders, "Indian Country" today is beset by grinding poverty, overwhelmed institutions, and obstructed opportunities, all-too-often exacerbated

https://doi.org/10.1037/0000319-014
APA Handbook of Research Methods in Psychology, Second Edition: Vol. 2. Research Designs: Quantitative, Qualitative, Neuropsychological, and Biological, H. Cooper (Editor-in-Chief)

by hapless national policies. Not even the most talented tribal leaders can be expected to chart a smooth way forward in service to transformative community revitalization and collective self-determination. And yet, in a supposedly rational and resourced "first world" context such as the Unites States, "fourth world" Indigenous communities need not "go it alone," as the problems of AIAN communities might in theory be taken up by the best and brightest minds throughout the nation. In this respect, research psychologists would seem to have a crucial role to play. Specifically, AIANs suffer from long-standing health and mental health disparities that shape life and livelihood in these settings in visible, pronounced, and heartrending fashion. Many AIAN communities grapple with epidemic levels of substance abuse, interpersonal violence, posttraumatic stress, relational dysfunction, and suicidal behavior (Gone & Trimble, 2012). Although these pathologies are perhaps best conceived as "postcolonial disorders" (Good et al., 2008), it typically falls to mental health professionals—including licensed psychologists—to provide community-based services in the effort to remedy these vexing problems. Thus, as the only mental health specialty that requires substantive research training as part of its professional credentialing process, disciplinary psychology has both the greatest investment as well as the greatest obligation to ensure appropriate inquiry in community-based research as it seeks a proper foundation of knowledge to effectively ameliorate these rampant health disparities (Trimble et al., 2010).

Current discussions of Indigenous psychology take as their point of departure the coloniality of Indian Country. That is, Indigenous persistence into the 21st century was scarcely imaginable at the outset of the 20th century, given the sweeping impacts of colonization that led Americans to conceive of AIANs as a "vanishing race." In this *Handbook* chapter, I review issues, approaches, and strategies for psychology research with contemporary AIAN communities whose "survivance" (a portmanteau of *survival* and *resistance*; Vizenor, 1999) was most improbable. First, I canvas the legacy of irrelevant and even exploitative research

by behavioral and health scientists, the recommendations for remedy that have been proposed, and the reparative implications of a shift to a relational ethics in psychology research. Second, I delve more deeply into processes of participatory engagement that follow from adoption of a relational ethics to ensure that psychology research is relevant and useful for AIAN populations. Finally, I consider Indigenous knowledge traditions and research methodologies with respect to the politics of knowledge production in psychology pursuant to AIAN resurgence and futurity. In this chapter, I center the experiences and realities of AIAN communities in the United States, but (because knowledge travels) I necessarily draw on observations and ideas from other Indigenous contexts and settings (especially from Canada, Australia, and New Zealand). In offering these observations for the discipline, it is my hope to make psychologists aware of specific research concerns in AIAN communities, to convey expansive conceptions of research ethics with respect to these communities, and to establish useful foundations for novel research approaches and partnerships that may also extend to other vulnerable and historically marginalized populations as well.

RENDING AND REPAIR IN INDIGENOUS RESEARCH

Striking narratives about exploitative researchers and detrimental research circulate routinely in AIAN communities, testifying to a rending of research relationships. So widespread is this discourse that a robust literature has emerged in the behavioral and health sciences to describe, analyze, remedy, and repair this history of "unethical research abuses" (Hodge, 2012).

Rending of Research Relationships

Six examples feature prominently in AIAN accounts of the misuses and abuses of research (see Freeman et al., 2006): (a) In the early 20th century, anthropologist Alfred Kroeber sent the brain of his deceased "informant" named Ishi to the Smithsonian Institution for preservation and study without anyone's permission (Starn, 2004); (b) not long thereafter, an Alaska Native man who died while visiting the Smithsonian was cremated with his child as witness, except the cremation was staged and his body was kept by the Smithsonian for its research collections (Starn, 2004); (c) between 1942 and 1952, Canadian nutrition experts conducted experiments on malnourished Indigenous people—including pupils attending residential schools—without consent to explore health outcomes associated with nutritional supplements (Mosby, 2013); (d) in the 1950s, the U.S. Air Force administered radioactive iodine to Alaska Natives to study acclimation to cold weather (Lanzarotta, 2020); (e) in the 1970s, Foulks reported on high alcoholism rates for an Alaska Native community that was picked up by the national news and resulted in a downgrading of the community's bond rating (Klausner & Foulks, 1979); and (f) in the "oughts," Havasupai tribal members provided genetic material that was subsequently analyzed for purposes (e.g., patterns of "inbreeding" or historical migration from Asia) that neither participants nor tribal authorities had approved or consented to (Mello & Wolf, 2010). This is not even to consider the repugnant tradition of early anthropological trafficking in AIAN remains through grave robbery and deceit (Thomas, 2000). Indeed, the father of American anthropology, Franz Boas, wrote about his own practice of stealing, collecting, and selling Indigenous skulls to museums to make ends meet (Appiah, 2020).

Thus, among the social sciences, anthropology has come up for the most withering of Indigenous critiques (Biolsi & Zimmerman, 1997), but psychology has not escaped unscathed. For example, Darou et al. (1993) recounted the experiences of the James Bay Cree communities of northern Quebec—comprising a population of about 10,000 people—with 13 research projects addressed to psychological topics. Of the six psychologists to have undertaken most of these studies, five were ejected from the Cree territories because research respondents felt "exploited and mistreated." In the wake of these stunning breakdowns in relationships, the James Bay Cree communities have "forbidden the conduct of further psychological research" in their midst (p. 325). This example illustrates some of the common reasons for AIAN dissatisfaction with academic research, which include the inattention, opportunism, and even arrogance of outside researchers; the denigration and disrespect shown for Indigenous lifeways; the sterility and irrelevance of the resultant knowledge; and the wasteful allocation of scarce community resources. In response, a burgeoning literature addressed to critical reimagination of research in Indian Country has emerged during the past few decades (Mihesuah, 1993; Wax, 1991). Only more recently have these critiques appeared in psychology publications (Trimble & Fisher, 2006). A March 2021 search in the PsycInfo bibliographic database returned 97 journal articles at the intersection of *Indigenous populations* and *research methodology* (using official thesaurus terms for these major concepts, as "exploded" for maximum inclusion), and 53 journal articles at the intersection of *Indigenous populations* and *research ethics* (not an official thesaurus term). Most articles in the latter corpus were not about Indigenous populations in the Unites States and/or were not published in psychology journals proper.

Repair in Research Relationships

One of the earliest Indigenous intellectuals to warn against the misuse of scholarly research in the social sciences was Vine Deloria, Jr. (1980), a founder of American Indian Studies. Since then, AIAN communities (with support from advocates and allies) have adopted various progressive measures to promote greater awareness, education, authority, and control over research efforts undertaken in their midst. The National Congress of American Indians (NCAI)—the United Nations of Indian Country—developed and disseminated numerous documents that provide guidance to Tribal Nations with respect to educating tribal leaders (NCAI, 2009) and tribal members (Sahota, 2010) about building tribal research relationships (NCAI Policy Research Center & MSU Center for Native Health Partnerships, 2012), reviewing research studies (Sahota, 2009a), and regulating research (Sahota, 2009b). A major component of this endeavor is the creation of independent research review boards (RRBs) by Tribal Nations. Despite significant capacity limitations, many AIAN communities have established such boards, the purview and power of which usually extend well beyond the familiar mandate to protect human subjects. Indeed, in response to criteria originating in Canada (Snarch, 2004), many AIAN RRBs pursue self-determination in expansive fashion with respect to OCAP principles. *OCAP* refers to tribal assertion of ownership, control, access, and possession concerning research materials, data, processes, and products. For example, many tribal RRBs require review and approval of any manuscripts written by researchers prior to submission for scholarly publication (and sometimes of associated presentation proposals prior to their submission for conferences). These exercises of AIAN sovereignty are becoming normative in Indian Country, and frequently entail entry by researchers into formalized (i.e., contractual) research arrangements that are increasingly governed by research codes adopted by Tribal Nations (American Indian Law Center, 1999).

Thus, in the name of AIAN community protections from harmful or exploitative research, recent decades have witnessed a tangible shift in authority and control over research away from autonomous and unaccountable researchers to sovereign and self-determining AIAN Tribal Nations. Concurrently, there have been proposals for a shift in ethical frameworks that might guide such research. As psychologists know, research regulation with respect to human subjects protections is founded on *The Belmont Report* (National Commission for the Protection of Human Subjects of Biomedical and Behavioral Research, 1979), including its three principles of *respect for persons* (undergirding practices of informed consent), *beneficence* (undergirding practices of risk-benefit analysis), and *justice* (undergirding practices of fair sample selection). With respect to research in AIAN communities, however, the application of these ethical principles and practices falls short owing to an associated

style of reasoning that is relentlessly individualist in orientation. This premise of *ontological individualism* (Wendt, 2010) has shaped ethical reasoning about research in ways that circumvent researcher accountability to tribal polities. The proposed remedies for this ethical incongruity include a shift away from a deontic rationale to a relational rationale (C. B. Fisher, 1999) and from an individualist orientation to a group-based orientation (Saunkeah et al., 2021). Importantly, neither of these shifts entails a formal rejection of the Belmont principles, but rather an expansion of these tenets that better accords with AIAN community sensibilities and commitments. Development of these expansive approaches have entailed a critical assessment of the cultural and epistemological limitations of the received (and reigning) paradigm of ethical reasoning that governs psychological inquiry.

Ethical Reasoning for Research Relationships

In this respect, C. B. Fisher (1999) delineated 10 ethical assumptions of normative scientific research with "vulnerable populations." Examples of these assumptions include knowledge gathering is unconditionally and fundamentally good, scientific knowledge production should aspire to be value-free, researchers are entitled to use humans in their pursuit of knowledge, the principle of individual autonomy (i.e., respect for persons) can trump the principles of beneficence and justice when obtaining consent, the absence of research benefits is acceptable so long as the research does no harm, and ethical decision making in research is the proper purview of professionals (whether researchers, ethicists, or institutional review board officials). Fisher considered several sobering challenges to these assumptions and concluded that reigning ethical codes are products of the scientific establishment that predominantly reflect Eurocentric philosophical conceptions (e.g., context-free principles, rational-deductive reasoning, libertarian assessments of the "good life"). In contrast, Fisher advanced an expansive *relational ethics* with explicit reference to the shift in moral reasoning advocated by Gilligan (1982) in response to Kohlberg (1984), namely, that ethical reasoning is not only about "principle-based justice ethics" but also about "relational-based care ethics." In this latter approach, proponents have "traditionally taken relationships as fundamental, viewed care as an obligation, focused on how one can achieve individual freedom without violating moral obligations to others, and stressed the construction of moral injunctions to protect relationships" (Fisher, 1999, p. 30). Fisher thus identified the source of AIAN suspicion and anger toward researchers and research: Although it would be difficult to overstate the importance of a relational orientation for everyday life in most AIAN communities (indeed, "being Indian" is fundamentally about one's kinship ties within a tribal polity), the ethical commitments that have guided psychology research in our communities have privileged deontic principles that have routinely resulted in an absence of care.

Thus, a relational ethics requires assessment of research not only with respect to autonomy, beneficence, and justice in abstracted and decontextualized (i.e., deontic) terms, but also with respect to considerations of power and vulnerability, contribution and accountability, and local conceptions of that which is true, beautiful, and good. Specifically, C. B. Fisher (1999) championed the importance of partnership between researchers and research participants (underscoring research as an interpersonal endeavor) in which learning is bidirectional and in which complementarity (if not symmetry) of status is a cherished outcome of research. With respect to research partnerships with AIAN communities in particular, Saunkeah and colleagues (2021) echoed this expansive ethical shift beyond the Belmont principles to recognition not just of individual autonomy but of group autonomy. In the AIAN research context, they promoted the importance of both *sovereignty* as the expression of respect for persons at the group-based level of Tribal Nations and *solidarity* as the expression of tribal commitments to protecting not just tribal members but collective tribal interests and cultural integrity. Moreover, in an extensive project that was years in the making, professional members of the Society of

Indian Psychologists collaboratively developed a critical commentary on the extant Ethics Code of the American Psychological Association (APA). Drawing on similarly expansive commitments to ethical reasoning—albeit originating from principles and approaches that prevail in AIAN community life—the commentary (García & Tehee, 2014) expressed limited confidence in the ability of the APA Ethics Code to resolve several important ethical issues. Instead, the commentary urged APA to consider lessons drawn from Indigenous values, including relationality and storytelling, in revising its code.

Summary

AIAN communities have experienced disrespectful, irrelevant, and even exploitative research in their midst, and, thus, frequently maintain a skeptical stance toward researchers. Although AIAN communities in the United States have not experienced researcher abuses akin to Nazi medical experiments or the Tuskegee syphilis study, AIAN communities have taken great offense at the routine failures of researchers to engage in proper partnerships with our communities, typically modeled on local conceptions of kinship that privilege core values such as relationship, responsibility, reciprocity, and redistribution (Americans for Indian Opportunity, n.d.). In consequence, AIAN communities have responded by establishing RRBs that assert sweeping authority over community research, demanding in many instances that researchers accede to tribal authority and oversight with respect to ownership, control, access, and possession of research data, materials, and products. Concurrently, ethicists have been rethinking the reigning paradigm that governs social and psychological research, critiquing it for its tacit commitments to abstract, individualist, and Eurocentric philosophical foundations with utterly inadequate attention to the expansive values of relationality and care. In contrast, a relational ethics seeks to express care through research partnerships that are responsive and responsible to research participants. Importantly, AIAN communities have also been acknowledged as collectivities that express both sovereignty and solidarity with respect to research. Thus, psychological inquiry concerning AIAN life and experience is now recognized to entail ethical commitments beyond the Belmont principles to a broader ethos of collaboration, partnership, and interaction as "good relatives."

RELATIONALITY AND RECONCILIATION IN INDIGENOUS RESEARCH

The success of this shift from a deontic individualist ethics to a relational and group-based ethics ultimately hinges on the adoption of *participatory engagement* by psychologists with AIAN community partners. Fortunately, a participatory approach to psychological inquiry has percolated and proliferated in the discipline for several decades.

Participatory Traditions in Research

Participatory traditions in behavioral science research have emerged from diverse historical antecedents. Brown and Tandon (1983) compared two such approaches—action research and participatory research—in search of commonalities and distinctions. Action research (as promoted by scholars such as Kurt Lewin, Chris Argyris, and Eric Trist) was an applied endeavor originating in the United States that entails cycles of analysis in which social scientists collaborate with people in organizations (e.g., business firms) to solve practical problems (e.g., workplace injuries) while contributing to new knowledge. Participatory research (as championed by scholars such as Paulo Freire, Bud Hall, and Marja-Liisa Swantz) was an emancipatory endeavor originating in the Global South that entails colearning and consciousness building in which teams of inquirers work together to achieve structural transformations for improving lives (e.g., analysis of local landowning patterns for political mobilization to remedy unfair tax advantages). According to Brown and Tandon, both approaches value useful knowledge and developmental change but differ with respect to their ideologies. Whereas action research stresses the individual (often in a larger group context), draws on a consensus-based social theory, and centers on problems of growth

and efficiency, participatory research stresses a societal analysis (e.g., economic conditions), draws on a conflict-based social theory, and centers on problems of oppression and equity. Thus, the political economies that shape action research and participatory research, respectively, differ in important ways. The principal distinction is that the former involves working within systems to develop solutions that would presumably benefit everyone in the system, while the latter involves allying with marginalized or oppressed constituencies to develop solutions that might benefit these constituencies by upending unjust systems and the status quo.

Although Brown and Tandon (1983) traced distinctive origins, attributes, and commitments of these applied research traditions, the reality for contemporary inquiry in psychology is that these approaches have been selectively adopted, adapted, blended, transformed, and circulated in the discipline since their emergence after World War Two. In terms of visible formations within contemporary psychology in the United States, these approaches endure in social, organizational, feminist, critical, and liberationist psychology. The subfield of psychology that is perhaps most closely aligned with participatory traditions of inquiry is community psychology (Kloos et al., 2021). Community psychology was born at the Swampscott conference of 1965, in which almost 40 psychologists (including just one woman) convened to chart a disciplinary path forward with respect to community mental health (Kelly, 1987; Walsh, 1987). Dissatisfied with the medicalizing tenets of both clinical psychology and psychiatry as well as with the lab-based conventions of social psychology, community psychologists embraced an expansive view of community mental health and pursued broad-based social interventions for preventing maladaptation, promoting well-being, and remedying social injustice in U.S. society. Throughout its 50 years as a recognized subfield of psychology (Tebes, 2016), community psychology has promoted psychological inquiry that is contextualized (rather than reductive), system-focused (rather than person-centered), ecologically embedded (rather than individuated), diversity-oriented (rather than universalizing), strengths-based (rather than deficit-based), collaborative (rather than expert-driven), empowering (rather than victim blaming), preventative (rather than rehabilitative), and values-driven (rather than disengaged).

Consequently, the sine qua non of community psychology is participatory engagement with people in their communities. Long cultivated within this subfield, *participatory action research* (PAR; see Brydon-Miller, 1997; Chevalier & Buckles, 2019) is one influential, integrative approach to such community-engaged inquiry. Kidd and Kral (2005) described PAR as a "macro method" that entails "creation of a context in which knowledge development and change might occur" (p. 187). PAR depends on a cyclical spiraling of reflecting, planning, acting, and observing for which the "process is, in effect, the method" (p. 189). Effective PAR fundamentally depends on proper attitudes among researchers and explicitly integrates three commitments: *participation*, requiring efforts to share power; *action*, requiring efforts to induce social change; and *research*, requiring efforts to produce new knowledge. Importantly, however, the generation of knowledge in PAR is not an end in itself but rather a means to transformative social change. In this sense, "knowledge is thus derivative" (p. 189). Finally, with respect to broader disciplinary obsessions with method, rigor, and science, PAR subsumes the selection and application of specific research methods both to the problems at hand and to the preferences of local partners. In a recent update, Kidd and colleagues (2018) acknowledged that shifting societal trends such as the assertion of greater agency by marginalized communities may require a rethinking of some aspects of PAR. One example includes reimagining the nature of participation for communities that have asserted greater control over research in their midst. These authors also acknowledged the challenge of describing "how to do a PAR 'project'," even wondering whether the field needs to envision "PAR careers rather than PAR projects" (p. 78).

Despite the perhaps inherent resistance of participatory approaches to procedural "how to" instructions or recommendations (cf. Chapter 15 in this volume), the principles that might guide such research have been thoroughly articulated in recent years in the field of public health. Israel and colleagues (2013) designated nine such principles for community-based participatory research: (a) acknowledge the community as the unit of identity, (b) build on community strengths and resources, (c) facilitate a collaborative and equitable partnership that entails power-sharing and attends to social disadvantage in all phases of the research, (d) foster among all partners both colearning and capacity building, (e) balance the mutual benefits of knowledge generation and intervention for everyone involved, (f) focus locally on the relevance of public health and ecological perspectives to attend to multiple determinants of health, (g) engage in systems development through cyclical and iterative processes, (h) disseminate research findings to partners and engage them in knowledge dissemination, and (i) prepare for a long-term process that commits to sustainability. Based on these principles, it should be clear that participatory engagement in psychological research requires attitudes, orientations, and preparations by researchers that differ from workaday knowledge production in the discipline. Participatory research requires that researchers prepare to interact with community partners much more intensively and proactively than is customary, dispense with the usual expert-layman distinctions by acknowledging the contributions of all partners, provide additional resources to community partners to assist with their engagement in research and commitment to the partnership, and consider issues of sustainability of solutions from the very beginning of the partnership.

Participatory Research With Indigenous Communities

Given the misuses and abuses in past research with AIAN communities, it is unsurprising that participatory approaches have risen to the fore in psychological inquiry with Indigenous community partners. P. A. Fisher and Ball (2003) promoted tribal participatory research, which builds on principles and practices of PAR while tailoring these for partnerships with AIAN communities. Specifically, Fisher and Ball recognized two facets of AIAN community experiences that require research accommodation: historical trauma (i.e., colonial oppression and post/colonial suffering; Hartmann et al., 2019) and intertribal cultural diversity. The authors identified four mechanisms to accommodate these facets. The first is *tribal oversight of research*, which includes three components: (a) a formal resolution authorizing the research from the tribal governing body, (b) oversight committees appointed by the tribal government to regulate research activities, and (c) a tribal research code that sets forth research regulations. The second is the *use of a facilitator* to manage the relationships between academic researchers and tribal committee/staff members in meetings to ensure balance among interests and perspectives. The third is the employment and training of AIAN *community members as project staff*, which is essential for building local research capacity in Indian Country. A final mechanism is the adoption of *culturally specific methods for assessment and intervention* in research projects. This entails the local vetting of possible or proposed interventions—along with similar review of tests and measures for assessing intervention impacts—with respect to their relevance and resonance with community values, orientations, and sensibilities. Fisher and Ball also explored the implications of these mechanisms, which frequently require expansions in project timelines, budgetary considerations, outcomes assessments, and researcher-community relationships.

Interestingly, key features of tribal participatory research (and participatory research in general) have found their way into research policies concerned with Indigenous populations in other nations. One striking instance of the institutionalization of a participatory approach occurred when the Canadian Institutes for Health Research (Canadian Institutes for Health Research, 2007) formally adopted as its official funding policy the *Guidelines for Health Research Involving Aboriginal People*. Among its 15 articles was an explicit requirement that "communities should be given the option of a participatory-research approach" (p. 3). Other articles in these *Guidelines* addressed researcher respect for Indigenous worldviews and cultural protocols, community jurisdiction over research, community control of access to traditional knowledge, community involvement in interpretation of data and review of findings, community rights to its intellectual property, protection of community anonymity, assurances of community benefit (including local education and training about research), and credit for contributions by community members. In 2010, the *Guidelines* were superseded by the Tri-Council Policy Statement for *Ethical Conduct for Research Involving Humans* (Canadian Institutes for Health Research et al., 2014), which continues to govern not just health research but all government-funded research in Canada. Importantly, the ethical commitments conveyed in the 2007 *Guidelines* are largely preserved in Chapter Nine of the Tri-Council Policy, including requirements for community engagement. One of the 22 articles in this chapter stated that "researchers and communities should consider applying a collaborative and participatory approach as appropriate to the nature of the research, and the level of ongoing engagement desired by the community" (p. 128). Clearly, as expressed in these policies, Canada has taken serious measures to remedy the legacy of irrelevant, offensive, and exploitative research in Indigenous communities.

With respect to AIAN community research, the U.S. National Institutes of Health (NIH) has not adopted formal policies that are specific to these communities, but in 2015 it established a Tribal Health Research Office within the Office of the Director at NIH to ensure consultation and collaboration with Tribal Nations regarding NIH policies and programs. This requires coordination and support of tribal health research-related activities across NIH, including the convening of annual tribal consultation sessions and support for a Tribal Advisory Committee. Comprising representatives appointed by AIAN tribal governments, the purpose of this committee is to ensure that NIH research funding helps to address the health inequities of Indian Country. Moreover, in recent years, the NIH has issued requests for applications for research funding that are explicitly designated for AIAN health issues (including addiction and suicide) and that encourage community engagement and participation for ensuring acceptable and useful research projects. Beyond such occasional requests for applications, NIH also funds the Native American Research Centers for Health portfolio. Supported through an NIH partnership with the federal Indian Health Service, these research grants are designated for competitive award directly to AIAN governments (or associated tribal organizations) for administering projects in partnership with academic researchers of their own choosing. Created to support tribal health priorities, community capacity building, and engagement of academic researchers in AIAN health research, these grants reflect a distinctive federal commitment to promote AIAN participation in community research. NIH also supports the Intervention Research to Improve Native American Health program, which is designed to support health intervention research in partnership with AIAN communities (K. Etz, personal communication, March 19, 2021).

Beyond NIH, the National Science Foundation in the United States, which funds social science research (including psychology research), primarily addresses AIAN research through funding to bolster the number of AIAN-identified researchers in the science, technology, engineering, and mathematics fields. It also supports a small Tribal College and University Program to fund research in these institutions. Finally, federal funding is also available to AIAN communities for health surveillance and program evaluation from the Centers for Disease Control and Prevention (which funds most costs for the national network of Tribal Epidemiology Centers, which are explicitly tasked with supporting Tribal Nations) and the Substance Abuse and Mental Health Services Administration (which routinely requires collection of basic information pertaining to the health programs it funds throughout the nation, including in Indian Country). In comparison with Canada, then, the United States lags in adopting formal research policies that mandate participatory approaches in funded research, even though the amount of research funding to and for Indigenous communities is higher in the United States (which, of course, has a larger Indigenous population).

Contextual Realities of Indigenous Research

Again, the promise of participatory approaches in research with AIAN communities is to repair the rending of relationships by past researchers in pursuit of contemporary reconciliation through new kinds of academic-community collaborations. To that end, initial discussions between academic researchers and community partners are likely to benefit from frank exchange concerning priorities, sensitivities, values, and expectations by all parties. These arise from and are situated within respective academic and AIAN community contexts, the implications of which are not always self-evident to the various partner constituencies. There are at least four summary contextual realities that academic researchers need to understand about AIAN communities. First, owing to past colonial subjugation, AIAN communities are sensibly sensitive to issues of autonomy and exploitation in research partnerships, which heightens the need for researcher awareness, respect, transparency, communication, and accountability (and, indeed, the need for contemporary reconciliation in research collaborations). Second, owing to cultural difference in the context of enduring power asymmetries, AIAN communities are committed to notions of what is good, right, proper, or fair (i.e., ethics) in ways that differ from those governing psychology research (motivating the shift, already described, from a deontic to a relational ethics). Third, AIAN communities are increasingly dedicated to celebrating and protecting Indigenous traditional knowledge and practices (Battiste, 2007). Owing to routine (and offensive) Euro-settler misappropriation of these, AIAN communities experience great ambivalence about whether and how to share such knowledges and practices, desiring to signal the centrality of these traditions for modern-day health and life but needing to protect these vulnerable traditions from ongoing misappropriation. Balancing these trade-offs requires close consultation and mutual trust. Finally, AIAN communities frequently contend with grave challenges and scarce resources, meaning that there is too much to be done by too few with too little support and funding. Although managing researchers and research in our midst is clearly necessary, doing so remains another demand on limited resources. It is, thus, important for academic researchers to recognize that the incentives for AIAN communities to engage in research partnerships include alignment of research with tribal priorities, utility of results, accessibility of findings, contribution of resources to the community (e.g., employment of research staff), and general efficiency of research activities, processes, and products.

In a parallel sense, in the spirit of relationality and reconciliation, there are at least four summary contextual realities that AIAN community partners would benefit from understanding about academic researchers and research. First, most academic researchers are typically conscientious and responsible people who do not intend to offend or distress others; it is unfair to generalize from the attitudes and behaviors of a few "bad apples" to all researchers. Consequently, within a relational frame, a proper response to lapses by academic researchers may be to seek contextual explanations for such lapses rather than to presume negative character attributes, with the immediate goal being to pursue communication, negotiation, recommitment, and remedy on all sides. Second, for most academic researchers, the primary reward for engaging in research is not primarily income, prestige, or power, but rather pursuit of intellectual questions or interests within the domain of one's professional expertise. One implication is that academic researchers may be unable or unwilling to accommodate every conceivable research request by AIAN communities. Importantly, a norm in some sectors of academia is the pursuit of one's intellectual interests as an entrepreneurial endeavor, and academic researchers can become

accustomed to exercising immense freedom and control in their research efforts. Adoption of a participatory approach to research clearly upends these norms, but it does so against a backdrop of extensive researcher autonomy. Third, research universities are run by their faculty, resulting in a wide range of competing obligations for academic researchers. In this sense, scholars at research universities are metaprofessionals who must juggle responsibility for research, teaching, and service. Balancing so many professional obligations and personal commitments is challenging. Moreover, those who undertake time-consuming participatory research are often disadvantaged in their research productivity relative to many colleagues. Thus, on occasion, efforts by academic researchers to manage multiple responsibilities beyond research proper falters, and lapses in project partnerships can result. Finally, the professional reputation of academic researchers is based on prominent publication of research findings. Appraisal of research quality is tied to methodological rigor and independence of analysis, and failure to publish the right number of articles in the right kinds of journals using the right forms of analysis in one's discipline can result in disapproval by one's colleagues. Again, participatory approaches entail alternative norms, but even dedicated academic researchers who embrace a relational ethics must contend with the broad pressures and sanctions associated with the academic context.

Most analyses of research with Indigenous populations focus on observations, analyses, and recommendations targeting academic research and researchers more so than focusing on AIAN communities. As an Indigenous research psychologist, I close this section with a few additional words for AIAN communities who are considering entry into participatory research with academic partners. The frame for these suggestions and recommendations is the shift beyond a deontic ethics to a relational ethics (as already discussed). First, I suggest that AIAN communities should partner with researchers based on researcher reputation, experience, and understanding of community priorities. Partnerships with new or unknown researchers should unfold carefully to afford community appraisal of researcher attitudes, values, and commitments in relational fashion. Second, I suggest that AIAN community partners should make clear their expectations of researchers early on to ensure researcher awareness of tribal plans for much greater involvement in research oversight. Indeed, mention of tribal RRBs rather than "tribal IRBs" may help to prevent researcher misimpressions that AIAN communities are only concerned with protecting human subjects in a narrow sense. Third, I suggest that AIAN community partners should recognize and respect the need for intellectual integrity in research publications by engaging in relational fashion to negotiate creative ways to address any community concerns about research findings. Usually, in good participatory fashion, communities and researchers can settle on consensual resolution of such concerns in research reporting. Finally, I suggest that AIAN community partners should interact with researchers not primarily through by-the-book procedures or contractual adherence but rather through open-minded, individually tailored acts of interactive problem-solving and mutual goodwill. Indeed, within a participatory approach, it is the relationships rather than the rules, the interpersonal dynamics rather than the rote procedures, that matter most for success (in fact, an obsession with bureaucracy may be a salient vestige of the colonial legacy in our communities).

METHODOLOGY AND METHOD IN INDIGENOUS RESEARCH

As I have already conveyed, psychology research with AIAN communities requires an alternative (or alter-Native) disposition and orientation if it is to prevent harm, promote reconciliation, and provide benefit in the wake of long histories of colonial subjugation. That is, for psychological inquiry to proceed in anticolonial fashion with Indigenous community partners, commitments to relationality and repair are fundamental. Thus far, I have considered legacies of misuse and abuse by researchers, an expansive shift in ethical frames, and the importance of participatory engagement in future AIAN research partnerships. These are

principally concerned with attitude, approach, and interaction in research activities, but what are the implications of these commitments for the adoption of specific methodologies (i.e., rationales or logics of inquiry) and methods (i.e., systematic procedures for analyzing "data") in psychological inquiry? Guba and Lincoln (1994) elaborated on the distinctions between *methodology* and *method*, in which the former arise from paradigmatic commitments by researchers to certain ontological (i.e., concerning the nature of reality) and epistemological (i.e., concerning the nature of knowledge) tenets, while the latter entail systematic procedures of reducing and transforming observations into findings. Importantly, such procedures can be adopted or incorporated across a variety of methodological paradigms (e.g., positivism, constructivism). The diversity and pluralism of knowledge production in psychology with respect to these distinctions is already evident across the various sections of this handbook. For my purposes, I will consider important trends in Indigenous research with respect to methodology and method, all of which emerge from an awareness of and sensitivity to the postcolonial politics of knowledge production.

Decolonizing Methodologies

Academic knowledge production entails the exercise of expertise and authority that is premised on access to resources and status (i.e., "loot and clout"; Ryan, 1976). Scholars with tenure in research universities occupy coveted positions of privilege and autonomy. By virtue of our standing, such researchers can disproportionately influence others through our ideas, analyses, and findings. In short, we exercise power in society. But many voices, visions, and viewpoints are not well represented in academic research, including those of AIAN people. For these reasons, knowledge production is inherently political: Research entails the asymmetrical exercise of power by privileged constituencies who hold differing—even conflicting—perspectives about issues of concern to marginalized others, including Indigenous communities. Past colonial subjugation deliberately sought the eradication and displacement of

Indigenous knowledges as uncivilized or savage, so AIAN communities today are deeply committed to the preservation and protection of remnant traditional knowledges and see value in these for charting self-determined, postcolonial futures. Beyond the political act of reclaiming Indigenous knowledge traditions proper, AIAN communities also seek to adopt (and adapt) modern knowledge practices in their own ways and on their own terms to meet pressing needs. It is for these purposes that knowledge and inquiry in psychology seems most relevant for AIAN lives, especially in practical domains such as education, health, leadership, and governance. Individual tribal members and distinct tribal communities must determine for themselves whether and how research activities and analyses pertain to their immediate situations, yielding interesting possibilities for agentic adoption, selective adaptation, or sweeping rejection of research.

A seminal contribution pertaining to these issues was the 1999 publication of *Decolonizing Methodologies* by the Maori scholar Linda Tuhiwai Smith. Writing about social research and Indigenous peoples in her homeland of Aotearoa (New Zealand), Smith (2012) synthesized and summarized global trends in research about Indigenous populations in critical fashion with an eye toward decolonizing such research. Importantly, she observed:

> Decolonization, however, does not mean and has not meant a total rejection of all theory or research or Western knowledge. Rather, it is about centering our concerns and worldviews and then coming to know and understand theory and research from our own perspectives and for our own purposes. (p. 41)

Thus, Smith (2012) provided a sensitive, nuanced, and elegant argument for wresting authority and control over Indigenous research away from autonomous (and unaccountable) academic researchers and instead for recentering such research predominantly within the realm of Indigenous self-determination. Using a metaphor of ocean tides, Smith depicted an Indigenous research agenda that includes explicit reference to psychological issues in three interrelated process domains: decolonization, transformation, and healing (p. 121). With respect to methodology in psychology proper, Wendt and Gone (2012) identified four features of qualitative inquiry that might advance decolonization in AIAN community research. Specifically, they observed that qualitative research could contextualize AIAN experiences within the colonial legacy, center AIAN cultural commitments, privilege insider (i.e., emic) AIAN perspectives, and preserve AIAN voice in psychology research.

Since then, attention to decolonization—as a self-conscious commitment to undo the legacies of colonization as these continue to structure modern life—has begun to circulate more widely in psychology (Bhatia, 2017; Goodman & Gorski, 2014), including in special issues of psychology journals (Adams et al., 2015; Barnes & Siswana, 2018; Carolissen & Duckett, 2018; Seedat & Suffla, 2017). Concurrently, some Indigenous scholars have contested the adoption of this term for "metaphorical" purposes (Tuck & Yang, 2012), in which *decolonization* is applied to broad antioppression or emancipatory projects (as in "decolonizing research," "decolonizing methodologies," "decolonizing psychology") rather than to formal restoration of Indigenous relationships to land (including a literal return of dispossessed lands to Indigenous control). In a recent special issue of the *Journal of Counseling Psychology* dedicated to research methods, I proposed that decolonization was best conceived as an approach to research that "is methodological without being a methodology" (Gone, 2021, p. 260). I adopted this approach to recover a specific domain of colonized knowledge, namely, traditional American Indian therapeutic expertise. By recounting the healing career of the 19th-century medicine man Bull Lodge among my own *Aaniiih* people and explicating the implicit therapeutic rationale that structured his doctoring practices, I grounded this tradition in longstanding tribal conceptions of land (and relationships to land). I then traced the significance of these conceptions and relationships for method, power, and process in the decolonial reclamation of AIAN therapeutic traditions prior to charting the general implications of a decolonization agenda for advancing social justice through knowledge, practice, and training in professional psychology.

Indigenous Knowledge Traditions

Indigenous psychology (in contrast to local or ethnopsychologies that are "indigenous" to all human communities) emerges at the confluence of psychology and Indigenous peoples. There are at least four domains circumscribed by this concept: (a) descriptive formulations of mind, mentality, and behavior in particular Indigenous communities (i.e., cultural psychologies of Indigenous peoples; see Gone, 2019b); (b) illuminating explanations of Indigenous life that privilege these formulations (e.g., "loneliness" as the Salish Flathead idiom for clinical depression; O'Neill, 1998); (c) creative application of these formulations in local programs, interventions, and services (e.g., ceremonial practices as treatment for addiction; Gone & Calf Looking, 2011, 2015); and (d) novel contributions to psychological knowledge based on Indigenous "ways of knowing" (Deloria et al., 2018). Each domain entails the apprehension, elucidation, and/or application of Indigenous knowledges, but the latter domain is perhaps most directly tied to methodologies and methods in AIAN community research. Indigenous knowledges refer to the diverse knowledge preferences and practices of Indigenous peoples, whether modern or traditional, but even modern Indigenous knowledges typically trace some continuity with the Indigenous past. By way of brief background, Indigenous knowledge traditions (IKTs) can be characterized with respect to at least four attributes: (a) IKTs are usually described as originating prior to European contact and colonization; (b) IKTs were altered, disrupted, suppressed, and sometimes even eradicated during European colonization; (c) despite such historical adversity, some features and forms of IKTs persist in AIAN communities today; and (d) such modern expressions of IKTs reflect these long histories of contact, subjugation,

and exchange (for additional explication, see Gone, 2019a).

Castellano (2000) identified three sources and five characteristics of ITKs. Sources of ITKs include: (a) *traditional teachings* that are reproduced across generations in Indigenous communities, such as various myths and tales (as illustrated in Gone, 2019b) and technological know-how (e.g., tepee construction, hide tanning); (b) *empirical knowledge* that accumulated across experiences and over time through careful observation (e.g., migration patterns of animal relatives); and (c) *revealed knowledge* of a sacred or mystical quality that is spiritually obtained through dreams and visions (e.g., Black Elk's grand vision, as discussed in Gone, 2016). For purposes of psychological inquiry with AIAN communities, the sources of principal interest would be relevant empirical knowledge and traditional teachings (especially as these address familiar psychological domains such as cognition, motivation, development, identity, maladaptation, and behavior change), but usually not revealed knowledge owing to its spiritual or religious character. Castellano also described the following five attributes of IKTs: (a) *personal*—tied to the integrity and perceptiveness of the knower rather than to the general and abstract claims of unknown others; (b) *oral*—communicated in-person (within the broader context of interpersonal responsibility for transfers of sacred power) as opposed to written or recorded for sharing with unknown others; (c) *experiential*—subjectively felt, richly interpreted, and implicitly self-referential as opposed to abstracted and removed from lived experience; (d) *holistic*—comprehended in integrative fashion across all domains of the self (physical, intellectual, emotional, and spiritual) as opposed to merely rationally considered; and (e) *narratively conveyed*—shared through stories (in keeping with diverse genres employing oblique instruction) as opposed to delineating abstract principles and propositions (or rendering admonitions and judgments).

Vine Deloria, Jr. (2001) explained that "the key to understanding Indian knowledge of the world is to remember that the emphasis was on the particular, not on general laws and explanations of how things worked" (p. 22). This observation captures the divergences that can appear between remnant IKTs and dominant scientific knowledge practices in psychology. Notable characteristics of the former are that salient knowledge preferences and practices are: personal and particular rather than abstract and general; holistically experienced across rational, emotional, and intuitive registers; valued for their subjective, introspective, and self-relevant qualities; evaluated with respect to the authority, influence, and reputation of the knower; and disseminated within a context of relationships and responsibilities. In contrast, notable characteristics of the latter are that salient knowledge preferences and practices in psychology are: probabilistic, abstract, and general (i.e., nomothetic) rather than deterministic, concrete, and particular (i.e., idiographic); rationally assessed in skeptical fashion; valued for their "objective" (i.e., distanced and unbiased) qualities; evaluated with respect to their reliance on rigorous and robust research designs and subsequent replication of findings; and disseminated through publication as journal articles following anonymous interrogation and critique by peers. Despite the reductive hazards of drawing sharp contrasts (e.g., IKTs are themselves integrative of other knowledge traditions, disciplinary psychology has been marked by methodological pluralism since its inception), such divergences in knowledge characteristics present certain philosophical, methodological, and practical challenges to psychology research in AIAN communities. And yet, in the past 2 decades, Indigenous scholars—mostly outside of psychology—have sought to harness IKTs for their methodological potential to contribute to academic knowledge production.

Indigenous Research Methodologies

Smith (2012) initially set forth the conceptual and political terms for decolonizing methodologies in Indigenous research. In directly addressing the politics of knowledge, she allowed that appropriate research with Indigenous communities need not exclude "Western" ideas and approaches but rather resituated these within a broad pro-Indigenous ethos or ethic in service to Indigenous self-determination. Subsequent attention to *Indigenous research methodologies* (IRMs) has emerged from Indigenous scholars, primarily in the fields of Indigenous Studies or Indigenous education. Most summary accounts (e.g., Windchief & San Pedro, 2019) trace the origins of IRMs to Smith, as elaborated by the Canadian Cree scholar Shawn Wilson and the Canadian Cree/Saulteaux scholar Margaret Kovach. In *Research Is Ceremony*, Wilson (2008) considered the distinctive conceptual foundations of Indigenous research, explaining that the shared and defining quality of Indigenous ontology and epistemology is *relationality* (which, he noted, constitutes reality) and that the shared and defining quality of Indigenous axiology and methodology is *accountability to relationships*. He outlined the practical implications on relationality and accountability for inquiry as sequentially determining the selection of what to study (i.e., topic), how to gather information (i.e., methods), how to interpret information (i.e., analysis), and how to transfer knowledge (i.e., presentation). He concluded that research is ceremonial in the sense that "the purpose of any ceremony is to build stronger relationships or bridge the distance between aspects of our cosmos and ourselves . . . that allows us a raised level of consciousness and insight into our world" (p. 11). Wilson modeled such relationality in his book through copious incorporation of conversations, dialogues, and exchanges with others in presenting these ideas.

Defining IRMs as "the theory and method of conducting research that flows from an Indigenous epistemology" (p. 20), Kovach (2009) noted the resemblance and overlap between IRMs and various qualitative methodologies even while asserting that "there is a need for methodologies that are inherently and wholly Indigenous" (p. 13) and that such "Indigenous approaches to seeking knowledge are not of a Western worldview" (p. 21). She reinforced many of the same ideas discussed by Smith (2012) and Wilson (2008), such as the importance of relationality, the adoption of a decolonizing lens, and the resituating of research within Indigenous community priorities and interests. Beyond this, Kovach also delineated a Plains Cree epistemology based on the pre-reserve traditional practice of bison hunting. Kovach's signature contribution, however, was her emphasis on narrative as an IRM (i.e., on "story as both method and meaning" [p. 94]). Specifically, Kovach described storytelling as the primary Indigenous modality for disseminating knowledge. Although narrative features prominently in all human societies, she observed that Indigenous stories stand out for their anchoring to particular places rather than their orientation to linear time (cf. Gone, 2008). Moreover, according to Kovach, Indigenous storytelling preserves a holistic relationality that ties speaker and listener within immediate and unfolding context, presenting problems for researchers when transferring these accounts from oral to literate form. Finally, for Kovach, Indigenous storytelling enacts and contributes to collective memory. Each of these attributes renders storytelling as a preferred means for undertaking Indigenous research that requires an "understanding [of] their form, purpose, and substance from a tribal perspective" so as not to "miss the point, possibly causing harm" (p. 97).

More recently, Drawson et al. (2017) conducted a systematic review of IRMs and identified 64 peer-reviewed journal articles from 11 bibliographic databases that they organized into five themes: general Indigenous frameworks, Western methods in an Indigenous context, community-based participatory research, storytelling, and culture-specific methods. They noted that the term *method* was used somewhat ambiguously across this literature to refer both to framework and procedure, with the former giving rise to the first thematic category. Beyond this, the authors classified photovoice, autoethnography, mixed methods, and Kovach's (2009) conversational method as those most familiar within a "Western" context, and catalogued a variety of culture-specific methods that emerged from or were tied to specific Indigenous communities (e.g., offering tobacco ties or participating in talking circles). From this latter category, one method that has circulated widely

is *Two-Eyed Seeing*, which entails "learning to see from one eye with the strengths of Indigenous knowledges and ways of knowing, and from the other eye with the strengths of Western knowledges and ways of knowing, and to using both these eyes together" (Bartlett et al., 2012, p. 335). For example, Hutt-McLeod and colleagues (2019) adopted a Two-Eyed Seeing approach in First Nations youth mental health, thereby offering youth "the choice between standard Western mental health services, or Indigenous methods of improving well-being, or a combination of the two" (p. 42). Drawson and colleagues concluded that "research done in collaboration with Indigenous Peoples cannot only reveal knowledge, but also decolonize, rebalance power, and provide healing" (p. 12). IRMs are, thus, conceived as an eclectic variety of methodological frameworks and procedures—all inspired by, originating in, or connected to Indigenous communities—that remain closely associated with existing critical, qualitative, and contextual inquiry in the behavioral sciences. What differentiates these, however, is their adoption, deployment, and promotion in accordance with a relentlessly relational ethos that is heralded as emancipatory for AIAN communities.

Promotion of IRMs is still relatively new and has thus far rarely appeared in psychology. A March 2021 search for "Indigenous methodologies" in PsycInfo returned 122 journal articles. Most of these did not appear in psychology journals and did not substantively address or incorporate IRMs per se. In the context of mental health, Lucero (2011) deconstructed scientific methodologies to advocate for AIAN therapeutic traditions as evidence-based practices in decolonizing fashion. Drawing on Smith (2012), she advocated for adoption of qualitative methods and narrative forms of data collection for outcome assessment in AIAN health organizations. Three other articles appeared in community psychology journals. Chung-Do and colleagues (2019) described a Native Hawaiian community–academic partnership that committed to participatory approaches and IRMs (but they did not discuss procedures associated with data collection or analysis).

Furness and colleagues (2016) described a similar partnership in a Maori setting and noted that a non-Maori researcher undertook interviews about adult literacy education in a conversational style with attention to the discursive and reflexive aspects of data collection. Gone (2017) discussed the ethics and dynamics of discussions of AIAN sacred knowledge in IRMs. Finally, only three articles appeared in any of the 90 psychology journals published by the APA. Dennis (2016) adopted Kovach's (2009) conversational method to interview Lakota elders about their traumatic experiences (she analyzed these interviews using familiar thematic analysis). Hill and colleagues (2010) sought to decolonize personality assessment by undertaking a "quantitative-qualitative-Indigenous" mixed methods study, in which their "quantitative results guided the qualitative approach," as "heavily informed and directed by Indigenous methodologies which privilege the perspective of the colonized" (p. 17). Lopez (2021) adopted an "Indigenous quantitative methodology"—the embedding of psychometric analysis within a pro-Indigenous ethic—to assess the construct validity of a new scale based on responses from members of the Quechan and Cocopah Tribal Nations.

In sum, IRMs are holistic and relational, situated and contextualized, practical and relevant, responsible and accountable, anchored in lived experience, dependent on personal narratives, and expressive of Indigenous language and worldview. In application they may sometimes seem indistinguishable from data collection and analysis elsewhere in the qualitative social sciences, but they may also feature adaptations and augmentations that enhance or underscore relationships between researchers and respondents (and relevant others) and between content and context. Elsewhere, I have reviewed several misgivings about the ways in which IRMs are sometimes promoted (including occasional engagement in untenable ethnoracial and cultural essentialism, insulation of Indigenous research from critical scrutiny, emphasis on aesthetic forms more than substantive findings, or obscuring intellectual debts to "Western" critical theories

and approaches; Gone, 2019a). Nevertheless, it would be reckless to overlook the potential for IRMs to contribute to an expansive knowledge in psychology. IRMs seem readily compatible with (some forms of) qualitative inquiry (when these methods are deployed in pro-Indigenous fashion) and appear to "stand in" for practices associated with "primary orality" (Ong, 2012). Indeed, much of what has been claimed about IKTs and IRMs is recognizable from Ong's (1986) systematic comparisons of orality and literacy, in which "primary oral culture"

> keeps its thinking close to the human life world, personalizing things and issues, and storing knowledge in stories. Categories are unstable mnemonically. Stories you can remember. In its typical mindset, the oral sensibility is out to hold things together, to make and retain agglomerates, not to analyze (which means to take things apart). (p. 25)

In consequence, IRMs invite Indigenous scholars and other researchers to forge a new methodological synthesis that might bridge oral tradition and academic knowledge production even as it elucidates connections between parts and wholes that may afford more integrative perspectives on important psychological domains in AIAN communities.

CLOSING

Indigenous communities in the United States have improbably survived centuries of European colonization. Persisting within a settler nation–state, contemporary AIANs endeavor to chart robust futures in the context of ongoing poverty, marginality, and discrimination. AIAN communities frequently express marked ambivalence (or outright anger) toward psychosocial research, recognizing that past research has been irrelevant, insensitive, or even exploitative. And yet, Indigenous survivance stands to benefit from appropriate research across multiple psychological domains, including the design of strengths-based community prevention programs, the tracing of psychosocial impacts from the legacy of colonization, the amelioration of postcolonial pathologies and mental health problems, the formation of resurgent cultural identities in the context of societal racism and discrimination, and so on. In this chapter, I reviewed the history of AIAN communities and psychosocial research, the promise of a relational research ethics to provide greater benefit for these communities, the politics of Indigenous knowledge in the context of postcolonial surviv-ance, and the methodological innovations that might arise through a synthesis of modern academic and Indigenous traditional approaches to knowing and knowledge production. In so doing, I aimed to promote academic-community partnerships that will empower AIAN communities as they vigorously exercise sovereignty in service to relentlessly self-determined futures.

References

Adams, G., Dobles, I., Gómez, L. H., Kurtiş, T., & Molina, L. E. (2015). Decolonizing psychological science: Introduction to the special thematic section. *Journal of Social and Political Psychology*, *3*(1), 213–238. https://doi.org/10.5964/jspp.v3i1.564

American Indian Law Center. (1999). *Model tribal research code, with materials for tribal regulation for research and checklist for Indian health boards* (3rd ed.). American Indian Law Center.

American Psychological Association. (2017). Ethical principles of psychologists and code of conduct (2002, amended effective June 1, 2010, and January 1, 2017). https://www.apa.org/ethics/code/

Americans for Indian Opportunity. (n.d.). *4-R's core cultural values*. https://aio.org/about-the-aio-ambassadors-program/4-rs-core-cultural-values/

Appiah, K. A. (2020, May 28). The defender of differ-ences: On Franz Boas and his critics. *The New York Review of Books*. https://www.nybooks.com/articles/2020/05/28/franz-boas-anthropologist-defender-differences/

Barnes, B., & Siswana, A. (2018). Psychology and decolonisation: Introduction to the special issue. *South African Journal of Psychology. Suid-Afrikaanse Tydskrif vir Sielkunde*, *48*(3), 297–298. https://doi.org/10.1177/0081246318798735

Bartlett, C., Marshall, M., & Marshall, A. (2012). Two-Eyed Seeing and other lessons learned within a co-learning journey of bringing together Indigenous and mainstream knowledges and ways of knowing.

Journal of Environmental Studies and Sciences, *2*(4), 331–340. https://doi.org/10.1007/s13412-012-0086-8

Battiste, M. (2007). Research ethics for protecting Indigenous knowledge and heritage. In N. K. Denzin & M. D. Giardina (Eds.), *Ethical futures in qualitative research: Decolonizing the politics of knowledge* (pp. 111–132). Routledge.

Bhatia, S. (2017). *Decolonizing psychology: Global-ization, social justice, and Indian youth identities*. Oxford University Press. https://doi.org/10.1093/oso/9780199964727.001.0001

Biolsi, T., & Zimmerman, L. J. (Eds.). (1997). *Indians and anthropologists: Vine Deloria, Jr., and the critique of anthropology*. University of Arizona Press.

Brown, L. D., & Tandon, R. (1983). Ideology and political economy in inquiry: Action research and participatory research. *The Journal of Applied Behavioral Science*, *19*(3), 277–294. https://doi.org/10.1177/002188638301900306

Brydon-Miller, M. (1997). Participatory action research: Psychology and social change. *Journal of Social Issues*, *53*(4), 657–666. https://doi.org/10.1111/j.1540-4560.1997.tb02454.x

Canadian Institutes for Health Research. (2007). *Guidelines for health research involving Aboriginal people*. https://cihr-irsc.gc.ca/e/29134.html

Canadian Institutes for Health Research, Natural Sciences and Engineering Research Council of Canada, and Social Sciences and Humanities Research Council of Canada. (2014). *Tri-council policy statement: Ethical conduct for research involving humans*. https://ethics.gc.ca/eng/policy-politique_tcps2-eptc2_2018.html

Carolissen, R. L., & Duckett, P. S. (2018). Teaching toward decoloniality in community psychology and allied disciplines: Editorial introduction. *American Journal of Community Psychology*, *62*(3–4), 241–249. https://doi.org/10.1002/ajcp.12297

Castellano, M. B. (2000). Updating Aboriginal traditions of knowledge. In G. J. Sefa Dei, B. L. Hall, & D. G. Rosenberg (Eds.), *Indigenous knowledges in global contexts: Multiple readings of our world* (pp. 21–36). University of Toronto Press.

Chevalier, J. M., & Buckles, D. J. (2019). *Participatory action research: Theory and methods for engaged inquiry* (2nd ed.). Routledge. https://doi.org/10.4324/9781351033268

Chung-Do, J. J., Ho-Lastimosa, I., Keaulana, S., Ho, K., Jr., Hwang, P. W., Radovich, T., Albinio, L., Rogerson, I., Keli'iholokai, L., Deitschman, K., & Spencer, M. S. (2019). Waimanalo Pono Research Hui: A community–academic partnership to pro-mote Native Hawaiian wellness through culturally grounded and community-driven research and programming. *American Journal of Community Psychology*, *64*(1–2), 107–117. https://doi.org/10.1002/ajcp.12355

Darou, W. G., Hum, A., & Kurtness, J. (1993). An investigation of the impact of psychosocial research on a Native population. *Professional Psychology, Research and Practice*, *24*(3), 325–329. https://doi.org/10.1037/0735-7028.24.3.325

Deloria, P. J., Lomawaima, K. T., Brayboy, B. M. J., Trahant, M. N., Ghiglione, L., Medin, D., & Blackhawk, N. (2018). Unfolding futures: Indigenous ways of knowing for the twenty-first century. *Daedalus*, *147*(2), 6–16. https://doi.org/10.1162/DAED_a_00485

Deloria, V., Jr. (1980). Our new research society: Some warnings for social scientists. *Social Problems*, *27*(3), 265–271. https://doi.org/10.2307/800245

Deloria, V., Jr. (2001). Power and place equal personality. In V. Deloria, Jr. & D. R. Wildcat (Eds.), *Power and place: Indian education in America* (pp. 21–28). American Indian Graduate Center/Fulcrum Resources.

Dennis, M. K. (2016). "I guess we survived": Insights into traumatic experiences of Lakota elders. *Traumatology*, *22*(1), 9–18. https://doi.org/10.1037/trm0000054

Drawson, A. S., Toombs, E., & Mushquash, C. J. (2017). Indigenous research methods: A systematic review. *International Indigenous Policy Journal*, *8*(2). https://doi.org/10.18584/iipj.2017.8.2.5

Fisher, C. B. (1999). Relational ethics and research with vulnerable populations. In National Bioethics Advisory Commission (Ed.), *Research involving persons with mental disorders that may affect decision making capacity* (Vol. II, pp. 29–49). National Bioethics Advisory Commission. https://govinfo.library.unt.edu/nbac/capacity/volumeii.pdf

Fisher, P. A., & Ball, T. J. (2003). Tribal participatory research: Mechanisms of a collaborative model. *American Journal of Community Psychology*, *32*(3–4), 207–216. https://doi.org/10.1023/B:AJCP.0000004742.39858.c5

Freeman, W. L., Romero, F. C., & Kanade, S. (2006). Community consultation to assess and minimize group harms. In E. A. Bankert & R. J. Amdur (Eds.), *Institutional review board: Management and function* (2nd ed., pp. 134–139). Jones & Bartlett.

Furness, J., Nikora, L. W., Hodgetts, D., & Robertson, N. (2016). Beyond ethics to morality: Choices and relationships in bicultural research settings. *Journal of Community & Applied Social Psychology*, *26*(1), 75–88. https://doi.org/10.1002/casp.2239

García, M. A., & Tehee, M. (Eds.). (2014). *Society of Indian Psychologists commentary on the American Psychological Association's (APA) Ethical Principles of Psychologists and Code of Conduct*. Society of Indian Psychologists.

Gilligan, C. (1982). *In a different voice*. Harvard University Press.

Gone, J. P. (2008). "So I can be like a Whiteman": The cultural psychology of space and place in American Indian mental health. *Culture and Psychology*, *14*(3), 369–399. https://doi.org/10.1177/1354067X08092639

Gone, J. P. (2016). Alternative knowledges and the future of community psychology: Provocations from an American Indian healing tradition. *American Journal of Community Psychology*, *58*(3–4), 314–321. https://doi.org/10.1002/ajcp.12046

Gone, J. P. (2017). "It felt like violence": Indigenous knowledge traditions and the postcolonial ethics of academic inquiry and community engagement. *American Journal of Community Psychology*, *60*(3–4), 353–360. https://doi.org/10.1002/ajcp.12183

Gone, J. P. (2019a). Considering Indigenous research methodologies: Critical reflections by an Indigenous knower. *Qualitative Inquiry*, *25*(1), 45–56. https://doi.org/10.1177/1077800418787545

Gone, J. P. (2019b). "The thing happened as he wished": Recovering an American Indian cultural psychology. *American Journal of Community Psychology*, *64*(1–2), 172–184. https://doi.org/10.1002/ajcp.12353

Gone, J. P. (2021). Decolonization as methodological innovation in counseling psychology: Method, power, and process in reclaiming American Indian therapeutic traditions. *Journal of Counseling Psychology*, *68*(3), 259–270. https://doi.org/10.1037/cou0000500

Gone, J. P., & Calf Looking, P. E. (2011). American Indian culture as substance abuse treatment: Pursuing evidence for a local intervention. *Journal of Psychoactive Drugs*, *43*(4), 291–296. https://doi.org/10.1080/02791072.2011.628915

Gone, J. P., & Calf Looking, P. E. (2015). The Blackfeet Indian culture camp: Auditioning an alternative indigenous treatment for substance use disorders. *Psychological Services*, *12*(2), 83–91. https://doi.org/10.1037/ser0000013

Gone, J. P., & Trimble, J. E. (2012). American Indian and Alaska Native mental health: Diverse perspectives on enduring disparities. *Annual Review of Clinical Psychology*, *8*(1), 131–160. https://doi.org/10.1146/annurev-clinpsy-032511-143127

Good, M.-J. D., Hyde, S. T., Pinto, S., & Good, B. J. (Eds.). (2008). *Postcolonial disorders*. University of California Press.

Goodman, R. D., & Gorski, P. C. (Eds.). (2014). *Decolonizing "multicultural" counseling through social justice*. Springer.

Guba, E. G., & Lincoln, Y. S. (1994). Competing paradigms in qualitative research. In N. K. Denzin & Y. S. Lincoln (Eds.), *Handbook of qualitative research* (pp. 105–117). SAGE.

Hartmann, W. E., Wendt, D. C., Burrage, R. L., Pomerville, A., & Gone, J. P. (2019). American Indian historical trauma: Anticolonial prescriptions for healing, resilience, and survivance. *American Psychologist, 74*(1), 6–19. https://doi.org/10.1037/amp0000326

Hill, J. S., Pace, T. M., & Robbins, R. R. (2010). Decolonizing personality assessment and honoring indigenous voices: A critical examination of the MMPI-2. *Cultural Diversity & Ethnic Minority Psychology, 16*(1), 16–25. https://doi.org/10.1037/a0016110

Hodge, F. S. (2012). No meaningful apology for American Indian unethical research abuses. *Ethics & Behavior, 22*(6), 431–444. https://doi.org/10.1080/10508422.2012.730788

Hutt-MacLeod, D., Rudderham, H., Sylliboy, A., Sylliboy-Denny, M., Liebenberg, L., Denny, J. F., Gould, M. R., Gould, N., Nossal, M., Iyer, S. N., Malla, A., & Boksa, P. (2019). Eskasoni First Nation's transformation of youth mental healthcare: Partnership between a Mi'kmaq community and the ACCESS Open Minds research project in implementing innovative practice and service evaluation. *Early Intervention in Psychiatry, 13*(Suppl. 1), 42–47. https://doi.org/10.1111/eip.12817

Israel, B. A., Eng, E., Schulz, A. J., & Parker, E. A. (2013). Introduction to methods for CBPR for health. In B. A. Israel, E. Eng, A. J. Schulz, & E. A. Parker (Eds.), *Methods for community-based participatory research for health* (2nd ed., pp. 3–37). Jossey-Bass.

Kelly, J. G. (1987). Some reflections on the Swampscott conference. *American Journal of Community Psychology, 15*(5), 515–517. https://doi.org/10.1007/BF00929904

Kidd, S., Davidson, L., Frederick, T., & Kral, M. J. (2018). Reflecting on participatory, action-oriented research methods in community psychology: Progress, problems, and paths forward. *American Journal of Community Psychology, 61*(1–2), 76–87. https://doi.org/10.1002/ajcp.12214

Kidd, S. A., & Kral, M. J. (2005). Practicing participatory action research. *Journal of Counseling Psychology, 52*(2), 187–195. https://doi.org/10.1037/0022-0167.52.2.187

Klausner, S., & Foulks, E. (1979). *Alcohol and the future of Ukpeagvik.* Center for Research on the Acts of Man.

Kloos, B., Hill, J., Thomas, E., Case, A. D., Scott, V. C., & Wandersman, A. (2021). *Community psychology: Linking individuals and communities* (4th ed.). American Psychological Association.

Kohlberg, L. (1984). *Essays on moral development* (Vol. 2). Harper & Row.

Kovach, M. (2009). *Indigenous methodologies: Characteristics, conversations, and contexts.* University of Toronto Press.

Lanzarotta, T. (2020). Ethics in retrospect: Biomedical research, colonial violence, and Iñupiat sovereignty in the Alaskan Arctic. *Social Studies of Science, 50*(5), 778–801. https://doi.org/10.1177/0306312720943678

Lopez, J. D. (2021). Examining construct validity of the scale of Native Americans giving back. *Journal of Diversity in Higher Education. 14*(4), 519–529. https://doi.org/10.1037/dhe0000181

Lucero, E. (2011). From tradition to evidence: Decolonization of the evidence-based practice system. *Journal of Psychoactive Drugs, 43*(4), 319–324. https://doi.org/10.1080/02791072.2011.628925

Mello, M. M., & Wolf, L. E. (2010). The Havasupai Indian tribe case—Lessons for research involving stored biologic samples. *The New England Journal of Medicine, 363*(3), 204–207. https://doi.org/10.1056/NEJMp1005203

Mihesuah, D. A. (1993). Suggested guidelines for institutions with scholars who conduct research on American Indians. *American Indian Culture and Research Journal, 17*(3), 131–139. https://doi.org/10.17953/aicr.17.3.630943325746p3x4

Mosby, I. (2013). Administering colonial science: Nutrition research and human biomedical experimentation in Aboriginal communities and residential schools, 1942–1952. *Histoire Sociale, 46*(91), 145–172. https://doi.org/10.1353/his.2013.0015

National Commission for the Protection of Human Subjects of Biomedical and Behavioral Research. (1979). *The Belmont report: Ethical principles and guidelines for the protection of human subjects of research.* Department of Health Education and Welfare. https://www.hhs.gov/ohrp/regulations-and-policy/belmont-report/read-the-belmont-report/index.html

NCAI. (2009). *Research that benefits Native people: A guide for tribal leaders.* NCAI Policy Research Center. https://www.ncai.org/policy-research-center/research-data/NCAIModule1.pdf

NCAI Policy Research Center, & MSU Center for Native Health Partnerships. (2012). *"Walk softly and listen carefully": Building research relationships with tribal communities.* NCAI Policy Research Center & MSU Center for Native Health Partnerships. https://www.ncai.org/resources/ncai_publications/walk-softly-and-listen-carefully-building-research-relationships-with-tribal-communities

O'Nell, T. D. (1998). *Disciplined hearts: History, identity, and depression in an American Indian community.* University of California Press.

Ong, W. J. (1986). Writing is a technology that restructures thought. In G. Bauman (Ed.), *The written word: Literacy in translation* (pp. 23–50). Clarendon Press.

Ong, W. J. (2012). *Orality and literacy: The technologizing of the word* (30th anniversary ed.). Routledge. (Original work published 1982)

Pevar, S. L. (2012). *The rights of Indians and tribes* (4th ed.). Oxford University Press.

Ryan, W. (1976). *Blaming the victim* (Revised ed.). Vintage.

Sahota, P. C. (2009a). *Research regulation in American Indian/Alaska Native communities: A guide to reviewing research studies.* NCAI Policy Research Center. https://www.ncai.org/policy-research-center/initiatives/research-regulation

Sahota, P. C. (2009b). *Research regulation in American Indian/Alaska Native communities: Policy and practice considerations.* NCAI Policy Research Center. https://www.ncai.org/policy-research-center/initiatives/Research_Regulation_in_AI_AN_Communities_-_Policy_and_Practice.pdf

Sahota, P. C. (2010). *Community-based participatory research in American Indian and Alaska Native communities.* NCAI Policy Research Center. https://www.academia.edu/download/31187422/CBPR_Paper_FINAL.pdf

Saunkeah, B., Beans, J. A., Peercy, M. T., Hiratsuka, V. Y., & Spicer, P. (2021). Extending research protections to tribal communities. *The American Journal of Bioethics, 21*(10), 5–12. https://doi.org/10.1080/15265161.2020.1865477

Seedat, M., & Suffla, S. (2017). Community psychology and its (dis)contents, archival legacies and decolonisation. *South African Journal of Psychology. Suid-Afrikaanse Tydskrif vir Sielkunde, 47*(4), 421–431. https://doi.org/10.1177/0081246317741423

Smith, L. T. (2012). *Decolonizing methodologies: Research and Indigenous Peoples* (2nd ed.). Zed Books.

Snarch, B. (2004). Ownership, control, access, and possession (OCAP) or self-determination applied to research: A critical analysis of contemporary First Nations research and some options for First Nations communities. *Journal of Aboriginal Health, 1*(1), 80–95.

Starn, O. (2004). *Ishi's brain: In search of America's last "wild" Indian.* W. W. Norton & Co.

Tebes, J. K. (2016). Reflections on the future of community psychology from the generations after

Swampscott: A commentary and introduction to the Special Issue. *American Journal of Community Psychology, 58*(3–4), 229–238. https://doi.org/10.1002/ajcp.12110

Thomas, D. H. (2000). *Skull wars: Kennewick Man, archeology, and the battle for Native American identity.* Basic Books.

Thornton, R. (1987). *American Indian holocaust and survival: A population history since 1492.* University of Oklahoma Press.

Trimble, J. E., & Fisher, C. B. (2006). Our shared journey: Lessons from the past to protect the future. In J. E. Trimble & C. B. Fisher (Eds.), *The handbook of ethical research with ethnocultural populations & communities* (pp. xv–xxix). SAGE. https://doi.org/10.4135/9781412986168

Trimble, J. E., Schárron-del-Rio, M. R., & Bernal, G. (2010). The itinerant researcher: Ethical and methodological issues in conducting cross-cultural mental health research. In D. C. Jack & A. Ali (Eds.), *Silencing the self across cultures: Depression and gender in the social world* (pp. 73–95). Oxford University Press. https://doi.org/10.1093/acprof:oso/9780195398090.003.0004

Tuck, E., & Yang, K. W. (2012). Decolonization is not a metaphor. *Decolonization, 1*(1), 1–40. https://jps.library.utoronto.ca/index.php/des/article/view/18630

Vizenor, G. (1999). *Manifest manners: Narratives on postindian survivance.* University of Nebraska Press.

Walsh, R. T. (1987). A social historical note on the formal emergence of community psychology. *American Journal of Community Psychology, 15*(5), 523–529. https://doi.org/10.1007/BF00929906

Wax, M. L. (1991). The ethics of research in American Indian communities. *American Indian Quarterly, 15*(4), 431–456. https://doi.org/10.2307/1185363

Wendt, D. C. (2010). *The Belmont Report: A philosophical, historical, and cultural contextualization* [Unpublished manuscript].

Wendt, D. C., & Gone, J. P. (2012). Decolonizing psychological inquiry in Native American communities: The promise of qualitative methods. In D. K. Nagata, L. Kohn-Wood, & L. A. Suzuki (Eds.), *Qualitative strategies for ethnocultural research* (pp. 161–178). American Psychological Association. https://doi.org/10.1037/13742-009

Wilson, S. (2008). *Research is ceremony: Indigenous research methods.* Fernwood Publishing.

Windchief, S., & San Pedro, T. (Eds.). (2019). *Applying Indigenous research methods: Storying with peoples and communities.* Routledge. https://doi.org/10.4324/9781315169811

PARTICIPATORY ACTION RESEARCH AS MOVEMENT TOWARD RADICAL RELATIONALITY, EPISTEMIC JUSTICE, AND TRANSFORMATIVE INTERVENTION: A MULTIVOCAL REFLECTION

Urmitapa Dutta, Jesica Siham Fernández, Anne Galletta, and Regina Day Langhout

Critical approaches to research and inquiry are grounded in an ethical responsibility to disrupt the status quo; namely, to understand and address injustice in particular contexts. Critical inquiry involves a number of threshold commitments and intentional actions: to expand the possibility of who can participate in socially sanctioned research; to empirically investigate intersubjective, lived realities that are shaped by complex relationships to history, place, and power, to commit to transformative social and systemic change, bridging the gap between "what is" to "what could or must be." Participatory action research (PAR) is one such approach where the research questions are codetermined by collaborators who might not be trained in conventional research methods. Yet, through their shared experiential knowledge, innovative strategies to wield and leverage power, and persistence toward self and collective determination, thriving, and well-being, they anchor their efforts in desire, imagination, and actions for transformative justice and systemic change. In this chapter, we affirm PAR as a generative paradigm and we engage our embodiment, subjectivity, and shared dialogical reflections, which we offer through featured stories and writings.

INTRODUCING OURSELVES: OUR SCHOLAR ACTIVISM TRAJECTORIES AND PARTICIPATORY ACTION RESEARCH

We begin first by introducing you, the reader, to us, a group of scholar–activists.

Jesica

I, Jesica, am an immigrant, born in México and raised between there and the Central Valley of California to a transmigrant farm working family. As a Chicana, cisgender person, and first-generation college graduate with a PhD, as well as community-engaged researcher, organizer, and teacher–scholar, I am grounded in a decolonial feminist praxis that strives to unsettle my relationship to coloniality as an uninvited occupant living and working in the land that rightfully belongs to the Ohlone and Muwekma Ohlone. Although

https://doi.org/10.1037/0000319-015
APA Handbook of Research Methods in Psychology, Second Edition: Vol. 2. Research Designs: Quantitative, Qualitative, Neuropsychological, and Biological, H. Cooper (Editor-in-Chief)

people often determine my legitimacy as a scholar–writer–thinker by my degrees and institutional affiliation, currently as an assistant professor of ethnic studies at a private Jesuit Institution in one of the most segregated areas in the country, the Silicon Valley, academe defines neither who I am nor the values and principles that guide my praxis. I come from a legacy of matriarchs who pursued and actualized their dreams of migration, education, and self-determination.

My goals and intentions when writing are to share what I know, reflect and connect, and expand, broaden, and nuance my own understandings in order to remain open to the practice of relational critical reflexivity as fundamental to colearning (Fernández, 2018). With regard to writing, and since completing my graduate studies, when I write I keep three audiences or readers in mind. These readers are not listed in any particular order of priority as I see all three as important in shaping my writing. The community partners who I am accountable to, the first audience, are always at the forefront of my writing as it is the community that offers me sources of strength or courage to write. Community partners are the group with whom I am in relationship, and these partners help inform what I am writing. Students are my second audience, specifically, the budding scholars within the disciplines I am engaged, and what it is that I hope for them to understand, or connect with that could contribute to unsettling or critically deepening the discipline. Lastly, my colleagues, mentors, and accompanying comrades who share a critical standpoint, who can offer guidance, resources, and support to help inform my process of unlearning/relearning. Community partners, students, and colleagues-mentors are the three audiences I keep in mind as a way to engage a practice of humility. I am hoping that by sharing what I learn, often through experience and in dialogue with others in the context of PAR, the writings or knowledge discerned can be put to action in emancipatory and humanizing praxes.

Anne

In writing about who I am and what I bring to my teaching and approaches to inquiry and social action, I write autobiographically of the notion of home. For me home was a space of affection, omissions, silences, and much said. It was a ritual of meeting and benefitting from measuring up to white[1] racialized and gendered notions of self and other. Asking questions about social arrangements, if it were possible to think outside the construction of normal as white, middle class, and heteropatriarchal, was viewed as impolite and not what one did. The presumed neutrality of my location in the world precluded understanding of how I embodied race and class privilege. In the segregated Long Island suburbs of my young adulthood, my occasional questioning of whiteness resulted in either awkward silence, impatience with my inability to find words for an unrealized language, or my own or others' flight from the dissonance of seeing the world from another's eyes.

In many ways, my writing about who I am and what I bring to my teaching and research is an unsettling of home and a transgressing of systems of meaning imparting privilege and exclusion within institutions, such as family, school, and the academy. Even as I have moved within and outside of these formative spheres, I continue to feel the imposition of heteropatriarchy and white racialized notions of self and others. I am not detached from these structures of power. Who I am and how I am understood reflect degrees of subjectivity and positionality, and they influence the caution I bring to PAR as I have witnessed the repercussions of my omissions and the ways in which I continue to find myself complicit in forms of structural violence. The persons and groups with whom I collectively engage in critical inquiry and social action reflect and embody disparate histories, languages, identities, and encounters with systems of authority. In university classrooms or high school hallways and cafeterias, libraries, or other public spaces, we construct ways of knowing and being in relation that reflect criticality and curiosity, deep tensions and points of connection, deliberateness and serendipity, and reflection and action.

[1]Our use of lowercase here and elsewhere is intended to decenter the power of whiteness and white supremacy; "white" is lowercased to affirm that whiteness is a power structure as opposed to an ethnic group (see Hurtado, 1996).

Regina (Henceforth, Gina)

I am a white cisgender woman who is mostly able bodied and mostly straight. I grew up working class and am a veteran of the first Gulf War. More of my cousins have gone to jail or prison than to college. I am a first-generation college student who grew up in Modesto, a conservative city in the central valley of California, and one of the least formally educated and most polluted places in the United States. I have been aware of social injustices since I was little. This includes many instances. One early memory is my parents enrolling me in karate when I was in kindergarten because they feared a skinny little white girl with blond hair would be picked on by the Brown youth in the neighborhood. These youth were siblings of my classmates and friends, which I found confusing. A much later memory is of my high school guidance counselor asking me what I wanted to do after high school. I told her I wanted to go to Stanford and become a lawyer. She told me kids like me do not go to Stanford and become lawyers, and I should instead go to Stanislaus State University and become a paralegal. I did not apply to Stanford.

Now, I teach at a public university that is an Hispanic-Serving Research Institution. I engage in PAR, but mostly youth participatory action research (yPAR), out of solidarity, anger, love, hope, and responsibility. I seek to support critical conversations that are already happening, often through opening a space in schools or neighborhoods where there is no institutional support for such critical reflection. I engage in PAR because it is the only way I can be in the academy and because I view PAR as an intervention into university spaces and ways of knowing, while also recognizing that the university gave me the space to work to understand myself and society from a more critical standpoint. I write in an attempt to unlearn "the social lie" (Martín-Baró, 1994)— or hegemonic dominant narratives that normalize dominance and oppression—and to try to grasp a more relational way of being. Accordingly, I position myself as a critical scholar–activist who is comfortable in a critical/transformative ontological paradigm. I am also currently flirting

with critical realism as another appropriate ontological fit. Moreover, I am actively working to understand how a white person whose ancestors were settler colonialists three generations ago, and who now benefits from coloniality, can position myself in relation to decoloniality; I currently prefer the term *anticoloniality* given my social positioning.

Urmitapa (Henceforth, Urmi)

My relationship to research was shaped by my experiences growing up in the Northeastern borderlands of India—by ancestral legacies of displacement and struggle. Research was not part of my vocabulary growing up; it was a distant and amorphous activity carried out by "experts" in mainland India and/or from the Global North. Yet, my lived experiences alerted me to the seemingly irreconcilable gap between our lives and meaning making processes versus how we were theorized and represented in mainstream academic discourse. At the time, I did not know the terms *epistemic violence* or *epistemic justice* (Fricker, 2007), but I had an embodied understanding of the former and a deep aspiration for the latter—manifested as the desire to tell our everyday stories in all their complexities and contradictions. Against the backdrop of these experiences, the notion of PAR, that we—communities who are most impacted by the issues at hand—can be knowledge producers and facilitators of self-determined action was radical and revolutionary! At the same time, PAR felt like stepping into an oddly familiar place.

Over the years, my PAR praxis has grown with my shifting geopolitical locations and political intimacies. An important part of this shift was my racialization as a Brown South Asian woman in the United States, which uncovered complex layers of marginality and complicity in relation to transnational vectors of oppression (e.g., coloniality, settler colonialism, racism, casteism, heteropatriarchy, imperialism). Wading through these messy terrains underscored the need to center Global South people's struggles and resistance as critical forms of antioppressive knowledges. In recent years, these commitments have shaped my solidarity with Miya people in Northeast India as they build communities of resistance against protracted colonial, structural, and epistemic violence; the most recent being the (ongoing) mass disenfranchisement and detention of Miya people. Our collective work is rooted in radical relationality—relationships that are not strategically cultivated around research collaborations/projects that tend to replicate institutional boundaries or binary logic such as researcher–researched or university–community. Rather, we are connected by shared histories, decolonial love, care, desire, and resistance. As part of our work together, we have created the Miya Community Research Collective (www.miyacommunityresearchcollective.org) to build a people's archive that documents state violence and its psychosocial impacts on Miya communities, explores culturally meaningful responses to intergenerational trauma, and uplifts Miya people's aspirations and desires. Notably, Miya community workers have been doing this work long before we formed the research collective, which represents a more concerted effort to build a repository of nonhegemonic knowledge. Consequently, our community research collective is neither housed in nor solely affiliated with Global North universities. In fact, our collective PAR work, while critical, is only one of manifold principled actions to build communities of resistance against transnational webs of persecution and dehumanization.

A MULTIVOCAL/MULTIVOICED APPROACH TO RESEARCH AND WRITING

We engaged in a multivocal/multivoiced process of writing to produce this chapter. *Multivocality* is an approach to writing that is inclusive and characterized by "many voices" that collectively create a whole—piecing together connections of threaded written and spoken dialogues (Einola et al., 2020; Pullen & Rhodes, 2008). Although we are differentially positioned on account of our identities and histories, we engage PAR through our embodied subjectivities. Our chapter is, therefore, a multivocal/multivoiced text informed

by a process of writing that is dialogical, emergent, and reflexive, as well as aligned with the collaborative relational elements of PAR. We began our collaborative process with free-writings, journaling, and sharing vignettes that featured our stories, biographies, and experiences with PAR. Multivocal/multivoiced writing allowed us to highlight both the immutability and the complexities or nuances of our PAR process, specifically the practice and ethics we engage in this work. In this way, we describe PAR often through our own stories, positionalities, and ethics. This process illustrates that with PAR, there is no "one size fits all." PAR praxis is most meaningful when considered in relation to our embeddedness in specific contexts, communities, or struggles.

A multivocal/multivoiced approach is well suited for and reflects the participatory process of PAR. Specifically, no one voice is more valuable than another, and each perspective we offer is grounded in theory and praxis, as well as community struggles, which often reflect our own histories and sociopolitical contexts. We are not implying a hierarchical distinction between local and transnational but instead are emphasizing that liberatory/transformative praxis must be necessarily informed by a critical *translocality*—simultaneously knowing the local and its transcendence (Tsing, 2005). To understand the generative power and potential of PAR, we look at local PAR praxis, where local does not imply small scale or isolation but a form of rootedness—working from a rooted place and connecting to others who are also rooted (Esteva, 2020). The generative potential of PAR emerges through these active dialogues and connections that transgress binaries and hierarchies of scale, reason, knowledge, and humanity. In this way, we are contributing to recent calls in feminist scholarship to approach academic writing as a mode of dialogical "embodied connections," and as a "form of activism and resistance" that refuses the hegemony of academic writing as solitary, disembodied, and positivistic (Gilmore et al., 2019; Mandalaki & Pérezts, 2022; Pullen et al., 2020).

We begin our more formal discussion of PAR with an introduction to how we conceptualize it, anchoring our discussion in the liberatory roots of PAR. We note its collective nature whereby relationships and multiple lived realities are ontologically central to the inquiry. We also note the epistemic aims of PAR to produce knowledge through engagement that unsettles structures of dominance and subjugation, some of which are starkly visible and others deeply masked. We then discuss three areas of focus that capture the dimensions and liberatory roots of PAR. In this way, we conceptualize PAR in terms of fostering, and in forms of working toward, radical relationality, epistemic justice, and intervention, which are linked by a deep and enduring commitment to ethics of justice, care, and resistance. We conclude the chapter by posing a set of questions and pro-vocations for readers as they consider and contend with various facets of PAR, its meaning, theories that undergird PAR, ethical imperatives, and practice.

LIBERATORY ROOTS OF PARTICIPATORY ACTION RESEARCH

PAR is more of a perspective, process, and way of being than a concept that can be easily defined. Yet, there is some commonality across those who engage in PAR. First, PAR researchers participate in a process whereby the group collaboratively decides the issue to be studied and then engages in inquiry about it, decides on an action to take and takes it, and then evaluates if the action made a difference (Fals-Borda, 1985; Rahman, 1993; Vio Grossi, 1981). In this way, PAR is iterative and grounded/embedded in the community where the process is taking place. Second, who the researchers are is broadly defined. A researcher could be someone who is part of the community engaging in PAR, someone outside of that community, and/or someone who is liminally situated, both inside and outside of the community engaging in the process. A PAR researcher might view themselves as someone who accompanies, witnesses, works against hegemony, and/or holds space for plurality.

PAR is, therefore, best understood as an ontoepistemological and ethical approach to inquiry and knowledge production, with deep roots in liberatory and decolonial movements in the majority world (Fals-Borda, 1985; Rahman, 1993; Vio Grossi, 1981). Those engaged in PAR (and allied approaches such as community-based participatory research, participatory development, and action research) trace their work to different lineages (for some examples, see Fine & Torre, 2019; Lykes, 2017). This very act of tracing our lineages to particular repositories of knowledge is itself a process of legitimation—one that has historically upheld colonially configured knowledge production, while excluding, delegitimizing, and at times, completely erasing subaltern knowledges (Ahmed, 2006; Khatun, 2018; Reyes Cruz, 2008). By *coloniality*, we mean ongoing processes, structures, and ideologies rooted in histories and ongoing practices of settler, imperial, and psychological colonization that have served to maintain hegemonic power, along with racialized capitalism (Maldonado-Torres, 2016; Robinson, 2020). Decoloniality then is about resisting, deconstructing, and challenging colo-nialism and colonial ways of thinking and being that manifest through hegemonic discourses, actions, structures, and practices. Decolonization and anticolonialism not only challenge the coloniality of power but also involve taking principled actions that recognize a shared humanity. Thus, *decoloniality* is a critical movement toward the restoration of love and understanding and against violence, dehumani-zation, and oppression (Lugones, 2014).

As an intervention, we begin by honoring the roots of PAR praxis in legacies of people's movements and struggles for justice in the majority world. The work of scholar–activists and organizers in Latin America and South Asia has been particularly influential in the development of PAR as responses to oppressive social structures aimed at reclaiming people's power (e.g., Fals-Borda, 1985; Freire, 1970/2000; Martín-Baró, 1994; Rahman, 1993; Vio Grossi, 1981). Orlando Fals-Borda (1985) defined people's power as

> the capacity of the grassroots groups
> which are exploited socially and

economically to articulate and systematize knowledge (both their own and that which comes from outside) in such a way that they can become protagonists in advancement of their society and in defence of their own class and group interests. (p. 94)

For Fals-Borda (1985) and others, PAR is a way to democratize and leverage knowledge production in larger struggles for justice and transformative social change.

We refer to PAR as an ontoepistemological approach because we understand PAR not simply as a methodological stance, but as lived and learned ways of being in the world that are oriented toward justice. Consider the following vignette from Jesica:

> Growing up in the California Central Valley with migrant farm working parents, I saw them organize in their own ways with migrant families in the fields and at church to demand better pay, working conditions, and resources for youth in the Migrant Education Program. They held *talleres*, *platicas*, and *paros* to support their organizing. Often these events and gatherings involved parents sharing stories/testimonios, getting signatures for petitions, and doing encuestas (short and informal surveys) often outside of church/mass and the mercado. Through their work, I understood the importance of (a) organizing—which my father described as "sin acción no hay transformación" (without action there is no transformation), (b) communities—relationships and settings/physical spaces—and (c) acting/serving/contributing to the betterment of our communities (Latinx, Mexican, immigrant, farm-working, low-income). My parents have always been involved in the church, even after they left working in the fields, and I suppose that it is

also through them that I learned the value of working with and alongside rather than for or on behalf of others. Bringing this history with me, and then learning about PAR and community-engaged research paradigms was affirming. I began to see a connection between what my parents did and how academics/researchers were doing something similar. I then began to see myself as a researcher, or at the very least as someone who could utilize research as a tool and strategy to support community struggles for change, well-being, and power.

Today, our understanding and practice of PAR is sharpened by knowledge generated in movement as we witness and/or engage in uprisings against oppression such as the Black Lives Matter movement in the United States, Indigenous people's movements in Chile, unprecedented mobilization of farmers in India, transnational Dalit movements against racialized and caste-based violence, Black-Palestinian solidarities against apartheid and settler colonial occupation, mutual aid for Asian American and Pacific Islander communities experiencing hate crimes in the United States, and many others. These movements are forms of practical labor and ways of being that lead to new knowledges—in contrast to assumptions of a unidirectional flow of knowledge from academic research to social transformation (Dutta, 2016; Mohanty, 2003).

Based on this broader orienting context, PAR is rooted in three key interrelated ethical considerations that are designed to democratize knowledge and decenter whiteness and coloniality: radical relationality, epistemic justice, and intervention toward social justice. Each consideration will be taken up in greater detail later in this chapter, but we offer a birds-eye view now, to help orient the reader to the broader conceptual orientation. PAR is deeply committed to humanizing and recognizing dignity, or *radical relationality*, not as abstract or universalizing values, but as they are expressed in specific projects or struggles. PAR enables a critique of the relationships governing conventional knowledge production, which are seeded in the ideological foundations of colonial and structural violence (Bulhan, 1985). PAR facilitates epistemic justice through collective inquiry, the intervention of collective social action based on self-determined priorities, and the imperative to work toward a rehumanized conception of the world (Lugones, 2014; Maldonado-Torres, 2016). Finally, PAR facilitates interventions at multiple levels, including in the research process given the focus on epistemic justice, as well as at the level of social change, given the emphasis on social action.

In our PAR endeavors, we are particularly indebted to decolonial, Indigenous, Women of Color, queer, and transnational feminists whose intellectual, affective, creative, and embodied political labor have powerfully demonstrated ways of being, knowing, and relating that do not subscribe to colonial modalities (e.g., Anzaldúa, 2017; brown, 2017; hooks, 1994; Khatun, 2018; Lugones, 2014; Mohanty, 2003; Pérez, 1999; Sandoval, 1990; Smith, 2012). Following in this tradition, PAR is an invitation to simultaneously disrupt and transform the roots of inquiry. The disruption of the colonial and neoliberal relationships governing knowledge production—relationships that lend ideological support to injustice and oppression—is fundamental to PAR (Rahman, 1993). As already mentioned, we will expand on all three—radical relationality, epistemic justice, and intervention—of these considerations. Before doing so, however, a cautionary note is in order, to warn against the co-optation of PAR.

Because of U.S. histories of coloniality and empire, the call to disrupt and work toward transformation via PAR can be easily misunderstood and co-opted. This is most likely to happen when PAR is used under positivist/postpositivist scientific frameworks because the assumptions of these objectivist constructions of science (Crotty, 1998) are in conflict with a PAR onto-epistemology. Briefly, postpositivism includes apprehending a reality that can be probabilistically understood, with the goal of finding generalizable

and universal laws that help explain human behavior (Riemer, 2020). Within this framework, the researcher is to be neutral and disinterested in the results. To increase rigor, the researcher should work to reduce bias in order to decrease contamination of the research. These assumptions are in conflict with radical relationality, epistemic justice, and social intervention toward justice, and when these positivist assumptions are overlaid with PAR, it often leads to tokenization and epistemic violence. Thus, established notions of what is real and possible, which in psychology includes the fetishizing of science as "truth," not only fail to see/name transformative practices but also preclude the emergence of radically alternative visions based in people's realities (brown, 2017; Escobar, 2020).

PARTICIPATORY ACTION RESEARCH AS RADICAL RELATIONALITY

PAR is relational and inquiry-based, where the collectives in which inquiry and action ensue may be themselves a site of liberatory struggle "not as a closed world from which there is no exit, but as a limiting situation which [we] can transform" (Freire, 1970/2000, p. 49). Relationality may involve people immersed in the setting and others connected in varied ways. Psychologists may share cultural and/or ancestral roots with communities confronting an issue, or they may live in the same neighborhood or work in a university/institution implicated in the problem or may be drawn to a desire for liberation. Relationships matter in approaching inquiry in a participatory manner because people bring knowledge of their lived conditions and willingness to collectively construct meaning toward actions for justice and liberation.

To challenge the hegemony of positivist/postpositivist research, we underscore the value of relationality in PAR. For us, PAR is a labor of love, never only a research project that is left at the office when we head home for the day. It includes joy, inspiration, and tension often sitting side by side, even in the same moment. Coming together is itself subject to constraints in that the relations of colonial power associated with forms of precarity and material dispossession outside the collective get reflected and activated *within* it. Commitments to a consciousness of power-sharing implies what Torre (2009) referred to as a contact zone in which PAR members acknowledge different levels of power and privilege. It is attention to the power differentials and how they may operate within the PAR collective and inform their inquiry that assists in not reproducing inequities while valuing and honoring each member's contributions. The shock of displacement that is viscerally experienced may be repeated in symbolic and embodied ways. Enactments of whiteness, heteropatriarchy, and social-class privilege may become a related source of study in PAR, offering analytical and often discomforting pathways to structural forces at work in institutions and contexts. Feelings may arise based on ontology, ethics, cooptation, building anew, recovering historical memory, and/or troubling identities, or for other reasons. Thus, having the courage to experience and express relationality, through an ethic of love, is essential to the praxis called for in PAR (Freire, 1970/2000). Love is action infused with the recognition that we are all interconnected. An ethic of love acknowledges our mutuality, interdependence, and humanity. In psychology, PAR is grounded in feminist, critical, decolonial frameworks that move toward liberation and accompaniment (Ayala et al., 2018) through enactments of love, which are central to the principle of radical relationality that characterizes our PAR process.

Conceptualizing Radical Relationality

Cultivating and sustaining relationships can support community power and characterizes radical relationality. This is especially the case when engaging in and with one's community, where one is rooted and connected in contexts of direct struggle and resistance (Atallah & Dutta, 2021; Dutta, 2021). PAR affirms that lived experience, as well as historical, local, and experiential knowledge that often unfolds through relationships can help guide actions for liberation. Unlike other research paradigms, a critical ethical reflexivity

can aid in the development of relationality rooted in accompaniment, as well as commitment, transparency, and sociocultural humility (Fernández, 2018; Pillow, 2003). Through radical relationality, all involved in the PAR process can come to intentionally and purposefully acknowledge and understand each other. Relating can help make visible how historic events, sociopolitical discourses, and local contexts impact communities at multiple levels, from the individual to the social, structural, and systemic. To cultivate radical relationality, however, we must strive to engage three interconnected principles: critical ethical reflexivity, relational power, and a praxis of solidarity.

First, PAR is oriented toward critical ethical reflexivity that involves action through interactive cycles of reflection and dialogue, often at every phase of the PAR process (i.e., discerning an area of focus, taking action, and evaluating the action). Specifically, it is essential to critically examine the roles and identities of all involved, and the subjectivities that shape collaboration and the research trajectory. Reflexivity is imperative for decentering hegemonic power, and ensuring that actions align with community desires (Fernández, 2018; Silva, 2017). Without a critical ethical reflexivity there is an even greater risk in reproducing the conditions of oppression and hegemony that PAR is designed to deconstruct. PAR may often be informed by people's positionalities or the knowledge that develops through being, coexisting, and witnessing in community. To illustrate, Anne offers a story of how the beginnings of a multiracial PAR collective of youth, high school teachers, and university students came together in response to the closure of a high school the youth attended. This occurred after several years of involvement with the youth and teachers from the high school.

> Our inquiry involves sitting in classrooms with students in January and hearing with them that their school is to be shuttered by June. It means making use of what is available to hold the things said and unsaid in our

words and bodies at that moment. It requires responding to the moment by providing comfort, sharing anger, and asking questions.

For Anne, radical relationality is facilitated through the affectivity of accompaniment and responsibility to each other. It foregrounds the struggles and conditions in need of transformation. Critical reflexivity creates the ethical space to individually and collectively feel and apprehend what is happening. It speaks to what Laura (2013) referred to as an ethic of love involving witnessing, "the deliberate attendance to people, seeing and taking notice of that which they believe is meaningful" (p. 290) and engaging in problem-posing and raising questions about the issues important to those with whom we inquire and the ways in which we are engaged in the inquiry (Guishard et al., 2018).

Expanding on the importance of reflexivity toward relationality, Anne describes how the inquiry is situated within the everyday unpredictability associated with the consequences of material dispossession, precarity, and resistance against the erasure of relationships and loss of public space. In her words,

> It involves being in the space and moment, reflecting on it, and drawing on what else can be known. What are the particular ways the school closure is presented to the community? What is the discourse of its justification? How might we distance ourselves from the prevailing views of education reform? What other frames of analysis exist for understanding this problem? How does local history, some of which remains untold, inform this moment? These and other questions allow for problem-posing to get at the event itself and its role in a larger set of unjust social arrangements.

The problem-posing process that Anne describes allows for relationality where all involved in PAR have an opportunity to share connections to a concern or an issue needing to be addressed. Mutual recognition of a challenge or struggle can help foster relationality and the actions necessary to support change.

Second, PAR strives to cultivate shared relational power (Ayala et al., 2018). Instead of having power lie in the hands of a few who are the decision makers, arbitrators, or even interlocutors for some community-based collaborators, PAR recognizes that at different points within the research process distinct skills, perspectives, and resources are needed. This can help sustain a *heterarchical* PAR collaboration where all are engaged and differentially participating based on their expertise—not passively involved. *Heterarchy* is distinct in its meaning and its practice from hierarchy and, therefore, more closely reflects the dimensions of PAR. Through this process, each person, with their unique positionalities and experiences, can exercise their agency and hold different roles, responsibilities, and power, which also shift depending on the task at hand (Tebes et al., 2014). Through a syncretic process, all involved in PAR can contribute and act together as part of a whole (Kincheloe, 2009; Tuck, 2009). All involved in PAR have the power to determine the problem and engage in gathering data, discerning results, and acting in a manner that is informed from their interpretation. Actions may involve access to decision making, redistributing resources, making visible an experience occluded or denied by prevailing social arrangements, or inquiring into histories known by local communities that reframe how problems are understood. Together, these processes constitute a form of strong objectivity (Fine & Torre, 2019; Harding, 1991). Power must be intentionally shared and deliberately engaged by all research collaborators through jointly deciding and directing the research process and practices, as well as leveraging resources—institutional, social, and otherwise—to support and advance community struggles. In this way, the relational dimensions of PAR shape actions and the power to address a shared concern.

To demonstrate shared relational power, Jesica recalls her collaboration with a group of Mexican immigrant women, who refer to themselves as *madres*. This collaboration began as a PAR course that was offered free of charge to members of a low-income, working-class community experiencing gentrification in the South Bay region of the Silicon Valley. The course was taught by Jesica, and as the weeks unfolded the madres developed their research skills in relation to their leadership and community organizing. In learning about their community's needs and strengths, the madres identified murals as important for representing their culture and the history of their neighborhood. For these reasons, and as a way to widely share via visual representations the outcomes of their research, they decided to create a community mural at the elementary school most of their children attended. As the relationship among us formed beyond the context of the PAR course, the madres saw themselves as members of a collective group and PAR project by the name of *Madres Emprendedoras*.

When shared relational power is not upheld by those involved, the outcome can be problematic. To illustrate this, Jesica describes the following:

> In deciding what to illustrate in their community mural, the madres agreed that they were not going to acquiesce to the mural design draft offered by the muralist. The muralist was a collaborator in the mural making process, however he was not involved in every step of the PAR process or in fostering deep and authentic relationships with the madres. The madres saw the muralist as an experienced artist, yet they were critical about the process the muralist followed to design the draft, which did not involve most of the madres in the drafting phase. The muralist, understanding themselves as an expert muralist yet unfamiliar with PAR, challenged the cultivation of shared relational power. In refusing the muralist's design, the madres stepped into their power, claiming ownership of their stories

and how they wanted to be represented. The madres wielded their knowledge, and the outcomes of their research to support their goals.

When hegemonic power is challenged it can provide an opportunity for all involved in the PAR process to build relationality. Indeed, shared relational power has the potential to influence the PAR process and outcomes in positive and/or problematic ways. Radical relationality grounded in mutuality and sustaining connections that support communities is one of the positive aspects associated with PAR. In the project described, for instance, the madres claiming their power through opportunities that included sharing stories, gathering and disseminating data, and owning and directing the outcomes of what they produced was a positive outcome. The imposition of the muralist's vision and the disregard for the madres having a say in the process illustrates, on the other hand, how relationships despite the best of intention can often obfuscate the cultivation of shared relational power, affecting whose voices, perspectives, and desires are centered/decentered. It was problematic for the muralist to assume that because of his expertise and a positive interpersonal relationship with the madres that they would approve of a mural design that did not involve them.

Third, PAR is a praxis of solidarities built on mutuality and critical connections, instead of transactional relationships. Returning to Jesica's reflection, similar to the muralist, Jesica was often viewed by the madres as an expert yet she troubled how she was positioned by reflecting and grounding herself in her ethics, the sources of knowledge and ignorance, and how her PAR training supported or challenged her relationship with the madres in a community that resembled her own—where she grew up and now lives and works. For the university-affiliated PAR researcher, questioning our positionalities, who we are in solidarity with and accountable to, is critical to PAR; there must be an honest commitment to being accountable to the community. Accountability means having a shared understanding of implicability, a commitment to mutual equitable engagement, and even risk that recognizes that each person matters in the PAR process. Relationality formed through solidarities about the issues at hand, and the possible solutions or actions to address them, is what a PAR process must consistently foster, especially among those involved who are liminaly situated within systems of power, or whose positionalities are complicated by their actual or presumed expertise. To ensure that community voices and experiences are amplified, solidarities that involve taking or sharing risk and joy and hope toward what is possible must be centered, while institutional agendas are resisted.

Implications of Radical Relationality

We recognize the pluriversality of who a PAR researcher is and how each person is distinctly positioned. Furthermore, we underscore the importance of decentering the power of the university/academic researcher, who is often presumed to be a holder of knowledge or expertise. Universities that are highly visible or explicit of their community involvement often purport solidarities. Yet the risks and accountability can often be performative or exercised in hegemonic ways. Relational solidarities of shared power are important for actualizing theories of change that develop with and within research collaborators from the bottom up. What this looks like is a research praxis committed to relational solidarity via accompaniment, critical ethical reflexivity, and connections that acknowledge and embrace complexities and struggles as these are challenged by members of the PAR collaborative who are most impacted by social issues. It is about approaching research with the humility to listen, reflect, and dialogue, as well as share the risks and joys along the way.

The three principles herein described caution people involved in the PAR process from subscribing to theories of change that may not reflect the ontological foundations and desires of PAR collaborators directly engaged in redressing injustices or that may unintentionally reproduce bifurcations or binaries, such as those of reform versus transformation or revolution. PAR implies a process of closeness where we work together to coconstruct knowledge and in this way acknowledge how we are often bound and brought together to redress an injustice. Echoing this point, Jesica offers a reflection:

> Most of my PAR work develops organically through connections formed in community organizing spaces that I am involved in—often as a member of the community, and/or as someone who is concerned about certain issues impacting the communities with which I identify. My commitments as a PAR-doer are always with my community partners. I align my values and actions to support communities I am connected to, and I engage PAR with the intention to cultivate connections—radical relationalities—that can guide actions toward transformative justice, liberation and well-being, and imagining what could be.

The boundedness that Jesica describes keeps PAR collaborators connected through experiences of struggle, tension, joy, and even love. In the PAR process each person may bring different perspectives and hold distinct positionalities, yet there is intention to build radical relationalities of shared power toward liberatory and reciprocally humanizing solidarities. Justice is actualized when those most impacted by conditions of oppression determine what and how structures must change; we, therefore, turn to this point next.

PARTICIPATORY ACTION RESEARCH AS EPISTEMIC JUSTICE

Epistemic justice refers to processes of radically transforming the meaning and politics of knowledge production. This includes but is not limited to critical interrogations of who is (or could be) a knower and what are the terms of knowledge production (e.g., what constitutes valid knowledge). Epistemic justice is a central concern in

PAR, which is premised on interrogation and reconfiguration of the idea of who constitutes the knower/researcher, as well as disrupting the monopoly on forms of knowledge and modes of knowledge production (Appadurai, 2006; Fals-Borda & Rahman, 1991; Lykes, 2017). Thus, PAR is not only anchored in principles of epistemic justice, but it also represents a powerful strategy for promoting epistemic justice.

The links between epistemic (in)justice and other forms of colonial/material domination have been extensively theorized (e.g., Fals-Borda, 1985; Galván-Álvarez, 2010; Kessi, 2017). Core to this linkage is the understanding that to be denied one's capacity as a knower violates an essential quality of being human, a form of dehumanization codified and systematized by colonial and settler colonial modes of knowledge production (Byskov, 2020; Fricker, 2007; Pérez, 1999). Epistemic justice is integral to decoloniality, where "the damné emerges as a questioner, thinker, theorist, writer, and communicator" (Maldonado-Torres, 2016, p. 24). Here, *damné* refers to colonized and subaltern subjects who are reduced to objects of knowledge production within colonial and imperialist knowledge schemas; they cannot occupy the position of knowledge producers. Thus, epistemic justice is not simply a project of "including" excluded perspectives but one that requires a fundamental transformation of the very meaning and terms of *inclusion*. In fact, Kincheloe (2009) warned that without a "critical epistemological and transformative politics of knowledge the story of the colonized will continue to be told by the colonizer" (p. 119). As in the African proverb tracing lines of power within historical narratives, Kincheloe noted, "Reclaiming these stories and this history is a central task of critical PAR" (p. 119). In this section, we discuss how PAR and epistemic justice are interwoven in our praxis: from interrogating the politics of knowledge production to uplifting storytelling as a means of disrupting established knowledge hierarchies; from honoring complex personhoods to adopting an ethical stance of refusal against processes/practices that perpetuate epistemic violence.

Interrogating Politics of Knowledge Production

PAR seeks to break down hierarchies and exclusions based on the historical imposition of values, knowledges, and worldviews (Kessi, 2017; Walker et al., 2020). Those hierarchies and underlying worldviews are deeply implicated in determining who gets a say in how to address which sociopolitical and economic concerns; those who are epistemically advantaged have privileged access to shape public and political discourse according to their interests (Byskov, 2020). Gina offers a story that exemplifies this aspect of PAR and epistemic justice:

> In my experience, epistemic justice for children, especially youth and children of color and working-class children, is especially powerful because this intersectional position is one that is rarely listened to or taken seriously in dominant U.S. society (Rogoff, 2003; Vaccarino-Ruiz et al., 2021). As a PAR researcher, I do my best to practice radical listening, or listening carefully to youth and children. For example, in one yPAR project with middle school youth, we were focusing on photovoice (a methodology sometimes used in PAR where people take pictures based on a prompt, write narratives about the photo, and discuss the photo in a group setting (Wang & Burris, 1997). We were sitting in a small group, in a circle, in classroom desk/chair units, pushed off to one side of the classroom so as not to bother another group also engaging in a photovoice discussion. In our group, a Latinx boy had been doing his best to make his friends laugh during the session. When I asked the question "What do you see here?" he said that he saw "zombies, vampires, and monsters," none of which were in the picture. He looked at his friends and laughed.

I then asked him if he was trying to tell me that there were people in his community who felt like they did not belong. He became instantly serious, looked me directly in the eye, and said yes, this was his point. We then went on to have a deep conversation about (lack of) belonging in the community and what this meant for Latinx youth.

As this example illustrates, PAR approaches can disrupt unjust discursive structures by revealing the ways in which hegemonic epistemic frameworks legitimize oppressive ideologies and practices, while also building counter framings/ narratives/analyses of pressing sociopolitical and economic concerns—analyses that would otherwise be obscured by the machinations of colonial and neoliberal power that undergird the politics of "expertise."

Storytelling and Honoring Complex Personhood

PAR may be leveraged to render visible complex personhood and explore the plurality of possibilities for those at the margins of the state and institutions (Tuck, 2009). These explorations are often facilitated through processes of collective storytelling. For Miya communities in Northeast India—who have borne legacies of persecution, violence, social exclusion, and cultural erasures since the colonial era—epistemic justice involves uplifting their knowledges, experiences, and resistance that are systematically excluded from hegemonic discourse (Dutta et al., 2022). Recognizing the utmost significance of telling their stories on their own terms, Miya grassroots organizers have created the digital community media platform Ango Khabar (Our News; https://www.facebook.com/angokhabarassam) to build a repository of stories that span the infinite horizon of Miya people's humanity—their pain, struggles, desires, art, history, culture, and their rebellion. Urmi shares the following vignette about witnessing Miya people step into their power as knowers:

An important part of my role early in our work together was to support capacity-building of Miya community workers in digital storytelling. During one of our numerous multiday digital storytelling sessions, I invited community workers to share their storylines. In the matter of minutes, the small room was charged with myriad emotions evoked by the stories as well the act of telling them. We listened, we saw, and we deeply felt the stories that Miya people carry with them at all times; stories that are metabolized from their own pains and from the struggles they witness as they accompany their communities. There were some stories that were fully formed— years in the making—waiting to be told. Some stories began as an idea and were woven into a powerful narrative as multiple people contributed threads. Yet other stories emerged from disjuncture and contradiction.

This is the kind of rebellious, embodied, evocative expression that Audre Lorde (1984/2012) alludes to in *The Transformation of Language Into Silence and Action*:

> What are the words you do not yet have? What do you need to say? What are the tyrannies you swallow day by day and attempt to make your own, until you will sicken and die of them, still in silence? (p. 41)

Although it was extraordinarily powerful to witness Miya community workers move into their power as knowers and storytellers, such shifts are not limited to organized PAR sessions. In fact, the Ango Khabar team are seeing such shifts in Miya communities living in char areas or ecologically fragile riverine islands. Rejecting objectifying rhetoric, char dwellers are not only owning their stories but are also mobilizing to create spaces for storytelling in their localities and communities. For Miya people then, storytelling constitutes a critical dimension of activating their collective power and reclaiming their dignity from the realm of subhuman invisibility (Dutta et al., 2022).

An Ethic of Refusal

The linkage between PAR and its potential for epistemic justice is crucially mediated by stances of refusal. Refusal in research are intentional endeavors to subvert, interrogate, disrupt, or otherwise place limits on the colonially configured parameters of knowing and knowability (Atallah & Dutta, 2021; Tuck & Yang, 2014a). Participatory or voice-centered ethics of PAR does not, in and of itself, mitigate ethical issues of representation, voice, consumption, and voyeurism (Tuck & Yang, 2014b). Refusal is characterized by a perpetual consciousness and confrontation of coloniality and the settler colonial logic of hegemonic research (Tuck & Yang, 2014a). It involves excavating and exposing metanarratives of knowledge that uphold oppressive vectors of coloniality, capitalism, and heteropatriarchy. Refusal aligns with and is imperative to actualizing epistemic justice because it is the intentional act of refusing to participate in coproducing oppressive realities. These acts may involve resisting standardized norms and expectations of research that so often perpetuate harm by overlooking and/or commodifying trauma, pain, and oppression.

A stance of refusal can also help clarify social justice ethics in PAR, as is illustrated in this example by Gina:

> My team and I had to choose between changing the trajectory of a yPAR program, where youth wanted to focus on ICE (Immigration and Customs Enforcement) accountability and abolition after ICE raids in their neighborhoods, and possibly ending the yPAR program. In this case, school leadership encouraged me to shift the children's focus from the ICE raids and accountability to student friendships in the school. To make such a shift, however, would have been

epistemically unjust and, therefore, a form of violence within a community that had already experienced state violence and silencing around that violence. Because of the process of PAR and the relationships I developed with the children and their families, I had no doubt that I would not participate in this act of violence and erasure because I had seen in the children the healing that had come through epistemic validation of being supported in wanting to research ICE violence, making plans to hold ICE accountable for their behavior during the raids, such as breaking windows, sinks, and physically harming people, and dreaming of a world without ICE.

A stance of refusal involves critical inquiry and reflection into what research is, what and who it is for, and the why to such inquiries that often lend themselves to voyeuristic pursuits that leave the coloniality of power in knowledge and relationships intact. Refusal requires us to embrace desire-based frameworks that entail "working inside a more complex and dynamic understanding of what one, or a community, comes to know in (a) lived life" (Tuck & Yang, 2014b, p. 231). A desire-based framework is a marked departure from overly simplified and truncated narratives—whether these are overdetermined narratives of trauma or idealized narratives of resilience. For Global South scholar–activists whose work is rooted in their own communities, a desire-based approach includes refusal to engage the researcher-researched binary configured by colonial and imperialist regimes (see Dutta, 2021, for an illustration). In the following paragraph, Urmi outlines some of these challenges:

> For me, this means continually facing the challenge of representing my people and communities (including our relationalities) in ethical and discursively complex ways, at the same time as my "insider" or "invested"

status are viewed as an impediment to "rigor." At other times, our Global North locations/affiliations are privileged in ways that situate us as the "expert" or "outsider" to our own communities, robbing us of the non-binary complexities inherent in our transnational and transborder lives. Refusal in this context can mean collective self-determined decision-making, for example, what aspects of our work, stories, and relationality may be made intelligible to the academy. In my work alongside and in solidarity with Miya communities, this stance is paramount. The entirety of our relationships is neither inherently knowable nor automatically open to scrutiny for the academy—assumptions/expectations we are subjected to as Global South peoples. This does not preclude critical interrogation and reflection on our praxis. In fact, our praxis, at every step, is defined by an unwavering ethical commitment to complex (and at times shifting) configurations of justice, self-determination, and complex personhood of those with whom we are in struggle and/or solidarity (Dutta et al., 2022). Furthermore, we continually and laboriously nurture political intimacies and transnational solidarities to bolster our moral and ethical compass in this work. These are the decolonial and liberatory ethics and accountabilities we prioritize over disciplinary-focused and institutionalized ethics that tend to privilege Global North lens/frameworks.

Refusal is a critical intervention into research. Stances of refusal also require us to trouble the very idea of research as inherently valuable or self-justified. As is evident across a number of vignettes/examples above, research is not the only mode of intervention. We do not have to designate an action as research for it to be legitimate. In fact, there are times when we actively refuse the mantle of research to center political intimacies and radical relationality (Atallah & Dutta, 2021). Along similar lines, we must trouble, decenter, and question the very foundations of the researcher-researched binary. PAR, when engaged from a standpoint of refusal, can advance epistemic justice by mitigating neoliberal modes of cooptation and commodification, as well as cocreating counter-hegemonic knowledges, humanizing relationships, and effecting individual, collective, and systemic transformations. Epistemic justice manifested as these forms of emancipatory praxes have the potential to restitute the sovereignty, dignity, and power of communities to shape conditions of collective thriving.

As we collectively sculpted the shape and content of this chapter, Jesica spoke about the level of heat needed to bring particular ingredients in a meal to a structural change in food chemistry, producing deeply rich and complex textures and tastes. Each element, when combined, builds toward the wholeness of what is produced—to be shared and enjoyed in a wholesome way. Similarly, each of the elements' features as we have described thus far characterize our PAR praxis and approach. In the next section, we discuss the nature of troubling and questioning, creating heat and change, revealing complexity in the generative heat of radical relationality and guidance of epistemic justice.

PARTICIPATORY ACTION RESEARCH AS INTERVENTION/TRANSFORMATION

Through processes of collective reflection and action among those close to the experience central to the inquiry, PAR offers forms of intervention that open up possibilities for transformation. The term *intervention* has theoretical roots in the work of Brazilian critical educator and philosopher Paulo Freire who worked with adults in Northeast Brazil who came to literacy through inquiring and acting upon the conditions affecting their lives. In this way, intervention suggests liberatory processes occurring in relationship with others to analyze the historical and contemporary conditions of a particular problem or situation (Freire, 1970/2000). At the individual, collective, and systemic levels, intervention creates openings and brings into focus how dehumanization, colonialism, coloniality, white supremacy, and anti-Blackness mask and sustain oppression. The dialogic process of questioning reframes, reimagines, and generates new ways of knowing and being in relationship as it disrupts injustice and creates possibilities for change. This, as we demonstrate through our stories and discussion of the elements of PAR, creates space for alternative processes of critical inquiry.

Creating Alternative Processes of Inquiry

In analyzing the historical and contemporary conditions of a particular problem or situation, PAR involves the interrogation of structural and cultural violence. *Structural violence* refers to systems and forms of inequality and oppression (often based on invidious categories such as race, gender, and class) that become seemingly endemic or naturalized to society and are no longer questioned. Structural violence is sustained by cultural violence, or dominant ideologies and dehumanizing discourses (e.g., via popular media, literature and arts, education, research, and policy) that construct particular groups of people as inferior, which serves to normalize, justify, and/or legitimize oppressive practices and collective indifference (Bell, 2018; Dutta et al., 2016; Langhout & Vaccarino-Ruiz, 2021). The critical theoretical perspective invoked in the notion of interrogation suggests the practice of questioning and of decoding discourse, institutional routines, social arrangements, unspoken assumptions, and predominant cultural givens. The practice of questioning orients from the understanding that silence, invisibility, and afterthoughts are mechanisms of symbolic and material exclusion and cultural marginalization. In this light, PAR—with its emphasis on interrogating social inequality and building emancipatory, locally relevant, and collectively produced

knowledge—can be used to intervene in cycles of structural/cultural violence (Lykes, 2017; McIntyre, 2000). Thus, PAR can be leveraged to name and analyze the ways in which the identified "problems" are structural concerns, and how they come to be associated with those who bear the brunt of the issues (Cahill, 2007; Tuck, 2009). Collective inquiry occurs through a critical recovery of non-Eurocentric, Indigenous, and/or community-centered subjugated histories, use of popular culture and storytelling, production of new knowledge, and sustained ownership of this knowledge by the people themselves (Fals-Borda & Rahman, 1991). In this way, PAR could help disrupt the conditions and narratives that preserve the linkages between oppressive social structures and people's daily struggles.

The construction of the problem as defined and determined in community and collaboration is dynamic and ongoing, and open to revision and complexity as communities deepen their engagement with the problem. In a multiracial PAR collective with youth and adults from Cleveland, Anne notes there were many iterations of problem posing concerning the experience of youth following the closure of their high school and the continued use of urban school district reform efforts that relied on metrics of high-stakes state testing to categorize and classify students, teachers, and schools by degrees of excellence or failure.

> To understand how students were experiencing these reforms, the collective developed and administered a survey for ninth-grade students on transitioning from K–8 schools into high schools. The process of analyzing survey results and using creative products to report back to youth in the district the collective's interpretation of the data reflected dialogic engagement. Throughout the project, the collective used creative forms of play—poetry, role play, performed scenes, and music—to get at meaning and forms of action to deepen the

collective's understanding and that of a wider public (jones et al., 2015, pp. 141–143).

In exploring the findings, one group performed two videotaped scenes. The first portrayed how a student grew increasingly exasperated over her teacher's rapid delivery of the steps to solve an algebra problem. In very little time, the situation escalated with the strong words and actions on the part of both teacher and student. The second videotaped scene is a direct contrast with the first. In this case, the teacher receives the student's questions as reflecting a desire to learn, and the teacher responds with care and clarity. While these video-taped scenarios reflected the survey results on teachers and students not getting along, they also seemed to point to existing discourses about uncaring and incompetent teachers or deviant students. These discourses, however, were sometimes inconsistent with the experiences of the youth who made the videos.

In this PAR collective's dialogue on what the two videotaped scenarios side by side conveyed about the survey results, the focus moved from interpretations of individual behaviors of students and teachers to a broader set of conditions these individuals were experiencing within the school system (Galletta, 2019). It also involved a look at the city's history of racial segregation and current reform policies distant from the experiences of the youth and their families. A serendipitous discovery of a set of rocks in Anne's office, homogenous in color on the outside while vibrant in layers of color on the inside led to a playful commentary and a metaphor within the video for analyzing on several structural levels, producing forms of discursive intervention for what initially appeared to be a straightforward problem at the level of the individual student and teacher (Galletta & Torre, 2019). Freire described this form of inquiry as problem posing

and a form of "intervention in reality—historical awareness itself," which results in a deepening of critical awareness, or *conscientização* (Freire, 1970/2000, p. 103). Everisto Benyera (2021) called this epistemic freedom, "to think, to historize, and theorize from where one is located," which he argues results in a decentering of privileged Eurocentric forms of knowledge. In this way, PAR efforts offer a "social mirror," as described by social psychologist Ignacio Martín-Baró (1994), who used public opinion polls to offer Salvadorans a way to "confront their own image, to see their own opinions and attitudes objectified" and "to examine with a more critical eye the contrast between what they are living and thinking and what the prevailing discourse is pronouncing" (p. 192). In the case of the PAR collective noted here, the students who took the survey could actually see their experience reflected back to them.

In the aforementioned example, many forms of analysis and interpretation are employed to look at the problem in different ways and creatively understand its dimensions. Reflecting on stories told through the use of video and audio recordings of what's been said and how it's been told, written transcripts analyzed through role play, thematic coding through graffiti walls, followed by interpretation of meaning through poetry, and further dialogue, opens up pathways for understanding (Cammarota & Fine, 2008). The process of becoming aware of what is at stake in the focus of inquiry occurs, then, at the individual and collective level, moving toward modes of reflection and consciousness of where and how change is necessary. As noted in the stories below, actions taken in PAR projects not only disrupt the regularity of practices and policies that maintain structural violence and colonizing interests, but they also produce change in the social and material experiences of people's lives.

Disrupting Injustice and Generating Change

PAR places inquiry and action for social justice in an interdependent relationship such that knowledge production and actions taken to end violence and dehumanization inform each other.

Here, intervention suggests not only disruption but also generative processes and creating spaces of possibility. It offers a way into understanding as noted by Gloria Anzaldúa and highlighted by Ayala et al. (2018) as *EntreMundos*, or a borderlands between separate worlds, in the following ways:

> an alternate space between social worlds that traverses cultural and psychological boundaries of aquí and allá; of U.S. and Latin America, of gender, class, and sexualities . . . a space of uncertainty and creativity, where people gather threads from different social worlds to make their own identity tapestries . . . [i]t is a hybrid form that is messy, ambiguous, and embodies conceptual/personal/social passions with little space for distance. (p. 7)

The generative potential of PAR interventions produces tensions, which can also be theorized to help understand systems-level change. Kohfeldt and colleagues (2011) focused on this process by discussing tension in the PAR process. They empirically demonstrate how tensions as the unit of analysis enable the group to assess if they are applying pressure on underlying systems and structures. Through the examination of their elementary school-based yPAR after-school program, they argue that even relatively small programs, housed within larger bureaucratic structures, can move the larger system toward second order change (i.e., changing norms, values, beliefs, and/or role relationships). Pressure can be applied through leveraging yPAR to draw attention to violations in assumptions, which then allows conversations around implicit structures and power, such as assumptions around the category of childhood, or which theory of social change should be followed (Kohfeldt et al., 2011).

Gina speaks of her experience with children in a yPAR project over many years in a school with Latinx students, most from immigrant families, whose knowledge of encounters with ICE come into conflict with white supremacist narratives of migrants as dangerous, and deserving of being detained and expelled from the lands of their ancestors.

The children bring knowledge to their PAR project, including their experience of a violent ICE raid involving 92 ICE/DHS/HSI (Immigration and Customs Enforcement/Department of Homeland Security/Homeland Security Investigations) officers and at least 21 city police officers. The children's understanding of the raid, which took place before dawn, with high-powered and militarized weaponry, opens up dialogue among them and the adult members of the project and creates space for "dangerous seeing" (Taylor, 1997). This seeing centers children's observations of their families' encounter with the structures of violence in policing and border control. Yet, these conversations are threatening to adults who understand schools to be environments for teaching and learning academic subjects in isolation of the children's lived experience.

PAR as intervention destabilizes structural racism and creates opportunities for healing and agency. In this case, the children decided to create artwork and a documentary to tell the story of what happened in their neighborhoods, making the case for ICE abolition. They showed their artwork and documentary at several venues in town, including to city council members, community organizers, activists, and others running for office. As Gina notes,

> Seeing and refusing to turn away creates a rupture or an opening for solidarity and mobilization because seeing creates connection and with it, opportunities for critical consciousness development (Bell, 2016). Specifically, those who see, either individually or collectively, decode the fictions told about subordinated

groups (Langhout & Vaccarino-Ruiz, 2021, p. 932).

Furthermore,

> The youth researchers refused to look away from what had happened to them, their families, and the broader community. In refusing to look away, they recognized their own actions as important forms of resistance. They also imagined ways individuals and groups could mobilize. Indeed, they created possibilities for coalition and solidarity work across social movements, and envisioned a more liberatory future. (Langhout & Vaccarino-Ruiz, 2021, p. 941)

In another example, Urmi speaks about Voices, a participatory and community action research project in the Garo Hills region of Northeast India—a border region where people's daily lives are shaped by intersecting colonial, structural, and cultural violence. Against this backdrop, Urmi facilitated a PAR project with 10 college students across diverse ethnic groups in Garo Hills to explore possibilities for belonging and critical community engagement beyond the trappings of state-sponsored ethnic identity categories (Dutta, 2017). Together with these young people, she worked to build a collective of local community researchers. In the tradition of Ignacio Martín-Baró (1994), they utilized social science research (e.g., archival research, key stakeholder interviews, public opinion surveys) to acquire a critical understanding of local issues and use those understandings to speak truth to power. Calling themselves Voices, the community action research team disseminated their findings at local venues, such as relevant community and university events and the local television channel. Across these various activities and actions, the Voices team perforated notions of intractability ascribed to ethnic conflict and then transformed those gaps into spaces for self-determined and collective action. Thus, this example highlights how young people conceptualize research as a collective resource to deepen their understanding of their sociopolitical context and use it as a way of exploring possibilities and advocating for community-level change.

CLOSING REFLECTIONS: ENGENDERING A MOVEMENT INTO RADICAL HOPE AND FREEDOM DREAMING

Motivated by our urgency to make visible the ethics, values, and principles that guide PAR toward more humanizing, just, and liberatory praxis, we have coauthored this chapter in the midst of physical isolation. Within a pandemic context that exacerbates our apprehension of loss and grief, and in response to the disturbing regularity with which Black, Indigenous, and Brown people of all genders encounter lethal state violence, we have forged moments of reprieve, care, political agitation, and community. With this in mind, we have written with a longing to uncover and articulate across our experiences the dimensions of PAR that reflect its resistance to injustice, as well as its liberatory roots. Indeed, PAR is more than a paradigm or an approach to research and scholarly engagement. It is a way of approaching critical inquiry and knowledge, learning and unlearning with humility, curiosity, and connectivity.

Through stories and expressed commitments that reflect three interrelated principles—radical relationality, epistemic justice, and intervention—we have described PAR as a valuable, and necessary paradigm toward actualizing transformative justice and liberation. In practicing PAR, we have also reflected upon our multiple ways of knowing and being in relation to ourselves and with those with whom we inquire, take action, and live in community. Through the multivoiced descriptions that we weaved throughout this chapter via our stories, we have sought to bring unique and complex subjectivities to the forefront that reveal how differently we are situated in relation to racial capitalism, coloniality, dehumanization, migration, and displacement. We have noted these in our opening statements to make visible who we are and why we pursue PAR with the

323

commitment and integrity that we do. Furthermore, in doing so we have aimed for a style of writing that reflects the collaborative, as well as relational and epistemically just elements of engaging in PAR. Writing is or can be a mode of intervention that agitates toward change and transformation; it is with this spirit, heart, and intention that we have written this chapter. In doing so, we bring forward, through our stories and reflections, radical relationality, epistemic justice, and liberatory interventions embedded in PAR. How do our stories speak to you? What do they evoke? What do they resonate with and what do they trouble in relation to your understanding and practice of PAR or of research? How do YOU, as our readers, trouble our ideas and praxis? What are your emerging questions and critiques?

The use of first-person plural in our writing joins us in our intentionality toward meeting the threshold commitments of democratizing inquiry, connecting intersubjective lived realities within contexts of history and power, and bridging the gap between "what is" and "what could be." Our intentionality is facilitated and complicated by who each of us is in our relationship to those with whom we collaborate. Our identities and histories inform how we understand, and are understood, within and outside of PAR sites of struggle and joy. A considerable degree of ethical and methodological complexity is present as we engage in our work. For example, our relationships within PAR collectives may be cultivated by a memorandum of understanding (MOU) at various junctures, or no MOU at all, other than the mutual reciprocal understanding that we are more than collaborators—we are friends, neighbors, and more—who will approach differences in positionality and power with the intentionality to cultivate relationships of justice, equity, and liberation. As we strive to trouble dynamics and conditions that may reinforce epistemic and ontological distance in the researcher-researched binary, we turn to and seek guidance from those who share similar critical, decolonial, and feminist praxes or from those in kinship with the communities of which we are a part or with whom we

are in solidarity. Where might you as our reader enter into this complexity? How do you envision your PAR praxis as ways of disrupting colonial difference and striving toward justice, equity, and liberation in your own communities/contexts? How do you position yourself in your research and how do you navigate different accountabilities (e.g., relational, community, political)?

Participatory action research often starts with creating counternarratives or oppositional stories of identities, experiences, issues, interests, and needs. The act of creating a counter-narrative is an emancipatory process when considered in light of the ways in which people who are Black, Indigenous, and Brown, and many Global South communities are portrayed largely as sites of damage, despair, and disinvestment (Gonzales, 2020; Kessi, 2017; Tuck, 2009). As we have elaborated across multiple vignettes, PAR processes can facilitate the coproduction of narratives that perforate and dismantle accepted oppressive ideologies perpetuated through dominant cultural, policy, or social scientific discourses. What are some dominant narratives upheld by cultural, policy, and/or social scientific discourses in the context of your work? What are the implications of these narratives for varied stakeholders? How might PAR help produce counter-narratives that challenge the hegemony, and contribute to emancipatory narratives?

The coproduction and centering of narratives encompasses an aspiration for, as Robin D. G. Kelley (2002) said, freedom dreaming, which he described as the capacity of the Black radical imagination to "dream out loud" in a way that engages consciousness and the aesthetics, history from the margins, transnational solidarities, and political struggle. In generating possibilities for subaltern groups to reclaim their stories on their own terms, and restore their humanity, PAR can intervene in the cultural violence that undergirds particular configurations of oppression and injustice. Intervening in cultural violence often lays the foundation for addressing structural and direct violence, which can change material conditions (e.g., better funding for schools, affordable housing). Thus, as our stories and multivocal writings demonstrate, we understand PAR as a praxis toward radical relationality, epistemic justice, and intervention that aims to center an ethic of care—of love, radical hope, freedom dreaming, and imagination—that is implicated in the process of disruption and resistance in order to create conditions of liberation, justice, and humanizing recognition.

References

Ahmed, S. (2006). *Queer phenomenology: Orientations, objects, others.* Duke University Press.

Anzaldúa, G. (2017). *Borderlands/la frontera: The new mestiza* (4th ed.). Aunt Lute Books.

Appadurai, A. (2006). The right to research. *Globalisation, Societies and Education, 4*(2), 167–177. https://doi.org/10.1080/14767720600750696

Atallah, D. G., & Dutta, U. (2021). 'Creatively in coalition' from Palestine to India: Weaving stories of refusal and community as decolonial praxis. *Journal of Social Issues,* josi.12460. Advance online publication. https://doi.org/10.1111/josi.12460

Ayala, J., Cammarota, J., Berta-Áliva, M. I., Rivera, M., Rodríguez, L. F., & Torre, M. E. (Eds.). (2018). *PAR EntreMundos: A pedagogy of the Américas.* Peter Lang. https://doi.org/10.3726/b11303

Bell, D. (2016). Retrieving psychosocial signs of structural violence in postcolonial Jamaica. *Community Psychology in Global Perspective, 1*(2), 114–126.

Bell, D. (2018). The indifferent. *Qualitative Research in Psychology, 15*(2–3), 140–155. https://doi.org/10.1080/14780887.2018.1429841

Benyera, E. (2021, April 27). *Decoloniality, ontology, and the structure of racism* [Paper presentation]. The Bahá'í Chair for World Peace, College Park, MD, United States. https://www.youtube.com/watch?v=Kh5c-A0kdkE&t=3369s

brown, m. (2017). *Emergent strategy: Shaping change, changing worlds.* AK Press.

Bulhan, H. A. (1985). Black Americans and psychopathology: An overview of research and theory. *Psychotherapy: Theory, Research, & Practice, 22*(2S), 370–378. https://doi.org/10.1037/h0085517

Byskov, M. F. (2020). What makes epistemic injustice an "injustice"? *Journal of Social Philosophy.* Advance online publication. https://doi.org/10.1111/josp.12348

Cahill, C. (2007). Repositioning ethical commitments: Participatory action research as a relational praxis of social change. *ACME: An International Journal for Critical Geographies, 6*(3), 360–373.

Cammarota, J., & Fine, M. (2008). *Revolutionizing education: Youth participatory action research in motion.* Routledge. https://doi.org/10.4324/9781003115700

Crotty, M. (1998). *The foundations of social research: Meaning and perspective in the research process.* Routledge.

Dutta, U. (2016). Prioritizing the local in an era of globalization: A proposal for decentering community psychology. *American Journal of Community Psychology, 58*(3–4), 329–338. https://doi.org/10.1002/ajcp.12047

Dutta, U. (2017). Creating inclusive identity narratives through participatory action research. *Journal of Community & Applied Social Psychology, 27*(6), 476–488. https://doi.org/10.1002/casp.2328

Dutta, U. (2021). The politics and poetics of "fieldnotes": Decolonizing ethnographic knowing. *Qualitative Inquiry, 27*(5), 598–607. https://doi.org/10.1177/1077800420935919

Dutta, U., Azad, A. K., & Hussain, S. M. (2022). Counterstorytelling as epistemic justice: Decolonial community-based praxis from the Global South. *American Journal of Community Psychology, 69*(1-2), 59–70. https://doi.org/10.1002/ajcp.12545

Dutta, U., Sonn, C. C., & Lykes, M. B. (2016). Situating and contesting structural violence in community-based research and action. *Community Psychology in Global Perspective, 2*(2), 1–20.

Einola, K., Elkina, A., Gao, G., Hambleton, J., Kaasila-Pakanen, A. L., Mandalaki, E., Zhang, L. E., & Pullen, A. (2020). Writing multi-vocal intersectionality in times of crisis. *Gender, Work & Organization: Feminist Frontiers, 28*(4), 1600–1623. https://doi.org/10.1111/gwao.12577

Escobar, A. (2020). *Pluriversal politics.* Duke University Press.

Esteva, G. (2020). Alternative paths of transformation. *Globalizations, 17*(2), 225–231. https://doi.org/10.1080/14747731.2019.1670959

Fals-Borda, O. (1985). *Knowledge and people's power: Lessons with peasants in Nicaragua, México and Colombia.* Indian Social Institute.

Fals-Borda, O., & Rahman, M. A. (Eds.). (1991). *Action and knowledge: Breaking the monopoly with participatory action-research.* Apex Press. https://doi.org/10.3362/9781780444239

Fernández, J. S. (2018). Toward an ethical reflective practice of a theory in the flesh: Embodied subjectivities in a youth participatory action research mural project. *American Journal of Community Psychology, 62*(1–2), 221–232. https://doi.org/10.1002/ajcp.12264

Fine, M., & Torre, M. E. (2019). Critical participatory action research: A feminist project for validity and solidarity. *Psychology of Women Quarterly*, *43*(4), 433–444. https://doi.org/10.1177/0361684319865255

Freire, P. (2000). *Pedagogy of the oppressed* (M. B. Ramos, Trans.). Continuum International Publishing Group. (Original work published 1970)

Fricker, M. (2007). *Epistemic injustice: Power and the ethics of knowing*. Oxford University Press. https://doi.org/10.1093/acprof:oso/9780198237907.001.0001

Galletta, A. (2019). Critical layering in participatory inquiry and action: Praxis and pedagogy in seeking educational change. In K. C. O'Doherty & D. Hodgetts (Eds.), *The SAGE handbook of applied social psychology* (pp. 467–488). SAGE. https://doi.org/10.4135/9781526417091.n23

Galletta, A., & Torre, M. E. (2019). *Educational politics and policy, educational theories and philosophies, education and society. Participatory action research in education*. Oxford Research Encyclopedias. https://doi.org/10.1093/acrefore/9780190264093.013.557

Galván-Álvarez, E. (2010). Epistemic violence and retaliation: The issue of knowledges in "Mother India." *Atlantis*, *32*(2), 11–26.

Gilmore, S., Harding, N., Helin, J., & Pullen, A. (2019). Writing differently. *Management Learning*, *50*(1), 3–10. https://doi.org/10.1177/1350507618811027

Gonzales, T. I. (2020). Ratchet-Rasquache activism: Aesthetic and discursive frames within Chicago-based women-of-color activism. *Social Problems*. *69*(2), 380–397. https://doi.org/10.1093/socpro/spaa034

Guishard, M., Halkovic, A., Galletta, A., & Li, P. (2018). Toward epistemological ethics: Centering communities and social justice in qualitative research. *Forum Qualitative Social Research*, *19*(3), Article 27. https://doi.org/10.17169/fqs-19.3.3145

Harding, S. (1991). *Whose science? Whose knowledge? Thinking from women's lives*. Cornell University Press.

hooks, b. (1994). *Teaching to transgress: Education as the practice of freedom*. Routledge.

Hurtado, A. (1996). *The color of privilege: Three blasphemies on race and feminism*. University of Michigan Press.

jones, v., Stewart, C., Ayala, J., & Galletta, A. (2015). Expressions of agency: Contemplating youth voice and adult roles in participatory action research. In J. Conner, R. Ebby-Rosin, & A. Slattery (Eds.), *National Society for the Study of Education yearbook: Student voice in American educational policy* (pp. 135–152). Teachers College Press.

Kelley, R. D. G. (2002). *Freedom dreams: The Black radical imagination*. Beacon Press.

Kessi, S. (2017). Community social psychologies for decoloniality: An African perspective on epistemic justice in higher education. *South African Journal of Psychology. Suid-Afrikaanse Tydskrif vir Sielkunde*, *47*(4), 506–516. https://doi.org/10.1177/0081246317737917

Khatun, S. (2018). *Australianama: The South Asian Odyssey in Australia*. Oxford University Press.

Kincheloe, J. L. (2009). Critical complexity and participatory action research: Decolonizing "democratic" knowledge production. In D. Kapoor & S. Jordan (Eds.), *Education, participatory action research, and social change* (pp. 107–121). Palgrave. https://doi.org/10.1057/9780230100640_8

Kohfeldt, D., Chhun, L., Grace, S., & Langhout, R. D. (2011). Youth empowerment in context: Exploring tensions in school-based yPAR. *American Journal of Community Psychology*, *47*(1–2), 28–45. https://doi.org/10.1007/s10464-010-9376-z

Langhout, R. D., & Vaccarino-Ruiz, S. S. (2021). "Did I see what I really saw?" Violence, percepticide, and dangerous seeing after an Immigration and Customs Enforcement raid. *Journal of Community Psychology*, *49*(4), 927–946. https://doi.org/10.1002/jcop.22336

Laura, C. T. (2013). Intimate inquiry: Love as "data" in qualitative inquiry. *Cultural Studies ↔ Critical Methodologies*, *13*(4), 289–292.

Lorde, A. (1984/2012). *Sister outsider: Essays and speeches*. Crossing Press.

Lugones, M. (2014). *Indigenous movements and decolonial feminism*. Seminario de grado y posgrado, Department of Women's, Gender and Sexuality Studies, The Ohio State University. https://wgss.osu.edu/sites/wgss.osu.edu/files/LugonesSeminarReadings.pdf

Lykes, M. B. (2017). Community-based and participatory action research: Community psychology collaborations within and across borders. In M. A. Bond, I. Serrano-García, C. B. Keys, & M. Shinn (Eds.), *APA handbook of community psychology: Methods for community research and action for diverse groups and issues* (pp. 43–58). American Psychological Association. https://doi.org/10.1037/14954-003

Maldonado-Torres, N. (2016). *Outline of ten theses on coloniality and decoloniality*. Frantz Fanon Foundation. https://caribbeanstudiesassociation.org/docs/Maldonado-Torres_Outline_Ten_Theses-10.23.16.pdf

Mandalaki, E., & Pérezts, M. (2022). It takes two to tango: Theorizing inter-corporeality through nakedness and eros in researching and writing organizations. *Organization*, *29*(4), 596–618. https://doi.org/10.1177/1350508420956321

Martín-Baró, I. (1994). *Writings for a liberation psychology*. Harvard University Press.

McIntyre, A. (2000). Constructing meaning about violence, school, and community: Participatory action research with urban youth. *The Urban Review, 32*(2), 123–154. https://doi.org/10.1023/A:1005181731698

Mohanty, C. T. (2003). "Under western eyes" revisited: Feminist solidarity through anticapitalist struggles. *Signs: Journal of Women in Culture and Society, 28*(2), 499–535. https://doi.org/10.1086/342914

Pérez, E. (1999). *The decolonial imaginary: Writing Chicanas into history.* Indiana University Press.

Pillow, W. (2003). Confession, catharsis, or cure? Rethinking the uses of reflexivity as methodological power in qualitative research. *International Journal of Qualitative Studies in Education: QSE, 16*(2), 175–196. https://doi.org/10.1080/0951839032000060635

Pullen, A., Helin, J., & Harding, N. (Eds.). (2020). *Writing differently.* Emerald Group Publishing. https://doi.org/10.1108/S2046-6072202004

Pullen, A., & Rhodes, C. (2008). Dirty writing. *Culture and Organization, 14*(3), 241–259. https://doi.org/10.1080/14759550802270684

Rahman, M. A. (1993). The theoretical standpoint of PAR [Participatory Action-Research]. In O. Fals-Borda & M. A. Rahman (Eds.), *Action and knowledge: Breaking the monopoly with participatory action-research* (pp. 13–23). Apex Press.

Reyes Cruz, M. (2008). What if I just cite Graciela? Working toward decolonizing knowledge through a critical ethnography. *Qualitative Inquiry, 14*(4), 651–658. https://doi.org/10.1177/1077800408314346

Riemer, M. (2020). Framing community-engaged research. In M. Riemer, S. M. Reich, S. D. Evans, G. Nelson, & I. Prilleltensky (Eds.), *Community psychology* (3rd ed.). Macmillan International.

Robinson, C. J. (2020). *Black Marxism: The making of the Black radical tradition* (3rd ed.). University of North Carolina Press.

Rogoff, B. (2003). *The cultural nature of human development.* Oxford University Press.

Sandoval, C. (1990). Feminism and racism: A report on the 1981 National Women's Studies Association Conference. In G. Anzaldúa (Ed.), *Making face, making soul/Haciendo caras: Creative and critical perspectives by feminists of color* (pp. 55–71). Aunt Lute Books.

Silva, J. M. (2017). When research "Unravels": One community psychologist's tale of becoming a Nepantlera. *American Journal of Community Psychology, 59*(1–2), 239–251. https://doi.org/10.1002/ajcp.12122

Smith, L. T. (2012). *Decolonizing methodologies.* Zed Books.

Taylor, D. (1997). *Disappearing acts: Spectacles of gender and nationalism in Argentina's dirty war.* Duke University Press.

Tebes, J. K., Thai, N. D., & Matlin, S. L. (2014). Twenty-first century science as a relational process: From eureka! to team science and a place for community psychology. *American Journal of Community Psychology, 53*(3–4), 475–490. https://doi.org/10.1007/s10464-014-9625-7

Torre, M. E. (2009). Participatory action research and critical race theory: Fueling spaces for nos-otras to research. *The Urban Review, 41*(1), 106–120. https://doi.org/10.1007/s11256-008-0097-7

Tsing, A. L. (2005). *Friction: An ethnography of global connections.* Princeton University Press. https://doi.org/10.1515/9781400830596

Tuck, E. (2009). Re-visioning action: Participatory action research and Indigenous theories of change. *The Urban Review, 41*(1), 47–65. https://doi.org/10.1007/s11256-008-0094-x

Tuck, E., & Yang, K. W. (2014a). R-words: Refusing research. In D. Paris & M. T. Winn (Eds.), *Humanizing research: Decolonizing qualitative inquiry with youth and communities* (pp. 223–248). SAGE.

Tuck, E., & Yang, K. W. (2014b). Unbecoming claims: Pedagogies of refusal in qualitative research. *Qualitative Inquiry, 20*(6), 811–818. https://doi.org/10.1177/1077800414530265

Vaccarino-Ruiz, S. S., Gordon, D. L., & Langhout, R. D. (2021). Toward the democratization of knowledge: Using photovoice, social biography, and the "five whys" in YPAR with children. *Cultural Diversity and Ethnic Minority Psychology, 28*(2). https://doi.org/10.1037/cdp0000457

Vio Grossi, F. (1981). Socio-political implications of participatory research. *Convergence (Toronto), 14*(3), 43–51.

Walker, M., Martinez-Vargas, C., & Mkwananzi, F. (2020). Participatory action research: Towards (non-ideal) epistemic justice in a university in South Africa. *Journal of Global Ethics, 16*(1), 77–94. https://doi.org/10.1080/17449626.2019.1661269

Wang, C., & Burris, M. A. (1997). Photovoice: Concept, methodology, and use for participatory needs assessment. *Health Education & Behavior, 24*(3), 369–387. https://doi.org/10.1177/109019819702400309

SAMPLING ACROSS PEOPLE AND TIME

CHAPTER 16

INTRODUCTION TO SURVEY SAMPLING

Roger Tourangeau and Ting Yan

One of the many things that distinguishes psychology from the other social sciences is its reliance on experiments as a key methodological tool and its relative neglect of surveys of members of well-defined populations. Political scientists and sociologists are more likely than psychologists to use data from survey samples, although psychologists do sometimes analyze data from population surveys, often taking advantage of publicly available data sets. Relative to laboratory experiments, surveys based on large, representative samples are expensive to conduct. In part, these costs reflect the size and geographic scope of survey samples. For example, the monthly employment figures released by the Bureau of Labor Statistics are derived from the Current Population Survey (CPS), a monthly survey conducted by the U.S. Census Bureau that collects information from about 60,000 households clustered in 824 sites around the country (U.S. Bureau of the Census, 2006). (In survey parlance, a *household* is a group of people living together; the place where they live is referred to as a *housing unit* or *dwelling unit*.) Each state and the District of Columbia are represented by multiple sites and households in the monthly CPS samples. National surveys featuring face-to-face interviews (like the CPS) can easily cost more than $1,000 per case.

PROBABILITY AND NONPROBABILITY SAMPLING

Survey statisticians distinguish between different types of samples. A fundamental distinction is the one between probability and nonprobability samples. A *probability sample* (often called a *random sample*) is a sample in which each element of the population has a known (or at least calculable) and nonzero probability of selection. Our focus in this chapter is on probability samples—more specifically, on probability samples of households rather than businesses or other institutions. *Nonprobability samples* (which encompass all other kinds of samples) are ones in which a selection probability cannot be assigned to every unit in the population. Traditionally, the main subtypes of nonprobability sample are *samples of convenience* (such as the samples of volunteers that figure so prominently in psychological research), *purposive samples* (which are selected deliberately to meet some goal, often nonstatistical), and *quota samples* (in which interviewers recruit and interview an assigned number of cases from each of several subgroups). Recently, two other types of nonprobability samples have gained popularity among researchers. *Opt-in web panels* are samples of volunteers who agree to respond to web surveys. *Respondent-driven samples* (RDS) start with a

https://doi.org/10.1037/0000319-016

APA Handbook of Research Methods in Psychology, Second Edition: Vol. 2. Research Designs: Quantitative, Qualitative, Neuropsychological, and Biological, H. Cooper (Editor-in-Chief)

convenience sample of people with some characteristic of interest, who in turn recruit other people with that characteristic. Under certain assumptions, this method can yield unbiased population estimates (e.g., Heckathorn, 2011, which also explores how this more rigorous method evolved from snowball sampling). RDS is usually used for rare or hidden populations (e.g., illicit drug users).

Definition of Probability Sampling

Probability sampling is sufficiently unfamiliar to most psychologists that it will be useful to unpack the standard definition. First, the requirement that a selection probability can be assigned to every element in the population presupposes that there is some well-defined population from which the sample is drawn and is intended to represent. Sampling statisticians refer to this population as the *target population* for the survey. The target population for the CPS is the civilian household population (age 15 and older) for the 50 states of the United States and the District of Columbia at a specific time period (the calendar week that includes the 12th day of the target month). Like many general population surveys, the CPS excludes people living in institutions (such as the prison population or students living in dormitories). All surveys that use probability sampling have (sometimes only implicitly) a well-defined target population that they are trying to characterize. For example, the target population for a telephone survey may be all persons in households that can be reached by telephone. A political poll may attempt to characterize all adults who are registered to vote or all those who are likely to vote. Often the sampling or survey procedures consistently omit some portion of the target population, a problem referred to as *undercoverage*. For example, telephone surveys in the United States omit the (shrinking) portion of the U.S. household population that does not have a telephone.

The definition of probability sampling also requires that the sample be selected using some clearly defined sampling procedure that allows the assignment of a selection probability to each member of the population. This requirement is most easily met when there is a list of the entire population. Although some surveys use *list samples* (e.g., researchers conducting a survey of employees at a firm may select the sample from a list of the firm's employees), most surveys rely on more complicated sampling strategies needed when, as is typically the case, there is no list of the target population. Still, regardless of whether the sampling procedure is relatively simple or complicated, the sampling procedure must consist of some objective but random method for selecting a portion of the full population as members of the sample.

Apart from a well-defined population and an objective selection procedure, probability sampling requires that (a) a selection probability can be calculated for each sample member (and for the nonsample members as well, although this is rarely done in practice) and (b) that selection probability is nonzero for every element in the target population. With sample designs that allow multiple pathways into the sample, it may be difficult to determine the selection probability for a specific unit. For example, many people now have both a landline telephone and a cellular telephone, giving them at least two chances of being selected into a telephone sample that includes both. Making unbiased estimates from such a sample requires either a more complex calculation of the selection probabilities for a given member of the sample (reflecting the multiple pathways by which a person might have come into the sample) or a more complex estimation procedure. Besides the requirement that the selection probability can, in principle, be calculated for every member of the target population, that probability must be greater than zero. If the selection probabilities for some portion of the population are zero, this means that that portion of the population has been excluded by design and that sample estimates may be biased.

It is often thought that probability samples must give every member of the target population the same selection probability, but unequal probability samples are probably the rule rather than the exception in federal and other high-quality surveys. There are many reasons for selecting different elements with different probabilities. One of the most common is to increase the sample size for small, but analytically important, subgroups of the population. Giving members of these subgroups higher selection probabilities increases their representation in the sample and allows analysts to produce reasonably precise estimates for these *oversampled* subgroups.

Types of Nonprobability Samples

Most social science studies do not use probability samples but rely instead on less rigorous methods. In this section, we describe four types of nonprobability sample.

Convenience and purposive samples. Most psychological studies involve experiments with student samples. These samples are typically self-selected samples of volunteers, meeting some course requirement or lured by a cash payment. In the language of survey sampling, such samples are *samples of convenience*, and they lack all the earmarks of probability samples. They are not drawn from any well-defined population of interest, they are not selected through some objective random procedure, and they do not allow researchers to calculate the probability that any given participant would end up in a given study.

At least one alternative to probably sample has had considerable intuitive appeal over the years. That alternative—*purposive* or *judgment* sampling—involves selecting a set of units deemed to be typical or representative of the target population. It often seems counterintuitive that a randomly selected sample can accurately capture the diversity of a large population; it might seem more sensible to construct a microcosm of the population by having experts handpick a representative sample. As late as the 1920s, there was controversy about the relative merits of purposive and probability sampling (e.g., Jensen, 1926), and it was not until some years later that the advantages of probability sampling were clearly demonstrated (Neyman, 1934).

Opt-in web samples. Although nonprobability samples are now largely shunned by the federal statistical agencies that sponsor many of the large-scale surveys conducted in the United States, they have made something of a comeback with the advent of web surveys. Many online survey firms offer samples selected from panels of volunteers that may number in the millions; the panels themselves are just very large samples of convenience (see Couper, 2000, for a discussion of web surveys and their samples). As survey costs have risen and response rates have fallen (National Research Council, 2013), the appeal of these online panels has increased dramatically. A thousand interviews with members of a nationally representative probability sample can easily cost more than $1 million; a thousand completed surveys from members of an online panel can cost less than $10,000. As a result, many (if not most) election polls rely partly or wholly on opt-in web panels (Kennedy et al., 2016, Figure 3). Still, opt-in web panels have been shown to differ systematically from the population as a whole (e.g., Cornesse et al., 2020; Kennedy et al., 2016), and estimates from surveys using opt-in panel members are subject to potentially large biases. The popularity of these panels has prompted concern among survey professionals, and one of the leading survey journals, the *Journal of Survey Statistics and Methodology,* published a special issue in 2020 on this topic.

Respondent-driven sampling. One other type of nonprobability sample is worth mentioning—respondent-driven sampling (RDS). A respondent-driven sample begins with a convenience sample of a few members of some rare or hidden population (jazz musicians, illicit drug users) for which no frame exists. These initial recruits (or "seeds") are asked to recruit a fixed number of additional members of the target population ("alters"); these new recruits are, in turn, asked to recruit additional population members and so on until the desired sample size is reached (see Heckathorn, 1997, 2002). Such samples can be used to estimate the size of the population or to give some indication of the characteristics of a population that would be nearly impossible to sample using probability methods. As with other methods for selecting nonprobability samples, the potential for bias in the resulting estimates is quite high—the initial sample of seeds may be unrepresentative, the recruitment of alters is nonrandom, recruited members of the population may not actually participate, and so on (Gile & Handcock, 2010).

Comparisons of probability and nonprobability samples. Several researchers have made systematic comparisons between nonprobability online panels and probability samples, addressing the issue of how well volunteer online panels can be used to characterize the general population. A review of empirical research comparing estimates from surveys using probability and nonprobability samples had two main findings (Cornesse et al., 2020). First, estimates from probability samples were generally more accurate than those from nonprobability samples; accuracy was assessed by comparing the survey estimates to trusted external benchmarks, such as figures from the decennial census. This finding held for surveys on different topics, conducted in different countries, and at different times. Second, although weighting could reduce the errors in estimates from nonprobability samples, even after weighting, the probability samples still produced more accurate estimates. The failure of the British polls in the 2015 elections in the United Kingdom also seems to have reflected the reliance of British pollsters on nonprobability samples (Sturgis et al., 2016).

The rest of this chapter covers probability sampling for household surveys in detail. We start by describing the different types of lists (or *frames*) from which such samples are selected. The next two sections of the chapter then turn to the major classes of sample design. The simplest probability sample design is a *simple random sample*, which is rarely used in practice but provides a convenient foundation for discussing the more complex sample designs covered in the next section of the chapter. The final two sections discuss methods for weighting sample data and for measuring sampling errors for statistics from surveys with complex sample designs.

SAMPLING FRAMES

Survey samples start with a *sampling frame*, a list or procedure that identifies all the elements making up the target population. Lessler and Kalsbeek's (1992) more detailed definition provides a useful starting point for our discussion of sampling frames:

> The frame consists of materials, procedures, and devices that identify, distinguish, and allow access to the elements of the target population. The frame is composed of a finite set of units to which the probability sampling scheme is applied. Rules or mechanisms for linking the frame units to the population elements are an integral part of the frame. The frame also includes auxiliary information (measures of size, demographic information). (p. 44)

The ideal frame would be a list of all members of the population, along with addresses and telephone numbers that could be used to locate and contact them. For some populations, such as students at a particular university or employees at a given company, such frames exist. But, although some European countries have population registries, the United States lacks a list of all its residents. As a result, for general population surveys in the United States, households are usually the sampling units. Households are typically identified and sampled through either their addresses or telephone numbers; thus, the two major types of sampling frames used for general population surveys in the United States are *area frames* and *telephone frames*. Both rely on a set of rules that link households or individuals to frame elements (that is, addresses or telephone numbers).

Frames for Area Samples

Many surveys sample addresses rather than directly selecting households. The frame for such samples typically begins with a list of areas, or an area frame. Area frames, together with area probability sampling, were widely used in the early stages of survey research (Kish, 1965), and this combination is still used in many federal surveys, including the CPS. With area probability samples, the sample is often selected in stages, beginning with relatively large areas (such as counties or metropolitan areas), then proceeding to progressively smaller areas at successive stages (U.S. Census Tracts or blocks), and finally to individual addresses.[1]

Separate frames are needed for each stage of sampling. The frame for the first stage of selection is typically a list of counties and metropolitan areas, along with population figures and geographic definitions for each. Once a sample of counties or other first-stage units has been selected, frames for the sampling units at the next stage must be obtained. In many surveys, the second-stage frame consists of lists of Census Tracts or blocks. Information about counties, metropolitan areas, Census Tracts, and blocks is available from the U.S. Census Bureau. Once relatively compact areas like blocks have been selected, the next step is to compile a list of addresses within those areas.

There are two main options for developing these lists. The traditional approach was to send field staff (or *listers*) to list addresses for the housing units in the sample areas, following a strict protocol. For instance, listers were generally be trained to canvass each selected area starting at a specified point (typically, the northwest corner) and continuing clockwise; the lister was supposed to record an address or description of every housing unit he or she found. The lists were then compiled and sampling of addresses carried out. Thus, the frame at this stage consisted of a set of area maps along with the lists of addresses for the housing units in each area. This process is referred to as *traditional listing*, *field listing*, or *on-site enumeration*. The other option is relatively new; it involves using the address list maintained by the U.S. Postal Service (USPS), which is available through various vendors (see https://www.aapor.org/Education-Resources/Reports/

Address-based-Sampling.aspx#SECTION%202 for details). The USPS address list is called the *delivery sequence file* (DSF); it lists residential addresses served and updated by mail carriers. It is ordered by zip code, carrier route, and walk sequence number, and these codes uniquely identify every delivery point in the country. *Address-based sampling* (ABS) entails using the DSF as the sampling frame, and it has become increasingly popular for survey samples. Studies indicate the DSF includes 97% of U.S. households (Iannacchione et al., 2003; O'Muircheartaigh et al., 2002) and, thus, provides a viable alternative to field listing for surveys of the general household population.

Frames for Telephone Samples

Random-digit-dial sampling. Most surveys use some form of random-digit-dial (RDD) to sample households for telephone surveys (Wolter et al., 2009). RDD takes advantage of the structure of U.S. telephone numbers, which can be represented as NPA-NXXabcd. The initial three digits (NPA) represent number plan areas or, to use more familiar terminology, area codes; these tend to be nested within states but do not have a straightforward correspondence with any other unit of geography. The three digits represented by NXX are called exchange codes or prefixes. Finally, the last four digits (abcd) are the suffix. Most forms of RDD sampling are based on a unit called the *100-bank*. A 100-bank consists of the 100 possible telephone numbers that begin with a given combination of the first eight digits (i.e., NPA-NXX-ab). With any given 100-bank, all the numbers may be assigned to landline telephones, to cellular telephones, or to a mix of both. Only a fraction of the 100 possible numbers may have been assigned, with the rest yet to be assigned. A list of all the active NPA-NXX combinations can be obtained from Telcordia Technologies or sampling vendors such as Survey Sampling, Inc., or the Marketing Systems Group.

---

[1]The Office of Management and Budget is charged with defining official metropolitan areas, which consist of a central city (with at least 50,000 residents) and one or more adjacent counties or countylike units (e.g., parishes, boroughs).

Telephone sampling faces two important but conflicting challenges. On the one hand, many potential numbers within active area code-prefix combinations are not working residential numbers (WRNs); in fact, the overall proportion of WRNs is less than 10% and falling (see Boyle et al., 2009, Table 5). Thus, a good deal of effort can be wasted dialing unassigned or business numbers. Unassigned numbers are not necessarily linked to a recorded message and, thus, can be hard to identify. On the other hand, sampling only listed telephone numbers would yield a much higher hit rate of WRNs but would omit a substantial portion of the telephone population—around 30% (Brick et al., 1995).

To cope with the problems of low hit rates and low population coverage, many survey researchers use a method called *list-assisted* sampling. A paper by Casady and Lepkowski (1993) examined the statistical properties of a method that generates random numbers only within 100-banks associated with at least one listed residential number. Listed-assisted sampling became practical once databases that included all the listed telephone numbers throughout the United States were commercially available. Subsequent empirical work by Brick et al. (1995) showed that the exclusion of 0-banks (banks with no residential listings) from list-assisted RDD samples led to little bias, in part because the 0-banks included so few WRNs—less than 4% of the total. List-assisted sampling of 1+-banks (that is, 100-banks with at least one residential listing) is now the most widely used method of sampling landline telephones in government and academic surveys.

Dual-frame samples. As cellular telephones have supplanted landline telephones as the most popular form of telephone service, telephone sampling has had to adjust. Banks with at least one listed residential number appear to include a shrinking proportion of landline WRNs, with one study (Fahimi et al., 2009) suggesting that as many as 20% of all WRNs may be in 0-banks (Boyle et al., 2009, provided a more optimistic assessment of the coverage of 1+ banks; they estimated that these banks still include about

95% of all WRNs). Even worse, a growing proportion of the population only has cell telephone service; as of 2019, more than 60% of adults and 70% of children lived in cell-only households (Blumberg & Luke, 2020).

To address these concerns, dual-frame sampling has been adopted as a means of including both landline and cell numbers in telephone samples. A dual-frame telephone sample draws independent samples of landline and cell phone numbers. This gives two (or more) chances of selections to households or individual who have both types of service (*dual users*). One approach for dealing with this issue, the screening approach, attempts to remove any dual users through screening. For instance, households sampled from the cell phone frame would be screened out during the data collection and dropped from the sample if they reported also having a landline (e.g., Brick et al., 2007). This approach simplifies weighting—it removes the overlap units from one frame—but is more expensive because of the added costs of calling and screening the sample cell phone numbers. Most dual-frame surveys take a different tack. Dual users are retained in the sample regardless of whether they were sampled from the landline frame or the cell phone frame. At the estimation stage, the weights of overlap units are adjusted to compensate for their multiple chances of selection. (We return to this issue later, in our discussion of survey weights.)

In dual-frame surveys, a key design decision involves the allocation of the sample across the two frames—the researchers must decide what proportion of the final sample should be cell phone numbers and what proportion landline numbers. This decision has cost implications, since it is more expensive to interview respondents with cell phone numbers than those with landlines. In addition, differences across frames in the rate of eligibility for the survey and the likelihood of completing an interview are major considerations in determining the optimal sample allocation.

Cell-only samples. The prevalence and use of cell phones in the United States has increased steadily since 2000. By 2021, 97% of American adults owned a cell phone of some kind (https://www.pewresearch.org/internet/fact-sheet/mobile/). The standard frames for generating RDD samples of cell phone numbers are lists of all possible cell telephone numbers; these are generally based on industry databases that identify types of service provided by 1,000-blocks (that is, groups of 1,000 potential numbers that share an area code and three-digit prefix). The frames are available from most sample suppliers. Typically, *full RDD* samples are drawn from the cell phone frame. Full RDD involves appending a randomly generated four-digit suffix to a sample of 1,000-blocks. As the general population coverage of cell phone frames continues to improve, many surveys will doubtless begin to field cell-only samples.

Still, cell phone frames present some challenges. One is ported numbers. U.S. consumers can keep their cell phone numbers when moving from one place to another. As a result, determining the geographic location associated with a cell phone number based on the number alone is not always straightforward. The Behavioral Risk Factor Surveillance System (BRFSS)—one of the largest RDD surveys done in the United States—reviewed the geographic locations of sample cell phone numbers and found 7% were misclassified by state and 42% by county (Pierannunzi et al., 2019). This is important in the BRFSS, which consists of separate telephone samples for each state. In addition, surveys need to modify their usual procedures for landline surveys when calling cell phones (American Association for Public Opinion Research, 2018). The Telephone Consumer Protection Act prohibits cold calls to cell phone numbers. In addition, it is standard to ask respondents not to answer if answering the survey questions would put their safety at risk (e.g., when they are driving).

Registered voter samples.   Voter files are national databases built by commercial organizations using publicly available voter registration data. The voter files may be enriched with information from other sources (e.g., data from credit bureaus). An evaluation of five voter files found that,

although the files had relatively high coverage overall, they were less likely to include politically disengaged segments of the public, such as younger, Hispanic, and more mobile voters (Igielnik et al., 2018). In addition, although some variables (race or party affiliation) on the voter files were quite accurate, others (e.g., income, education) were often missing. Thus, these lists are better suited as frames for surveys of registered voters than of the general population.

Probability Web Samples

Probability web panels start with a probability sample of the target population, often selected via ABS, and the panel members are recruited via offline modes of contact, such as mail, face-to-face, or telephone. Once recruited, the panel members are asked to fill out survey questionnaires online (or by mail if the member lacks internet access). Compared with nonprobability web panels (the opt-in samples described earlier), probability web panels tend to be smaller but have better coverage of the population. In the United States, there are several probability web panels: the KnowledgePanel, maintained by Ipsos (https://www.ipsos.com/en-us/solutions/public-affairs/knowledgepanel); the AmeriSpeak Panel, maintained by NORC at the University of Chicago (https://amerispeak.norc.org/Pages/default.aspx); the American Trends Panel maintained by the Pew Research Center (https://www.pewresearch.org/methods/u-s-survey-research/american-trends-panel/); the Understanding America Study Panel, maintained by the University of Southern California (https://uasdata.usc.edu/index.php); the American Life Panel maintained by RAND (https://www.rand.org/research/data/alp.html); and the SSRS probability panels (SSRS Opinion Panel and SSRS Text Message Panel, https://ssrs.com/services/). There are also several probability web panels in Europe. A weakness shared by these samples is the low cumulative response rate for any given survey; nonresponse occurs in the initial recruitment of panel members, over time as panel members drop out, and in requests to complete specific surveys.

FRAME PROBLEMS AND COVERAGE ERRORS

In a perfect world, a sampling frame would satisfy four requirements: (a) Every population element would appear on the frame; (b) every population element would appear as a separate frame element; (c) every population element would appear only once; and (d) the frame would contain nothing but population elements (Kish, 1965; see also Lessler & Kalsbeek, 1992). That is, with a perfect frame, there would be a one-to-one correspondence between the frame elements and the elements in the target population. Any departures from a one-to-one correspondence between the sampling frame and target population create potential coverage problems; these problems include undercoverage, ineligibility, duplication, and clustering.

Undercoverage

Undercoverage refers to the omission of some members of the target population from the sampling frame. No frame is perfect, but area frames are thought to provide the best coverage of the general population, with some under-coverage because of the exclusion of the homeless population, missed housing units, and within-household omissions. This last form of under-coverage reflects the failure to include all members of the household on the household roster used to select a respondent, either because of deliberate concealment (Tourangeau et al., 1997) or confusion about who should be included (Martin, 1999). Every survey misses a portion of the population and many surveys have higher rates of undercoverage among particular demographic subgroups, such as young Black or Hispanic males.

For means and proportions, coverage bias results when the population elements that are included on the sampling frame differ from those that are not on the frame on the characteristic of interest.

$$Bias = P_{Exc}\left(\bar{Y}_{Cov} - \bar{Y}_{Exc}\right), \qquad (16.1)$$

in which P_{Exc} is the proportion of the target population that is excluded from the frame,

$\bar{Y}_{Cov}$ is the mean (or proportion) among the portion of the population that is covered, and $\bar{Y}_{Exc}$ is the mean (or proportion) among those who are excluded. Intuitively, the bias gets worse as the proportion of the population that is left out gets larger and as the excluded portion differs more markedly from the portion that is represented on the variable of interest.

Coverage bias is obviously not desirable, and survey researchers do their best to reduce the extent of undercoverage—the P_{Exc} term in the bias equation—to a minimum. For example, when one frame is clearly inadequate, the survey researchers may sample from a second frame to improve coverage; telephone surveys may, thus, include samples of both landline and cell telephone numbers. Or interviewers assigned to cases in an area sample may be instructed to look for missed units linked to the sample addresses (a method known as the *half-open interval* procedure) and to add some portion of these omitted addresses to the sample.

Ineligible, Blank, or Foreign Elements

The first potential problem is that the frame may not include enough elements, excluding some members of the target population. But the opposite problem is also common: The frame includes too many elements, including some that do not belong to the target population. For example, many potential telephone numbers are nonworking or business numbers. Survey researchers attempt to purge such elements from the frame before sampling or at least before fielding the sample. For example, the vendors of telephone samples often put the sample numbers through autodialers that can identify unassigned numbers by their rings; this allows them to cull out some of the unassigned numbers before the sample is fielded. Unoccupied dwellings are the analogue to unassigned numbers in the context of area samples but are difficult to identify without actually knocking on the door. Ineligible units are generally less of a problem than undercoverage, because they do not contribute to error if they are dropped from the sample. Still, the presence of many ineligibles in a sample can lead to smaller-than-expected sample sizes and add to data collection costs. Researchers can allow for ineligibility by selecting a larger initial sample if the rate of ineligibility is known or can be estimated.

Duplication (or Multiplicity)

When a population element is associated with more than one element on the sampling frame, the frame is said to have duplicates. *Duplication* (or *multiplicity*) is quite common in surveys. For example, in telephone surveys, someone with a cell phone and a landline phone has at least two chances for inclusion in the sample. Similarly, in area frames, households with more than one residence constitute duplicates. A population element linked to two frame elements has twice the probability of being selected as the other population elements, leading to bias in the survey estimates if there is a correlation between the rate of duplication and the variables of interest. Multiplicity can be handled in several ways. Sometimes the frame can be deduplicated before sampling. Or rules can be adopted to identify and remove duplicate elements at the time of sample selection or data collection. For instance, a rule can be imposed to accept only the first eligible element and treat the later duplicated frame elements as ineligibles. (Of course, this in turn requires a rule for defining one of the frame elements as the first.) The most common solution is to apply weights after data collection to compensate the overrepresentation of population units linked to two or more frame elements. In the simplest case, the weighting factor is the inverse of the number of frame elements linked with the population element.

Clustering

The final frame problem is clustering, which arises when a frame element corresponds to multiple population elements. For instance, an address is shared by all members of the household. Therefore, if the survey samples adults via their addresses, it runs into the problem of the clustering of adults who share that address. Although it is possible to select all of the eligible elements within the cluster, this is often difficult operationally, especially if each member is supposed to respond for himself or herself. Still, some surveys (including the CPS) do gather information about all eligible members of sample households.

The alternative is to subsample within the household. In the case of household surveys, within-household respondent selection procedures can be used to select (randomly or nonrandomly) one eligible member of the household. As noted, this can lead to coverage problems, when household members are left off of the rosters that are used to select a single member as the respondent (Martin, 1999; Tourangeau et al., 1997). Streamlined within-household selection procedures are often used in telephone surveys (such as asking for the adult with the most recent birthday), but these can also lead to undercoverage problems (Gaziano, 2005; Yan, 2009).

To conclude our discussion of frames, we note that coverage problems are problems with sampling frames. As a result, they exist *before* the sample is drawn. Any biases that might be produced would still arise even if we did a census of the frame elements rather than drawing a sample. Thus, they are not problems with any specific sample but are likely to affect all samples selected from the frame.

SIMPLE RANDOM SAMPLING

Most discussions of sampling procedures begin by describing simple random sampling; it is mathematically the simplest procedure, and it provides the key building blocks for other designs that are more common in practice. Sampling texts usually follow certain notational conventions that we also adopt here. Population values and parameters are represented by capital letters and the corresponding sample quantities by lower case letters. For example, the population size is N and the sample size is n. Likewise, the vector of population values for a given variable is represented by $Y_1, Y_2, Y_3, \ldots, Y_N$; the vector of sample values is represented by $y_1, y_2, y_3, \ldots, y_n$. In general, we follow the notation used by Kalton (1983; see also Lohr, 2022).

A simple random sample is a sample with a fixed size, n, in which each element has the same probability of selection (n/N) and each *combination* of n elements has the same probability of selection as every other combination of n elements. Sometimes, selection procedures are used that allow the same population element to be selected more than once, a design referred to as unrestricted random sampling or simple random sampling with replacement (*srswr*). We focus on simple random sampling without replacement (or *srswor*).

The population mean ($\bar{Y}$) and sample mean ($\bar{y}$) are defined in the usual ways:

$$\bar{y} = \sum_{i-1}^{n} y_i$$

$$\bar{Y} = \sum_{i-1}^{N} Y_i. \tag{16.2}$$

And the sample element variance is also defined in the familiar way:

$$s^2 = \frac{\sum_{i=1}^{n}(y_i - \bar{y})^2}{n-1}. \tag{16.3}$$

But, in the sampling literature, the expression for the population element variance typically uses $N-1$ rather than N in the denominator:

$$S^2 = \frac{\sum_{i=1}^{N}(Y_i - \bar{Y})^2}{N-1}. \tag{16.4}$$

When N is used in place of $N-1$, the population element variance is denoted by σ^2 rather than by S^2. The statistical properties of a given statistic depend both on the form of the estimator and the sample design; reflecting this, sampling texts often use subscripts to denote statistics from a particular sample design. Thus, the sample mean from a simple random sample is denoted $\bar{y}_0$. With a sample random sample, $\bar{y}_0$ is an unbiased estimator of the population mean.

Because the sample is drawn from a finite population with a fixed population total (denoted by Y), there is a slight negative covariance among the elements in a simple random sample. This covariance is reflected in the sampling variance for the mean:

$$V(\bar{y}_0) = (1 - n/N)\frac{S^2}{n}$$

$$= (1 - f)\frac{S^2}{n}. \tag{16.5}$$

Equation 16.5 is similar to the formula for the variance of a mean that is familiar to most psychologists but introduces a new element—the factor $1 - f$, or the *finite population correction*. (In addition, Equation 16.5 uses S^2 in place of σ^2) The variance in Equation 16.5 measures the variance of the means from all possible simple random samples drawn from the population. According to the equation, the variance depends on the variance of the elements, the size of the sample, and the portion of the population that is selected into the sample. It makes sense that the mean would vary less across samples as the samples included larger and larger proportions of the population; f, the *sampling fraction*, represents the proportion of the population that is included in the sample, and $1 - f$ represents the reduction in variance that results from selecting a nonnegligible share of the population. At the limit, there will be no variation across samples when the sample includes the entire population so that the survey is a complete census (that is, when $f = 1$). When population is infinite or when the sample is selected with replacement, the finite population correction term drops out (because $f = 0$) and $S^2 = \sigma^2$ so that Equation 16.5 reduces to the more familiar σ^2/n.

The sample element variance is an unbiased estimate of S^2 (not of σ^2), so that the expression in Equation 16.6 gives an unbiased estimator of the variance of a mean derived from a simple random sample:

$$v(\bar{y}_0) = (1 - f)\frac{s^2}{n}. \tag{16.6}$$

Again, the lower case v indicates that the quantity in Equation 16.6 is a sample estimate. Similarly, the usual estimator for the standard error of y_0 is the square root of the quantity in Equation 16.6:

$$se(\bar{y}_0) = \left[(1 - f)\frac{s^2}{n}\right]^{1/2}. \qquad (16.7)$$

When the variable of interest (y) is dichotomous, the mean becomes a proportion. The sample proportion (p_0) provides an unbiased estimate of the population proportion (P). An unbiased estimator of the sampling variance of p_0 is given by

$$v(p_0) = (1 - f)\frac{p_0(1 - p_0)}{n - 1}. \qquad (16.8)$$

Relative to other sampling designs, simple random samples have several noteworthy properties: (a) The samples are element samples (i.e., they are selected in a single stage directly from a list frame for the target population); (b) the selection probabilities for any one population element do not depend on those of any other population element; (c) they make no attempt to control the size of the samples for different subpopulations (or, in sampling parlance, different *sampling strata*); (d) the samples are equal probability samples (i.e., every element in the population has the same selection probability);[2] and (e) because they are equal probability samples, the resulting data do not require any weighting to produce unbiased estimates of population means or proportions (assuming that all sample members respond to the survey).

These properties of simple random sampling are mostly absent from the sample designs that are used to draw large national samples in practice. Still, simple random samples provide a useful starting point for discussing more complex designs, and the efficiency of statistics from other designs is often compared with those from simple random samples.

When simple random sampling can be used, the simplest practical method (assuming that the frame exists as an electronic data file) is to (a) generate a random variable for each element on the frame, (b) sort the file by this file by this randomly generated variable, and (c) select the first n cases from the sorted frame file. In an earlier era, tables of random numbers would have been used in place of random number generators to select the sample.

MORE COMPLEX SAMPLE DESIGNS

Most actual samples depart from simple random sampling for three main reasons. The first has to do with the absence of sampling frames that provide adequate coverage of the target population. In the United States, for example, there is no complete list of individuals or households that could be used to cover the general population and the costs of developing such a list frame would be prohibitive.[3] Instead, most samples are selected via frames of *clusters* of people, such as lists of counties or smaller geographic units, like blocks. A second reason for the relative popularity of cluster samples is that they can sharply reduce the cost of data collection. Even if one could select a simple random sample of adults in the United States, it would be extremely expensive to interview the members of the sample because they would be scattered at random across the United States. It is a lot more cost-effective to carry out in-person interviews with sample cases that are clustered—say, within a set of sample blocks. The final reason that simple random samples are seldom selected in practice is that they are not just expensive but can be statistically inefficient as well. Because simple random samples do not ensure representation to key population subgroups, the estimates derived from them can have higher variances than similar estimates

---

[2]The class of equal probability sampling designs is often referred to as *epsem* designs in the sampling literature (e.g., Kish, 1965); epsem is an acronym for equal probability of selection methods.

[3]The closest thing to such a frame in the United States is the Master Address File (MAF) compiled by the U.S. Census Bureau; the MAF is the list of residential addresses used for the decennial census of the population. It is thought to have nearly complete coverage, but by law it is not available to researchers outside the U.S. Census Bureau. The USPS address list, or DSF, is available to survey researchers (through licensed vendors), but the coverage is less complete than that of the MAF, which supplements the DSF addresses with data from other sources.

from stratified sample designs. Simple random samples guarantee unbiased estimates in the long run, but other designs that build in greater control over subgroup sample sizes offer greater intuitive appeal (the samples look more like cross-sections of the population) and can produce unbiased estimates with lower standard errors.

Stratification

Stratification refers to dividing the population into nonoverlapping subgroups and then selecting separate samples within each subgroup (or *stratum*). It makes sense that stratified samples would produce less variability than simple random samples of the same overall size because stratified samples control the stratum sample sizes, implying that certain unrepresentative samples are impossible in a stratified design rather than just unlikely (e.g., all the samples in which no cases are selected from one or more strata). The reduced sampling variance relative to simple random sampling reflects this feature of stratified sampling (e.g., Neyman, 1934). Another way of looking at the gains from stratification is to think of the overall sampling variance in a survey estimate as consisting of two components—one reflecting random fluctuations across samples in the mix of cases by strata and the other reflecting random fluctuations in the sample means within each stratum. Stratified sampling eliminates the first component of the sampling variance.

Most sampling texts use the subscript h to denote a specific stratum; we follow that convention here. We denote the size of the stratum population by N_h, the stratum sample size by n_h, the stratum population mean by $\bar{Y}_h$, the stratum mean by $\bar{y}_h$, and so on. The proportion of the overall population in stratum h is denoted by W_h ($= N_h/N$). The overall sample estimate (for a mean or proportion) is a weighted sum of the stratum means (or proportions):

$$\bar{y}_{str} = \sum_{h=1}^{H} W_h \bar{y}_h. \qquad (16.9)$$

Because the samples in each stratum are selected independently from each other, the variance of $\bar{y}_{str}$ is given by Equation 16.10:

$$V(\bar{y}_{str}) = \sum_{h=1}^{H} W_h^2 v(\bar{y}_h). \qquad (16.10)$$

If the samples within each stratum are selected via simple random sampling, the variance becomes

$$V(\bar{y}_{str}) = \sum_{h=1}^{H} W_h^2 (1 - f_h) \frac{s_h^2}{n_h}, \qquad (16.11)$$

in which f_h is the sampling fraction in stratum h (that is, n_h/N_h) and s_h^2 is the within-stratum element variance. The latter quantity can be estimated by the sample within-stratum variance, s_h^2, leading to Equation 16.12:

$$v(\bar{y}_{str}) = \sum_{h=1}^{H} W_h^2 (1 - f_h) \frac{s_h^2}{n_h}. \qquad (16.12)$$

There are two major types of stratified sample—proportionate and disproportionate. In a proportionate stratified sample, the proportions of the sample in each stratum are the same as the population proportions (i.e., $\frac{n_h}{n} = \frac{N_h}{N} = W_h$). A proportionate allocation, thus, yields a sample that is a microcosm of the population, with the same mix of elements by stratum as the population. It also means that the sample is selected with equal probabilities (since $f_h = \frac{n_h}{N_h} = \frac{W_h n}{W_h N} = \frac{n}{N} = f$).

When the sample follows a proportionate stratified design, the estimator for the sampling variance given in Equation 16.12 simplifies even further:

$$v(\bar{y}_{str}) = \frac{(1 - f)}{n} \sum_{h=1}^{H} W_h s_h^2. \qquad (16.13)$$

The expression in Equation 16.13 is quite similar to the one in Equation 16.6, but the weighted sum of within-stratum element variances replaces the overall element variance. Because the overall variance is the sum of the within and between components, the variance of a mean from a proportionate stratified cannot be larger than that from a simple random sample and can be much smaller. The gains from stratification vary from variable to variable and depend on the ratio of the within-stratum element variance for that variable $(S_w^2 = \sum_{h=1}^{H} W_h S_h^2)$ to the total element variance (S^2).

Given the clear advantages of proportionate allocation—greater apparent representativeness, increased precision of the estimates, and greater computational ease (because weights are not needed)—one might wonder why anyone would use disproportionate allocation across strata. There are two main reasons that disproportionate allocation is often used in practice. First, additional sample cases are sometimes needed to increase the precision of estimates involving one of the strata. For example, the CPS sample design might allocate more than the proportionate sample size for a particular state so that the unemployment rate figures for that state meet a specified precision goal. A related purpose for departing from proportionate allocation is to improve the precision of estimates of the *difference* between means for two of the strata $(\bar{y}_1 - \bar{y}_2)$. Difference estimates tend to achieve the highest efficiency when the two strata have near-equal sample sizes (for a more thorough discussion, see Kalton, 1983, p. 25).

The second reason for using a disproportionate allocation is that it can lower the variance of an estimate for the entire population even more than a proportionate allocation. The proportionate allocation puts the sample cases where the population is—that is, $n_h \propto W_h$. The optimal allocation takes uncertainty and costs per case into account as well:

$$\frac{n_h}{n} = \frac{W_h S_h / \sqrt{c_h}}{\sum_{h=1}^{H} W_h S_h / \sqrt{c_h}}, \qquad (16.14)$$

in which S_h is the within-stratum standard deviation and c_h is the cost per case for data collection within stratum h. The optimal allocation allots cases where the population is largest, where the uncertainty is greatest, and where the costs per case are lowest. When the data collection costs do not differ by stratum, then the optimal stratum sample sizes are proportional to the product of the stratum weight and the within-stratum standard deviation $(n_h \propto W_h S_h)$, an allocation often referred to as the *Neyman allocation* (Neyman, 1934). And when the stratum standard deviations are also the same, then the proportionate allocation is also optimal.

The best stratification variables are those for which there is substantial variation across strata (and minimal variation within strata) on the key survey variables; these produce the largest reductions in the variances of the estimates. Still, there are practical limitations on the likely effectiveness of stratification in practice. First, the stratification variables need to be available for all members of the population; this means that the stratification variables are usually limited to variables available on the sampling frame. In addition, most surveys involve multiple estimates, and the stratification variables (and the allocation of sample cases by strata) that are best for one estimate may not be best for another. Thus, in practice, the variables that are used to stratify the sample tend to be ones that are weakly related to all the variables in the survey. For example, in an area probability sample, the sample areas are likely to be stratified geographically (by Census region or finer levels of geography) and by level of urbanization (e.g., urban vs. rural). Similarly, in a telephone survey, the stratification variables are also likely to be geographic variables, reflecting information that is available about the area covered by the area code or prefix of the sample numbers. In a business survey, it is sometimes possible to find better stratification variables because richer data tend to be available for businesses. Because the frame data may offer only limited choices for stratification variables, surveys sometimes select a large initial sample and conduct short screening interviews with the members of that initial sample. These screening data are used to classify the cases by strata, and a stratified subsample is selected for more detailed data collection. The screening interviews allow the researchers to collect better stratification data than are available on the frame. This technique is referred to a *two-phase* or *double* sampling.

Systematic Sampling

Before the era of high-speed computers, it was often necessary to select samples by hand, and one method that reduced the labor involved was systematic sampling. *Systematic sampling* entails selecting every *k*th element on the list, beginning with an element selected at random from among the first *k* (Madow & Madow, 1944). When the sampling interval (the value of *k*) is not an integer, it is still easy to use systematic sampling. One method is simply to truncate the result obtained by successively adding *k* to previous sums beginning with the random starting value. For example, suppose the goal is to select a sample of 100 students from a population of 1,623 students at specific high school. The sampling interval is then 16.23 (= 1,623/100). A random start is selected (i.e., a random number is generated in the range from 0.01 to 16.23); let us say that this starting value is 2.55. The first selection is the second student on the list (the integer portion of 2.55); the next selection is the 18th student on the list (corresponding to the truncated value of 2.55 plus 16.23, or the integer portion of 18.78); the third student selected is the 35th student on the list (corresponding to the truncated value of 2.55 plus 16.23 plus 16.23, or the integral portion of 35.01); and so on down the list until 100 students are selected. If the integer portion of the initially selected random start is zero, then one just adds the sampling interval to that random start and begins over from there. For example, had the initial random start been 0.35, the new random start would be 16.58 (i.e., 0.35 plus 16.23) and the first selection would be the 16th student on the list.

Even though computational burden is no longer a consideration, many sampling statisticians still use systematic sampling to select samples. One reason is that this selection algorithm is easy to program and check. The method is also flexible. One way to select a simple random sample is to generate a random variable for each element on the list, sort the elements by this random value, and then select a systematic sample. The first two steps put the elements into a random order and the third step selects an equal probability sample of them. Systematic sampling also offers a simple method for selecting a proportionate stratified sample; just sort the elements by the stratum variables and then select a systematic sample from the sorted list. (When the strata are formed by sorting the file in this way, the strata are said to be *implicit*.) This eliminates the work of selecting separate samples from each stratum.

Systematic sampling is also a simple way to build relatively complex stratification into a sample design. Once the elements have been sorted into their respective strata, they can be further sorted within the strata by some continuous variable. For example, areas can be sorted into strata based on their Census region and level of urbanization; areas can then be sorted further within these strata according to the percentage of residents who are minority group members. It is often easier to take advantage of the frame variables in this way than to group elements into refined explicit strata.

The major drawback to systematic sampling is that is sharply reduces the number of possible samples that can be selected and sometimes those samples can be highly unrepresentative. Suppose the sampling interval is an integer, say, 100. This means that, no matter how large the population is once the frame file has been sorted, only 100 distinct samples can be selected. If the order of the elements on the frame follows some underlying periodicity, this can also create problems. For example, consider a list in which husbands and wives alternate, with the wife always coming first; then, if *k* is an even integer, half the possible samples will consist exclusively of wives and the other half exclusively of husbands. The limited number of potential samples means that it can be difficult to find an unbiased estimator of the variance for statistics derived from systematic samples; Wolter (2007) provided a good discussion of these difficulties. Making the last sort variable, a randomly generated value helps alleviate these problems by increasing the number of potential samples.

Cluster Sampling

As we noted at the outset of this section, it is often more cost effective to pick nearby bunches of cases rather than individuals. For example, the members of a sample may be clustered within a set of sample blocks or sample schools. The advantage of selecting the sample in this way is that it can lead to large reductions in the data collection costs, allowing the survey to have a much larger sample than otherwise possible.

The simplest version of cluster sampling involves selecting a set of clusters and then including all of the individuals within that cluster as part of the sample (Hansen et al., 1953). More complicated versions involve subsampling units within the selected clusters. Large national samples often involve multiple levels of clustering; the sample is selected in several stages, with smaller clusters selected at each successive stage. The CPS sample is an example. It is selected in three stages. The first-stage units are metropolitan areas and individual counties; a total of 824 such areas are included in the CPS sample. Within the sample first-stage areas, clusters of housing units are then selected; these second-stage units typically consist of four nearby housing units. Sometimes these clusters are larger than expected and a third stage of sampling is carried out to select a subsample of the housing units. Data are gathered for all of the eligible residents at the sample housing units (U.S. Bureau of the Census, 2006). Many national area probability samples follow similar strategies, selecting counties or metropolitan areas in the first stage, blocks in the second, addresses in the third, and individuals in the final stage of selection.

The clustering of the sample can complicate the estimation of even simple statistics, like means or proportions. Let's start with the simplest case, in which the sample consists of a clusters, selected from a population of A clusters via simple random sampling and all the clusters include the same number of elements (B). Under these assumptions, the mean for the population is

$$\bar{Y} = \frac{\displaystyle\sum_{\alpha=1}^{A}\sum_{\beta=1}^{B} Y_{\alpha\beta}}{AB}$$

$$= \frac{\displaystyle\sum_{\alpha=1}^{A} \bar{Y}_{\alpha}}{A}, \qquad (16.15)$$

in which $\bar{Y}_{\alpha}$ represents the population mean for the cluster. If there is no subsampling within clusters (so that the cluster sample size, b, equals B), then the overall sample mean ($\bar{y}_{clu}$) is an unbiased estimator of the population mean:

$$\bar{y}_{clu} = \frac{\displaystyle\sum_{\alpha=1}^{A}\sum_{\beta=1}^{B} y_{\alpha\beta}}{aB}$$

$$= \frac{\displaystyle\sum_{\alpha=1}^{a} \bar{y}_{\alpha}}{a}. \qquad (16.16)$$

In effect, this design selects a simple random sample of a clusters out of a population of A clusters and the estimator for the overall mean is an average of the means for the sample clusters. The sample mean for a cluster is also its *population* mean since all B elements in the cluster were sampled (so $\bar{y}_{\alpha} = \bar{Y}_{\alpha}$). The variance of $\bar{y}_{clu}$ can thus be estimated with a variant of the estimator in Equation 16.6:

$$v\left(\bar{y}_{clu}\right) = \left(1 - f\right)\frac{s_{\bar{a}}^2}{a}$$

$$s_{\bar{a}}^2 = \frac{\displaystyle\sum_{\alpha=1}^{a}\left(\bar{y}_{\alpha} - \bar{y}_{clu}\right)^2}{a-1}. \qquad (16.17)$$

In Equation 16.17, the sample estimate of the variation in the cluster means ($s_{\bar{a}}^2$) replaces the estimate of the element variance in Equation 16.6 because, in effect, the sample observations are cluster means rather than individual data points. By the same logic, the number of sample clusters (a) replaces the overall sample size (n, or in this case aB). The sampling fraction (f) can be seen either as the proportion of clusters included in the sample (a/A) or the proportion of individuals (n/N, because $n = aB$ and $N = AB$).

The relative efficiency of this whole-cluster design can be compared with that of a simple random sample by comparing the estimated variances for the same statistic (such as a sample mean), assuming the same sample sizes:

$$Deff_{clu} = \frac{V(\bar{y}_{clu})}{V(\bar{y}_0)}$$

$$= \frac{(1-f)\dfrac{S_a^2}{a}}{(1-f)\dfrac{S^2}{n}} = B\frac{S_a^2}{S^2}. \qquad (16.18)$$

The design effect (or *Deff*) is the ratio of the expected variances under the two designs, and its value depends on the amount of between-cluster variation expressed as a proportion of the total variation in the survey variable y.

The design effect, because of the clustering of the sample, can also be expressed in terms of the similarity of the elements from the same cluster as measured by the intraclass correlation statistic, or ρ:

$$Deff_{clu} = 1 + (B-1)\rho. \qquad (16.19)$$

Roughly speaking, ρ is the expected correlation between any two elements from the same cluster. If subsampling is used to select elements from the sample clusters, the subsample size (b) replaces the cluster size (B) in Equation 16.19. Either way, the loss of efficiency because of clustering reflects the degree to which the data provided by different members of the same cluster are redundant with each other (with the redundancy indexed by ρ) and the number of sample cases per cluster. At the limit—if every sample member selected from a cluster provides the same information—the design effect is b, or the mean from the clustered sample is b times more variable than the mean from a simple random sample of the same overall size, where b is the number of sample cases per cluster. Equation 16.19 seems reasonable because the sample includes only a independent data points to characterize the population, not n.

Although whole cluster sampling is sometimes used in practice (as when students are sampled via the selection of intact classrooms), it is more common to subsample the elements in a cluster, in a two-stage or multistage design. And, of course, most naturally occurring populations come in clusters of unequal sizes rather than clusters of the same size. We deal briefly with each of these complications.

The simplest multistage design features two stages of sampling—the first selects a simple random sample of a clusters and the second stage selects simple random subsamples consisting of b elements apiece from each of the sample clusters. The overall sample size is then ab. The sample mean ($\bar{y}_{2s}$) still provides an unbiased estimator of the population mean:

$$\bar{y}_{2s} = \frac{\displaystyle\sum_{\alpha=1}^{a}\sum_{\beta=1}^{b} y_{\alpha\beta}}{ab}$$

$$= \frac{\displaystyle\sum_{\alpha=1}^{a} \bar{y}_\alpha}{a}, \qquad (16.20)$$

but the sample cluster means ($\bar{y}_\alpha$) are now estimates, based on the b sample elements from the cluster, not on all B elements in the cluster. The overall estimate of the mean is subject to sampling error both in the selection of the clusters and in the selection of elements within sample clusters. The expected variance of a mean from a two-stage sample reflects both sources of sampling error:

$$V(\bar{y}_{2s}) = \left(1 - \frac{a}{A}\right)\frac{S_a^2}{a} + \left(1 - \frac{b}{B}\right)\frac{S_b^2}{ab}$$

$$S_b^2 = \frac{\displaystyle\sum_{\alpha=1}^{A}\sum_{\beta=1}^{B}(Y_{\alpha\beta} - \bar{Y}_\alpha)^2}{A(B-1)}. \qquad (16.21)$$

The new term is the within-cluster variance (S_b^2), averaged across all clusters. When whole-cluster sampling is used, the second term in the variance equation drops out, leading to the variance estimator presented in Equation 16.17.

Because the variation in the *sample* means for the clusters itself reflects both sources of sampling error, the unbiased estimator for the variance of $\bar{y}_{2s}$ does not fully parallel the expression in Equation 16.21:

$$v(\bar{y}_{2s}) = \left(1 - \frac{a}{A}\right)\frac{s_a^2}{a} + \left(1 - \frac{b}{B}\right)\frac{a}{A}\frac{s_b^2}{ab}. \qquad (16.22)$$

The second term in Equation 16.22 involving the within-cluster variation (s_b^2) is multiplied by the sampling fraction at the first stage of selection (a/A); because this factor is often quite small, $v(\bar{y}_{2s}) \approx \dfrac{s_a^2}{a}$ is often used instead of the expression in Equation 16.22. Kalton (1983, pp. 34–35) gave a fuller justification for the use of this approximation to estimate the variance of a mean from a two-stage sample.

When there is subsampling at the second stage of a two-stage sample design, the question naturally arises as to how many elements should be selected from each cluster—that is, how large should b be? On the basis of a simple cost model in which the total data-collection costs for the survey reflects the costs per cluster, or C_a, and the costs per element, or C_b, we can derive the optimal cluster size (b'):

$$b' \sqrt{\frac{C_a(1-\rho)}{C_b\rho}}. \qquad (16.23)$$

If the cost of adding a new cluster is 10 times that of adding a case within an existing cluster (i.e., $C_a/C_b = 10$) and if the value of ρ is .05, then the optimal sample size for a cluster is about 14. If the cost ratio drops to 5, then the optimal cluster size drops to about 10. For a fixed ratio of costs, the higher the value of ρ, the smaller the optimal cluster sample size. With a cost ratio of 10, the optimal cluster size is about 15 when $\rho = .04$, but it is about 31 when $\rho = .01$.

Unequal Cluster Sizes

In the designs discussed so far, the sample size is fixed and is not itself subject to sampling fluctuations. One complication introduced by clusters of unequal sizes is that it is more difficult to control the final size of the sample, which partly depends on which clusters are selected. When both the numerator and denominator of the sample mean are subject to sampling error, a ratio estimator (r) is generally used instead of the simple mean to estimate the population mean ($\bar{Y}$):

$$r = \frac{y}{x}. \qquad (16.24)$$

In Equation 16.24, y represents the sample total and x the sample size (which is a random variable). In practice, both y and x are typically weighted totals. An estimator of the variance of the ratio mean (based on Taylor series approximation) is:

$$v(r) \approx \frac{1}{x^2}\left[v(y) + r^2 v(x) - 2r\,\text{cov}(x, y)\right], \qquad (16.25)$$

in which $\text{cov}(x, y)$ represents the covariation between the sample totals and the sample sizes. The variance terms ($v(y)$ and $v(x)$) are estimated from the variation in the cluster totals around the average cluster total; the covariance term is estimated in the same way. For example, in a stratified design, the estimator for $v(y)$ is as follows:

$$v(y) = \sum_{h=1}^{H} a_h s_{yh}^2$$

$$s_{yh}^2 = \sum_{\alpha=1}^{a_h} \frac{\left(y_{h\alpha} - y_h/a_h\right)^2}{a_h - 1}, \qquad (16.26)$$

in which a_h is the number of first-stage units selected in stratum h, $y_{h\alpha}$ represents the sample total for the survey variable y in a first-stage unit from that stratum, and y_h is the stratum total. In many sampling textbooks (e.g., Kish, 1965; Lohr, 2022), the first-stage units are referred to as primary sampling units (or PSUs), the second-stage units as secondary sampling units (or SSUs), and so on.

PPS Sampling

Equation 16.25 highlights the impact of variation in the cluster sizes on the variance of a sample mean; the more the cluster sizes vary, the more the estimates vary. (That is the significance of the $v(x)$ term in the equation.) Moreover, the ratio mean is biased (though it is consistent) and the size of the bias also depends on the variation in the cluster sample sizes (Kish, 1965, pp. 208–209). As a result, it is important to try to control the fluctuations in the size of the samples across the different clusters in a two-stage or multistage sample.

One method for accomplishing this is to make the selection probabilities for all but the final stage units proportional to the size of the unit; typically, the size measure is an estimate of the number of elements in the cluster. In a two-stage sample, a first-stage units are selected, but their selection probabilities vary, depending on their estimated size:

$$Pr_1\left(FS_i\right) = \frac{a}{A}\frac{M_i}{\overline{M}},\qquad(16.27)$$

in which M_i is the estimated size of first-stage unit i, $\overline{M}$ is the average size of all the first-stage units in the population, and A is the total number of first-stage units. Equation 16.27 boosts the selection probabilities for larger-than-average clusters and reduces them for smaller-than-average units. At the second stage of sampling, within each of the sample first-stage units, an equal probability sample of elements is drawn; the sample size for the second-stage units (b) is the same within every sample first-stage unit:

$$Pr_2\left(FS_i\right) = b/M_i.\qquad(16.28)$$

It is apparent from Equations 16.27 and 16.28 that the overall selection probabilities across both stages of sampling are constant across all the elements in the population ($= \frac{ab}{A\overline{M}} = \frac{n}{N}$). In addition, the sample sizes in each cluster are also constant; they are all equal to b. Thus, PPS sampling simultaneously accomplishes two important

goals—it reduces (or, ideally, eliminates) variability in the cluster sample sizes and it achieves an equal probability sample.

PPS sampling can easily be extended to more than two stages of sampling. For example, in a three-stage sample, the first-stage units would be selected according to Equation 16.27 and the units at the second stage of selection would also be selected with probabilities proportional to size:

$$Pr_2\left(SS_{ij}\right) = \frac{b}{B_i}\frac{M_{ij}}{\overline{M}_i},\qquad(16.29)$$

in which M_{ij} is the size of the jth second-stage unit within first-stage unit i, M_i is the average size of all the second-stage units in that first-stage unit, and B_i is the total number of second-stage units within that first-stage unit. At the final stage of selection, c elements are selected at random from among the M_{ij} elements in that second-stage unit, yielding an equal probability sample of abc elements, with c sample elements selected within each second-stage cluster.

A couple of complications arise in practice. Equation 16.27 can yield selection probabilities that are greater than 1. When that happens, the unit is taken with probability 1 and is referred to as a *certainty* or *self-representing* selection. Sample sizes within these certainty selections may have to be adjusted to produce an equal probability sample overall. For example, in a national household sample with 100 first-stage selections, each sample first-stage unit is supposed to represent roughly one one-hundredth of the population. The largest metropolitan areas (e.g., the New York City area) may include more than that share of the overall population. To compensate, the number of units selected at the second stage of sampling would be increased proportionately. If the New York metropolitan area includes, say, three one-hundredths of the target population, the number of second stage units to be selected there would be increased by a factor of three. The second complication is that the measures of size are typically only estimates. For example, the measure of size for an area sample might be housing unit counts from the most recent decennial census. The actual number of housing units found at the time the survey is fielded may vary from that figure; as a result, the relevant equation (e.g., Equation 16.28) would be used to set the sampling *rates* (i.e., the sampling fraction within unit ij would be c/M_{ij}), but the actual sample sizes might vary somewhat from one area to the next, depending on how close the size estimate is to the actual count of elements.

WEIGHTING

Survey data are often weighted to make inferences from the sample to the population as close as possible. The weights serve three main purposes. They compensate for unequal selection probabilities, adjust for the effects of nonresponse, and correct for discrepancies between the sample characteristics and known population figures. These discrepancies from population benchmarks can reflect random sampling error or more systematic problems, like undercoverage. Often, the weights are computed in three steps, first adjusting for differential selection probabilities, then compensating for nonresponse, and finally bringing the sample into line with population benchmarks.

Base Weights

Under a probability sampling design, each sampled element has a known probability of selection whether or not the element eventually responds to the survey. The base weights (W_1) are simply the inverses of the selection probabilities:

$$W_{1i} = 1/\pi_i. \qquad (16.30)$$

Differences in selection probabilities are sometimes present by design, as when a disproportionate allocation is used. Groups sampled at higher-than-average sampling rates are said to be *oversampled*; those sampled at lower-than-average rates are said *undersampled*. The overrepresented groups get relatively small weights and the underrepresented groups relatively large ones. Another source of variation in the weights is the selection of a single respondent from

households with more than one eligible member. Often, samples are equal probability (or nearly equal probability) down to the household level but then select a single person to respond from among several eligible household members. Persons living alone have a higher final selection probability than those living in households with two or more members of the target population, and the base weights correct for this. When the weights are calculated according to Equation 16.30, the sum of the weights provides an estimate of the population size.

It is easy to show that the weighted sum of the sample observations yields an unbiased estimate of the population total:

$$\hat{Y} = \sum_{i=1}^{n} W_{1i} y_i. \qquad (16.31)$$

The estimate for the population mean usually takes the form of a ratio estimator (compare Equation 16.24):

$$r = \frac{\sum_{i=1}^{n} W_{1i} y_i}{\sum_{i=1}^{n} W_{1i}}. \qquad (16.32)$$

Adjustments to the Base Weights

Compensating for nonresponse. Unfortunately, the sample of cases that actually provide data (the *responding* cases) are generally only a subset of the cases selected for the sample. If the nonrespondents are missing completely at random (Little & Rubin, 2002), then the respondents are simply a random subsample of the initial sample, and nonresponse does not introduce any bias into the estimates. Unfortunately, nonresponse is rarely purely random; for example, response rates are almost always noticeably higher within some subgroups than within others. This implies that the mix of cases by subgroup is different for the respondents than for the sample as a whole and that some groups are unintentionally overrepresented or underrepresented.

The basic method for compensating for this differential nonresponse involves estimating the probability that each case will become a respondent. There are two main approaches for estimating these *response propensities*. The first method is to group the cases (both respondents and non-respondents) into nonresponse adjustment cells and to use the observed response rate within each cell as the estimated response propensity for the cases in that cell (see Oh & Scheuren, 1983, for an early discussion of this approach). The second approach is to fit a logistic regression (or similar) model, predicting which cases will become respondents (vs. nonrespondents) based on some set of covariates available for both (Ekholm & Laaksonen, 1991); for example, the model might be based on frame data available for both respondents and nonrespondents. Whichever method is used to estimate the response propensities, the adjusted weights for the responding cases (W_{2i}) are just the base weights defined in Equation 16.30 divided by the estimated response propensity ($\hat{p}_i$):

$$W_{2i} = W_{1i}/\hat{p}_i. \qquad (16.33)$$

The nonrespondents are dropped at this point (i.e., they receive adjusted weights of zero). The sum of the adjusted weights for the respondents should equal (exactly in the case of the nonresponse cell approach, approximately in the logistic regression approach) the sum of the unadjusted weights for the whole sample ($\sum_{i=1}^{r} W_{2i} = \sum_{i=1}^{n} W_{1i}$, where the first summation is across the *r* respondents and the second is across all *n* cases in the initial sample).

Nonresponse adjustments are effective at reducing bias to the extent that the variables used to form the adjustment cells (or the variables included in the logistic regression model for estimating propensities) are actually related to both the response propensities and to the survey variables of interest (Little & Vartivarian, 2005). With the adjustment cell approach, the nonresponse bias is completely removed when the respondents and nonrespondents within each adjustment cell have the same distribution on the survey variables. Both methods for computing nonresponse

adjustments require information on both respondents and nonrespondents. Thus, the calculation of nonresponse weights is often limited by what information is available for both, typically frame data or data collected in the process of attempting to carry out data collection (e.g., the number of calls made to the sample household). As a result, the nonresponse adjustments are unlikely to be fully successful at compensating for the biasing effects of nonresponse.

Adjusting to population figures. As a final step in developing weights, the weights assigned to the survey participants may be adjusted to bring them into line with external population figures, such as estimates from a recent census or from the American Community Survey (see https://www.census.gov/programs-surveys/acs). The American Community Survey is the largest survey done by the Census Bureau between decennial censuses. For example, the researchers may want to ensure that the weighted sample figures match the population in terms of the mix by gender or region. These same methods are also sometimes used to compensate for nonresponse bias (Kalton & Flores-Cervantes, 2003).

The first method for adjusting to population totals is known as *ratio adjustment, poststratification*, or *cell weighting*. It adjusts "the sample weights so that the sample totals conform to the population totals on a cell-by-cell basis" (Kalton & Flores-Cervantes, 2003, p. 84). The procedure is quite simple—the weight for each respondent (e.g., W_{2i} in Equation 16.33) in a weighting cell (or post-stratum) is multiplied by an adjustment factor:

$$W_{3ij} = \left(\frac{N_i}{\sum_{j=1}^{r_i} W_{2ij}} \right) W_{2ij}, \qquad (16.34)$$

in which W_{3ij} is the adjusted or poststratified weight and the adjustment factor (the factor in parentheses on the right side of Equation 16.34) is the ratio between the population total for cell *i* (N_i) and the sum of the current weights (the W_2's) for the respondents in that cell. Sometimes the population total is actually an estimate based on a large survey. After adjustment, the weighted sample totals for each cell exactly match the population totals. The adjustment factors are sometimes based on the population proportions rather than population totals; for example, the sample proportions by gender for the respondents may be aligned with the population proportions.

The other popular adjustment procedure is called *raking* (or *rim weighting*; Deming & Stephan, 1940). It adjusts the sample weights so that sample totals line up with external population figures, but the adjustment aligns the sample to the *marginal* totals for the auxiliary variables, not to the cell totals. For example, if population figures are available for males and females and for people living in cities and those living in rural areas, the adjusted sample weights would bring the sample totals into line with the population figures for males and females and for city dwellers and residents of rural areas but not for males living in cities or females living in rural areas. Raking might be preferable to poststratification when population figures are not available for every adjustment cell formed by crossing the auxiliary variables. Or there may be so few participants in a given cell that the adjustment factors become extreme and highly variable across cells. Or, finally, the researchers may want to incorporate too many variables in the weighting scheme for a cell-by-cell adjustment to be practical.

Raking is carried out via *iterative proportional fitting*. First, the sample weights are adjusted to agree with the marginal totals for one of the auxiliary variables, say, gender. The adjustment factor is computed in the same way as the one described in Equation 16.34, only the population targets are based on marginal totals (the total number of males and females). Then, the weights are adjusted to agree with the marginal totals for the next auxiliary variable (level of urbanization) and so on until adjustments have been made for each of the auxiliary variables. The adjustment process for later variables (urbanization) may have thrown off the totals for the earlier variables (gender) so the process is repeated until the weights no longer change. Convergence is usually rapid.

Occasionally, more sophisticated adjustments are applied to survey weights, such as generalized regression weighting, that take further advantage of the external data (e.g., Lee & Valliant, 2009). All three of these methods for adjusting weights to external figures—poststratification, raking, and generalized regression weighting—are members of a single family of techniques called *calibration estimation* (Deville & Sarndal, 1992).

It is common in longitudinal surveys to produce additional weights for each wave of the survey. These added weights adjust the final weight from the first wave to compensate for nonresponse in subsequent waves of the survey (i.e., panel attrition).

Weighting for dual-frame samples. As we noted in our discussion of dual-frame samples, the sample design may give multiple chances of selection to some members of the population (e.g., dual users in a telephone sample). There are three general approaches for dealing with the issue of cases that are on both frames (the *overlap cases*). The first, the screening approach, eliminates the problem by dropping overlap cases selected from one of the frames. For example, in a telephone survey, numbers selected from the cell phone frame would be dropped if the respondent reported that they also has a landline telephone. Under this approach, dual users can come into the sample only if they are selected from the landline frame. This approach has the drawback that it "wastes" potential respondents and is rarely used in practice. A second approach is to modify the base weights so that they reflect the selection probabilities from each frame:

$$W_{1i} = 1/\pi_i^L + 1/\pi_i^C - 1/(\pi_i^L \pi_i^C), \qquad (16.35)$$

where π_i^L and π_i^C are the selection probabilities for case i from the landline frame and cell phone frame, respectively. The final approach (due to Hartley, 1974) treats the overlap cases selected from each frame as independent samples and constructs on overall estimate for the overlap portion of the population as a weighted average of these two sample estimates. For example, the estimator for a total would take this form:

$$\hat{Y} = \hat{Y}_l + \hat{Y}_c + \theta\hat{Y}_{lc}^L + (1-\theta)\hat{Y}_{lc}^C. \quad (16.36)$$

$\hat{Y}_{lc}^L$ and $\hat{Y}_{lc}^C$ represent the estimated totals based on the overlap cases (e.g., the dual users) selected from the landline frame and the cell frame, respectively; θ is the weight given to the estimate based on selections from the landline frame; and $(1 - \theta)$ is the weight given to the estimate based on the cell frame. Although more sophisticated choices are available for θ (Baffour et al., 2016), in practice, researchers have gravitated to one half or to the relative sample sizes for the two samples:

$$\theta = \frac{n_{lc}^L}{n_{lc}^L + n_{lc}^M}, \quad (16.37)$$

in which, n_{lc}^L and n_{lc}^M represent the raw (or effective) sample sizes for the two samples of overlap cases. (The effective sample size is the actual number of cases divided by the design effect.) The estimator in Equation 16.37 gives more weight to the estimate with lower variance. If effective sample sizes are used to calculate the compositing factor, θ, they should be based on the average design effect for a range of estimates. The final weight for a given case from the overlap portion of the sample would be its adjusted weight (e.g., W_3 from Equation 16.34) times the compositing factor, θ or $(1 - \theta)$.

Drawbacks to weighting. Although weights are usually needed for unbiased estimates, as the weights become more variable, the variance of the estimates can increase. For example, in a sample that consists of several hundred cases each with a weight of 1 and a single case with a weight of 10,000, the estimates will largely reflect the value for the single high-weight observation. Effectively, the sample size is close to 1. Sampling statisticians sometimes attempt to gauge the impact of the weights on the variability of the estimates by calculating a design effect due to weighting. A popular approximation is that the weights increase the variance of means and

proportions by a factor equal to $1 + L$ (where L is the relative variance of the weights). To reduce this impact, extreme weights may be scaled back or trimmed. *Trimming* refers to establishing maximum weight and setting any weights that exceed this value to the maximum. Of course, the $1 + L$ formula is only an approximation, and weighting adjustments sometimes reduce the variance of the estimates even as they increase the variance of the weights (Little & Vartivarian, 2005).

VARIANCE ESTIMATION

Because they depart from simple random sampling in various ways (e.g., unequal selection probabilities, clustering, use of stratification), survey samples require different procedures for estimating sampling errors from the procedures outlined in introductory statistics texts. Those texts for the most part assume simple random sampling with replacement. Earlier we discussed the notion of a design effect, or the ratio of the sampling variance of a statistic from a more complex design to the variance under a simple random sample (e.g., Equations 16.18 and 16.19). Clustering, unequal-size clusters, and unequal selection probabilities tend to increase the sampling variances of survey statistics relative to a simple random sample; stratification tends to reduce the variances. The net effect of these features of most national samples is to increase the variability of the estimates, generally substantially, relative to the corresponding estimates from a simple random sample. National samples often produce statistics with design effects ranging from 2 to 3 or higher. Clearly, treating survey sample data as though they came from simple random samples can produce very misleading conclusions.

Because the usual formulas cannot be used to estimate variances, sampling statisticians have developed several alternative approaches for use with survey data instead. We briefly describe the five main approaches—Taylor series approximation, the random groups procedure, balanced repeated replication, jackknife repeated replication, and bootstrapping.

Taylor Series Approximation

The estimators used in surveys are often nonlinear combinations of the observations, such as the ratio mean in Equation 16.24 or correlation and regression coefficients, and unbiased estimators of their sampling variance are not always available (Wolter, 2007). The Taylor series approach (or delta method) is to replace the nonlinear estimators with linear approximations of them; variance estimators are then applied to the linear approximation (Hansen et al., 1953, Volume 2, Chapter 4). Sometimes exact variance expressions are available for the linear approximation (as with Equation 16.25) or sometimes another approach must be used to estimate the variance of the approximation. Linear approximations have been worked out for many standard survey statistics and many of the software packages available for estimating variances for survey data from complex samples are based on these approximations.

Random Groups

Conceptually, a straightforward method for estimating the variation from one sample to the next would be to select multiple samples and observe the actual variation across samples. This insight is the basis for another approach for estimating the variance of statistics from survey samples—the random group approach. The random group method entails selecting two or more samples from the population under the same sampling design. Estimates of a given population parameter are made from each sample and from the combination of all samples. Then, these estimates are compared. Historically, this was one of the first techniques developed to simplify the variance estimation for complex sample surveys (Wolter, 2007).

When the random groups are selected independently, a reasonable estimator for the combined sample is the unweighted average of the estimates from the different random groups:

$$\hat{\bar{\theta}} = \sum_{\alpha=1}^{k} \hat{\bar{\theta}}_{\alpha} / k, \qquad (16.38)$$

in which $\hat{\bar{\theta}}$ is the overall estimate for some parameter and $\hat{\bar{\theta}}_{\alpha}$ is the estimate for that parameter from random group α. The variance estimator for $\hat{\bar{\theta}}$ reflects the variation across the random group estimates:

$$v\left(\hat{\bar{\theta}}\right) = 1/k \sum_{\alpha=1}^{k} \frac{\left(\hat{\theta}_{\alpha} - \hat{\bar{\theta}}\right)^2}{k-1}. \qquad (16.39)$$

Sometimes an overall estimate ($\hat{\theta}$) is calculated by combining the random groups into a single large sample. This overall estimate is used instead of the average of the estimates from the random groups; the expression in Equation 16.39 is still used as the variance estimator. (The two overall estimators—$\hat{\theta}$ and $\hat{\bar{\theta}}$—can be identical but do not have to be.) The random groups may be selected as independent samples, but more often a single sample is selected and then divided at random into subsamples; the subsamples are the random groups for variance estimation purposes. The subsamples must preserve the key features of the original sample design. Typically, each subsample includes one or more first-stage units randomly selected from each stratum in the full sample design.

Balanced and Jackknife Repeated Replication

A limitation of the random groups approach is that the number of random groups available for variance estimation is typically quite small, and the stability of the variance estimate depends in part on k, the number of random groups. Some sample designs attempt to gain the maximum possible benefits from stratification by including just two first-stage selections in each stratum. (Any fewer selections would make it impossible to come up with an unbiased estimator of the sampling variance.) At this lower limit, only two subsamples can be created, each a half-sample that includes one of the two selections from each stratum.

Balanced repeated replication (BRR) is an attempt to get around this limitation. With a total of H strata in the design, each with two first-stage selections, one could, in principle, form a total of $2H$ different half-samples. The squared difference between the estimate from each half-sample and the corresponding full-sample estimate is an unbiased estimate of the variance of the full-sample estimate (Wolter, 2007, p. 110). The trick is to improve the stability of this variance estimate by computing multiple half-sample estimates. This is what BRR does. With BRR, multiple half-samples are formed in a balanced way, so that the estimates from the different half-samples are uncorrelated (McCarthy, 1969).

The basic procedure for constructing an estimate and estimating its variance is similar to the procedure in the random group method. First, a number of half-samples are formed. (To maintain full balance, the number of half-samples must be a multiple of four greater than or equal to the number of strata.) For each one, an estimate is computed based on the elements included in that half-sample ($\hat{\theta}_\alpha$). This typically involves doubling the weights of the cases in the half-sample. Next, the overall estimate is computed as an average of the half-sample estimates ($\bar{\hat{\theta}}$). Finally, the variance of the overall estimate is computed as follows:

$$v\left(\hat{\theta}\right) = \sum_{\alpha=1}^{k} \frac{\left(\hat{\theta}_\alpha - \hat{\theta}\right)^2}{k}. \qquad (16.40)$$

Typically, the full-sample estimate ($\hat{\theta}$) rather than the mean of the half-sample estimates ($\bar{\hat{\theta}}$) is used to calculate the variance. Forming a half-sample necessarily entails forming a complementary half-sample at the same time, and alternative versions of the BRR variance estimator in Equation 16.40 make use of the data from the complementary half-sample.

Jackknifing follows an approach similar to BRR (Durbin, 1959). It forms replicates by dropping a sample first-stage unit within each stratum and then weighting up the remaining first-stage selections to maintain the overall stratum weight. If there are two first-stage selections in each stratum (as BRR assumes), this amounts to forming a replicate by dropping one of the selections

from a stratum and then doubling the weight for the other selection in that stratum. Typically, $2H$ replicates are formed, with each first-stage unit dropped from the sample in turn. The jackknife variance estimator for a stratified sample takes this form:

$$v_J\left(\hat{\theta}\right) = \sum_{h=1}^{H} \frac{m_h - 1}{m_h} \sum_{\alpha=1}^{m_h} \left(\hat{\theta}_{h\alpha} - \hat{\theta}\right)^2, \qquad (16.41)$$

in which m_h is the number of first-stage selections in stratum h (often two) and $\hat{\theta}_{h\alpha}$ is the estimate that results when unit α is dropped from stratum h.

Bootstrapping

Random groups, BRR, and jackknife repeated replication are all examples of replication procedures for variance estimation. That is, they assess the variation in the estimates derived from the one sample that was actually selected by mimicking the selection of multiple samples and measuring the variation across these pseudosamples, or *replicates*. The random groups procedure forms the replicates by dividing the original sample into subsamples that preserve the stratification and clustering in the original. BRR forms half-samples by repeatedly taking one selection from each stratum; it attempts to make the estimates from these half-samples orthogonal to each other. Jackknife repeated replication forms replicate by deleting one first-stage selection from each stratum in turn.

With bootstrapping (Efron, 1979), the replicate samples are formed by taking simple random samples *with replacement* from the full sample. If the full sample is a stratified multistage sample, then the bootstrap involves repeatedly selecting samples including m_h of the a_h first-stage sample units within each stratum. The units selected into the bootstrap sample are reweighted. In the simplest case, the bootstrap sample includes $a_h - 1$ selections from stratum h (i.e., $m_h = a_h - 1$), some of them possibly selected more than once. The new weight for a given selection is as follows:

$$w_{hi}^* = w_{hi} \frac{a_h}{a_h - 1} d_{hi}, \qquad (16.42)$$

in which d_{hi} represents the number of times unit hi was selected; units that were not selected in a given bootstrap sample, thus, get a weight of zero. The new weights for a given bootstrap replicate are used to generate an estimate ($\hat{\theta}_\alpha$). As in Equation 16.40, the variance estimate for the full-sample estimate is the average squared deviation of the bootstrap estimates from the full-sample estimate across the k bootstrap replicates. The performance of the bootstrap improves as k gets larger.

Software for Variance Estimation

At least three general statistical analysis packages (SAS, SPSS, and STATA) allow users to take complex sample design features, like clustering and unequal selection probabilities, into account using the Taylor series approach and replication methods. For example, the SAS survey procedures allow both BRR and jackknifing as well as Taylor series estimates of variances for survey statistics, such as means, proportions, and logistic regression coefficients (https://support.sas.com/rnd/app/stat/procedures/SurveyAnalysis.html). In addition, at least two specialized packages were developed specifically for the analysis of survey data—SUDAAN developed at RTI International (https://www.rti.org/impact/sudaan-statistical-software-analyzing-correlated-data) and WesVar developed at Westat (https://www.westat.com/capability/information-technology/wesvar). (RTI International and Westat are two of the U.S. largest survey firms.) The "survey" package in R can also be used to analyze complex survey data by taking into account clustering, stratification, and weighting (http://cran.fhcrc.org/web/packages/survey/survey.pdf). All of these packages are well documented and handle most statistics that analysts are likely to use (means, proportions, linear and logistic regression coefficients, etc.). Since variation across first-stage units is generally an essential component for estimating variances, the programs can sometimes stumble when there is only a single selection from a stratum; this can occur for various reasons, such as nonresponse. In such cases, it may be necessary to "collapse" strata—treating first-stage selections from similar strata as though they were selected from the same stratum.

Empirical comparisons of the different variance estimation approaches (and of the different software packages) have not revealed major differences across the approaches for many types of statistics (e.g., Kish & Frankel, 1974). Now that computational resources are cheap, bootstrapping has become a more attractive option; it does well with all types of estimates and all types of sample design. The era when analysts had difficulty locating software for analyzing survey data is long past. There is little excuse for not using appropriate methods to estimate the variances in survey statistics, and inappropriate procedures can lead to biased results.

CONCLUSION

Although the mathematics of survey sampling are mostly well established, important changes are still taking place in the practice of sampling. The frames used for area and telephone samples are in a state of flux. Address lists based on the U.S. Postal Service's DSF provide an alternative to traditional field listing, and as more people move away from landline telephone service, new methods of telephone sampling are being widely adopted. It is not yet clear how samplers will ultimately adjust to these new realities. Falling response rates have encouraged samplers to use more sophisticated weighting procedures, such as calibration estimation, to reduce the biases in survey statistics. On a more positive note, popular packages like SAS and SPSS have incorporated modules that allow analysts to accurately gauge the variance of survey estimates. And more sophisticated model-based estimation procedures are constantly being developed to improve the estimates from survey data. These new methods are likely to play an ever-larger role as survey costs continue to rise and the representativeness of survey samples continues to decline.

References

American Association for Public Opinion Research (AAPOR). (2018). *Spam flagging and call blocking and its impact on survey research.*

https://www.aapor.org/Education-Resources/Reports/Spam-Flagging-and-Call-Blocking-and-Its-Impact-on.aspx

Baffour, B., Haynes, M., Western, M., Pennay, D., Misson, S., & Martinez, A. (2016). Weighting strategies for combining data from dual-frame telephone surveys: Emerging evidence from Australia. *Journal of Official Statistics, 32*(3), 549–578. https://doi.org/10.1515/jos-2016-0029

Blumberg, S. J., & Luke, J. V. (2020). *Wireless substitution: Early release of estimates from the National Health Interview Survey, July–December 2019.* https://www.cdc.gov/nchs/nhis.htm

Boyle, J., Bucuvalas, M., Piekarski, L., & Weiss, A. (2009). Zero banks: Coverage error and bias in RDD samples based on hundred banks with listed numbers. *Public Opinion Quarterly, 73*(4), 729–750. https://doi.org/10.1093/poq/nfp068

Brick, J. M., Edwards, W. S., & Lee, S. (2007). Sampling telephone numbers and adults, interview length, and weighting in California Health Interview Survey Cell Phone Pilot Study. *Public Opinion Quarterly, 71*(5), 793–813. https://doi.org/10.1093/poq/nfm052

Brick, J. M., Waksberg, J., Kulp, D., & Starer, A. (1995). Bias in list-assisted telephone samples. *Public Opinion Quarterly, 59*(2), 218–235. https://doi.org/10.1086/269470

Casady, R. J., & Lepkowski, J. M. (1993). Stratified telephone survey designs. *Survey Methodology, 19,* 103–113.

Cornesse, C., Blom, A. G., Dutwin, D., Krosnick, J. A., de Leeuw, E. D., LeGleye, S., Paske, J., Pennay, D., Philips, B., Sakshaug, J. W., Struminskaya, B., & Wenz, A. (2020). A review of conceptual approaches and empirical evidence on probability and nonprobability sample survey research. *Journal of Survey Statistics and Methodology, 8*(1), 4–36. https://doi.org/10.1093/jssam/smz041

Couper, M. (2000). Web surveys: A review of issues and approaches. *Public Opinion Quarterly, 64*(4), 464–494. https://doi.org/10.1086/318641

Deming, W. E., & Stephan, F. F. (1940). On a least squares adjustment of a sample frequency table when the expected marginal totals are known. *Annals of Mathematical Statistics, 11*(4), 427–444. https://doi.org/10.1214/aoms/1177731829

Deville, J.-C., & Sarndal, C.-E. (1992). Calibration estimators in survey sampling. *Journal of the American Statistical Association, 87*(418), 376–382. https://doi.org/10.1080/01621459.1992.10475217

Durbin, J. (1959). A note on the application of Quenouille's method of bias reduction to the estimation of ratios. *Biometrika, 46*(3–4), 477–480. https://doi.org/10.1093/biomet/46.3-4.477

Efron, B. (1979). Bootstrap methods: Another look at the jackknife. *Annals of Statistics, 7*(1), 1–26. https://doi.org/10.1214/aos/1176344552

Ekholm, A., & Laaksonen, S. (1991). Weighting via response modeling in the Finnish Household Budget Survey. *Journal of Official Statistics, 7*(3), 325–337.

Fahimi, M., Kulp, D., & Brick, J. M. (2009). A reassessment of list-assisted RDD methodology. *Public Opinion Quarterly, 73*(4), 751–760. https://doi.org/10.1093/poq/nfp066

Gaziano, C. (2005). Comparative analysis of within-household respondent selection techniques. *Public Opinion Quarterly, 69*(1), 124–157. https://doi.org/10.1093/poq/nfi006

Gile, K. J., & Handcock, M. S. (2010). Respondent-driven sampling: An assessment of current methodology. *Sociological Methodology, 40*(1), 285–327. https://doi.org/10.1111/j.1467-9531.2010.01223.x

Hansen, M. H., Hurwitz, W. N., & Madow, W. G. (1953). *Sample survey methods and theory.* Wiley.

Hartley, H. O. (1974). Multiple frame methodology and selected applications. *Sankhyā C, 36,* 99–118.

Heckathorn, D. D. (1997). Respondent-driven sampling: A new approach to the study of hidden populations. *Social Problems, 44*(2), 174–199. https://doi.org/10.2307/3096941

Heckathorn, D. D. (2002). Respondent-driven sampling II: Deriving valid population estimates from chain-referral samples of hidden populations. *Social Problems, 49*(1), 11–34. https://doi.org/10.1525/sp.2002.49.1.11

Heckathorn, D. D. (2011). Comment: Snowball versus respondent-driven sampling. *Sociological Methodology, 41*(1), 355–366. https://doi.org/10.1111/j.1467-9531.2011.01244.x

Iannacchione, V. G., Staab, J. M., & Redden, D. T. (2003). Evaluating the use of residential mailing addresses in a metropolitan household survey. *Public Opinion Quarterly, 67*(2), 202–210. https://doi.org/10.1086/374398

Igielnik, R., Keeter, S., Kennedy, C., & Spahn, B. (2018). *Commercial voter files and the study of U.S. Politics: Demystifying the digital databases widely used by political campaigns.* Pew Research Center. https://www.pewresearch.org/methods/2018/02/15/commercial-voter-files-and-the-study-of-u-s-politics/

Jensen, A. (1926). The representative method in practice. *Bulletin of the International Statistical Institute, 22,* 359–380.

Kalton, G. (1983). *Introduction to survey sampling.* SAGE. https://doi.org/10.4135/9781412984683

Kalton, G., & Flores-Cervantes, I. (2003). Weighting methods. *Journal of Official Statistics, 19*(2), 81–97.

Kennedy, C., Mercer, A., Keeter, S., Hatley, N., McGeeney, K., & Gimenez, A. (2016). *Evaluating online nonprobability surveys.* Pew Research Center. https://www.pewresearch.org/methods/2016/05/02/evaluating-online-nonprobability-surveys/

Kish, L. (1965). *Survey sampling.* Wiley.

Kish, L., & Frankel, M. R. (1974). Inference from complex samples. *Journal of the Royal Statistical Society: Series B. Methodological, 36*(1), 1–22. https://doi.org/10.1111/j.2517-6161.1974.tb00981.x

Lee, S., & Valliant, R. (2009). Estimation for volunteer panel web surveys using propensity score adjustment and calibration adjustment. *Sociological Methods & Research, 37*(3), 319–343. https://doi.org/10.1177/0049124108329643

Lessler, J. T., & Kalsbeek, W. D. (1992). *Nonsampling error in surveys.* Wiley.

Little, R. J., & Rubin, D. B. (2002). *Statistical analysis with missing data* (2nd ed.). Wiley. https://doi.org/10.1002/9781119013563

Little, R. J., & Vartivarian, S. (2005). Does weighting for nonresponse increase the variance of survey means? *Survey Methodology, 31*, 161–168.

Lohr, S. L. (2022). *Sampling: Design and analysis* (3rd ed.). CRC Press.

Madow, W. G., & Madow, L. H. (1944). On the theory of systematic sampling. *Annals of Mathematical Statistics, 15*(1), 1–24. https://doi.org/10.1214/aoms/1177731312

Martin, E. (1999). Who knows who lives here? Within-household disagreements as a source of survey coverage error. *Public Opinion Quarterly, 63*(2), 220–236. https://doi.org/10.1086/297712

McCarthy, P. C. (1969). Pseudoreplication: Half-samples. *Review of the International Statistical Institute, 37*(3), 239–264. https://doi.org/10.2307/1402116

National Research Council. (2013). *Nonresponse in social science surveys: A research agenda.* The National Academies Press.

Neyman, J. (1934). On the two different aspects of the representative method: The method of stratified sampling and the method of purposive selection.

Journal of the Royal Statistical Society, 97(4), 558–625. https://doi.org/10.2307/2342192

O'Muircheartaigh, C., Eckman, S., & Weiss, C. (2002). *Traditional and enhanced field listing for probability sampling.* http://www.asasrms.org/Proceedings/y2002/Files/JSM2002-001047.pdf

Oh, H. L., & Scheuren, F. (1983) Weighting adjustments for unit nonresponse. In W. G. Madow, I. Olkin, & D. Rubin (Eds.), *Incomplete data in sample surveys: Vol. 2. Theory and bibliographies* (pp. 143–184). Academic Press.

Pew Research Center. (2011). *Americans and their cell phones.* https://www.pewresearch.org/internet/2011/08/15/americans-and-their-cell-phones/

Pierannunzi, C., Gamble, S., Locke, R., Freedner, N., & Town, M. (2019). Differences in efficiencies between ABS and RDD samples by mode of data collection. *Survey Practice, 12*(1). https://doi.org/10.29115/SP-2019-0006

Sturgis, P., Baker, N., Callegaro, M., Fisher, S., Green, J., Jennings, W., Kuha, J., Lauderdale, B., & Smith, P. (2016). *Report of the inquiry into the 2015 British general election opinion polls.* Market Research Society and British Polling Council.

Tourangeau, R., Shapiro, G., Kearney, A., & Ernst, L. (1997). Who lives here? Survey undercoverage and household roster questions. *Journal of Official Statistics, 13*(1), 1–18.

U.S. Bureau of the Census. (2006). *Design and methodology: Current population survey* (Technical Report 66). U.S. Department of Commerce.

Wolter, K. (2007). *Introduction to variance estimation* (2nd ed.). Springer.

Wolter, K., Chowdhury, S., & Kelly, J. (2009). Design, conduct, and analysis of random-digit dialing surveys. In D. Pfeffermann & C. R. Rao (Eds.), *Handbook of statistics: Vol. 29A. Sample surveys: Design, methods and applications* (pp. 125–154). Elsevier. https://doi.org/10.1016/S0169-7161(08)00007-2

Yan, T. (2009, May 14–17). *A meta-analysis of within-household respondent selection methods* [Paper presentation]. Annual Meeting of the American Association for Public Opinion Research, Hollywood, FL, United States.

CHAPTER 17

EPIDEMIOLOGY

Rumi Kato Price and Heidi H. Tastet

Epidemiology is a broad discipline that investigates the distributions of health and illness in populations and factors affecting these conditions. *Distributions* can be defined as a range of observable, and sometimes latent, measures of how a specific health or illness condition is spread or contained; relevant factors include both etiological and confounding factors that mask the true etiology. In modern epidemiology, surveillance and prevention of diseases are also considered as applications of epidemiology (Last, 2001). Health and illness encompass a wide range of phenotypes (outcomes), including clinically defined diseases and injuries, various types of health-related problems, and normal or healthy behaviors as well. The study population is most frequently a human population. However, depending on the types of phenotype and topic areas, the unit of analysis (observation) may be nonhuman species, such as a rat (e.g., effect of chronic stress on a rat's hippocampal volume), or the unit can be any quantifiable one, such as a geographic unit (e.g., alcohol outlet density in census block groups affecting the rate of motor vehicle accidents). Because epidemiology often serves as a foundation for providing the evidence base and logic for both treatment and preventive intervention, epidemiology is considered to be an integral part of both medicine and public health.

Epidemiologic methods, including biostatistics, provide basic tools for biomedical, psychological, and public health research. As seen in this chapter, the modern origin of epidemiology is usually traced to infectious diseases that involved identification of infectious agents (e.g., *Plasmodium* parasites that cause malaria) and the vectors (e.g., anopheline mosquitoes) or hosts (e.g., humans) that carry these agents. However, contemporary epidemiology has expanded in scope to include a large number of chronic noninfectious conditions, such as diabetes mellitus, obesity, and most psychiatric disorders. Epidemiology as a discipline, in fact, has proliferated so much that it is difficult to think of a phenotype to which epidemiology is irrelevant; it is probably best thought of as a multidisciplinary science that allows studies in many applied fields within public health (Ahrens et al., 2014). This chapter, however, is written primarily for psychologists and other behavioral and social scientists, teachers, and students who are interested in psychosocial studies that employ epidemiological methods.

The first section of this chapter provides a brief history of epidemiologic research. Next, we provide basics of epidemiologic methods. The methods include main concepts of epidemiology and note how they relate to contemporary

Preparation for this chapter was supported in part by a Washington University Institute for Public Health faculty grant to the first author.

https://doi.org/10.1037/0000319-017

APA Handbook of Research Methods in Psychology, Second Edition: Vol. 2. Research Designs: Quantitative, Qualitative, Neuropsychological, and Biological, H. Cooper (Editor-in-Chief)

epidemiologic methods; basic and commonly used measures, including measures of occurrence, association, impact, predictive utility, and disease burden; traditional and hybrid study designs; and selected topics in sampling methods. Fuller descriptions of some topics introduced here are provided in other chapters (e.g., for genetic epidemiology, see Chapter 37 of this volume; for survey sampling, see Chapter 16 of this volume; for internet use for data collection, see Chapter 19 of this volume). Although this chapter provides basic information on measures of association, more elaborate quantitative data analysis strategies are given separately over several commonly used methods in Volume 3, Part I, of this handbook. For excellent further in-depth reading and reference books on epidemiology, readers may also consult with Morabia (2004a), Susser and Stein (2009), Ahrens and Pigeot (2014), Bhopal (2016), and Lash et al. (2021); Oakes and Kaufman (2017) include methods to illuminate socioeconomic status, race, segregation and health inequalities.

BRIEF HISTORY OF EPIDEMIOLOGY

The word *epidemic* means "something that falls upon people" in ancient Greek (*epi*, upon, and *demos*, the people). This original meaning still is in evidence in contemporary epidemiology because the essence of epidemiology involves examining diseases and conditions at the population level. The second basic idea, studying disease distribution, may stem from Hippocrates' distinction of *epidemic* (diseases that are visited upon) from *endemic* (reside within). The third idea of *etiology* or *causes* can also be traced back to such early writings by ancient Greek and Roman philosophers and practitioners of medicine, including Hippocrates (ca. 460–375 BCE) and Galen (or Galenus; 129–199/217) (see Ahrens et al., 2014; Susser & Stein, 2009).

A modern use of the term *epidemiology* is believed to have first appeared in Madrid circa 1802 (Greenwood, 1932). Throughout the 19th century and up to middle of the 20th century, however, use of this term was restricted to studies of

epidemics of infectious disease origin (Greenwood, 1932). The best-known example of the practice of epidemiology in this regard is the work on the 1854 London cholera outbreak by a British physician, John Snow. Snow identified the source of transmission for the cholera outbreak as the Broad Street water pump by tracking fatal cases during a short span of approximately 45 days. This example illustrates several basic concepts, such as incident cases, ratios, relative risk, and case-control design (see the Fundamentals of Epidemiologic Methods section for details of these measures and designs). Modifying a cause (removing the handle of the suspected water pump) further illustrated the connection of epidemiology to etiology that leads to intervention and prevention. It was 17 years later, however, when the causative agent *Vibrio cholerae* was finally identified and publicized (Brock, 1999; Snow, 1854; see also the John Snow website created by the UCLA School of Public Health: https://www.ph.ucla.edu/epi/snow.html#YOUTH). The fact that effective action can be taken even in the absence of knowledge of a specific etiological factor is an important concept in modern public health.

The connection of epidemiology to statistics originates in population thinking. In England and France, devastating plague epidemics stimulated the interest in population data collection. The etymology of the word *statistics* shows the word was derived from New Latin *statisticum collegiums* (council of state), Italian *statista* (statesman), and German *Statistik*, or in a contemporary term, *population statistics* (Morabia, 2004b; Rosen, 1958). The occurrence of disease in populations was first measured in ratios, proportions, and a rudimentary mortality ratio as early as late 17th century (e.g., Graunt's plague statistics; Rothman, 1996). William Farr, superintendent of the General Register Office for England and Wales from 1842–1879, is often credited for advancing epidemiologic statistics at a time when multiple epidemics of infectious diseases such as cholera and phthisis (pulmonary tuberculosis) plagued England (Farr, 2004; Susser & Adelstein, 1975; Susser & Stein, 2009). The development of later, more refined epidemiologic measures reflects the evolution of methodology for studying diseases and conditions over the past 2 centuries and is introduced in the section Commonly Used Basic Epidemiologic Measures.

Emergence of large-scale epidemiologic studies examining psychiatric and psychological outcomes coincided with the emergence and dominance of chronic disease epidemiology in the latter half of the 20th century. Psychosocial and psychiatric epidemiology became a subfield of epidemiology and contributed to advances of chronic disease epidemiology methods over the past 70 years. It is usual to separate landmark studies to first generation (before World War II), second generation (after World War II to about 1980), third generation (1980–2000), and more recent fourth generation (Tohen et al., 2000). Most of the commonly used epidemiologic measures and study designs were developed and refined with second- and third-generation studies. Because this chapter focuses on epidemiologic methods, we provide a summary of four landmark psychosocial and psychiatric epidemiology studies in Appendix 17.1. Social Class and Mental Illness (Faris & Dunham, 1939, 1960) provided an example of pre–World War II record examination study. The Epidemiologic Catchment Area (ECA) study (Robins & Regier, 1991) was a classic general population psychiatric epidemiology study carried out in 1980s. The International Study of Schizophrenia (ISoS) was an example of a clinical-sample-based multicountry series carried out in Europe (Hopper et al., 2007; Leff et al., 1992). The National Vietnam Veterans Readjustment Study (NVVRS; Kulka et al., 1990; Schlenger et al., 1992) provided an example of another classic study but focused on a special population (U.S. military veterans).

Although Appendix 17.1 focuses on classic epidemiologic studies prior to the turn of the century, there have been many more recent, large-scale, landmark studies. These newer studies have even more ambitious scopes of inquiry and larger sample sizes than those listed in Appendix 17.1, which reflects both increased computational power and methodological advances. Examples of the newer generation of studies include the National Comorbidity Study (NCS) series (e.g., Kessler et al., 2004); National Epidemiologic Survey on Alcohol and Related Conditions (NESARC) series (e.g., Grant et al., 2015); and the Army Study to Assess Risk and Resilience in Service Members (Army STARRS; e.g., Ursano et al., 2016) to name a few. Most recently, the National Institute on Drug Abuse (NIDA) and several other Institutes from the National Institutes of Health (NIH) launched the Adolescent Brain Cognitive Development (ABCD) study (Volkow et al., 2018). This unprecedented program is the largest long-term study of brain development and child health in the United States to date. The scope of standardized and harmonized assessments is also unprecedented, covering neurocognition, physical and mental health, social and emotional functions, culture, and environment, as well as integrating brain imaging and bioassays to interview data.

FUNDAMENTALS OF EPIDEMIOLOGIC METHODS

In the remainder of this chapter, we describe the fundamentals of epidemiologic concepts, frequently employed epidemiologic measures, epidemiologic study designs, and common sampling methods. Because statistical techniques have proliferated in 21st-century psychological research, other chapters in Volume 3 of this handbook detail a variety of current analytic techniques.

Concepts of Epidemiology

Epidemiology is often thought of not as a distinctive scientific discipline (such as medicine) but as an allied methodological field based heavily in statistics. However, several epistemological concepts distinguish epidemiology from other fields (e.g., clinical medicine). As noted, population thinking is the foundation of epidemiology, and study populations include individuals, dyads, families, groups, communities, states, and nations at macro levels.

The second fundamental concept is variation. Examining variations is an essential aspect of inquiry in most science fields; epidemiology focuses on patterns of diseases and other health conditions. Variations can be across time, between subgroups, or across place. The importance of this concept rests on the assumption that understanding such variations lead to new knowledge on the etiology of a disease or health condition, thus in turn leading to intervention and prevention of disease (Bhopal, 2016). Early emphasis on natural history (observational study of disease process) is related to the history of epidemiology being tied to disease epidemics. Thus, by understanding the disease epidemic pattern, one hoped to identify the causative agent (e.g., *Vibrio cholerae*) or source of transmission (e.g., water pump in John Snow's case). As the field expanded to endemic or chronic diseases, interest in natural history shifted toward identifying underlying factors that yield the observed patterns of disease over time, that is, developmental or life-course perspectives (Ben-Shlomo & Kuh, 2002; Berkman & Kawachi, 2014).

The third fundamental concept is causal inference. Although not unique to epidemiology, historically, epidemiology is considered the discipline that "discovered" and further articulated the concept of causal relationship in the area of health and disease (Rothman & Greenland, 2014). Epidemiology contributed to establish distinctions such as necessary and sufficient conditions (Greenwood, 1932) and association and causation (Hill, 1961). Epidemiologists and quantitative methodologists also elaborated multiple causation models (Morris, 1964) and web of causation mechanisms (MacMahon & Pugh, 1970). It is believed that William McDougall was among the first psychologists to hypothesize differential sensitivity to alcohol based on personality traits (McDougall, 1929). Such a hypothesis is called an interaction or moderator effect in the more contemporary methodology literature. Distinctions between interaction and moderator effects, which are often confusing, may be in part attributable to types of measurements. When the relationship between X and Y is dependent on categorical measure, say Z_1 (in the above example personality traits), we frequently use "interaction" of Z_1 on X to Y; on the other hand, if the relationship depends on a dimensional measure, Z_2, on X to Y, we frequently use the term "moderation" effect. However, some argue that while "interaction" is a statistical term that does not imply causal sequence, moderation implies a causal sequence from X to Y. A further potential confusion in the literature relates to the distinction between "moderation" and "mediation." Moderation refers to a differential relationship depending on the value of the mediating variable; while mediation refers to the situation of the variable, Z_3 is causally impacted by X and in turn impacts Y (Baron & Kenny, 1986; Wu & Zumbo, 2008).

The fourth fundamental concept is sometimes referred to as the epidemiologic triangle of agent, host, and environment (Ahrens et al., 2014; Bhopal, 2016). The model can be considered as crudely corresponding to "what" (agent), "who" (host), and "where" (environment), which are the key variables in understanding the spread of disease. An additional factor is time, which is often placed in the center of the triangle. Agents are necessary for diseases to occur (biological, physical, chemical); host factors are those that influence the chance for the disease to express and affect the severity of the disease; and, finally, environments are external conditions that contribute to the disease process. The idea is that an epidemic occurs when three factors are not in balance (homeostasis). This model is most suitable for studying outbreaks of epidemics such as infectious diseases. However, the model may not be well suited for use when host factors are complex and the disease process is chronic (or endemic; Ahrens et al., 2014; Songer, 2010).

These fundamental concepts are summarized in Table 17.1. Each concept is summarized with respect to its meaning, historical origin, and role for methodological development. Several other related concepts not listed in Table 17.1 are often found in introductory textbooks of epidemiology. For example, Zhang and colleagues (2004) analyzed eight textbooks on epidemiology published over the past century and summarized the evolution

---

TABLE 17.1

Basic Concepts in Epidemiology

Concept	What it means	Historical origin	How they relate to epidemiologic methods
Population thinking	Finding a cause of disease requires examining the whole population, not just individuals	Can be traced back to Hippocrates (Buck et al., 1998); modern origins can be traced to British epidemiologists such as William Farr and John Snow (examined by Susser & Stein, 2009, Chapter 7)	Sampling techniques, study designs, prevalence, incidence
Stochastic variation	Disease expression is not constant but varies by groups, place, and time; and that expression is not perfect and comes with a random element	Modern origin in epidemiology can be traced to John Snow with comparisons of rates across three places	Measures of occurrence, association, and multivariate modeling are based on the notion of random error; modern-day statistics used in epidemiology are almost always stochastic
Causal inference	Identifying the relationship between factors (causes) and disease occurrence	Can be traced back to Aristotle (384–322 B.C.), Hippocrates (ca. 460–375 B.C.), and Galen (ca. 129–199/217); modern prototypes, Lind's report on scurvy (ca. 1753) (from Carpenter, 1986) and Snow's study on cholera (1854)	Necessary vs. sufficient causes, confounding, interaction, mediators, moderators, statistical controls
Epidemiologic triangle	Disease expression depends on three factors of agent (what), host (who), and environment (where) and considered a basic model of causation	19th-century microbiologists such as Robert Koch and Louis Pasteur (examined by Susser & Stein, 2009, Chapters 10 and 11)	Multilevel, multivariate, and interaction analysis; prevention models

of six concepts of epidemiology: confounding, bias, cohort, case-control, causal inference and interaction. Other concepts involving study designs and sampling are more fully discussed in the section Study Designs and the section Sampling Methods and Issues.

Commonly Used Basic Epidemiologic Measures

We now introduce some basic measures of occurrence, association, impact, predictive utility, and disease burden used in a wide range of epidemiologic research. These measures provide different ways in which associations (relationship between cause, risk factor, and outcome) are quantitatively assessed. Intended as an introductory section, measures specific to multivariate

analysis are omitted here. However, some measures, such as risk ratio and odds ratio, are also applicable in the context of multivariate statistics. Also, it should be noted that the majority of this discussion involves dichotomous measures reflecting a disease orientation of epidemiologic outcomes.

Measures of occurrence. Prevalence and incidence measures are the most commonly used measures of occurrence. Prevalence rate can be classified into point prevalence and period prevalence. Point prevalence is calculated as follows:

(Number of existing cases on a specific date)/

(Population number in the particular date). (17.1)

Psychiatric epidemiology most frequently uses period prevalence, which is the frequency of occurrence during a given time period. Lifetime prevalence is the cumulative prevalence up to the point of assessment and is often asked by *ever* questions (i.e., "Have you ever . . .?"). A shorter period prevalence can be 30 days, past month, past 12 months, or some other unit of time. Incidence rate (cumulative incidence) is calculated as follows:

$$(\text{Number of new cases in a given period})/$$
$$(\text{Population at risk for the given period}). \quad (17.2)$$

When the denominator is the product of Person × Time of at-risk population (e.g., Person × Number of Years Disease Free), this is usually called the *incidence density rate*. The latter measure may be more suitable when individuals in populations are observed for varying durations over time in a cohort-based study. In a fixed population, (Prevalence) = (Incidence) × (Average Duration of Disease). However, in a dynamic population (e.g., a human population over time), this equivalence cannot be assumed. Although they are not identical and serve different purposes, the hazard rate, $h(t)$, is considered synonymous with incidence; therefore, hazard rate is sometimes called the incidence intensity. It is the instantaneous rate of developing disease in a short interval Δ around time t; thus, as a shorthand, it can be written nonmathematically as follows (cf. Bhopal, 2002, p. 168):

$$\text{Hazard rate} = (\text{Probability that disease-free}$$
$$\text{person at } t \text{ will develop}$$
$$\text{disease between } t \text{ and } t + \Delta t)/$$
$$(\text{Time from } t \text{ to } t + \Delta t), \quad (17.3)$$

where Δt is a small change in t.

If time interval is assumed to be constant, incidence rate is an estimate of the hazard rate. One might prefer the use of incidence for acute and short-duration diseases, whereas prevalence may be more preferable for chronic and noncyclical diseases. Use of incidence cases is often better suited for studying causes of disease because it is easier to identify causal etiology based on temporal patterns that are independent of confounding factors. Hazard rate is an essential function for estimating failure time as in death and prevention studies (Benichou & Palta, 2014; Bhopal, 2016; Mausner & Kramer, 1985).

Measures of association. Relative risks (RR) and odds ratio (OR) remain the most frequently used measures of association. In a prospective cohort study, RR is defined as the ratio of incidence rate in the exposed group as compared with incident rate in the unexposed group. Using a standard 2 × 2 table (see Table 17.2), RR is as follows:

$$\text{RR} = [a/(a+b)]/[c/(c+d)]. \quad (17.4)$$

A retrospective study (e.g., case control) is usually able to estimate RR of prevalent cases. OR is theoretically more appropriate in case-control or cross-sectional studies, although RR and OR are often used interchangeably and distinctions depend on a number of design factors (Knol et al., 2008). In the epidemiological context, OR estimates the relative odds of being diseased (or exposed) compared with not diseased (or exposed). Using the same 2 × 2 table, OR is typically reported in the format of $(a \times d)/(b \times c)$, but this does not show its intended meaning

---

TABLE 17.2

Risk Ratio and Odds Ratio Computation Table

Exposure classification	Disease cases	Nondiseased (or controls)	Total
Present	a	b	M1 (a + b)
Absent	c	d	M2 (c + d)
Total	M3 (a + c)	M4 (b + d)	N = M1 + M2 = M3 + M4 = a + b + c + d

because its equivalent forms are more intuitive to understand the meanings of ORs:

$$OR = (a \times d)/(b \times c) = (a/c)/(b/d)$$
$$= (a/b)/(c/d). \tag{17.5}$$

The formula $(a/c)/(b/d)$ is the exposure ratio in cases as compared with nondiseased controls; the formula $(a/b)/(c/d)$ shows the disease ratio among exposed as compared with nonexposed. In a simple 2×2 table, the confidence interval can be even be manually computed from the four cell numbers using the log odds ratio, $Ln(OR)$, which is approximately normally distributed ($L \sim N(\log(OR), \sigma^2)$):

$$Ln(OR) \pm 1.96SE[Ln(OR)]$$
$$= Ln(OR) \pm (1/a + 1/b + 1/c + 1/d)^{1/2}. \tag{17.6}$$

ORs asymptotically approach RRs for a less common disease or condition (less than 10% incidence rate). When certain assumptions are met, an OR can be adjusted to provide an estimate of RR using the following:

$$RR = OR/[(1 - P^0) + (P^0 \times OR)], \tag{17.7}$$

where P^0 is the incidence rate.

Cautions are needed, however, when making inferences from the confidence intervals (or standard errors) using this adjustment because confidence intervals appear to be substantially narrower than the true values (McNutt et al., 2003; Zhang & Yu, 1998). It is not entirely clear why OR has become a standard measure of association. One reason may be the symmetric nature (with respect to disease and nondisease), although such symmetry is only true if there are no additional covariates in the model. The ease of interpretation of ORs in multiple logistic regression may have contributed substantially to the current wide use of OR in epidemiologic and psychosocial studies (Benichou & Palta, 2014; Bhopal, 2016; Kahn & Sempos, 1989).

Measures of impact. Traditional epidemiologic measures of association are useful for pinpointing a relative effect of exposure and or any risk factors. For a controlled experiment of clinical trial, the measure of risk difference (RD) may be a simple and intuitive way to assess the absolute effect of a risk factor or the excess risk of disease among those who have a risk factor (exposure) compared to those who do not. Risk difference over a specified time period is simply:

$$RD = R_e - R_u, \tag{17.8}$$

where R_e is the rate or risk (e.g., incidence rate, cumulative incidence, prevalence) among the group exposed to a risk factor; and R_u is the rate or risk among the group unexposed to the same risk factor (Aschengrau & Seage, 2003, p. 62). The aforementioned RR and OR provide a measure of the strength of the association, while the RD provides a measure of the clinical or public health impact. For a binary outcome in a clinical trial study (such as efficacy of a medical procedure on death), reporting both absolute and relative effect sizes is recommended, as in the statement by the Consolidated Standards of Reporting Trials (CONSORT), a group of scientists dedicated to improving the quality of randomized clinical trial reporting. Such a recommendation is based on the understanding that either of the two alone is insufficient to provide a complete picture of the effect and more importantly implications for clinical trial efficacy (Moher et al., 2010).

Attributable risk (AR), sometimes called *attributable fraction*, was originally intended to quantify the impact of a well-known cause on disease outcome (e.g., smoking on cancer; Levin, 1953). Although AR is sometimes used interchangeably with RD, they are different in that while RD compares the absolute difference between the exposed and unexposed, AR measures the difference between the exposed and the unexposed in the group, which is then conditioned the incident rate among the exposed. In a general term,

$$AR = [Pr(D) - Pr(D/E)]Pr(D), \tag{17.9}$$

where $Pr(D)$ is the probability of a disease in the group; $Pr(D/E)$ is the probability among the nonexposed in the group, so the intent is to measure the fraction of the difference, taking into consideration how common the disease (or condition) is occurring in the community. AR can be interpreted in several ways; for example, proportion of excess risk or proportion of a preventable disease; consequently, a number of derived formulas are used with each having different interpretations (Levine, 2007; Rockhill et al., 1998). To see the connection with the RR, the original formula can be rewritten as (cf. Bhopal, 2016, Table 8.12, p. 278):

$$AR = (\text{Incidence in exposed})$$
$$- (\text{Incidence in unexposed})/$$
$$(\text{Incidence in exposed})$$
$$= RR(\text{exposed}) - RR(\text{unexposed})/$$
$$RR(\text{exposed})$$
$$= (RR - 1)/RR. \tag{17.10}$$

Population attributable risk (PAR), sometimes called *population attributable fraction*, measures the proportion of disease in the population as a whole that is attributable to exposure or a risk factor:

$$PAR = [(\text{Incidence in total population})$$
$$- (\text{Incidence in unexposed population})]/$$
$$(\text{Incidence in total population})$$
$$= P(\text{exposed})(RR - 1)/$$
$$[1 + P(\text{exposed})(RR - 1)]. \tag{17.11}$$

Thus, RR or OR, when appropriate, can be used even for a cross-sectional study to obtain PAR (e.g., Prigerson et al., 2002). The PAR has gained popularity as an alternative or an addition to traditional measures of association, in part because PAR allows making a choice of prevention(s) targeted to specific risk factor(s) and choice of disease, in cases in which a prevention should have the greatest reduction in the future if that

prevention were to be implemented. Nonetheless, AR and PAR rates are estimates of the amount of risk reduction that could potentially be achieved. Data do not usually allow confirming the causality of a risk factor; thus, AR and PAR should be considered the theoretical upper-limit estimates. An experimental trial is needed to assess the validity of a specific estimate. More extensive discussion on usefulness and potential pitfalls of AR and PAR is found in Benichou and Palta (2014) and Bhopal (2016).

Predictive utility. More relevant for performance of a screening test, sensitivity and specificity relate to basic epidemiologic concepts of error specifications (Type I error concerns false positive rate, and Type II error concerns false negative rate). An exposure or a risk factor can be equated with a screening test (positive and negative). Sensitivity (true positive rate) and specificity (true negative rate), respectively, are as follows:

$$Sensitivity = [\text{Number of true positives (diseased)}]/$$
$$\{[\text{Number of true positives (diseased)}]$$
$$+ [\text{Number of false negatives}$$
$$(\text{screen/exposure/risk factor}$$
$$\text{negatives who are/have become}$$
$$\text{disease})]\} = a/(a + c),$$
$$Specificity = [\text{Number of true negatives}$$
$$(\text{nondiseased})]/\{[\text{Number of true}$$
$$\text{negatives (nondiseased)}] + [\text{Number}$$
$$\text{of false positives (screen/exposure/}$$
$$\text{risk positives who are/remain}$$
$$\text{nondiseased})]\} = d/(d + b), \tag{17.12}$$

where a, b, c, and d are the cell numbers used identically to those in Table 17.2.

Although they can be applied to cross-sectional results, the concepts are designed to predict the future outcomes. Associated measures include positive predictive value (PPV) = (Number of true positives)/[(Number of true positives) + (Number of false positives)] = $a/(a + b)$; and negative predictive value (NPV) = (Number of true negatives)/[(Number of true negatives) + (Number of false negatives)] = $d/(d + c)$. The false discovery rate (FDR) derives from a simple formula $b/(b + a) = 1 - $ PPV (Bhopal, 2016). FDR is often used in multiple hypothesis testing in genetic analysis, when hypothesis testing is used instead of a screening measure typical in clinical epidemiology.

For use as a clinical screening tool, one would want to maximize the value of sensitivity (pick up all who become diseased), but as a cost-efficient screening device, one would want to maximize the value of specificity (screen out those who are likely to be disease free). To counterbalance sensitivity and specificity, the receiver (relative) operating characteristic (ROC) curve has been used for a wide range of topics, including radiology, psychology, medicine (Weinstein & Fineberg, 1980), and, more recently, machine learning. ROC can be used to determine the optimal utility of a predictive measure, for example, finding the best cutoff of dimensional symptom measures (Robins & Price, 1991), optimal choice and recode for biomarkers (Perkins & Schisterman, 2006), or choosing an optimal screening instrument for the general-population survey (Kessler et al., 2003). The ROC plots the sensitivity (true positives, y-axis) and $1 - $ specificity (false positives, x-axis), which provides a visual aid in deciding the optimal screening tool or cutoffs.

The most commonly used summary statistic is the area under the curve (AUC), which varies between .5 and 1 (where .5 is random prediction). This can be computed by constructing trapezoids under the curve as an approximation; however, a maximum likelihood estimator is also available. The AUC contains some attractive features, such as its close relationship to Wilcoxon test of ranks and Gini coefficients (Hand & Till 2001). To find the optimal screening cutoff point (e.g., level of symptoms or biomarker levels), the distance to the left top corner, d, is often used, although a number of alternative measures are available (Perkins & Schisterman, 2006). This Euclidean distance is: $d = [(1 - \text{sensitivity})^2 + (1 - \text{specificity})^2]^{1/2}$, and the smaller, the more optimal cutoff.

Unlike sensitivity, specificity, PPV, and NPV, AUC is independent of cutoff score, which contributes to their utility for comparing predictive power across measures derived from different survey instruments. Because AUC provides nonparametric statistics, it is a suitable and visually intuitive summary measure for evaluating nonparametric or semiparametric modeling approaches to decision making (e.g., Price et al., 2000).

Disease burden.   For public health and health impact assessment for multifactorial chronic illnesses, traditional epidemiologic measures geared toward association and etiology may not provide the needed tools for priority assessment of intervention and prevention. A number of population-based disease burden measures utilize information on mortality and estimates of lives' worth when compromised by disease or other health conditions. For example, potential years of life lost (PYLL), or years of potential life lost (YPLL), is a simple measure for premature mortality and estimates the average number years a person would have lived had they not died prematurely. PYLL for a particular population in the given year is a summation over all deaths in the population in that year. With cause of death information, PYLL can be computed for cause-specific mortality, such as PYLL attributable to alcohol (Rehm et al., 2006). Slow-progressing chronic diseases are likely to produce some excess mortality, but the personal and societal impacts may be greater during the years still living but not in good health. Such may be the case for a number of debilitating psychiatric disorders, such as depression (unless it leads to suicide).

More commonly used today, the disability-adjusted life years (DALY) was developed initially by the World Health Organization (Murray, 1996) with the intent to create overall disease burden estimates to be comparable across countries. DALY takes into account both premature deaths and the impact of disability during years alive and is expressed as follows:

$$DALY = (YLL) + (YLD), \qquad (17.13)$$

where YLL, years life lost, is the number of years "lost" because of premature mortality and YLD, years lived with disability, is life years still alive but living in a less-than-healthy condition. In its simplest form, $YLL = \sum d \times e$, where d is fatal case, e is individual life span, and summation is over the health outcomes of the disease; and YLD is years lived with disability adjusted for severity, $YLD = \sum n \times t \times w$, where n is a case, t is the duration of the disease, w is the disability weight, and summation is again over all health outcomes (Murray, 1994).

Both PYLL and DALY, unlike the measures described thus far in the chapter, are derived within the tradition of mortality and morbidity statistics with the use of life tables. Critics of DALY pointed out that the underlying assumption that disability means loss of productivity may not be appropriate. Methodologically, computation of DALY has required several assumptions, such as age weighting and discount rate (discount coming from health benefit in the same sense that financial investment now is worth more in the future; Prüss-Üstüm et al., 2003). The need to make such assumptions made DALY estimates sensitive to values of assumptions (Fox Rushby & Hanson, 2001). The Global Burden of Disease (GBD) Study 2010 discontinued the use of discounting parameters with the use of Bayesian meta-regression analytical methodology (Vos et al., 2012), and thus estimates are believed to be more accurate, compared with estimates derived from previous deterministic modeling. Using more refined analytical methods, recent GBD studies demonstrated the huge societal costs of psychiatric illnesses: mental and behavioral disorders account for the largest portion (over 22%) of global years lived with disability (YLD) both in 1990 and 2010 (Becker & Kleinman, 2013).

Study Designs

Five basic study designs are most frequently used in epidemiological research: case series, cross-sectional, case-control, cohort, and trial studies (Bhopal, 2016). In contemporary research, case series—an observational study using medical records for a given outcome or tracking a small number of patients with a known exposure—are mostly used for surveillance by government or health care sectors (hospital case surveillance) and thus are omitted here. Clinical trials and other experimental designs are enormously important for medication development and environmental prevention research. The clinical trial design can be considered a combination of case-control and cohort design with experimental manipulation. (Details are found in Chapters 27 of this volume and, thus, are omitted here.)

Cross-sectional study.   This design is conceptually the most simple. A population is defined at a particular point in time and, most frequently, in a geographically or politically defined boundary (e.g., contiguous states of the United States). Once the population is defined and the sample is drawn (or the whole population is studied, as in the example of the U.S. Census), counting cases will provide prevalence rates. Cross-sectional studies also allow examinations of differences in rates among subgroups as well as associations between the outcomes and risk factors and, in some cases, protective factors. These comparisons and associational examinations enable researchers to generate hypotheses regarding underlying etiology of disease expression, and if expressed, its severity. The natural history of an illness can be examined in a limited way in a cross-sectional study by retrospectively assessing the timing of onset and recurrence. Incidence rates can also be obtained in theory if the population is assumed to be closed (no population attrition or migration). For psychosocial conditions and psychiatric illnesses, however, obtaining incidence rates from a cross-sectional study is problematic. If they are obtained using self-report, the accuracy of timing is questionable. If they are obtained from archival data, record searches are often incomplete and case definitions may vary across various record sources. Moreover, a cross-sectional study is not suitable for measuring changes over time. By design it is a snapshot in which it is difficult to discern causal relationships. Thus, hypothesis testing for multiple potential explanations in cross-sectional studies is difficult, if not impossible (Bhopal, 2016; Kelsey et al., 1996). Despite these disadvantages, most large-scale surveys use a cross-sectional design in large part because of relative cost-efficiency. In particular, when the prevalence is expected to be low, cross-sectional studies afford accurate and reliable estimates of population prevalence, which is useful for policy purposes.

Cohort study. Believed to be first introduced by Frost (1935), a *cohort study* is designed to examine the study population, usually at the time of exposure to one or more risk factors and track that population over a period of time to observe differences in outcomes. This type of study is also called a *follow-up*, *longitudinal*, or *prospective* study. In contrast to a cross-sectional study, data are collected at least at two time points from the same individuals. A prospective cohort study is the most commonly used design in contemporary epidemiology. Use of a retrospective cohort study has also been common, however, and they are advantageous when historical records are available for the defined cohort (e.g., occupational group; Bhopal, 2016; Comstock, 2004; Doll, 2004; Mausner & Kramer, 1985). In reality, most prospective cohort studies use some historical records, such as medical records, that existed before baseline data collection. Retrospective cohort studies can easily be expanded to prospective studies after baseline data are collected to test the hypothesis developed from the retrospective data. Most prospective cohort studies collect data in a follow-up period over a preceding period. In short, the retrospective–prospective dichotomy, although conceptually important, share more features than may be superficially obvious. A clear advantage of prospective cohort studies is the ability to observe outcomes via self-report, direct medical examinations, or assay collection. When case definition is well established, incidence rates can be obtained as part of examining the natural history of the disease in question.

Disadvantages include the labor-intensive nature of data collection, various forms of attrition that can bias results, and the inability to assess cohort-specific effects, for example, a youth cohort established in the Depression era may be different from a youth cohort of the same age range established during the 1960s with respect to illicit drug use, even though individual risk factors may be similar (Bhopal, 2016; Mausner & Kramer, 1985; Miller et al., 2014).

Case-control study. The *case-control study*, sometimes called a *retrospective study*, examines the association between disease and hypothesized risk factors of past exposure by comparing diseased cases and unaffected control samples at risk of developing disease. The case-control design arose in the context of infectious diseases in 19th-century England. Doll and Hill's (1950) classic study on the relationship between cigarette smoking and lung cancer is considered a model case-control investigation. Although this design has a number of strengths (e.g., relative ease and cost-efficient data collection, straightforward data analysis scheme, clinical relevance of results), it has several major limitations, including results being more dependent on accurate case definition, incomplete case records, adequacy of control selection, and selection bias in prevalent cases (Breslow, 2014; Mausner & Kramer, 1985). For those reasons, a cohort study design is usually considered superior by many epidemiologists and the case-control design has fallen out of favor in recent years in observational epidemiology. Nevertheless, a study of a rare disorder or condition would require an extremely large cohort study. For such a disorder, practically only a case-control design may be feasible. The case-control design became a preferred design for genetic epidemiology of psychiatric disorders (Andrieu & Goldstein, 1998) compared with the family-based association study or general-population cohort study. This is in part because cost containment is necessary, which is required for large sample sizes, and extreme cases are preferable to identify gene variants with modest effect size. In fact, the case-control design is a standard in the genome-wide association study (GWAS), which has become the most dominant design since the turn of the 21st century—so much so that, by 2018, about 3,700 studies had accumulated (Mills & Rahal 2019). However, genetic linkage analysis is reemerging in part because of a limited coverage of variants in GWAS (Tam et al., 2019); moreover, linkage analysis is advantageous for identifying rare but high-penetrant variants that are associated with complex traits such as psychiatric disorders (Ott et al., 2015).

Hybrid designs. Many hybrid study designs that combine elements of different designs have been developed. An obvious motivation is to improve design efficiency and reduce disadvantages associated with each of the major basic designs described thus far. For example, the repeated cross-sectional design repeats a cross-sectional data collection multiple times on, in principle, different individuals. This design is used in government-sponsored annual surveys (Johnston et al., 2020; Substance Abuse and Mental Health Services Administration, 2017) and is usually designed to *not* include the same respondents. This design is helpful not only for monitoring trends over time but also for separating developmental or age effects from cohort and period effects (Yang & Land, 2008). Use of the repeated cross-sectional design may be more advantageous than a longitudinal cohort design when the population is in flux because a cohort design is restricted to the initial sample recruited at the baseline survey. However, this design still does not allow making inferences regarding changing behaviors over time (Yee & Niemeier, 1996).

In a classic paper, Mantel and Haenszel (1959) discussed the interconnectedness of different study designs. In fact, they argued that studies using different designs should reach the same conclusions. For example, case-control and cohort studies can be seen as two sides of the same coin: Whereas the case-control study selects cases and controls by which to associate exposure in the past to risk factors, the cohort-study sample may be ascertained based on exposure and risk factors by which to estimate

disease incidence and prevalence in the future (Mausner & Kramer, 1985, p. 158). Thus, a hybrid study design can be chosen from a large cohort or cross-sectional study to conduct a case-control substudy (Doll, 2004). This is referred to as a *nested case-control study* or sometimes called *two-stage sampling* (Breslow, 1996; White, 1982). For example, Price et al. (2009) studied differences in coping behaviors in midlife between those who had a suicide attempt or suicidal ideation (cases) and those who scored very low in the combined risk scale for suicidality obtained in preceding years (controls) from a cohort of Vietnam veterans who had been followed up since 1972. Because those veterans were all at higher risk of psychological problems in middle age, to get contrasting results in coping behaviors, we considered a nested case-control design to be scientifically better and more economical than following up all of the cohort members. As in this case, an obvious advantage of a cohort-based nested case-control design is the knowledge of all cohort members. This design may be particularly efficient for an uncommon disorder or condition (e.g., suicide attempt). It is also an efficient strategy when the budget is limited. For example, it would not be economical to obtain data on all cohort members when omitted members may not provide information that is as informative as selected cases and controls (Tager, 2000). A potential problem with a nested case-control design is that the choice of a control group is often dependent on the choice of cases, especially when selecting matched controls. When multiple phenotypes are of interest, drawing several matched control groups would defeat the merit of a nested case-control design because a case may be a case for one phenotype but may be a control for another phenotype, or an uninformative sample for yet another phenotype. In such a case, it would be more scientifically sound to follow up all cohort members.

An alternative is the *case-cohort design* (also called *case-base design*), in which the control group is randomly selected from the entire cohort, thus serving as a control for multiple outcomes

(Prentice, 1986). This is an unmatched nested case-control design in which a control is drawn at the onset of cohort study. The choice between a case-cohort and nested case-control design should be made based on the purpose of the study (e.g., narrowly defined single outcome versus need to investigate multiple outcomes). For some measures (e.g., incidence rate ratio), analysis becomes more complex and requires variance adjustments. An apparent lack of consensus for correct variance estimators appears to hinder a wider use of this hybrid design, despite the considerable potential to assess incidence of comorbid psychiatric disorders (Barlow et al., 1999; Kass, 2014; Langholz & Thomas, 1990; Sharp et al., 2014).

Although the case-cohort or nested case-control designs try to retain the advantage of the cohort study design without the costs required for following up all cohort members, a hybrid design can be developed to reduce scientific weaknesses of a cohort design, even though it may increase the costs and labor. A *cohort sequential design,* also referred to as an *accelerated longitudinal design,* is particularly labor-intensive by combining cross-sectional and longitudinal cohort sampling (Schaie, 1965). *Cohort* usually refers to age cohort; this design is aimed at measuring samples of multiple age groups at multiple times of measurements. This design is thus suitable for developmental studies in which age-related changes are considerable, a large age span needs to be studied, or potential period and cohort effects could complicate interpretations of simple cohort designs. Although labor and cost intensive, the lead investigators can complete a large project with a span of their productive time period. Furthermore, depending on model specification, longitudinal and cross-sectional trends can be separated out via a combination of unique parameters (Galbraith et al., 2017). When age-graded changes are hypothesized to be predominantly biological and can be considered under genetic control, a cohort-sequential design can be informative and time efficient as in studies of behavioral genetics (Heath et al., 1999).

The *case-crossover design* is another hybrid design first introduced in 1991 to study transient effects on the risk of acute events, using only cases (Maclure, 1991). The idea is to capture a case's exposure immediately before or during the case-defining event within the same person (i.e., the person serving as their matched control; Lu & Zeger, 2007). It is a variation of repeated-measures longitudinal design and can be considered as an alternative to the case-control design. The crossover design is often associated with clinical trial studies or pharmaco-epidemiology because of its ability to measure the association of drug exposure with acute outcomes (Delaney & Suissa, 2009) since this design is best suited for studies of intermittent and/or short-duration exposures and transient acute effect (Mittleman & Mostofsky, 2014). Most recently, a placebo crossover design has been suggested to assess the efficacy durability of the potent mRNA vaccines against infection and more severe endpoints of SARS-COV-2, the virus that causes COVID-19 (Fintzi & Follmann, 2021). An original double-blinded randomized clinical trial is then "rebranded" to assess the post-crossover estimates of time-dependent hazard rate (e.g., vaccine efficacy that may wane over time). Additionally, such a design can "bypass" ethical controversies surrounding continuing a placebo-controlled clinical trial when the treatment or prevention is determined to be very efficacious (Rid et al., 2021).

The crossover design is also suitable for certain observational epidemiology studies—for example, effect of alcohol consumption on injury within a defined time after consumption (Spurling & Vinson, 2005). An advantage of this design is its ability to remove the effect of unmeasured time-invariant (between-subject) confounders. It is a conceptually attractive alternative to a case-control study, for which obtaining controls are logistically or theoretically difficult, or ethically undesirable. A disadvantage is its "carryover" effect. For example, if the past drinking affects the drinking on the day of injury, the results would be biased, which would be applicable to heavy drinkers (Kass, 2014).

Table 17.3 summarizes the aims of each design (types of knowledge gain), advantages,

TABLE 17.3

Basic and Hybrid Epidemiological Designs: Advantages, Disadvantages, and When to Use

Design	Knowledge gain	Advantages	Disadvantages	Classic or landmark studies
Cross-sectional	■ Prevalence ■ Disease burden ■ Group difference ■ Association with risk factors (odds ratios) ■ Generate hypotheses	■ Relatively cost-effective ■ Ability to provide generalizable estimates ■ Allows analysis of many different outcomes ■ Data collection commitment short	■ Access to sampling frame needed ■ Data collection time frame short ■ Difficult to make causal inference ■ Selection bias due to nonresponse ■ Analytical adjustments most likely needed to provide generalizable results	■ Major landmark psychiatric epidemiology studies ■ Epidemiologic Catchment Area (ECA) Wave 1; (Robins & Regier, 1991) ■ National Comorbidity Study [NCS] Wave 1; (Kessler et al., 1994) ■ National Epidemiologic Survey on Alcohol and Related Conditions [NESARC] Wave 1; (Grant, 1997) ■ National Vietnam Veterans Readjustment Study (Kulka et al., 1990; Schlenger et al., 1992)
Cohort	■ Incidence ■ Burden of disease ■ Risk factor analysis (relative risks) ■ Temporal or causal analysis	■ Ability to observe changes ■ Ability to discern cause-effect better than cross-sectional ■ Complete information on all members of the sample ■ Allow analysis of many different outcomes	■ Labor-intensive ■ Costs high ■ Long-term research commitment ■ Confidentiality issues high with small sample size ■ Selection bias due to differential attrition ■ Difficult to change measures over the course of study ■ Results are cohort specific ■ May not be suitable for rare diseases ■ Complex analysis to adjust within-individual correlations	■ Classical life course studies (e.g., Oakland Growth Study; Elder, 1974) ■ Follow-up surveys of general population cross sectional studies (e.g., NESARC longitudinal) ■ Special population longitudinal (e.g., Millennium cohort study; Ryan et al., 2007) ■ Genetic epidemiology (e.g., Vietnam Era Twin Registry, Goldberg, True, Eisen, & Henderson, 1990; Denedin Longitudinal Study, Caspi et al., 2003)
Case-control	■ Clinical knowledge ■ Risk factor analysis (odds ratios) ■ Generate hypothesis ■ Potential discovery of agent	■ Cost-effective ■ Straightforward analysis	■ Sensitive to case definition ■ May not be suitable for dimensional outcomes ■ Criteria for appropriate control often difficult to assess ■ Greater risk for confounding ■ Difficult to make causal inferences ■ Results in potential bias due to stratification	■ Earlier clinical epidemiology studies ■ Early generation genetic association studies

TABLE 17.3

Basic and Hybrid Epidemiological Designs: Advantages, Disadvantage, and When to Use (*Continued*)

Design	Knowledge gain	Advantages	Disadvantages	Classic or landmark studies
Repeated cross-sectional	■ Same as single-point cross-sectional ■ Allows multipoint trend analysis	■ Same advantages of cross-sectional	■ Same disadvantages of single-point cross-sectional ■ Difficult to change conceptual and analytical framework corresponding to paradigmatic or cultural changes	■ Large-scale trend monitoring surveys (National Survey on Drug Use and Health)
Nested case-control (two-stage sampling)	■ Same as case-control ■ Potential for discovery greater (e.g., gene variants) ■ Causal inference potential greater with knowledge of cohort as a whole	■ More cost-effective than collecting data from all cohort members or the whole original case-control sample members	■ Same disadvantage as case-control ■ Ability to make population causal inference substantially reduced	■ Based on large hospital or agency records (Graham et al., 2005) ■ Genetic epidemiology (e.g., genome-wide association study; Bierut et al., 2008)
Case-cohort	■ Same as case-control	■ Control drawn from the whole cohort reduce costs for drawing cases for multiple substudies ■ Results not dependent on definition of control ■ Multiple outcomes can be studied simultaneously	■ Variance estimation technique complex for some measures ■ Various models of multiple outcomes (Cologne et al., 2012)	■ Incidence study of large cohort studies (Salomaa et al., 1999) ■ Genetic epidemiology (Kulathinal et al., 2007)
Cohort-sequential	■ Able to document nonmonotonic and relatively rapid changes (e.g., age graded)	■ Combined advantage of cohort and repeated panel data collection ■ Shorter duration of data collection commitment ■ Ability to separate cohort effects from developmental changes	■ Labor- and cost-intensive ■ Normative history graded influence still a confounder	■ Normal developmental studies in behavior genetics (e.g., early to adolescent development) ■ Child developmental studies
Case cross-over	■ Disease burden ■ Impact of short-term exposure ■ Ability to draw causal inference greater than regular cohort studies	■ Cost-effective ■ No control needed (within-subject control) ■ Remove time-invariant confounding	■ Carryover effect contaminate results ■ Suitable only for transient types of exposure	■ Pharmaco-epidemiologic applications (e.g., acute drug effect) ■ Injury prevention (e.g., alcohol intoxication and resultant injuries)

Note. These are commonly used designs in observational epidemiology. Clinical case series (uncommon research design) and clinical trial (experimental design) are not included.

disadvantages, and example studies for the three basic and five hybrid study designs introduced thus far (for more detailed comparisons of several designs, see Bhopal, 2016; Kass, 2014).

Sampling Methods and Issues

Covering all aspects of sampling techniques is beyond the scope of this review. For those readers interested in further detail, see comprehensive and introductory books on sampling, including Fuller (2009), as well as Chapter 16 of this volume. Within the traditional sampling techniques, systematic sampling techniques are most applicable to cross-sectional design and its variations. Cohort study sampling uses the same sampling technique as a cross-sectional design at baseline data collection. Follow-up sampling is dependent on design and attrition scheme and others that are study specific. For case-control design, matching methods become more important. Simple random sampling is possible for a reasonably well-defined small population or sampling frame (such as a class of university). Most large-scale psychiatric epidemiology survey sampling applies more complex survey techniques. Here in this chapter, select topics at the level of introductory epidemiology are discussed.

Multistage sampling for large cross-sectional surveys. We briefly describe here the steps involved in complex sampling and the analytical consequences of complex survey design applied to household surveys. As an illustration, the National Survey on Drug Use and Health, one of the most complex survey designs, defines the population as civilian, noninstitutionalized, ages 12 or older, and residing in the United States and the District of Columbia. The basic sampling scheme since 2014 (simplified version here) is that the first-level stratum is U.S. states with different target sample sizes (37 states and D.C., each with a target sample of 960, to states as large as California, with a target sample of 4,560). Each state is divided into sampling regions with census tracts selected within each state sampling region; then the census tracts are partitioned into compact clusters of dwelling units (DUs), which

are termed *segments*. Each segment is selected within each sampled census tract with probability proportionate to size. It is this segment for which a complete list of all eligible DUs are compiled to determine the minimum number of DUs in each segment. Sample DUs are selected and a roster of all persons residing in DUs are compiled. Multiple persons can be selected from each DU (CBHSQ, 2015).

This example shows that multiple strata (state, region) and multiple sampling stages (census tracts, segment, DUs, and selection of person in DU) affect the probability of a person being chosen. Sampling weights are derived accordingly and include nonresponse adjustment. Thus, weights are used to adjust for unequal probability selection in that weighted point estimates correspond to the estimates as if simple random sampling had been applied. Remaining problems relate to variance estimates because the weighted number of observations is different from actual sample size and complex sampling produces correlated data. Most commonly used has been the Taylor series linearization method, which uses an infinite sum of terms calculated from the values of its derivatives at a single point (Lohr, 1999). This method derives a linear approximation of variance estimates based on the variance of the linear terms of the Taylor expansion for a particular statistic of interest. Other well-known replication methods (e.g., jackknife, balanced repeated replication) also regained popularity in part because of the simplicity of statistics based on repeated resampling (Rust & Rao, 1996; Wolter, 1985). Corrections on standard errors are customarily done thanks to the availability of easy-to-use software (e.g., Brick & Morganstein, 1996; Research Triangle Institute, 2001) that can handle more than two strata and are particularly suitable for multistage sampling used in large-scale government annual surveys. When sample stratification structure is relatively simple, other estimators (such as the Huber-White estimator) provide consistent variance estimates (Rogers, 1993). Major statistical packages, such as SAS Institute's survey procedures (e.g., Lewis, 2018) and Mplus (Muthén & Muthén, 1998–2017), allow for the inclusion of complex sampling weights and variance adjustments.

Sampling controls in the case-control design. Three basic principles for control selection are to reduce ascertainment, confounding, and information biases (Wacholder et al., 1992). The principle for case-cohort design is to randomly select controls from disease-free sample members of the sample (if no random control is possible, an appropriate control can be selected to ensure representativeness of the exposure); the deconfounding principle is to choose controls to be as similar as possible to the cases with respect to the distribution of one or more confounders by stratification or matching (Breslow, 2014), and comparable accuracy refers to uniform exposure and outcome measures between cases and controls. Of those principles, methods to achieve the deconfounding principle by matching are perhaps the most controversial. The basic justification for matching is that underlying factors used for matching are hypothesized to be associated with exposure. Thus, ideal matching should result in the distribution of exposure in the matched control group to be similar to that of the case group. Several justifications can be made for the necessity of matching. For example, matching can improve efficiency, and matching methods such as cotwin control and sibling control intended to control for multiple factors that are difficult to measure (e.g., quantitative genetics). Matching introduces several problems, however. Matching on underlying risk factors may reduce the variability in exposure variables of interest and thus reduce efficiency. Such is the case with overmatching. Overmatching is more serious beyond loss of efficiency when an intermediate confounder, which is affected by exposure and is an etiological factor, is used for matching. Such intermediate confounders mask the true nature of the causal relationship and lead to statistical bias (Breslow, 2014; Kupper et al., 1981). In general, stratification of the control sample with broad demographics (e.g., age group, gender) should be sufficient to achieve comparability of cases and controls without unnecessary overmatching.

In the United States and elsewhere in high- and middle-income countries, large-scale cross-sectional surveys are routinely conducted by the government on health and illness, including mental health and substance abuse. The propensity score matching methods allow mimicking some characteristics of a randomized controlled trial using data from an observational (nonrandomized) study, such as a cross-sectional general population survey (Austin, 2011). Formalized by Rosenbaum and Rubin (1983), the propensity score is the conditional probability of treatment assignment, given a set of covariates (but not effects of the treatment). This is expressed as:

$$ln\left(\left(\text{propensity score}\right)/1-\left(\text{propensity score}\right)\right)$$
$$= \beta_0 + \beta_1 X_1 + \ldots + \beta_p X_p, \qquad (17.14)$$

where β_0 is an intercept, β_i is a regression coefficient and, X_i is a covariate, as in a regression equation. However, "treatment" needs not be a clinical treatment in a traditional sense, for example, causal effect of exposure to firearm violence on violent behavior, which is not appropriate, ethically or technically, for a randomized experimental study (Bingenheimer et al., 2005).

Through a propensity score matching method, one hopes to reduce or eliminate the effects of confounding in an observational study data because "treatment" selection is most likely influenced by characteristics of study participants. There are several matching methods that can result in a different degree of bias in the estimation of the effect of treatment. Propensity score matching methods are limited to measured covariates only, even though a major strength of propensity score matching is to be able to utilize an observational study, which is often more representative of the population than that of a randomized clinical trial study. Furthermore, when some of the baseline individual-level covariates affect both the outcome and treatment/exposure, estimated treatment or exposure effect will result in an increased bias, although several solutions (some inconsistent with others) were introduced to remedy this weakness (Brookhart et al., 2006).

Sampling bias. Sampling bias, which is also called *ascertainment bias* in genetic epidemiology, arises when sampling is not random. Numerous sources contribute to selection bias, but examples include self-selection such as using only volunteers without the use of a sampling frame, nonresponse, and refusal. In epidemiology, a classic example of Berkson's bias (Berkson, 1946) involved a retrospective study examining a risk factor for a disease in a hospital in-patient sample. If a control group is also obtained from the in-patient population, a difference in hospital admission rates for the case versus control sample can result in a spurious association between the disease and the risk factor. In a more general term, Berkson bias occurs when the sampling fractions depend jointly on exposure and disease. Another example is the healthy worker effect that is often found in occupationally defined follow-up or case-control studies for which controls or unexposed groups come from different occupational or nonworking groups (Li & Sung, 1999). For example, veterans are in general healthier than their general population counterpart because of military eligibility criteria. Thus, even though they may have suffered from combat-related psychological injuries, their morbidity and mortality may not be significantly different from those among a civilian-matched control.

In genetic epidemiology, ascertainment (sampling) bias often resides in specific sampling strategies. For example, sampling of affected (diseased) probands to obtain pedigree data would produce an upward bias favoring positive familial association with the trait of interest. Another ascertainment bias more akin to genetic association studies is population stratification bias in which estimates of genetic effect are subject to confounding when cases and controls differ in their ethnic backgrounds (Hellwege et al., 2017). Potential bias by population stratification appears pronounced when allele frequencies and phenotypes both vary by ethnicity (e.g., DRD2 and alcoholism; Thomas & Witte, 2002).

Having been focused primarily on the populations of European ancestry to date, scholars of the genome-wide association studies (GWAS) of psychiatric disorders acknowledge the need for and benefits of obtaining human genomics data from more diverse populations (racial, ethnic, and ancestral diversity). Currently, two approaches are used: one combining all individuals regardless of ancestry and the other, a stratifying approach of separate population specific analysis followed by cross-ancestry meta-analysis (Peterson et al., 2019). The latter approach requires even larger sample sizes than has been used, for example, GWAS meta-analyses of cannabis use disorders utilized a total sample of over 384,000 with an impressive array of genomic as well as phenotypic association findings; however, authors noted that the African ancestry sample was still underpowered (Johnson et al., 2020).

Sampling for online surveys. Internet or web-based surveys and more recently smartphone-based surveys have exploded over time. Especially with arrival of the COVID-19 pandemic, researchers have been adapting to these types of surveys compared to the traditional in-person surveys. More detailed examination of the new modes of survey administration are explored more fully in Chapter 19 in this volume. Relevant for sampling considerations for web-based or smartphone surveys, most notable distinction, compared to traditional modes of surveys, is that the population is restricted to those with reliable and inexpensive access to the internet or a smartphone. Another is self-completion, which could affect response rate—an issue similar to a mailed survey. Another distinction of the online survey is less controlled access to participation. More generally, although there is a general consensus that online surveys will lower costs, shorten the delivery time and eliminate interviewer bias, disadvantages of web-based or smartphone surveys include computer literacy, substantial margin for sample bias, lower response rates, as well as less complete response, which can affect point estimates (Nayak & Narayan, 2019). Detailed interviews that would require interviewers, such as for a psychiatric diagnostic assessment, may be less suitable for web-based surveys (Fricker & Schonlau, 2002; Heiervang & Goodman, 2011).

Zhao and Jin (2006) listed a dozen sampling approaches unique to online survey, including hypertext links, pop-up surveys, and banner invitations (others, such as harvested addresses, have a telephone equivalence). These methods are useful in drawing a random sample, although the sampling frame is restricted to site visitors. When a closed population is appropriate (e.g., organization, company), drawing a probability sample for an email or web survey is not much different from sampling for use with more conventional survey media. Currently, probability sampling for a general population for web-based surveys still depends on preexisting conventional lists and use of emails for the first contact. Since email lists of general population for recruitment are not generally available, drawing a sampling frame would be near impossible at the population level (Fricker, 2016). Although these methods have been widely available for more than two decades, there is still a dearth of comprehensive reviews and comparative analyses on the methodology and assessment of online surveys to answer a number of practical questions such as how to enhance response rate, optimal length of survey, optimal methods for reminders, and how to maximize representativeness of the sample (Menon & Muraleedharan, 2020). Use of internet-based surveys, which had already been expanding rapidly more than a decade prior to the COVID-19 pandemic, was further accelerated by the pandemic.

This trend will continue beyond the pandemic, in part because digitalization allows the big science to get even bigger through wider collaboration, but also clinical trials and human experiment studies as well shifted online to a large extent out of necessity during the pandemic (Aschwanden, 2021).

CONCLUSION

This chapter has introduced epidemiologic concepts and basic methods. A brief history of epidemiologic research and main concepts of epidemiology has shown that the development of methods was historical in nature, reflecting the historical focus of diseases of the time. Method development was closely tied to basic concepts; major studies contributed greatly to development and refinement of the contemporary study design and methods. Many of the basic epidemiologic measures are linked with each, conceptually and often mathematically, and serve different purposes for stages of epidemiologic inquires. Use of particular measures requires knowledge of advantages and disadvantages of study designs as well as the properties of the measures. Confusion still exists even for basic measures with respect to how to use particular measures in the most appropriate fashion. Careful consideration is needed for choosing the most appropriate measure among those that have similar properties.

APPENDIX 17.1.   EXAMPLES OF LANDMARK PSYCHOSOCIAL AND PSYCHIATRIC EPIDEMIOLOGIC STUDIES IN THE 20TH CENTURY

Name	Why landmark?	Epidemiologic methods used	Major findings and impacts
Social Class and Mental Illness	Represents the first-generation psychiatric epidemiology studies; application of Chicago school ecological perspective to mental illness	Used record examination; ecological analyses by developmental zones; no individual data	Downward drift hypothesis supported; spurred a generation of studies examining social causation vs. social selection theory to explain the association between socioeconomic status and mental illness
Epidemiologic Catchment Area	Then the largest general-population psychiatric epidemiology study; first major multisite study; development of standardized psychiatric assessment to arrive at diagnostic criteria; all major Axis I disorders assessed	General population cross-sectional and 1-year follow-up design; multistage cluster sampling; several oversample schemes; subset clinical samples; Diagnostic Interview Schedule (Robins et al., 1981) used by lay interviewers; built-in mental health services assessment	Psychiatric disorder is common (one third of U.S. adult population experience a clinical psychiatric syndrome sometime in their lifetime); comorbidity rates are high; standardized instrument, careful cluster sampling, assessment of comorbidity became norms of subsequent large-scale studies such as National Comorbidity Study (Kessler et al., 1994) and National Epidemiologic Survey on Alcohol and Related Conditions (Grant et al., 2004)
International Study of Schizophrenia (ISOS)	World Health Organization initiatives in instrument development and multi-nation coordination; focus on cross-cultural similarities and differences; focus on schizophrenia, an extreme spectrum of psychiatric disorders	A total of 12 countries involved; use of clinical samples utilizing existing clinical infrastructure; admission-based ascertainment; careful cross-cultural equivalence examination; follow-up assessments	The International Pilot Study of Schizophrenia and the ISoS both confirm differences in long-term prognosis of schizophrenia; recovery rates better in developing than industrial countries; focus on prognosis and disability in contrast to accurate prevalence/incidence estimation continues to enlighten mainstream U.S. psychiatric epidemiology
National Vietnam Veterans Readjustment Study	The then-largest special population (veteran) study; first major attempt to accurately assess the rates of posttraumatic stress disorder (PTSD) among Vietnam veterans	Cross-sectional; cluster sampling to obtain representative samples; three comparison groups— deployed, nondeployed era veteran, and civilian control	Lifetime prevalence rate of PTSD 31% among veterans; war-zone exposure definite risk factor; a majority appear to have adjusted relatively well to civilian lives; study spurred a generation of studies on war and other traumas and PTSD; became customary to assess psychological stress in military research

References

Ahrens, W., Krickeberg, K., & Pigeot, I. (2014). An introduction to epidemiology. In W. Ahrens & I. Pigeot (Eds.), *Handbook of epidemiology* (2nd ed., pp. 3–41). Springer. https://doi.org/10.1007/978-0-387-09834-0_42

Ahrens, W., & Pigeot, I. (Eds.). (2014). *Handbook of epidemiology* (2nd ed.). Springer. https://doi.org/10.1007/978-0-387-09834-0

Andrieu, N., & Goldstein, A. M. (1998). Epidemiologic and genetic approaches in the study of gene-environment interaction: An overview of available methods. *Epidemiologic Reviews, 20*(2), 137–147. https://doi.org/10.1093/oxfordjournals.epirev.a017976

Aschengrau, A., & Seage, G. R., III. (2003). *Essentials of epidemiology in public health.* Jones and Bartlett Learning.

Aschwanden, C. (2021). How COVID is changing the study of human behaviour. *Nature, 593*(7859), 331–333. https://doi.org/10.1038/d41586-021-01317-z

Austin, P. C. (2011). An introduction to propensity score methods for reducing the effects of confounding in observational studies. *Multivariate Behavioral Research, 46*(3), 399–424. https://doi.org/10.1080/00273171.2011.568786

Barlow, W. E., Ichikawa, L., Rosner, D., & Izumi, S. (1999). Analysis of case-cohort designs. *Journal of Clinical Epidemiology, 52*(12),

1165–1172. https://doi.org/10.1016/S0895-4356(99)00102-X

Baron, R. M., & Kenny, D. A. (1986). The moderator-mediator variable distinction in social psychological research: Conceptual, strategic, and statistical considerations. *Journal of Personality and Social Psychology, 51*(6), 1173–1182. https://doi.org/10.1037/0022-3514.51.6.1173

Becker, A. E., & Kleinman, A. (2013). Mental health and the global agenda. *The New England Journal of Medicine, 369*(1), 66–73. https://doi.org/10.1056/NEJMra1110827

Ben-Shlomo, Y., & Kuh, D. (2002). A life course approach to chronic disease epidemiology: Conceptual models, empirical challenges and interdisciplinary perspectives. *International Journal of Epidemiology, 31*(2), 285–293. https://doi.org/10.1093/ije/31.2.285

Benichou, J., & Palta, M. (2014). Rates, risks, measures of association and impact. In W. Ahrens & I. Pigeot (Eds.), *Handbook of epidemiology* (2nd ed., pp. 123–185). Springer. https://doi.org/10.1007/978-0-387-09834-0_3

Berkman, L., & Kawachi, I. (2014). A historical framework for social epidemiology: Social determinants of population health. In L. Berkman, I. Kawachi, & M. Glymour (Eds.), *Social epidemiology* (2nd ed., pp. 1–16). Oxford University Press.

Berkson, J. (1946). Limitations of the application of fourfold table analysis to hospital data. *Biometrics, 2*(3), 47–53. https://doi.org/10.2307/3002000

Bhopal, R. (2002). *Concepts of epidemiology: An integrated introduction to the ideas, theories, principles, and methods of epidemiology.* Oxford University Press.

Bhopal, R. (2016). *Concepts of epidemiology: An integrated introduction to the ideas, theories, principles, and methods of epidemiology* (3rd ed.). Oxford University Press. https://doi.org/10.1093/med/9780198739685.001.0001

Bierut, L. J., Stitzel, J. A., Wang, J. C., Hinrichs, A. L., Grucza, R. A., Xuei, X., Saccone, N. L., Saccone, S. F., Bertelsen, S., Fox, L., Horton, W. J., Breslau, N., Budde, J., Cloninger, C. R., Dick, D. M., Foroud, T., Hatsukami, D., Hesselbrock, V., Johnson, E. O., . . . Goate, A. M. (2008). Variants in nicotinic receptors and risk for nicotine dependence. *The American Journal of Psychiatry, 165*(9), 1163–1171. https://doi.org/10.1176/appi.ajp.2008.07111711

Bingenheimer, J. B., Brennan, R. T., & Earls, F. J. (2005). Firearm violence exposure and serious violent behavior. *Science, 308*(5726), 1323–1326. https://doi.org/10.1126/science.1110096

Breslow, N. E. (1996). Statistics in epidemiology: The case-control study. *Journal of the American Statistical Association, 91*(433), 14–28. https://doi.org/10.1080/01621459.1996.10476660

Breslow, N. E. (2014). Case-control studies. In W. Ahrens & I. Pigeot (Eds.), *Handbook of epidemiology* (2nd ed., pp. 293–323). Springer. https://doi.org/10.1007/978-0-387-09834-0_7

Brick, J. M., & Morganstein, D. (1996). WesVarPC: Software for computing variance estimates from complex designs. In *Proceedings of the 1996 Annual Research Conference* (pp. 861–866). U.S. Bureau of the Census.

Brock, T. (1999). *Robert Koch: A life in medicine and bacteriology.* ASM Press.

Brookhart, M. A., Schneeweiss, S., Rothman, K. J., Glynn, R. J., Avorn, J., & Stürmer, T. (2006). Variable selection for propensity score models. *American Journal of Epidemiology, 163*(12), 1149–1156. https://doi.org/10.1093/aje/kwj149

Buck, C., Llopis, A., Najera, E., & Terris, M. (Eds.). (1998). *The challenge of epidemiology: Issues and selected readings* (Scientific Publication No. 505). Pan American Health Organization.

Carpenter, K. (1986). *The history of scurvy and vitamin C.* Cambridge University Press.

Caspi, A., Sugden, K., Moffitt, T. E., Taylor, A., Craig, I. W., Harrington, H., McClay, J., Mill, J., Martin, J., Braithwaite, A., & Poulton, R. (2003). Influence of life stress on depression: Moderation by a polymorphism in the 5-HTT gene. *Science, 301*(5631), 386–389. https://doi.org/10.1126/science.1083968

Center for Behavioral Health Statistics and Quality. (2015). *National survey on drug use and health: 2014 and 2015 redesign changes.* Substance Abuse and Mental Health Services Administration.

Cologne, J., Preston, D. L., Imai, K., Misumi, M., Yoshida, K., Hayashi, T., & Nakachi, K. (2012). Conventional case-cohort design and analysis for studies of interaction. *International Journal of Epidemiology, 41*(4), 1174–1186. https://doi.org/10.1093/ije/dys102

Comstock, G. (2004). Cohort analysis: W. H. Frost's contributions to the epidemiology of tuberculosis and chronic disease. In A. Morabia (Ed.), *A history of epidemiologic methods and concepts* (pp. 223–230). Birkhaser Verlag. https://doi.org/10.1007/978-3-0348-7603-2_12

Delaney, J. A., & Suissa, S. (2009). The case-crossover study design in pharmacoepidemiology. *Statistical Methods in Medical Research, 18*(1), 53–65. https://doi.org/10.1177/0962280208092346

Doll, R. (2004). Cohort studies: History of the method. In A. Morabia (Ed.), *A history of epidemiologic methods and concepts* (pp. 243–274). Birkhaser Verlag. https://doi.org/10.1007/978-3-0348-7603-2_14

Doll, R., & Hill, A. B. (1950). Smoking and carcinoma of the lung; preliminary report. *British Medical Journal, 2*(4682), 739–748. https://doi.org/10.1136/bmj.2.4682.739

Elder, G. (1974). *Children of the great depression: Social change in life experience.* University of Chicago Press.

Faris, R., & Dunham, H. (1939). *Mental disorders in urban areas: An ecological study of schizophrenia and other psychosis.* University of Chicago Press.

Faris, R., & Dunham, H. (1960). *Mental disorders in urban areas: An ecological study of schizophrenia and other psychosis* (2nd ed.). Hafner.

Farr, W. (2004). On prognosis. In A. Morabia (Ed.), *A history of epidemiologic methods and concepts* (pp. 159–178). Birkhaser Verlag. https://doi.org/10.1007/978-3-0348-7603-2_5

Fintzi, J., & Follmann, D. (2021). Assessing vaccine durability in randomized trials following placebo crossover. *Statistics in Medicine, 40*(27), 5983–6007. https://doi.org/10.1002/sim.9001

Fox Rushby, J. A., & Hanson, K. (2001). Calculating and presenting disability adjusted life years (DALYs) in cost-effectiveness analysis. *Health Policy and Planning, 16*(3), 326–331. https://doi.org/10.1093/heapol/16.3.326

Fricker, R. D. (2016). Sampling methods for online surveys. In N. G. Fielding, R. M. Lee, & G. Blank (Eds.), *The SAGE handbook of online research methods* (2nd ed., pp. 195–217). SAGE Publications. https://doi.org/10.4135/9781473957992

Fricker, R., & Schonlau, M. (2002). Advantages and disadvantages of internet research surveys: Evidence from the literature. *Field Methods, 14*(4), 347–367. https://doi.org/10.1177/152582202237725

Frost, W. (1935). The outlook for the eradication of tuberculosis. *American Review of Tuberculosis, 32,* 644–650.

Fuller, W. (2009). *Sampling statistics.* Wiley. https://doi.org/10.1002/9780470523551

Galbraith, S., Bowden, J., & Mander, A. (2017). Accelerated longitudinal designs: An overview of modelling, power, costs and handling missing data. *Statistical Methods in Medical Research, 26*(1), 374–398. https://doi.org/10.1177/0962280214547150

Goldberg, J., True, W. R., Eisen, S. A., & Henderson, W. G. (1990). A twin study of the effects of the Vietnam War on posttraumatic stress disorder. *JAMA, 263*(9), 1227–1232. https://doi.org/10.1001/jama.1990.03440090061027

Graham, D. J., Campen, D., Hui, R., Spence, M., Cheetham, C., Levy, G., Shoor, S., & Ray, W. A. (2005). Risk of acute myocardial infarction and sudden cardiac death in patients treated with cyclo-oxygenase 2 selective and non-selective non-steroidal anti-inflammatory drugs: Nested case-control study. *The Lancet, 365*(9458), 475–481. https://doi.org/10.1016/S0140-6736(05)17864-7

Grant, B. F. (1997). Prevalence and correlates of alcohol use and *DSM-IV* alcohol dependence in the United States: Results of the National Longitudinal Alcohol Epidemiologic Survey. *Journal of Studies on Alcohol, 58*(5), 464–473. https://doi.org/10.15288/jsa.1997.58.464

Grant, B. F., Goldstein, R. B., Saha, T. D., Chou, S. P., Jung, J., Zhang, H., Pickering, R. P., Ruan, W. J., Smith, S. M., Huang, B., & Hasin, D. S. (2015). Epidemiology of *DSM-5* alcohol use disorder: Results from the National Epidemiologic Survey on Alcohol and Related Conditions III. *JAMA Psychiatry, 72*(8), 757–766. https://doi.org/10.1001/jamapsychiatry.2015.0584

Grant, B. F., Stinson, F. S., Dawson, D. A., Chou, S. P., Dufour, M. C., Compton, W., Pickering, R. P., & Kaplan, K. (2004). Prevalence and co-occurrence of substance use disorders and independent mood and anxiety disorders: Results from the National Epidemiologic Survey on Alcohol and Related Conditions. *Archives of General Psychiatry, 61*(8), 807–816. https://doi.org/10.1001/archpsyc.61.8.807

Greenwood, M. (1932). *Epidemiology: Historical and experimental.* Johns Hopkins Press.

Hand, D. J., & Till, R. J. (2001). A simple generalization of the area under the ROC curve for multiple class classification problems. *Machine Learning, 45*(2), 171–186. https://doi.org/10.1023/A:1010920819831

Heath, A. C., Madden, P. A., Grant, J. D., McLaughlin, T. L., Todorov, A. A., & Bucholz, K. K. (1999). Resiliency factors protecting against teenage alcohol use and smoking: Influences of religion, religious involvement and values, and ethnicity in the Missouri Adolescent Female Twin Study. *Twin Research, 2*(2), 145–155. https://doi.org/10.1375/twin.2.2.145

Heiervang, E., & Goodman, R. (2011). Advantages and limitations of web-based surveys: Evidence from a child mental health survey. *Social Psychiatry and Psychiatric Epidemiology, 46*(1), 69–76. https://doi.org/10.1007/s00127-009-0171-9

Hellwege, J., Keaton, J., Giri, A., Gao, X., Velez Edwards, D. R., & Edwards, T. L. (2017). Population stratification in genetic association studies. *Current Protocols in Human Genetics 95,* 1.22.1–1.22.23. https://doi.org/10.1002/cphg.48

Hill, A. (1961). *Principles of medical statistics.* Oxford University Press.

Hopper, K., Harrison, G., Janca, A., & Sartorius, N. (2007). *Recovery from schizophrenia: An international perspective—A report from the WHO Collaborative Project, the International Study of Schizophrenia.* Oxford University Press.

Johnson, E. C., Demontis, D., Thorgeirsson, T. E., Walters, R. K., Polimanti, R., Hatoum, A. S., Sanchez-Roige, S., Paul, S. E., Wendt, F. R., Clarke, T. K., Lai, D., Reginsson, G. W., Zhou, H., He, J., Baranger, D. A. A., Gudbjartsson, D. F., Wedow, R., Adkins, D. E., Adkins, A. E., . . . Agrawal, A., & the Psychiatric Genomics Consortium Substance Use Disorders Workgroup. (2020). A large-scale genome-wide association study meta-analysis of cannabis use disorder. *The Lancet Psychiatry*, 7(12), 1032–1045. https://doi.org/10.1016/S2215-0366(20)30339-4

Johnston, L., Miech, R. A., O'Malley, P., Bachman, J., Schulenberg, J., & Patrick, M. (2020). *Monitoring the future national survey results on drug use 1975–2019: Overview, key findings on adolescent drug use.* Institute for Social Research, University of Michigan. https://doi.org/10.3998/2027.42/162579

Kahn, H., & Sempos, C. (1989). Relative risk and odds ratio. In H. A. Kahn & C. T. Sempos (Eds.), *Statistical methods in epidemiology* (pp. 45–71). Oxford University Press.

Kass, P. H. (2014). Modern epidemiologic study designs. In W. Ahrens & I. Pigeot (Eds.), *Handbook of epidemiology*, (2nd ed., pp. 325–363). Springer. https://doi.org/10.1007/978-0-387-09834-0_6

Kelsey, J., Whittemore, A., Evans, A., & Thompson, W. (1996). *Methods in observational epidemiology* (2nd ed.). Oxford University Press.

Kessler, R. C., Barker, P. R., Colpe, L. J., Epstein, J. F., Gfroerer, J. C., Hiripi, E., Howes, M. J., Normand, S. L., Manderscheid, R. W., Walters, E. E., & Zaslavsky, A. M. (2003). Screening for serious mental illness in the general population. *Archives of General Psychiatry*, 60(2), 184–189. https://doi.org/10.1001/archpsyc.60.2.184

Kessler, R. C., Berglund, P., Chiu, W. T., Demler, O., Heeringa, S., Hiripi, E., Jin, R., Pennell, B. E., Walters, E. E., Zaslavsky, A., & Zheng, H. (2004). The US National Comorbidity Survey Replication (NCS-R): Design and field procedures. *International Journal of Methods in Psychiatric Research*, 13(2), 69–92. https://doi.org/10.1002/mpr.167

Kessler, R. C., McGonagle, K. A., Zhao, S., Nelson, C. B., Hughes, M., Eshleman, S., Wittchen, H. U., & Kendler, K. S. (1994). Lifetime and 12-month prevalence of *DSM-III-R* psychiatric disorders in the United States. Results from the National Comorbidity Survey. *Archives of General Psychiatry*, 51(1), 8–19. https://doi.org/10.1001/archpsyc.1994.03950010008002

Knol, M. J., Vandenbroucke, J. P., Scott, P., & Egger, M. (2008). What do case-control studies estimate? Survey of methods and assumptions in published case-control research. *American Journal of Epidemiology*, 168(9), 1073–1081. https://doi.org/10.1093/aje/kwn217

Kulathinal, S., Karvanen, J., Saarela, O., & Kuulasmaa, K. (2007). Case-cohort design in practice—Experiences from the MORGAM Project. *Epidemiologic Perspectives & Innovations*, 4, 15. https://doi.org/10.1186/1742-5573-4-15

Kulka, R., Schlenger, W., Fairbanks, J., Hough, R., Jordan, B., Marmar, C., & Grady, D. A. (1990). *Trauma and the Vietnam War generation: Report of findings from the National Vietnam Veterans Readjustment Study.* Brunner Mazel.

Kupper, L. L., Karon, J. M., Kleinbaum, D. G., Morgenstern, H., & Lewis, D. K. (1981). Matching in epidemiologic studies: Validity and efficiency considerations. *Biometrics*, 37(2), 271–291. https://doi.org/10.2307/2530417

Langholz, B., & Thomas, D. C. (1990). Nested case-control and case-cohort methods of sampling from a cohort: A critical comparison. *American Journal of Epidemiology*, 131(1), 169–176. https://doi.org/10.1093/oxfordjournals.aje.a115471

Lash, T. L., VanderWeele, T. J., Haneause, S., & Rothman, K. (2021). *Modern epidemiology* (4th ed.). Lippincott Williams & Wilkins.

Last, J. (2001). *A dictionary of epidemiology* (4th ed.). Oxford University Press.

Leff, J., Sartorius, N., Jablensky, A., Korten, A., & Ernberg, G. (1992). The International Pilot Study of Schizophrenia: Five-year follow-up findings. *Psychological Medicine*, 22(1), 131–145. https://doi.org/10.1017/S0033291700032797

Levin, M. L. (1953). The occurrence of lung cancer in man. *Acta—Unio Internationalis Contra Cancrum*, 9(3), 531–541.

Levine, B. (2007). What does the population attributable fraction mean? *Preventing Chronic Disease*, 4(1), A14.

Lewis, T. H. (2018). *Complex survey data analysis with SAS.* CRC Press Chapman and Hall.

Li, C.-Y., & Sung, F.-C. (1999). A review of the healthy worker effect in occupational epidemiology. *Occupational Medicine* 49(4), 225–229. https://doi.org/10.1093/occmed/49.4.225

Lohr, S. L. (1999). Variance estimation in complex surveys. In *Sampling: Design and analysis* (pp. 289–318). Duxbury Press.

Lu, Y., & Zeger, S. L. (2007). On the equivalence of case-crossover and time series methods in environmental epidemiology. *Biostatistics*, 8(2), 337–344. https://doi.org/10.1093/biostatistics/kxl013

Maclure, M. (1991). The case-crossover design: A method for studying transient effects on the risk of acute events. *American Journal of Epidemiology*, *133*(2), 144–153. https://doi.org/10.1093/oxfordjournals.aje.a115853

MacMahon, B., & Pugh, T. (1970). *Epidemiology: Principles and methods*. Little, Brown.

Mantel, N., & Haenszel, W. (1959). Statistical aspects of the analysis of data from retrospective studies of disease. *Journal of the National Cancer Institute*, *22*(4), 719–748.

Mausner, J., & Kramer, S. (1985). *Epidemiology: An introductory text* (2nd ed.). Saunders.

McDougall, W. (1929). The chemical theory of temperament applied to introversion and extroversion. *Journal of Abnormal and Social Psychology*, *24*(3), 293–309. https://doi.org/10.1037/h0075883

McNutt, L.-A., Wu, C., Xue, X., & Hafner, J. P. (2003). Estimating the relative risk in cohort studies and clinical trials of common outcomes. *American Journal of Epidemiology*, *157*(10), 940–943. https://doi.org/10.1093/aje/kwg074

Menon, V., & Muraleedharan, A. (2020). Internet-based surveys: Relevance, methodological considerations and troubleshooting strategies. *General Psychiatry*, *33*(5), e100264. https://doi.org/10.1136/gpsych-2020-100264

Miller, A. B., Goff, D. C., Bammann, K., & Wild, P. (2014). Cohort studies. In W. Ahrens & I. Pigeot (Eds.), *Handbook of epidemiology* (2nd ed., pp. 259–292). Springer. https://doi.org/10.1007/978-0-387-09834-0_6

Mills, M. C., & Rahal, C. A. (2019). Scientometric review of genome-wide association studies. *Communications Biology*, *2*, 9. https://doi.org/10.1038/s42003-018-0261-x

Mittleman, M. A., & Mostofsky, E. (2014). Exchangeability in the case-crossover design. *International Journal of Epidemiology*, *43*(5), 1645–1655. https://doi.org/10.1093/ije/dyu081

Moher, D., Hopewell, S., Schulz, K. F., Montori, V., Gøtzsche, P. C., Devereaux, P. J., Elbourne, D., Egger, M., & Altman, D. G. (2010). CONSORT 2010 explanation and elaboration: Updated guidelines for reporting parallel group randomised trials. *BMJ*, *340*, c869. https://doi.org/10.1136/bmj.c869

Morabia, A. (2004a). *A history of epidemiologic methods and concepts*. Birkhaser Verlag. https://doi.org/10.1007/978-3-0348-7603-2

Morabia, A. (2004b). Part I: Epidemiology: An epistemological approach. In A. Morabia (Ed.), *A history of epidemiologic methods and concepts* (pp. 3–125). Birkhaser Verlag. https://doi.org/10.1007/978-3-0348-7603-2_1

Morris, J. (1964). *Uses of epidemiology*. Livingstone.

Murray, C. J. L. (1994). Quantifying the burden of disease: The technical basis for disability-adjusted life years. *Bulletin of the World Health Organization*, *72*(3), 429–445.

Murray, C. J. L. (1996). Rethinking DALYs. In C. J. L. Murray & A. D. Lopez (Eds.), *The global burden of disease* (pp. 1–98). Harvard School of Public Health on behalf of the World Health Organization and the World Bank.

Muthén, L. K., & Muthén, B. O. (1998–2017). *Mplus user guide* (8th ed.). https://www.statmodel.com/download/usersguide/MplusUserGuideVer_8.pdf

Nayak, M. S. D. P., & Narayan, K. A. (2019). Strengths and weakness of online surveys. *IOSR Journal of Humanities and Social Science 24*, 5, Ser. 5, 31–38.

Oakes, J., & Kaufman, J. (Eds.). (2017). *Methods in social epidemiology*. Jossey-Bass.

Ott, J., Wang, J., & Leal, S. M. (2015). Genetic linkage analysis in the age of whole-genome sequencing. *Nature Reviews. Genetics*, *16*(5), 275–284. https://doi.org/10.1038/nrg3908

Perkins, N. J., & Schisterman, E. F. (2006). The inconsistency of "optimal" cutpoints obtained using two criteria based on the receiver operating characteristic curve. *American Journal of Epidemiology*, *163*(7), 670–675. https://doi.org/10.1093/aje/kwj063

Peterson, R. E., Kuchenbaecke, K., Walters, R. K., Chen, C.-Y., Popejoy, A. B., Periyasamy, S., Lam, M., Iyegbe, C., Strawbridge, R. J., Brick, L., Carey, C., Martin, A., Meyers, J. L., Su, J., Chen, J., Edwards, A. C., Kalungi, A., Koen, N., Majara, L., . . . Duncan, L. E. (2019). Genome-wide association studies in ancestrally diverse populations: Opportunities, methods, pitfalls, and recommendations. *Cell*, *179*(3), 589–603. https://doi.org/10.1016/j.cell.2019.08.051

Prentice, R. (1986). A case-cohort design for epidemiologic cohort studies and disease prevention trials. *Biometrika*, *73*(1), 1–11. https://doi.org/10.1093/biomet/73.1.1

Price, R. K., Chen, L.-S., Risk, N. K., Haden, A. H., Widner, G. A., Ledgerwood, D. M., & Lewis, C. L. (2009). Suicide in a natural history study: Lessons and insights learned from a follow-up of Vietnam veterans at risk for suicide. In D. Buchanan, C. Fisher, & L. Gable (Eds.), *Research with high-risk populations: Balancing science, ethics, and law* (pp. 109–132). American Psychological Association. https://doi.org/10.1037/11878-005

Price, R. K., Spitznagel, E. L., Downey, T. J., Meyer, D. J., Risk, N. K., & el-Ghazzawy, O. G. (2000). Applying artificial neural network models to clinical decision making. *Psychological Assessment, 12*(1), 40–51. https://doi.org/10.1037/1040-3590.12.1.40

Prigerson, H. G., Maciejewski, P. K., & Rosenheck, R. A. (2002). Population attributable fractions of psychiatric disorders and behavioral outcomes associated with combat exposure among US men. *American Journal of Public Health, 92*(1), 59–63. https://doi.org/10.2105/AJPH.92.1.59

Prüss-Üstüm, A., Mathers, C., Corvalán, C., & Woodward, A. (2003). *Introduction and methods: Assessing the environmental burden of disease at national and local levels.* Geneva, World Health Organization (WHO Environmental Burden of Disease Series, No. 1), Chapter 3, pp. 27–40.

Rehm, J., Patra, J., & Popova, S. (2006). Alcohol-attributable mortality and potential years of life lost in Canada 2001: Implications for prevention and policy. *Addiction, 101*(3), 373–384. https://doi.org/10.1111/j.1360-0443.2005.01338.x

Research Triangle Institute. (2001). *SUDAAN user's manual* (Release 8.0). Research Triangle Institute.

Rid, A., Lipsitch, M., & Miller, F. G. (2021). The ethics of continuing placebo in SARS-COV-2 vaccine trials. *JAMA, 325*(3), 219–220. https://doi.org/10.1001/jama.2020.25053

Robins, L. N., Helzer, J. E., Croughan, J., & Ratcliff, K. S. (1981). National Institute of Mental Health Diagnostic Interview Schedule. Its history, characteristics, and validity. *Archives of General Psychiatry, 38*(4), 381–389. https://doi.org/10.1001/archpsyc.1981.01780290015001

Robins, L. N., & Price, R. K. (1991). Adult disorders predicted by childhood conduct problems: Results from the NIMH Epidemiologic Catchment Area project. *Psychiatry, 54*(2), 116–132. https://doi.org/10.1080/00332747.1991.11024540

Robins, L. N., & Regier, D. (1991). *Psychiatric disorders in America: The Epidemiological Catchment Area Study.* Free Press.

Rockhill, B., Newman, B., & Weinberg, C. (1998). Use and misuse of population attributable fractions. *American Journal of Public Health, 88*(1), 15–19. https://doi.org/10.2105/AJPH.88.1.15

Rogers, W. (1993). Regression standard errors in clustered samples. *Stata Technical Bulletin, 13,* 19–23.

Rosen, G. (1958). *A history of public health.* MD Publications. https://doi.org/10.1037/11322-000

Rosenbaum, P. R., & Rubin, D. B. (1983). The role of the propensity score in observational studies for causal effect. *Biometrika, 70*(1), 41–55. https://doi.org/10.1093/biomet/70.1.41

Rothman, K. J. (1996). Lessons from John Graunt. *The Lancet, 347*(8993), 37–39. https://doi.org/10.1016/S0140-6736(96)91562-7

Rothman, K. J., & Greenland, S. (2014). Basic concepts. In W. Ahrens & I. Pigeot (Eds.), *Handbook of epidemiology* (2nd ed., pp.75–122). Springer. https://doi.org/10.1007/978-0-387-09834-0_44

Rust, K. F., & Rao, J. N. (1996). Variance estimation for complex surveys using replication techniques. *Statistical Methods in Medical Research, 5*(3), 283–310. https://doi.org/10.1177/096228029600500305

Ryan, M. A. K., Smith, T., Smith, B., Amoroso, P., Boyko, E., Gray, G., & Hopper, T. I. (2007). Millennium cohort: Enrollment begins a 21-year contribution to understanding the impact of military service. *Journal of Clinical Epidemiology, 60,* 181–191. https://doi.org/10.1016/j.jclinepi.2006.05.009

Salomaa, V., Matei, C., Aleksic, N., Sansores-Garcia, L., Folsom, A. R., Juneja, H., Chambless, L. E., & Wu, K. K. (1999). Soluble thrombomodulin as a predictor of incident coronary heart disease and symptomless carotid artery atherosclerosis in the Atherosclerosis Risk in Communities (ARIC) Study: A case-cohort study. *The Lancet, 353*(9166), 1729–1734. https://doi.org/10.1016/S0140-6736(98)09057-6

Schaie, K. W. (1965). A general model for the study of developmental problems. *Psychological Bulletin, 64*(2), 92–107. https://doi.org/10.1037/h0022371

Schlenger, W. E., Kulka, R. A., Fairbank, J. A., Hough, R. L., Jordan, B. K., Marmar, C. R., & Weiss, D. S. (1992). The prevalence of post-traumatic stress disorder in the Vietnam generation: A multimethod, multisource assessment of psychiatric disorder. *Journal of Traumatic Stress, 5*(3), 333–363. https://doi.org/10.1002/jts.2490050303

Sharp, S. J., Poulaliou, M., Thompson, S. G., White, I. R., & Wood, A. M. (2014). A review of published analyses of case-cohort studies and recommendations for future reporting. *PLOS ONE, 9*(6), e101176. https://doi.org/10.1371/journal.pone.0101176

Snow, J. (1854). *On the mode of communication of cholera.* Churchill.

Songer, T. (2010). *Introduction to the fundamentals of epidemiology.* https://www.pitt.edu/~super1/lecture/lec19061/001.htm

Spurling, M. C., & Vinson, D. C. (2005). Alcohol-related injuries: Evidence for the prevention paradox. *Annals of Family Medicine, 3*(1), 47–52. https://doi.org/10.1370/afm.243

Substance Abuse and Mental Health Services Administration. (2017). *Key substance use and mental health indicators in the United States: Results from* the 2016 National Survey on Drug Use and Health (HHS Publication No. SMA 17-5044, NSDUH Series H-52). Center for Behavioral Health Statistics and Quality, Substance Abuse and Mental Health Services Administration. https://www.samhsa.gov/data

Susser, M., & Adelstein, A. (1975). An introduction to the work of William Farr. *American Journal of Epidemiology, 101*(6), 469–476. https://doi.org/10.1093/oxfordjournals.aje.a112117

Susser, M., & Stein, Z. (2009). *Eras in epidemiology: The evolution of ideas.* Oxford University Press. https://doi.org/10.1093/acprof:oso/9780195300666.001.0001

Tager, I. B. (2000). Current view of epidemiologic study designs for occupational and environmental lung diseases. *Environmental Health Perspectives, 108*(Suppl. 4), 615–623.

Tam, V., Patel, N., Turcotte, M., Bossé, Y., Paré, G., & Meyre, D. (2019). Benefits and limitations of genome-wide association studies. *Nature Reviews. Genetics, 20*(8), 467–484. https://doi.org/10.1038/s41576-019-0127-1

Thomas, D. C., & Witte, J. S. (2002). Point: Population stratification: A problem for case-control studies of candidate-gene associations? *Cancer Epidemiology, Biomarkers & Prevention, 11*(6), 505–512.

Tohen, M., Bromet, E., Murphy, J. M., & Tsuang, M. T. (2000). Psychiatric epidemiology. *Harvard Review of Psychiatry, 8*(3), 111–125. https://doi.org/10.1080/hrp_8.3.111

Ursano, R. J., Kessler, R. C., Stein, M. B., Naifeh, J. A., Aliaga, P. A., Fullerton, C. S., Wynn, G. H., Vegella, P. L., Ng, T. H., Zhang, B. G., Wryter, C. L., Sampson, N. A., Kao, T. C., Colpe, L. J., Schoenbaum, M., McCarroll, J. E., Cox, K. L., Heeringa, S. G., & the Army STARRS Collaborators. (2016). Risk factors, methods, and timing of suicide attempts among US Army soldiers. *JAMA Psychiatry, 73*(7), 741–749. https://doi.org/10.1001/jamapsychiatry.2016.0600

Volkow, N. D., Koob, G. F., Croyle, R. T., Bianchi, D. W., Gordon, J. A., Koroshetz, W. J., Pérez-Stable, E. J., Riley, W. T., Bloch, M. H., Conway, K., Deeds, B. G., Dowling, G. J., Grant, S., Howlett, K. D., Matochik, J. A., Morgan, G. D., Murray, M. M., Noronha, A., Spong, C. Y., Wargo, E. M., . . . Weiss, S. (2018). The conception of the ABCD study: From substance use to a broad NIH collaboration. *Developmental Cognitive Neuroscience, 32,* 4–7. https://doi.org/10.1016/j.dcn.2017.10.002

Vos, T., Flaxman, A. D., Naghavi, M., Lozano, R., Michaud, C., Ezzati, M., Shibuya, K., Salomon, J. A., Abdalla, S., Aboyans, V., Abraham, J., Ackerman, I., Aggarwal, R., Ahn, S. Y., Ali, M. K., AlMazroa, M. A., Alvarado, M., Anderson, H. R., Anderson, L. M., . . . Murray, C. J. L. (2012). Years lived with disability (YLDs) for 1160 sequelae of 289 diseases and injuries 1990–2010: A systematic analysis for the Global Burden of Disease Study 2010. *The Lancet, 380*(9859), 2163–2196. https://doi.org/10.1016/S0140-6736(12)61729-2

Wacholder, S., McLaughlin, J. K., Silverman, D. T., & Mandel, J. S. (1992). Selection of controls in case-control studies. I. Principles. *American Journal of Epidemiology, 135*(9), 1019–1028. https://doi.org/10.1093/oxfordjournals.aje.a116396

Weinstein, M. C., & Fineberg, H. V. (1980). *Clinical decision analysis.* Saunders.

White, J. E. (1982). A two stage design for the study of the relationship between a rare exposure and a rare disease. *American Journal of Epidemiology, 115*(1), 119–128. https://doi.org/10.1093/oxfordjournals.aje.a113266

Wolter, K. (1985). *Introduction to variance estimation.* Springer-Verlag.

Wu, A. D., & Zumbo, B. D. (2008). Understanding and using mediators and moderators. *Social Indicators Research, 87*(3), 367–392. https://doi.org/10.1007/s11205-007-9143-1

Yang, Y., & Land, K. (2008). Age-period-cohort analysis of repeated cross-section surveys: Fixed or random effects? *Sociological Methods & Research, 36*(3), 297–326. https://doi.org/10.1177/0049124106292360

Yee, J., & Niemeier, D. (1996). *Advances and disadvantages: Longitudinal vs. repeated cross-section surveys.* https://rosap.ntl.bts.gov/view/dot/13793

Zhang, F. F., Michaels, D. C., Mathema, B., Kauchali, S., Chatterjee, A., Ferris, D. C., James, T. M., Knight, J., Dounel, M., Tawfik, H. O., Frohlich, J. A., Kuang, L., Hoskin, E. K., Veldman, F. J., Baldi, G., Mlisana, K. P., Mametja, L. D., Diaz, A., Khan, N. L., . . . Morabia, A. (2004). Evolution of epidemiologic methods and concepts in selected textbooks of the 20th century. *Sozial- und Praventivmedizin, 49*(2), 97–104. https://doi.org/10.1007/s00038-004-3117-8

Zhang, J., & Yu, K. F. (1998). What's the relative risk? A method of correcting the odds ratio in cohort studies of common outcomes. *JAMA, 280*(19), 1690–1691. https://doi.org/10.1001/jama.280.19.1690

Zhao, W., & Jin, Y. (2006). A study of sampling method for internet survey. *International Journal of Business and Management, 1,* 69–77.

CHAPTER 18

COLLECTING LONGITUDINAL DATA: PRESENT ISSUES AND FUTURE CHALLENGES

Simran K. Johal, Rohit Batra, and Emilio Ferrer

One of the most common types of data collection in psychological research involves assessing individuals (their families, schools, or other entities) at multiple measurement occasions. These longitudinal data are particularly useful to examine questions about processes that unfold over time and to study change at the individual level. Despite the value and widespread use of longitudinal data, collecting such data is not always straightforward. In this chapter, we review some of the important issues regarding the planning and collection of various types of longitudinal data in psychological research, and make note of certain issues that might arise during the analysis stage. We end with some practical recommendations for researchers.

LONGITUDINAL DATA

Longitudinal data consist of repeated assessments of the same entity (e.g., individuals, families, schools) over time. Such repeated assessments can span short or long periods of time and can involve many types of data, such as observations, self-reports, psychophysiological signals, brain imaging, or digital footprint, just to name a few.

Generally, longitudinal data exhibit a number of features. First, some of the same entities are observed at repeated occasions. As we describe in the following sections, not all the entities are required to be observed at each occasion; very often, for example, some individuals who participate at the initial assessment in a study do not return for all subsequent assessments. Second, the measurement and scaling of observations are known. For example, one must understand the measurement properties of the variables, so that analyses can be performed to determine that the same construct is being measured at all occasions. If so, changes over time can be interpreted as quantitative changes in the construct of interest rather than qualitative changes in the nature of the construct, or changes in the measuring instrument, as when the meaning of words changes over time. Third, the ordering and metric of the time underlying the observations are known. This time metric depends on the research question and the type of data and can range from milliseconds to decades. Whatever the metric, it needs to be well characterized to make appropriate inferences about sequences and time-related changes.

Simran K. Johal and Rohit Batra share first authorship of this chapter.

This chapter is a revised version of the chapter entitled "Issues in Collecting Longitudinal Data" that appeared in the first edition of *APA Handbook of Research Methodology in Psychology*, of which Dr. Kevin Grimm was a coauthor. We would like to thank Dr. Grimm for his valuable contributions to that chapter.

https://doi.org/10.1037/0000319-018
APA Handbook of Research Methods in Psychology, Second Edition: Vol. 2. Research Designs: Quantitative, Qualitative, Neuropsychological, and Biological, H. Cooper (Editor-in-Chief)

Goals of Longitudinal Data and Longitudinal Research

Few, if any, would argue the need for longitudinal data in examining changes in a process. Collecting such data, however, presents a number of challenges. The first of these challenges concerns the purpose of the study. That is, what kind of longitudinal data are most suitable to answer the desired research questions? Or, alternatively, what types of questions can one address with longitudinal data? This seemingly trivial question is often overlooked in the early stages of planning a study, thus reducing the chances of collecting data that are appropriate to the questions at hand. One helpful way to conceptualize issues related to longitudinal data collection is through Baltes and Nesselroade's (1979) objectives of longitudinal research. Although now 40 years old, these objectives remain relevant and can be useful in determining the types of questions one can investigate and, consequently, the types of data to be collected.

The first objective is the identification of intraindividual change. Many longitudinal studies aim to examine changes at the group level, without a direct translation to any given individual (e.g., Molenaar, 2004). Change at the individual level can take different forms, including systematic long-term trends or short-term fluctuations. Either way, the focus is the individual and the way change manifests for each person. Examining this goal requires multiple occasions of measurement (for instance, collecting data with high density if the questions pertain to fluctuations) and statistical models specified at the individual level or, in some cases, models that consider the individual to be the primary unit of analysis. In subsequent sections, we describe various research designs, statistical models, and issues associated with the objective of capturing intraindividual change.

The second objective in Baltes and Nesselroades's (1979) principles is the direct identification of interindividual differences in intraindividual change. That is, not only do we examine change for each person, but we also evaluate whether those changes vary across individuals. Such differences can

be systematic and possibly associated with—or explained by—other variables of interest. Addressing questions related to this objective would require collecting repeated measures data from multiple individuals together with covariates that can be used to relate to the changes in the outcomes of interest.

The third objective concerns the analysis of interrelationships in change. Imagine, for example, that one is interested in studying the development of reading and overall intellectual abilities. Pertinent questions here would include how each of these processes unfolds over time, say, during childhood and adolescence, and whether they are related to each other. It is possible that both processes help each other over time (e.g., Ferrer et al., 2010), and such influences can be either unidirectional, from one process to another, or bidirectional, where both influence each other simultaneously. Alternatively, both processes could develop jointly as a result of a third factor or simply independently. Whatever the dynamics, this third objective focuses on the interrelations between the changes of two or more variables. To accomplish this goal, researchers need longitudinal data on two or more variables. Of particular importance here is the choice of the right statistical model, as different models focus on different aspects of the interrelations at work. For example, some models allow researchers to identify associations between changes in two variables (e.g., bivariate growth curves), whereas other models specify such interrelations in terms of lead-lagged dynamic sequences (e.g., latent change score models). For this, the researcher must decide what type of question to address and then specify a model according to the hypothesis of change (e.g., Ferrer & McArdle, 2010; Grimm, 2007; McArdle, 2009; Singer & Willett, 2003).

The fourth objective refers to the analysis of causes (or determinants) of intraindividual change, and the fifth concerns the analysis of causes (or determinants) of interindividual differences in intraindividual change. These goals denote the identification of mechanisms (i.e., time-related associations, dynamic sequences) that explain within-person changes and differences in such changes across people. Examining research questions within these goals requires collecting repeated data on both the outcomes and the covariates of interest for multiple individuals. In addition, identifying the desired mechanisms entails the use of specific models of change, typically dynamic models.

Again, these objectives pertain to longitudinal research and, thus, should help researchers identify the right questions to be examined in the study. We believe these questions will, in turn, guide the choice of the optimal research design for data collection, the type and amount of data to be collected, and the statistical model employed to analyze such data.

Benefits and Challenges of Longitudinal Data

Longitudinal data have a number of advantages over cross-sectional data or repeated cross-sectional data. They have become essential for understanding how a process unfolds over time, and its association with other relevant dimensions (e.g., Baltes & Nesselroade, 1979; Bollen & Curran, 2006; Grimm et al., 2016; Hertzog & Nesselroade, 2003; Singer & Willett, 2003).

The advantages of longitudinal over cross-sectional designs are many and varied. As described in the previous sections, they allow the researcher to address multiple questions about change, processes, and dynamics. Examining such questions with cross-sectional data would be limited at best and simply not plausible at worst. For example, longitudinal data allow the direct estimation of within-person change over time. Similarly, they allow the estimation of variation in such change across individuals, as some individuals change more or less than others. Moreover, longitudinal data permit estimating associations between within-person changes and other covariates of interest (e.g., development of reading achievement as related to parental education) and the interrelations between two processes as they unfold over time (e.g., for depressed mood and sleep disorders see, Ferrer & Ghisletta, 2011; and Schaie & Hofer, 2001, for discussions about benefits of longitudinal over cross-sectional data).

Longitudinal data are necessary to study change, but often such change is approximated by cross-sectional differences (e.g., Grimm & Ram, 2009). For example, cognitive development between ages 3 and 4 can be studied longitudinally by measuring a sample of 3-year-olds, waiting a year, and measuring them again when they are 4 years old. These changes could be approximated with cross-sectional data by measuring a group of 3-year-olds and another group of 4-year-olds simultaneously. The differences between these two groups can approximate the longitudinal changes if the sample of 4-year-olds represents what the 3-year-old sample would be in one year. However, this assumption can be invalid, as the two groups likely vary in their cognitive development and other important factors. To this extent, cross-sectional differences are a poor estimation of longitudinal changes. Furthermore, even when the assumption is valid and cross-sectional differences are a good approximation of longitudinal changes, they are only a good estimate of the average amount of change (at the population level) and do not provide any information regarding variation in changes across individuals.

A second important limitation of cross-sectional data as an estimate of longitudinal change concerns its lack of information about the mechanisms underlying the observed change. Often, such change is being driven by many factors, including external variables. For example, some important facets in a given developmental process include a set of initial conditions describing the onset of the process, information about how quickly the process changes, how acceleration and deceleration influence the change process, and how the process enters and leaves different phases of change (Grimm et al., 2010). For complex developmental processes that involve multiple variables, cross-sectional data simply average over the many important aspects of change, thus missing the complexity of the process (McArdle, 2009). For example, a cross-sectional study may be able to demonstrate that a process declines over time but cannot show whether this relation holds for each individual participant, or whether the process fluctuates, or perhaps even increases over time within participants.

Although the advantages of longitudinal data are obvious, such data present a number of challenges and issues. Some of these features are logistic, such as deciding the number of assessments, the time interval between them, and how to best allocate one's budget to optimize sample size and measurement occasions (Estrada & Ferrer, 2019). These questions can be evaluated before data collection. Other decisions take place while the data are being collected, such as maximizing retention of participants. Yet others are of a methodological nature and need to be addressed once the data have already been collected (e.g., attrition, cohort effects, and retest effects). We discuss each of these issues in subsequent sections.

Types of Longitudinal Data

The most traditional type of longitudinal study is the panel design, where a sample of individuals is measured repeatedly at certain intervals over the course of the study. Although useful, this type of design is often unfeasible for studying processes over very long periods. For example, if a researcher were interested in studying development from childhood into adolescence, the number of years required for the study would not only be financially costly, but it is unlikely that all participants would remain in the study for that time, leading to loss of data.

One proposed alternative to avoid some of the problems of the traditional panel design is the *accelerated longitudinal design* (ALD, also known as cohort-sequential design; Bell, 1953, 1954; T. E. Duncan et al., 1996). In this design, researchers recruit a cross-sectional sample of participants with a wide age range and then repeatedly measure these participants on the variables of interest for only a few measurement occasions. Although each person is assessed only a few times, the sample covers the entire period of interest. Figure 18.1 includes examples of four different cohort-sequential designs intended to cover the age span of 5 to 19 years. In Design 1, individuals are measured twice, with an interval of one year, and the age range at the first

occasion is 5 to 17 years. In Design 2, individuals are measured three times, every other year. In Design 3, individuals are also measured three times but in consecutive years. Finally, Design 4 also includes three measures per individual but alternates the retest interval between cohorts. For instance, individuals entering the study at age 5 have their second assessment the following year, when they are 6, and then two years later. Those entering at age 6, on the other hand, have their first retest 2 years later, when they are 8, and then the following year. A cohort-sequential design allows multiple options, depending on a variety of factors such as the period the researcher intends to cover (e.g., childhood, life-span), length of the study (e.g., 5 years), sample size, and number of occasions (Estrada & Ferrer, 2019; McArdle et al., 2002; Milojev & Sibley, 2017).

Panel and cohort-sequential designs, due to their long-term nature, are well suited to address questions about how a process changes over time (e.g., how memory develops from childhood into adulthood). However, many researchers may be less interested in studying the average trajectory of a process and more interested in studying fluctuations and short-term interrelations (i.e., how a process fluctuates over time within an individual, whether and how various processes fluctuate together). Technological advances have allowed researchers to more easily collect *intensive longitudinal data* (ILD). ILD is characterized by a high frequency of measurement occasions, with such measurements often separated by only days or even milliseconds. The intensive nature of this data allows greater insight into the within-person processes over time, affording the opportunity to explore differences in intraindividual variability in greater depth.

ILD can take different forms, with the main distinction being the time frame at which the variables of interest operate. Psychophysiological and neuroimaging data, for example, operate on very short time frames (anywhere from milliseconds to minutes), whereas ecological momentary assessment (EMA) studies (also known as experience sampling method [ESM] studies) may

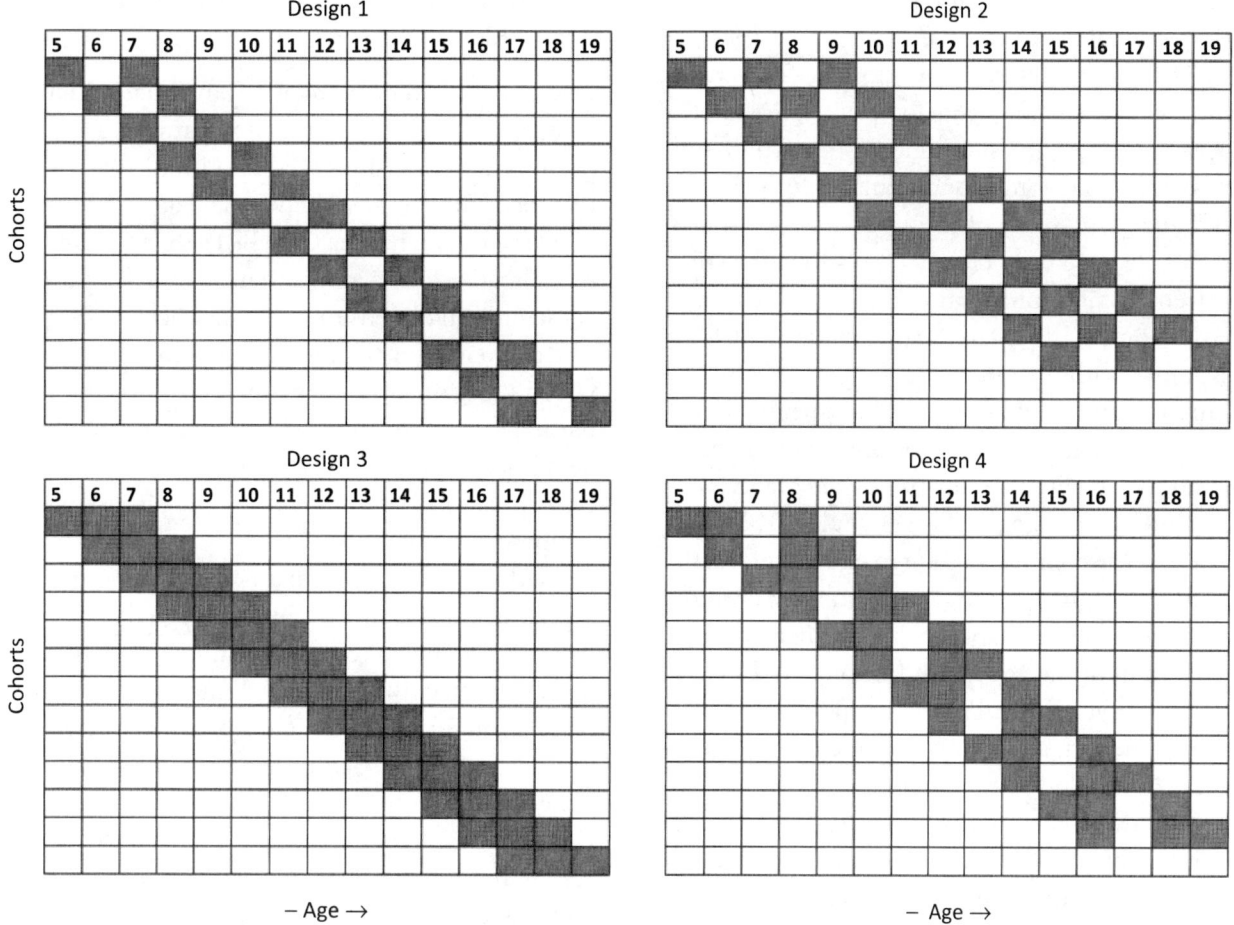

FIGURE 18.1. Four cohort-sequential designs covering an age span of 5 to 19 years are shown. The horizontal axis represents the age while the vertical axis is the different cohorts based on when the individuals entered the study. Colored boxes indicate measurement occasions. The four designs have 13, 11, 13 and 12 cohorts, respectively.

require multiple measurements per day over the course of a few weeks. Increasingly sophisticated techniques for acquiring imaging data allow researchers to collect signals related to brain structure and brain function at higher and higher resolution, both spatial and temporal. Similarly, psychophysiological data can be collected simultaneously on multiple dimensions (e.g., heart rate variability, respiration, skin conductance, blood pressure) while participants engage in laboratory tasks or go about their daily lives. For an EMA study, participants are typically asked to respond to questionnaires (often prompted by a smartphone or other device) at random times of the day or to reflect and report at the end of the day on feelings and behaviors that occurred during

that day (Csikszentmihalyi & Larson, 1987; Larson & Csikszentmihalyi, 1983).

EMA studies in particular are thought to improve the ecological validity of participant responses by asking them about their thoughts, emotions, or behaviors in naturalistic contexts. Moreover, they may be less affected by recall bias than traditional longitudinal designs, as participants are asked to report on behaviors that occurred within a more recent timeframe (i.e., in the past few hours as opposed to the past 6 months; Bolger & Laurenceau, 2013; Sonnentag et al., 2012). Maximizing the potential of such rich data requires decisions regarding data collection, such as which tasks best map onto the hypotheses, the duration of the study, and the appropriate time resolution to capture enough information about the signal for data analyses.

This technological innovation has also created a massive reserve of digital footprint. Every motion performed on one's smartphone—every tap, text, or swipe—is recorded and available for collection and analyses. Aware of these possibilities, social scientists have been creating tools to gather this extremely rich information (Hilbert & López, 2011; Ram et al., 2020; Reeves et al., 2020). For example, with the use of web scraping, researchers can now automatically "harvest" specific data from the world wide web or simply collect what is on the screen on one's smartphone as any moment leading to *screenomics* (Reeves et al., 2020). They can also use computer vision to extract information from digital images or videos. Similarly, current advances in technology allow researchers to collect data on multiple genes, with the goal of linking them to psychological processes, psychiatric disorders, health, and aging to name a few (Glahn et al., 2013; Kao et al., 2010).

Given the many possibilities for the collection of intensive data over multiple dimensions, and the resulting complexity of information, researchers need to think carefully about the questions to be addressed, as well as the type of data to gather and the optimal design to address their scientific queries. In some instances, specific hypotheses can be used to guide this process; in other instances, however, the lack of a priori hypotheses makes this more difficult. In the former, researchers may be able to select specific types of data under precise conditions. They can then implement data analyses aimed at evaluating such well-defined hypotheses. In the latter, researchers might need to cast a wider net in their search for information and then use techniques designed to discover patterns in their data. Very often, researchers combine these two possibilities in both data collection and analyses. That is, in addition to data selected on theoretical premises, they also gather broader information and then analyze these combined data using confirmatory techniques together with exploratory methods such as machine learning, natural language processing, or other artificial intelligence techniques.

MEASUREMENT OCCASIONS, VARIABLES, AND PERSONS

One of the main challenges in any longitudinal design is the selection of data regarding variables, persons, and occasions. Cattell (1988) illustrated this idea with the so-called basic data relations box (Figure 18.2, after Cattell, 1988, and Ram & Nesselroade, 2007), a hypothetical sample space containing all dimensions of experimental designs. The challenge for the researcher is to select which individuals (how many and who) should participate in the study, which variables should be measured, and on how many occasions (see Nesselroade, 1988, for an extensive discussion on these issues).

With regard to participants, two important aspects to consider are whether enough participants have been selected to provide sufficient statistical power to detect the effect(s) of interest, and which persons ought to be selected from the population of interest to avoid sampling bias. A similar concern relates to the selection of variables. Here, the researcher faces issues related to multivariate representation and measurement of the constructs of interest. Finally, with regard to measurement occasions, critical decisions involve the number of assessments (and the interval between them) necessary to examine change and once again provide sufficient statistical power. Of course, this selection is not limited to occasions,

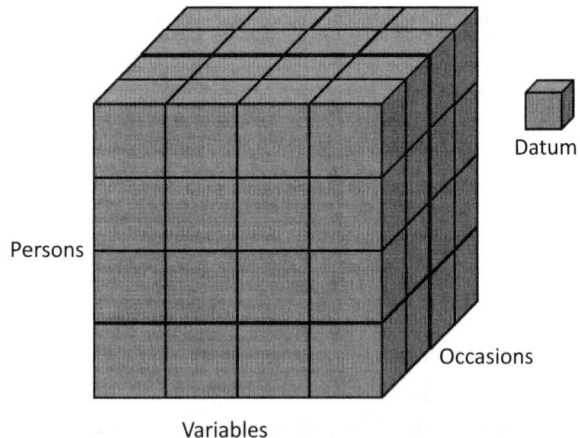

FIGURE 18.2. A data box containing all hypothetical variables, persons, and measurement occasions.

variables, and persons. Other domains are relevant and worth considering. For example, one might think about the relevant context for data collection, whether it is the home, the school, or the neighborhood. Similarly, the unit of analysis is a key piece in the data box. This could be the individual, the dyad (e.g., mother-child, teacher-student), the family, or some other, more complex system. We elaborate on each of these aspects of data collection in subsequent sections of the chapter.

Selection of Occasions

Regardless of the type of longitudinal data a researcher plans to collect, one key decision is how many measurement occasions are needed, together with the time interval between them. This decision is critical, both to obtain enough measurements at the optimal frequency to understand the change of the given process, and to ensure adequate power for later statistical analyses (Hertzog et al., 2006; Muthén & Curran, 1997). The minimum number of time points needed for a longitudinal study is only two, and two occasions might be selected due to budget constraints or because that is all that is needed to answer the research question (such as in a pre- and posttest design). Two occasions might be the most informative when used in the context of an ALD. In this scenario, the focus would not be on the change across the two measurement occasions but on the change across the entire age span (e.g., McArdle et al., 2002).

Having more than two occasions of data is preferred, as using only two occasions creates some limitations in both the design (e.g., O. D. Duncan, 1975; Rogosa, 1988) and in the ability to study change (Cronbach & Furby, 1970; cf. Nesselroade & Cable, 1974). In particular, change scores calculated using more than two occasions of data are more reliable than those from only two occasions, and having more than two occasions helps improve the estimation process by increasing the data density.

Once the decision has been made to collect three or more occasions of data, the specific number of occasions mostly depends on the characteristics of the process being studied

(see Nesselroade & Boker, 1994). A rapidly changing process, such as those seen in neuro-imaging or psychophysiological data, needs more frequent measurements to capture the features of that process (e.g., trend and amplitude). Too few measurement occasions can miss important aspects of the signal or the underlying dynamics of the process altogether (e.g., Adolph et al., 2008). For example, if a process is completely cyclic, then too few measurement occasions may mistakenly lead researchers to believe that the process is completely stable and does not change at all (Nesselroade & Boker, 1994). If, on the other hand, the process is stable or changes slowly, then fewer measurement occasions are required. Therefore, it is important to have some information about the change features in order to select the number of occasions and interval between them. If possible, pilot data might help researchers get a sense of how quickly the process is changing; else, a general recommendation is to sample more frequently to avoid the risk of not adequately capturing the trajectory of the process (Adolph et al., 2008).

Considering the appropriate frequency of and length between assessments is even more necessary in an EMA study, where a greater number of measurements are being taken over a smaller timespan. In general, the length of a study depends in large part on the sampling scheme chosen by the researcher (Bolger & Laurenceau, 2013). In daily diary studies, participants are measured (as the name implies) once per day (e.g., Ferrer et al., 2012); in signal-contingent sampling, participants are asked to respond multiple times per day in response to a randomly occurring prompt (Bolger & Laurenceau, 2013). The choice of sampling scheme influences the total duration of the study—daily diary studies are seen as less burdensome to participants because they are only required to respond once per day. This decreased burden means that participants are more likely to comply with the study protocol (and perhaps be more careful in their responses, improving the quality of the collected data). The study, therefore, can have a longer duration without placing an undue burden on the participant or compromising data quality (O'Laughlin, 2020). Regardless of the total duration of the study, having just one assessment per day may miss fluctuations in a variable that occur over the course of the day, which may be of interest to the researcher.

Signal-contingent designs are better suited for collecting information on variables that are believed to fluctuate more rapidly, perhaps multiple times a day, but this design places a higher burden on participants due to multiple measurement occasions per day and, therefore, tends to have a shorter duration (typically only days or weeks). Much like in traditional longitudinal studies, researchers may be able to use pilot or previously collected data to inform how quickly the process under study is changing and how frequently assessments are needed. Using techniques such as variance decomposition (Shiyko & Ram, 2011), previously collected data can be used to roughly determine how often the process of interest fluctuates, as well as whether it varies mostly within or between days. If the process mostly fluctuates across days, and not within a day, then a daily diary study might be enough to capture the relevant characteristics. On the other hand, a rapidly fluctuating process that changes more within each day might require a signal-contingent design to capture its behavior more accurately.

When employing a signal-contingent sampling scheme, researchers also need to decide how often participants should be prompted throughout the day. More frequent measurements may be viewed as intrusive by the participants but could provide more accurate responses due to asking about events, thoughts, or emotions that occurred more recently (and, therefore, are less subject to recall bias) and could more adequately capture the dynamics of the construct under study. However, some researchers might accept a trade-off of having fewer measurement occasions per day in order to lessen the risk of noncompliance and careless responding, leading to an overall improvement in participants' response quality (Bolger & Laurenceau, 2013; Janssens et al., 2018). In some cases, even relatively frequent measurements can lead to acceptable compliance rates, and an

experimental manipulation of the number of assessments per day in a sample of university students found no relation to participants' feelings of burden, their compliance, or the quality of their responses (Eisele et al., 2022; Rintala et al., 2019). Therefore, having a higher sampling frequency may be preferable, as this does not seem to affect participants' responses and results in finer-grained data to better examine within-individual changes.

As mentioned in a previous section, EMA studies can provide information on the dynamics of a process and how these change within an individual, whereas panel designs are better-suited for answering questions on the average change of a process over time. The two are not mutually exclusive and often are combined in a measurement-burst design (Nesselroade, 1991; Ram & Gerstorf, 2009). Measurement-burst designs involve collecting intensive longitudinal data from participants for a period of time (the "burst") and then allowing some time to pass (e.g., months or a year) before collecting another burst of data from those same participants. In this way, researchers can examine both how a process changes within an individual (through the burst data), as well as how the process changes over time, often with more precision than traditional panel designs (Sliwinski, 2008).

Such measurement-burst designs have also been proposed for examining the interrelations between two variables that operate on different timescales (O'Laughlin, 2020; Ram et al., 2014). For example, researchers may be interested in studying the relation between stress levels (which fluctuate daily) and hormone levels (which are more stable) or between mood and physical activity. The study can be designed so that the faster-changing process is captured by the more frequent measurements within each burst, and bursts are separated by a period of days or weeks (as opposed to years) to capture the slower-moving process.

Selection of Variables

Another essential consideration, along with the frequency of assessments, is selecting the correct variables to measure over the course of the study. Although the choice of the measures depends on the research question, a general premise is that they need to capture the construct of interest and be sensitive to changes in that construct. Similarly, they need to show relevant psychometric properties, including various forms of validity and reliability (e.g., Little et al., 1999). To guarantee the variables are psychometrically sound, researchers often use statistical techniques such as factor analyses, structural equation modeling with latent variables, and item response models. Similarly, the variables ought to show sensitivity to measure systematic change with precision (e.g., for within-person reliability, see Cranford et al., 2006).

An important concern regarding measures in a longitudinal study is the possibility that they change through the course of the study. For example, suppose that a researcher is interested in understanding the development of mathematical skills from childhood through adolescence. Over the course of the study, the researcher may wish to switch out the measures to account for the participants' maturation, improvement in math skills, and because some measures are no longer age-appropriate. Although the interest in studying the same underlying construct (mathematical skills) remains, the exact measures used may have changed during the study, which adds an additional challenge to measuring change over time. To deal with this, linkage using factor or item response models and ideas behind factorial invariance are typically required to ensure the intended construct is equivalent over time (see Bauer & Hussong, 2009; Curran et al., 2008; McArdle et al., 2009). We expand on this issue in the section on factorial invariance, but one key point is having measures that overlap at successive measurement occasions.

Overlapping variables are also important for researchers who are interested in pooling data from multiple studies in order to perform secondary analysis. This technique, known as integrative data analysis (IDA), may afford researchers the opportunity to study change over a longer time span than afforded by any single study, as well as incorporating multiple operationalizations of a construct (Curran & Hussong, 2009). When combining multiple data sets, different instruments are often used in each study to assess the same underlying construct; however, having some items be the same across the different studies is useful for later linking the studies together. Therefore, when researchers are planning their own longitudinal study, it may be helpful to consider including measurement instruments that can aid future researchers who hope to use that study within an IDA framework. For example, having multiple indicators of the same construct, or including an instrument that is commonly used within other studies that examine the same or similar age range, can increase the chances of shared items across studies and assist in IDA.

Although the selection of measures depends on the study context, some general recommendations can be made in specific situations, such as in EMA studies employing questionnaires. Just as researchers are concerned with the frequency of measurements increasing the burden placed on their participants, there is a similar concern regarding the effect of longer questionnaires (Galesic & Bosnjak, 2009; Rolstad et al., 2011). However, meta-analysis attempts have come to mixed conclusions and either found a negative effect of questionnaire length or no effect at all (Eisele et al., 2022). In their study, Eisele et al. (2022) manipulated the questionnaire length to be either long (60 items) or short (30 items) and found that the longer questionnaire was associated with greater burden, lower compliance, and lower data quality due to careless responding. Since the reliabilities of a longer versus shorter questionnaire are likely to be similar (e.g., a 60-item questionnaire is not much more reliable than a 30-item questionnaire), it is recommended that researchers conducting an EMA study keep their questionnaires short in order to decrease the burden placed on their participants.

Statistical Power

Referring to Cattell's data box (1988), the task of selecting which individuals (how many and who) should participate in the study has become even more challenging. Before starting a study, researchers need to consider issues related to statistical power (how many individuals are necessary to detect an effect?) and sampling bias (which individuals should be selected so results pertain to the population of interest?). In this section, we focus on the issue of statistical power and describe work relating power analysis to the specific research design.

Ensuring that a longitudinal study has adequate statistical power to detect the intended effects is not only important in and of itself but also for the later replicability of the research findings. The power of a longitudinal study depends on a number of study features: the number of participants, the number of assessments, the time interval between assessments, and the total duration of the study. Furthermore, the goal of the longitudinal investigation (e.g., determining the average rates of change for different age-groups and detecting differences between those age-groups, or evaluating individual processes and characterizing differences between individuals) and the particular statistical model used in later analyses can also affect statistical power (Schlesselman, 1973a, 1973b).

Determining sample size in the context of power is further complicated in studies with intensive longitudinal data, as having observations be so close in time introduces temporal dependency between measurements at nearby time points (Bolger et al., 2012; Lafit et al., 2020). Furthermore, in intensive longitudinal data, power can be increased in a number of ways, such as by increasing the number of participants *or* increasing the number of measurements from each participant (Bolger et al., 2012; Lane & Hennes, 2018). The choice of whether to maximize the number of time points or the number of persons depends in part on the research goal. For example, if the goal is detecting interindividual differences in intraindividual change, then both the sample size and number of assessments should be high (Lafit et al., 2020). However, simulation studies have shown that increasing the number of participants might result in greater power and more accurate estimates than simply increasing the

number of assessments (Lane & Hennes, 2018; Schultzberg & Muthén, 2018). One possible explanation for more participants being able to compensate for shorter time series is that during the estimation process, information can be "borrowed" from other participants to estimate the within-person effects of interest (Hecht & Zitzmann, 2021; Schultzberg & Muthén, 2018).

Unfortunately, there is no one-size-fits-all approach to calculating the sample size or frequency of assessments needed to reach a certain value of power. As previously mentioned, such calculations depend on the statistical model used and the main goal of the investigation. Fortunately, there has been much work evaluating how to conduct power analyses in longitudinal studies (Basagaña & Spiegelman, 2010; Fan, 2003; Hertzog et al., 2006; Kelley & Rausch, 2011; Maxwell et al., 2008; Muthén & Curran, 1997; Rast & Hofer, 2014; Raudenbush & Xiao-Feng, 2001; Tu et al., 2007; Winkens et al., 2006; Zhang & Wang, 2009), as well as the development of corresponding software and applications to make such calculations easier. Some of these programs include RMASS2 (Hedeker et al., 1999), Mplus (Muthén & Muthén, 2002), Optimal Design (Raudenbush et al., 2011), PinT (Bosker et al., 2007), ML-DEs (Cools et al., 2008), and PowerAnalysisIL (Lafit et al., 2020), to name a few. We, therefore, refer interested readers to these sources that can serve as a guide to conduct their power analysis before starting data collection.

FACTORIAL INVARIANCE OVER TIME

A critical aspect of measurement in longitudinal data is factorial invariance over time. Factorial invariance is a measurement property that helps a researcher test that the assessment tool is consistently measuring the same construct (Meredith, 1993). In longitudinal designs, establishing *longitudinal invariance* (also called *factorial invariance*) for measures collected on a construct across time is important. Structural equation modeling and latent variables require a clear understanding that the measures have the same functional relationship to the hypothesized construct over the study period. This condition ensures that the latent construct has an equivalent definition and scale across measurement occasions (Meredith, 1993; Ferrer et al., 2008; Sayer & Cumsille, 2001; Widaman et al., 2010). Such a condition is necessary to identify quantitative changes in the construct over time (Nesselroade et al., 2007). Although checking for invariance across time is typically addressed at the phase of data analysis, in this section, we cover some of the important underpinnings of factorial invariance that might help inform the study planning and data collection phase.

Based on the work by (Meredith 1993; Meredith & Horn, 2001), a practical approach to factorial invariance was proposed by Widaman and Reise (1997). They distinguished a number of increasingly restrictive models for assessing invariance. The first of such models was configural invariance, indicating that the same observed variables of the latent construct are specified at each occasion, independent of the numerical values. The second model was weak metric invariance, indicating that the factor loading of each indicator has the same value across all occasions. The third model was strong factorial invariance, in which the restriction is further increased by specifying an invariant intercept of each indicator across all occasions. The last model, strict factorial invariance, requires invariant unique variances for each observed variable over time. To assess all these invariance assumptions step-by-step and confidently model growth of a latent variable, it is important to have multiple variables at the measurement level.

Longitudinal invariance is a multivariate property and, thus, having only one observed variable at the measurement level makes it impossible to test for invariance (Widaman et al., 2010). In such univariate situations, invariance must be assumed, so caution should be taken regarding the development of the latent variables (Ferrer et al., 2008). When possible, researchers should collect measures with multiple indicators and implement analyses as such (e.g., Ferrer et al., 2008; Hancock et al., 2001; McArdle, 1988; Widaman et al., 2010). These multivariate models

(also called second-order models) have been shown to increase precision and power to assess change estimates (e.g., see Hertzog et al., 2006).

Establishing at least strong invariance allows one to estimate the means at the structural level in longitudinal models. Often, however, such criteria are difficult to meet with empirical data. In situations when these conditions are too restrictive for their data, investigators occasionally free constraints and allow some of the model parameters to vary across occasions (e.g., some of the factor loadings are not invariant across all occasions). This type of invariance, often called *partial invariance*, is not always considered a sufficient compromise. To overcome some of the difficulties posed by invariance, Nesselroade et al. (2007) proposed that invariance be met at the level of the interfactor relationships instead of the indicators. Moreover, a newer solution to this problem that approximates measurement invariance is the Bayesian structural equation modeling (BSEM) framework (Muthén & Asparouhov, 2013; Winter & Depaoli, 2020).

Longitudinal invariance is relevant in longitudinal studies where the measures need to be changed across assessments, as described in a previous section. This can occur, for example, when a measure is no longer appropriate to assess the development of a construct. If this issue is foreseen during the phase of study planning, then one solution is to have overlapping measures across measurement occasions when transitioning from one occasion to the next. Under assumptions of longitudinal invariance, this approach allows defining a single construct across all occasions (see McArdle et al., 2009). Figure 18.3 illustrates this idea with a hypothetical example of mathematics skills during grade school. In particular, this figure is a path diagram of a second-order linear growth curve model (Ferrer et al., 2008; Hancock et al., 2001; McArdle, 1988) with observed variables that change across time, matching the progression of math skills in school. The goal is to model math skills from first to fourth grade. For this, a researcher uses four measures: addition, subtraction, multiplication, and division. At each

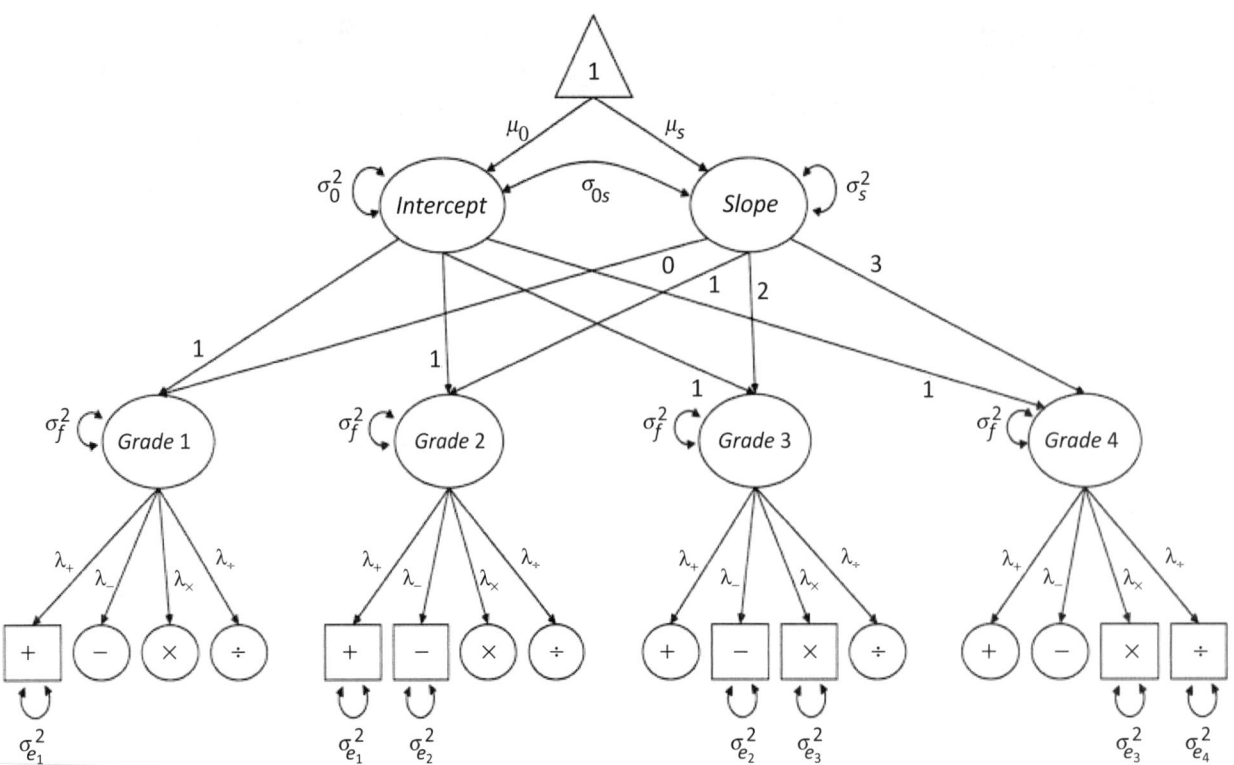

FIGURE 18.3. Path diagram of second-order growth curve of math skills from Grade 1 to Grade 4 using four observed measures: addition, subtraction, multiplication, and division. Following the conventions of path diagrams, squares represent observed variables, while circles represent unobserved or latent variables.

grade, a latent factor is specified to represent math skills using measures relevant for that grade. For example, at Grade 1, only addition might be an appropriate measure of math skills if the students have not been exposed to other aspects of mathematics. At Grade 2, both addition and subtraction are appropriate, so a measure of subtraction is included. At Grade 3, addition becomes obsolete because it is too easy for students, so it is removed. Instead, multiplication is introduced alongside subtraction as the appropriate measures. Finally, at Grade 4, multiplication and division are the only age-appropriate measures, with subtraction becoming obsolete. Here, factorial invariance cannot be formally assessed because the four measures are not present at all occasions. However, under invariance assumptions, the use of a measurement model with transitions in the measures (Grades 2 and 3) enables the evaluation of change at the factor level.

A similar transitioning strategy can be applied at the item level (McArdle et al., 2009). Instead of

measures transitioning in and out across occasions, the items can be altered (see Edwards & Wirth, 2009). This approach of transitioning items or variables has some drawbacks. Such models do not allow testing for factorial invariance, which compromises the examination of change. In addition, these models can be difficult to fit to data from cohort-sequential designs or to sparse data across assessments.

Finally, longitudinal invariance can also be influenced by the type of data collected. For example, traditional approaches for testing incremental invariance do not produce optimal parameter estimates when ordered-categorical data are treated as continuous variables (Rhemtulla et al., 2012). Using an incremental approach similar to the traditional invariance tests, Liu et al. (2017) used thresholds of ordered items to establish invariance while taking into account the sparsity in the response categories. For example, for a Likert-type item with response categories of 1 to 5, participants may endorse 1 to 5 at the first occasion, whereas at the second occasion they may endorse categories 2 to 5, which affects the thresholds across the two assessments.

CHALLENGES DURING COLLECTION OF LONGITUDINAL DATA

Even after selecting the number of occasions and participants and which measures to use, researchers still must consider issues that can arise during collection of the longitudinal data, particularly when these issues may impact later statistical analyses. Such issues can include missing data, as well as the consideration of cohort and retest effects.

Missing Data

One of the first phases where missing data can occur is during the initial sampling and contact of participants. Lack of representativeness in the sampling, lack of response to outreach, and refusal by participants to begin participation in the study are all significant forms of incomplete data that are often overlooked and unstudied. These factors ought to be considered during the planning of the study before data collection.

The main mechanism leading to missing data in longitudinal studies is attrition. Attrition can be due to the participants' refusal to complete parts of a questionnaire or take part in an experimental task, or, most importantly, due to participants dropping out of the study (either temporarily or permanently). Reasons for dropout include fatigue, aversion to or dissatisfaction with the study, relocation, health, and, in studies involving older individuals, death. Many of these issues are difficult to prevent, but other aspects can be thought out before data collection to minimize the loss of data. The main consequences of attrition are the reduction in statistical power and bias of parameter estimates. The former is associated with data loss, while the latter is particularly worrisome when the dropout is nonrandom— that is, those individuals who continue in the study are systematically different from those who withdraw. This is particularly relevant in studies involving older populations: those who tend to

remain in the study are typically healthier, more motivated, and more highly functioning than those who drop out (see Ferrer & Ghisletta, 2011; Schaie & Hofer, 2001).

When attrition is not related to the study in any systematic way, the missing data can be ignored. However, when data loss is related to variables in the study (e.g., participants in a study about health cannot take part in an assessment because of illness), accounting for the incompleteness is more complicated. Sometimes information about the reasons for missing data is related to measured variables and can be taken into consideration in the statistical analyses. Other times, although the missing data are related to variables in the study, such information is not available so statistical models are limited—or ineffective—in accounting for the missing data (for comprehensive reviews on analyses of incomplete data, see Graham, 2009; Schafer & Graham, 2002).

One fundamental consideration for researchers collecting longitudinal data is how to minimize attrition. For this, tracking participants over time and keeping them involved in the study is essential. Some common techniques to track participants over time include collecting contact information from the participants as well as from two or three other contact individuals. These other contacts can help locate the participants in case, say, they move from their original residence. It is always useful, particularly in studies that last several years, to check from time to time to ensure that the records are up to date. Retention can also be improved by keeping participants involved and engaged in the study. Some methods to facilitate this include periodic contact with the participants via newsletters, postcards, birthday cards, and the use of various incentives. In most longitudinal studies, participants are paid or offered some incentives for their continued participation. Incentives—monetary or not— often increase over time, so participants receive higher incentives the longer they stay in the study. In addition to such payments, it is a good idea to regularly send information about the findings and progress of the study to the partici- pants. This can be done, for example, through newsletters or summary reports that contain key findings written in nontechnical language so that participants can see the application of the research and the relevance of their participation.

Accelerated longitudinal designs represent a form of missing data that has been planned into the study design. By design, all participants are missing data at multiple ages. In contrast, other types of incomplete data can lead to biased results. To avoid such issues, researchers can occasionally take steps before and during data collection to help minimize the loss of data; in other situations, particularly for data that has been already collected, statistical models are needed to account for the types and patterns of missingness in the data.

Cohort Effects

A *cohort* is defined as a group of individuals "entering the specified environment at the same point in time" (Schaie & Hertzog, 1982, p. 92) and is typically based on birth year (i.e., individuals born in the same year or in some time interval are classified as part of the same cohort). However, birth year is not the only way to define cohorts (see Table 1 in Schaie, 1984, for examples), and some other definition of cohort may be used, depending on what is most relevant to the study.

Regardless of how cohorts are defined, it is important to take potential cohort effects into consideration when designing a longitudinal study, particularly ALDs. The sampling design of an ALD assumes that each of the cohorts share the same longitudinal trajectory—that is, if all individuals had been measured for the entire age range of the study, their longitudinal trajectories would be the same and there would be no systematic differences between individuals of different cohorts. Cohort effects exist when this assumption—called *convergence* or *cohort equivalence* (Estrada et al., 2021)— is violated, and different cohorts have different longitudinal trajectories. An example of this nonconvergence is shown in Figure 18.4, which depicts three different cohorts defined by their age of entry into the study, with older cohorts having higher intercept values. Failing to account for these potential cohort effects can introduce

bias into the parameter estimates and affect the validity of the analyses (Estrada & Ferrer, 2019; Sliwinski et al., 2010). Luckily, the assumption of cohort equivalence can often, but not always, be tested during data analysis (Estrada et al., 2021; Miyazaki & Raudenbush, 2000).

Although detecting cohort effects is especially important in ALDs, there is the concern that such effects can be confounded. In particular, a participant's response can be due to their age (which is often the primary effect of interest in longitudinal research), their cohort, and the time at which they were measured. Although all three effects may be of interest to researchers, only two of these effects can ever be studied at a time, and the third would always be confounded with the two that are studied (Baltes et al., 1979; Schaie, 1965; for more on the statistical methodology behind age-period-cohort analysis, or empirical examples, see Mason & Fienberg, 1985; Yang & Land, 2013). In an ALD, researchers are able to study the effects due to age versus cohort, but such effects are confounded with any effects due to time of measurement. This can cause concern if there is the potential for retest effects in the data—not only can retest effects lead to a lack of convergence (Sliwinski et al., 2010), but cohort effects can compromise the estimation of retest effects (Hoffman et al., 2011). This is because any approach to estimating retest effects—either design or statistical analyses—relies on the assumption of equivalence across samples. In other words, the compared samples should only differ with respect to the number of measurement occasions and age (or some other time-related variable). When cohort effects accentuate the differences between samples, the estimation of retest effects is confounded.

Retest Effects

Another important issue associated with the collection of longitudinal data concerns retest effects. Cohort, selection, maturation, and retest effects represent a major threat to validity in longitudinal studies (e.g., see Baltes et al., 1979; Schaie, 1986). Depending on the measurement instrument used, the number of occasions may

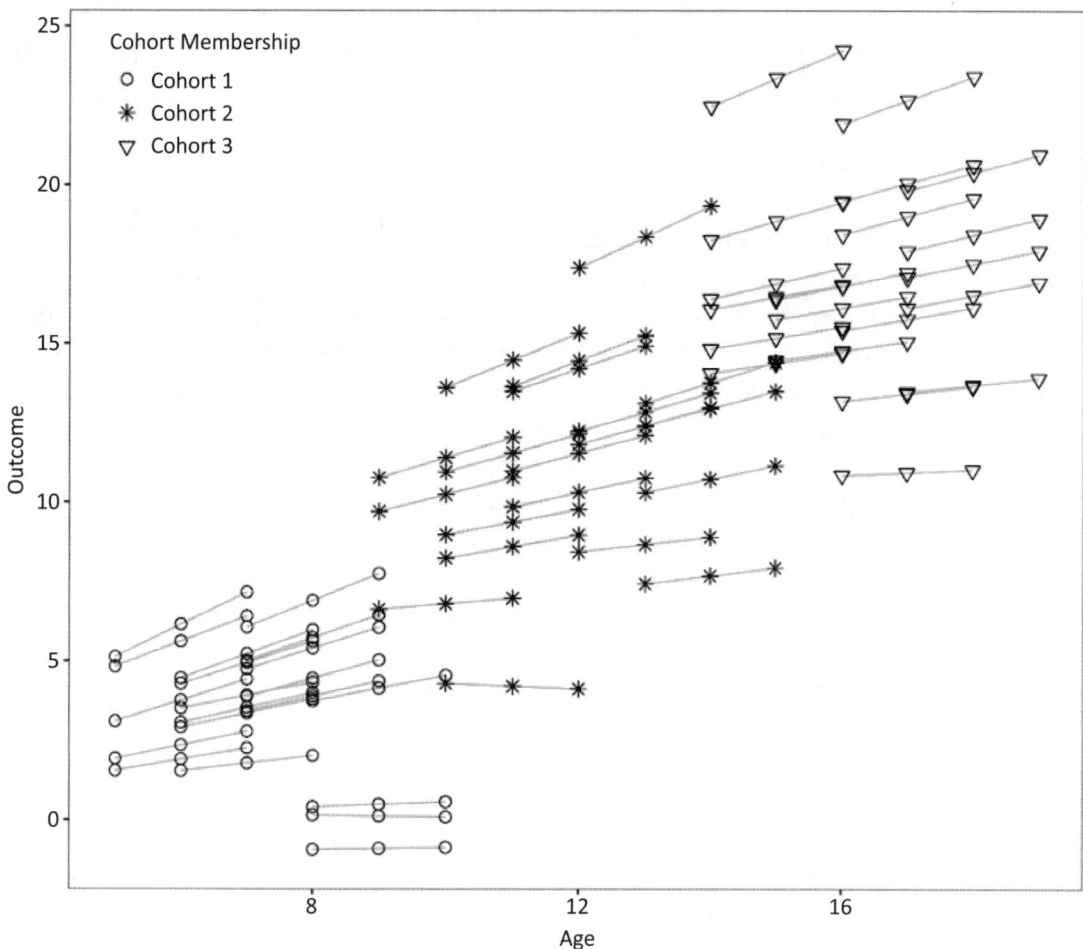

FIGURE 18.4. Linear trajectories of individuals in three age-related cohorts, each with a different intercept.

not be related to the attribute in question. For instance, for physical growth, every new assessment indicates how much a participant grows irrespective of the number of measurement occasions or the measurement tool used. For other variables, however, the repeated measurement may interfere with the assessment of the attribute.

Imagine, for instance, a sample of individuals responding to a battery of measures related to memory at repeated occasions. The mere completion of the tests at a given occasion may influence the participants' performance at the next assessment. This could be due to a number of factors, such as familiarity with the setting, practice from repeated exposure to the same tests, time between assessments, and the nature of the attribute being measured (e.g., Cattell, 1957;

McArdle & Woodcock, 1997). Here, the repeated measurement is contaminating the assessment of the process under investigation. That is, in the illustration, improvements in memory could be due to both developmental maturation (usually coded as age) and practice effects. Empirical findings of this phenomenon indicate that performance in cognitive tests tend to improve over repeated occasions, varying in degree across variables (e.g., Rabbitt et al., 2001; Wilson et al., 2002; cf. Schaie, 1988), across persons (Ferrer et al., 2004; Ferrer et al., 2005), and across occasions (Lövdén et al., 2004; Rabbitt et al., 2001).

There are two possible stages in a study where retest effects can be avoided or minimized. The first stage is during the planning of the study and data collection. If the researcher anticipates that retest effects might occur, they can employ so-called *refreshment samples*. These are samples with the same characteristics and structure with respect to important variables (e.g., age, gender, socioeconomic status) as the main sample at the initial assessment and are included at any repeated occasion. If the samples are truly equivalent with respect to important sampling characteristics, differences in the scores of each sample can be attributed to retest effects (cf. Schaie, 1988). However, collecting refreshment samples at every new assessment can be a costly affair. Also, the assumption that each new cohort coming into the study has the same important characteristics might be unfeasible for the amount of heterogeneity that exists among the participants.

The other stage in a study where we can account for retest is after the data has already been collected, during the stage of data analysis. In this phase, there are several important factors that can influence the retest estimated in a model, including the design of the data (i.e., is there enough variation in the retest interval for estimates of retest to be disentangled from other within-person effects?), the time metric of analytic model (if models based on measurement occasions are used, then each new occasion can be confounded with retest), the number of measures (i.e., as each measure might follow a different scale and in turn can have different retest effects), and the assumption of retest effects imposed across individuals (i.e., do individuals follow the same trajectory in their practice gains or are there individual differences with retest?).

Typically, longitudinal studies are used to investigate the development (e.g., time course, age-related changes) of a given attribute. It is important that the changes related to development or maturation are separated from the changes related to retest (i.e., reflecting practice and experience). But age is not the only confounder with practice. Retest effects can also be confounded with other important factors in longitudinal studies, such as attrition and cohort effects (Hoffman et al., 2011; Schaie, 1988). Interested readers are referred to the existing literature in the area where different models are proposed to

separate the variance due to age and retest (e.g., Batra et al., 2021; Ferrer et al., 2004; McArdle & Woodcock, 1997; Rabbitt et al., 2001).

ESTABLISHING CAUSALITY IN LONGITUDINAL STUDIES

In his work on causality, Pearl (2009) enumerated the different stages of developing a structural model and the importance of a priori assumptions about the variables under study before a researcher can establish causal relations among them. It is important to consider, for instance, the possibility of unobserved (confounder) variables that might cause both the predictor and the outcome, a situation called *confounding*. Another important consideration is the different values that an outcome might take for the same value of the predictor, a comparison strategy between alternate "realities" called *counterfactual theory*. Pearl's work also addressed the issue of identification in observational studies, an important step for establishing direct and indirect causal paths. This is achieved when a number of criteria are met within both parametric and nonparametric frameworks (Pearl, 2014). If the paths are not properly identified in this way, they cannot be causally interpreted.

The concepts outlined in Pearl's original theory on causal reasoning change slightly when working with longitudinal models. Here, many times researchers use dynamic modeling techniques when a variable at any given point is being predicted by itself at the previous time point, the so-called *autoregressive relation*. In this instance, the concept of counterfactual relates to keeping the past history fixed at the observed value and considering the different values that the current time could take given that fixed predictor. Regarding longitudinal data, Arjas and Parner (2004) built on Pearl's work and highlighted the idea that a "cause has to precede the effect" is not enough to make causal inferences from a longitudinal design; many other factors, such as confounders and counterfactuals, need to be considered.

One final point regarding causality during the planning of a study concerns mediating variables.

In a simple study design, there is a single outcome and a single predictor, and then there is a mediator that transmits the effect of the predictor on the outcome (MacKinnon, 2008). Extending this logic into longitudinal studies is complex and has resulted in various approaches. We refer interested readers to the literature on various statistical methods available to deal with mediator variables in longitudinal studies for the goal of causal inference (e.g., Albert & Nelson, 2011; MacKinnon et al., 2009; Maxwell & Cole, 2007; O'Laughlin et al., 2018; Preacher, 2015; Roth & MacKinnon, 2012; Selig & Preacher, 2009).

RECOMMENDATIONS AND PRACTICAL GUIDELINES

Planning and carrying out a longitudinal study is no easy undertaking, especially considering the time and financial resources required. To optimize these resources, several factors need to be considered simultaneously during the planning of the study, and researchers may wish to consider the following questions to help guide their study planning.

1. **Is the focus on the overall trajectory of a psychological process or the within-person fluctuations of the process?** Making this choice helps researchers decide the type of longitudinal study design needed as well as the aspects of the change process to focus on. Researchers who are interested in evaluating how a process changes over time across all individuals might find a more traditional panel design or accelerated longitudinal design suits their needs. The longer time frame of such studies better allows for the examination of the overall trajectory of a process. In this case, the relevant aspects of the change process might be features such as the initial level and rate of change, or other characteristics in nonlinear trajectories (Grimm et al., 2011). Conversely, if the focus is on how the process fluctuates within an individual or its dynamics with other variables, then a study design that relies on intensive longitudinal data might be best. The relevant change aspects

in such a design may be the amplitude of the fluctuations or the temporal dependency in the data (e.g., autoregressive coefficients). Finally, researchers who are interested in exploring both the group level changes and individual level changes may consider employing a measurement-burst design that combines aspects of both panel and intensive longitudinal designs.

2. **How rapidly does the process change?** This question can help determine how frequently the construct needs to be measured, and the length of time between assessments. More rapidly changing processes, such as moods or physiological states, would require more frequent measurements that occur closer together. On the other hand, a stable or slower-changing process would require fewer measurements, although additional assessments could provide a more accurate understanding of the underlying construct and its stability. When the rate of change in the process is not known, researchers can try to approximate it with preliminary data. In general, researchers are recommended to sample more frequently to avoid missing important aspects of the change process (Adolph et al., 2008) but should not add additional measurement occasions for the sake of collecting more data—there is a "diminishing return" associated with additional assessments, such that extra assessments do not substantially increase the precision of the obtained estimates but require more time and resources to be put into the study (Timmons & Preacher, 2015).

3. **How can the construct best be measured?** This question pertains to choosing appropriate measures for the constructs under study. In longitudinal studies, researchers often administer the same battery of measures at each assessment, with the idea that using the same battery leads to a more accurate study of individual change. However, researchers need to consider whether those measures are measuring the same construct in the same way at all occasions or ages (i.e., assess factorial

invariance), or whether measures need to be transitioned out for more age-appropriate ones as the study progresses. Additionally, it is important that the full range of the desired construct be covered at each measurement occasion, as studying change becomes difficult when data have floor and ceiling issues. Whenever possible, researchers should use multiple indicators to measure a construct.

4. **Does the planned study have sufficient power?** The answer to this question is often tied to the decision of sample size and frequency of assessments, as both can influence power in longitudinal studies. Once again, preliminary data can prove useful here. Estimates from pilot studies can help calculate the power for different combinations of sample size and measurement occasions, allowing researchers to optimize their resources to study their hypotheses with sufficient power. However, researchers should also account for possible attrition in their study and conduct the power analysis accordingly. As mentioned previously, power analyses for longitudinal studies are specific to the statistical models that are used later to answer the research questions.

5. **Considerations for Open Science.** In line with current practices for Open Science, researchers should consider preregistering their study. Although having explicit hypotheses and anticipated findings is often difficult, this exercise could be beneficial to avoid biases, reduce the probability of Type I errors, increase the probability of replication, enhance critical thinking about the design, variables, and analytic strategies, and be explicit about the research questions. Researchers should also consider making the details of their study available, including design, data, and analytic models. Doing so could help other researchers and facilitate the dissemination of science.

CONCLUSION

Longitudinal data are necessary to study development processes, change, and intraindividual variability and dynamics. The appropriate planning of longitudinal studies can allow researchers to optimize their resources and alleviate difficulties that would otherwise limit or be dealt with during analysis. Longitudinal data collection carries a heavy cost and, thus, should be given appropriate time to plan and optimize resources.

References

Adolph, K. E., Robinson, S. R., Young, J. W., & Gill-Alvarez, F. (2008). What is the shape of developmental change? *Psychological Review*, *115*(3), 527–543. https://doi.org/10.1037/0033-295X.115.3.527

Albert, J. M., & Nelson, S. (2011). Generalized causal mediation analysis. *Biometrics*, *67*(3), 1028–1038. https://doi.org/10.1111/j.1541-0420.2010.01547.x

Arjas, E., & Parner, J. (2004). Causal reasoning from longitudinal data. *Scandinavian Journal of Statistics*, *31*(2), 171–187.

Baltes, P. B., Cornelius, S. W., & Nesselroade, J. R. (1979). Cohort effects in developmental psychology. In J. R. Nesselroade & P. B. Baltes (Eds.), *Longitudinal research in the study of behavior and development* (pp. 61–87). Academic Press.

Baltes, P. B., & Nesselroade, J. R. (1979). History and rationale of longitudinal research. In J. R. Nesselroade & P. B. Baltes (Eds.), *Longitudinal research in the study of behavior and development* (pp. 1–39). Academic Press.

Basagaña, X., & Spiegelman, D. (2010). Power and sample size calculations for longitudinal studies comparing rates of change with a time-varying exposure. *Statistics in Medicine*, *29*(2), 181–192. https://doi.org/10.1002/sim.3772

Batra, R., Bunge, S. A., & Ferrer, E. (2021). Modeling retest effects in developmental processes using latent change score models. *Structural Equation Modeling*, *29*(2), 295–309. https://doi.org/10.1080/10705511.2021.1946807

Bauer, D. J., & Hussong, A. M. (2009). Psychometric approaches for developing commensurate measures across independent studies: Traditional and new models. *Psychological Methods*, *14*(2), 101–125. https://doi.org/10.1037/a0015583

Bell, R. Q. (1953). Convergence: An accelerated longitudinal approach. *Child Development*, *24*(2), 145–152. https://doi.org/10.2307/1126345

Bell, R. Q. (1954). An experimental test of the accelerated longitudinal approach. *Child Development*, *25*(4), 281–286. https://doi.org/10.2307/1126058

Bolger, N., & Laurenceau, J.-P. (2013). *Intensive longitudinal methods: An introduction to diary and experience sampling research*. Guilford Press.

Bolger, N., Stadler, G., & Laurenceau, J.-P. (2012). Power analysis for intensive longitudinal studies. In M. R. Mehl & T. S. Conner (Eds.), *Handbook of research methods for studying daily life* (pp. 285–301). Guilford Press.

Bollen, K. A., & Curran, P. J. (2006). *Latent curve models: A structural equation perspective*. Wiley.

Bosker, R. J., Snijders, T. A. B., & Guldemond, H. (2007). *PinT (Power in two-level designs): Estimating standard errors of regression coefficients in hierarchical linear models for power calculations* (Version 2.12) [Computer software].

Cattell, R. B. (1957). *Personality and motivation structure and measurement*. World Book.

Cattell, R. B. (1988). The data box. In J. R. Nesselroade & R. B. Cattell (Eds.), *Handbook of multivariate experimental psychology* (pp. 69–130). Springer.

Cools, W., Van den Noortgate, W., & Onghena, P. (2008). ML-DEs: A program for designing efficient multilevel studies. *Behavior Research Methods*, *40*(1), 236–249. https://doi.org/10.3758/BRM.40.1.236

Cranford, J. A., Shrout, P. E., Iida, M., Rafaeli, E., Yip, T., & Bolger, N. (2006). A procedure for evaluating sensitivity to within-person change: Can mood measures in diary studies detect change reliably? *Personality and Social Psychology Bulletin*, *32*(7), 917–929. https://doi.org/10.1177/0146167206287721

Cronbach, L. J., & Furby, L. (1970). How we should measure "change": Or should we? *Psychological Bulletin*, *74*(1), 68–80. https://doi.org/10.1037/h0029382

Csikszentmihalyi, M., & Larson, R. (1987). Validity and reliability of the experience-sampling method. *The Journal of Nervous and Mental Disease*, *175*(9), 526–536. https://doi.org/10.1097/00005053-198709000-00004

Curran, P. J., & Hussong, A. M. (2009). Integrative data analysis: The simultaneous analysis of multiple data sets. *Psychological Methods*, *14*(2), 81–100. https://doi.org/10.1037/a0015914

Curran, P. J., Hussong, A. M., Cai, L., Huang, W., Chassin, L., Sher, K. J., & Zucker, R. A. (2008). Pooling data from multiple longitudinal studies: The role of item response theory in integrative data analysis. *Developmental Psychology*, *44*(2), 365–380. https://doi.org/10.1037/0012-1649.44.2.365

Duncan, O. D. (1975). Some linear models for two-wave, two-variable panel analysis with one-way causation and measurement errors. In H. M. Blalock (Ed.), *Quantitative sociology: International perspectives on mathematical and statistical modeling* (pp. 285–306). Academic Press.

Duncan, T. E., Duncan, S. E., & Hops, H. (1996). Analysis of longitudinal data within accelerated longitudinal designs. *Psychological Methods*, *1*(3), 236–248. https://doi.org/10.1037/1082-989X.1.3.236

Edwards, M. C., & Wirth, R. J. (2009). Measurement and the study of change. *Research in Human Development*, *6*(2–3), 74–96.

Eisele, G., Vachom, H., Lafit, G., Kuppens, P., Houben, M., Myin-Germeys, I., & Viechtbauer, W. (2022). The effects of sampling frequency and questionnaire length on perceived burden, compliance, and careless responding in experience sampling data in a student population. *Assessment*, *29*(2), 136–151. https://doi.org/10.1177/1073191120957102.

Estrada, E., Bunge, S. A., & Ferrer, E. (2021). Controlling for cohort effects in accelerated longitudinal designs using continuous- and discrete-time dynamic models. *Psychological Methods*. Advance online publication. https://doi.org/10.1037/met0000427

Estrada, E., & Ferrer, E. (2019). Studying developmental processes in accelerated cohort-sequential designs with discrete- and continuous-time latent change score models. *Psychological Methods*, *24*(6), 708–734. https://doi.org/10.1037/met0000215

Fan, X. (2003). Power of latent growth modeling for detecting group differences in latent growth trajectory parameters. *Structural Equation Modeling*, *10*(3), 380–400. https://doi.org/10.1207/S15328007SEM1003_3

Ferrer, E., Balluerka, N., & Widaman, K. F. (2008). Factorial invariance and the specification of second-order latent growth models. *Methodology*, *4*(1), 22–36. https://doi.org/10.1027/1614-2241.4.1.22

Ferrer, E., & Ghisletta, P. (2011). Methodological and analytical issues in the psychology of aging. In K. W. Schaie & S. L. Willis (Eds.), *Handbook of the psychology of aging* (pp. 25–39). Elsevier Academic Press. https://doi.org/10.1016/B978-0-12-380882-0.00002-4

Ferrer, E., & McArdle, J. J. (2010). Longitudinal modeling of developmental changes in psychological research. *Current Directions in Psychological Science*, *19*(3), 149–154. https://doi.org/10.1177/0963721410370300

Ferrer, E., Salthouse, T. A., McArdle, J. J., Stewart, W. F., & Schwartz, B. S. (2005). Multivariate modeling of age and retest in longitudinal studies of cognitive abilities. *Psychology and Aging*, *20*(3), 412–422. https://doi.org/10.1037/0882-7974.20.3.412

Ferrer, E., Salthouse, T. A., Stewart, W. F., & Schwartz, B. S. (2004). Modeling age and retest processes in longitudinal studies of cognitive abilities. *Psychology and Aging, 19*(2), 243–259. https://doi.org/10.1037/0882-7974.19.2.243

Ferrer, E., Shaywitz, B. A., Holahan, J. M., Marchione, K., & Shaywitz, S. E. (2010). Uncoupling of reading and IQ over time: Empirical evidence for a definition of dyslexia. *Psychological Science, 21*(1), 93–101. https://doi.org/10.1177/0956797609354084

Ferrer, E., Steele, J., & Hsieh, F. (2012). Analyzing dynamics of affective dyadic interactions using patterns of intra- and inter-individual variability. *Multivariate Behavioral Research, 47*(1), 136–171. https://doi.org/10.1080/00273171.2012.640605

Galesic, M., & Bosnjak, M. (2009). Effects of questionnaire length on participation and indicators of response quality in a web survey. *Public Opinion Quarterly, 73*(2), 349–360. https://doi.org/10.1093/poq/nfp031

Glahn, D. C., Kent, J. W., Jr., Sprooten, E., Diego, V. P., Winkler, A. M., Curran, J. E., McKay, D. R., Knowles, E. E., Carless, M. A., Göring, H. H., Dyer, T. D., Olvera, R. L., Fox, P. T., Almasy, L., Charlesworth, J., Kochunov, P., Duggirala, R., & Blangero, J. (2013). Genetic basis of neurocognitive decline and reduced white-matter integrity in normal human brain aging. *Proceedings of the National Academy of Sciences of the United States of America, 110*(47), 19006–19011. https://doi.org/10.1073/pnas.1313735110

Graham, J. W. (2009). Missing data analysis: Making it work in the real world. *Annual Review of Psychology, 60*, 549–76. https://doi.org/10.1146/annurev.psych.58.110405.085530

Grimm, K. J. (2007). Multivariate longitudinal methods for studying developmental relationships between depression and academic achievement. *International Journal of Behavioral Development, 31*(4), 328–339. https://doi.org/10.1177/0165025407077754

Grimm, K. J., & Ram, N. (2009). Nonlinear growth curve models in Mplus and SAS. *Structural Equation Modeling, 16*(4), 676–701. https://doi.org/10.1080/10705510903206055

Grimm, K. J., Ram, N., & Estabrook, R. (2010). Nonlinear structured growth mixture models in M plus and OpenMx. *Multivariate Behavioral Research, 45*(6), 887–909. https://doi.org/10.1080/00273171.2010.531230

Grimm, K. J., Ram, N., & Estabrook, R. (2016). *Growth modeling: Structural equation and multilevel modeling approaches.* Guilford Press.

Grimm, K. J., Ram, N., & Hamagami, F. (2011). Nonlinear growth curves in developmental research. *Child Development, 82*(5), 1357–1371. https://doi.org/10.1111/j.1467-8624.2011.01630.x

Hancock, G. R., Kuo, W., & Lawrence, F. R. (2001). An illustration of second-order latent growth models. *Structural Equation Modeling, 8*, 470–489. https://doi.org/10.1207/S15328007SEM0803_7

Hecht, M., & Zitzmann, S. (2021). Sample size recommendations for continuous-time models: Compensating shorter time series with larger numbers of persons and vice versa. *Structural Equation Modeling, 28*(2), 229–236. https://doi.org/10.1080/10705511.2020.1779069

Hedeker, D., Gibbons, R. D., & Waternaux, C. (1999). Sample size estimation for longitudinal designs with attrition: Comparing time-related contrasts between two groups. *Journal of Educational and Behavioral Statistics, 24*(1), 70–93. https://doi.org/10.3102/10769986024001070

Hertzog, C., Lindenberger, U., Ghisletta, P., & Oertzen, T. (2006). On the power of multivariate latent growth curve models to detect correlated change. *Psychological Methods, 11*(3), 244–252. https://doi.org/10.1037/1082-989X.11.3.244

Hertzog, C., & Nesselroade, J. R. (2003). Assessing psychological change in adulthood: An overview of methodological issues. *Psychology and Aging, 18*(4), 639–657. https://doi.org/10.1037/0882-7974.18.4.639

Hilbert, M., & López, P. (2011). The world's technological capacity to store, communicate, and compute information. *Science, 332*(6025), 60–65. https://doi.org/10.1126/science.1200970

Hoffman, L., Hofer, S. M., & Sliwinski, M. J. (2011). On the confounds among retest gains and age-cohort differences in the estimation of within-person change in longitudinal studies: A simulation study. *Psychology and Aging, 26*(4), 778–791. https://doi.org/10.1037/a0023910

Janssens, K. A. M., Bos, E. H., Rosmalen, J. G. M., Wichers, M. C., & Riese, H. (2018). A qualitative approach to guide choices for designing a diary study. *BMC Medical Research Methodology, 18*(1), 140. https://doi.org/10.1186/s12874-018-0579-6

Kao, W. T., Wang, Y., Kleinman, J. E., Lipska, B. K., Hyde, T. M., Weinberger, D. R., & Law, A. J. (2010). Common genetic variation in Neuregulin 3 (NRG3) influences risk for schizophrenia and impacts NRG3 expression in human brain. *Proceedings of the National Academy of Sciences of the United States of America, 107*(35), 15619–15624. https://doi.org/10.1073/pnas.1005410107

Kelley, K., & Rausch, J. R. (2011). Sample size planning for longitudinal models: Accuracy in parameter estimation for polynomial change parameters. *Psychological Methods, 16*(4), 391–405. https://doi.org/10.1037/a0023352

Lafit, G., Adolf, J. K., Dejonckheere, E., Myin-Germeys, I., Viechtbauer, W., & Ceulmans, E. (2020). Selection of the number of participants in intensive longitudinal studies: A user-friendly Shiny app and tutorial to perform power analysis in multilevel regression models that account for temporal dependencies. *Advances in Methods and Practices in Psychological Science, 4*(1), 1–24. https://doi.org/10.1177/2515245920978738

Lane, S. P., & Hennes, E. P. (2018). Power struggles: Estimating sample size for multilevel relationships research. *Journal of Social and Personal Relationships, 35*(1), 7–31. https://doi.org/10.1177/0265407517710342

Larson, R., & Csikszentmihalyi, M. (1983). The experience sampling method. In H. T. Reis (Ed.), *New directions for methodology of social and behavioral science* (pp. 41–56). Jossey-Bass.

Little, T. D., Lindenberger, U., & Nesselroade, J. R. (1999). On selecting indicators for multivariate measurement and modeling with latent variables: When "good" indicators are bad and "bad" indicators are good. *Psychological Methods, 4*(2), 192–211. https://doi.org/10.1037/1082-989X.4.2.192

Liu, Y., Millsap, R. E., West, S. G., Tein, J. Y., Tanaka, R., & Grimm, K. J. (2017). Testing measurement invariance in longitudinal data with ordered-categorical measures. *Psychological Methods, 22*(3), 486–506. https://doi.org/10.1037/met0000075

Lövdén, M., Ghisletta, P., & Lindenberger, U. (2004). Cognition in the Berlin Aging Study (BASE): The first 10 years. *Aging, Neuropsychology, and Cognition, 11*(2–3), 104–133. https://doi.org/10.1080/13825580490510982

MacKinnon, D. P. (2008). *Introduction to statistical mediation analysis.* Taylor & Francis Group.

MacKinnon, D. P., & Fairchild, A. J. (2009). Current directions in mediation analysis. *Current Directions in Psychological Science, 18*(1), 16–20. https://doi.org/10.1111/j.1467-8721.2009.01598.x

Mason, W. M., & Fienberg, S. (Eds.). (1985). *Cohort analysis in social research: Beyond the identification problem.* Springer-Verlag. https://doi.org/10.1007/978-1-4613-8536-3

Maxwell, S. E., & Cole, D. A. (2007). Bias in cross-sectional analyses of longitudinal mediation. *Psychological Methods, 12*(1), 23–44. https://doi.org/10.1037/1082-989X.12.1.23

Maxwell, S. E., Kelley, K., & Rausch, J. R. (2008). Sample size planning for statistical power and accuracy in parameter estimation. *Annual Review of Psychology, 59*(1), 537–563. https://doi.org/10.1146/annurev.psych.59.103006.093735

McArdle, J. J. (1988). Dynamic but structural equation modeling of repeated measures data. In J. R. Nesselroade & R. B. Cattell (Eds.), *Handbook of multivariate experimental psychology. Perspectives on individual differences* (pp. 561–614). Springer. https://doi.org/10.1007/978-1-4613-0893-5_17

McArdle, J. J. (2009). Latent variable modeling of differences and changes with longitudinal data. *Annual Review of Psychology, 60*(1), 577–605. https://doi.org/10.1146/annurev.psych.60.110707.163612

McArdle, J. J., Ferrer-Caja, E., Hamagami, F., & Woodcock, R. W. (2002). Comparative longitudinal structural analyses of the growth and decline of multiple intellectual abilities over the life span. *Developmental Psychology, 38*(1), 115–142. https://doi.org/10.1037/0012-1649.38.1.115

McArdle, J. J., Grimm, K. J., Hamagami, F., Bowles, R. P., & Meredith, W. (2009). Modeling life-span growth curves of cognition using longitudinal data with multiple samples and changing scales of measurement. *Psychological Methods, 14*(2), 126–149. https://doi.org/10.1037/a0015857

McArdle, J. J., & Woodcock, R. W. (1997). Expanding test–retest designs to include developmental time-lag components. *Psychological Methods, 2*(4), 403–435. https://doi.org/10.1037/1082-989X.2.4.403

Meredith, W. (1993). Measurement invariance, factor analysis and factorial invariance. *Psychometrika 58*, 525–543. https://doi.org/10.1007/BF02294825

Meredith, W., & Horn, J. (2001). The role of factorial invariance in modeling growth and change. In L. M. Collins & A. G. Sayer (Eds.), *New methods for the analysis of change* (pp. 203–240). American Psychological Association. https://doi.org/10.1037/10409-007

Milojev, P., & Sibley, C. G. (2017). Normative personality trait development in adulthood: A 6-year cohort-sequential growth model. *Journal of Personality and Social Psychology. 112*(3), 510–526. https://doi.org/10.1037/pspp0000121

Miyazaki, Y., & Raudenbush, S. W. (2000). Tests for linkage of multiple cohorts in an accelerated longitudinal design. *Psychological Methods, 5*(1), 44–63. https://doi.org/10.1037/1082-989X.5.1.44

Molenaar, P. C. (2004). A manifesto on psychology as idiographic science: Bringing the person back into scientific psychology, this time forever. *Measurement, 2*(4), 201–218. https://doi.org/10.1207/s15366359mea0204_1

Muthén, B., & Asparouhov, T. (2013). BSEM measurement invariance analysis. *Mplus Web Notes, 17,* 1–48.

Muthén, B. O., & Curran, P. J. (1997). General longitudinal modeling of individual differences in experimental designs: A latent variable framework for analysis and power estimation. *Psychological Methods, 2*(4), 371–402. https://doi.org/10.1037/1082-989X.2.4.371

Muthén, L. K., & Muthén, B. O. (2002). How to use a Monte Carlo study to decide on sample size and determine power. *Structural Equation Modeling, 9*(4), 599–620. https://doi.org/10.1207/S15328007SEM0904_8

Nesselroade, J. R. (1988). Sampling and generalizability: Adult development and aging research issues examined within the general methodological framework of selection. In K. W. Schaie, R. T. Campbell, W. Meredith, & S. C. Rawlings (Eds.), *Methodological issues in aging research* (pp. 13–42). Springer.

Nesselroade, J. R. (1991). The warp and woof of the developmental fabric. In R. Downs, L. Liben, & D. Palermo (Eds.), *Visions of development, the environment, and aesthetics: The legacy of Joachim F. Wholwill* (pp. 213–240). Erlbaum.

Nesselroade, J. R., & Boker, S. M. (1994). Assessing constancy and change. In T. Heatherton & J. Weinberger (Eds.), *Can personality change?* (pp. 121–147). American Psychological Association. https://doi.org/10.1037/10143-006

Nesselroade, J. R., & Cable, D. G. (1974). "Sometimes, it's okay to factor difference scores"—The separation of state and trait anxiety. *Multivariate Behavioral Research, 9*(3), 273–284. https://doi.org/10.1207/s15327906mbr0903_3

Nesselroade, J. R., Gerstorf, D., Hardy, S. A, & Ram, N. (2007). Idiographic filters for psychological constructs. *Measurement, 5*(4), 217–235. https://doi.org/10.1080/15366360701741807

O'Laughlin, K. D. (2020). *Integration of multiple time-scales in psychology: Considerations for study design, sampling, and data analysis* (Publication No. AAI27829059) [Doctoral Dissertation, University of California, Davis]. ProQuest Information and Learning.

O'Laughlin, K. D., Martin, M. J., & Ferrer, E. (2018). Cross-sectional analysis of longitudinal mediation processes. *Multivariate Behavioral Research, 53*(3), 375–402. https://doi.org/10.1080/00273171.2018.1454822

Pearl, J. (2009). *Causality*. Cambridge University Press.

Pearl, J. (2014). Interpretation and identification of causal mediation. *Psychological Methods, 19*(4), 459–481. https://doi.org/10.1037/a0036434

Preacher, K. J. (2015). Advances in mediation analysis: A survey and synthesis of new developments. *Annual Review of Psychology, 66*(1), 825–852. https://doi.org/10.1146/annurev-psych-010814-015258

Rabbitt, P., Diggle, P., Smith, D., Holland, F., & Mc Innes, L. (2001). Identifying and separating the effects of practice and of cognitive ageing during a large longitudinal study of elderly community residents. *Neuropsychologia, 39*(5), 532–543.

Ram, N., Conroy, D. E., Pincus, A. L., Lorek, A., Rebar, A., Roche, M. J., Coccia, M., Morack, J., Feldman, J., & Gerstorf, D. (2014). Examining the interplay of processes across multiple time-scales: Illustration with the Intraindividual Study of Affect, Health, and Interpersonal Behavior (iSAHIB). *Research in Human Development, 11*(2), 142–160. https://doi.org/10.1080/15427609.2014.906739

Ram, N., & Gerstorf, D. (2009). Time-structured and net intraindividual variability: Tools for examining the development of dynamic characteristics and processes. *Psychology and Aging, 24*(4), 778–791. https://doi.org/10.1037/a0017915

Ram, N., & Nesselroade, J. R. (2007). Modeling intraindividual and intracontextual change: Rendering developmental contextualism operational. In T. D. Little, J. A. Bovaird, & N. A. Card (Eds.), *Modeling contextual effects in longitudinal studies* (pp. 325–342). Lawrence Erlbaum Associates.

Ram, N., Yang, X., Cho, M. J., Brinberg, M., Muirhead, F., Reeves, B., & Robinson, T. N. (2020). Screenomics: A new approach for observing and studying individuals' digital lives. *Journal of Adolescent Research. 35*(1), 16–50. https://doi.org/10.1177/0743558419883362

Rast, P., & Hofer, S. M. (2014). Longitudinal design considerations to optimize power to detect variances and covariances among rates of change: Simulation results based on actual longitudinal studies. *Psychological Methods, 19*(1), 133–154. https://doi.org/10.1037/a0034524

Raudenbush, S.W., Spybrook, J., Congdon, R., Liu, X., Martinez, A., Bloom, H., & Hill, C. (2011). Optimal Design Plus Empirical Evidence (Version 3.0) [Computer software]. https://wtgrantfoundation.org/resource/optimal-design-withempirical-information-od

Raudenbush, S. W., & Xiao-Feng, L. (2001). Effects of study duration, frequency of observation, and sample size on power in studies of group differences in polynomial change. *Psychological Methods, 6*(4), 387–401. https://doi.org/10.1037/1082-989X.6.4.387

Reeves, B., Robinson, T. N., & Ram, N. (2020). Time for the human screenome project. *Nature, 577,* 314–317. https://doi.org/10.1038/d41586-020-00032-5

Rhemtulla, M., Brosseau-Liard, P. É., & Savalei, V. (2012). When can categorical variables be treated as continuous? A comparison of robust continuous and categorical SEM estimation methods under suboptimal conditions. *Psychological Methods*, *17*(3), 354–373. https://doi.org/10.1037a0029315

Rintala, A., Wampers, M., Myin-Germeys, I., & Viechtbauer, W. (2019). Response compliance and predictors thereof in studies using the experience sampling method. *Psychological Assessment*, *31*(2), 226–235. https://doi.org/10.1037/pas0000662

Rogosa, D. (1988). Myths about longitudinal research. In K. W. Schaie, R. T. Campbell, W. Meredith, & S. C. Rawlings (Eds.), *Methodological issues in aging research* (pp. 171–209). Springer Publishing Company.

Rolstad, S., Adler, J., & Rydén, A. (2011). Response burden and questionnaire length: Is shorter better? A review and meta-analysis. *Value in Health*, *14*(8), 1101–1108. https://doi.org/10.1016/j.jval.2011.06.003

Roth, D. L., & MacKinnon, D. P. (2012). Mediation analysis with longitudinal data. In J. Newsom, R. N. Jones, & S. M. Hofer (Eds.), *Longitudinal data analysis: A practical guide for researchers in aging, health, and social sciences* (pp. 181–216). Routledge.

Sayer, A. G., & Cumsille, P. E. (2001). Second-order latent growth models. In L. M. Collins & A. G. Sayer (Eds.), *New methods for the analysis of change* (pp. 179–200). American Psychological Association. https://doi.org/10.1037/10409-006

Schafer, J. L., & Graham, J. W. (2002). Missing data: Our view of the state of the art. *Psychological Methods*, *7*(2), 147–177. https://doi.org/10.1037/1082-989X.7.2.147

Schaie, K. W. (1965). A general model for the study of developmental problems. *Psychological Bulletin*, *64*(2), 92–107. https://doi.org/10.1037/h0022371

Schaie, K. W. (1984). Historical time and cohort effects. In K. A. McCluskey (Ed.), *Life-span developmental psychology: Historical and generational effects* (pp. 1–16). Elsevier. https://doi.org/10.1016/B978-0-12-482420-1.50006-4

Schaie, K. W. (1986). Beyond calendar definitions of age, time, and cohort: The general developmental model revisited. *Developmental Review*, *6*(3), 252–277.

Schaie, K. W. (1988). Internal validity threats in studies of adult cognitive development. In M. L. Howe & C. J. Brainerd (Eds.), *Cognitive development in adulthood. Springer Series in Cognitive Development.* Springer. https://doi.org/10.1007/978-1-4612-3852-2_8

Schaie, K. W., & Hertzog, C. (1982). Longitudinal methods. In B. B. Wolman (Ed.), *Handbook of developmental psychology* (pp. 91–115). Prentice-Hall.

Schaie, K. W., & Hofer, S. M. (2001). Longitudinal studies in aging research. In J. E. Birren & K. W. Schaie (Eds.), *Handbook of the psychology of aging* (pp. 53–77). Academic Press.

Schlesselman, J. J. (1973a). Planning a longitudinal study: I. Sample size determination. *Journal of Chronic Diseases*, *26*, 553–560. https://doi.org/10.1016/0021-9681(73)90060-X

Schlesselman, J. J. (1973b). Planning a longitudinal study. II. Frequency of measurement and study duration. *Journal of Chronic Diseases*, *26*(9), 561–570. https://doi.org/10.1016/0021-9681(73)90061-1

Schultzberg, M., & Muthén, B. (2018). Number of subjects and time points needed for multilevel time-series analysis: A simulation study of dynamic structural equation modeling. *Structural Equation Modeling*, *25*(4), 495–515. https://doi.org/10.1080/10705511.2017.1392862

Selig, J. P., & Preacher, K. J. (2009). Mediation models for longitudinal data in developmental research. *Research in Human Development*, *6*(2–3), 144–164. https://doi.org/10.1080/15427600902911247

Shiyko, M. P., & Ram, N. (2011). Conceptualizing and estimating process speed in studies employing ecological momentary assessment designs: A multilevel variance decomposition approach. *Multivariate Behavioral Research*, *46*(6), 875–899. https://doi.org/10.1080/00273171.2011.625310

Singer, J. D., & Willett, J. B. (2003). *Applied longitudinal data analysis: Modeling change and event occurrence*. Oxford University Press. https://doi.org/10.1093/acprof:oso/9780195152968.001.0001

Sliwinski, M., Hoffman, L., & Hofer, S. M. (2010). Evaluating convergence of within-person change and between-person age differences in age-heterogeneous longitudinal studies. *Research in Human Development*, *7*(1), 45–60. https://doi.org/10.1080/15427600903578169

Sliwinski, M. J. (2008). Measurement-burst designs for social health research. *Social and Personality Psychology Compass*, *2*(1), 245–261. https://doi.org/10.1111/j.1751-9004.2007.00043.x

Sonnentag, S., Binnewies, C., & Ohly, S. (2012). Event-sampling methods in occupational health psychology. In R. R. Sinclair, M. Wang, & L. E. Tetrick (Eds.), *Research methods in occupational health psychology: Measurement, design, and data analysis* (pp. 208–228). Routledge.

Timmons, A. C., & Preacher, K. J. (2015). The importance of temporal design: How do measurement intervals affect the accuracy and efficiency of parameter estimates in longitudinal research? *Multivariate Behavioral Research*, *50*(1), 41–55. https://doi.org/10.1080/00273171.2014.961056

Tu, X. M., Zhang, J., Kowalski, J., Shults, J., Feng, C., Sun, W., & Tang, W. (2007). Power analyses for longitudinal study designs with missing data. *Statistics in Medicine, 26*(15), 2958–2981. https://doi.org/10.1002/sim.2773

Widaman, K. F., Ferrer, E., & Conger, R. D. (2010). Factorial invariance within longitudinal structural equation models: Measuring the same construct across time. *Child Development Perspectives, 4*(1), 10–18.

Widaman, K. F., & Reise, S. P. (1997). Exploring the measurement invariance of psychological instruments: Applications in the substance use domain. In K. J. Bryant, M. Windle, & S. G. West (Eds.), *The science of prevention: Methodological advances from alcohol and substance abuse research* (pp. 281–324). American Psychological Association. https://doi.org/10.1037/10222-009

Wilson, R. S., Beckett, L. A., Barnes, L. L., Schneider, J. A., Bach, J., Evans, D. A., & Bennett, D. A. (2002). Individual differences in rates of change in cognitive abilities of older persons. *Psychology and Aging, 17*(2), 179–193. https://doi.org/10.1037/0882-7974.17.2.179

Winkens, B., Schouten, H. J. A., van Breukelen, G. J. P., & Berger, M. P. F. (2006). Optimal number of repeated measures and group sizes in clinical trials with linearly divergent treatment effects. *Contemporary Clinical Trials, 27*(1), 57–69. https://doi.org/10.1016/j.cct.2005.09.005

Winter S. D., & Depaoli, S. (2020). An illustration of Bayesian approximate measurement invariance with longitudinal data and a small sample size. *International Journal of Behavioral Development. 44*(4):371–382. https://doi.org/10.1177/0165025419880610

Yang, Y., & Land, K. C. (2013). *Age-period-cohort analysis: New models, methods, and empirical applications.* Chapman and Hall/CRC. https://doi.org/10.1201/b13902

Zhang, Z., & Wang, L. (2009). Statistical power analysis for growth curve models using SAS. *Behavior Research Methods, Instruments, & Computers, 41*(4), 1083–1094. https://doi.org/10.3758/BRM.41.4.1083

CHAPTER 19

USING THE INTERNET TO COLLECT DATA

Ulf-Dietrich Reips

The internet is not one single, monolithic medium. It consists of many services with different functions and needs for input, even more than the medium *telephone* varies between clunky devices made from wood that we sometimes see in old movies,[1] the iPad, smartphones, and Voice-over-Internet Protocol.

Using the internet can mean writing and receiving emails that may be purely text based or rich in media. It can mean to surf using a web browser on a desktop computer, laptop, or smartphone. Driving a car also often automatically means using the internet, as information about the location of the car is sent to satellites and databases connected via the internet. The *internet of things*, one of the next steps in the internet revolution, will connect more and more of the world to the internet. However, this will need to happen in sensible and privacy-protecting ways. The Gartner Group projected in 2009 that by the end of 2012, physical sensors would generate 20% of nonvideo internet traffic: "The extent and diversity of real-time environmental sensing is growing rapidly as our ability to act on and interpret the growing volumes of data to capture valuable information increases" (Plummer et al., 2009). They now write of the importance of

> how these devices are increasing and forming the foundations for smart spaces, and move key applications and services closer to the people and devices that use them. By 2023, there could be more than 20 times as many smart devices at the edge of the network as in conventional IT roles. (Panetta, 2020, "Trend No. 6: The Empowered Edge")

Universal addressability of things and people (sometimes called the *semantic web*[2]) (Berners-Lee et al., 2001; World Wide Web Consortium, 2010) allows internet-based data collection even about people and things that are not connected to the internet. Other agents refer to them by sending their location, images, etc. A case vividly demonstrating this principle is *Google Street View*, which combines location information with panoramic images creating a highly informative and immersive tool to explore the world at a human scale (i.e., with the eyes of a traveler). The future combination of visual location information with the internet of things will create

---

[1]Examine some example images of phones at http://www.sparkmuseum.com/TELEPHONE.HTM and http://www.museumofyesterday.org/museum/page3.htm
[2]From the definition favored by the World Wide Web Consortium you may gather that the semantics of the Semantic Web are not generally agreed upon: "The term 'Semantic Web' refers to W3C's vision of the Web of linked data. Semantic Web technologies enable people to create data stores on the Web, build vocabularies, and write rules for handling data." (World Wide Web Consortium [W3C], 2010)

https://doi.org/10.1037/0000319-019
APA Handbook of Research Methods in Psychology, Second Edition: Vol. 2. Research Designs: Quantitative, Qualitative, Neuropsychological, and Biological, H. Cooper (Editor-in-Chief)

a more and more tightly meshed representation of the world on the internet.

This chapter shows the major steps in collecting data on the internet. The first section, Internet-Based Research, briefly narrates the short history of internet-based data collection methods in psychological research, describes their characteristics, and presents a systematic overview of the four basic types of methods. Some notions about planning internet-based research lead to the second section, Generating a Web Experiment, which describes an example and provides the reader with the opportunity to become active and experience internet-based data collection methods by creating and conducting a web experiment in a step-by-step fashion. The example introduces the important concepts of *client-side* versus *server-side* and illustrates a number of important techniques. The third section, Pretesting, emphasizes the need to take extra care in preparing the materials and procedure, and evaluate their usability. Useful procedures in pretesting internet-based data collection are introduced, and how these prevent methodological problems is explained. In the fourth section, Recruitment, the pros and cons of various ways of attracting participants to internet-based studies are explained, concluding with the use of games as research environments on the internet. Data Analysis explains a number of important issues such as raw data preservation, paradata, inclusion criteria, and technical variance. Furthermore, the section introduces several specific methods, including log file analysis. The concluding section summarizes ethical considerations in internet-based research and looks at future trends and the continuing evolution of internet-based methods and their use in behavioral and social research.

INTERNET-BASED RESEARCH

Data collection methods in internet-based research, despite its short history, naturally depend on its quickly evolving technologies and spread. For example, mobile research, that is, research that depends on mobile phones, has greatly increased in frequency. The present chapter describes characteristics and methods of internet-based research as they persisted and changed over time.

General Issues and History

The first psychological questionnaires on the World Wide Web (WWW) appeared in 1994 following the introduction of interactive form elements in the scripting language, HTML, that underlies the WWW (Musch & Reips, 2000). Krantz et al. (1997) and Reips (1997) conducted the first internet-based experiments in the summer of 1995, and Reips opened the first virtual laboratory for internet-based experiments in September, 1995 (Web Experimental Psychology Lab: https://www. wexlab.eu/[3]). Their results had also been presented at the Society for Computers in Psychology (SCiP) conference in Chicago in 1996 (http://psych. hanover.edu/SCiP/sciprg96.html) (see Smith & Leigh, 1997). Several studies in most areas of internet-based data collection such as surveying, web experimentation, data mining, and social network analysis online, were presented at the German Online Research conference in Cologne in 1997 (http://www.gor.de/gor97/abstracts.htm). The number of studies conducted via the internet has grown exponentially since then (Krantz & Reips, 2017).

To find examples of psychological studies archived or currently in progress on the web, the reader may visit studies linked at the Web Experimental Psychology Lab or at the following web sites:

- Web experiment list (Reips & Lengler, 2005): http://wexlist.net/; and web experiment list 2.0 (Reips & Shevchenko, 2021): https://wexlist. uni-konstanz.de (Figure 19.1)
- Web survey list: http://www.wexlist.net/ browse.cfm?action=browse&modus=survey
- Psychological Research on the Net by John Krantz: http://psych.hanover.edu/research/ exponnet.html

---

[3]Because web addresses (URLs) may change, the reader may use a search engine like Google (http://www.google.com/) to access the web pages mentioned in this chapter if a link does not work. In the present case, typing "web experimental psychology lab" into the search field returns the link to the laboratory as the first result listed after the Wikipedia entry.

The web experiment list - welcome!

An interactive Web-based hotspot and archive for Internet-based experiments and surveys.

Support science, take part in an experiment here. Go to a random current study here.

As a researcher, add your Internet-based experiments and surveys here.

A related publication

Reips, U.-D., & Lengler, R. (2005). The Web Experiment List: A Web site for the recruitment of participants and archiving of Internet-based experiments. Behavior Research Methods, 37, 287-292.

Links

Find the previous version here. http://wexlist.net/

Check out more of our tools: iscience.eu

iscience   We are the iScience group - iscience.uni.kn

FIGURE 19.1.   Front page of the Web Experiment List. From *The Web Experiment List*, by iScience, n.d. (https://wexlist.uni-konstanz.de/). Copyright by iScience. Reprinted with permission.

- Online Social Psychology Studies by Scott Plous: http://www.socialpsychology.org/expts.htm
- Decision Research Center by Michael Birnbaum: http://psych.fullerton.edu/mbirnbaum/decisions/thanks.htm

Types of Internet-Based Research

Generally speaking, there are four types of internet-based data collection: (a) nonreactive internet-based methods, (b) internet-based surveys and interviews, (c) internet-based tests, and (d) internet-based experiments (Reips, 2006).

Nonreactive internet-based methods and *data mining* refer to the use and analysis of existing databases and collections of materials on the internet (e.g., open forum contributions, server log files, tweets, or picture repositories). The internet provides many opportunities for nonreactive data collection. The sheer size of internet corpora multiplies the specific strengths of this type of methods: Nonmanipulable events can be studied as they happen in natural behavior on the internet (navigating, searching, selecting, chatting, reading, timing of these behaviors, etc.), facilitating the examination of rare behavioral patterns or integrating behavioral traces in useful ways (e.g., for television program recommendations [Van Aart

et al., 2009]). Many of these "user behaviors" are stored in server log files or data bases. Thus, log file analysis is an important example of a nonreactive web-based method (Reips & Stieger, 2004).

Nonreactive methods have a long tradition in psychological research (e.g., Fritsche & Linneweber, 2006; Webb et al., 1966), and they were used early on in the internet. In 1996 and 1997 Stegbauer and Rausch (2002) studied the communicative behavior among members of several mailing lists. In this early example of the use of nonreactive data on the internet the authors researched so-called *lurking behavior* (i.e., passive membership in mailing lists, newsgroups, forums, and other social Internet services). They analyzed the number and time of postings and the interaction frequencies pertaining to email headers in contributions (without much need for filtering: it certainly helped that "spam" was a rare phenomenon at the time). Several questions regarding the lurking phenomenon could thus be clarified empirically. For example, about 70% of subscribers to mailing lists could be classified as lurkers, and "among the majority of users, lurking is not a transitional phenomenon but a fixed behavior pattern [within the same social space]" (Stegbauer & Rausch, 2002, p. 267). The behavioral pattern, however, is specific to a mailing list: The analysis of individuals' contributions to different mailing lists showed a sizeable proportion of people may lurk in one forum but are active in another. "With this result, Stegbauer and Rausch empirically supported the notion of so-called 'weak ties' as a basis for the transfer of knowledge between social spaces" (Reips, 2006, p. 74).

The most widely used services on the internet are search engines. With billions of searches performed every day, it is obvious that these searches contain much information about many aspects of human life. A simple measure is *search engine count estimates* that you may have seen as an opener of a slide presentation ("Googling X returns 1.2 million links"). Janetzko (2008) has shown good quality (objectivity, validity, reliability)

for search engine count estimates as estimates of relative importance of searched items. Several search engine providers have recently moved beyond frequencies and subjected their data to higher order algorithms for mining, as the following examples show.

During the writing of the first edition of this handbook the knowledge about then-new search-based prediction services had not been disseminated widely to the population, so it was possible to generate relatively manipulation-free (and, thus, accurate) predictions. For example, Google's Eurovision site (Google Eurovision, 2010) generated a prediction from searches for performers in the yearly Eurovision song contest that correctly predicted the winner in 2009. Figure 19.2 shows

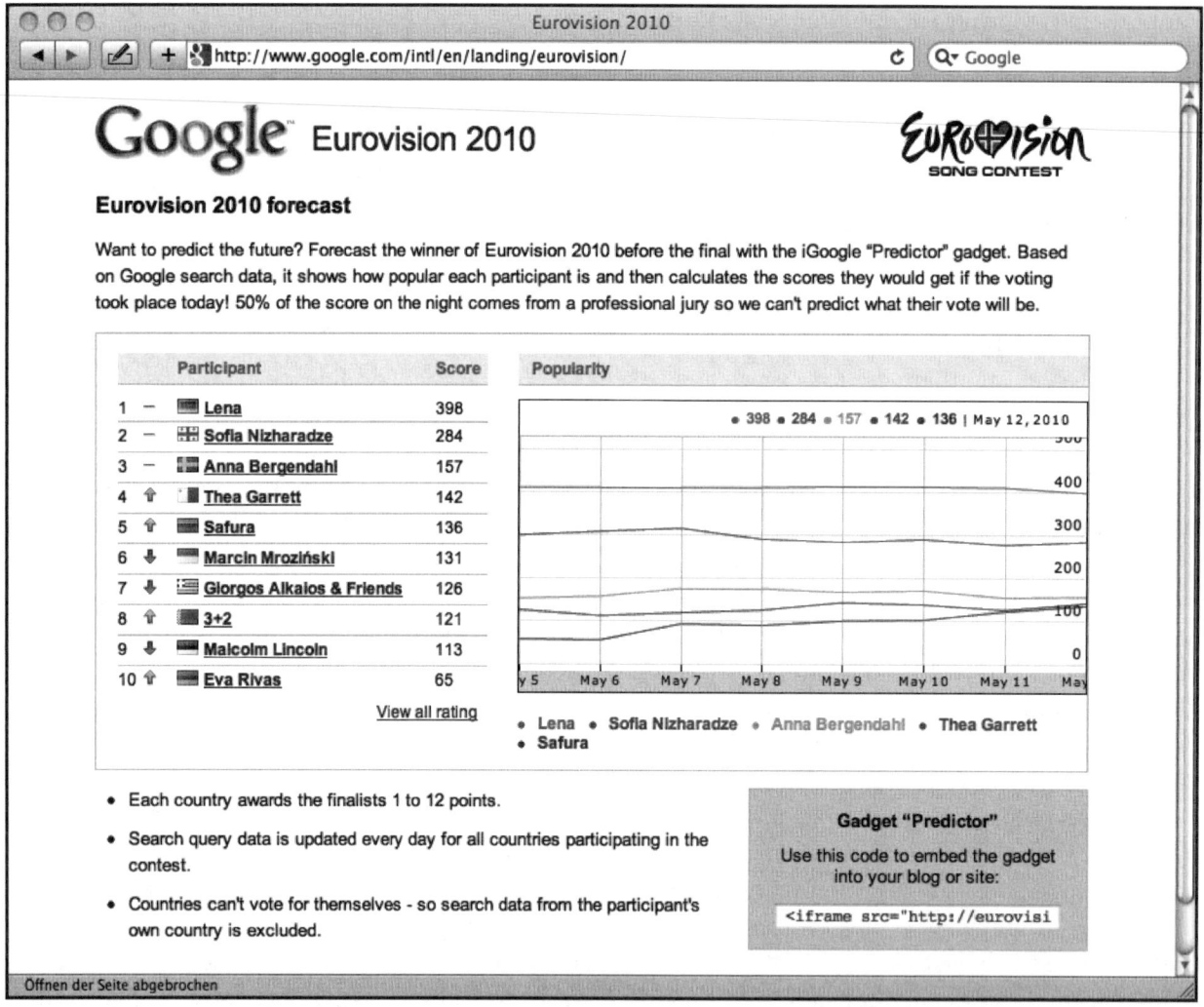

FIGURE 19.2. Using Google Analytics to predict the results of the Eurovision Contest. As in 2009, the prediction correctly identified the winner. Retrieved from http://www.google.com/intl/en/landing/eurovision.

the prediction for the 2010 contest at the time of the writing of this chapter in the first edition on May 12, 2010. Indeed, this prediction was again correct, Lena won. However, once this prediction site became more widely known upon its success (also with the help of the Eurovision song contest site, https://eurovision.tv/story/google-projects-winner-based-on-search-results), thousands of fans, in an apparent attempt to reverse causality, went to the site and tried boosting the search count for their favorite performer. Thus, the predictive power broke down, and in 2011 the Google Eurovision prediction was far off, following Campbell's (1979) statement:

> The more any quantitative social indicator is used for social decision-making, the more subject it will be to corruption pressures and the more apt it will be to distort and corrupt the social processes it is intended to monitor. (p. 85)

Subsequently, Google abandoned the Eurovision prediction tool. A similar fate hit Google's Oscar winner prediction attempts (McGee, 2011), another specific trend prediction site. Google Trends (http://www.google.com/trends) as a general trend prediction site merged with formerly separate Google Insights, both of which have been used to predict a rise in influenza (Ginsberg et al., 2009) and local unemployment rates (Askitas & Zimmermann, 2009). Psychologists working in health care, social services, or advertising may benefit directly from these new intelligent data mining tools. They can get more time for preparing for the events predicted for their area, psychological researchers may use the tools to mine searches for certain terms or combinations of terms, in combination with filters like geolocation or time frame (Reips, 2009b). One freely available tool that was developed for researchers to mine messages sent on the social networking platform Twitter is *iScience Maps* (http://tweetminer.eu). Reips and Garaizar (2011), who developed and published the tool, were able to replicate an older study on personality characteristics associated with first names and discover the frequencies

of first names as a confound that explains the results of the original study. Using *iScience Maps* to conduct the study took only about 2 hours, even though the replication was conducted for both the Western part of the United States and the United Kingdom including Ireland, compared with weeks for the original study, which was conducted in Los Angeles only. Data from websites for psychologists may also be mined to discover megatrends, for example, changes in the topics studied in psychological research (Reips, 2009a; Reips & Lengler, 2005).

Social websites have become valuable sources for social-behavioral research that is based on nonreactive data collection. David Crandall and colleagues from Cornell University (http://www.cs.cornell.edu/~Crandall/) created detailed maps by analyzing the location information of approximately 35 million geo-tagged photos that had previously been uploaded to *flickr*, a website dedicated to photo sharing. The locations of the motifs show the relative interest in places, and because the sea is always an attractive motive, as a result the shapes of continents appeared on the maps (see Barras, 2009; Figure 19.3). This information may lead to applications in tourism, city planning, ecology, and economics. For example, city planners may trace the location maps over long periods and, thus, identify areas to be developed or to be made accessible via public transportation.

The most commonly used internet-based assessment method is the *internet-based survey*. The frequent use of surveys on the internet can be explained by the apparent ease with which web questionnaires can be constructed, conducted, and evaluated. However, web survey methodology is a difficult matter, if one aims at generalizing results from a sample to a particular population. Work by Dillman and his group (Dillman & Bowker, 2001; Dillman et al., 2008; Smyth et al., 2006), among others, has shown that many web surveys are plagued by problems of usability, display, coverage, sampling, nonresponse, or technology. Decisions already made at the invitation stage may influence results (e.g., Selkälä et al., 2021). Joinson and Reips (2007) have shown through experiments that the degree of

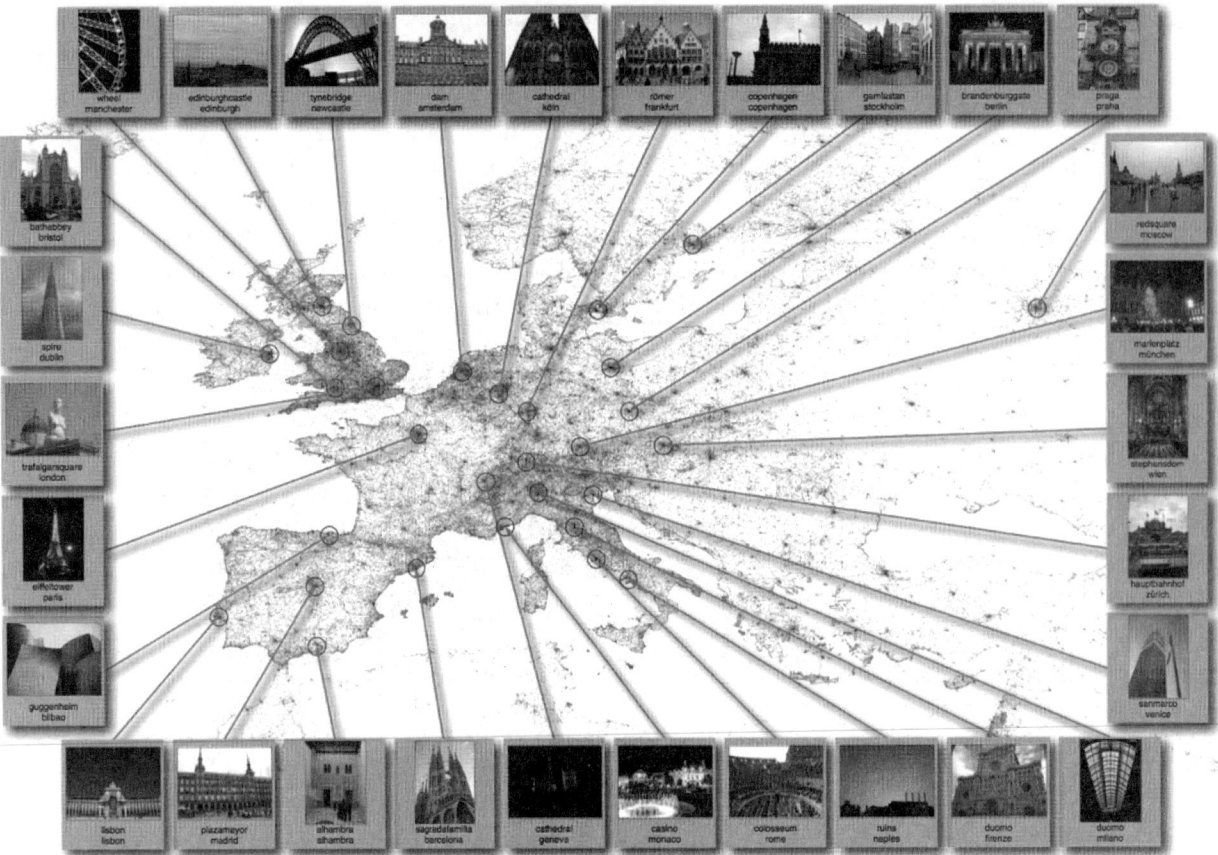

FIGURE 19.3. Map of Europe generated from information embedded in Flickr photographs. From "Gallery: Flickr Users Make Accidental Maps," by G. Barras, April 27, 2009, *New Scientist* (https://www.newscientist. com/article/dn17017-galleryflickr-user-tracesmake-accidental-maps.html). Image created by David Crandall. Reprinted with permission.

personalization and the power attributable to the sender of an invitation to participate in the survey can have an impact on survey response rates. Data quality can be influenced by degree of anonymity, and this factor as well as information about incentives also can influence the frequency of dropout (Frick et al., 2001). The impression of anonymity on the internet is particularly helpful in the investigation of sensitive topics. For example, already in 1997, Coomber used web surveys to conduct research with drug dealers. Mangan and Reips (2007) described two web surveys on the sensitive and rare condition sexsomnia that reached more than 5 times as many participants from the target population than all nine previous studies from 20 years of research combined.

Design factors like the decision whether a "one item, one screen" procedure is applied or not may trigger context effects that turn results upside down (Reips, 2002a, 2010). Any aspect of a web survey that may annoy participants, such as forcing a response, will likely create psychological reactance (Brehm, 1966) and subsequently lead to an increase in random answering behavior, nonresponse, and possibly even dropout (Stieger et al., 2007). Despite these findings, converging evidence shows that web-based survey methods result in qualitatively comparable results to traditional surveys, even in longitudinal studies (Hiskey & Troop, 2002). Recently, mobile experience sampling methodology as one particular type of longitudinal research has been flourishing due to the proliferation of smartphones (Shevchenko & Reips, 2022) and survey researchers have begun to explore options of mixed-mode surveys (e.g., De Leeuw, 2005, and the meta analysis by

Shih & Fan, 2007). Very good sources for research and advice on web surveying are the web survey methodology website at http://websm.org and Callegaro et al. (2015).

Web-based psychological testing constitutes one specific subtype of web surveying (Reips, 2021) that involves psychometric measurement. Buchanan and Smith (1999), Buchanan (2001, 2007), Preckel and Thiemann (2003), and Wilhelm and McKnight (2002), among others, have shown that web-based testing is possible if the particularities of the internet situation are considered (e.g., computer anxiety may keep certain people from responding to a web-based questionnaire), and tests are used that were validated for use on the internet. Buchanan and Smith found that an internet-based, self-monitoring test not only showed similar psychometric properties to its conventional equivalent but compared favorably as a measure of self-monitoring. Similarly, Buchanan et al. (2005) modified an International Personality Item Pool (http://ipip.ori.org/) inventory. In their evaluation, it showed to have satisfactory psychometric properties as a brief online measure of the domain constructs of the five-factor model. Across two studies using different recruitment techniques, they observed acceptable levels of internal reliability and significant correlations with relevant criterion variables. Psychometric equivalence of paper-and-pencil versions of questionnaires with their web-based counterparts is not always the case, however. For instance, Buchanan et al. (2005) could only recover two of four factor-analytically derived subscales of the Prospective Memory Questionnaire with a sample of $N = 763$ tested via the internet. Buchanan and Reips (2001) showed that technical aspects of how the web-based test is implemented may interact with demography or personality and, consequently, introduce a sampling bias. In their study, they showed that the average education level was higher in web-based assessment if no JavaScript was used to code survey and website, and that Mac users scored significantly higher on the personality dimension "openness to experience" (appreciation for art, adventure, curiosity, emotion, unusual ideas, and variety of experience)

than PC users. Götz et al. (2017) showed that personality differences also exist for users of different types of smartphones, but they seem to be smaller than the differences for desktop and laptop computers that Buchanan and Reips found in their 2001 study.

Via the iScience server at http://iscience.eu, the author of this chapter offers use of the five-factor personality test ("Big 5 Personality Test") for use on the internet. Researchers may simply append the test to their own study by redirecting participants to a study-specific URL. The English and German versions of the test were previously validated for use on the internet by Buchanan et al. (2005) and Hartig et al. (2003). Validation of the version in Spanish is under way.

Web experiments show several basic differences from experiments conducted in the laboratory or in the field (e.g., Honing & Reips, 2008; Reips, 2000, 2002d; Reips et al., 2015; Reips & Krantz, 2010). However, the underlying logic is the same as that in the other experimental methods. Hence, the definition of *experiment* used here requires manipulation of the independent variable(s), repeatability, and random assignment to conditions. Likewise, a web quasi-experiment would involve nonrandom assignment of subjects to conditions (see Campbell & Stanley, 1963; Kirk, 1995). Birnbaum (2007) further discussed representative and systextual experiment designs.

Web experiments offer a chance to validate findings that were acquired using laboratory experiments and field experiments. The number of participants is notoriously small in many traditional studies because researchers set the Type I error probability to a conventional level (and, therefore, the power of these studies is low; Faul et al., 2009). One of the greatest advantages in web research is the ease with which large numbers of participants can be reached. The Web Experimental Psychology Lab, for instance, was visited by several thousand people per month (Reips, 2001, 2007) and web experimenters still report ease of recruitment as a chief advantage of internet-based experimenting (Krantz & Reips, 2017). On the internet the participants may leave at any time, and the experimental situation is usually free of the subjective pressure to stay often inherent in experiments conducted for course credit with students. Because web experiments are often visible on the internet and remain there as a documentation of the research method and material, overall transparency of the research process is increased.

Planning an Internet-Based Study

In planning an internet-based study, many of the topics covered in this handbook are important. For example, regarding the measurement of psychological constructs (Part III in Volume 1, this handbook) on the internet, we need to consider measurement scales, behavior observation (Volume 1, Chapter 13, this handbook), and use of computers (Volume 1, Chapter 17, this handbook). Regarding psychological tests we need to consider the various subtypes of tests (Volume 1, Chapters 18–20, this handbook) and brief instruments and short forms (Volume 1, Chapter 21, this handbook).

In the following section, I focus on planning and generating a web experiment, but many of the issues apply to all types of internet-based data collection.

GENERATING A WEB EXPERIMENT

Creating a web-based study requires knowledge about methodology and technology, as well as practical routines. In the present chapter, I summarize important techniques and show by example how experiment generator software supports creating a web-based study.

Important Techniques

For anyone using the internet for research purposes, they should know that there is a growing body of research on methods and techniques ("tricks") (e.g., Reips, 2002d, 2007, 2009a; Reips et al., 2015) and the impact of design features of web-based studies. For example, when choosing a response format for questions one has many options, some of which are not available in paper-and-pencil format (Reips, 2002a, 2010). Figure 19.4 shows a slider scale, a radio

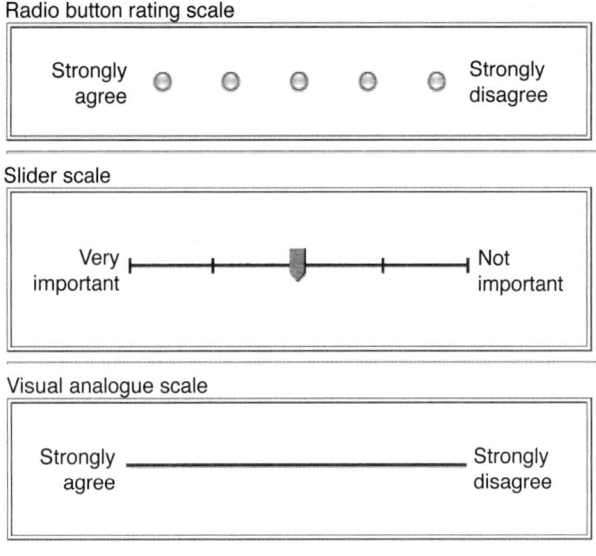

FIGURE 19.4. From top to bottom: A radio button scale, a slider scale, and a visual analogue scale.

button scale, and a visual analogue scale. Funke et al. (2011) found slider scales to lead to significantly higher break-off rates than radio button scales (odds ratio 6.9) and to substantially higher response times. Problems with slider scales were especially prevalent for participants with less than average education, suggesting the slider scale format is more challenging in terms of previous knowledge needed or cognitive load. The finding resonates well with the general principle that low-tech solutions are to be preferred for the design of web-based data collection (Buchanan & Reips, 2001; Reips, 2007, 2010).

Reips (2002c) proposed 16 standards or guidelines that may help researchers and reviewers of manuscripts that are based on internet-mediated research. While a number of standards define choices and procedures that we discuss later in this chapter, the proposed standards that refer to techniques are now explained.

Standard 5. Link your study to multiple sites. Consider linking your web study to several internet sites and services (multiple site entry technique) to determine effects of self-selection or sampling and estimate generalizability. The multiple-site entry technique is implemented by identifying each source for participants by using a slightly modified link, for example,

- "https://wextor.eu:8080/yourname/yourstudy/ index.html?so=clinic1ar." For patients from Clinic 1; two random characters are added after the "1" so as to not allow anyone to change the URL to a real existing link like ". . . clinic2".
- "https://wextor.eu:8080/yourname/yourstudy/ index.html?so=clinic2gi." For patients from Clinic 2.
- "https://wextor.eu:8080/yourname/yourstudy/ index.html?so=psstudents." For psychology students.
- "https://wextor.eu:8080/yourname/yourstudy/ index.html?so=frfam." For friends and family.
- "https://wextor.eu:8080/yourname/yourstudy/ index.html?so=onr." A forum for online researchers.

The resulting data table contains a column named "so" containing the values "clinic1ar," "clinic2gi," "frfam," "onr," and so on, so analyses can be done by source. Following Standard 5, thus, usually results in a win–win situation: either the results are replicated for all sources and samples, therefore strengthening the argument that both do not play a role in obtaining these specific results, or, some sources and samples may deviate systematically (maybe even theoretically predictable) from the rest—opening up interesting investigations into the reasons for the deviation.

Standards 7 to 9. Possible strategies to deal with dropout.   If dropout is to be avoided, Standard 7 suggests the use of a *warm-up technique*, that is, the actual experimental manipulation only happens several pages deep into the material, after the typical initial spike in dropout, so a high compliance is already established. Any dropout or other nonresponse behavior occurring before the experimental manipulation cannot be attributed to the manipulation. Thus, the results are immune to dropout-related criticisms. For example, in a web experiment on list context effects by Reips et al. (reported in Reips, 2002c, 2003b), the target category number was experimentally manipulated in a categorizing task only after 31 other items had been categorized to the nonmanipulated categories "flower," "female," and "vegetable," resulting in a dropout of only about 2%. Usually,

dropout rates are at about 35% in web experiments (Musch & Reips, 2000).

Standard 8 says to use dropout to determine whether there is *motivational confounding*, that is, the confounding of the motivation to continue participating in the experiment with levels of the independent variable(s). For example, in the case of one experimental condition being more boring than another, a difference in results from the two conditions could simply come from the difference in "boringness" (Reips, 2007).

Standard 9 suggests the use of the *high-hurdle technique*, *incentive information*, and *requests for personal information* to influence time and degree of dropout. The high-hurdle technique seeks to provoke an early drop in participants who likely would have dropped later during a study (Reips, 1997, 2000; but see discussion between Frauendorfer & Reips, 2009, and Göritz & Stieger, 2008). Incentive information is known to have an influence on response rates and dropout (Frick et al., 2001; Göritz, 2006; Musch & Reips, 2000) such that a small amount of money or a chance to win a raffle in the sense of a token of appreciation seems to be the optimal strategy. Requests for personal information at the beginning of a study were shown to increase compliance with study instructions, including a reduction in dropout and other nonresponse (Frick et al., 2001). This is in line with Standard 10.

Standard 10. Ask filter questions (e.g., seriousness of participation, expert status, language skills) at the beginning of the experiment to encourage serious and complete responses.   The "seriousness check" (Aust et al., 2013; Reips, 2000) has become one of the most successful techniques in increasing the quality of data in internet-based data collection. A simple, albeit very effective strategy: Participants are asked at the very beginning of the study whether they "are intending to seriously participate now" or whether they "just want to take a look." Including only the data of those who chose the first option dramatically improves the quality of data. For example, Reips (2005) repeatedly found dropout rates to differ markedly between serious (about 15% dropout) and other (about 75% dropout) participants. Aust et al. (2013) found that restricting analyses to serious participants allowed a more valid forecast of election results. Moreover, serious participants answered attitudinal questions in a more consistent manner than other participants.

Standard 11. Check for obvious naming of files, conditions, and, if applicable, passwords. During the process of creating a study, many researchers tend to use names for files and folders that help them remember the meaning of conditions and files or sequences of screens. However, these names are visible to participants via the browser's location window. Consider for example an URL like "http://somesite.edu/psych/survey3/controlcond/page4.html." Participants here would be able to jump pages by exchanging the 4 in "page4" for a different number, similarly they could investigate previous surveys by changing "survey3." From "controlcond" they would think they were sent to the control condition, etc. (Reips, 2002b). Using web services for scientists that were constructed with these issues in mind (e.g., WEXTOR.eu) will support the scientist in avoiding such frequent errors, for example, by mixing logical with random sequences of characters.

Standard 12. Consider avoiding multiple submissions by exclusively using participant pools and password techniques. Multiple submissions are a rare phenomenon—who would like to fill in a questionnaire repeatedly after all? Internet scientists observed that repeated submissions mostly happen right after the first submission (Birnbaum, 2000; Reips & Birnbaum, 2011). However, to make sure that each participant joins the study only one time, one can send out emails to a predefined list of participants. Each of the emails contains a unique URL to the study that works only a single time. Furthermore, by building and maintaining a participant pool (or "online panel," Göritz, 2007) for recurring participation requests to the same pool of people, one exerts a higher degree of control of participation than in open recruitment on the Internet.

Standard 13. Perform consistency checks. For example, items with slightly different wording but identical meaning should be answered in the same way, and participants claiming to have a high educational degree should be of a certain age.

Meta tagging. Meta tags are information snippets in the headers of web pages that inform web browsers, caches, and proxy servers about various issues related to the page. Exhibit 19.1, for example shows several meta tags suitable for pages following the entry page in internet-based research studies. The *robot* tag tells search engines not to process the content of the page, so no participant can enter the study via this page. The *pragma* tag tells caches and proxy servers not to save the content (so no outdated content is served). The *expires* tag tells caches and proxy servers to consider the content expired (the date lies in the past); thus, it is not stored.

Client versus server. Reactive data collection techniques on the internet can be categorized into server-side and client-side processing (Schmidt, 2000, 2007).

Server-side processing means that all necessary computing is done at the researcher's web server, including receiving and sending hypertext transfer protocol (HTTP) requests (communication with participant computers), recording and computing of data, communication with a database application, writing logs, and dynamic selecting and creating materials that may depend on a user's input. Because dynamic procedures are performed on the server, server-side processing is less subject to platform dependent issues. Sometimes,

---

EXHIBIT 19.1

Use of Meta Tags for Internet-Based Research Studies in Pages Following the Entry Page

---

```
<HTML>
<HEAD>
<meta name="author" content="Experimenter">
<meta name="robots" content="none">
<meta http-equiv="pragma" content="no-cache">
<meta http-equiv="expires" content="Thursday, 1-Jan-1991
    01:01:01 GMT">
<TITLE></TITLE>
</HEAD>
(insert the body of the Web page here)
```

---

however, the server may resemble a bottleneck, causing delays.

Client-side methods distribute most tasks to the processing power of the participants' computers. Therefore, time measurements do not contain error from network traffic and problems with server delays are less likely. Client-side processing relies on the participants' computer configurations, however, and, therefore, is subject to issues of technical variance (Schmidt, 2007). Although there are potential security issues with client-side processing (Amoroso, 2020), they would generally only slightly affect study results, because of the decentralized character of client-side processing. Server-side and client-side processing methods can be combined, and they can be used to estimate technical error variance by comparison of measurements.

Experiment generators: The example of WEXTOR. Several experiment generators and study builders for the internet have come and gone (e.g., ibex farm, https://spellout.net/ibexfarm/; lab.js, Henninger et al., 2022; Tatool, von Bastian et al., 2013). One of the longest standing, WEXTOR (available at https://wextor.eu), was developed by Reips and Neuhaus (2002) and recently upgraded to version 2022, which features responsive design (automatic optimal adaptation to the devices used, e.g., touch devices). It is a web-based tool that can be used to design laboratory and web experiments in a guided step-by-step process. It dynamically creates the customized web pages and JavaScript needed for the experimental procedure and provides experimenters with a print-ready visual display of their experimental design and code plan. WEXTOR flexibly supports complete and incomplete factorial designs with between-subjects, within-subjects, and quasi-experimental factors as well as mixed designs. It implements server- and client-side response time measurement and includes a content wizard for creating interactive materials, as well as dependent measures (e.g., Likert-type scales, visual analog scales, multiple-choice items) on the experiment pages.

Many of the methodological solutions discussed in this chapter were built into WEXTOR.

As a web service, WEXTOR can be used to design and manage experiments from anywhere on the internet using a login/password combination. For support, there are tutorials, a frequently asked questions page, and feedback and bug report forms. Figure 19.5 shows a version of WEXTOR's entry page. The reader is encouraged to download the step-by-step-tutorial available from http://wextor.eu/wextor_docs/WEXTOR_tutorial.pdf and recreate a web experiment as explained.

The process of creating an experimental design and procedure as a self-contained folder of all materials and scripts for an experiment with WEXTOR involves 10 steps. An experimenter logs on to WEXTOR and clicks on the link to "Create/modify an experimental design," then enters number and names of within- and between-subjects and quasi-experimental factors and their levels. The experimenter then specifies the number of web pages (screens) and adds information about the type of design (e.g., complete or incomplete), the assignment to conditions, counterbalancing, and so on. Text, stimuli (for a discussion of stimulus delivery, see Krantz, 2001), and measures of various kinds can be added, including visual analogue scales that were shown to produce better measurements than radio button scales (Funke & Reips, 2012; Reips & Funke, 2008). Any object can be integrated with the experimental materials, including, for example, images or video content (for more information on using media in internet-based research, see Krantz & Williams, 2010).

WEXTOR produces an organized visual and textual representation of the experimental design and the web pages and associated JavaScript and cascading style sheet files required to implement that design. Furthermore, a code plan is generated. In the final step, one can then download the experimental materials in a compressed archive that contains all directories (folders), scripts, and Web pages. Among true experiment builders, with this material structure WEXTOR is the only one that provides an intuitive one-to-one correspondence of the screens visible to the participants as files and folders.

FIGURE 19.5. WEXTOR at https://wextor.eu is a web service to generate and host experiments that can be conducted in the lab and/or on the internet.

After decompressing the archive, the resulting web pages created in WEXTOR can be viewed and tested for their functionality, even when not connected to the internet. After further optional editing in a hypertext markup language (HTML) editor, the whole folder with all experimental materials can be uploaded onto the WEXTOR server or to a personal web server. Then the experiment is ready to go.

Many techniques for internet-based experimenting mentioned in this chapter were built into WEXTOR to automatically avoid common errors found in internet-based data collection. Among these techniques are meta tags, the seriousness check technique, the multiple-site entry technique, and the high-hurdle technique (see the section Important Techniques). Flexible timing out of individual pages and soft form validation can be applied to the web pages. Skins are available to flexibly change the appearance of all web pages in the entire experiment at once. Figure 19.6 shows options for the implementation of the high-hurdle technique (Reips, 2000, 2002c), response time measurement, session identification, and form validation in Step 9 in WEXTOR.

For experiments hosted at the WEXTOR website, data preparation can optionally be done on the server, so that data can then be downloaded and opened in spreadsheet programs like Excel or SPSS. The downloaded data file contains a column showing the path taken by each participant (e.g., to see use of the back button) and both server-side and client-side measurements of response time for each page that was accessed.

PRETESTING

Pretesting for an internet-based study involves gathering information about several aspects that combine to make the study materials accessible and understandable to participants, for example, the usability of the websites involved.

Steps and Procedures

It is best to follow several steps during a pretest phase. First, test your study offline on your own computer and read the form entries in the location window. Second, test the study online and remember to mark the entries or record the time

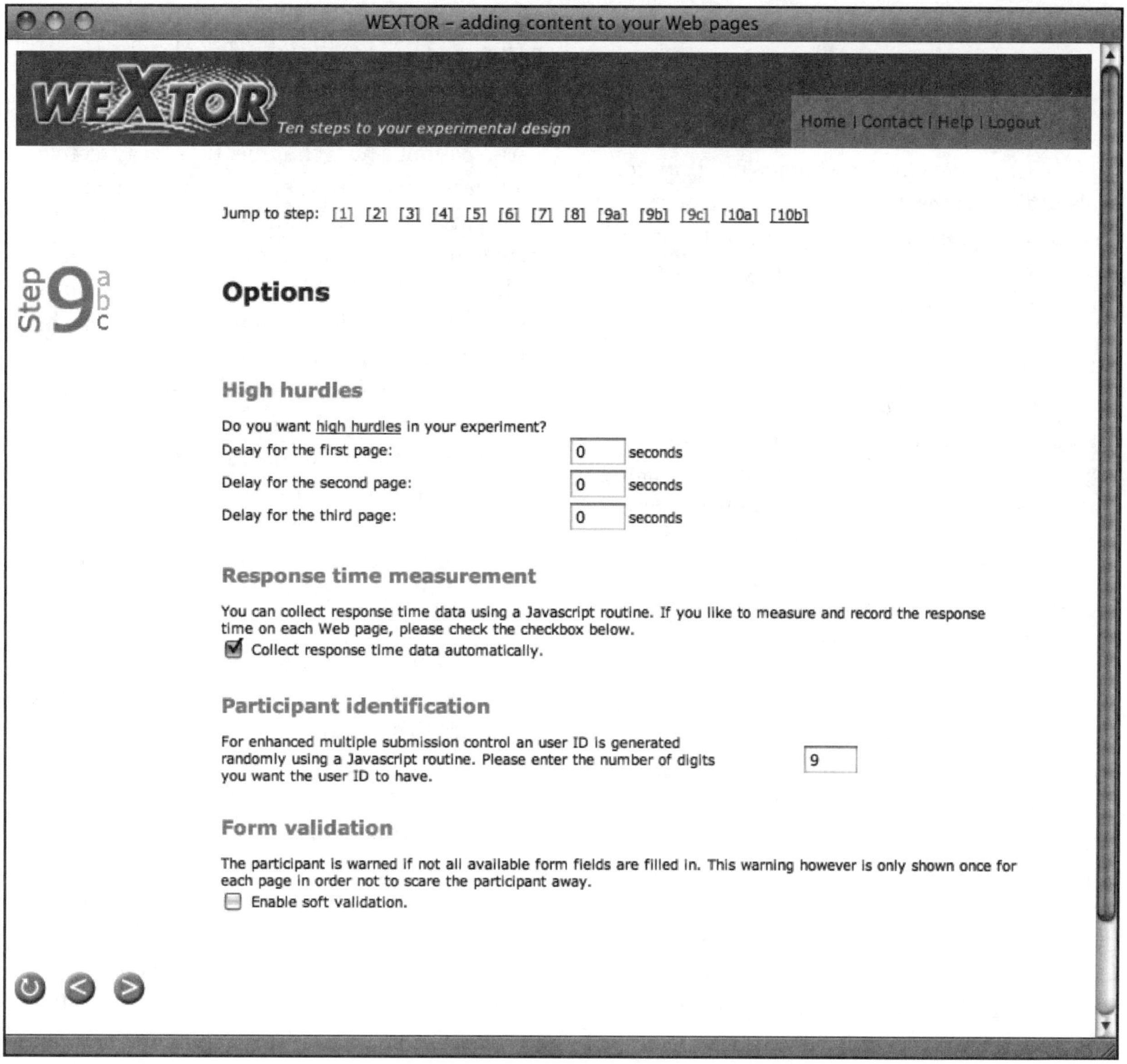

FIGURE 19.6. Step 9c in WEXTOR, showing implementation of the high hurdle, double collection of response times, session ID, and soft validation.

for later exclusion of test data. Third, ask a few colleagues and friends to test the study, and possibly observe some of them to see where they seem to have problems or get stuck. A good procedure is to ask participants to think aloud (speak out what they are thinking, while they are thinking), which often reveals the worst usability problems.

In studies that require a particular sample (e.g., children, participants not native in English), pretest a few people from the target population. Finally, check comments and data after the first two dozen or so participants (do not recruit several hundred or more testers at once).

Preventing Methodological Problems

To prevent running into methodological problems, ask experts for advice (e.g., see the website of the Society for Computation in Psychology, https://computationinpsych.com). Internet-savvy colleagues may help detect technical issues, and those trained in internet-based research may be able to give advice on designs and procedures.

RECRUITMENT

In this section, I describe ways of finding and contacting participants for internet-based research, such as *portals and lists* on the web, *mailing lists, forums, and newsgroups, participant pools and online panels, search engines and banners,* and *job and recruitment markets,* I discuss their pros and cons and offline recruitment as well as gaming as alternatives.

Portals and Lists

Portals and list sites such as the web experiment list and others mentioned in this chapter are a good way to recruit people who are interested in taking part in research. These sites are accurately referred to by many other places on the web as research sites that welcome participants. Over time, they have gained a stable reputation and are used and recommended by many universities around the world.

Mailing Lists, Forums, and Newsgroups

One very effective way of recruiting participants are emails to mailing lists, newsgroups, and forums (newsgroups were popular in the early internet, forums are more of a recent development) of people who, in principle, are open to receiving invitations to participate in studies. Of course, this depends on a number of factors, for example whether the study is related to the topic or membership/clientele of the mailing list, newsgroup, or forum, or whether the invitation is endorsed by the moderator. At a conference he attended, Reips (2003a) heard an interesting paper on the first day of the conference and decided to replicate that study overnight. Within 8 hours, complete data sets from 162 participants (compared with 64 in the original study) were recorded in the web experiment, most of whom were recruited via three mailing lists of which he is a member. He included the results in his talk on the second day of the conference, in order to demonstrate how efficient internet-based data collection can be.

Participant Pools and Online Panels

A recruitment option for institutions and for researchers who want to follow a long-term strategy in managing one's participants is the participant pool technique. People who sign up for this pool provide the web experimenter with their demographic data and can be paid for participation. The technique, thus, is attractive for researchers who want to know much about their participants, including who participated in which web experiments. Consequently, the technique allows for drawing stratified samples (Reips, 2000). Following a naming tradition in survey research, participant pools are in much of the literature on online research now called *online panels*—unfortunately suggesting to reviewers that the participants in the research at hand may have been a small group of experts discussing an issue in a small group meeting. Göritz has published extensively on online panels (Göritz, 2007, 2009; Göritz et al., 2002).

Search Engines and Banners

Search engines may be used to recruit participants to studies that remain on the internet for lengthy periods of time, for example, when testing an item pool for the development of a new test, or for the recruitment of people who are interested in a particular phenomenon. Exhibit 19.2 shows how meta tags can be used to inform search engines, in this case, the study entrance page (and it should be only that one—as the researcher does not want to have participants enter a study later).

EXHIBIT 19.2

Use of Meta Tags to Recruit via Search Engine

```
<HTML>
<HEAD>
<META NAME="keywords" CONTENT="micronations,ruler,
   survey,head of state,psychology,research,">
<META NAME="description" CONTENT="research psychologists
   invite rulers of micronations to complete a survey of
   experiences that we hope will contribute to understanding
   the needs of micronations">
<TITLE>Survey of Rulers of Micronations</TITLE>
</HEAD>
(Further information on the study and a link to the study would
   be placed here)
</BODY>
</HTML>
```

In the example, the study appears high in searches for "micronations" associated with terms like *ruler*, *survey*, *head of state*, *psychology*, and *research*.

The meta tag <META NAME="description" CONTENT=""> informs searches that "research psychologists invite rulers of micronations to complete a survey of experiences that we hope will contribute to understanding the needs of micronations," so this very particular audience, but not many others, will receive an invitation by search.

A supplementary option to guide search engines for proper handling of web-based studies is the Sitemaps protocol that was introduced by Google in 2005 (Sitemaps, 2010). Like the robots.txt file, it allows a webmaster to inform search engines about URLs on a website that are available for crawling. Improving on the robots.txt file, Sitemap allows for the inclusion of additional information about each URL: last update, frequency of changes, and relative importance to other URLs in the site. This information allows search engines to crawl the site more intelligently. According to Sitemaps, "Sitemaps are particularly beneficial on websites where . . . some areas of the website are not available through the browsable interface, or webmasters use rich Ajax, Silverlight, or Flash content that is not normally processed by search engines" (Sitemaps, 2010).

Sitemaps containing all accessible URLs on a site can be submitted to search engines. Because the major search engines use the same protocol, having a Sitemap would let these search engines have the updated pages and links information. However, the Sitemaps protocol does not guarantee that web pages will be included in search indexes.

Banners ads were shown to generate only few responses despite their cost and, thus, this method is not recommended (Tuten et al., 2000). Furthermore, any recruitment that takes the form of commercial ads may throw a negative light on the research, even on research in general.

Offline Recruitment

One way to recruit participants for internet-based data collection is often overlooked: traditional media and other offline routes. Simply handing out flyers or printing a study URL in documents accessed by potential participants from the desired population can be very successful. The case of the BBC internet study (Reimers, 2007) illustrated just how successful recruitment via mostly traditional media like radio and television can be in terms of large numbers: Reimers and the BBC collected data from around 255,000 participants.

Other Sources and Techniques in Recruitment

To assess internet users' privacy concerns Paine et al. (2007) used a Dynamic Interviewing Programme (Stieger & Reips, 2008) to survey users of an instant messaging client (ICQ, "I seek you") using both closed- and open-question formats. Even though their final analysis was based on data from only 530 respondents, the Dynamic Interviewing Programme automatically contacted 79,707 ICQ users who indicated in the instant messaging service that they were open to being contacted.

Participant recruitment has also been placed on markets. Amazon's Mechanical Turk (https://www.mturk.com/) is a large job market that equally values and shows job seekers and job openings. Because the jobs can be very small and short in scale, the site seems an ideal place to recruit participants and have the payment arranged via Amazon's well-established and trusted services. However, results from a study by Reips et al. (2011) showed that participants recruited via Mechanical Turk provide lower quality data than participants from traditional sources for internet-based data collection: for example, shorter and less variable response times per item (which one would expect to vary widely, if participants think about the items) and more responses to the middle of scales in 50 out of 64 items. At the root of these findings may be that "Mturkers" sign up as workers. Workers respond to be paid, whereas other research participants respond to help with research. A second reason why Mturkers provide lower-quality data may be tied to the forums they have established where jobs are discussed, including online studies. It may well be that rumors and experiences shared in these forums lead to a decrease in data quality.

A third reason is artificial Mturkers that have appeared on the site; these are computer scripts or "bots," not humans (Dreyfuss, 2018), ironically replacing the "hidden humans" in the machine by machines (Reips, 2021).

After initial widespread enthusiasm about Amazon's Mechanical Turk among researchers, the site and its concept subsequently has received much criticism. Stewart et al. (2015) calculated that with more and more laboratories in the behavioral sciences moving to MTurk, the total size of the actual participant pool for all studies approaches just 7,300 people rather than the hundreds of thousands in the past. Anderson et al. (2019) showed for social and personality psychology as an example how dominant recruitment via MTurk became just within a few years.

Game Scenarios

Many potential participants of research studies are more easily recruited if they believe that participating will be fun. Consequently, a way to create internet-based research is to use game scenarios as covers or design feature. The iScience server at http://iscience.eu has one link to a web service named "idex" on it. Researchers and students can create their own Stroop-like web experiments, then invite participants, and later download the data from the site (Figure 19.7).

DATA ANALYSIS

Scientific investigation relies on the principle of preserving raw data. Raw data need to be saved for investigations by other researchers from the community (American Psychological Association, 2020), for example, to aid in deeper understanding of the research, in reanalysis or meta-analysis. This principle applies to internet-based data collection as well. Raw data in internet-based data collection can be results from searches, server log files, or whole data bases (Reips, 2007; Reips & Stieger, 2004).

It may be difficult to retain raw data if data collection or parts thereof are delegated to web services, especially those that may not allow easy download of all data. Figure 19.8 shows *Google Analytics*, a very useful free service for collecting, analyzing, and visualizing statistics about visitors to web sites. However, collecting data with Google Analytics may be difficult, because Google follows a strategy that requires the owner of a Google Analytics account to login frequently to view and save the data.

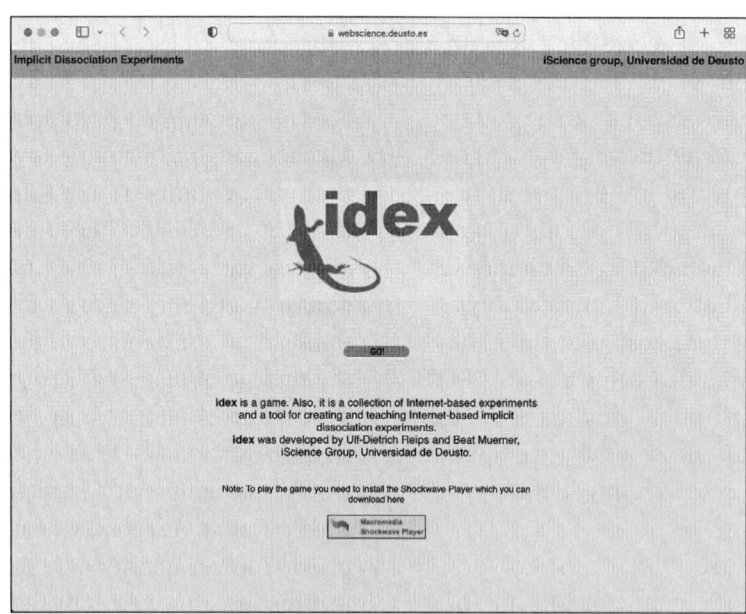

FIGURE 19.7. **An example of using the web to create experiments, invite participants, and download data. From idex (https://webscience.deusto.es/idex/). Reprinted with permission.**

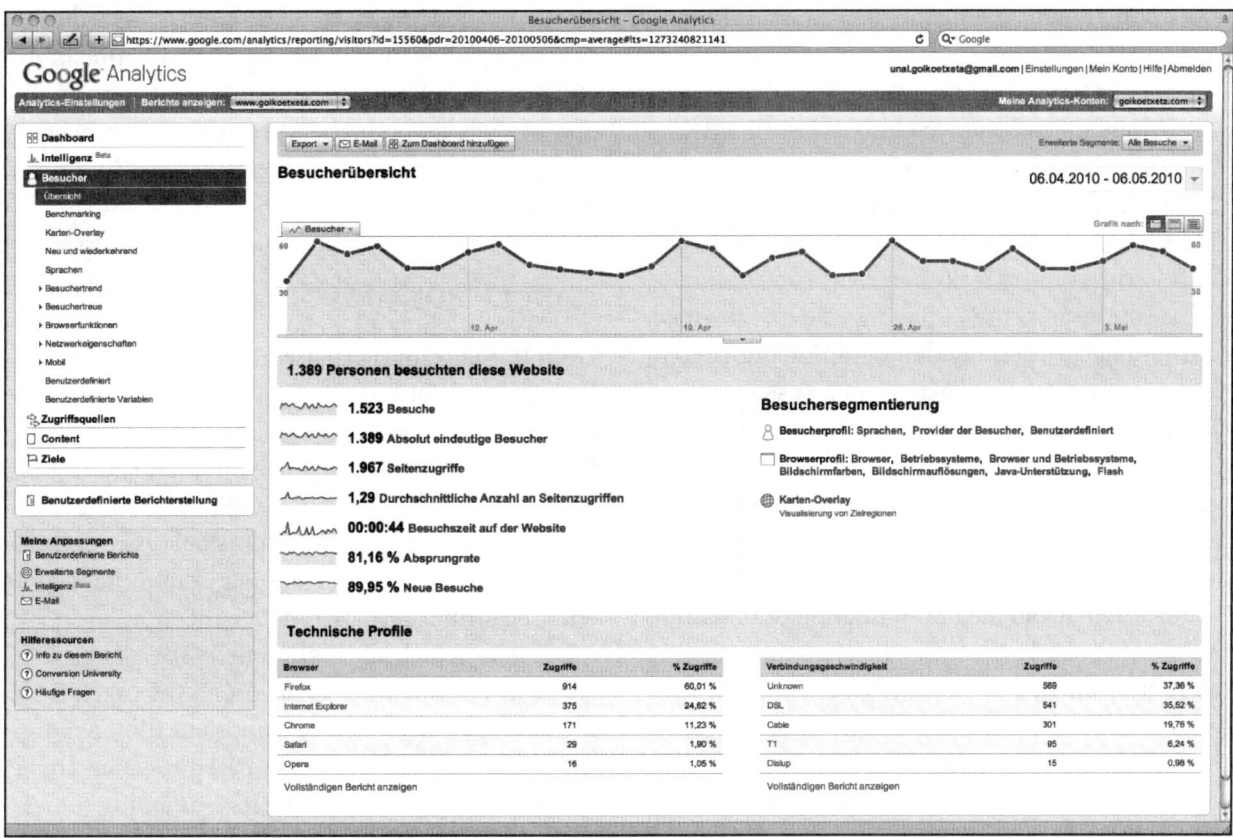

FIGURE 19.8. Google Analytics freely collects, analyzes, and visualizes statistics about visitors to websites. Retrieved from Google Analytics (https://www.google.com/analytics/reporting/visitors).

Paradata

Stieger and Reips (2010) developed a tool, the *UserActionTracer*, that allows the recording and later reconstruction of paradata, such as timing, clicks, scrolling, and so on, as a reconstructed video sequence. They applied *UserActionTracer* to a large web sample ($N = 1,046$) in an online questionnaire of average length and found that 10.5% of participants showed more than five single behaviors (out of 132 theoretically possible) that have a clearly negative impact on data quality.

Despite claims that web-based study builders show "excellent timing performance across systems" (Henninger et al., 2022), response time is likely one of the few issues where measurement is actually increasingly unreliable and difficult to achieve. Garaizar and Reips (2019) showed that today's complicated multilayer technology and highly frequent updating of many browsers fulfill high-resolution timing requirements less and less, compared to the early days of internet-based research. At the root of this problem are diverging interests of browser vendors (speed, sales, versatility) versus scientists (validity, objectivity, precision, accuracy).

Inclusion Criteria

Data collected on the internet in their raw form usually contain a number of entries that resemble "noise" and are not to be included in data analysis, for example, accesses from automatic scripts that are used by search engines to assess the content of web pages. Also, because participants on the web exert much more freedom to withdraw their participation, criteria should be preset in each internet-based data-collection effort as to which entries are to be included and which not. For example, a preset inclusion criterion may be that at least half of all items in a questionnaire have to be answered. The following is a typical

425

series of inclusion–exclusion steps in an internet-based study.

The number of hits is taken of the very first page. Then, all cases are excluded that ended here, that is, no further pages were accessed.[4] This exclusion step may also be defined with a different threshold, for example, the first major point in the study was not reached. Such major points can be agreeing to having read an informed consent page, providing demographic information (e.g., so a minimum age can be assumed), distributing to experimental conditions, displaying the instructions, and so on. Next, only those participants are included who answered positively to the seriousness check (possibly also excluding those who did not respond at all to the check). Exclusions to avoid data from multiple submissions can conservatively be determined on the basis of internet protocol (IP) numbers, even though two or more different participants may be assigned the same number by a large provider. Further criteria for inclusion or exclusion may include the following: whether the browser back button was used, whether a certain proportion of items was answered, whether particularly important items were answered, whether a certain minimum or maximum time was reached, or whether a longer break was taken.

Checking for Technical Variance

In a typical internet-based study, the participants access the materials using hundreds of combinations of computers, operating systems, versions and types of web browsers, and network speeds. Information about these can be gathered, many are part of the HTTP (operating systems, version and type of web browsers) and others can be computed (network speeds) or gathered via JavaScript (e.g., size and resolution of screen used).

The impact of technical variance can then be checked by analyzing the data via analysis of variance, using the technology parameters as factors. Often, one finds well-established differences, such as different results on personality tests for Mac versus PC users and JavaScript turned on or off depending on level of education (Buchanan & Reips, 2001). It depends on the aim of the study whether any other differences that may appear are a challenge or an asset to the hypothesis at hand.

CONCLUSION AND OUTLOOK

Even though internet-based data collection has been around for more than 25 years and is widely accepted, there are still ongoing debates in some fields about whether this new method should be accepted (e.g., Kendall, 2008, vs. Honing & Reips, 2008, for the field of musicology). In the meantime, numerous articles appeared that report data from internet-based data collection, even in areas in which the technique is still debated (such as Egermann et al., 2009, in the case of musicology research). An important dimension in discussions about internet-based research are ethical considerations. Some long-standing topics, such as deception, may require new adjustments online, see, for example, Hilbig and Thielmann (2021). Cases of data leaks and misuse of data (e.g., in the Cambridge Analytica scandal) have alerted the research community and wider public.

Internet-based research can raise particular, sometimes nonobvious, challenges in adhering to ethics principles in research. Often researchers are not experts in internet technologies and security systems and, thus, may not fully understand how to secure confidentiality of participant data, for example, if data are stored on servers that are maintained by third parties or designed for other purposes, too. Deidentified data sets may potentially become reidentified when combined with other information that is available. Patterns of information in otherwise anonymous data sets could reveal identities if combined with other data that are available on the internet. Even though the likelihood for breaches is relatively low, researchers need to be aware that it is in many cases impossible to maintain absolute

---

[4]If the meta tags for the exclusion of search engine spiders are used as advised elsewhere in this chapter, then no one will enter the study materials after the first page.

confidentiality. Ethics codes by many professional organizations for researchers have been updated to include the particularities of internet-based research and provide advice; furthermore, there are specific guides by online researchers (e.g., Barchard & Williams, 2008; Hewson & Buchanan, 2013).

The internet of things will gain more room and become more of a topic for the general public as well as for researchers over the next years and decades. It will be a question whether and when issues of privacy with various internet services that recently were discussed more broadly will lead to a compromise between internet penetration of daily life and the desire and legal requirement of anonymity and privacy.

With this chapter, I hope to have contributed to the spreading of helpful information that counters two popular misconceptions (Reips, 2002c): Internet-based data collection is neither just like offline data collection nor completely different from offline data collection.

References

American Psychological Association. (2020). *Publication manual of the American Psychological Association* (7th ed.).

Amoroso, E. (2020). *A client-side perspective on web security.* https://www.helpnetsecurity.com/2020/04/07/threats-web-security/

Anderson, C. A., Allen, J. J., Plante, C., Quigley-McBride, A., Lovett, A., & Rokkum, J. N. (2019). The MTurkification of social and personality psychology. *Personality and Social Psychology Bulletin, 45*(6), 842–850. https://doi.org/10.1177/0146167218798821

Askitas, N., & Zimmermann, K. F. (2009). Google econometrics and unemployment forecasting. *Applied Economics Quarterly, 55*(2), 107–120. https://doi.org/10.3790/aeq.55.2.107

Aust, F., Diedenhofen, B., Ullrich, S., & Musch, J. (2013). Seriousness checks are useful to improve data validity in online research. *Behavior Research Methods, 45*(2), 527–535. https://doi.org/10.3758/s13428-012-0265-2

Barchard, K. A., & Williams, J. (2008). Practical advice for conducting ethical online experiments and questionnaires for United States psychologists. *Behavior Research Methods, 40*(4), 1111–1128. https://doi.org/10.3758/BRM.40.4.1111

Barras, G. (2009). Gallery: Flickr users make accidental maps. *New Scientist.* http://www.newscientist.com/article/dn17017-gallery-flickr-user-traces-make-accidental-maps.html

Berners-Lee, T., Hendler, J., & Lassila, O. (2001). The semantic web: A new form of web content that is meaningful to computers will unleash a revolution of new possibilities. *Scientific American, 284*(5), 34–43. https://doi.org/10.1038/scientificamerican0501-34

Birnbaum, M. H. (2000). Decision making in the lab and on the web. In M. H. Birnbaum (Ed.), *Psychological experiments on the internet* (pp. 3–34). Academic Press. https://doi.org/10.1016/B978-012099980-4/50002-2

Birnbaum, M. H. (2007). Designing online experiments. In A. Joinson, K. McKenna, T. Postmes, & U.-D. Reips (Eds.), *The Oxford handbook of internet psychology* (pp. 391–403). Oxford University Press.

Brehm, J. W. (1966). *A theory of psychological reactance.* Academic Press.

Buchanan, T. (2001). Online personality assessment. In U.-D. Reips & M. Bosnjak (Eds.), *Dimensions of internet science* (pp. 57–74). Pabst Science.

Buchanan, T. (2007). Personality testing on the Internet: What we know, and what we do not. In A. N. Joinson, K. McKenna, T. Postmes, & U.-D. Reips (Eds.), *Oxford handbook of internet psychology* (pp. 447–459). Oxford University Press.

Buchanan, T., Johnson, J. A., & Goldberg, L. R. (2005). Implementing a five-factor personality inventory for use on the Internet. *European Journal of Psychological Assessment, 21*(2), 115–127. https://doi.org/10.1027/1015-5759.21.2.115

Buchanan, T., & Reips, U.-D. (2001). Platform-dependent biases in online research: Do Mac users really think different? In K. J. Jonas, P. Breuer, B. Schauenburg, & M. Boos (Eds.), *Perspectives on internet research: Concepts and methods.* https://www.uni-konstanz.de/iscience/reips/pubs/papers/Buchanan_Reips2001.pdf

Buchanan, T., & Smith, J. L. (1999). Research on the Internet: Validation of a world-wide web mediated personality scale. *Behavior Research Methods, Instruments, & Computers, 31*(4), 565–571. https://doi.org/10.3758/BF03200736

Callegaro, M., Manfreda, K. L., & Vehovar, V. (2015). *Web survey methodology.* SAGE. https://doi.org/10.4135/9781529799651

Campbell, D. T. (1979). Assessing the impact of planned social change. *Evaluation and Program Planning, 2*(1), 67–90. https://doi.org/10.1016/0149-7189(79)90048-X

Campbell, D. T., & Stanley, J. (1963). *Experimental and quasi-experimental designs for research.* Houghton Mifflin.

Coomber, R. (1997). Using the internet for survey research. *Sociological Research Online, 2*(2), 49–58. https://doi.org/10.5153/sro.73

De Leeuw, E. D. (2005). To mix or not to mix data collection modes in surveys. *Journal of Official Statistics, 21*(2), 233–255.

Dillman, D. A., & Bowker, D. K. (2001). The web questionnaire challenge to survey methodologists. In U.-D. Reips & M. Bosnjak (Eds.), *Dimensions of internet science* (pp. 159–178). Pabst Science.

Dillman, D. A., Smyth, J. D., & Christian, L. M. (2008). *Internet, mail, and mixed-mode surveys: The tailored design method.* Wiley.

Dreyfuss, E. (2018). A bot panic hits Amazon's Mechanical Turk. *Wired.* https://www.wired.com/story/amazon-mechanical-turk-bot-panic/

Egermann, H., Nagel, F., Altenmüller, E., & Kopiez, R. (2009). Continuous measurement of musically-induced emotion: A web experiment. *International Journal of Internet Science, 4*(1), 4–20. https://www.ijis.net/ijis4_1/ijis4_1_egermann_pre.html

Faul, F., Erdfelder, E., Buchner, A., & Lang, A. G. (2009). Statistical power analyses using G*Power 3.1: Tests for correlation and regression analyses. *Behavior Research Methods, 41*(4), 1149–1160. https://doi.org/10.3758/BRM.41.4.1149

Frauendorfer, D., & Reips, U.-D. (2009). *Investigating the high hurdle technique* [Paper presentation]. 11th General Online Research conference, Vienna, Austria, April 6–8, 2009.

Frick, A., Bächtiger, M. T., & Reips, U.-D. (2001). Financial incentives, personal information, and drop-out in online studies. In U.-D. Reips & M. Bosnjak (Eds.), *Dimensions of Internet science* (pp. 209–219). Pabst Science.

Fritsche, I., & Linneweber, V. (2006). Nonreactive methods in psychological research. In M. Eid & E. Diener (Eds.), *Handbook of multimethod measurement in psychology* (pp. 189–203). American Psychological Association. https://doi.org/10.1037/11383-014

Funke, F., & Reips, U.-D. (2012). Why semantic differentials in web-based research should be made from visual analogue scales and not from 5-point scales. *Field Methods, 24*(3), 310–327. https://doi.org/10.1177/1525822X12444061

Funke, F., Reips, U.-D., & Thomas, R. K. (2011). Sliders for the smart: Type of rating scale on the Web interacts with educational level. *Social Science Computer Review, 29*(2), 221–231. https://doi.org/10.1177/0894439310376896

Garaizar, P., & Reips, U.-D. (2019). Best practices: Two Web-browser-based methods for stimulus presentation in behavioral experiments with high-resolution timing requirements. *Behavior Research Methods, 51*(3), 1441–1453. https://doi.org/10.3758/s13428-018-1126-4

Ginsberg, J., Mohebbi, M. H., Patel, R. S., Brammer, L., Smolinski, M. S., & Brilliant, L. (2009). Detecting influenza epidemics using search engine query data. *Nature, 457*(7232), 1012–1014. https://doi.org/10.1038/nature07634

Google Eurovision. (2010). *Eurovision 2010 forecast.* https://web.archive.org/web/20100521034540/https://www.google.com/intl/en/landing/eurovision/

Göritz, A. S. (2006). Incentives in web studies: Methodological issues and a review. *International Journal of Internet Science, 1*(1), 58–70. https://www.ijis.net/ijis1_1/ijis1_1_goeritz_pre.html

Göritz, A. S. (2007). Using online panels in psychological research. In A. N. Joinson, K. Y. A. McKenna, T. Postmes, & U.-D. Reips (Eds.), *The Oxford handbook of internet psychology* (pp. 473–485). Oxford University Press.

Göritz, A. S. (2009). Building and managing an online panel with phpPanelAdmin. *Behavior Research Methods, 41*(4), 1177–1182. https://doi.org/10.3758/BRM.41.4.1177

Göritz, A. S., Reinhold, N., & Batinic, B. (2002). Online panels. In B. Batinic, U.-D. Reips, & M. Bosnjak (Eds.), *Online social sciences* (pp. 27–47). Hogrefe & Huber.

Göritz, A. S., & Stieger, S. (2008). The high-hurdle technique put to the test: Failure to find evidence that increasing loading times enhances data quality in web-based studies. *Behavior Research Methods, 40*(1), 322–327. https://doi.org/10.3758/BRM.40.1.322

Götz, F. M., Stieger, S., & Reips, U.-D. (2017). Users of the main smartphone operating systems (iOS, Android) differ only little in personality. *PLOS ONE, 12*(5), e0176921. https://doi.org/10.1371/journal.pone.0176921

Hartig, J., Jude, N., & Rauch, W. (2003). *Entwicklung und Erprobung eines deutschen Big-Five-Fragebogens auf Basis des International Personality Item Pools (IPIP40)* [Development and testing of a German Big Five questionnaire that is based on the International Personality Item Pool (IPIP40)]. Arbeiten aus dem Institut für Psychologie der Johann Wolfgang Goethe-Universität.

Henninger, F., Shevchenko, Y., Mertens, U. K., Kieslich, P. J., & Hilbig, B. E. (2022). lab.js: A free, open, online study builder. *Behavior Research Methods. 54*(2), 556–573. https://doi.org/10.3758/s13428-019-01283-5

Hewson, C., & Buchanan, T. (2013). *Ethics guidelines for Internet-mediated research*. The British Psychological Society.

Hilbig, B. E., & Thielmann, I. (2021). On the (mis)use of deception in web-based research: Challenges and recommendations. *Zeitschrift für Psychologie*, 229(4), 225–229. https://doi.org/10.1027/2151-2604/a000466

Hiskey, S., & Troop, N. A. (2002). Online longitudinal survey research: Viability and participation. *Social Science Computer Review*, 20(3), 250–259. https://doi.org/10.1177/089443930202000303

Honing, H., & Reips, U.-D. (2008). Web-based versus lab-based studies: A response to Kendall (2008). *Empirical Musicology Review*, 3(2), 73–77. https://doi.org/10.18061/1811/31943

Janetzko, D. (2008). Objectivity, reliability, and validity of search engine count estimates. *International Journal of Internet Science*, 3(1), 7–33. https://www.ijis.net/ijis3_1/ijis3_1_janetzko_pre.html

Joinson, A. N., & Reips, U.-D. (2007). Personalized salutation, power of sender and response rates to web-based surveys. *Computers in Human Behavior*, 23(3), 1372–1383. https://doi.org/10.1016/j.chb.2004.12.011

Kendall, R. (2008). Commentary on "The potential of the internet for music perception research: A comment on lab-based versus web-based studies" by Honing & Ladinig. *Empirical Musicology Review*, 3(1), 8–10. https://doi.org/10.18061/1811/31693

Kirk, R. E. (1995). *Experimental design: Procedures for the behavioral sciences* (3rd ed.). Brooks/Cole.

Krantz, J. H. (2001). Stimulus delivery on the web: What can be presented when calibration isn't possible? In U.-D. Reips & M. Bosnjak (Eds.), *Dimensions of internet science* (pp. 113–130). Pabst Science.

Krantz, J. H., Ballard, J., & Scher, J. (1997). Comparing the results of laboratory and world-wide web samples on the determinants of female attractiveness. *Behavior Research Methods, Instruments, & Computers*, 29(2), 264–269. https://doi.org/10.3758/BF03204824

Krantz, J. H., & Reips, U.-D. (2017). The state of web-based research: A survey and call for inclusion in curricula. *Behavior Research Methods*, 49(5), 1621–1629. https://doi.org/10.3758/s13428-017-0882-x

Krantz, J. H., & Williams, J. E. (2010). Using graphics, photographs, and dynamic media. In S. Gosling & J. A. Johnson (Eds.), *Advanced methods for behavioral research on the internet* (pp. 45–61). American Psychological Association. https://doi.org/10.1037/12076-004

Mangan, M. A., & Reips, U.-D. (2007). Sleep, sex, and the web: Surveying the difficult-to-reach clinical population suffering from sexsomnia. *Behavior Research Methods*, 39(2), 233–236. https://doi.org/10.3758/BF03193152

McGee, M. (2011). *Google asks: Can search trends predict the Oscars?* https://searchengineland.com/google-asks-can-search-trends-predict-the-oscars-64912

Musch, J., & Reips, U.-D. (2000). A brief history of Web experimenting. In M. H. Birnbaum (Ed.), *Psychological experiments on the internet* (pp. 61–87). Academic Press. https://doi.org/10.1016/B978-012099980-4/50004-6

Paine, C., Reips, U.-D., Stieger, S., Joinson, A., & Buchanan, T. (2007). Internet users' perceptions of 'privacy concerns' and 'privacy actions.' *International Journal of Human-Computer Studies*, 65(6), 526–536. https://doi.org/10.1016/j.ijhcs.2006.12.001

Panetta, K. (2020). *Gartner top 10 strategic technology trends for 2020*. https://www.gartner.com/smarterwithgartner/gartner-top-10-strategic-technology-trends-for-2020/

Plummer, D. C., Hafner, B., Hill, J. B., Redman, P., Brown, R. H., Dulaney, K., Clark, W., Willis, D. A., Lee, C. G., Smulders, C., Dayley, A., & Rosser, B. (2009). *Gartner's top predictions for IT organizations and users, 2009 and beyond: Where is the money?* Gartner Group. http://www.gartner.com/DisplayDocument?id=874312

Preckel, F., & Thiemann, H. (2003). Online versus paper-pencil version of a high potential intelligence test. *Swiss Journal of Psychology/Schweizerische Zeitschrift für Psychologie/Revue Suisse de Psychologie*, 62, 131–138.

Reimers, S. (2007). The BBC internet study: General methodology. *Archives of Sexual Behavior*, 36(2), 147–161. https://doi.org/10.1007/s10508-006-9143-2

Reips, U.-D. (1997). Das psychologische Experimentieren im Internet [Psychological experimenting on the internet]. In B. Batinic (Ed.), *Internet für Psychologen* (pp. 245–265). Hogrefe.

Reips, U.-D. (2000). The web experiment method: Advantages, disadvantages, and solutions. In M. H. Birnbaum (Ed.), *Psychological experiments on the Internet* (pp. 89–117). Academic Press. https://doi.org/10.1016/B978-012099980-4/50005-8

Reips, U.-D. (2001). The web experimental psychology lab: Five years of data collection on the Internet. *Behavior Research Methods, Instruments, & Computers*, 33(2), 201–211. https://doi.org/10.3758/BF03195366

Reips, U.-D. (2002a). Context effects in web surveys. In B. Batinic, U.-D. Reips, & M. Bosnjak (Eds.), *Online social sciences* (pp. 69–79). Hogrefe & Huber.

Reips, U.-D. (2002b). Internet-based psychological experimenting: Five dos and five don'ts. *Social Science Computer Review, 20*(3), 241–249. https://doi.org/10.1177/089443930202000302

Reips, U.-D. (2002c). Standards for Internet-based experimenting. *Experimental Psychology, 49*(4), 243–256. https://doi.org/10.1026/1618-3169.49.4.243

Reips, U.-D. (2002d). Theory and techniques of conducting web experiments. In B. Batinic, U.-D. Reips, & M. Bosnjak (Eds.), *Online social sciences* (pp. 229–250). Hogrefe & Huber.

Reips, U.-D. (2003a, August 25–27). *Seamless from concepts to results: Experimental internet science* [Paper presentation]. "Decision Making and the Web." Swiss Federal Institute of Technology 19th Biannual Conference on Subjective Probability, Utility, and Decision Making, Zurich, Switzerland. https://iscience.uni-konstanz.de/archive/reips/SPUDM_03/pages/slide1.html

Reips, U.-D. (2003b). Web-Experimente: Eckpfeiler der Online-Forschung [Web experiments: cornerstones in online research]. In A. Theobald, M. Dreyer, & T. Starsetzki (Eds.), *Online-Marktforschung: Beiträge aus Wissenschaft und Praxis* (Rev. ed., pp. 73–89). https://doi.org/10.1007/978-3-663-10948-8_6

Reips, U.-D. (2005, November 10). *Collecting data in surfer's paradise: Internet-based research yesterday, now, and tomorrow* [Paper presentation]. Society for Computers in Psychology Conference, Toronto, Ontario, Canada.

Reips, U.-D. (2006). Web-based methods. In M. Eid & E. Diener (Eds.), *Handbook of multimethod measurement in psychology* (pp. 73–85). American Psychological Association. https://doi.org/10.1037/11383-006

Reips, U.-D. (2007). The methodology of Internet-based experiments. In A. Joinson, K. McKenna, T. Postmes, & U.-D. Reips (Eds.), *The Oxford handbook of internet psychology* (pp. 373–390). Oxford University Press.

Reips, U.-D. (2009a). Internet experiments: Methods, guidelines, metadata. *Human Vision and Electronic Imaging XIV. Proceedings of the Society for Photo-Instrumentation Engineers, 7240*(1), 724008. https://doi.org/10.1117/12.823416

Reips, U.-D. (2009b). Schöne neue Forschungswelt: Zukunftstrends [Beautiful new world of research: Future trends]. In C. König, M. Stahl, & E. Wiegand (Eds.), *Nicht-reaktive Erhebungsverfahren* [Non-reactive data collection methods] (pp. 129–138). GESIS Schriftenreihe, Band 1.

Reips, U.-D. (2010). Design and formatting in internet-based research. In S. Gosling & J. Johnson (Eds.), *Advanced internet methods in the behavioral sciences* (pp. 29–43). American Psychological Association. https://doi.org/10.1037/12076-003

Reips, U.-D. (2021). Web-based research in psychology: A review. *Zeitschrift für Psychologie, 229*(4), 198–213. https://doi.org/10.1027/2151-2604/a000475

Reips, U.-D., & Birnbaum, M. H. (2011). Behavioral research and data collection via the internet. In R. W. Proctor & K.-P. L. Vu (Eds.), *The handbook of human factors in web design* (2nd ed., pp. 563–585). Erlbaum.

Reips, U.-D., Buchanan, T., Krantz, J. H., & McGraw, K. (2015). Methodological challenges in the use of the Internet for scientific research: Ten solutions and recommendations. *Studia Psychologica (Warszawa), 2*(15), 139–148. https://doi.org/10.21697/sp.2015.14.2.09

Reips, U.-D., Buffardi, L., & Kuhlmann, T. (2011, March). Using Amazon's Mechanical Turk for the recruitment of participants in internet-based research. *13th General Online Research* [Meeting]. University of Düsseldorf, Germany. https://doi.org/10.13140/RG.2.2.19049.34402

Reips, U.-D., & Funke, F. (2008). Interval-level measurement with visual analogue scales in internet-based research: VAS Generator. *Behavior Research Methods, 40*(3), 699–704. https://doi.org/10.3758/BRM.40.3.699

Reips, U.-D., & Garaizar, P. (2011). Mining twitter: A source for psychological wisdom of the crowds. *Behavior Research Methods, 43*(3), 635–642. https://doi.org/10.3758/s13428-011-0116-6

Reips, U.-D., & Krantz, J. (2010). Conducting true experiments on the web. In S. Gosling & J. Johnson (Eds.), *Advanced internet methods in the behavioral sciences* (pp. 193–216). American Psychological Association. https://doi.org/10.1037/12076-013

Reips, U.-D., & Lengler, R. (2005). The web experiment list: A web service for the recruitment of participants and archiving of internet-based experiments. *Behavior Research Methods, 37*(2), 287–292. https://doi.org/10.3758/BF03192696

Reips, U.-D., & Neuhaus, C. (2002). WEXTOR: A web-based tool for generating and visualizing experimental designs and procedures. *Behavior Research Methods, Instruments, & Computers, 34*(2), 234–240. https://doi.org/10.3758/BF03195449

Reips, U.-D., & Shevchenko, Y. (2021). *The web experiment list 2.0* [Manuscript submitted for publication]. Department of Psychology, University of Konstanz.

Reips, U.-D., & Stieger, S. (2004). Scientific LogAnalyzer: A web-based tool for analyses of server log files in psychological research. *Behavior Research Methods, Instruments, & Computers, 36*(2), 304–311. https://doi.org/10.3758/BF03195576

Schmidt, W. C. (2000). The server-side of psychology web experiments. In M. H. Birnbaum (Ed.), *Psychological experiments on the internet* (pp. 285–310). Academic Press. https://doi.org/10.1016/B978-012099980-4/50013-7

Schmidt, W. C. (2007). Technical considerations when implementing online research. In A. Joinson, K. McKenna, T. Postmes, & U.-D. Reips (Eds.), *The Oxford handbook of internet psychology* (pp. 461–472). Oxford University Press.

Selkälä, A., Viinamäki, L., Suikkanen, A., & Reips, U.-D. (2021). Web survey entry selection by a mailed invitation letter. *Survey Practice, 14*(1), 1–13. https://doi.org/10.29115/SP-2021-0003

Shevchenko, Y., & Reips, U.-D. (2022). How to prepare and conduct an Experience Sampling study via mobile phones [how-to guide]. *SAGE Research Methods: Doing Research Online*. Sage. https://doi.org/10.4135/9781529610116

Shih, T.-H., & Fan, X. (2007). Response rates and mode preferences in web-mail mixed-mode surveys: A meta-analysis. *International Journal of Internet Science, 2*(1), 59–82. https://www.ijis.net/ijis2_1/ijis2_1_shih_pre.html

Sitemaps. (2010, May 8). In *Wikipedia, The Free Encyclopedia*. https://en.wikipedia.org/w/index.php?title=Sitemaps&oldid=360892548

Smith, M. A., & Leigh, B. (1997). Virtual subjects: Using the internet as an alternative source of subjects and research environment. *Behavior Research Methods, Instruments, & Computers, 29*(4), 496–505. https://doi.org/10.3758/BF03210601

Smyth, J. D., Dillman, D. A., Christian, L. M., & Stern, M. J. (2006). Effects of using visual design principles to group response options in web surveys. *International Journal of Internet Science, 1*(1), 6–16. https://www.ijis.net/ijis1_1/ijis1_1_smyth_pre.html

Stegbauer, C., & Rausch, A. (2002). Lurkers in mailing lists. In B. Batinic, U.-D. Reips, & M. Bosnjak (Eds.), *Online social sciences* (pp. 263–274). Hogrefe & Huber.

Stewart, N., Ungemach, C., Harris, A. J., Bartels, D. M., Newell, B. R., Paolacci, G., & Chandler, J. (2015). The average laboratory samples a population of 7,300 Amazon Mechanical Turk workers. *Judgment and Decision Making, 10*(5), 479–491.

Stieger, S., & Reips, U.-D. (2008). Dynamic Interviewing Program (DIP): Automatic online interviews via the instant messenger ICQ. *Cyberpsychology & Behavior, 11*(2), 201–207. https://doi.org/10.1089/cpb.2007.0030

Stieger, S., & Reips, U.-D. (2010). What are participants doing while filling in an online questionnaire: A paradata collection tool and an empirical study. *Computers in Human Behavior, 26*(6), 1488–1495. https://doi.org/10.1016/j.chb.2010.05.013

Stieger, S., Reips, U.-D., & Voracek, M. (2007). Forced-response in online surveys: Bias from reactance and an increase in sex-specific dropout. *Journal of the American Society for Information Science and Technology, 58*(11), 1653–1660. https://doi.org/10.1002/asi.20651

Tuten, T. L., Bosnjak, M., & Bandilla, W. (2000). Banner-advertised web surveys. *Marketing Research, 11*(4), 17–21.

Van Aart, C., Siebes, R., Buser, V., Aroyo, L., Raimond, Y., Brickley, D., Schreiber, G., Minno, M., Miller, L., Palmisano, D., & Mostarda, M. (2009, October 25). *The NoTube beancounter: Aggregating user data for television programme recommendation* [Paper presentation]. 8th International Semantic Web Conference, Washington, DC, United States. https://ceur-ws.org/Vol-520/paper01.pdf

von Bastian, C. C., Locher, A., & Ruflin, M. (2013). Tatool: A Java-based open-source programming framework for psychological studies. *Behavior Research Methods, 45*(1), 108–115. https://doi.org/10.3758/s13428-012-0224-y

Webb, E. J., Campbell, D. T., Schwartz, R. D., & Sechrest, L. (1966). *Unobtrusive measures: Nonreactive research in the social sciences.* Rand McNally.

Wilhelm, O., & McKnight, P. E. (2002). Ability and achievement testing on the world wide web. In B. Batinic, U.-D. Reips, & M. Bosnjak (Eds.), *Online social sciences* (pp. 151–180). Hogrefe & Huber.

World Wide Web Consortium (W3C). (2010). *Semantic web.* https://www.w3.org/standards/semanticweb/

PART IV

BUILDING AND TESTING MODELS

CHAPTER 20

STATISTICAL MEDIATION ANALYSIS IN PSYCHOLOGICAL RESEARCH

David P. MacKinnon, JeeWon Cheong, Angela G. Pirlott, and Heather L. Smyth

Mediating variables are central to psychology because they explain the processes of psychological phenomenon. As a field, psychology focuses on how an organism is intermediate in the link between a stimulus and the response to that stimulus. This focus on the organism that intervenes between stimulus and behavior was recognized early in psychology in the stimulus-to-organism-to-response model (Woodworth, 1928). In this model, the organism, a person for example, translates a stimulus into a response by means of mediating processes within the individual. For example, when a list of words (S) is presented, the person (O) memorizes them, and then later recalls (R) the words. This S-O-R model has been extended to understand mediating processes for other units besides individuals such as schools, teams, and communities and is now widely used to develop and refine prevention and treatment programs (Kazdin, 2009; MacKinnon, 2008).

Psychological theories specify mediating mechanisms that may explain psychological phenomena. For example, the theory of reasoned action (Fishbein & Ajzen, 1975) in social psychology, postulates that attitudes cause intentions, which in turn cause behavior. Applying this theory to intervention research for smoking, an intervention must first change the attitudes toward the consequences of smoking, intentions to smoke, and perceptions of efficacy toward quitting, so that the person can eventually stop smoking. In cognitive psychology, memory processes mediate the transmission of information into a response. When a number of words are presented, using pictorial cues may be more effective for word recall than memorizing the words in the presented order. Social learning theory describes how various behaviors are learned in social settings. For example, when a child watches a model being reinforced for performing a certain behavior, the child later produces the same behavior under the same circumstances as a result of this learning process (Bandura et al., 1963). In clinical psychology, a cognitive theory of depression suggests that changing cognitive attributions about the self or the world reduces depression (Beck et al., 1979). In developmental psychology, a theory of attachment postulates that deprivation at birth leads to developmental deficits that lead to poor subsequent parenting behavior (Arling & Harlow, 1967).

In the simplest mediation theory, the investigation of mediation specifies a chain of relations by which an antecedent variable affects a mediating variable that in turn affects a dependent variable. Mediating variables can be behavioral, biological, psychological, or social constructs that transmit the effect of one variable to another

https://doi.org/10.1037/0000319-020
APA Handbook of Research Methods in Psychology, Second Edition: Vol. 2. Research Designs: Quantitative, Qualitative, Neuropsychological, and Biological, H. Cooper (Editor-in-Chief)

variable. There are two overlapping applications of mediation theory. One major application of mediating variables is after an effect is observed and researchers investigate how this effect occurred. This application arises from Lazarsfeld's (1955) and Hyman's (1955) outlines of elaboration methodologies. In this framework, a third variable is inserted into the analysis of an $X \rightarrow Y$ relation in order to improve understanding of the relation, that is, to determine whether the relation is due to a mediator or is spurious. The most notable citation for this approach to mediation theory is the classic Baron and Kenny (1986) article, which clarified the steps to assess mediation described in earlier references (Hyman, 1955; Judd & Kenny, 1981a, 1981b; Lazarsfeld, 1955). Another type of application of mediation theory is selecting the mediating variables for intervention based on the theories specifying the causes of the dependent variable or prior research demonstrating that these are candidate causal variables of the dependent variable. If the mediating variables are causally related to the dependent variable, then changing the mediating variables changes the dependent variable. For example, in drug prevention programs mediating variables such as social norms or expectations about drug use are targeted to change in order to change a dependent variable such as drug use. Many researchers have emphasized the importance of considering mediation in treatment and prevention research (Baranowski et al., 1998; Judd & Kenny, 1981a, 1981b; Kazdin, 2009; Kraemer et al., 2002; MacKinnon, 1994; Weiss, 1997). Evaluating mediation to explain an observed effect is probably more susceptible to chance findings than evaluating mediation by design because the mediators in the former case are often selected after the study, while the mediators in the latter case are selected in advance based on theory and prior empirical research. Most programs of research investigating mediating variables employ both mediation by design and mediation for explanation approaches (MacKinnon, 2008, Chapter 2).

Because of the importance of identifying mediating variables in psychological research, methods to assess mediation are an area of active research. The overall purpose of this chapter is to outline current thinking about mediation analysis in psychology, but the length of the chapter precludes addressing all new developments, which can be found in other sources (MacKinnon, 2008; MacKinnon, in press; MacKinnon, Fairchild, & Fritz, 2007; VanderWeele, 2015). This revision of a chapter first published in 2010 includes sections outlining new developments in causal mediation analysis and the refinement of methods for more complicated models including multilevel, longitudinal, and models with moderation and mediation. This chapter defines mediation and other third-variable effects. Statistical mediation methods using a single mediator case are then described in order to clarify the extensions of the single mediator model discussed in the rest of the chapter. Assumptions of the single mediator model are then addressed, followed by sections on the latest research on statistical testing of mediated effects, such as longitudinal mediation models, mediator and moderator models, and modern causal inference for mediation models. Next, various experimental designs for investigating mediation are described, and directions for future research are discussed.

DEFINITIONS

The simplest mediation model involves an *independent variable*, X, a *mediating variable*, M, and a *dependent variable*, Y. As described elsewhere (MacKinnon, 2008), there are several different types of third variable effects. In its simplest form, mediation represents the addition of a third variable to an $X \rightarrow Y$ relation so that the causal sequences can be modeled such as X causes the mediator, M, and M causes Y, that is, $X \rightarrow M \rightarrow Y$. Although the mediation relation may appear simple, it has several complications. One of these complications is that mediation is one of several relations that may be present when a third variable is included in the analysis of a two-variable relationship. The third variable is a confounding variable if it causes both X and Y; ignoring the third variable leads to an inaccurate inference about the relation of X and Y. If the third variable is related to X and/or Y so that information about the third variable improves prediction of Y by X, but including the third variable in the analysis does not substantially alter the relation of X to Y, the third variable is a covariate. If the third variable modifies the relation of X to Y such that the X to Y relation differs at different values of the third variable, the third variable is a moderator. A third variable may be another measure of X or Y, so it provides redundant information and is best included as an additional indicator of X or Y. Finally, a collider third-variable is caused by X and Y, so it should not be adjusted in analysis. *Collider variables* have received greater attention recently (Elwert & Winship, 2014) and are the opposite of *confounders*—a confounder must be adjusted in statistical analysis and a collider must not be adjusted in statistical analysis. Adjustment by a collider variable introduces bias in the X to Y relation. A mediator differs from each of these other third variable effects in that the mediator is in a causal chain such that X causes M and M causes Y (Kraemer et al., 2002; MacKinnon et al., 2000; MacKinnon & Lamp, 2021; Robins & Greenland, 1992, for more information on the third variable effects).

Mediation Regression Equations

The single mediator model for X, M, and Y is shown in Figure 20.1 and in Equations 20.1 to 20.3:

$$Y = i_1 + cX + e_1 \qquad (20.1)$$

$$Y = i_2 + c'X + bM + e_2 \qquad (20.2)$$

$$M = i_3 + aX + e_3 \qquad (20.3)$$

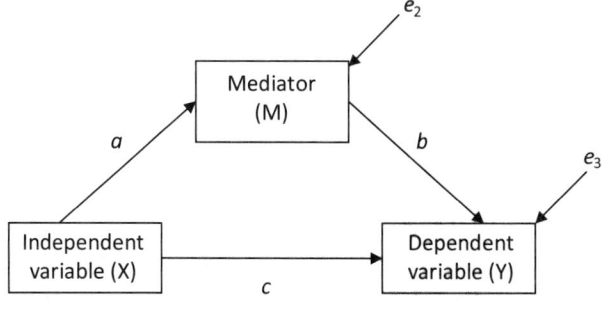

FIGURE 20.1.   Single mediator model.

where Y is the dependent variable, X is the independent variable, and M is the mediator; the parameters i_1, i_2, and i_3 are intercepts in each equation; and e_1, e_2, and e_3 are residuals. In Equation 20.1, the coefficient c represents the total effect, that is, the total effect that X can have on Y. In Equation 20.2, the parameter c' denotes the relation between X and Y controlling for M, representing the direct effect, that is, the effect of X on Y that is not intervened by M. The parameter b denotes the relation between M and Y controlling for X. Finally, in Equation 20.3, the coefficient a indicates the relation between X and M. Equations 20.2 and 20.3 are represented in Figure 20.1 which shows how the total effect of X on Y is separated into a direct effect relating X to Y and a mediated effect where X has an indirect effect on Y through M. The current practice of statistical mediation analysis can be grouped to three approaches, that is, (a) causal steps, (b) difference in coefficients, and (c) product of coefficients (MacKinnon, Lockwood, et al., 2002), which are all based on the information from the regression equations for testing the single mediator model.

The first approach to statistical mediation analysis, called the *causal steps approach*, is based on the influential work of Baron and Kenny (1986; also Kenny et al., 1998) and Judd and Kenny (1981a, 1981b), originating in Hyman (1955) and Lazarsfeld (1955). In this approach, a researcher conducts four steps of analyses to establish mediation and estimate all three equations described earlier. First, the independent variable X should be significantly related to the dependent variable Y, resulting in the significant coefficient c in Equation 20.1. Second, the independent variable X should be significantly related to the hypothesized mediating variable M, producing a significant coefficient a in Equation 20.3. Third, the mediating variable M must be significantly related to the dependent variable Y, controlling for the independent variable X, thus finding a significant coefficient b in Equation 20.2. Finally, the relation between the independent variable X and the dependent variable Y should be weaker when the mediating variable M is added to the model.

Thus, the coefficient c' should be smaller than the coefficient c, that is, $c - c' > 0$. In the causal steps approach, the conditions by which a potential mediator is identified as a significant mediator are clearly established, but the mediated effect is not directly estimated.

The other two approaches, the *difference in coefficients* and the *product of coefficients* approaches, involve estimation of the mediated or indirect effect and its standard error, allowing formal tests for significance of the mediated effects (MacKinnon, Lockwood, et al., 2002). In the difference in coefficients approach, the mediated effect is estimated by comparing the relations between the independent variable X and the dependent variable Y from Equations 20.1 and 20.2, where the effect of X on Y is estimated with and without adjusting for the mediator M. The idea is that the mediation effect can be estimated by the difference between the total effect and the direct effect that is not attributable to the mediator, $\hat{c} - \hat{c}'$. In the product of coefficients approach, the mediated effect is estimated by the product of $\hat{a}$ and $\hat{b}$, $\hat{a}\hat{b}$ (Alwin & Hauser, 1975), from Equations 20.2 and 20.3. Thus, the mediated effect reflects the extent to which the independent variable X changes the mediator M and the extent to which the mediator changes the dependent variable Y. The quantities in Equations 20.1 to 20.3 can also be presented in a plot as described in MacKinnon (2008).

The mediated effect estimated in the difference in coefficients approach, $\hat{c} - \hat{c}'$, is algebraically equivalent to the mediated effect obtained in the product of coefficients approach, $\hat{a}\hat{b}$, under the normal theory, ordinary least squares and maximum likelihood estimation, as long as the same sample is used for Equations 20.1 to 20.3 (MacKinnon et al., 1995). When the mediated effect is assessed in multilevel models (Krull & MacKinnon, 1999), logistic or probit regression (MacKinnon & Dwyer, 1993), the two estimates of the mediated effect, $\hat{a}\hat{b}$ and $\hat{c} - \hat{c}'$, are not always equivalent and can sometimes be greatly discrepant (MacKinnon, 2008).

Although the statistical mediation analysis is straightforward under the assumption that the model is correctly specified, the identification of mediation relations has several complications that can only be addressed in a program of research (MacKinnon, 2008). For example, like all statistical analyses, it is often helpful to consider two models, the population or true model and the sample model. The population model represents the true relations among variables, those relations that we would see if we had the entire population. As a sample of data represents one of many different samples from the population, sample estimates of population parameters vary from sample to sample. Generally, it is assumed that the equations and variables specified in the sample model are the same equations in the population model. There are qualifications even to this sample/population dichotomy. For example, causal inference approaches to mediation suggest another superpopulation model that represents the true causal relations among variables with all assumptions validated, similar to the theoretical mediation model described by MacCorquodale and Meehl (1948). The challenge of using sample data to uncover mediation relations is that evidence for mediation must come from a program of research including a variety of designs and approaches to uncovering true mediation relations.

Standard Error of the Mediated Effect

One of the most frequently used standard errors of the mediated effect is the first-order solution derived by Sobel (1982, 1986) using the multivariate delta method (Bishop et al., 1975) as follows:

$$\sigma_{\hat{a}\hat{b}} = \sqrt{\sigma_{\hat{a}}^2 \hat{b}^2 + \sigma_{\hat{b}}^2 \hat{a}^2} \qquad (20.4)$$

where $\hat{a}$ and $\hat{b}$ are estimated regression coefficients and $\sigma_{\hat{a}}^2$ and $\sigma_{\hat{b}}^2$ are the squared standard error of $\hat{a}$ and $\hat{b}$ from Equations 20.2 and 20.3. The formula shown in Equation 20.4 is implemented in various structural equation modeling programs, such as EQS (Bentler, 1997) and Mplus (Muthén & Muthén, 1998–2007), for testing significance of mediated or indirect effects. Alternative formulas for the standard error for different approaches can be found in MacKinnon, Lockwood, et al. (2002) and MacKinnon (2008).

Confidence Limits for the Mediated Effect

Confidence limits of the mediated effects can be constructed using the estimated mediated effect and its standard error. The upper and lower confidence limits are as follows:

upper confidence limit (UCL)

$$= \text{mediated effect} + z_{Type\ I\ error}(\sigma_{\hat{a}\hat{b}}) \qquad (20.5)$$

lower confidence limit (LCL)

$$= \text{mediated effect} - z_{Type\ I\ error}(\sigma_{\hat{a}\hat{b}}) \qquad (20.6)$$

For example, when the mediated effect is calculated by the product of the coefficients, $\hat{a}\hat{b}$, and the standard error is estimated by Equation 20.4, the confidence limits are obtained as follows:

$$\hat{a}\hat{b} \pm z_{Type\ I\ error} * \sigma_{\hat{a}\hat{b}} \qquad (20.7)$$

As the mediated effect is the product of two regression coefficients, its distribution most closely follows the distribution of the product of the two normally distributed random variables, which may not be normally distributed (Springer, 1979). As a result, more accurate confidence limits can be obtained by using the distribution of the product of the two random variables to obtain critical values (MacKinnon et al., 2004). PRODCLIN (MacKinnon, Fritz, et al., 2007; Tofighi & MacKinnon, 2016) provides critical values of the distribution of the product of the two random variables and computes confidence intervals for the mediated effects (see the shiny app for distribution of the product confidence limits [https://rdrr.io/cran/RMediation/man/RMediation-package.html]).

Alternatively, resampling methods such as bootstrapping can be used to compute confidence intervals that adjust for the nonnormal distribution of the product of coefficients (Bollen & Stine, 1990; MacKinnon et al., 2004; Preacher & Hayes, 2004; Shrout & Bolger, 2002). From the original sample data, repeated samples are obtained and based on the mediation effects estimated from these repeated samples, an empirical sampling distribution is formed to determine the significance of the mediated effect and construct the confidence intervals (Efron & Tibshirani, 1993; Manly, 1997). Resampling methods are useful when assumptions of statistical methods are not met, such as data with nonnormal distributions, and provide confidence limits for more complex mediation models. More on resampling methods for mediation is described in MacKinnon (2008, Chapter 12).

Significance Testing

A statistical significance test for the mediated effect can be conducted in several ways. One way is to assess whether the confidence interval includes 0. When 0 is not included in the confidence interval, the mediated effect is statistically significant or the hypothesized mediator is considered a statistically significant mediator. Another way to test the significance of the mediation effect is to obtain the ratio of the estimated mediated effect to its standard error and compare the ratio to the critical values under the normal distributions. For example, $\hat{a}\hat{b}$ is divided by the standard error in Equation 20.4 and this ratio is compared to ±1.96. If the ratio is greater than 1.96 or smaller than −1.96, the mediated effect is significantly different from 0. In simulation studies (MacKinnon, Lockwood, et al., 2002; MacKinnon et al., 2004) of the statistical performance of 14 commonly used methods for testing the significance of mediation, the most widely used causal step methods showed quite low power and low Type I error rates. Power was also low for the methods that assume the normal distribution of mediated effect, in which the estimated mediated effect ($\hat{a}\hat{b}$ or $\hat{c} - \hat{c}'$) is divided by its respective standard error and the ratio is compared to the critical values of z or t distribution. Testing the significance of $\hat{a}$ and $\hat{b}$ and considering there to be significant mediation if both tests are statistically significant (i.e., joint significance test) showed a good balance between Type I and Type II errors as did methods based on the distribution of the product of two regression coefficients or bootstrap resampling.

The low power of most methods for testing mediation can be explained in several ways.

The low power of the causal steps approach results from the requirement of the first step that the relation between X and Y be significant, especially in the case of complete mediation (i.e., direct effect c' is 0). There are cases where the mediated effect is statistically significant, even if the relation between X and Y in Equation 20.1 is not significant, such as in opposing mediation, where the direction of the mediated effect is the opposite to the direction of the direct effect. O'Rourke and MacKinnon (2015) describe situations in which the power to detect the mediated effect is greater than the power to detect the total effect and recommend that researchers conduct mediation analysis whether or not the total effect is nonsignificant (O'Rourke & MacKinnon, 2018). Investigating the overall relation of X and Y is often the most important test for some research, but requiring the significant relation between X and Y for mediation to exist substantially reduces power to detect real mediation effects for the causal steps approach. The low power of the methods using the product of the coefficients and the difference in the coefficients is due to the nonnormality of the distribution of the mediated effects (MacKinnon et al., 2004). This nonnormality issue can be resolved with resampling methods and the methods based on the distribution of the product of ab described earlier.

COMPLETE VERSUS PARTIAL MEDIATION

As described earlier, the total effect c is the sum of the mediated effect (ab or $c - c'$) and the direct effect c'. Complete mediation is defined as a case in which the total effect is completely explained by the mediator. In this case, the total effect is equal to the mediated effect (i.e., $c = ab$) and the direct effect is statistically non-significant (i.e., $c' = 0$). Partial mediation refers to a case where the relation between the independent and the dependent variables is not completely accounted for by the mediator. In this case, both the mediated effect and the direct effect are statistically significant (i.e., $ab \neq 0$ and $c' \neq 0$), indicating that the mediator significantly accounts for part of the relation between the independent

and the dependent variables, and yet there are some other variables that may explain the relation. Considering the complexity of the behaviors studied in social science research, there may be a variety of causes of those behaviors, and, thus, it is often more realistic to expect that a single mediator would only partially explain the relation between the independent and the dependent variables (Baron & Kenny, 1986). James and colleagues (James et al., 2006) argued for the specification of complete or partial mediation prior to study and first testing for complete mediation. The test for complete mediation does not include the c' parameter in the model, and, as a result, inadequate model fit in covariance structure analysis suggests incomplete mediation. If theory predicts complete mediation, this approach provides a straightforward way to test mediation.

MEDIATION EQUATIONS WITH TWO MEDIATORS

The two-mediator model is described here because it helps to compare the causal steps, difference in coefficients, and product of coefficients approaches to testing mediation in more complicated models. When the mediation model includes two mediators, the regression equations can be expanded as follows (MacKinnon, 2008):

$$Y = i_1 + cX + e_1 \qquad (20.8)$$

$$Y = i_2 + c'X + b_1 M_1 + b_2 M_2 + e_2 \qquad (20.9)$$

$$M_1 = i_3 + a_1 X + e_3 \qquad (20.10)$$

$$M_2 = i_4 + a_2 X + e_4 \qquad (20.11)$$

where X is the single independent variable, M_1 and M_2 are two mediators, and Y is the dependent variable. The coefficients a_1 and a_2 represent the relations between the independent variable and the two mediators, respectively. The coefficients b_1 and b_2 represent the relations between each mediator and the dependent variable controlling for the independent variable and the other mediator. Again, an estimator of the mediated effect can be obtained by the difference between the total effect and the direct effect, that is, $c - c'$ or by the product of the relevant coefficients, that is, a_1b_1 and a_2b_2. The estimator of $c - c'$ is the total mediated effect, that is, the mediated effect via both M_1 and M_2. On the other hand, the estimators of a_1b_1 and a_2b_2 are the mediated effects uniquely attributable to M_1 and M_2, respectively.

The two-mediator Equations 20.8, 20.9, 20.10, and 20.11 demonstrate the superiority of the product of coefficients approach compared to the causal steps and difference in coefficients tests. Each method is relatively easily applied to the case of a single mediator; however, only the product of coefficients method is directly applicable to more complicated models. Causal steps and difference score methods could be applied but are more cumbersome. With two mediators, there are now three mediated effects, the effect of X on Y through M_1, the effect of X on Y through M_2, and the total mediated effect of X on Y through M_1 and M_2, called the *total indirect effect*. With the causal steps method, it is possible to test the significance of the a and b paths corresponding to each mediated effect, but there is not a direct test of the total mediated effect, the sum of a_1b_1 and a_2b_2. The other limitation of the causal steps method is that there is not a direct point estimate and standard error useful for confidence limits and effect size calculation. However, with the product of coefficients method it is much more straightforward to test whether the total mediated effect, the sum of a_1b_1 and a_2b_2, is statistically significant either by forming the ratio of the estimate to estimated standard error or by creating confidence limits via a resampling method. The difference score method is appropriate to test the total indirect effect because it is the difference between the relation of X on Y before and after adjustment for both mediators, $c - c'$. The standard error of this difference for the total indirect effect is given in MacKinnon (2008). However, the difference in coefficients method is quite cumbersome for testing the specific indirect effects, a_1b_1 or a_2b_2, as it is not clear which coefficients would be compared. These problems with causal steps and difference in coefficients methods

are magnified in more complicated models. These quantities can be obtained in a straightforward manner with the product of coefficients method.

CONSISTENT AND INCONSISTENT MEDIATION MODELS

Consistent or inconsistent mediation models are determined by the signs of the mediated and the direct effects. For consistent mediation models, all the mediated and the direct effects in a model have the same sign. Inconsistent mediation models, on the other hand, include at least one mediated effect having the opposite sign to the other mediated or direct effects in the model (Blalock, 1969; Davis, 1985; MacKinnon et al., 2000). When the signs of the mediated effect(s) and the direct effect are inconsistent, the overall relation between the independent and the dependent variables, that is, the total effect, may not be statistically significant, as described in MacKinnon et al. (2000).

The two-mediator model also is helpful to demonstrate inconsistent mediation effects. Sheets and Braver (1999) hypothesized that an overall relation between social dominance and sexual harassment would be 0 because of opposing mediation effects via harasser's power (M_1) and desirability (M_2). Murayama and Elliot (2012) explain inconsistent effects for competition on performance because competition increases avoidance goals that reduces performance and competition increases approach goals that increase performance. There are other hypothetical examples of possible opposing effects. For example, an abstinence program may increase intentions to abstain but participating in the program may also increase interest in sexual activity leading to a null program effect because of opposing mediators. For another example, incarceration in prison may lead to rehabilitation, which reduces recidivism, but exposure to fellow inmates in prison may also engender a norm more favorable towards criminal activity, which then increases recidivism. It is possible that any intervention would have opposing mediation effects when the program is composed of multiple components designed to change the outcome. The opposing mediation effects would be observed more easily if multiple mediator models are estimated.

EFFECT SIZE MEASURES OF MEDIATION

Effect size in mediation models can be specified for each path involved in the mediation pathway and for the entire mediated effect. To specify the effect size of each path, correlations, partial correlations, and standardized coefficients are used. There are several ways to define the effect size of the entire mediated effect. One of the most commonly used effect size measures is the proportion mediated, which is obtained by the ratio of the mediated effect to the total effect, that is, $ab/(ab + c')$. The proportion mediated has heuristic value, in that researchers can gauge the effect size in terms of the proportion of the total effect that is mediated. Limitations of the proportion mediated effect include the large sample size requirements (Mackinnon et al., 1995), ambiguity when effects are small, and ambiguity in interpretation for inconsistent mediation models where the mediated and the direct effects have the opposite signs (taking absolute values of all the effects before calculating the proportion mediated may be helpful in this case; see Alwin & Hauser, 1975). Other measures of effect size for the entire mediated effect are the ratio of the mediated effect to direct effect, ab/c', R-squared measures (Fairchild et al., 2009), and effect standardized by standard deviation of the dependent variable (see Miočević et al., 2018, for information on mediation effect size measures).

ASSUMPTIONS OF THE SINGLE MEDIATOR MODEL

Most current developments in mediation analysis address statistical and inferential assumptions of the mediation model. For the $\hat{ab}$ estimator of the mediated effect, several simultaneous regression analysis assumptions are required, including that the mediator and the residual in Equation 20.2 are independent and that the residuals in Equations 20.2 and 20.3 are independent (MacKinnon, 2008; McDonald, 1997). It is also assumed that there is not an interaction between X and M in Equation 20.3, although this interaction can be tested and in some cases may be expected based on theory as outlined below. The temporal order of the variables in the model is also assumed to be correctly specified (e.g., X→ M → Y rather than Y → M → X). The sample is assumed to be a random sample from the population of interest. Several other types of model specification are assumed to be correct, including self-containment that no variables related to the variables in the mediation equations are left out of the estimated model and that coefficients estimate causal effects. It is also assumed that the model has minimal errors of measurement (Holland, 1988; James & Brett, 1984; McDonald, 1997).

Assumption of No Interaction Between X and M

The X-by-M interaction could be included in Equation 20.2, which would suggest a moderator effect such that the b coefficient differs across the levels of X. Different b coefficients across levels of X may reflect that an experimental manipulation may have changed the relation of M to Y (MacKinnon et al., 2020). For example, a smoking prevention program may remove a relation between offers to use tobacco (M) and subsequent tobacco use (Y) in the program group but not for participants in the control group, because persons exposed to the program learned skills to refuse offers of tobacco so that offers are not significantly related to tobacco use (Judd & Kenny, 1981a). Significant XM interactions may also be obtained when there are other nonlinear relations in the model. If a program increases M to a value so that the relation between M and Y differs from the relation at other levels of M, the XM interaction would be statistically significant, because of a nonlinear relation between X and Y. If there is some other variable that is an important mediator, it is possible that this variable may predict both M and Y, leading to a statistically significant XM interaction.

Assumption of Correct Model Specification

There have been many important recent extensions to address limitations of the standard mediation analysis described earlier. First, more complicated models are often hypothesized. These models may include multiple independent variables, multiple mediators, and multiple outcomes. With these more comprehensive models, the relations among variables in the mediation model may be more explicitly specified and the mediation effects may be more accurately estimated. Second, when the data are clustered, methods for testing mediation within and across levels have been developed to accommodate the statistical issues in multilevel analysis and to explore the rich information in multiple levels of analysis (Krull & MacKinnon, 1999, 2001; Preacher et al., 2010). Third, mediation effects may differ by subgroups defined by moderator variables both within (such as M or Y) the mediation model and outside (variables other than M or Y) the mediation model (Fairchild & MacKinnon, 2009; Muller et al., 2005; Preacher et al., 2010). Fourth, mediation requires temporal precedence clarifying that X affects M that affects Y in a longitudinal or temporal order (Gollob & Reichardt, 1991; Kraemer et al., 2002; MacKinnon, 2008). Finally, developments in the causal interpretation of mediation studies (Holland, 1988; Robins & Greenland, 1992) provide a useful framework to describe the strengths and limitations of possible causal inferences from a mediation study. Estimates of causal mediation effects for the case of continuous M and Y variables correspond to traditional mediation analysis without an XM interaction, and causal mediation effects correspond to simple mediation and simple direct effects if the XM interaction is present (MacKinnon et al., 2020). The correspondence between traditional effects and causal effects does not correspond for all effects when the M and Y variables are categorical (Rijnhart, Valente, MacKinnon, et al., 2021; Rijnhart, Valente, Smyth, et al., 2021).

MEDIATION WITH CATEGORICAL OUTCOMES

In some mediation studies the dependent variable is categorical, such as whether a person suffered a heart attack or died or not. In such cases, Equations 20.1 and 20.2 must be rewritten for logistic or probit regression, so that the dependent variable is a latent continuous variable that has been dichotomized for the analysis. Because the residual variances in logistic or probit regression are fixed, the parameters c, c', and b depend on the other predictor variables in the model. So, the differences in coefficients across models could reflect real differences, but they could also be artificial effects due to the fixed error variance (MacKinnon, 2008), which is also known as a *lack of collapsibility* (Rijnhart, Valente, MacKinnon, et al., 2021). For example, the estimator $\hat{c} - \hat{c}'$ for mediation may be incorrect because the parameter estimate of $\hat{c}'$ depends on the true relation of the mediator to the outcome and the scaling of Equations 20.1 and 20.2 (MacKinnon & Dwyer, 1993). A solution to this discrepancy is to standardize regression coefficients prior to estimating mediation (MacKinnon, Lockwood, et al., 2007; Winship & Mare, 1983), which brings the two estimates of the mediated effect closer in value. More accurate methods can be obtained with application of causal mediation methods (Rijnhart, Valente, MacKinnon, et al., 2021; Rijnhart, Valente, Smyth, et al., 2021; Rijnhart, Valente, & MacKinnon, 2022; Valeri & VanderWeele, 2013) to be described below.

MEDIATION WITH COUNT OUTCOMES

Mediation analysis has been extended to models with count data, where M and/or Y are count variables (Coxe & MacKinnon, 2010; Geldhof et al., 2018; O'Rourke & Vazquez, 2019; Wang & Albert, 2012). Many outcomes in psychology are count variables (e.g., frequency of aggressive behaviors, days of drinking for a typical month, number of errors in memory test), and such models can be handled in the *generalized linear modeling (GLM)* framework (Volume 3, Chapter 9, this Handbook). The GLM framework allows for different link functions that can relate the observed outcome scores to the predicted scores so that the relations between the predicted outcome scores and the explanatory variables (predictors) can be estimated in a linear way. In addition, GLM has a flexible error structure, which makes it suitable for the analysis of count outcomes whose conditional error distributions are not normal.

Applying Poisson regression to conventional mediation analysis for count variable Y, Coxe and MacKinnon (2010) demonstrated that mediated effects estimated by $\hat{a}\hat{b}$ and estimated by $\hat{c} - \hat{c}'$ both were biased, although bias decreased as sample size increased. In addition, similar to the mediation for binary outcomes, the bias was larger when the mediated effects were estimated by $\hat{c} - \hat{c}'$ than estimated by $\hat{a}\hat{b}$. Other studies on conventional mediation analysis for count outcomes focused on the interpretation of the mediated effects. GLM estimates a linear relation between the predictor and the predicted outcome (i.e., log of counts); however, the relation between the predictor and the observed outcome is non-linear, and, thus, the effect of the predictor is not constant. It was suggested, therefore, that the mediated effects obtained by $\hat{a}\hat{b}$ be examined at various levels of X, resulting in evaluating several mediated effects obtained by the product of a coefficient and the first partial derivative of Equation 20.2 with respect to M, that is, $\hat{a}\hat{b}(e^{i_2+bM+c'X})$ (Geldhof et al., 2018; O'Rourke & Vazquez, 2019). Drawing on causal mediation literature (Imai et al., 2010; Valeri & VanderWeele, 2013), causal mediated effects for models with count variable M and/or count variable Y can be estimated using the GLM coefficients and exponentiating the relevant quantity needed to obtain causal effects (e.g., MacKinnon, in press; Muthén et al., 2016).

The flexibility of GLM allows for handling mediation models with mediator and/or outcome with excess zeros, that is, zero-inflated (ZI) count variables, where a substantial number of participants have a zero-response value while the rest have positive values, resulting in positively skewed, over-dispersed distributions (e.g., binge drinking episodes, frequency of sexually trans-mitted infections). Note that not all zeroes are excess zeros, for example, for a question asking about alcohol use, some drinkers report zero drinks in the last week and nondrinkers also report zero drinks. Models for the count variables with ZI distributions, such as ZI-Poisson, ZI-negative binomial, and ZI-hurdle models, simultaneously estimate the prediction of zero (vs. non-zero) responses, that is, binary process, and the prediction

of counts, that is, count process. These models may be beneficial when investigating differential mediat-ing mechanisms for the two processes. For example, hypothesized mediators may work for prevent-ing adolescents from drinking, for reducing the frequency of alcohol use among drinkers, or both.

LONGITUDINAL MEDIATION MODELS

With longitudinal data assessed over time on the same individuals, researchers can examine more complex questions regarding meditation mechanisms. The time ordering of X, M, and Y can be specified in the mediation model. Longitudinal data also allows researchers to investigate media-tion in terms of within-individual changes. For example, mediation can be modeled as X causes changes in M between pre- and posttest, which, in turn, causes changes in Y between pre- and posttest. In addition, one can examine the stability of effects across time, such as whether the effect of X on M or the effect of M on Y are stable across time, and test the stability of mediation effects. However, it is challenging to determine the optimal timing of measurements to accurately assess when longitudinal relations occur. Also, researchers need to pay more attention to the potential mis-specification of the model, such as omitted variables or paths, and hypothesizing correct mediation pathways (Cheong, 2011; Cole & Maxwell, 2003; Collins et al., 1998).

Although there are various ways of modeling longitudinal mediation relations (MacKinnon, 2008), we present four approaches: (a) auto-regressive models, (b) latent growth curve models, (c) latent difference scores models, and (d) person-oriented longitudinal models. Besides these approaches, one can combine autoregressive and latent growth models (LGM; Bollen & Curran, 2004) or specify the model parameters in a contin-uous time metric to reflect different time intervals between measurements (Boker & Nesselroade, 2002; Fritz, 2007). Similarities and differences between these different modeling approaches applied to two waves of data are described in Valente and MacKinnon (2017). More general discussion of longitudinal mediation modeling strategies with applications are described in Goldsmith et al. (2018) and Krull et al. (2016).

Autoregressive Mediation Model

In the typical autoregressive mediation models, relations among X, M, and Y one measurement occasion apart are specified. In autoregressive mediation models, researchers have several options for modeling mediation. First, one can focus only on the relations consistent with longitudinal mediation, such as $X_{T1} \rightarrow M_{T2} \rightarrow Y_{T3}$, assuming that mediation would not occur within the same wave. Another possibility is to add contemporary mediation relations (e.g., $X_{T2} \rightarrow M_{T2}$, $M_{T2} \rightarrow Y_{T2}$) to the longitudinal autoregressive mediation model and estimate the contemporary mediation effect within each wave, except the first wave, where the relations among X, M, and Y are typically specified as correlated. A third type of autoregressive mediation model includes any possible relations among X, M, and Y, including longitudinal relations based on time ordering (e.g., $M_{T1} \rightarrow X_{T2}$, $Y_{T2} \rightarrow M_{T3}$), which may be counterintuitive in that the directions of the relations among X, M, and Y are the opposite to the hypothesized mediation model. This type of model, however, may be realistic, considering that X, M, and Y are interrelated. It is possible that M_{T2} is predicted by Y_{T1} because Y_{T1} is related to M_{T1}. Regardless of the type of autoregressive model, the estimated mediation effect and its standard error can be obtained in the usual way, using the relevant path coefficients and their estimates of standard errors, to test the significance of the point estimate of mediation and construct confidence intervals. More details on autoregressive mediation models can be found in Cole and Maxwell (2003), Gollob and Reichardt (1991), and MacKinnon (2008).

Autoregressive mediation models are useful because they can provide information about time-specific mediation effects, such as when the mediation effects start to occur or when they stop working. However, it is a common practice to estimate autoregressive models only using covariance structure without mean structure, resulting in mediated effects estimated based on between-individual differences in the variables, rather than within-individual changes over time (see also Dwyer, 1983, and Rogosa, 1988). In addition, with many potential mediation effects, it may not be easy to determine which mediation relation represents the true model.

Latent Growth Mediation Model

When LGM is applied to mediation analysis, the mediation process is typically modeled using parallel process models (see Muthén & Curran, 1997; Singer & Willett, 2003, for more on latent growth modeling), where the growth trajectories of X, M, and Y are estimated in three distinctive growth trajectories and the mediation is hypothesized in the relations among the growth factors. Typically, researchers examine whether the slope of X affects the slope of M and whether the slope of M, in turn, affects the slope of Y. Alternatively, mediation can be evaluated in the relations among the initial level of X, the slope of M, and the slope of Y. As in the mediation models described in earlier sections, the relation between the trajectory of X and the trajectory of Y has two sources: the indirect effect via the trajectory of M and the direct effect on the trajectory of Y. The unique aspect of testing mediation in LGM framework is that the mediation is modeled based on within-individual changes.

When the mediation effect is examined based on the relations of slope factors of X, M, and Y that are measured across the same time periods, causal explanation is limited because the relations among the slopes of the three trajectories are concurrent. When the variable X represents randomized group status, the effect of X on the slope of M can be interpreted as causal, but the relation between the slope of M and the slope of Y is still correlational. One way to improve causal explanation in the LGM mediation model is using the two-stage piecewise parallel process model (Cheong et al., 2003), in which X affects the growth of M at an earlier phase, which then affects the growth of Y at a later phase.

Latent Change Score Model

As in the LGM approach to mediation, latent change score (LCS) models also examine the relations among the changes in X, M, and Y. While the changes in the LGM approach are estimated as an average change per time unit (e.g., per year) based on several waves of data, the changes estimated in the LCS approach are based the changes between the pairs of adjacent·waves (Ferrer & McArdle, 2003; McArdle, 2001; McArdle & Nesselroade, 2003; O'Rourke et al., 2021). Again, the relation between the change in X and the change in Y are composed of two parts, that is, the indirect effect via the change in M and the direct effect, and the interpretation of mediation is similar to the LGM approach: the change in X affects the change in M, which then affects the change in Y.

In the LCS modeling, the true scores at each wave and the change scores between waves are estimated using latent variables and fixed parameters. Once the change scores are obtained, these change scores are then analyzed using the same equations as for cross-sectional models. LCS mediation models with more than two waves of data are particularly informative when researchers expect different mediation mechanisms for changes at different waves of measurement. For example, the treatment program may change adolescent drug use via change in parental monitoring at early adolescence but via change in peer norms at later adolescence. In addition, researchers can test time specific mediation, as in autoregressive mediation models, based on within-individual changes. Furthermore, one can examine the change in the difference scores in LCS models and specify the models to represent moving averages.

Person-Oriented Longitudinal Models

Several different approaches have been suggested for identifying subgroups of persons based on their values of the independent variable, mediating variable, and dependent variable. Typically, binary latent variables are created to indicate individuals' status, that is, to signify whether the individual's responses are consistent with a hypothesized mediation pattern or not. Three original approaches are based on trajectory classes (Muthén & Muthén, 1998–2007), staged response across

trials (Collins et al., 1998), and configural frequency analysis (Smyth & MacKinnon, 2021; von Eye et al., 2009; Wiedermann & von Eye, 2021). These models represent several new ways to understand both individual-level mediating processes as well as group-level mediating processes (von Eye et al., 2009). A related approach to identifying mediational processes is to focus on single-subject data with repeated measures. For example, mediation relations observed with one subject are tested with future subjects to provide cumulative evidence for a mediation relation. Another single-subject approach involves conducting permutation and randomization tests with the repeated measures data (MacKinnon et al., 2021; Taylor & MacKinnon, 2012). In some research areas where sample sizes are small such as some clinical populations, single-subject methods may be the only reasonable approach.

MODERATION AND MEDIATION

The strength and form of mediation relations may depend on other variables. For example, the relation of X to M (*a* path) and/or M to Y (*b* path) may differ across levels of a moderator variable, resulting in different mediated effect (*ab*) across levels of moderator variable. The moderator variable may be either an experimentally manipulated factor or a naturally occurring variable such as gender or ethnicity. These types of models have been an active area of research in the last few decades (Hays, 2022; Fairchild & MacKinnon, 2009; MacKinnon, 2008; Muller et al., 2005). One way to organize the different types of mediation analysis with moderator variables is to consider two different types of cases, (a) moderation of a mediated effect and (b) mediation of a moderator effect.

Moderation of a Mediated Effect

In the first case, moderation of a mediation relation, the X-to-M, M-to-Y, or the entire mediation relation may differ across levels of a moderator variable, such as subgroups of participants (e.g., cohorts, ages, or sexes). For a single mediator case, the application of moderation of a mediation analysis consists of estimating the same mediation model for each subgroup and then comparing the X-to-M relation, M-to-Y relation, and the mediated effect across subgroups. The equivalence of the mediated effect across groups can be tested (MacKinnon, 2008). Tests of the equality of $\hat{a}$, $\hat{b}$, and $\hat{c}'$ coefficients provide information about the invariance of action theory (how the program changes mediators) and the invariance of conceptual theory (how mediators are related to the outcome) across groups. The moderation of a mediation effect is more complex when the moderator variable is continuous. Although the regression equations are the same as for the categorical moderator case, the interpretation of results may be complicated for the continuous moderator case because of the large number of values of the moderator at which mediation relations may potentially differ. One approach is to apply a multilevel mediation model to these data (Asparouhov & Muthén, 2008; Muthén & Muthén, 1998–2007).

Mediation of a Moderator Effect

In a second type of mediation and moderation analysis, mediation of a moderator effect may be investigated. In this situation, a mediating variable is sought to explain how an interaction between two variables is related to a dependent variable, that is, to investigate evidence that the mediator transmits the relation from an interaction to a dependent variable. One common example from the treatment and prevention literature is that program effects are greater for high-risk subjects, so that there is an interaction effect of program exposure and risk status. In this case, the interaction may affect a mediating variable of social norms that then affects drug use. The purpose of mediation of a moderator analysis is to assess whether the mediating variable(s) explains the interaction effect. Investigation of these effects consists of estimating a series of regression equations where the main effect of a covariate and the interaction of the covariate and the independent variable are included in both Equations 20.2 and 20.3.

To date, models investigating mediation and moderation have been largely independent, which

is not surprising given the complexity of investigating mediation and moderation alone. This separation in the theory and statistical testing between moderation and mediation has contributed to some ambiguity regarding the substantive motivation and statistical testing of these models. A critical goal of future research for mediation and moderation models will be to further develop and evaluate a general model in which each of the models is a special case (Fairchild & MacKinnon, 2009; MacKinnon, 2008; Muller et al., 2005).

CAUSAL INFERENCE

As an explanatory method, the goal of mediation analysis is to investigate how one variable transmits its effects to another. Fundamentally, this is a question of causation; however, traditional estimation methods are insufficient on their own in providing evidence for causal inference. Causal mediation methods, such as potential outcomes and graphical models (Pearl, 2012, 2014; VanderWeele, 2015; VanderWeele & Vansteelandt, 2009) provide the necessary framework to advance causal inference in mediation analysis. Methods for testing mediation that are based on regression and structural equation modeling approaches have been criticized from the perspective of counterfactual approaches to causal analysis of the relations among variables (MacKinnon, 2008, Chapter 13). Limitations to mediation models in particular and structural equation models in general have been outlined in social science (Morgan & Winship, 2007; James et al., 2006; Holland, 1988;) and epidemiological literature (Robins & Greenland, 1992). One widely known limitation of these models is the equivalent model criticism. Applied to the mediation model, if X, M, and Y are measured at the same time, there are other equivalent models (e.g., $Y \rightarrow M \rightarrow X$) that would explain the data equally well and are often indistinguishable without more information (Spirtes et al., 1993). Another limitation is the temporal precedence assumption. Cross-sectional data require additional assumptions if they are to be interpreted in a causal fashion. A third limitation is the aforementioned assumption of no omitted variables.

When X represents randomization to conditions, inference regarding X-to-M and X-to-Y relations is less problematic because it is clear that X came before M and Y. With randomization of a sufficient number of units to levels of X, all unmeasured covariates are assumed to be balanced between groups at baseline, and, thus, the relation of X to M and the relation of X to Y (that is not adjusted for M) can be attributed to the randomized manipulation. However, inference regarding the M to Y and X to Y adjusted for M relations is problematic because individuals are not randomly assigned to the levels of M, and, thus, omitted variables may seriously affect the interpretation of the b and c' paths.

Most causal mediation approaches are based on the *potential outcomes model*, which considers all possible conditions in which a participant could serve in addition to the condition that the participant did serve in. The specification of actual and counterfactual conditions provides a general framework for defining causal effects. For the two group X and Y design, the target causal estimand is the difference between the Y score for the same person in each group. It is not possible to simultaneously measure performance in both groups, but the difference in the average Y in each group from a randomized design provides a causal estimate of the group effect. The potential outcomes including a mediating variable are more complex because both the level of M and the level of Y is specified, for example, Y for a person in the treatment group if their mediator variable is changed from what they would get in the control to what they would get in the treatment group. That is, causal effects are defined as the difference between potential outcomes formed by changing the value of the mediator from the value in one group to the value that would have been obtained in the other group (MacKinnon, in press). For example, the pure natural indirect effect is the change in the Y score when the mediator value is changed from the control to the treatment group. Methods of estimation of these causal effects based on regression (Valeri & VanderWeele, 2013), imputation based methods (Vansteelandt et al., 2012) and weighting (Hong, 2015) are available

and all seek to estimate causal effects based on contrasts between potential outcomes. For the case of continuous M and continuous Y, the traditional and causal mediation methods give the same results under certain assumptions (MacKinnon et al., 2020). If the assumptions are violated or for categorical M and Y, results differ between the two methods.

Another strength of modern causal inference approaches is that they suggest strategies for investigating assumptions of the statistical methods, especially the ambiguity regarding the interpretation of the M-to-Y relation. When X represents random assignment to conditions, causal interpretation of mediating variables is improved (Holland, 1988; Robins & Greenland 1992) because X must causally precede M and Y. Holland showed that under some assumptions, the regression coefficient for the intervention effect on Y, $\hat{c}$, and the intervention effect on M, $\hat{a}$, are estimators of the true causal effect, because of the randomization of units to treatment. In contrast, the regression coefficient, $\hat{b}$, is not an accurate causal effect estimator because this relation is correlational, because participants are not directly randomized to scores on the mediator. Along the same logic, the estimator, $\hat{c}'$, is also not an accurate causal estimator of the direct effect because this relation is also correlational. These approaches provide an instrumental variable approach, whereby an estimate of the true causal relation between M and Y is the extent to which the predicted scores in the X-to-M relation, M', are related to Y, assuming a linear additive relation of M to Y and assuming that there is no direct effect of X on Y, that is, complete mediation. Several new approaches to causal inference for mediation have added to this original work. These methods use additional information such as covariates or specifying types of persons based on their response to any intervention, in order to improve causal inference of mediation effects. One of these alternatives, principal stratification, specifies the different ways in which participants could respond to an intervention and the mediated effect is estimated within stratifications defined by the different ways that participants could respond (Angrist et al., 1996; Frangakis & Rubin, 2002; Jo, 2008). For example, different types of persons are identified, such as persons who would acquire the mediator if exposed to the treatment and persons who would not get the mediator regardless of whether exposed to the treatment or not. The mediated effect is obtained in these models by comparing the outcome measure between strata of persons who could get the mediator but did or did not receive the mediator. Sobel (2008) enhanced the Holland instrumental variable method to further investigate assumptions of the method. Other alternatives use randomization approaches based on covariates to model observed and counterfactual data (Lynch et al., 2008; Pearl, 2009; Robins, 1994; Ten Have et al., 2007), weighting observations by measured confounding (Coffman & Zhong, 2012) and estimation of the direct effect and indirect effect based on all of the potential outcomes (MacKinnon & Pirlott, 2015; Vansteelandt, 2009).

Another strategy to improve causal inference is to assess sensitivity of mediated effects to unmeasured confounding of the M-to-Y relation, measurement error in the mediator, or both confounding and measurement error (Cox et al., 2013; Fritz et al., 2016; Imai et al., 2010). The fact that the M-to-Y relation in the mediation model is considered the weakest link is interesting from the perspective of theories in psychology. In most psychological studies, the M-to-Y relation is specified based on theory, extensive prior research, and a variety of information besides statistical analysis, and mediators are selected because of this information. The emphasis on ambiguity of the M-to-Y relation may be reduced in psychology because it is generally much easier to conduct replication and extension experiments in psychology compared to some other disciplines, such as medicine, where conducting studies is often more expensive and requires extensive follow-up for disease processes to emerge. The application of causal inference approaches in psychology remain an important and active area of research because it illuminates untested assumptions in mediation theory. Regarding the causal interpretation of mediation relations, researchers have several

options based on current research practice. First, new models of causal inference can be applied to mediation analysis, although this may be difficult given the paucity of clear, concrete examples of their application in psychology. Second, one can treat the results of the mediation analysis as descriptive information, rather than true underlying causal mediation relations, especially for the M-to-Y relation, and address the variety of limitations of such a mediation analysis. Third, one can plan future experimental studies to provide evidence for the consistency and specificity of mediation relations as described below. These future studies may also include qualitative methods and clinical observations. In particular, a program of research that repeatedly tests mediator theory including testing mediation theory in other contexts provides the most convincing evidence for mediation.

EXPERIMENTAL DESIGNS TO INVESTIGATE MEDIATION

The mediation relationship presumes a causal relationship from X to M to Y. However, most designs randomly assign participants to levels of X and measure M and Y. Given that M is not randomized, the true causal relationship of M to Y cannot be inferred, given other variables confounded with M could be causing the M-to-Y relationship and only experiments can provide evidence of causality. Most of these designs are encouragement designs where participants are randomized to conditions that encourage participants to take up an activity that changes a mediator rather than direct random assignment to the level of a mediator (Holland, 1988). For example, randomization to study more hours does not randomize participants to the number of hours of study but encourages more study overall. However, researchers have been increasingly using experimental approaches to demonstrate the causal effect of the mediator (MacKinnon, Taborga, & Morgan-Lopez, 2002; Spencer et al., 2005; West & Aiken, 1997). Pirlott and MacKinnon (2016) provided experimental approaches to investigate the causal effect of the mediator. Specifically, they discussed two approaches to manipulate the mediator—experimental manipulations demonstrating a causal effect of the mediator and experimental manipulations targeting the effect of the mediator—and three types of designs that include mediator manipulations—double randomization designs, concurrent double randomization designs, and parallel designs. We summarize these approaches in the following section; examples of the manipulations in the upcoming section and designs and an assessment of their pros and cons can be found in Pirlott and MacKinnon (2016).

Types of Manipulation-of-Mediator Manipulations

Several types of manipulations attempt to randomly assign participants to levels of a mediating construct. Below we differentiate between manipulations that seek to demonstrate a causal effect of the mediator versus manipulations that seek to change the *magnitude* of the mediator's effect.

Manipulations demonstrating a causal effect of the mediator. Manipulations that look to demonstrate a causal relationship of the mediator on the dependent variable randomize participants to levels of the mediator and measure its effects on the dependent variable, akin to a typical experiment, with the main difference being that the randomization is to the theoretically proposed mediator. Measured differences in the dependent variable across levels of the manipulation provide evidence of the causal effect of the mediator. Including a manipulation check measuring the mediator that shows mean differences corresponding to the manipulation demonstrates the effectiveness of the manipulation. The manipulation of the mediator could be operationalized as a present versus absent operationalization of the mediator or as a high versus low operationalization of the mediator, although Imai et al. (2013) argued that mediators cannot be truly manipulated in an absolute present versus absent operationalization (perhaps aside from physiological interventions) but can instead be encouraged or discouraged.

As an example (discussed in Pirlott & MacKinnon, 2016) in which the mediator was

encouraged versus discouraged was used by Li et al. (2012). Their model predicted that belief in a soul (M) mediates the difference between Catholics and Protestants (X) in internal attributions (Y). They randomly assigned Protestants to either write an essay suggesting souls do or do not exist (thus encouraging or discouraging belief in a soul) and then measured internal attributions. Comparing internal attributions between the "high" and "low" belief in a soul conditions revealed a differentiated pattern of internal attributions suggesting that belief in a soul causally affected internal attributions.

Manipulations targeting the magnitude of the effect of the mediator. Designs that manipulate the *effect* of the mediator attempt to either increase or decrease the effect of the mediator in conjunction with an experimental manipulation of X. These designs randomly assign participants to one level of X and one level of the mediator. The manipulation of the mediator includes a control condition in which the mediator is allowed to vary freely relative to the experimental condition, which seeks to either increase or decrease the effect of the mediator.

Blockage manipulation. The blockage manipulation of the mediator attempts to block the mediator from operating or reduce its effect. It eliminates or minimizes the systematic variance in the mediator caused by X by controlling or blocking the mediator from varying as a function of X. Accordingly, there should be no mean differences in Y as a function of X because the mediator was blocked from varying. This is compared to the control condition in which the mediator was allowed to vary freely. Mean differences in Y should exist as a function of X because the mediator was allowed to vary.

Enhancement manipulation. The enhancement manipulation of the mediator attempts to increase the effect of the mediator by increasing the systematic variance in the mediator caused by X. As in the blockage manipulation, the enhancement condition is compared to the control condition in which the mediator was allowed to vary freely. Accordingly, there should be larger mean differences in Y as a function of X in the enhancement condition relative to the pattern of mean differences in Y as a function of X in the control condition.

As described in Pirlott and MacKinnon (2016), Cooper et al. (1978) used a blockage and enhancement manipulation in conjunction with a cognitive dissonance model, in which counterattitudinal behaviors (X) elicit dissonance arousal (M) that causes attitude change (Y). They blocked, enhanced, or did not change the variance in the mediator by randomly assigning participants to receive a stimulant, depressant, or placebo, respectively, and randomly assigning participants to the counterattitudinal condition. In the placebo condition in which the mediator was allowed to vary naturally, the predicted effect occurred in which attitudes differed between counterattitudinal conditions. In the depressant condition, the mediator (arousal) was blocked from varying, thus, there appeared to be no effect of the counterattitudinal manipulation on attitudes, that is, no difference in attitudes between counterattitudinal conditions. Lastly, in the stimulant condition, the effect of the mediator (arousal) was enhanced, such that it produced a larger attitude change than in the placebo condition.

Types of Manipulation-of-Mediator Designs

The previous section discussed methods to manipulate the mediator. Below, we discuss overarching study designs that include manipulations of the mediator.

Double randomization designs. Double randomization designs involve two experiments. In the first experiment, researchers manipulate X and measure M and Y, which enables a causal inference of the X-to-M and X-to-Y paths. Then in the second experiment, researchers manipulate the mediator and, thus, randomly assign participants to levels of the manipulated mediator and measure Y. As suggested above, also measuring the mediator provides additional evidence of the construct validity of the manipulation.

Concurrent double randomization designs. The concurrent double randomization design simultaneously manipulates X and M, thus yielding, minimally, a 2×2 experimental design. This allows for the causal inference of X on Y and M on Y. This could demonstrate a main effect of X on Y, a main effect of M on Y, and/or an interaction between X and M to effect Y. Again, measuring the mediator would also provide evidence that X affects M, given this design is otherwise a moderation design.

Parallel designs. Imai et al. (2013) proposed parallel designs, in which participants are randomly assigned to one of two studies: one that manipulates X and measures M and Y or one that concurrently manipulates X and M and measures Y. The two studies in tandem can provide convergent validity of the mediator as the causal factor linking X and Y. Furthermore, by randomly assigning participants to the particular study, any differences in the effects can solely be attributed to the type of design (e.g., manipulation of mediator versus measurement of mediator) and not due to other confounds that is a strength beyond the double randomization design.

GUIDELINES FOR REPORTING MEDIATION ANALYSIS

The purpose of this section is to provide a number of guidelines for reporting the research study on mediation relations in psychology. Guidelines for reporting mediation analysis for randomized trials and observational studies have recently been described (Lee et al., 2021). Most of the characteristics of mediation studies are the same as for any research study in psychology. First, describe the theoretical and empirical basis for hypothesized mediation relation prior to conducting the study. Describing the mediation theory clarifies the overall purpose of the study and forces consideration of alternative interpretations of the results of the study leading to better research design. If the mediation theory is complex, explicitly indicate which mediated effect or combinations of mediated effects are to be investigated in the study as well as the pattern of effects in the mediation model. Discuss how the mediators targeted for study are the critical mediators based on prior research. Second, describe results of each link in the mediation chain and report the estimated mediated effect, standard errors, and confidence limits, as well as effect size measures. If there are more links in the chain, then significance tests for each link in the chain help clarify the accuracy of mediation theory. Calculation of confidence limits and significance tests for the mediated effect should be conducted using a method that incorporates the nonnormal distribution of the product, either based on the distribution of the product or resampling methods. Third, clear discussion of how the study assessed the specified temporal relation among variables is necessary. If longitudinal data are not available, defense of the ordering in the analysis may be more difficult but potentially more important both to bolster evidence for a mediation relation and to help guide the design of future longitudinal studies. Fourth, discuss how omitted variables may alter conclusions and provide some indication of the sensitivity of the observed results to additional confounding variables. Fifth, directly address problems with interpreting the M-to-Y relation. As emphasized in causal inference approaches, randomization is central to defending a hypothesized mediation relation. Thus, the extent to which M can be considered randomized should be addressed by considering counterfactual cases such as how the relation between M and Y may differ across experimental groups. Also, detailed discussion of the mediator investigated in the study is useful. Is the mediator you measured the actual mediator? Is there a more fine-grained mediator that may actually be the most important in changing Y? Similarly, if you could measure additional mediators what would they be? Is there evidence of overlap in the measures of the mediator and outcome? Sixth, describe additional designs and research findings that could be used to further clarify a mediation relation. In particular, future experimental studies to investigate the consistency and specificity of the mediation relation are necessary to provide convincing evidence for mediation. Overall, the identification of mediation relations requires a sustained program of research including many different types of information including

qualitative, quantitative, and clinical information. During this process it may be useful to incorporate prior information on mediation relations in a sequential Bayesian perspective (Yuan & MacKinnon, 2009; Wurpts et al., 2022) and to report results in a manner suitable for meta-analysis studies of mediation processes (Cheung, 2015).

SUMMARY AND FUTURE DIRECTIONS

Extensive interest in statistical analysis of mediation relations is understandable considering that psychological theories focus on the process by which phenomena occur. Mediation relations are also of interest in many other fields including epidemiology, public health, and medicine. Mediating processes are critically important for intervention and prevention research because they provide information that can be used to make these interventions more efficient and powerful. Demonstration of mediation relations is a difficult and challenging process but there has been considerable recent development in methods to accurately assess mediation (MacKinnon et al., 2018). Significance tests for mediation based on the nonnormal distribution of the product are most accurate, including tests directly based on the distribution of the product and methods that model the distribution of the product such as the bootstrap or resampling methods. Multiple mediator and models that are more comprehensive allow for consideration of omitted and additional variables that may be central to test mediation. Alternative longitudinal mediation models provide important opportunities to test temporal relations among variables in the mediation model. Complementary investigation of mediation relations with person-oriented models provides more evidence for true mediation relations. Developments in causal inference for mediation relations are rapidly increasing, thereby providing an accurate assessment of the limitations and strengths of contemporary mediation methods. New approaches to test the sensitivity of tests of mediation to violations of assumptions should add greatly to the identification of true mediation relations. An important characteristic of psychological research is that it is often easier to conduct randomized replication studies than in other fields such as sociology or epidemiology. This opportunity for replication is ideal for testing mediation theory in the variety of applications necessary to demonstrate the consistency and specificity of theoretical mediating process fundamental to psychology.

References

Alwin, D. F., & Hauser, R. M. (1975). The decomposition of effects in path analysis. *American Sociological Review, 40*(1), 37–47. https://doi.org/10.2307/2094445

Angrist, J. D., Imbens, G. W., & Rubin, D. B. (1996). Identification of causal effects using instrumental variables (with commentary). *Journal of the American Statistical Association, 91*(434), 444–455. https://doi.org/10.1080/01621459.1996.10476902

Arling, G. L., & Harlow, H. F. (1967). Effects of social deprivation on maternal behavior of rhesus monkeys. *Journal of Comparative and Physiological Psychology, 64*(3), 371–377. https://doi.org/10.1037/h0025221

Asparouhov, T., & Muthén, B. (2008). Multilevel mixture models. In G. R. Hancock & K. M. Samuelsen (Eds.), *Advances in latent variable mixture models* (pp. 27–51). Information Age Publishing.

Bandura, A., Ross, D., & Ross, S. A. (1963). Vicarious reinforcement and imitative learning. *Journal of Abnormal and Social Psychology, 67*(6), 601–607. https://doi.org/10.1037/h0045550

Baranowski, T., Anderson, C., & Carmack, C. (1998). Mediating variable framework in physical activity interventions. How are we doing? How might we do better? *American Journal of Preventive Medicine, 15*(4), 266–297. https://doi.org/10.1016/S0749-3797(98)00080-4

Baron, R. M., & Kenny, D. A. (1986). The moderator-mediator variable distinction in social psychological research: Conceptual, strategic, and statistical considerations. *Journal of Personality and Social Psychology, 51*(6), 1173–1182. https://doi.org/10.1037/0022-3514.51.6.1173

Beck, A. T., Rush, A. J., Shaw, B. F., & Emery, G. (1979). *Cognitive therapy of depression.* Guilford Press.

Bentler, P. M. (1997). *EQS for Windows (Version 5.6)* [Computer program]. Multivariate Software.

Bishop, Y. M. M., Fienberg, S. E., & Holland, P. W. (1975). *Discrete multivariate analysis: Theory and practice.* MIT Press.

Blalock, H. M. (1969). *Theory construction: From verbal to mathematical formulations.* Prentice-Hall.

Boker, S. M., & Nesselroade, J. R. (2002). A method for modeling the intrinsic dynamics of intra-individual variability: Recovering the parameters of simulated oscillators in multi-wave panel data. *Multivariate Behavioral Research, 37*(1), 127–160. https://doi.org/10.1207/S15327906MBR3701_06

Bollen, K. A., & Curran, P. J. (2004). Autoregressive latent trajectory (ALT) models: A synthesis of two traditions. *Sociological Methods & Research, 32*(3), 336–383. https://doi.org/10.1177/0049124103260222

Bollen, K. A., & Stine, R. A. (1990). Direct and indirect effects: Classical and bootstrap estimates of variability. *Sociological Methodology, 20,* 115–140. https://doi.org/10.2307/271084

Cheong, J. (2011). Accuracy of estimates and statistical power for testing meditation in latent growth modeling. *Structural Equation Modeling, 18*(2), 195–211. https://doi.org/10.1080/10705511.2011.557334

Cheong, J., MacKinnon, D. P., & Khoo, S. T. (2003). Investigation of mediational processes using parallel process latent growth curve modeling. *Structural Equation Modeling, 10*(2), 238–262. https://doi.org/10.1207/S15328007SEM1002_5

Cheung, M. W.-L. (2015). *Meta-analysis: A structural equation modeling approach.* Wiley.

Coffman, D. L., & Zhong, W. (2012). Assessing mediation using marginal structural models in the presence of confounding and moderation. *Psychological Methods, 17*(4), 642–664. https://doi.org/10.1037/a0029311

Cole, D. A., & Maxwell, S. E. (2003). Testing mediational models with longitudinal data: Questions and tips in the use of structural equation modeling. *Journal of Abnormal Psychology, 112*(4), 558–577. https://doi.org/10.1037/0021-843X.112.4.558

Collins, L. M., Graham, J. J., & Flaherty, B. P. (1998). An alternative framework for defining mediation. *Multivariate Behavioral Research, 33*(2), 295–312. https://doi.org/10.1207/s15327906mbr3302_5

Cooper, J., Zanna, M. P., & Taves, P. A. (1978). Arousal as a necessary condition for attitude change following induced compliance. *Journal of Personality and Social Psychology, 36*(10), 1101–1106. https://doi.org/10.1037/0022-3514.36.10.1101

Cox, M. G., Kisbu-Sakarya, Y., Miočević, M., & MacKinnon, D. P. (2013). Sensitivity plots for confounder bias in the single mediator model. *Evaluation Review, 37*(5), 405–431. https://doi.org/10.1177/0193841X14524576

Coxe, S., & MacKinnon, D. P. (2010). Mediation analysis of Poisson distributed count outcomes.

Multivariate Behavioral Research, 45(6), 1022–1022. https://doi.org/10.1080/00273171.2010.534375

Davis, J. A. (1985). *The logic of causal order.* SAGE Publications.

Dwyer, J. H. (1983). *Statistical models for the social and behavioral sciences.* Oxford.

Efron, B., & Tibshirani, R. J. (1993). *An introduction to the bootstrap.* Chapman & Hall/CRC Press. https://www.hms.harvard.edu/bss/neuro/bornlab/nb204/statistics/bootstrap.pdf

Elwert, F., & Winship, C. (2014). Endogenous selection bias: The problem of conditioning on a collider variable. *Annual Review of Sociology*, 40(1), 31–53. https://doi.org/10.1146/annurev-soc-071913-043455

Fairchild, A. J., & MacKinnon, D. P. (2009). A general model for testing mediation and moderation effects. *Prevention Science*, 10(2), 87–99. https://doi.org/10.1007/s11121-008-0109-6

Fairchild, A. J., MacKinnon, D. P., Taborga, M. P., & Taylor, A. B. (2009). R2 effect-size measures for mediation analysis. *Behavior Research Methods*, 41(2), 486–498. https://doi.org/10.3758/BRM.41.2.486

Ferrer, E., & McArdle, J. J. (2003). Alternative structural models for multivariate longitudinal data analysis. *Structural Equation Modeling*, 10(4), 493–524. https://doi.org/10.1207/S15328007SEM1004_1

Fishbein, M., & Ajzen, I. (1975). *Belief, attitude, intention, and behavior: An introduction to theory and research.* Addison-Wesley.

Frangakis, C. E., & Rubin, D. B. (2002). Principal stratification in causal inference. *Biometrics*, 58(1), 21–29. https://doi.org/10.1111/j.0006-341X.2002.00021.x

Fritz, M. S. (2007). *An exponential decay model for mediation* [Unpublished doctoral dissertation]. Arizona State University.

Fritz, M. S., Kenny, D. A., & MacKinnon, D. P. (2016). The combined effects of measurement error and omitting confounders in the single-mediator model. *Multivariate Behavioral Research*, 51(5), 681–697. https://doi.org/10.1080/00273171.2016.1224154

Geldhof, G. J., Anthony, K. P., Selig, J. P., & Mendez-Luck, C. A. (2018). Accommodating binary and count variables in mediation: A case for conditional indirect effects. *International Journal of Behavioral Development*, 42(2), 300–308. https://doi.org/10.1177/0165025417727876

Goldsmith, K., MacKinnon, D. P., Chalder, T., White, P. D., Sharpe, M., & Pickles, A. (2018). Tutorial: The practical application of longitudinal structural equation mediation models in clinical trials. *Psychological Methods*, 23(2), 191–207. https://doi.org/10.1037/met0000154

Gollob, H. F., & Reichardt, C. S. (1991). Interpreting and estimating indirect effects assuming time lags really matter. In L. M. Collins & J. L. Horn (Eds.), *Best methods for the analysis of change: Recent advances, unanswered questions, future directions* (pp. 243–259). American Psychological Association. https://doi.org/10.1037/10099-015

Hays, A. F. (2022). *Introduction to mediation, moderation, and conditional process models* (3rd ed.). Guilford Press.

Holland, P. W. (1988). Causal inference, path analysis, and recursive structural equation models. *Sociological Methodology*, 18(1), 449–484. https://doi.org/10.2307/271055

Hong, G. (2015). *Causality in a social world: Moderation, mediation, and spill-over.* Wiley. https://doi.org/10.1002/9781119030638

Hyman, H. H. (1955). *Survey design and analysis: Principles, cases, and procedures.* Free Press.

Imai, K., Keele, L., & Tingley, D. (2010). A general approach to causal mediation analysis. *Psychological Methods*, 15(4), 309–334. https://doi.org/10.1037/a0020761

Imai, K., Tingley, D., & Yamamoto, T. (2013). Experimental designs for identifying causal mechanisms. *Journal of the Royal Statistical Society. Series A (Statistics in Society)*, 176(1), 5–51. https://doi.org/10.1111/j.1467-985X.2012.01032.x

James, L. R., & Brett, J. M. (1984). Mediators, moderators, and tests for mediation. *Journal of Applied Psychology*, 69(2), 307–321. https://doi.org/10.1037/0021-9010.69.2.307

James, L. R., Mulaik, S. A., & Brett, J. M. (2006). A tale of two methods. *Organizational Research Methods*, 9(2), 233–244. https://doi.org/10.1177/1094428105285144

Jo, B. (2008). Causal inference in randomized experiments with mediational processes. *Psychological Methods*, 13(4), 314–336. https://doi.org/10.1037/a0014207

Judd, C. M., & Kenny, D. A. (1981a). *Estimating the effects of social interventions.* Cambridge University Press.

Judd, C. M., & Kenny, D. A. (1981b). Process analysis: Estimating mediation in treatment evaluations. *Evaluation Review*, 5(5), 602–619. https://doi.org/10.1177/0193841X8100500502

Kazdin, A. E. (2009). Understanding how and why psychotherapy leads to change. *Psychotherapy Research*, 19(4–5), 418–428. https://doi.org/10.1080/10503300802448899

Kenny, D. A., Kashy, D. A., & Bolger, N. (1998). Data analysis in social psychology. In D. T. Gilbert, S. T. Fiske, & G. Lindzey (Eds.), *The handbook of social psychology* (Vol. 1, pp. 233–265). Oxford University Press.

Kraemer, H. C., Wilson, G. T., Fairburn, C. G., & Agras, W. S. (2002). Mediators and moderators of treatment effects in randomized clinical trials. *Archives of General Psychiatry, 59*(10), 877–883. https://doi.org/10.1001/archpsyc.59.10.877

Krull, J. L., Cheong, J., Fritz, M. S., & MacKinnon, D. P. (2016). Moderation and mediation in inter-individual longitudinal analysis. In D. Cicchetti (Ed.), *Developmental psychopathology: Theory and method* (pp. 922–985). John Wiley & Sons. https://doi.org/10.1002/9781119125556.devpsy121

Krull, J. L., & MacKinnon, D. P. (1999). Multilevel mediation modeling in group-based intervention studies. *Evaluation Review, 23*(4), 418–444. https://doi.org/10.1177/0193841X9902300404

Krull, J. L., & MacKinnon, D. P. (2001). Multilevel modeling of individual and group level mediated effects. *Multivariate Behavioral Research, 36*(2), 249–277. https://doi.org/10.1207/S15327906MBR3602_06

Lazarsfeld, P. F. (1955). Interpretation of statistical relations as a research operation. In P. F. Lazarsfeld & M. Rosenberg (Eds.), *The language of social research: A reader in the methodology of social research* (pp. 115–125). Free Press.

Lee, H., Cashin, A., Lamb, S., Hopewell, S., Vansteelandt, S., VanderWeele, T., MacKinnon, D., Collins, G., Golub, R., McAuley, J., & the AGReMA Group. (2021). A guide for reporting mediation analyses of randomized trials and observational studies: The AGReMA Statement. *Journal of the American Medical Association, 326*(11), 1045–1056. https://doi.org/10.1001/jama.2021.14075

Li, Y. J., Johnson, K. A., Cohen, A. B., Williams, M. J., Knowles, E. D., & Chen, Z. (2012). Fundamental(ist) attribution error: Protestants are dispositionally focused. *Journal of Personality and Social Psychology, 102*(2), 281–290. https://doi.org/10.1037/a0026294

Lynch, K. G., Cary, M., Gallop, R., & Ten Have, T. R. (2008). Causal mediation analyses for randomized trials. *Health Services and Outcomes Research Methodology, 8*(2), 57–76. https://doi.org/10.1007/s10742-008-0028-9

MacCorquodale, K., & Meehl, P. E. (1948). On a distinction between hypothetical constructs and intervening variables. *Psychological Review, 55*(2), 95–107. https://doi.org/10.1037/h0056029

MacKinnon, D. P. (1994) Analysis of mediating variables in prevention intervention studies. In A. Cazares & L. A. Beatty (Eds.), *Scientific methods for prevention intervention research: NIDA research monograph 139* (DHHS Pub. 94–3631, pp. 127–153). U.S. Department of Health and Human Services.

MacKinnon, D. P. (2008). *Introduction to statistical mediation analysis*. Routledge.

MacKinnon, D. P. (in press). *Introduction to statistical mediation analysis* (2nd ed.). Routledge.

MacKinnon, D. P., & Dwyer, J. H. (1993). Estimation of mediated effects in prevention studies. *Evaluation Review, 17*(2), 144–158. https://doi.org/10.1177/0193841X9301700202

MacKinnon, D. P., Fairchild, A. J., & Fritz, M. S. (2007). Mediation analysis. *Annual Review of Psychology, 58*(1), 593–614. https://doi.org/10.1146/annurev.psych.58.110405.085542

MacKinnon, D. P., Fritz, M. S., Williams, J., & Lockwood, C. M. (2007). Distribution of the product confidence limits for the indirect effect: Program PRODCLIN. *Behavior Research Methods, 39*(3), 384–389. https://doi.org/10.3758/BF03193007

MacKinnon, D. P., Krull, J. L., & Lockwood, C. M. (2000). Equivalence of the mediation, confounding and suppression effect. *Prevention Science, 1*(4), 173–181. https://doi.org/10.1023/A:1026595011371

MacKinnon, D. P., & Lamp, S. (2021). A unification of mediator, confounder, and collider effects. *Prevention Science, 22*(8), 1185–1193. https://doi.org/10.1007/s11121-021-01268-x

MacKinnon, D. P., Lockwood, C. M., Brown, C. H., Wang, W., & Hoffman, J. M. (2007). The intermediate endpoint effect in logistic and probit regression. *Clinical Trials, 4*(5), 499–513. https://doi.org/10.1177/1740774507083434

MacKinnon, D. P., Lockwood, C. M., Hoffman, J. M., West, S. G., & Sheets, V. (2002). A comparison of methods to test mediation and other intervening variable effects. *Psychological Methods, 7*(1), 83–104. https://doi.org/10.1037/1082-989X.7.1.83

MacKinnon, D. P., Lockwood, C. M., & Williams, J. (2004). Confidence limits for the indirect effect: Distribution of the product and resampling methods. *Multivariate Behavioral Research, 39*(1), 99–128. https://doi.org/10.1207/s15327906mbr3901_4

MacKinnon, D. P., & Pirlott, A. G. (2015). Statistical approaches for enhancing causal interpretation of the M to Y relation in mediation analysis. *Personality and Social Psychology Review, 19*(1), 30–43. https://doi.org/10.1177/1088868314542878

MacKinnon, D. P., Smyth, H. L., Somers, J., Ho, E., Norget, J., De Paepe, A., & Miočević, M. (2021). A permutation test for single subject mediation. *Evaluation and the Health Professions, 45*(1), 54–65. https://doi.org/10.1177/01632787211070811

MacKinnon, D. P., Taborga, M. P., & Morgan-Lopez, A. A. (2002). Mediation designs for tobacco prevention research. *Drug and Alcohol Dependence, 68*(Suppl. 1), S69–S83. https://doi.org/10.1016/S0376-8716(02)00216-8

MacKinnon, D. P., Valente, M. J., & Gonzalez, O. (2020). The correspondence between causal and traditional mediation analysis: The link is the mediator by treatment interaction. *Prevention Science, 21*(2), 147–157. https://doi.org/10.1007/s11121-019-01076-4

MacKinnon, D. P., Valente, M. J., & Wurpts, I. C. (2018). Benchmark validation of statistical mediation analysis: Application to imagery and memory theory. *Psychological Methods, 23*(4), 854–671. https://doi.org/10.1037/met0000174

MacKinnon, D. P., Warsi, G., & Dwyer, J. H. (1995). A simulation study of mediated effect measures. *Multivariate Behavioral Research, 30*(1), 41–62. https://doi.org/10.1207/s15327906mbr3001_3

Manly, B. F. J. (1997). *Randomization and Monte Carlo methods in biology* (2nd ed.). Chapman and Hall.

McArdle, J. J. (2001). A latent difference score approach to longitudinal dynamic structural analysis. In R. Cudeck, S. du Toit, & D. Sörbom (Eds.), *Structural equation modeling: Present and future. A festschrift in honor of Karl Jöreskog* (pp. 341–380). Scientific Software International.

McArdle, J. J., & Nesselroade, J. R. (2003). Growth curve analysis in contemporary research. In J. Schinka & W. Velicer (Eds.), *Comprehensive handbook of psychology, Vol. II: Research methods in psychology* (pp. 447–480). Pergamon Press.

McDonald, R. P. (1997). Haldane's lungs: A case study in path analysis. *Multivariate Behavioral Research, 32*(1), 1–38. https://doi.org/10.1207/s15327906mbr3201_1

Miočević, M., O'Rourke, H. P., MacKinnon, D. P., & Brown, H. C. (2018). Statistical properties of four effect-size measures for mediation models. *Behavior Research Methods, 50*(1), 285–301. https://doi.org/10.3758/s13428-017-0870-1

Morgan, S. L., & Winship, C. (2007). *Counterfactuals and causal inference: Methods and principles for social research.* Cambridge University Press. https://doi.org/10.1017/CBO9780511804564

Muller, D., Judd, C. M., & Yzerbyt, V. Y. (2005). When moderation is mediated and mediation is moderated. *Journal of Personality and Social Psychology, 89*(6), 852–863. https://doi.org/10.1037/0022-3514.89.6.852

Murayama, K., & Elliot, A. J. (2012). The competition-performance relation: A meta-analytic review and test of the opposing processes model of competition and performance. *Psychological Bulletin, 138*(6), 1035–1070. https://doi.org/10.1037/a0028324

Muthén, B. O., & Curran, P. J. (1997). General longitudinal modeling of individual differences in experimental designs: A latent variable framework for analysis and power estimation. *Psychological Methods, 2*(4), 371–402. https://doi.org/10.1037/1082-989X.2.4.371

Muthén, B. O., Muthén, L., & Asparaouhov, T. (2016). *Regression and mediation analysis using Mplus.* Muthén & Muthén.

Muthén, L. K., & Muthén, B. O. (1998–2007). *Mplus user's guide* (5th ed.). Muthén & Muthén.

O'Rourke, H. P., Fine, K. L., Grimm, K. J., & MacKinnon, D. P. (2021). The importance of time metric precision when implementing bivariate latent change score models. *Multivariate Behavioral Research, 1*–19. https://doi.org/10.1080/00273171.2021.1874261

O'Rourke, H. P., & MacKinnon, D. P. (2015). When the test of mediation is more powerful than the test of the total effect. *Behavior Research Methods, 47*(2), 424–442. https://doi.org/10.3758/s13428-014-0481-z

O'Rourke, H. P., & MacKinnon, D. P. (2018). Reasons for testing mediation in the absence of an intervention effect: A research imperative in prevention and intervention research. *Journal of Studies on Alcohol and Drugs, 79*(2), 171–181. https://doi.org/10.15288/jsad.2018.79.171

O'Rourke, H. P., & Vazquez, E. (2019). Mediation analysis with zero-inflated substance use outcomes: Challenges and recommendations. *Addictive Behaviors, 94,* 16–25. https://doi.org/10.1016/j.addbeh.2019.01.034

Pearl, J. (2009). *Causality: Models, reasoning, and inference* (2nd ed.). Cambridge University Press.

Pearl, J. (2012). The causal mediation formula—A guide to the assessment of pathways and mechanisms. *Prevention Science, 13*(4), 426–436. https://doi.org/10.1007/s11121-011-0270-1

Pearl, J. (2014). Interpretation and identification of causal mediation. *Psychological Methods, 19*(4), 459–481. https://doi.org/10.1037/a0036434

Pirlott, A. G., & MacKinnon, D. P. (2016). Design approaches to experimental mediation. *Journal of Experimental Social Psychology, 66,* 29–38. https://doi.org/10.1016/j.jesp.2015.09.012

Preacher, K. J., & Hayes, A. F. (2004). SPSS and SAS procedures for estimating indirect effects in simple mediation models. *Behavior Research Methods, Instruments, & Computers*, 36(4), 717–731. https://doi.org/10.3758/BF03206553

Preacher, K. J., Zyphur, M. J., & Zhang, Z. (2010). A general multilevel SEM framework for assessing multilevel mediation. *Psychological Methods*, 15(3), 209–233. https://doi.org/10.1037/a0020141

Rijnhart, J. J. M., Valente, M. J., & MacKinnon, D. P. (2022). *Total effect decomposition in mediation analysis in the presence of non-collapsibility* [Manuscript submitted for publication]. Department of Epidemiology, University of South Florida.

Rijnhart, J. J. M., Valente, M. J., MacKinnon, D. P., Twisk, J. W. R., & Heymans, M. W. (2021). The use of traditional and causal estimators for mediation models with a binary outcome and exposure-mediator interaction. *Structural Equation Modeling*, 28(3), 345–355. https://doi.org/10.1080/10705511.2020.1811709

Rijnhart, J. M., Valente, M. J., Smyth, H., & MacKinnon, D. P. (2021). Statistical mediation analysis for models with a binary mediator and binary outcome: The differences between causal and traditional mediation analysis. mediator interaction. *Prevention Science*, https://doi.org/10.1007/s11121-021-01308-6

Robins, J. (1994). Correcting for non-compliance in randomized trials using structural nested mean models. *Communications in Statistics. Theory and Methods*, 23(8), 2379–2412. https://doi.org/10.1080/03610929408831393

Robins, J. M., & Greenland, S. (1992). Identifiability and exchangeability for direct and indirect effects. *Epidemiology*, 3(2), 143–155. https://doi.org/10.1097/00001648-199203000-00013

Rogosa, D. R. (1988). Myths about longitudinal research. In K. W. Schaie, R. T. Campbell, W. M. Meredith, & S. C. Rawlings (Eds.), *Methodological issues in aging research* (pp. 171–209). Springer.

Sheets, V. L., & Braver, S. L. (1999). Organizational status and perceived sexual harassment: Detecting the mediators of a null effect. *Personality and Social Psychology Bulletin*, 25(9), 1159–1171. https://doi.org/10.1177/01461672992512009

Shrout, P. E., & Bolger, N. (2002). Mediation in experimental and nonexperimental studies: New procedures and recommendations. *Psychological Methods*, 7(4), 422–445. https://doi.org/10.1037/1082-989X.7.4.422

Singer, J. D., & Willett, J. B. (2003). *Applied longitudinal data analysis: Modeling change and event occurrence.*

Oxford University Press. https://doi.org/10.1093/acprof:oso/9780195152968.001.0001

Smyth, H. L., & MacKinnon, D. P. (2021). Statistical evaluation of person-oriented mediation using configural frequency analysis. *Integrative Psychological & Behavioral Science*, 55(3), 593–636. https://doi.org/10.1007/s12124-020-09519-2

Sobel, M. E. (1982). Asymptotic confidence intervals for indirect effects in structural equation models. *Sociological Methodology*, 13, 290–312. https://doi.org/10.2307/270723

Sobel, M. E. (1986). Some new results on indirect effects and their standard errors in covariance structure models. *Sociological Methodology*, 16, 159–186. https://doi.org/10.2307/270922

Sobel, M. E. (2008). Identification of causal parameters in randomized studies with mediating variables. *Journal of Educational and Behavioral Statistics*, 33(2), 230–251. https://doi.org/10.3102/1076998607307239

Spencer, S. J., Zanna, M. P., & Fong, G. T. (2005). Establishing a causal chain: Why experiments are often more effective than mediational analyses in examining psychological processes. *Journal of Personality and Social Psychology*, 89(6), 845–851. https://doi.org/10.1037/0022-3514.89.6.845

Spirtes, P., Glymour, C., & Scheines, R. (1993). *Causation, prediction, and search*. Springer-Verlag. https://doi.org/10.1007/978-1-4612-2748-9

Springer, M. D. (1979). *The algebra of random variables*. John Wiley and Sons.

Taylor, A. B., & MacKinnon, D. P. (2012). Four applications of permutation methods to testing a single-mediator model. *Behavior Research Methods*, 44(3), 806–844. https://doi.org/10.3758/s13428-011-0181-x

Ten Have, T. R., Joffe, M. M., Lynch, K. G., Brown, G. K., Maisto, S. A., & Beck, A. T. (2007). Causal mediation analyses with rank preserving models. *Biometrics*, 63(3), 926–934. https://doi.org/10.1111/j.1541-0420.2007.00766.x

Tofighi, D., & MacKinnon, D. P. (2016). Monte Carlo confidence intervals for complex functions of indirect effects. *Structural Equation Modeling*, 23(2), 194–205. https://doi.org/10.1080/10705511.2015.1057284

Valente, M. J., & MacKinnon, D. P. (2017). Comparing models of change to estimate the mediated effect in the pretest-posttest control group design. *Structural Equation Modeling*, 24(3), 428–450. https://doi.org/10.1080/10705511.2016.1274657

Valeri, L., & VanderWeele, T. J. (2013). Mediation analysis allowing for exposure-mediator interactions and causal interpretation: Theoretical assumptions and implementation with SAS and SPSS macros. *Psychological Methods, 18*(2), 137–150. https://doi.org/10.1037/a0031034

VanderWeele, T. (2015). *Explanation in causal inference: Methods for mediation and interaction.* Oxford University Press.

VanderWeele, T. J., & Vansteelandt, S. (2009). Conceptual issues concerning mediation, interventions and composition. *Statistics and Its Interface, 2*(4), 457–468. https://doi.org/10.4310/SII.2009.v2.n4.a7

Vansteelandt, S. (2009). Estimating direct effects in cohort and case-control studies. *Epidemiology, 20*(6), 851–860. https://doi.org/10.1097/EDE.0b013e3181b6f4c9

Vansteelandt, S., Bekaert, M., & Lange, T. (2012). Imputation strategies for the estimation of natural direct and indirect effects. *Epidemiologic Methods, 1*(1), 130–158. https://doi.org/10.1515/2161-962X.1014

von Eye, A., Mun, E. Y., & Mair, P. (2009). What carries a mediation process? Configural analysis of mediation. *Integrative of Psychological and Behavioral Science, 43*(3), 228–247. https://doi.org/10.1007/s12124-009-9088-9

Wang, W., & Albert, J. M. (2012). Estimation of mediation effects for zero-inflated regression models. *Statistics in Medicine, 31*(26), 3118–3132. https://doi.org/10.1002/sim.5380

Weiss, C. H. (1997). How can theory-based evaluation make greater headway? *Evaluation Review,* 21(4), 501–524. https://doi.org/10.1177/0193841X9702100405

West, S. G., & Aiken, L. S. (1997). Toward understanding individual effects in multiple component prevention programs: Design and analysis strategies. In K. Bryant, M. Windle, & S. West (Eds.), *The science of prevention: Methodological advances from alcohol and substance abuse research* (pp. 167–209). American Psychological Association. https://doi.org/10.1037/10222-006

Wiedermann, W., & von Eye, A. (2021). A simple configural approach for testing person-oriented mediation hypotheses. *Integrative Psychological & Behavioral Science, 55*(3), 637–664. https://doi.org/10.1007/s12124-020-09598-1

Winship, C., & Mare, R. D. (1983). Structural equations and path analysis for discrete data. *American Journal of Sociology, 89*(1), 54–110. https://doi.org/10.1086/227834

Woodworth, R. S. (1928). Dynamic psychology. In C. Murchison (Ed.), *Psychologies of 1925* (pp. 111–126). Clark University Press.

Wurpts, I. C., Miočević, M., & MacKinnon, D. P. (2022). Sequential Bayesian data synthesis for mediation and regression analysis. *Prevention Science, 23*(3), 378–389. https://doi.org/10.1007/s11121-021-01256-1

Yuan, Y., & MacKinnon, D. P. (2009). Bayesian mediation analysis. *Psychological Methods, 14*(4), 301–322. https://doi.org/10.1037/a0016972

CHAPTER 21

STRUCTURAL EQUATION MODELING WITH LATENT VARIABLES

Rick H. Hoyle and Nisha C. Gottfredson

The focus of this chapter is a family of statistical methods and strategies collectively referred to as *structural equation modeling* (SEM), of which path analysis is a special case. These range from the relatively straightforward and familiar to the complex and new. Our goal in the current treatment is threefold and reflected in the structure of the presentation: In the first section of the chapter, we develop a context for understanding the origins of SEM by tracing its emergence and positioning it among the statistical methods that are familiar to many psychological scientists. In the second section, which constitutes the core of the chapter, we describe and illustrate the steps involved in using SEM. In the third and final section, we present an array of prototypic models that illustrate the range of structures and processes that could be modeled using SEM. A firm grasp of material presented in the chapter will prepare readers to understand most published reports of SEM analysis in psychological science and position them to make an informed decision about whether their own research agenda could benefit from using SEM.

BACKGROUND AND CONTEXT

Structural equation modeling is a growing family of multivariate statistical methods for modeling data. SEM is substantially more flexible than statistical methods that have dominated data analysis in psychological science since the early 20th century. It allows for multiple independent and dependent variables, which may be observed or implied by the combination or pattern of associations among observed variables. Directional relations, as in analysis of variance (ANOVA) and multiple regression analysis, can be modeled between independent variables and between dependent variables. Complex models of the latent structure underlying a set of observed variables (i.e., unmeasured sources of influence and their interrelations) can be evaluated. These models can be estimated from continuous or ordered categorical data and include correlations between variables, direct and indirect effects, and focus on both relations between variables and patterns of means between groups or over time. The flexibility of SEM permits modeling of data in ways that are not possible with other, more commonly used, statistical methods.

While writing this chapter, the first author was supported by National Institute on Drug Abuse (NIDA) Grant P30 DA023026. Its contents are solely the responsibility of the author and do not necessarily represent the official views of NIDA.

https://doi.org/10.1037/0000319-021
APA Handbook of Research Methods in Psychology, Second Edition: Vol. 2. Research Designs: Quantitative, Qualitative, Neuropsychological, and Biological, H. Cooper (Editor-in-Chief)

For this reason, SEM both facilitates tests of hypotheses not adequately tested by other methods and suggests hypotheses that might not otherwise be considered for lack of a framework within which to venture them.

Historical Context

The roots of contemporary SEM can be traced to the earliest form of path analysis, Wright's (1934) method of path coefficients. Wright, a geneticist, developed path analysis for the purpose of modeling the relative influence of heredity and environment on the color of guinea pigs (Wright, 1920). These influences were assumed to be causal, and Wright referred to his use of path analysis, which uses observed covariances (unstandardized zero-order correlations) as input, as a means of testing causal effects when "more direct attempts" (i.e., randomized experiments) were not feasible. The unfortunate result of this cooccurrence of nonexperimental design and causal inference is that, from the outset, path analysis and SEM have been misconstrued as providing evidence for causality based on correlational data (Denis & Legerski, 2006). Although such inferences could be defended for many of Wright's models, given their focus on genetic influences, such is not the case for the lion's share of models that are tested using path analysis and SEM in the social and behavioral sciences.

Wright also is credited with the invention of the path diagram, the widely used graphic means of representing models. His (and, therefore, the) first path diagram was a stylized depiction of the concurrent influences of the genetic contribution of a sire and a dam, environmental factors, and chance on the color of guinea pig offspring (Wright, 1920). From this stylized depiction, Wright developed a more formal and general diagram that could be used to depict the full array of relations between variables in a "system of causes and effects" (Wright, 1920, p. 330). Wright's *system* corresponds to the contemporary notion of a model. An important feature of Wright's diagram was the inclusion of *path coefficients* (a term coined by Wright) on paths indicating the magnitude and direction of statistical relations in the system.

In a description that captures well the activity of SEM as elaborated later in this chapter, Wright (1920) characterized path analysis as the activity of "expressing the known correlations in terms of unknown path coefficients" (p. 330).

Although there is evidence that social and behavioral scientists were aware of Wright's innovation relatively soon after his seminal publications (e.g., Burks, 1928), it was not until the 1960s that a wave of interest began to build. The stimulus was an important book by Blalock (1964), *Causal Inferences in Nonexperimental Research*, which seemed to underscore the inference that researchers drew from Wright's work—that path analysis/SEM could be used to test causal hypotheses using data from correlational research (a misinterpretation of both Wright's and Blalock's writing). Sociologists extended the use of path analysis to longitudinal models and, though the methodology for including latent variables (i.e., unmeasured sources of influence) had not yet been fully developed, sociologists indicated an awareness of the importance of accounting for unmeasured variables (Tomer, 2003). It was a sociologist who published the first article in a psychology journal highlighting the potential of path analysis/SEM for psychological research (Duncan, 1969). By 1970, there was evidence that path analysis had begun to find traction in psychological science (Werts & Linn, 1970). Preceding and overlapping developments by methodologists in sociology were important developments by econometricians. Perhaps the most important of these concerned the method by which parameters (e.g., regression weights, factor loadings) were estimated. As early as the 1940s, it became evident that ordinary least squares was inadequate for estimating parameters in multiequations systems and that maximum likelihood could be used effectively (e.g., Mann & Wald, 1943). Goldberger and Duncan (1973) integrated the sociological approach to path analysis with the simultaneous equations approach in economics and the factor analytic approach in psychology (e.g., Duncan, 1975; Goldberger, 1971), yielding the generalization of path analysis now known as SEM (described by Bentler, 1986b, as "the literal grafting of a factor analytic model upon a simultaneous equation model," p. 41). This general model was formalized and extended in the 1970s by Jöreskog (1973), Keesling (1972), and Wiley (1973), producing what became known as the LISREL (*linear structural relations*) model.

Bentler (1986b) credited the "spread from the methodology laboratory to the research laboratory with unusual rapidity" to the fact that SEM allows researchers "to effectively study substantive problems that could not easily be investigated using alternative approaches" (p. 35). The effectiveness of SEM was introduced to psychologists primarily by Bentler and colleagues in an early set of publications that used SEM to evaluate complex multivariate hypotheses in a unified and efficient matter (e.g., Bentler & Speckart, 1979; Huba & Bentler, 1982). These and other compelling demonstrations (e.g., Maruyama & McGarvey, 1980) coupled with the growing accessibility of LISREL, the primary computer program for implementing SEM at the time (Jöreskog, 1973), and the introduction of Bentler's (1985) more user-friendly EQS program fueled the early growth in the use of SEM in psychological science.

By the late 1980s, developments in SEM methods and reports of substantive research using SEM were appearing with increasing frequency. During the period from 1987 to 1994, the overall number of such publications increased from 80 to 185. During that period, the number of SEM methods–focused articles remained steady, whereas the number of substantive articles increased nearly threefold (Tremblay & Gardner, 1996). This pattern of growth continued during the period from 1994 to 2001, with the number of substantive publications almost doubling and the number of different psychology journals in which a report of research using SEM appeared increasing as well (Hershberger, 2003). The breadth of models and data types for which SEM is appropriate continues to increase (Matsueda, in press; Tarka, 2018), enabling researchers to use a single analytic model for diverse hypothesis tests and exploratory analyses in a program of research. Importantly, across the period of these reviews, substantive publications reporting results

from analyses using other multivariate methods (e.g., multivariate analysis of variance, factor analysis, and cluster analysis) remained steady or declined (Hershberger, 2003; Tremblay & Gardner, 1996). Within a relatively short period of time, SEM has moved from relative obscurity and use by a small number of methodologically minded researchers to its current status as a well-known multivariate method used by researchers across the spectrum of psychological science.

Statistical Context

An effective way to begin developing an understanding of SEM is to compare and contrast it with more familiar statistical methods, each of which can be viewed as a special case of SEM. An overly simplistic, but useful, view of SEM as typically applied is as a hybrid of multiple regression analysis and factor analysis. Some readers will be familiar with the two-step strategy of using factor analysis to determine the latent influences in a set of variables, and then using factor scores or unit-weighted composites to focus the data analysis on the latent influences. In SEM, these two steps are accomplished simultaneously in such a way that actual scores for the latent influences are not needed. Instead, those influences in the form of latent variables (i.e., factors) are estimated from the data when they are included as predictors or outcomes in a set of regression-like equations. Importantly, however, unlike multiple regression analysis, for which outcomes are addressed one at a time, multiple, possibly latent, outcomes can be included in a single model. Moreover, predictive relations between the outcomes can be modeled if there is reason to do so. Variables that are predicted by other variables in a model are differentiated from variables that are not by the qualifiers endogenous and exogenous, respectively.

With this general idea in mind, we can see how SEM is a generalization of a host of narrower, more familiar, statistical methods. For example, the *t* test is a special case of ANOVA, which is, in turn, a special case of multiple regression analysis. As noted, multiple regression analysis is a special case of SEM. Focusing on the latent variable component of SEM, covariances also are a special case of SEM, though they also are the building blocks for factor analysis. SEM can be used to model categorical latent variables (i.e., latent classes), which are an extension of methods based on contingency tables as well as latent class and latent transition analysis (e.g., Kaplan, 2009; Marsh et al., 2009). To this set of capabilities can be added the modeling of patterns of means as in trend analysis in ANOVA. And, when the means are from repeated assessments of a sample of individuals, these patterns of means can be treated as predictors or outcomes in multilevel models (e.g., Curran, 2000). The end result for SEM is a very general model that includes components of many narrower statistical models with which psychological scientists are familiar but, bringing them together in a single framework, allows for models and hypothesis tests not possible using those narrower models.

BASIC CONCEPTS

An initial understanding of a number of features of SEM sets the stage for a more detailed description of the steps involved in using SEM. In each of the short sections that follow, we juxtapose a feature of SEM against a comparable feature typical of statistical methods commonly used by psychological scientists. The goal is not to show that one is superior to the other but rather to highlight the features of SEM that are likely to be unfamiliar to most readers.

Modeling Versus Analyzing Data

Psychological scientists are accustomed to analyzing data. By *analyze*, we mean test specific differences (e.g., *t* test, ANOVA) and coefficients (e.g., correlation, regression), typically against zero, using tailored methods that involve relatively little concern for the full array of influences apparent in the data. Modeling data, on the other hand, involves accounting for features of the research design and substantive influences that explain the pattern of relations across a set of variables (for a fuller treatment of this distinction, see Rodgers, 2010). Whereas the outcome of analysis typically is evidence for or against a posited difference or coefficient, the outcome of modeling is a statement about the correspondence between a system of relations between variables specified by the researcher, such as a conceptual model based on the researcher's theoretical model, with a set of observed data on those variables. Psychological scientists occasionally engage in exploratory modeling, as in factor analysis, in which the goal is to discover a plausible model to explain the relations between a set of variables, or *hierarchical multiple regression analysis* (not to be confused with *hierarchical linear modeling*, which is also called *multilevel* or *mixed modeling*), in which the goal is to incrementally build a model of the relations that produce variance in a single outcome; however, psychological scientists, in the main, are data analysts. As is evident from its name, SEM is a strategy and set of methods for modeling. Thus, its use requires a shift in thinking about hypothesis testing.

Covariances Versus Raw Scores as Data

Whether analyzing or modeling data, the goal of most statistical methods is to account for variability in observed data. The degree to which the difference or relation tested by the model does not account for the data is termed *error*; thus, the goal of data analysis or modeling might be conceptualized as an exercise in minimizing error. (We discuss the error concept in the context of modeling data in a section on model estimation later in the chapter.) SEM differs from methods to which psychological scientists are accustomed in its definition of error. In least squares methods such as multiple regression analysis, the goal is to find the set of coefficients that minimize the difference between each individual's observed value on the outcome variable and the value predicted for them by the regression line on the basis of their scores on the predictor variables. The focus, then, is on the correspondence between observed and predicted case-level data. In SEM, the data of interest typically are the observed variances and covariances of the variables (although means are sometimes of interest). The adequacy of a model is judged by the correspondence between the observed variances and covariances and those predicted by the model. For this reason, SEM is sometimes referred to as *covariance structure analysis*. The interpretation and use of SEM requires a shift in focus from accounting for observed scores on a single outcomes to accounting for observed covariances among all variables in a model.

Specification of a Model Versus Running an Analysis

Most of the data-analytic strategies with which psychological scientists are familiar are, to use a computer analogy, "plug and play." All that is required to run an analysis is choosing the variables, in some cases indicating which are independent and which are dependent variables, and identifying them as such in the computer program of choice. Because of the narrow and tailored nature of the methods, relatively few, if any, decisions need to be made beyond which variables to include and where to include them. The execution of an SEM analysis is substantially more involved. This is, in part, a by-product of the high degree of flexibility afforded by the method. In SEM, there is no default model. The selection and designation of variables is just the first in a series of steps involved in specifying a model. As will become apparent later in the chapter, any number of models might be specified for a set of variables. Indeed, for a large number of variables, the number of models that might be specified is extremely large. The important point is that computer programs for running SEM analyses are not "plug and play." Rather, the researcher must make a potentially large number of decisions about which variables in a set are related to each other and how. Collectively, these decisions are referred to as model specification. Psychological scientists occasionally engage in specification (without using the label), as in choosing how many factors to extract and how to rotate them in a factor analysis, choosing the random effect structure in multilevel models, or deciding how to group variables and the order in which groups are entered in hierarchical multiple regression analysis. In SEM, all analyses require specification.

All Parameters Versus a Select Few

In commonly used methods such as ANOVA and multiple regression analysis, the researcher typically is provided with, or elects to attend to, only a subset of the parameters that are estimated. This is because many of the parameters involved in the analysis are neither under the control of, nor typically of interest to, the researcher. Thus, for example, the variances of predictors and the covariances between them in multiple regression analysis are rarely seen when that analysis is run, except during diagnostics for colinearity. The uniquenesses, variance in variables not accounted for by the factors in a factor analysis, are not routinely provided in computer output. In SEM, every parameter in a model is "in play." In fact, a decision must be made about how every parameter is handled in the estimation of the model. Although this requirement adds to the work required before a model can be estimated using SEM, it suggests a potentially large number of hypotheses that might be tested but routinely are not formally considered.

Goodness of Fit Versus Difference From Zero

As noted, the typical focus of data analysis in psychological science is the question of whether a particular difference or coefficient differs from zero. Although these differences and coefficients may be thought of as continuous variables that vary in magnitude, it remains the case that, in many quarters of the discipline, they are categorical variables that can take on two values—significant or nonsignificant. Furthermore, although some statistical methods allow for testing of a set of relations, as in tests of R^2 in multiple regression analysis, most focus on individual relations (e.g., main effects and interactions in ANOVA). In SEM, the primary focus is a system of relations as specified in a model. Tests of specific coefficients are consulted only after the question of whether the model provides an acceptable account of the data has been addressed. By "acceptable account," we mean the degree to which the covariances implied by the researcher's specified model mirror the observed covariances. When the two sets of covariances are statistically equivalent, the model fits the data. Thus, a key difference between methods to which psychological scientists are accustomed and SEM, is that SEM focuses on the collective adequacy of the system of relations in a model. The magnitude of specific coefficients within the model, although related to the adequacy of the model as a whole, typically is of secondary interest.

Latent Versus Observed Variables

A hallmark of SEM is the ability to specify relations between latent variables, or factors. Latent variables are unobserved sources of influence that typically are inferred from the pattern of relations between a set of observed variables, referred to as *indicators*. Although, as noted, relations between latent variables sometimes are approximated by a piecemeal strategy using factor or principal components analysis followed by ANOVA or multiple regression analysis using factor scores, this combination is implemented seamlessly in SEM. As illustrated in the final section of the chapter, the ability to model and test hypotheses about latent variables is the basis for a number of rigorous and sophisticated strategies for decomposing variance in observed variables. The most straightforward benefit, however, is the ability to estimate relations between variables from which unreliability has been removed. This approach not only results in larger coefficients indexing relations between variable but also, because of the dependency between coefficients in a model, it sometimes results in smaller coefficients (e.g., as in mediation models; Hoyle & Kenny, 1999). In both cases, the coefficients are assumed to better approximate the true relation between constructs than coefficients between fallible observed variables.

STEPS IN THE USE OF STRUCTURAL EQUATION MODELING

Although many types of models can be evaluated using SEM, the steps involved in applying SEM are virtually always the same. These steps are used to implement SEM in the service of one of

three goals (Jöreskog, 1993). In a *strictly confirmatory* use of SEM, the goal is to evaluate the degree to which a single, a priori model accounts for a set of observed relations. Alternatively, instead of focusing on a single model, SEM might be used to compare two or more competing models in an *alternative models* strategy. Finally, a use of SEM might have a *model-generating* focus. If, for example, an a priori model does not adequately account for the observed data, rather than abandoning the data, the researcher might use it to generate an exploratory model (McArdle, 2011). Of course, using the data to generate a model of the data is inferentially risky (MacCallum et al., 1992); however, careful modification of a poor-fitting a priori model with the goal of finding a model that accounts for the data can lead to discoveries that, if replicated, increase understanding of a psychological structure or process. Regardless of the goal, an application of SEM follows an ordered set of steps that begins with specification and concludes with interpretation.

We illustrate those steps with an empirical example. The data are from two waves of a longitudinal study of problem behavior among middle school students (Harrington et al., 2001). A total of 1,655 students from 14 schools participated in the study. Students first completed the self-report survey early during the academic year when they were from 11 to 13 years old. They completed the survey a second time near the end of the academic year, about eight months later. (An intervention and a third wave of data detract from the illustrative benefits of the data set and are, therefore, ignored for this example.) The analysis data set includes 10 observed variables measured on two occasions and assumed to reflect three latent variables. The focal outcome is *problem behavior*, for which indicators are past 30-day drug use (dichotomized due to heavy zero inflation), a composite score of sexual activity (ranging from affectionate physical contact to sexual intercourse), and a composite score of interpersonal aggression (ranging from teasing to physical fighting). These three problem behavior indicators were measured at baseline and at Time 2. Having a baseline measure of problem behavior allows us to estimate the effect of risk and protective factors on residualized change in problem behavior. The latent variable *risk* is indicated by composite scores on three individual differences: impulsive decision making, sensation seeking, and (low) self-esteem. The other latent predictor, *protection*, is reflected by four composite scores on scales designed to tap values and lifestyle variables assumed to be incompatible with problem behavior. These variables include bonding to school, a personal and public commitment to avoid problem behavior, an assumption that prevailing norms are not to engage in problem behavior, and the view that problem behavior interferes with a productive and otherwise desirable lifestyle. Additional information about the data set, including the management of missing data, can be found in the published report by Harrington et al. (2001).

MODEL SPECIFICATION

All applications of SEM begin with the specification of a model. Model specification involves three sets of decisions that stem from questions about a model:

1. Which variables will be included and in what form (observed or latent)?
2. Which variables will be interrelated and how?
3. Which parameters (i.e., coefficients) will be estimated, and which will be set to specific values?

Before detailing how these questions are addressed in SEM, let us consider how they are addressed in familiar methods such as ANOVA, multiple regression, and factor analysis. Although each of these statistical methods, when applied to research questions, involve specification, most aspects of specification in these are established by convention and imposed by computer programs used to analyze data. The exception would be the first question, which typically is addressed directly by the researcher without consulting the data, although some data-reduction and data-mining methods involve consulting the data to decide which variables are to be included in a model. A decision about variables that is key in SEM is whether latent variables will be included and, if so, how many. In factor analysis, the decision to extract factors is a decision to include latent variables, and the decision about how many to extract is a decision about how many to include. As with data-reduction and data-mining methods, this decision about including latent variables typically is made on the basis of patterns in the data. In SEM, the decision about whether to include latent variables and how many can be made before data have been collected and certainly should be made before the data have been consulted.

The second question involved in model specification is which variables will be interrelated and how they will be interrelated. Again, restricting our discussion to methods familiar to psychological scientists, these decisions often are part and parcel of using a particular statistical method. For instance, a 2×2 factorial design yields 3 degrees of freedom for specifying a model that captures the pattern of means. In the default specification, 1 degree of freedom is used for each main effect, and 1 is used for the interaction. The remaining $(n - 1) - 3$ degrees of freedom is the divisor in the error term. Even with this simple design, other specifications are possible. These alternative specifications would require defining sets of contrasts that differ from those implied by the standard main-effects-and-interaction specification. With more complex designs, the number of sets of such contrasts is large. In factor analysis, the decision to use an orthogonal rotation method is a decision to not allow factors to correlate with each other; the use of an oblique rotation allows those correlations. A final component, one that is particularly salient in SEM, is the direction of influence between variables assumed to be directionally related. In analyses of data from randomized experiments, this decision is straightforward: Influence runs from the manipulated variables to variables assessed in the experimental context after the manipulation. In data from quasi- or nonexperimental studies, the decision is not straightforward. In its simplest form, it involves deciding, for instance, whether a particular variable will be positioned on the predictor or outcome side of a multiple regression equation. Such decisions constitute model specification within the rather restrictive data-analytic frameworks of methods such as ANOVA and multiple regression analysis. When the causal relationship between two constructs is unclear, one can specify a correlation instead of a directional path. In our example, we use temporality to determine the position of our variables in the model; variables measured at baseline predict problem behavior at Time 2, whereas variables measured at baseline are allowed to correlate freely with no directional assumptions.

The final question is which parameters in the model will be estimated and which will be fixed to a specific value and, therefore, not estimated. This aspect of specification is less apparent than identifying variables and their interrelations, but it is no less important in defining models. Examples of parameters that generally are estimated include regression coefficients and factor loadings. Parameters that are fixed are less obvious. For example, in exploratory factor analysis, the uniqueness components of indicators are independent; that is, the covariances between them are fixed to 0. As noted, an orthogonal rotation specifies uncorrelated factors, which is equivalent to fixing the covariances between the factors to 0. There is relatively little room to fix parameters in the standard statistical methods used by psychological scientists, but every parameter in a model to be estimated and tested using SEM can be fixed to a particular value, given certain mathematical constraints.

Before discussing and illustrating model specification in SEM, it is worth considering what constitutes a *model* in SEM. This consideration is particularly important when drawing inferences from the results from estimating and testing a model in SEM. One interpretation of a model is as a literal reflection of reality as captured by the data. Of course, "reality" is remarkably complex, impossible to fully grasp, and, on some counts, simply uninteresting, rendering this idea of a model less than appealing. An alternative interpretation

is that a model is anchored in reality but includes only those aspects relevant to a research question (although accounting for salient features of research design, such as confounding variables). This view of a model assumes that the models of interest to psychological scientists never fully accounts for a set of data. Rather, the models provide a parsimonious account of relations evident in a set of data with reference to an interesting and potentially useful set of constructs and theoretical relations. Consistent with this idea, Box (1979) famously quipped, "All models are wrong, but some are useful" (p. 201). In other words, the goal of model specification is the identification of a model that is testable and useful, even if it fails to account for all aspects of the reality that produced the data. Pearl (2000) offered a definition that will guide our thinking in the remainder of the chapter. A model is "an idealized representation of a reality that highlights some aspects and ignores others" (p. 202).

Now, let us focus specifically and concretely on model specification in SEM by returning to the example introduced at the beginning of this section. Recall that a large sample of middle-school students provided information on 13 observed variables. Although the research question might focus on the contribution of each of the three risk and four protective factors to each of the three problem behaviors, the focus is broader: To what extent do risk and protection evident in certain dispositional, perceptual, and attitudinal constructs, effect change in problem behavior, broadly defined? To address this question, we need three latent variables that reflect the general constructs of risk, protection, and problem behavior. Thus, in terms of identifying variables, we include 17 variables—13 observed variables and four latent variables (problem behavior is observed on two occasions).

Having designated the variables to be included in the model, we now need to specify the relations between variables. We provide additional detail later in this section, but for now we can describe the set of relations in general terms. We intend to explain the commonality among impulsive decision making, sensation seeking, and low self-esteem with a latent variable labelled risk. A second latent variable, protection, accounts for the commonality among bonding to school, commitment to avoid problem behavior, belief that problem behavior is not the norm, and belief that problem behavior interferes with success. And we model the commonality among drug use, sexual activity, and interpersonal aggression as a third latent variable, problem behavior. *Commonality* is defined as the proportion of variance in a set of items explained by a common factor. These relations and any correlations between latent variables constitute a subcomponent of the model referred to as the *measurement model.* As outlined in Table 21.1, the measurement component of the model links measured indicators to latent variables and includes several types of parameters: loadings, item intercepts, (co)variances of latent variables, latent variable means and intercepts, and unexplained variance in indicators, or uniquenesses. Each of these parameters must

be designated as fixed (i.e., set at a specific value) or free (i.e., to be estimated from the data). We outline considerations involved in these designations in the next section.

In the model of interest, the measurement model is not an end in itself. Although we need to establish empirically that the observed variables reflect the latent variables in the pattern we have proposed, our ultimate goal is estimating the structural relations between the latent variables. Because this is a longitudinal model and temporality is established, we are particularly interested in the directional relation between each variable at Time 1 and problem behavior at Time 2. These paths and the correlations between the latent variables at Time 1 constitute the *structural model.* The parameters included in the structural model are listed and described in the lower portion of Table 21.1. As with the measurement model, each of these parameters must be designated as fixed or free.

TABLE 21.1

Parameters to Be Considered When Specifying a Model

Parameter	Description	Greek symbol
Measurement component		
Measured variables		
Loadings	Coefficient resulting from the regression of an indicator on a latent variable	λ
Intercepts	Item mean when the latent variable(s) on which it loads equal(s) 0	ν
Thresholds	For ordinal items, the z-score value that corresponds to a 50% probability of increasing response categories (thresholds are not independently identifiable from intercepts)	τ
Variance, uniqueness	Variance in the indicator not attributable to latent variable(s)	ε_x, δ_y
Latent variables		
Mean	Mean of the latent variable	μ
(Co)variances	Variances of, and covariances among, latent variables	ϕ
Structural component		
Variance, exogenous variables	Variance of a measured or latent exogenous variable	ϕ
Variance, endogenous disturbance	Variance unaccounted for by predictors in a measured or latent endogenous variable	ζ
Means	Latent or observed variable mean (for exogenous variables)	μ
Intercept	Latent or observed variable mean when predictors equal 0 (for endogenous variables)	α
Covariances	Covariance among exogenous variables or endogenous disturbances	ϕ
Directional path (exogenous origin)	The regression coefficient relating an exogenous measured or latent predictor to the dependent measured or latent variable	γ
Directional path (endogenous origin)	The regression coefficient relating an endogenous measured or latent predictor to the dependent measured or latent variable	β

Path Diagrams

One means of formalizing the specification of a model to be analyzed using SEM is the path diagram. A path diagram of our example model is shown in Figure 21.1. This example includes all the components necessary to fully specify all but a few highly specialized models. First, note the squares, labeled x_1 to x_{10} and y_1 to y_3. These represent observed variables, in this case, the 13 variables described earlier. Variables x_1 to x_{10} were measured at Time 1, and variables y_1 to y_3 were measured at Time 2. Next, notice the four large ovals, labeled ξ_1, ξ_2, ξ_3, and η, which include the names of the constructs on which the model is focused. These ovals designate latent variables, or factors. The exogenous factors are labelled with ξ, and the endogenous factor is labelled with η. Smaller circles indicate variances of two types. Attached to each indicator, labeled ε or δ for x-side and y-side measures, respectively, are uniquenesses. These,

too, are latent influences on the indicators. The uniquenesses reflect both variance attributable to random processes and variance attributed to processes specific to that indicator. For example, variance in an indicator of past month alcohol use may be partially due to problem behavior (the common factor), partially due to depression (a specific factor), and partially due to variation in when the measure happened to be administered (randomness). A lone small circle, labeled ζ, is attached to the Time 2 problem behavior latent variable. Typically referred to as a *disturbance*, this latent influence reflects all processes that contribute to variance in η that are not attributable to ξ_1, ξ_2, and ξ_3. The straight lines indicate directional influence, either between latent variables and indicators (λ) or between independent and dependent latent variables (γ). The curved arrow between ξ ξ variables indicate covariances (ϕ). The sharply curved, double-headed arrows pointing to the uniquenesses,

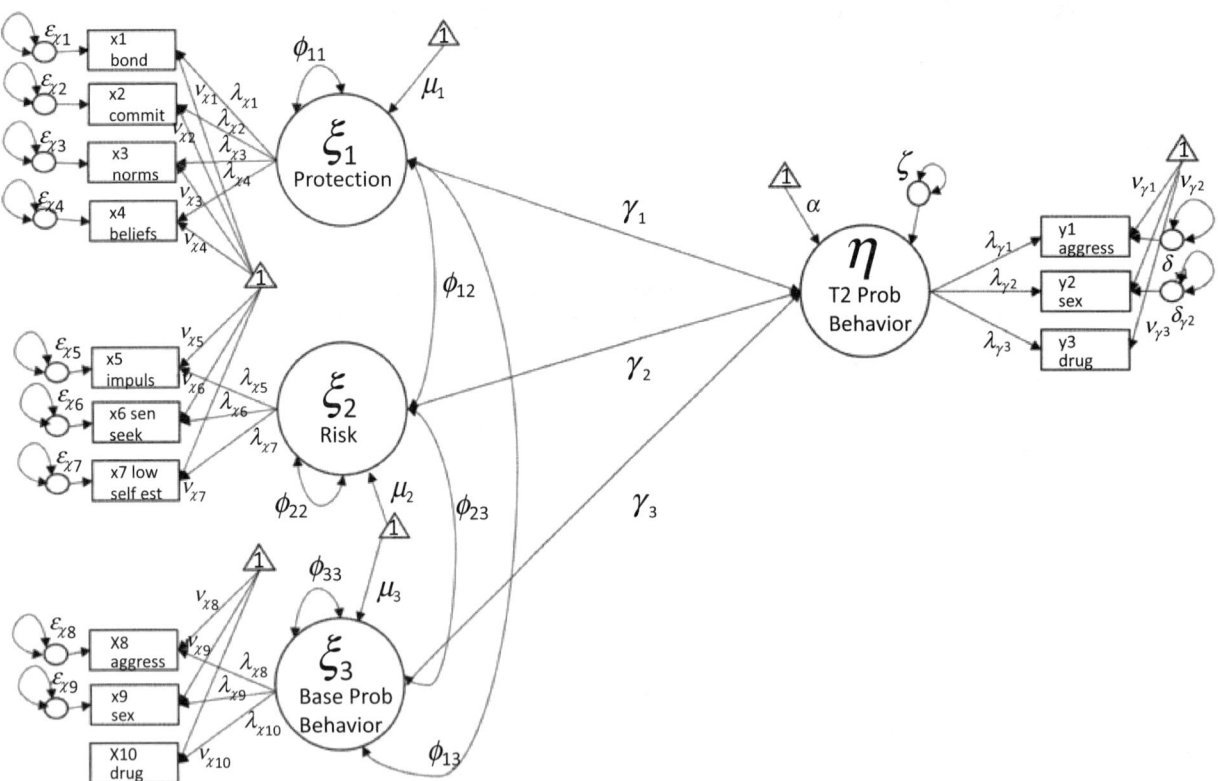

FIGURE 21.1. Path diagram illustrating all of the structural and measurement components of path diagrams, including parameter labels, from the empirical example.

the disturbance, and the independent latent variables indicate variances (σ^2, ϕ, ζ).

Some readers might be surprised to see paths in the measurement component of the model running from the latent variables to their indicators. This specification corresponds to the common factor model, which assumes that the commonality among a set of variables is attributable to one or unmeasured influences. These influences are assumed to account for a portion of the variance in the indicators. In SEM terms, indicators related to latent variables in this way are referred to as reflective indicators; they are fallible reflections of the underlying variable of interest. Virtually all latent variables in psychological science are related to their indicators in this way. Nonetheless, it bears mention that an alternative specification reverses the direction of the arrows so that the latent variables are assumed to be caused by its indicators. In this case, the observed variables are referred to as *formative indicators*. In that alternative specification, each measured indicator is assumed to represent a unique component that, when added to the other components, yields the latent variable. Such models pose significant estimation challenges and this, coupled with their rarity in psychological research, justifies our focus solely on reflective indicators in the remainder of the chapter (for an informative discussion of this distinction, see Bollen & Hoyle, in press). In our view, when applied researchers encounter a situation for which formative indicators are more appropriate, such as the measurement of socioeconomic status, they may decide that it is most expedient to use a composite score of the items instead of estimating a latent variable model.

It is common to establish one "anchor item" per latent variable and to fix its factor loading to 1.0. Alternatively, latent variables can be standardized with a fixed mean and variance. While we could write these constraints on the path diagram (e.g., by labelling a factor loading as "1" instead of as its Greek label), path diagrams do not make other types of constraints explicit.

For instance, the absence of paths between uniquenesses implies that the covariances between them have been fixed to 0. Each indicator is specified to load on only one latent variable, meaning that its loadings on the other two latent variables have been fixed to 0 (the absence of cross-loadings is sometimes called "simple structure"). Thus, although the path diagram is an appealing means of presenting a model, a significant weakness in terms of model specification is that parameters fixed at 0 are generally not shown. Of course, the paths we have identified could be added to the model with coefficients of 0 associated with them; however, such a diagram would be too cluttered to communicate effectively about the basic features of the model (e.g., imagine a path running from η_3 to γ_1).

Matrix Notation

Another approach to model specification is through matrix notation. Although it may be more tedious and intimidating for those who are new to SEM, model specification using matrix notation has two significant advantages over path diagrams. First, except for certain shortcuts, every parameter, fixed and free, is explicitly shown. Second, matrix notation is the means by which new developments in SEM typically are communicated. As such, an understanding of how models are communicated using matrix notation is essential for keeping abreast of the new developments. Of importance to researchers working on questions that cross disciplinary boundaries is the fact that matrix notation is used to communicate specifications and findings from substantive research in some disciplines.

Measurement model. The matrix equation for measured indicators of latent variables follows the following form, where i represents an individual subject. Bold font is used to indicate the use of vectors and matrices, rather than scalars.

$$\mathbf{x}_i = \boldsymbol{\nu}_x + \boldsymbol{\xi}_i \boldsymbol{\lambda}_x + \boldsymbol{\varepsilon}_i$$

$$\mathbf{y}_i = \boldsymbol{\nu}_y + \boldsymbol{\eta}_i \boldsymbol{\lambda}_y + \boldsymbol{\delta}_i \qquad (21.1)$$

Unpacking these equations further makes specific parameters explicit. Equation 21.2 expands the top line of Equation 21.1. The matrix specification allows us to see the fixed 0 loadings.

$$\begin{bmatrix} x_1 \\ x_2 \\ x_3 \\ x_4 \\ x_5 \\ x_6 \\ x_7 \\ x_8 \\ x_9 \\ x_{10} \end{bmatrix} = \begin{bmatrix} v_{x1} \\ v_{x2} \\ v_{x3} \\ v_{x4} \\ v_{x5} \\ v_{x6} \\ v_{x7} \\ v_{x8} \\ v_{x9} \\ v_{x10} \end{bmatrix} + \begin{bmatrix} \lambda_{11} & 0 & 0 \\ \lambda_{21} & 0 & 0 \\ \lambda_{31} & 0 & 0 \\ \lambda_{41} & 0 & 0 \\ 0 & \lambda_{61} & 0 \\ 0 & \lambda_{62} & 0 \\ 0 & \lambda_{72} & 0 \\ 0 & 0 & \lambda_{83} \\ 0 & 0 & \lambda_{93} \\ 0 & 0 & \lambda_{103} \end{bmatrix} \begin{bmatrix} \xi_1 \\ \xi_2 \\ \xi_3 \end{bmatrix} + \begin{bmatrix} \varepsilon_1 \\ \varepsilon_2 \\ \varepsilon_3 \\ \varepsilon_4 \\ \varepsilon_5 \\ \varepsilon_6 \\ \varepsilon_7 \\ \varepsilon_8 \\ \varepsilon_9 \\ - \end{bmatrix}$$

(21.2)

Residual variances (i.e., variances of ε) are usually represented as a vector because we generally do not allow residual terms to covary. However, it is sometimes appropriate to allow residual covariances, and, in this case, one would use a square matrix with residual variances along the diagonal, like the following:

$$\begin{bmatrix} \sigma_1^2 & & & & & & & & \\ 0 & \sigma_2^2 & & & & & & & \\ 0 & 0 & \sigma_3^2 & & & & & & \\ 0 & 0 & 0 & \sigma_4^2 & & & & & \\ 0 & 0 & 0 & 0 & \sigma_5^2 & & & & \\ 0 & 0 & 0 & 0 & 0 & \sigma_6^2 & & & \\ 0 & 0 & 0 & 0 & 0 & 0 & \sigma_7^2 & & \\ 0 & 0 & 0 & 0 & 0 & 0 & 0 & \sigma_8^2 & \\ 0 & 0 & 0 & 0 & 0 & 0 & 0 & 0 & \sigma_9^2 \\ - & - & - & - & - & - & - & - & - \end{bmatrix}$$

(21.3)

For our purposes, the advantage of providing the matrix of residual variances is that it makes clear that a host of model parameters are fixed at 0 in the specification. There are times when it makes sense to correlate residuals, such as when one needs to account for method or reporter variance that affects multiple indicators.

At this point, the reader may be wondering why there is no residual term ε_{10}. The reason is that x_{10} corresponds to a binary variable: any drug use in the past 30 days. We will account for the binary nature of this indicator using a probit link (a logit link would also be acceptable). Randomness is introduced into the distribution via probability within the link function, so the residual term corresponding to this variable is not uniquely estimated. (For information about ordered categorical indicators, of which there are none in our example, see Bovaird & Koziol, in press.)

The measurement model is completed by specifying the variances for the latent variables and any covariances between them. For exogenous latent variables, means are specified in the vector $\boldsymbol{\mu}$ and variances and covariances are specified in the matrix, $\boldsymbol{\phi}$, which for our model takes the form

$$\begin{bmatrix} \xi_1 \\ \xi_2 \\ \xi_3 \end{bmatrix} \sim N \left(\begin{bmatrix} \mu_1 \\ \mu_2 \\ \mu_3 \end{bmatrix}, \begin{bmatrix} \phi_{11} & & \\ \phi_{21} & \phi_{22} & \\ \phi_{31} & \phi_{32} & \phi_{33} \end{bmatrix} \right).$$

(21.4)

The diagonal elements are variances, and the off-diagonal elements are the covariances among exogenous latent variables.

In the measurement model phase of model estimation, all latent constructs are treated as exogenous and all are allowed to covary. The purpose of this stage is to arrive at a good-fitting measurement model because a poorly fitting measurement model leads to a poorly fitting structural model. We describe what it means to have a good-fitting model later, but common changes to the measurement model include dropping indicators that load poorly, allowing cross-loadings of an item onto multiple factors, changing the number of factors or the pattern of loadings, or allowing residual variances to correlate. Once the measurement models achieve satisfactory fit, the analyst moves on to specifying directional relationships amongst variables, and this is where the exogenous/endogenous distinction becomes important.

Structural model. Relations between latent variables specified in these matrices are specified in the structural equation

$$\boldsymbol{\eta}_i = \boldsymbol{\alpha} + \boldsymbol{\xi}_i\boldsymbol{\Gamma} + \boldsymbol{\eta}_i\boldsymbol{\beta} + \boldsymbol{\zeta}_i. \qquad (21.5)$$

Notice that we allow for endogenous latent variables to be regressed on other endogenous latent variables (as in a mediation analysis). For our example, this equation is expanded to reveal individual parameters and their status in the model

$$[\eta_i] = [\alpha] + \begin{bmatrix} \xi_{1i} & \xi_{2i} & \xi_{3i} \end{bmatrix} \begin{bmatrix} \gamma_1 \\ \gamma_2 \\ \gamma_3 \end{bmatrix} + [\zeta_i]. \qquad (21.6)$$

The only remaining parameter to be specified is the variance of the disturbance. Variances of disturbances and any covariances between them are specified in the matrix ψ, which in the example model is simply $[\psi_{11}]$.

Any of these strategies—path diagrams, matrix notation, or equations—allow for specification of a model. Each indicates the observed and latent variables to be included in the model, their relative positions in the model, the relations among them, and the various fixed and free parameters that characterize those relations. Regardless of the method used, once a model has been formally specified, assuming data are available for the observed variables, it can be estimated.

ESTIMATION OF PARAMETERS

The goal of estimation is finding the optimal set of estimates for free parameters in a model given the observed data and the relations specified in the model. By "optimal," we mean a statistical criterion targeted by an estimator. As an example, consider the ordinary least squares estimator, which is typically used to find the optimal, or best-fitting, regression line in multiple regression

analysis. The criterion targeted by that estimator is the minimization of the average squared distance between the observed value on the dependent variable for each case and the value predicted for them given the regression line. Several alternative estimators are available. These generally fall into one of three categories: mean and variance-adjusted weighted least squares (WLSMV), full information maximum likelihood (FIML), or Bayesian estimation. All of these estimators allow for categorical response options, but the WLSMV estimator assumes that an unobserved normal distribution underlies a coarsely measured categorical variable. Additionally, weighted least squares requires stricter missing data assumptions than FIML or Bayesian estimators (unless the analyst also uses multiple imputation to handle missing data or has complete data). Because a complete discussion of missing data is beyond the scope of this chapter, we refer the interested reader to comprehensive treatments of this topic, such as those written by Enders (in press) and Graham (2009). Benefits of weighted least squares include computational speed and the straightforward provision of goodness-of-fit statistics for a wide array of models. Models estimated using FIML or Bayesian estimators sometimes produce relative fit indices, such as the Bayesian information criterion (BIC), but not model-specific goodness-of-fit.

Before returning to the example, we briefly treat an important consideration in estimation: *identification*. In general, identification concerns the degree to which a unique estimate can be obtained for each parameter in a model. Although identification typically is discussed at the global level (i.e., for the model as a whole), if any parameter in a model is not identified (i.e., local identification status), then the model is not identified. Importantly, if it is not identified, attempts at estimation will not meet the criterion inherent in most estimators—minimizing the difference between the observed data and the data implied by the model.

With regard to identification, the status of a model is referred to in one of three ways. An identified model is one in which a single, unique value can be obtained through at least one set of manipulations of other parameters in the model given the data. If the value of one or more parameters can be obtained in more than one way, then the model is *overidentified* and subject to testing for model fit. If the value of each parameter can be obtained in exactly one way, then the model is *just identified*. Although the parameter estimates in just identified models are valid, such models cannot be tested. Finally, a model in which a single, unique value for each parameter cannot be obtained is underidentified, or simply, *unidentified*.

Determining the identification status of a specified model can be a challenge, sometimes requiring the determination of whether the specification meets one or more technical criteria. Those criteria are detailed in comprehensive treatments of SEM (e.g., Bollen, 1989). In some instances, those criteria manifest as relatively straightforward rules of thumb. For instance, for the distribution of a latent variable to be defined, it must either be fixed (e.g., as $N(0,1)$) or anchored to one of the indicators, which typically is accomplished by fixing the loading for that indicator to a value of 1 (Steiger, 2002). Another rule of thumb concerns the number of indicators per latent variable. If a latent variable is modeled as uncorrelated with other variables in a model (e.g., a one-factor model or a model with orthogonal factors), it must have at least three indicators to be identified. This is because of the general identification rule that a model cannot have more free parameters than the number of nonredundant elements in the observed covariance matrix. For present purposes, it is important only to understand that, although SEM is flexible in terms of the kinds of relations between variables that can be specified, that flexibility can be limited somewhat by technical considerations having to do with how parameters are estimated.

We now illustrate the estimation process using our running example and describe, in context, additional considerations. Recall that a relatively large sample of middle school students provided data on 10 variables at baseline and three at follow-up. We hypothesized that the 10 observed variables were indicators of three latent variables of interest at baseline, and that three observed variables measured at Time 2 were indicators of one latent variable. We want to know whether variability in a latent variable for problem behavior at Time 2 is prospectively predicted by latent variables for personal characteristics that reflect risk for and protection from problem behavior, over and above baseline problem behavior. Displayed in Figure 21.2 is a path diagram depicting the set of relations in the model with the observed variables omitted from the diagram. The reason for their omission is twofold: (a) Their inclusion, as shown in Figure 21.1, yields a figure too cluttered to be of use to convey the main study hypotheses to an applied audience, and (b) although the measurement model is a component of the model, for this specific model, it is not the component of greatest interest. The structural component, which specifies the direction relations between the latent variables, is of primary substantive interest, and it is this component shown in the figure.

Because the figure shows only the structural component of the model to be estimated, it does not provide full detail regarding model specification. The part of the model not shown concerns the relations and parameters in the measurement component. In our model, these fall into four categories: (a) the relations between indicators and latent variables, (b) item intercepts (or thresholds), (c) uniquenesses associated with indicators, and (d) covariances between uniquenesses. Referring to Figure 21.1, it is apparent that the 10 observed variables at Time 1 are arrayed so that four reflect protection, three reflect risk, and three reflect problem behavior. It also is evident that, with the exception of the binary measure of drug use, a uniqueness is associated with each indicator. What we did not show in Figure 21.1 are nonzero covariances between selected uniquenesses in the model. These are illustrated for repeated indicators of problem behavior in Figure 21.3. Notice the curved arrow between the errors of each indicator measured at the two waves of data collection. These autocorrelations are not substantively interesting—they merely reflect the fact that any

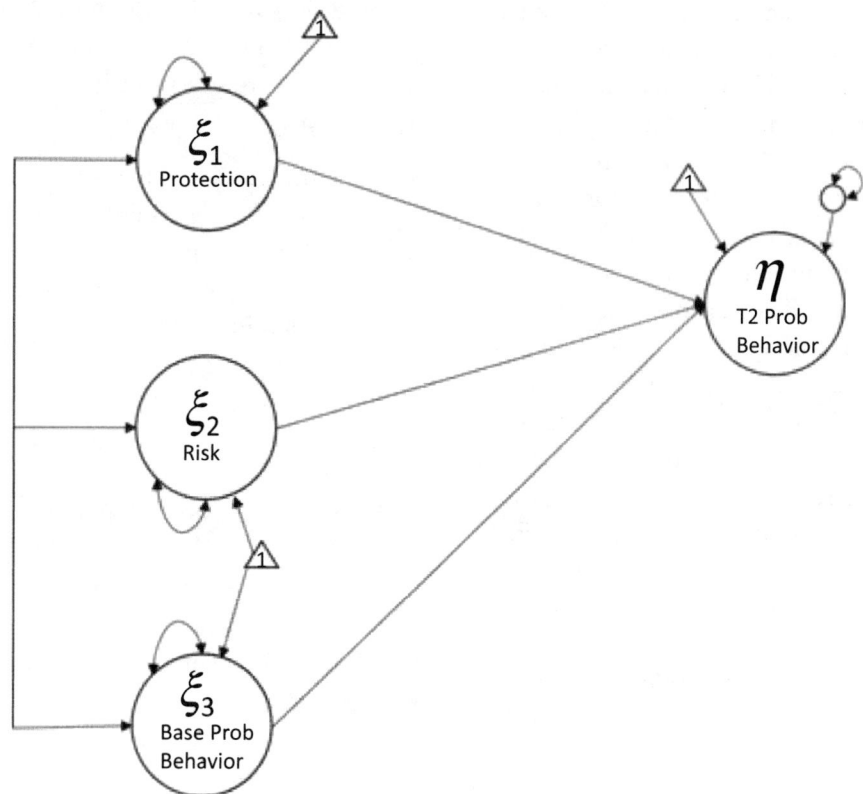

FIGURE 21.2. Simplified path diagram depicting structural model components only with no parameter labels.

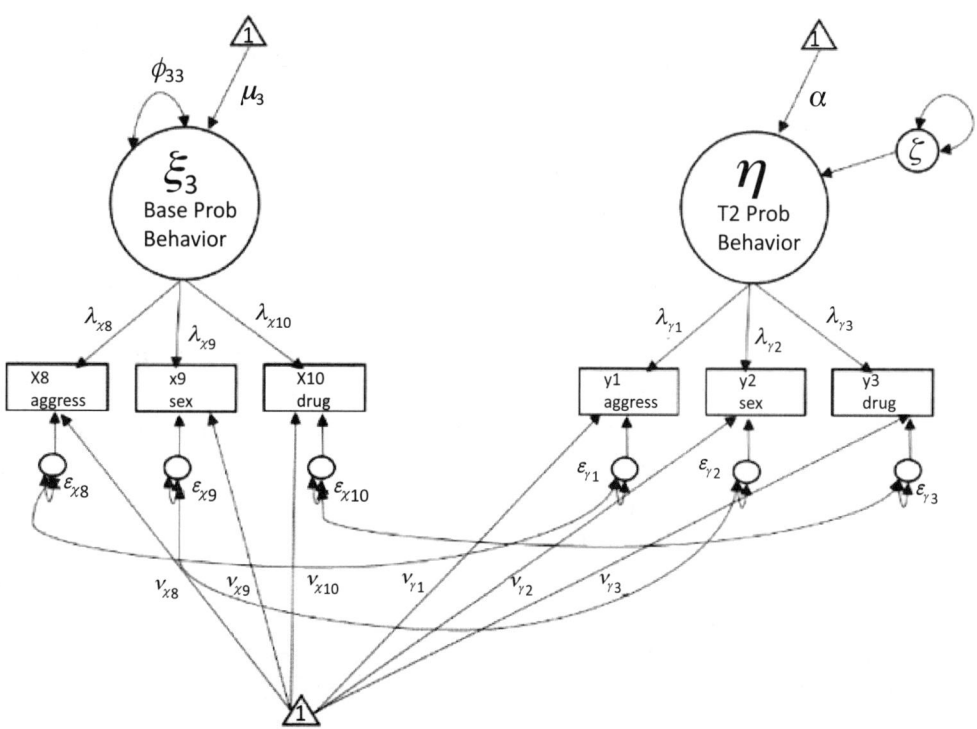

FIGURE 21.3. Portion of the example model illustrating autocorrelated uniquenesses.

unique, nonrandom variance in an observed variable at one point in time should be evident at other points in time. The astute reader may notice that our binary indicator, "drug," has a residual in Figure 21.3. Although the residual variances are not unique from the factor loading and factor (co)variances, they are fixed values (either to 1.0 with a probit link or to $\pi^2/3$ with a logit link), and it still is possible to identify a residual correlation amongst binary indicators even if the residual variances are not free parameters in the model (Muthén & Asparouhov, 2002). However, the user must be willing to assume that a latent normal distribution underlies categorical item responses to capitalize on this approach. An alternative, but much more computationally burdensome, approach is to include an orthogonal method factor onto which the binary indicators load. In this approach, the factor loadings are fixed to 1.0 and the variance of the method factor is equivalent to the residual covariance.

In models that include constructs measured repeatedly over time, the analyst may wish to impose equality constraints on the measurement models over time. Doing so ensures the desirable property that the latent variables have the same meaning over time. In our case, this would mean imposing the following constraints: $\lambda_{x8} = \lambda_{y1}$, $\lambda_{x9} = \lambda_{y2}$, $\lambda_{x10} = \lambda_{y3}$, $v_{x8} = v_{y1}$, $v_{x9} = v_{y2}$, and $v_{x10} = v_{y3}$. In general, it is neither necessary nor appropriate to constrain residual variances to be equal. It is good practice to evaluate whether constraining the measurement models to be equal produces a significant decrement in model fit. We discuss this process in the Measurement Invariance section of this chapter.

As noted, the goal of estimation is to obtain values for the free parameters that, when coupled with the fixed parameters, minimize the discrepancy between the observed data and the data implied by the model. Moreover, these values are obtained iteratively, beginning with a guess based on convention and values in the data and culminating in the optimal estimates. The processes of estimation are best understood by dissecting an example.

First, it is useful to pinpoint all of the free parameters to be estimated in a model. In our model there are 42. Their locations in the model are as follows:

- 7 loadings at Time 1 (recall that one is fixed on each latent variable)
- 0 loadings at Time 2 (2 if loadings for T2 problem behavior are not equated to the T1 loadings)
- 9 uniquenesses at Time 1
- 2 uniquenesses at Time 2
- 3 covariances to reflect autocorrelated errors (as in Figure 19.3)
- 3 covariances among latent variables measured at Time 1
- 3 variances of latent variables measured at Time 1
- 3 paths from Time 1 to Time 2 latent variables
- 1 disturbance at Time 2
- 10 item intercepts at Time 1
- 0 item intercepts at Time 2 (3 if intercepts for T2 problem behavior items are not equated to the T1 intercepts)
- 1 latent variable intercept at Time 2

Unless explicitly requested, means of exogenous latent variables are not part of the model and do not count toward the degrees of freedom. For this illustration, we use the WLSMV (Asparouhov & Muthén, 2010) within Mplus to estimate and evaluate our model. As we noted previously, we could have used a FIML estimator instead. However, we have no missing data in our data set, and we would not get some of the most important model fit indices if we used FIML estimation. These indices are not currently available when FIML is used with categorical data because the fit indices are based on observed and model-implied covariances, which can only be estimated by invoking polychoric correlations used by WLSMV. Our final reason for selecting WLSMV is that we want to be able to correlate the residuals of the repeated, binary drug use items, so we already need to assume that a continuous latent variable underlies participant responses to drug use.

Although we use WLSMV, we briefly explain FIML estimation. The FIML estimation algorithm works by assigning a random start value to each free parameter. The user may wish to override the default random start values by providing them manually, but this is only necessary to do for very complex models. An expectation maximization (EM) algorithm is used to iterate from the start values to the maximum likelihood solution. Although the EM algorithm is known to converge to the maximum likelihood solution (Dempster et al., 1977), it is sometimes assisted by a quasi-Newton-based iteration that leads to a larger jump in parameter values, thereby accelerating the process of reaching the FIML solution (Jamshidian & Jennrich, 1997). The WLSMV estimator is an extension of standard weighted least squares estimators and related "robust" weighted-least-squares approaches (see Flora & Curran, 2004). Like FIML, WLSMV minimizes the distance between the observed and implied data, but it relies on polychoric correlation matrices to handle categorical data.

Sometimes estimation fails to converge. A *failure to converge* is a relative term, because an upper bound ordinarily is imposed on the number of iterations to be attempted. Although it is possible that an attempt at estimation would converge if allowed additional iterations (which can be done by overriding the computer program's default), this typically is not the case. A failure to converge can result from the presence of one or more unidentified parameters in a model or ill-conditioned data. In some cases, a model may be identified in terms of specification, but because a parameter estimate is in effect 0 (equivalent to having fixed the path to 0 in the specification), it is not. Such models are empirically unidentified. Otherwise, failures to converge often occur in complex models or with data that are not normally distributed. A failure to converge is a signal to reevaluate the model specification and, if no problems are identified there, to reexamine the scaling and distribution of variables in the data set. One might also consider using an alternative estimator or maximization algorithm.

EVALUATION OF FIT

Once a set of optimal parameter estimates has been obtained, the fit of a model can be evaluated. In theory, this evaluation can be done in a standard, null-hypothesis statistical testing framework. That is, a null hypothesis can be posed and either be rejected or not using some test statistic. In the case of SEM, the null hypothesis is

$$H_0 : \Sigma = \Sigma(\hat{\Theta}), \qquad (21.7)$$

where Σ is the population covariance matrix, estimated by the observed covariance matrix, and $\Sigma(\hat{\Theta})$ is that matrix written as a function of the model parameter values, or the implied covariance matrix. The desired statistical outcome is to fail to reject this null hypothesis or, in statistical test terms, to find a probability greater than .05 associated with the test statistic. The minimized value of the fitting function can be used to produce a value that, under certain circumstances, is distributed as a χ^2 statistic with degrees of freedom equal to the difference between the number of nonredundant elements in the covariance matrix and the number of free parameters in the model. In theory, using this value and the appropriate reference distribution, one can conclude that a specified model either fits or does not fit the data.

For two principal reasons, this hypothesis test is, in practice, not useful. Most fundamentally, the conditions necessary for the value on the basis of the minimized value of the fit function to approximate a χ^2 statistic are never met in substantive applications of SEM. These conditions include multivariate normal data, a sample large enough to ensure that the asymptotic properties of the estimator are realized, and a model that is correct in the population. Even if the conditions were met in typical applications, the test suffers from the shortcoming of all null-hypothesis statistical tests: Unless the implied and observed covariance matrixes are identical, the null hypothesis can, with enough power, be rejected. Conversely, the implied and observed covariance matrices can be nontrivially different, but if power is sufficiently low, the null hypothesis cannot be rejected. Thus, the statistical test, even if valid on theoretical grounds, is as much a reflection of power as it is of meaningful difference between the implied and observed covariance matrices.

Because of these limitations, alternative means of evaluating model fit have been developed. A prevalent strategy, pioneered by Bentler and Bonett (1980), involves comparing the fit of a specified model with the fit of a model that specifies no relations among the variables (referred to as the null, baseline, or independence model). These comparisons typically yield a value between 0 and 1 that is interpreted as a proportion. The resultant values are indices, not statistics, and, therefore, are descriptive rather than inferential. Two widely used indices are the comparative fit index (CFI; Bentler, 1990) and the Tucker-Lewis index (TLI; also called nonnormed fit index, NNFI; Tucker & Lewis, 1973). An alternative strategy is to index the absolute fit of a model by summarizing the differences between corresponding elements in the implied and observed covariance matrixes (i.e., the residuals). The root-mean-square error of approximation (RMSEA) is a commonly used index of this sort (Steiger & Lind, 1980). The RMSEA has the additional benefits of including a correction for model complexity and an interpretation that allows for tests of close, rather than exact, fit (Browne & Cudeck, 1993).

The omnibus fit indices just described provide information about the goodness-of-fit of a single model. However, it is best practice to compare alternative plausible models. For nested models, this can be done by performing a likelihood ratio test using change in the model deviance, which is distributed as chi-square with degrees of freedom equal to the difference in the number of parameters between the two alternative models. When models are not nested, they can be compared using information criteria indices, Akaike information criterion (AIC) and BIC. There are no formal statistical comparisons for the AIC and BIC; rather, the model with the lower AIC or BIC value is preferred.

Returning now to the running example, we illustrate the general activity of evaluating fit and the use of omnibus fit indices. As noted, we obtain a deviance value that often is interpreted with reference to the χ^2 distribution. This value, which is directly proportional to the sample size, is referenced against the χ^2 distribution for the number of degrees of freedom in the model. That value, as noted, corresponds to the difference between the number of elements in the covariance matrix (computed as $p(p + 1)/2$, where p is the number of observed variables) plus the number of item means and the number of free parameters in the model. For our example, there are 91 observed variances and covariances, 13 item means, and 42 free parameters in the model, which typically would yield 62 degrees of freedom. However the WLSMV adjusts the degrees of freedom due to the use of a scaling correction, so our degrees of freedom were 60. The critical value for $p < .05$ for 60 degrees of freedom is 79.1, well below our observed value of 651.8. Assuming the unrealistic assumptions described earlier are met, this outcome indicates that the data implied by our model do not match the observed data within the sampling error.

Before moving to alternative means of evaluating fit, it will be useful to look more closely at the values reflected in the residual covariances. For illustrative purposes, focusing only on that portion of the model relevant to the Time 1 protection latent variable, we have the residual covariance matrix (calculated as the model-implied minus the observed values) in Table 21.2. Our model accounts for item covariances through the specification of the latent variable ξ_1. If this specification is sufficient to explain the pattern

TABLE 21.2

Residual Covariance Matrices for Indicators of One Latent Variable in the Example Model

Variable	V_1	V_2	V_3	V_4
V_1	.00			
V_2	−.01	.00		
V_3	−.01	.00	.00	
V_4	.00	−.01	.01	.00

of covariances, the parameter estimates should yield an implied, or reproduced, covariance matrix very close to the observed matrix. Looking first to the diagonal, the values are 0. This reflects the fact that we fully account for variance in the variables in the model, either by the influence of the latent variable or the influence of a uniqueness component. The values of most interest are the off-diagonal elements, the observed and implied covariances between the variables. For models that do not provide an acceptable account of the data as reflected in the values of fit indexes, examination of the residual matrix can be useful in pointing to specific relations that are over- or, more typically, underestimated in the specified model. In this case, the off-diagonal elements are very small, reflecting good fit (at least for this portion of the model).

Returning now to the evaluation of fit, given the well-documented concerns about the validity of the χ^2 variate, we could consult one of a number of alternative indexes that have been proposed and evaluated and that generally have found support for most modeling circumstances. The typical recommendation is to choose at least two, each from a different class of index. As noted earlier, we favor CFI and TLI, which index incremental, or comparative fit, and RMSEA (with confidence intervals), which reflects absolute fit. Values of CFI and TLI can range from 0 to 1, with higher values indicating better fit. The value for a specified model is interpreted as the proportionate improvement in fit of the specified model over the null, or independence, model. Although values of .90 and higher are commonly interpreted as indicative of acceptable fit, simulation studies indicate that .95 is a more appropriate lower bound, with values between .90 and .95 interpreted as marginal fit (Hu & Bentler, 1999). The value of CFI for the example model is .95, and the value of TLI is .94, indicating that the specified model provides a marginal-to-acceptable account of the data.

RMSEA indexes the degree of misspecification in a model per degree of freedom. To explain, a model can only imply data different from the observed data if it is more parsimonious than the unstructured data. To wit, a just-identified

model that has the same number of free parameters as elements in the observed covariance matrix perfectly reproduces the observed data. Such a model has 0 degrees of freedom. Fixing a parameter yields a degree of freedom, but it also requires introducing an assumption in the model that is not born out in the data. To the extent the value of the fixed parameter is incorrect, it results in a poorer fit of the model to the data because of misspecification. RMSEA captures this property across the model. Thus, as noted, our example model has 60 degrees of freedom, which can be interpreted as 60 ways in which an assumption was imposed on the model that could be incorrect. RMSEA addresses the question of whether, on average, these assumptions are tenable given the data. If the assumptions imposed by fixed parameters are perfectly consistent with the observed data, they result in no misspecification and yield a value for RMSEA of 0, indicating perfect model fit. Unlike χ^2, RMSEA typically is interpreted with reference to a criterion of close fit. Thus, values of .08 or less are viewed as indicative of acceptable model fit. Values from .08 to .10 indicate marginal fit, and values greater than .10 indicate poor fit. The standard error of RMSEA is known, and, therefore, a confidence interval can be put on the point estimate. It is customary to report the upper and lower limits of the 90% confidence interval. In such cases, the focus is on the degree to which the upper limit falls beneath the .08 and .10 criterion values. For the example model, the point estimate of RMSEA is .077, and the 90% confidence limits are .072 and .083. Because the upper confidence limit is above .08, RMSEA indicates a marginal fit of the model to the data.

If support for the overall fit of a model is obtained, then attention turns to the values of the parameter estimates. If fit is marginal or poor, the analyst should consider model modifications to achieve good model fit before interpreting parameter estimates. The reason is that questionable model fit indicates that results are not trustworthy. Moving beyond omnibus fit, it is possible for a model to provide acceptable fit to the observed data but not yield parameter estimates that are consistent with expectation. The most basic question about model parameter estimates is whether they differ from zero, a hypothesis tested, as in other contexts, by the ratio of the parameter estimate to its standard error. The resulting statistic, the critical ratio, is interpreted as a z statistic. Other questions that can be addressed about parameter estimates are their difference from other assumed values (e.g., .30) and their difference from each other.

Because of the number of free parameters in the example model, we present parameters in the measurement and structural components separately. Parameter estimates for the measurement component are presented in Table 21.3. For each parameter, we include the estimated (or fixed) value, the standard error, and the standardized estimate. The estimate is an unstandardized value, the equivalent of an unstandardized regression coefficient or a covariance. The standardized estimate is the value psychological scientists are inclined to present and interpret from multiple regression analyses and factor analyses. The standardized estimates for loadings are the equivalent of factor loadings in exploratory factor analysis. As is apparent from the large values for the critical ratio, all factor loadings at both time points are significantly different from 0. The standardized values range from .42 for the loading of low self-esteem on risk (λ_{x1}) to .89 for the loading of commitment to avoid problem behavior on protection (λ_{x6}). The moderate-to-large loadings indicate that the observed variables for each construct share considerable commonality, which is presumed to reflect the construct of interest. The estimated residual covariances for the problem behavior constructs measured at baseline and Time 2 are highly significant, suggesting that, had these paths been omitted from the specification, the fit to the data would have been poor. The standardized estimates are correlation coefficients, and their magnitudes make clear that there is considerable and stable nonrandom variance in the indicators not explained by the latent variables.

The estimates of greatest interest are those that index the relations between latent variables. Those estimates, and other estimates within the

TABLE 21.3

Parameter Estimates and Standard Errors for Measurement Component of Example Model

	Unstandardized estimate	Standard error	Standardized estimate
Factor loadings			
λ_{x1}	1.00	Fixed	.42
λ_{x2}	1.81	.13	.53
λ_{x3}	1.35	.05	.72
λ_{x4}	1.00	Fixed	.72
λ_{x5}	.95	.03	.75
λ_{x6}	1.33	.04	.89
λ_{x7}	.82	.04	.59
$\lambda_{x8} = \lambda_{y1}$	1.00	Fixed	.76/.71
$\lambda_{x9} = \lambda_{y2}$	.20	.01	.60/.59
$\lambda_{x10} = \lambda_{y3}$	.71	.02	.72/.73
Item intercepts			
v_{x1}	1.81	.01	3.39
v_{x2}	3.11	.02	4.02
v_{x3}	2.21	.01	5.21
v_{x4}	.05	.02	.09
v_{x5}	1.28	.01	.11
v_{x6}	.05	.02	.08
v_{x7}	.06	.02	.10
$v_{x8} = v_{y1}$	1.28	.01	3.66/3.55
$v_{x9} = v_{y2}$	.93	.01	.69/.63
$v_{x10} = v_{y3}$	−.91	.03	−.92/−.94
Residual variances			
σ^2_{x1}	.23	.01	.82
σ^2_{x2}	.44	.02	.73
σ^2_{x3}	.09	.01	.48
σ^2_{x4}	.16	.01	.48
σ^2_{x5}	.12	.01	.44
σ^2_{x6}	.08	.01	.22
σ^2_{x7}	.21	.01	.65
σ^2_{x8}	.08	.01	.64
σ^2_{x9}	.79	.04	.43
σ^2_{y1}	.09	.01	.66
σ^2_{y2}	1.08	.05	.50
Residual covariances			
$\sigma_{x8,y1}$	.03	.01	.42
$\sigma_{x9,y2}$	.51	.03	.56
$\sigma_{x10,y3}$	.22	.03	.47

structural component of the model, are provided in Table 21.4. Moving toward the bottom of Table 21.4, the high correlations between the latent variables at Time 1 are apparent. Correlation coefficients are disattenuated in structural equation modeling, meaning that they tend to be higher

TABLE 21.4

Parameter Estimates and Test Statistics for Structural Component of Example Model

Parameter	Estimate	Standard error	Standardized estimate
Regression paths			
γ_1	.62*	.32	.14
γ_2	−.10	.69	−.04
γ_3	.67*	.31	.66
Latent variable variances and disturbance			
ζ	.36***	.03	.34
ϕ_{11}	.05***	.01	1.00
ϕ_{22}	.17***	.01	1.00
ϕ_{33}	1.04***	.06	1.00
Covariances, latent variables			
ϕ_{12}	−.08***	.01	−.83
ϕ_{13}	.19***	.01	.84
ϕ_{23}	−.41***	.02	−.97
Latent variable intercept			
α	.18***	.03	.17

*$p < .05$; **$p < .01$; ***$p < .001$.

than what the reader may be used to. Even so, the correlations among our Time 1 factors are very high and we should be cautious in interpreting our regression coefficients given this degree of multicollinearity.

We can now move to the directional relations between the latent variables at Time 1 and Time 2. First, we consider the autoregressive path, γ_3, which reflects the stability of the latent problem behavior variable over the period of time covered by the study, about 8 months. As would be expected, there is fairly high stability in problem behavior over time.

Moving now to the predictive paths, we find that the effect of Time 1 protection on Time 2 problem behavior (γ_2), over and above Time 1 problem behavior and risk, is nonsignificant. There is a significant, positive path between Time 1 risk and Time 2 problem behavior (γ_3). The standardized estimate tells us that a one standard deviation increase in risk at Time 1 is associated with a .66 standard deviation increase in Time 2 problem behavior, over and above Time 1 protection and Time 1 problem behavior.

We began the section by outlining Jöreskog's (1993) discussion of the different approaches to using SEM. To this point, it would appear that we are using SEM in a strictly confirmatory manner. We could, however, consider alternatives to the specified model that might serve to increase our confidence that the model affords the best account of the data. Use of these alternative models approach is most effective when the models to be compared are nested. One model is nested in another when its free parameters are a subset of the free parameters in another model. We can produce a model nested in our example model by fixing some of its parameters. To illustrate this process, we consider the validity of the equality constraints imposed on the problem behavior measurement model. Removing the original equality constraints provides a test of whether the parameters in the repeated measurement models are significantly different. By constraining the two loadings and three intercepts for problem behavior to equality, we reduced the number of parameters to be estimated because the parameters constrained to be equal are treated as one parameter. If we remove the constraint, we increase the number of degrees of freedom by five. We can compare the two models using the χ^2-difference test (with a scaling factor correction that is necessary with the WLSMV estimator; Satorra & Bentler, 2001). The χ^2-difference test was highly significant, I $\chi^2 = 26.71$ ($df = 5$), $p < .001$, indicating that at least one of the equality constraints was inconsistent with the data. When we examine the output of the unconstrained model, it appears that the intercept for involvement in sexual activity is higher at the second time point. This finding makes sense from an adolescent development perspective: over time, sexual involvement may be less indicative of underlying problem behavior, and more indicative of normative development. Indeed, when we compare a model that constrains aggressive-behavior and drug-use parameters, but not sexual involvement, we find that the partially noninvariant model is much better than the fully constrained model (I $\chi^2 = 18.59$ ($df = 2$), $p < .001$), but that the unconstrained model is only slightly better than the partially noninvariant model ($I \chi^2 = 8.92$ ($df = 3$), $p = .03$). The reader may have expected that the degrees of freedom for the test comparing the partially noninvariant model to the fully constrained model would be 3. However, since sexual involvement was our anchor item (with a factor loading constrained to 1), we had to select a different anchor item in order to allow its factor loading to vary over time. We ended up constraining the factor loadings for aggressive behaviors to be fixed to 1.

Model Modification

Specified models, including the alternatives to which they are compared, do not always provide an acceptable account of the data. That is, they yield values for the fit indexes of choice that fail with reference to a priori criteria (e.g., CFI or TLI < .95, RMSEA > .10). In such cases, if the researcher is using SEM in a strictly confirmatory or alternative models manner, the analysis is completed and the model or models declared inadequate as a description of the processes that produced the observed data. Yet, data typically are acquired at considerable effort and expense, leading most researchers to respond to evidence of unacceptable fit by asking, "What if?" which shifts them to using SEM for model generation. The what-if question might concern the observed variables: What if certain variables were dropped from the model or new variables added to it? It is generally the case, however, that the variables in a model are of sufficient interest that dropping one or more would leave a set that does not map well onto the original research question or conceptual model guiding the research. Typically, the what-if question concerns the relations between variables in a model and can be phrased in terms of fixed and free parameters. What if certain parameters that were originally fixed are freed? Or, what if one or more free parameters were fixed?

The consideration of whether model fit might be improved by changing the status of parameters in a model is termed *specification searching*. As the term indicates, the goal of specification searching is to find and address the misspecification in the original model that resulted in its lack of

acceptable fit to the data. Specification searching typically takes one of two forms, each of which involves consulting the results from the initial estimation and testing. In *manual specification searching*, the researcher consults the tests of specific parameter to determine whether parameters that were free in the model could be fixed to 0 or consults the residual matrix to determine whether one or more observed covariances were not sufficiently accounted for by the free parameters in a model. In *automated specification searching*, a computer program evaluates all fixed or free parameters and returns a list of those parameters that are contributing to the size of the model χ^2 relative to its degrees of freedom.

Returning to the example model, you will recall that the upper bound of the confidence interval for the RMSEA exceeded .08, and the TLI was .94. Therefore, it may prove useful to evaluate whether any adjustments to the model would result in a better account of the data. We first examine tests of individual parameters. Referring to Table 21.4, the effect of protection on problem behavior at Time 2 (γ_2) was not significant, suggesting that fixing this path to 0 would simplify the model without significantly reducing fit. With $\gamma_2 = 0$, it makes sense to remove other parameters associated with ξ_2 from the model: $\phi_{22}, \phi_{12}, \phi_{23} = 0$. The resultant model has CFI =.97, TLI =.95, and the 90% confidence interval for RMSEA = [.06, .07]. Thus, we have moved from marginal fit to acceptable fit. In addition to the slight improvement in fit, these adjustments to the model reduce the problem of multicollinearity that we identified previously.

We next consult the residual matrix to determine whether there is evidence that any covariances have been underestimated because certain parameters were fixed at 0. Recall that the residual matrix is constructed by subtracting corresponding elements in the observed and implied covariance matrixes. Relatively large values raise the value of the fitting function and, thereby, reduce the favorability of fit indexes. Manually evaluating the residuals can be relatively straightforward for small models; however, for a model based on 13 observed variables, scanning the 78 residual covariances, even their more readily interpretable standardized form, often does not suggest obvious ways in which a model might be modified to improve its fit. Indeed, the only thing clear from scanning the residuals is that the relation between low self-esteem and a number of the remaining observed variables is underestimated. Given the number of these residuals and the position of relevant parameters across the model, there are no obvious fixed parameters that, if freed, would significantly improve the fit of the model.

An alternative strategy, one better suited to larger models such as our example, is *automated specification searching*. Automated searching typically focuses on fixed parameters in a model (although some computer programs allow a focus on free parameters as well). The computer program, in effect, frees each fixed parameter and returns, in the form of a *modification index*, the amount by which the model χ^2 would be reduced if the parameter were freed (Bentler, 1986a; Sörbom, 1989). Some programs order these from highest to lowest, allowing a quick determination of which modifications would produce the greatest improvement in fit. As noted, however, each modification ripples through the model, affecting estimates of some, if not all, of the other parameters. Thus, for example, it may appear that model fit would improve if two fixed parameters were freed; however, freeing the first yields a model in which freeing the second offers no additional improvement in fit. Because of the dependency among parameters, a better approach is to use the multivariate approach to automated searching, in which the full set of modification indexes is evaluated in search of the set of modifications that, together, would produce the maximum improvement in fit. Although automated specification searching for the example models suggests a number of fixed parameters that, if freed, would improve the fit of the model, none are theoretically justifiable. For instance, the largest model improvement would be generated by allowing the residual of sensation seeking to correlate with low self-esteem.

Because adjustments to the original specification were made with reference to the data,

the likelihood of Type I error is unacceptably high, and, therefore, fit statistics and indexes resulting from data-driven model modifications cannot be taken at face value (MacCallum et al., 1992). Thus, although researchers working in model generation mode might be tempted to confidently interpret the results from estimation of respecified models that produce acceptable values of fit indexes, they should instead proceed with caution because the likelihood is unacceptably high (i.e., > .05) that the model that fits the data in hand would not fit another set of data from the same population. As such, the results can only be interpreted with reference to the current sample. In summary, there is a good chance that data-driven modifications will not replicate (MacCallum et al., 1992), so data-driven, post-hoc adjustments are generally frowned upon. Unless a modification results in a very substantial improvement in model fit and can be justified on conceptual or design grounds, respecified models should not be interpreted until they are cross-validated.

Regardless of whether one uses data-driven modification indices to alter a model, cross-validation is always a good idea, particularly given the many stages of model building and multiple decision points along the way. If the sample is reasonably large (approximately $N = 600$ or higher), we recommend randomly selecting about half to two thirds of the sample to serve as the *calibration sample*, and using the remaining one third to one half of the sample as the *validation sample*. Once the final form of the model has been determined in the calibration sample, the analyst should test the fit of the final model using the validation sample. An alternative strategy would be to draw a unique sample from the same population to validate the original model that was built on the original sample.

INTERPRETATION

Once support has been obtained for an informative model, the focus moves to the final step in using SEM—interpretation and reporting. Interpretation begins with presentation. Although what is presented and, to some extent, how it is presented is constrained by the medium and forum, a number of principles apply whether the findings are presented in a journal article, a book, or an oral presentation. The observed data, code used to read and prepare it for input, code used for all analyses, and output from which results were extracted should be made available for access. Ideally, the data would be available in a format that could be read by any SEM software (e.g., csv, txt) to allow for evaluations of reproducibility. Access to these files should be by a persistent link such as a digital object identifier or a link provided by a stable repository such as Open Science Framework or Inter-University Consortium for Political and Social Research (ICPSR). (The raw data, input, and output files for the example used in this chapter can be accessed at https://osf.io/5wmgf.) In addition, an accurate accounting of the focal model as well as any alternatives and modifications should be included. For many models, a path diagram suffices. Regardless of the format in which the model is presented, a thorough accounting for degrees of freedom should be offered. The estimation method should be made explicit and its use justified. A set of fit indexes and criteria for their interpretation should be offered (see Hu & Bentler, 1999, for a useful overview). Parameter estimates should be provided. For simple models, these can be included on a path diagram and flagged for statistical significance. For more complex models, tables such as Tables 21.3 and 21.4 should be used. In our presentation of findings from the example analysis, we listed all parameters and provided unstandardized and standardized values as well as statistical test information. We would be unlikely to provide that level of detail in a journal article; however, the estimates and tests of the focal parameters should be given in full. When multiple alternative models are specified a priori, it is useful to table the fit statistics for each model, which facilitates comparisons between models. Finally, if modifications are made to the originally specified model or an alternative specified alternative, it should be made clear to the reader the basis on which the model was modified,

including how many consultations of the data were required to produce the model to be interpreted. Additional detail regarding these aspects of presentation can be found in a number of articles and chapters focused specifically on the presentation of results from SEM analyses (e.g., Boomsma et al., 2012; Hoyle & Isherwood, 2013; McDonald & Ho, 2002; Schreiber et al., 2006).

The substantive interpretation of SEM results refers to information provided in the presentation. Care should be taken to distinguish between comparative and absolute fit, unstandardized and standardized parameters estimates, and a priori and post hoc components of a model. As with any multivariate model, specific relations should be described with reference to other relations in the model.

Beyond these specific guidelines for presenting and interpreting the statistical results of an SEM analysis, two broader considerations should receive attention. A key consideration in interpretation is the extent to which a statistically defensible model provides a uniquely satisfactory account of the data. That is, for many well-fitting models, it is possible to generate one or more alternative models that are, statistically speaking, equivalent to the specified model (Breckler, 1990; MacCallum et al., 1993). For example, in a simple study involving two variables, x and y, the model that specifies x as a cause of y cannot be distinguished in terms of fit from a model that specifies y as a cause of x or x and y as simply correlated. A set of basic respecification rules can be used to generate possible alternatives to a specified model when they are less obvious (Williams, 2012). Sometimes the inferential conundrum produced by equivalent models can be resolved through design (e.g., x is manipulated) or a consideration of what the variables represent (e.g., x is a biological characteristic). Otherwise, the researcher can only infer that the results provide necessary, but not sufficient, support for the focal model.

Perhaps the most controversial aspect of interpreting results from SEM analyses is the inference of causality (e.g., Baumrind, 1983; cf. Bollen & Pearl, 2013). Although the judicious application of SEM can strengthen causal inferences when they are otherwise warranted, SEM cannot overcome the significant limitations of nonexperimental designs, particularly when all data are gathered at one point in time. Because of its capacity for isolating putative causal variables and modeling data from longitudinal designs, SEM offers a stronger basis for inferring causality than commonly used statistical techniques (Pearl, in press). In the end, however, statistics yield to design when it comes to causal inferences, and, therefore, data generated by experimental or carefully designed quasi-experimental designs with a longitudinal component are required (Hoyle & Robinson, 2003).

Prototypic Models

Except for limitations associated with research design (e.g., temporal order of variables in longitudinal models) and model identification, there is considerable flexibility in model specification for SEM analyses. Indeed, as the number of observed variables increases, the number of models one might construct from them increases dramatically (e.g., Raykov & Marcoulides, 2001). For that reason, it is not possible to review all, or even a substantial proportion, of the models psychological scientists might construct and evaluate using SEM. Rather, to give a sense of the kinds of models psychological scientists might evaluate using SEM, we briefly describe a number of prototypic models. These generally fall into one of two categories: (a) models focused primarily on latent variables without particular concern for how they relate to each other, and (b) models focused primarily on structural paths, whether they involve observed or latent variables.

At several points in the presentation of these models, we refer to comparisons between groups. Because such comparisons can be undertaken for any model evaluated using SEM, we describe the basic strategy for making such comparisons before presenting the models. In multigroup SEM, data are available on all of the observed variables for two or more groups of cases for which a comparison would be of interest. For instance, the example data set referenced throughout the

chapter includes female and male middle-school students in sufficient numbers that parameters in the model could be estimated separately for the two groups and compared individually or in sets. To compare a model across groups, we either need to produce separate covariance matrices for each group to be compared or ensure that the raw data includes a variable that designates group membership. A single model is simultaneously fit data from these groups, permitting the use of equality constraints to compare parameters between groups. For example, we could fit the example model to data from female and male students, constraining corresponding regression paths to be equal. That model is nested in and has three more degrees of freedom than a model in which the parameters are free to vary between groups. The χ^2-difference test evaluates whether the set of constraints are consistent with the data. If the difference is significant, one or more of the equality constraints is inconsistent with the data, indicating a difference in the parameter(s) for female and male students. Such multiple group comparisons are the equivalent of tests of statistical interaction because a significant between-group difference indicates that the relation between two variables differs across levels of a third variable—in this case, the grouping variable (for a general treatment of between-group comparisons, see Hancock, 2004).

Models Focused on Latent Variables

Although the model used to illustrate the steps involved in using SEM included latent variables, the primary focus of the model was the directional relation between problem behavior from Time 1 to Time 2. Such is not always the case. For example, it might be the case the latent variables—protection, risk, and problem behavior—are not sufficiently well-defined to warrant tests of hypotheses about the relations between them. Or perhaps the constructs are generally well-defined, but there is reason to believe the relations between the indicators and latent variables differ across groups or time (e.g., if we found evidence that none of the factor loadings or item intercepts could be constrained to equality for the repeated assessments of problem behavior). These and a host of additional questions of potential interest to psychological scientists can be addressed in measurement models. We illustrate the possibilities by describing two latent-variable focused models.

Measurement Invariance

When latent variables are included in a model and mean levels on those variables or their relations with other variables are to be compared across samples from different populations (e.g., native English speakers versus nonnative speakers) or within a sample across time, a key concern is whether the meaning of the latent variables is consistent across the units to be compared. To the extent that the measurement model for a latent variable is consistent across samples or time, it is *invariant* with respect to measurement (for a review, see Widaman & Olivera-Aguilar, in press).

SEM is an appealing strategy for evaluating measurement invariance, because of the flexibility with which models can be specified and estimated, and the ease with which parameters can be compared across groups or time. For instance, consider the question of measurement invariance with respect to the risk construct in the example used throughout the chapter. Perhaps our concern is the degree to which dispositional risk influences problem behavior for young women and men. A meaningful comparison of this influence assumes that the indicators of risk function similarly for females and males. We can simultaneously estimate the measurement model for risk for females and males, using equality constraints to compare any or all parameters in the model. For instance, it would be important to show that responses on the indicators (e.g., impulsive decision making) are influenced by the latent variable to a similar degree for the two groups (i.e., the factor loadings and intercepts are comparable). This evaluation is done within a multigroup context in which the models are simultaneously fit to separate sub-samples. If we constrain all of the factor loadings and intercepts to be equal for females and males, and the fit is equivalent to the fit of a model in which the loadings are allowed to vary, we infer

that the loadings and intercepts are equivalent. When intercepts and loadings can be constrained to equality, we say that the measurement model is "strongly invariant"; if only the factor loadings, but not the intercepts, are invariant, we say the measurement model is *weakly invariant* (Millsap & Tein, 2004). If, as in our case with measuring problem behavior over time, some of the items are invariant and some are not, we call this *partial invariance*. The same strategy could be used to compare uniquenesses (though there is generally not a good rationale for constraining uniquenesses across groups), the variance of the latent variable, or any parameter in the measurement model. Before making group comparisons regarding latent variable means, it is essential to check for measurement invariance. This is because undetected measurement noninvariance can cause what appear to be mean differences on the latent construct, when the reality is that items are measuring the constructs differently across groups (Millsap, 1998).

Latent Growth Models

The addition of the mean structure to a model makes possible another class of specialized models of relevance to phenomena studied by psychological scientists—latent growth models (also referred to as latent curve models). Like trend analysis in repeated measures ANOVA, latent growth models focus on modeling patterns of means over time. For instance, returning to the illustrative example, if a sample of adolescents completed our bonding to school measure at the beginning of each of their last 2 years in middle school and their first 2 years of high school, we could examine the trajectory, or growth curve, of school belonging during these transitional years. As in repeated measures ANOVA, we can evaluate the first $k - 1$ order curves, with k indicating the number of repeated assessments.

A virtue of latent growth modeling in the SEM context is the ability to focus on individual growth (Bollen & Curran, 2006; McArdle, 2012). For instance, in the school-bonding example, let us assume that, generally speaking, the trajectory during the period we are studying is linear.

This outcome would be determined by observing acceptable fit of relevant portions of a model in which the means are fit to a straight line. If estimation indicates support for this model, then the focus turns to variability in growth parameters—the slope and intercept of the linear trajectory. These growth parameters are modeled as variances of latent variables, hence, the label *latent* growth modeling. If, for instance, there is in effect no variability in the slope parameter, we might infer that the observed trajectory is normative. If there is variability in this parameter or the intercept parameter, then we can move to an interesting set of questions that concern the explanation or consequences of this variability (Willett & Sayer, 1994). At this point, the model is referred to as a conditional growth model because we are acknowledging that the growth parameters vary across individuals as a function of some characteristic of those individuals or the circumstances in which they live. This general strategy—determining the shape of the trajectory of change in a construct over time and then attempting to explain individual variability in trajectories—is particularly useful for studying development or the time course of a process.

MODELS FOCUSED ON STRUCTURAL PATHS

As with the example used throughout the chapter, SEM frequently is used to model the relations between variables. Although, as in path analysis, the relations can involve only measured variables, the most beneficial use of SEM is to model directional relations between latent variables. In this section, we highlight the benefits of modeling relations in this way.

Cross-Lagged Panel Models

Panel models are those in which the same variables are assessed at multiple points in time. The simplest case, two variables and two waves of data, illustrates the logic and benefits of cross-lagged panel models as analyzed using SEM. Modeling the two variables as latent variables ensures that no path coefficients are attenuated because of measurement error. This is a particular

advantage in this context because path coefficients are to be compared, and it is important that any observed differences in coefficients be attributable to differences in the actual strength of the relations between constructs as opposed to differential attenuation of path coefficients because of measurement error. Another concern is that the cross-lagged path coefficients are estimated controlling for between-person stability. The random intercept cross-lagged panel model achieves this control by decomposing scores into grand mean, between-person, and within-person components, the latter of which allows for unconfounded tests of cross-lagged effects (Hamaker et al., 2015; Mulder & Hamaker, 2021).

In the prototypic cross-lagged panel model, we are interested in the absolute and the relative magnitudes of the coefficients associated with the cross-lagged paths. In absolute terms, we are interested in whether, after controlling for stability and between-person differences in the constructs, there is evidence of an association between them. This is determined by testing whether the cross-lagged path coefficients differ from 0. In relative terms, we are interested in whether one of the cross-lagged path coefficients between two variables is larger than the other. This is determined by constraining the coefficients to be equal and determining whether the fit of the model declines significantly. If it does, then the constraint must be relaxed and the inference is that the two coefficients differ. If one cross-lagged coefficient is larger than the other, particularly if the smaller coefficient is not significantly different from 0, then the evidence supports a causal relation in the direction of the path associated with the larger coefficient (Mulder & Hamaker, 2021, cover additional tests possible in cross-lagged panel models estimated using SEM).

Mediation

A distinguishing feature of theories in psychological science is their prescription of the processes or mechanisms by which one construct exerts a causal influence on another. Competing theories may agree about the causal relation but offer differing accounts of the process or mechanisms, prompting research focused specifically on the explanation for the effect. Variables that capture the putative explanations are *mediators*, and models in which their explanation of an effect is estimated are *mediation models*. Although such models can be estimated and tested by a series of multiple regression equations (Baron & Kenny, 1986), the inability to deal effectively with measurement error in multiple regression analysis, although always a concern, is particularly problematic for tests of mediation.

The simplest mediation model includes three directional effects: the direct effect of a causal variable on an outcome, the direct effect of the cause on a mediator, and the direct effect of the mediator on the outcome. The latter two effects, together, constitute the indirect effect of the cause on the outcome. The product of the path coefficients for these two paths indexes the indirect, or mediated, effect. In this simple model, the direct and indirect paths are perfectly correlated. As one increases, the other decreases. Moreover, the strongest evidence in support of a putative mediator is a significant indirect effect and a nonsignificant direct effect of the cause on the outcome. Although a number of conditions might lead to the underestimation of the indirect effect, one that is addressed well by SEM is unreliability in the mediator (Hoyle & Kenny, 1999). As the degree of unreliability in the mediator increases, the indirect effect is increasingly underestimated and the direct effect is overestimated. SEM offers a means of estimating these effects with unreliability removed from the mediator. When multiple indicators are available, this is accomplished by modeling the mediator as a latent variable. When only one indicator is available, unreliability can be removed from the mediator by modeling it as a latent variable with a single indicator whose uniqueness is fixed to reflect an estimate of unreliability in the indicator. Using either strategy ensures that the indirect effect is not underestimated, the direct effect is not overestimated, and, as a result, evidence for mediation by the proposed process or mechanism is not missed when it should be found. As with many applications of SEM, assumptions are often

made about causal direction in mediation models that might not be tenable given the research design. In such cases, care must be taken to rule out models that offer a statistically equivalent account of the data but imply directions of influence inconsistent with the favoured model (Pek & Hoyle, 2016).

Latent Interaction

Measurement error is similarly problematic for tests of moderation, or interaction, in which the effect of one variable on another is assumed to vary across levels of a third variable. The effects of measurement error are compounded in tests of moderation because those tests often involve the product of two variables, each of which may be measured with error. The reliability of the product term typically is lower than the reliability of either of the individual variables, increasing the likelihood that a model that includes the main effects and interaction will yield support only for the main effects. When multiple indicators of the variables are available, unreliability can be effectively removed from the individual variables and their product by modeling them as latent variables using SEM.

Although the basic approach to using SEM in this way was documented in the mid-1980s (Kenny & Judd, 1984), it has seen limited use. Until the early 2000s, this could be attributed to the complexity involved in specifying the latent interaction variable—which increases as the number of indicators of each individual variable increases beyond two. This complexity stems from the fact that indicators of the latent interaction variable are the cross-products of the indicators of the two variables (e.g., two latent variables with three indicators each yields nine indicators of the latent interaction variable) and their relation to both the latent variable and their uniqueness term is nonlinear. The complexities associated with manual specification of latent interaction variables have been reduced (Marsh et al., 2004) or eliminated (Klein & Moosbrugger, 2000). The latent moderated structural equations approach, which uses the mixture distribution to estimate latent interaction effects, does not require the specification of latent interaction variables to estimate latent interaction effects and is implemented in widely available SEM software (e.g., Cortina et al., 2021; Klein & Muthén, 2007). As a result, it is now straightforward to address the attenuating effect of compounded unreliability in interaction variables, significantly increasing the likelihood of detecting moderation when it is present.

CONCLUSION

The flexibility and increasing generality of SEM make it an attractive alternative to traditional statistical methods such as ANOVA, multiple regression analysis, and exploratory factor analysis for psychological scientists. Although those methods have been, and will continue to be, well suited to many hypothesis tests in psychology, they significantly limit the range of hypotheses than can be considered. SEM, with its focus on modeling rather than analyzing data, affords new ways of studying the measurement of complex constructs and the relations between them. The ability to embed latent variables in any model is perhaps the most important feature of SEM and, as we have demonstrated, can be used to considerable benefit when the observed variables are measured with error. If the possibilities described and illustrated in this chapter have piqued your interest, we recommend building on the foundation provided here by consulting one or more of the detailed treatments offered in the growing array of textbooks (e.g., Bollen, 1989; Kaplan, 2009; Kline, 2016; Little, 2013; Schumacker & Lomax, 2016) and edited volumes (e.g., Hancock & Mueller, 2013; Hoyle, in press).

References

Asparouhov, T., & Muthén, B. O. (2010). *Computing the strictly positive Satorra-Bentler chi-square test in Mplus*. https://www.statmodel.com/examples/webnotes/webnote12.pdf

Baron, R. M., & Kenny, D. A. (1986). The moderator-mediator variable distinction in social psychological research: Conceptual, strategic, and statistical considerations. *Journal of Personality and Social Psychology, 51*(6), 1173–1182. https://doi.org/10.1037/0022-3514.51.6.1173

Baumrind, D. (1983). Specious causal attributions in the social sciences: The reformulated stepping-stone theory of heroin use as exemplar. *Journal of Personality and Social Psychology, 45*(6), 1289–1298. https://doi.org/10.1037/0022-3514.45.6.1289

Bentler, P. M. (1985). *Theory and implementation of EQS: A structural equations program*. BMDP Statistical Software.

Bentler, P. M. (1986a). *Lagrange multiplier and Wald tests for EQS and EQS/PC*. BMDP Statistical Software.

Bentler, P. M. (1986b). Structural equation modeling and psychometrika: An historical perspective on growth and achievements. *Psychometrika, 51*(1), 35–51. https://doi.org/10.1007/BF02293997

Bentler, P. M. (1990). Comparative fit indexes in structural models. *Psychological Bulletin, 107*(2), 238–246. https://doi.org/10.1037/0033-2909.107.2.238

Bentler, P. M., & Bonett, D. G. (1980). Significance tests and goodness-of-fit in the analysis of covariance structures. *Psychological Bulletin, 88*(3), 588–606. https://doi.org/10.1037/0033-2909.88.3.588

Bentler, P. M., & Speckart, G. (1979). Models of attitude–behavior relations. *Psychological Review, 86*(5), 452–464. https://doi.org/10.1037/0033-295X.86.5.452

Blalock, H. M. (1964). *Causal inferences in non-experimental research*. University of North Carolina Press.

Bollen, K. A. (1989). *Structural equations with latent variables*. Wiley. https://doi.org/10.1002/9781118619179

Bollen, K. A., & Curran, P. J. (2006). *Latent curve models: A structural equation approach*. Wiley.

Bollen, K. A., & Hoyle, R. H. (in press). Latent variables in structural equation modeling. In R. H. Hoyle (Ed.), *Handbook of structural equation modeling* (2nd ed.). Guilford Press.

Bollen, K. A., & Pearl, J. (2013). Eight myths about causality and structural equation models. In S. L. Morgan (Ed.), *Handbook of causal analysis for social research* (pp. 301–328). Springer. https://doi.org/10.1007/978-94-007-6094-3_15

Boomsma, A., Hoyle, R. H., & Panter, A. T. (2012). The structural equation modeling research report. In R. H. Hoyle (Ed.), *Handbook of structural equation modeling* (pp. 341–358). Guilford Press.

Bovaird, J. A., & Koziol, N. A. (in press). Measurement models for ordered categorical indicators. In R. H. Hoyle (Ed.), *Handbook of structural equation modeling* (2nd ed.). Guilford Press.

Box, G. E. P. (1979). Robustness in the strategy of scientific model building. In R. L. Lawner &

G. N. Wilkinson (Eds.), *Robustness in statistics* (pp. 201–236). Academic Press. https://doi.org/10.1016/B978-0-12-438150-6.50018-2

Breckler, S. J. (1990). Applications of covariance structure modeling in psychology: Cause for concern? *Psychological Bulletin, 107*(2), 260–273. https://doi.org/10.1037/0033-2909.107.2.260

Browne, M. W., & Cudeck, R. (1993). Alternative ways of assessing model fit. In K. A. Bollen & J. S. Long (Eds.), *Testing structural equation models* (pp. 136–162). SAGE.

Burks, B. S. (1928). The relative influence of nature and nurture upon mental development: A comparative study of foster parent–foster child resemblance and true parent–true child resemblance. In G. M. Whipple (Ed.), *The twenty-seventh yearbook of the National Society for the Study of Education* (pp. 219–316). Public School Publishing Company.

Cortina, J. M., Markell-Goldstein, H. M., Green, J. P., & Chang, Y. (2021). How are we testing interactions in latent variable models? Surging forward or fighting shy? *Organizational Research Methods, 24*(1), 26–54. https://doi.org/10.1177/1094428119872531

Curran, P. J. (2000). A latent curve framework for studying developmental trajectories of adolescent substance use. In J. Rose, L. Chassin, C. Presson, & J. Sherman (Eds.), *Multivariate applications in substance use research* (pp. 1–42). Erlbaum.

Dempster, A. P., Laird, N. M., & Rubin, D. B. (1977). Maximum likelihood from incomplete data via the EM algorithm. *Journal of the Royal Statistical Society. Series B. Methodological, 39*(1), 1–22. https://doi.org/10.1111/j.2517-6161.1977.tb01600.x

Denis, D. J., & Legerski, J. (2006). Causal modeling and the origins of path analysis. *Theory and Science, 7.* https://theoryandscience.icaap.org/content/vol7.1/denis.html

Duncan, O. D. (1969). Some linear models for two-wave, two-variable panel analysis. *Psychological Bulletin, 72*(3), 177–182. https://doi.org/10.1037/h0027876

Duncan, O. D. (1975). *Introduction to structural equation models.* Academic Press.

Enders, C. K. (in press). Missing data in structural equation modeling. In R. H. Hoyle (Ed.), *Handbook of structural equation modeling* (2nd ed.). Guilford Press.

Flora, D. B., & Curran, P. J. (2004). An empirical evaluation of alternative methods of estimation for confirmatory factor analysis with ordinal data. *Psychological Methods, 9*(4), 466–491. https://doi.org/10.1037/1082-989X.9.4.466

Goldberger, A. S. (1971). Econometrics and psychometrics: A survey of commonalities. *Psychometrika, 36*(2), 83–107. https://doi.org/10.1007/BF02291392

Goldberger, A. S., & Duncan, O. D. (Eds.). (1973). *Structural equation models in the social sciences.* Academic Press.

Graham, J. W. (2009). Missing data analysis: Making it work in the real world. *Annual Review of Psychology, 60*(1), 549–576. https://doi.org/10.1146/annurev.psych.58.110405.085530

Hamaker, E. L., Kuiper, R. M., & Grasman, R. P. P. P. (2015). A critique of the cross-lagged panel model. *Psychological Methods, 20*(1), 102–116. https://doi.org/10.1037/a0038889

Hancock, G. R. (2004). Experimental, quasi-experimental, and nonexperimental design and analysis with latent variables. In D. Kaplan (Ed.), *The handbook of quantitative methodology for the social sciences* (pp. 317–334). SAGE. https://doi.org/10.4135/9781412986311.n17

Hancock, G. R., & Mueller, R. O. (Eds.). (2013). *Structural equation modeling: A second course* (2nd ed.). Information Age.

Harrington, N. G., Giles, S. M., Hoyle, R. H., Feeney, G. J., & Yungbluth, S. C. (2001). Evaluation of the All Stars character education and problem behavior prevention program: Effects on mediator and outcome variables for middle school students. *Health Education & Behavior, 28*(5), 533–546. https://doi.org/10.1177/109019810102800502

Hershberger, S. L. (2003). The growth of structural equation modeling: 1994–2001. *Structural Equation Modeling, 10*(1), 35–46. https://doi.org/10.1207/S15328007SEM1001_2

Hoyle, R. H. (Ed.). (in press). *Handbook of structural equation modeling* (2nd ed.). Guilford Press.

Hoyle, R. H., & Isherwood, J. C. (2013). Reporting results from structural equation modeling analyses in *Archives of Scientific Psychology. Archives of Scientific Psychology, 1*(1), 14–22. https://doi.org/10.1037/arc0000004

Hoyle, R. H., & Kenny, D. A. (1999). Sample size, reliability, and tests of statistical mediation. In R. H. Hoyle (Ed.), *Statistical strategies for small sample research* (pp. 195–222). SAGE.

Hoyle, R. H., & Robinson, J. I. (2003). Mediated and moderated effects in social psychological research: Measurement, design, and analysis issues. In C. Sansone, C. Morf, & A. T. Panter (Eds.), *Handbook of methods in social psychology* (pp. 213–233). SAGE.

Hu, L.-T., & Bentler, P. M. (1999). Cutoff criteria for fit indexes in covariance structure analysis: Conventional criteria versus new alternatives. *Structural Equation Modeling, 6*(1), 1–5. https://doi.org/10.1080/10705519909540118

Huba, G. J., & Bentler, P. M. (1982). On the usefulness of latent variable causal modeling in testing theories of naturally occurring events (including adolescent drug use): A rejoinder to Martin. *Journal of Personality and Social Psychology, 43*(3), 604–611. https://doi.org/10.1037/0022-3514.43.3.604

Jamshidian, M., & Jennrich, R. I. (1997). Acceleration of the EM algorithm by using quasi-Newton methods. *Journal of the Royal Statistical Society. Series B, Statistical Methodology, 59*(3), 569–587. https://doi.org/10.1111/1467-9868.00083

Jöreskog, K. G. (1973). A general method for estimating a linear structural equation system. In A. S. Goldberger & O. D. Duncan (Eds.), *Structural equation models in the social sciences* (pp. 85–112). Academic Press.

Jöreskog, K. G. (1993). Testing structural equation models. In K. A. Bollen & J. S. Long (Eds.), *Testing structural equation models* (pp. 294–316). SAGE.

Kaplan, D. (2008). An overview of Markov chain methods for the study of stage-sequential developmental processes. *Developmental Psychology, 44*(2), 457–467. https://doi.org/10.1037/0012-1649.44.2.457

Kaplan, D. (2009). *Structural equation modeling: Foundations and extensions* (2nd ed.). SAGE. https://doi.org/10.4135/9781452226576

Keesling, J. W. (1972). *Maximum likelihood approaches to causal analysis* [Unpublished doctoral dissertation]. University of Chicago.

Kenny, D. A., & Judd, C. M. (1984). Estimating the nonlinear and interactive effects of latent variables. *Psychological Bulletin, 96*(1), 201–210. https://doi.org/10.1037/0033-2909.96.1.201

Klein, A., & Moosbrugger, H. (2000). Maximum likelihood estimation of latent interaction effects with the LMS method. *Psychometrika, 65*(4), 457–474. https://doi.org/10.1007/BF02296338

Klein, A., & Muthén, B. O. (2007). Quasi-maximum likelihood estimation of structural equation models with multiple interactions and quadratic effects. *Multivariate Behavioral Research, 42*(4), 647–673. https://doi.org/10.1080/00273170701710205

Kline, R. B. (2016). *Principles and practice of structural equation modeling* (4th ed.). Guilford Press.

Little, T. D. (2013). *Longitudinal structural equation modeling*. Guilford Press.

MacCallum, R. C., Roznowski, M., & Necowitz, L. B. (1992). Model modifications in covariance structure analysis: The problem of capitalization on chance. *Psychological Bulletin, 111*(3), 490–504. https://doi.org/10.1037/0033-2909.111.3.490

MacCallum, R. C., Wegener, D. T., Uchino, B. N., & Fabrigar, L. R. (1993). The problem of equivalent models in applications of covariance structure

analysis. *Psychological Bulletin, 114*(1), 185–199. https://doi.org/10.1037/0033-2909.114.1.185

Mann, H. B., & Wald, E. (1943). On the statistical treatment of linear stochastic difference equations. *Econometrica, 11*(3/4), 173–220. https://doi.org/10.2307/1905674

Marsh, H. W., Lüdtke, O., Trautwein, U., & Morin, A. J. S. (2009). Classical latent profile analysis of academic self-concept dimensions: Synergy of person-and variable-centered approaches to theoretical models of self-concept. *Structural Equation Modeling, 16*(2), 191–225. https://doi.org/10.1080/10705510902751010

Marsh, H. W., Wen, Z., & Hau, K.-T. (2004). Structural equation models of latent interactions: Evaluation of alternative estimation strategies and indicator construction. *Psychological Methods, 9*(3), 275–300. https://doi.org/10.1037/1082-989X.9.3.275

Maruyama, G., & McGarvey, B. (1980). Evaluating causal models: An application of maximum-likelihood analysis of structural equations. *Psychological Bulletin, 87*(3), 502–512. https://doi.org/10.1037/0033-2909.87.3.502

Matsueda, R. L. (in press). Key advances in the history of structural equation modelling. In R. H. Hoyle (Ed.), *Handbook of structural equation modeling* (2nd ed.). Guilford Press.

McArdle, J. J. (2011). Some ethical issues in factor analysis. In A. T. Panter & S. Sterba (Eds.), *Handbook of ethics in quantitative methodology* (pp. 313–339). Taylor & Francis.

McArdle, J. J. (2012). Latent curve modeling of longitudinal growth data. In R. H. Hoyle (Ed.), *Handbook of structural equation modeling* (pp. 547–570). Guilford Press.

McDonald, R. P., & Ho, M.-H. R. (2002). Principles and practice in reporting structural equation analyses. *Psychological Methods, 7*(1), 64–82. https://doi.org/10.1037/1082-989X.7.1.64

Millsap, R. E. (1998). Group differences in regression intercepts: Implications for factorial invariance. *Multivariate Behavioral Research, 33*(3), 403–424. https://doi.org/10.1207/s15327906mbr3303_5

Millsap, R. E., & Tein, J. Y. (2004). Assessing factorial invariance in ordered-categorical measures. *Multivariate Behavioral Research, 39*(3), 479–515. https://doi.org/10.1207/S15327906MBR3903_4

Mulder, J. D., & Hamaker, E. L. (2021). Three extensions of the random intercept cross-lagged panel model. *Structural Equation Modeling, 28*(4), 638–648. https://doi.org/10.1080/10705511.2020.1784738

Muthén, B. O., & Asparouhov, T. (2002). *Latent variable analysis with categorical outcomes: Multi-group and growth modeling in Mplus.* https://www.statmodel.com/download/webnotes/CatMGLong.pdf

Pearl, J. (2000). *Causality: Models, reasoning, and inference.* Cambridge University Press.

Pearl, J. (in press). The causal foundations of structural equation modeling. In R. H. Hoyle (Ed.), *Handbook of structural equation modeling* (2nd ed.). Guilford Press.

Pek, J., & Hoyle, R. H. (2016). On the (in)validity of tests of simple mediation: Threats and solutions. *Social and Personality Psychology Compass, 10*(3), 150–163. https://doi.org/10.1111/spc3.12237

Raykov, T., & Marcoulides, G. A. (2001). Can there be infinitely many models equivalent to a given covariance structure model? *Structural Equation Modeling, 8*(1), 142–149. https://doi.org/10.1207/S15328007SEM0801_8

Rodgers, J. L. (2010). The epistemology of mathematical and statistical modeling: A quiet methodological revolution. *American Psychologist, 65*(1), 1–12. https://doi.org/10.1037/a0018326

Satorra, A., & Bentler, P. M. (2001). A scaled difference chi-square test statistic for moment structure analysis. *Psychometrika, 66*(4), 507–514. https://doi.org/10.1007/BF02296192

Schreiber, J. B., Nora, A., Stage, F. K., Barlow, E. A., & King, J. (2006). Reporting structural equation modeling and confirmatory factor analysis results: A review. *The Journal of Educational Research, 99*(6), 323–338. https://doi.org/10.3200/JOER.99.6.323-338

Schumacker, R. E., & Lomax, R. G. (2016). *A beginner's guide to structural equation modeling* (4th ed.). Erlbaum.

Sörbom, D. (1989). Model modification. *Psychometrika, 54*(3), 371–384. https://doi.org/10.1007/BF02294623

Steiger, J. H. (2002). When constraints interact: A caution about reference variables, identification constraints, and scale dependencies in structural equation modeling. *Psychological Methods, 7*(2), 210–227. https://doi.org/10.1037/1082-989X.7.2.210

Steiger, J. H., & Lind, J. C. (1980, May). *Statistically based tests for the number of common factors* [Paper presentation]. Annual Meeting of the Psychometric Society, Iowa City, IA, United States.

Tarka, P. (2018). An overview of structural equation modeling: Its beginnings, historical development, usefulness and controversies in the social sciences. *Quality & Quantity, 52*(1), 313–354. https://doi.org/10.1007/s11135-017-0469-8

Tomer, A. (2003). A short history of structural equation models. In B. H. Pugesek, A. Tomer, & A. von Eye (Eds.), *Structural equation modeling: Applications in ecological and evolutionary biology* (pp. 85–124). Cambridge University Press. https://doi.org/10.1017/CBO9780511542138.005

Tremblay, P. F., & Gardner, R. C. (1996). On the growth of structural equation modeling in psychological journals. *Structural Equation Modeling, 3*(2), 93–104. https://doi.org/10.1080/10705519609540035

Tucker, L. R., & Lewis, C. (1973). A reliability coefficient for maximum likelihood factor analysis. *Psychometrika, 38*(1), 1–10. https://doi.org/10.1007/BF02291170

Werts, C. E., & Linn, R. L. (1970). Path analysis: Psychological examples. *Psychological Bulletin, 74*(3), 193–212. https://doi.org/10.1037/h0029778

Widaman, K. F., & Olivera-Aguilar, M. (in press). Investigating measurement in variance using confirmatory factor analysis. In R. H. Hoyle (Ed.), *Handbook of structural equation modeling* (2nd ed.). Guilford Press.

Wiley, D. E. (1973). The identification problem for structural equation models with unmeasured variables. In A. S. Goldberger & O. D. Duncan (Eds.), *Structural equation models in the social sciences* (pp. 69–83). Academic Press.

Willett, J. B., & Sayer, A. G. (1994). Using covariance structure analysis to detect correlates and predictors of individual change over time. *Psychological Bulletin, 116*(2), 363–381. https://doi.org/10.1037/0033-2909.116.2.363

Williams, L. J. (2012). Equivalent models: Concepts, problems, alternatives. In R. H. Hoyle (Ed.), *Handbook of structural equation modeling* (pp. 247–260). Guilford Press.

Wright, S. (1920). The relative importance of heredity and environment in determining the piebald pattern of guinea-pigs. *Proceedings of the National Academy of Sciences of the United States of America, 6*(6), 320–332. https://doi.org/10.1073/pnas.6.6.320

Wright, S. (1934). The method of path coefficients. *Annals of Mathematical Statistics, 5*(3), 161–215. https://doi.org/10.1214/aoms/1177732676

CHAPTER 22

MATHEMATICAL PSYCHOLOGY

Parker Smith, Yanjun Liu, James T. Townsend, and Trisha Van Zandt

This chapter defines mathematical psychology and presents a scientific history of its formation as a subdiscipline within psychology. It also provides examples of its contributions to research in cognitive psychology and current issues in the field. Mathematical psychology is not, per se, a distinct branch of psychology. Indeed, mathematical psychologists can be found in any area of psychology. Rather, mathematical psychology characterizes the approach that mathematical psychologists take in their substantive domains. Mathematical psychologists are concerned primarily with developing theories and models of behavior that permit quantitative prediction of behavioral change under varying experimental conditions. There are as many mathematical approaches within psychology as there are substantive psychological domains. As with most theorists of any variety, the mathematical psychologist typically starts by considering the psychological phenomena and underlying structures or processes that they wish to model.

A mathematical model or theory (and we do not distinguish between them here) is a set of mathematical structures including a set of *linkage* statements. These statements relate variables, equations, and so on with components of the psychological process of interest, and possibly also aspects of the stimuli or environment. Regardless of the domain, then, the first step in a mathematical approach is to quantify the variables, both independent and dependent, measured to study a psychological process. Quantification permits variables to be represented as parameters in a mathematical equation or statistical expression, the goal and defining feature of the mathematical psychology enterprise.

Mathematical psychologists, then, construct mathematical and statistical models of the processes they study. Some domains, such as vision, learning, and memory and judgment and decision making, which frequently measure easily quantifiable performance variables like accuracy and response time, exhibit a greater penetration of mathematical reasoning and a higher proportion of mathematical psychologists than other domains. Processes such as the behavior of individual neurons, information flow through visual pathways, evidence accumulation in decision making, and language production or development have all been subjected to a great deal of mathematical modeling. However, even problems like the

This work was supported by the National Science Foundation under grant no. BCS-0738059, the National Institute of Mental Health under grant no. 57717-04A1, and the Air Force Office of Special Research grant no. FA9550-07-1-0078. This material is based upon work while Trisha Van Zandt was serving at the National Science Foundation. Any opinion, findings, and conclusions or recommendations expressed in this material are those of the authors and do not necessarily reflect the views of the National Science Foundation.

https://doi.org/10.1037/0000319-022
APA Handbook of Research Methods in Psychology, Second Edition: Vol. 2. Research Designs: Quantitative, Qualitative, Neuropsychological, and Biological, H. Cooper (Editor-in-Chief)

dynamics of mental illness, problems falling in the domains of social or clinical psychology, have benefitted from a mathematical modeling approach (see, e.g., the special issue on modeling in clinical science in the *Journal of Mathematical Psychology*, Vol. 54).

The power of the mathematical approach arises when unrealized implications of particular model structures become obvious after the mathematical representation of the model has been written down. By contrast, while verbal models might possess logical structure, the inability to interpret concepts in a mathematical fashion means that we cannot derive their logical implications. The ability to make such derivations for mathematical representations leads to better testability of theories, improved experimental designs targeting specific model predictions, and better data analyses—such analyses frequently being rooted in the statistical properties of the model variables.

Mathematical modeling is the foundation of many of the physical sciences. In comparison to these, psychology is often described as a "young" science; as Laming (1973) described several decades ago, psychologists are still often focused on the questions of what is happening rather than why it is happening. Mathematical psychologists, pointing to the role that mathematics has played in the advancement of the physical sciences, have argued that advancement in psychology (and other social sciences) depend on the extent to which mathematical theorizing is applied to psychological issues. A testament to this argument is the fact that while not all "important" psychological models are mathematical a great many of them are.

Psychology, however, differs from a physical science in more than its age, and the use of mathematical models does not, on its own, carry psychology forward. First, the systems studied by psychologists are far more complex than comparable systems in the physical sciences; and second, relationships between psychological variables are obscured by intrinsic variability in these complex systems. Thus, progress in psychology is tied to progress in statistics, as well as technological developments that improve our ability to measure behavior. Even the best mathematical tools may not improve our understanding of some quirk of human behavior if we are unable to measure that behavior or discriminate between changes in that behavior and random fluctuations— fluctuations in either our measurements or the cognitive system we are studying.

The remainder of this chapter consists of three sections. The first outlines the history of mathematical psychology. The second describes its influence in modern experimental psychology (i.e., all those empirically driven and nonapplied fields of psychological study). The third discusses some ongoing issues in the field.

HISTORY

Though a cornerstone of modern psychology, the origins of mathematical psychology came long after the original discipline's conceptual founding. Thus begins our examination of mathematical psychology's origins.

Foundations

Mathematical psychology traces its roots to before the beginning of experimental psychology, the latter usually dated from the 1879 establishment of Wilhelm Wundt's (1832–1920) laboratory in Leipzig, Germany. Eighteenth-century astronomers were well aware of the "personal equation" that characterized variations in observers' times to estimate when celestial objects moved past wires on a grid. These estimates were made with the assistance of a metronome. Thus, the estimates depended on the time the astronomer needed to refocus attention from the visual to the auditory modality. Clearly, the reliability of astronomical measurements were, therefore, heavily dependent on the degree to which observers differed from each other or, indeed, from one observation to the next.

Many astronomers were, thus, naturally concerned about precisely measuring the personal equation so that equipment could be appropriately recalibrated for different observers. Astronomer and mathematician Friedrich Bessel (1784–1846), however, was further interested in why such timing issues arose. He formulated a hypothesis that a second stimulus (whether the auditory click of the metronome or visual movement of the star) produced a disturbance in the perceptual system already processing the first stimulus (Duncombe, 1945). This was perhaps the first formalization of what was later to be known as the *psychological refractory period* (Rabbitt, 1969), or the *doctrine of prior entry* (Shore & Spence, 2005).

Recent historical research, however, suggests that even the embryonic experimental psychology of the 19th century was much more laden with mathematical thinking than was previously appreciated (see Murray & Link, 2021). The earliest modeling applied to actual experimentation lay within the field of psychophysics.

Psychophysics. While the interesting question of the personal equation focused on the speed with which people can perform a task, a different historical branch began with how frequently people make different kinds of responses. Physiologist Ernst Weber (1795–1878) asked people to make yes/no judgments about whether the perceived weights of two objects were different. Holding the mass of the first object constant, he gradually increased the mass of the second object until people said "yes" ("different"). He was then able to define the *just noticeable difference*, the smallest increase in weight, ΔI, that a person could detect, and found that it was not a constant but instead a function of the weight I of the first object, or

$$\Delta I = kI.$$

Weber found that the value of k that determined the just noticeable difference was a constant for most values of I, establishing what we now refer to as *Weber's law*. This law holds for a wide range of intensities, I, and across different stimulus modalities.

Gustav Theodor Fechner (1801–1887), founder of the field of psychophysics and the first true mathematical psychologist, was inspired by Weber's work (Fechner, 1860/1889). Although trained as a physicist, Fechner yearned to solve one of philosophy's central and long-standing puzzles, namely, the relationship of the mind to

the outside world and the physiological body itself. This giant of philosophical enigmas is known as the *mind–body problem*, which continues even now to attract attention from philosophers and cognitive scientists. Fechner tried to solve the mind–body problem by establishing a connection, via an equation, between events in the physical world and the psychological experience they evoked. In modern mathematical psychology, this problem is one of foundational measurement (see the upcoming paragraphs): How can psychological experience be quantified and related to physical intensity? While Weber's work proposed a relationship between changes in a physical dimension and a person's ability to detect that change, of their experience, Fechner sought a lawful and mathematical relationship between physical intensity and the experience itself.

Fechner had the clever idea of employing Weber's law by making the assumption that the psychological experience of a just noticeable difference is the same for all values of I. That is, if the change in the psychological effect $\Delta S = c$ is equal to the same constant c for all just noticeable differences ΔI, then

$$\frac{\Delta S}{\Delta I} = \frac{c}{kI}, \text{ or, in the limit,}$$

$$dS = \frac{c}{kI} dI.$$

Applying the rules of calculus to solve this differential equation leads to the expression we now call *Fechner's Law*: Psychological effects, S, are a logarithmic function of physical intensity, I, or

$$S = K \log\left(I/I_0\right),$$

where I_0 is the absolute threshold (the stimulus value such that the person detects it 50% of the time) and K is some positive constant. Perhaps because of the slowing decaying links with philosophy, no one thought at the time of experimentally testing the logarithm function prediction of Fechner's law. It was not until much later that Stevens (1957) tried and tested other formulas for the relation of sensation to stimulation. In fact, Stevens proposed a power law of the form $S = KI^a$ where K is again a positive constant and "a" is also a positive number characterizing the physical dimension and, possibly, the individual perceiver. We meet up with Stevens again under the topic Foundvational Measurement.

Mental chronometry.   While Weber and Fechner were laying the foundations of psychological measurement and psychophysics, the great 19th-century scientist Hermann von Helmholtz (1821–1894) was busy measuring the speed of nerve conduction in a frog's leg (Helmholtz, 1850). In addition to his massive achievements in physics, such as conservation of energy, he contributed to many fields of science, including sensory physiology and psychology (see Helmholtz, 1877/1912).

The realization that neural events take measureable time spurred F. C. Donders (1818–1889) to develop a system for mental chronometry, the measurement of the time required to perform cognitive tasks (Donders, 1868/1969). Donders asked people to perform three tasks involving two lights. Each task required three different cognitive components. We now refer to these tasks as *simple reactions* (respond when any light is perceived), *go–no-go reactions* (respond when one specific light is perceived), and *choice reactions* (respond one way when one light is perceived and a different way when the other light is perceived). The cognitive components involved are perception, stimulus discrimination, and response selection. For simple reactions, only perception is required; for go–no-go reactions, perception and stimulus discrimination are required; for choice reactions, perception, stimulus discrimination, and response selection are required.

Donders measured the response times for each task and then estimated the duration of the stimulus discrimination and response selection components by subtraction. The difference between simple reaction and go–no-go reaction times gave an estimate of stimulus discrimination time. The difference between go–no-go reaction and choice reaction times gave an estimate of response selection time. Donders's *method of subtraction*

was the foundation of the idea, now fundamental in cognitive psychology, that differences in response time provide information about cognitive architecture—how the brain structures tasks to achieve different levels of performance. It has been used in a variety of experimental paradigms over the past 150 years and set the stage for such techniques of analysis as Sternberg's (1969) *additive factors method.*

Sternberg's approach proposed to determine whether two subprocesses involved in a psychological task were arranged in a strict series with one starting and finishing before the other (a serial process). Subsequent mathematical work extended the additive factors method in such a way that a very large class of potential mental architectures (including parallel processing, where task subprocesses are executed simultaneously) could also be directly tested (Schweickert, 1978; Schweickert & Townsend, 1989; Townsend, 1984).

Psychometrics.   Experimental psychology took a sharp turn in 1914 with the publication of a landmark book by John B. Watson (1878–1958). This book (Watson, 1914) heralded the dominance of the psychological school of behaviorism, which holds that behavior can be explained without reference to mental events. The *school of behaviorism* was beneficial to psychology by helping the nascent field break away from its sometimes-murky philosophical roots. However, it relegated Fechner's psychological measurement and Donders's mental chronometry to the realm of pseudoscience and inhibited developments in the study of cognition for several decades. This did not entirely stop the growth of mathematical psychology as it was applied to behavior, however. In fact, one of the later so-called neo-behaviorists, Clark Leonard Hull (1884–1952), used mathematics in his mission to form a general theory of learning and motivation (see, e.g., Hull, 1952).

Applied concerns also required the development of psychologically motivated quantitative methods to solve problems in human engineering and measurement. Much of psychology strives to unearth laws of thinking and behavior that apply to almost everyone; however, the domain of psychometrics concentrated from its beginnings to study individual differences. This strain of psychological research was powerfully motivated by Darwin's seminal results, especially influencing Francis Galton, who attempted to explain these differences via evolutionary theory. While ultimately arguably leading to considerable interest to society, it also unfortunately helped succor the dangerous excesses of eugenics (see Gould, 1981).

Yet, the desire of colleges and the military and ultimately almost all sectors of society, to measure human intelligence and aptitude and even psychological pathologies, led to the rise of standardized testing and psychometrics just as the behaviorism movement was getting off the ground. Even before Darwin and Galton, using tests to assess knowledge and aptitude had a history that extends back to ancient China (Elman, 2002). At the turn of the 20th century, the first intelligence tests were published (e.g., Binet, 1905/1916), and the College Entrance Examination Board (now the College Board) was founded, providing colleges and universities a way to test fitness of applicants to complete their curriculum. Similarly, the military has always been concerned about fitting soldiers to jobs for which they are well-suited, and the demand for large-scale answers to problems of psychological measurement began at the beginning of the First World War.

L. L. Thurstone (1887–1955), founder and first president of the Psychometric Society, made significant contributions to the theory of measurement and psychophysics.

His work was concentrated on the problem of quantifying human ability—intelligence, primarily, and he worked closely with the Army and the Institute for Government Research writing civil service exams (Thurstone, 1952). His *law of comparative judgment* (Thurstone, 1927) was the first to establish the concept of a psychological continuum, a range of quantifiable psychological experience that could be used as the basis for psychophysical judgments. He later expanded this continuum to attitudes and ability, and it became the forerunner to the Bradley–Terry–Luce and Rasch models of psychometrics, as well as signal detection theory (see the next section).

The Rise of Modern Mathematical Psychology

Modern mathematical psychology stems from three innovations in psychology and engineering: (a) the first application of signal detection theory to human performance (Swets et al., 1961), (b) the application of information theory to encoding and decoding messages in the human cognitive system (Attneave, 1954), and (c) two milestone publications in mathematical learning theory (Bush & Mosteller, 1955; Estes, 1950). Together these three areas of research laid the groundwork for the idea that remains central in cognitive psychology today: the human being, as they make their way through the world, operates like an information processing device. Information from the external world is encoded by sensory transducers; this information is operated upon by various brain mechanisms to produce their perception of the world and to allow them to select appropriate responses to the world; finally, if necessary, they can activate their response effectors to manipulate the state of their external world.

Signal detection theory, born from the problems of communications engineers during World War II, borrows its fundamentals from a nice, and rather elegant confluence of statistical decision theory with applied physics. An observer is presented with a low-amplitude signal tone in a burst of white noise and must determine if the signal is present. This stimulus gives rise to some sensory effect (perceived intensity) that varies randomly each time it is presented. This randomness is attributed to the inherent variability of sensory transduction or noise in the cognitive channel. Randomness means that signals (in which a tone is present) may sometimes have the same sensory effect as noise alone. Signal or noise decisions are made by evaluating either the likelihood that a particular sensory experience resulted from a signal or noise stimulus or by evaluating the magnitude of the sensory effect relative to some minimum criterion required to call a stimulus a signal. The applied physics part of the approach told the researchers how the mathematical operations that describe a detection filter can, with the aid of the complementary statistical theory, prescribe an optimal decision criterion.

The important contribution of signal detection theory to psychology, which now forms the heart of many modern models of perception, cognition, and action, is that it provides a method for separating effects of response bias (how the likelihood or magnitude of experience is evaluated) from the discriminability of the stimulus.

Information theory also derived from work in statistics and communications engineering (see, e.g., Shannon & Weaver, 1949). It is a way of quantifying the information or uncertainty of a signal from the probabilities associated with each possible stimulus for that signal. Communications engineers were concerned with how signals could be compressed and how much information could be transmitted over a noisy communications channel. The analogy to the human decision maker was immediately obvious to psychologists (see, e.g., Attneave, 1954; Garner, 1974). Not only could information theory be used to quantify sets of stimuli and collections of responses, but it could be used to measure how much information the cognitive system could transmit.

Information theory contributed to the "intelligent machine revolution," represented best perhaps by Wiener's influential book *Cybernetics; or, Control and Communication in the Animal and the Machine* (1948). Cybernetics, the science of feedback control systems applied to biological systems, influenced our treatment of the human as an information processor but had its greatest impact on research in artificial intelligence. It also encouraged the application of general systems theory (and nonlinear dynamics) in cognitive modeling (see the upcoming section Neural Modeling).

From information theory came a tremendous amount of research exploring the processing limitations of humans, and led to one of the first links between the dependent variables of response frequency and response time. The *Hick-Hyman law* of response time states that response time, *RT*, is a linear function of the amount of information *H* (measured in *bits*) transmitted through the system, or

$$RT = a + bH,$$

where *b* is the channel capacity of the human (Hick, 1952; Hyman, 1953). Later, Miller (1956) reviewed the channel capacity literature that encompassed a number of different tasks. In his classic paper, "The Magical Number Seven Plus or Minus Two: Some Limits on Our Capacity for Processing Information," he argued that people were limited in their ability to process and transmit information to approximately 2.5 bits.

An outcome of Miller's work was the realization that information contained in a set of items might be less important than the size of the set itself. This, together with other work demonstrating that information theory did not provide a useful explanation for how information was processed (e.g., Leonard, 1959), arguably led to a decline in the use of information theory in cognitive modeling (see also Luce, 2003). However, it still remains a useful way to quantify psychological and behavioral concepts (e.g., Strange et al., 2005). In addition, the general concept that humans can be studied as perceptual, cognitive, and action systems through which information flows led to the rise of the *information processing approach*, which continues to dominate much of experimental psychology today.

Signal detection and information theory both suggested ways that stimuli could be quantified. Furthermore, signal detection theory suggested what a perceptual representation of stimuli might look like, pointing the way to a cognitive theory of stimulus discrimination. At this time, new theories of learning were presented (Bush & Mosteller, 1955; Estes, 1950, 1957). Bush and Mosteller's (1955) work derived from the prevailing behavioristic view of animal learning. Their theories focused solely on changes in the observer's response probability over time. For example, Bush and Mosteller's approach employed a simple difference equation for learning. Consider a task in which an animal must learn to make one particular response. Letting $q(n)$ be the probability of an error on trial n, the simplest Bush and Mosteller model specified that $q(n) = aq(n-1)$, where *a* is greater than 0 and less than 1. The straightforward solution of this elementary difference equation is simply $q(n) = a^{(n-1)}q(1)$ where $q(1)$ is the probability of an error on trial 1. This means that the likelihood of an error decreases over trials, that is, the animal learns.

Consistent with behavioristic dogma, Bush and Mosteller's learning models did not speculate about the internal mental states of the observer. However, Estes's (1950, 1957) stimulus sampling theory, like signal detection theory, diverged from this philosophy by representing stimuli as being composed of smaller "elements" that could be sampled and possibly conditioned (i.e., learned) by the observer (e.g., Atkinson & Estes, 1963). In contrast to Bush and Mosteller's approach, Estes' models made a large impact not only on research in learning but also on research in memory. Many modern memory models have taken advantage of his conception of stimulus elements and the idea that stimulus elements become associated to various components of a task structure (e.g., Shiffrin & Steyvers, 1997).

The following decades saw the publication of several books that established mathematical psychology as a formal discipline. The first were the three volumes of the *Handbook of Mathematical Psychology* (Luce et al., 1963–1965a), followed by two volumes of *Readings in Mathematical Psychology* (Luce et al., 1963–1965b). These volumes were targeted primarily toward researchers active in the field.

Atkinson et al. published the more elementary *An Introduction to Mathematical Learning Theory* in 1966, but it wasn't until the publication of Coombs et al.'s (1970) *Mathematical Psychology* that there existed an introductory textbook suitable for undergraduates in psychology This text covered a broad set of topics, including signal detection, information and learning theory, as well as judgment and decisions, psychological measurement and game theory. The year 1970 saw yet another introductory book, this one by Restle and Greeno (1970). In addition to some topics overlapping with other texts, this one was somewhat prescient in beginning to consider critical problems in model testing including notions of parameter identifiability.

In 1973, Laming published a more advanced *Mathematical Psychology* text, one that focused on models that could predict response times, a neglected domain in texts up until that time. His models tended to be tightly linked with generalizations of signal detection theory to across-time signal-sampling procedures.

Professional Societies and Journals Devoted to Mathematical Psychology

The branch of quantitative psychology oriented toward the measurement of individual differences, psychometrics, had already, by 1935, established its own society (Psychometric Society) and begun publishing its journal, *Psychometrika*. As noted earlier, mathematical psychology per se got its formal start several decades later.

Nonetheless, by 1960, there were at least a large handful of truly mathematical psychologists. As Estes (2002) described, some of these psychologists regularly participated in what are now called the Social Science Research Council's Knowledge Institutions. These particular Institutions were held at Stanford University for the purposes of training social scientists in mathematical and statistical techniques. Stanford meetings alternated with similar summer conclaves at the University of Pennsylvania. The main nuclei in mathematical psychology during the 1960s were Stanford, University of Pennsylvania, University of Michigan, and Indiana University.

In 1963, the idea was proposed to begin a new journal devoted to the publication of theoretical, mathematical articles in psychology; in 1964, the first issue of the *Journal of Mathematical Psychology* was published. Richard C. Atkinson, Robert R. Bush, Clyde H. Coombs, William K. Estes, R. Duncan Luce, William J. McGill and George A. Miller served on the first Editorial Board of the *Journal*.

Several years later, mathematical psychologists began meeting informally in the summer to give papers and symposia. The first such meeting was held at Stanford in 1968. After a number of years, in 1976, the Editorial Board of the *Journal* decided to organize the Society for Mathematical Psychology. Bylaws were drafted by Estes and

Luce, together with William H. Batchelder and Bert F. Green; in 1977 the Society was formally incorporated. The Society has now, for over 40 years, hosted an annual meeting each summer at which students and researchers from a wide range of disciplines have presented papers, posters, and symposia highlighting the application of mathematical and statistical models to problems in psychology, cognitive science, neuroscience, and cognitive engineering.

By the time the Society was getting underway in the United States, a similar organization had already been formed in Europe, the European Mathematical Psychology Group. The Group, although never formally incorporated, has met every year since it was founded by Jean-Claude Falmagne in 1971. The British Psychological Association began publishing the *British Journal of Mathematical and Statistical Psychology* in 1965, which was an offshoot of the *British Journal of Psychology: Statistical Section* (1947–1952) and later the *British Journal of Statistical Psychology* (1953–1964). The papers appearing in the *British Journal* are from researchers in both psychometrics and mathematical psychology, and so it is in these pages that we can see most strongly the links between these two branches of quantitative psychology.

In 2018, the Society launched a new journal, *Computational Brain and Behavior.* This journal serves as an outlet for work that is less mathematical and more computational. Many important approaches to studying the mind and brain use statistical models and computer simulation, approaches that do not have a natural home in the *Journal of Mathematical Psychology* but that form a critical part of the research conducted by members of the Society. *Computational Brain and Behavior* publishes work in psychology and neuroscience, as well as related disciplines such as computer science, mathematics, and linguistics.

In the southern hemisphere, another meeting, the Australasian Mathematical Psychology Conference, has taken place annually in Australia for several decades. In 2021, the conference organizers and attendees, including Scott Brown, Erin Walsh, John Dunn, Paul Garrett and Rachel Stephens, formed the Australian Society for Mathematical Psychology. This organization includes members from Australia and countries in Asia, as well as other countries around the world.

MODERN MATHEMATICAL PSYCHOLOGY

If one sampled a mathematical psychologist at random, one would find that they could be roughly categorized along four (nonorthogonal) dimensions. First of all, we might determine whether their modeling is strictly axiomatic or more loosely formulated. Next, we could determine whether they takes primarily a deterministic or a stochastic modeling approach. Then, we could ask whether their approach is primarily analytic or computational. Finally, their work may be primarily empirical or theoretical.

At the risk of oversimplification, an axiomatic approach is one where the modeler writes down some primary definitions and then statements (axioms) about what should be true. For example, the modeler may specify mathematical definitions based on the desire to represent situations in which people are presented with stimulus pairs, and that their task is to choose the stimulus in the pair with the greatest perceived magnitude. An axiom might then be that, when presented with two tones (the stimulus pair), people should be able to identify correctly the one that is louder with probability greater than or equal to 0.5. These axioms, then, permit the association of mathematical variables and formulas to psychological concepts. Given a set of axioms, the modeler can go on to make logical inferences about what people should do under different conditions.

Axiomatic theorems can be either *deterministic* or *stochastic*. Deterministic models (whether posited in an axiomatic systems or not) must perforce produce the same result time after time (a good example from physics is Newton's theory of mechanics). A stochastic model, by contrast, can produce very different results even when the parameters and the stimulus are fixed (think of quantum mechanics as an example from physics). Models of cognitive processing are frequently stochastic. Sequential sampling models, such as those reviewed by Ratcliff and Smith (2004), are perfect examples of the stochastic approach. Predictions about behavior are often focused on how dependent variables are distributed, and how the parameters of those distributions change with changes in experimental procedures.

We have to be a bit careful with defining *analytic*. One major use in mathematics comes from *analysis*, which in the math domain implies the huge set of tools and content related to calculus and the continuum. A slightly more general interpretation adds the employment of algebra to the topics. We do *not* intend either of these meanings here.

A rather distinct definition, if sometimes a bit fuzzy, is intended to distinguish explicit formulas, theorems, and proofs and so on as opposed to numerical procedures, approximations, computational methods like simulation, and so forth. Of course, these may overlap. For example, one can often prove theorems about numerical procedures. Another example is the branch of mathematics that deals with chaos. Beautiful proofs of phenomena involving matters like how fast a deterministic system evolves to appear completely at random can be forged (for a rigorous, but elementary introduction to chaos, see Townsend, 1992).

An example of an analytical approach is one where a dependent variable Y can be written as an analytical expression involving a independent variable X, or $Y = g(X)$ for a function g that does not require any messy numerical calculations (like taking a limit or integrating). The general linear model employed in regression is one example of an analytic expression. The expressions providing finishing time distributions for serial (one-at-a-time processing of items) and parallel (items processed simultaneous) processing systems (e.g., Townsend, 1972, 1976; also see upcoming paragraphs) are other examples.

In contrast, a nonanalytic expression does not allow one to write $Y = g(X)$ and generate predictions for Y algebraically; instead, a computer must be used to simulate the model or solve for Y. Thus, an alternative in studying parallel versus serial processes would be to write a computer program that simulated a serial or parallel system (each trial a new datum is created concerning the output of such systems).

Often, the more complex the issue being addressed, the more likely it is that a computational approach is necessary. Techniques for model comparison (Pitt et al., 2002), Bayesian model fitting (Lee, 2008), and models devoted to particularly intractible problems like text comprehension or language processing (e.g., Dennis & Kintsch, 2007) often require a computational approach.

Finally, many mathematical psychologists are also empiricists: They collect data to test their models. However, there is a subset of mathematical psychologists who rarely or never collect data; their work is primarily theoretical. When theoretical work suggests a certain empirical approach, they either collaborate with empiricists or, if it is available, they reanalyze already-published data. These mathematical psychologists make theoretical contributions that suggest new mathematical representations of different psychological problems, or methodological contributions that provide new techniques of analysis. They are rather akin to theoretical physicists, some of whom had remarkable insights about the nature of things but were notoriously inept in the laboratory.

Foundational Measurement

Foundational measurement is axiomatic, analytic, mostly deterministic, and has been for the most part theoretical. Its goal is to find measurement systems capable of quantifying psychological experience—to measure such experience. In the physical world, we measure objects frequently. We weigh ourselves, we compute distance, we mark time. Such physical quantities are based in extensive measurement, which requires the existence of a ratio scale (one with a true zero). We are so accustomed to making measurements of this sort that it seems natural to extend this kind of logic to psychological problems. However, the axioms of extensive measurement may not be justified for the measurement of psychological experience (cf. Narens, 1996).

In a sense, measurement represents the first and oldest approach to applying mathematical reasoning to psychological problems. Measuring individual differences, as discussed earlier, and underpinning the field of psychometrics, precedes in history even most of the 19th-century advances in psychophysics.

Foundational measurement was birthed somewhat informally in a number of suppositions by the earlier-mentioned 20th-century psychophysicist S. S. Stevens. Assume that the term *scale* refers to the set of numbers associated with the sensation accorded to a set of, usually one-dimensional, stimuli. Now, Stevens posited that there existed primarily four echelons of scale from the strongest *absolute* to *ratio*, to *interval*, and finally, the weakest, *ordinal*. He noted that as the scales become weaker, one may change the numbers on the scale in a less and less constricted way. Thus, an absolute scale is very strong but brooks no alterations at all. An example is measuring by counting. Virtually any arithmetic comparison is allowed. The second strongest, ratio, permits meaningful ratios, differences, and so on and allows only changes via multiplication by a positive number (therein changing the scale unit). The primary dimensions in classical physics—length, mass, time—lie on a ratio scale. The third, interval, introduces so called *affine transformations* (change of scale unit plus addition of a real number [changing the origin]) and prohibits comparison of ratios but does feature ratios of differences. Celsius and Fahrenheit temperatures are interval variables. The next strongest, *ordinal* scales, only afford comparison of magnitude (greater than or less than), but their values can be subjected to any monotonic transformation with harm to such comparisons. The final one put forth by Stevens hardly deserves being designated as a scale since *nominal numbers* have no quantitative meaning outside of being distinct from one another and, therefore, only useful for identification.

Stevens thought this was all rather obvious, and he believed his invented psychophysical methods, such as magnitude estimation (tell the person to assign a number to each stimulus level) automatically yielded a true ratio scale.

That this was incorrect became one of the main goals of the early work in foundational measurement and involved a great deal of axiomatic treatment. These approaches recede in history at least to the famous tome by von Neuman and Morgenstern that created modern utility theory. However, the first rigorous efforts that began to axiomatize the Stevens-like approach introduced earlier, was undoubtedly a paper by the Stanford philosophers Suppes and Scott in 1958. Suppes, alluded to earlier, was one of the true pioneers in mathematical psychology and led a team of fellow mathematical psychologists in establishing foundational measurement as an important subfield of the terrain (Suppes et al., 1989). One of the first tutorials was a chapter in Volume 1 of the *Handbook of Mathematical Psychology* (Suppes & Zinnes, 1963). A book by the mathematician Fred Roberts (1979) is still a worthy textbook that is mathematically meticulous but eminently readable by folks with at least some calculus, algebra, and set theory or logic in their quantitative quiver. Likewise, Townsend and Ashby (1984) offered the typical psychologist a set of reasons why we all should be observant as to the main tenets and strictures imposed by the lessons provided by foundational measurement.

In many ways, foundational measurement set the tone for the utmost rigor possible in mathematical work in psychology and especially in psychophysics and decision making. R. Duncan Luce brought the mathematics developed for foundational measurement to bear on problems both in psychophysics and decision making, leading to some of the field's most impressive contributions extending from the 1950s until the present day (Luce, 1959, 2004; Narens & Luce, 1986; Steingrimsson & Luce, 2005a, 2005b, 2006, 2007).

Psychophysics is amenable to a measurement approach because the physical quantity of interest is usually very easy to measure (e.g., frequency of a tone) and there is a corresponding continuum of psychological experience (e.g., pitch). A fairly large body of beautiful mathematics has been developed to represent the psychological experience of magnitude in detection and discrimination tasks (e.g., Colonius & Dzhafarov, 2006; Falmagne, 1985; Krantz et al., 1971; Luce et al., 1990; Suppes et al., 1989).

For decision making, the goal of foundational measurement has been to derive scales of preference for objects based on the frequency with which people choose one object over another. An axiomatic approach provides a basis for predicting what people should prefer in various circumstances. Violations of these predicted preferences point to incorrect axioms, which in turn leads to a greater understanding of how people make decisions. Tversky and Kahneman's work (e.g., Tversky & Kahneman, 1974, 1981) demonstrated above all that perfectly sensible axioms such as those underlying expected utility theory do not apply in many decision-making environments. Their work led to Kahneman's Nobel Prize in Economics in 2002. One of the emerging useful tools in these arenas, particularly in psychophysics and decision making, has been the *theory of functional equations* (not to be confused with *functional analysis*). J. C. Falmagne one of the second-generation pioneers in mathematical psychology (and the founder of the European Mathematical Psychology Group) has continued to make progress, especially in employment of functional equations, up to the present day (e.g., Falmagne, 1986).

Work in foundational measurement is generally deterministic, meaning that it deals primarily with the algebraic and nonprobabilistic properties of different measurement systems (though random utility theory does contain probabilistic elements). This fact means that, although mathematically quite elegant, measurement theories can be quite removed from empirical treatments and, indeed, may be difficult or impossible to empirically evaluate because the variability of real data obscure and distort the relationships predicted by the theories (Luce, 2005; Narens & Luce, 1993). While there have been several promising inroads to formulating stochastic approaches to foundational measurement over the past decade or so (Falmagne et al., 1997; Heyer & Niederée, 1989;

Myung et al., 2005), as yet there is no completely satisfactory solution.

Cognitive Modeling

Mathematical approaches to modeling cognitive processes are now fairly well ingrained in mainstream cognitive psychology. These approaches are equally balanced between analytic and computational models but are primarily stochastic and almost always empirical. It will not be possible for us to give a comprehensive treatment of every area in cognitive psychology where mathematical modeling is important, for this task would require many books. We focus on memory, categorization, choice response time, and neural modeling.

Memory.   Nowhere else in experimental psychology has mathematical work had a greater impact than in the development of models for memory. Mathematical models of recognition and recall now set the standard for theoretical developments in this area and have driven empirical research before them. Memory models no longer follow the early examples set by statistical learning theory and models of information processing. It became obvious in the late 60s and early 70s that the complexity of the process to be modeled was not adequately captured by linearly decomposing it into a sequence of subtasks (e.g., Sternberg, 1966). This led to the development of connectionist models (see the upcoming section, Neural Modeling) and machine-learning-inspired models that incorporate learning, problem solving, and language comprehension (e.g., Dennis, 2005; Jilk et al., 2008; Kintsch et al., 2007). Signal detection theory still plays a very important role in most memory models.

Older strength theories (Atkinson & Juola, 1973; Murdock, 1965; Parks, 1966) relied on the signal detection framework as the basis for the "old"/"new" judgment. Newer global memory models such as those proposed by Murdock (1982), Hintzman (1988), and Gillund and Shiffrin (1984), and even more recent models such as REM (Shiffrin & Steyvers, 1997), developed encoding, storage, and retrieval architectures explaining how memory traces are established, maintained, and decay over time, and how different memory traces become associated with each other and to the context in which they were experienced. Each of these models requires, however, an evaluation of memory strength for a recognition decision, and this evaluation is assumed to be performed within a signal-detection framework.

While global memory models go some way toward explaining how memory strength contributes to recognition performance, many researchers have explored the contributions of other memory processes, often lumped together under the term *recall*. In this sense, recall is the ability to remember specific details of the remembered item, and this ability requires conscious effort. In contrast, recognition is based only on perceived strength, which happens effortlessly. Some memory work is focused on separating these different cognitive contributions to recognition decisions (e.g., Wixted, 2007). The receiver operating characteristic curve from signal detection is used to try to separate the signal detection recognition component from the recall component. Dual-process memory theories, thus, combine the signal detection approach with a less-quantitatively specified recall component.

Another theoretical avenue to multiprocess memory models are the multinomial processing-tree models explored by Batchelder and Riefer (1999). This general approach provides a way to explore many different structures producing categorical measurements of behavior. The multinomial processing tree model considers how different components of a task depend on each other (e.g., if recall fails, evaluate familiarity) but does not explain the mechanisms by which each component operates. So while signal detection theory might explain the probability that a subject calls an item "old," the multinomial approach only assumes that such a probability exists. The approach allows for a consideration of different latent structures and comparisons between different model architectures. It has been applied to a wide range of problems, most recently in the evaluation of cognitive deficits (e.g., Batchelder & Riefer, 2007). It lends itself well to Bayesian analysis and is closely linked

to measurement problems in psychometrics (Batchelder, 2010).

Categorization. Categorization tasks ask observers to classify stimuli according to their types. These types may be quite concrete (e.g., chairs, dogs, diseases) or very abstract. As in memory research, several very influential mathematical models of categorization have set a standard for explanations of categorization behavior, and much of the empirical work in categorization over the last few decades has been driven by these models.

The first class of these models assumes that subjects construct a mental representation of different categories and that categorization decisions are made based on the psychological distances (often referred to as similarities) between a stimulus and other objects (exemplars) in the mental space (Nosofsky, 1988; Nosofsky & Palmeri, 1997). These models take much inspiration from early work in multidimensional scaling (Torgerson, 1958), which was used to derive scales that could measure multidimensional stimuli and place them in relation to each other.

The second class of these models assumes that categories of stimuli can be represented as probability distributions in multidimensional space (Ashby, 1992; Ashby & Gott, 1988). Categorization judgments are made based on a stimulus's location in that space relative to multidimensional discriminant functions (lines, planes, hyperplanes) that divide the space into categories. These models are called *decision bound models*, and they are very closely related to signal detection models. They preserve the ideas of discriminability, bias, optimality, and so forth from signal detection, but the interest is more on how different stimulus dimensions are perceived and how those perceptions influence the placement of decision bounds.

Choice response time. Signal detection theory also motivated most of the current, most successful mathematical models of simple choice, including Ratcliff's diffusion model (e.g., Ratcliff & Smith, 2004), Usher and McClelland's (2001) leaky competing accumulator model, the Poisson race model (Pike, 1973; Van Zandt et al., 2000),

Vickers's accumulator model (Smith & Vickers, 1988; Vickers, 1979), and the linear ballistic accumulator (Brown & Heathcote, 2008). These models address how simple choices are made in most cognitive experiments. The theory from which all these *sequential sampling* models derive is quite simple: To make a decision, an observer engages a process of information gathering. Information is obtained by repeated sampling from the stimulus (if it is present) or from its mental representation (if it is not). Information is modeled as a continuum of sensory effect, and the stimulus representation from which information is sampled is provided by the signal detection framework.

Each sample of information supports one of the two possible responses and is stored appropriately. The characteristics of this information (discrete or continuous), the time course of the sampling process (discrete or continuous) and the nature of the storage mechanisms (separate as in a race model or combined as in a random walk or diffusion), define the differences between the sequential sampling models. The important contribution of these models is their explanation of the speed-accuracy tradeoff, an explanation that pulls the dependent variables of response time and frequency together within the same mechanism. To make a decision requires "enough" information—a threshold. If a decision must be made quickly, it must be made on the basis of less information, which will lead to less accurate decisions.

Not only do these models explain changes in both response time and response frequency, but the stochastic processes upon which they are based are (usually) simple enough that we can write down analytic expressions for the response time distributions and the response probabilities as functions of the parameters of the process. These models presently stand as the most successful explanations of response selection in simple tasks. We have some neurophysiological evidence that the brain uses neural modules as information collectors (Schall, 2003), which has encouraged continued application of these models across cognitive, clinical, and developmental psychology (Ratcliff, 2008; White et al., 2009).

In addition, these models are being brought to bear on classic problems in judgment and decision making (e.g., Busemeyer & Diederich, 2002; Busemeyer & Townsend, 1993; Merkle & Van Zandt, 2006; Pleskac & Busemeyer, 2010; Ratcliff & Starns, 2009; Trueblood et al., 2014; Van Zandt, 2000). In particular, the sequential sampling framework is being extended to judgments of confidence, leading to the simultaneous prediction of three dependent measures. This body of research, together with other models for judgment and decision making, has been named *cognitive decision theory*.

Neural modeling. Efforts to construct models of brain activity really got underway with "Dynamic Models in Biology and Psychology" (Rashevsky, 1936). Subsequent years saw more innovations including results more in line with new theories of automata, such as the *perceptron* by McCulloch and Pitts (1943), popularized by Rosenblatt (1957) and others. Neural theorizing arguably suffered a rather serious setback for some years when Minsky and Papert (1969) showed that linear perceptrons, serving as pattern recognizers, could not even solve certain elementary topological problems (e.g., divining topological closure). One of the few stalwarts of neural theorizing who continued his output during these lean years has been Stephen Grossberg (see Grossberg, 1980, 2021).

A prominent development of the 1980s was a resurrection of neural modeling by way of the advent of computational models inspired by neural processing mechanism. These quantitative constructions were dubbed *parallel-distributed processing* or *connectionist models* (McClelland & Rumelhart, 1986; Rumelhart & McClelland, 1986). The computational tools provided by connectionism have been widely applied to complex cognitive problems such as speech and pattern recognition (e.g., Norris & McQueen, 2008) and even decision making (e.g., Roe et al., 2001). They have been used in engineering applications including computer vision, handwriting recognition, textual analysis, and quality control. Indeed, they still form a major segment of so-called *neural net approaches* in the venues of machine learning called *deep learning.*

Yet again came a backlash in the late 1980s against the use of connectionist models for cognition, a backlash rooted in the argument that connectionist models were simply associationism (à la behaviorism) in disguise (Pinker & Mehler, 1988). Also, many cognitive psychologists argued that connectionist models, while they may provide reasonable explanations of how the brain performs computations, they do not necessarily make predictions about overt behavior (Fodor & Pylyshyn, 1988). Consequently, although neural modeling is an important and rapidly advancing enterprise, it does not look much like the cognitive connectionism of the early 1980s.

To model the brain well requires a deeper understanding of neuroanatomy than most cognitive psychologists possess, a set of skills that might include animal laboratory work that cognitive psychologists do not usually possess, and measuring devices (e.g., multiprobe electrode arrays and *functional magnetic resonance imaging*) that were not available at the advent of connectionism. These deficiencies inspired new training programs designed to provide future researchers with these skills and to encourage collaboration between neuroscientists and behavioral scientists. There is now a huge body of research exploring neural models of cognition and brain function, models that are fundamentally quantitative in nature (e.g., Hasselmo, 2009; Howard & Kahana, 2002; O'Reilly & Frank, 2006), published in journals such as the *Journal of Computational Neuroscience* and *Neural Computation.*

At the time connectionist models became popular, there was a wave of enthusiasm for nonlinear dynamics as applied to problems in many of the domains in psychology and cognition (e.g., Port & van Gelder, 1998). This enthusiasm was driven not only by the obvious nonlinear dynamics of connectionist models (at least outside the traditional linear perceptrons) but also by *ecological psychology*, which is motivated by the idea that the human brain operates not only within the head but also within the environment (Gibson,

1950). The complex interactions between neural modules and the ever-changing external world can be modeled with general systems theory (Klir, 1969).

General systems theory encompasses the mathematics of catastrophe and chaos theory, which were the focus of much excitement and many symposia in the 1980s, but catastrophe and chaos theory never led to a revolution in mathematical cognitive modeling. The nonlinear dynamics approach, however, has led to an important bridge between mathematical biology and cognitive science and to the focus on complex systems in psychology represented by the important work of Turvey (1990, 2009), Kelso (1995), and others (e.g., Large & Jones, 1999; Schmidt et al., 1990).

CURRENT ISSUES IN MATHEMATICAL MODELING

As mathematical psychology continues to mature, with the inevitable growing pains that process engenders, there has been some navel-gazing about where the discipline is headed (Luce, 1999, 2005; Townsend, 2008). In the heady 1950s and 1960s, mathematical psychology seemed the road toward a physical science of psychology, but perhaps the road did not go to the places the field's founders anticipated it would. If true, there might be several reasons for this, one being that (of course) one's children never grow up to become what one thought they would. Mathematical psychology prospers, even though it hasn't quite followed in its parents' footsteps.

Mathematical psychology is currently tackling two major issues, and both are focused primarily on methodology: (a) how to distinguish between different models of the same subsystem, and (b) constructing Bayesian methods for the analysis of behavioral data. We discuss each of these before closing the chapter.

Model Testing, Evaluation and Comparisons

Verbal theories are notorious in the social sciences for being tough to test decisively against one another. During the 1930s and 1940s, two giants of neobehaviorism, Clark Hull and Edwin Tolman, battled ferociously through countless well-designed experiments. Ultimately, theory (somewhat loosely defined, though Hull's concepts were typically more rigorously formulated quantitatively) really won out. Nonetheless, even though mathematical theorizing renders concepts clearer and more straightforward to test, the field is a long way from heaven in this regard.

A challenge faced by any scientist employing mathematical models with one or more free parameters is that of *parameter identifiability*. The scientist must be wary of data sets that do not uniquely specify a set of parameters. "Too many parameters" is the usual cause of this affliction. We mentioned earlier, one of the very first texts, especially at an introductory level, to discuss that issue, was the introduction to mathematical psychology by Restle and Greeno (1979).

More directly related to models testing is the important area in mathematical psychology, which addresses the problem of how to discriminate between different models. This is a long-standing problem in any field that constructs mathematical and statistical models, including statistics, where this issue is dealt with by considering issues of goodness of fit, variance accounted for, information criteria, Bayes factors, and so forth. In addition, the possibility that models based on very different psychological principles or mechanisms might be mathematically similar or even identical, the challenge of *model mimicking* can generate a formidable threat to the uncovering of psychological laws. These and other important topics are outlined in this section.

Mathematical psychologists have recently focused on the issue of *model complexity*. That is, one model may fit data better than another not because it is a better model but only because it is more complex. Complexity is not just a question of how many parameters a model has. Two models may have the same number of parameters yet one of them (the more complex one) may be able to accommodate a wider range of data patterns than the other. Even in basic psychophysics, it became apparent that the first model to predict how the

magnitude of a physical stimulus related to sensation, the Fechner log function, was less complex than the much later Stevens power law (see the section Psychophysics; Townsend, 1974).

A down-to-earth example of this is a comparison of two models of object recognition (e.g., letters, faces) that predict *confusion matrices* of success and error rates. The popular *similarity choice model* (Luce, 2003) possesses exactly the same number of parameters as the less well-known *overlap model* but has been shown to be significantly more complex than the latter (Townsend & Ashby, 1983, 1984).

Dealing with this issue borrows ideas from computer science and has its roots in information theory. Computer scientists have developed numerical techniques for quantifying complexity, opening the way for a different perspective on model selection. Pitt and colleagues (2006, 2008) applied these techniques to a number of different problems, including the optimization of experimental designs for model testing and explorations of model parameter spaces.

Another method for model testing and selection is the powerful *state-trace analysis* methodology invented by Donald Bamber (1979) and recently made popular by John Dunn (2008). This technique is applied to problems where the goal is to determine how many processes are contributing to the performance of a task (see, e.g., the discussion of dual-process memory models mentioned earlier). Many empirical pursuits try to answer the question of "how many processes" by looking for dissociations in patterns of data. That is, situations where one experimental variable moves a dependent variable in the opposite direction (or not at all) of another variable. This finding is sometimes called *selective influence*, and it is used to argue that one variable affects one process whereas another variable affects a different process independent from the first. State trace analysis is a simple technique based on minimal assumptions. In particular, no particular probability distributions, other mathematical functions, or parameters are required. On the basis of this technique, Dunn and colleagues have argued that, in many situations, dissociations do not provide strong evidence for multiple processes (e.g., Dunn, 2004, 2008; Newell & Dunn, 2008).

Ashby and Bamber (2022) recently provided theorems covering a number of important topics in state trace analysis. Space precludes broad coverage here, but their findings rule out the possibility that this methodology can, except in one extreme case, identify the number of underlying systems.

Another approach to model testing uses the "strong inference" philosophy described by John R. Platt (1964). The fundamental idea requires the scientist to set up a series of two or more juxtaposed hypotheses, rather than the more typical "there is a (predicted) effect" versus "there is no effect." For example, we might first test whether a psychological phenomenon takes place within short-term versus long-term memory and then follow that with a test of whether the coding system in that memory is verbal or spatial. Or we might formulate two or more entire classes of models that obey contrasting fundamental principles. The scientist first tests among these and in a second stage of research, begins to test among more specific models within the "winning" class.

Research on serial versus parallel processing of elements in visual and memory search illustrates the challenges of model mimicking (e.g., Townsend, 1972, 1974; Townsend & Ashby, 1983), as well as the opportunity for implementation of strong inference (e.g., Townsend, 1984). For instance, parallel and serial models can, for some popular experimental designs, produce exactly the same predictions and, thus, be totally indiscriminable (e.g., Townsend, 1972). Townsend and colleagues (e.g., Townsend & Nozawa, 1988; Townsend & Wenger, 2004) however, presented mathematical formulations for large classes of parallel and serial models, formulations that highlight empirically distinguishable, through the tool mentioned earlier of selective influence, aspects of the different structures. They then used these class differences as assays to test the models. The strategies we mentioned earlier for identification of even more complex architectures (Schweickert, 1978; Schweickert & Townsend, 1989) also adhere to this type of strategy. With these assays, juxtaposed models can be refined to be more and more specific so that, for example, if the assays suggest that processing is parallel, then we might go on to test, say, a diffusion process (e.g., Ratcliff, 1978) versus a counting mechanism (e.g., Smith & Van Zandt, 2000).

Finally, we note that the central tools of systems, identification and selective influence, have evolved in scope and rigor over the past several decades and will very likely continue that progress. In rough order of development we have Sternberg (1969), Townsend (1984), Townsend and Nozawa (1988), Schweickert (1978), Townsend and Schweickert (1989), Townsend (1990), Dzhafarov (2003), and Townsend and Liu (2022).

The issue of how to select between different mathematical models of a process will never be one that may be considered "solved," any more than the perfect statistical procedure for all circumstances will be discovered. As models change over the years, techniques for testing and selecting them will necessarily evolve.

The IID Problem and Bayesian Modeling

When subjects participate in a psychological experiment, they are usually asked to make more than one response. This is because one measurement does not allow the researcher to make inferences; intrinsic variability makes the measurement unreliable. A large number of responses from (usually) a large number of subjects across different conditions is collected to overcome this problem.

Although multiple observations solve the problem of statistical power, from a scientific perspective, they create another, entirely different problem. The measurement we obtain from a subject at one point in time is a function of all that has happened to that subject in the past. In particular, it is a function of the other measurements the subject has provided in our experiment. It is not possible to obtain repeated measurements under exactly the same conditions, even if the stimulus conditions remain exactly the same from trial to trial.

Nonetheless, we treat our data as independent and identically distributed observations from the same data-generating mechanism. Often, we assume the data are independent and identically distributed even if the observations are coming from different subjects. We blithely average, combine, and collapse, even knowing that such operations can distort the shape of any underlying function relating independent to dependent variables (Estes & Maddox, 2005).

This is the independent and identically distributed problem, and it is presently being tackled by the application of hierarchical Bayesian modeling techniques to established processing models (Craigmile et al., 2010; Lee, 2008; Peruggia et al., 2002; Rouder & Lu, 2005; Rouder et al., 2005). As in most Bayesian analyses, the goal is to determine the posterior distribution of some model parameters given a specified prior and the model itself (the likelihood). In a hierarchical model, the parameters for each subject are assumed to be drawn from common hyperdistributions, so that the posterior hyperdistributions are informed by all the data from all the subjects. Thus, each subject's data are fit in a way that allows for individual differences, but inferences about effects of independent variables are made on the hyperparameter posteriors, which have been "learned" from all the subjects' data combined.

Bayesian modeling has the potential to eliminate the problem of individual differences as well as order and other confounding effects (e.g., Craigmile et al., 2010), but it is a computationally difficult issue to address. There is currently a great deal of interest in treating response time data as time series (e.g., Thornton & Gilden, 2005; Van Orden et al., 2005), an approach that recognizes that repeated observations from a single subject are correlated. At this time, however, the techniques usually employed for such analyses can be criticized, as well as the conclusions that result from them (Wagenmakers et al., 2004).

Replication Crisis and Responses

Another core issue in mathematical psychology rose to further prominence around the mid 2010s with what has come to be termed the *replication crisis* (Shrout & Rodgers, 2018). A great number of papers began to fail statistical muster upon

being replicated, leading to a greater focus on statistical rigor and further scrutiny on the statistical tools and rationale utilized by researchers. The most common topics among this include a practice known as "*p*-hacking" (Head et al., 2015), as well misconceptions on proper modeling, and reeducation on fundamental topics in statistics (e.g., *p* values; Chambers, 2019). Thus, those well-practiced in mathematical psychology are being called on to refine statistical tools and to reeducate psychologists on proper research methods as well as on what conclusions can be reasonably inferred from data.

One other response to these growing concerns is the push for "open science" initiatives, which include preregistration and ready access to papers that are published in the field (e.g., preprints). Preregistration is a practice that allows researchers to publish publicly their predictions and planned analyses, reducing possible posthoc analyses and further transparency. Preprints also allow for papers to be critiqued by the community before review, once again aiding in the circulation of ideas regardless of whether it is accepted. Notably, there are differing opinions as to the extent the practices are needed; however, they ultimately are becoming a staple of the community.

Machine Learning

Alongside this greater focus on statistical tools comes the growing popularity of machine learning approaches to handling incoming data, as well as a new focus on descriptive rather than inferential studies in psychology. *Machine learning* is the modern name for what was, for many years referred to as *pattern recognition* (e.g., Fukanaga, 1990) Eventually, the name, used early on by Nilsson (1965), "learning machines," took center stage. Some authors nowadays use "pattern recognition" to refer to the program that ends up doing the classification and "machine learning" to designate the learning process that attempts to optimize (in some sense) the recognition process (see Bishop, 2006).

Neural networks, often in the guise of *deep learning* continues to play a significant role in these fields of computer science and engineering and, perhaps due to the provocative name, tend to be dominant in the popular mind. However, so-called *support vector machines* have been a strong competitor in recent times, partly because they do not tend to possess as many local optima as nonlinear neural networks often do. This challenge probably stems from the greater complexity in many of the multilayer neural networks. Also, the mathematics and investigations of support vector machines tends to be comprehended better than that of neural networks in general. Yet, a massive limitation in the former is that in the rigorous theory, they are confined to binary classifications (one needs to assemble successions of binary problem solution-algorithms).

As computing power increases, so too does the accessibility and allure of machine learning practices within mathematical research. These approaches are applied in numerous branches of behavioral research from clinical psychology (Dwyer, 2018) to neuroscience (Vu et al., 2018) and often provide reliable predictive power. Frequently, these connectionist models can arrive at predictions quickly and (when well trained) boast a rather high predictive power (Rosenbusch et al., 2021). These approaches, however, are removed from a tradition predictive approach because results from machine learning can lack the ability to explain how these predictions arise or how/why specific weights between nodes are assigned. Thus, a philosophical difference in focus between describing what behavior/response is likely to occur and understanding why it is occurring has also risen (Yarkoni & Westfall, 2017).

CONCLUSION

Modern mathematical psychology is a critical component of modern experimental psychology. From its earliest inception, mathematical psychology has made important contributions to our understanding of learning, memory, perception, and choice behavior; mathematical models continue to guide research in these areas as well as language acquisition and comprehension, problem solving, categorization, and judgment. Although modest in number, mathematical

psychologists appear as leaders in many psychological disciplines, especially in cognition and neuroscience. They have been elected to the most esteemed societies in experimental psychology as well as to the elite National Academy of Science. Several mathematical psychologists (Herbert Simon, Patrick Suppes, William K. Estes, and R. Duncan Luce) have received the United States' highest scientific honor, the National Medal of Science.

As experimental psychology matures, it is likely that our current definition for what constitutes mathematical psychology will change. Eventually, we hope, experimental psychologists will all use mathematical reasoning and develop mathematical models, and so everyone will be mathematical psychologists under the definition we have provided in this chapter. However, just as there remain specifically mathematical subdisciplines in the physical and life sciences (e.g., physics, chemistry, and biology), we anticipate that mathematical psychology will endure as a unique endeavor among the different subdisciplines that make up the science of psychology.

References

Ashby, F. G., & Bamber, D. (2022). State trace analysis: What it can and cannot do. *Journal of Mathematical Psychology, 108*, 102655. https://doi.org/10.1016/j.jmp.2022.102655

Ashby, F. G. (Ed.). (1992). *Multidimensional models of perception and cognition*. Lawrence Erlbaum.

Ashby, F. G., & Gott, R. E. (1988). Decision rules in the perception and categorization of multidimensional stimuli. *Journal of Experimental Psychology: Learning, Memory, and Cognition, 14*(1), 33–53. https://doi.org/10.1037/0278-7393.14.1.33

Atkinson, R. C., Bower, G. H., & Crothers, E. J. (1966). *An introduction to mathematical learning theory*. John Wiley.

Atkinson, R. C., & Estes, W. K. (1963). Stimulus sampling theory. In R. D. Luce, R. R. Bush, & E. Galanter (Eds.), *Handbook of mathematical psychology* (Vol. 2, pp. 121–268). Wiley Press.

Atkinson, R. C., & Juola, J. F. (1973). Factors influencing the speed and accuracy of word recognition. In S. Kornblum (Ed.), *Attention and performance IV* (pp. 583–612). Academic Press.

Attneave, F. (1954). *Applications of information theory to psychology: A summary of basic concepts, methods, and results*. Holt, Rinehart, and Winston.

Bamber, D. (1979). State-trace analysis: A method of testing simple theories of causation. *Journal of Mathematical Psychology, 19*(2), 137–181. https://doi.org/10.1016/0022-2496(79)90016-6

Batchelder, W. H. (2010). Cognitive psychometrics: Using multinomial processing tree models as measurement tools. In S. E. Embretson (Ed.), *Measuring psychological constructs: Advances in model-based approaches* (pp. 71–93). American Psychological Association. https://doi.org/10.1037/12074-004

Batchelder, W. H., & Riefer, D. M. (1999). Theoretical and empirical review of multinomial process tree modeling. *Psychonomic Bulletin & Review, 6*(1), 57–86. https://doi.org/10.3758/BF03210812

Batchelder, W. H., & Riefer, D. M. (2007). Using multinomial processing tree models to measure cognitive deficits in clinical populations. In R. W. J. Neufeld (Ed.), *Advances in clinical cognitive science: Formal modeling of processes and symptoms* (pp. 19–50). American Psychological Association. https://doi.org/10.1037/11556-001

Binet, A., & Simon, T. (1916). New methods for the diagnosis of the intellectual level of subnormals. In A. Binet & T. Simon (Eds.), *The development of intelligence in children* (E. S. Kite, Trans.). Williams & Wilkins. (Original work published 1905)

Bishop, C. M. (2006). *Pattern recognition and machine learning*. Springer.

Brown, S. D., & Heathcote, A. (2008). The simplest complete model of choice response time: Linear ballistic accumulation. *Cognitive Psychology, 57*(3), 153–178. https://doi.org/10.1016/j.cogpsych.2007.12.002

Busemeyer, J., & Diederich, A. (2002). Survey of decision field theory. *Mathematical Social Sciences, 43*(3), 345–370. https://doi.org/10.1016/S0165-4896(02)00016-1

Busemeyer, J. R., & Townsend, J. T. (1993). Decision field theory: A dynamic–cognitive approach to decision making in an uncertain environment. *Psychological Review, 100*(3), 432–459. https://doi.org/10.1037/0033-295X.100.3.432

Bush, R. R., & Mosteller, F. (1955). *Stochastic models for learning*. Wiley. https://doi.org/10.1037/14496-000

Chambers, C. (2019). *The seven deadly sins of psychology: A manifesto for reforming the culture of scientific practice*. Princeton University Press.

Colonius, H., & Dzhafarov, E. N. (Eds.). (2006). *Measurement and representation of sensation*. Lawrence Erlbaum Associates.

Coombs, C. H., Dawes, R. M., & Tversky, A. (1970). *Mathematical psychology: An elementary introduction*. Prentice-Hall.

Craigmile, P. F., Peruggia, M., & Van Zandt, T. (2010). Hierarchical Bayes models for response time data.

Psychometrika, 75(4), 613–632. https://doi.org/10.1007/s11336-010-9172-6

Dennis, S. (2005). A memory-based theory of verbal cognition. *Cognitive Science, 29*(2), 145–193. https://doi.org/10.1207/s15516709cog0000_9

Dennis, S., & Kintsch, W. (2007). The text mapping and inference rule generation problems in text comprehension: Evaluating a memory-based account. In F. Schmalhofer & C. A. Perfetti (Eds.), *Higher level language processes in the brain: Inference and comprehension processes* (pp. 105–132). Lawrence Erlbaum Associates.

Donders, F. C. (1969). On the speed of mental processes (W. G. Koster, Trans.). *Acta Psychologica, 30*, 412–431. https://doi.org/10.1016/0001-6918(69)90065-1

Duncombe, R. L. (1945). Personal equation in astronomy. *Popular Astronomy, 53*, 2–13, 63–76, 110–121.

Dunn, J. C. (2004). Remember-know: A matter of confidence. *Psychological Review, 111*(2), 524–542. https://doi.org/10.1037/0033-295X.111.2.524

Dunn, J. C. (2008). The dimensionality of the remember-know task: A state-trace analysis. *Psychological Review, 115*(2), 426–446. https://doi.org/10.1037/0033-295X.115.2.426

Dwyer, D. B., Falkai, P., & Koutsouleris, N. (2018). Machine learning approaches for clinical psychology and psychiatry. *Annual Review of Clinical Psychology, 14*, 91–118. https://doi.org/10.1146/annurev-clinpsy-032816-045037

Dzhafarov, E. N. (2003). Selective influence through conditional independence. *Psychometrika, 68*, 7–25. https://doi.org/10.1007/BF02296650

Elman, B. (2002). *A cultural history of civil examinations in late imperial China*. University of California Press.

Estes, W. K. (1950). Toward a statistical theory of learning. *Psychological Review, 57*(2), 94–107. https://doi.org/10.1037/h0058559

Estes, W. K. (1957). Of models and men. *American Psychologist, 12*(10), 609–617. https://doi.org/10.1037/h0046778

Estes, W. K. (2002). Traps in the route to models of memory and decision. *Psychonomic Bulletin & Review, 9*(1), 3–25. https://doi.org/10.3758/BF03196254

Estes, W. K., & Maddox, W. T. (2005). Risks of drawing inferences about cognitive processes from model fits to individual versus average performance. *Psychonomic Bulletin & Review, 12*(3), 403–408. https://doi.org/10.3758/BF03193784

Falmagne, J.-C. (1985). *Elements of psychophysical theory*. Oxford University Press.

Falmagne, J.-C. (1986). Psychophysical measurement and theory. In K. R. Boff, L. Kaufman, & J. P. Thomas (Eds.), *Handbook of perception and performance* (Vol. 1.). John Wiley.

Falmagne, J.-C., Reggenwetter, M., & Groffman, B. (1997). A stochastic model for the evolution of preferences. In A. A. J. Marley (Ed.), *Choice, decision, and measurement: Essays in honor of R. Duncan Luce* (pp. 111–130). Lawrence Erlbaum Associates.

Fechner, G. T. (1889). *Elemente der psychophysik* [*Elements of psychophysics*]. Breitkopf and Härtel. (Original work published 1860)

Fodor, J. A., & Pylyshyn, Z. W. (1988). Connectionism and cognitive architecture: A critical analysis. *Cognition, 28*(1–2), 3–71. https://doi.org/10.1016/0010-0277(88)90031-5

Fukanaga, K. (1990). *Introduction to statistical pattern recognition* (2nd ed.). Academic Press.

Garner, W. R. (1974). *The processing of information and structure*. Lawrence Erlbaum Associates.

Gibson, J. J. (1950). *The perception of the visual world*. Houghton Mifflin.

Gillund, G., & Shiffrin, R. M. (1984). A retrieval model for both recognition and recall. *Psychological Review, 91*(1), 1–67. https://doi.org/10.1037/0033-295X.91.1.1

Gould, S. J. (1981). *The mismeasure of man*. W. W. Norton.

Grossberg, S. (1980). How does a brain build a cognitive code? *Psychological Review, 87*(1), 1–51. https://doi.org/10.1007/978-94-009-7758-7_1

Grossberg, S. (2021). *Conscious mind, resonant brain: How each brain makes a mind*. Oxford University Press.

Hasselmo, M. E. (2009). A model of episodic memory: Mental time travel along encoded trajectories using grid cells. *Neurobiology of Learning and Memory, 92*(4), 559–573. https://doi.org/10.1016/j.nlm.2009.07.005

Head, M. L., Holman, L., Lanfear, R., Kahn, A. T., & Jennions, M. D. (2015). The extent and consequences of p-hacking in science. *PLOS Biology*. https://doi.org/10.1371/journal.pbio.1002106

Helmholtz, H. (1850). Vorläufiger Bericht über die Fortpflanzungsgeschwindigkeit der nervenreizung [Preliminary Report on the Speed of Propagation of the Nerve Stimulus]. *Archiv für Anatomie, Physiologie und Wissenschaftliche Medizin, 71*.

Helmholtz, H. (1912). *On the sensations of tone as a physiological basis for the theory of music* (3rd ed.). Longmans, Green. (Original work published 1877)

Heyer, D., & Niederée, R. (1989). Elements of a model-theoretic framework for probabilistic measurement. In E. E. Roskam (Ed.), *Mathematical psychology in progress* (pp. 99–112). Springer. https://doi.org/10.1007/978-3-642-83943-6_7

Hick, W. E. (1952). On the rate of gain of information. *The Quarterly Journal of Experimental Psychology, 4*(1), 11–26. https://doi.org/10.1080/17470215208416600

Hintzman, D. L. (1988). Judgments of frequency and recognition memory in a multiple-trace memory model. *Psychological Review, 95*(4), 528–551. https://doi.org/10.1037/0033-295X.95.4.528

Howard, M. W., & Kahana, M. J. (2002). A distributed representation of temporal context. *Journal of Mathematical Psychology, 46*(3), 269–299. https://doi.org/10.1006/jmps.2001.1388

Hull, C. L. (1952). *A behavior system; an introduction to behavior theory concerning the individual organism*. Yale University Press.

Hyman, R. (1953). Stimulus information as a determinant of reaction time. *Journal of Experimental Psychology, 45*(3), 188–196. https://doi.org/10.1037/h0056940

Jilk, D. J., Lebiere, C., O'Reilly, R. C., & Anderson, J. R. (2008). SAL: An explicitly pluralistic cognitive architecture. *Journal of Experimental & Theoretical Artificial Intelligence, 20*(3), 197–218. https://doi.org/10.1080/09528130802319128

Kelso, S. J. A. (1995). *Dynamic patterns: The self-organization of brain and behavior*. MIT Press.

Kintsch, W., McNamara, D. S., Dennis, S., & Landauer, T. K. (2007). LSA and meaning: In theory and application. In T. K. Landauer, D. S. McNamara, S. Dennis, & W. Kintsch (Eds.), *Handbook of latent semantic analysis* (pp. 467–479). Lawrence Erlbaum Associates.

Klir, G. J. (1969). *An approach to general systems theory*. Van Nostrand Reinhold.

Krantz, D. H., Luce, R. D., Suppes, P., & Tversky, A. (1971). *Foundations of measurement* (Vol. I). Academic Press.

Laming, D. R. (1973). *Mathematical psychology*. Academic Press.

Large, E. W., & Jones, M. R. (1999). The dynamics of attending: How people track time-varying events. *Psychological Review, 106*(1), 119–159. https://doi.org/10.1037/0033-295X.106.1.119

Lee, M. D. (2008). Three case studies in the Bayesian analysis of cognitive models. *Psychonomic Bulletin & Review, 15*(1), 1–15. https://doi.org/10.3758/PBR.15.1.1

Leonard, J. A. (1959). Tactile choice reactions. *The Quarterly Journal of Experimental Psychology, 11*(2), 76–83. https://doi.org/10.1080/17470215908416294

Luce, R. D. (1959). *Individual choice behavior: A theoretical analysis*. Wiley Press.

Luce, R. D. (1999). Where is mathematical modeling in psychology headed? *Theory & Psychology*, *9*(6), 723–737. https://doi.org/10.1177/0959354399096001

Luce, R. D. (2003). Whatever happened to information theory in psychology? *Review of General Psychology*, *7*(2), 183–188. https://doi.org/10.1037/1089-2680.7.2.183

Luce, R. D. (2004). Symmetric and asymmetric matching of joint presentations. *Psychological Review*, *111*(2), 446–454. https://doi.org/10.1037/0033-295X.111.2.446

Luce, R. D. (2005). An open measurement problem of interest. *Journal of Mathematical Psychology*, *49*(6), 440–442. https://doi.org/10.1016/j.jmp.2005.05.001

Luce, R. D., Bush, R. R., & Galanter, E. (Eds.). (1963–1965a). *Handbook of mathematical psychology: Vols. 1, 2, and 3*. Wiley Press.

Luce, R. D., Bush, R. R., & Galanter, E. (Eds.). (1963–1965b). *Readings in mathematical psychology: Vols. 1 and 2*. Wiley Press.

Luce, R. D., Krantz, D. H., Suppes, P., & Tversky, A. (1990). *Foundations of measurement* (Vol. 3). Academic Press.

McClelland, J., & Rumelhart, D. (1986). *Parallel distributed processing: Explorations in the microstructure of cognition: Vol. 2. Psychological and Biological Models*. MIT Press.

McCulloch, W., & Pitts, W. (1943). A logical calculus of ideas immanent in nervous activity. *Bulletin of Mathematical Biophysics. 5*(4), 115–133. https://doi.org/10.1007/BF02478259

Merkle, E. C., & Van Zandt, T. (2006). An application of the poisson race model to confidence calibration. *Journal of Experimental Psychology: General*, *135*(3), 391–408. https://doi.org/10.1037/0096-3445.135.3.391

Miller, G. A. (1956). The magical number seven plus or minus two: Some limits on our capacity for processing information. *Psychological Review*, *63*(2), 81–97. https://doi.org/10.1037/h0043158

Minsky, M. L., & Papert, S. A. (1969). *Perceptrons*. MIT Press.

Murdock, B. B., Jr. (1965). Signal-detection theory and short-term memory. *Journal of Experimental Psychology*, *70*(5), 443–447. https://doi.org/10.1037/h0022543

Murdock, B. B. (1982). A theory for the storage and retrieval of item and associative information. *Psychological Review*, *89*(6), 609–626. https://doi.org/10.1037/0033-295X.89.6.609

Murray, D., & Link, S. W. (2021). The creation of scientific psychology. In S. W. Link & J. T. Townsend (Eds.), *Scientific psychology series*. Routledge.

Myung, J. I., Karabatsos, G., & Iverson, G. J. (2005). A Bayesian approach to testing decision making axioms. *Journal of Mathematical Psychology*, *49*(3), 205–225. https://doi.org/10.1016/j.jmp.2005.02.004

Narens, L. (1996). A theory of ratio magnitude estimation. *Journal of Mathematical Psychology*, *40*(2), 109–129. https://doi.org/10.1006/jmps.1996.0011

Narens, L., & Luce, R. D. (1986). Measurement: The theory of numerical assignments. *Psychological Bulletin*, *99*(2), 166–180. https://doi.org/10.1037/0033-2909.99.2.166

Narens, L., & Luce, R. D. (1993). Further comments on the "nonrevolution" arising from axiomatic measurement theory. *Psychological Science*, *4*(2), 127–130. https://doi.org/10.1111/j.1467-9280.1993.tb00475.x

Newell, B. R., & Dunn, J. C. (2008). Dimensions in data: Testing psychological models using state-trace analysis. *Trends in Cognitive Sciences*, *12*(8), 285–290. https://doi.org/10.1016/j.tics.2008.04.009

Nilsson, N. J. (1965). *Learning machines: Foundations of trainable pattern-classifying systems*. McGraw-Hill.

Norris, D., & McQueen, J. M. (2008). Shortlist B: A Bayesian model of continuous speech recognition. *Psychological Review*, *115*(2), 357–395. https://doi.org/10.1037/0033-295X.115.2.357

Nosofsky, R. M. (1988). Exemplar-based accounts of relations between classification, recognition, and typicality. *Journal of Experimental Psychology: Learning, Memory, and Cognition*, *14*(4), 700–708. https://doi.org/10.1037/0278-7393.14.4.700

Nosofsky, R. M., & Palmeri, T. J. (1997). Comparing exemplar-retrieval and decision-bound models of speeded perceptual classification. *Perception & Psychophysics*, *59*(7), 1027–1048. https://doi.org/10.3758/BF03205518

O'Reilly, R. C., & Frank, M. J. (2006). Making working memory work: A computational model of learning in the prefrontal cortex and basal ganglia. *Neural Computation*, *18*(2), 283–328. https://doi.org/10.1162/089976606775093909

Parks, T. E. (1966). Signal-detectability theory of recognition-memory performance. *Psychological Review*, *73*(1), 44–58. https://doi.org/10.1037/h0022662

Peruggia, M., Van Zandt, T., & Chen, M. (2002). Was it a car or a cat i saw? An analysis of response times for word recognition. *Case Studies in Bayesian Statistics*, *167*, 319–334. https://doi.org/10.1007/978-1-4612-2078-7_17

Pike, R. (1973). Response latency models for signal detection. *Psychological Review*, *80*(1), 53–68. https://doi.org/10.1037/h0033871

Pinker, S., & Mehler, J. (Eds.). (1988). *Connections and symbols*. MIT Press. https://doi.org/10.7551/mitpress/2103.001.0001

Pitt, M. A., Kim, W., Navarro, D. J., & Myung, J. I. (2006). Global model analysis by parameter space partitioning. *Psychological Review, 113*(1), 57–83. https://doi.org/10.1037/0033-295X.113.1.57

Pitt, M. A., Myung, I. J., & Zhang, S. (2002). Toward a method of selecting among computational models of cognition. *Psychological Review, 109*(3), 472–491. https://doi.org/10.1037/0033-295X.109.3.472

Pitt, M. A., Myung, J. I., Montenegro, M., & Pooley, J. (2008). Measuring model flexibility with parameter space partitioning: An introduction and application example. *Cognitive Science, 32*(8), 1285–1303. https://doi.org/10.1080/03640210802477534

Platt, J. R. (1964). Strong inference: Certain systematic methods of scientific thinking may produce much more rapid progress than others. *Science, 146*(3642), 347–353. https://doi.org/10.1126/science.146.3642.347

Pleskac, T. J., & Busemeyer, J. R. (2010). Two-stage dynamic signal detection: A theory of choice, decision time, and confidence. *Psychological Review, 117*(3), 864–901. https://doi.org/10.1037/a0019737

Port, R. F., & van Gelder, T. (1998). *Mind as motion: Explorations in the dynamics of cognition*. MIT Press. https://doi.org/10.7551/mitpress/4622.001.0001

Rabbitt, P. (1969). Psychological refractory delay and response-stimulus interval duration in serial, choice-response tasks. *Acta Psychologica, 30*, 195–219. https://doi.org/10.1016/0001-6918(69)90051-1

Rashevsky, N. (1936). Mathematical biophysics and psychology. *Psychometrika, 1*, 1–26. https://doi.org/10.1007/BF02287920

Ratcliff, R. (1978). A theory of memory retrieval. *Psychological Review, 85*(2), 59–108. https://doi.org/10.1037/0033-295X.85.2.59

Ratcliff, R. (2008). Modeling aging effects on two-choice tasks: Response signal and response time data. *Psychology and Aging, 23*(4), 900–916. https://doi.org/10.1037/a0013930

Ratcliff, R., & Smith, P. L. (2004). A comparison of sequential sampling models for two-choice reaction time. *Psychological Review, 111*(2), 333–367. https://doi.org/10.1037/0033-295X.111.2.333

Ratcliff, R., & Starns, J. J. (2009). Modeling confidence and response time in recognition memory. *Psychological Review, 116*(1), 59–83. https://doi.org/10.1037/a0014086

Restle, F., & Greeno, J. G. (1970). *Introduction to mathematical psychology*. Addison-Wesley.

Roberts, F. S. (1979). *Discrete mathematical models: With applications to social, biological, and environmental problems*. Pearson.

Roe, R. M., Busemeyer, J., & Townsend, J. T. (2001). Multialternative decision field theory: A dynamic artificial neural network model of decision making. *Psychological Review, 108*(2), 370–392. https://doi.org/10.1037/0033-295x.108.2.370

Rosenblatt, F. (1957). *The perceptron—a perceiving and recognizing automaton*. Cornell Aeronautical Laboratory.

Rosenbusch, H., Soldner, F., Evans, A. M., & Zeelenberg, M. (2021). Supervised machine learning methods in psychology: A practical introduction with annotated R code. *Social and Personality Psychology Compass, 15*(2). https://doi.org/10.1111/spc3.12579

Rouder, J. N., & Lu, J. (2005). An introduction to Bayesian hierarchical models with an application in the theory of signal detection. *Psychonomic Bulletin & Review, 12*(4), 573–604. https://doi.org/10.3758/BF03196750

Rouder, J. N., Lu, J., Speckman, P., Sun, D., & Jiang, Y. (2005). A hierarchical model for estimating response time distributions. *Psychonomic Bulletin & Review, 12*(2), 195–223. https://doi.org/10.3758/BF03257252

Rumelhart, D., & McClelland, J. (1986). *Parallel distributed processing: Explorations in the microstructure of cognition: Vol. 1. Foundations*. MIT Press.

Schall, J. D. (2003). Neural correlates of decision processes: Neural and mental chronometry. *Current Opinion in Neurobiology, 13*(2), 182–186. https://doi.org/10.1016/S0959-4388(03)00039-4

Schmidt, R. C., Carello, C., & Turvey, M. T. (1990). Phase transitions and critical fluctuations in the visual coordination of rhythmic movements between people. *Journal of Experimental Psychology: Human Perception and Performance, 16*(2), 227–247. https://doi.org/10.1037/0096-1523.16.2.227

Schweickert, R. (1978). A critical path generalization of the additive factor methods analysis of a Stroop task. *Journal of Mathematical Psychology, 18*(2), 105–139. https://doi.org/10.1016/0022-2496(78)90059-7

Schweickert, R., & Townsend, J. T. (1989). A trichotomy method: Interactions of factors prolonging sequential and concurrent mental processes in the stochastic PERT networks. *Journal of Mathematical Psychology, 33*(3), 328–347. https://doi.org/10.1016/0022-2496(89)90013-8

Scott, D. S., & Suppes, P. (1958). Foundational aspects of theories of measurement. *The Journal of Symbolic Logic, 23*(2), 113–128. https://doi.org/10.2307/2964389

Shannon, C. E., & Weaver, W. (1949). *The mathematical theory of communication.* University of Illinois Press.

Shiffrin, R. M., & Steyvers, M. (1997). A model for recognition memory: REM-retrieving effectively from memory. *Psychonomic Bulletin & Review, 4*(2), 145–166. https://doi.org/10.3758/BF03209391

Shore, D. I., & Spence, C. (2005). Prior entry. In L. Itti, G. Rees, & J. K. Tsotsos (Eds.), *Neurobiology of attention* (pp. 89–95). Elsevier. https://doi.org/10.1016/B978-012375731-9/50019-7

Shrout, P. E., & Rodgers, J. L. (2018). Psychology, science, and knowledge construction: Broadening perspectives from the replication crisis. *Annual Reviews of Psychology, 69,* 487–510. https://doi.org/10.1146/annurev-psych-122216-011845

Smith, P. L., & Van Zandt, T. (2000). Time-dependent Poisson counter models of response latency in simple judgment. *British Journal of Mathematical & Statistical Psychology, 53*(2), 293–315. https://doi.org/10.1348/000711000159349

Smith, P. L., & Vickers, D. (1988). The accumulator model of two-choice discrimination. *Journal of Mathematical Psychology, 32*(2), 135–168. https://doi.org/10.1016/0022-2496(88)90043-0

Steingrimsson, R., & Luce, R. D. (2005a). Evaluating a model of global psychophysical judgments: I. Behavioral properties of summations and productions. *Journal of Mathematical Psychology, 49*(4), 290–307. https://doi.org/10.1016/j.jmp.2005.03.003

Steingrimsson, R., & Luce, R. D. (2005b). Evaluating a model of global psychophysical judgments: II. Behavioral properties linking summations and productions. *Journal of Mathematical Psychology, 49*(4), 308–319. https://doi.org/10.1016/j.jmp.2005.03.001

Steingrimsson, R., & Luce, R. D. (2006). Empirical evaluation of a model of global psychophysical judgments: III. A form for the psychophysical function and intensity filtering. *Journal of Mathematical Psychology, 50*(1), 15–29. https://doi.org/10.1016/j.jmp.2005.11.005

Steingrimsson, R., & Luce, R. D. (2007). Empirical evaluation of a model of global psychophysical judgments: IV. Forms for the weighting function. *Journal of Mathematical Psychology, 51*(1), 29–44. https://doi.org/10.1016/j.jmp.2006.08.001

Sternberg, S. (1966). High-speed scanning in human memory. *Science, 153*(3736), 652–654. https://doi.org/10.1126/science.153.3736.652

Sternberg, S. (1969). The discovery of processing stages: Extensions of Donder's method. In W. G. Koster (Ed.), *Attention and performance II* (pp. 276–315). North-Holland. https://doi.org/10.1016/0001-6918(69)90055-9

Stevens, S. S. (1957). On the psychophysical law. *Psychological Review, 64*(3), 153–181. https://doi.org/10.1037/h0046162

Stevens, S. S. (1961). To honor Fechner and repeal his law: A power function, not a log function, describes the operating characteristic of a sensory system. *Science, 133*(3446), 80–86. https://doi.org/10.1126/science.133.3446.80

Strange, B. A., Duggins, A., Penny, W., Dolan, R. J., & Friston, K. J. (2005). Information theory, novelty and hippocampal responses: Unpredicted or unpredictable? *Neural Networks, 18*(3), 225–230. https://doi.org/10.1016/j.neunet.2004.12.004

Suppes, P., Krantz, D. H., Luce, R. D., & Tversky, A. (1989). *Foundations of measurement.* Academic Press.

Suppes, P., & Zinnes, J. (1963). Basic measurement theory. In R. D. Luce, R. R. Bush, & E. Galanter (Eds.), *Handbook of mathematical psychology* (pp. 1–76). John Wiley and Sons.

Swets, J., Tanner, W. P., Jr., & Birdsall, T. G. (1961). Decision processes in perception. *Psychological Review, 68*(5), 301–340. https://doi.org/10.1037/h0040547

Thornton, T. L., & Gilden, D. L. (2005). Provenance of correlations in psychological data. *Psychonomic Bulletin & Review, 12*(3), 409–441. https://doi.org/10.3758/BF03193785

Thurstone, L. L. (1927). A law of comparative judgement. *Psychological Review, 34*(4), 273–286. https://doi.org/10.1037/h0070288

Thurstone, L. L. (1952). L. L. Thurstone. In E. G. Boring, H. S. Langfeld, & H. W. R. M. Yerkes (Eds.), *A history of psychology in autobiography* (Vol. IV, pp. 295–321). Clark University Press.

Torgerson, W. S. (1958). *Theory and methods of scaling.* Wiley.

Townsend, J. T. (1972). Some results concerning the identifiability of parallel and serial processes. *British Journal of Mathematical & Statistical Psychology, 25*(2), 168–199. https://doi.org/10.1111/j.2044-8317.1972.tb00490.x

Townsend, J. T. (1974). Issues and models concerning the processing of a finite number of inputs. In B. H. Kantowitz (Ed.), *Human information processing: Tutorials in performance and cognition* (pp. 133–168). Lawrence Erlbaum.

Townsend, J. T. (1976). Serial and within-stage independent parallel model equivalence on the minimum completion time. *Journal of Mathematical Psychology, 14*(3), 219–238. https://doi.org/10.1016/0022-2496(76)90003-1

Townsend, J. T. (1984). Uncovering mental processes with factorial experiments. *Journal of Mathematical*

Psychology, 28(4), 363–400. https://doi.org/10.1016/0022-2496(84)90007-5

Townsend, J. T. (1990). Truth and consequences of ordinal differences in statistical distributions: Toward a theory of hierarchical inference. *Psychological Bulletin, 108*(3), 551–567.

Townsend, J. T. (1992). Chaos theory: A brief tutorial and discussion. In A. F. Healy, S. M. Kosslyn, & R. M. Shiffrin (Eds.), *From learning theory to connectionist theory: Essays in honor of William K. Estes* (Vol. 1, pp. 65–96). Lawrence Erlbaum Associates.

Townsend, J. T. (2008). Mathematical psychology: Prospects for the 21st century: A guest editorial. *Journal of Mathematical Psychology, 52*(5), 269–280. https://doi.org/10.1016/j.jmp.2008.05.001

Townsend, J. T., & Ashby, F. G. (1983). *The stochastic modeling of elementary psychological processes.* Cambridge University Press.

Townsend, J. T., & Ashby, F. G. (1984). Measurement scales and statistics: The misconception misconceived. *Psychological Bulletin, 96*(2), 394–401.

Townsend, J. T., & Nozawa, G. (1988). Strong evidence for parallel processing with simple dot stimuli. *Bulletin of the Psychonomic Society, 26*(6), 515–515.

Townsend, J. T., & Liu, Y. (2022). Varieties of selective influence: Toward a more complete taxonomy and implications for systems identification. *Mathematics, 10*(7), 1059. https://doi.org/10.3390/math10071059

Townsend, J. T., & Schweickert, R. (1989). Toward the trichotomy method: Laying the foundation of stochastic mental networks. *Journal of Mathematical Psychology, 33*, 309–327.

Townsend, J. T., & Wenger, M. J. (2004). The serial-parallel dilemma: A case study in a linkage of theory and method. *Psychonomic Bulletin & Review, 11*(3), 391–418. https://doi.org/10.3758/BF03196588

Trueblood, J. S., Brown, S. D., & Heathcote, A. (2014). The multiattribute linear ballistic accumulator model of context effects in multialternative choice. *Psychological Review, 121*(2), 179–205. https://doi.org/10.1037/a0036137

Turvey, M. T. (1990). Coordination. *American Psychologist, 45*(8), 938–953. https://doi.org/10.1037/0003-066X.45.8.938

Turvey, M. T. (2009). On the notion and implications of organism-environment system: Introduction. *Ecological Psychology, 21*(2), 97–111. https://doi.org/10.1080/10407410902877041

Tversky, A., & Kahneman, D. (1974). Judgment under uncertainty: Heuristics and biases. *Science, 185*(4157), 1124–1131. https://doi.org/10.1126/science.185.4157.1124

Tversky, A., & Kahneman, D. (1981). The framing of decisions and the psychology of choice. *Science,* *211*(4481), 453–458. https://doi.org/10.1126/science.7455683

Usher, M., & McClelland, J. L. (2001). The time course of perceptual choice: The leaky, competing accumulator model. *Psychological Review, 108*(3), 550–592. https://doi.org/10.1037/0033-295X.108.3.550

Van Orden, G. C., Holden, J. G., & Turvey, M. T. (2005). Human cognition and 1/f scaling. *Journal of Experimental Psychology: General, 134*(1), 117–123. https://doi.org/10.1037/0096-3445.134.1.117

Van Zandt, T. (2000). ROC curves and confidence judgements in recognition memory. *Journal of Experimental Psychology: Learning, Memory, and Cognition, 26*(3), 582–600. https://doi.org/10.1037/0278-7393.26.3.582

Van Zandt, T., Colonius, H., & Proctor, R. W. (2000). A comparison of two response time models applied to perceptual matching. *Psychonomic Bulletin & Review, 7*(2), 208–256. https://doi.org/10.3758/BF03212980

Vickers, D. (1979). *Decision processes in visual perception.* Academic Press.

Vu, M. T., Adalı, T., Ba, D., Buzsáki, G., Carlson, D., Heller, K., Liston, C., Rudin, C., Sohal, V. S., Widge, A. S., Mayberg, H. S., Sapiro, G., & Dzirasa, K. (2018). A shared vision for machine learning in neuroscience. *The Journal of Neuroscience, 38*(7), 1601–1607. https://doi.org/10.1523/JNEUROSCI.0508-17.2018

Wagenmakers, E.-J., Farrell, S., & Ratcliff, R. (2004). Estimation and interpretation of 1/f$^\alpha$ noise in human cognition. *Psychonomic Bulletin & Review, 11*(4), 579–615. https://doi.org/10.3758/BF03196615

Watson, J. B. (1914). *Behavior: An introduction to comparative psychology.* Henry Holt. https://doi.org/10.1037/10868-000

White, C., Ratcliff, R., Vasey, M., & McKoon, G. (2009). Dysphoria and memory for emotional material: A diffusion-model analysis. *Cognition and Emotion, 23*(1), 181–205. https://doi.org/10.1080/02699930801976770

Wiener, N. (2019). *Cybernetics; or, control and communication in the animal and the machine.* MIT Press. (Original work published 1948)

Wixted, J. T. (2007). Dual-process theory and signal-detection theory of recognition memory. *Psychological Review, 114*(1), 152–176. https://doi.org/10.1037/0033-295X.114.1.152

Yarkoni, T., & Westfall, J. (2017). Choosing prediction over explanation in psychology: Lessons from machine learning. *Perspectives on Psychological Science, 12*(6), 1100–1122. https://doi.org/10.1177/1745691617693393

CHAPTER 23

COMPUTATIONAL MODELING

Adele Diederich

Over the last 50 years or so, computational modeling has become a rapidly growing approach in many scientific disciplines. In psychology, computational modeling is more recent but has had an exponential growth. It has predominantly been applied in cognitive psychology, in particular, in learning, memory, categorization, pattern recognition, psycholinguistics, vision, decision making and lately, developmental psychology, social psychology, and even clinical psychology took interest in the approach. It is also bridging the neurosciences and the behavioral sciences.

In the last 15 years, several (introductory) books have been written on how to do computational modeling in psychology and in neuroscience. For instance, Sun (2008a) devoted an entire handbook to computational modeling in psychology; Busemeyer and Diederich (2010) provided a tutorial that reviews the methods and steps used in cognitive modeling; in the same vein, Lewandowsky and Farrell (2011) outlined the principles and practice of computational modeling in cognition; Farrell and Lewandowsky (2018) updated their textbook, extended it to newer modeling practice, and added examples of models in psychology and neuroscience to demonstrate the steps typically involved in computational modeling. Besides many journal articles on

specific technics of computational modeling, a psychological journal—*Computational Brain and Behavior*—has been founded recently as another outlet for the growing work in this field.

Given that mathematical psychology (Chapter 22, this volume) has been an established field since the middle of the last century, the questions arise whether computational modeling is different from mathematical modeling; whether there is something like computational psychology; and if so, whether it is different from mathematical psychology.

To answer these questions, it is helpful to distinguish between mathematical/computational models and mathematical/computational modeling. In general, a *model* is an abstraction representing some aspects of a complex phenomenon or situation in the real world. A formal model applies mathematical and statistical methods, formal logic, or computer simulation to establish a correspondence between a particular set of empirical phenomena and a formal system reflecting the assumptions about specific entities or objects and their relations to each other. The model thereby may take on various structures such as algebraic or geometric, and forms such as axiomatic, systems of equations, algorithms, networks, and so on. They are static or dynamic, deterministic, or

This chapter is a revised version of Diederich and Busemeyer (2012).

https://doi.org/10.1037/0000319-023
APA Handbook of Research Methods in Psychology, Second Edition: Vol. 2. Research Designs: Quantitative, Qualitative, Neuropsychological, and Biological, H. Cooper (Editor-in-Chief)

probabilistic, linear or nonlinear in nature, and so forth. They are designed to describe internal presentations, processes, functions, mechanisms, and structures. The goal of a formal model is to derive predictions which can connect to data observed in the real world. These data are often obtained in experiments. Interpreting data in light of the model's prediction is crucial for the modeling process and often leads to a modification of the model. This entire process is referred to as mathematical modeling. When the phenomena of interest stem from psychological questions, the area is called *mathematical psychology* (Chapter 22, this volume), and the process often is called *cognitive modeling*.

Sometimes, a mathematical model representing the phenomena or situation is so complex that an analytical solution is not readily available or a closed-form solution does not even exist. Other times, experiments are too expensive or may not even be feasible to conduct. For those cases, a computational approach is considered as a valuable alternative. Computational approaches develop computer algorithms and programs, implement them on a computer, and the computer simulations derive the predictions of the model and also generate data. Instead of deriving an analytical solution to the problem, a computer simulation—that is, changing the parameters of the system in the computer—provides the basis for studying and evaluating the model by comparing the simulated data to the outcome of the experiments.

Many computational models are computer simulations of complex mathematical equations that cannot be solved in a simple form and must be simulated by computer. Some other computational models are simply based on if–then production rules and are harder to see as mathematical models. Technically, they are finite-state machines, or if a probabilistic selection of rules is applied, they technically become Markov models in a large state space. However, these types of computational models are never expressed mathematically, even though they could be. Models such as Act-R (Lebière & Anderson, 1993) or Clarion (Sun, 2009) use some mathematical

equations, such as power function decay, linear combinations of inputs to produce activation values, and mathematical reinforcement learning rules. But they are also heavily reliant on production rules. That is, technically, they could be formalized as mathematical models (dynamic systems, stochastic dynamic systems, finite-state machines, Markov processes); however, in practice, it is difficult to see the mathematics in some of them, such as pure production rule systems.

With this description of a computational approach in mind, are mathematical models then a subset of computational models, as Sun (2008b) claimed? Or are they merely a tool in mathematical psychology, one of many methods that can be applied in the modeling process, with the advantage that data can be simulated easily and extremely quickly? After all, computational models require a mathematically and logically formal representation of the problem and could therefore be considered as a subset of mathematical models.

In light of the many disciplines involved in computational modeling research, it seems impossible to come up with an agreed-upon definition. There are interesting discussions going on in some disciplines outside of psychology. Indeed, an entire subfield of computer science studies the relationships and differences between computational and mathematical models. I am not dwelling on it here further (Diederich & Busemeyer, 2012) and agree with Wilson and Collins (2019) that computational modeling in behavioral science use precise mathematical models.

Many formal models in (cognitive) psychology are functional in nature. They are built to describe and explain psychological mechanisms and processes and to predict (human) performance— that is, what can be expected to happen under various conditions. The (cognitive) architecture of a model reflects its structure and computational rules, that is, its functional organization. Cognitive architectures are classified as symbolic, subsymbolic (connectionist) or hybrid depending on the assumed properties of the models and the rules applied to the system.

Symbolic modeling has its origin in computer science, in particular, artificial intelligence, which focuses on building enhanced intelligence into computer systems. Patterns of reasoning, such as logical operations or processing systems with their respective specified rules, operate by using symbols. From early on, these models have attracted a broad range of disciplines from philosophy to engineering. They have been applied to semantic representation, language processing, knowledge representation, reasoning, speech recognition, computer vision, robotic, various expert systems, and many more (see Nilsson, 2010, for a history and achievement of artificial intelligence with a focus on engineering, and Boden, 2006, for a comprehensive work on a history of cognitive science, which also include the philosophical perspective of computational approaches).

Subsymbol or connectionist models use the analogy to neural networks as observed in the human brain. Activation patterns among large numbers of processing units (neurons) encode knowledge and specific content. Connectionist models are developed in many scientific disciplines from computer science to neuroscience, natural science, cognitive science, and behavioral sciences. They have been applied to speech recognition and speech generation, predictions of financial indices, identification of cancerous cells, automatic recognition to handwritten characters, sexing of faces and many more. Hybrid architectures combine both types of processing and become more interesting for cognitive modelers (Diederich & Busemeyer, 2012). Two simple connectionist types of models for categorical learning serve as examples of the modeling process later.

THE ADVANTAGE OF FORMAL MODELS AND MODELING

Modeling is part of the scientific method (e.g., Hepburn & Andersen, 2021; van Rooij & Baggio, 2021; Voit, 2019). Roughly, starting with an observation or a general theory, we formulate assumptions (or hypotheses), derive predictions, test them in the laboratory or in the field, and possibly modify our assumptions to give a better account of the data. Formal modeling has several advantages over a merely verbal modeling approach. First, it forces the researcher to give precise definitions and clear statements. This requires a high degree of abstraction: Assumptions about underlying processes, relations between entities, interactions between variables, and so on, all need to be mapped onto mathematical objects and operations. The language of mathematics minimizes the risk of making contradictory statements in the theory. Second, formal modeling allows deriving precise predictions from the underlying assumptions, thereby enabling empirical falsification of these assumptions. Furthermore, deriving predictions is particularly important and useful when they are not obvious. Testable predictions may be useful for deciding between competing theories of a given phenomenon. They are not necessarily quantitative but can also reflect qualitative patterns, which can be observable in the data. Third, mathematical modeling brings together theory and data; it facilitates the analysis and interpretation of complex data and helps generating new hypotheses. Fourth, even rather simple mathematical models often describe data better and are more informative than a statistical test of a verbally phrased hypothesis. Finally, formal models can provide a unifying language and methodology that can be used across disciplines ranging from experimental psychology to cognitive science, computer science, and neuroscience.

USAGE OF COMPUTATIONAL MODELS

Wilson and Collins (2019) identified the application of computational models predominantly in four different fields: simulation, parameter estimation, model comparison, and latent variable inference. These are parts of the modeling process. How to design a good computational/mathematical model is a different topic and goes beyond the scope of this chapter.

Simulation

Simulation, in this context, refers to generating (a) artificial data by inserting specific parameter values into the model, (b) qualitative and quantitative predictions of the model by inserting a wide range of different parameter values (combinations), or (c) a combination of both. Simulation is particularly important in the model-building phase (Fan, 2012). Wilson and Collins (2019) suggested also including qualitative properties of the model; it may give the modeler a better intuition for the model's behavior and may allow for specific predictions. For instance, take the popular diffusion model for binary choice options, which accounts simultaneously for (mean) choice response times and choice frequencies (Ratcliff, 2012). It assumes that all the information of the stimuli (provided in attributes or dimensions) is mapped onto one so-called drift rate, μ. It reflects the mean tendency to choose one alternative over the other. The better the two stimuli can be discriminated, the larger is μ. To account for specific choice patterns, additional (ad hoc) assumptions are necessary (Ratcliff, 2012). The multiattribute diffusion model for binary choice options (Diederich, 1997) on the other hand links attribute information sequentially to separate stages—that is, one piece of information delivered at t_0, a second piece of information at t_1, and so on. Diederich and Oswald (2014) showed that for two stages, only the relationship (larger, smaller) between the drift rate parameters of the first stage and the second stage is crucial for predicting a specific pattern between mean choice response time and choice probability, regardless of the parameters values. In particular, when drift rate μ_1 of the first stage of the process is larger than drift rate μ_2 of the second stage, predicted mean choice response time is always smaller for the more frequently chosen alternative than for the less frequently chosen alternative. On the other hand, when $\mu_1 < \mu_2$, then the predicted mean choice response time is always smaller for the less frequently chosen alternative than for the more frequently chosen alternative (fast error). Thus, when in an experimental setup more stimulus information is provided in a first stage than in a second while the data show fast errors, there is no rescue for this model.

Palminteri et al. (2017) argued that simulation, including visualization of the outcome, is a

decisive step in model falsification, showing that a computational cognitive model is unable to account for a specific (behavioral) phenomenon. This becomes even more important when several model candidates are compared (see the Model Comparison section). Navarro (2019, p. 234) argued that showing how the qualitative patterns in the empirical data emerge from a computational model is often more scientifically useful than presenting a quantified measure of its performance.

Simulation also includes parameter recovery; that is, when artificial data are produced with a specific set of parameters, and the model is fitted to those data (see below), the estimated parameters should be close to the ones that generated the artificial data.

Parameter Estimation

Starting with a particular model, the major interest is to find the set of parameters that best accounts for observed data. This is also referred to as fitting the model to the data. We distinguish between free (to be estimated) parameters and fixed parameters. Ideally, free parameters are related to psychological concepts and interpreted accordingly. They also may serve to summarize differences between experimental conditions and experimental groups. Some other parameters may be added to the model to improve the fit. They appear sometimes ad hoc and are not related to psychological concepts. Fixed parameters are set and often part of the model's genuine feature, for instance, in a diffusion process, the diffusion coefficient (randomness). Note that in cognitive sciences, the number of parameters is kept as small as possible so as not to have too flexible a model.

There are many different ways how to estimate the parameters from data. Indeed, Farrell and Lewandowsky (2018) devoted roughly half of their book to this topic.

Before selecting a particular method to estimate the free parameters from the data, we need to decide what kind of measure to take to minimize the deviance between the model's predictions and the data. In other words, we seek those parameters that maximize the similarity between the data and the model predictions. Clearly, this becomes an optimization problem, and the function that maximizes or minimizes an output value by systematically choosing input values—for example, selecting parameter values from a (predefined) set—is called an *objective function*.

Here the objective function itself may include a discrepancy measure such as the mean of the squared deviation between the data and the model prediction, the square root of it, or root mean square error of approximation (RMSEA), variations of chi-squared test formulas, or any goodness-of-fit measure that is appropriate (e.g., Browne & Cudeck, 1992; Chechile, 1999; Smith & Vickers, 1988). For instance, fitting the dynamic dual process model to a risky decision situation with two frames (gain and loss), two deadlines for making a decision (short and long) and nine gambles (probability and value combinations), Diederich and Trueblood (2018) minimized the function

$$\chi^2 = \sum_{i=1}^{72} \left(\frac{RT_{obs}^i - RT_{pred}^i}{SE_{RT_{obs}}^i} \right)^2 + \sum_{i=1}^{36} \left(\frac{Pr_{obs}^i - Pr_{pred}^i}{SE_{Pr_{obs}}^i} \right)^2 \tag{23.1}$$

for estimating the parameters from 72 mean choice response times (choice between sure option and lottery) and 36 choice frequencies for the lottery (or the sure option). RT_{obs}^i and RT_{pred}^i are the observed and the model's predicted mean response times related to condition I, respectively, $SE_{RT_{obs}}^i$ is the observed standard error for i. Similar notation holds for the choice probabilities (Pr). Note that for statistical testing, not rejecting the null hypothesis is the desired outcome for a fitted model.

Another approach to estimate parameters includes maximum likelihood estimation (MLE). It estimates the parameters of a probability distribution (rather than means, for instance) by maximizing a likelihood function. Assume that we observed a sample of n response times $y = \{(y)_1, y_2, \ldots, y_n)$, that is, realizations from random variables Y_i, and the model accounting for the observations includes k parameters $\boldsymbol{\theta} = (\theta_1, \theta_2, \ldots, \theta_k)$. The real-valued function

$$L(\boldsymbol{\theta}|y) = f(y|\boldsymbol{\theta}) \tag{23.2}$$

is called the likelihood function. That is, as a function of y with fixed $\boldsymbol{\theta}$, $f(y|\boldsymbol{\theta})$ is a probability (density/mass) function; as a function of $\boldsymbol{\theta}$ with fixed y, $f(y|\boldsymbol{\theta})$ is a likelihood function.

For a random sample (independent and identically distributed variables), it is the product of n individual functions

$$f(y|\boldsymbol{\theta}) = \prod_{i=1}^{n} f(y_i|\boldsymbol{\theta}),$$

and taking the logarithm, it becomes the log-likelihood

$$LL(\boldsymbol{\theta}|y) = \ln f(y|\boldsymbol{\theta}) = \sum_{i=1}^{n} \ln f(y_i|\boldsymbol{\theta}). \tag{23.3}$$

Maximum likelihood parameter estimation seeks to find those parameters that maximize the likelihood of the chosen model for the given set of data. This method plays a major role in Bayesian parameter estimation (Feinberg & Gonzales, 2007; Farrell & Lewandowsky, 2018, devote several chapters to it).

Parameter estimation techniques are computer algorithms, often as part of a computer program such as MATLAB, Python, R, and so on. That is, there is no need to develop a computer program for minimizing or maximizing the objective function. For instance, the MATLAB Optimization Toolbox offers a family of algorithms for solving optimization problems, including primal and dual simplex algorithms, originally based on the Nelder-Mead simplex method. The Python optimizing methods and the R package "optimization" also include the simplex methods (e.g., George & Raimond, 2013; Sun et al., 2019; for a survey of methods, Beasley & Rodgers, 2012).

Closely related to the previous two topics are model complexity and parameter recovery. Myung and Pitt (1997) defined *model complexity* or *model flexibility* as the model's ability to fit diverse patterns of data. They identified three dimensions of a model that contribute to its complexity: the number of parameters, the mode's functional form, and the extension of the parameter space.

Adding more parameters to the model typically gives a better fit of the data. To give a simple and intuitive example: the higher the degree of a polynomial model is, the better it can be fitted to even very noisy data. Several goodness-of-fit measures take the number of parameters into account. They penalize models with many parameters as compared to models with fewer parameters. Example of measures are listed in the next section on model comparison.

The functional form is defined as the way in which parameters are combined in the model equation. For instance, for psychophysical models mapping the intensity of a physical stimulus, I, onto the perceived magnitude, Steven's power law, $\psi(I) = k \cdot I^a$, is more complex than Fechner's law with the same number of parameters, $\psi(I) = k \cdot ln(I + a)$, because the parameter a in Steven's law can take on any value in R, and therefore allows for convex, concave, and linear functional curvatures whereas Fechner's law is only defined for $a \in R^+$, restricting it to concave functions (cf. Myung & Pitt, 1997; Townsend, 1975). Thus, Steven's law can account for a much broader pattern of data, and therefore, is more difficult to falsify. The third dimension of model complexity is extension of parameter space and demonstrated in the previous example. The parameter space may cover the entire real numbers or is restricted to a subset of it. Obviously, the more restrictions there are, the less flexible the model is.

Computational and statistical modeling are used as *explanations* or as *predictions* (Shmueli, 2010), in psychology also referred to as *measurements* (Farrell & Lewandowsky, 2018). In the context of statistical modeling, Shmueli (2010) defined the relationship between theory and data *explaining* as causal explanation and *explanatory modeling* as the use of models for testing causal explanations. The hypotheses are given in terms of theoretical constructs (p. 290).

When a model is used as measurement model (predictive model), conclusions are drawn from parameter estimates; the purpose here is to predict future observations. According to Shmueli (2010), predictions (measurements) include point or interval predictions, predictive regions, and predictive distributions (p. 291). When a model is used as measurement model, it is important to know whether the parameters are identifiable—that is, whether the set of parameter values can be determined from the set of data and whether the model can recover the parameters. Parameter recovery includes the following steps: The computational model simulates data with known parameter values. Then the model is fitted to these simulated data. Typically, this procedure is repeated for several sets of parameters. Ideally, the estimated parameters are identical (or close) to the ones that generated the data (see, e.g., Hübner & Pelzer, 2020; Kandil et al., 2014; van Ravenzwaaij & Oberauer, 2009; for examples of parameter recovery studies for different models).

Model Comparison

Science relies on accumulated knowledge, and the scientific method (see above) requires new empirical evidence to be built into the model. A new model may replace a previous one and/or compete with other models. Before answering the question of which model is best supported by the data, some of the issues addressed before need to be checked. Is the model falsifiable—that is, does the model make predictions that can be tested empirically? Are the model parameters identifiable—that is, is there a unique mapping between a specific set of parameters and a specific set of data? Does the model make qualitative predictions that reflect the patterns in the data? When the models meet these criteria, they are compared by goodness-of-fit measures that take the number of parameters into account. Some measures also deal with model flexibility. Most, if not all, goodness-of-fit measures have been developed in the context of testing structural equation models (see Cole & Ciesla, 2012; Flaherty & Kiff, 2012; Steyer et al., 2012).

Some widely used measures for computational models involving MLE (Equations 23.2 and 23.3) are the Akaike information criterion (AIC; Akaike, 1983) and the Bayesian information criterion

(BIC; Schwarz, 1978). The AIC for model i with k_i free parameters is

$$AIC_i = -2\widehat{LL}_i + 2k_i \qquad (23.4)$$

where $\widehat{LL}_i$ is the maximized value of the log-likelihood (Equation 23.3) for the ith-model with estimated parameter values $\hat{\theta}_i$ that maximized the likelihood function. The model with the smallest AIC should be chosen.

The BIC is similar to the AIC except that it also includes the number of observations n:

$$BIC_i = -2\widehat{LL}_i + k_i \ln n. \qquad (23.5)$$

For fewer than eight observations ($\exp(2) = 7.39$), BIC is smaller than AIC and grows slowly as n increases ($\ln(1000) = 6.91$). For a detailed discussion of both measures with respect to the philosophical background (information theory versus Bayesian theory) and statistical properties see Burnham and Anderson (2004) and Vrieze (2012).

Another goodness-of-fit measures is the RMSEA (R^*; Browne & Cudeck, 1992; Steiger, 1990):

$$R^* = \sqrt{\frac{F^*}{\upsilon}}. \qquad (23.6)$$

F^* is the Population Noncentrality Index (PNI), a measure of badness-of-fit (Steiger, 1990). As Steiger (n.d., p. 5) pointed out, model complexity is directly related to the number of free parameters and inversely to the number of degrees of freedom (υ). Therefore, dividing the PNI by the degrees of freedom accounts for model complexity and taking the square root of the ratio returns the index to the same metric as the original standardized parameters (Steiger, n.d., p. 5).

For example, Schubert et al. (2017) used this measure when fitting quantiles of a diffusion model to the empirical RT quantiles (Ratcliff, 2012). Using a χ^2 statistics (the squared difference between the observed and predicted quantile values, divided by the predicted quantile values and then summed up, slightly different from Equation 23.1) as objective function, the PNI

is defined as $F^* = \chi^2 - df$. The degrees of freedom are defined in terms of the number of experimental conditions, c, number of response bins, b, and number of free parameters, k—that is, $\upsilon = c(2b - 1) - k$. The number of participants, N, is also included in the denominator:

$$R^* = \sqrt{\frac{\max(F^*, 0)}{\upsilon(N-1)}}. \qquad (23.7)$$

Obviously, the smaller R^*, the better is the model fit. If χ^2 is smaller than υ, zero is taken. Summaries and evaluation of goodness-of-fit measures are provided by, for instance, Evren and Tuna (2012) based on statistical entropy, Steiger (n.d.), and many more. Farrell and Lewandowsky (2018) described Bayesian model comparison using Bayes factors in Chapter 11 of their book.

Besides comparing competing models on the basis of goodness-of fit measures, several other methods have been proposed, like cross-validation procedures likelihood ratio tests, in particular for nested models, and many more (Nezlek, 2012; Rindskopf, 2012).

EXAMPLE OF THE MODELING PROCESS WITH TWO COMPETING CONNECTIONIST MODELS

The following simple example demonstrates with two competing connectionist models for categorical learning how the modeling process is performed.

Categorizing (perceptual) objects or patterns in distinct classes is important to many real-life situations. Does the functional magnetic resonance imaging scan indicate disease A or B or none? Are these cells cancerous or not? Is this a female or male face? What ethnic group do these people belong to? Often, people are very successful in performing these and similar tasks, but sometimes they are not. How do we learn to categorize objects, and how do we generalize our knowledge to objects we have not seen before?

Step 1

The first step in the modeling process to answer these questions is to come up with a conceptual theoretical framework. This requires creativity on the part of the researcher and involves hard work. For the current demonstration two existing and competing theoretical frameworks for categorization are taken: a prototype model and an exemplar model. According to the prototype model, some members of a category are more central than others. The person extracts the central tendency (sometimes referred to as characteristic features) of the examples presented during a learning phase and uses these characteristic features to form a prototype, which serves as basis for categorizing new objects. That is, when a new target object is presented, it is compared with the prototypical object of each category, and the category with the most similar prototype is chosen. According to the exemplar model, the learner stores specific instances (*exemplars*) for each category. When a new target stimulus is presented, the similarity of the target to each stored example is computed for each category, and the category with the greatest total similarity is chosen.

Step 2

The second step is to describe the objects in an abstract formal way, translate the assumptions into equations, and describe the response also in a rigorous form. Here, we take a connectionist version of a prototype model and a connectionist version of an exemplar model (e.g., Nosofsky et al., 1992). There has been a long debate about which of these two models (prototype versus exemplar) best represents category learning, and some question whether it is possible to distinguish empirically.

Digression.   Before describing the models in more detail, we define the general framework of key features for connectionist processing (Rumelhart et al., 1986; Thomas & McClelland, 2008) to fix some notation.

1. A *set of processing units* u_i, organized in layers and often divided into input units, which receive the information to be processed; output units, which provide the results of the processing; and hidden units, in which specific computations necessary for the entire process

may be performed. The units can be interpreted as natural and artificial neurons and groups of neurons. For cognitive models, the input units may represent perceptual features, letters, faces, and so on, and output units may represent words, phonemes, or ethnic groups. All the processing is carried out by these units. The system is parallel, as many simple operations are carried out simultaneously. Units in a computer simulation are virtual entities and usually presented by circles.

2. A *state of activation* for each unit, a_i, at a given time $t, a_i(t)$. The state of a set of units at time t are organized in a vector, $a(t) = (a_1(t), a_2(t), \ldots, a_i(t) \ldots, a_n(t))$. The activation values can be any numeric value but often they are real numbers bounded between 0 and 1. The analogy to neural activity is the neuron's firing rate (rate of action potentials). A zero would indicate the least and a one the most possible activity of a neuron.

3. The *pattern of connectivity*. To make a network, units need to be connected. If units are analogous to neurons, connections are analogous to synapses. Connections are represented with lines and arrows indicate the flow of information from one unit to the next. In a standard, three-layer feedforward network (described later), activation is sent from all input units to all hidden units to all output units in a single direction—that is, a directed graph with nodes and intermodal connections. The strength or weakness of a connection between any two units determines the extent to which the activation state of one unit can affect the activation state of another unit and can be measured by a connection weight, w. The connections weights of all units are organized in a matrix $\mathbf{W} = \|w_{ij}\|$. Often connection weights are real numbers between -1 and 1. High connection weights represent a strong connection while low weights represent a weak connection, analogous to excitatory and inhibitory synapses.

4. The *propagation rule*. This rule determines how activation is propagated through the network. The activation values of the sending units

are combined with the connection weights to produce the net input into the receiving units, usually by a linear function. That is, the inputs from all sending units are multiplied by the connection weights and summed to get the overall input of the receiving units, that is, the net input for the receiving units is $net(t) = W \cdot a(t)$. The net input for a specific unit, i, is therefore, $net_i(t) = \sum_j w_{ij}\, a_j(t)$.

5. The *activation rule*. This rule specifies how the combined or net input of a given unit is transformed to produce its new activation state $a_i(t + 1)$, and is expressed in terms of a function F, such that $a_i(t + 1) = F(net_i(t))$. Typically, the activation F is chosen from a small selection of functions including $F(x) = \text{sgn}(x)$, producing binary (± 1) output; $F(x) = (sgn(x) + 1)/2$, producing binary (0/1) output; $F(x) = (1 + e^{-x})^{-1}$, the sigmoidal (logistic) nonlinearity, producing output between 0 and 1; $F(x) = \tanh(x)$, producing output between -1 and 1; and some other forms are also possible. The net input can take on any value and the function F ascertains that the new activation state does not exceed the maximum or minimum activation values (e.g., above 1 or below 0).

6. The *learning rule*. Learning in a neural network involves modifying the connection weights and finding the right weights is at the heart of connectionist models. The learning rule is an algorithm and specifies how the connectivity changes over time as a function of experience, that is, data. For instance, the simplest learning rule assumes that the weight w_{ij} between two units u_i and u_j changes proportional to the respective activation values—that is, I $w_{ij} = w_{ij}(t + 1) - w_{ij}(t) = \eta a_i a_j$, where the constant η is called *learning rate*. Basically, it determines the step size at each iteration. There is a variety of learning algorithms. They differ from each other in the way in which the adjustment of the connection weights of a unit is formulated (e.g., Haykin, 1999, for a detailed description of several algorithms). Specific learning rules depend on the architecture of the neural network. In addition, various learning para-

digms refer to models of the environment in which the neural network operates. Any given network architecture can usually be employed in any given learning paradigm.

7. *Network architectures*. There are three fundamentally different classes of network architectures:

   - *Single-layer feedforward networks*. The input layer of source nodes projects on an output layer of computational nodes but not vice versa. It is strictly feed-forward. The notion "single-layer" refers to the output layer of the computational nodes. The input layer is not counted since no computation takes place.

   - *Multilayer feedforward networks*. One or more hidden layers or hidden units are sandwiched between the input layer and the output layer. The hidden units intervene between the external input and the network output in some way. Typically, the units in each layer of the network have as their inputs the output signals of the preceding layer. If every node in each layer of the network is connected to every other node in the adjacent forward layer, the neural network is fully connected. If a connection is missing the neural network is partially connected.

   - *Recurrent networks*. The network has at least one feedback loop. The feedback loops may be self-feedback loops—that is, the output of a neuron is fed back into its own input or no self-feedback loops, for instance, when the output is fed back to the inputs of all the other neurons.

8. *Learning paradigms*. There are three major learning paradigms: supervised learning, unsupervised learning, and reinforcement learning.

   - *Supervised learning*, also referred to as *learning with a teacher*. In supervised learning, there is given a set of data, the training set, which consists of the input (e.g., object patterns) and the desired output (e.g., classification). That is, the input is given together with the correct output, also called target. The parameters of the network are gradually adjusted to match the input and desired output by going through the training set many times. The aim of the supervised neural network is to predict the correct answer to new data that were not included in the training set. That is, the network is expected to learn certain aspects of the input–output pairs in the training set and to apply to it new data.

- *Unsupervised learning*, also referred to as self-organized leaning or learning without a teacher. In unsupervised learning a correct or desired output is not known—that is, there is no input–output pair. This type of learning is often used to form natural groups or clusters of objects based on similarity between objects.

- *Reinforcement learning*. In reinforcement learning the only information given for each input–output pair is whether the neural network produced the desired result or not or the total reward given for an output response. The weights are updated based solely on this global feedback (that is, the Boolean values true or false or the reward value) (for details, see, e.g., Rojas, 1996).

As an example for a learning rule, consider the single-unit perceptron (Figure 23.1), which is the simplest version of a feed-forward neural network and classifies inputs into two distinct categories. That is, it maps a real-valued input

vector a (e.g., describing visual objects) to a binary output value y (e.g., category A or B). Furthermore, the neural network applies a reinforcement paradigm. The architecture of this model in the above introduced notation is

$$y = F\left(\sum_{j=1}^{n} w_j a_j(t) + w_0\right) = sgn\left(\sum_{j=1}^{n} w_j a_j(t) + w_0\right),$$
(23.8)

where w_0 is a bias factor. The bias has the effect of increasing or lowering the net input of the activation function, depending on whether it is positive or negative, respectively. Setting $a_0 \equiv 1$ the above equation can be written as

$$y = sgn\left(\sum_{j=0}^{n} w_j a_j(t)\right) = sgn(w'a(t)).$$
(23.9)

Denote the set of training or learning data as $D = \{[a(t), z(t)], t = 1, \ldots, m\}$, where $\{z(t)\}$ contains the binary classification variables ± 1, the desired activation state at time t and $a(t) = (a_0(t), a_1(t), \ldots, a_n(t))$ is the state activation vector for the observation at time t as before. Learning is modeled by updating the weight vector w during m iterations for all training examples. That is, for each pair in D and for each iteration t, the weight w is updated according to

$$\Delta w_j = w_j(t+1) - w_j(t) = \eta(z - y)a_j,$$
(23.10)

where the constant η (> 0) is the learning rate, and the learning rule is called the *delta rule*. The delta rule is related to a gradient descent type of method for optimization.

End of digression. For the two connectionist models for categorization, we assume very simple objects characterized by only two dimensions. These could be saturation and brightness, length and orientation, distance between eyes and length of mouth, and so on. The stimuli are conveniently described in forms of vectors. A stimulus is denoted $S = (s_1, s_2)$, where s_1 represents the value of the stimulus on the first dimension and s_2 represents the value of the stimulus on the second dimension. Consider the connectionist version of the prototype model first.

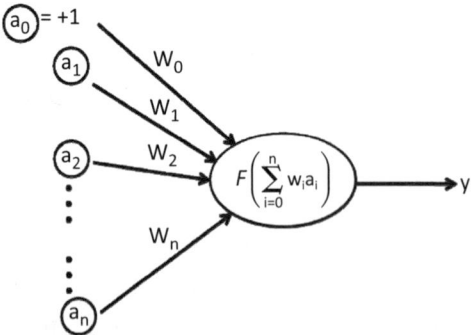

FIGURE 23.1. A simple single-unit perceptron, also known as McCulloch-Pitts neuron (McCulloch & Pitts, 1943).

Connectionist version of the prototype model.
The model assumes that a stimulus is represented
by two sets of input units: One set, u_1, is activated by the value of the stimulus on the first
dimension, s_1; and the other set, u_2, is activated
by the value of the stimulus on the second
dimension, s_2. The number of units in each set
is p, $u_i = \{u_{i1}, u_{i2}, \ldots, u_{ip}\}$, $i = 1, 2$, and so there
are a total of $2 \cdot p$ units. Obviously, this can be
written as $u_1 \cup u_2 = \{u_1, \ldots, u_p, u_{p+1}, \ldots, u_{2p}\}$.
Each unit within a set is designed to detect a
particular stimulus value, which is called the
ideal point of the unit. This may be considered in
analogy to neuronal tuning. Neurons responding
best to specific orientation, movement direction,
disparity, frequency, and the like are said to be
tuned to that orientation, movement direction,
disparity, frequency. The ideal point value of
each unit is not naturally given but needs to be
defined. These additional detailed assumptions
(called *ad hoc assumptions*) are necessary in order
to complete the model. That is, for the prototype
model, assumptions about what features should
be used to represent the stimuli to be categorized
need to be added and also formulated in an
abstract way.

The jth unit in the first set is designed to
detect a stimulus value, z_{1j}, that is, the ideal
point of that unit and the activation of this unit,
denoted $a_{1j}(t)$, is determined by the similarity
of s_i presented at trial t to the ideal point z_{1j}.
Analogously, the jth unit in the second set is
designed to detect a stimulus value, z_{2j}, and the
activation of this unit, denoted $a_{2j}(t)$, is determined
by the similarity of the ideal point z_{2j} to s_2 presented
at trial t.

How large the set U is, depends on how many
specific features are to be coded. For instance,
Le Cun et al. (1989) developed a network for
zip-code recognition, in which 7,291 handwritten
zip-code digits were processed such to fit into a
16×16 pixel image with grey levels in the range
of -1 to $+1$. Thus, the dimensionality of each
input is 256.

The similarity between the current stimulus
value s_i and the ideal point z_{ij}, for each unit j is
determined by the following function:

$$f_{sim}(z_{ij}, s_i) = \exp\left(-\left(\frac{z_{ij} - s_i}{\sigma}\right)^2\right),$$

$$i = 1, 2 \qquad j = 1, \ldots, p. \qquad (23.11)$$

The choice of this function is another
ad hoc assumption. Indeed, there are a variety
of similarity functions one can choose from.
The proposed one is related to Shepard's (1987)
so-called universal law stating that the perceived
similarity between two entities is an exponential
decay function of their distance. In the present
example the similarity function is Gaussian
(exponent is 2).

The parameter σ is called the *discriminability*
parameter, and it determines the width or spread
of the activation around the ideal point. A low
discriminability parameter (large σ) makes it
hard to discriminate differences between the
stimulus value and the ideal point, and a high
discriminability parameter (small σ) makes easy-
to-discriminate differences between the stimulus
value and the ideal point. That is, it determines
the rate at which similarity declines with distance.
The values of the function range between 0 and 1.
If the stimulus value s_i and the ideal point z_{ij} are
identical, the function takes on the value 1. If the
stimulus value s_i is far apart from the ideal point z_{ij},
the function approaches 0.

The input activation $a_{ij}(t)$ generated at the
jth unit is determined by the similarity of that
unit relative to the sum of the similarity of all
the units:

$$a_{ij}(t) = \frac{f_{sim}(z_{ij}, s_i)}{\sum_{j=1}^{p} f_{sim}(z_{ij}, s_i)},$$

$$i = 1, 2 \qquad j = 1, \ldots, p. \qquad (23.12)$$

The input units are connected to two output
units, one for each category. The activation
of the two category units is denoted $c_1(t)$ and
$c_2(t)$ for category C_1 and C_2, respectively. The
connection weight, w_{ijk}, connects the input
activation $a_{ij}(t)$ to the kth output unit, $k = 1, 2$.
The propagation rule—that is, the function
that combines the input activation with the

connection weights to produce the input to the output units—is

$$c_k(t) = \sum_{j=1}^{p} w_{1jk} a_{1j}(t) + \sum_{j=1}^{p} w_{2jk} a_{2j}(t), \qquad k = 1, 2.$$
(23.13)

This is the net input for unit k, such that $c_k(t) = net_k(t)$. The set of weights $\{w_{11k}, \ldots, w_{1pk};$ $w_{21k}, \ldots, w_{2pk}\}$ connecting the inputs to the output for category C_k forms a representation of the prototype pattern for category C_k. The more similar the input activation pattern is to these weights, the more likely the stimulus matches the prototype for category C_k.

The connection weights are updated according to the delta learning rule (Equation 23.10):

$$\Delta w_{ijk} = w_{ijk}(t+1) - w_{ijk}(t) = \eta \cdot [h_k(t) - c_k(t)] \cdot a_{ij},$$
(23.14)

where $h_k(t)$ is the indicator function with $h_k(t) = 1$ for the desired category and 0 otherwise.

The whole learning process begins with some initial weights, and usually these are randomly assigned to represent a state of ignorance at the beginning of the learning process. Alternatively, if some prior knowledge or training exists, then the initial weights can be set to values that represent this prior knowledge or training.

The architecture of the connectionist version of the prototype model is presented in Figure 23.2.

One essential step in computational modeling is to implement the model onto the computer—that is, writing codes and algorithms for training the model and estimating the parameters.

To do so it is convenient to rewrite the equations in matrix format. Computer languages such as MATLAB, Mathematica, Python, and R have built-in matrix operators, which allows effective programming leading to fast computations.

The deviation between the p ideal points and the stimulus value s_i in Equation 23.11 can be written as p-dimensional vector d_i, $i = 1, 2$ with

$$d_i = \frac{1}{\sigma}(z_i - s_i O),$$
(23.15)

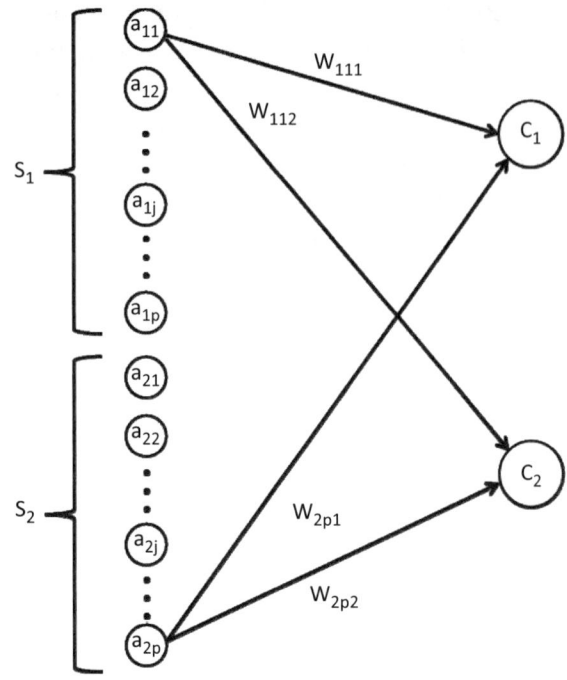

FIGURE 23.2. Architecture of the connectionist version of the prototype model.

where z_i is a vector of length p with the p ideal points for dimension i and O is a p-dimensional vector containing ones. The similarity function is

$$f_{sim}(z_i, s_i) = \exp(-d_i^{\cdot 2}),$$
(23.16)

where $\cdot 2$ means the elementwise square of the vector.

The activation function in Equation 23.12 is a p-dimensional vector with

$$a_i(t) = \frac{1}{O^T \cdot f_{sim}(z_i, s_i)} f_{sim}(z_i, s_i), \qquad i = 1, 2$$
(23.17)

where O^T is the transposed vector with ones, that is, a row vector. Note that $(O^T \cdot f_{sim}(z_i, s_i))$ is the inner product, which produces a scalar.

Obviously, the activation for both stimulus dimensions can be expressed in one vector of length 2p with $a(t) = \begin{pmatrix} a_1(t) \\ a_2(t) \end{pmatrix}$. The weights for each category are arranged in a $2 \times p$ matrix

$W = \begin{bmatrix} w_1^T \\ w_2^T \end{bmatrix}$. The propagation rule in Equation 23.6 can be written as

$$c(t) = Wa(t), \qquad (23.18)$$

where $c(t) = \begin{pmatrix} c_1(t) \\ c_2(t) \end{pmatrix}$ is a vector of length 2 with the activation of the two category units for category C_1 and C_2, respectively.

Finally, the delta rule (Equation 23.14) can be written as

$$\Delta W = W(t+1) - W(t) = \eta \cdot [h(t) - c(t)] \cdot a, \qquad (23.19)$$

where $h(t) = \begin{pmatrix} h_1(t) \\ h_2(t) \end{pmatrix}$ is the 2-dimensional vector of the indicator function with 1 for the desired category and 0 otherwise.

There are numerous ways to write the algorithms and programs for the model. A convenient one is to divide the program in several subprograms and address only those necessary for a specific purpose. For instance, estimating parameters from data require different steps than simulating predictions of the model over a set of predefined parameters. However, both routines involve the computational model. An example of the model written in MATLAB codes is found in Table 23.1. Subprograms in MATLAB are called "functions" and received input from, and provide output to, other parts of the program. For demonstrational reasons, the expressions are taken apart. For experienced programmers, they can be written more compactly. These functions are embedded in a larger frame where parameters such as the delta and sigma are defined, stimuli vectors are read, ideal points are defined, and so forth. For an example of a complete program, see Busemeyer and Diederich (2010).

Connectionist version of the exemplar model.
The model assumes that the inputs to the network form a square grid with p rows and p columns—that is, a $p \times p$ matrix. Each point on the grid,

TABLE 23.1

MATLAB Codes for Determining the Similarity Function and Weights for the Prototype Model

Program command	Comment
function[a] = protoac(Z,S, sigma,j);	Input and output of function
fsim=exp(-((Z-S(j))./sigma).^2);	Calculating similarity
a=fsim/sum(fsim);	Calculation activation
function[W] = prototype(eta,p)	
W = zeros(2,p)	Initial connection weights
for j=1:p	Loop for stimuli
[a1]=protoac(Z1,S1,sigma,j);	Activation for category 1
[a2]=protoac(Z2,S2,sigma,j);	Activation for category 2
c=W*[a1;a2];	Propagation
W1=eta*([1;0]-c)*a1;	Adjusting weights for c1
W2=eta*([0;1]-c)*a2;	Adjusting weights for c2
W=W+W1+W2;	Updating the weights
End	End of loop

that is, each cell of the matrix represents a single input unit. Each unit on the grid is designed to detect a pair of stimulus values. In particular, the unit on the grid point corresponding to row i and column j is designed to detect the value $z_{ij} = [z_i, z_j]$, which is the ideal point for this unit. The difference between the assumptions of the prototype model and the exemplar model is obvious. For the prototype model a unit is tuned to exactly one feature, but the exemplar model assumes that as unit is tuned to two (or possibly more) features. The stimulus $S = (s_1, s_2)$ activates a circular receptive field of grid points. Note that the analogy to neural structures in the brain is drawn, including the same terminology. A receptive field of a neuron in the visual system, for instance, is a restricted area of the retina that influences the firing rate of that neuron because of light. Receptive fields of ganglion cells have a concentric form with a center-surround organization. A receptive field in the context of artificial neural networks is a restricted network with local connections which may or may not be concentric. The centroid of the receptive field is located at the pair of stimulus values (s_1, s_2). The amount of activation of a nearby input unit declines as a function of the distance of the unit from this center. The activation of this unit, $a_{ij}(t)$, is determined by the similarity of the stimulus S to the ideal point z_{ij} denoted $f_{sim}(z_{ij}, S)$ and defined as

$$f_{sim}(z_{ij}, S) = \exp\left(-\left(\frac{z_i - s_1}{\sigma}\right)^2\right) \bullet \exp\left(-\left(\frac{z_j - s_2}{\sigma}\right)^2\right),$$

$$i = 1, \ldots, p \qquad j = 1, \ldots, p. \qquad (23.20)$$

This is a type of a bivariate Gaussian distribution and is used to form the receptive field. As for the prototype model the values of the function range between 0 and 1. If the stimulus values of both dimensions (s_1, s_2) and the ideal point (z_i, z_j) are identical, the function takes on the value 1. If the stimulus value of at least one dimension, s_i, $i = 1, 2$, is far apart from its ideal point, z_i, $i = 1, 2$, the function approaches 0, regardless of the difference between the stimulus value and its ideal point of the other dimension.

The parameter σ is interpreted as the discriminability parameter and has the same effect as it had before for the prototype model. Low discriminability (large values of σ) produces a large receptive field, which makes it hard to detect differences among stimuli. High discriminability (small values of σ) produces a small receptive field, which makes it easy to detect differences among stimuli.

The input activation $a_{ij}(t)$ generated at the unit in the ith row and jth column is determined by the similarity of that unit relative to the sum of similarity of all the units:

$$a_{ij}(t) = \frac{f_{sim}(z_{ij}, S)}{\sum_{i=1}^{p} \sum_{j=1}^{p} f_{sim}(z_{ij}, S)},$$

$$i = 1, \ldots, p \qquad j = 1, \ldots, p. \qquad (23.21)$$

A stimulus produces a bivariate distribution of input activations on the grid, which is centered around the pair of stimulus values. As before, the input units are connected to two category units, one for each category and the activation of the two category units are $c_k(t)$, $k = 1, 2$, for category $C_k(t)$, $k = 1, 2$. Each unit on the grid has a connection weight, w_{ijk}, which connects the input

activation $a_{ij}(t)$ to the kth output unit, $k = 1, 2$. The propagation rule for the exemplar model is

$$c_k(t) = \sum_{i=1}^{p} \sum_{j=1}^{p} w_{ijk} a_{ij}(t), \qquad k = 1, 2. \qquad (23.22)$$

This model is called an exemplar model because each receptive field of a training stimulus is associated with the output category units through a separate set of connection weights. Thus, the model simply associates each region of the stimulus space with a response, and similar examples get mapped to similar responses.

As for the prototype model, the connection weights are updated according to the delta learning rule:

$$\Delta w_{ijk} = w_{ijk}(t+1) - w_{ijk}(t) = \eta \bullet [h_k(t) - c_k(t)] \bullet a_{ij},$$

$$(23.23)$$

where $h_k(t)$ is the indicator function with $h_k(t) = 1$ for the desired category and 0 otherwise.

The architecture of the connectionist version of the exemplar model is presented in Figure 23.3.

The matrix form of the exemplar model is derived as follows. The deviations between the ideal points and the stimulus values on each dimension are the same as in Equation 23.15. The similarities for these deviations are the same as in Equation 23.16. The function in Equation 23.20 is one point on the grid (one input unit); all the elements on the $p \times p$ grid of input units can be computed by the Kronecker product $\otimes$:

$$f_{sim}(Z, S) = f_{sim}(z_1, s_1) \otimes f_{sim}(z_2, s_2). \qquad (23.24)$$

Note that $f_{sim}(Z, S)$ is a p^2 vector with elements as defined in Equation 23.21. This could have been arranged differently, as a $p \times p$ matrix, by setting $f_{sim}(Z, S) = f_{sim}(z_1, s_1) \bullet f_{sim}(z_2, s_2)^T$. It depends on what is more convenient for the remaining steps in the calculation but is also a matter of taste of the individual researcher.

The input activations for all the input units on the $p \times p$ grid are

$$a(t) = \frac{1}{O^T \bullet f_{sim}(z, S)} f_{sim}(z, S). \qquad (23.25)$$

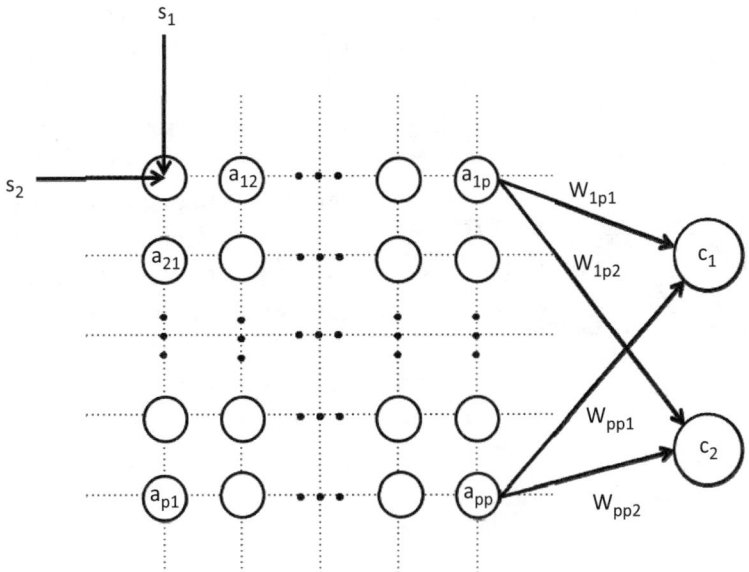

FIGURE 23.3.   Architecture of the connectionist version of the exemplar model.

$a(t)$ is a p^2 vector with elements as defined in Equation 23.22. The propagation rule and the delta rule are analogous to Equation 23.18 and Equation 23.19, respectively. The algorithm for this part of the model can be found in Table 23.2.

Step 3

The third step of the modeling process is to derive the predictions of the models. The predictions can be qualitative and quantitative. Although qualitative predictions do not require specific parameter values of the model (the predictions

hold for all possible parameter values), quantitative predictions do require specific values for the free parameters of the model. Probing the model includes both qualitative and quantitative tests. For a qualitative test, the model predicts characteristic patterns which are compared to patterns observed in data. For the quantitative test, the free parameters of the model are estimated from data and a goodness-of-fit measure (see above) provides information about how well the model describes the data in a statistical sense. (For a broader discussion on qualitative versus quantitative tests, see Busemeyer and Diederich, 2010.)

Both models make predictions with respect to two different transfer tests: a generalization test and a recognition test. For the generalization test, new stimuli, not previously presented in the training set are classified. For the recognition test, new and old stimuli—that is, those presented in the training set are mixed and classified as *new* and *old*.

For the generalization test, the models assume that the probability of choosing category C_k for a new stimulus S_{new} (i.e., not an element of the training set) is based on a ratio of strength of the output activations. After t trials of training,

TABLE 23.2

MATLAB Codes for Determining the Similarity Function and Weights for the Exemplar Model

Program command	Comment
function[a] = exempac(Z1,Z2,S1,S2, sigma,j);	Input and output of function
fsim1=exp(-((Z1-S1(j))./sigma).^2);	Calculating similarity
fsim2=exp(-((Z2-S2(j))./sigma).^2);	
fsim=kron(fsim1,fsim2);	
a=fsim/sum(fsim);	Calculation activation

the output for category $k = 1$ is $c_1(t)$ and the probability for choosing C_1 is

$$Pr[C_1|S_{new}] = \frac{\exp(\beta \cdot c_1(t))}{\exp(\beta \cdot c_1(t)) + \exp(\beta \cdot c_2(t))}$$

$$= \frac{1}{1 + \exp(-\beta(-c_1(t) + c_2(t)))} \quad (23.26)$$

and the probability for choosing C_2 is

$$Pr[C_2|S_{new}] = 1 - Pr[C_1|S_{new}]. \quad (23.27)$$

That is, the activation rule, which specifies how the net input of a given unit produces

its new activation state, is the logistic function $F(x) = (1 + e^{-x})^{-1}$, where $x = \beta(-c_1(t) + c_2(t))$. The coefficient, β, is called a sensitivity parameter. Increasing the sensitivity parameter decreases the value for $\exp(-\beta)$ and therefore increases the $F(x)$. That is, increasing the sensitivity increase the slope of the function that relates the choice probability to the activation of a category. Here it increases the probability for choosing C_1 with activation $c_1(t)$.

The predictions of both models over a range of parameters are presented in Figure 23.4. In particular, the sensitivity parameter β ranged from 0 to 15 in unit steps, the learning parameter η

a. Prototype: Generalization predictions

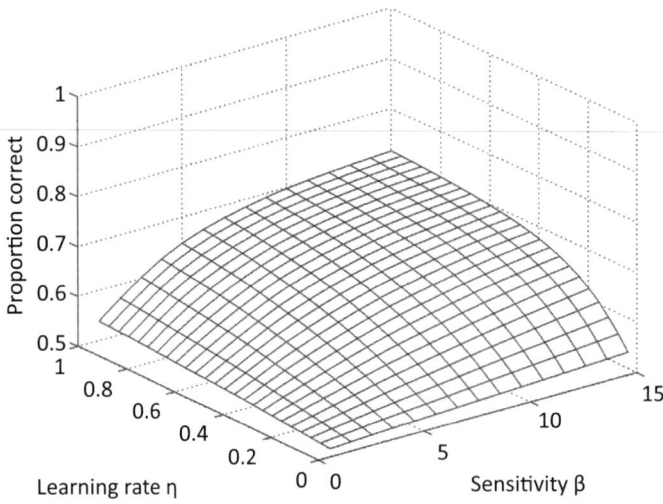

b. Exemplar: Generalization predictions

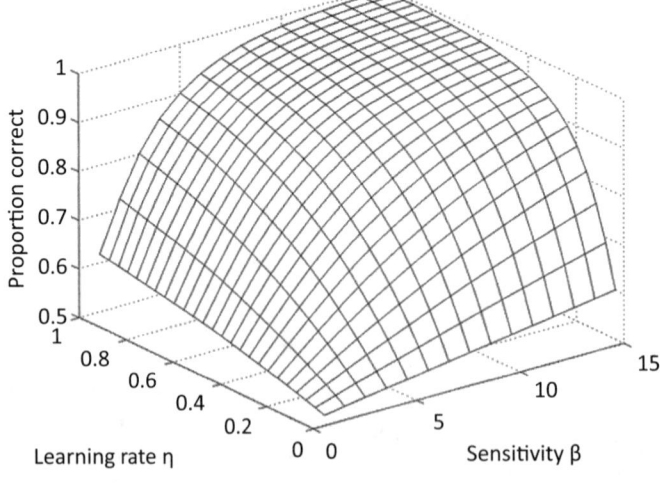

FIGURE 23.4.   Prediction of the prototype model (a) and the exemplar model (b) with respect to a generalization task.

from 0 to one in steps of 0.04, and σ in Equation 23.11 and Equation 23.20 is set to 5. Suppose the stimuli are defined by two dimensions, and let H and L be sets containing all possible values within the described dimension. Stimuli belonging to category C_1 have either low values, L, on both dimensions, $(S_1 \in L, S_2 \in L) = (l, l)$, or high values, H, on both dimensions, $(S_1 \in H, S_2 \in H) = (h, h)$. Stimuli belonging to category C_2 have low values on the first dimension and high values on the second dimension, $(S_1 \in L, S_2 \in H) = (l, h)$, or high values on the first dimension and low values on the second dimension, $(S_1 \in H, S_2 \in L) = (h, l)$. For the simulation, the stimuli are realizations from Gaussian distributions, $N(\mu, \varphi^2)$. In particular, stimuli belonging to category C_1 have low values on both dimensions, with mean $\mu_1 = 1$ for the first and $\mu_2 = 1$ for the second dimension, or high values on both dimensions, with mean $\mu_1 = 10$ for the first and $\mu_2 = 9$ for the second dimension; stimuli belonging to category C_2 have either a low and a high value on both dimensions with $\mu_1 = 2$ for the first and $\mu_2 = 10$ for the second dimension, or with $\mu_1 = 9$ for the first and $\mu_2 = 1$ for the second dimension. For all conditions, φ^2 is set to 1.

For a recognition task, the models assume that the probability of classifying a stimulus as *old*, that is, as previously presented in the training set, is an increasing function of the total amount of activation produced by the stimulus to both output units.

Again, a logistic function is used to relate total activation to old–new recognition response probability:

$$\Pr[old|S_{new}] = \frac{\exp(\gamma \bullet (c_1(t) + c_2(t)))}{\delta + \exp(\gamma \bullet (c_1(t) + c_2(t)))}$$

$$= \frac{1}{1 + \exp(-(\gamma \bullet (c_1(t) + c_2(t)) + \ln(\delta))}$$

(23.28)

and the probability for choosing *new* is

$$\Pr[new|S_{new}] = 1 - \Pr[old|S_{new}]. \quad (23.29)$$

The sensitivity parameter γ determines the recognition probability to the category activations. Increasing the sensitivity parameter causes the recognition probability to be more strongly influenced by the category activations.

The parameter δ is a background-noise constant (Nosofsky et al., 1992). Here, it can be interpreted as a response bias parameter representing the tendency to say *new* to any stimulus, and increasing δ increases the tendency to respond *new*.

Both models have five model parameters: the discriminability parameter σ which determines the width of the generalization gradients; the learning rate parameter η for the delta learning rule; the sensitivity parameter β for the categorization choice rule; and two parameters for the recognition response rule, the sensitivity parameter γ and the response bias parameter δ. The main difference between the two models is in terms of the input representation. The prototype model uses two univariate sets of input units, whereas the exemplar model uses a single bivariate grid of input units. The latter is plausible as many neurons are tuned to more than one feature. For instance, neurons in MT are tuned both to direction and spatial frequency or neurons in V1 and V2 are tuned both to orientation and spatial frequency (e.g., De Valois & De Valois, 1990; Mazer et al., 2002).

Step 4

The fourth step is to test the predictions of the model with data and to compare the predictions of competing models with respect to their ability to explain the empirical results. However, as Roberts and Pashler (2000) pointed out, showing that a model fits the data is not enough. As pointed out before, a major concern is that if a model is too flexible (fits too much) and does not constrain possible outcomes, then the fit is meaningless; if it is too flexible, it is necessary to penalize it for its complexity (Myung, 2000).

All models are an abstraction from a real-world phenomenon, and they focus only on essential aspects of a complex system. To be tractable and useful, models only reflect a simple and limited representation of the complex phenomenon.

That is, a priori, all models are wrong in some details, and a sufficient amount of data will always prove that a model is not true. The question is which among the competing models provides a better representation of the phenomenon under question. Within the present context, the question is which of the two models, the prototype model or the exemplar model provide a better explanation of how objects are categorized.

To empirically test competing models, it is crucial to design experiments that challenge the models. For instance, designing experimental conditions that lead to opposite qualitative predictions (categorical or ordinal) is an essential step in the model testing process. For example, the prototype model predicts that stimulus S is categorized in category C_1 most often, but the exemplar model predicts that stimulus S is categorized in category C_2 most often. Qualitative tests are parameter free in the sense that the models are forced to make these predictions for any value of the free parameters. The following briefly describes a design and shows a qualitative test for the two competing models.

Experiments in categorical learning typically are divided in two phases: a learning or training phase followed by a transfer test phase. During the training phase, the participants categorize objects in distinct classes and receive feedback about the performance. The transfer test is either a generalization test or a recognition test, both without feedback (see Step 3).

Assume that the participants accurately learned the category assignments for each of the four clusters of stimuli, $(S_1 \in L, S_2 \in L) = (l, l)$, $(S_1 \in H, S_2 \in H) = (h, h)$, $(S_1 \in L, S_2 \in H) = (l, h)$, $(S_1 \in H, S_2 \in L) = (h, l)$, during the training phase. According to the exemplar model, for the transfer test, when fixing the first dimension at a high value $(h, \cdot)$, the probability of choosing category C_2 decreases as the value of the second dimension increases, $(h, l \rightarrow h)$; however, fixing the first dimension at a low value $(l, \cdot)$, the probability of choosing category C_2 increases as the value of the second dimension increases $(l, l \rightarrow h)$. Thus, according to the exemplar model, the value of the second dimension has opposite effects on

response probability, depending on the value of the first dimension (Nosofsky et al., 1992). This crossover interaction effect is critical for a qualitative test of the two competing models. As it turns out, the prototype model cannot predict the crossover effect when fixing one dimension and varying only the second; the exemplar model, however, predicts this crossover for a wide range of parameter values (see Busemeyer & Diederich, 2010). For demonstration, let us take the same parameters for β, η, σ as in Step 3. The mean for the stimuli values, however, are set to $\mu_1 = 1$ and $\mu_2 = 1$ or $\mu_1 = 10$ and $\mu_2 = 10$ for category C_1, and $\mu_1 = 1$ and $\mu_2 = 10$ or $\mu_1 = 10$ and $\mu_2 = 1$ for category C_2. Figure 23.5 shows the simulation results. A dot indicates a combination of parameters that successfully reproduced the crossover. If the parameters are sufficiently large the exemplar model predicts the crossover, here in 337 out of 375 possible cases.

When we take the previous parameters $\mu_1 = 1$ and $\mu_2 = 1$ or $\mu_1 = 10$ and $\mu_2 = 9$ for category C_1 and $\mu_1 = 2$ and $\mu_2 = 10$ or $\mu_1 = 9$ and $\mu_2 = 1$ for category C_2, the simulation reproduces the crossover for both models as show in Figure 23.6.

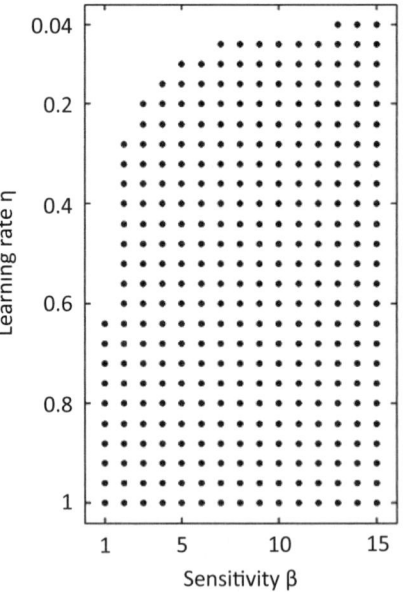

FIGURE 23.5. Predicted patterns of results for the exemplar model. Each dot indicates a combination of parameters that correctly reproduced the crossover interaction.

(A)

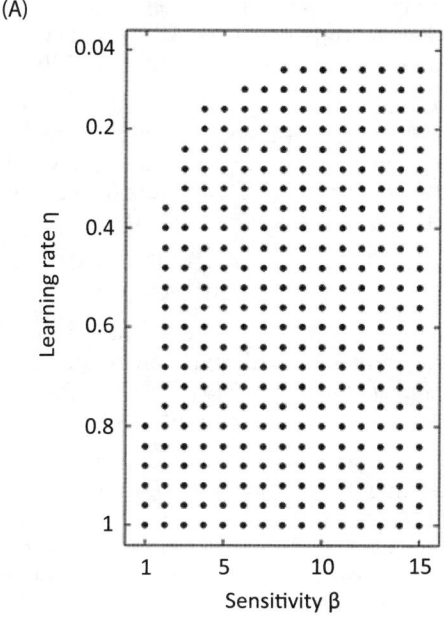

(B)

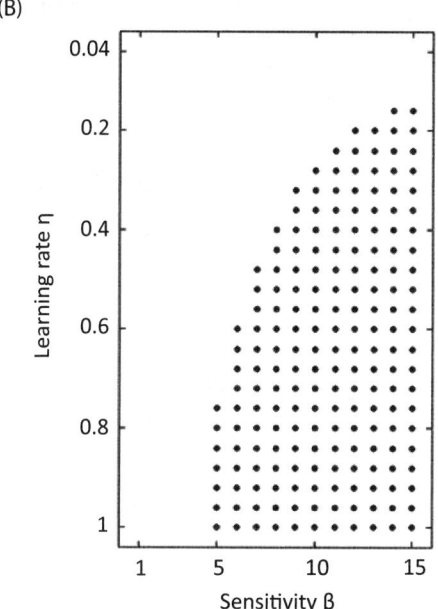

FIGURE 23.6.   **Predicted patterns
of results for the exemplar model (A)
and the prototype model (B). Each dot
indicates a combination of parameters
that correctly reproduced the crossover
interaction.**

The exemplar model (Fig. 23.6A) reproduces the
correct pattern in 325 out of 375 possible cases,
the prototype model reproduces it in 191 cases.

This example shows how crucial it is to design
a proper experiment to distinguish between two
competing models that make, in general, very
similar predictions. It is not always possible to
construct qualitative tests for deciding between
competing models.

For instance, a model may predict increasing
or decreasing functions depending on the specific
parameter values. Furthermore, a model might be
so complex that is it impossible to identify general
qualitative patterns. For example, an arbitrarily
large, hidden unit, nonlinear neural network model
can approximate a wide range of continuous
functions, and thus it is not constrained to predict
a general pattern that can be tested. Sometimes
it is also important to interpret specific parameter
values—for instance, when comparing patients and
healthy adults or younger and older participants.
For those cases, a quantitative test of the model or
a quantitative comparison of competing models is
appropriate. It is also necessary for a model to
make quantitative predictions that are more accurate than its competitors. Quantitative predictions
of a model are evaluated on the basis of an optimal
selection of parameters. Otherwise, a perfectly good
model could be rejected due to a poor selection of
parameters.

Step 5

The last step is in the modeling process is to
modify the model in light of the data. Sometimes
it is sufficient to make some adjustments to account
for the observed data. Sometimes it is necessary
to reformulate the theoretical framework—for
instance, modifying assumptions or by adding
new assumptions; sometimes it is inevitable to
abandon the model and construct a completely
new model based on the feedback obtained from
new experimental results. That is, new experimental findings pose new challenges to previous
models. New models trigger new experiments.
Modeling is a cyclic process, and progress in the
empirical and experimental sciences is made via
this cycle: theorizing about the phenomenon and
developing a model, deriving predictions from
the model, testing the model, revising the model
in light of empirical findings, testing the model
again, and so on. Thus, the modeling process
produces an evolution of models that improve
and become more powerful over time as the
science in a field progresses.

CONCLUSION

What are the advantages of having a computational model, what can they offer to the modeling cycle? D'Mello and Franklin (2011) pointed to two benefits. First, the process of model development is highly instrumental in obtaining a deep understanding of the phenomenon under consideration. It involves deciding on the functional requirements and goal of the model; separating the various individual components of the model; and inventing schemes that bring all this together in order to obtain the desired behavior. Second, insights can be obtained from basic computational principles that underlie the model. That is, any decision on a design made in the model-building process can be interpreted as a hypothesis that can be tested empirically.

References

Akaike, H. (1983). Information measures and model selection. *Bulletin of the International Statistical Institute, 50,* 277–290.

Beasley, W. H., & Rodgers, J. L. (2012). Bootstrapping and Monte Carlo methods. In H. Cooper, P. M. Camic, D. L. Long, A. T. Panter, D. Rindskopf, & K. J. Sher (Eds.), *APA handbook of research methods in psychology: Vol. 2. Research designs: Quantitative, qualitative, neuropsychological, and biological* (pp. 407–425). American Psychological Association. https://doi.org/10.1037/13620-022

Boden, M. A. (2006). *Mind as machine: A history of cognitive science.* The Clarendon Press.

Browne, M. W., & Cudeck, R. (1992). Alternative ways of assessing model fit. *Sociological Methods & Research, 21*(2), 230–258. https://doi.org/10.1177/0049124192021002005

Burnham, K. P., & Anderson, D. R. (2004). Multimodel inference: Understanding AIC and BIC in model selection. *Sociological Methods & Research, 33*(2), 261–304. https://doi.org/10.1177/0049124104268644

Busemeyer, J. R., & Diederich, A. (2010). *Cognitive modeling.* SAGE Publishing.

Chechile, R. A. (1999). A vector-based goodness-of fit metric for interval-scaled data. *Communications in Statistics. Theory and Methods, 28*(2), 277–296. https://doi.org/10.1080/03610929908832298

Cole, D. A., & Ciesla, J. A. (2012). Latent variable modeling of continuous growth. In H. Cooper, P. M. Camic, D. L. Long, A. T. Panter, D. Rindskopf, & K. Sher (Eds.), *APA handbook of research methods in psychology, Vol. 3. Data analysis and research publication* (pp. 309–322). American Psychological Association. https://doi.org/10.1037/13621-015

D'Mello, S., & Franklin, S. (2011). Computational modeling/cognitive robotics complements functional modeling/experimental psychology. *New Ideas in Psychology, 29*(3), 217–227. https://doi.org/10.1016/j.newideapsych.2009.07.003

De Valois, R. L., & De Valois, K. K. (1990). *Spatial vision.* Oxford University Press.

Diederich, A. (1997). Dynamic stochastic models for decision making with time constraints. *Journal of Mathematical Psychology, 41*(3), 260–274. https://doi.org/10.1006/jmps.1997.1167

Diederich, A., & Busemeyer, J. R. (2012). Computational modeling. In H. Cooper, P. M. Camic, D. L. Long, A. T. Panter, D. Rindskopf, & K. J. Sher (Eds.), *APA handbook of research methods in psychology: Vol. 2. Research designs: Quantitative, qualitative, neuropsychological, and biological* (pp. 387–405). American Psychological Association. https://doi.org/10.1037/13620-021

Diederich, A., & Oswald, P. (2014). Sequential sampling model for multiattribute choice alternatives with random attention time and processing order. *Frontiers in Human Neuroscience, 8,* 697. https://doi.org/10.3389/fnhum.2014.00697

Diederich, A., & Trueblood, J. S. (2018). A dynamic dual process model of risky decision making. *Psychological Review, 125*(2), 270–292. https://doi.org/10.1037/rev0000087

Evren, A., & Tuna, E. (2012). On some properties of goodness of fit measures based on statistical entropy. *International Journal of Research and Reviews in Applied Sciences, 13*(1), 192–205.

Fan, X. (2012). Designing simulation studies. In H. Cooper, P. M. Camic, D. L. Long, A. T. Panter, D. Rindskopf, & K. J. Sher (Eds.), *APA handbook of research methods in psychology: Vol. 2. Research designs: Quantitative, qualitative, neuropsychological, and biological* (pp. 427–444). American Psychological Association. https://doi.org/10.1037/13620-021

Farrell, S., & Lewandowsky, S. (2018). *Computational modeling of cognition and behavior.* Cambridge University Press. https://doi.org/10.1017/CBO9781316272503

Feinberg, F. M., & Gonzalez, R. (2007, March). *Bayesian modeling for psychologists: An applied approach* [Paper presentation]. Tutorial Workshop on Bayesian Techniques, University of Michigan, Ann Arbor, MI, United States.

Flaherty, B. P., & Kiff, C. J. (2012). Latent class and latent profile models. In H. Cooper, P. M. Camic, D. L. Long, A. T. Panter, D. Rindskopf, & K. Sher (Eds.), *APA handbook of research methods in psychology, Vol. 3. Data analysis and research publication* (pp. 391–404). American Psychological Association. https://doi.org/10.1037/13621-019

George, G., & Raimond, K. (2013). A survey on optimization algorithms for optimizing the numerical functions. *International Journal of Computers and Applications, 61*(6), 41–46. https://doi.org/10.5120/9935-4570

Haykin, S. (1999). *Neural networks: A comprehensive foundation* (2nd ed.). Prentice Hall.

Hepburn, B., & Andersen, H. (2021). Scientific method. In E. N. Zalta (Ed.), *The Stanford encyclopedia of philosophy.* https://plato.stanford.edu/archives/sum2021/entries/scientific-method/

Hübner, R., & Pelzer, T. (2020). Improving parameter recovery for conflict drift-diffusion models. *Behavior Research Methods, 52*(5), 1848–1866. https://doi.org/10.3758/s13428-020-01366-8

Kandil, F. I., Diederich, A., & Colonius, H. (2014). Parameter recovery for the time-window-of-integration (TWIN) model of multisensory integration in focused attention. *Journal of Vision, 14*(11), 1–20. https://doi.org/10.1167/14.11.14

Kruschke, J. K. (1992). ALCOVE: An exemplar-based connectionist model of category learning. *Psychological Review, 99*(1), 22–44. https://doi.org/10.1037/0033-295X.99.1.22

Le Cun, Y., Boser, B., Denker, J. S., Henderson, D., Howard, R. E., Hubbard, W., & Jackel, L. D. (1989). Backpropagation applied to handwritten Zip code recognition. *Neural Computation, 1*(4), 541–551. https://doi.org/10.1162/neco.1989.1.4.541

Lebière, C., & Anderson, J. R. (1993). A connectionist implementation of the ACT-R production system. In *Proceedings of the Fifteenth Annual Conference of the Cognitive Science Society* (pp. 635–640). Lawrence Erlbaum Associates.

Lewandowsky, S., & Farrell, S. (2011). *Computational modeling in cognition: Principles and practice.* SAGE Publications. https://doi.org/10.4135/9781483349428

Mazer, J. A., Vinje, W. E., McDermott, J., Schiller, P. H., & Gallant, J. L. (2002). Spatial frequency and orientation tuning dynamics in area V1. *Proceedings of the National Academy of Sciences of the United States of America, 99*(3), 1645–1650. https://doi.org/10.1073/pnas.022638499

McCulloch, W. S., & Pitts, W. (1943). A logical calculus of ideas immanent in nervous activity. *Bulletin of Mathematical Biophysics, 5,* 115–133. https://doi.org/10.1007/BF02478259

Myung, I. J. (2000). The importance of complexity in model selection. *Journal of Mathematical*

Psychology, 44(1), 190–204. https://doi.org/10.1006/jmps.1999.1283

Myung, I. J., & Pitt, M. A. (1997). Applying Occam's razor in modeling cognition: A Bayesian approach. *Psychonomic Bulletin & Review, 4*(1), 79–95. https://doi.org/10.3758/BF03210778

Navarro, D. J. (2019). Between the devil and the deep blue sea: Tensions between scientific judgment and statistical model selection. *Computational Brain & Behavior, 2*(1), 28–34. https://doi.org/10.1007/s42113-018-0019-z

Nezlek, J. B. (2012). Multilevel modeling for psychologists. In H. Cooper, P. M. Camic, D. L. Long, A. T. Panter, D. Rindskopf, & K. J. Sher (Eds.), *APA handbook of research methods in psychology: Vol. 3. Data analysis and research publication* (pp. 219–241). American Psychological Association. https://doi.org/10.1037/13621-011

Nilsson, N. J. (2010). *The quest for artificial intelligence: A history of ideas and achievements.* Cambridge University Press.

Nosofsky, R. M., Kruschke, J. K., & McKinley, S. C. (1992). Combining exemplar-based category representations and connectionist learning rules. *Journal of Experimental Psychology: Learning, Memory, and Cognition, 18*(2), 211–233. https://doi.org/10.1037/0278-7393.18.2.211

Palminteri, S., Wyart, V., & Koechlin, E. (2017). The importance of falsification in computational cognitive modeling. *Trends in Cognitive Sciences, 21*(6), 425–433. https://doi.org/10.1016/j.tics.2017.03.011

Ratcliff, R. (2012). Response time distributions. In H. Cooper, P. M. Camic, D. L. Long, A. T. Panter, D. Rindskopf, & K. J. Sher (Eds.), *APA handbook of research methods in psychology: Vol. 2. Research designs: Quantitative, qualitative, neuropsychological, and biological* (pp. 429–443). American Psychological Association. https://doi.org/10.1037/13620-021

Rindskopf, D. (2012). Generalized linear models. In H. Cooper, P. M. Camic, D. L. Long, A. T. Panter, D. Rindskopf, & K. J. Sher (Eds.), *APA handbook of research methods in psychology: Vol. 3. Data analysis and research publication* (pp. 191–206). American Psychological Association. https://doi.org/10.1037/13621-009

Roberts, S., & Pashler, H. (2000). How persuasive is a good fit? A comment on theory testing. *Psychological Review, 107*(2), 358–367. https://doi.org/10.1037/0033-295X.107.2.358

Rojas, R. (1996). *Neural networks. A systematic introduction.* Springer.

Rumelhart, D. E., McClelland, J. L., & the PDP Research Group. (1986). *Parallel distributed processing: Explorations in the microstructure of cognition: Vol. 1. Foundations.* MIT Press.

Schubert, A.-L., Hagemann, D., Voss, A., & Bergmann, K. (2017). Evaluating the model fit of diffusion models with the root mean square error of approximation. *Journal of Mathematical Psychology, 77*, 29–45. https://doi.org/10.1016/j.jmp.2016.08.004

Schwarz, G. (1978). Estimating the dimension of a model. *Annals of Statistics, 6*(2), 461–464. https://doi.org/10.1214/aos/1176344136

Shepard, R. N. (1987). Toward a universal law of generalization for psychological science. *Science, 237*(4820), 1317–1323. https://doi.org/10.1126/science.3629243

Shmueli, G. (2010). To explain or to predict? *Statistical Science, 25*(3), 289–310. https://doi.org/10.1214/10-STS330

Smith, P. L., & Vickers, D. (1988). The accumulator model of two-choice discrimination. *Journal of Mathematical Psychology, 32*(2), 135–168. https://doi.org/10.1016/0022-2496(88)90043-0

Steiger, J. H. (1990). Structural model evaluation and modification: An interval estimation approach. *Multivariate Behavioral Research, 25*, 173–180.

Steiger, J. H. (n.d.). *Measures of fit in structural equation modeling: An introduction.* https://www.statpower.net/Content/312/Handout/Measures%20of%20Fit%20in%20Structural%20Equation%20Modeling.pdf

Steyer, R., Geiser, C., & Fiege, C. (2012). Latent state–trait models. In H. Cooper, P. M. Camic, D. L. Long, A. T. Panter, D. Rindskopf, & K. Sher (Eds.), *APA handbook of research methods in psychology: Vol. 3. Data analysis and research publication* (pp. 291–308). American Psychological Association. https://doi.org/10.1037/13621-014

Sun, R. (2008a). *The Cambridge handbook of computational psychology.* Cambridge University Press.

Sun, R. (2008b). Introduction to computational cognitive modeling. In R. Sun (Ed.), *The Cambridge handbook of computational psychology* (pp. 3–19). Cambridge University Press.

Sun, R. (2009). Theoretical status of computational cognitive modeling. *Cognitive Systems Research, 10*(2), 124–140. https://doi.org/10.1016/j.cogsys.2008.07.002

Sun, S., Cao, Z., Zhu, H., & Zhao, J. (2019). *A survey of optimization methods from a machine learning perspective.* arXiv:1906.06821v2. https://doi.org/10.48550/arXiv.1906.06821

Thomas, M. S. C., & McClelland, J. L. (2008). Connectionist models of cognition. In R. Sun (Ed.), *The Cambridge handbook of computational psychology* (pp. 23–58). Cambridge University Press.

Townsend, J. T. (1975). The mind-body equation revisited. In C. Cheng (Ed.), *Philosophical aspects of the mind-body problem.* The University Press of Hawaii.

van Ravenzwaaij, D., & Oberauer, K. (2009). How to use the diffusion model: Parameter recovery of three methods: EZ, fast-dm, and DMAT. *Journal of Mathematical Psychology, 53*(6), 463–473. https://doi.org/10.1016/j.jmp.2009.09.004

van Rooij, I., & Baggio, G. (2021). Theory before the test: How to build high-verisimilitude explanatory theories in psychological science. *Perspectives on Psychological Science, 16*(4), 682–697. https://doi.org/10.1177/1745691620970604

Voit, E. O. (2019). Perspective: Dimensions of the scientific method. *PLOS Computational Biology, 15*(9), e1007279. https://doi.org/10.1371/journal.pcbi.1007279

Vrieze, S. I. (2012). Model selection and psychological theory: A discussion of the differences between the Akaike information criterion (AIC) and the Bayesian information criterion (BIC). *Psychological Methods, 17*(2), 228–243. https://doi.org/10.1037/a0027127

Wilson, R. C., & Collins, A. G. E. (2019). Ten simple rules for the computational modeling of behavioral data. *eLife, 8*, e49547. https://doi.org/10.7554/eLife.49547

CHAPTER 24

FUNDAMENTALS OF BOOTSTRAPPING AND MONTE CARLO METHODS

William Howard Beasley, Patrick O'Keefe, and Joseph Lee Rodgers

One of the most modern, and valuable, statistical innovations is the class of statistical procedures that uses simulations based on observed data to generate useful distributions, such as sampling distributions, and features of those distributions, such as standard errors. Until the development of modern, high-speed computing and effective software, such methods were intractable (and therefore undeveloped). Both Fisher and Gosset were aware of the value of simulation-based distributions in the early 20th century (see, e.g., Rodgers & Beasley, 2013), but were constrained to small and simple statistical settings by computational limitations. By mid-century, Tukey and colleagues were refining and expanding the range of such methods (e.g., Rodgers, 1999). In 1979, Efron developed the bootstrap, which has become the most popular and powerful of the simulation methods to define sampling distributions. Since then, simulation methods have become useful in the distributional requirements of Bayesian statistical settings, through methods such as the Metropolis-Hastings algorithm and Gibbs sampling. This chapter is designed to provide theoretical background, conceptual understanding, and examples so that applied researchers can use this broad and valuable class of statistical methods.

One hundred years ago, a researcher interested in a theoretical distribution or characteristics of that distribution, such as its mean, standard deviation, or 2.5 and 97.5 percentiles, was restricted practically by computing limitations to the types of theoretical distributions that are described by an explicit equation,[1] such as the binomial or multivariate normal distribution. Using mathematical models of distributions often requires considerable mathematical ability and imposes severe and often intractable assumptions (e.g., normality, independence, variance assumptions, and so on). Computer simulations now provide more flexibility specifying distributions, which in turn provide more flexibility specifying models.

Many modern methods rely on simulation. One contemporary simulation technique is Markov chain Monte Carlo (MCMC) simulation, which can specify arbitrarily complex and nested multivariate distributions. It can even combine different theoretical families of variates. Another contemporary technique is the bootstrap, which can construct sampling distributions of conventional statistics that are free from most (but not all) assumptions. It can even create sampling distributions for new or exotic test statistics that the researcher created for a specific experiment.

---

[1] Our present definition of *explicit equation* includes exact equations and well-defined series. An analytic solution relies only on explicit equations, although the definition's boundaries are fuzzy.

https://doi.org/10.1037/0000319-024
APA Handbook of Research Methods in Psychology, Second Edition: Vol. 2. Research Designs: Quantitative, Qualitative, Neuropsychological, and Biological, H. Cooper (Editor-in-Chief)

The field of simulation is a large one, and we try to cover only the aspects that have an immediate benefit for applied behavioral researchers. The field is very wide and extends into almost every area of statistics. It even extends beyond statistics; several influential techniques were developed by physicists in the 1940s and 1950s. The field has a history that itself is almost as long as modern statistics. Many of the founders of modern statistics conceptually described the benefits and justifications of simulations before they were pragmatically possible. The bootstrap and some useful simulation terminology are introduced in the chapter's first section. General simulations and MCMC simulations are covered in the second section.

R code for the chapter's examples is available at https://github.com/OuhscBbmc/beasley-simulation-methods-2 and can be viewed with a simple text editor. The first example has two versions. The first listing is intended to be a clear and direct translation of the described steps; the second listing is optimized for efficiency and produces the graphs used in this chapter.

THE BOOTSTRAP

The bootstrap is a resampling technique that uses an observed sample to construct a statistic's sampling distribution. Many founders of modern statistics actively developed and promoted resampling, including William Gosset (also known as Student), R. A. Fisher, and John Tukey.

Bootstrapping Univariate Observations

The bootstrap is a flexible tool that can provide inferences in a complicated multivariate space, but the opening example is a simple collection of five scalars.

Example 1a: Standard error of the median.

A psychologist collects waiting times in a sample of $N = 5$ subjects to gain insight into the larger population of people.[2] She believes the population's distribution is likely skewed and decides the research question is best addressed by the median

and its variability. Unfortunately, the median does not have a closed-form equation for a standard error. One convenient solution is to use a bootstrap, which has five stages.

Stage 1. Collect the sample and calculate the observed median, MD_{Obs}, from the N scores.

Stage 2. Prepare the sampling frame, which can be thought of as a pool of scores. In this example, all five observed scores are placed in the sampling frame.

Stage 3. Draw $N = 5$ scores *with replacement* from the sampling frame; this creates one *bootstrap sample*. Repeat this process many times, say $B = 9,999$.

Stage 4. The *bootstrap distribution* is formed by calculating the median of each bootstrap sample. Each bootstrapped statistic is denoted with an asterisk. The bootstrap distribution is the collection of B bootstrapped medians: $MD_1^*, MD_2^*, \ldots, MD_{9999}^*$.

Stage 5. The standard error of the median is estimated by the standard deviation of the bootstrap distribution.

$$\overline{se}_{MD} = \frac{1}{B-1} \sqrt{\sum_{b=1}^{B} \left(MD_b^* - MD_{Obs}^* \right)^2}, \quad (24.1)$$

where $MD_{Obs}^* = \frac{1}{B} \sum_{b=1}^{B} MD_b^*$.

Suppose the observed scores were 1, 4, 10, 50, and 80, and the summaries are $MD_{Obs} = 10$ and $\overline{X}_{Obs} = 29$. Table 24.1 illustrates possible simulation outcomes. In the first bootstrap sample, the values 4 and 50 were drawn twice, whereas 1 and 80 were never drawn. In the second-to-last sample, the five drawn scores were coincidentally the same as the observed sample. In the last sample, 4 was drawn almost every time.

In Stages 2 and 3, a *sampling frame* was formed and five scores were randomly drawn from it repeatedly. The goal was to mimic the median's variability that would occur if additional samples of $N = 5$ were drawn from the *population*. For many

---

[2]For a discussion of how to select a worthy research question, see Volume 1, Chapter 7, this handbook.

	TABLE 24.1	

Illustration of Bootstrapped Scores and Statistics

Bootstrap index	Bootstrapped sample (Stage 3)	Bootstrapped statistic (Stage 4)
1	4, 4, 50, 10, 50	$MD_1^* = 10$
2	10, 80, 10, 50, 80	$MD_2^* = 50$
3	50, 4, 4, 1, 80	$MD_3^* = 4$
. . .		
9,998	1, 4, 10, 50, 80	$MD_{9998}^* = 10$
9,999	4, 4, 4, 4, 50	$MD_{9999}^* = 4$

types of bootstraps, the best sampling frame is simply the observed sample.

In Stage 4, a bootstrap distribution of medians was built to make an inference about the median of the population. Using a sample's statistic to estimate a population parameter follows the *plug-in principle*; the median is the *plug-in statistic* in this example (Efron & Tibshirani, 1993, Chapter 4).

A statistic's standard error quantifies the variability in its sampling distribution. Instead of calculating the spread of a *theoretical* sampling distribution (closed-form mathematical solutions that exist for statistics such as $\bar{X}$, r, and t, but not for *MD*), we calculate the spread in an *empirical* sampling distribution in Stage 5.

Example 1b: Standard error of the mean. The researcher later reused the collected sample to address a different question—one that is better suited by the mean. The algorithm proceeds as in Example 1a, except the plug-in statistic is now the mean instead of the median.

Stage 1. Collect the sample and calculate the observed mean, $\bar{X}_{Obs}$, from the N scores.
Stage 2. Prepare the sampling frame, which is the five observed scores in this example.
Stage 3. Draw N scores with replacement from the sampling frame; this creates one bootstrap sample. Repeat this process many times, say $B = 9,999$.

Stage 4. A bootstrap distribution is formed by calculating the mean of each of the B bootstrap samples. The bootstrap distribution is the B bootstrapped means: $\bar{X}_1^*, \bar{X}_2^*, \ldots, \bar{X}_{9999}^*$.
Stage 5. The standard error of the mean is estimated by the standard deviation of the bootstrap distribution.

$$\overline{se}_{\bar{x}} = \frac{1}{B-1} \sqrt{\sum_{b=1}^{B} (\bar{X}_b^* - \bar{X}_{Obs}^*)^2}, \qquad (24.2)$$

where $\bar{X}_{Obs}^* = \frac{1}{B} \sum_{b=1}^{B} \bar{X}_b^*$.

The bootstrap samples from Example 1a can be reused to calculate the bootstrapped means.[3] The last column in Table 24.1 would be replaced with the values $\bar{X}_b^* = 23.6, 46, 27.8, \ldots, 29, 13.2$. Stage 5 then calculates the standard deviation of these 9,999 statistics (the reason for choosing $B = 9,999$ is discussed briefly in the section Bootstrap Sample Size).

There are many types of bootstraps, and the two just described are *nonparametric* in the sense that they require no assumptions about the sampling distributions (however, they do assume that the observed scores are drawn independently from the population of interest). A procedure is *parametric* when it relies on assumptions about the population distribution. The typical parametric standard error of the mean is

$$\text{Parametric } \overline{se}_{\bar{x}} = \frac{1}{\sqrt{N}} \sqrt{\frac{\sum_{i=1}^{N} (X_i - \bar{X})^2}{(N-1)}} = \frac{s}{\sqrt{N}}. \qquad (24.3)$$

The conventional standard error of the mean measures the variability in a sample (i.e., the standard deviation, s) to estimate the variability in the population of means.[4] It uses the central limit theorem to relate s to the $\overline{se}_{\bar{x}}$. Unfortunately, many useful statistics do not have a convenient theoretical relationship such as this. For the statistics that do, the required assumptions can

---

[3]We want to emphasize that this process is unaffected by the choice of plug-in statistic.
[4]When a large sample is drawn from a normally distributed population, the bootstrap standard error will be very close to the conventional standard error of the mean.

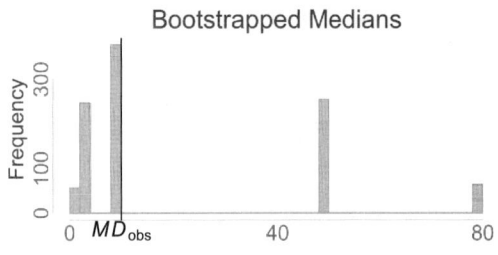
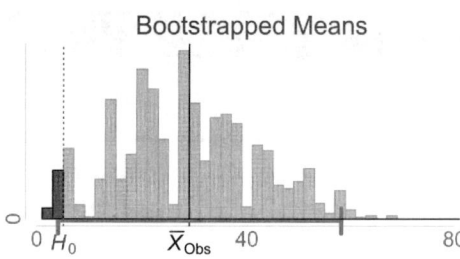

FIGURE 24.1. Bootstrap distributions. The right panel includes the bootstrap CI and *p* value (dark gray area).

be unreasonable in some applied scenarios. The bootstrap can help in both cases: calculating the standard error is simple even for complicated plug-in statistics. The choice of the plug-in statistic is very flexible, and this is discussed later.

Example 1c: Confidence interval for the mean. A 95% confidence interval (CI) for the mean[5] can be estimated from the bootstrap distribution created in Stage 4. The bootstrap samples and bootstrap distribution can be reused. Only the final stage is different.

Stages 1 to 4.

Proceed as in Example 1b.

Stage 5. Order the $B = 9,999$ bootstrapped statistics from smallest to largest.

The CI bounds are marked by the 250th smallest value and the 250th largest value (i.e., the .025 and .975 quantiles). The number of scores in each tail is calculated by $\alpha(B + 1)/2$; α is .05 with a 95% CI.

A CI determined from this type of bootstrap distribution has an additional advantage over a CI determined from a parametric, theoretical normal distribution. The parametric distribution relies on the central limit theorem for normality, and thus the tails are an equal distance from $\bar{X}$; the CI is defined by $\bar{X} \pm 1.96 \times \overline{se}_{\bar{x}}$. The parametric procedure can be justified as N grows infinitely large, but it can be misleading when a small sample is drawn from a skewed distribution. In fact, the parametric CI in this example is $(-1.4, 59.4)$,

which produces a nonsensical negative value for waiting time.

This bootstrap CI method has the appealing feature that it is *range-preserving*; in this case, the CI for waiting time will never be negative. The bootstrap CI is (4.0, 58.8); its boundaries are guaranteed to be values that could be observed in a sample (because they were calculated from values that were actually observed in a sample; Efron & Tibshirani, 1993, Section 13.7). The bootstrap distribution is shown in Figure 24.1, along with the CI.

Example 1d: The *p* value for the mean. A one-tailed *p* value is determined in an intuitive way, as the proportion of bootstrapped statistics that are more extreme than the value of the null hypothesis. A two-tailed *p* value is easy to determine as well but would not make theoretical sense with the waiting time example. If H_0: $time \leq 5$, the five stages are:

Stages 1 to 4. Proceed as in Example 1b.
Stage 5. Tally the number of $\bar{X}_b^*$ values equal to or less than the hypothesized value, expressed as

$$\#\{\bar{X}_b^* \leq time_{\text{Null}}\}. \tag{24.4}$$

The *p* value is $(1 + \#\{X_b^* \leq time_{\text{Null}}\})/(B + 1)$.

Notice that the choice of plug-in statistic in Stage 2 is unrelated to the choice of statistic that summarizes the bootstrap distribution in Stage 5. A standard deviation can be calculated on the *B* statistics regardless of plug-in equation used in

---

[5]A frequentist 95% CI is built so that 95% of similarly constructed CIs will contain the population parameter value.

Stage 2 (e.g., the median or mean). Similarly in Stage 5, the distribution of B means can be summarized in a variety of ways (e.g., standard error, CI, or p).

The code accompanying the chapter replicates the steps in our examples, including plotting simplified versions of the figures. These examples are intended to supplement the knowledge of novice bootstrappers (with limited exposure to R) and to provide a template for more complicated bootstraps that can arise in applied research. Software is further discussed at the end of the chapter.

Terminology. Before we move to slightly more complicated examples, we summarize the entities and notation. Typically, a researcher draws a sample X to gain insight into its population distribution of single scores, F (this F is unrelated to the analysis of variance [ANOVA] F distribution). If we are interested in the mean of the population, μ, the appropriate plug-in statistic is the mean of the sample, $\bar{X}$. An inferential procedure mimics F with a theoretical distribution called $\hat{F}$, to assess the accuracy of $\bar{X}$ (or any other plug-in statistic). Conceptually, $\hat{F}$ stands in for F because we don't know F, but we do know $\hat{F}$. In the world of resampling, $\hat{F}$ is more specifically called an empirical distribution. Examples 1b to 1d calculate three common expressions of the uncertainty in the estimate of μ: the standard error, CI, and p value.

The empirical distribution, $\hat{F}$, should not be confused with the bootstrap distribution, which is a type of empirical *sampling* distribution. For instance, in Example 1a, $\hat{F}$ is a distribution of N single *observations*, whereas the bootstrap distribution is a collection of B *statistics* (that were each calculated from a bootstrap sample of N scores randomly drawn from the sampling frame). The distinction between these different types of distributions is explained in detail in Rodgers (1999).

The sampling frame is the mechanism behind $\hat{F}$, because it is the pool of single points from which the bootstrap samples are drawn. The previous examples have used a sampling frame that was built directly from the observed sample. We will show three other types of bootstraps that are only indirect expressions of the sample. In the second half of the chapter, we discuss Monte Carlo methods, which are simulations in which $\hat{F}$ is entirely unconnected to an observed sample.

So far, the sampling frames produced empirical distributions that represent an observed population. We start using the notation $\hat{F}_{\text{Obs}}$ to distinguish it from an empirical distribution representing a null hypothesis, $\hat{F}_{\text{Null}}$. Examples 2a and 2b focus on this difference.

Bootstrapping With Novel Designs

The mean is a well-known statistic with an accessible theoretical sampling distribution—yet the bootstrap can help when the central limit theorem assumptions are not justifiable. The median is well known, but it does not have a good theoretical sampling distribution; the bootstrap can help by providing an accessible empirical sampling distribution.

In some scenarios, an established sampling distribution exists but does not fit the profile of an experimental design. For instance, the longitudinal, nested factorial design of Smith and Kimball (2010, Experiment 1) benefited from the flexibility of a bootstrap in two ways. First, a subject's final outcome was conditioned on their initial response in a way that prevented the ANOVA sampling distribution from representing it appropriately. This linking created correlated error terms for the linked observations, which invalidated the traditional ANOVA distribution as an appropriate sampling distribution (and we know that the ANOVA is not robust to violations of independence of errors). Second, there was substantial heterogeneity in the variability, making it difficult to model appropriately. After the sampling frame was customized to fit the researchers' specific contrasts, a bootstrap was able to test hypotheses with $N = 110$ subjects that a parametric generalized linear model or multilevel model could not.

The bootstrap's flexibility perhaps is demonstrated best when it provides a sampling distribution for a *new statistic* that is created for a specific design protocol. In fact, "subject to mild conditions," the selected bootstrapped statistic "can be the output of an algorithm of almost arbitrary complexity, shattering the naïve notion that a parameter is a Greek letter appearing in a probability distribution and showing the possibilities for uncertainty analysis for the complex procedures now in daily use, but at the frontiers of the imagination a quarter of a century ago." (Davison et al., 2003, p. 142).

It is difficult to give concise examples of this flexibility, because several paragraphs would be needed just to describe a novel design; advice and examples are found in Boos (2003) and Davison and Hinkley (1997).

To provide an approximation, and to stimulate the reader to think deeper about such a constructed statistic, consider the following setting. Tukey's (1977) H-spread was designed to measure the distance across the middle half of a distribution (often referred to as the interquartile range). Suppose a theory implies interest in another distance: the distance across the middle 20% of the distribution (a range-type measure even less influenced by extreme scores than the H-spread). This statistic is sensible and interesting, but in this case, the statistical community has no background or statistical theory to help the applied researcher. But the bootstrap is every bit as facile and useful in this previously undefined setting as it is in applications involving other well-known statistics like the mean, median, or H-spread.

Bootstrapping Multivariate Observations

When two scores are collected from a subject, our definition of an observation is expanded to a bivariate point, $u_i = (x_i, y_i)$.

Example 2a: $\hat{F}_{Obs}$ for a correlation. Diaconis and Efron (1983) bootstrapped a correlation by using the observed sample as the sampling frame. In Example 1, N univariate points were drawn from a sampling frame of N univariate points. Here, N bivariate points are drawn from a sampling frame of N bivariate points.

Stage 1. Collect the sample and calculate r_{obs} from the N data points (pairs of X, Y values).

Stage 2. Prepare the sampling frame. To produce $\hat{F}_{Obs}$ in this case, use the observed sample.

Stage 3. Randomly draw N pairs of scores with replacement while keeping the pairs intact. For instance, if x_3 is selected, the accompanying value must be y_3 (i.e., the x and y scores for the third subject). Repeat this stage to form B bootstrap samples.

Stage 4. Calculate $r_{Obs}*$ for each bootstrap sample drawn in Stage 3.

Stage 5. Calculate the CI$[r^*_{(250)}, r^*_{(9750)}]$ with $B = 9,999$. If a hypothesis test is desired, the null hypothesis can be rejected if ρ_{null} falls outside of the CI. As before, the standard error is the standard deviation of the B statistics in the bootstrap distribution.

Univariate Sampling Bootstrap

Example 2b: $\hat{F}_{Null}$ for a correlation. As early as 1935, Fisher (1970) developed a resampling method, called the *permutation test* or the *randomization test*. It is very similar to the bootstrap, except that it samples from the sampling frame *without replacement*.[6] Fisher did not intend to estimate the standard error but rather to calculate the p value of a null hypothesis, which is achieved by constructing a sampling frame that represents the null hypothesis.

In the case of a bivariate correlation, suppose the null hypothesis states that X and Y are linearly independent in the population. An interesting special case of linear independence (Rodgers et al., 1984) that is often tested is $\rho_{Null} = 0$. One approach is to conceptualize this as "every value of X has an equal chance of being associated with any value of Y." To reflect $\hat{F}_{Null}$, the sampling frame enumerates all possible X and Y pairs—creating a sampling frame with N^2 bivariate points (see Lee & Rodgers, 1998). Figure 24.2 portrays the two different sampling approaches.

This procedure for bootstrapping $\hat{F}_{Null}$ resembles Example 2a, with three exceptions. First, the sampling frame has N^2 points instead of N. Second,

---

[6]"[The bootstrap] was designed to extend the virtues of permutation testing" (Efron & Tibshirani, 1993, p. 218).

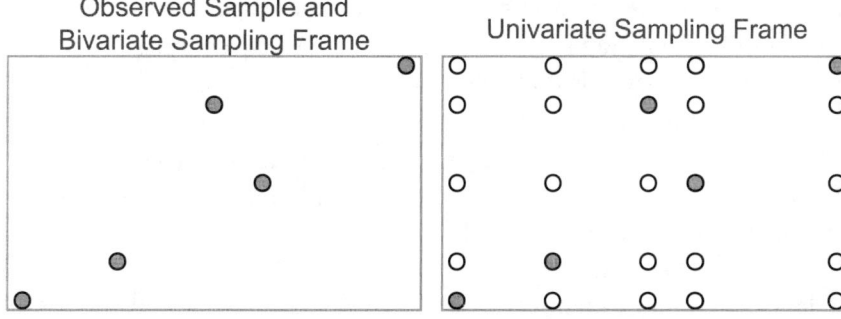

FIGURE 24.2. Scatter plots of a bivariate sampling frame based on $\hat{F}_{\text{Obs}}$ (left) and a univariate sampling frame based on $\hat{F}_{\text{Null}}$ (right).

each of these points has a $1/N^2$ probability of being selected on each draw, instead of $1/N$. Finally, a hypothesis is tested by comparing r_{Obs} with the CI, instead of comparing ρ_{Null} with the CI.

Stage 1. Collect the sample and calculate r_{Obs} from the N data points (pairs of X, Y values).

Stage 2. Prepare the univariate sampling frame by combining every x with every y value.

Stage 3. Randomly draw N pairs of scores with replacement from the N^2 possible points in the sampling frame. Repeat this stage to form $B = 9,999$ bootstrap samples.

Stage 4. Calculate r_{Obs}^* for each bootstrap sample drawn in Stage 3.

Stage 5. Calculate the $CI[r_{(250)}^*, r_{(9750)}^*]$. If a hypothesis test is desired, the null hypothesis can be rejected if r_{Obs} falls outside of the region of nonrejection defined by the CI. The standard error is again the standard deviation of the bootstrap distribution.

This CI (derived from $\hat{F}_{\text{Null}}$) represents the variability around ρ_{Null}, whereas the previous CI (derived from $\hat{F}_{\text{Obs}}$) represents the variability around r_{Obs}. The two contrasting *p*-value equations for H_0: $\rho > \rho_{\text{Null}}$ are $p_{\hat{F}_{\text{Obs}}} = \dfrac{1 + \#\left\{r_b^* < \rho_{\text{Null}}\right\}}{B+1}$ and

$p_{\hat{F}_{\text{Null}}} = \dfrac{1 + \#\left\{r_b^* < r_{\text{Obs}}\right\}}{B+1}$. Notice that the value of

ρ_{Null} is not present in the latter *p*-value equation because it is reflected within the sampling frame, which is constrained by its construction to have a correlation of zero.

The univariate sampling bootstrap is easily extended to cases where correlations are non-zero. Using a method called "diagonalization" the sampling frame produced by the univariate sampling framework can be shaped to exhibit any correlation a researcher might require. This is particularly useful in two ways. The first is to test non-nil null hypotheses. In some cases, simply rejecting the null hypothesis of no correlation may not be of interest. In order to use the univariate sampling bootstrap for this test of the non-nil null, the researcher can set the correlation in the sampling frame to the null hypothesized correlation coefficient. The bootstrap procedure then proceeds as before. This creates a null distribution *around the non-nil null*.

The second case where diagonalization of the univariate sampling frame is useful is when a confidence interval is desired. By diagonalizing the univariate sampling frame so that it has the same correlation as the originally observed data, and then bootstrapping as before, the resulting confidence interval is the confidence interval of the observed statistic.

While the alternative step of using the uni-variate sampling frame, instead of the raw data, may seem to be trivial, this alteration to the bootstrap has repeatedly shown itself to provide advantages over the traditional bootstrap, particularly with regards to Type I error rates. Research on correlation coefficients has demonstrated this in a number of settings (e.g., Beasley et al., 2007; Bishara & Hittner, 2012, 2017). Research for uses other than correlation coefficients has also recently found an advantage for the univariate sampling bootstrap over other bootstrap alternatives and some nonbootstrap CI methods (O'Keefe & Rodgers, 2020). Software implementations of the univariate bootstrap are available in R (e.g., Omisc) that manage the creation of the univariate sampling frame, diagonalization if desired, and the bootstrapping procedure itself.

Hutson (2019) defined an almost identical approach to the univariate sampling bootstrap and named it the *surrogate bootstrap*. (The only difference is his focus on defining the *p* value, instead of the confidence interval; if the confidence interval is used for hypothesis testing, the outcome must always be identical. Hutson noted in relation to the Lee and Rodgers, 1998, procedure that "the test can also be inverted to provide precise confidence interval for ρ"). Hutson provided mathematical justification for the univariate sampling bootstrap, along with additional simulation support for the excellent operating characteristics of this bootstrap method.

Example 3a: Parametric bootstrap.   The *parametric bootstrap* is similar to the nonparametric bootstrap in previous examples, except that $\hat{F}_{\text{Obs}}$ and its sampling frame have distributional assumptions. In a correlational setting, an analyst might be able to assume the variables approximately follow a bivariate normal distribution with a linear relationship of r_{Obs} (Efron & Tibshirani, 1993, Section 6.5). In this case, scores in the sampling frame do not contain any observed scores. The sample influences the sampling frame only thorough r_{Obs}. For a given bootstrap sample, the *N* bivariate points are generated as follows:

Stage 1. Collect the sample and calculate r_{Obs} from the *N* data points (pairs of *X*, *Y* values).
Stage 2. State the parametric form of the estimated population. A linear, normal distribution is

$$\begin{pmatrix} X \\ Y \end{pmatrix} \sim N\left(\begin{pmatrix} \bar{X} \\ \bar{Y} \end{pmatrix}, \begin{pmatrix} \sigma_X^2 & \sigma_{XY} \\ \sigma_{XY} & \sigma_Y^2 \end{pmatrix} \right). \quad (24.5)$$

Stage 3. Randomly draw *N* bivariate points. The random number generator produces a

unique point every draw. Repeat to form *B* bootstrap samples.
Stage 4. Calculate r_{Obs}^* for each bootstrap sample drawn in Stage 3.
Stage 5. If desired, calculate the CI and *p* value as in Example 2a (and not like Example 2b).

Although r_{Obs}^* is now parametric, the bootstrap distribution itself is still considered nonparametric. The shape of the collection of r_{Obs}^* values has no equation or restrictions. The parametric bootstrap can be a good tool when the population's characteristics can be reasonably assumed, but the statistic's characteristics are not well known. This situation occurs with statistics like the median (that lack a closed-form sampling distribution) or for novel statistics that are tailored to a specific experimental protocol (e.g., Boos, 2003).

Example 3b: Semiparametric bootstrap.   A *semiparametric* bootstrap draws observations from an $\hat{F}$ that is constructed from some parametric and some nonparametric assumptions. In a multiple regression setting, one could assume *F* has a linear relationship and the residuals are exchangeable but not assume the residuals are normally distributed. In this model, the *i*th subject's predicted score is $y_i = b_0 + b_1 x_{1,i} + b_2 x_{2,i} + e_i$, and e_i is their residual.

Stage 1. Collect the sample and calculate the sample coefficients (b_0, b_1, b_2) that estimate the population parameters (β_0, β_1, β_2).
Stage 2. The sampling frame is formed from the *N* residuals ($e_1, \ldots, e_N$).
Stage 3a. Randomly draw *N* residuals with replacement ($e_1^*, e_2^*, \ldots, e_N^*$).
Stage 3b. If the independent variables (the *x* values) are considered fixed, each bootstrap sample is

$$y_1^* = b_0 + b_1 x_{1,1} + b_2 x_{2,1} + e_1^* = \hat{y}_1 + e_1^*$$

$$y_2^* = b_0 + b_1 x_{1,2} + b_2 x_{2,2} + e_2^* = \hat{y}_2 + e_2^*$$

$$\cdots$$

$$y_N^* = b_0 + b_1 x_{1,N} + b_2 x_{2,N} + e_N^* = \hat{y}_N + e_N^*. \quad (24.6)$$

This creates a bootstrap sample of N values: $(y_1^*, y_2^*, \ldots, y_N^*)$. Repeat this stage to form B bootstrap samples.

Stage 4. Calculate b_0^*, b_1^*, and b_2^* with the same three-parameter linear model for each bootstrap sample created in Stage 3.

Stage 5. Calculate the desired statistics (similar to Example 2a) on the trivariate bootstrap distribution of (b_0^*, b_1^*, b_2^*).

The x values are considered fixed in this specific example, so they are not drawn randomly in Stage 3b. Bootstrap distributions of other plug-in statistics such as R^2 may better address the specific research question (e.g., Manly, 2007, Chapter 7). The linear model does not necessarily have to minimize squared error (e.g., it could minimize the median of absolute values of deviations). Semiparametric bootstraps can provide a foundation for many generalized linear models (Davison & Hinkley, 1997, Section 7.2) and exploratory approaches, such as loess curves and cubic splines (Hastie et al., 2009).

If additional assumptions are justifiable, a semiparametric bootstrap can model dependencies more naturally than a nonparametric bootstrap. Drawing residuals as if they were interchangeable requires the assumption of homogenous variance (drawing observed samples, as described in Examples 2a and 2b, does not). Adjustments such as standardizing the residuals may improve the robustness of semi-parametric approaches (for this and other techniques, see Davison & Hinkley, 1997, Sections 3.3, 6.2–6.3).

Bootstrapping data with dependencies. Bootstrapping is reasonably straightforward when the data are independently and identically distributed. However, psychological designs frequently model dependency among the observations (e.g., time series), variables (e.g., multiple regression, repeated measures designs), or sampling levels (e.g., multilevel models). Sometimes a nonparametric bootstrap may be unable to accommodate these designs because it is difficult to incorporate the appropriate dependency into the sampling frame and also avoid distributional assumptions; instead, parametric and semiparametric bootstraps can be used. For more strategies and applications, see Davison and Hinkley (1997) and Beasley and Rodgers (2009). Lahiri (2003) is a mathematically oriented book dedicated to dependent data.

Pragmatic Bootstrapping Issues

A statistical analysis can accommodate both bootstrap and parametric procedures. A researcher may believe a χ^2 distribution is appropriate for the fit statistic for testing a structural equation model (SEM), while also believing the CIs around the means and covariances are asymmetric. In this case, a parametric fit statistic can be complemented by bootstrapped standard errors. If a parametric distribution is problematic, the Bollen-Stine (Bollen & Stine, 1992) bootstrap distribution could be used instead (Enders, 2010, Sections 5.11 and 5.15). Another illustration of a heterogeneous strategy is using parametric standard error of the mean and a bootstrapped H-spread. In short, adopting the bootstrap can be a gradual transition.

Confidence interval adjustments. The CI calculated in Example 2 is commonly called the percentile CI. Its simple definition is that the percentile of the bootstrap distribution maps directly to the percentile of the inferred population. For instance, the 250th smallest r^* (out of $B = 9,999$) estimates the population's 2.5% percentile, assuming the null hypothesis is true. However, this effortless relationship can produce biased estimates in common conditions and several CI adjustments have been developed to have less bias and greater efficiency.

At least eight CI adjustments have been proposed (many authors frequently use ambiguous or conflicting names; surveyed in Beasley & Rodgers, 2009, pp. 372–375). We prefer the BCa (which stands for "bias-corrected and accelerated") adjustment because it has a favorable combination of efficiency, robustness, and wide applicability. It attempts to correct for bias in the bootstrap distribution and for heterogeneous variability in the plug-in statistic (Efron & Tibshirani, 1993, Chapter 14).

Bootstrap sample size. Nonparametric bootstraps are randomly drawn from the empirical sampling frame because complete enumeration of all possible bootstrap samples is rarely practical.[7] This randomness introduces simulation error (which can be thought of a type of sampling error from $\hat{F}$) and fortunately increasing B to a reasonable number makes this error negligible. All the chapter's bootstrap examples complete in less than 5 seconds, even when $N = 500$.

We recommend that at least 10^3 and 10^4 replications be run for standard errors and 95% CIs, respectively. Additional discussion and references are found in Beasley and Rodgers (2009, pp. 378–379), but reading this takes longer than completing $B = 99,999$. It may seem strange that our suggested B values have been chosen so that $(B + 1)\alpha$ is an integer (e.g., 9,999 instead of the more natural 10,000). Boos (2003) explained the "99 Rule" and how it slightly improves CI accuracy.

Additional bootstrap applications. Most psychological research questions and designs are more complex than the chapter's examples, but the principles remain the same. Examples and references to sophisticated designs and plug-in statistics are found in Beasley and Rodgers (2009, pp. 375–378). These include designs like time series, stratified samples, circular variables, and models like generalized linear models, multilevel linear models, survival models, Bayesian analysis, mediation models, and SEM. The resampling procedures that influenced the development of the bootstrap are also discussed, including the permutation test and jackknife (see also Rodgers, 1999).

Limitations. Two commonly encountered limitations of parametric procedures that apply to the bootstrap and are worth stating here. First, inferences can be misleading when dependencies in the data are not appropriately modeled. Second,

a flawed sampling process can produce problematic inferences (although the bootstrap may be less susceptible to this problem than traditional parametric procedures).[8]

The bootstrap does have problems if the plug-in statistic estimates a boundary, or a value close to a boundary, such as a minimum reaction time (Andrews, 2000). In this case, the estimate will be biased upward because the bootstrapped statistic of reaction time cannot be negative. Notice that it is acceptable to estimate a quantity near the boundary of a bootstrap distribution (such as the 2.5th percentile in Stage 5) but not near the boundary of the population distribution (Stage 4). Andrews (2000, Section 2) and LePage and Billiard (1992) discussed other potential concerns that are less likely to affect psychologists.

Beran (2003) wrote,

> Success of the bootstrap, in the sense of doing what is expected under a probability model for data, is not universal. Modifications to Efron's (1979) definition of the bootstrap are needed to make the idea work for estimators that are not classically regular. (p. 176)

When a novel plug-in statistic is developed (either bootstrap or parametric), good inferential performance is not assured. We advise that the new statistic be studied with a small simulation to assess if it has acceptable Type I error and adequate power, for the observed N. This proactive analysis (Steiger, 2007) should include several likely population values and nonnormal distributions. Many of the same tools and skills used to bootstrap can be applied to the proactive analysis.

We occasionally are asked whether the validity of bootstrap inferences suffers with small sample sizes. We feel that if one or more outliers, or even an unrepresentative sample caused by natural

---

[7]In Example 1, a small-data example, complete enumeration requires $5^5 = 3,125$ bootstrap samples, which actually requires less work than the suggested $B = 9,999$. However, this is rarely the case, because the sample size is usually larger than $N = 5$; if one more score had been collected, complete enumeration requires $B = 6^6 = 46,656$. Even a moderate size of $N = 30$ requires $B \approx 10^{44}$. This number can be reduced by accounting for and reweighting redundant samples (e.g., the sample {11, 11, 4} produces the same statistic as {4, 11, 11}), but programming these shortcuts would take much longer than running a large B, and the sample still may not be small enough to be practical.

[8]With respect to the correlation, the bootstrap outperformed parametric procedures in simulations of restricted range (Chan & Chan, 2004; Mendoza et al., 1991), nonnormal correlated populations (Beasley et al., 2007), and composite populations (Lee & Rodgers, 1998).

sampling variability, can mislead a bootstrap distribution, then it is likely to be even more disruptive to a parametric sampling distribution. For instance, parametric inferences were more susceptible than bootstrap inferences when a bivariate correlation was calculated from a sample of five observations (Beasley et al., 2007). With a multivariate normal population, the procedures had comparable Type I error, whereas the parametric had slightly better power than the bootstrap. However, when the assumptions were violated by using skewed populations, the parametric procedure had liberal Type I error (reaching 0.15), whereas the bootstrap did not. Summarizing across all simulated values of N, the parametric procedure benefited when its assumptions were met, but could be unreliable when they were not. Of course, it is irresponsible to claim this pattern will hold for all statistics and population distributions, which is another reason to perform a proactive analysis before using a novel plug-in statistic.

Software. Software for parametric procedures is much more available and user-friendly than for the equivalent bootstraps. The flexibility that empowers the bootstrap also prevents automation. Twenty years later, Fan's (2003) assessment of available bootstrapping software still applies. When bootstrapping a statistic, it is likely that writing code will be necessary.

R has the most complete support for two reasons. First, it has many concise routines useful to bootstrapping. For instance, the line `sample(x=obs, size=15, replace=TRUE)` randomly draws $N = 15$ scores from a vector called `obs`. Second, most developments and publications involving applied bootstrapping have come from statisticians (and especially biostatisticians) who publish their examples in this language. Examples and documentation

also can be found in Stata and SAS.[9] The SEM programs EQS and Mplus provide bootstrapping for better fit statistics and for more robust CIs (Enders, 2010, Table 11.1).

Two of the most popular bootstrap books use R and S-PLUS exclusively (Davison & Hinkley, 1997; Efron & Tibshirani, 1993).[10] They accommodate some common designs with less than 10 lines of code from the practitioner. The user defines their specific plug-in statistic, and then passes this definition to a reusable base routine provided by the package.

It can be tricky to define this specialized function, however, even for common analyses such as those that (a) incorporate multiple groups, (b) draw from $\hat{F}_{Null}$, or (c) use sampling frames that do not have exactly N points. If the base routine has trouble accommodating the plug-in function, we suggest that users create their own routine by starting with the code for a routine (like bcanon) in the bootstrap package and modifying it to fit the current design.[11]

The defined plug-in statistic needs to detect and react to atypical samples. In Example 2a, it is likely that one of the 9,999 bootstrap samples will have no variation, so that r^*_{Obs} is undefined. If unanticipated, this will either halt the program's execution or insert an undefined value into the bootstrap distribution (depending on the statistical software).

If the software supports a "Try-Catch" block, it can be used to recover from this event. One implementation of Example 2a catches the undefined statistic and forces another bootstrap sample to be drawn and calculated. Another implementation simply replaces the undefined values with zeros (which is much faster than having the computer construct a Try-Catch block). Even if this behavior is not ideal theoretically, it will happen too infrequently to have any noticeable effect.[12] If the software language does

---

[9] Good starting points are https://www.stata.com/help.cgi?bootstrap, Poi (2004), and https://support.sas.com/kb/24/982.html.

[10] Their routines are included in the "bootstrap" and "boot" packages. After loading the package, documentation appears after typing "?bootstrap" or "?boot". Both packages have good help files, with "boot" being slightly more thorough. Packages are discussed in "An Introduction to R," which is available on the help menu of R.

[11] In R, a routine's underlying code is presented when its name is entered by itself (e.g., "bcanon" when Efron & Tibshirani's, 1993, "bootstrap" package has been installed and loaded). Saving the code in a script allows it to be modified, executed, and saved.

[12] When $N = 5$ in Example 2a, roughly $5^{-4} = 0.16\%$ of bootstrap statistics will be undefined. When $N = 10$, this proportion drops to 10^{-9}. We believe this source of error is overwhelmed by sampling error and can be ignored.

not provide error handling (and zero is not an appropriate substitute value for the statistic), the custom code should anticipate and test for illegal conditions.

Despite the additional issues to consider, bootstrapping can be valuable to a practitioner when it holds a statistical advantage. The bootstrap is a good candidate when the desired statistic lacks a closed-form standard error equation, when necessary parametric assumptions are not met, or especially when small sample sizes are combined with the previous restrictions.

BROADER SIMULATION METHODS

When simulation uses repeated random sampling to build a distribution, it is frequently called a *Monte Carlo method*. The bootstrap is a specific type of Monte Carlo simulation. It can create a distribution of statistics that lacks an equation for the probability density function (pdf) and the cumulative distribution function (CDF; i.e., the integral of the pdf). Thus, in the bootstrap, a collection of B points are simulated and substituted for the desired pdf or CDF.

In most Monte Carlo simulations, the distribution of the relevant statistic(s) has a tractable pdf but an intractable CDF. In other words, equations are available to calculate the probability for a single parameter value (e.g., $p(\theta = 2)$) but not for a range of parameter values (e.g., $p(0 \leq \theta \leq 2)$ or $p(\theta \leq 1.7)$); the standard error and other moments typically are not available either. Like the bootstrap, the general Monte Carlo method builds a collection of B points as a substitute for the desired distribution. Simulation literature commonly calls this the *target distribution, f*.[13]

The following simulation techniques are general and can evaluate many types of distributions, although we will discuss them in the context of the posterior distribution. A Bayesian posterior distribution is proportional to the product of the prior and likelihood distributions (as explained in Chapter 26 of this volume). Many posterior distributions have an equation for the pdf, but not for the CDF or standard error, and so simulation methods are an attractive tool.

Before the 1990s, most Bayesian analysts had to choose their prior and likelihood distributions carefully, so that the posterior's CDF had a closed-form equation.[14] This was not a weakness of Bayesian theory but rather a limitation of available Bayesian methods. This restriction was a common inconvenience for single-parameter models, but it made the use of many multiparameter models completely intractable (especially when the posterior distribution included parameters from different families of distributions). With the development of simulation, Bayesian methods are now arguably more flexible than frequentist (i.e., standard parametric) methods.

General Simulation

Simulation is unnecessary when the posterior describes a small number of parameters. A distribution can be systematically partitioned into small areas, which are calculated separately before being recombined. This deterministic technique, called *numerical integration*, can be a rectangular approximation used to estimate the area under a curve and is taught to all calculus students before the more elegant *analytical integration*. Analytical integration is not possible with most posterior distributions used in research, however, and even numerical integration is not practical when the posterior has many parameters. A target distribution has one dimension for every parameter; it is common for f to have too many dimensions to integrate deterministically.

When analytical and numerical integration are not feasible, simulation can be the next best method. As Monahan (2001) said, "Monte Carlo should be viewed as just another way to compute an integral; numerical integration should be

---

[13]The target distribution, f, should not be confused with the bootstrap literature's F (or $\hat{F}$). F is the theoretical population distribution of single observations, whereas f is the desired distribution of statistics. If the simulation notation were applied to the bootstrap, f would be the bootstrap distribution.

[14]One common conjugate relationship is a Gaussian prior and a Gaussian likelihood, resulting in a Gaussian posterior. Another common relationship is a beta prior and a binomial likelihood, resulting in a beta posterior.

viewed as just another way to sample points in a space" (p. 235). Although our simple simulation examples include only one or two parameters, simulation's real benefit is evident in high-dimensional problems.

Example 4a: Rejection sampling with bounded support. *Rejection sampling* is a simple simulation technique in which points are generated and then accepted or rejected into the final collection of points (it is sometimes called *acceptance–rejection sampling*). To focus on rejection sampling, we will assume that the sample has been collected, and the prior and likelihood distributions have been defined so that the posterior's pdf can be found. Thus, the posterior pdf is the target distribution, f.

Suppose the researcher has found f for a parameter, θ, that ranges between $-.5$ and $+.5$. The height of f (the bimodal solid line in Figure 24.3, left panel) can be found directly, but not the area underneath it (say from $\theta = 0$ to $\theta = .2$). To find this area and other quantities, five stages are needed:

Stage 1. Specify and graph f (the curved solid line in Figure 24.3, left panel).

Stage 2a. Determine the *candidate bounds*, represented by the endpoints of the horizontal axis in Figure 24.3, left panel. It should cover the minimum and maximum values of the target parameter (which is $[-.5, .5]$).

Stage 2b. Determine the *density bounds*, $[0, c]$. It should start at zero and extend slightly

beyond the tallest point f. The height is called the *scaling constant*, c.

Stage 2c. Plot the box for the candidates and the densities. Stage 2a determines the horizontal coordinates of the box, and Stage 2b determines the vertical coordinates. It should completely envelope f.

Stage 3a. Draw a random uniformly distributed variate, x_b, from the candidate bounds $[-.5, .5]$ (i.e., the width of the dashed box). Repeat this B times to generate $x_1, x_2, \ldots, x_b, \ldots, x_B$.

Stage 3b. For every candidate, draw a uniformly distributed variate, y_b, from the density bounds $[0, c]$ (i.e., the height of the dashed box).

Stage 4. For every candidate, find the corresponding height of the target pdf, $f(x_b)$. Accept the candidate if $f(x_b) \geq y_b$. Accepted candidates are stored in a collection of target points. Plot each (x_b, y_b) point; in Figure 24.3, left panel, an accepted point is a dark gray circle, whereas a rejection is a light gray x.

Stage 5. Calculate the summary statistics of the distribution. Like the bootstrap, the inferences are estimated by calculating statistics on the distribution of accepted candidates. For instance, the estimated mean of the posterior is simply the mean of the accepted candidates. Similarly, the 95% Bayesian CI is marked by the .025 and .975 quantiles of the accepted candidates.

After the candidate and density bounds are established in Stage 2, a pair of random numbers

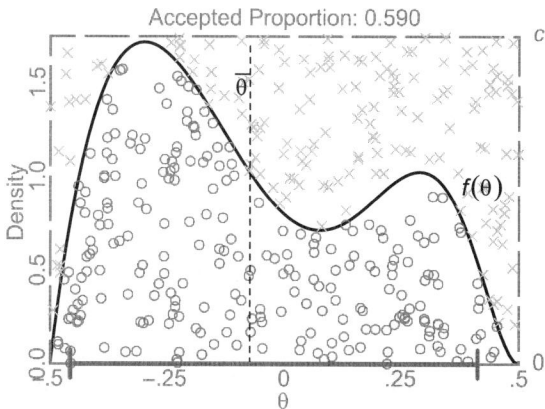 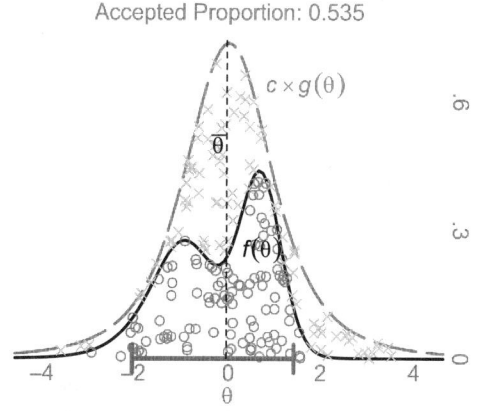

FIGURE 24.3. Rejection sampling of a bounded parameter (a) and unbounded parameter (b). The target distribution is solid, whereas the candidate distribution is dashed. A dark gray circle indicates an accepted candidate, whereas a light gray x is a rejected candidate.

is drawn for every candidate in Stage 3. The first variate is a parameter value (i.e., the point's horizontal position). The second variate is a density value (i.e., the vertical position). It is important that these variates can cover the range of both dimensions.

The target distribution is taller at $\theta = -.3$ than at $\theta = .1$, indicating that $-.3$ is more likely. Therefore, in Stage 4, we want more of the accepted candidates to be in the neighborhood of $-.3$ than in the neighborhood of $.1$. The height of f at $\theta = -.3$ is roughly 1.7 and c (the height of the dashed box) is 1.75. As a result, a candidate of $\theta = -.3$ has a 97% ($= 1.7/1.75$) chance of being accepted. For comparison, candidates in the neighborhood of $\theta = .1$ will be accepted 41% ($= .72/1.75$) of the time. When enough candidates are evaluated, the collection of accepted candidates will have more than twice as many values near $-.3$ than near $.1$. This allows the summary statistics calculated in Stage 5 to assess the properties of the posterior distribution.

The example's f was defined to be a proper probability distribution[15] (i.e., the total area under the curve, its integral, equals 1), which allows us to verify that the proportion of accepted candidates is approximately correct. The area of the box is 1.75 ($= (.5 - [-.5]) \times (1.75 - 0)$) and the area under the target distribution is 1; 57.1% ($= 1/1.75$) of candidates should be accepted. In this example 57.8% were accepted, which will vary slightly between simulation runs.

Example 4b: Rejection sampling with unbounded support. The parameter in Example 4a was bound by $[-.5, .5]$, which permitted a convenient box to be drawn around f. Two primary changes are necessary when θ is unbounded. First, an unbounded *candidate distribution*, g, is needed. In the previous example, the candidate distribution was the uniform distribution, $U(-.5, .5)$, but now g should be chosen more carefully. Second,

the density variate drawn in Stage 3b will depend on the candidate drawn in Stage 3a. It will no longer be fixed at $U(0, c)$. The range of the uniform distribution will differ for each candidate. For instance, sometimes it is $U(0, .35)$, and sometimes $U(0, 1.3)$.

Stage 1. Specify and graph the target distribution, f (the solid bimodal line in Figure 24.3, right panel). Because f extends $(-\infty, \infty)$, decide on reasonable bounds for the graph. The target's tails should practically be zero at the graph's boundaries.

Stage 2a. Choose an appropriate g. When f covers $(-\infty, \infty)$, g also should be unbounded.

Stage 2b. Choose the density bounds. The scaling constant, c, should be defined $f(\theta) \leq c \times g(\theta)$, at all points (i.e., the solid line never exceeds the dashed line).

Stage 2c. Plot the scaled candidate distribution, $c \times g(\theta)$. Make adjustments in Stages 2a to 2b until the candidate envelopes the target completely. In Figure 24.3, right panel, we ultimately settled on $g(\theta) = t_{df=3(\theta)}$ with $c = 2$.

Stage 3a. Draw random variate x_b from g. Repeat this B times.

Stage 3b. For every candidate, find the corresponding height of the dashed line (i.e., $c \times g(x_b)$). Draw the density variate y_b from $U(0, c \times g(x_b))$.

Stage 4. For every candidate, find $f(x_b)$. Accept and store the candidate if $f(x_b) \geq y_b$.

Stage 5. Calculate the desired summary statistics of the distribution as in Example 4a.

In Example 4a, the only explicit adjustment in Stages 2a to 2c was the c value because the candidate distribution already covered the range of the θ parameter. In this example, however, the analyst determines c and the family of the candidate distribution (along with distribution parameters like df). In practice, these are decided together with trial and error.[16]

---

[15]Rejection sampling can estimate improper probability distributions whose total area is not 1. The total area underneath does not matter, as long as the heights along f are correctly proportioned. This is useful in Bayesian statistics, in which the posterior is known only up to a proportional constant.

[16]Albert (2009, p. 99) provided an automatic way to find the scaling constant with a multivariate target distribution (although the candidate distribution and its parameter are still decided by a human). This approach improves efficiency because as c grows, more candidates are rejected and the simulation becomes less efficient. It also is useful with multivariate distributions where graphically determining c is difficult.

The choice of candidate distribution has three requirements. First, after it is multiplied by c, it must be equal to or greater than the target distribution for all values in the target. For this reason, a heavy tailed distribution is a good initial try (like a t with few degrees of freedom). Second, the target distribution should have a quick and accessible random number generator. Third, the height of the target distribution should be easily calculated. Most statistical software provides a function for producing random variates from a t distribution and calculating its pdf.

Markov Chain Monte Carlo

An MCMC simulation introduces dependencies between the B statistics. The theoretical justification and foundations of MCMC are covered in Robert and Casella (2004) and Gamerman and Lopes (2006). Only a few details differ between rejection sampling and the simplest MCMC.

Example 5a: Independent metropolis-hastings. Rejection sampling candidates are generated independently—for example, the 53rd candidate has no effect on the value or the rejection chances of the 54th candidate. This differs from the independent Metropolis-Hastings (IMH) sampler. On the bth step, there is a competition between the *incumbent*, z_b, and the candidate, x_b. The accepted candidate becomes the incumbent for the subsequent step, z_b+1. The sequence of z_b values is called a *chain*.

This example reuses f and g from Example 4b. The heights of these two distributions are $f(x_b)$ and $g(x_b)$ at point x_b.

Stage 1. Specify f.
Stage 2. Choose g. From g, draw the incumbent for the chain's first step, z_1.
Stage 3a. Draw the candidate x_b from g.
Stage 3b. Calculate a_b, which affects the candidate's chances of acceptance:

$$a_b = \frac{g(z_b)}{f(z_b)} \times \frac{f(x_b)}{g(x_b)}. \qquad (24.7)$$

This is the ratio of the incumbent at the candidate and target distribution, multiplied by the ratio of the new candidate at the target and candidate distribution.

Stage 4. If $a_b \geq 1$, the new candidate wins and becomes the incumbent for the next step (so, $z_b+1 = x_b$). If $a_b < 1$, there is a runoff election in which the new candidate's probability of winning is a_b. Draw y_b from $U(0, 1)$. The new candidate wins if $a_b > y_b$; otherwise, the incumbent is reelected and survives another step (so, $z_b+1 = z_b$).

Repeat *Stages 3a, 3b*, and *4* for $b = 1, 2, \ldots,$ B *steps*.

Stage 5. Calculate any summary statistics on the B incumbents, as in Example 4a.

As seen in the upper left panel of Figure 24.4, the candidate does not have to envelope the target distribution in an IMH. The histogram of the B accepted points matches the theoretical target distribution nicely. Compared with rejection sampling, it is less important to graph f and g because c does not exist. However, g is still required to support all possible values of f. For instance, if f supports $(-\infty, \infty)$, g cannot be $\chi^2_{(df=10)}$, which supports only $(0, \infty)$.

The top right panel identifies three points (D, E, F) to illustrate the logic of jumping. Assume the incumbent is D and the candidate is E at step 70. The first ratio in a_{70} (i.e., $g(z_{70})/f(z_{70})$) equals 1 because the target and candidate distribution are equal at the incumbent's position. Point E is at the mode of g incidentally, so it is the most likely position for a candidate. However, $g(E)$ would overestimate $f(E)$ by a factor of 2 if all candidates at E were accepted; to account for the disparity between the distributions, the second ratio in a_{70} (i.e., $f(x_{70})/g(x_{70})$) is roughly .5—indicating that half of the candidates are accepted.

Assume the candidate E was rejected at Step 70, and F is the new candidate for Step 71. The value x_{71} is guaranteed victory because the first ratio in a_{71} is one and the second ratio is greater than one. The MCMC's first 100 steps are shown in the bottom panel of Figure 24.4. Flat chain links indicate the incumbent was reelected. Notice there are many longtime incumbents with values

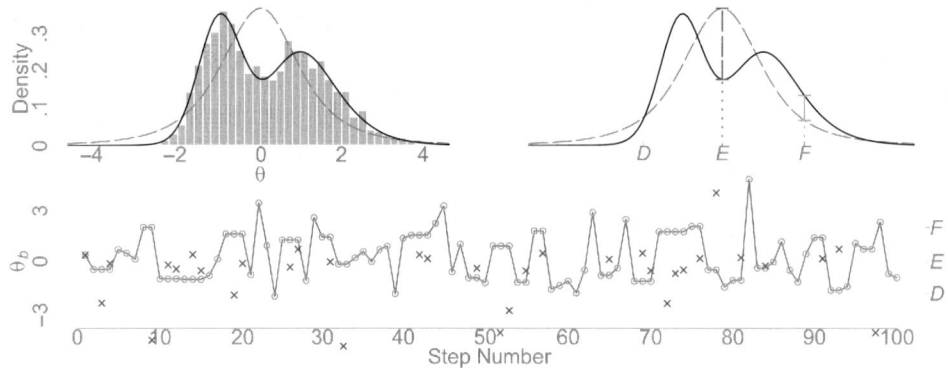

FIGURE 24.4. The target (*f*; solid) and candidate (*g*; dashed) distributions of an independent Metropolis-Hastings (top left). A histogram of the accepted candidates (top left) closely matches the target distribution (top right). In the bottom panel, the chain's history is overlaid with victorious candidates (light gray circles) and rejected new candidates (dark gray x symbols).

around point *F* (e.g., see the flat sequence for Steps 71–76). Furthermore, there are many candidates around point *E* but few victories (e.g., see the *x* values for Steps 11–17 and 71–76).

If *f* and *g* are equal at both x_b and z_b, then a_b equals 1 and a jump is guaranteed. If *f* and *g* are always equal, every jump is guaranteed. We later discuss the Gibbs sampler, which exploits this property in a multivariate context. In a univariate context, it would be better to simply draw x_b from *f* (instead of *g*) and always accept it. However, if it is possible to simulate directly from the univariate *f*, it is very likely that *f* has tractable equations for its CDF and standard error—so simulation is unnecessary.

The IMH is called *independent* because the candidate distribution never changes, and thus *g* is independent of z_b. The IMH may be practical when *f* is tight and has well-defined boundaries. However, when *f* is complex and highly dimensional, capturing "the main features of the target distribution is most often impossible" (Robert & Casella, 2004, p. 284). An MCMC can cover a multivariate space better if the candidate distribution is able to wander, which is a feature of the next sampler.

Example 5b: Metropolis-Hastings. In a Metropolis-Hastings (MH) sampler, the incumbent influences *g*. In Example 5a, *g* was unaffected by the previous step and remained centered on

$\theta = 0$; *g* could be expressed $g_0(x_b) = t(x_b|df = 3, mean = 0)$. The MH adds a location parameter to *g*: $g_z(x) = g(x_b|z_b) = t(x_b|df = 3, mean = z_b)$ and $g_x(z_b) = g(z_b|x_b) = t(z_b|df = 3, mean = x_b)$. Only two procedural changes are necessary. In Stage 3a, x_b is drawn from g_{zb}, which is centered around z_b. In Stage 3b, the acceptance variable is

$$a_b = \frac{g(z_b|x_b)}{f(z_b)} \times \frac{f(x_b)}{g(x_b|z_b)}. \qquad (24.8)$$

We revisit the scenario depicted Figure 24.4, upper right panel. When *D* is the incumbent at Steps 70 and 71, the candidates are generated from a t_3 distribution centered around *D*. When point *F* wins Step 71, g_z will shift right, and the next candidate will be drawn from a t_3 distribution centered around point *F*. The target distribution never moves. The candidate distribution jumps around for each x_b and z_b as it tries to recover a chain of points that are representative of the target.

Inferences are calculated directly from the chain's *B* points. For instance, a multilevel model uses no explicit formula for the shrinkage from a level-one parameter toward a level-two parameter (e.g., Gelman & Hill, 2007, Equation 12.1) when estimated with an MCMC. The challenging aspect of an MCMC is getting the chain to represent *f*. Like a bootstrap, the equations for the estimates are simply summary statistics.

The MH is the oldest and most general and flexible of the MCMC samplers. A seminal article by Metropolis and Ulam (1949) established the term *Monte Carlo method*. Newer MCMC samplers can be more efficient, but more knowledge of the target distribution is required.

Example 6: Gibbs sampler. The Gibbs sampler has two important differences from the MH. The basic MH changes every dimension at once, whereas Gibbs divides the problem into substeps and jumps in only one direction at a time. Every dimension has its own candidate distribution, which leads to the second difference between Gibbs and the MH—every candidate is accepted. The candidate and target distributions are identical, which permits direct simulation from f. When direct simulation is possible from conditional distributions, Gibbs *can* be more efficient than the MH. If f has four parameters $x = (x^{(1)}, x^{(2)}, x^{(3)}, x^{(4)})$, the Gibbs involves four substeps in every step:

Stage 1. Determine that the joint distribution of f exists (but it does not actually need to be specified).

Stage 2. Choose starting values for each parameter $(x_1^{(1)}, x_1^{(2)}, x_1^{(3)}, x_1^{(4)})$.

Stage 3. In each substep, draw a variables' candidate while fixing the other three variables:

$$x_b^{(1)} \sim f_1\left(x^{(1)} \middle| \quad\quad x_{b-1}^{(2)}, \quad x_{b-1}^{(3)}, \quad x_{b-1}^{(4)}\right)$$

$$x_b^{(2)} \sim f_2\left(x^{(2)} \middle| x_b^{(1)} \quad\quad, \quad x_{b-1}^{(3)}, \quad x_{b-1}^{(4)}\right)$$

$$x_b^{(3)} \sim f_3\left(x^{(3)} \middle| x_b^{(1)}, \quad x_b^{(2)}, \quad\quad\quad x_{b-1}^{(4)}\right)$$

$$x_b^{(4)} \sim f_4\left(x^{(4)} \middle| x_b^{(1)}, \quad x_b^{(2)}, \quad x_b^{(3)} \quad\quad\right). \quad (24.9)$$

Stage 4. Automatically accept the multivariate candidate, $z_b = x_b = (x_b^{(1)}, x_b^{(2)}, x_b^{(3)}, x_b^{(4)})$.

Repeat *Stages 3* and *4 for b = 2, 3, . . ., B steps.*

Stage 5. Calculate any summary statistics as in Example 4a.

Stage 3 exhibits a leapfrog pattern. Variables jump one at a time, and then they stay still in the updated position until the others complete their turn. The jump for the first variable in line, $x_b^{(1)}$, relies on the values from the previous step $(x_{b-1}^{(2)}, x_{b-1}^{(3)}, x_{b-1}^{(4)})$. The jump for the second variable, $x_b^{(2)}$, relies on the current step's value for $x^{(1)}$ but on the previous step's value for $x^{(3)}$ and $x^{(4)}$ because they have not been updated yet. This sequence continues until the last variable is updated entirely from values from the bth step.

Examples 5 and 6 have used a single chain. A recommended practice is to run at least four independent chains (e.g., Robert & Casella, 2004, Chapter 12). The algorithms are modified by running Stages 2 through 4 once for each chain. It is important that chains' positions do not affect each other. However, the summary statistics in Stage 5 combine the chains and treat their points as one large sample.

Metropolis within Gibbs. The Gibbs advantage can be exploited even when it is not possible to simulate directly from the joint f. Suppose f_1, f_2, and f_3 could produce their respective candidates, but f_4 could not. This last substep could use an MH to draw $x^{(4)}$, while $x^{(1)}$, $x^{(2)}$, and $x^{(3)}$ are temporarily fixed. In fact, each substep could be replaced by a different MH. Consider a typical growth model in which each subject has three parameters; a study with 100 subjects has a target distribution with more than 300 dimensions. Robert and Casella (2010) explained the advantage:

> It is most often the case that designing a Metropolis Hastings algorithm on a large-dimensional target is challenging or even impossible. The fundamental gain in using a Gibbs-like structure is that it breaks down a complex model into a large number of smaller and simpler targets, where local MH algorithms can be designed at little expense. (p. 230)

Pragmatic MCMC Issues

Expectations for learning the MCMC method are different from those for the bootstrap and rejection sampling. For a student or researcher with a solid graduate-level statistics background (say, two or more rigorous statistics courses), we believe 1 or 2 days is a reasonable amount of time to understand the basics of bootstrap theory, program some necessary routines, and competently interpret the results for a two-factor experiment. However, learning MCMC takes more investment. The techniques are not only more complicated—both conceptually and mathematically—but also usually applied to more complex experimental designs. But their power and flexibility should be obvious. With some (worthwhile) effort, readers can appreciate the capabilities of MCMC and understand applied articles containing an MCMC analysis.

Convergence and mixing. The MH and Gibbs are defined so that f is guaranteed to be recovered after an infinite number of steps. Most applications require fewer steps, but deciding how many are needed is somewhat subjective.

There are two milestones for an MCMC. The chains' starting values (specified in Stage 2) are not necessarily on f, especially when f has many dimensions. It is recommended to run a chain for several hundred (or several thousand) steps during a *warm-up* or *burn-in* period; these initial points are unlikely to represent f, so they are discarded and not considered by the Stage 5 statistics. Several indicators can assess different aspects of convergence, and the popular indicators are explained in MCMC and contemporary Bayesian books (e.g., Carlin & Louis, 2009; Gelman et al., 2013; Gelman et al., 2020; McElreath, 2020a; Robert & Casella, 2004).

After reaching the warm-up milestone, then determine how many steps are needed to adequately represent f. The primary concern is how well the chains continue to mix with each other and how quickly they cover f. Weak mixing can occur when successive points in a chain are strongly correlated or when a chain gets stuck in an isolated region of f, like a local maximum. One general strategy is to specify an equivalent model in which

the parameters are "as independent as possible" (Robert & Casella, 2004, p. 396; for many specific strategies, see Gelman & Hill, 2007, especially Chapter 19; Gelman et al., 2020).

Failing to converge is rarely a concern for a (properly specified) model that covers a few dimensions, because computers are powerful enough to generate a chain long enough to cover f decisively. But their brute-force nature is not ensured to be adequate for a target distribution with hundreds of dimensions (which occurs even for modest multilevel models, because each subject has multiple individual parameters).

MCMC software and resources. After running a bootstrap for 30 seconds, simulation error is usually negligible (and 1 second is adequate for most one-dimensional distributions). The duration of a nontrivial MCMC is much longer. Compared with bootstrapping, each simulation replication is less efficient and most MCMC models are much more complex. Models may require several minutes of computer time to get a rough estimate and 1 hour or more before simulation error is negligible. To reduce development time, we agree with Gelman and Hill (2007, p. 345) that similar models should be run initially with non-Bayesian software that uses maximum likelihood (ML; see also Gelman et al., 2020, Section 5).[17]

Most recent Bayesian books use Stan (plus R or Julia) for their computational examples.[18] Stan's syntax is flexible and can even address frequentist models that may be impossible to run in frequentist software. It decides many technical details; for instance, the user does not need to determine the posterior distribution—only the prior and likelihood equations that ultimately define it.

Typically, a researcher (1) manipulates the data set with R, (2) estimates the model with MCMC software (such as Stan, BUGS, or JAGS), and (3) diagnoses convergence and views the model

---

[17]Although MCMC is less computationally efficient, it has at least three benefits over typical ML approaches. First, ML cannot incorporate prior information. Second, ML approaches fix the estimates of variance parameters instead of allowing their uncertainty to inform lower level parameter estimates appropriately (Gelman & Hill, 2007, p. 345). Third, ML finds only the mode of the likelihood distribution, whereas MCMC can capture many features of the target distribution, like its mean, modes, and quantiles (Robert & Casella, 2004, Section 9.4).

[18]The BUGS and JAGS programs were the community's favorites before Stan's release in 2012. Their strengths and weaknesses are covered in Stan Development Team, 2023, Appendix; Lunn et al., 2009, and their subsequent discussion; and Plummer 2017, Appendix A. Software such as SAS and Mplus have released MCMC routines, although we expect most books will continue to target the Stan syntax.

results in R again. This workflow is demonstrated in most recent applied Bayesian books (e.g., Albert, 2009; Carlin & Louis, 2009; Gelman et al., 2013; Gelman et al., 2020; Gelman & Hill, 2007; Gill, 2008; McElreath, 2020a). Presently there exist a number of R packages that facilitate the use of Stan directly from R. Packages like the 'brms' and 'rstanarm' packages provide convenient "wrappers" for Stan, so that researchers can use familiar R syntax to conduct Bayesian analyses (Bürkner, 2018; Goodrich et al., 2020). The "rethinking" package, intended for use alongside *Statistical Rethinking* (McElreath, 2020a, 2020b) provides a syntax closer to actual Stan syntax. Finally, the 'cmdstanr' and 'rstan' packages provide full Stan functionality and use the full Stan syntax (Gabry & Češnovar, 2021; Stan Development Team, 2023). For most users, there will be little difference between the 'cmdstanr' and 'rstan' packages, although 'cmdstanr' is slightly ahead of the 'rstan' package in terms of available features and tends to use a slightly more current version of the Stan program. For non-R users, a variety of similar packages are available in other programs (e.g., Python).

There exist pedagogical and performance advantages to writing a sampler for a specific model, such as the code for Examples 5 and 6. R has many functions that make MCMC development more manageable, as well as packages such as MCMCpack that handle common details automatically but allow the user to specify the exact samplers (Martin et al., 2011; Gelman & Hill, 2007, Chapter 18). Regardless of the software, we recommend starting with the simplest possible model (e.g., the sample's grand mean) and incrementally increasing complexity (e.g., group- and subject-level covariates). Although this appears pedantic and tedious, any syntax and logic errors are more obvious when only one feature has changed. Common accidents like misspelling a variable or creating an unidentified model are easier to detect, and the overall process is less tedious.

Furthermore, an incremental approach naturally produces a sequence of nested models that can be statistically compared with one another

(see Rodgers, 2010, for a modeling rationale). The complexity of the specified model should be given careful thought. As Fisher (1970) wrote,

> No human mind is capable of grasping in its entirety the meaning of any considerable quantity of numerical data. The number of independent facts supplied by the data is usually far greater than the number of facts sought, and in consequence much of the information supplied by any body of actual data is irrelevant. It is the object of the statistical processes employed in the reduction of data to exclude this irrelevant information, and to isolate the whole of the relevant information contained in the data. (p. 6)

CONCLUSION

Simulation methods like MCMC and the bootstrap are tools that allow an applied researcher to approach questions that cannot be addressed with conventional analytic methods. The statistical tools required of well-trained behavioral science researchers now include traditional approaches such as ANOVA and categorical data analysis, along with more recently developed strategies for multilevel latent variable models and missing data. Simulation methods support the feasibility of these approaches. They provide access to many (underlying) distributions that were previously intractable, which permits statisticians to specify models that are more appropriate to their research goals.

References

Albert, J. (2009). *Bayesian computation with* R (2nd ed.). Springer. https://doi.org/10.1007/978-0-387-92298-0

Andrews, D. W. K. (2000). Inconsistency of the bootstrap when a parameter is on the boundary of the parameter space. *Econometrica, 68*(2), 399–405. https://doi.org/10.1111/1468-0262.00114

Beasley, W. H., DeShea, L., Toothaker, L. E., Mendoza, J. L., Bard, D. E., & Rodgers, J. L. (2007).

Bootstrapping to test for nonzero population correlation coefficients using univariate sampling. *Psychological Methods, 12*(4), 414–433. https://doi.org/10.1037/1082-989X.12.4.414

Beasley, W. H., & Rodgers, J. L. (2009). Resampling methods. In R. E. Millsap & A. Maydeu-Olivares (Eds.), *Quantitative methods in psychology* (pp. 362–386). SAGE.

Beran, R. (2003). The impact of the bootstrap on statistical algorithms and theory. *Statistical Science, 18*(2), 175–184. https://doi.org/10.1214/ss/1063994972

Bishara, A. J., & Hittner, J. B. (2012). Testing the significance of a correlation with nonnormal data: Comparison of Pearson, Spearman, transformation, and resampling approaches. *Psychological Methods, 17*(3), 399–417. https://doi.org/10.1037/a0028087

Bishara, A. J., & Hittner, J. B. (2017). Confidence intervals for correlations when data are not normal. *Behavior Research Methods, 49*(1), 294–309. https://doi.org/10.3758/s13428-016-0702-8

Bollen, K. A., & Stine, R. A. (1992). Bootstrapping goodness-of-fit measures in structural equation models. *Sociological Methods & Research, 21*(2), 205–229. https://doi.org/10.1177/0049124192021002004

Boos, D. D. (2003). Introduction to the bootstrap world. *Statistical Science, 18*(2), 168–174. https://doi.org/10.1214/ss/1063994971

Bürkner, P. (2018). Advanced Bayesian multilevel modeling with the R package brms. *The R Journal, 10*(1), 395–411. https://doi.org/10.32614/RJ-2018-017

Carlin, B. P., & Louis, T. A. (2009). *Bayesian methods for data analysis* (3rd ed.). Chapman & Hall/CRC.

Carpenter, B., Gelman, A., Hoffman, M. D., Lee, D., Goodrich, B., Betancourt, M., Brubaker, M., Guo, J., Li, P., & Riddell, A. (2017). Stan: A probabilistic programming language. *Journal of Statistical Software, 76*(1), 1–32. https://doi.org/10.18637/jss.v076.i01

Chan, W., & Chan, D. W. L. (2004). Bootstrap standard error and confidence intervals for the correlation corrected for range restriction: A simulation study. *Psychological Methods, 9*(3), 369–385. https://doi.org/10.1037/1082-989X.9.3.369

Davison, A. C., & Hinkley, D. V. (1997). *Bootstrap methods and their application.* Cambridge University Press. https://doi.org/10.1017/CBO9780511802843

Davison, A. C., Hinkley, D. V., & Young, G. A. (2003). Recent development in bootstrap methodology. *Statistical Science, 18*(2), 141–157. https://doi.org/10.1214/ss/1063994969

Diaconis, P., & Efron, B. (1983, May). Computer-intensive methods in statistics. *Scientific American, 248*(5), 116–130. https://doi.org/10.1038/scientificamerican0583-116

Efron, B. (1979). Bootstrap methods: Another look at the jackknife. *Annals of Statistics, 7*(1), 1–26. https://doi.org/10.1214/aos/1176344552

Efron, B., & Tibshirani, R. J. (1993). *An introduction to the bootstrap.* Chapman & Hall/CRC.

Enders, C. K. (2010). *Applied missing data analysis.* Guilford Press.

Fan, X. (2003). Using commonly available software for bootstrapping in both substantive and measurement analyses. *Educational and Psychological Measurement, 63*(1), 24–50. https://doi.org/10.1177/0013164402239315

Fisher, R. A. (1970). *Statistical methods for research workers* (14th ed.). Hafner.

Gabry, J., & Češnovar, R. (2021). cmdstanr: R Interface to 'CmdStan'. https://mc-stan.org/cmdstanr

Gamerman, D., & Lopes, H. F. (2006). *Markov chain Monte Carlo.* Chapman & Hall/CRC. https://doi.org/10.1201/9781482296426

Gelman, A., Carlin, J. B., Stern, H. S., Dunson, D. B., Vehtari, A., & Rubin, D. B. (2013). *Bayesian data analysis* (3rd ed.). Chapman & Hall. https://doi.org/10.1201/b16018

Gelman, A., & Hill, J. (2007). *Data analysis using regression and multilevel/hierarchical models.* Cambridge University Press.

Gelman, A., Hill, J., & Vehtari, A. (2020). *Regression and other stories.* Cambridge University Press. https://doi.org/10.1017/9781139161879

Gill, J. (2008). *Bayesian methods* (2nd ed.). Chapman & Hall.

Goodrich, B., Gabry, J., Ali, I., & Brilleman, S. (2020). rstanarm: Bayesian applied regression modeling via Stan (R package Version 2.21.1). https://mc-stan.org/rstanarm

Hastie, T., Tibshirani, R., & Friedman, J. (2009). *The elements of statistical learning: Data mining, inference, and prediction* (2nd ed.). Springer. https://doi.org/10.1007/978-0-387-84858-7

Hutson, A. D. (2019). A robust Pearson correlation test for a general point null using a surrogate bootstrap distribution. *PLOS ONE, 14*(5), e0216287. https://doi.org/10.1371/journal.pone.0216287

Lahiri, S. N. (2003). *Resampling methods for dependent data.* Springer. https://doi.org/10.1007/978-1-4757-3803-2

Lee, W., & Rodgers, J. L. (1998). Bootstrapping correlation coefficients using univariate and bivariate sampling. *Psychological Methods, 3*(1), 91–103. https://doi.org/10.1037/1082-989X.3.1.91

LePage, R., & Billiard, L. (Eds.). (1992). *Exploring the limits of bootstrap.* Wiley.

Lunn, D., Spiegelhalter, D., Thomas, A., & Best, N. (2009). The BUGS project: Evolution, critique and future directions. *Statistics in Medicine, 28*(25), 3049–3067. https://doi.org/10.1002/sim.3680

Manly, B. (2007). *Randomization, bootstrap and Monte Carlo methods in biology* (3rd ed.). Chapman & Hall.

Martin, A. D., Quinn, K. M., & Park, J. H. (2011). MCMCpack: Markov Chain Monte Carlo in R. *Journal of Statistical Software, 42*(9), 1–21. https://doi.org/10.18637/jss.v042.i09

McElreath, R. (2020a). *A Bayesian course with examples in R and Stan.* Chapman & Hall/CRC. https://doi.org/10.1201/9780429029608

McElreath, R. (2020b). *rethinking: Statistical rethinking course and book package* [Computer software]. https://github.com/rmcelreath/rethinking

Mendoza, J. L., Hart, D. E., & Powell, A. (1991). A bootstrap confidence interval based on a correlation corrected for range restriction. *Multivariate Behavioral Research, 26*(2), 255–269. https://doi.org/10.1207/s15327906mbr2602_4

Metropolis, N., & Ulam, S. (1949). The Monte Carlo method. *Journal of the American Statistical Association, 44*(247), 335–341. https://doi.org/10.1080/01621459.1949.10483310

Monahan, J. F. (2001). *Numerical methods of statistics.* Cambridge University Press. https://doi.org/10.1017/CBO9780511812231

O'Keefe, P., & Rodgers, J. L. (2020). A simulation study of bootstrap approaches to estimate confidence intervals in DeFries–Fulker regression models (with application to the heritability of BMI changes in the NLSY). *Behavior Genetics, 50*(2), 127–138. https://doi.org/10.1007/s10519-020-09993-9

Plummer, M. (2017). *JAGS Version 4.3.0 user manual.* https://people.stat.sc.edu/hansont/stat740/jags_user_manual.pdf

Poi, B. P. (2004). From the help desk: Some bootstrapping techniques. *Stata Journal, 4*, 312–328. https://journals.sagepub.com/doi/pdf/10.1177/1536867X0400400308

Robert, C. P., & Casella, G. (2004). *Monte Carlo statistical methods.* Springer. https://doi.org/10.1007/978-1-4757-4145-2

Robert, C. P., & Casella, G. (2010). *Introducing Monte Carlo methods with R.* Springer. https://doi.org/10.1007/978-1-4419-1576-4

Rodgers, J. L. (1999). The bootstrap, the jackknife, and the randomization test: A sampling taxonomy. *Multivariate Behavioral Research, 34*(4), 441–456. https://doi.org/10.1207/S15327906MBR3404_2

Rodgers, J. L. (2010). The epistemology of mathematical and statistical modeling: A quiet methodological revolution. *American Psychologist, 65*(1), 1–12. https://doi.org/10.1037/a0018326

Rodgers, J. L., & Beasley, W. H. (2013). Fisher, Gossett, and AHST: Bootstrapping multiple correlation alternative hypotheses. In M. Edwards & R. MacCallum (Eds.), *Current topics in the theory and application of latent variable models* (pp. 217–239). Routledge.

Rodgers, J. L., Nicewander, W. A., & Toothaker, L. (1984). Linearly independent, uncorrelated, and orthogonal variables. *The American Statistician, 38*(2), 133–134. https://doi.org/10.2307/2683250

Smith, T. A., & Kimball, D. R. (2010). Learning from feedback: Spacing and the delay-retention effect. *Journal of Experimental Psychology: Learning, Memory, and Cognition, 36*(1), 80–95. https://doi.org/10.1037/a0017407

Stan Development Team. (2023). *Stan modeling language users guide and reference manual* (Version 2.31). https://mc-stan.org

Steiger, J. H. (2007, August). *Statistical games we all should play* [Paper presentation]. 115th Annual Convention of the American Psychological Association, San Francisco, CA, United States.

Tukey, J. W. (1977). *Exploratory data analysis.* Addison-Wesley.

CHAPTER 25

DESIGNING SIMULATION STUDIES

Xitao Fan

This chapter provides a practical guide for designing Monte Carlo simulation studies. Simulation studies are often needed to provide empirical solutions to some problems in quantitative analysis. In this chapter, some quantitative techniques are used as illustrative examples, but the quantitative techniques themselves are not the focus of the chapter. Quantitative researchers from psychology and other social and behavioral sciences (e.g., education, sociology) are the intended audience.

WHAT IS A SIMULATION STUDY?

As defined in *Merriam-Webster's Online Dictionary* (2021), *Monte Carlo* relates to or involves "the use of random sampling techniques, and often the use of computer simulation, to obtain approximate solutions to mathematical or physical problems, especially in terms of a range of values each of which has a calculated probability of being the solution." Monte Carlo simulation may offer an empirical alternative to a theoretical approach (i.e., a solution based on statistical or mathematical theory), especially in situations where a theoretical approach can be difficult to implement or even unavailable.

The Monte Carlo simulation approach in quantitative analysis is increasingly possible and more popular because of the advances in computing technology, as Monte Carlo simulation typically requires intensive computing. Monte Carlo studies simulate sampling from a defined statistical population, generally for the purpose of estimating the sampling distribution of a statistic of interest. This approach can be applied to a variety of situations in different disciplines.

Situations Where Simulation Is Useful

The situations where a simulation study can be useful include, but are not limited to, assessing the consequences of assumption violations, understanding a sample statistic that has unknown distribution characteristics, evaluating the performance of a technique when statistical theory is weak or even nonexistent, and understanding the statistical power of a technique under some specified data conditions (Fan et al., 2002).

Consequences of assumption violations. Statistical techniques are classified into two broad categories: parametric and nonparametric. Parametric statistical methods have theoretical assumptions about data distributions. Although statistical theories are usually efficient, the validity of statistical results is contingent on some theoretical assumptions. When the assumptions are violated to some degree, the validity of the analysis

https://doi.org/10.1037/0000319-025
APA Handbook of Research Methods in Psychology, Second Edition: Vol. 2. Research Designs: Quantitative, Qualitative, Neuropsychological, and Biological, H. Cooper (Editor-in-Chief)

results may be in question. Statistical theory stipulates what the condition should be, but statistical theory does not provide clear indications about what the reality would be if the conditions are not satisfied in the data. As a result, statistical theory does not inform us about the seriousness of the consequences when some assumptions are violated. In this situation, simulation becomes a viable empirical approach to understanding these issues.

Understanding a sample statistic that has no theoretical distribution.   In some situations, theoretical sampling distribution of a statistic of interest may not be available (e.g., canonical function and structure coefficients, factor pattern coefficients in exploratory factor analysis). In such a situation, simulation can inform us about the distribution characteristics of the sample statistic for the specified data conditions.

Other situations.   There are other situations in which simulation is useful or even necessary. For example, in exploratory factor analysis, one prominent issue is to retain statistically meaningful factors. For this purpose, competing approaches are available: eigenvalue greater than 1, scree plot, parallel analysis, and so on. If we are interested in understanding how these approaches perform under different data conditions, a simulation study will be necessary. As another example, growth mixture modeling (GMM) has become widely used in longitudinal data modeling in psychological research, for exploring the possibility that unobserved subpopulations may have different longitudinal growth trajectories. How well do the different enumeration indexes in GMM perform in identifying the correct number of latent subpopulations in a data sample? How is the performance of GMM influenced by different data conditions (e.g., sample size, degree of separation among the subpopulations)? These and similar issues typically do not have theoretical or analytical solutions; instead, simulation is often useful and necessary for our understanding of these issues.

BASIC STEPS IN A SIMULATION STUDY

Simulation studies are designed for different purposes, and not surprisingly, they may be very different. Some basic steps, however, are common for most simulation studies, and here is a quick summary of these steps.

Asking Questions Suitable for a Simulation Study

This may appear to be too obvious to warrant discussion, but this initial step is often important enough to shape the simulation study under consideration. Unless you ask the right question(s), it may not be possible or necessary to do a simulation study in the first place. As discussed above, simulation is usually concerned with the empirical sampling distribution characteristics of a statistic of interest, especially in situations where statistical theory is weak (e.g., discriminant function and structure coefficients in canonical correlation analysis; Thompson, 1991), or some important assumptions underlying the statistical theory are not viable and are violated to varying degrees (e.g., Type I error control of an independent-sample t test when the assumption of equal population variances is violated). In a general sense, simulation is suitable for questions to which there are either no analytical and theoretical solutions, or no trustworthy ones.

Simulation Study Design

Once the question(s) for a simulation study are identified (e.g., how well does an independent sample t test control Type I error when the assumption of equal population variances is violated?), a simulation study needs to be carefully designed to provide answers to the question(s). In a simulation design, the major factors that may potentially affect the outcome of interest should be included and manipulated. For example, in the context of an independent-sample t test when the equal population variance assumption is violated, it would be obvious that the design needs to include conditions with both equal and unequal population variances. In addition, the degree of unequal variances also needs to be varied. A reasonable design should include a range of unequal variance conditions ranging from "minor" (e.g., two-population variance ratio of 2:1) to "severe" levels (e.g., two-population variance ratio of 8:1), with several intermediate levels in between.

It should be noted, however, that there do not appear to be "rules of thumb" in defining the magnitude of difference between groups' variances (e.g., ratio of 2:1, 3:1, or some ratios) as too problematic, because this factor would interact with the factor of equal/unequal group sizes to be described below. So the "minor" or "severe" unequal variance conditions described here is for operational convenience only, but not for suggesting that these were guidelines for this condition. Glass and Hopkins (1996; Chapter 12) provided a concise summary of the intertwined issues of equal/unequal group variances and equal/unequal group samples sizes in the context of independent *t* tests, and interested readers may consult that chapter for more information related to this issue.

In addition, group sample size may also be considered in this design, both in terms of equal–unequal samples sizes of the two groups, and in terms of how the two groups with unequal sample sizes are paired with larger–smaller variance conditions. Furthermore, the total sample size is another factor that can be manipulated. Assuming that these are the only three factors to be considered in a simulation, and the three factors are fully crossed, we may have the schematic representation of the design in Table 25.1.

The design for this seemingly simple problem (i.e., Type I error control of independent-sample *t* test with violation of equal population variance assumption) could be more complex if we are willing to consider either more levels of each manipulated factor (e.g., other unequal sample-size variations in addition to 0.7:0.3 ratio), or if we are to expand the design to cover additional factors such as data normality conditions (e.g., normally distributed data condition, mildly to severely nonnormal data conditions). These

TABLE 25.1

Schematic Design Representation of an Independent *t* Test Simulation Study

N	Two-group variance ratio	Two group sample size ratio		
		Equal	Unequal (1)[a] 0.7 : 0.3	Unequal (2)[b] 0.3 : 0.7
30	1:1	1,000[c]	1,000	1,000
	2:1	1,000	1,000	1,000
	4:1	1,000	1,000	1,000
	8:1	1,000	1,000	1,000
60	1:1	1,000	1,000	1,000
	2:1	1,000	1,000	1,000
	4:1	1,000	1,000	1,000
	8:1	1,000	1,000	1,000
120	1:1	1,000	1,000	1,000
	2:1	1,000	1,000	1,000
	4:1	1,000	1,000	1,000
	8:1	1,000	1,000	1,000

[a]The larger sample size group has larger population variance. [b]The larger sample size group has smaller population variance. [c]Number of replications in each cell condition.

potential factors to be included in the design, and their levels of variation require careful consideration, as guided by the research literature, by practical constraints (e.g., realistically manageable scope of a simulation project), and by some other considerations (e.g., desired degree of generalizability of the findings).

Data Generation

Once the design issues in a simulation study are settled, the next step is to generate sample data to which a statistical technique of interest (e.g., independent-sample *t* test) will be applied. Data generation is the most important step in any simulation study, because the validity of simulation findings hinges upon the validity of the data-generation process implemented in a simulation. In this sense, the importance of data generation in a simulation study can never be overemphasized. Depending on the complexity of a simulation study, the data-generation process may involve some or all the following steps.

Generation of univariate sample data. Initially, sample data are generated on a univariate basis, even though multiple variables may be involved in a simulation. Univariate sample data generation can be accomplished with an appropriate random number generator (for a normally distributed variable, for a uniformly distributed variable, and so on) commonly available in many statistical software packages. Once the univariate random variables are generated for the specified sample size conditions, some transformation(s) may follow so that the sample data will reflect the targeted data distribution shapes specified in a simulation study.

Transformation of univariate sample data. In most situations, the initial univariate sample data generated may not have the statistical properties (e.g., the four statistical moments: mean, standard deviation, skewness, kurtosis) that we desire in our simulation design. Thus, data transformation is often needed to reflect the variables' population characteristics as specified in a simulation design. For this purpose, there are two major types of transformation. The first is linear transformation, through which the univariate sample data will reflect the first two moments (population mean and standard deviation of a variable) of the population parameters of the variable as specified in a design. This transformation is straightforward. For a sample of a random normal univariate X_i, the transformed variable $X_{i\,new}$ will be:

$$X_{i_{new}} = X_i \sigma_{population} + \mu_{population},\qquad(25.1)$$

where $\sigma_{population}$ and $\mu_{population}$ are the specified population standard deviation and mean, respectively, for the variable.[1]

The second type of transformation involves nonlinear transformation, through which the sample data will reflect the third and fourth moments (i.e., skewness and kurtosis) of the population data parameters as specified in a simulation design. This transformation is necessary if issues related to data nonnormality are of interest in a simulation study. This transformation (i.e., nonlinear transformation for achieving a specified degree of nonnormality of a variable as defined by its third and fourth moments of skewness and kurtosis) is more complicated and will be discussed later.

Transformation to multivariate sample data. Linear and nonlinear transformations involve univariate sample data. In most situations, multiple variables are involved in statistical analyses, and these multiple variables have the specified intervariable correlation pattern. Procedures are needed to transform the sample data of *independent* variables to sample data of *correlated* variables that reflect the specified population correlation pattern. Procedures for implementing this transformation are discussed later.

Accumulation of the Statistic(s) of Interest

Most simulation studies in psychology and other related disciplines focus on the performance characteristics of some type(s) of statistical techniques. Once a data sample is generated based on the specified population parameters and other considerations (e.g., sample size) in a simulation design, the relevant statistical technique is applied to the data sample for analysis, and the statistic(s) of interest from such an analysis will be computed from the data sample. The statistic(s) of interest *from each random sample* is obtained, and each statistic of interest needs to be accumulated across the random samples that are repeatedly generated under the specified conditions (e.g., 1,000 random samples under each cell condition in Table 25.1). This process continues until the statistic of interest is obtained and accumulated across all random samples under all design conditions. What the "statistic of interest" is in a simulation context depends on what the researcher is focusing on. In the

---

[1]This transformation step may not be obvious because in most statistical programs (e.g., R), the desired population mean and standard deviation can be directly specified in the data generation process. Behind the scenes, however, there are two steps: (a) generation of standard random normal variate, and (b) transformation of this standard normal variate to the targeted population mean and standard deviation.

independent *t* test example, the researcher might be interested in the distribution characteristics (e.g., mean, standard deviation) of the *t* statistic itself under different data conditions. If so, the main statistic of interest would be the *t* statistic, which would be accumulated from all the random samples for later analyses. On the other hand, a researcher could focus on whether or not a sample *t* statistic exceeded a certain probability level (e.g., "statistically significant" at the level of .05 or .01), and the sample *t* statistic itself is not really the main focus. In reality, however, we typically have multiple "statistics of interest" in mind, and we accumulate as much information as possible from each random sample for later analyses. For this reason, both the sample *t* statistic and its associated significance level could of our interest.

For the illustrative design in Table 25.1, from each random sample, the statistic of interest is whether the *t* statistic has reached the statistical significance level of our definition (e.g., $\alpha = 0.05$). This is a dichotomous outcome, with $p < \alpha$ representing a Type I error under the *true* null hypothesis condition from which the sample data were generated, and $p \geq \alpha$ representing a correct decision. From Table 25.1, there are 36 unique cell conditions with 1,000 replications in each, and the total number of the statistic of interest will be 36,000 *t*-test outcomes (e.g., 1 for Type I error, and 0 for correct decision), with each outcome associated with the three other variables designating the three design conditions (total sample size, variance ratio, and group-size ratio).

Analysis of the Accumulated Statistic(s) of Interest

Once the statistic of interest from all the samples under all design conditions has been accumulated, the simulation process is complete. Depending on the nature of the question(s) in a simulation study, the follow-up data analyses may be simple or complicated. For the simulation represented in Table 25.1, data analysis can be simple descriptive analysis, such as tabulating the Type I error rate under each unique cell condition. Alternatively, a more sophisticated analysis approach could be considered, such as using logistic regression

analysis to model the dichotomous outcome (Type I error or not) to examine how, and to what extent, different design conditions could predict the occurrence of Type I error.

Drawing Conclusions

Ultimately, we conduct a simulation study to answer questions about some statistical analysis outcomes of our interest and about what data conditions may affect such outcomes. The simulation design and analyses of simulation results described thus far should be conducive to providing answers to the question(s) that motivated the simulation study in the first place. The validity of the conclusions drawn from a simulation study largely hinges on the simulation design (relevant design conditions included, appropriate levels of each design condition implemented, and so on) and on the validity of the data-generation process. For the hypothetical simulation design in Table 25.1, we can draw some tentative conclusions about how unequal group variances may affect the Type I error rate of an independent sample *t* test, and how such an impact may be moderated by other conditions, such as how group sample size condition is paired with unequal variance condition (e.g., the Type I error rate may be more severe when the smaller group has larger variance).

Our conclusions, however, must be limited to the design conditions implemented in the simulation design; extrapolation beyond these conditions and their levels should be avoided. To increase the generalizability of simulation study findings, not only the relevant conditions should be included, but the levels of each condition should also cover a meaningful range of levels, including extreme levels when possible. Not having sufficient levels of a design condition limits the generalizability of simulation findings.

DATA GENERATION IN A SIMULATION STUDY

This section provides a concise description of the major steps in data generation. In addition, some common issues in data generation process are noted.

Common Random Number Generators

There are different random number generators[2] corresponding to different probability density functions, such as binomial distribution, Cauchy distribution, exponential distribution, gamma distribution, Poisson distribution, normal distribution, uniform distribution, and so on. In simulation studies in psychology and related disciplines, the most common random number generators are probably those for normal, uniform, and binomial distributions, and these random number generators are readily available in statistical software packages (e.g., SAS, SPSS, R).

Simulating Univariate Sample Data

Most Monte Carlo studies involve multiple variables. However, to generate sample data of a single variable is the foundation for data generation involving multiple variables. Simulating sample data from a standard normal distribution is straightforward, whereas simulating sample data for a population with some specified degree of nonnormality is more challenging. Because many analytical techniques assume data normality, the impact of data normality assumption violation on the validity of statistical results often becomes an area of focus for empirical investigations. Consequently, data nonnormality is often an important area of research interest in Monte Carlo simulation studies.

Normally distributed sample data with specified first two moments.   All statistical software packages have a normal variate generator to generate data samples from a normally distributed statistical population with a mean of 0 and standard deviation of 1 [i.e., z scores ~ N (0, 1)]. Through a simple linear transformation, these sample z scores can then be transformed to a variable with specified first two moments (i.e., mean and standard deviation) of a population distribution. Linear transformation changes only the first two moments (i.e., mean and variance) of a distribution, but not the shape of the distribution as defined by the third and fourth statistical moments (i.e., skewness and kurtosis). The linear transformation takes the following form:

$$X' = \mu_{X'} + z(\sigma_{X'}), \qquad (25.2)$$

where X' is the transformed variable; $\mu_{X'}$ is the desired population mean of the transformed variable; z is the z score values generated through a random normal variate generator; and $\sigma_{X'}$ is the desired population standard deviation of the transformed variable.

In many statistical software packages, this transformation is an automated process, and the user only needs to specify the values of $\mu_{X'}$ and $\sigma_{X'}$ when using the random normal variate generator.

Sample data generation from a nonnormal distribution.   Although it is relatively easy to generate sample data from a normal distribution, it is considerably more complicated to generate data from a nonnormal distribution. Different algorithms, such as the generalized lambda distribution (GLD) approach by Ramberg and Schmeiser (1974) and the power transformation approach by Fleishman (1978), have been developed to simulate nonnormality distribution conditions (Burr, 1973; Fleishman, 1978; Johnson, 1949, 1965; Johnson & Kitchen, 1971; Pearson & Hartley, 1972; Ramberg & Schmeiser, 1974; Ramberg et al., 1979; Schmeiser & Deutch, 1977). Of the competing approaches, Fleishman's power transformation approach, as described below, is widely known and used.

Fleishman's power transformation method. Fleishman (1978) introduced a polynomial transformation method (third order power polynomial) to transform a normally distributed variable to a variable with specified degrees of skewness and kurtosis. The polynomial transformation takes the following form:

$$Y = a + bZ + cZ^2 + dZ^3, \qquad (25.3)$$

where Y is the transformed nonnormal variable with specified population skewness and kurtosis;

---

[2]As discussed in Fan et al. (2002), all random number generators are based on uniform distribution, and other distributions can be obtained from a uniform distribution through some transformation process. See Chapter 3 in Fan et al. for details.

Z is unit normal variate, that is, normally distributed variable with population mean of zero and variance of one; and a, b, c, and d are coefficients needed for transforming the unit normal variate to a nonnormal variable with specified degrees of population skewness and kurtosis. Of the four coefficients, $a = -c$.

The coefficients (a, b, c, d) needed for the transformation are tabulated in Fleishman (1978) for selected combinations of skewness and kurtosis values. Table 25.2 presents a small example set of Fleishman power transformation coefficients for skewness of .75 and for kurtosis ranging from $-.20$ to $+3.20$. The Fleishman method for generating sample data from nonnormal distributions is easy to implement in simulation because the coefficients needed for the nonnormal transformation are tabulated in his 1978 article for many selected combinations of skewness and kurtosis. If nonnormality conditions other than those tabulated in Fleishman (1978) are needed, Fan et al. (2002, Chapter 4) provided SAS codes for generating these coefficients once the targeted skewness and kurtosis are specified.

TABLE 25.2

Coefficients for Selected Nonnormality Conditions

Skew[a]	Kurtosis	b	c	d
.75	−0.20	1.173302916	.207562460	−.079058576
.75	0.00	1.112514484	.173629896	−.050334372
.75	0.40	1.033355486	.141435163	−.018192493
.75	0.80	0.978350485	.124833577	.001976943
.75	1.20	0.935785930	.114293870	.016737509
.75	1.60	0.900640275	.106782526	.028475848
.75	2.00	0.870410983	.101038303	.038291124
.75	2.40	0.843688891	.096435287	.046773413
.75	2.80	0.819604207	.092622898	.054275030
.75	3.20	0.797581770	.089386978	.061023176

Notes. Coefficient $a = -c$. Adapted from *SAS for Monte Carlo Studies: A Guide for Quantitative Researchers* (p. 67), by X. Fan, A. Felsovalyi, S. A. Sivo, and S. Keenan, 2002, SAS Institute. Copyright 2002 SAS Institute Inc. Adapted with permission.
[a]For negative skewness, reverse the signs of coefficient c and coefficient a.

Because positive and negative skewness can be considered symmetrical, the tabulated transformation coefficients in Fleishman (1978) did not list negative skewness conditions. But the coefficients for negative skewness conditions can be obtained simply by reversing the signs of c and a.

The Fleishman (1978) method, similar to other approaches such as the GLD method (Ramberg & Schmeiser, 1974), does not cover the entire space of possible combinations of skewness and kurtosis. In other words, this approach cannot generate nonnormal data for certain skewness and kurtosis conditions (Fleishman, 1978; Tadikamalla, 1980). The comparative study by Tadikamalla (1980) indicated that the GLD approach by Ramberg and Schmeiser (1974) and the power transformation approach by Fleishman cover approximately the same parameter space of nonnormality as defined by skewness and kurtosis, but the Fleishman method is more efficient. More important, the Fleishman method is easier to use when *multivariate* nonnormal data conditions are desired in Monte Carlo simulation, as will be discussed in the next section. The fifth-order power polynomial method discussed in Headrick and Sawilowsky (1999) provides more flexibility in covering the parameter space of nonnormality, and the details of this approach can be found in the Headrick (2009). Readers interested in this issue may consult these references about the approximate parameter space (nonnormality conditions as defined by skewness and kurtosis) for which the method can generate nonnormal data.

Simulating Multivariate Sample Data

In most Monte Carlo simulation studies, it is typical to involve multiple variables. For example, in any regression analysis, there must be at least two correlated variables: the dependent variable (Y) and one predictor (X). Thus, the researcher not only must control the univariate distributional characteristics but also must control the population intervariable relationship pattern. The degree of complexity in generating multiple variables with a specified intervariable relationship pattern largely depends on whether the individual variables involved are normally distributed. This discussion is divided into two sections: The first section covers normally distributed variables, and the second section covers nonnormal variables.

Sample data from a multivariate normal distribution. When all variables are normally distributed, it is relatively straightforward to impose a specified population intercorrelation pattern on the sample data of multiple variables. Kaiser and Dickman (1962) presented a matrix decomposition procedure that imposes a specified correlation matrix on a set of otherwise-uncorrelated random normal variables. Given a specified population intercorrelation matrix R, the basic matrix decomposition procedure takes the following form (Kaiser & Dickman, 1962):

$$Z_{(k \times k)} = F_{(kk)} \times X_{(k \times N)}, \qquad (25.4)$$

where k is the number of variables; N is the number of observations in a sample (sample size N); X is a $k \times N$ data matrix, with N observations, each with k uncorrelated random normal variables (mean of 0 and standard deviation of 1); F is a $k \times k$ matrix containing principal component factor pattern coefficients obtained by applying principal component factorization to the given population intercorrelation matrix R; Z is the resultant $k \times N$ sample data matrix (N observations on k variables), as if sampled from a population with the given population intercorrelation matrix R; and $k \times N$ are matrix dimensions (k rows and N columns).

Procedurally, to generate sample data of k variables with the desired population inter-correlation pattern as specified in R, take the following steps:

1. For a specified population intercorrelation matrix R, conduct a factor analysis using principal components as the factor extraction method (the default option in statistical software packages, such as SAS or SPSS), requesting the option to keep the same number of factors as the number of variables in the specified population correlation matrix R, and obtain the matrix of factor pattern coefficients F.

2. Generate k uncorrelated random normal variables ($\mu = 0$, $\sigma = 1$), each with N observations. The dimension of this matrix was originally $N \times k$. It is then transposed to a $k \times N$ dimensions matrix X, that is, the matrix has k rows representing k variables, and N columns representing N observations.

3. Premultiply the uncorrelated sample data matrix X with the factor pattern matrix F. The resultant Z matrix ($k \times N$) contains N observations on k correlated variables, as if the N observations were sampled from a population with a population intercorrelation pattern represented by R. This correlated data matrix is then transposed back to an $N \times k$ dimension sample data matrix for later statistical analysis in the simulation loop.

When individual variables are univariate normal, the multivariate data generated through this matrix decomposition procedure are multivariate normal (Vale & Maurelli, 1983). The procedural steps can be implemented in statistical software packages that have matrix computation capabilities (e.g., SAS, SPSS). Fan et al. (2002, Chapter 4) provided SAS illustrative examples for these procedural steps.

Sample data from multivariate nonnormal distribution. Although it is relatively straightforward to simulate sample data from a multivariate normal distribution with a desired population intervariable correlation pattern, it is considerably more difficult to simulate sample data from a multivariate nonnormal distribution. The following provides a brief discussion on the relevant issues and procedures for accomplishing this goal.

Interaction between nonnormality and intervariable correlations. As discussed in previous sections, simulating sample data from a univariate nonnormal distribution can be accomplished through several procedures, and Fleishman's (1978) power transformation method was one of them. As pointed out, Fleishman's method has some limitation because it does not cover the entire space of nonnormality as defined by all possible combinations of skewness and kurtosis. Fleishman's method, however, does offer "an advantage over the other procedures in that it can easily be extended to generate multivariate random numbers with specified intercorrelations and univariate means, variances, skews, and kurtoses" (Vale & Maurelli, 1983, p. 465). In other words, to simulate sample data from a *multivariate* nonnormal distribution with specified population univariate skewness and kurtosis, and specified population intervariable correlation pattern among the variables, Fleishman's approach is usually the method of choice.

To generate multivariate nonnormal data, Vale and Maurelli (1983) showed that the application of a matrix decomposition procedure for controlling the intervariable correlations among the variables is not as straightforward as was demonstrated earlier. On the surface, the goal of simulating multivariate nonnormal data can be accomplished by (a) generating multivariate normal data with specified intervariable correlations through the matrix decomposition procedure, and (b) transforming each variable to the desired distributional shapes as defined by the specified univariate skewness and kurtosis. Unfortunately, the two processes interact, and the resultant multivariate nonnormal data generated will have an intervariable correlation pattern that differs from that specified in the matrix decomposition procedure.

Intermediate correlations. The intermediate correlation procedure by Vale and Maurelli (1983) demonstrated that, for multiple correlated variables, simple implementation of matrix decomposition procedures does not work as expected when the variables are not normally distributed. To counter the effect of nonnormal conditions on the intervariable correlations in the process of data generation, intervariable correlations that are different from those specified as population intervariable correlations must be derived and used in the matrix decomposition procedure. These derived correlations are called *intermediate correlations*, and the derivation of these intermediate correlations is based on the specified population intervariable correlation pattern and on the specified univariate nonnormality conditions as defined by the univariate skewness and kurtosis.

Derivation of intermediate correlations. Derivation of all *pairwise* intermediate correlations is essential for simulating nonnormal data conditions. The derivation process takes into account both the originally specified population correlation between two variables and the population non-normality conditions of the two variables as defined by univariate skewness and kurtosis. In this situation, the Fleishman (1978) power transformation method becomes very useful, as the coefficients in Fleishman's power transformation can readily be used to derive the needed intermediate correlation coefficients. As Vale and Maurelli (1983) discussed, it is not obvious that other nonnormality transformation procedures (e.g., GLD approach; Ramberg & Schmeiser, 1974) can have the same direct extension to multivariate non-normality data situations.

As discussed, any two normal variates, Z_1 and Z_2, can be transformed through Fleishman's (1978) power transformation method into two nonnormal variables X_1 and X_2, each with its own known skewness and kurtosis:

$$X_1 = a_1 + b_1 Z_1 + c_1 Z_1^2 + d_1 Z_1^3 \text{ and}$$

$$X_2 = a_2 + b_2 Z_2 + c_2 Z_2^2 + d_2 Z_2^3. \qquad (25.5)$$

Once the degrees of skewness and kurtosis are specified, the coefficients (a_i, b_i, c_i, and d_i, for $i = 1, 2$) are known (e.g., by consulting Fleishman's table in the original article or by using the SAS program codes provided in Fan et al., 2002, Chapter 4). The targeted population correlation between the two nonnormal variables X_1 and X_2 can be specified as $R_{X_1 X_2}$. Vale and Maurelli (1983) demonstrated that the following relationship exists:

$$RX_1 X_2 = \rho(b_1 b_2 + 3b_1 d_2 + 3d_1 b_2 + 9d_1 d_2)$$
$$+ \rho^2 (2c_1 c_2) + \rho^3 (6d_1 d_2), \qquad (25.6)$$

where ρ is the intermediate correlation coefficient. Here, all elements are known except the intermediate correlation coefficient ρ. The bivariate intermediate correlation coefficient ρ must be solved for all possible pairs of the variables involved. These intermediate correlation coefficients are then assembled into an intermediate correlation matrix, which is then factor analyzed to obtain the factor pattern matrix needed to transform uncorrelated variables into correlated ones (i.e., matrix decomposition procedure by Kaiser & Dickman, 1962).

There is no direct algebraic solution to solve the polynomial function for ρ; as a result, an iterative estimation approach is needed to arrive at an estimated solution. As an illustrative example, we have a three-variable situation with the specified univariate skewness and kurtosis conditions and the specified population intervariable correlation pattern, as shown in Table 25.3.

Appendix 25.1 provides SAS program codes (Fan et al., 2002, Chapter 4) using the Newton-Raphson method to solve for the intermediate correlation ρ between X_1 and X_2. Using this SAS program, all three pairwise intermediate correlation coefficients could be solved. After solving for each pairwise intermediate correlation coefficient among the three variables and assembling the resultant three intermediate correlation coefficients, we have the intermediate correlation matrix, as shown in Exhibit 25.1.

EXHIBIT 25.1

Intermediate Correlation Matrix for Table 23.3 Data Conditions

X_1	1.0000		
X_2	0.7402	1.0000	
X_3	0.2054	0.4173	1.0000

This intermediate intervariable correlation matrix is then factor analyzed (decomposed). The resultant factor pattern matrix is then used in the matrix decomposition procedure to impose the specified population intervariable correlation pattern on a set of nonnormal variables. The result is a correlated multivariate nonnormal sample data that has the population intervariable correlation pattern as originally specified.

Checking the Validity of Data-Generation Procedures

Data generation is probably the most important component of a simulation experiment, as the validity of the results from a Monte Carlo simulation experiment hinges on the validity of the

---

TABLE 25.3

Three Nonnormal Variables for Simulation

Variables	Targeted population parameters						
	M	*SD*	Skew	Kurtosis	Correlation matrix		
X_1	100	15	.75	0.80	1.00		
X_2	50	10	−.75	0.80	0.70	1.00	
X_3	0	1	.75	2.40	0.20	0.40	1.00

Variables	Fleishman coefficients for the three variables			
	a	*b*	*c*	*d*
X_1	−.124833577	.978350485	.124833577	.001976943
X_2	.124833577	.978350485	−.124833577	.001976943
X_3	−.096435287	.843688891	.096435287	.046773413

Note. Adapted from *SAS for Monte Carlo Studies: A Guide for Quantitative Researchers* (p. 84), by X. Fan, A. Felsovalyi, S. A. Sivo, and S. Keenan, 2002, SAS Institute. Copyright 2002 SAS Institute Inc. Adapted with permission.

TABLE 25.4

Comparison Between Population Parameters and Sample Statistics (in Parentheses) From a Large Sample ($N = 1,000,000$)

Variables	*M*	*SD*	Skew	Kurtosis	Correlation matrix		
X_1	100 (99.99)	15 (14.99)	.75 (.75)	0.80 (0.80)	1.00		
X_2	50 (49.99)	10 (10.01)	−.75 (−.75)	0.80 (0.81)	0.70 (0.70)	1.00	
X_3	0 (−.00)	1 (1.00)	.75 (.76)	2.40 (2.42)	0.20 (0.20)	0.40 (0.40)	1.00

sample data-generation process. Because of this, it is important to empirically verify the data-generation procedures first before implementing the simulation experiment. This can be done by generating sample data for some limited conditions and comparing sample data characteristics against the targeted population parameters.

As an example of data simulation verification, assuming that a planned Monte Carlo simulation experiment would involve three multivariate nonnormal variables shown in Table 25.3. Using the Fleishman coefficients for the targeted univariate nonnormal conditions, and after obtaining all the "intermediate" correlation coefficients (see Appendix 25.1 and Exhibit 25.1), we may do a quick data-generation verification by generating a large sample of 1 million observations (i.e., $N = 1,000,000$) using the SAS program codes in Appendix 25.2.[3] For such a large sample, we expect that the sample statistics should be very close to the population parameters (e.g., mean, standard deviation, skewness, kurtosis, and intervariable correlation coefficients).

One execution of the SAS program in Appendix 25.2 provided the comparison between the population parameters and the sample statistics (in parentheses) shown in Table 25.4. The sample statistics (in parenthesis) are very close, if not identical, to the population parameters for all the parameters (mean, standard deviation, skewness, kurtosis, and the intervariable correlations). This information provides assurance that the data-generation procedures implemented indeed produced sample data as defined by the population parameters.

Although the results from the quick verification as shown in Table 25.5 are comforting, a more rigorous verification check would involve examining the *empirical* sampling distribution characteristics of the simulated data samples relative to the population parameters. For examining the sampling distribution characteristics, we may select one or more sample size condition(s) (e.g., $N = 100$), generate repeated samples (e.g., 1,000 replications) under that sample size condition, and then examine the sampling distributions of various sample statistics of interest (e.g., sample mean, sample skewness, sample kurtosis) relative to the population parameters. This more rigorous verification process is especially important in situations in which the simulation procedures may be relatively new (e.g., involving some relatively new algorithms), thus uncertainty may exist about the simulation outcomes.

In a simulation experiment, depending on the mathematical–statistical software and the platform used, how the data-generation procedures are implemented may be very different. In some cases (e.g., SPSS, SAS), the researcher needs to implement and program the components for data generation. In some others (e.g., Mplus), the software has built-in data-generation procedures, and the researcher may need to specify only the targeted population parameters of a model. In such a case, it is the researcher's responsibility to verify the validity of the data-generation procedures.

---

[3]Use of the SAS program is not required; such verification can be carried out in any other programs, such as R or SPSS.

TABLE 25.5

Population Parameters for Two Groups for Selected Conditions

Group variance ratio	Group difference (*d*)	Group sample size ratio[a]	Population parameters	
			Group 1 (μ_1, σ_1^2, n_1)	Group 2 (μ_2, σ_2^2, n_2)
1:1	.00	0.5:0.5	50, 100, 60	50, 100, 60
		0.7:0.3	50, 100, 84	50, 100, 36
	.50	0.5:0.5	50, 100, 60	45, 100, 60
		0.7:0.3	50, 100, 84	45, 100, 36
2:1	.00	0.5:0.5	50, 100, 60	50, 50, 60
		0.7:0.3	50, 100, 84	50, 50, 36
	.50	0.5:0.5	50, 100, 60	45.67, 50, 60
		0.7:0.3	50, 100, 84	45.39, 50, 36

[a]This illustrative example only includes the condition of larger group with larger variance.

OTHER CONSIDERATIONS

In addition to the major steps in simulation process as discussed in the previous section, there can be some other issues that a researcher needs to be consider. Some common ones are described here.

Design Factors and Manipulation Levels

In a typical simulation experiment, careful consideration should be given to the population conditions to be simulated. In general, population conditions should include the major factors relevant for the outcome of interest, and each factor should vary to cover a reasonable and realistic range of values to enhance the generalizability of findings. If a relevant, or even important, factor is missing in the design, our understanding about the phenomenon would be limited, as we would know nothing about the influence of that factor on the outcome of interest. For each factor to be manipulated in the simulation, an appropriate range of levels should be covered so as to increase the generalizability of findings from the simulation experiment.

As an example, we may be interested in understanding both Type I error control and statistical power of independent *t* test under the conditions of (a) equal versus nonequal group variances, and (b) data normality versus nonnormality conditions.

A cursory planning for this simulation experiment could lead us to five dimensions that can be manipulated: equal versus unequal group variances, data normality versus nonnormality conditions, group difference on the outcome variable (as defined by effect size), total sample size (two groups combined), and equal versus unequal group sample sizes. These factors are included in the design for manipulation because we believe that each factor could have potential effect on the outcome of interest (i.e., Type I error control, or statistical power). Such a belief could be based on theoretical considerations (statistical power is related to sample size; violation of data normality assumption may affect the performance of *t* test, etc.) or based on some previous findings in the field (e.g., consequence of the violation of equal variance assumption is related to unequal sample sizes of two groups; Glass et al., 1972). In other words, there should be a reasonable rationale about why a factor is included in a simulation experiment.

Once the factors to be manipulated in a simulation experiment are determined, the levels for each factor should be carefully considered. The primary consideration is that each factor should cover a reasonable and realistic range of levels so that the findings from the study will have a reasonable degree of generalizability. Although it is generally true that a wider range of a factor, and more levels within the range, would lead to better generalizability, a researcher needs to strike a balance between the desire to achieve better generalizability and the scope and manageability of a simulation experiment. For our hypothetical example concerning an independent group's *t* test, some deliberation about the levels of the multiple factors could lead to the following tentative decisions about the levels on each of the five factors:

1. For equality and nonequality of group variances, the group variance ratios could be
   1 : 1
   2 : 1
   4 : 1
   8 : 1
2. For data normality:
   normality (i.e., skew = 0, kurtosis = 0)
   slight nonnormality (e.g., skew = |1|,
        kurtosis = |1|)
   severe nonnormality (e.g., skew > |2|,
        kurtosis > |3|)
3. For group difference on the dependent variable to be tested (defined as standardized mean difference of *d*):
   $d = 0.0$ (no difference; for Type I error control)
   $d = 0.2$ (small effect size)
   $d = 0.5$ (medium effect size)
   $d = 0.8$ (large effect size)
4. For total sample size *N* (two groups combined):
   $N = 30$
   $N = 60$
   $N = 120$
   $N = 240$
5. For equal versus unequal group sample sizes (group sample size ratio for a given total *N*):
   equal ratio: 0.5 : 0.5
   #1 unequal ratio: 0.7 : 0.3 (larger group has larger population variance)
   #2 unequal ratio: 0.3 : 0.7 (smaller group has larger population variance)

For some factors, the choice of the levels may be well-grounded in theory or in research practice. For example, for #3 above (group difference on the dependent variable to be tested), the four levels represent no difference, difference of small effect ($d = 0.20$), of medium effect ($d = 0.50$), and of

large effect ($d = 0.80$), respectively, and these are widely used benchmarks in social science research (Cohen, 1988). On the other hand, for some factors, there may be some uncertainty and ambiguity regarding the levels to be implemented. For example, for the data normality dimension (#2 above), the operationalization of *slight* and *severe* nonnormality levels are more subjective. In a real simulation experiment, the researcher may need a literature review concerning how, and to what extent, nonnormality conditions could be operationalized in a similar situation, and then make the informed decisions about the levels of nonnormality (as defined by skewness and kurtosis) to be implemented in the experiment. In short, to the fullest extent possible, the selected levels of a factor in a simulation design should be grounded either in theory or in practice.

From Simulation Design to Population Data Parameters

Once simulation design issues are settled, the design (i.e., the factors, and levels within each factor) needs to be translated into population data parameters that statistically conform to the design conditions, so that it is possible to simulate data of random samples under the specified design conditions. Depending on the complexity of the design, the statistical technique, and some other considerations (e.g., software used for simulation), specification of population data parameters for simulation implementation may or may not be a straightforward process. In this section, two hypothetical simulation situations are discussed as illustrations of this process.

For the independent groups *t* test simulation example described in the previous section, for the sake of simplicity, assume that we only consider normal data and total *N* of 120 (i.e., combined total sample size of 120). Furthermore, we only consider some selected conditions of group variance ratio (1:1 and 2:1), group difference on the dependent variable to be tested ($d = 0.00$ and $d = 0.50$), and group sample size ratio (for unequal group sample sizes, only the situation of larger group with larger variance). For these design conditions, the population parameters, that is, μ and σ^2 for the dependent variable, and the group sample sizes are shown in Table 25.5.

In this example, Group 1 is specified to have population parameters of $\mu_1 = 50$ and $\sigma_1^2 = 100$. Once Group 1's parameters are known, and Group 2's population parameters are worked out for the selected design conditions in the table. The specification of Group 2's parameters is based on the following simple algorithms:

$$d = \frac{\mu_1 - \mu_2}{\sigma_{pooled}}, \qquad (25.7)$$

where

$$\sigma_{pooled} = \sqrt{\frac{(n_1 - 1)\sigma_1^2 + (n_2 - 1)\sigma_2^2}{n_1 + n_2 - 1}}. \qquad (25.8)$$

Once the design conditions are given, the only parameter that needs to be worked out is μ_2, whereas all others (μ_1, d, σ_{pooled}) are already known. The parameter μ_2 can be worked out as follows:

$$\mu_2 = \mu_1 - d * \sigma_{pooled}. \qquad (25.9)$$

This example illustrates that it may take some work to translate the design conditions to population parameters to implement data simulation. Depending on the complexity of the design and some other factors (e.g., statistical techniques involved in the simulation experiment), this process could be considerably more complicated and time-consuming than illustrated here.

As a more complicated example, we are interested in assessing the potential adverse impact (e.g., biased estimates of growth model parameters) of mis-specifying the residual structure in growth modeling analysis. In growth modeling analysis, it is common to assume that the residuals (ε_1 to ε_6) of the repeated measurements have homoscedastic ($var(\varepsilon_i) = var(\varepsilon_j)$) and uncorrelated ($Cov_{ij} = 0$) residuals, as shown in Figure 25.1a. However, the repeated measurements may have more complicated residual structure (e.g., Sivo et al., 2005), such as heteroscedastic ($var(\varepsilon_i) \neq var(\varepsilon_j)$) and correlated ($Cov_{ij} \neq 0$) residuals, as shown in Figure 25.1b. What would the potential adverse impact be if the true residual structure as in Figure 25.1b was erroneously modeled as the simpler residual structure as in Figure 25.1a in growth modeling analysis? A simulation study may be designed to examine this issue (e.g., You et al., 2006).

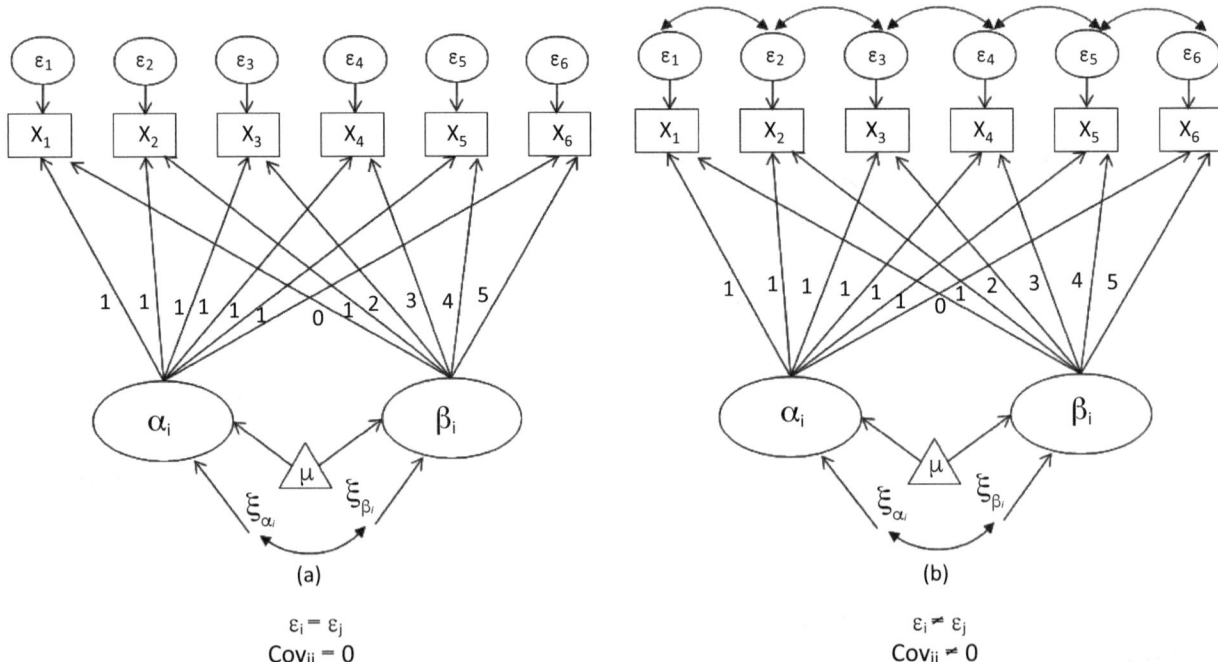

(a)

$\varepsilon_i = \varepsilon_j$

$Cov_{ij} = 0$

(b)

$\varepsilon_i \neq \varepsilon_j$

$Cov_{ij} \neq 0$

FIGURE 25.1. Linear growth models: (a) homoscedastic and independent residuals; (b) heteroscedastic and correlated residuals.

Assuming that for one simulation condition, the growth model has the following model parameters:

1. Residual variances of the repeated measurements increase by an equal increment of 2.0, with the initial residual variance (of ε_1) being 20, and the largest (of ε_6) to smallest (of ε_1) ratio is 1.5, we, therefore, have the following residual variances for the six repeated measures: 20, 22, 24, 26, 28, and 30.
2. Correlation between adjacent residuals is 0.15: $r_{\varepsilon_i, \varepsilon_{i+1}} = 0.15$, and between nonadjacent residuals is 0.
3. Intercept is 50, with intercept variance of 100.
4. Slope is 2, with slope variance of 0.25.
5. Correlation between intercept and slope is 0.2.

From these model parameters, we have the following matrices (using Linear Structural Relations [LISREL] notations):

$$\Lambda_X = \begin{bmatrix} 1 & 0 \\ 1 & 1 \\ 1 & 2 \\ 1 & 3 \\ 1 & 4 \\ 1 & 5 \end{bmatrix}, \qquad (25.10)$$

$$\Phi = \begin{bmatrix} 100 & 1.0 \\ 1.0 & .25 \end{bmatrix}, \qquad (25.11)$$

$$\Theta_\delta = \begin{bmatrix} 20 & 3.15 & 0 & 0 & 0 & 0 \\ 3.15 & 22 & 3.45 & 0 & 0 & 0 \\ 0 & 3.45 & 24 & 3.75 & 0 & 0 \\ 0 & 0 & 3.75 & 26 & 4.05 & 0 \\ 0 & 0 & 0 & 4.05 & 28 & 4.35 \\ 0 & 0 & 0 & 0 & 4.35 & 30 \end{bmatrix}, \qquad (25.12)$$

and

$$\kappa = \begin{bmatrix} 50 \\ 2 \end{bmatrix}, \qquad (25.13)$$

where

Λ_X is the matrix for the intercept and slope coefficients;
Φ contains the variances and the covariance for the intercept and slope;
Θ_δ is the variance/covariance matrix of the residuals; and
κ contains the intercept (initial level) and slope (growth rate) values.

In Φ and Θ_δ above, the off-diagonal elements are covariances. The relationship between covariance (COV_{ij}) and correlation (r_{ij}) is as follows:

$$r_{ij} = \frac{COV_{ij}}{\sigma_i \sigma_j}. \qquad (25.14)$$

When the correlation (r_{ij}) and the variances of two variables (σ_i^2, σ_j^2) are known, the standard deviations of the variables (σ_i, σ_j) are defined, and we can obtain the covariance between the two variables:

$$COV_{ij} = r_{ij}\sigma_i\sigma_j. \qquad (25.15)$$

Once the four matrixes $(\Lambda_X, \Phi, \Theta_\delta, \text{and } \kappa)$ are defined for the specified condition of the growth model, the parameters (covariance matrix and mean vector) of the six repeated measurements $(X_1 – X_6)$ can be obtained:

$$COV_X = \Lambda_X \Phi \Lambda_X' + \Theta_\delta. \qquad (25.16)$$

$$\mu_X = \Lambda_X \kappa. \qquad (25.17)$$

For this particular simulation condition, the resultant population means, standard deviations, and correlation matrix of the six repeated measures are shown in Table 25.6. This represents only one condition of the simulation design; potentially, there are many other conditions that vary, for example, the correlation of adjacent residuals, the degree of heteroscedasticity of residual variances, and so on. For each unique combination defined by the design dimensions, such population parameters need to be worked out so that random samples from the defined population can be simulated.

TABLE 25.6

Repeated-Measure Parameters for the Growth Model Condition

Parameters	X_1	X_2	X_3	X_4	X_5	X_6
μ	50	52	54	56	58	60
σ	10.9544	11.1467	11.3578	11.5866	11.8321	12.0933

Correlations

1.0000					
0.8529	1.0000				
0.8198	0.8447	1.0000			
0.8115	0.8110	0.8377	1.0000		
0.8023	0.8036	0.8036	0.8318	1.0000	
0.7925	0.7956	0.7972	0.7975	0.8270	1.0000

These two hypothetical examples show that translating simulation design conditions to data population parameters may involve a considerable amount of careful work.

Accumulation and Analysis of the Statistic(s) of Interest

By definition, a simulation experiment involves drawing many random samples from a defined population. From each sample, some statistic(s) of interest need to be collected and saved for later analysis. Depending on the nature of the study, from each random sample, there may be only a very limited number of statistic(s) of interest, or there may be many statistics of interest. For the hypothetical example of Type I error control and statistical power of independent t test discussed above, the statistic of interest may only be the statistical significance level of the t test from each random sample. For the growth modeling example, however, the purpose is to examine the potential adverse effect of mis-specified residual structure on other model parameter estimates. In this situation, there may be many statistics of interest, such as the estimates of growth model intercept, slope, intercept and slope variance–covariance, model fit indexes, and so on.

The process of accumulation of the statistic(s) of interest over repeated random samples and across all the design conditions can be straight-forward or complicated, or anywhere in between,

depending on many factors, such as the statistical software used, the analytical technique involved, and the statistic(s) of interest to be accumulated. In general, this is typically not an automated process by default; instead, it usually involves careful planning and execution, and it may involve some programming. Because various platforms exist to implement a simulation experiment, it is difficult to discuss about a specific example. For the SAS environment, Fan et al. (2002) provided detailed simulation examples for this and other aspects of a simulation experiment; interested readers may consult this source for more details.

Once the statistic(s) of interest from all the random samples across all design conditions have been accumulated, the simulation process itself is complete. Depending on the nature of the research question(s) in a simulation study, follow-up data analysis may be simple or sophisticated. Considerations for follow-up data analysis are not different from many other data analysis situations. For the simulation represented in Table 25.1, data analysis can be simple descriptive analysis involving tabulations of Type I error rate under each unique cell condition. A more sophisticated analysis approach could also be considered. For example, one may consider using logistic regression to model the dichotomous outcome (1 for Type I error or 0 for no Type I error in a sample) to assess how and to what extent different design conditions and their interactions have influenced the occurrence of Type I error.

For the illustrative growth modeling example discussed above, in addition to descriptive results to be presented in tabular format, one may consider inferential analysis by obtaining bias estimates (bias = sample estimate – parameter) for different parameters (intercept, slope, intercept and slope variances, intercept and slope covariance, etc.), and then using a general linear model analysis to model the bias estimate as an outcome, with design dimensions, and their potential interactions, as independent variables (e.g., You et al., 2006).

Presentation and Drawing Conclusions

A simulation experiment typically involves multiple factors in the simulation design, with each factor having a range of levels. As a result, the number of unique conditions can be quite large. This often poses challenges for presenting simulation findings. Commonly, findings are presented in simple tabular format, and the results are shown in tables for all the conditions in the simulation design. But when a large number of tables are presented, the presentation and the subsequent discussion may easily become robotic and repetitive. As a result, the important messages from the study may be muddied or buried in all these numbers and tables.

A better approach for presenting simulation findings is to focus on *representativeness* and *exceptions*. Representativeness means the general trends observed in the simulation results; exceptions are those findings that are different from the general trends under certain conditions. It would be far more effective to present findings from some carefully selected conditions to illustrate the representativeness and exceptions, and to discuss about the extent to which the findings

from other conditions are aligned with these two different observations.

Whenever possible, graphic representation, which is usually more concise and more condensed in terms of information content, should be used for presentation, as a good picture may be more effective than multiple tables. Graphic representation is effective both for showing the general trends and for illustrating exceptions in the simulation findings, as shown in Fan and Sivo (2007).

The validity and generalizability of the conclusions drawn from a simulation study depend on the adequacy and appropriateness of the simulation design (e.g., relevant design factors included, appropriate levels of each design factor implemented) and on the validity of the data-generation process (e.g., simulated sample data indeed reflect the intended population parameters as defined by the simulation design conditions). The conclusions should be limited to the conditions (i.e., design factors and the levels of the factors) implemented in the simulation design; extrapolation beyond these conditions should be avoided. To increase the generalizability of simulation study findings, not only the relevant design factors should be included, but also the levels of each design factor should be carefully planned to cover a meaningful range of levels, including extreme levels when possible. Failure to include a relevant factor (e.g., data nonnormality) in a simulation design excludes the possibility of drawing any conclusions about that factor. But for a factor included in the design, failure to implement a sufficient range of levels (e.g., for data nonnormality, only very minor nonnormality conditions were implemented in the design) limits, sometimes severely, the generalizability of simulation findings.

APPENDIX 25.1. SAS CODES FOR DERIVING INTERMEDIATE CORRELATION BETWEEN X_1 AND X_2 IN TABLE 25.3

```
DATA D1;
B1=.978350485; C1=-.124833577; D1=.001976943; * use Fleishman coefficients;
B2=.978350485; C2= .124833577; D2=.001976943;
```

```
TARGET=.70; * target population correlation;
R=.5; * starting value for iteration;
DO I=1 TO 5;
FUNCTION=(R**3*6*D1*D2+R**2*2*C1*C2+R*(B1*B2+3*B1*D2+3*D1*B2+9*D1*D2)-TARGET);
DERIV=(3*R**2*6*D1*D2+2*R*2*C1*C2+(B1*B2+3*B1*D2+3*D1*B2+9*D1*D2));
RATIO=FUNCTION/DERIV;
R_TEMP = R - RATIO;
IF ABS(R_TEMP - R)>.00001 THEN R = R_TEMP; OUTPUT;
END;
PROC PRINT; WHERE I=5; * print intermediate correlation r for the last iteration;
VAR I RATIO R;
RUN;
```

Note. From *SAS for Monte Carlo Studies: A Guide for Quantitative Researchers* (p. 84), by X. Fan, A. Felsovalyi, S. A. Sivo, and S. Keenan, 2002, SAS Institute. Copyright 2002 SAS Institute Inc. Reprinted with permission.

APPENDIX 25.2. SAS PROGRAM FOR DATA GENERATION VERIFICATION FOR TABLE 25.3 DATA CONDITIONS

```
DATA A (TYPE=CORR); _TYPE_='CORR'; INPUT X1-X3;
CARDS; * these are 'intermediate' correlation coefficients;
1.0000 . .
.7402 1.0000 .
.2054 .4173 1.0000
;
* obtain factor pattern matrix for data generation;
PROC FACTOR N=3 OUTSTAT=FACOUT;
DATA PATTERN; SET FACOUT;
IF _TYPE_='PATTERN';
DROP _TYPE_ _NAME_;
RUN;
PROC IML;
USE PATTERN; * read in the factor pattern as a matrix 'F';
READ ALL VAR _NUM_ INTO F;
F=F';
DATA=RANNOR(J(1000000,3,0)); *** generate data matrix (1000000×3);
DATA=DATA'; *** transpose data matrix (3×1000000);
Z = F*DATA; *** impose intercorrelations;
Z = Z'; *** transpose data matrix back (1000000×3); * Fleishman nonnormality
transformation;
X1 = -.124833577 + .978350485*Z[,1] + 124833577*Z[,1]##2 + .001976943*Z[,1]##3;
X2 = .124833577 + .978350485*Z[,2] - 124833577*Z[,2]##2 + .001976943*Z[,2]##3;
X3 = -.096435287 + .843688891*Z[,3] + 096435287*Z[,3]##2 + .046773413*Z[,3]##3;
```

```
X1=X1*15 + 100; * linear transformation for mean & std;
X2=X2*10 + 50;
X3=X3;
Z=X1||X2||X3;
CREATE A FROM Z [COLNAME={X1 X2 X3}]; * output a SAS working data 'A';
APPEND FROM Z;
* obtaining descriptive stats for sample data;
PROC MEANS DATA=A N MEAN STD SKEWNESS KURTOSIS; VAR X1 X2 X3;
PROC CORR DATA=A NOSIMPLE NOPROB; VAR X1 X2 X3;
RUN; QUIT;
```

Note. From *SAS for Monte Carlo Studies: A Guide for Quantitative Researchers* (p. 86), by X. Fan, A. Felsovalyi, S. A. Sivo, and S. Keenan, 2002, SAS Institute. Copyright 2002 SAS Institute Inc. Reprinted with permission.

References

Burr, I. W. (1973). Parameters for a general system for distributions to match a grid of α_3 and α_4. *Communications in Statistics*, 2(1), 1–21. https://doi.org/10.1080/03610927308827052

Cohen, J. (1988). *Statistical power analysis for the behavioral sciences* (2nd ed.). Erlbaum.

Fan, X., Felsovalyi, A., Sivo, S. A., & Keenan, S. (2002). *SAS for Monte Carlo studies: A guide for quantitative researchers*. SAS Institute.

Fan, X., & Sivo, S. (2007). Sensitivity of fit indices to model misspecification and model types. *Multivariate Behavioral Research*, 42(3), 509–529. https://doi.org/10.1080/00273170701382864

Fleishman, A. I. (1978). A method for simulating non-normal distributions. *Psychometrika*, 43(4), 521–532. https://doi.org/10.1007/BF02293811

Glass, G. V., & Hopkins, K. D. (1996). *Statistical methods in education and psychology* (3rd ed.). Allyn & Bacon.

Glass, G. V., Peckham, P. D., & Sanders, J. R. (1972). Consequences of failure to meet assumptions underlying the fixed-effects analysis of variance and covariance. *Review of Educational Research*, 42(3), 237–288. https://doi.org/10.3102/00346543042003237

Headrick, T. C. (2009). *Statistical simulation: Power method polynomials and other transformations*. CRC Press. https://doi.org/10.1201/9781420064919

Headrick, T. C., & Sawilowsky, S. S. (1999). Simulating correlated multivariate nonnormal distributions: Extending the Fleishman power method. *Psychometrika*, 64(1), 25–35. https://doi.org/10.1007/BF02294317

Johnson, N. L. (1949). Systems of frequency curves generated by methods of translation. *Biometrika*, 36(1–2), 149–176. https://doi.org/10.1093/biomet/36.1-2.149

Johnson, N. L. (1965). Tables to facilitate fitting S_u frequency curves. *Biometrika*, 52(3–4), 547–558. https://doi.org/10.1093/biomet/52.3-4.547

Johnson, N. L., & Kitchen, J. O. (1971). Tables to facilitate fitting S_B curves. *Biometrika*, 58, 223–226.

Kaiser, H. F., & Dickman, K. (1962). Sample and population score matrices and sample correlation matrices from an arbitrary population correlation matrix. *Psychometrika*, 27(2), 179–182. https://doi.org/10.1007/BF02289635

Merriam-Webster's Online Dictionary. (2021). Monte Carlo [adjective]. https://www.merriam-webster.com/dictionary/Monte%20Carlo

Pearson, E. S., & Hartley, H. O. (Eds.). (1972). *Biometrika tables for statisticians* (Vol. 2). Cambridge University Press.

Ramberg, J. S., Dudewicz, E. J., Tadikamalla, P. R., & Mykytka, E. F. (1979). A probability distribution and its use in fitting data. *Technometrics*, 21(2), 201–214. https://doi.org/10.1080/00401706.1979.10489750

Ramberg, J. S., & Schmeiser, B. W. (1974). An approximate method for generating asymmetric random variables. *Communications of the ACM*, 17(2), 78–82. https://doi.org/10.1145/360827.360840

Schmeiser, B. W., & Deutch, S. J. (1977). A versatile four parameter family of probability distributions suitable for simulation. *AIIE Transactions*, 9(2), 176–182. https://doi.org/10.1080/05695557708975140

Sivo, S., Fan, X., & Witta, L. (2005). The biasing effects of unmodeled ARMA time series processes on latent growth curve model estimates. *Structural Equation Modeling, 12*(2), 215–231. https://doi.org/10.1207/s15328007sem1202_2

Tadikamalla, P. R. (1980). On simulating non-normal distributions. *Psychometrika, 45*(2), 273–279. https://doi.org/10.1007/BF02294081

Thompson, B. (1991). Invariance of multivariate results: A Monte Carlo study of canonical function and structure coefficients. *Journal of Experimental Education, 59*(4), 367–382. https://doi.org/10.1080/00220973.1991.10806573

Vale, C. D., & Maurelli, V. A. (1983). Simulating multivariate nonnormal distributions. *Psychometrika, 48*(3), 465–471. https://doi.org/10.1007/BF02293687

You, W., Fan, X., & Sivo, S. A. (2006, April). *Assessing the impact of failure to adequately model the residual structure in growth modeling* [Paper presentation]. Annual Meeting of American Educational Research Association, San Francisco, CA, United States.

CHAPTER 26

BAYESIAN MODELING FOR PSYCHOLOGISTS: AN APPLIED APPROACH

Fred M. Feinberg and Richard Gonzalez

Bayesian methods offer new insights into standard statistical models and provide effective procedures for problems common in psychological research, such as missing data and latent variables. Appeals for Bayesian methods are often made from a dogmatic, theory-based standpoint concerning the philosophical underpinnings of statistical inference, the role of prior beliefs, claims about how one should update beliefs given new information, and foundational issues, such as the admissibility of a statistical decision. Although such a rhetorical approach is academically rigorous, it usually is not the kind of argument a practicing researcher wants to read about. Researchers care about analyzing their data in a rigorous manner that leads to clear, defensible conclusions. In this chapter, we address the reader who wants to learn something about what all the Bayesian fuss is about and whether the Bayesian approach offers useful tools to incorporate into one's data analytic toolbox. We hope this chapter prompts readers to learn more about what Bayesian statistical ideas have to offer in standard data analytic situations. Throughout the chapter, we highlight important details of the Bayesian approach; how it differs from the frequentist approach typically used in psychological research; and most important, where it offers practical advantages, particularly concerning custom model-building, over the methods most commonly used by academic researchers in psychology and cognate disciplines.

SOME GENTLE PRELIMINARIES

Practicing research psychologists wish to understand and explain a variety of behaviors in humans and animals. Statistical methods and reasoning sharpen insight into experimental design and avoid the potential pitfalls of lay examination of data patterns. Deserving special mention is a point often missed in substantively focused studies: The purpose of statistical inference is to replace intuitions based on a mass of data with those achievable from examination of *parameters*, the "unknown constants" in a statistical model, usually characterizing some distribution, like the mean, variance, or functions thereof (e.g., mean differences in two populations). Except in nonparametric settings relatively rare in psychological and other social science research, understanding one's data relies on critically choosing an appropriate statistical model and both estimating and examining the distributions of its parameters. By this we typically mean the so-called *marginal distribution* (examining one parameter at a time) or *joint distribution* (several parameters at a time)— that is, everything we can say about a model's parameter once our data have been accounted for.

https://doi.org/10.1037/0000319-026
APA Handbook of Research Methods in Psychology, Second Edition: Vol. 2. Research Designs: Quantitative, Qualitative, Neuropsychological, and Biological, H. Cooper (Editor-in-Chief)

To examine their hypotheses, researchers often, either out of convention or convenience, rely on classical statistical methods that—explicitly or implicitly—enact certain assumptions. The most common of these assumptions is that the number of respondents is "large enough" for the central limit theorem to kick in, but can also manifest in (to take but a few examples), presuming equal variances in analysis of variance (ANOVA) designs, making various untested assumptions about (lack of) correlation in errors and variables, or requiring balanced designs. Each of these requirements is necessary because the commonly used classical statistical tests do not achieve "nice" forms when their assumptions are violated. Imagine instead a world in which researchers can simply collect a data set and let the chosen statistical model summarize everything of interest it contains; the only assumptions one makes concern the underlying model generating the data and not aspects of the data set itself (e.g., balance, lack of error correlation, and so on); missing values do not mean either throwing out a subject's data entirely or deciding among a variety of imputation methods; individuals can differ in their parameters; and covariates, like age and gender, can be used to describe how and why parameters differ across respondents.

Classical methods, such as nonparametric tests, can sometimes be used in the sorts of situations in which standard assumptions (like underlying normality) are known (or suspected) to be violated. But they typically come at a cost in power: the ability to detect incorrect hypotheses. Bayesian statistical methods, however, provide a general framework that is adaptable to many different types of data, for the relatively modest—and steadily decreasing over time—price of additional computational effort. As we emphasize throughout this chapter, Bayesian methods dramatically expand a researcher's ability to work with real data sets and explain what they have to tell us. Bayesian methods do this by yielding both joint and marginal distributions for all parameters of interest, not merely summary measures like means and variances that are only asymptotically valid, and with fewer presumptions

about model forms and large-sample properties of estimators.

For these and other reasons, we advocate the increased adoption of Bayesian methods by the psychological community. In this chapter, we take a first relatively nontechnical step in explaining how this might come about and what such methods might offer the practicing psychologist. Before starting, however, it is important to emphasize that both classical and Bayesian methods often work with (nearly) exactly the same model, but differ in terms of how parameters *in* that model are estimated and summarized. For whole classes of models— for example, hierarchical linear models (HLMs) widely used in social science—powerful classical programs offer most or essentially all the advantages of the Bayesian approach, and additional ones of speed and scalability for very large data sets. It is not our purpose here to suggest that classical statistical methods are inappropriate, wrongheaded, or misleading; rather, they can make it difficult to recover actual parameter distributions and engage in the sort of custom model-building that modern Bayesian programs—as discussed later in this chapter—readily accommodate.

Many treatments of Bayesian statistics that have been written for (or by) psychologists have focused on the more philosophical issues. Practicing research psychologists rarely need to grapple with the theory underlying conventional statistical inference, for example, how one interprets the usual *p*-value (as reflecting the probability of observing some sample statistic under the null hypothesis), "significance" (McShane et al., 2019), or the classical confidence interval as the frequency of intervals that contain the true population parameter value. It is in this context that Bayesian techniques are usually discussed as an alternative way of thinking about so-called "confidence" intervals (credible intervals in Bayesian parlance) and hypothesis testing, one that seems more conceptually straightforward for its avoidance of the notion of hypothetical replication. It has similarly been argued that the Bayesian approach provides an alternative methodology and philosophical foundation for hypothesis testing (e.g., Jaynes, 1986), although we do not take up such issues here, focusing instead on practical advantages in estimation, inference, and model-building.

A simple way of conceptualizing the distinction between the two approaches is about how one views uncertainty. A classical statistician views uncertainty as residing in the data one happens to observe: One needs to think about all the other observations that could have been made, under the hypothesized model, and base one's statistical test on the resulting distribution, which often achieves a "nice" form (e.g., one that can be looked up in a table). An example of this kind of logic is seen in the Fisherian interpretation of the *p*-value (the probability of possible results that are "more extreme" than the observed result) and in some standard tests like the Fisher exact test for contingency tables, which uses the hypergeometric distribution to compute the probability of all contingency tables that are "more extreme" than the one that was actually observed.

The Bayesian approach places uncertainty not in the observations but rather in one's lack of knowledge. For a Bayesian, the observed data are not uncertain—you observed what you observed. But uncertainty must be addressed somewhere in the analysis. A Bayesian places the uncertainty in our lack of knowledge about *parameters* and operationalizes that lack of knowledge in terms of a (joint) probability distribution over all unknown quantities—that is, parameters. Before any data are observed, the Bayesian summarizes everything known about the model's parameters in just such a distribution, called the *prior distribution*. This can include information from previously conducted studies, common-sense reasoning (e.g., gaining an inch in height will, all else being equal, entail an upswing in weight), or even seemingly inviolable facts about parameters (e.g., correlations must fall between –1 and 1). The prior distribution is then combined with (often called *updated by*) the likelihood, which is common from the usual frequentist analysis, to yield the *posterior* distribution.

As we will see, literally everything researchers might wish to say about their data—estimation, testing, prediction, and so on—can be extracted, in a natural and direct way, from this posterior. In a sense, it replaces the entire canon of specialized test procedures covered in introductory statistics courses with one simple conceptual object. This key object—the posterior—may be simple to conceptualize and use, but can rarely be obtained in closed-form, and so requires methods for numerically estimating it. So, in a sense, the Bayesian replaces the difficulty in classical statistics of *fashioning an appropriate test procedure* with one of *simulating the posterior*. As we hope to convince readers in this chapter, the once-tedious task of simulating the sought-after posterior has been largely automated in the last decade through both commercial and open-source software, dramatically lowering the entry costs of Bayesian analysis for the practicing researcher.

In the next section, we refine and illustrate some of these issues, using elementary examples common to statistics texts of both the frequentist and Bayesian varieties. We also provide references to some presently available software and a few comprehensive, book-length treatments of Bayesian statistical methods. Throughout, we eschew formulas and other mainstays of *rigor* for a more user-oriented discussion, one especially geared to the practicing researcher in psychology.

THE NITTY-GRITTY OF THE BAYESIAN APPROACH

We begin with a relatively simple example, one common throughout statistical inference, in psychology and elsewhere: estimating the proportion of times a particular event occurs.

Estimating a Proportion

To provide a specific context, consider a dependent variable that codes whether a couple has divorced within their first 20 years of marriage. The data set includes 10 couples, six of whom were divorced within the 20-year window. Of course, any beginning student knows that this sample can be used to estimate the divorce rate: simply divide the number of divorces by the total number of couples, $6/10 = 0.6$. But how do we know that is the best estimate of the true divorce rate in the population? How do we assess the uncertainty of this estimate?

To handle such questions within the classical framework, one reverts to the likelihood principle (i.e., "all the information in our sample is contained in the likelihood function"), makes an assumption about the independence of those 10 observations, and assumes the binomial model for the observed outcomes. To derive the usual maximum likelihood estimator for the proportion, we take the first derivative of the likelihood, set it to zero, and solve for any unknown parameters, of which in our present example there is only one. Some of the computations in maximum likelihood estimation are simpler if one works with the logarithm of the likelihood—which, as a monotonic transformation, leaves the maximum intact—thus converting products to sums. In our exposition, we focus primarily on the likelihood itself, because that is more convenient for Bayesian derivations, and point out when the log likelihood is used instead.

It is a common quip that the likelihood is the only thing about which both Bayesians and frequentists agree, and it is true that the likelihood plays a critical role in both accounts of statistical inference. In simple language, the likelihood function tells us how likely the parameters are to take one set of values, compared with any other. It is not a probability itself (indeed, it can even be greater than 1) but a relative statement, so that the likelihood ratio, a common concept in hypothesis testing, is a simple way to assess the comparative degree of appropriateness for any two given sets of parameters. In general, the likelihood is defined by

$$L(\theta|Y) = f(Y|\theta), \qquad (26.1)$$

where Y represents the observations, θ represents the unknown parameters, and f is some probability density function. It is necessary to assume a distribution f, such as the binomial or normal (perhaps the two most common statistical models), to write down a likelihood function that converts

probability statements into statements about *parameters*. It is therefore critical to conceptualize parameters as belonging to a specific model; it is the form of the model's likelihood function that allows the parameters to be estimated, regardless of whether the estimation is classical (usually, seeking the "maximum likelihood") or Bayesian (metaphorically speaking, "sampling from" the likelihood) in nature.

To return to our sample problem, the likelihood for binomial data is given by

$$L(\pi|Y) = \binom{N}{k} \pi^k (1-\pi)^{N-k}, \qquad (26.2)$$

where π is the population proportion that is being estimated (in the binomial case, the unknown parameter θ is traditionally denoted as π). The number of trials (N) and the number of successes k (which are the sum of our binary observations, Y) are held fixed, and one searches for values of π that maximize the value of Equation 26.2. We say values because many likelihood functions—although not the one in Equation 26.2, which is unimodal and in fact has a simple formula for its lone maximum—can have multiple *local maxima*, only one of which is the true global maximum, that is, the single best choice of parameter(s). It is for this reason that maximum likelihood is conceptualized in terms of a "search" for unknown parameter(s), which in practice can be quite complex in the classical approach, because multivariate optimization can be computationally intensive.

Although the likelihood of Equation 26.2 may look just like an elementary statement about the probability of observing a particular set of data, in actuality, the inference is done in the other direction; that is, we infer parameter π given the data Y. (We note here that the actual binary observations, Y, can be replaced by their sum, k, in this particular model, since the latter is a sufficient statistic for the former, meaning the original data are no longer needed for inference about the underlying parameter, π.) For this particular model, both the "best" value of the parameter ($\pi = k/n$) and its variance ($\pi(1-\pi)/n$)

can be written down exactly. But, more generally, in the classical estimation approach, the standard error of the parameter emerges by calculating the Hessian (the matrix of second derivatives) of the log likelihood at its maximum value. The logic justifying the use of the Hessian for this purpose involves imposing assumptions—most notably that the curvature of the log likelihood can be approximated by a multivariate Taylor series, up through its quadratic term. This is the underlying rationale for the typical approach taken by psychologists: computing a point estimate and constructing a confidence interval around that estimate. The classical approach focuses nearly exclusively on the maximum value of the likelihood (the point estimate) and approximates uncertainty (via the Hessian); all other details of parameter estimation are de-emphasized or even discarded. In this way, the classical statistician is forced to rely on a number of asymptotic (i.e., large sample) assumptions, without any practical way to verify them. It is only when these assumptions are valid that the usual properties of estimators, like normality, can be shown to hold. When a problem comes along for which none of the typical distributions (z, t, F, chi-square, etc.) are provable asymptotic approximations, defensible inferences from the data become far more difficult. As we shall see, the Bayesian is not hampered by this restriction because Bayesian analysis yields the actual distributions of any desired set of parameters (or functions of them) and rarely needs to rely on the common distributions covered in first courses on statistical inference.

It is important to emphasize that both classical and Bayesian estimation do share one bedrock set of assumptions: those that lead to the likelihood itself. Where they differ—and where we believe Bayesian methods offer a distinct advantage—is how the parameters of the likelihood are characterized and summarized. That is, the Bayesian approach also analyzes the likelihood (Equation 26.1 in general, or Equation 26.2 for our

binomial example) but differs in how it is used. Although the classical statistician *maximizes*[1] the likelihood by choosing the best parameter values θ, the Bayesian instead converts the problem into a statement about the (posterior) distribution θ.

To keep notation simple and avoid having to keep track of different density functions, we use so-called bracket notation, which has become the standard way to represent useful properties and rigorous derivations in Bayesian analysis. Instead of picking arbitrary functional notation, like $f(X)$ or $g(Y)$, it focuses instead on the dependence relationships among variables themselves. So, for example, $[Y]$ would simply be the distribution of the variable Y, while $[Y|X]$ would be the distribution of Y at a particular value of X, that is, its conditional distribution. As we will see, because densities integrate to 1, it is convenient to only keep track of *functional* relationships, and simply ignore constants (like $(2\pi)^{-1/2}$ appearing in the Gaussian density), and consequently replace equality of distributions (=) with proportionality ($\propto$). As mentioned earlier, a key Bayesian property is that the posterior distribution is proportional to the product of the likelihood and prior distribution; using our bracket notation, this will be denoted as

$$[\theta|y] \propto [y|\theta][\theta]. \qquad (26.3)$$

The prior distribution $[\theta]$ reflects what we know (or do not know) about the parameters θ *before* consulting the data; the posterior distribution $[\theta|y]$ reflects what we know about the parameters θ after combining both the observed data and the information contained in the prior. The change in reference turns out to be the key property of the Bayesian approach: rather than work only with the likelihood $[y|\theta]$, as in the classical approach, Bayesians work with the posterior distribution $[\theta|y]$ (which classical statisticians also seek to make inferences about, but work in reverse through the likelihood).

---

[1]We have conflated classical estimation with maximum likelihood because it is overwhelmingly the most common approach in practice. However, other approaches exist, most notably, (Generalized) Method of Moments, which is a common strategy in econometrics, and these typically enact fewer assumptions in parameter estimation.

Under this approach, the posterior tells us literally everything we can know about the parameters θ once the data *y* are observed. The Bayesian merely has to *explore* the posterior and use it for inference. This is simple, at least in theory, but we need to explain what we mean by exploring the posterior.

We must also stress that it is not the case that Bayesians have the extra step of imposing a prior distribution, whereas classical statisticians do not. There is a sense in which, when viewed through Bayesian eyes, classical statistics presumes that all values of a parameter are equally likely, what is called a "flat," "uniform," or sometimes "noninformative" prior in the Bayesian context (we return to the last of these later, since the distinction can be subtle, but have nonsubtle consequences). A Bayesian with a flat prior works with the same functional information as a classical statistician and has an analogous approach to such key issues as the interval constructed around a parameter estimate. The reason is that, with a flat prior, the Bayesian posterior is functionally the same as the classical likelihood. So, as long as the Bayesian acts on the posterior in the same way as the classical statistician (e.g., computes the maximum, also called the *mode*), then the two approaches yield identical results. Bayesians, however, provide a different, and some would say more nuanced, description of uncertainty by numerically capturing an impression of the entire posterior, not merely the small region surrounding its mode.

The Bayesian framework also provides a language that is more natural to empirical researchers. For example, the Bayesian tradition does not promote the *Gedankenexperiment*-type language of how to interpret a confidence interval (i.e., the percentage of such intervals that contain the true population value) and can more directly talk about an interval as representing a 95% degree of confidence (*credibility*) for the value of the unknown parameter. In our experience, students first encountering statistics are put off by counter-factual notions concerning what might happen if similar data were collected many times under identical circumstances. Rather, they ask conceptually direct questions about what can be said

using *this* data set, as it is. Bayesian inference refers to the data one has, not the data one might obtain were the world to replay itself multiple times.

Conjugate Priors

One way to simplify calculating and sampling from the posterior—the main practical challenges in most Bayesian analyses—is by careful selection of the prior distribution (although, as we discuss later, recent advances in Bayesian algorithm design and computation make this less critical). There are well-known prior-likelihood pairs, as on the right-hand side of Equation 26.3, that yield posteriors with the same form as the prior (i.e., the prior and posterior fall into the same distributional family, differing only in their parameters). For example, for binomial data, a beta prior distribution (i.e., beta-binomial pair) leads to a beta posterior distribution. Such conjugate priors make the overall Bayesian analysis easier to work with, both in terms of derivation and computation (Box & Tiao, 1973/1992).

To continue with our earlier (binomial) example, the beta distribution has two parameters, α and β, in its "functional" portion (i.e., leaving out constants that allow it to integrate to 1), $x^{\alpha-1}(1-x)^{\beta-1}$. Different values of α and β lead to different prior distributions over the unknown parameter π of the binomial distribution, making some values more likely than others before recourse to the actual data. For instance, the parameter pair α = 1 and β = 1 produces a beta distribution that is uniform over [0, 1], meaning that the prior presumes all values of the unknown binomial parameter π are equally likely; α = 2 and β = 2 makes values of π near one half somewhat more likely; and α = 101 and β = 201 makes values of π near one third quite a bit more likely (all these statements can be verified by simply graphing $x^{\alpha-1}(1-x)^{\beta-1}$ for the values in question). One then conducts an empirical study and observes *Y* successes out of *N* trials, such as in the example of six divorces in 10 couples (equivalently, six divorces and four nondivorces). The posterior distribution, when using a conjugate prior (i.e., the prior is beta and the likelihood is binomial), will also be a beta distribution, but the posterior parameters characterizing the posterior distribution are $\alpha + Y$ and $\beta + N - Y$, respectively. In other words, the posterior beta distribution has parameters that consist of both the prior parameter and the data (e.g., the first parameter of the posterior distribution is the sum of the prior parameter α and the observed number of divorces Y, and the second parameter is the sum of the prior parameter β and the number of nondivorces, $N - Y$). So, for our ongoing example, a uniform prior over the [0, 1] interval (all proportions are equally likely), leads to a posterior that is a beta distribution with parameters 7 and 5 (i.e., $\alpha = \beta = 1$, $Y = 6$, $N = 10$). For reasons that can now be clearly seen, this process is often referred to as *updating* the prior, using the data to obtain the posterior from which all Bayesian inference follows.

The mode (i.e., the most likely value, where the density function reaches its largest value) of the beta distribution is $(\alpha - 1)/(\alpha + \beta - 2)$. So, the mode of the posterior for our ongoing divorce example using a uniform prior distribution is 0.60 (i.e., the posterior has parameters $\alpha = 7$ and $\beta = 5$, so the mode is 0.60), the same value as the maximum likelihood estimator. Other summary measures of the posterior distribution are also possible. The mean of a beta distribution is $\alpha/(\alpha + \beta)$, so a Bayesian could take the estimate of the proportion to be $7/12 = 0.58$, rather than the classically derived maximum likelihood estimate of $6/10 = 0.60$ (Figure 26.1).

One general feature of Bayesian estimation is that inferences depend on both the prior and the data ("likelihood"). Consequently, as the sample size gets larger, the impact of the particular choice of the prior becomes less influential, as nearly any reasonable prior will be progressively overwhelmed by ever more data. If we had 600 couples divorce out of 1,000, then the posterior mean would be $601/1002 = 0.5998$, which is very close to the maximum likelihood estimate of 0.60. (The mode remains 0.60 for the uniform prior distribution.)

We note that the classical and Bayesian estimates for the proportion also coincide when the Bayesian uses a beta prior distribution with parameters α and β both very close to zero (note that α and β must be positive to give rise to a nondegenerate distribution; a so-called

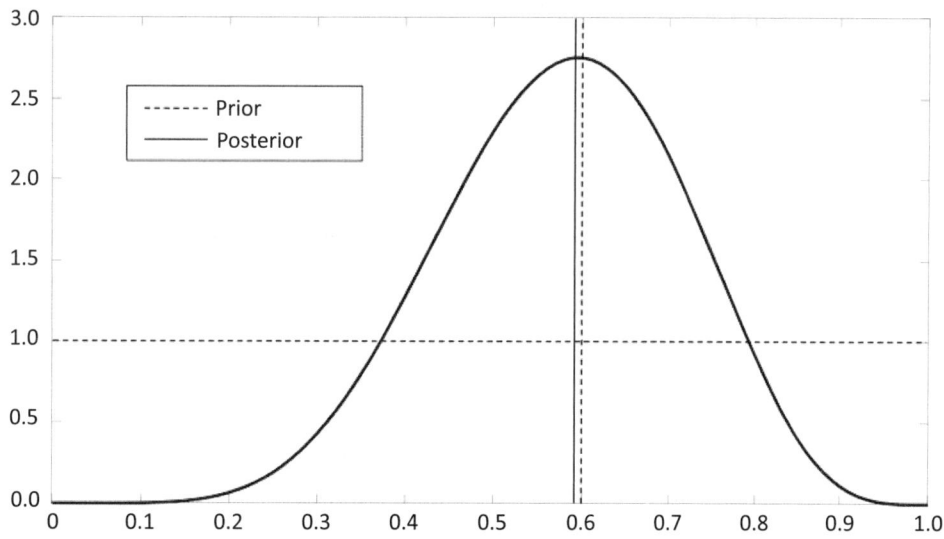

FIGURE 26.1. An example of six divorces out of 10 couples. The solid vertical line is the Bayesian estimate for the unknown proportion given a uniform prior (dotted horizontal line) and posterior distribution (thick solid curve). The theoretical posterior distribution is a beta; the thick solid curve is the estimated posterior distribution from MCMC sampling. The dashed vertical line is the maximum likelihood estimate and the mode of the posterior (0.6).

improper prior results if one literally sets both to zero because the functional part of the beta density, $x^{-1}(1-x)^{-1}$, does not have a finite integral over $[0, 1]$). Such an improper prior corresponds to a flat or uniform prior over the logit scale—that is, every value of the logit transform of π, or $\log[\pi/(1-\pi)]$, is equally likely—which can be used to provide a Bayesian justification for using logistic regression in the case of data that follow a binomial distribution. Note that we have avoided calling such priors "noninformative": Although the prior is flat over the logit scale (and so would appear to say all such values are equally likely), it is *extremely* informative over the scale of the proportions themselves, putting ever more weight on values closer to 0 and 1. Thus, one need be careful in deeming a prior "noninformative," since what can be minimally influential in one parameterization can have very different effects in an alternative parameterization of the very same problem (Seaman et al., 2012).

The prior distribution has other effects on the analysis as well. For example, the prior can define the feasible search space while exploring the posterior distribution. Many statistical models impose restrictions on possible parameter values, such as that variances cannot be negative, which would seem to be an inviolable property that need not be specified, or even checked. Under classical estimation routines, however, negative variances can and do occur, even in common models like one-way random effects ANOVA, but especially in the case of latent variable models and mixture models, as users of programs that estimate such models soon discover. The prior distribution can address these issues by defining the effective feasible region for the unknown variance to be non-negative (i.e., forcing the prior distribution to have mass only over nonnegative values).

Conjugate priors (e.g., such as the "beta-binomial" example above, the posterior of which is a "named" distribution that offers closed-form expressions for the mean, mode, and variance) can be helpful for pedagogical purposes and simplify by-hand derivations. Yet they do create a needless constraint, as there is nothing in the Bayesian framework that requires or even favors conjugacy. Indeed, the elegance of the Bayesian approach is that one can utilize more general priors that may be particularly suitable for the data analytic problem. Modern Bayesian software such as Stan (discussed later in this chapter) and its underlying "Hamiltonian" algorithm works roughly equally well for conjugate and nonconjugate priors, allowing the analyst to focus on choosing an appropriate model, not on whether the prior will simplify computation.

THE WHOLE DISTRIBUTION AND NOTHING BUT THE WHOLE DISTRIBUTION

The previous subsection sells the Bayesian approach short. Comparing the Bayesian posterior mean to the parameter that emerges from the classical maximum likelihood framework is playing to the strength of the classical approach, which provides the estimate of the mean, and with a little more work and a few additional assumptions, a symmetric standard error (based again on asymptotic assumptions) emerges. The Bayesian approach has much more to offer, however. Instead of providing a point estimate and a standard error for a given parameter, the Bayesian approach provides its entire posterior distribution. This is available in the form of a sample drawn from the posterior, from which any quantity of interest can be computed. In some (all too rare) instances, as in the case of conjugate priors, closed-form solutions are possible, and so the entire posterior distribution takes a known form, and sample draws from the posterior are not needed. But, even when the posterior does not take such a known form—and this is the case in the vast majority of real-world applications—the researcher can, using the posterior, readily compute not only the mean but also the median or any quantile one would like (e.g., the lower or upper 2.5%), even estimate the entire shape of the distribution. Knowledge of the posterior distribution allows one to construct intervals for parameters of interest without making specific, potentially unfounded, assumptions, like symmetry (too often assumed, particularly so for bounded and skewed quantities like variances). Indeed, if the posterior distribution is asymmetric, one can easily construct an interval that accurately reflects this asymmetry; in fact, the customary "highest density region" (HDR) commonly provided by Bayesian software takes advantage of this property by producing the narrowest interval likely to contain the parameter at a given "confidence" level, which is typically not symmetric.

Furthermore, when the unknown parameter θ is a vector, the posterior distribution becomes multidimensional. The classical approach to a parameter vector θ is to work with point estimates for each parameter separately, calculate a covariance matrix across parameters (via the Hessian), and rely on asymptotic results to make inferences. The Bayesian tackles the entire multivariate posterior distribution head on, however, by taking large samples from it directly. A few decades ago, this was rather difficult to do for real-world data sets and models. Modern computers, along with some sampling techniques that emerged from statistical mechanics problems in physics (e.g., Gibbs sampling, simulated annealing), have revolutionized how an analyst can explore a posterior distribution. As mentioned, the solution turns out to be "Monte Carlo" sampling: the analyst takes a sample as large as needed from the posterior distribution and uses it for inference and model comparison.

It is important to distinguish the Bayesian approach to sampling from the posterior from well-known *resampling* procedures, such as the bootstrap or the jackknife. The Bayesian approach produces samples of the unknown parameters, whereas other approaches to estimation or inference that make use of sampling involve sampling either the observations themselves or quantities from a model-fitting procedure. For example, to bootstrap slopes in a regression equation, one can either create bootstrap samples of the original data set and compute regression parameters on each of those bootstrap samples (in which case there are as many regressions as bootstrap samples), or one can take bootstrap samples of the residuals after having fit a regression model to the original data (in which case only one

regression is estimated). In neither case is the sampling done from the joint posterior distribution for all unknown model quantities (i.e., the joint distribution of the intercept, the slope, and the variance of the residuals), the cornerstone of Bayesian estimation.

Once the multivariate distribution of the parameter vector θ is in hand, one can use it in creative ways to resolve some nontrivial problems. As mentioned, one can compute the mean or median of the posterior distribution of each parameter. More interesting, one can compute functions of the unknown parameters. For example, one common test statistic used in mediation analysis is the product of two unknown parameters: the slope of the predictor to the mediator and the slope of the mediator to the dependent variable (where the latter slope is computed in the context of a regression that also includes the predictor). The prospect of a well-behaved statistical test on the product of two regression slopes is nearly hopeless using frequentist techniques because it cannot be guaranteed to have a *standard* distribution. But the Bayesian perspective provides a well-behaved and reasonable solution. The analyst simply multiplies the samples of the two regression slopes (i.e., multiplies draws from the posterior distributions for both quantities) and instantly has a new posterior distribution for the product. One can then work with that posterior distribution in the usual way, such as compute the mean or median, or the 2.5% and 97.5% quantiles, to construct an interval that can be used to assess whether mediation has occurred (as indicated by the computed product being suitably far from zero). One works with the posterior distribution directly without having to assume symmetry in the sampling distribution (as the classical approach requires, which is suspect in any case because the distribution of a product of random variables is not, in general, symmetric; Yuan & MacKinnon, 2009, provided an introductory account of how to implement this idea for testing mediation in normally distributed data).

It is relatively straightforward to extend this Bayesian approach to mediation to more complicated situations, such as when the mediator or the outcome (or both) involves binary data. In this setting, it is necessary to use a generalized linear model, such as logistic regression, for mediation, and the inference within the classical approach for products of parameters across two such general regressions becomes even more difficult. The Bayesian approach can easily handle mediation models in cases in which predictor, mediator, and outcome are on different scales (e.g., normally distributed, binary, ordinal, count, or survival data), and it can even be extended into new territories that have not been fully explored within the classical framework (e.g., a mixture model for mediation in which the analysis partitions the sample into different subgroups exhibiting different mediation patterns; Feinberg 2012). So long as we can sample from the posterior, we can construct any interval or test of interest with little additional effort.

Another example that is relatively simple within the Bayesian approach is the statistical test for a random effect term. Many multilevel modeling programs provide a classical test for the variance for a random effect term against the null value of 0. Unfortunately, the classical test does not apply when testing a parameter at its boundary (i.e., variances are bounded below by 0). So, testing the variance against a null of 0 corresponds to a test that technically does not exist and erroneously produces significant results in all but very small samples.[2] Thus, most tests for the variance of the random effect term that appear in popular programs are, if not overtly incorrect, potentially misleading. Some attempts have been made to address this issue using frequentist methods, but a Bayesian approach handles this problem directly, by yielding the posterior distribution of the variance term under a prior that is properly defined over the feasible range of the variance (a common one being a noninformative prior for the log of the variance). Bayesian testing procedures can compare measures of model fit for a model with a random effect to one without it,

akin to the classical likelihood ratio test but valid for testing any set of candidate models against one another, not merely parametrically related (i.e., nested) ones. (We discuss model comparison at length later in this chapter.)

Data, Parameters, and Missingness

The shorthand notation of θ to denote the unknown parameters masks the strength of the Bayesian approach. Any and all unknown quantities can be incorporated into the vector θ. For instance, missing data can be construed as unknown parameters and included in θ. The Bayesian practice of estimating the joint distribution enables one to properly capture the effect of missing data on the parameters of interest, such as a mean or regression slope; the overall uncertainty resulting from *all* unknown quantities are jointly modeled. Other unknowns that can enter the vector θ include terms representing random effects and latent variables as well as terms representing proportions or latent class indicators in mixture models. For each of these features of the Bayesian approach, the entire posterior distribution for all unknowns is estimated: We have not only the point estimate for the missing data but also their posterior distribution, and all other parameters are adjusted for the uncertainty because of the entire *pattern of missingness*. By comparison, options built into older frequentist statistical programs common in psychological analyses— casewise or listwise deletion, or the downright dangerous option to replace missing data by means—appear almost primitive, although frequentist methods to "correct for" missing data, such as expectation-maximization (EM) and multiple imputation, can be quite sophisticated, effective, and computationally scalable (Dong & Peng, 2013; Little & Rubin, 2019).

Although this chapter lacks space for a full explication of these ideas, one of the major conceptual and computational advantages of the Bayesian approach is its recognition of just

---

[2]Here we avoid the long-standing debate in statistics regarding testing point hypotheses like $\mu = 0$, which the Bayesian takes to mean whether the data are more consistent with a model in which this is true from one in which μ is estimated along with the posterior distribution for all other model parameters.

two kinds of quantities: those you know (data), and those you do not know (parameters). Gone are the tedious distinctions between data types, latent variables, limited–censored–truncated, dependent versus independent, missing points or covariates, and the entire menagerie of specialized techniques one must master to deal with them. A Bayesian can simply treat anything not observed as a parameter in the model and, in a rigorous and natural way, numerically integrate over it (even if, in practice, the computations can be complex and time-consuming). So, missing data include not only literal morsels of unavailable information but also other unobservables such as latent variables or mixing parameters in a mixture model. Using a technique called *data augmentation* that fills in any missing values (which are treated as parameters) on each pass of the numerical simulator, dramatic simplifications in programming the likelihood are possible. As stated, a full description is well beyond the frame of this chapter. In our view, the ability of Bayesian analysis to seamlessly handle missing data is among its most powerful practical advantages, once researchers properly conceptualize the notion of missingness. We refer the interested reader to the classic texts by Little and Rubin (2019) and Gelman et al. (2013).

Techniques for Sampling From the Posterior Distribution

The idea of sampling from the posterior, and using the sample to compute summary measures such as expected value (means) and the distribution of parameters θ, is the modern contribution of the Bayesian framework. Bayesian computations were extremely difficult before this development of dedicated simulation techniques, which is one reason why the use of conjugate priors was so prominent in the early applications of Bayesian statistics (Box & Tiao, 1973/1992).

The key innovation in the Bayesian toolbox is the general technique of Markov chain Monte Carlo (MCMC) methods. The basic idea is to sample each unknown parameter in turn (including those that reflect missing data), sequentially cycling through each unknown many times, always conditional on the latest draws for all the others. Under fairly general conditions (which are both technical and satisfied in the vast majority of actual research settings), theorems show that the sampling will reach a *stationary distribution* for the parameters of interest. One of the complexities of Bayesian analysis is that one can only rarely sample from the desired posterior distribution immediately because this would require knowing approximately where it is largest. Instead, one can choose a start point at random, let the simulation go, and, usually within several thousand iterations (and often much sooner), a stationary distribution is reached, after which everything produced by the simulator can be used for testing, inference, and forecasting.

Several diagnostic tests are available to identify when such a stationary distribution has been reached. Within the Bayesian framework, the stationary distributions are reached by sampling from the so-called conditional densities (i.e., probability densities for one or a set of parameters given specific values for all the others), but the researcher is interested in—and obtains—samples from the entire joint distribution for all unknown quantities (parameters). Samples from the stationary distribution then serve to estimate parameters and the uncertainty in each as well as assess model fit. The availability of the joint distribution allows for tests that are sometimes very difficult within the standard framework. For example, if one wants to test the distribution of a product of two unknown parameters (a situation that arises in testing mediation models, as discussed earlier), it is straightforward to have the product distribution merely by multiplying the samples of the two unknown distributions (Yuan & MacKinnon, 2009). Additionally, it is trivial for the researcher to place a priori constraints on parameters, for example, specifying that an estimated correlation is positive. This can be done via the prior or within the sampling scheme, simply by setting any parameter or function of them to a specific value, like zero, and sampling for all the others conditional on the constraints. The analogous procedure in a frequentist analysis can be quite difficult, as such constraints can wreck asymptotic normality, making it tricky to derive standard error estimators. But this poses no problems for Bayesians, who need not bother about asymptotics and presumptions of standard distributional forms.

Different methods lie within the MCMC family of algorithms, the dominant ones being Gibbs sampling and Metropolis-Hastings sampling. Loosely put, the former is used when conditional densities take "nice" forms (known distributions relatively easy to sample from), the latter when they do not. (For a review of these methods, see Tanner, 1993.) Bayesian algorithm design is complex and technical, so we cannot provide anything close to a complete description of the subject here; the interested practitioner can consult dedicated articles that lay out the details in an accessible manner (e.g., Jackman, 2000), or several of the texts discussed later in the chapter. We can, however, readily convey the flavor of what is involved in a nontechnical way. The primary goal of Bayesian analysis is generating a sample from the posterior distribution. This means that the probability that a point (i.e., a set of parameter values) is in the sample is proportional to the height of the posterior distribution at that point. Or, more usefully, the ratio of the probability of any two points being in the sample is the ratio of the posteriors at those points. This is very close to the foundational insight of the dominant algorithm, Metropolis-Hastings, used in Bayesian analysis: if one is at a point that has already been accepted into the sample, one jumps to another point on the basis of whether its posterior is higher or lower. If it is higher, one jumps; if not, one jumps with probability related to the ratio of the posteriors. (There are some technicalities involving how one generates potential jumps as well, but this would take us far afield.)

This simple algorithm can, in principle, be used to navigate high-dimensional parameter spaces, that is, to estimate statistical models with dozens or even hundreds of parameters. In practice, there are many techniques used to make it efficient, like jumping along one dimension at a time, taking small steps (which make jumping more likely), and using special schemes to choose where to jump. If one can calculate closed-form expressions for particular densities (describing where to jump), it is possible to prove that one always jumps, eliminating a potentially long series of staying put.

When a large number, usually several tens of thousands, of such jumps have been made, one has that many drawn parameter values that can be used for inference. Unfortunately, these draws are often highly autocorrelated. In simple language, this means they do not jump around the distribution randomly, but rather move across it slowly, because where you jump *to* depends on where you jump *from*. One approach to this problem is *thinning*, that is, retaining only every 10th, 20th, or 50th draw, although this can discard information and is sometimes frowned upon. Even with thinning, the researcher will typically have many thousands of points to use for inference, and this is ordinarily sufficient to trace out a close approximation to the true marginal distribution of any subset of parameters of interest, even for missing values (which, as explained, are treated as parameters). And if one does not have enough draws, it is simple to keep taking more, until one does. More recent innovations involving the *Hamiltonian* (implemented in the Stan analysis language, as detailed later) have the proposed jumps follow special contours related to the geometry of the log-likelihood surface, greatly reducing the autocorrelation often encountered with very large parameter spaces and thereby allowing efficient estimation.

Evaluating the Convergence of the Sampling Process

MCMC methods pose several practical questions that need to be addressed when analyzing data. What starting values should be used to initiate the sampling? How long should the burn-in (the initial "warmup" draws that help approach the stationary distribution, but that must be discarded) period be? Which algorithms will be efficient in terms of run time?

Rather than provide full answers to all these implementation issues, we will focus on one key aspect of the sampling process: the traceplot.

This plot focuses on a single parameter and plots its drawn value against the iteration number. In the previously introduced case of the binomial proportion (of six divorces out of 10 couples), we use MCMC sampling to generate, say, 10,000 samples from a beta posterior (which arises from the conjugate beta prior and a binomial likelihood). Each of these samples represents a draw from the distribution. They can be plotted against iteration number, and one can inspect whether there are systematic deviations or other obvious patterns. One looks for general stability in the traceplot, that is, for little evidence of systematic deviation (e.g., several hundred samples near $\pi = 1$, then several hundred near $\pi = 0$, both of which are endpoint values, indicating extreme deviations from a stable, interior solution). Figure 26.2 represents a well-behaved traceplot resulting from sampling from the posterior beta for our example of six divorces out of 10 couples. The sample was thinned by retaining only every

10th observation, hence 1,000 iterations are plotted out of 10,000 draws.

A more interesting example than estimating a simple proportion is using Bayesian methods to estimate the latent growth curve. This sort of model allows for two types of heterogeneity, for both slope and intercept (and higher order terms, too, given a sufficient number of time points per individual). Each subject is therefore allowed their own slope and intercept, but the regressions are estimated simultaneously both for efficiency and for proper modeling of the error term. The latent growth model can be estimated either in a multilevel model using random terms for the slope and intercept (time points are nested within subject) or in a structural equations model using latent variables for slope and intercept (raw data are the indicators, paths are fixed to correspond to the unit vector for the intercept and the linear contrast for the slope). To illustrate, we borrowed a data set from one of our collaborators, involving

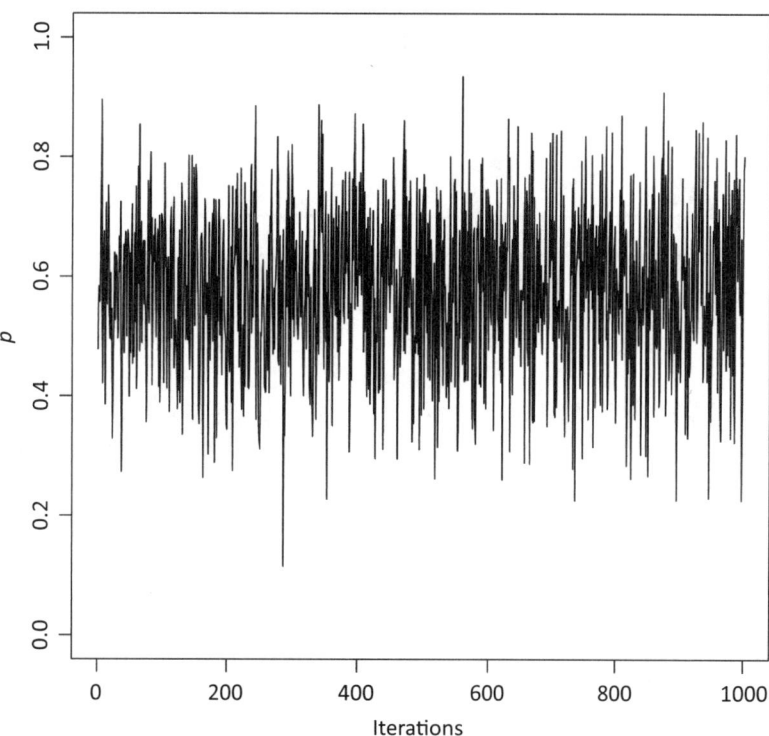

FIGURE 26.2. An example of a traceplot following the posterior density in Figure 26.1. The samples were thinned by 10. This example did not have a burn-in period because the sampling was done directly from the posterior beta with parameters 7 and 5, per the conjugate prior.

591

five time points for each participant on the same dependent variable. We estimated a latent intercept and latent linear slope using the Bayesian estimation routine in the R package brms (discussed further in a later section regarding software). The posterior distribution and the traceplot appear in Figure 26.3. We used 50,000 iterations for burn-in, then estimated 50,000 samples, thinning by keeping every fourth observation, running such four chains, resulting in 50,000 samples (the choice of thinning proportion is left to the researcher on the basis of the autocorrelation of the samples from the posterior; diagnostics appear in many programs to aid in this choice). The estimate of the linear latent variable is –0.06

(this is the posterior mean); the 95% (credible) interval is (–.10, –.02). The maximum likelihood estimate for this sample is –0.06 with a standard error of 0.022 (the estimate corresponds to the fixed-effect term for the slope in the multilevel model). We do not present the complete output for the other parameters, such as the intercept and the random effect variances and covariances, but similar densities and traceplots are produced for every other parameter.

Model Comparison: Bayes Factors and Deviance Information Criterion

Among the many conceptual and pragmatic difficulties of the classical approach is model

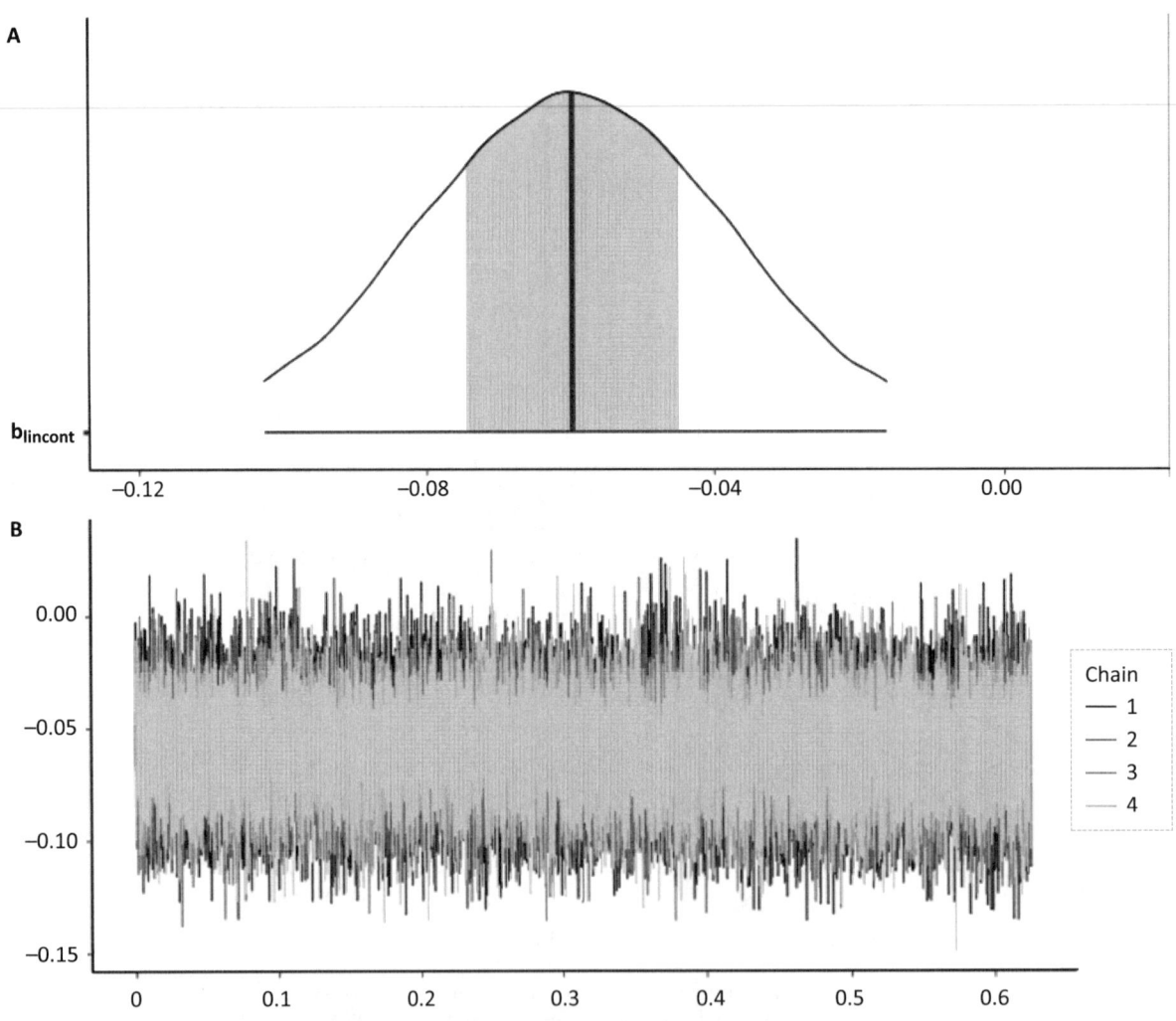

FIGURE 26.3. Example of a latent growth curve model. Results for the mean of the latent variable representing the linear term. The posterior density plot appears in panel A; the traceplot appears in panel B.

comparison. In some sense, determining which model best fits given data is among the key problems in all of scientific inference. Although there are a number of specialized approaches to making this determination in classical statistics, they hold primarily for nested models. By contrast, Bayesian inference provides a general procedure for comparing *any* set of candidate models in terms of how well they are supported by the data: the Bayes factor.

Given two models, the Bayes factor quantifies how much more strongly the data favor one model over the other. Its calculation depends on one's ability to determine the so-called marginal likelihood for a model, which can be challenging in practical applications. Philosophically, the procedure is akin to the standard likelihood-ratio (LR) test in classical statistics, although the LR test depends on maximizing both model likelihoods, whereas the Bayes factor averages them over all parameters via integrating over the prior distribution. Although it is not obvious, this one change pays great benefits: Not only can the Bayes factor compare any two candidate models, but it also penalizes overparameterized models for needless complexity; by contrast, classical methods often do so via various synthetic measures, such as the Akaike information criterion (AIC) and the Bayesian information criterion (BIC), that penalize "nonparsimonious" models (those with many parameters), although in practice they can point to different models as the best tradeoff between fit and complexity.

Because marginal likelihoods and Bayes factors can be difficult to calculate, Bayesian statisticians have sought other comparison metrics that are easily computed from standard simulation output (i.e., the draws themselves). Among the most commonly applied of these is the deviance information criterion (DIC). DIC sums two terms, the first assessing model lack-of-fit and the second assessing model complexity (i.e., effective number of parameters). Large values of DIC therefore indicate high lack of fit, high complexity, or both, and therefore a less desirable model. DIC is known to be valid only when the log-likelihood is itself approximately multivariate normal, and thus

must be used with caution, although it is built into many Bayesian statistical programs, simplifying model comparison considerably.

Making Predictions

It is often argued, with some justification, that real-world users of statistics have little use for parameters in and of themselves. What real users care about is using a statistical model to run what-if analyses, that is, to make predictions. Predictions can address what will happen for those units (e.g., experimental subjects, longitudinal survey respondents, and so on) already in the data or new units, the likelihood of attrition or missingness, or even the future values of parameters themselves (e.g., are the animals becoming less sensitive to stimuli over time?). In the classical, frequentist approach, this is done via prediction intervals, at least in the standard regression or general linear models framework. But this, again, is highly dependent on asymptotic normality (or other such distributional assumptions), which may not hold for a particular data set. A secondary issue is that predictions are often made from a frequentist model using point estimates for its parameters, even though those parameters may have a complex, and relatively loose (i.e., high variance), joint distribution of their own.

Once again, the Bayesian approach supplies a complete and conceptually appealing solution to prediction: A prediction is, like everything else, simply a distribution, one that we can calculate from the posterior (not including the new observation about which we are trying to make predictions), and all available data. In simple terms, we integrate over the posterior of the parameters in the model. In symbols,

$$P(Y_{new}|Y) = \int P(Y_{new}|\theta)P(\theta|Y)d\theta. \qquad (26.4)$$

This tells us that if we wish to know the distribution for a *new* observation, Y_{new}, we must consider all the data we already have, Y. And the way to incorporate this existing data is via the posterior probability of the parameters of the model, $P(\theta|Y)$. We simply average this (i.e., integrate) over the entire parameter space, θ.

Once we have this *posterior predictive distribution*, $P(Y_{new}|Y)$, we can use it like any other distribution, to calculate means, modes, variance, quartiles, or more exotic functions. There is no guarantee that this predictive distribution will look like any of the standard distributions of elementary statistics. In fact, when this happens, it indicates that the prediction problem would have been difficult or impossible using frequentist tools alone. A simple lesson arising from this example is that the posterior distribution for the parameters, $P(\theta|Y)$, is a powerful object that can be used to readily obtain a great deal more information of use in practical statistical settings, especially so in forecasting.

Learning More About the Bayesian Approach

Many excellent textbooks and review articles provide detailed information about both Bayesian inference and estimation for the practicing researcher. Among the classics is Box and Tiao (1973/1992); as much a research monograph as a textbook, it provided detailed derivations of theoretical results in a Bayesian framework, although it did not cover modern MCMC-based approaches to Bayesian computation. Similarly, an early paper by Edwards et al. (1963) made a strong case for use of Bayesian inference in psychological research, while a recent systematic review of the psychological literature found hundreds of articles availing of Bayesian methodology (van de Schoot et al., 2017).

Practicing researchers hoping to learn more about and apply Bayesian methods are almost spoiled for choice, with many excellent full-scale review articles, book-length treatments, and thoroughly documented software packages available. We would direct the general reader first to a comprehensive guide for "Bayesian statistics and modelling" (van de Schoot et al., 2021) in *Nature Reviews Methods Primers*, with an extensive bibliography pointing to the primary research literature, including key articles in psychology proper. Similarly, a recent trio of articles lays out the fundamentals of Bayesian inference in a manner specifically targeted to researchers in academic psychology (Etz & Vandekerckhove

2018; Wagenmakers, Love, et al., 2018; Wagenmakers, Marsman, et al., 2018).

Contemporary approaches to Bayesian estimation rely heavily on MCMC algorithms that sample the joint distribution of parameters. Such techniques have been adapted to many novel model and data types, and there are numerous contemporary textbooks on the details of various Bayesian algorithms as well as general introductions, some geared to specific software packages. Perhaps the most influential general introduction is Gelman et al. (2013), providing comprehensive coverage of all aspects of Bayesian model-building, estimation, testing, and inference, as well as an archive for teaching materials (https://stat.columbia.edu/~gelman/book/) and code for several software platforms.

The practicing psychologist interested in applying Bayesian methods empirically will probably wish to learn it in the context of specific programs meant to streamline Bayesian analysis, so we restrict out purview to textbooks with that aim. Among recent treatments are McElreath (2020), which emphasizes a computational approach to estimation, multilevel modeling, and causal inference using R and Stan, including its own "rethinking" package to help implement popular classes of Bayesian models; Kruschke (2014), which takes a step-by-step approach of introducing the Bayesian workflow for researchers using R, JAGS, and Stan; and Congdon (2007, 2014), with an emphasis on model-building in WinBUGS.

Software

Although software to implement and conduct Bayesian analyses came about relatively slowly, this picture has changed over the last 2 decades, with many excellent choices. We recognize that software (and associated textbook) recommendations are always a moving target, so we restrict the discussion to current capabilities, with the caveat that these will deepen over time. Among the most general of the early frameworks is WinBUGS (https://www.mrc-bsu.cam.ac.uk/software/bugs/the-bugs-project-winbugs/)—and its successors OpenBUGS and JAGS—which, as mentioned earlier, is covered by multiple introductory textbooks, including Ntzoufras (2011) and Gelman and Hill's (2006) classic text on multilevel and hierarchical modeling.

More recently, Bayesian tools have become widely available due to the open-source language and model development platform, Stan (mc-stan.org). Stan leverages a special type of Bayesian algorithm, *Hamiltonian Monte Carlo* (HMC; see Neal, 2011 or Betancourt, 2017), that is suitable for high-dimensional parameter spaces and complex, nonlinear (log)likelihoods. Like WinBUGS, Stan frees the analyst from custom-programming densities, and offers a flexible language for simply stating model priors and likelihoods; it also features visualization tools, via the "shinystan" graphical user interface (GUI), to explore all model estimation results. Such is the power of Stan that several front-end interfaces have emerged to harness its power to estimate broad swaths of models of particular interest to empirical researchers, without requiring familiarity with Stan itself. Two such are brms (cran.rstudio.com/web/packages/brms/) and rstanarm (cran.r-project.org/web/packages/rstanarm), both of which run within the open-source statistical package R (https://www.r-project.org); brms, in particular, replicates much of the functionality of the popular lme4 package for linear mixed-effects models (Bürkner, 2017).

For researchers who wish to remain within their customary analysis environment, a fortunate development is the wide appearance of Bayesian methods and algorithms within popular, widely-adopted programs. For example, SAS offers a broad range of Bayesian options, including the finite mixture models, generalized linear models, and Cox regressions, simply by adding a "BAYES" statement to standard code; and "natively Bayesian" procedures, including generalized linear mixed and discrete choice models (e.g., multinomial logit/probit, nested logit), as well as a general MCMC procedure for user-specified priors and likelihoods. Stata has been similarly expansive, with over 50 likelihood models and free choice of priors for a variety of linear, nonlinear, and mixed models, as well as a "bayesmh" command for user-defined models. SPSS has likewise added

a variety of basic Bayesian tests and models, including for regression, ANOVA, and log-linear models; MLwiN has enabled Bayesian estimation throughout, with an attractive GUI for model-building, parametric restrictions, and output monitoring; and the structural equation modeling programs Amos and Mplus support Bayesian estimation.

Lastly, there is now also a substantial choice of "general-purpose" Bayesian software besides WinBUGS and Stan, including JAGS, NIMBLE, and PyMC3, as well as entire programming languages suitable for Bayesian inference, like Julia, MATLAB, R, Pyro, and Tensorflow, that are used widely in industry, government, and academia. And, within languages like R, specialized packages of particular importance have emerged, for example, (a) BANOVA, which greatly generalizes the range of ANOVA models available to research psychologists by allowing unbalanced designs, numerous outcome variable types (e.g., binary or count), and a full hierarchical (i.e., mixed model) set-up and (b) blavaan, which provides Bayesian estimation of structural equations models. In short, Bayesian analysis "has come to a program near you" and allows practicing researchers to implement popular models out of the box, or build their own as their projects require.

TWO RICHER EXAMPLES ILLUSTRATING THE USEFULNESS OF THE BAYESIAN APPROACH

In this section, we discuss two examples that we use to explore, at a deeper level, the concepts presented earlier in this chapter. The first is a general discussion of a canonical problem throughout the social sciences, and the second shows how a Bayesian approach can allow researchers to estimate a fairly complex model, for a real research problem, using modern-day software tools.

Multilevel Models: A Bayesian Take on a Classic Problem

We illustrate how Bayesian ideas can come into play when understanding multilevel or random effect models. Many areas of psychology have seen some form of multilevel or random effect (we will use the terms interchangeably) model come to the forefront in the past decade. Developmental psychologists use multilevel models to account for individual differences in growth-curve trajectories. Clinical psychologists use latent factors to model individual differences in scale response. Cognitive neuroscientists using functional magnetic resonance imaging in their research invoke a two-level model to account for both the intraindividual time course of the blood-oxygen-level dependence response and inter-individual differences in parameters. These random effect and multilevel ideas are not new, having been developed actively since the 1940s, if not earlier. They appear in many of the early experimental design textbooks in chapters with such titles as "Random and Nested Effects" (e.g., Winer, 1971). An important special case of this framework is the repeated measures analysis of variance, in which observations are nested within subject, each subject is assigned a parameter, and data are not treated as independent observations. The correlated structure of the repeated measures is modeled through random effect terms.

Among the major limitations of the early developments in random effect and multilevel modeling was that the problem was tractable (in closed form) only for balanced designs—that is, an equal number of subjects across conditions were needed to derive formulas—and for either linear or general linear models. The major advance in the past 30 years has been the development of specialized algorithms to handle the general problem of multilevel and random effect models for a rich variety of model and data types. The new algorithms can work with unequal number of subjects (e.g., not all classrooms have to contain the same number of pupils), missing data, and so-called latent variable formulations (e.g., random utility models) and can accommodate both predictors of the random effect terms and the use of the random effect terms to predict other parameters in the model.

An important issue in working with multilevel and random effect models is that to compute estimates and standard errors, it is necessary to average over the random effect terms. That is, to estimate parameters in the classic statistical framework, it is necessary to compute the likelihood of the data at each value of the hypothesis, weight the likelihood by a function of the value of the hypothesis, and sum the products over all possible hypotheses. Typical data sets involve multiple independent observations, so the overall likelihood is taken as the product of each observation's individual likelihood. The multiplication of likelihoods (one for each observation) is justified because of the independence assumption, just as we multiply the probability of independent coin tosses to compute the joint probability of outcomes over multiple independent coin tosses. In symbols, we denote the product over multiple observations and use an integral to denote the average over the random effect term:

$$\int \prod_i f(y_i|u) g(u) \, du, \qquad (26.5)$$

where the product is taken over observations i, with likelihood $f(y_i|u)$ for a single observation, and distribution $g(u)$ over random effect u. This is a standard way to write the likelihood in the classical approach. One can then use well-known, specialized maximum likelihood techniques to estimate parameters and their standard errors directly from this likelihood (e.g., McCulloch & Searle, 2001), under suitable asymptotic assumptions.

The basic point we want to communicate is that the use of random effects involves some fairly complicated mathematical operations that do not lend themselves to easy descriptions. Equation 26.5 communicates the notion that there is a kind of averaging over the likelihood, where the likelihoods are weighted by the distribution $g(u)$ of the random effects. Equation 26.5 presents some difficult computational challenges, too. It is necessary to use specialized numerical algorithms to maximize this kind of likelihood, which contains an integral, and compute terms necessary in the classical framework, such as standard errors of the parameter estimates. There are several ways of performing a maximization over such an average, including quadrature methods and Laplace transforms, each with its pros and cons (e.g., McCulloch & Searle, 2001).

We use Equation 26.5 to make a simple point about the relation between Bayesian and classical methods. Equation 26.5 highlights a difficulty that has plagued statisticians for decades, spurring a cottage industry of ingenious computational techniques, all to more efficiently compute multilevel and random effect model parameters. Although frequentist statisticians have made great strides in surmounting the challenges that Equation 26.5 presents (e.g., using the same sort of Monte Carlo techniques that Bayesians rely on), it nonetheless entails a nasty integral, one that makes it impossible to write general, closed-form solutions, such as with unequal sample sizes or errors that are not normally distributed.

Bayesians looking at Equation 26.5 immediately spot a connection to a concept highly tractable within their framework. Equation 26.5 is proportional to the posterior distribution (e.g., Rossi & Allenby, 2003):

$$p(u|y) \propto \int \prod_i f(y_i|u) g(u) du. \qquad (26.6)$$

Although the classical statistician looks at the right-hand side of Equation 26.6 and frets about developing numerical procedures to maximize over a thorny integral, the Bayesian statistician instantly knows how to work with it, via well-established techniques for sampling from posterior distributions, such as MCMC. In addition, a set of useful tools for selecting a model, handling missing data, and assessing predictions comes along with the approach. There are a few drawbacks to the Bayesian approach. These include, for instance, having to write specialized code for specific problems (except for the simplest problems, one gives up the canned, off-the-shelf statistical package concept), to work with new concepts that emerge from algorithms that use stochastic simulation, and to choose a prior

distribution. We do not view these as deal-breakers for using the Bayesian approach, as such issues also arise in a classical setting. For example, in a frequentist analysis, one assumes an underlying distribution and makes simplifying assumptions, such as equality of variances, to make a problem tractable; in a Bayesian setting, one selects a prior distribution. There are parallels in both cases, and in mathematical models one never completely gets away from assumptions. The key issue concerns which assumptions are more reasonable to make, which assumptions become irrelevant because of robustness issues, and which model makes difficult problems tractable.

We like this multilevel modeling example because it illustrates that there is a connection between the classical and Bayesian approaches in the case of random effect and multilevel models. The approaches turn out to be very similar: The classical statistician chooses to work with the right-hand side of Equation 26.6 and tackles the nasty integral directly, whereas the Bayesian chooses to work with the left-hand side, samples the posterior distribution to estimate parameters, and uses the posterior distribution to assess parametric uncertainty. They both work with the same idea; they just approach it using different methods, which we view as one of the major lessons of this chapter.

Research Example

To illustrate the power of Bayesian analysis, we present an example from published work that formulated a "bespoke" model for a self-report based on a latent psychological phenomenon, that is, one unavailable as a pre-programmed option in any extant software package (although, as we discuss below, it is possible to estimate it using frequentist tools by building the model in such programs as MLwiN, R:glmm, and HLM). We choose this example not only because it involves a data type—intent, measured on an ordinal scale—common in psychological research, but also because all data and programs for analysis were made available by the authors: cumulativetimedintent.com contains illustrative data in several formats, along with Bayesian and classical code in WinBUGS, MLwiN, and SAS, so the reader can verify results directly. For this chapter, we also supplement the code using the modern Bayesian modeling language, Stan, and compare its results.

At the heart of the project was a need to better predict what people would purchase on the basis of their stated intentions. Studies relating intentions to behavior have been conducted for many years; the one we examine here (van Ittersum & Feinberg, 2010) introduced a new technique for eliciting individuals' intentions, by asking them to state their intent at multiple time periods on a probability scale. For example, "What is the likelihood [on an imposed 0%, 10%, 20%, . . . , 90%, 100% scale] you will have purchased this item 6 [and 12, 18, 24] months from now"? Each respondent's data looks like a nondecreasing sequence of stated, scaled probabilities, over time. That is, can we merely *ask* people when they might purchase something and relate it, statistically, to whether and when they actually do?

In essence, this is a random effects model, but one not handled out of the box by classical estimation software. It is, however, readily amenable to Bayesian treatment. Of note for psychologists is that we can posit that each individual has some growth curve, which is taken to be linear in time (and perhaps other predictor variables as well). The key is how to relate these individual-level, latent growth curves to (a) the observable (stated probability on an ordinal scale), (b) covariates, and (c) one another. It turns out that each of these is natural in the Hierarchical Bayes approach, which is nothing more than a (nonlinear) hierarchical model, estimated using Bayesian techniques.

Suppose that the latent adoption *propensity* for subject i at time t is given by a simple linear expression,

$$\text{Propensity}_{it} = \beta_0 + \beta_{1i} t. \qquad (26.7)$$

This specifies how the propensity changes over time for an individual but not how it varies *across* individuals. This is accomplished via a heterogeneity, or multilevel, model,

$$\beta_{1i} = \Delta z_i + u_i \qquad (26.8)$$

$$u_i \sim N(0, \Omega_u). \qquad (26.9)$$

This models slopes (β_{1i}) as a function of individual-level covariates (z_i) and coefficients (Δ); for simplicity of exposition and presentation of results, we have only taken these slopes to be random, but the analysis could easily accommodate random intercepts (β_0) as well. So-called unobserved heterogeneity, represented by u_i, is presumed normal, its degree measured by Ω_u. So far, this is exactly in keeping with standard practice in HLMs and would in fact be equivalent to the standard formulation—which is amenable to frequentist analysis—except that we do not observe the propensity directly, but something related to it, with measurement error. Specifically, propensity, on an unbounded scale, must be functionally related to adoption probability on the unit scale. We choose a probit transform because of its conjugacy properties for Bayesian analysis, noting that the Stan language does not "reward" models that have conjugate priors, allowing researchers to mix-and-match priors and likelihoods according to the phenomena in question:

$$\pi_{it} = \Phi(\text{Propensity}_{it}). \qquad (26.10)$$

Because this resulting probability (π_{it}) is continuous, but our observable stated intent lies on a discrete scale, one more model stage is required. Given probability π_{it}, we can employ an especially parsimonious transformation, the *rank-ordered binomial* (Rost, 1985), to map from continuous latent, to discrete $(1, \ldots, K)$ observed, probabilities, which in this example has $K = 11$ (corresponding to values 0%, 10%, . . . , 100%); this yields a binomial distribution, albeit one that looks slightly different owing to the convention of numbering outcomes starting with $k = 1$, not 0:

$$p(Y_{it} = k) = \binom{K-1}{k-1} \pi_{it}^{k-1} (1 - \pi_{it})^{K-k}, \quad k = 1, \ldots, K.$$
$$(26.11)$$

Conjoining all model stages yields the following hierarchical Bayes formulation:

Level I:

$$p(Y_{it} = k) = \binom{K-1}{k-1} \pi_{it}^{k-1} (1 - \pi_{it})^{K-k}, \quad k = 1, \ldots, K$$

$$\text{Probit}(\pi_{it}) = \beta_0 + \beta_{1i} t \qquad (26.12)$$

Level II:

$$\beta_{1i} = \Delta z_i + u_i$$

$$u_i \sim N(0, \Omega_u). \qquad (26.13)$$

Whereas early Bayesian analyses would have required tedious specialized derivations and laborious programming, nowadays one can write such a model in statistical language directly. Here, we illustrate this in two ways: via MLwiN (which allows an array of variations on generalized linear models), as well as Stan (which allows models of arbitrary complexity in a fully general modeling language). In both cases, coupled with noninformative priors, the resulting output includes samples from the posterior density for all model parameters. Automatically generated diagnostics help determine model convergence and provide plots of all marginal distributions, which do *not* have to be normal, and inferences about parameters proceed off these density plots.

For example, we may wish to make inferences about parameters in both the Level II (heterogeneity, or dealing with the distribution of individual-level parameters) and Level I (dealing with individuals' parameters, or latent growth curves) models. Actual MLwiN output for this model, using real data, includes the following, which the program provides written in full statistical notation:

$$\text{probit}(\pi_{it}) = -1.970(0.031)\text{CONS} + \beta_{1i} t$$

$$\beta_{1i} = 0.753(0.065) + u_{1i}$$

$$[u_{1i}] \sim N(0, \Omega_u): \Omega_u = [0.508(0.078)]$$

Prior Specifications:

$$P(\beta_0) \infty 1, P(\beta_0) \infty 1$$

$$p(1/\sigma_u^2) \sim \text{Gamma}(0.001, 0.001).$$

While parts of the model appear to be immediately recognizable as the estimated values of both the Level I and Level II parameters, with standard errors in parentheses, these are not merely point estimates in the usual sense, but the result of taking the mean and standard deviation of 100,000 draws from the posterior distribution. The program automatically simulates the marginal distribution for each parameter of interest, and uses it to estimate the parameter's mean and standard deviation (the frequentist's standard error), with the critical distinction that the standard deviation is *not* merely an approximation from the Hessian (i.e., the matrix of second derivatives of the log-likelihood, as in frequentist analyses) but rather comes from the simulated marginal distribution directly. The program also shows that it uses flat priors for the regression parameters (β_0 and β_1), and a fairly noninformative (i.e., very high variance) inverse gamma prior, a popular choice, for the variance (σ_u^2), which is sometimes equivalently written as a gamma prior on the "precision", $1/\sigma_u^2$.

While programs like MLwiN are useful for models that fall into certain natural classes, they are not meant to deal with those of arbitrary complexity. We therefore continue our analysis using Stan, a powerful Bayesian modeling language that allows the analyst to lay out the model part by part, with all sampling algorithms, diagnostics, and graphics generated automatically. Because Stan utilizes a newer sampling based on "Hamiltonian" Monte Carlo, it is suitable for models with hundreds or even thousands of parameters, with which older Bayesian algorithms like Metropolis-Hastings can struggle.

To demonstrate the power and flexibility of Stan, we write out the key portions of the same model using that language (see Exhibit 26.1).

Let us proceed through the code line-by-line. Line 1 tells us that we will first deal with parameters; lines 2–4 say there are three parameters, $\{\beta_0, \beta_1, \sigma_u^2\}$, to be estimated, the third of which is positive. Lines 5–6 say there are R units (individuals) and that each will have its own coefficient "beta_1" and deviation "u". (If one doesn't specify a prior on a particular parameter,

EXHIBIT 26.1 Stan Code for Hierarchical Propensity Model

```
01 parameters {
02 real beta_0;
03 real beta_1_mu;
04 real<lower = 0> u_sigma_2;
05 row_vector[R] beta_1;
06 row_vector[R] u;}
07 model {
08 u_sigma_2 ~ inv_gamma(0.001,0.001);
09 beta_1 ~ normal(beta_1_mu, sqrt(u_sigma_2));
10 for (r in 1:R) {
11 for (s in 1:S) {
12 prop[r, s] ~ binomial(10, Phi(beta_0 + X[r,s] * beta_1[r]));}}}
```

like "beta_0", Stan will just assume it is flat.) Line 7 starts off the section about the "model"; line 8 suggests there is the same gamma distribution on the inverse of σ_u^2; line 9 that the individual-level "beta_1" are normally distributed about their mean; and lines 10–12 that the likelihood is binomial. We note three key elements here: first, that the one piece of real work for the analyst is figuring out how to specify this likelihood, but even that is straightforward; second, that the analyst could have specified any distribution for the "random coefficients" ("beta_1"), not merely the usual assumption that they are normally distributed; and, lastly, that changing any element of the model, including the priors and likelihood, requires simply inputting a formula, and the estimation algorithm does the hard work of extracting all posterior distributions, *irrespective*

of whether these assumptions are standard or not. This is among the main attractions of the Bayesian approach: the ability to simulate a posterior for *any* model the analyst can write down for the problem and data at hand.

Estimation results from the model are as follows (Table 26.1), and are quite close to those obtained from MLwiN.

We might interpret the model as follows. Each individual has a latent propensity to purchase (π_{it}), and the probit transform of that probability is linear in time, with an intercept of −1.983 ($SE = 0.034$), and a coefficient (β_{1i}) with a mean of 0.767 ($SE = 0.072$). However, there is some degree of *variation* in the value of this coefficient across respondents. The mean across respondents, as we have seen, is 0.767, but the variance is estimated to be 0.497 ($SE: 0.081$). We include

TABLE 26.1

Parameters for a Hierarchical Propensity Model Estimated in MLwiN

Parameter	Mean	SE	2.5%	25%	50%	75%	97.5%	R_{hat}	N_{eff}
β_0	−1.983	0.034	−2.049	−2.006	−1.983	−1.960	−1.916	1.001	867
β_1	0.767	0.072	0.625	0.720	0.767	0.815	0.907	1.000	3363
σ_u^2	0.497	0.081	0.360	0.439	0.488	0.547	0.677	1.001	2639
$\beta_{1,1}$	0.824	0.068	0.690	0.778	0.824	0.870	0.955	1.000	3012
$\beta_{1,2}$	1.819	0.120	1.586	1.737	1.818	1.901	2.059	1.001	3370
(etc.)									

R_{hat} = potential scale reduction factor; N_{eff} = Effective Sample Size.

information on the slopes for the first two individuals, $\{\beta_{1,1}, \beta_{1,2}\}$, finding them to be quite different, suggesting that *slope heterogeneity* is substantial here (as captured by $\sigma_u^2 = 0.497$, or $\sigma_u \approx 0.7$), with 95% of the density lying between the 2.5 and 97.5 percentiles of $[0.625, 0.907]$. The program also includes two other useful quantities for each parameter: R_{hat}, a measure of how well the different chains converged on the same answer, which should ideally be less than 1.05; and N_{eff}, the "effective sample size", that is, how many *independent* draws-worth of information is contained in that parameter's sample draws. Both appear quite good here.

We would also wish to check that the traceplot for each of these parameters looked reasonable, meaning like a sequence of independent draws—roughly speaking, if it is already on one side of the mean, it does not tend to stay there long—with no patterns obvious to the eye. These appear in Figure 26.4, also as generated automatically in

Stan, for the last 10,000 draws for each parameter; we have also included kernel density plots to get a sense of how "unimodal" each might be, finding them to be quite so. Because we can access all these draws, and indeed have them for each of the respondent's individual slope coefficients (β_{1i}), we can calculate latent growth curves for each, error bars around them, and in fact *any* function of their parameters, all by operating on the posterior draws directly.

Although this model can be estimated using classical techniques—indeed, one can program it using PROC NLMIXED in SAS, with some patience, by writing out the model likelihood directly—the Bayesian approach allows all parameters of interest to be calculated to any desired degree of accuracy. Moreover, we obtain a *distribution* for each of these parameters, and an arbitrarily large number of draws from each one, meaning that *any prediction we want to make from the model automatically carries the appropriate*

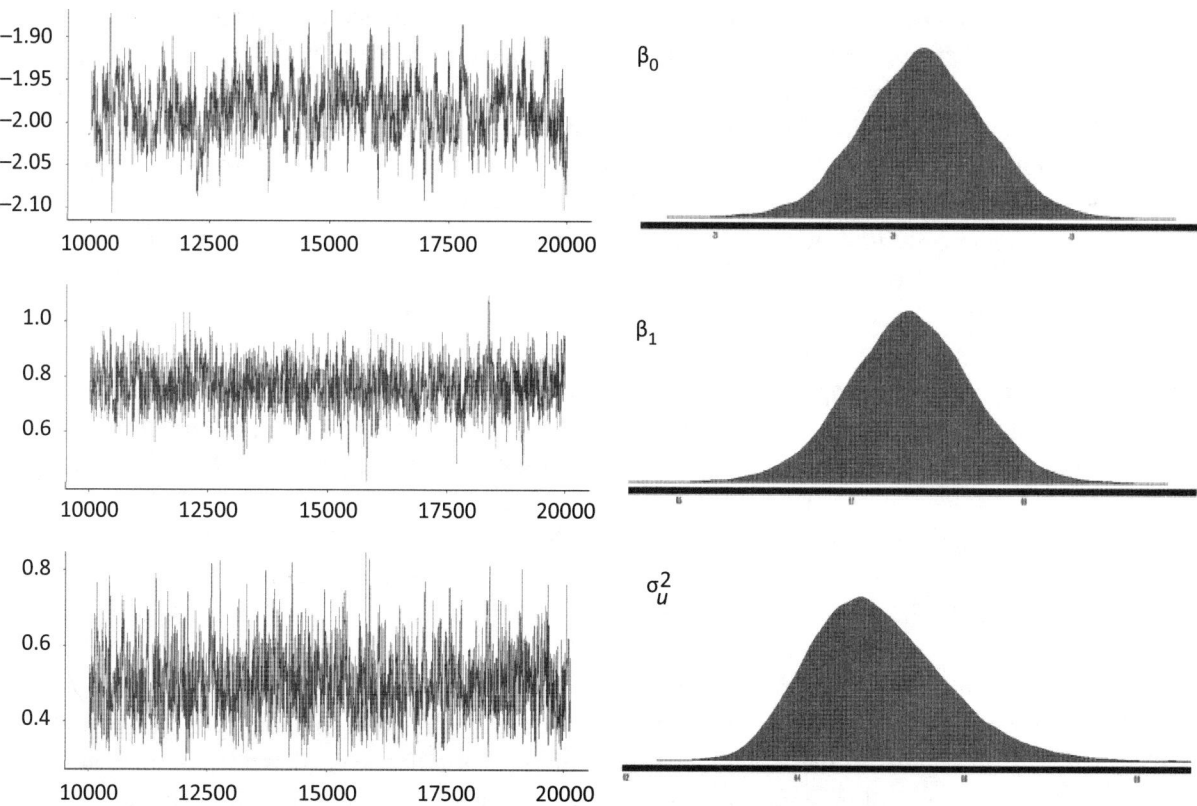

FIGURE 26.4. Traceplots and kernel densities for three parameters from a latent purchase intent model, generated in Stan.

degree of uncertainty coded into this full posterior. In practical terms, this means that the analyst is freed from making any assumptions about the asymptotic behavior of parameters and can perform on-the-fly postestimation tests on complex functions of the problem's parameters (as we pointed earlier, for example, in the case of mediation analyses). This is well beyond what frequentist techniques can easily offer, yet it is natural and straightforward using Bayesian estimation.

CONCLUSION

Some readers will get the sense that our views about Bayesian statistics are not entirely mainstream. Partisans will undoubtedly feel we did not portray their vantage point with sufficient detail. The classical statistician may take issue with superficial attention to the problem of defining one's prior. "Ambiguity over selecting a prior distribution is the Achilles' heel of the Bayesian approach," a classically inclined researcher may say. Bayesians may be incensed that we lump their elegant, comprehensive formalism with the classical approach by saying they both act the same when the Bayesian assumes a noninformative prior. "But you miss the important differences between how we interpret the results," will be shouted from the Bayesian rooftops. Let us be the first to acknowledge that some of the subtle details have been omitted. But that was completely intentional. We want to bring more researchers to the discussion, expose more people to the underpinnings of both classical and Bayesian approaches, and show researchers some new tools. We believe (and we have a pretty sharp prior on that belief) that the best way to accomplish this is by outlining the similarities of the approaches and the advantages each offers.

We hope this chapter has been a readable and accessible introduction to the basic notions of Bayesian statistics and that it provides a straightforward way to formulate some of the tools that the Bayesian tradition offers. In these relatively few pages we cannot cover all the ins and outs of conducting different types of Bayesian analyses—there are books, online courses (e.g., Coursera,

MIT OpenCourseWare), and in fact entire series of hands-on, widely accessible videos that do that (e.g., by Ben Lambert's, 2018, "A Student's Guide to Bayesian Statistics" and David Draper's, 2013, course at Google, "Bayesian Modeling, Inference, Prediction, and Decision-Making," both available on YouTube). If the reader's interest is piqued sufficiently to seek out some of the reference books and explore some of the software we mention, then this chapter has been successful.

We feel compelled to point out that, while we feel the Bayesian approach is the "correct" one for statistical inference—obtaining the full posterior distribution is always advantageous if it can be extracted at reasonable computational cost—this by no means invalidates frequentist estimation. Both approaches need to coexist, and each has a domain of practical superiority. To take but one compelling example, machine learning models can have parameters numbering in the billions (e.g., the recent GPT-3 model for the English language has roughly 175 billion), and the focus in estimation is on predictive accuracy, not quantifying uncertainty. In such situations, the speed and scalability of frequentist approaches wins out over the advantages of drawing a full posterior sample via Bayesian methodology. Similarly, although *in theory* frequentist methods can offer up nearly all the advantages of Bayesian analyses, *in practice* inference relies on large-sample properties like asymptotic normality which may not hold for particular models, data sets, and parameters; in such cases, the analyst would do well to turn to Bayesian methods.

Some areas of psychology have already started to apply modern Bayesian methods. For example, models in item response theory have used Bayesian ideas to estimate multivariate, multilevel, second-order, item-response theory models (e.g., Duncan & MacEachern, 2008; Fox & Glas, 2001; Sheng & Wikle, 2008). Bayesian approaches can also be used as part a study's experimental design, such as in choosing the next query or stimulus presentation to the participant; for an example of Bayesian adaptive testing procedures in the context of judgment and decision making research, see Cavagnaro et al. (2013), or for more efficiently running experimental trials in general, Berry et al. (2010). We hope these and other examples will provide the inspiration to seek new ways to test your research ideas and that Bayesian methods provide some useful tools to carry out those tests.

References

Berry, S. M., Carlin, B. P., Lee, J. J., & Muller, P. (2010). *Bayesian adaptive methods for clinical trials.* CRC Press. https://doi.org/10.1201/EBK1439825488

Betancourt, M. (2017). *A conceptual introduction to Hamiltonian Monte Carlo.* arXiv preprint. https://arxiv.org/abs/1701.02434

Box, G. E. P., & Tiao, G. C. (1992). Bayesian inference in statistical analysis. John Wiley & Sons. (Original work published 1973) https://doi.org/10.1002/9781118033197

Bürkner, P. C. (2017). brms: An R package for Bayesian multilevel models using Stan. *Journal of Statistical Software, 80*(1), 1–28. https://doi.org/10.18637/jss.v080.i01

Cavagnaro, D. R., Pitt, M. A., Gonzalez, R., & Myung, J. I. (2013). Discriminating among probability weighting functions using adaptive design optimization. *Journal of Risk and Uncertainty, 47*(3), 255–289. https://doi.org/10.1007/s11166-013-9179-3

Congdon, P. (2007). *Bayesian statistical modelling* (2nd ed.). John Wiley & Sons.

Congdon, P. (2014). *Applied Bayesian modelling* (2nd ed.). John Wiley & Sons.

Dong, Y., & Peng, C. Y. J. (2013). Principled missing data methods for researchers. *SpringerPlus, 2*(1), 222. https://doi.org/10.1186/2193-1801-2-222

Draper, D. (2013, July 16). *Bayesian modeling, inference, prediction, and decision-making* [Video]. https://www.youtube.com/watch?v=KCF6b8sYuZk

Duncan, K., & MacEachern, S. (2008). Nonparametric Bayesian modeling for item response. *Statistical Modelling, 8*, 41–66. https://doi.org/10.1177/1471082X0700800104

Edwards, W., Lindman, H., & Savage, L. (1963). Bayesian statistical inference for psychological research. *Psychological Review, 70*(3), 193–242. https://doi.org/10.1037/h0044139

Etz, A., & Vandekerckhove, J. (2018). Introduction to Bayesian inference for psychology. *Psychonomic Bulletin & Review, 25*(1), 5–34. https://doi.org/10.3758/s13423-017-1262-3

Feinberg, F. M. (2012). Mediation analysis and categorical variables: Some further frontiers. *Journal of Consumer Psychology, 22*(4), 595–598. https://doi.org/10.1016/j.jcps.2012.03.007

Fox, J.-P., & Glas, C. (2001). Bayesian estimation of a multilevel IRT model using Gibbs sampling. *Psychometrika, 66*(2), 271–288. https://doi.org/10.1007/BF02294839

Gelman, A., Carlin, J. B., Stern, H. S., Dunson, D., Vehtari, A., & Rubin, D. B. (2013). *Bayesian data analysis* (3rd ed.). CRC Press. https://doi.org/10.1201/b16018

Gelman, A., & Hill, J. (2006). *Data analysis using regression and multilevel/hierarchical models.* Cambridge University Press. https://doi.org/10.1017/CBO9780511790942

Jackman, S. (2000). Estimation and inference via Bayesian simulation: An introduction to Markov chain Monte Carlo. *American Journal of Political Science, 44*(2), 375–404. https://doi.org/10.2307/2669318

Jaynes, E. (1986). Bayesian methods: General background. In J. H. Justice (Ed.), *Maximum entropy and Bayesian methods in applied statistics* (pp. 1–25). Cambridge University Press. https://doi.org/10.1017/CBO9780511569678.003

Kruschke, J. (2014). *Doing Bayesian data analysis: A tutorial with R, JAGS, and Stan.* Elsevier. https://doi.org/10.1016/B978-0-12-405888-0.09999-2

Lambert, B. (2018, April 30). *A student's guide to Bayesian statistics* [Video]. https://www.youtube.com/watch?v=P_og8H-VkIY&list=PLwJRxp3blEvZ8AKMXOy0fc0cqT61GsKCG

Little, R. J., & Rubin, D. B. (2019). *Statistical analysis with missing data* (Vol. 793). John Wiley & Sons.

McCulloch, C. E., & Searle, S. R. (2001). *Generalized, linear, and mixed models.* Wiley.

McElreath, R. (2020). *Statistical rethinking: A Bayesian course with examples in R and Stan.* CRC Press. https://doi.org/10.1201/9780429029608

McShane, B. B., Gal, D., Gelman, A., Robert, C., & Tackett, J. L. (2019). Abandon statistical significance. *The American Statistician, 73*(Suppl. 1), 235–245. https://doi.org/10.1080/00031305.2018.1527253

Neal, R. M. (2011). MCMC using Hamiltonian dynamics. In S. Brooks, A. Gelman, G. Jones, & X.-L. Meng (Eds.). *Handbook of Markov chain Monte Carlo* (pp. 113–162). Chapman & Hall/CRC. https://doi.org/10.1201/b10905-6

Ntzoufras, I. (2011). *Bayesian modeling using WINBUGS.* Wiley. https://onlinelibrary.wiley.com/doi/book/10.1002/9780470434567

Rossi, P. E., & Allenby, G. M. (2003). Bayesian statistics and marketing. *Marketing Science, 22*(3), 304–328. https://doi.org/10.1287/mksc.22.3.304.17739

Rost, J. (1985). A latent class model for rating data. *Psychometrika, 50*(1), 37–49. https://doi.org/10.1007/BF02294146

Seaman, J. W., III, Seaman, J. W., Jr., & Stamey, J. D. (2012). Hidden dangers of specifying noninformative priors. *The American Statistician, 66*(2), 77–84. https://doi.org/10.1080/00031305.2012.695938

Sheng, Y., & Wikle, C. (2008). Bayesian multidimensional IRT models with a hierarchical structure. *Educational and Psychological Measurement, 68*(3), 413–430. https://doi.org/10.1177/0013164407308512

Tanner, M. A. (1993). *Tools for statistical inference* (Vol. 3). Springer.

van de Schoot, R., Depaoli, S., King, R., Kramer, B., Märtens, K., Tadesse, M. G., Vannucci, M., Gelman, A., Veen, D., Willemsen, J., & Yau, C. (2021). Bayesian statistics and modelling. *Nature Reviews Methods Primers, 1*(1), 1–26. https://doi.org/10.1038/s43586-020-00001-2

van de Schoot, R., Winter, S. D., Ryan, O., Zondervan-Zwijnenburg, M., & Depaoli, S. (2017). A systematic review of Bayesian articles in psychology: The last 25 years. *Psychological Methods, 22*(2), 217–239. https://doi.org/10.1037/met0000100

Van Ittersum, K., & Feinberg, F. M. (2010). Cumulative timed intent: A new predictive tool for technology adoption. *Journal of Marketing Research, 47*(5), 808–822. https://doi.org/10.1509/jmkr.47.5.808

Wagenmakers, E. J., Love, J., Marsman, M., Jamil, T., Ly, A., Verhagen, J., Selker, R., Gronau, Q. F., Dropmann, D., Boutin, B., Meerhoff, F., Knight, P., Raj, A., van Kesteren, E. J., van Doorn, J., Šmíra, M., Epskamp, S., Etz, A., Matzke, D., . . . Morey, R. D. (2018). Bayesian inference for psychology. Part II: Example applications with JASP. *Psychonomic Bulletin & Review, 25*(1), 58–76. https://doi.org/10.3758/s13423-017-1323-7

Wagenmakers, E. J., Marsman, M., Jamil, T., Ly, A., Verhagen, J., Love, J., Selker, R., Gronau, Q. F., Šmíra, M., Epskamp, S., Matzke, D., Rouder, J. N., & Morey, R. D. (2018). Bayesian inference for psychology. Part I: Theoretical advantages and practical ramifications. *Psychonomic Bulletin & Review, 25*(1), 35–57. https://doi.org/10.3758/s13423-017-1343-3

Winer, B. J. (1971). *Statistical principles in experimental design* (2nd ed.). McGraw-Hill.

Yuan, Y., & MacKinnon, D. P. (2009). Bayesian mediation analysis. *Psychological Methods, 14*(4), 301–322. https://doi.org/10.1037/a0016972

PART V

DESIGNS INVOLVING EXPERIMENTAL MANIPULATIONS

DESIGNS WITH DIFFERENT PARTICIPANT ASSIGNMENT MECHANISMS

CHAPTER 27

RANDOMIZED DESIGNS IN PSYCHOLOGICAL RESEARCH

Larry Christensen, Lisa A. Turner, and R. Burke Johnson

Designs that use random assignment have generally been attributed to the British biometrician Ronald A. Fisher (1928). It is true that Fisher repeatedly stressed the need to randomly assign participants to groups to validly apply the statistical technique of analysis of variance (ANOVA). Random assignment of participants to groups, however, predated the development of the designs Fisher discussed.

Active experimentation and comparing the performance of experimental and control groups has been a tradition in psychological research from about the 1870s, when researchers were conducting psychophysical studies (Dehue, 2001). Psychophysical researchers even constructed randomized orders to control for participant expectations of which stimuli would be presented next (Dehue, 1997). It was not until the 1920s, however, that random assignment of participants to experimental and control conditions was proposed as a way to cancel out unwanted variation (Dehue, 2001). The emphasis that Fisher (1935) placed on the need for random assignment to validly apply his statistical technique and his elaboration of designs using random assignment provided a forceful argument and encouraged researchers to not only make use of the designs he elaborated on but also to use random assignment of participants to treatment conditions.

The arguments made by Fisher (1935) and the credible evidence that these designs have produced are supported by the fact that such designs are considered to be the gold standard in the field of medicine for identifying causal relationships (e.g., Hariton & Locascio, 2018; Salmond, 2008) and that various government agencies have given priority to studies that use randomized designs as a component of their research strategy (Donaldson, 2009). This is because designs using random assignment have high internal validity, although they are not immune from all threats. While some authors today recommend that randomized designs be combined with additional methods (e.g., Clay, 2010; Johnson & Schoonenboom, 2016), we focus on randomized designs in this chapter. Prior to presenting the basic randomized designs, it is important to consider the different ways that independent variables can be manipulated and the designs that result from these different types of manipulation.

BASIC EXPERIMENTAL RESEARCH DESIGNS

Research design refers to the outline, plan, or strategy that is used to seek an answer to a research question. Experimental designs are designs that represent the outline, plan, or strategy used to

https://doi.org/10.1037/0000319-027
APA Handbook of Research Methods in Psychology, Second Edition: Vol. 2. Research Designs: Quantitative, Qualitative, Neuropsychological, and Biological, H. Cooper (Editor-in-Chief)

identify causal relationships by manipulating the independent variable (or variables). For this purpose, and to be considered a strong experimental design, this plan or strategy must incorporate control over all components of the study, including the random assignment of participants to groups, determination of who gets what treatment condition and in what order, and how much or what type of treatment each participant gets. In other words, the researcher must have control over all facets of the experiment to identify a causal relationship between the independent variable and dependent variable (denoted IV and DV in this chapter). Researchers use two basic types of designs when conducting experimental studies. They are traditionally referred to as between- and within-subjects, or more recently, as between- and within-participants designs.

Between-Participants Designs

A *between-participants design* is an experimental research design that is characterized by the fact that each treatment condition is administered to a different group of participants. For example, in a *randomized* between-participants experiment testing the efficacy of a new drug for treating depression, the set of participants are randomly assigned to the two conditions: One group receives the new drug and the other group receives the placebo. It is important to note that random assignment is not required for all between-participants designs, but it is very strongly recommended if one is interested in making a claim of cause and effect. In Figure 27.1, we illustrate a randomized controlled trial (RCT; in medical research, sometimes called a randomized clinical trial). In this traditional and strong design, the treatment condition mean is compared with the control group mean to determine efficacy of the new drug. The control group (receiving the placebo or inert substance) provides the estimate of the *counterfactual,* which is defined as how the participants in the treatment group would be expected to perform if they had *not* received the active treatment. The hypothetical study illustrated in Figure 27.1 is seeking to answer the question of whether the drug is more effective than the

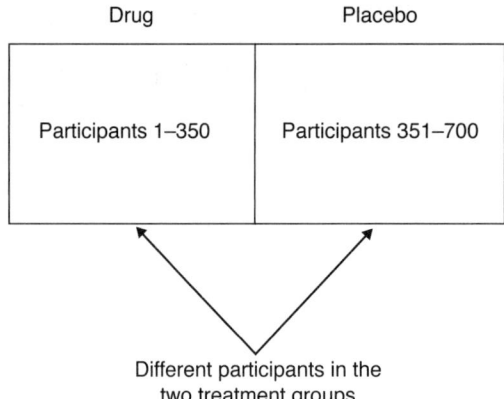

FIGURE 27.1.   Illustration of a between-participants design. Different participants are randomly assigned to the two conditions.

placebo in treating depression *between* the two different groups of participants—hence the label *between-participants design.*

Within-Participants or Repeated-Measures Designs

A *within-participants design* is an experimental design in which each participant experiences every treatment condition as illustrated in Figure 27.2. All participants are, therefore, repeatedly measured

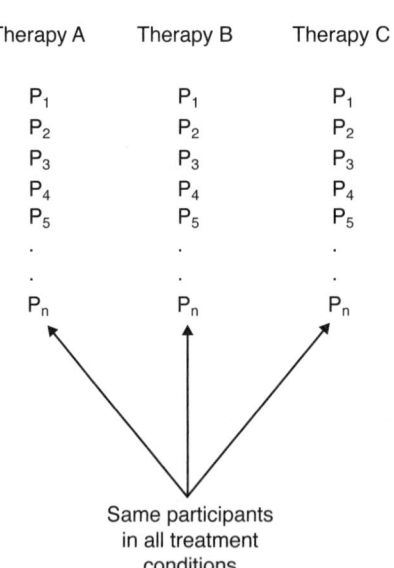

FIGURE 27.2.   Within-participants design. The same participants were studied in all three therapy conditions.

under all treatment conditions, which is why this design is also referred to as a *repeated-measures design*. From Figure 27.2 you can see that the within-participants design compares the effectiveness of the three approaches to therapy by comparing the effect each therapy has on the same group of participants. In this design, all participants receive all therapies, but the conditions are usually presented in different orders to control for order and carryover effects (discussed later in the chapter). The participants are measured on the outcome variable after receiving each treatment condition, and before being administered the next treatment condition. When using a within-participants design the question being asked is, "Which treatment is most effective *within* the same group of participants?"—hence the label *within-participants design*.

Advantages and Limitations of the Between- and Within-Participants Designs

The between- and within-participants designs represent the basic experimental designs used by researchers. Although both can be excellent designs, each has limitations and advantages. The between-participants design has the advantages of being relatively easy to understand, design, and analyze. It is especially strong for establishing the presence of causal effects when random assignment (also called randomization) is used to equate the groups. The primary disadvantage of the between-participants design is that each of the treatment conditions has different participants.

This one characteristic of the between-participants design has several implications. The first is that more participants are needed when using this design versus the within-participants design to achieve the same level of statistical power. The variability in participants within groups contributes to the error term. This is not the case in within-participants designs where the error term only includes variability due to the participants × treatment interaction (Keppel & Zedeck, 1989). This increased error variability means that the between-participants design is not as sensitive as the within-participants design in terms of

detecting a treatment effect. Finally, having different participants in each treatment condition introduces the possibility that differences between the groups are due to systematic differences on one or more extraneous variables confounded with the IV in addition to any differences caused by the IV. Random assignment is required to rule out this differential selection threat.

The within-participants design has advantages over the between-participants design in terms of creating equivalence of participants in the various treatment groups, increasing the sensitivity of the study to detecting a treatment effect, and in economy of participants. The advantage in terms of economy of participants is readily apparent because the number of participants needed in a within-participants study is equal to the number needed in one experimental treatment condition because all participants take part in all treatment conditions. For example, in a within-participants study investigating the relative effectiveness of three approaches to therapy the a priori sample size recommended for sufficient statistical power might require each therapy condition be administered to 50 participants. If a between-participants design were used, 150 participants (50 in each condition) would be needed.

When using a within-participants design, there is no need to worry about equivalence of the participants in the various treatment conditions because the same participants are used in every treatment condition. Therefore, there is perfect matching of the participants in all treatment conditions. In other words, the participants serve as their own control because variables such as age, education, prior experience, and motivation remain constant across the conditions in the experiment.

Statistically speaking, the within-participants design has the advantage of being more sensitive to detecting a real treatment effect because participants serve as their own control. When the same participants take part in every treatment condition, there is less variability in the data from one treatment condition to the next because variation caused by individual differences among participants is statistically removed from the error term in the data analysis. This also increases the probability of a real treatment effect being detected. This increased sensitivity to detecting a real effect makes the within-participants design a popular choice when it can be used effectively.

One additional advantage of the within-participants design involves an issue of research ethics. Consider that you are planning to conduct a simple randomized between-participants design, where you have one IV with two levels: an active treatment condition and a no-treatment, control condition. If there is a strong chance that the treatment will be highly effective, an ethical issue arises in whether it is ethical to withhold the treatment from the control participants in the research study. This is a question often asked by institutional review boards at universities. If it is considered unethical to withhold the treatment, then one might use a cross-over within-participants design where all participants receive both the treatment and control conditions, but in different orders. This provides a test of the effectiveness of the treatment and also ensures that all participants have access to the treatment condition.

With all of these advantages, it might seem that the within-participants design is the experimental design of choice. However, the within-participants design has some rather significant limitations. The most serious limitation of within-participants designs is that they are open to the confounding influence of a sequencing effect. A *sequencing* effect is an effect that occurs when the same participants participate in more than one treatment condition. There are actually two different types of sequencing effects that can occur. An *order* effect arises from the order in which the treatment conditions are administered. As a participant experiences first one and then another treatment condition, they may experience increased fatigue, boredom, and familiarity with or practice with reacting to the IV or responding to the DV. Any of these could affect the participants' responses to the DV and confound the results of the study. It is important to remember that the changes in the participants' responses caused by order effects

are independent of the actual treatment condition or the sequence in which the treatment conditions are administered. Order effects occur in the same ordinal position regardless of the sequence in which the treatment conditions are administered.

The second type of sequencing effect is a carryover effect. A *carryover* effect occurs when the effect of one treatment does not dissipate before the presentation of the next treatment but rather carries over and influences the response to the next treatment condition. For example, a carryover effect would exist if participants were given Drug A, and Drug A was still having an effect on the participants when they were given Drug B. The measured effect of Drug B, therefore, would include the effect of Drug B plus the effect of Drug A that was carried over to the Drug B treatment condition.

There are experiments, such as learning, transfer of training, and forgetting experiments, in which carryover and order effects are expected and desirable. In most studies, however, these effects are confounding variables that must be controlled. The most common way of controlling for sequencing effects is to incorporate some form of counterbalancing in the design of the study. Counterbalancing is an effective method of control when sequencing effects are linear. When differential carryover effects occur, counterbalancing is not an effective method of control. This issue is explained later in this chapter.

BASIC BETWEEN-PARTICIPANTS RANDOMIZED DESIGNS

The *basic randomized design* is a design in which a group of participants are randomly assigned to the levels of the IV. The IV can have two or more levels, but often there are two levels, such as a treatment and control group. The response of the participants in these different conditions on the DV is then compared to determine whether the treatment condition produced different results than the control condition as illustrated in Figure 27.3. If a statistically significant difference does exist, then it is

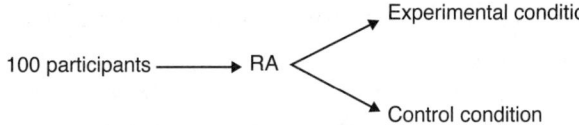

FIGURE 27.3. Structural representation of the basic randomized design. RA indicates random assignment of participants to treatment conditions.

inferred that the treatment condition caused the difference.

It is the random assignment of participants to the treatment conditions that makes this design so powerful because it is this component that provides maximum assurance that the groups are equated on all known and unknown extraneous variables.

Random assignment of participants to conditions is such an important component because it is essential that the participants in the experimental and control conditions be as similar as possible at the outset of the study to make a credible causal inference. The reason the control and experimental groups must be very similar at the outset of the experiment is because the control condition represents the effect that exists in the absence of the experimental treatment. By comparing the effect of the absence of the treatment (no-treatment control condition) with the presence of the treatment (experimental condition), an inference can be made about the effect of the treatment condition.

The term *random* refers to the equiprobability of events. *Random assignment* refers to any procedure that assigns participants to the comparison groups on the basis of chance. Random assignment, therefore, not only assigns the participants to the various groups by chance but all of the characteristics and variables associated with these participants are distributed randomly and should therefore be equated across the groups. This means that groups that are created by means of random assignment will have the greatest probability of being similar to each other on both known and unknown sources of variation. The various groups will, on average (in the long run and given a sufficient sample size), be similar at the outset of the study, which means that any differences observed

between the various groups at the end of the study are likely to be due to the IV. A researcher can, therefore, draw a causal inference because the samples are "randomly similar to each other" (Shadish et al., 2002, p. 248) on all variables except the treatment condition.

Random assignment can take several different forms. In simple random assignment, one randomly assigns participants to the groups or levels of the IV. For example, one can assign a number to all participants (1 to N) and then use a random number generator to assign them to the different groups. Here are two of the many randomization programs: https://www.random.org and https://www.randomizer.org. Sometimes the researcher may want to make random assignment even more precise than simple random assignment. If there are one or more variables for which one wants to make sure the groups are similar, then *stratified random assignment* is useful. With this approach, the researcher determines the stratification variable(s) (e.g., sex) and then randomly assigns the participants in the categories of the stratification variable to the treatment conditions. In the case of a quantitative stratification variable such as age, the researcher orders the participants by age, and then if there are two treatment conditions, the first two participants (the two oldest) should be randomly assigned to Condition 1 and Condition 2, the next two oldest should be randomly assigned to the two conditions, and this process is continued through the last two participants (the youngest) in the participant sample. If one has three treatment conditions, then the first three participants are randomly assigned to the three treatment conditions, the next three are assigned to the three treatment conditions, until one reaches the last participants who are randomly assigned. For some additional and older types of random assignment, see Alferes (2012). One additional kind of random assignment is called *cluster random assignment*. In this case, one starts with a set of clusters (e.g., classrooms, families, study sites) and then randomly assigns these clusters to the treatment conditions. We discuss this last kind of random assignment in more detail later in this chapter.

Random assignment equates the treatment groups at the outset of the experiment, but much thought must be given to the experience of the participants in the control group. For the control condition or any comparison group to function effectively as a contrasting condition, it must be as similar as possible to the experimental group on all variables that could affect the observed outcome. This means that you must identify the variables that need to be controlled and maximally ensure that the control and experimental group are as similar as possible on all of these variables. Statistically speaking, any variable that is related to both the IV and the DV is a confounding variable and therefore must be controlled. For example, if you were conducting a study testing the effect of a particular type of psychotherapy in treating depression, the experimental condition would involve the administration of the psychotherapeutic technique to depressed individuals and the control condition would involve an absence of the psychotherapeutic technique. However, many other variables other than the psychotherapeutic technique could affect the outcome of the experiment. Variables such as the time spent with a therapist, the attention provided by the therapist, or the fact that the participants are paying for a service and may be given tasks to accomplish between therapy sessions could also affect the outcome of such a study. Such variables must be controlled.

The key issue is identification of what needs to be controlled. This is an important issue in all studies because it is impossible to identify all variables that could have an effect on the outcome of the experiment. There are many types of control groups that could be formed to account for many of the extraneous variables. Shadish et al. (2002), Nock et al. (2008), and Freedland et al. (2019) provided excellent discussions of control groups and the various types of control groups that are appropriate to different experimental situations. Selection of the appropriate control group is essential for eliminating many of the threats to internal validity. Although an appropriately constructed control group is needed to control for many extraneous variables, there are many

variables on which participants differ such as age, intelligence, and various personality characteristics that are not effectively controlled just by including a control group. These participant characteristics are controlled by the use of random assignment to groups.

One additional characteristic of the most basic between-participants randomized design is that it does not include a pretest but rather relies on the random assignment of participants to provide assurance that the experimental and control groups are similar. This is a reasonable assumption if the study includes a sufficiently large number of participants. From an internal validity perspective, the absence of a pretest is also desirable if pretesting might differentially sensitize the participants to the experimental treatment condition causing the groups to become different; random assignment makes this unlikely. From an external validity perspective, designs without a pretest might better generalize to groups that have not been pretested.

Although the absence of a pretest is important in some studies, in others, the inclusion of a pretest is important. One common benefit of including a pretest is that it provides for a more sensitive test of the IV (this logic is commonly used in analysis of covariance). Additionally, a control variable is sometimes included at the pretest to provide further evidence about a plausible alternative explanation. Another reason for including a pretest surrounds the issue of attrition.

Attrition is a common occurrence in many field and therapy studies. *Attrition* occurs when participants who are scheduled for participation in a study do not complete the study because they either fail to show up at the scheduled time and place or do not complete all phases of the study. Attrition is a problem for claims of causation when it is *differential* (affecting the groups differently) because it can compromise the benefit derived from random assignment. Random assignment creates similar groups of participants at the outset of an experiment, and this similarity is assumed to carry over to the posttest. However, when attrition exists in a study, the presumed equivalence may not carry over to posttesting because attrition may not be a random event. When differential attrition occurs, the benefit that is derived from random assignment is compromised, and it can no longer be assumed that the participants in the various treatment groups who were similar at the outset of the experiment are still similar at the end of the study. Another way of saying this is that there may be nonrandom correlates of attrition that may influence the DV and thereby contribute to any observed posttest difference that may exist between the experimental and control conditions. For example, perhaps in an experimental study of the effects of induced stress, highly depressed participants in the stress induction treatment group find the research too difficult, and many drop out of the study. However, because of the lack of stress induction in the control group, highly depressed participants may remain. The result is that random assignment to groups is now null and void. The experimental group no longer includes highly depressed participants and the control group does include highly depressed participants. In such situations, the ability to infer that the treatment condition produced the observed group differences at the posttest is compromised.

The best situation is to conduct an experiment in which attrition does not occur. In many studies, especially in longitudinal studies, however, attrition is a fact of life. When attrition does occur, it is important to understand the extent to which it threatens the internal validity of the study. Shadish et al. (2002) discussed several methods for analyzing the effect of attrition. These methods make use of pretest scores, which is another reason why pretesting is important in some studies. If pretesting is part of the experimental design you plan to use, random assignment of participants to the comparison groups is still essential to have the most robust experiment.

In sum, the advantages of this between-participants randomized design are that it includes a control group and the participants are randomly assigned to the groups (i.e., levels of the IV). These two factors provide maximum control of threats to the internal validity of the experiments. In the presence of random assignment, the standard

threats to internal validity are usually controlled in this design; however, *without* random assignment, *differential selection* (sometimes called *selection*) becomes a severe threat to internal validity because the groups are now different on some (many?) extraneous variables in addition to just the levels of the IV (Christensen et al., 2020; Shadish et al., 2002). The importance of random assignment cannot be overemphasized. It is also true that although random assignment maximizes the probability of control of confounding extraneous variables, this assurance is not guaranteed. Even with random assignment of participants, it is possible that the needed control of extraneous confounding variables has not been accomplished. This is particularly true when the number of participants being randomly assigned is too small. When conducted correctly, randomized designs are generally thought of as providing more credible evidence of causal relationships than other designs because they reduce the likelihood of systematic bias (cf. Blair, 2004; Cook, 2018).

Between-Participants Designs With More Than Two Levels of the IV

The simplest extension of the basic between-participants randomized design is a design that has more than two levels of the IV, in which level refers to the number of different variations of the independent variable. There are many situations in which it would be appropriate to investigate a number of different levels of a single IV. Drug research is one area for which it would be advantageous to determine not only whether the drug produced a result different from a placebo (or different drug) condition but also whether differing amounts of the experimental drug produced different reactions. In such a case, participants would be randomly assigned to as many groups as there were experimental drug and control conditions. If there were four drug groups in addition to the no-treatment control condition, or five levels of variation of the IV, participants would be randomly assigned to five groups as illustrated in Figure 27.4. A statistical

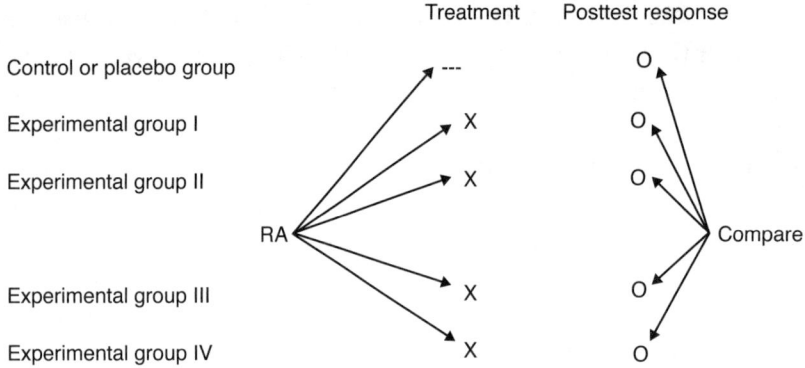

FIGURE 27.4. Randomized design with five levels of variation of the independent variable. RA indicates that the participants were randomly assigned to groups, X refers to the treatment condition, and O refers to the posttest response.

test would then be used to determine whether the amount of drug given makes a difference. However, there is an additional step; if there is a statistically significant effect of the IV, the researcher follows up with additional analyses to determine which groups differed from each other on the DV. Sometimes, the researcher will skip the overall or omnibus test and instead directly test for differences that are hypothesized before analyzing the data (i.e., via planned comparisons). In addition, effect sizes (indicators of magnitude of difference or strength of relationship) and confidence intervals (often around the effect sizes) are *strongly* recommended in psychological research (American Psychological Association, 2020, Chapter 3; Appelbaum et al., 2018).

This type of study is sometimes called a *dose-response study*, as it indicates the response to different dosages of the drug. The advantage of such a study is that it provides a more fine-grained assessment of the effect of different drug dosages. The term dose-response is also used outside of medical research. In these areas, one generally expects a stronger outcome given a stronger amount of the active experimental treatment; that is, the more treatment, the more effect.

This design is excellent for investigating the effect that exists from varying a number of different amounts of one IV. However, it provides only a one-dimensional view of behavior. In most psychology research, we are interested in

the effect of multiple IVs acting independently and in concert to provide a richer multivariable view of causation. Randomized designs that include *at least two* independent variables, and at least one of the IVs is manipulated, are called *factorial designs*.

FACTORIAL DESIGNS

A *factorial design* is a design that investigates the independent and interactive effect of two or more IVs on the DV. By definition, in a factorial design, at least one of the IVs must be manipulated and random assignment must be used for at least one manipulated IV. Factorials may be fully between-participants, where all IVs are between-participants variables; fully within-participants, where all IVs are within-participants variables; or mixed, where at least one IV is between-participants and at least one IV is within-participants.

Without factorial designs, we are often left with incomplete knowledge or even a mischaracterization of the effect of an independent variable. For example, a single variable might show no effect, when in fact, there are different effects for different groups. That is, the exclusion of a moderator variable can cause a single-variable design to be misleading. The ability to study interaction (moderator) effects is a *major* advantage of factorial designs.

In factorial designs, the IVs are also referred to as *factors*. For example, assume you wanted to compare the effect of three different induced mood states (depressive, neutral, and elated) and two stimulus presentation modes (visual and auditory) on recall of material studied for an hour. In this hypothetical study, there are two factors: induced mood state (Factor A) and presentation mode (Factor B). The different variations of each factor are often referred to as the *levels* of the factor. Figure 27.5, which depicts this design, reveals that there are three different variations of the induced mood state factor, so there are three levels of this factor: A_1, A_2, and A_3. There are two levels of the presentation mode factor because this factor includes visual and auditory presentation: B_1 and B_2. Therefore, this design has six combinations of the two factors: A_1B_1, A_1B_2, A_2B_1, A_2B_2, A_3B_1, and A_3B_2. When a factorial design contains all possible combinations of the two factors, such as is the case with this design, it is referred to as a *completely crossed design*.

The description of a factorial design is often based on the number of factors included and the number of levels of each of the factors. In this example, there are two factors with three levels of one factor and two levels of the other factor, so this design would be described as a 3×2 factorial design. If the design included a third factor with two levels of the third factor, then the design would be described as a $3 \times 2 \times 2$ factorial design.

Each one of the treatment combinations in a factorial design is referred to as a *cell*. Thus, in the design depicted in Figure 27.5, there are six cells. In this example of a fully randomized factorial, each participant receives the combination of treatments corresponding to one cell. For example, participants randomly assigned to the A_1B_2 cell would have a depressed mood state induced and would experience a visual presentation mode, whereas a participant randomly assigned to the A_3B_1 cell would have an elated mood state induced and experience an auditory presentation mode. It is essential to understand that strong conclusions about causation in a factorial design apply only to the IV or IVs that are manipulated and randomized. For example, if one IV, such as presentation mode, is manipulated and randomized but not another IV, such as personality type, then one must be very cautious in making a claim about a causal effect of personality type on the DV because it is likely that the participants with different personality types were also different on other extraneous variables. It is optimal when all IVs are manipulated and randomized.

Factorial designs are frequently used in psychological research because they are rich in the information they provide. There are two types of information that are obtained from a factorial design: main effects and interaction effects. A *main effect* is the effect of one factor. All factorial designs contain more than one factor and the separate effect of each of these factors can be identified. This means that a factorial design contains within it a subset of single-factor effects. In the design depicted in Figure 27.5, there are two single-factor effects—the effect of the induced mood factor and

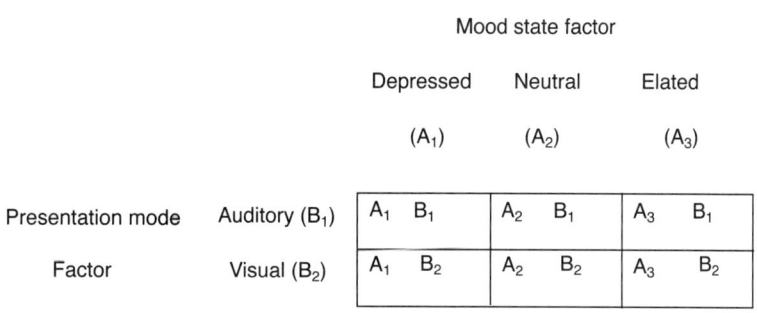

FIGURE 27.5. Illustration of a factorial design with three levels of one factor (mood state) and two levels of a second factor (presentation mode).

the effect of the presentation mode factor. Each of these is referred to as a separate main effect, so, potentially, there is a mood main effect and a presentation mode main effect. The mood main effect tells us whether the different induced mood states (ignoring or averaging across the levels of the presentation mode factor) produced different recall rates, and the presentation mode factor tells us whether different presentation modes (averaging across the levels of the mood factor) produced different recall rates.

Although main effects provide information about specific factors, the information they provide refers to the average effect of each factor, which can miss important information. It does not tell you whether the effect of one factor depends on the level of the other factor. This information can only be derived from an interaction effect. An *interaction* occurs when the effect of one factor varies over the levels of another factor. That is, an interaction is present when the relationship between one factor and the DV *depends* on the levels of the other factor. When an interaction occurs, we state that moderation occurs and one of the IVs is also called a *moderator variable*. For example, an interaction would exist if the material studied using a visual mode resulted in recall of 10% of the material when depressed, 20% when in a neutral mood state, and 30% when elated; however, when using an auditory mode,

30% of the material was recalled when depressed, 20% when in a neutral mood state, and only 10% when elated. In this instance, the effect of mood state on the percentage of material recalled fully depended on whether one was using a visual or auditory presentation mode. Figure 27.6 presents a visual representation of this classic interaction effect and also reveals that the effect of mood state on recall of material depended on whether one used a visual or auditory presentation mode. It is essential to understand that in a two-variable factorial, (a) not all interaction graphs show an X pattern (see ordinal vs. disordinal interactions in Johnson & Christensen, 2020) and (b) any combination of main effects and interactions are empirically possible, such as, for example, no main effects and an interaction effect, two main effects and no interaction, one main effect and an interaction, and so forth.

This discussion of factorial designs has focused on a design with two factors. Mathematically and statistically speaking, there is no limit to the number of factors that can be included. Practically speaking, there is difficulty associated with increasing the number of factors. As the number of factors increases, the number of cells in the design increases, which means that more participants are needed. A 3 × 2 factorial design has six cells; if 30 participants were required per cell, 180 participants would be needed.

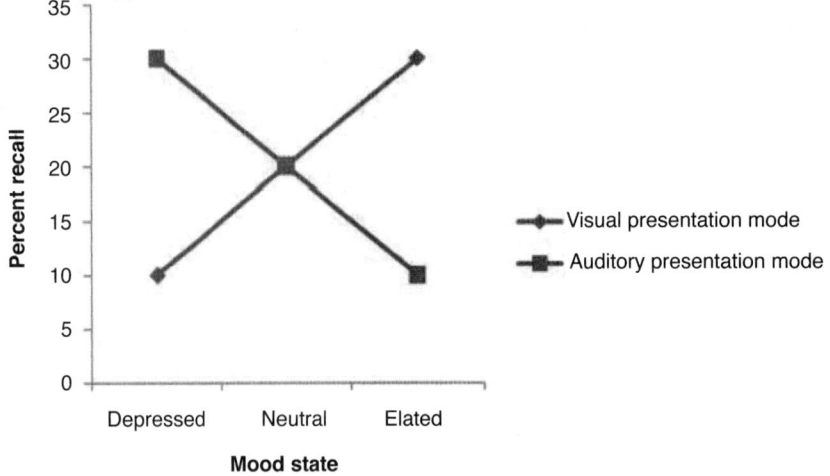

FIGURE 27.6. Illustration of an interaction between mood state and presentation mode.

However, just adding a third factor with two levels makes it a $3 \times 2 \times 2$ factorial design with 12 cells, so this design would require 360 participants.

An additional issue is that manipulating the combination of factors becomes more difficult as more factors are included. It would be harder to simultaneously manipulate mood state, presentation mode, quality of tutoring, and anxiety level (a four-factor design) than it would be to manipulate only mood state and presentation mode. A final difficulty with factorial designs is that the interpretation of the interactions is more difficult as the number of factors increases. An interaction between the two factors of mood state and presentation mode would be easier to interpret than would an interaction between the three factors of mood state, presentation mode, and anxiety level. A three-way interaction is present when a two-way interaction varies across the levels of the third IV.

In spite of these difficulties, factorial designs are popular and used frequently because of the advantages they afford when used properly. The first advantage is that the effect of more than one factor can be tested, which means that more than one hypothesis can be tested. In the basic between-participants randomized design, only one hypothesis can be tested. However, in a factorial design, you can test hypotheses relating to each main effect and each interaction effect.

A second advantage of factorial designs is that control of a potentially confounding variable can be created by building it into the design of the experiment. Whether an extraneous variable (e.g., intelligence level) should be included as a factor in the design of an experiment depends largely on the research question. If there is reason to suspect that the variable intelligence would interact with the other IV(s), it may be important to include it in the design. When including the extraneous variable in the design, you have the advantages of (a) obtaining a more statistically powerful test of the factor of interest by removing variation that would otherwise be part of the estimate of error variance, (b) enabling the researcher to study the effect of the other IV on the DV, and (c) testing for interactions between the original variable and other IV(s). Testing for interaction effects is perhaps the most important advantage of factorial designs. This enables us to investigate the complexity of behavior because it reveals how the effect of one factor changes with the different levels of another factor. The importance of the presence of an interaction between the factors in a factorial design is apparent when you recognize that this means that the main effects (or lack of main effects) alone do not fully describe the outcome of the experiment. In fact, the presence of interactions means that the main effects are insufficient (Keppel & Wickens, 2004) and that attention should be focused on the interaction to better understand the results of the study.

Although interactions are important because they reveal the complexity of behavior, they are often more difficult to detect than main effects (Shadish et al., 2002). This means that larger sample sizes (size to be determined by a priori power analysis) might be necessary when interactions are the focus of attention. However, interactions often provide the richest and most valuable information, which is why this is the most important advantage of factorial designs.

Mixed Factorial Designs

There are many times in psychological research when interest exists in one or more variables that fit into a randomized or between-participants type of design and other variable(s) fit into a repeated-measure or within-participants type of design. When this type of situation exists, a mixed factorial design is needed because a *mixed factorial design* combines the characteristics of a between-participants design with the characteristics of a within-participants design. The simplest form of a mixed factorial design is one that includes one between-participants factor and one within-participants factor, as illustrated in Figure 27.7. From Figure 27.7 it can be seen that there are two factors, A and B, and that there are three levels of Factor A and two levels of Factor B. Figure 27.7 also reveals that participants are randomly assigned to the two levels of Factor B and that all participants take each of

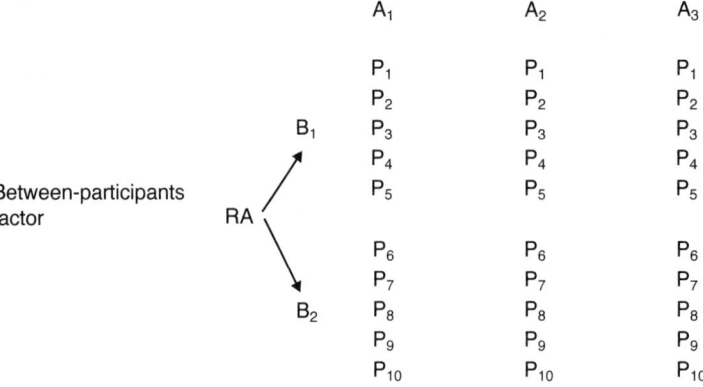

FIGURE 27.7.   Mixed factorial design in which A represents the three levels of the within-participants or repeated-measures variable and B represents the two levels of the between-participants variable. RA indicates that the participants were randomly assigned to the two groups.

the three levels of Factor A. Therefore, Factor B is a between-participants factor with random assignment of participants and Factor A is a within-participants or repeated-measures factor.

Ugwuanyi et al. (2020) employed a mixed factorial in their investigation of the effect of cognitive behavior therapy (CBT) on academic procrastination of university students. Students were randomly assigned to the treatment or control groups and all participants were assessed at three time points (pretest, posttest, and follow-up). This study used a mixed factorial design because it included one between-participants factor (CBT treatment vs. control) and one within-participants or repeated-measures factor (time of assessment).

A mixed factorial design is a popular design because it combines some of the advantages of both the between- and within-participants designs. When using this design, you can test for the main effect of both the between and within factors as well as the interaction between these factors. This design also has the advantage of needing fewer participants than a between-participants factorial design because all participants take all levels of the within factor. Therefore, the number of participants needed is a multiple of the number of levels of only the between factor. It also gives a more sensitive test of the within

factor. The within factor in this design is usually "time," where you are interested in testing for a potential change across levels of the time factor. However, for other within-participants factors, counterbalancing may be needed for the within-factor conditions in each of the between-participants groups.

This discussion of mixed factorial designs has focused on only one between and one within factor. This design can be extended to include more than one between or within factor. As many factors as can be incorporated into the design as are considered necessary. These factors can be any combination of within and between factors. For example, if a study was conducted using three factors, two of these factors could be within factors and one could be a between factor. Conversely, two could be between factors and one could be a within factor. The essential requirement for a mixed factorial design is that it includes at least one within and at least one between factor.

CLUSTER RANDOMIZED DESIGNS (AND NESTING)

Sometimes random assignment occurs at different levels when dealing with research questions at organizational levels like classrooms, schools, businesses, and hospitals. In these cases, people are naturally nested into groups or clusters, and the cluster becomes the object (or unit) of random assignment. For example, to test the effectiveness of a new educational curriculum on academic performance, classrooms might be randomly assigned to the treatment (the new curriculum) and control (standard procedure or varied procedure) groups. The classrooms include already existing groups of students. When this occurs, there *should be* statistical independence of the clusters, given the use of random assignment but not the individuals within the clusters. The "should be" qualifier entails assuming these clusters are themselves not nested in a higher order unit (e.g., districts) in a meaningful way.

Now, we briefly review the concept of statistical dependence within some given cluster. Statistical independence means that no single observation about a participant should tell you something about another participant. However, in the case of cluster random assignment of classrooms, participants within a classroom are not independent of each other—they likely share much in common (e.g., daily experiences, background characteristics, school culture). Therefore, observations of these students in the same classroom cannot be considered statistically independent. The dependent variable scores of students in each cluster are not independent of each other, and there is a factor, other than treatment exposure, that should be handled in the analyses. In this case, an independent samples *t* test or ANOVA would not work because an important assumption on which it depends, statistical independence, cannot be made; therefore, a different analytic technique is needed.

In the case of nested designs (clustering), the use multilevel modeling (cf. HLM) can help account for statistical dependence. The strategy entails assessing the degree of dependence (usually called intraclass correlations or, for purposes of this discussion, intracluster correlations), which is estimated and accounted for in statistical modeling. For an empirical example of a cluster randomized (nested) design using multilevel modeling, Jitendra et al. (2015) tested

the effectiveness of a mathematics intervention by randomly assigning teachers to either the treatment or control group. Student participants were nested within teacher classrooms. By using multilevel modeling, these researchers were able to examine the effect of the treatment along with student and teacher characteristics. The Level 1 or student variables included student characteristics (e.g., race, sex), and the Level 2 variables included the manipulated treatment variable and nonmanipulated teacher variables, such as years of teaching math and number of math courses completed in college. Multilevel modeling is a commonly used technique when there are multiple levels of variables of interest. Some benefits are (a) the standard errors will be correct, and (b) it recognizes the levels and nesting that are present in the research design.

Our last point here is that rather than using traditional GLM approaches to statistical analysis in the presence of clusters and nesting, we recommend the use of the newer and more accurate approaches of multilevel modeling. There are many useful references for learning more about multilevel modeling (e.g., Garson, 2020; Hoffman & Rovine, 2007; Raudenbush & Bryk, 2002; Robson & Pevalin, 2016).

WITHIN-PARTICIPANTS/REPEATED MEASURES DESIGNS

The primary strength of a within-participants design is that the same participants are administered all levels of the IV. However, the challenge of this design is to present the conditions in a way that controls for carryover and order effects. Most within-participants designs use some form of *counterbalancing* to equally distribute order and carryover effects across the different conditions. Only when these sequencing effects are balanced across the various levels of the factor being studied can the effect of that factor be measured.

The simplest within-participants design is one that includes one within-participants IV with two levels. This design produces two sequences (i.e., orders of presentation of the conditions) as illustrated in Figure 27.8. From this figure,

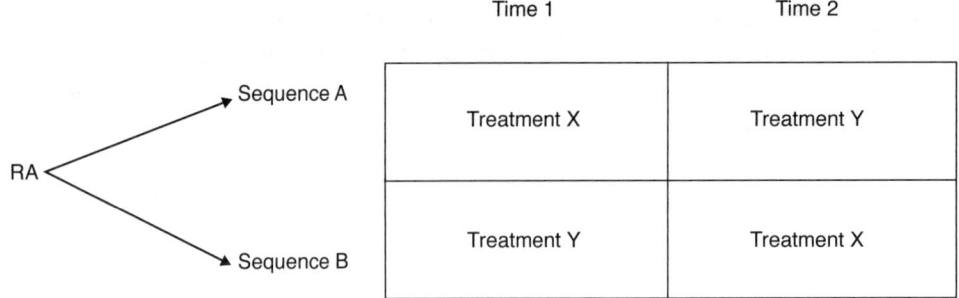

FIGURE 27.8.   Illustration of a within-participants design with two levels of the independent variable condition. RA represents random assignment of participants to the two sequences.

you can see that there are two sequences of the treatment conditions: treatment condition X followed by treatment condition Y, and treatment condition Y followed by treatment condition X. Participants are randomly assigned to one of the two sequences, and each randomly assigned participant then takes their assigned sequence of the two treatment conditions. This is sometimes called a *crossover design* because participants "cross-over" from one condition to the next. As mentioned earlier, when testing the efficacy of a treatment, this design has the ethical advantage that all participants receive the treatment.

Centola et al. (2020) employed a within-participants design in their investigation of the effect of alcohol consumption on driving behaviors in a simulated driving task. Each participant was randomly assigned to one of two test sequences. Half of the participants were first tested in the alcohol condition and then in the placebo condition. The others were first tested in the placebo condition and then in the alcohol condition. Therefore, each group received the treatment and control conditions but in a different sequence. As predicted, risky driving behaviors were greater when participants were in the alcohol condition.

The primary advantage of a within-participants design is the increased power to detect a true treatment effect because the comparison between conditions is made within-participants. That is, each participant is tested in each condition. With counterbalancing, order and carryover effects are controlled (equally distributed across the conditions) because each condition occurs

in each position an equal number of times and each condition follows and precedes the other condition an equal number of times. For example, as seen in Figure 27.8, condition X occurs first in order once and second in order once; also, condition Y occurs first in order once and second in order once. Furthermore, X precedes Y once and Y precedes X once. When you obtain a mean for treatment X (across the two orders) and a mean for treatment Y across the orders, the order and carryover effects are controlled. (See the next paragraph for the exception.)

There are some cases where this design is not appropriate. If there are differential carryover effects or if a treatment condition causes a relatively permanent change in the participants, then a within-participants design is not appropriate. *Differential carryover* refers to the case where a carryover effect varies depending on which condition follows it (Maxwell & Delaney, 2018). In the case of two conditions, the carryover from treatment X to treatment Y may be different than the carryover from treatment Y to treatment X. In the case of three conditions, the carryover from treatment X to treatment Y may be different from the carryover of treatment X to treatment Z. If this is the case, counterbalancing does not control for differential carryover effects and within-participants designs should not be used. For some treatments, such as drug studies, a wash-out period may be sufficient to eliminate any carryover effect. *Wash-out* refers to adding a period of time between the conditions to allow the effects of the prior treatment to be eliminated (washed out) before introducing the next condition. In cases where a treatment has resulted in a relatively permanent change in behavior, a wash-out period is insufficient, and within-participants designs should not be used.

Before leaving this section on the two-condition within-participants crossover design, we do want to mention that there are other sequences that could be used in addition to the XY and YX sequences. Jones and Kenward (2003) elaborated in detail on two-treatment designs with more than two sequences or more than two time periods. A two-treatment design could, for example, include the following four sequences: XX, YY, XY, and YX, or it might include two sequences but three time periods producing the following sequences: XYY and YXX. Wager et al. (2017) used a similar approach when assessing the validity of telephone interviews compared to mailed questionnaires. All participants completed two assessments. The orders were Telephone/Telephone, Mail/Mail, Telephone/Mail, and Mail/Telephone. Jones and Kenward pointed out that such designs have the advantage of obtaining estimators of carryover effects or a treatment by time period interaction. If you use a crossover design and think you might have carryover or a treatment by time period interaction and do not want to use a between-participants design, consult Jones and Kenward.

Within-Participants With More Than Two Levels of the IV

Although many experiments focus on comparing the effect of two conditions, the focus of other experiments is on comparing the effect of more than two conditions. When there are more than two conditions, counterbalancing to control for order and carryover effects may gradually become more cumbersome. There are three primary counterbalancing strategies: randomized counterbalancing, complete counterbalancing, and incomplete counterbalancing. With *randomized counterbalancing*, you will use a computer to randomly assign each participant to a randomly generated sequence of conditions. This works well when it is practical for the researcher to administer a sequence of conditions (e.g., via a computer screen) to each individual rather than to groups of individuals. There also must be a sufficient number of participants for this probabilistic strategy to control for carryover and order effects (Maxwell & Delaney, 2018).

The next two counterbalancing approaches are deterministic and use the logic of a Latin Square. A *Latin square* is an $n \times n$ table filled with n different symbols in such a way that each symbol occurs exactly once in each row and exactly once in each column as shown in Figure 27.9. From this figure, you can see that each of the letters, A, B, and C, occur once in each row and column and that a Latin square really represents a form of counterbalancing.

Complete counterbalancing employs all possible orders of conditions (i.e., sequences). The crossover design described above used complete counterbalancing. When there are two levels of the IV (X and Y), there are two possible sequences (X followed by Y and Y followed by X). When there are three levels of the IV, there

FIGURE 27.9.   Illustration of a Latin square.

are six possible sequences. Using complete counterbalancing with three levels of the IV, each participant would be randomly assigned to one of six sequences. As the number of levels of the IV increase, the number of sequences becomes substantially larger. In complete counterbalancing, the number of sequences can be calculated by *N!* where *N* is the number of sequences and *N* is multiplied by each number below it (e.g., in the case of four levels of the IV, *N!* would be equal to $4 \times 3 \times 2 \times 1$ or 24 sequences). As the number of sequences required by complete counterbalancing becomes large, it is often advisable to use incomplete counterbalancing instead.

Incomplete counterbalancing requires fewer sequences but makes use of a balanced Latin Square. The specific properties that must exist are (a) each treatment must occur the same number of times in each ordinal position and (b) each treatment condition must precede and follow every other treatment an equal number of times. A Latin square created in this manner is said to be *diagram balanced* (Keppel & Wickens, 2004). Here is a formula that can be used for incomplete counterbalancing. The first sequence is 1, 2, *n*, 3, (*n* – 1), 4, (*n* – 2), 5, and so forth, until reaching the total number of conditions. For example, if the within-participants IV has four levels, the first sequence would be 1, 2, 4, 3. If the within-participants IV has six conditions, the first sequence will be 1, 2, 6, 3, 5, 4. To obtain the remaining sequences, the researcher will increment each value in the preceding sequence by 1. In our example with four levels, the resulting set of sequences for the study are as follows:

Sequence (using letters for the numbers)
A B D C
B C A D
C D B A
D A C B

If the within-participants IV has an odd number of conditions, it is necessary to use the generated diagram balanced Latin square and also a mirror image of it. Once the set of sequences is identified for a research design, the participants are randomly assigned to the sequences, with an equal number of participants falling in each sequence.

DESIGNING RANDOMIZED STUDIES

Experimental studies use one of the designs or a combination of the designs and the design features discussed in this chapter. However, conducting a good experimental study that provides the most credible evidence requires much more than just selecting and using a specific randomized design found in a methods book. This is why Donald Campbell and his colleagues shifted over time from providing lists of particular designs (with the common threats to internal validity listed) to discussing key design categories and threats and having researchers use or construct an appropriate design. This point is seen in a comparison of Campbell and Stanley (1963) with Cook and Campbell (1979) and Shadish et al. (2002). It is also seen in published empirical research where the researchers often (usually) do not use specific design names and, instead, explain the design components and how they were used together in the research study.

We have explained the logic behind the pieces of experimental research design. The following key design components of an experimental research design should be considered and combined appropriately by the researcher on a study-by-study basis: (a) constructing appropriate treatment condition(s); (b) constructing the control group or other comparison conditions; (c) use of a between-participants, a within-participants, or a mixed design; (d) the use of pretests and posttests; and (e) determine appropriate the type of random assignment. All of these issues have been discussed. Now we briefly address one additional issue in the following section.

Expanding Randomized Experimental Designs

The randomized experiment is the strongest way to obtain evidence of causation. That is why it is often referred to as the gold standard. Multivariable randomized experiments can include multiple manipulated and nonmanipulated variables, which adds important information, such as how IVs interact, which can be missed in single variable experiments. Experiments can be conducted in laboratory and field settings, with the former providing the most control over the conditions in which human behavior occurs and the latter offering information about behavior in more "real world" settings and conditions. Experiments can also be used to study outcomes that operate at multiple levels (and analyzed via multilevel modeling).

This last brief section in this chapter takes the prior statement as a crucial starting point. Here, we want to suggest a few possibilities for *adding to* what the powerful experimental methodology usually provides. Shadish et al. (2002) pointed out that experiments are the most powerful method for causal description (i.e., did a variable have a causal impact on an outcome variable). They contrasted this with causal explanation, which involves the study of mediating/intervening variables, and causal process, which may be more difficult to manipulate in experiments. Causal explanation can be studied quantitatively (e.g., SEM research), but qualitative data (e.g., interviews, observations) can enhance causal explanation and strengthen theory development (Johnson et al., 2019).

If a researcher does not obtain statistical significance in a simple randomized experiment, important additional information might be obtained with qualitative data. For example, perhaps an omitted moderator variable is identified via interviews, helping the researcher identify why a main effect was not found. As a general rule, qualitative data (interviews, observations, open-ended questionnaires, conduct of case studies) can help one see complexities in the world that hypotheses testing simple main effects or even interaction effects do not address. Exploratory approaches can be used along with experimental (confirmatory) approaches to determine complexity occurring for the different participants. It might

be that there are different ways to reach the same outcome (equifinality) that are not easily investigated in basic experiments.

Strong science operates in both inductive or exploratory and deductive or confirmatory directions. Science requires both theory discovery/generation and theory testing, and there are many systematic methods available for both of these goals. Traditional experimental science has focused on the testing of models and hypotheses. Ultimately this is most important for obtaining strong claims about "what works." At the same time, qualitative and mixed methods approaches can be helpful in knowing what works, for whom, in what situations and contexts, and how it works.

Mixed methods may have something to add before, during, and after some experiments (Johnson & Schoonenboom, 2016). This is especially true in applied psychology, in field studies, social programs, and longitudinal studies. *Before the experiment*, exploratory data can sometimes help experimenters improve their understanding of conceptual, cultural, and contextual factors that might be theoretically relevant to fully understanding the phenomenon or theory. Preexperimental exploration might also help the experimenter in making practical decisions about data collection instruments and measurement that is appropriate for the kinds of participants in the study. Experimenters can attempt to check some of their assumptions about the participants in relation to the experiment being planned and designed. Some knowledge might also be obtained about how to best engage the participants. *During the experiment*, one might collect additional information that will sometimes help document theoretical process. *After the experiment*, additional data might be collected for a manipulation check (is what occurred what the researcher planned to occur?). The researcher might also retrospectively discuss with participants what occurred, and some data may be obtained about process (e.g., see the causal process literature and literature on mixed methods grounded theory: Johnson et al., 2019; Shim et al., 2021).

Here are a few possible recommendations that sometimes might be appropriate as supplements to traditional experimental designs:

1. Understand and include researchers', participants', and stakeholders' views and values about the experiment/program/ intervention (e.g., need/fit, context, DVs of concern, meaningful instruments, reasons for attrition, perceptions of outcomes, views about future directions).
2. Include participants' experiences with the experiment/intervention and program participation.
3. Examine context-specific characteristics.
4. Attempt to gain some understanding of the individual/idiographic level effects and the effect seen at the group/nomothetic level (study variance among individuals as cases, and document complexity through individual cases).
5. Explore differences among participant subgroups (e.g., look for subpopulations, success cases and nonsuccess cases).
6. Explore and explain the process underlying the effect (open up the "black box" and turn it into a "clear box," identify intervening processes to explain relationship).
7. Search for unforeseen results in addition to the hypothesized effect (i.e., add a discovery/ generative dimension to the experiment).
8. Better ground the effect in additional obtained data (i.e., collect additional thick, deep, and multiple perspectival data).
9. Scrutinize underlying assumptions (Is the relationship spurious? Is the measurement reliable and valid? Are there any omitted variables invalidating the analysis? Were the participants honest?).

CONCLUSION

In this chapter, we have defined and explained the major types of experiments in empirical research. We have focused on experiments that include random assignment because it is the best way to control for alternative explanations due to group differences. It "equates the groups" on all known and unknown extraneous variables. It is the task of empirical researchers to thoughtfully and creatively mix and match the experimental design components discussed in this chapter on a study-by-study basis to produce strong designs suited to their particular research questions and hypotheses. Experimental research has a long and cherished history in psychology because it provides the strongest evidence of causation. The use of strong experiments produces rigorous and trustworthy empirical research which contributes to the advancement of the science of psychology. We look forward to continued advancements in the use of randomized experiments in psychology.

References

Alferes, V. R. (2012). *Methods of randomization in experimental design*. Sage. https://doi.org/10.4135/9781452270012

American Psychological Association. (2020). *Publication manual of the American Psychological Association* (7th ed.). https://doi.org/10.1037/0000165-000

Appelbaum, M., Cooper, H., Kline, R. B., Mayo-Wilson, E., Nezu, A. M., & Rao, S. M. (2018). Journal article reporting standards for quantitative research in psychology: The APA Publications and Communications Board task force report. *American Psychologist, 73*(1), 3–25. https://doi.org/10.1037/amp0000191

Blair, E. (2004). Gold is not always good enough: The shortcomings of randomization when evaluating interventions in small heterogeneous samples. *Journal of Clinical Epidemiology, 57*(12), 1219–1222. https://doi.org/10.1016/j.jclinepi.2004.06.003

Campbell, D., & Stanley, J. (1963). *Experimental and quasi-experimental designs for research*. Wadsworth.

Centola, C., Tagliabue, M., Spoto, A., Palpacelli, M., Giorgetti, A., Giorgetti, R., & Vidotto, G. (2020). Enhancement of unsafe behaviors in simulated moped-riding performance under the influence of low dose of alcohol. *Accident; Analysis and Prevention, 136*, 105409. https://doi.org/10.1016/j.aap.2019.105409

Christensen, L. B., Johnson, R. B., & Turner, L. A. (2020). *Research methods: Design and analysis*. Pearson.

Clay, R. (2010). More than one way to measure. *Monitor on Psychology, 41*(8), 52. https://www.apa.org/monitor/2010/09/trials

Cook, T. D. (2018). Twenty-six assumptions that have to be met if single random assignment experiments are to warrant "gold standard" status: A commentary on Deaton and Cartwright. *Social Science & Medicine, 210*, 37–40. https://doi.org/10.1016/j.socscimed.2018.04.031

Cook T. D., & Campbell D. T. (1979). *Quasi-experimentation: Design and analysis issues for field settings.* Rand McNally.

Dehue, T. (1997). Deception, efficiency, and random groups: Psychology and the gradual origination of the random group design. *Isis, 88*(4), 653–673. https://doi.org/10.1086/383850

Dehue, T. (2001). Establishing the experimenting society: The historical origin of social experimentation according to the randomized controlled design. *The American Journal of Psychology, 114*(2), 283–302. https://doi.org/10.2307/1423518

Donaldson, S. I. (2009). In search of the blueprint for an evidence-based global society. In S. I. Donaldson, C. A. Christie, & M. M. Mark (Eds.), *What counts as credible evidence in applied research in evaluation practice?* (pp. 2–18). SAGE. https://doi.org/10.4135/9781412995634.d6

Fisher, R. A. (1928). *Statistical methods for research workers.* Oliver & Boyd.

Fisher, R. A. (1935). *The design of experiments.* Oliver & Boyd.

Freedland, K. E., King, A. C., Ambrosius, W. T., Mayo-Wilson, E., Mohr, D. C., Czajkowski, S. M., Thabane, L., Collins, L. M., Rebok, G. W., Treweek, S. P., Cook, T. D., Edinger, J. D., Stoney, C. M., Campo, R. A., Young-Hyman, D., Riley, W. T., & the National Institutes of Health Office of Behavioral and Social Sciences Research Expert Panel on Comparator Selection in Behavioral and Social Science Clinical Trials. (2019). The selection of comparators for randomized controlled trials of health-related behavioral interventions: Recommendations of an NIH expert panel. *Journal of Clinical Epidemiology, 110*, 74–81. https://doi.org/10.1016/j.jclinepi.2019.02.011

Garson, G. D. (2020). *Multilevel modeling: Applications in STATA, IBM SPSS, SAS, R., & HLM.* SAGE.

Hariton, E., & Locascio, J. J. (2018). Randomized controlled trials—The gold standard for effectiveness research. *BJOG, 125*(13), 1716. https://doi.org/10.1111/1471-0528.15199

Hoffman, L., & Rovine, M. J. (2007). Multilevel models for the experimental psychologist: Foundations and illustrative examples. *Behavior Research Methods, 39*(1), 101–117. https://doi.org/10.3758/BF03192848

Jitendra, A. K., Harwell, M. R., Dupuis, D. N., Karl, S. R., Lein, A. E., Simonson, G., & Slater, S. C. (2015). Effects of a research-based intervention to improve seventh-grade students' proportional problem solving: A cluster randomized trial. *Journal of Educational Psychology, 107*(4), 1019–1034. https://doi.org/10.1037/edu0000039

Johnson, R. B., & Christensen, L. B. (2020). *Educational research: Quantitative, qualitative, and mixed approaches* (7th ed.). SAGE.

Johnson, R. B., Russo, F., & Schoonenboom, J. (2019). Causation in mixed methods research: The meeting of philosophy, science, and practice. *Journal of Mixed Methods Research, 13*(2), 143–162. https://doi.org/10.1177/1558689817719610

Johnson, R. B., & Schoonenboom, J. (2016). Adding qualitative and mixed methods research to health intervention studies: Interacting with differences. *Qualitative Health Research, 26*(5), 587–602. https://doi.org/10.1177/1049732315617479

Jones, B., & Kenward, M. G. (2003). *Design and analysis of cross-over trials.* Chapman & Hall/CRC. https://doi.org/10.1201/9781420036091

Keppel, G., & Wickens, T. D. (2004). *Design and analysis: A researcher's handbook.* Pearson Prentice Hall.

Keppel, G., & Zedeck, S. (1989). *Data analysis for research designs: Analysis of variance and multiple regression/correlation approaches.* Worth Publishers.

Maxwell, S. E., & Delaney, H. D. (2018). *Designing experiments and analyzing data: A model comparison perspective.* Erlbaum.

Nock, M. K., Janis, I. B., & Wedig, M. M. (2008). Research designs. In A. M. Nezu & C. M. Nezu (Eds.), *Evidence-based outcome research: A practical guide to conducting randomized controlled trials for psychosocial interventions* (pp. 201–218). Oxford University Press.

Raudenbush, S. W., & Bryk, A. S. (2002). *Hierarchical linear models: Applications and data analysis methods.* SAGE.

Robson, K., & Pevalin, D. (2016). *Multilevel modeling in plain language.* SAGE. https://doi.org/10.4135/9781473920712

Salmond, S. S. (2008). Randomized controlled trials: Methodological concepts and critique. *Orthopaedic Nursing, 27*(2), 116–124. https://doi.org/10.1097/01.NOR.0000315626.44137.94

Shadish, W. R., Cook, T. D., & Campbell, D. T. (2002). *Experimental and quasi-experimental designs for generalized causal inference.* Houghton Mifflin.

627

Shim, M., Johnson, R. B., & Gasson, S. (2021). A mixed methods-grounded theory for producing more refined theoretical models. *Journal of Mixed Methods Research, 15*(1), 61–86. https://doi.org/10.1177/1558689820932311

Ugwuanyi, C. S., Gana, C. S., Ugwuanyi, C. C., Ezenwa, D. N., Eya, N. M., Ene, C. U., Nwoye, N. M., Ncheke, D. C., Adene, F. M., Ede, M. O., Onyishi, C. N., & Ossai, V. O. (2020). Efficacy of cognitive behaviour therapy on academic procrastination behaviours among students enrolled in physics, chemistry, and mathematics education (PCME). *Journal of Rational-Emotive & Cognitive Therapy, 38*(4), 522–539. https://doi.org/10.1007/s10942-020-00350-7

Wager, J., Barth, F., Stahlschmidt, L., & Zernikow, B. (2017). Testing the validity of telephone interviews to assess chronic pain in children and adolescents: A randomized cross-over trial. *European Journal of Pain (London, England), 21*(10), 1707–1716. https://doi.org/10.1002/ejp.1081

CHAPTER 28

NONEQUIVALENT COMPARISON GROUP DESIGNS

Henry May and Zachary K. Collier

This chapter focuses on research designs in which the effects of a treatment or intervention are estimated by comparing outcomes of a treatment group and a comparison group but without the benefit of random assignment. In psychology and other social sciences, these designs often involve self-selection, in which the members of the treatment group are those who volunteered or otherwise sought to receive the treatment, whereas the comparison group members did not. Alternatively, assignment to the treatment group may be made through a subjective decision process. This is common in education research when an intervention targets schools or students and district or school staffs select whom to assign to the treatment. More generally, a nonequivalent comparison group design involves any comparison of treatment and control groups in which the treatment assignment mechanism cannot be modeled explicitly, and the treatment and comparison groups are likely to exhibit pretreatment differences on measured or unmeasured factors.

Given the probable and often obvious preexisting differences between the treatment and comparison groups in this design, it is normally imprudent to draw strong causal inferences about the effects of an intervention. The suitability of a nonequivalent group as a counterfactual

(i.e., a group that tells you what would have happened to the treatment group in the absence of the treatment) is difficult to ensure and impossible to guarantee in a nonequivalent comparison group design. Therefore, much of the literature on this design revolves around the question of how to estimate the treatment's effect in the absence of random assignment. Nevertheless, because it is applicable in so many circumstances, the nonequivalent groups design is one of the most commonly implemented research designs in the social sciences (Campbell & Stanley, 1963; Shadish et al., 2002; Reichardt, 2019).

Much has been written about the nonequivalent comparison groups design, and the introduction to this chapter continues with a brief review of major contributions to that prior literature. The remainder of the chapter delves more deeply into key methodological issues and recent advances in analytical techniques. In the review of prior literature, readers will likely notice the ubiquitous contributions of Donald T. Campbell. His publications over several decades, along with those of his collaborators, created and refined the experimental–quasi-experimental paradigm and the framework of threats to internal and external validity that continues to guide the design of countless social science research projects.

https://doi.org/10.1037/0000319-028
APA Handbook of Research Methods in Psychology, Second Edition: Vol. 2. Research Designs: Quantitative, Qualitative, Neuropsychological, and Biological, H. Cooper (Editor-in-Chief)

The seminal text by Campbell and Stanley (1963), entitled *Experimental and Quasi-Experimental Designs for Research*, defined the nonequivalent control group design as involving a comparison of treatment and comparison groups that were "as similar as availability permits, but yet not so similar that one can dispense with the pretest" (p. 47). They advocated strongly for the use of a pretest to (a) evaluate the similarity of the treatment and control groups prior to treatment and (b) statistically adjust for preexisting differences when estimating treatment impacts. In a discussion of the nonequivalent groups design's inferential validity, they also noted that pretesting both groups removes preexisting differences across groups, ostensibly. This effectively mitigates many basic threats to internal validity (see the Key Threats to Internal Validity section) in that these threats must now operate on pre–post changes (i.e., not just the posttest), and they must operate differently for the treatment and control groups (i.e., they must interact with selection). Although Campbell and Stanley (1963) used the term *control group* in their label for this design, others prefer the term *comparison group* to better differentiate this design from a randomized experiment and to place clear emphasis on the nonequivalence of the comparison group. Following that logic, this chapter will hereafter refer to the nontreatment group in this design as the *comparison* group.

In their 1963 text, Campbell and Stanley also introduced a simple and intuitive notation for describing this and other research designs in terms of group equivalence and timing of observations and treatments. Their notation for the nonequivalent control group design is as follows:

$$
\begin{array}{ccc}
\text{O} & \text{X} & \text{O} \\
\hline
\text{O} & & \text{O}
\end{array}
\qquad (28.1)
$$

The horizontal line in this notation differentiates the treatment and control groups, whereas the use of a dashed line signifies that the two groups are not equivalent. Outcomes are assessed (with each instance denoted by O) for both groups before and then again after the introduction of the treatment (X) in one group. Campbell and Stanley (1963) pointed out that the assignment of the treatment to one group or the other is "assumed to be random and under the experimenter's control" (p. 47).[1] However, given the prevalence of volunteering and subjective allocation of the treatment in applied settings, this assumption is probably violated in most studies using the nonequivalent comparison group design. Fortunately, violations of this assumption have few practical implications for analysis or interpretation of results—even with random assignment at the group level, the groups are still nonequivalent. The presence of volunteering or subjective allocation may make the nonequivalence overt (making specific threats to validity easier to identify), but group-level random assignment with only two groups does little to address either overt or hidden selection bias. Such a scenario would not improve validity unless the study can be repeated numerous times, which would be analogous to a cluster randomized experiment (see Boruch et al., 2004) using randomization within matched pairs of groups.

There exist numerous statistical methods to address group nonequivalence, and a thorough discussion of classical analytic issues was written by Reichardt (1979), which appeared as a chapter in the book edited by Cook and Campbell entitled *Quasi-Experimentation: Design and Analysis Issues for Field Settings*. Reichardt's chapter substantiated the need for a pretest in this design, and it reviewed a number of alternative methods for analyzing the pre–post data from a nonequivalent groups design. Unfortunately, the choice of preferred statistical model for producing unbiased effect estimates is not simple, and it is not consistent across applications of the nonequivalent groups design. Although the present chapter reviews the key methodological considerations raised by Reichardt (see the section Classical Statistical

---

[1]Random assignment of two existing groups is different from random assignment of participants. For example, an experimenter might be able to assign a reading treatment randomly to one of two classrooms but not have control of which students were in each class.

Adjustments), the reader is directed to Reichardt's 1979 chapter and more recent book (Reichardt, 2019) for a detailed discussion of issues regarding unbiased effect estimates produced via classical statistical models.

Shadish et al. (2002) built on these two prior works by reframing the discussion around a comprehensive theory of generalized causal inference. Their discussion of the nonequivalent comparison group design (Shadish et al., 2002, pp. 136–153) largely parallels that from Cook and Campbell (1979, pp. 103–133); however, this more recent work includes design enhancements that improve validity by combining multiple comparison groups with treatment replications or nonequivalent dependent variables (Shadish et al., 2002, pp. 153–161). The relevant chapter in their book also included an appendix that briefly reviewed recent advances in statistical approaches to dealing with selection bias, including propensity score modeling (see Volume 1, Chapter 2, this handbook), control function and instrumental variables analyses, and latent variable–structural equation modeling (see Chapter 21 of this volume).

To best reflect the continuous improvements in methodological theory, this chapter includes a concise discussion of key issues and perspectives from these prior works, followed by a more comprehensive discussion of recent advances in statistical and econometric methods that are directly applicable to the nonequivalent comparison groups design. Because this chapter provides a relatively nontechnical and broad discussion of theories and methodologies related to the nonequivalent groups design, the essential elements of each topic are presented in nontechnical language and are supported by references to more technical publications. The interested reader is directed to these references for more detail on the theory behind and procedures for each method.

The structure of the remainder of this chapter includes three main sections. The first section describes an illustrative example of a nonequivalent comparison group design, which will then be used as a foundation for discussing the methods and issues raised in subsequent sections. The second section includes a review of key threats to internal validity of the nonequivalent groups design, leaning heavily on the prior work of Campbell and colleagues. The third section focuses on the use of baseline measures to address selection issues and is divided into three parts: classical statistical adjustments (e.g., analysis of covariance [ANCOVA]), statistical models for controlling observable bias (e.g., regression, stratification, matching), and econometric techniques for controlling unobservable bias (e.g., instrumental variables analysis). Finally, the fourth section focuses on design enhancements, including extensions to the simple two-group pre–post design, cohort comparison groups, moderation–mediation analysis, and sensitivity analysis.

AN ILLUSTRATIVE EXAMPLE

A classic question in the clinical psychology literature has focused on the relative value of medication for patients participating in psychotherapy for depression. The basic question is, when a patient receives effective psychotherapy, is there any added benefit achieved (or harm inflicted) by augmenting the therapy with an antidepressant medication? Perhaps the medication improves the efficacy of the psychotherapy. Or, perhaps the medication does not improve the efficacy of the psychotherapy but increases the risk of suicide. Unfortunately, the truth is not easily ascertained without random assignment because myriad selection mechanisms are at work that determine who does or does not receive antidepressant medication. For example, the selection process may look something like the following. First, individuals suffering from clinical depression must be referred to or otherwise seek psychotherapeutic treatment. Of those seeking treatment, some will visit a psychologist and others will visit a psychiatrist, depending on a number of factors, including the relative availability of these two types of practitioners, relative costs, and personal preferences and beliefs. Of those who visit a psychologist, only a portion will visit a psychologist able to prescribe antidepressant medications, a possibility that currently exists in only a select number of states. Alternatively, patients enrolled in health management organization plans may receive a prescription for an antidepressant from their primary care physician along with a referral to a psychologist for psychotherapy, or they may receive only the referral for psychotherapy. The act of prescribing a medication will depend on a number of factors, including medical history, the time frame and severity of the depression, and the relative liberality with which the psychiatrist, psychologist, or physician issues such prescriptions. But this complicated process likely represents only a fraction of the mechanisms that determine whether a psychotherapy patient also receives an antidepressant medication. So we are left with a situation in which a simple comparison of patients receiving only psychotherapy to patients receiving psychotherapy plus medication is somewhat like comparing apples and oranges. Yes, the two groups are similar in many ways, but they are also different in many important ways that could exert significant influence on their outcomes.

In the simplest nonequivalent comparison group design, we would capture preexisting differences in outcomes between the psychotherapy and psychotherapy plus medication groups by collecting pretest data on the severity of depression (i.e., using a reliable and valid standardized measure) before the initiation of any treatment. Then, at some point after the treatment begins (e.g., 12 weeks later), we would collect posttest data on the severity of depression. The basic idea is that by measuring preexisting differences in depression, one can adjust impact estimates accordingly. Of course, this is a simplistic approach to dealing with selection bias, and there are many reasons to believe that simply measuring preexisting differences in the severity of depression will fail to account for all of the important factors that influence differences in outcomes. For example, there may be no detectable differences in severity of depression between patients who visit a psychiatrist and those who visit a psychologist, but the treatment they receive (independent of the medication) may end up looking very different. In the sections that follow,

key issues and analytic methods relevant to the nonequivalent groups design are discussed, with illustrations intertwined throughout that tie back to this hypothetical study of the efficacy of antidepressant medication.

KEY THREATS TO INTERNAL VALIDITY

The nonequivalent comparison group design deals effectively with many basic threats to internal validity as long as a pretest is employed for both groups. It accomplishes this by focusing the impact analysis not on simple posttest differences between the treatment and comparison groups but on differences between the groups in their pre–post changes. The issue of selection as a main effect is addressed to the extent that pretreatment differences between the two groups are captured by the pretest, and these preexisting differences are subsequently factored out when calculating posttest impact estimates. In other words, any posttreatment differences attributable to the main effect of selection are subtracted (or statistically adjusted) from the final impact estimate under the assumption that pretreatment differences would persist in the posttest measure. For selection bias to persist, the key issues of history, maturation, testing, instrumentation, regression to the mean, and mortality (now called attrition) must interact with selection to explain away differences in pre–post changes (Campbell & Stanley, 1963, p. 48). For example, maturation is an issue whenever natural improvement would occur even without a treatment. In a simple pre–post study without a comparison group, a main effect of maturation could explain completely a simple pre–post change (i.e., subjects were already improving without the treatment). In a study that includes a comparison group but no pretest, a main effect of selection could explain a difference in posttest scores between treatment and comparison groups (i.e., subjects in the two groups would have had different outcomes even without the treatment). With the inclusion of both a pretest and comparison group in a nonequivalent comparison group design, however, any main effect of maturation will be evident in the pre–post change of the comparison group as well and can be adjusted out of the impact estimate. For example, in our hypothetical study of antidepressants, all patients may be expected to improve because they are all participating in psychotherapy, and this general improvement (i.e., maturation) that happens regardless of whether one receives an antidepressant would be evident in the pre–post changes in the comparison group and could be adjusted out when calculating the impact of the antidepressants on the treatment group. On the other hand, if the rates of improvement without the treatment are different for the treatment and comparison groups (i.e., the maturation effect interacts with selection), it is impossible to determine whether differences in pre–post changes across the two groups are attributable to the treatment or to preexisting differences in maturation rates. For example, if those patients receiving antidepressants were already improving at a faster (or slower) rate than the comparison group, their average pre–post change would be larger (or smaller) even without the antidepressants. In general, we need to be concerned whether one group experiences improvement in their depression that was unrelated to whether they received a drug and instead attributable to other preexisting differences between the groups. Alternatively, if we can assume that the average rates of change (or lack thereof) without the treatment would be similar for subjects in the treatment and comparison groups, then differences in the pre–post changes of the two groups are more directly attributable to the effect of the treatment.

The logic of this approach is similar to that of difference-in-differences models from the econometric literature (Greene, 1993). This model, also known as a *change score* analysis or a *fixed-effects model* with two time points, is said to control for all time-invariant confounds. In other words, confounding factors will introduce bias only to the extent that they influence pre–post changes differentially between treatment and comparison groups. If the factors differentiating the groups are consistent over time and are unrelated to differences in pre–post change (i.e., they do not interact with time), then the difference-in-differences model will produce unbiased estimates of the treatment effect.

Beyond maturation-selection interactions, numerous other selection interactions may threaten the validity of inferences from the nonequivalent comparison group design. A history-selection interaction would occur whenever an event occurs between the pretest and posttest for one group but not the other (or more or less for one group). In essence, this "intrasession history" (Campbell & Stanley, 1963, p. 14) acts as an additional treatment, whose effects cannot be distinguished from the effects of the treatment of interest. For example, perhaps those patients seeing a psychiatrist are more likely to receive medication but also tend to have shorter psychotherapy sessions. If the antidepressants had a positive effect, it could be hidden by the diminished effect of less-intensive psychotherapy. Alternatively, if the antidepressants had no effect, the diminished effect of less intensive psychotherapy could even make the drugs appear harmful.

A testing-selection interaction would occur whenever repeated testing bias affects the two groups differently. In general, members of the comparison group receiving no treatment may become more fatigued by repeated testing, causing their posttest performance to worsen and resulting in a positive bias in the impact estimate. An instrumentation-selection interaction would occur whenever the accuracy of measurement improved or degraded differently for the two groups. For example, observers may become bored when rating the comparison group given an absence of desired outcomes, resulting in a positive bias in the impact estimate. An attrition-selection interaction would occur whenever the treatment and comparison groups exhibited differential rates of loss of participants. In our hypothetical antidepressant study, if the drugs were beneficial and those not receiving them were more likely to discontinue treatment (thus missing the posttest), the treatment effect would be underestimated. This is because the outcomes for the psychotherapy-only group could have been biased upward (i.e., less severe depression on average) given that more patients with severe depression and less effective treatment would discontinue treatment and miss the posttest. Finally, a regression-selection interaction would occur whenever one group was selected from a more extreme position in a distribution of prior outcomes. In this case, posttest outcomes for the more extreme group would be expected to exhibit greater regression to the mean, resulting in either a positive or negative bias in the impact estimate. This is especially plausible in our hypothetical study of antidepressants given that drugs are most likely to be prescribed to those patients with the most severe pretreatment depression symptoms.

As Campbell and Stanley (1963) pointed out, regression-selection interactions are problematic in studies in which individuals self-select into a treatment, and attempts to create a comparison group by matching those who self-select into a treatment with those who did not is likely to introduce substantial regression-selection inter-action bias (p. 49). This is because the members of the comparison group would likely represent an extreme group relative to the population of potential controls. In other words, of those who did not seek out the treatment, those selected for inclusion in the comparison group are likely to be quite unusual relative to the rest of that group. On the other hand, those who self-selected into the treatment group are probably not unusual relative to the population of potential treatment recipients. Thus, because the members of the comparison group are more extreme relative to the population from which they were drawn, the comparison group would be expected to exhibit greater regression to the mean.

Although the nonequivalent group design with a pretest of treatment and comparison groups does much to address threats to internal validity, there is no guarantee that selection interactions will be sufficiently controlled. In fact, for most studies utilizing this design, it is relatively easy to imagine a selection issue that weakens the credibility of causal inferences from those studies. There are a number of design and analytic steps that one can take to strengthen the validity of

a nonequivalent groups comparison. However, without the benefit of random assignment, this can prove to be a complicated and often impossible task.

STATISTICAL AND ECONOMETRIC METHODS TO ADDRESS SELECTION ISSUES

The use of a pretest measure is a key component in addressing selection bias in the nonequivalent comparison group design. Unfortunately, the most effective analytic methods for dealing with selection bias are not necessarily consistent from one study to the next. This section provides a description of the rationale and assumptions under-lying three classes of techniques for dealing with selection bias in nonequivalent group comparisons. The first approach relies on classical statistical analyses intended to adjust posttest outcomes for differences in pretest measure. The second approach attempts to explicitly control for factors confounded with treatment assignment and the outcome. Finally, the third approach attempts to deal directly with omitted variable bias (i.e., the bias attributable to unmeasured confounds not included in the model) by isolating the difference in the outcome that is unconfounded with other factors and thus is attributable solely to the impact of the treatment.

Classical Statistical Adjustments

For decades, the most common statistical analysis performed in conjunction with the nonequivalent comparison group design has been ANCOVA. The theory behind this method is that by includ-ing the pretest measure as a covariate in the model, the estimated impact of the treatment equals the difference between the treatment and comparison groups, after holding pretest scores constant. In other words, the ANCOVA seeks to estimate the expected difference in posttest scores between subjects who started with the same pretest score. In our hypothetical study of antidepressants, this is analogous to comparing the severity of depression at posttest for patients receiving or not receiving antidepressants who had identical severity of depression before treatment.

In an ANCOVA model, the relationship between pretest and posttest scores is captured in a regression equation, and the difference in intercepts between the regression lines for the treatment and comparison groups serves as the estimate of the treatment effect.[2] Figure 28.1 depicts this relationship using ovals to approximate the location of data points for the treatment and comparison groups, solid lines to depict the regression lines, and a dashed box to illustrate the idea of holding the pretest constant when estimating the posttest difference.

Although the ANCOVA approach may be intuitively appealing, it has a number of significant shortcomings.[3] All of these shortcomings can cause the model to adjust inappropriately, either too much or too little, for preexisting differences between the groups. This leads to bias in the treatment effect, and this bias may be either positive or negative.

One likely source of bias is unreliability in the pretest measure, which is certain to occur in our study of antidepressants given that severity of depression cannot be measured with perfect reliability. Because the pretest–posttest relationship is estimated using a regression equation, the slope of that equation is subject to bias associated with measurement error in the pretest scores. It is well known that measurement error in an independent variable in a regression model will result in attenuation of the slope estimate toward zero proportionate to the unreliability in that predictor variable—the estimated slope will equal the true slope multiplied by the reliability of the predictor (i.e., $\beta_{Obtained} = \beta_{True} \times \rho_{xx}$). When unreliability attenuates the pretest slope in an ANCOVA model used to estimate impacts for a nonequivalent groups design, the estimate of the treatment effect will be biased whenever there are differences in the mean pretest scores of the treatment and comparison groups. Figure 28.2 presents a case

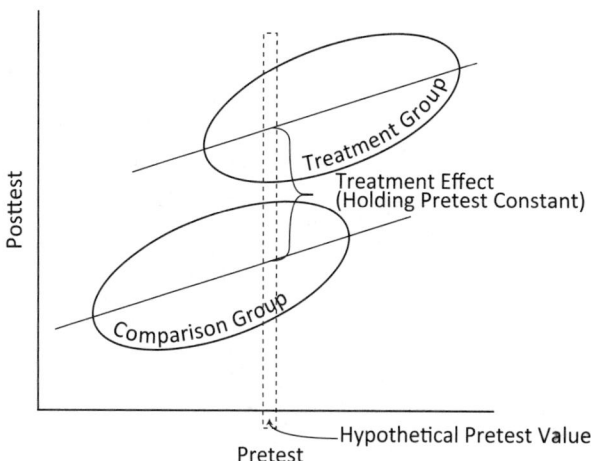

FIGURE 28.1. The logic of analysis of covariance in estimating treatment effects in a nonequivalent comparison group design.

in which the treatment and comparison groups are sampled from different ends of the same population and the effect of the treatment is zero.

The attenuation in the pre–post regression slope is evident in the slope of the dashed lines, which is less steep than the slope for the full population (i.e., the solid line). This attenuation results in separation of the intercepts for the two groups, thus giving the illusion of a treatment effect. As demonstrated by Reichardt (1979, p. 163; 2019, pp. 127–130), as unreliability in the pretest increases, the degree of adjustment induced by the ANCOVA decreases, resulting in a failure to remove all of the preexisting differences from the impact estimate. Therefore, when measurement error exists in the pretest, a preexisting difference favoring the treatment group would result in a positively biased impact estimate, whereas a preexisting difference favoring the comparison group would result in a negatively biased impact estimate. If there is no pretest difference between treatment and comparison groups (e.g., as in a randomized experiment), then the attenuation in

---

[2]The standard ANCOVA model assumes parallel pretest–posttest slopes in the treatment and comparison groups. This is referred to as the *homogeneity of regression assumption* (Wildt & Ahtola, 1978). This assumption can be relaxed by including an interaction between the pretest variable and the treatment indicator, although doing so makes interpretation of results in nonequivalent comparison designs very problematic (Reichardt, 1979, p. 170).

[3]These shortcomings also apply to the technique of linear regression with a pretest control variable and a group indicator, since this approach is mathematically equivalent to ANCOVA.

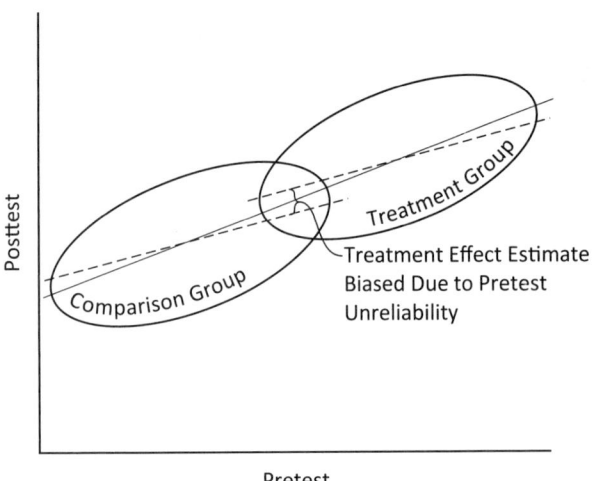

FIGURE 28.2. **Measurement bias in the regression slope under an analysis of covariance model of treatment impact in a nonequivalent comparison group design.**

slope would cause both regression lines to pivot on the same fulcrum (i.e., the overall mean). Thus, no difference in intercepts would result from pretest unreliability if there were no preexisting difference on the pretest.

Naturally, one might conclude that the bias in the ANCOVA's pre–post slope could be easily removed by dividing the estimated slope by the reliability of the pretest measure. In practice, the procedure for adjusting ANCOVA for unreliability in the pretest is slightly different but also simple. Consider that the regression slope coefficient represents the expected change in Y (i.e., the dependent variable) for each one-unit change in X (i.e., the independent variable). Because the biased regression coefficient in an ANCOVA is underestimated to a degree equal to the reliability in the pretest measure (i.e., r_{xx}), one way to increase the size of the slope coefficient by that exact amount is to change the scale of the X variable by that same amount. This is accomplished by rescaling the pretest scores by the reliability coefficient using the formula:

$$X_{adj} = \overline{X}_j + \rho_{xx}\left(X_{ij} - \overline{X}_j\right), \qquad (28.2)$$

where $\overline{X}_j$ is the mean score for group j (e.g., treatment or comparison group), X_{ij} is the unadjusted

pretest score for subject i in group j, and ρ_{xx} is the reliability of the pretest measure. This adjustment must be calculated separately for each group in the ANCOVA in order to shift the slopes but not the intercepts. Essentially, the adjustment shrinks the pretest scores toward their respective group means by an amount proportionate to the amount of unreliability in the pretest measure. This effectively changes the scale of the pretest measure in the ANCOVA so that what had originally been a one-unit change in the X variable is now only a ρ_{xx}-unit change in the X_{adj} variable. This translates to an increase in the slope coefficient equal to $1/\rho_{xx}$. Porter (1967) and Porter and Chibucos (1974) referred to this technique as the *estimated true scores adjustment* to ANCOVA.

Because the problem of unreliability and attenuation of the pretest slope is an artifact of regression analysis, another way to avoid this problem (but perhaps create other problems) is to forgo the regression aspect of covariance adjustment and analyze simple pre–post change scores instead. This is the approach taken by the difference-in-differences analysis mentioned earlier that is popular in econometric literature (Greene, 1993). When the data contain only two time points (i.e., pretest and posttest), the results are the same whether group differences in change scores are estimated after subtracting each subject's pretest score from their posttest score or, alternatively, fixed-effects (i.e., dummy variables) for subjects are included in a model that includes both pretest and posttest scores in the dependent variable (i.e., with two records, pretest and posttest, in the data set for each subject). Furthermore, the realized model is also equivalent to an ANCOVA model when the pretest slope has been fixed at a value of one. The implication of this is that a model analyzing change scores assumes that the pretest difference between treatment and comparison groups would persist in identical direction and magnitude in the absence of a treatment effect (e.g., a 10-point difference in the pretest would result in exactly a 10-point difference in the posttest). In our hypothetical study of antidepressants, this implies that the mean difference in depression scores between those receiving and not receiving medication would be identical in the pretest and posttest, if the medication had no effect. This requires that depression be measured on a perfectly interval scale (so that a difference of X has the same interpretation at any point on the scale) and that the effect of psychotherapy alone is identical regardless of the pretest depression score (e.g., every patient's depression score is expected to drop by 20 points, regardless of where they started). In our example, these assumptions are difficult to justify.

Figure 28.3 illustrates the parallel trends assumption in change score and difference-in-difference models. The dotted lines and italicized labels represent the unobserved potential outcomes (e.g., the posttest outcome for the treatment group, had the treatment not been delivered). Unfortunately, this assumption of parallel trends in potential outcomes is often violated in social science research. Factors that deflate the transfer of pretest differences to posttest scores include pre–post construct shift and construct nonequivalence. These terms refer to situations in which the meaning of what is measured changes slightly (i.e., a shift) or completely (i.e., nonequivalence) from pretest to posttest. For example, if identical or equated measures of depression severity are not used at pretest and posttest, then posttest differences cannot be expected to equal pretest differences.

Factors that can inflate or deflate the transfer of pretest differences to posttest scores include changes in measurement scale and pre–post changes in score variance (e.g., posttest scores may be more variable than pretest scores). Furthermore, the assumption that the pre–post change for the comparison group serves as a good counterfactual for the treatment group can also be violated by any of the selection interactions mentioned thus far. These selection-interaction validity threats affect both change score and ANCOVA analyses.

Simply put, both ANCOVA and change score models have substantial potential for bias when estimating treatment effects in conjunction with

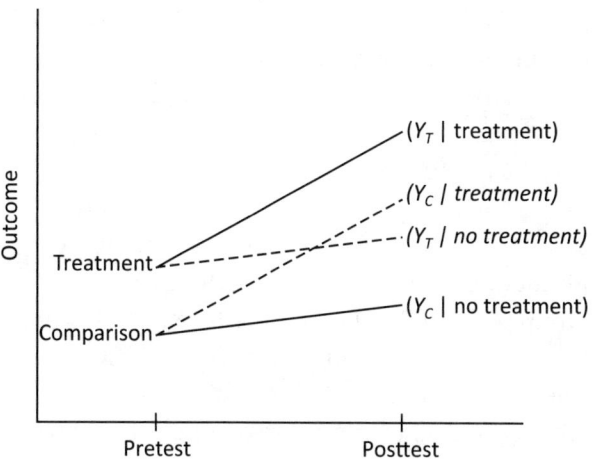

FIGURE 28.3. The parallel trends assumption of change score and fixed-effects analysis of treatment impacts in a nonequivalent comparison group design.

a nonequivalent comparison group design. The choice between these two approaches has long been a topic of discussion, and although the problem has largely been solved, the news is not good. Although there are clear circumstances under which the ANCOVA works best and there are other circumstances under which the change score analysis works best, these circumstances are restrictive. Unfortunately, most circumstances involving a nonequivalent comparison group design in reality will induce bias in both analyses, and the two methods will often yield different results. The difference in results produced by these two analyses was originally presented as Lord's (1967) paradox. It is a paradox in that it is perplexing that the two methods so often produce different results despite the fact that they are intended to answer the same research question (i.e., "What is the treatment effect?"). Holland and Rubin (1983) were the first to solve Lord's paradox by evaluating the problem in the context of Rubin's potential outcomes framework for causal inference (Holland, 1986; Rubin, 1974).[4] Their key revelation was that the decision to use ANCOVA versus change score analysis was driven by untestable assumptions about the potential outcomes for the two groups. In the context of

---

[4]See West and Thoemmes (2010) for a comparative discussion of Campbell's and Rubin's perspectives on causal inference.

a nonequivalent groups design, the implicit assumptions are whether the posttest scores for the treatment group, had the treatment not been delivered, are better approximated by adding the average change for the comparison group to the pretest scores of the treatment group (Option A), or using a within-group regression model to predict posttest outcomes for the treatment group (Option B). Option A leads to change score analysis, whereas Option B leads to ANCOVA. These assumptions are entirely untestable without additional data (e.g., multiple pretests), and the choice between these two analytical alternatives is not necessarily obvious.

Fortunately, choosing between ANCOVA and change score analysis becomes a little less perplexing when one realizes that the two approaches target different analytical questions (Hand, 1994; Wainer, 1991; Wright, 2006). The change score analysis simply seeks to determine whether, on average, one group experienced a larger pretest–posttest difference. Contrast this with the ANCOVA, which seeks to determine whether the posttest scores of subjects from the treatment group were, on average, higher or lower than those of comparison group subjects who had equivalent pretest scores. This logic also helps us understand when one approach may be more appropriate than the other. For example, whenever it is unreasonable to calculate a change score by subtracting the pretest from the posttest score (e.g., when the pretest and posttest are not on the same scale), the change score analysis can be eliminated as a viable option. On the other hand, the change score analysis may be less biased than the ANCOVA whenever it is reasonable to expect that in the absence of the treatment, the posttest scores will approximately equal the pretest scores. In the case of our hypothetical study of antidepressants, every patient's depression score is expected to change given that they are receiving psychotherapy, and there is no reason to believe that psychotherapy will yield the same degree of change for every value of the pretest

measure, so ANCOVA is likely the better approach. However, ANCOVA is still not guaranteed to produce unbiased estimates in our case. Although being specific about the analytic questions and assumptions may help a researcher decide between ANCOVA and change score analysis in a nonequivalent groups study, the fact that the assumptions behind the choice are untestable suggests that the estimated treatment effect will not necessarily be unbiased.

To reach a higher level of certainty, one must go beyond the specificity of analytic questions and focus also on the ability of the analytic model to properly account for the treatment assignment mechanism. Maris (1998) used Rubin's causal model to present a mathematical explanation of the differences between ANCOVA and change score analyses and to show how their ability to produce unbiased treatment effects is related to the treatment assignment mechanism. Using empirical simulation, Wright (2006) verified and further illustrated Maris's results, which are as follows. Both ANCOVA and change score analysis produce unbiased results when assignment to treatment is random (i.e., as in a randomized experiment). When the pretest is used to assign subjects to the treatment, either using a cutoff (i.e., as in a regression discontinuity design; see Chapter 29 of this volume) or using blocked random assignment (i.e., all subjects with the same pretest score have the same probability of assignment to treatment), then ANCOVA is unbiased, whereas change score analysis is biased. When the probability of assignment to treatment is correlated with the pretest, but the pretest does not precisely determine assignment probability (i.e., all subjects with the same pretest score do not have an identical probability of assignment to treatment), then ANCOVA is always biased and change score analysis will be unbiased only if the pre–post trends are independent of the groups.[5] Lastly, when treatment assignment is correlated with (but not determined by) the pretest and also with errors of measurement contained in the pretest

[5]This is analogous to the *parallel trends assumption* (see Figure 28.3), which implies that the comparison group trend can be used to estimate the change for the treatment group in the absence of the treatment, and the treatment group trend can be used to estimate the change for the comparison group if they had received the treatment.

(or other factors exhibiting the same measurement biases as the pretest), then both ANCOVA and change score analyses are biased. Unfortunately, this last case is most likely applicable to our example study of antidepressants, so we may be better served by seeking out other ways to address selection bias.

Matching to Address Overt Bias

An alternative to model-based adjustments for pretest differences involves the use of blocking or matching on pretreatment covariates. The logic here is that posttest comparisons are restricted to those subjects in the treatment and comparison groups that had similar pretreatment characteristics. This approach is similar to that of ANCOVA; however, blocking or matching does not usually rely on a linear regression to model equivalence.

In the simplest case of blocking, subjects in the treatment and comparison groups might be grouped into blocks on the basis of similar scores on the pretest. For example, in our hypothetical study of antidepressants, we might group patients with similar pretest depression scores into homogeneous blocks. As the number of blocks increases, the reduction of selection bias approaches that of the ANCOVA model after relaxing the assumptions of linearity or homogeneity of regression. Cochran (1968) demonstrated that the vast majority of selection bias associated with a covariate can be removed using as few as five blocks.

An alternative to blocking involves pair matching or caliper matching (Cochran & Rubin, 1973). Instead of categorizing subjects into broad groups, each subject in the treatment group is either matched to a subject from the comparison group with the same pretest score (i.e., pair matching) or is matched to a subject from the comparison group who has a pretest score that is close to the treatment subject's pretest score (i.e., caliper matching). Cochran and Rubin (1973) showed that the vast majority of selection bias associated with a pretest difference can be removed using a caliper as large as one half of a standard deviation.

Unfortunately, blocking and matching on the pretest is subject to the same sources of bias that threaten ANCOVA analyses, including measure-

ment bias and selection interactions (Maris, 1998; Reichardt, 1979). Furthermore, because the pretest blocking or matching approaches can never perform better than an ANCOVA that appropriately models nonlinear and nonparallel regression trends, the value of blocking or matching on the pretest is limited.

One area in which matching holds greater promise is in multivariate matching using multiple pretreatment variables. For our hypothetical study of antidepressants, we could imagine measuring and then matching patients on initial severity of depression, age, gender, race, income, type of insurance, place of residence (e.g., city vs. suburbs), and various other factors related to the outcome. Rosenbaum (2002, 2010, 2020) presented several methods for matching on multiple covariates. Each of these methods relies on a distance matrix to evaluate the relative proximity of treatment and comparison group members on the multiple covariates. These matching methods can be distinguished on the basis of the method of linking treatment and comparison subjects and the number of treatment or comparison subjects that may be linked. Methods include caliper matching, greedy matching, and optimal matching. Multivariate caliper matching links subjects that have proximal values on all covariates. Greedy matching links subjects to the nearest neighbor matches and moves sequentially through the data set. Greedy matching is so named because once a match is made, it is not broken, even if a chosen match would be better matched to another subject farther down in the data set. In our hypothetical study of antidepressants, a greedy matching algorithm might match a subject in the treatment group to a control with a similar pretest score, despite the fact that that pretest score for that particular control was even closer to the pretest score for another treatment group member farther down in the data set. Alternatively, optimal matching links subjects in such a way that the total distance between matches is minimized. In other words, matches can be rearranged during the matching process so that the end result produces the closest matched set possible.

The different approaches to the number of links made in multivariate matching include pair matching, multiple control matching, and full matching. Pair matching links each treatment group member to one comparison group member, whereas multiple control matching links each treatment group member to at least one comparison group member. For example, each patient taking antidepressants may be matched to one comparison patient (with pair matching) or to two or more comparison patients (with multiple matching) who were not taking antidepressants but who were similar in other respects. Lastly, full matching links each treatment group member to at least one comparison group member and also allows each comparison group member to be matched to multiple treatment group members, although each subject appears in only one matched group. For example, patients taking antidepressants who are similar on other characteristics may be matched to the same comparison patients, thus producing a group that is consistent on measured covariates but varied in terms of antidepressant treatment.

The objective of any matching method is to create blocks or strata that include at least one member of the treatment group and at least one member of the comparison group where the members in any given group are similar on all observed covariates. Among these matching methods, the most effective approach for balancing preexisting differences is optimal full matching, although matching using the propensity score (see the following four paragraphs) may provide even better covariate balance (Gu & Rosenbaum, 1993).

Recall from the previous section that the solution to Lord's (1967) paradox requires an understanding of the relationship between the pretest and the treatment assignment mechanism. To ensure unbiased estimation of the treatment effect, comparisons of outcomes should be restricted to only those subjects with equal probability of assignment to the treatment. In other words, unbiased estimation of the treatment effect can be ensured only when the use of covariates in the analytical model serves to create a blocked random assignment design. Extending this logic, Rosenbaum and Rubin (1983) defined the *propensity score* as the probability that an individual is or was assigned to the treatment group. When an analysis compares outcomes for subjects with identical propensity scores, it mimics a blocked random assignment design, and the estimate of the effect of the treatment is unbiased.

In randomized experiments, the values of the individual propensity scores are known. If simple random assignment is used, then the propensity scores equal .5 if half of the study sample is assigned to the treatment. If blocked random assignment is used, then the propensity scores in each block are equal to the proportion of subjects that were assigned to the treatment from that block. In nonrandomized studies, the propensity scores are unknown, but they may be estimated using observed covariates. This is typically accomplished by building a statistical model predicting treatment assignment (i.e., $Y_i = 1$ if treated; $Y_i = 0$ if untreated) on the basis of observed pretreatment covariates. In our study of antidepressants, we could imagine using all of the covariates and matching factors previously mentioned as predictors of whether a patient receives antidepressant medication. The predicted probabilities from this model can serve as estimates of the individual propensity scores in an observational study. In general, the propensity score model includes all available covariates and may also include interactions and nonlinear terms. Because the objective is to maximize the precision and accuracy of the estimated propensity scores, it is advisable to include all available covariates related to the treatment assignment and the outcome, even if they do not meet the traditional criteria for statistical significance (Rosenbaum, 2002, 2010; Rubin, 1997; Rubin & Thomas, 1996).[6] The objective is to build a propensity score model

---

[6]It is important that none of the predictors included in the propensity score model are caused by the treatment or the outcome. This suggests that mediators and other intermediate outcomes should be excluded from the propensity score model. The best way to ensure exclusion of intermediate and secondary outcomes may be to use only pretreatment variables, measured before the intervention, as predictors in the propensity score model.

that includes all relevant confounds such that the assignment to treatment is independent, conditional on the propensity score, of the potential outcomes. In other words, the objective is to remove all confounding between treatment assignment and any covariates related to the outcome. There are several modeling strategies for estimating propensity scores. The simplest of these is logistic regression, but this can exhaust the available degrees of freedom when it includes many covariates. This potentially restricts the model to a subset of available covariates and greatly reduces the estimate's precision (McCaffrey et al., 2004). Another major limitation of regression approaches is the assumption of linearity between the dependent variable and the independent variables. Disregard for distributional assumptions may result in not achieving covariate balance (Rubin, 2010). If a model does not achieve covariate balance, the researcher should modify the propensity score model before moving forward with the analysis (Collier et al., 2021).

Recent literature suggests data mining is a promising alternative for propensity score estimation. For example, neural networks are helpful to propensity score estimation because they can automatically detect complex interactions involving a large number of covariates and may outperform logistic regression in nonlinear settings (Collier & Leite, 2021). But some literature suggests that data mining techniques tend to overfit in real-data analyses and are computationally expensive (Alam et al., 2019). Overfitting occurs when a propensity score model predicts the treatment precisely, which leads to a violation of positivity (Ju et al., 2019).

After satisfactory propensity score estimates are produced, it is common practice to estimate treatment–comparison group differences after implementing paired, multiple, or full matching using the propensity score as a single matching variable (see Rosenbaum, 2010). Alternatively, propensity score stratification may be used to group subjects by their propensity scores, much like blocking on the pretest. And, similar to blocking on the pretest, Rosenbaum and Rubin (1984) also cited Cochran (1968) in support of their recommendation for five strata when using propensity score stratification. Furthermore, Rubin (2004) recommended including covariates in the statistical model of program impacts, even after matching on the propensity score. Lastly, the propensity score may also be used as a covariate in an ANCOVA, although this approach imposes the assumption of a linear relationship between the propensity score and the outcome.[7]

Although the propensity score may be intuitively appealing, perhaps even ingenious, as a method for improving causal inference in nonexperimental studies, it has a number of important limitations. For example, as the number of relevant covariates increases, and the predictive power of the model improves, there is increased separation in estimated propensity scores between the treatment and comparison groups. This suggests that as the propensity score model improves in precision, the overlap in estimated propensity scores between the treatment and comparison groups diminishes, and the availability of suitable propensity score matches decreases. In other words, a propensity score model with very high predictive power may confirm that the treatment and comparison groups are, in fact, incomparable. Imagine if the logistic regression model predicting which patients do and do not receive antidepressant medication has such high predictive power that the estimated propensity scores for nearly all of those receiving medication were close to 1 and for nearly all of those not receiving medication were close to zero. This would suggest that (a) we could predict quite well (albeit not perfectly) who did and did not receive medication, and (b) the differences in the propensities of these two groups were so large that they are simply incomparable.

Even when there is substantial overlap in the distributions of propensity scores, there is no

---

[7] A curvilinear relationship may also be modeled by including a quadratic term for the propensity score. However, stratification is better able to handle many forms of nonlinearity in the relationship between the propensity score and the outcome.

guarantee that stratification or matching will produce balance on all of the observed covariates. Even though the propensity score is remarkably effective when used as a single matching variable, it is imperative that covariate balance be evaluated by testing for treatment–control differences within strata or by comparing absolute differences in covariates within pairs or strata (see Rosenbaum, 2010, pp. 187–190). Shadish et al. (2002) pointed out that the propensity score model requires large samples (e.g., hundreds, if not thousands, of subjects in each group), lack of overlap in the distribution of propensity scores can limit analytic sample size and generalizability of results, the likelihood of missing data across many covariates complicates the estimation of propensity scores, and the ability of the propensity score approach to produce unbiased estimates is dependent on the availability of all relevant confounding variables (i.e., those covariates related to treatment assignment and potential outcomes). This last point is crucial. If any unmeasured covariates exist that are related to both treatment assignment and the outcome after controlling for other observed covariates, the impact estimate will still be biased even after conditioning on the propensity score. In our hypothetical study of antidepressants, the sheer number of factors that are related to depression outcomes and that also influence whether a patient receives an antidepressant is so large that a propensity score model is unlikely to account for all aspects of selection bias—can we really expect to measure everything that determines whether a patient receives antidepressants and is also related to posttreatment outcomes? When propensity score models do not meet the assumption of no unmeasured confounders, researchers need to determine if the lack of data has a strong influence on the analysis. That is, determining if there is a strong correlation between the unmeasured covariate(s) and the outcome variable, after conditioning on observed covariates. Bayesian modeling with informative priors and multiple imputation are examples of approaches that may help to determine the impact of an unmeasured covariate on the propensity score analysis (Uddin et al., 2016).

Using Instrumental Variables to Address Hidden Bias

The problem of potential hidden bias plagues the nonequivalent comparison group design. In any such study, the validity of the conclusions may be questioned because there may be an uncontrolled confound that explains away the relationship between the treatment and the outcome. In most nonequivalent group designs, it is not hard to conjecture about specific unmeasured confounds that might exist, and the methods discussed up to this point can only hope to control those confounds that were actually measured. What is needed is a method that can control for both observed bias and also hidden bias associated with unobserved confounds. Recall that for the difference-in-differences model, it was argued that analysis of change scores removes the selection bias attributable to any time-invariant confounding variable. In that case, the effects of these variables might be controlled, even without explicitly measuring them. The econometric instrumental variables (IV) technique promises to do the same thing in the analysis of treatment effects in a nonequivalent groups design. Unfortunately, the literature on IV is highly technical and relies on notation and vocabulary that, until recently, was inaccessible to noneconomists. The purpose of the following section is to provide a brief, minimally technical description of the theory and assumptions behind IV and describe common methods for producing IV-adjusted impact estimates.

To understand the IV technique, one must focus on one crucial, but often ignored, assumption underlying unbiased estimation in statistical modeling. That crucial assumption is that the predictor variables in a model must be uncorrelated with the model error term. In this case, the error term does not refer to model residuals. Although residuals are estimates of the errors, they will be biased estimates of the errors if the model itself is biased. To illustrate this, consider a simple regression model of a treatment impact:

$$Y_i = \beta_0 + \beta_1 T + \varepsilon_i, \tag{28.3}$$

in which Y_i is the outcome for individual i, β_0 is the model intercept representing the mean outcome under the control condition, β_1 is the effect of treatment T (coded one for the treatment group and zero for the comparison group), and ε_i is the variability in the outcome for individual i that is attributable to random error and any other unmeasured covariates. Because ε_i includes the influence of all unmeasured covariates, we could imagine separating ε_i into two parts. The first part, ξ_i, represents random error that is uncorrelated with anything. The second part, π, is a set (i.e., a vector) of regression slopes, which is multiplied by a set of relevant covariates X_i measured on each individual i. After substitution, our regression model looks like this:

$$Y_i = \beta_0 + \beta_1 T + (\pi X_i + \xi_i), \qquad (28.4)$$

and the problem should start to become clear. If we were to actually measure all of the X variables and include them as controls in this model, the original estimate of the effect of T would change if T is correlated with any of the X variables. That is the nature of control variables and confounding in statistical models.[8] If the X variables are unmeasured, then the parameter estimate for T remains unadjusted (i.e., biased). Furthermore, because the T variable is correlated with at least one of the X variables, and the effects of the unmeasured X variables are subsumed in the error term, then T is correlated with the error term. This is a very bad situation if the objective is to estimate the causal effect of T on Y. If we estimate a naive model that does not include all of the relevant X variables as controls, then the part of the error term that is correlated with T is included in our estimate of the impact β. In other words, the naïve model does a bad job of properly attributing variation in the outcome

to T versus the error term, and part of what should be attributed to unmeasured covariates and included in the error is attributed to the treatment.

IV techniques offer an opportunity to get around this problem under certain circumstances. For those readers already familiar with mediation analysis (Baron & Kenny, 1986), the logic of IV may sound somewhat familiar. In fact, IV analysis can be thought of as somewhat like a backward mediation analysis. First, the researcher must identify an *instrument*, which is a measurable variable that is (a) correlated with the treatment variable (i.e., it predicts treatment assignment); (b) through its correlation with the treatment, also correlated with the outcome; and (c) uncorrelated with any other covariate related to the outcome. In other words, a valid instrument has a significant relationship with the outcome variable but only as a result of its correlation with treatment assignment.[9] From a mediation perspective (i.e., in which the effect of one variable happens indirectly through its effect on an intermediate outcome), the effect of the instrument is mediated by the treatment; however, unlike in mediation analysis, we do not care about the direct or indirect effects of the instrument. We simply want to use the instrument to remove the influence of selection bias and adjust the estimated treatment effect to produce an unbiased causal effect.

The logic of how an IV analysis produces an unbiased estimate is shown in Figure 28.4. Here the causal effect on the outcome Y of the treatment T is equal to β. An additional covariate X is also related to the outcome, with a regression slope equal to π. The correlation between T and X is equal to ρ. If we were to estimate a naïve model with only T predicting Y, then our estimate of the slope for T would actually equal $\beta + \pi\rho$, which is clearly biased unless either ρ or π equal zero.[10]

---

[8]For more information on control variables, confounding, and unbiased parameter estimation in linear statistical models, see Neter et al. (1996).

[9]This is referred to in the econometric literature as the *exclusion restriction* because the instrument can be excluded from the causal model if the X's are observed.

[10]Either π or ρ would be equal to zero only if X were uncorrelated with either Y or T, respectively. If that were true, then X would not be confounded with the effect of T, and we would be able to estimate the effect of T without any adjustment. Of course, having no confounding variables is only likely to happen in a randomized experiment.

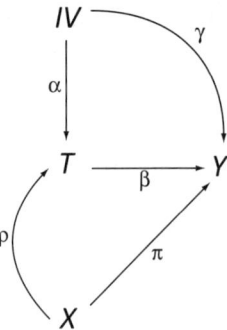

FIGURE 28.4. The logic of instrumental variables (IV) analysis and omitted variable bias in estimating the effect of a treatment (*T*) on an outcome (*Y*).

Unfortunately, we cannot use this formula to adjust our estimate of β because neither ρ nor π can be estimated since *X* has not been measured. However, if the relationship between the IV and *Y* occurs only because of the relationship between the IV and the treatment, then we can estimate β using our knowledge of α and γ. This is because a simple linear regression predicting *Y* only on the basis of the IV will yield a slope estimate γ, which is equal to the direct effect of the IV on *Y* (which we assume is zero because the IV's relationship with *Y* happens exclusively through *T*) plus an amount equal to the product of α and γ (i.e., $\gamma = 0 + \alpha\beta$). This follows from the same formula used to show the bias in the naïve impact estimate. Thus, with a little algebra, we can calculate β directly as γ/α. This is the IV estimate of the impact of *T* on *Y*.

Estimation of the IV model is typically done through two-stage least squares, in which both the regression of *T* on the IV and the regression of *Y* on the IV are estimated in a simultaneous equations process. Using simultaneous equations ensures that the standard errors of the IV estimate are unbiased. Structural equation modeling and maximum likelihood techniques can also be used to estimate the simultaneous equations in an IV analysis. Unfortunately, because of the stringent requirements of the exclusion restriction, good instruments are often hard to find.[11] For example, a good instrument has a strong correlation with the treatment variable. If the instrument has a low correlation with the treatment variable, then the denominator in the IV calculation is small, resulting in an unstable and usually biased estimate. This is referred to as having a *weak instrument* (Bound et al., 1995). Even more common may be violations of the assumption that the instrument is uncorrelated with other confounding covariates. Angrist and Pischke (2009) pointed out that this assumption is analogous to saying that "the instrument is as good as randomly assigned" (p. 117). That means that the instrument is essentially random in relation to the unobserved covariates and potential outcomes while it is strongly correlated with treatment assignment. Obviously, finding such a variable may be impossible. Angrist and Krueger (2001) explained the problem of identifying good instruments and provided numerous examples. In general, the most promising IVs are often those that are associated with a policy or circumstance that limits or enhances access to a treatment but that does so fairly arbitrarily (e.g., month of birth, policy differences across adjacent municipalities, and distance to a facility).

In our hypothetical study of antidepressants, there are at least a couple of candidates for use as an IV. First, consider the relative prevalence of psychiatrists or psychologists with prescribing privileges in a geographic area. If we first restrict our analyses to those patients who do not receive a prescription for an antidepressant from their primary care physician, then the likelihood of receiving an antidepressant is related to the likelihood of visiting or being referred to a practitioner with prescribing privileges and that is dependent on the availability of such practitioners in the area. Furthermore, it may be reasonable to expect that prescribing practitioners are relatively randomly distributed across geographic areas. Given this, we could calculate for each patient, the relative prevalence of practitioners with prescribing privileges within 10 miles of the patient's residence. We would then

---

[11]For more on the assumptions of IV and assessment of the IV assumptions, see the following: Angrist et al. (1996); Bound et al. (1995); Buse (1992); Staiger & Stock (1997).

use simultaneous equations estimation to regress the depression posttest scores on the IV (to estimate γ) and also regress the treatment indicator (1 = antidepressant; 0 = no antidepressant) on the IV (to estimate α). Finally, β is calculated as γ/α.

As a potential IV, our measure of the prevalence of practitioners with prescribing privileges within 10 miles of the patient's residence is likely to meet the relevance assumption (i.e., it is related to the probability of receiving an antidepressant and hence is not a weak instrument); however, it is unlikely to meet the exclusion assumption. That is, the correlation between the number of prescribing practitioners near a patient's residence and that patient's depression posttest scores is unlikely to be solely attributable to whether that patient received a prescription for an antidepressant. For example, if practitioners with prescribing privileges are less likely to open offices in impoverished areas (because of crime, uninsured residents, and so on) and poverty is correlated with severity of depression, then the relationship between our IV and depression posttest scores may be attributable to an unmeasured confound (i.e., poverty), thus violating the exclusion restriction.

Another potential IV is whether different insurance carriers have different policies regarding their coverage for antidepressant medications. If some patients are forced to pay higher copayments for their antidepressants, they may be less likely to take the medication. Therefore, this potential IV is related to the probability of taking an antidepressant, but it may be otherwise uncorrelated with posttest depression scores. In other words, the relationship between the amount of the copayment and posttest depression scores is due solely to whether the patient fills the prescription. Of course, one could imagine violations of the exclusion restriction if the size of copayments was related to other confounding variables like income or age.

OTHER DESIGN ENHANCEMENTS TO ADDRESS SELECTION BIAS

This section briefly reviews a few additional design enhancements that are especially promising for improving the validity of nonexperimental com-

parison group designs. These enhancements are designed to do one of three things. First, they may address directly specific threats to internal validity, such as a probable selection-maturation interaction. Second, they may improve internal validity by explicitly testing a series of hypothesized causal relationships, thereby evaluating not just the overall impact of a program but its entire theory of action. Third, they may seek to quantify the potential for selection bias to establish a plausible range for the impact of a treatment.

Using Multiple Pretests

Recall that a key assumption in the analysis of pretest–posttest data from a nonequivalent groups design is that the pre–post trend for the comparison group (represented either with a simple change score or a pre–post regression model) represents what would have happened in the treatment group if the intervention had not been delivered (i.e., the counterfactual). In the case of a change score model, this implies that the pre–post difference for the comparison group can simply be added to the pretest for the treatment group to produce the expected outcome for the treatment group under the counterfactual. In the case of an ANCOVA model, this implies that the pooled within-groups pre–post regression can be used to extrapolate the expected posttest scores, given the observed pretest score, for the treatment group under the counterfactual.

With only two waves of data (i.e., the pretest and the posttest), these assumptions are untestable. If an additional pretest were available, with the time difference between the two pretests being similar to the time difference between the last pretest and the posttest, then one could explicitly test these assumptions. The objective is to demonstrate that there is no difference in the pretest-one to pretest-two trend between the treatment and comparison groups. This helps to confirm that there is no selection-maturation interaction and that the two groups were experiencing similar trends before the introduction of the intervention.

In our hypothetical antidepressant study, multiple pretests would only be feasible if the antidepressants were not prescribed for several weeks after psychotherapy began. If that were the case, we could estimate the pretest-one to pretest-two change in depression scores to check for differences in trends before the start of antidepressant therapy in a subset of patients.

The statistical model used to test for differences in pretest trends could take several forms. The simplest approach is to estimate separate models for pretest trends and pre–post trends. The first model would use the second pretest as the outcome and the first pretest as a baseline in a change score model or as a covariate in an ANCOVA. A finding of no significant difference between treatment and comparison groups would support a conclusion of no difference in pretest trends. Once this is confirmed, a second model would be estimated to calculate treatment impact on posttest scores. An alternative to running separate models would be to extend the impact model to include repeated measures (including appropriate terms for autocorrelation of errors to model correlations in repeated measures over time) and to test simultaneously for differences in pretest-one to pretest-two trends as well as differences in pretest-two to posttest trends between the treatment and comparison group.

Even when using multiple pretests confirms a selection-maturation interaction through differential pretest trends, it may be that the pretreatment difference in trends does not explain completely the observed posttest difference between treatment and comparison groups. If the trend in the comparison group remains consistent over time, then the treatment estimate may be parameterized as the difference between treatment and comparison groups in pretest–posttest trends above and beyond the difference in trends that existed before the introduction of the treatment. This situation is far less desirable than having confirmed similar pretest trends, but it does help to remove at least some of the bias attributable to a selection-maturation interaction. More specifically, for selection-maturation to persist as a threat to validity, it must take the form of a three-way interaction between selection, maturation, and time. That is, the difference in maturation rates would need to be changing over time to explain away a treatment effect manifested as differences in changes in trends between the treatment and comparison groups.

Cohort Comparisons

Another design enhancement that can improve the internal validity of the nonequivalent comparison group design involves the use of one or more untreated cohorts as a comparison group. This is often possible when treatments are delivered to eligible persons on the basis of age (e.g., education interventions, health interventions, interventions related to age-based policies such as drinking or voting). The basic idea is that when an intervention is implemented or discontinued, adjacent cohorts differ in their access to the intervention—one cohort gets access whereas the prior cohort did not or vice versa.

There are multiple advantages to the cohort comparison approach. First, the treatment and comparison cohorts may be more likely to be similar on measured and unmeasured covariates. Second, the cohort comparison group design does not prevent the delivery of the treatment to any eligible participant (i.e., the treatment can be delivered to everybody). Third, when the treatment is not delivered to everyone but delivery is restricted to only those in certain cohorts (e.g., subjects in eligible cohorts self-select into the treatment), then cohort membership may be useful as an instrumental variable. Assuming the cohorts are similar on measured and unmeasured covariates, the subjects can be thought of as randomly assigned to cohorts (i.e., the instrument is uncorrelated with covariates), but cohort membership is highly correlated with participation in the treatment because only certain cohorts get access to the treatment (i.e., cohort membership is a strong instrument). In this case, using cohort membership as an instrument for the effect of the treatment has a good chance of producing a valid causal impact estimate.

In our hypothetical study of antidepressants, we could imagine a cohort comparison in a state that is about to enact new legislation allowing psychologists to prescribe antidepressants and other psychotropic medications. By comparing the outcomes of patients from cohorts receiving treatment just before and after enactment of this legislation, we can estimate an unbiased treatment effect as the differences in posttest depression scores so long as the patients in these two cohorts are comparable in all other respects. One clear example of how this assumption might be violated is if the enactment of the legislation coincided with an economic downturn or recovery. In that case, it would be impossible to distinguish the effects of the policy from the effects of changes in the economic situation.

Causal Modeling, Moderation, and Mediation Analyses

Cochran and Chambers (1965) reflected on advice given by Sir Ronald Fisher regarding causal inference in observational studies, "make your theories elaborate" (p. 252). By this, Fisher meant that one should conceptualize and design a study in such a way that the hypothesized effects of an intervention could be tested on multiple outcomes and under multiple scenarios to establish consistent trends in results that support (or disconfirm) the theory of action behind an intervention. The logic of this perspective is evident in the literature on causal path modeling (Asher, 1983; Pearl, 2009) and mediation and moderation analyses (Baron & Kenny, 1986). In causal path modeling of data from a nonequivalent comparison group design, a series of structural equations are used to estimate simultaneous relationships between treatment conditions and characteristics (e.g., dosage), covariates, intermediate outcomes, and final outcomes. The intent of this approach is to establish evidence of a causal chain that begins with the treatment. In our hypothetical study of antidepressants, we might include multiple outcomes in addition to posttreatment depression scores that are related to depression, such as motivation, concentration, sleep patterns (e.g., insomnia, hypersomnia), libido, appetite, and suicidal thoughts or actions. By exploring the relationships between antidepressant treatment and changes in these outcomes, we may better

understand the mechanisms by which the drugs achieve their effects, if there are any.

Similarly, mediation and moderation analyses also use structural models to examine effects of interventions. One intent is to identify mediator variables, which are essentially intermediate outcomes on the causal pathway between the intervention and the outcome. In a mediation analysis, one is able to explore the degree to which the effect of an intervention on an outcome may follow directly from the effect of the intervention on one or more intermediate outcomes. A second intent is to identify moderator variables, which interact with the treatment to produce differential effects depending on the level of the moderator variable. For example, one might use moderation analysis to identify those factors that support or impede the impacts of an intervention. In the case of our antidepressant study, moderation analysis can be used to test for different levels of effectiveness of the drugs across subgroups of patients.

Although a well-designed path analysis or structural model for mediation or moderation may substantiate a theory of action behind an intervention, the model alone does little to address threats to internal validity. This is because these models typically operate in ways similar to that of simple ANCOVA or change score analyses. Thus, the same issues and threats to validity persist. The common practice of trying to "control for" many covariates in a multiple regression or a path model can even lead to exacerbated bias if confounders, mediators, and moderators are not properly identified and modeled appropriately (Pearl, 2009; Cinelli et al., 2020). Therefore, when causal path analysis and mediation or moderation analyses are used, it can be advantageous to combine them with other techniques for addressing overt or hidden bias, such as propensity score matching and instrumental variables analysis.

Sensitivity Analysis

In a nonequivalent comparison group design, regardless of the steps taken to address threats to validity, there is always the possibility of an unmeasured confound that might explain any treatment effect. Even though the existence of potential unmeasured confounds cannot be debated, it is important to recognize that all confounds are not equal. Although every confound, if controlled, might change the results of an impact analysis in a nonequivalent groups study, minor confounds would change the results only slightly, whereas major confounds can change results in dramatic ways. Rosenbaum (2002, 2010) advocated that sensitivity analyses be conducted in any observational study to determine the magnitude of uncontrolled selection bias that would need to exist to substantially reduce or render insignificant the estimate of impact.

The logic of such a sensitivity analysis begins with the notion that comparisons in a properly designed nonequivalent groups design have been appropriately matched, blocked, or modeled so that the treatment effect estimate is based on comparisons of subjects who have equal propensity scores. Under this assumption, it is helpful to think of the magnitude of selection bias in terms of the relative difference in propensity scores if the *matched* subjects did not in fact have equal probabilities of assignment to treatment. For example, two subjects with estimated propensity scores of .70 may actually have true propensity scores of .90 and .60, with the failure of the propensity score model to capture this difference because a key covariate was unobserved. In this situation, the actual propensity scores of .90 and .60, when converted to an odds ratio (i.e., $[.90/(1 - .90)]/[.60/(1 - .60)] = 6$), suggest that one subject is actually 6 times more likely to have experienced the treatment than their matched counterpart. This is a large potential bias.

A sensitivity analysis for a nonequivalent groups design reveals the magnitude of hidden bias (i.e., the odds ratio of propensity scores) required to reduce or eliminate the estimated effect of the treatment. If a sensitivity analysis yielded a figure of 6 as in the example, then one would conclude that to dismiss the estimate of treatment effect as being caused by selection bias, one or more unmeasured confounds would need to exist that would make the subjects in the treatment group at least 6 times more likely to experience the treatment than those in the comparison group. Given that odds ratios of 6 are quite uncommon in social science research, it is reasonable to conclude that the unobserved selection bias would need to be gigantic in order to dismiss the estimated treatment effect. The calculations behind sensitivity analyses are detailed in Rosenbaum (2002, Chapter 4); however, these calculations are applicable only to nonparametric analyses (i.e., McNemar's test, Wilcoxon's signed rank test, Hodges-Lehmann point estimate). While Rosenbaum's (2002) sensitivity analysis is the most popular, numerous other approaches for addressing bias caused by unobserved confounding may perform better and rely on fewer assumptions (Rudolph & Stuart, 2018).

In our hypothetical study of antidepressants, it is reasonable to expect that the best predictor of prescription of antidepressants is the pretreatment severity of depression. Imagine then that the odds ratio for a one–standard deviation increase in depression severity is 3, suggesting that the likelihood of receiving an antidepressant triples with each standard deviation increase in pretreatment depression severity. Following that, if a sensitivity analysis revealed that an unmeasured confound would need to produce differences in propensity scores analogous to an odds ratio of 6, then that confound would need to have a predictive effect on the receipt of an antidepressant that was twice as large as the pretreatment severity of depression. Such a confound is unlikely to exist, thus bolstering the confidence with which results from this nonequivalent comparison group design can be interpreted.

CONCLUSION

Light et al. (1990) claimed, "You can't fix by analysis what you bungled by design" (p. v). Although that statement is generally true regarding nonequivalent comparison group designs, there are clearly a number of rather powerful tools that can enhance the validity of inferences from this design. Through explicit controls for measured confounds, enhancements to address validity threats, instrumental variables to remove hidden bias, and elaborate theories to test hypotheses, there is the potential for nonexperimental designs to provide useful information about the effects of interventions. In some cases, the accuracy of that information may rival that from a randomized experiment. Yet, even when the potential for selection bias persists, we can use sensitivity analysis to evaluate the robustness of the findings against likely or hypothetical confounding factors.

The recommendations that follow from this discussion of methods are similar to those proposed by Rubin (2004). First, a researcher should implement as many design enhancements as possible to address probable threats to valid inference. Second, the researcher should collect both pre- and posttreatment data on as many relevant covariates, treatment indicators, intermediate outcomes, and final outcomes as feasible. Third, the researcher should use propensity score methods, matching, or blocking to account for major differences between treatment and comparison groups and remove most observable selection bias. Fourth, the researcher should use covariance analysis, regression modeling, and instrumental variables analysis (when feasible) to increase precision and provide additional control of observed and perhaps unobserved covariates not yet completely balanced. Last, the researcher should conduct sensitivity analyses to determine the extent to which unmeasured confounds may create selection biases large enough to substantially alter the impact estimates.

Although nonequivalent comparison group studies are quite susceptible to bias, the ability to extract useful information is especially important because many interventions are not amenable to study through an experimental design or a well-controlled quasi-experiment. In these cases, we are often forced to simply compare those who received the treatment with those who did not. Thankfully, we have several methods at our disposal that can help avoid apples to oranges comparisons and perhaps even turn lemons into lemonade.

References

Alam, S., Moodie, E. E. M., & Stephens, D. A. (2019). Should a propensity score model be super? The utility of ensemble procedures for causal adjustment. *Statistics in Medicine, 38*(9), 1690–1702. https://doi.org/10.1002/sim.8075

Angrist, J., & Krueger, A. B. (2001). Instrumental variables and the search for identification: From supply and demand to natural experiments. *The Journal of Economic Perspectives, 15*(4), 69–85. https://doi.org/10.1257/jep.15.4.69

Angrist, J., & Pischke, S. (2009). *Mostly harmless econometrics: An empiricists' companion.* Princeton University Press. https://doi.org/10.1515/9781400829828

Angrist, J. D., Imbens, G. W., & Rubin, D. B. (1996). Identification of causal effects using instrumental variables. *Journal of the American Statistical Association, 91*(434), 444–455. https://doi.org/10.1080/01621459.1996.10476902

Asher, H. (1983). *Causal modeling.* SAGE. https://doi.org/10.4135/9781412983600

Baron, R. M., & Kenny, D. A. (1986). The moderator-mediator variable distinction in social psychological research: Conceptual, strategic, and statistical considerations. *Journal of Personality and Social Psychology, 51*(6), 1173–1182. https://doi.org/10.1037/0022-3514.51.6.1173

Boruch, R. F., May, H., Turner, H. M., Lavenberg, J., Petrosino, A., De Moya, D., Grimshaw, J., & Foley, E. (2004). Estimating the effects of interventions that are deployed in many places: Place randomized trials. *American Behavioral Scientist, 47*(5), 608–633. https://doi.org/10.1177/0002764203259291

Bound, J., Jaeger, D. A., & Baker, R. M. (1995). Problems with instrumental variables estimation when the correlation between the instruments and the endogenous explanatory variables is weak. *Journal of the American Statistical Association, 90*(430), 443–450. https://doi.org/10.1080/01621459.1995.10476536

Buse, A. (1992). The bias of instrumental variable estimators. *Econometrica, 60*(1), 173–180. https://doi.org/10.2307/2951682

Campbell, D. T., & Stanley, J. C. (1963). *Experimental and quasi-experimental designs for research.* Houghton Mifflin.

Cinelli, C., Forney, A., & Pearl, J. (2020, September 9). *A crash course in good and bad controls.* https://doi.org/10.2139/ssrn.3689437

Cochran, W. G. (1968). The effectiveness of adjustment by subclassification in removing bias in observational studies. *Biometrics, 24*(2), 295–313. https://doi.org/10.2307/2528036

Cochran, W. G., & Chambers, S. P. (1965). The planning of observational studies of human populations (with discussion). *Journal of the Royal Statistical Society. Series A (General), 128*(2), 234–266. https://doi.org/10.2307/2344179

Cochran, W. G., & Rubin, D. B. (1973). Controlling bias in observational studies: A review. *Sankhya Series A, 35*, 417–446.

Collier, Z. K., & Leite, W. L. (2021). A tutorial on artificial neural networks in propensity score analysis. *Journal of Experimental Education.* Advance online publication. https://doi.org/10.1080/00220973.2020.1854158

Collier, Z. K., Leite, W. L., & Karpyn, A. (2021). Neural networks to estimate generalized propensity scores for continuous treatment doses. *Evaluation Review, 0*(0). https://doi.org/10.1177/0193841X21992199

Cook, T. D., & Campbell, D. T. (1979). *Quasi-experimentation: Design and analysis issues for field settings.* Rand McNally.

Greene, W. H. (1993). *Econometric analysis* (2nd ed.). Macmillan.

Gu, X. S., & Rosenbaum, P. R. (1993). Comparison of multivariate matching methods: Structures, distances, and algorithms. *Journal of Computational and Graphical Statistics, 2*(4), 405–420. https://doi.org/10.1080/10618600.1993.10474623

Hand, D. J. (1994). Deconstructing statistical questions. *Journal of the Royal Statistical Society: A, 157*, 317–356. https://doi.org/10.2307/2983526

Holland, P. W. (1986). Statistics and causal inference. *Journal of the American Statistical Association, 81*(396), 945–960. https://doi.org/10.1080/01621459.1986.10478354

Holland, P. W., & Rubin, D. B. (1983). On Lord's paradox. In H. Wainer & S. Messick (Eds.), *Principles of modern psychological measurement* (pp. 3–35). Erlbaum.

Ju, C., Schwab, J., & van der Laan, M. J. (2019). On adaptive propensity score truncation in causal inference. *Statistical Methods in Medical Research, 28*(6), 1741–1760. https://doi.org/10.1177/0962280218774817

Light, R. J., Singer, J. D., & Willett, J. B. (1990). *By design: Planning research on higher education.* Harvard University Press. https://doi.org/10.4159/9780674040267

Lord, F. M. (1967). A paradox in the interpretation of group comparisons. *Psychological Bulletin, 68*(5), 304–305. https://doi.org/10.1037/h0025105

Maris, E. (1998). Covariance adjustment versus gain scores—Revisited. *Psychological Methods, 3*(3), 309–327. https://doi.org/10.1037/1082-989X.3.3.309

McCaffrey, D. F., Ridgeway, G., & Morral, A. R. (2004). Propensity score estimation with boosted regression for evaluating causal effects in observational studies. *Psychological Methods, 9*(4), 403–425. https://doi.org/10.1037/1082-989X.9.4.403

Neter, J., Kutner, M. H., Nachtsheim, C. J., & Wasserman, W. (1996). *Applied linear statistical models* (4th ed.). McGraw-Hill.

Pearl, J. (2009). *Causality: Models, reasoning, and inference* (2nd ed.). Cambridge University Press. https://doi.org/10.1017/CBO9780511803161

Porter, A. C. (1967). *The effects of using fallible variables in the analysis of covariance* [Unpublished doctoral dissertation]. University of Wisconsin, Madison.

Porter, A. C., & Chibucos, T. R. (1974). Selecting analysis strategies. In G. Borich (Ed.), *Evaluating educational programs and products* (pp. 415–464). Educational Technology Press.

Reichardt, C. S. (1979). The statistical analysis of data from nonequivalent group designs. In T. D. Cook & D. T. Campbell (Eds.), *Quasi-experimentation: Design and analysis issues for field settings* (pp. 147–205). Rand McNally.

Reichardt, C. S. (2019). *Quasi-experimentation: A guide to design and analysis.* Guilford Press.

Rosenbaum, P., & Rubin, D. B. (1983). The central role of the propensity score in observational studies for causal effects. *Biometrika, 70*(1), 41–55. https://doi.org/10.1093/biomet/70.1.41

Rosenbaum, P. R. (2002). *Observational studies.* Springer-Verlag. https://doi.org/10.1007/978-1-4757-3692-2

Rosenbaum, P. R. (2010). *Design of observational studies.* Springer-Verlag. https://doi.org/10.1007/978-1-4419-1213-8

Rosenbaum, P. R. (2020). Modern algorithms for matching in observational studies. *Annual Review of Statistics and Its Application, 7*(1), 143–176. https://doi.org/10.1146/annurev-statistics-031219-041058

Rosenbaum, P. R., & Rubin, D. B. (1984). Reducing bias in observational studies using subclassification on the propensity score. *Journal of the American Statistical Association, 79*(387), 516–524. https://doi.org/10.1080/01621459.1984.10478078

Rubin, D. B. (1974). Estimating causal effects of treatments in randomized and non-randomized studies. *Journal of Educational Psychology, 66*(5), 688–701. https://doi.org/10.1037/h0037350

Rubin, D. B. (1997). Estimating causal effects from large data sets using propensity scores. *Annals of Internal Medicine, 127*(8 Pt. 2), 757–763. https://doi.org/10.7326/0003-4819-127-8_Part_2-199710151-00064

Rubin, D. B. (2004). Teaching statistical inference for causal effects in experiments and observational studies. *Journal of Educational and Behavioral Statistics, 29*, 103–116. https://doi.org/10.3102/10769986029001103

Rubin, D. B. (2010). Propensity score methods. *American Journal of Ophthalmology, 149*(1), 7–9. https://doi.org/10.1016/j.ajo.2009.08.024

Rubin, D. B., & Thomas, N. (1996). Matching using estimated propensity scores: Relating theory to practice. *Biometrics, 52*(1), 249–264. https://doi.org/10.2307/2533160

Rudolph, K. E., & Stuart, E. A. (2018). Using sensitivity analyses for unobserved confounding to address covariate measurement error in propensity score methods. *American Journal of Epidemiology, 187*(3), 604–613. https://doi.org/10.1093/aje/kwx248

Shadish, W. R., Cook, T. D., & Campbell, D. T. (2002). *Experimental and quasi-experimental designs for generalized causal inference*. Houghton Mifflin.

Staiger, D., & Stock, J. H. (1997). Instrumental variables regression with weak instruments. *Econometrica, 65*(3), 557–586. https://doi.org/10.2307/2171753

Uddin, M. J., Groenwold, R. H., Ali, M. S., de Boer, A., Roes, K. C., Chowdhury, M. A., & Klungel, O. H. (2016). Methods to control for unmeasured confounding in pharmacoepidemiology: An overview. *International Journal of Clinical Pharmacy, 38*(3), 714–723. https://doi.org/10.1007/s11096-016-0299-0

Wainer, H. (1991). Adjusting for differential base rates: Lord's Paradox again. *Psychological Bulletin, 109*(1), 147–151. https://doi.org/10.1037/0033-2909.109.1.147

West, S. G., & Thoemmes, F. (2010). Campbell's and Rubin's perspectives on causal inference. *Psychological Methods, 15*(1), 18–37. https://doi.org/10.1037/a0015917

Wildt, A. R., & Ahtola, O. T. (1978). *Analysis of covariance*. SAGE. https://doi.org/10.4135/9781412983297

Wright, D. B. (2006). Comparing groups in a before-after design: When *t* test and ANCOVA produce different results. *The British Journal of Educational Psychology, 76*(3), 663–675. https://doi.org/10.1348/000709905X52210

CHAPTER 29

REGRESSION DISCONTINUITY DESIGNS

Charles S. Reichardt and Gary T. Henry

Regression discontinuity (RD) designs are quasi-experiments and, like all quasi-experiments, are used to estimate the effects of treatments, programs, or interventions. Regression discontinuity designs are generally considered the most rigorous of the quasi-experimental designs, capable of producing unbiased estimates of treatment effects under reasonable assumptions. While it appears these designs are underutilized in psychology, the strengths of regression discontinuity designs are becoming widely known in the social sciences, especially in economics. This chapter explicates the logic of RD designs, methods for analyzing data from RD designs, potential sources of bias, and ways to assess and cope with the biases. The chapter also describes strengths and weaknesses of RD designs compared to other designs.

THE LOGIC OF THE REGRESSION DISCONTINUITY DESIGN

The prototypical RD design compares the effects of two treatment conditions which could consist of a novel intervention and a standard treatment. Or one of the treatments could consist of a control condition where no treatment is provided. For simplicity, we shall refer to one of the treatments as the *experimental condition* and the other treatment as the *comparison condition*. The units

assigned to the different treatments will be called *participants*.

The distinguishing feature of an RD design is that assignment to treatment conditions is determined by a specified cutoff score on a measured variable, called the quantitative assignment variable (QAV or, in some disciplines, the forcing variable), on which each participant has been assessed. Those participants with a QAV score on one side of a cutoff are assigned to the experimental treatment while participants with a QAV score on the other side of the cutoff score are assigned to the comparison condition. Following the assignment of participants to conditions, the two treatment conditions are implemented and, after the treatments have had a chance for their effects to be observable, the participants in both groups are assessed on an outcome variable. The effects of the treatments are then assessed by regressing the outcome scores onto the QAV, separately in each of the treatment groups. A treatment effect is evidenced by a discontinuity in the two regression lines at the cutoff score, hence the name of the design.

The intuition behind the RD design is that the outcomes of the participants near the cutoff in the experimental treatment and those near but on the other side of the cutoff are expected to differ significantly only due to the exposure to different treatments. Another way to understand the logic of the RD design is pictorially. Figure 29.1 presents

https://doi.org/10.1037/0000319-029
APA Handbook of Research Methods in Psychology, Second Edition: Vol. 2. Research Designs: Quantitative, Qualitative, Neuropsychological, and Biological, H. Cooper (Editor-in-Chief)

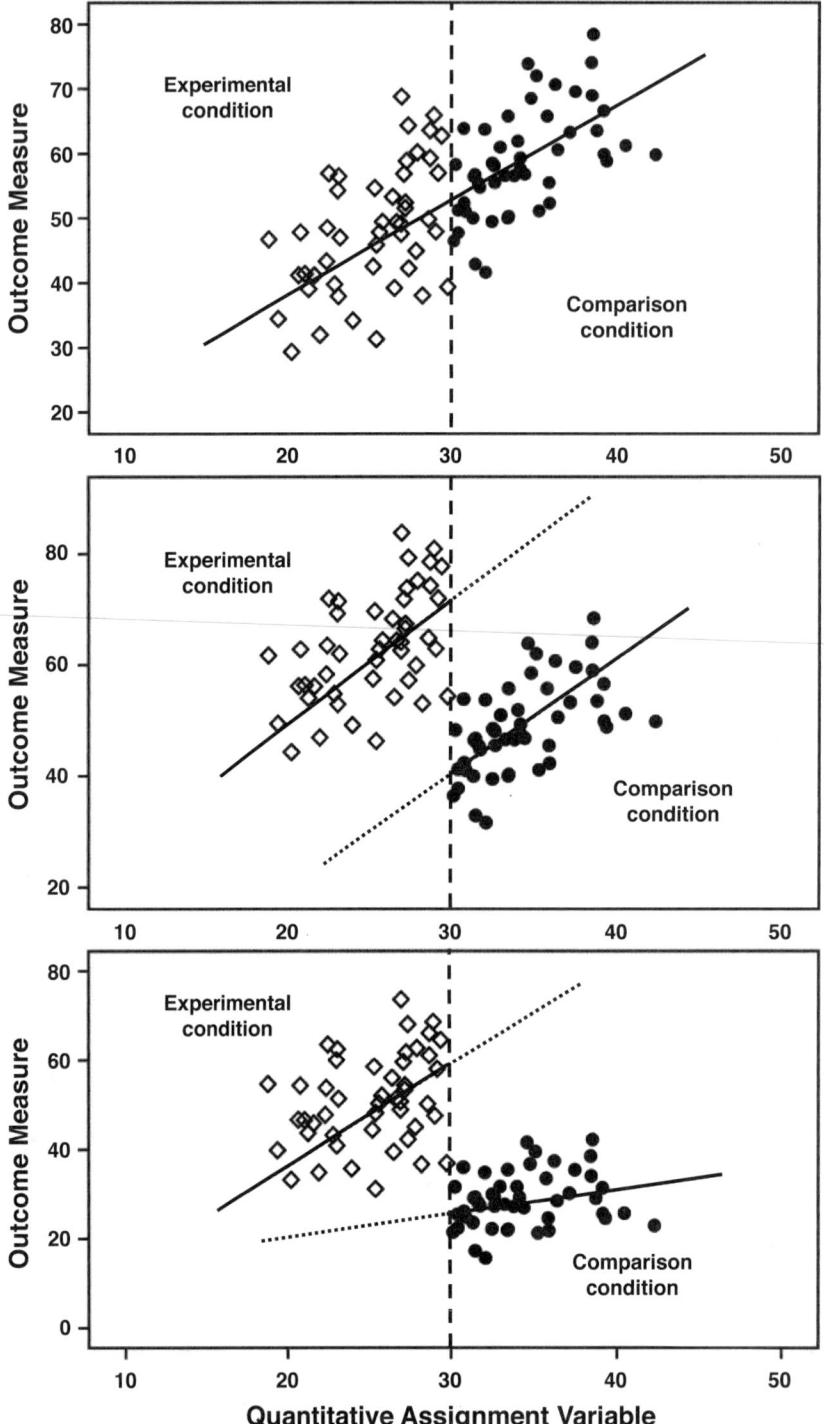

FIGURE 29.1. Hypothetical data showing potential effects of treatments in the regression discontinuity design.

three potential outcomes of an RD design. Each panel of the figures displays scatterplots of the scores of the participants in the treatment and comparison conditions. In each panel, scores on the QAV are plotted along the horizontal axis while scores on the outcome variable are plotted along the vertical axis. The cutoff score falls at the value of 30 on the QAV as represented in the figures by a vertical line at the score of 30 on the horizontal axis. Participants with a score on the QAV below 30 were assigned to the experimental condition and their scores in the figures are denoted by diamonds. Participants with a QAV score above 30 were assigned to the comparison condition and their scores in the figures are denoted by circles. The sloped lines in the figures are the regression lines that pass through the scatter of the data points in the two conditions.

In the top panel in Figure 29.1, the experimental treatment is assessed to have no effect compared to the comparison treatment because the regressions in the two conditions fall on the same line. Absence of a discontinuity between the regression lines at the cutoff—or for this case, identical regression lines—indicates the lack of a treatment effect. In the middle panel in Figure 29.1, the experimental treatment has a positive effect compared to the comparison treatment because the regression line in the experimental group is displaced upwardly (positively) compared to the regression line in the comparison group. In other words, the presence of a break or discontinuity between the regression lines in the experimental and comparison conditions at the cutoff score reveals the presence of a treatment effect. Alternatively, it is possible for the experimental treatment to have a negative effect compared with the comparison condition wherein the regression line in the experimental condition would be shifted downward compared with the regression line in the comparison condition. Because the regression lines in the two conditions are parallel, the treatment also appears to have the same effect for participants with scores at all values along the QAV, as indicted by the extension of the dotted regression lines on each side of the cutoff score.

The bottom panel in Figure 29.1 depicts yet another potential outcome of an RD design. As in the middle panel, the regression line in the experimental group in the bottom panel is displaced vertically at the cutoff score compared with the regression line in the comparison group, which reveals that the experimental condition has a positive effect compared to the comparison condition at the cutoff score. But unlike in the middle panel, the regression lines in the two groups in the bottom panel are not parallel, which suggests the experimental treatment has a different effect for participants with different QAV scores. That is, the degree of vertical displacement between the two regression lines in the bottom panel depends on the score on the QAV. Were the regression lines from each condition to be extrapolated to the opposite side of the cutoff score (as shown by the dotted lines for each group), the vertical discrepancy between the regression line from the experimental group and the regression line from the comparison group would be larger for participants with higher QAV scores. This means an interaction between the treatment and the QAV is present. A discontinuity or break in the regression lines at the cutoff point, as illustrated in both the middle and bottom panels in Figure 29.1, is called an effect due to a change in level while nonparallel regression lines, as illustrated in the bottom panel, is called an effect due to a change in slope.

The Quantitative Assignment Variables (QAV)

Any quantitative measure can be used as the quantitative assignment variables (QAV) in an RD design, though the What Works Clearinghouse (WWC, 2020) requires a minimum of four unique values with actual observations in the data on each side of the cutoff (and more than four is usually much to be preferred). If the experimental treatment is intended to address a problem or deficit, the QAV could be a measure of the participants' need for the ameliorative intervention or their risk of negative outcomes in the absence of such an intervention, with the treatment given to those who reveal the greatest need or risk on the QAV (e.g., Henry & Harbatkin, 2020).

Alternatively, the experimental treatment could be a reward (such as a scholarship), the QAV could be a measure of merit, and the treatment could be given to those who exhibit the greatest merit on the QAV (e.g., Leeds & DesJardins, 2015).

In addition to measures of need, risk, or merit, other types of QAVs could be used to determine eligibility for a treatment in an RD design. For example, a treatment allocated on the basis of first come, first served could be assessed in an RD design using either time of arrival or time of application for the treatment as the QAV (e.g., Pinotti, 2017). If different treatments are made available to people residing in different geographical regions that have sharp boundaries, the physical distance from the boundary could be used as the QAV in an RD design (e.g., Black, 1999). Or consider Lipsey et al. (2015), who estimated the effects of the first year of school using age as the QAV and the minimum age required to enroll a child in school as the cutoff score.

The QAV could be derived from subjective judgments as long as such judgments are given numerical values so participants can be ordered, a cutoff value specified, and (for WWC approval) at least four unique values occur with actual observations on each side of the cutoff. If desired, the QAV could also be a composite of several separate measures where each measure is differentially weighted. For example, Henry et al. (2010) created an RD design where the lowest-scoring school districts were assigned to treatments using an index of educational advantage composed of four separate variables: teacher stability, teacher experience, children not living in poverty, and students meeting state proficiency standards. All that is required is that the separate measurements be combined quantitatively into a single index, which is used as the QAV. Also note that neither the QAV nor any of the separate measures used in its composition need be free of measurement error. The primary requirement is that the QAV, however fallibly measured, be used to assign participants to treatment conditions according to a cutoff value on that fallible measure (Cappelleri et al., 1991; Reichardt et al., 1995; Trochim et al., 1991).

Statistical precision and power increase as the correlation between QAV and the outcome measure increases in absolute value. Using a QAV that is operationally identical to the outcome measure, measured prior to the assignment to treatment, is often advantageous because it maximizes the correlation between the two. An example of operationally identical measures would be a pretest measure of cognitive ability being used to assign students to a remedial educational program and a posttest measure of the same test being used as the outcome assessment. But the logic of the RD design holds regardless of the correlation between the QAV and the outcome measure.

The Problem of Nonlinearities

The relationship between the QAV and the outcome must be modeled correctly to obtain an unbiased estimate of the treatment effect. In Figure 29.1, the regression surfaces in each of the treatment conditions are linear. However, the regression surfaces might be nonlinear rather than straight lines. Figure 29.2 illustrates how fitting straight lines in the presence of curvilinearity could bias the estimate of the treatment effect. To make the illustration as simple as possible, the scatter in the data has been removed, so the data points all fall directly on top of the regression lines. As Figure 29.2 shows, the regression surface is curvilinear with no discontinuity at the cutoff score of 40 on the QAV. A model that fits the proper curvilinear regression surfaces would correctly estimate the treatment effect to be zero because there is no discontinuity between the two curvilinear regression surfaces. But if straight lines were fit to the data, as shown in Figure 29.2, a discontinuity at the cutoff would be found along with a treatment effect interaction. In other words, an improper analysis that fit straight, rather than curved, regression lines would produce both a discontinuity and a treatment effect interaction, when in fact neither effect is present.

Curvilinearity can arise because the true underlying relationship between two constructs is nonlinear or because anomalies of the measurement process introduce twists and turns into an observed relationship. For example, measurement

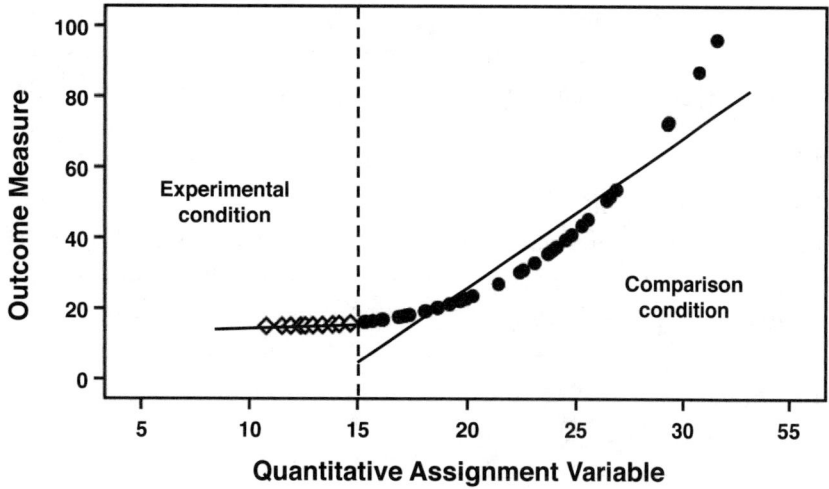

FIGURE 29.2.   Bias resulting from fitting straight lines to a curvilinear relationship.

nonlinearities due to floor and ceiling effects can make an otherwise linear relationship curvilinear.

Creating a scatterplot showing the relationship between the QAV and outcome scores can help in modeling nonlinearities properly. Plot the data before statistical analyses are conducted to diagnose the nature of any nonlinearity that exists, and plot the residuals after analyses have been conducted to see if the models have properly fit the nonlinearity that was present. Including both straight and best-fitting lines in the plots can help point out departures from linearity. Best-fitting lines can be plotted using locally weighted (loess) regression, which uses proximate subsets of the data to plot the best-fitting regression line for each point along the QAV. Alternatively, other forms of smoothing, such as mean or median smoothing, can be used to view the relationship between the QAV and outcome variable (see Jacob et al., 2012; and Lee & Lemieux, 2010, for other smoothing options). Note that outliers in the plots can be particularly worrisome because of their influential effects on regression fits.

Global Regression Analysis

Two approaches to statistical analysis are frequently used to analyze data and estimate treatment effects in an RD design: global regression and local regression. The difference between the two approaches is that the global analysis uses all the available data while the local analysis uses only a subset of the data. The analysis of covariance (ANCOVA) model (which is a special case of multiple regression) is the classic method for analyzing data from an RD design in both the global and local approaches. Nonparametric approaches such as kernel regression, spline regression, and generalized additive models are also possible, but are beyond the scope of this chapter. The present section describes the global analysis. A subsequent section introduces the local analysis.

Change in level.   The simplest ANCOVA model for the analysis of data from an RD design is

$$Y = a + B_t T + B_x (X - X') + E. \qquad (29.1)$$

The model contains three observed variables: Y, T, and X. The Y variable is the participants' scores on the outcome measure, T is an indicator variable representing assignment either to the treatment condition ($T = 1$) or to the comparison condition ($T = 0$), X is the participants' scores on the QAV, and X' is the value of the cutoff score on the QAV. In the top and middle panels in Figure 29.1, the cutoff score is 30, so X' equals 30. The notation $(X - X')$ means that the value of X' is subtracted from all the QAV scores before these scores are entered into the model as an independent variable. The model could be fit using either an ANCOVA option in a statistical package or a multiple regression option where Y is regressed onto T and $X - X'$.

The model in Equation 29.1 specifies that the regression of Y onto $X - X'$ (which represents the QAV scores) is a straight line that has the same slope in the two treatment groups. According to the model, the effect of the experimental treatment does nothing more than displace the regression line in the experimental group upward or downward compared to the regression line in the comparison group. This means the treatment effect is constant across the QAV. The value of B_t is the size of the vertical displacement of the regression line in the experimental group compared to the comparison condition at the cutoff, X'. Because assignment to the experimental treatment is based on the values of the QAV (X), the assignment to treatment is perfectly modeled in the equation and, if the assumptions hold, B_t is an unbiased estimate of the effect of the experimental treatment. The value of B_x is the slope of the two parallel regression lines. This model would well fit the data in the top and middle panels in Figure 29.1, where the regression surfaces in the two groups are straight and parallel lines, and the treatment has either no effect or a constant effect across the values of the QAV. Note that the value of the "a" parameter in Equation 29.1 is the intercept of the regression slope in the comparison condition and is usually of little interest in the analysis. The "E" variable in the model is the disturbance or error term, and represents all factors not included in the regression that influence each participant's score on Y and allows the individual data points, such as in Figure 29.1, to scatter around the regression lines.

Treatment effect interactions. A slightly more complex model is required to fit the data in the bottom panel in Figure 29.1 and should be tested in any RD study, since the true nature of the relationship between the QAV and outcome is unknown. This model allows for the treatment effect to alter both the level and the slope of the regression line in the experimental group compared with the regression line in the comparison group. The more complex model is

$$Y = a + B_t T + B_x(X - X') + B_{tx} T(X - X') + E. \quad (29.2)$$

The notation $T(X - X')$ means a variable is created that is the product of the indicator variable T and the $(X - X')$ variable. In this model, the value of B_t is the size of the vertical displacement of the regression lines at the cutoff score. Note that if the regression lines are not parallel, as in bottom panel in Figure 29.1, the size of the vertical displacement between the two regression lines depends on where the displacement is measured along the QAV. By including the QAV scores scaled as $(X - X')$ in Equation 29.2, the model estimates the vertical displacement at the cutoff score on the QAV. If the value of X' is not subtracted from the value of X, the vertical displacement between the regression lines will be estimated at the point where the QAV equals 0, which is likely to be uninformative or even misleading. To estimate the vertical displacement at a different value along the QAV, such as at QAV equal to X'', create the new variable $X - X''$ and enter that variable in place of $X - X'$ in the two places it appears in Equation 29.2.

The value of B_x in Equation 29.2 is the slope of the regression line in the comparison group. The value of B_{tx} is the difference between the slopes in the experimental and comparison groups, which represents the effect of a treatment interaction. A positive value of B_{tx} means the slope in the experimental group is steeper than in the comparison condition.

In the presence of a treatment effect interaction, methodologists often suggest placing more emphasis on the estimate of the vertical displacement at the cutoff score on the QAV than on the estimate of the vertical displacement at any other point along the QAV (West et al., 2014; see also Wing & Bello-Gomez, 2018). This is because estimating the vertical displacement at the cutoff score requires minimal extrapolation of the regression lines in the two groups. To estimate the vertical displacement of the regression lines at any other point along the QAV would require extrapolation of the regression line from one of the treatment groups into a region where there is no data from that group. For example, to estimate the vertical displacement for a value of the QAV less than X' in the bottom panel in Figure 29.1, the regression line for the comparison group would have to be extrapolated to the left of the cutoff point, where no data from the comparison group exists. Estimates of treatment effects based on such extrapolations tend to be both less powerful and less credible than estimates of effects at the cutoff score.

Adding polynomial terms. If the regression surfaces in the two treatment groups are curvilinear (as in Figure 29.2), that curvilinearity should be taken into account in the statistical model to avoid bias in the estimates of a treatment effect. The most common approach is to model curvilinearity by adding polynomial terms to the ANCOVA equation. For example, the following model adds a quadratic term:

$$Y = a + B_t T + B_x (X - X') + B_{tx} T (X - X')$$
$$+ B_{x2} (X - X')^2 + E. \qquad (29.3)$$

Equation 29.3 is the same as Equation 29.2, except the quadratic term $B_{x2}(X - X')^2$ has been added. This term allows the regression surfaces in the two groups to take on a quadratic curvature. Equation 29.4 adds an interaction term to allow the quadratic curvature in the regression surfaces to differ across the treatment groups, which would be evidence of a treatment effect interaction:

$$Y = a + B_t T + B_x (X - X') + B_{tx} T (X - X')$$
$$+ B_{x2} (X - X')^2 + B_{tx2} T (X - X')^2 + E. \quad (29.4)$$

Higher order polynomial terms with or without interaction terms could be added as well. For example, both a cubic term $B_{x3}(X - X')^3$ and a cubic interaction term $B_{tx3}T(X - X')^3$ could be added to allow the regression surface to take on a cubic curvature and to allow for a treatment effect interaction in the shape of the cubic curvature. Note that all polynomial terms are entered with the QAV variable scaled as $(X - X')$. Norming the

X variable in this fashion means any change in level due to the treatment effect is estimated at the cutoff score. To estimate the change in level at an alternative location along the QAV variable (say at X'' rather than X'), the value of X' should be replaced everywhere by X''.

In theory, any curvilinear shape can be fit perfectly if enough polynomial terms are added to the model. In practice, however, there are limits to the number of polynomial terms that can reasonably be added because of limits imposed by sample size, multicollinearity, and instability. Adding polynomial terms can increase the power of the statistical analysis to the extent they better fit the true regression surface. But adding polynomial terms also tends to reduce statistical power because of multicollinearity—that is, because the polynomial terms are correlated both among themselves and with the treatment assignment. Expert opinion appears to be changing, with recommendations now appearing against using polynomials beyond quadratic because of the potential overfitting of the regression surface, which can lead to inappropriate estimates of treatment effects (Gelman & Imbens, 2019).

Fitting Models to the Data

The task in performing a global analysis is to decide which interaction and polynomial terms, if any, to add to the model. Our presentation began with the simplest ANCOVA model and built up to more complex models. Such an approach can be used in practice when determining which model to use. In particular, a researcher would start with the simplest model and add interaction and polynomial terms, one at a time, until they are no longer statistically significant, stopping with the last statistically significant term. The reverse process is also recommended by some. With the alternative procedure, the researcher starts with the most complex model that would seem necessary from a visual inspection of the data and then drops terms, one at a time, if they are not statistically significant (Cappelleri & Trochim, 2015).

Yet a third strategy is to rely on indices of model fit (Jacob et al., 2012; Lee & Lemieux, 2010). Indicator variables, which represent intervals of the QAV scores, are added to the model (see the discussion of bins below). Further interaction or polynomial terms are added to the statistical model to the extent these indicator variables account for variation in the data (such as reflected in the R-squared of the model fit).

Underfitting the model by including too few terms can lead to bias, but overfitting by including too many terms can reduce the power of the analysis due to multicollinearity. It is important to use diagnostics such as the variance inflation factor to understand the effects of multicollinearity. Perhaps most importantly, researchers should attend to the size of the treatment effect estimates. The analyst can place most confident in the results if the treatment effect estimates vary little across different models as terms are added or omitted. If the sizes of the treatment effect estimates vary meaningfully as terms are dropped, even if the dropped terms are not statistically significant, it is possible a term is not statistically significant because of low power to detect its importance rather than because the term is not needed to model the data correctly. Examine residuals, and if the residuals reveal lack of adequate fit, add interaction and polynomial terms. The best trade-off, according to some researchers, is to favor overfitting rather than underfitting the model (Cappelleri & Trochim, 2015; Trochim, 1984; Wong et al., 2012).

In the same vein, note how difficult it can be to distinguish between a model that fits a curvilinear relationship and a model that fits straight lines plus a treatment effect interaction. Such a difficulty would arise, for example, with the relatively subtle degree of curvilinearity that exists in Figure 29.2. If the data points in that figure scattered widely around the best fitting line rather than falling directly on top of the line, both a curvilinear model and a linear model with an interaction would account for the data quite well if these two models were fit separately, therefore making it difficult to choose between them. Because of the difficulty of distinguishing between linear interactions and curvilinearity, some methodologists have suggested that an apparent interaction should not be taken as

evidence of a treatment effect unless a discontinuity in level exists at the cutoff score (Campbell, 1984). But such a restriction would not solve the problem of misinterpretation in Figure 29.2, where curvilinearity, if improperly modeled, can masquerade as both a linear treatment interaction and a discontinuity in level. The ambiguity of correctly specifying the relationship between the QAV and an outcome variable has led many researchers to prefer a local regression analysis to fit the data.

Local Regression Analysis

Local regression analysis ignores data from participants who have QAV scores a certain distance or more from the cutoff value (Hahn et al., 2001; Imbens & Lemieux, 2008; Jacob et al., 2012). That is, only data from participants who have QAV scores close to the cutoff (i.e., within a narrow bandwidth on each side of the cutoff score) are included in the analyses. The statistical analysis of the data uses the same ANCOVA models as in the global analysis. The intuition behind the RD design fits well with a local regression approach that includes data only near the cutoff score in the study sample to estimate the relationship between outcome scores and QAV. Within the bandwidth, the relationship is more likely linear than curvilinear so bias due to improperly fitting a model to take account of curvilinearity is minimized. Nonetheless, plots of the data can still be used to assess the quality of model fit and polynomial terms can still be added to the ANCOVA model as needed. Sensitivity checks can also be performed by varying both the number of polynomial terms and the bandwidth to see if the treatment effect estimates remain stable across analyses. For narrower bandwidths, a simple linear ANCOVA model is more likely to fit the data well without need for polynomial terms (Angrist & Pischke, 2009). As the bandwidth widens to include more data, the local regression approach converges on the global approach and makes the assumption of linearity more questionable.

The global and local regression approaches make counterbalancing tradeoffs. Because it uses all the available data, the global approach can increase the statistical power of hypothesis tests and yield a more precise estimate of treatment effects when compared to the local approach. But the global approach is also more susceptible to bias because of misspecification of curvilinearity. In particular, the global approach can be unduly influenced by misspecification of the model far from the cutoff score. To minimize bias, it is most important to fit the data close to the cutoff score. That is what the local approach does. A task with the local approach is to determine the optimal bandwidth or range of the QAV within which the treatment effect is estimated that produces the best tradeoff between precision and bias (Calonico et al., 2014; Imbens & Lemieux, 2008; Jacob et al., 2012; Thoemmes et al., 2017). The optimal bandwidth depends on the sample size. Smaller sample sizes make the optimal bandwidth larger thus trending toward the global approach. Conversely, the larger the sample size (especially with substantial data near the cutoff score) the less the researcher needs to worry about imprecision and can focus on bias reduction by using the local approach.

In any case, uncertainty about which model correctly fits the data will virtually always be present. The best recommendation is to use a variety of plausible models (both global and local) to try to bracket the estimate of the treatment effect within a range of plausible values. The more likely it is that the variety of models include ones with appropriate specifications of the shape of the regression surface, the more confidence the researcher can have that the range of estimates includes the true size of the treatment effect (Imbens & Lemieux, 2008; Lee & Lemieux, 2010; Reichardt & Gollob, 1987; Wong et al., 2012). Some sources, such as the WWC (2020), advocated estimating the effects using three bandwidths such as the optimal bandwidth, half the optimal bandwidth, and twice the optimal bandwidth.

Fuzzy RD Designs

Thus far, we have assumed that research participants assigned to the different treatment conditions have received the treatment conditions as assigned. But that might not be the case because of noncompliance with (or nonadherence to) treatment assignment, which can take either of two forms. Some participants (called no-shows) who are assigned to the treatment condition might not receive the treatment (perhaps because they did not attend treatment sessions). Conversely, some participants who are assigned to the comparison condition might receive the experimental treatment instead. Together, both types of participants are called crossovers. For example, administrators or researchers might respond to pressure to admit participants into a desired treatment when their QAV scores fall just on the opposite side of the cutoff score needed to be assigned to that treatment because those participants are particularly deserving or demanding of the desired treatment. Or participants assigned to the comparison condition might arrange to receive the experimental treatment from a source outside the study. In the presence of a degree of noncompliance, the RD design is called a fuzzy RD design.

To assess the pattern and degree of fuzziness, researchers can calculate the probability of receipt of the experimental treatment across scores on the QAV. Such a calculation is best accomplished by dividing the data into intervals (called bins) according to scores on the QAV. For example, if the QAV runs from 0 to 100 with a cutoff score of 30, scores could be grouped into bins of width 5. In this scenario, participants with scores of 0–4 would be put in one bin, participants with scores of 5–9 would be put in another bin, participants with scores of 10–14 would be put in another bin, and so on. The proportion of participants in each bin who received the treatment would be calculated. If there is no fuzziness, the bin proportions would be equal to 1 on the treatment side of the cutoff score and equal to 0 on the comparison side of the cutoff score. If fuzziness is present, the proportions would deviate from 1 and 0 in some of the bins. The most common pattern of fuzziness is for the proportions to be close to 1 and 0 in bins at the extremes of the QAV scores and deviate more from 1 and 0 in bins near the cutoff score on the QAV (because participants with scores close to the cutoff will most likely feel they should have been assigned to the alternative treatment condition). An example (with a detailed graph) is provided in Henry and Harbatkin (2020).

Analysis of the Fuzzy RD Design

A variety of analysis strategies have been proposed for addressing the problems introduced by noncompliance (Jacob et al., 2012; Sagarin et al., 2014). One simple strategy is to ignore fuzziness and analyze the data according to how participants were assigned to the treatment conditions, rather than according to the condition they actually received (Boruch, 1997). Such an analyze-as-assigned-rather-than-as-treated strategy is called the intention-to-treat (ITT) analysis or the treatment-as-assigned analysis. The ITT estimate is an underestimate of the effect of the treatment for those who complied with treatment assignment. But the ITT analysis can either under or overestimate the effect of the treatment on all participants had treatment receipt been as assigned. For example, the ITT analysis would underestimate the treatment effect if those who were no-shows would have benefited most from the treatment. Alternatively, the ITT analysis would overestimate the treatment effect if those who were no-shows would have benefited least from the treatment. The ITT estimate can even be positive when the treatment effect is negative and negative when the treatment effect is positive (Sagarin et al., 2014). Some experts consider ITT estimates more realistic effect estimates if compliance with assignment is not compelled when the intervention is fully implemented. In some contexts, the complier average causal effect (CACE) analysis that is considered next can be preferred but frequently both analyses are reported to provide a more complete picture of the potential effects.

The CACE is also known as the local average treatment effect. The CACE estimates the treatment effect at the cutoff score for those participants who complied with treatment assignment (Hahn et al., 2001; Jacob et al., 2012; Reichardt, 2019; van der Klaauw, 2002, 2008). The CACE

analysis requires a number of restrictive assumptions, including that crossovers would perform the same regardless of the treatment condition to which they were assigned.

One way to conceptualize and perform the analysis is as a two-stage least squares regression. In the first stage, an indicator variable representing receipt of the treatment is regressed onto both the QAV and an indicator variable representing treatment assignment. In the second stage, the outcome variable is regressed onto both the QAV and the estimate of the outcome variable from the first stage (i.e., the estimated indicator variable representing receipt of the treatment). The CACE estimate of the treatment effect is the regression coefficient for the estimated indicator variable representing the probability of receipt of the treatment in the second stage. The CACE analysis can also be conceptualized as an instrumental variable analysis where the indicator variable for treatment assignment serves as an instrument for the indicator variable representing treatment receipt. The CACE estimate assumes that the noncompliance is not correlated with the outcome variable.

Discontinuities in the Absence of a Treatment Effect

The analysis of data from an RD design assumes the regression of the outcome variable on the QAV would be continuous (rather than discontinuous) at the cutoff score in the absence of a treatment effect. The results of the RD analysis would be biased if the regression surface would have been discontinuous at the cutoff point in the absence of a treatment effect. A discontinuity not due to the treatment could arise in a variety of ways.

History Including Co-occurring Treatments

A discontinuity in the absence of a treatment effect could be introduced if another treatment were implemented concurrently with the treatment under study. For example, imagine estimating the effects of Medicaid insurance payments that are made available to anyone with income below the poverty line when, at the same time as Medicaid is introduced, other transfer payments, such as food stamps, are also introduced using the same eligibility criterion of income below the poverty line. In that case, the RD design would be estimating the joint of effects of Medicaid and the other transfer payments rather than the effects of Medicaid alone.

Differential Attrition

Participants sometimes drop out of research studies once they have begun or fail to complete the outcome measurements (Wong & Wing, 2016). Such participants produce incomplete or missing data, which can bias estimates of treatment effects. A bias is especially likely when data are missing because participants drop out differentially across the treatment conditions, such as because participants who fail to qualify for the desired experimental treatment decide not to show up for the study. A bias would be introduced, for example, if the less capable participants dropped out from the less desirable treatment condition more than from the desirable condition. The means of preventing attrition and coping with missing data are much the same in RD designs as in randomized experiments (Reichardt, 2019).

Manipulation of QAV or Cutoff Scores

Some participants might manipulate their QAV scores so they can be assigned to a desired treatment condition (Hallberg et al., 2013; Wong & Wing, 2016; Wong et al., 2012). Such manipulation is most likely to occur when the participants know the cutoff score before QAV scores are obtained and the values of the QAV scores are reported by the participants rather than measured independently by researchers. But service staff or data collectors can also manipulate QAV scores to advantage certain participants, perhaps to keep particularly vocal participants from complaining or to get clients deemed worthy into a treatment the staff believe to be most effective. Such QAV manipulation can bias estimates of the treatment effect if the most motivated or desperate participants tend to be incorrectly assigned more to one treatment condition than to the other, and are therefore underrepresented in one group and

overrepresented in the other (Gleason et al., 2018). For example, administrators might manipulate the cutoff score so that participants deemed more likely to have positive outcomes are placed into the experimental treatment conditions.

Both differential attrition and manipulation of the QAV scores will tend to alter the distribution of scores on the QAV on one side of the cutoff score as compared with the other side. In particular, differential attrition would be expected to produce a localized dip in the height of the distribution of the QAV scores on one side or the other of the cutoff score. And manipulation of the QAV scores is likely to produce a bulge in the frequency distribution of the QAV scores on one side of the cutoff score and a dip in the other side. Therefore, evidence of bias due to differential attrition or manipulation of the QAV scores can be obtained by plotting the frequency distribution of the QAV scores and looking for a discontinuity at the cutoff score. McCrary (2008) and Cattaneo et al. (2018) provided a test of the statistical significance of such a discontinuity in the QAV frequency distribution.

Elaborations of the Prototypical RD Design

The preceding sections have considered only the simplest RD design. However, the simple RD design can be embellished in a variety of ways to better tailor the design to the demands of the research setting and to improve credibility (Reichardt, 2006, 2019).

Covariates

Variables that are measured prior to the administration of the treatment or that do not vary over time can be used as covariates in statistical analyses. The power of the statistical analysis, which can be an issue with RD studies, is maximized when the covariates are highly related to the outcome variable but little related to the QAV. Note that including covariates in RD studies is not intended to address selection bias as it might be in other quasi-experimental designs but rather to improve statistical power and precision of the effect estimates.

Let *pretest* be used as a label for a covariate that is operationally identical to the outcome variable and measured before the treatment is introduced and *posttest* be used as the label for the true outcome measure. Then a pretest can be used to assess the presence of spurious discontinuities at the cutoff score. Because treatment effects cannot be present in the pretest, any discontinuity in the relationship between the pretest and the QAV cannot be due to the treatment. Assuming the true outcome scores would behave much the same as a pretest, absence of spurious discontinuities in the pretest relationship with the QAV would foretell the absence of spurious discontinuities in the posttest relationship.

In a similar fashion, a pretest could be used to assess the likely presence of nonlinearities in the relationship between posttest and the QAV (Hallberg et al., 2013; Wing & Cook, 2013). Lack of nonlinearity in the relationship between a pretest and the QAV would suggest absence of nonlinearity between the posttest and the QAV. And the presence of nonlinearities in the pretest-QAV relationship could help with the specification of nonlinearities in the relationship between the true outcome and the QAV.

It has also been suggested that pretest and posttest data be analyzed together to create a pretest-supplemented RD design (Angrist & Rokkanen, 2015; Kisbu-Sakarya et al., 2018; Tang & Cook, 2018; Wing & Cook, 2013). Such a combination analysis (called a comparative RD design) could increase power and precision, as well as aid in the extrapolation of the regression line for the posttest data in the comparison condition into the region of the QAV for the experimental condition. Such an improved extrapolation could increase the credibility of estimates of treatment effects at points along the QAV other than at the cutoff score.

Nonequivalent Groups and Nonequivalent Dependent Variables

Evidence of the presence or absence of nonlinearities and spurious discontinuities might also be obtained using data from a nonequivalent group of participants, perhaps from a neighboring locale, where the experimental treatment was not available (Hallberg et al., 2013; Tang et al., 2018; Wong et al., 2012). Again, a pattern of discontinuities or nonlinearities that was or was not present in the data from the nonequivalent participants would suggest the same pattern of discontinuities and nonlinearities in the RD design using the experimental participants.

In addition, Tang et al. (2018) suggested analyzing the data from an RD design together with the data from the nonequivalent group in a single analysis. Such a combined analysis (also called a comparative RD design) using a nonequivalent group could have the same benefits as a combined analysis using a pretest (as explained in the preceding section).

A nonequivalent dependent variable can also be used to good effect. A nonequivalent dependent variable is a measure taken at the same time as the posttest but not expected to be influenced by the treatment. Lack of a spurious treatment effect in the nonequivalent dependent variable would suggest lack of a spurious treatment effect in the posttest variable (Angrist & Pischke, 2015).

RD Designs Combined With Randomized Experiments

An RD design can be combined with a randomized experiment (Boruch, 1975; Moss et al., 2014; Shadish et al., 2002). When comparing two treatment conditions, one combination of designs would use two cutoff scores to create two extreme groups of participants based on their QAV scores. One of the extreme groups on the QAV measure would receive the comparison condition, the other extreme group would receive the experimental condition, and those in the middle (in between the two cutoff scores) would be randomly assigned to the treatment conditions. This design (called a tie-breaking experiment) could satisfy a desire by administrators to assign most participants to treatments based on need or merit, while acknowledging that, because measures of need or merit are fallible, it would be most equitable to give all the participants who fell within a middle range on the QAV an equal chance of receiving the experimental treatment.

Another design option, using a single cutoff score, would be to assign participants with QAV scores on one side of the cutoff to one of the treatment conditions and assign participants with QAV scores on the other side of the cutoff score to one of the two treatment conditions at random. For example, everyone with scores at one end of the QAV could be given the comparison condition while those with scores on the other side of the cutoff could be assigned to the experimental and comparison conditions at random.

Designs that combine randomized experiments with RD designs are likely to be more powerful and produce results that are more credible than produced either by RD designs without random assignment or by random assignment without the additional data from the RD portion of a design where participants are not assigned to treatments at random.

Cluster Designs

Cluster RD designs arise when clusters of people, such as in schools, classrooms, or clinics, are assigned to treatment conditions. In cluster RD designs, assignment to treatment conditions is based on a QAV measured at the cluster level so all the people in a given cluster are assigned to the same treatment condition (Henry et al., 2010; Henry & Harbatkin, 2020; Pennel et al., 2011). In cluster designs where outcomes are measured on people, but treatments are assigned to clusters of people, multilevel models can maximize the power of the analysis to detect treatment effects. When cluster RD designs are implemented, the Calonico et al. (2014) calculation for the optimal bandwidth adjusts for the clustering.

Relative Strengths and Weaknesses of the RD Design

Nonequivalent group (NEG; Reichardt, 1979) designs are described in Chapter 28 in the present volume. NEG designs tend to be easier to implement than RD designs. The reason is that NEG designs place no restrictions on how units are assigned to treatment conditions, while RD designs require that participants be assigned according to a cutoff score on the QAV.

In addition, an RD design may have less statistical power than an NEG design. Because an RD design allows no overlap between the treatment groups on the QAV while the treatment groups in a NEG design could overlap substantially on covariates, the power of RD designs, which often includes multiple terms involving the QAV (see Equations 29.2–29.4), tends to be reduced by multicollinearity more than the power of NEG designs.

However, estimates of effects from RD designs tend to be more credible than estimates from NEG designs, especially in light of fewer assumptions required by the RD design and evidence comparing estimates of effects from RD designs to those from randomized experiments and NEG designs (Cook et al., 2008). The nature of initial differences between treatment groups is known in RD designs because RD designs impose a quantitative assignment rule and including the QAV in the estimation equation breaks up any correlation between the treatment indicator and the disturbance terms, assuming correct specification of the relationship between the QAV and outcome variable. In contrast, the nature of the effects of initial differences is usually less well understood in NEG designs, so the specification and modeling of initial differences is more difficult and leads to less credible estimates.

Estimates of treatment effects derived from randomized experiments can be more credible than estimates from RD designs. The reason is two-fold. First, the effects of initial differences must be modeled in RD designs by using the QAV as a covariate in a regression analysis. Using an improper model (e.g., fitting linear regression surfaces when the true regression shape is nonlinear) can bias the estimates of treatment effects. In randomized experiments, initial differences between groups are random which can be taken into account without having to fit a proper regression surface, so there is less chance of bias. Second, estimating treatment effect interactions (where the effect of the treatment varies across QAV scores) in RD designs involves extrapolating the regression line from the comparison condition into a region on the QAV which contains no data from the comparison group and extrapolating the regression line from the experimental condition into a region on the QAV which contains no data from the experimental condition. In contrast, treatment effect interactions in randomized experiments can be estimated without extrapolating regression surfaces into regions that do not contain relevant data. As a result, estimates of treatment effect interactions tend to be more precise in randomized experiments than in RD designs.

The results from RD designs are also less precise and statistically less powerful than from randomized experiments due to the inherent correlation of the QAV and the treatment-assignment indicator variable in the RD design. In contrast, any covariates included in the analysis of data from a randomized experiment are uncorrelated with the treatment-assignment indicator variable and therefore can't diminish precision and power due to multicollinearity. To obtain the same precision and power as in a randomized experiment, an RD design must have more than 2 times as many participants (Cappelleri et al., 1994; Goldberger, 1972, 2008; Jacob et al., 2012; Schochet, 2008, 2009). In addition, a larger sample size is needed in an RD design, as compared to a randomized experiment, to ensure the regression surface between the QAV and outcome score is modeled correctly. However, randomized experiments can be more difficult to implement than RD designs. Whether for ethical or practical reasons, situations arise where administrators and participants are more likely to resist the random assignment of a desirable treatment than assignment based on a measure of need or merit. In addition, randomized experiments can suffer from their own biases because it is often impossible to implement them as well in practice as in theory. The point is that the choice between randomized experiments and RD designs must depend on how well they can be implemented in practice.

A large literature has developed wherein the results of well-implemented randomized experiments are compared with the results of well-implemented RD designs (Chaplin et al., 2018; Cook et al., 2008; Cook & Wong, 2008; Wong et al., 2018). The general conclusion is that well-implemented RD designs can produce results that have little, if any, bias compared with well-implemented randomized experiments.

If well implemented and the data well analyzed, the RD design is eligible to receive the highest rating (i.e., meeting standards without reservations) by the WWC in the Institute of Education Sciences (WWC, 2020). And funding agencies, such as the Institute for Educational Sciences of the U.S. Department of Education, have given the RD design special status compared to other quasi-experiments that allows RD designs to serve as acceptable replacements when randomized experiments are not practical. In addition, the WWC has promulgated and regularly updates specific tests that must be met by RD designs to meet their standards with and without reservations (WWC, 2020). These standards offer practical guidance for conducting validity tests that strengthen the credibility of effect estimates from RD studies. The WWC (2020) *Handbook* includes four standards for all RD design studies, including examination of the integrity of the QAV, attrition, other discontinuities along the QAV, and the specification of the functional form and/or selection of the bandwidth used to estimate the effect estimates. A fifth standard applies only to "fuzzy" RD studies and examines the strength of the first stage estimates of the probability of compliance with the assignment to treatment conditions.

CONCLUSION

The RD design was originally invented by Thistlethwaite and Campbell (1960). The design was relatively neglected at first but was resurrected in the 1990s in economics and since then has experienced a substantial resurgence in its use. Because of its many advantages, the RD design is receiving increased attention and stature in producing rigorous estimates of the effects of interventions from funding agencies such as the Institute for Educational Science (Cook & Wong, 2008). But in spite of its potential advantages compared with NEG designs and randomized experiments, the RD design has been used relatively infrequently in psychological research.

The primary reason, we suspect, is that many psychological researchers are simply unaware of the design and its advantages. We suspect the RD design is poised for a renewal of interest among research psychologists, especially in applied areas of research where randomized experiments are not always practical or can't be implemented without risk of substantial bias. Further details about the design and analysis of the RD design can be found in Reichardt (2019).

References

Angrist, J. D., & Pischke, J.-S. (2009). *Mostly harmless econometrics: An empiricist's companion.* Princeton University Press. https://doi.org/10.1515/9781400829828

Angrist, J. D., & Pischke, J.-S. (2015). *Mastering 'metrics: The path from cause to effect.* Princeton University Press.

Angrist, J. D., & Rokkanen, M. (2015). Wanna get away? Regression discontinuity estimation of exam school effects away from the cutoff. *Journal of the American Statistical Association, 110*(512), 1331–1344. https://doi.org/10.1080/01621459.2015.1012259

Black, S. E. (1999). Do better schools matter? Parental valuation of elementary education. *The Quarterly Journal of Economics, 114*(2), 577–599. https://doi.org/10.1162/003355399556070

Boruch, R. F. (1975). Coupling randomized experiments and approximations to experiments in social program evaluation. *Sociological Methods & Research, 4*(1), 31–53. https://doi.org/10.1177/004912417500400103

Boruch, R. F. (1997). *Randomized experiments for planning and evaluation: A practical guide.* SAGE. https://doi.org/10.4135/9781412985574

Calonico, S., Cattaneo, M. D., & Titiunik, R. (2014). Robust nonparametric confidence intervals for regression-discontinuity designs. *Econometrica, 82*(6), 2295–2326. https://doi.org/10.3982/ECTA11757

Campbell, D. T. (1984). Forward. In W. M. K. Trochim (Ed.), *Research design for program evaluation: The regression-discontinuity approach* (pp. 15–43). SAGE.

Cappelleri, J. C., Darlington, R. B., & Trochim, W. M. K. (1994). Power analysis of cutoff-based randomized clinical trials. *Evaluation Review, 18*(2), 141–152. https://doi.org/10.1177/0193841X9401800202

Cappelleri, J. C., & Trochim, W. M. K. (2015). Regression discontinuity design. In J. D. Wright (Ed.), *International encyclopedia of the social & behavioral sciences* (2nd ed., Vol. 20, pp. 152–159). Elsevier. https://doi.org/10.1016/B978-0-08-097086-8.44049-3

Cappelleri, J. C., Trochim, W. M. K., Stanley, T. D., & Reichardt, C. S. (1991). Random measurement error does not bias the treatment effect estimate in the regression-discontinuity design: I. The case of no interaction. *Evaluation Review, 15*(4), 395–419. https://doi.org/10.1177/0193841X9101500401

Cattaneo, M. D., Jansson, M., & Ma, X. (2018). Manipulation testing based on density discontinuity. *The Stata Journal, 18*(1), 234–261. https://doi.org/10.1177/1536867X1801800115

Chaplin, D. D., Cook, T., Zurovac, J., Coopersmith, J., Finucane, M. M., Vollmer, L. N., & Morris, R. (2018). The internal and external validity of the regression discontinuity design: A meta-analysis of 15 within-study-comparisons. *Journal of Policy Analysis and Management, 37*(2), 403–429. https://doi.org/10.1002/pam.22051

Cook, T. D., Shadish, W. R., & Wong, V. C. (2008). Three conditions under which experiments and observational studies produce comparable causal estimates: New findings from within-study comparisons. *Journal of Policy Analysis and Management, 27*(4), 724–750. https://doi.org/10.1002/pam.20375

Cook, T. D., & Wong, V. C. (2008). Empirical tests of the validity of the regression discontinuity design. *Annales d'Economie et de Statistique, 91/92*, 127–150. https://doi.org/10.2307/27917242

Gelman, A., & Imbens, G. (2019). Why high-order polynomials should not be used in regression discontinuity designs. *Journal of Business & Economic Statistics, 37*(3), 447–456. https://doi.org/10.1080/07350015.2017.1366909

Gleason, P., Resch, A., & Berk, J. (2018). RD or not RD: Using experimental studies to assess the performance of the regression discontinuity approach. *Evaluation Review, 42*(1), 3–33. https://doi.org/10.1177/0193841X18787267

Goldberger, A. S. (1972). *Selection bias in evaluating treatment effects: Some formal illustrations* (Discussion Paper 123-72). University of Wisconsin, Institute for Research on Poverty.

Goldberger, A. S. (2008). Selection bias in evaluation treatment effects: Some formal illustrations. In T. Fomby, R. C. Hill, D. L. Millimet, J. A. Smith, & E. J. Vytlacil (Eds.), *Modeling and evaluating treatment effects in economics* (pp. 1–31). JAI Press. https://doi.org/10.1016/S0731-9053(07)00001-1

Hahn, J., Todd, P., & van der Klaauw, W. (2001). Identification and estimation of treatment effects with a regression-discontinuity design. *Econometrica,*

69(1), 201–209. https://www.econometricsociety.org/publications/econometrica/2001/01/01/identification-and-estimation-treatment-effects-regression

Hallberg, K., Wing, C., Wong, V., & Cook, T. D. (2013). Experimental design for causal inference: Clinical trials and regression discontinuity designs. In T. D. Little (Ed.), *The Oxford handbook of quantitative methods in psychology* (Vol. 1, pp. 223–236). Oxford University Press. https://doi.org/10.1093/oxfordhb/9780199934874.013.0012

Henry, G. T., Fortner, C. K., & Thompson, C. L. (2010). Targeted funding for educationally disadvantaged students: A regression discontinuity estimate of the impact on high school student achievement. *Educational Evaluation and Policy Analysis, 32*(2), 183–204. https://doi.org/10.3102/0162373710370620

Henry, G. T., & Harbatkin, E. (2020). The next generation of state reforms to improve their lowest performing schools: An evaluation of North Carolina's school transformation intervention. *Journal of Research on Educational Effectiveness, 13*(4), 702–730. https://doi.org/10.1080/19345747.2020.1814464

Imbens, G. W., & Lemieux, T. (2008). Regression discontinuity designs: A guide to practice. *Journal of Econometrics, 142*(2), 615–635. https://doi.org/10.1016/j.jeconom.2007.05.001

Jacob, R., Zhu, P., Somers, M.-A., & Bloom, H. (2012). *A practical guide to regression discontinuity.* Manpower Demonstration Research Corporation.

Kisbu-Sakarya, Y., Cook, T. D., Tang, Y., & Clark, M. H. (2018). Comparative regression discontinuity: A stress test with small samples. *Evaluation Review, 42*(1), 111–143. https://doi.org/10.1177/0193841X18776881

Lee, D. S., & Lemieux, T. (2010). Regression discontinuity designs in economics. *Journal of Economic Literature, 48*(2), 281–355. https://doi.org/10.1257/jel.48.2.281

Leeds, D. M., & DesJardins, S. L. (2015). The Effect of Merit Aid on Enrollment: A Regression Discontinuity Analysis of Iowa's National Scholars Award. *Research in Higher Education, 56*(5), 471–495. https://doi.org/10.1007/s11162-014-9359-2

Lipsey, M. W., Weiland, C., Yoshikawa, H., Wilson, S. J., & Hofer, K. G. (2015). The prekindergarten age-cutoff regression-discontinuity design. *Educational Evaluation and Policy Analysis, 37*(3), 296–313. https://doi.org/10.3102/0162373714547266

McCrary, J. (2008). Testing for manipulation of the running variable in the regression discontinuity design. *Journal of Econometrics, 142*(2), 698–714. https://doi.org/10.1016/j.jeconom.2007.05.005

Moss, B. G., Yeaton, W. H., & Lloyd, J. E. (2014). Evaluating the effectiveness of developmental mathematics by embedding a randomized experiment within a regression discontinuity design. *Educational Evaluation and Policy Analysis, 36*(2), 170–185. https://doi.org/10.3102/0162373713504988

Pennel, M. L., Hade, E. M., Murray, D. M., & Rhoda, D. A. (2011). Cutoff designs for community-based intervention studies. *Statistics in Medicine, 30*(15), 1865–1882. https://doi.org/10.1002/sim.4237

Pinotti, P. (2017). Clicking on heaven's door: The effect of immigrant legalization on crime. *The American Economic Review, 107*(1), 138–168. https://doi.org/10.1257/aer.20150355

Reichardt, C. S. (1979). The statistical analysis of data from nonequivalent group designs. In T. D. Cook & D. T. Campbell (Eds.), *Quasi-experimentation: Design and analysis issues for field settings* (pp. 147–205). Rand McNally.

Reichardt, C. S. (2006). The principle of parallelism in the design of studies to estimate treatment effects. *Psychological Methods, 11*(1), 1–18. https://doi.org/10.1037/1082-989X.11.1.1

Reichardt, C. S. (2019). *Quasi-experimentation: A guide to design and analysis.* Guilford Press.

Reichardt, C. S., & Gollob, H. F. (1987). Taking uncertainty into account when estimating effects. In M. M. Mark & R. L. Shotland (Eds.), Multiple methods for program evaluation. *New Directions for Program Evaluation, 35* (pp. 7–22). Jossey-Bass. https://doi.org/10.1002/ev.1456

Reichardt, C. S., Trochim, W. M. K., & Cappelleri, J. C. (1995). Reports of the death of regression-discontinuity analysis are greatly exaggerated. *Evaluation Review, 19*(1), 39–63. https://doi.org/10.1177/0193841X9501900102

Sagarin, B. J., West, S. G., Ratnikov, A., Homan, W. K., Ritchie, T. D., & Hansen, E. J. (2014). Treatment noncompliance in randomized experiments: Statistical approaches and design issues. *Psychological Methods, 19*(3), 317–333. https://doi.org/10.1037/met0000013

Schochet, P. Z. (2008). *Technical methods report: Statistical power for regression discontinuity designs in education evaluations.* Institute for Education Sciences, National Center for Education Evaluation and Regional Assistance, NCEE.

Schochet, P. Z. (2009). Statistical power for regression discontinuity designs in education evaluations. *Journal of Educational and Behavioral Statistics, 34*(2), 238–266. https://doi.org/10.3102/1076998609332748

Shadish, W. R., Cook, T. D., & Campbell, D. T. (2002). *Experimental and quasi-experimental designs for generalized causal inference.* Houghton Mifflin.

Tang, Y., & Cook, T. D. (2018). Statistical power for the comparative regression discontinuity design with a pretest no-treatment control function: Theory and evidence from the National Head Start Impact Study. *Evaluation Review, 42*(1), 71–110. https://doi.org/10.1177/0193841X18776117

Tang, Y., Cook, T. D., & Kisbu-Sakarya, Y. (2018). Statistical power for the comparative regression discontinuity design with a nonequivalent comparison group. *Psychological Methods, 23*(1), 150–168. https://doi.org/10.1037/met0000118

Thistlethwaite, D. L., & Campbell, D. T. (1960). Regression-discontinuity analysis: An alternative to the ex-post-facto experiment. *Journal of Educational Psychology, 51*(6), 309–317. https://doi.org/10.1037/h0044319

Thoemmes, F., Liao, W., & Jin, Z. (2017). The analysis of the regression-discontinuity design in R. *Journal of Educational and Behavioral Statistics, 42*(3), 341–360. https://doi.org/10.3102/1076998616680587

Trochim, W. M. K. (1984). *Research designs for program evaluation: The regression-discontinuity approach.* SAGE.

Trochim, W. M. K., Cappelleri, J. C., & Reichardt, C. S. (1991). Random measurement error does not bias the treatment effect estimate in the regression-discontinuity design: II. When an interaction effect is present. *Evaluation Review, 15*(5), 571–604. https://doi.org/10.1177/0193841X9101500504

van der Klaauw, W. (2002). Estimating the effect of financial aid offers on college enrollment: A regression discontinuity approach. *International Economic Review, 43*(4), 1249–1287. https://doi.org/10.1111/1468-2354.t01-1-00055

van der Klaauw, W. (2008). Regression discontinuity analysis: A survey of recent developments in economics. *LABOUR, 22*(2), 219–245. https://doi.org/10.1111/j.1467-9914.2008.00419.x

West, S. G., Cham, H., & Liu, Y. (2014). Causal inference and generalizations in field settings: Experimental and quasi-experimental designs. In H. T. Reis & C. M. Judd (Eds.), *Handbook of research methods in social and personality psychology* (2nd ed., pp. 49–80). Cambridge University Press.

What Works Clearinghouse (WWC). (2020). *Standards Handbook, Version 4.1.* Institute of Education Sciences, U.S. Department of Education.

Wing, C., & Bello-Gomez, R. A. (2018). Regression discontinuity and beyond: Options for studying external validity in an internally valid design. *The American Journal of Evaluation, 39*(1), 91–108. https://doi.org/10.1177/1098214017736155

Wing, C., & Cook, T. D. (2013). Strengthening the regression discontinuity design using additional design elements: A within-study comparison. *Journal of Policy Analysis and Management, 32*(4), 853–877. https://doi.org/10.1002/pam.21721

Wong, V. C., Steiner, P. M., & Anglin, K. L. (2018). What can be learned from empirical evaluations of nonexperimental methods? *Evaluation Review, 42*(2), 147–175. https://doi.org/10.1177/0193841X18776870

Wong, V. C., & Wing, C. (2016). The regression discontinuity design and the social corruption of quantitative indicators. *Observational Studies, 2,* 183–209. https://doi.org/10.1353/obs.2017.0006

Wong, V. C., Wing, C., Steiner, P. M., Wong, N., & Cook, T. D. (2012). Research designs for program evaluation. In J. A. Schinker, W. F. Velicer, & I. B. Weiner (Eds.), *Handbook of psychology: Vol. 2. Research methods in psychology* (2nd ed., pp. 316–341). Wiley.

EXPERIMENTAL MANIPULATIONS IN APPLIED SETTINGS

CHAPTER 30

TREATMENT VALIDITY FOR INTERVENTION STUDIES

Dianne L. Chambless and Steven D. Hollon

That psychologists conduct sound research is important whatever their research areas, but it is especially important when the results of this research have a substantial impact on people's lives. This is the case for intervention research, the findings of which may influence the type of treatments people receive. Sound intervention research is critical for determining what treatments are beneficial and what treatments are ineffective or even harmful. Moreover, intervention research is typically very expensive to conduct, with a single project often taking 5 to 7 years to complete and costing well over $1 million. This means that relatively little psychosocial intervention research is conducted, making the validity of each trial that much more important.

Intervention research is challenging, and during such a study (often called a *trial*), investigators will be faced with many events they could not have foreseen. Common problems in treatment research are predictable, however, and many potential difficulties in interpretation can be avoided with proper attention to design before the trial begins. In this chapter, we review the most common design questions in intervention research and specify the basic elements we believe must be present to permit researchers to draw valid conclusions from their data.

ASSESSMENT

Assessment is something of a stepchild for intervention researchers. Researchers often pay inadequate attention to whether the measures they select assess are reliable and valid for the constructs they wish to measure. There is a tendency to choose measures simply because they are in widespread use or because their names suggest that they represent the constructs of interest. Without valid and appropriate measurement, the results of a study are severely compromised, if not meaningless, and time spent up-front on selection of appropriate measures will pay off in the end. This is not a task to hand off to an inexperienced research assistant.

Several types of assessment are important. First, how will the investigator determine that the participants represent the types of people to whom this research is supposed to generalize (a critical aspect of the external validity of the study)? In prevention research, the potential participant pool may be everyone who was exposed to some stressor such as a hurricane or all couples attending a given church who are engaged to be married. In such cases, the definition of the sampling frame may be relatively straightforward, although in cases of exposure to stressors,

https://doi.org/10.1037/0000319-030
APA Handbook of Research Methods in Psychology, Second Edition: Vol. 2. Research Designs: Quantitative, Qualitative, Neuropsychological, and Biological, H. Cooper (Editor-in-Chief)

the researcher will want to carefully assess the degree of exposure. In psychotherapy research, it is common, although not mandatory, for the participant pool to be defined in terms of the primary diagnosis conferred (or group of related diagnoses in the case of transdiagnostic approaches; Dalgleish et al., 2020), with predefined exclusions of those who have other conditions that might render the proposed treatment inappropriate. For example, investigators typically exclude patients with a history of psychosis from trials of nonpsychotic disorders. In such research, the researcher needs to convince readers that the diagnoses were reliably and validly made. For studies of psychiatric disorders, this generally means that structured diagnostic interviews were used and that the researcher demonstrated satisfactory interrater reliability by having a randomly selected sample of diagnostic interviews repeated or rated by a second diagnostician who is not informed of the first diagnostician's decisions. Alternatively, participants may be selected on the basis of their scores on self-report measures. For example, couples may be selected for marital therapy on the basis of their stated desire for couples therapy and their falling below some threshold of marital satisfaction on a psychometrically sound inventory. In a research report, investigators were encouraged to report clearly the reasons that potential participants were excluded from the study, decided against participation, or later dropped out, along with numbers for each category, perhaps using a chart advocated by the CONSORT guidelines to standardize the report (Schultz et al., 2010). Figure 30.1, taken from Striegel-Moore et al.'s (2010) study on guided self-help for recurrent binge eating, provides an example of a CONSORT chart.

Second, how will the investigator know whether the intervention had the desired effect? Here is it crucial to select reliable and valid outcome measures appropriate to the sample being studied. Because each method of measurement captures only a part of the latent variable the researcher wants to assess, it is preferable to use multiple methods of assessment, including,

for example, self-report, interviewer, and observational or behavioral measures. In research on children, it is desirable to obtain ratings from parents and teachers as well as from the children themselves (Kraemer et al., 2003; Makol et al., 2020). When researchers use interviewer and observational measures, they must demonstrate adequate interrater reliability for all occasions of assessment (e.g., pretest, posttest, follow-up). If, as is usually the case, it is too expensive to have reliability ratings for every participant assessed, investigators should randomly sample from all occasions of assessment for reliability ratings and report these findings using measures of reliability appropriate for the level of measurement (Shrout & Fleiss, 1979).

Third, how will the investigators know whether the intervention works for the reasons that they propose? Reliable and valid measurement is required to test such process or mediational questions (Chapter 20, this volume). For example, if the researcher proposes that psychotherapy works because the client forms a close working alliance with the therapist, a good measure of the working alliance must be included.

Careful determination of all the constructs that need to be assessed in the study and selection of appropriate means of measurement are critical to the ultimate success of the trial. Attention to the validity of assessment speaks to the construct validity of the research.

SELECTION OF THE RESEARCH DESIGN

Single-case and quasi-experimental designs are covered in other chapters. Here we concentrate on the randomized controlled trial (RCT), which permits the strongest inferences of causality, that is, allows the investigator to say with the most confidence that any changes observed are due to the intervention (Shadish et al., 2002).

Randomization

In a randomized study design, each participant is assigned at random to an intervention condition; alternatively, randomization occurs at some group level. For example, classrooms of children may be

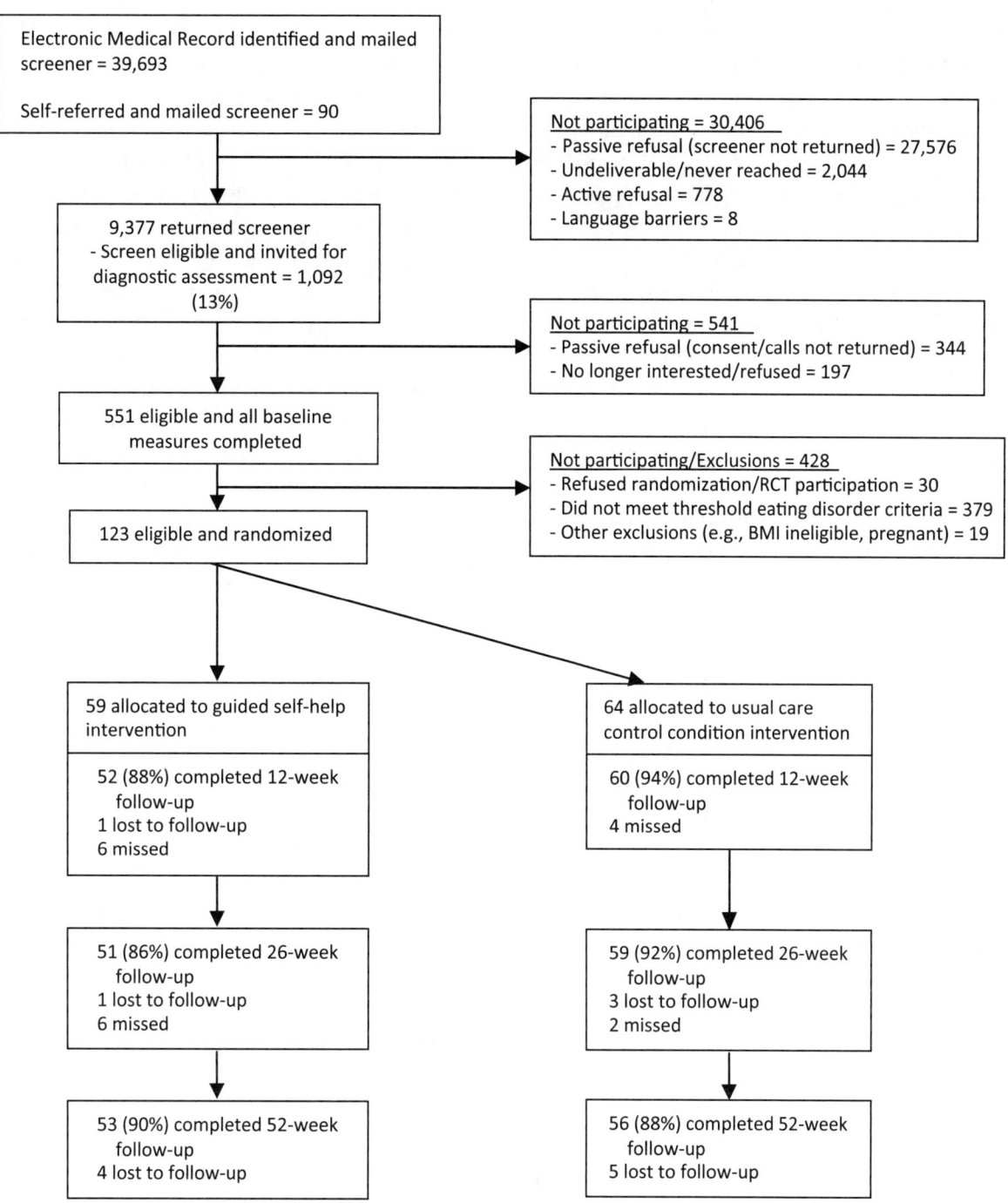

FIGURE 30.1.   An example of a CONSORT flowchart. RCT = randomized controlled trial; BMI = body mass index. From "Cognitive Behavioral Guided Self-Help for the Treatment of Recurrent Binge Eating," by R. H. Striegel-Moore, G. T. Wilson, L. DeBar, N. Perrin, F. Lynch, F. Rosselli, and H. C. Kraemer, 2010, *Journal of Consulting and Clinical Psychology*, 78(3), p. 314 (https://doi.org/10.1037/a0018915). Copyright 2010 by the American Psychological Association.

assigned at random to a prevention program or alternative condition, or wards of a hospital may be assigned at random to an experimental procedure, whereas other wards serve as a control condition. This approach to assignment is sometimes called *cluster randomized assignment* (see Campbell et al., 2012, for a discussion of methodological issues in such studies). Randomization is the best method for guarding against *selection* effects (Shadish et al., 2002), the presence of systematic differences between groups that imperil the investigator's ability to draw the conclusion that the intervention rather than pre-existing differences between groups led to the observed difference in outcome.

When very large numbers of participants are involved, the experimenter can be relatively confident that randomization will ensure that treatment conditions will not differ on important variables other than receipt of the intended intervention. However, intervention trials are often not so large, and fairly frequently treatment groups will be found to differ significantly on one or more variables before treatment. For this reason, investigators would do well to consider in advance the presence of other variables that might be related to outcome and on which participants might differ. For example, suppose the investigator believes that patients with borderline personality disorder are likely to do worse in treatment for major depressive disorder than patients without such personality pathology. In this case the investigator might block or stratify the patients on presence or absence of borderline personality disorder before randomization and then conduct randomization within blocks. Such a practice makes it more likely that each treatment condition will have roughly equal numbers of patients with this personality disorder, particularly if the researcher uses procedures to foster balance across conditions or blocks within conditions, among the most common of which is *urn randomization* (Wei & Lachin, 1988). In urn randomization, the probability that subsequent patients will be assigned to a specific treatment condition is adjusted on an ongoing basis to reflect the number and type of patients previously

assigned to that condition. Urn randomization is used to decrease the likelihood that randomization will fail (distribute uneven numbers or types of patients across the treatment conditions) simply on the basis of chance. Knowledge of the literature on factors associated with treatment outcome will guide the investigator in the selection of the most important blocking variables, in that it is not possible to stratify on numerous factors.

In implementing randomization, the researcher needs to separate knowledge of eligibility from knowledge of the randomization sequence. Randomization should occur only after it has been determined that a patient meets eligibility criteria. Otherwise, the investigator risks having unintentional biases creep in. For example, suppose the investigator is handling random assignment and knows that the next patient in the randomization sequence will be assigned to his or her preferred treatment. When that patient proves to be a difficult case—one the investigator suspects will not do well—the investigator might unintentionally find a reason this patient is not eligible for the study. Procedures should be in place to prevent such temptation, for example, by having someone not involved in eligibility determination (e.g., the project data manager) maintain the randomization sequence in secret, providing the patient's treatment condition assignment only once a firm decision has been made regarding eligibility, and the patient's status on any blocking variables is known (Efron, 1971). With the increased importance of meta-analytic reviews, it is important not only to implement the randomization adequately but to describe clearly what procedures were followed to allow others to rate the trial for risk of bias (Sterne et al., 2019).

The Comparison Group

Selection of the appropriate comparison group should be determined by the research question. Do we simply want to know whether a treatment is beneficial? If so, the control condition for the RCT can be a waiting list control group that accounts for potential confounding variables, such as the effects of the assessment procedures and the passage of time, during which the problem might run its course or be affected by healing agents in the patient's natural environment. Such a design tells us whether our treatment has *efficacy*, that it is better than no treatment. We might prefer to know whether our treatment works better than some placebo or basic treatment. If it does, then we say it has *specificity*. Designs testing for specificity allow the investigator to control for additional variables, such as hope and expectancy of change, a caring relationship with a professional, and education about one's disorder.

Why do we care whether a treatment is specific? Is it not enough to know that it works? From a practical standpoint, we care because interventions are often costly and require extensive training and supervision of the interventionists. If patients benefit as much from regular meetings with a caring counselor as from a more elaborate and expensive intervention, then we have no need for a more complex intervention requiring extensive training. From a theoretical standpoint, we care because we wish to understand why change occurs, and we base our interventions on hypotheses about the critical changes processes. If our treatment fares no better than a nonspecific control, we need to question our beliefs about the necessary ingredients for change. Thus, tests of specificity speak to the issue of construct validity.

Finally, the investigator might wish to test for *superiority* relative to one or more rival interventions in the treatment or prevention of a given disorder. This is the most ambitious type of trial to mount because it requires large numbers of participants (see discussion on power in the section Appropriate Statistical Analysis). Such trials might involve the comparison of different schools of psychotherapy or of psychotherapy versus pharmacotherapy (Mohr et al., 2009). Note that each successive design subsumes the other like Russian nesting dolls; superiority perforce subsumes specificity, and specificity perforce subsumes efficacy.

Special concerns arise when the comparison condition the investigator selects is care-as-usual (CAU; Cuijpers et al., 2021). Such designs are especially common in effectiveness studies, in which investigators transport research clinic-

tested treatments to clinical settings in the community. In such a design, in contrast to efficacy designs, the investigator does not dictate the contents of the comparison condition but relies on ordinary care at the clinical setting where the research is conducted or refers the participants randomized to CAU to community resources. Such studies have substantial external validity, in that they tell us whether the treatment in question is superior to what patients would otherwise have gotten, while avoiding the ethical problem of withholding treatment from someone who seeks it. However, construct validity problems can make their results easy to misinterpret: In many cases, the CAU group receives very little intervention, and any superiority of the new treatment may be due simply to the fact that the participants in that condition actually got treatment. For example, a culturally adapted behavioral intervention recently outperformed "enhanced usual care" in a primary care setting in rural India (Patel et al., 2017). However, fewer than 5% of the participants in the control condition got any depression treatment at all, even though investigators informed the primary care physicians that their patients were depressed and provided guidance on medication. In addition, the therapists in the new treatment may receive special training and supervision, creating excitement that can lead to a Hawthorne effect (i.e., improvement from the mere fact of being studied vs. improvement for the hypothesized reasons; Shadish et al., 2002). In other cases, there are problems in generalization of the results because the investigator fails to determine what sort of treatment the participants in the CAU condition received. Lacking this knowledge, how can we guess whether a new treatment that was superior to CAU in Clinic A will be similarly superior in Clinic B where CAU services are better? Only if the investigator has the resources to study CAU in a large number of clinics that represent adequately the range of services in the community does it become possible to conclude that on average the new treatment is better than typical practice.

Design issues for the investigator do not end with selection of the proper control group for the research question. To what degree should the investigator favor realistic conditions in the research versus tight control of factors such as amount of time in therapy? For example, patients in the community receiving psychotherapy for their depression generally meet with their therapists for 45 to 50 minutes at least once weekly. If they are in pharmacotherapy, however, after initial sessions they would rarely see their physician for more than 15-minute sessions. Should the investigator constrain both treatment interventions to 45- to 50-minute sessions, even though this would not mimic real-world conditions and would be expensive in terms of the increase in physicians' time in the study? We have seen a change in this choice over our decades in the intervention field, where earlier researchers and reviewers favored carefully equating treatments on amount of time, but more recently, delivery of the treatments permits differences in amount of time and attention consistent with the way treatments are delivered in the field. As such, psychotherapy researchers have moved from a more rigid adherence to maintenance of internal validity (by equating all conditions tightly on time in treatment) to permitting more focus on external validity (matching more closely what happens in the clinic) (Nathan et al., 2000). There is no right answer to this dilemma. Rather, investigators must carefully consider the match of the design with the research question and clearly describe any limitations in the interpretation of findings that follow from this choice in the discussion section of any report of the trial.

When two or more psychotherapy conditions are compared, the investigator must decide whether therapists are to be crossed or nested within treatments. When therapists are crossed with treatment condition, each therapist delivers all treatment conditions. When therapists are nested within treatment, each implements only one of the treatment conditions. In the crossed case, the investigator can be sure that, if two treatments are found to differ, it is not because particularly good therapists were more likely to be assigned to one treatment condition than another. However, the more the treatments are

theoretically distinctive and require extensive training and commitment, the less likely it is that any one therapist can carry out each with equal competence and commitment. For example, a committed cognitive therapist might not do a credible job of psychodynamic psychotherapy or might communicate to patients in psychodynamic therapy that they are receiving the less preferred treatment. The nested condition avoids this problem if the investigator recruits therapists who are equally skilled in and committed to their treatment approach for each condition— not an easy thing to do given the difficulty in assessing therapist competence reliably and validly (Waltz et al., 1993) and in finding skilled adherents of each treatment condition in many geographic areas. However, it leaves open the concern that the investigators may have unintentionally selected skilled therapists for their preferred condition and less adequate ones for the other(s). In addition, investigators might have provided less than adequate supervision for the less favored treatment(s) (see, e.g., Coffman et al., 2007).

ATTRITION

Attrition in intervention research is a common source of threats to both the internal and external validity of the findings. External validity is affected by a form of attrition that arises before potential participants ever begin the program. Who met criteria for entry to the study but chose not to participate? The larger the refusal rate, the less able we are to generalize the results of the study to the population of interest. The investigator can help the reader determine external validity in this sense by reporting how many suitable people were offered admission to the trial but refused and what reasons they gave for their rejection, perhaps using a flow chart such as that in Figure 30.1 to make attrition across the course of the trial easy to assess. Such a chart provides valuable information but does not reveal one important form of attrition: It is virtually impossible to determine how many potential participants learned of the procedures of the trial and decided against application for what might be important reasons that speak to a treatment's acceptability.

Once participants enter the study, the problem of maintaining their cooperation with the data collection effort and retaining them in treatment arises. The longer the study, the more likely it is that participants will fail to continue with treatment, assessment, or both. Dropouts are a problem even in pretest–posttest designs, but attrition is especially problematic at follow-up, when participants no longer have the incentive of receipt of the intervention to maintain their adherence with assessment procedures. The more people drop out of a research trial, the less representative the data are of the average person who enters treatment—a threat to external validity (Shadish et al., 2002). This can be addressed by providing financial incentives for continuing to take part in ongoing assessments and by using duration of sustained improvement as the primary outcome in a survival analysis (DeRubeis et al., 2020). Survival analyses give participants credit for the length of time they maintain their improvement and differentiate those who relapse versus those who drop out or are otherwise lost to follow-up via censoring the latter.

Problems with attrition are even graver when attrition is differential (Shadish et al., 2002). Here internal validity is threatened. Differential attrition is obvious when dropout rates are higher in one intervention condition than another. It is more subtle, but equally dangerous, when different kinds of people drop out of one condition than another. Imagine two treatment conditions for which one condition is arduous but effective for those who stay the course, whereas the other condition is less demanding but also less effective. It is possible that for those people who complete treatment, the arduous treatment is more effective than the comparison condition, but that the less motivated people drop out of the demanding treatment. A comparison of treatment completers then yields findings that do not represent the results for the group of patients who started treatment; the investigators have lost the benefits of random assignment because there are now systematic differences between people in different treatment conditions (more motivated participants are in one condition than another), and internal validity is threatened. We address the problems of attrition further when we discuss statistical conclusion validity. For now, we note only that the reader of any report based on completer rather than intention-to-treat analyses (Hollis & Campbell, 1999) should be very wary, and that investigators should make every attempt to continue to collect data on people who drop out of treatment (Lavori, 1992), for example, by using financial incentives to keep participants involved.

MODERATION AND MEDIATION

Researchers are usually not content to know simply whether a treatment works. They also want to know for whom it works and how it works when it works. The first question concerns moderation and the second mediation (Baron & Kenny, 1986).

Moderation

Many psychotherapists believe it is important to select a treatment that matches a client in some important regard, and the search for client characteristics that predict better outcomes for different patients in different treatments has become something of a quest for the Holy Grail in psychotherapy research. Moderation comes in two types, both represented as patient-by-treatment interactions (PTIs) in statistical tests. In disordinal interactions, different patients respond differentially to different treatments. Such interactions would suggest that "all have won" but for different people. From our reading of the literature, disordinal interactions are rarely found and less often replicated, perhaps because the sample sizes typical of psychotherapy trials generally provide inadequate power to detect interaction effects unless quite large. (Lack of perfect reliability in measurement of a typical moderator variable and the fact that interactions can only claim variance after the main effects have been accounted for combine to lower power for interaction terms; Aiken & West, 1991.)

Or perhaps they are truly rare. The failure of Project MATCH (Project MATCH Research Group, 1997) represents a sad example: This very large, very expensive, and well-conducted study was explicitly designed to test matching hypotheses in a sample of more than 1,700 patients with alcoholism. Previous findings from literature with alcohol-abusing or -dependent patients largely failed to replicate.

Ordinal interactions apply to some but not all patients. In our reading of the literature, these are more common than disordinal interactions. We suspect that they are most likely to be found among patients who show specificity of response, since that implies the operation of some causal mechanism that goes beyond the generic. For example, because psychotherapy is only superior to nonspecific controls among more severely depressed patients (Driessen et al., 2010), it is unlikely that anyone will do better in the non-specific control than the active intervention. Patients with more severe depressions may show different specific responses to different interventions that would manifest as ordinal interactions on different indices (some patients show a specific response to Treatment A, whereas others show a specific response to Treatment B) or a disordinal interaction on the same baseline variable. Studying only patients with more severe depressions, DeRubeis et al. (2014) found cognitive therapy and medication treatment were comparable to one another and each superior to pill-placebo (thereby demonstrating specificity for each) but also found a number of interactions that, taken in aggregate, indicated that different thirds of the sample would have done better in one treatment than the other.

When moderator variables are selected after the trial has been conducted (at which point the researcher has knowledge of the results) rather than a priori, the investigator needs to be especially cautious in interpreting the findings, which may capitalize on chance (Kraemer et al., 2002). Until replicated, the results should be seen as heuristic for future research rather than definitive. For example, in the Treatment of Depression Collaborative Research Program (TDCRP),

post hoc moderation analyses found that cognitive therapy was not as effective as antidepressant medication for patients with severe depression (Elkin et al., 1989). This effect was widely cited, but the authors' caution that the moderation results were merely exploratory was often forgotten. Subsequent trials with more adequate implementation typically have found cognitive therapy to be as efficacious as antidepressant medications and each superior to pill-placebo (e.g., DeRubeis et al., 2005).

Some experts hold that investigators should consider as potential moderators only those variables that can be assessed before treatment (Kraemer et al., 2002). In our view, this is too restrictive and risks overlooking important findings. For example, Addis et al. (2006) randomly assigned therapists in a health maintenance organization to training in cognitive behavior therapy (CBT) for panic disorder or to a waiting list for training. Panic disorder patients who saw the specially trained therapists improved significantly more than patients who saw the waiting list therapists, but only when patients received at least eight sessions of treatment. When patients received fewer than eight sessions, there were no differences between conditions—a moderation effect. Note that in this study, Addis et al. did not experimentally assign patients to different numbers of sessions. Accordingly, this part of the report is quasi-experimental in nature and does not have the force of an investigation in which patients were randomly assigned to more or fewer sessions.

With the advent of sophisticated machine learning (artificial intelligence) approaches there is renewed interest in generating precision treatment rules (PTRs) that can be used to predict in advance the optimal treatment for a given patient (Cohen & DeRubeis, 2018). There are a variety of strategies that can be used, but the essence is that machine learning can be applied to large data sets to identify combinations of baseline indices that identify the optimal treatment for a given individual or to time-varying outcomes to guide adaptive or stepped care decisions (Kessler, 2018). Rather than searching for univariate indices one at a time, these sophisticated analytic strategies combine multiple indices often in a nonlinear fashion in a manner that optimizes the prescriptive information in the data. Samples need to be dauntingly large to stabilize the PTRs (usually 300–500 patients per condition; Luedtke et al., 2019), checks built in to avoid overfitting, and replicability tested in independent samples (Cohen et al., 2021). The consensus is that the field stands on the threshold of realizing Gordon Paul's (1967) classic dictum: "*What* treatment, by *whom*, is most effective for *this* individual with *that* specific problem, and under *which* set of circumstances?" (p. 111).

Mediation

Mediation analyses cut deeper still and test not just whether patients have changed on clinical endpoints but what processes might account for that change. In essence, tests of mediation are tests of causal agency or proposed mechanisms. What components of the larger treatment package played a causal role in bringing about the change in outcomes observed, and what mechanisms in the patient played a causal role in transmitting the impact of treatment to the outcomes of interest? Such tests speak to the construct validity of the research. For example, it goes without saying that cognitive therapists believe that changing patients' maladaptive cognitions is the central curative process in psychotherapy. In treatment research, mediation is tested by determining whether changes in the outcome variable over time or differences in treatment efficacy between two treatment conditions (e.g., CBT vs. placebo) can be statistically accounted for by changes in the mediator (e.g., cognitive change; Kraemer et al., 2002). For example, Smits and colleagues (2006) collected data across 15 exposure trials from patients in treatment for social phobia, assessing cognitive variables before each exposure trial and fear after each trial. The authors demonstrated that reductions in patients' predictions that they would look anxious, stupid, and so forth statistically accounted for reductions in fear across trials. A critical factor in the appropriate test of mediation is the researcher's ability to demonstrate that change in the mediator preceded change on the outcome variable. Otherwise, the mediator could just as easily have been caused by the outcome as the converse or be a time-varying third variable not causally related to the outcome at all. We return to this point with a specific example in the Alliance section.

Moderation and mediation are not wholly unrelated (Kraemer, 2016). Whenever patients respond differentially to different treatments (moderation) they are perforce adhering to different mechanisms (mediation) (Kazdin, 2007). The implication is that tests of mediation that do not include PTIs necessarily water down the signal regarding the causal mechanisms (Vanderweele & Vansteelandt, 2009). For example, since severity moderates the specific effect of psychotherapy in the treatment of depression, whatever mechanisms are responsible for the changes observed over and above generic nonspecific change can only be detected among those patients who show a specific response. This phenomenon is called *moderated mediation* and can be addressed by including PTIs in the tests of mediation (or better still, PTRs developed via machine learning) in those terms (Preacher et al., 2007).

STATISTICAL CONCLUSION VALIDITY

Investigators may have selected appropriate measures and good research designs but undercut the validity of their research by their statistical approach. Here we consider some of the common pitfalls we have observed in psychotherapy research.

Type I and II Errors

Perhaps because the opportunity to collect data in an intervention trial is precious, investigators tend to want to collect data on many variables, including outcome variables. This is understandable but runs the risk of Type I error. Investigators have been known to test 20 or more outcome variables, all with an alpha level of .05, and then interpret a smattering of significant effects as indicating they have demonstrated efficacy for the treatment tested. Worse yet, the investigator might report only those measures that yielded findings consistent with the hypothesis. After the fact, it is tempting to conclude that the measures yielding significant outcomes are the most valid measures.

Using a large number of outcomes and then adopting stringent Bonferroni-corrected alpha values, or even more lenient approaches such as the Benjamini-Hochberg approach (1995), is not a reasonable strategy for intervention research, in which each additional participant is costly and difficult to recruit (Nakagawa, 2004). The necessary sample sizes for testing large numbers of outcomes with experiment-wise corrections to *p* values are unlikely to be achieved. Rather, the investigator should select the best measure(s) as the primary measure(s) of outcome (a judicious number of other variables can still be tested as secondary outcomes) or seek to cut the number of outcome variables by reducing the data before hypothesis testing (Rosenthal & Rosnow, 2008), for example, by conducting a principal components analysis of the outcome variables and using the component scores rather than individual variables for hypothesis testing. Kraemer et al. (2003) provided suggestions for combining data from multiple informants.

The problem of Type II error also plagues intervention research. If a treatment is genuinely effective, most often it will be found to be statistically significantly different from a waiting-list condition. Comparisons with an active treatment are another matter, however, because effect sizes in this case are likely to be no more than medium. Psychotherapy research trials are typically underpowered to detect this sort of difference (Kazdin & Bass, 1989), and researchers and readers frequently make the mistake of concluding there is no difference between treatments when from the outset the sample size precluded differences of a medium size from being statistically significant. With increased awareness of this problem, researchers have banded together across centers to conduct multisite trials to obtain the sample sizes they need to test important questions of differential efficacy. This, of course, introduces another set of challenges in ensuring that methods are comparable across two or more sites (Kraemer, 2000).

Noninferiority and Equivalence Testing

Often in intervention research, the investigator's goal is not to test whether one intervention is better than another but rather to test whether some new intervention is as good as a well-established treatment. Perhaps this new intervention is briefer, less costly, or easier to implement than the standard treatment. A frequent mistake is for the researcher to conduct standard tests for statistically significant differences between interventions' impact, find none, and declare that the two procedures are comparable in their efficacy. This is not correct; they were just not statistically significantly different in this trial. To conduct a proper test of the investigator's hypothesis requires a test of noninferiority (the new intervention is no worse than the standard intervention) or of equivalence (the new intervention is neither worse than nor better than the standard intervention; Stegner et al., 1996).

To conduct such tests, the investigators must identify in advance what effect they consider so small as to be clinically irrelevant (Piaggio et al., 2012). It is best if the field has some consensus on how small that difference should be and on what outcome variable it should be tested. The investigators then conduct statistical tests for equivalence or noninferiority (Stegner et al., 1996), depending on which fits best with their research question. These tests involve rejecting the null hypothesis that the two interventions are different in their efficacy rather than the usual null hypothesis of no difference. Equivalence and noninferiority trials have become common in biomedical research but not in psychological research, in part because the large sample sizes required for this approach are rare in psychotherapy research. Because sloppy research can lead investigators to find no difference between treatments when such a difference does exist (error swamps the treatment effect), equivalence and noninferiority trials must be exquisitely conducted with an eye to internal validity for confident interpretation.

Effect Size and Clinically Significant Change

A common error for researchers and research consumers is to state that the treatment effect was really big because the *p* value was very small. Despite decades of exhortations that psychologists should report and interpret the effect sizes derived from their findings (e.g., Wilkinson & Task Force on Statistical Inference, 1999), researchers and consumers of research still confuse the interpretation of a *p* value with the size of the effect. Because the *p* value is highly dependent on not only the size of the effect but also the sample size, we cannot determine how big the difference was between two intervention conditions by a report of the *p* value alone. To give the consumer an idea of how big the difference is in a way that is not dependent on the scale of the particular outcome measure used, the researcher should report an effect size, commonly given in standard deviation units, although this varies with the type of statistical analysis (Cohen, 1988).

Even the effect size, however, can be hard to interpret, as changes will be bigger on measures that are more reliable (because the standard deviation will be smaller). Patients might change substantially according to average effect sizes on a very reliable measure but still be quite impaired. Accordingly, if the investigator wishes to report how many of the patients are doing well, it is best to incorporate an additional approach. These approaches might include reporting what percentage of patients in each group no longer meet diagnostic criteria for the primary diagnosis at the end of treatment or reporting what percentage of patients in each group meet criteria for clinically significant change (Jacobson & Truax, 1991). The calculation of clinically significant change as cited includes determining whether a given patient has changed to a statistically reliable degree, and whether they are more likely to fall in the distribution of the scores of a normal sample rather than a sample of people with the disorder under investigation.

Research groups in some areas have developed conventions for what they consider recovery in their field that are based on yet different criteria.

For example, researchers in major depression in the United States have adopted a set of criteria for the definition of recovery from a major depressive episode (Rush, Kraemer, et al., 2006). Whatever method researchers choose, they may then test whether the intervention groups differ on the percentage of patients recovered, although this test will generally be less powerful than tests of the continuous variables.

Once some metric of success has been established, the investigator may then report the results using an effect size from biomedical research that has become increasingly popular in psychiatric research, that is, *number needed to treat* (NNT). NNT is the number of patients one would have to treat to achieve one more successful case than if an equal number of patients received the comparison or control. The smaller the NNT, the larger the treatment effect size. For example, the results of a meta-analysis of psychotherapy versus waiting-list control groups recast as NNT by Kraemer and Kupfer (2006) suggested that for every 3.1 patients who received psychotherapy rather than being on a waiting list, one more patient would improve. Kraemer and Kupfer also described methods for converting continuous measures of outcome into NNT.

Appropriate Statistical Analysis

Standards for the statistical analysis of data from intervention research are ever higher, and readers of older research papers may find procedures that would lead a manuscript to be rejected for publication in the 21st century. Several common issues arise.

First, as noted, missing data are common in longitudinal research. Patients drop out of treatment, and participants fail to complete all assessment points. The investigator who conducts only *completer analyses* of people who provide all data and who complete treatment is analyzing data that are unrepresentative of the sample that was randomized to intervention conditions. Once awareness of this problem developed, researchers began to use a procedure called *last observation carried forward* (LOCF) to cope with missing data (Shao & Zhong, 2003). For example, if the client drops out of treatment or refuses posttest assessment, their pretest score (or most recent score available) is substituted for the missing datum at posttest. Although this may be a better approach than a completer analysis, it may underestimate treatment effects, in that people sometimes disappear from trials because they are doing well and feel no further need for assistance. (See Lavori, 1992, for a further critique of the LOCF approach.)

Accordingly, the development of more sophisticated approaches to missing data has been a boon to intervention research. The approach variously called hierarchical linear modeling, random regression modeling, and multilevel modeling allows the investigator to model the trajectory across time on the outcome variable for each subject on the basis of however many data points that subject completed (Bryk & Raudenbush, 1987). The trajectories for the individual subjects then become the data for between-group analysis. If data are missing at random or missing completely at random, multilevel modeling approaches can cope well with less than complete data (Hedeker & Gibbons, 1997). To get the greatest benefit from this approach, the investigator would do well to collect outcome data at multiple points across the trial rather than just at pretest, posttest, and follow-up. Multiple data points not only provide greater statistical power (de Jong et al., 2010) but also allow a better determination of the individual trajectories and are especially helpful in the case of dropout.

Multilevel modeling allows the investigator to address readily a second common statistical problem in intervention research, that of nesting. Usually a given therapist sees multiple patients in a trial, and to the degree that there are any differences across therapists in how effective they are, patients seen by a particular therapist share some variance in their outcomes that is due to the therapist. Other forms of nesting include the group in trials of group therapy, the classroom and the school in interventions conducted in education settings, and the site in multisite trials. When nesting is ignored in the analyses, Type I error can increase dramatically (de Jong et al., 2010).

Multilevel modeling allows the researcher to build such nesting into the statistical analysis. A particularly thorny issue in studies involving nesting is whether to treat therapists, for example, as fixed or random effects. To treat therapists as fixed effects in the analyses means that the investigator cannot generalize the results of the trial beyond these specific therapists—a point largely ignored in the treatment literature. If therapists are treated as a random effect, it is reasonable to generalize the results of the study to similar therapists with comparable training (Crits-Christoph et al., 2003). Because inclusion of therapists as a random effect diminishes statistical power, investigators are loath to do this (Crits-Christoph et al., 2003).

The third common problem we will mention arises when full randomization is not possible because the investigator is conducting quasi-experimental research or when the investigator randomizes intact groups (e.g., schools) to an intervention program. In such cases, it is likely that there will be pretreatment differences between intervention conditions. Given large enough sample sizes, the investigator can overcome the problems represented by the preintervention differences with propensity score analysis (Joffe & Rosenbaum, 1999). In this approach, logistic regression is used to predict treatment group assignment by all possible covariates to yield a predicted probability of being in one group versus the other. This resulting probability score can then be used as a single covariate in the analyses of outcome. Alternatively, the propensity score may be used to form strata within which participants are closely matched, then the analyses are conducted within strata. The latter approach clearly requires a very large sample to execute with adequate power. If the investigator has collected data on all the important covariates, then propensity score analysis is effective in diminishing selection effects (Shadish et al., 2002).

CONSTRUCT VALIDITY OF AN EXPERIMENT

Construct validity refers to the extent to which one can make inferences from the procedures of a study to the higher order constructs they were intended to represent (Shadish et al., 2002). With respect to RCTs, that means the extent to which the investigator has accurately identified the causally active components of the treatment manipulation. Most treatments consist of multiple components, some specified by theory and others common to the treatment enterprise. Construct validity asks whether we understand the causally active components of the intervention and the mechanisms through which they operate.

As previously described in the section on selection of control groups, different types of control groups allow for increasingly greater confidence that the theory as specified was adequately tested. For example, cognitive therapy is predicated on a theory that states that teaching patients to examine the accuracy of their beliefs should reduce distress. If we were to compare cognitive therapy to its absence, we might very well produce an internally valid difference that could be attributed to the experimental manipulation (and thereby establish its efficacy), but it would not do much to convince a skeptic that it did so by targeting inaccurate beliefs. It could just as well have been the nonspecific aspects of the treatment package (expectation for change and personal contact with the therapist) that were responsible for the change observed. Construct validity would be enhanced if cognitive therapy were found to be superior to a nonspecific control that was equated for the mobilization of expectations and therapist contact. Construct validity would be enhanced even further if change in cognition was linked to subsequent change in distress in a manner suggestive of causal mediation. The issue, then, with respect to construct validity is whether the experiment conducted provides an adequate test of the underlying substantive theory. To do so, it must implement the treatment in question in an adequate fashion and control for other alternative explanations not specified by theory.

Treatment Manuals

Treatment manuals represent an attempt to specify the underlying principles and specific behaviors that together constitute a treatment intervention. Manuals differ in the extent to which they constrain the therapist's behavior: some provide considerable latitude for the clinician to respond to the specific needs of the client as they unfold over time, whereas others go so far as to specify the actual dialogue that the therapist is supposed to follow across the course of treatment. Treatment manuals serve a useful purpose in communicating what is done in a given intervention and facilitate dissemination to other researchers and therapists in other settings. They also reduce variability between therapists within a trial (Crits-Christoph et al., 1991), thereby enhancing the extent to which the essential aspects of a treatment are implemented (construct validity) and increasing the likelihood that treatment differences will be detected relative to controls.

Nonetheless, treatment manuals are neither necessary nor sufficient to ensure that an intervention has been adequately implemented in a given trial. In the classic Temple study, experienced psychoanalytic therapists operated without a formal treatment manual but were able to instantiate dynamic treatment in a representative fashion nonetheless, due no doubt to years of training and their experience (Sloane et al., 1975). At the same time, despite training all to a manual, the National Institute of Mental Health (NIMH) TDCRP found that therapists with prior experience with cognitive therapy got considerably better results than those who had none (Jacobson & Hollon, 1996). To assure the research consumer that the treatment was faithfully and well conducted, additional steps are required of the investigator. We turn to those next.

Therapist Adherence

Adherence refers to the extent that therapists implement the therapy as intended. A study would have little construct validity if therapist behavior bore no relationship to what was intended by theory. Adherence can be measured on the basis of therapist self-report or the completion of postsession checklists, but the preferred manner is by actual direct observation of the session itself, often in the form of ratings of audio or video tapes (Chevron & Rounsaville, 1983). Such methods require observers trained to recognize the behaviors specified by theory but do not necessarily require that those observers be competent to implement the therapy themselves. For example, Hill et al. (1992) found that cognitive therapy could readily be distinguished from interpersonal psychotherapy and each from clinical management of pharmacotherapy by nonprofessional raters listening to audiotapes from the TDCRP.

Therapist Training and Competence

Competence refers to the extent to which therapists perform the intended therapy in a skillful fashion. Competence is related to adherence (you cannot perform a therapy well if you are not performing the therapy) but can be differentiated at least in theory; it is possible to implement the various components of a treatment in a highly recognizable manner that is neither skillful nor responsive to the needs of the patient at a given moment. To use an analogy, it is possible to play a musical piece in a manner that others could recognize without doing so in a manner that is pleasing to the ear. In the TDCRP, adherence unexpectedly functioned as a suppressor variable, the inclusion of which enhanced the relation between competence and outcome in cognitive therapy, suggesting that at least some of the therapists were adherent to the approach without being competent in its execution (Shaw et al., 1999). Like adherence, competence can be rated in a variety of ways but most often is rated by expert therapists working from actual session tapes.

Adherence and competence are not fixed factors that a therapist obtains and retains for all cases and all time. For example, patient characteristics (e.g., interpersonal aggression; Boswell et al., 2013) may affect a therapist's performance, such that the therapist becomes what some have called *unskilled* with particularly challenging cases.

Therapist training is intended to enhance adherence and especially competence. Just how much training is required and how best it is accomplished is a matter of some debate, but it seems fair to say that the strategies pursued

should match the purposes of the study. In the typical efficacy trial, the goal is usually to determine whether a given treatment has a causal impact under ideal conditions. In such a trial, it seems reasonable to ask that the therapists be trained to the point at which they can implement the therapy in a manner specified by theory. In other types of trials, especially some types of effectiveness studies, the goal may be to see how much change can be produced by therapists trained to whatever level of competence is allowed given the pragmatic constraints in the natural environment. Either level of training is fine so long as it is clear what was going on, and causal inferences are drawn in an appropriate manner.

Training is often supplemented by subsequent supervision that may continue through the duration of the trial, as adherence and competence may deteriorate even over the course of the treatment of a given patient, and therapists may need additional supervision for maintaining their skills in the face of particularly challenging patients (Boswell et al., 2013). Again, just how to supervise and how much supervision to provide should be determined by the questions being asked in the particular trial, and problems arise only when the inferences drawn do not match the implementation. For example, in the TDCRP, therapists with varying levels of prior experience with and commitment to cognitive therapy were provided with several days of training and intensive supervision while working with several practice cases each. Once the study proper started, supervision was cut back unless ratings on a competence measure dropped below a preset cutoff (Shaw, 1984). What the investigators found was that rated levels of competence dropped from the training phase into the study proper (Shaw et al., 1999) and that cognitive therapy was less efficacious than medications and no better than pill-placebo for patients with more severe depressions (Elkin et al., 1995). By way of contrast, in a subsequent trial DeRubeis et al. (2005) selected experienced cognitive therapists at one site and, at a second site, continued intensive training throughout the course of the study proper for that site's less experienced cognitive therapists. The investigators found that cognitive therapy was as efficacious as medications and superior to pill-placebo in the treatment of patients with depressions of comparable severity. Although both trials were intended to speak to the efficacy of cognitive therapy as specified by theory, they differed considerably in the nature of the therapists they selected and the quality and intensity of the training and supervision that they provided—differences that appear to be reflected in the outcomes that they generated.

Allegiance

Investigator allegiance is an important correlate of variance in outcomes across the treatment literature (Luborsky et al., 1999). Treatments usually do better in the hands of investigators who are invested in their outcomes, and comparisons between different treatments often rise and fall on the basis of who carries out the study. There are at least two possible interpretations: First, it may be that investigators with a vested interest cannot or will not conduct a fair trial and that bias (unintended or otherwise) colors the results. Second, it could be that some investigators are simply more competent when it comes to implementing some treatments than others and that differential outcome across studies reflects differential competence of the investigators. For example, cognitive therapy was found to be superior to antidepressant medications in a study conducted at the site where the psychosocial treatment was first developed (Rush et al., 1977). However, pharmacotherapy was not adequately implemented: Dosages were marginal, and tapering was begun before the end of treatment. Subsequent studies that did a better job of implementation typically found cognitive therapy as efficacious as but no better than medication at the end of treatment (e.g., DeRubeis et al., 2005), although with an enduring effect following treatment termination that medications simply could not match (e.g., Hollon et al., 2005).

Unintended bias can be addressed by adherence to principles of good research design (random assignment and blinded evaluators), but differential competence can be resolved only by including

investigators in the research team who have expertise and investment in each of the modalities tested. This is the principle of *adversarial collaboration* that has been described in the cognitive psychology literature to offset the operation of bias (Mellers et al., 2001). It is important that this allegiance and expertise permeate all aspects of the study, starting with the investigator team and including the therapists who provide the respective interventions.

Expectancy

Patients enter treatment in the hope that it will make things better, and expectations of improvement have been shown to have a powerful effect on outcomes in their own right. Some treatments do a better job of mobilizing expectations for change than others, and differences in expectations can influence the comparisons between conditions. To the extent that the mobilization of expectations can be considered an inherent part of a given intervention, then expectancies pose no threat to the internal validity of the design. An effect is an effect and can be attributed to the intervention regardless of how it was produced.

Isolating the contribution of expectancy effects, however, can play a major role in determining whether a treatment works for the reasons specified by theory, a matter of construct validity. For example, it is routine to test new medications against a pharmacologically inert pill-placebo that controls for all the psychological aspects of medication-taking, including the expectation of change. Only if the novel medication exceeds that pill-placebo control in a beneficial fashion is it allowed to be marketed to patients. The pill-placebo control is presumed to generate similar expectations for relief to those generated by the actual medication (as well as other nonspecific benefits of contact with a treating professional), and any differences observed are presumed to be the consequence of the pharmacological properties of the medication. Similar steps are often taken in psychotherapy research to determine whether comparison conditions are equated for the expectations that they generate at the outset of treatment, and studies are sometimes criticized for including intent-to-fail controls if they cannot be shown to be equated for initial expectations (Baskin et al., 2003). We suspect that expectancy differences may be one result of differences in allegiance to different treatments. That is, if investigators compare some alternative treatment to their preferred treatment, they may inadvertently do so in a way that communicates to patients and therapists which treatment is expected to be inferior (e.g., by their enthusiasm, the quality of the training materials, and supervision provided).

Alliance

Patients not only have expectations regarding treatment outcomes but also form relationships with their therapists. The quality of the working alliance represents one attempt to operationalize the quality of the therapeutic relationship, and the term is often used in a generic fashion to refer to the larger construct of relatedness between patient and therapist (Goldfried, 1980). It has long been noted that various measures of alliance predict treatment outcome (Horvath & Symonds, 1991). What is not so clear, however, is whether the therapeutic alliance plays a causal role in producing those outcomes. In most instances, alliance is rated periodically across treatment and correlated with treatment outcome. This means that early change in symptoms could be driving the quality of the relationship rather than the other way around.

Feeley et al. (1999) tested this hypothesis by assessing symptom change before and after therapy sessions that were rated for techniques specific to cognitive therapy and for nonspecific quality of the therapeutic alliance. After they controlled for prior symptom change, adherence to cognitive therapy in early sessions predicted subsequent change in depression, whereas ratings of the therapeutic alliance did not. Moreover, rated quality of the therapeutic alliance improved over time as a consequence of prior symptom change. These findings suggest that for cognitive therapy (as practiced in their sample), adherence to the techniques specified by theory drove subsequent symptom change

and that change in turn drove the rated quality of the therapeutic alliance. At the same time, other studies that have controlled for prior symptom change in a similar fashion have found that rated quality of the alliance does predict subsequent symptom change (Flückiger et al., 2020), although effect sizes are lower than in studies in which the temporal sequence problem was ignored. What seems likely is that the therapeutic alliance may be either a cause or a consequence of improvement in treatment and that it is important to control for the temporal relations between treatment process and symptom change whenever investigating such effects (Flückiger et al., 2020). Even so, it is important to keep in mind that the most sophisticated analyses controlling for temporal relations between treatment process and symptom change are still correlational in nature and not sufficient to establish a causal effect.

Exclusion of Medication or Medication Stability

One issue that is sometimes confronted in psychotherapy research is what to do about patients who enter a study already on medications. On the one hand, patients often are reluctant to give up medications that they are already taking, and excluding those patients from the trial would reduce the external validity of the design. On the other hand, patients are taking medications precisely because they think they make a difference, and to the extent this is true, such effects can obscure (or facilitate) the effects of psychotherapy.

Some investigators resolve this dilemma by asking patients to discontinue any psychoactive medications before entering the trial (and losing at least some potential patients who refuse to do so), whereas others are willing to allow patients to remain on stable doses of existing medications. Either strategy represents a reasonable accommodation to the practical realities of conducting clinical trials with patients who can choose to not participate, and causal inferences can still be drawn so long as they are tempered by recognition of the possible influences of concurrent medication usage. For example, Barlow et al. (2000)

found that successfully treated patients with panic disorder who had received medication plus CBT during treatment did worse in the follow-up period after medication was withdrawn than those who had received CBT alone or CBT plus placebo. While these patients were randomized to treatment conditions, it seems likely that this effect would hold for those who enter on medication. In such situations, it is particularly important to monitor what medications patients are taking and to conduct secondary analyses that control for medication usage. Changes in medication usage that occur after randomization are particularly problematic because they could be a consequence of differential treatment.

Exclusion of Other Treatment

Similar issues are raised by allowing patients to pursue other psychosocial treatment during the course of the study. As was the case for off-protocol medication treatment, excluding patients who refuse to give up ongoing psychotherapy threatens the external validity of the design, whereas allowing such patients in the trial presents problems for construct validity (if comparable in nature across conditions) or internal validity (if differential across the conditions). Moreover, having patients in two different kinds of psychotherapies risks having them working at cross-purposes. What many investigators do is to ask that patients discontinue any outside psychotherapy directed at the disorder under study for the duration of the trial, but they often make exceptions for psychosocial interventions directed at other issues, such as marital therapy.

Adequacy of Dose of Treatment

The essence of construct validity is that the underlying constructs are tested in a manner specified by theory. That suggests that what constitutes an adequate dose of treatment is determined by the question being addressed. There is nothing inherent in any given dose of treatment, but the doses selected for testing ought to be consistent with what is specified by theory. For example, neither the early study that compared cognitive therapy to inadequate doses of medication treatment

(Rush et al., 1977) nor the subsequent NIMH TDCRP that left the implementation of cognitive therapy in the hands of relatively inexperienced therapists (Elkin et al., 1989) provided an adequate basis for comparing the relative efficacy of the two modalities as each is ideally practiced. Meta-analytic reviews suggested that each is comparable to the other when each is adequately implemented (Cuijpers, 2017). However, those same meta-analytic reviews also showed an advantage for full-strength medication treatment over relatively abbreviated courses of psychotherapy in managed care settings. It seems fair to conclude from these reviews that medication treatment is superior to psychotherapy when the number of sessions of the latter must be restricted because of pragmatic constraints, so long as one does not conclude that that relative inferiority reflects anything other than those pragmatic constraints.

EXTERNAL VALIDITY

External validity refers to the extent that treatment outcomes observed in controlled trials can be generalized to populations and settings of interest (Shadish et al., 2002). Several aspects of generalizability need to be considered, including but not limited to variation across patients, therapists, and settings. External validity is closely related to the notion of clinical utility and may be considered in conjunction with cost (American Psychological Association [APA], 2002).

Continuum of Efficacy–Effectiveness Research

It has become commonplace in recent years to differentiate between efficacy and effectiveness research (Nathan et al., 2000). According to this distinction, efficacy research is said to be conducted in highly controlled settings using carefully selected patients who are randomly assigned to treatment by highly trained therapists. Conversely, effectiveness research is thought to be conducted in real-world settings in which random assignment to differential treatment is not always feasible and in which presumably more complicated patients are treated by less experienced therapists working under pragmatic constraints imposed by their many clinical demands (Seligman, 1995). Although there is some truth to these perceptions, we think it is unwise to draw too sharp a distinction between efficacy and effectiveness and prefer instead to think in terms of internal and external validity. Any given study can be evaluated with respect to how it scores on each dimension. The goal is to determine how well a given intervention works in the real-world settings in which it needs to be applied to wholly representative patients.

Treatment outcomes are largely a function of two sets of factors: patients and procedures. Patients' characteristics are fixed at the time they first present for treatment, but procedures (including therapist skills and setting considerations) can be changed if there is sufficient reason. That is why we think that it is especially important to conduct research on wholly representative patient samples. If a treatment does not work for the patients for whom it is intended, then there is little that can be done to improve the situation. In contrast, there can be great value in first establishing that something works under ideal conditions even if it does not initially generalize well to real-world settings, because therapists can be better trained and contexts modified if there is sufficient reason to do so. That is why we emphasize internal validity over external validity and selecting representative patients (rather than therapists or settings) in early trials.

Generalizability

Beautifully conducted research may be of great interest to scientists, but psychotherapy research is also meant to be of applied interest. Thus, we care about whether the results obtained are pertinent for other patients, those who were not enrolled in the research trial. This is a question of generalizability.

To patients in clinical settings.   It is important to know whether treatments that are efficacious in research settings generalize to the kinds of applied settings in which most patients are treated.

Applied settings can vary with respect to the caseload expected, the length of treatment that is feasible, and the demands on clinician time (Weisz & Addis, 2006). For example, we were once informed by therapists who worked for a large managed-care organization that they could see patients as often as they thought appropriate, just so long as they started six new patients a week. Although no constraint was placed on the number of sessions that could be offered to any given patient, the pressure to add so many new patients effectively limited the number of possible sessions.

To patients in community settings.   There is a widespread perception that patients treated in efficacy studies in research settings are necessarily less complicated or comorbid than patients found in community settings (Westen et al., 2004). Although this may have been the case in early analogue studies, there is no necessary reason why complex and comorbid patients must be excluded from controlled trials. For example, two-thirds of the patients selected on the basis of meeting criteria for major depressive disorder in an earlier efficacy trial in a research clinic also met criteria for one or more additional Axis I disorders, half met criteria for one or more Axis II disorders, and one-third met criteria for substance abuse or dependence (DeRubeis et al., 2005).

Conversely, when Stirman et al. (2003) matched information found in community outpatients' charts to the inclusion and exclusion criteria used in published trials, they found nearly 80% of the diagnosed patients in community settings would have qualified for inclusion in one or more published RCTs. The major reason patients would have been excluded from RCTs was not that they were too complicated or comorbid. Rather, their conditions were not severe enough, in that many carried diagnoses of adjustment disorder. Such disorders are by definition transient and will likely never warrant the conduct of an RCT. It also is likely that at least some of these patients would have met criteria for Axis I or Axis II disorders if diagnosed according to strict research criteria; clinicians in applied settings often give diagnoses of adjustment disorder to avoid stigma. If so, then an even larger proportion of the patients seen in applied settings would likely qualify for inclusion in one or more controlled clinical trials. Clearly, research needs to be done with the kinds of patients found in applied community settings, but it is not clear that they will prove to be all that different from patients found in clinical research sites.

To clinicians in community settings. Clinicians in community settings are likely to be less experienced with specific disorders and less highly trained than clinicians in research settings. It is an open question just how well these clinicians can implement the kinds of treatments developed in research settings and tested in efficacy studies. On the one hand, there is little evidence that experience or professional status necessarily guarantees superior performance (Jacobson & Christensen, 1996), but on the other, much of the variability in outcomes across different studies appears to be related to the competence with which the therapists can perform the given interventions (Jacobson & Hollon, 1996). It is likely that years of experience and professional status are not particularly good markers of competence with a particular approach.

It is not clear just how much training is required to allow community clinicians to perform with the same level of proficiency as research therapists or how feasible such training is to provide in community settings. What does appear to be clear is that the provision of treatment manuals and brief workshops are not sufficient to help community therapists reach a reasonable level of proficiency; ongoing supervision is required for some period of time (Miller et al., 2006).

To patients of diverse backgrounds. It is important to include a diverse array of patients with respect to race, ethnicity, and socioeconomic status (SES) in research trials to determine whether study findings generalize to such patients. For example, in cognitive processing therapy for posttraumatic stress disorder, Lester et al. (2010) found that Black patients were more likely to

drop out of treatment than White ones but nonetheless had equivalent treatment outcomes in intention-to-treat analyses. Minority patients tend to be few in number in clinical trials not only because they are fewer in number overall but also because they may be suspicious of the motives of clinical researchers (with considerable historical justification). Language can be a barrier for many ethnic patients, and patients with low SES often face barriers to participation with respect to transportation and childcare. It is often the case that special efforts must be made to recruit and retain such patients in controlled trials (Miranda et al., 2003). Such efforts are required to address longstanding health disparities minority patients have suffered (Atdjian & Vega, 2005). Research in global mental health serves as a reminder that race and ethnicity are largely social constructs; most of the interventions that work in high-income countries work as well (if culturally adapted) in low- and middle-income countries (Singla et al., 2017).

To other research settings. Treatments typically are developed by a single individual or group and tested in the sites at which they were first developed. This means that early studies typically are done by groups that are invested in the treatment they are testing. Replication is a key principle in science, and if a treatment is truly efficacious, then other investigators at other sites should be able to replicate the findings generated in those initial trials. Some shrinkage is to be expected, as it is unlikely that other groups will be as expert in a given modality as the people who developed it. Nonetheless, if a treatment is to have value in real-world applications, then it must perform well in the hands of other groups at other sites. At the same time, the principle of replication implies that those other groups put in a good faith effort to learn how to implement the treatment in a reasonable fashion. Replication means that we should be able to reproduce the earlier findings if we implement the same procedures: With respect to treatment trials, this means that we must implement the treatment in question with reasonable fidelity.

Feasibility

Feasibility refers to the ease with which treatment can be delivered to actual patients in the settings in which they are typically treated (APA, 2002). Feasibility incorporates such factors as acceptability, patients' willingness and ability to adhere to the requirements of the intervention, ease of dissemination, and cost-effectiveness. We examine each in turn.

Acceptability and patient-preference designs.

For a treatment to be applied in practice, it must be acceptable to patients and other relevant parties, including therapists and administrators. There are many reasons why individual patients may prefer not to receive particular treatments, and these preferences need to be respected (APA Presidential Task Force on Evidence-Based Practice, 2006). At the same time, patients often have trouble accepting the very interventions that are most likely to be useful to them. For example, exposure therapy is the best established psychological treatment for obsessive–compulsive disorder, yet it is frightening to most patients because it calls for them to do exactly those things that they most fear.

Therapists also may be reluctant to implement treatments, like exposure, that they find threatening or distasteful and omit them or implement them poorly when they believe, for example, that patients cannot tolerate the initial distress of exposure or, worse, will decompensate during treatment (e.g., Deacon et al., 2013). Moreover, some go so far as to ignore empirically supported interventions in favor of more traditional approaches that they find more compelling or in which they are already trained. The recent APA clinical practice guideline on the treatment of PTSD provides an example. Despite clear empirical evidence supporting the superiority of exposure-based approaches that involved reliving the traumatic event over other more traditional approaches, over 40,000 practitioners petitioned the APA to rescind the guideline because it did not reflect their preferred approaches (Hollon & Teachman, 2019).

Acceptability also plays a role in the decision to randomize. Given that patients differ in terms of how they are likely to change over time in the absence of treatment, we have argued in the section on Randomization that random assignment to intervention conditions is essential if any differences observed in outcomes are to be attributed to the experimental manipulation.

That being said, no one likes to be randomized, and no one likes to randomize someone else to treatment. Prospective patients dislike the notion of leaving their fates to chance, and clinicians typically assume, rightly or wrongly, that they have the experience and expertise to select the best treatment for a given patient. Some have gone so far as to say that randomization may turn out to be worse than useless: Choice is itself curative, and patients may adhere better if they get the treatment they prefer (Seligman, 1995). A number of potential solutions have been proposed, from relying on retrospective surveys of patient satisfaction to the use of quasi-experimental designs that attempt to control for some of the threats to internal validity, to the use of benchmarking in which the results of open trials in applied settings are compared with those obtained in randomized controlled trials. Retrospective surveys are wholly uncontrolled and highly susceptible to the risk of confounding patient characteristics with treatment effects, quasi-experimental designs provide some protection against threats to internal validity but that protection is only partial, and benchmarking is interpretatively ambiguous because any similarities or differences observed could be the product of differences in patients or procedures.

These concerns have led to an interest in the patient-preference design. Brewin and Bradley (1989) proposed a comprehensive cohort design that restricts randomization to only those patients who are willing to accept it; those who refuse are provided with the treatment they prefer. Others have proposed a two-stage randomization design in which patients are randomized to be (a) randomized to condition or (b) allowed to pick their treatment (Wennberg et al., 1993). Neither approach is wholly satisfying because causal inferences can be drawn with any confidence only for patients who were randomized to the respective treatment conditions. The comprehensive cohort design does allow randomized patients to be benchmarked against those who refused and got their preferred treatment, and the two-stage randomized design does allow causal inferences to be drawn about the effects of patient choice. It remains unclear just how great a problem this is. A systematic meta-analytic review of patient-preference designs found that patient preferences led to substantial rates of refusal; prospective patients who are employed and well educated were especially likely to refuse randomization (King et al., 2005). This suggests that patient preferences are a threat to the external validity of the typical RCT. At the same time, there was little evidence that patient preferences compromised the conclusions drawn from the studies: Differences in outcomes between randomized and preference groups typically were small (especially in larger studies) and, when they were evident in smaller trials, were inconsistent in direction. The preference problem may not be as big as some believe.

The NIMH-funded Sequenced Treatment Alternatives to Relieve Depression (STAR*D; Rush, Trivedi, et al., 2006) project used a particularly interesting strategy called equipoise stratified randomization in which patients or clinicians were allowed to rule out treatment strategies that they found unacceptable. Patients were subsequently randomized to the remaining options and only included in analyses that compared patients who accepted randomization to a given option. For example, patients who showed a partial response to their initial medication could choose to not be switched, and patients who were unable to tolerate their initial medication could choose to not have their medication augmented. This approach appears to be the most compelling of the patient-preference strategies and has generated some enthusiasm in the field. Still, it is not without its problems. Rates of refusal were suspiciously high for some conditions (less than one third of the participants were willing to be randomized to cognitive therapy because they had to pay for therapy). Permitting patients to opt out of specific strategies might encourage greater rates of refusal

than might otherwise have occurred. Moreover, treating clinicians often have even stronger preferences than their patients, which may inflate rates of refusal. Nonetheless, equipoise stratified randomization is an interesting approach that warrants further consideration.

Clients' adherence to treatment requirements. Even the most efficacious treatment will not work if the client does not implement the necessary steps. This issue is closely related to acceptability but is slightly more subtle. Patients may readily accept a treatment but not necessarily carry through with all the steps required to derive maximum benefit. Both the quality and the quantity of the homework patients complete has been found to predict treatment outcomes (Kazantzis et al., 2016). Similarly, it would be inappropriate to say that a medication does not work if a patient does not take it. From a methodological standpoint, it is important to assess adherence to permit accurate conclusions about treatment efficacy. For example, we once monitored medication adherence in patients assigned to continuation treatment and conducted secondary analyses in which we censored patients who were less than fully adherent in the several weeks before a relapse (Hollon et al., 2005). Whereas the primary analysis that left such relapses uncensored provided the best estimate of how patients actually did on continuation medication, the secondary analyses provided an estimate of how those patients would have done if they all had been adherent.

Ease of dissemination. Some treatments are easier to learn than others and, therefore, easier to disseminate. Classical psychoanalysis requires a training analysis of many years' duration, and even those aiming to practice psychoanalytically oriented psychotherapy are encouraged to pursue personal therapy as part of the training process. It is likely that such requirements contributed to the gradual decline in the number of such practitioners across recent decades (Norcross et al., 2005). No intervention grew so rapidly over the last quarter of the last century as CBT, whereas the number of practitioners professing an allegiance to more purely behavioral therapies has stayed relatively constant over that same interval. That may be subject to change in years to come as the so-called third-wave behavioral approaches gain greater credibility in the treatment community, fueled in part by the perception that it is easier to learn to do simple behavioral interventions than to also learn more complicated cognitive strategies. From a methodological perspective, it is important to report just what was required to implement the treatment(s) in a given study, including who the therapists were, how they were selected, how much training was required, and what kind of supervision was provided.

Cost-effectiveness.　Consideration of the costs of treatment should be conceptually distinct from the scientific evidence for its effectiveness, but costs need to be considered nonetheless (APA, 2002). Costs include the expense to the patient and the health care professional as well as the cost of any technology or equipment involved in the intervention. Clearly, those interventions that produce the same outcome at a lower cost than others are to be preferred. It becomes more difficult to decide on the appropriate course of action when the most expensive treatments are also the most efficacious. Health care economists have developed ways to quantify the costs of leaving problems unresolved (e.g., how much is a depression-free day worth?), and it is often possible to evaluate the relative costs of an intervention against the value it provides. Conducting a sophisticated cost-effectiveness analysis requires collecting information not just on the direct costs of treatment but also on the indirect costs incurred, such as time lost from work and child care and transportation expenses. Moreover, given that costs are often not normally distributed (a single hospitalization can be extremely expensive), the sample sizes required to conduct a sophisticated cost–benefit analysis are often exponentially larger than those required to detect a treatment effect. Nonetheless, information regarding the differential costs and benefits of different treatments can be valuable in evaluating the relative merits of different treatments.

Relative cost-effectiveness also can be influenced by the health care system in which it is embedded. In the United States, health care organizations often have little incentive to provide preventive interventions even when they are cost-effective over the long run, because job change happens with sufficient frequency that third-party payers rarely profit from the long-term benefits of preventive care (Stricker et al., 1999). Conversely, with the incentive of its single-payer system, Great Britain invested £700 million to train therapists to provide the cognitive and behavioral interventions shown to have enduring effects that make them more cost-effective than ongoing medication treatment (Clark, 2018). This means cost-effectiveness is not absolute and must be considered in the context of the larger economic system in which it is embedded.

Implementation.　Related to and overlapping with some of the topics we have raised in this section on generalization are developments in implementation science (Brown et al., 2017). In this burgeoning field, the outcome variables are no longer how well patients respond to treatment but how well systems adopt treatments developed in efficacy and effectiveness trials. Thus, implementation science concerns itself with whether a given treatment is used in, for example, community agencies, how well it is implemented in those agencies, what barriers exist to its uptake, and what strategies might be most successful in making changes in agencies' use of an effective treatment. To further these ends, implementation scientists use the full array of research designs, including, for example qualitative and survey research to identify barriers to uptake, and experimental and quasi-experimental designs to test different implementation strategies. From our reading of the literature, they are more likely to use stepped-wedge designs (Hemming et al., 2018) than are efficacy and effectiveness researchers. Such a design allows all participating agencies to ultimately receive the selected intervention but in a staggered fashion. Thus, one cluster of agencies might receive an implementation strategy after a suitable baseline data collection interval, whereas the second cluster continues in baseline until a later period, the third cluster in yet a later period, and so forth. Once each cluster of agencies starts the intervention phase, they continue in it until the end of the trial. Such trials are statistically complicated but likely encourage agencies' participation, as all will benefit ultimately from the implementation strategy, with the length of the lags determined by the amount of time required for implementation and assessment of its effect.

Representativeness. Seligman (1995) argued that psychotherapy as practiced in RCTs lacks external validity because it is unrepresentative of community practice; in such settings, if a client fails to respond to treatment, practitioners change the treatment approach rather than administering the monotherapy of an RCT. Whether that consistently happens in routine practice we cannot say, but certainly it should. How are such practices to be captured in controlled research? An important innovation in treatment research design is the adaptive trial, one example of which is the SMART design (Sequential Multiple Assignment Randomized Trial; Lei et al., 2012). Such a design maintains much of the rigor of the

RCT but adapts treatment according to clients' initial response. In such a trial, clients who show unsatisfactory response to an intervention are randomized to a second intervention, whereas those who are showing good benefit remain with the original approach. Such designs can get quite complex and require specialized statistical approaches, but they can offer rich results of great interest to practitioners. The critical elements of a SMART design are (a) a set of sequential decisions about a client's care, (b) development of a set of interventions that can be used at each sequential decision point, (c) identification of variables that indicate when a change in treatment should occur (e.g., poor early response), and (d) clear if–then decision rules to be made at each critical decision point (Lei et al., 2012). Typically, a SMART is conducted only when there are two or more intervention approaches that have each proved efficacious in RCTs. Figure 30.2 provides an example from Pelham et al.'s (2016) comparison of behavior modification, medication, and their combination for children with ADHD. On the main outcome variable, children who received low-dose behavior modification followed by high-dose behavior modification if insufficient response ("B-then-B" in Figure 30.2) showed the best results.

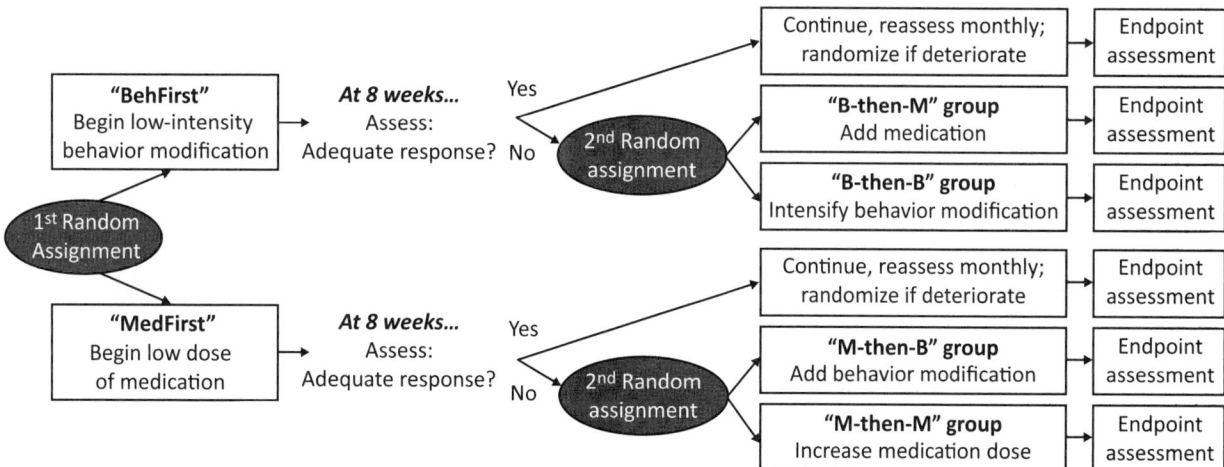

FIGURE 30.2. Example of a SMART (Sequential Multiple Assignment Randomized Trial) design. From "Treatment Sequencing for Childhood ADHD: A Multiple-Randomization Study of Adaptive Medication and Behavioral Interventions," by W. E. Pelham, Jr., G. A. Fabiano, J. G. Waxmonsky, A. R. Greiner, E. M. Gnagy, W. E. Pelham III, S. Coxe, J. Verley, I. Bhatia, K. Hart, K. Karch, E. Konijnendijk, K. Tresco, I. Nahum-Shani, and S. A. Murphy, 2016, *Journal of Clinical Child & Adolescent Psychology*, 45(4), p. 401 (https://doi.org/10.1080/15374416.2015.1105138). Copyright 2016 by Taylor and Francis. Reprinted with permission.

CONCLUSION

Methodology for intervention research necessarily cuts across many of the topics of other chapters in these volumes, and we have only touched on complex issues that deserve prolonged discussion. We refer the reader to other chapters in these volumes for additional information and to excellent texts such as Shadish et al. (2002) and Kazdin (2017) on research design and MacKinnon (2008) on mediation. In addition, we believe the reader will find it useful to refer to the CONSORT statements on non-inferiority and equivalence trials (Piaggio et al., 2012), RCTs (Boutron et al., 2017; Schultz et al., 2010), and stepped-wedge trials (Hemming et al., 2018), as well as the TREND statement on quasi-experiments (Des Jarlais et al., 2004), and APA's paper on journal article reporting standards (Appelbaum et al., 2018). Although these statements are designed to encourage uniform reporting of critical design features, being reminded of what these features are when planning the research rather than after the fact facilitates the conduct of sound research.

References

Addis, M. E., Hatgis, C., Cardemil, E., Jacob, K., Krasnow, A. D., & Mansfield, A. (2006). Effectiveness of cognitive-behavioral treatment for panic disorder versus treatment as usual in a managed care setting: 2-year follow-up. *Journal of Consulting and Clinical Psychology*, 74(2), 377–385. https://doi.org/10.1037/0022-006X.74.2.377

Aiken, L. S., & West, S. G. (1991). *Multiple regression: Testing and interpreting interactions*. SAGE.

American Psychological Association. (2002). Criteria for evaluating treatment guidelines. *American Psychologist*, 57(12), 1052–1059. https://doi.org/10.1037/0003-066X.57.12.1052

APA Presidential Task Force on Evidence-Based Practice. (2006). Evidence-based practice in psychology. *American Psychologist*, 61(4), 271–285. https://doi.org/10.1037/0003-066X.61.4.271

Appelbaum, M., Cooper, H., Kline, R. B., Mayo-Wilson, E., Nezu, A. M., & Rao, S. M. (2018). Journal article reporting standards for quantitative research in psychology: The APA Publications and Communications Board task force report. *American Psychologist*, 73(1), 3–25. https://doi.org/10.1037/amp0000191

Atdjian, S., & Vega, W. A. (2005). Disparities in mental health treatment in U.S. racial and ethnic minority groups: Implications for psychiatrists. *Psychiatric Services*, 56(12), 1600–1602. https://doi.org/10.1176/appi.ps.56.12.1600

Barlow, D. H., Gorman, J. M., Shear, M. K., & Woods, S. W. (2000). Cognitive-behavioral therapy, imipramine, or their combination for panic disorder: A randomized controlled trial. *JAMA*, 283(19), 2529–2536. https://doi.org/10.1001/jama.283.19.2529

Baron, R. M., & Kenny, D. A. (1986). The moderator-mediator variable distinction in social psychological research: Conceptual, strategic, and statistical considerations. *Journal of Personality and Social Psychology*, 51(6), 1173–1182. https://doi.org/10.1037/0022-3514.51.6.1173

Baskin, T. W., Tierney, S. C., Minami, T., & Wampold, B. E. (2003). Establishing specificity in psychotherapy: A meta-analysis of structural equivalence of placebo controls. *Journal of Consulting and Clinical Psychology*, 71(6), 973–979. https://doi.org/10.1037/0022-006X.71.6.973

Benjamini, Y., & Hochberg, Y. (1995). Controlling the false discovery rate: A practical and powerful approach to multiple testing. *Journal of the Royal Statistical Society: Series B. Methodological*, 57(1), 289–300. https://doi.org/10.1111/j.2517-6161.1995.tb02031.x

Boswell, J. F., Gallagher, M. W., Sauer-Zavala, S. E., Bullis, J., Gorman, J. M., Shear, M. K., Woods, S., & Barlow, D. H. (2013). Patient characteristics and variability in adherence and competence in cognitive-behavioral therapy for panic disorder. *Journal of Consulting and Clinical Psychology*, 81(3), 443–454. https://doi.org/10.1037/a0031437

Boutron, I., Altman, D. G., Moher, D., Schulz, K. F., & Ravaud, P. (2017). CONSORT statement for randomized trials of nonpharmacologic treatments: A 2017 update and a CONSORT extension for nonpharmacologic trial abstracts. *Annals of Internal Medicine*, 167(1), 40–47. https://doi.org/10.7326/M17-0046

Brewin, C. R., & Bradley, C. (1989). Patient preferences and randomised clinical trials. *British Medical Journal*, 299(6694), 313–315. https://doi.org/10.1136/bmj.299.6694.313

Brown, C. H., Curran, G., Palinkas, L. A., Aarons, G. A., Wells, K. B., Jones, L., Collins, L. M., Duan, N., Mittman, B. S., Wallace, A., Tabak, R. G., Ducharme, L., Chambers, D., Neta, G., Wiley, T., Landsverk, J., Cheung, K., & Cruden, G. (2017). An overview of research and evaluation designs for dissemination and implementation. *Annual*

Review of Public Health, *38*, 1–22. https://doi.org/10.1146/annurev-publhealth-031816-044215

Bryk, A. S., & Raudenbush, S. W. (1987). Application of hierarchical linear models to assessing change. *Psychological Bulletin*, *101*(1), 147–158. https://doi.org/10.1037/0033-2909.101.1.147

Campbell, M. K., Piaggio, G., Elbourne, D. R., & Altman, D. G. (2012). CONSORT 2010 statement: Extension to cluster randomised trials. *BMJ*, *345*, e5661. https://doi.org/10.1136/bmj.e5661

Chevron, E. S., & Rounsaville, B. J. (1983). Evaluating the clinical skills of psychotherapists: A comparison of techniques. *Archives of General Psychiatry*, *40*(10), 1129–1132. https://doi.org/10.1001/archpsyc.1983.01790090091014

Clark, D. M. (2018). Realizing the mass public benefit of evidence-based psychological therapies: The IAPT Program. *Annual Review of Clinical Psychology*, *14*(1), 159–183. https://doi.org/10.1146/annurev-clinpsy-050817-084833

Coffman, S. J., Martell, C. R., Dimidjian, S., Gallop, R., & Hollon, S. D. (2007). Extreme nonresponse in cognitive therapy: Can behavioral activation succeed where cognitive therapy fails? *Journal of Consulting and Clinical Psychology*, *75*(4), 531–541. https://doi.org/10.1037/0022-006X.75.4.531

Cohen, J. (1988). *Statistical power analysis for the behavioral sciences* (2nd ed.). Erlbaum.

Cohen, Z. D., Delgadillo, J., & DeRubeis, R. J. (2021). Personalized treatment approaches. In M. Barkham, W. Lutz, & L. G. Castonguay (Eds.), *Bergin and Garfield's handbook of psychotherapy and behavior change* (7th ed., pp. 673–704). Wiley Blackwell.

Cohen, Z. D., & DeRubeis, R. J. (2018). Treatment selection in depression. *Annual Review of Clinical Psychology*, *14*, 209–236. https://doi.org/10.1146/annurev-clinpsy-050817-084746

Crits-Christoph, P., Baranackie, K., Kurcias, J. S., Beck, A. T., Carroll, K., Perry, K., Luborsky, L., McLellan, A., Woody, G., Thompson, L., Gallagher, D., & Zitrin, C. (1991). Meta-analysis of therapist effects in psychotherapy outcome studies. *Psychotherapy Research*, *1*(2), 81–91. https://doi.org/10.1080/10503309112331335511

Crits-Christoph, P., Tu, X., & Gallop, R. (2003). Therapists as fixed versus random effects-some statistical and conceptual issues: A comment on Siemer and Joormann (2003). *Psychological Methods*, *8*(4), 518–523. https://doi.org/10.1037/1082-989X.8.4.518

Cuijpers, P. (2017). Four decades of outcome research on psychotherapies for adult depression: An overview of a series of meta-analyses. *Canadian Psychology*, *58*(1), 7–19. https://doi.org/10.1037/cap0000096

Cuijpers, P., Quero, S., Papola, D., Cristea, I., & Karyotaki, E. (2021). Care-as-usual control groups across different settings in randomized trials on psychotherapy for adult depression: A meta-analysis. *Psychological Medicine*, *51*(4), 634–644. https://doi.org/10.1017/S0033291719003581

Dalgleish, T., Black, M., Johnston, D., & Bevan, A. (2020). Transdiagnostic approaches to mental health problems: Current status and future directions. *Journal of Consulting and Clinical Psychology*, *88*(3), 179–195. https://doi.org/10.1037/ccp0000482

de Jong, K., Moerbeek, M., & van der Leeden, R. (2010). A priori power analysis in longitudinal three-level multilevel models: An example with therapist effects. *Psychotherapy Research*, *20*(3), 273–284. https://doi.org/10.1080/10503300903376320

Deacon, B. J., Farrell, N. R., Kemp, J. J., Dixon, L. J., Sy, J. T., Zhang, A. R., & McGrath, P. B. (2013). Assessing therapist reservations about exposure therapy for anxiety disorders: The Therapist Beliefs about Exposure Scale. *Journal of Anxiety Disorders*, *27*(8), 772–780. https://doi.org/10.1016/j.janxdis.2013.04.006

DeRubeis, R. J., Cohen, Z. D., Forand, N. R., Fournier, J. C., Gelfand, L. A., & Lorenzo-Luaces, L. (2014). The Personalized Advantage Index: Translating research on prediction into individualized treatment recommendations. A demonstration. *PLOS ONE*, *9*(1), e83875. https://doi.org/10.1371/journal.pone.0083875

DeRubeis, R. J., Hollon, S. D., Amsterdam, J. D., Shelton, R. C., Young, P. R., Salomon, R. M., O'Reardon, J. P., Lovett, M. L., Gladis, M. M., Brown, L. L., & Gallop, R. (2005). Cognitive therapy vs. medications in the treatment of moderate to severe depression. *Archives of General Psychiatry*, *62*(4), 409–416. https://doi.org/10.1001/archpsyc.62.4.409

DeRubeis, R. J., Zajecka, J., Shelton, R. C., Amsterdam, J. D., Fawcett, J., Xu, C., Young, P. R., Gallop, R., & Hollon, S. D. (2020). Prevention of recurrence after recovery from a major depressive episode with antidepressant medication alone or in combination with cognitive behavior therapy: Phase 2 of a 2-phase randomized clinical trial. *JAMA Psychiatry*, *77*(3), 237–245. https://doi.org/10.1001/jamapsychiatry.2019.3900

Des Jarlais, D. C., Lyles, C., Crepaz, N., & the TREND Group. (2004). Improving the reporting quality of nonrandomized evaluations of behavioral and public health interventions: The TREND statement. *American Journal of Public Health*, *94*(3), 361–366. https://doi.org/10.2105/AJPH.94.3.361

Driessen, E., Cuijpers, P., Hollon, S. D., & Dekker, J. J. M. (2010). Does pretreatment severity moderate the efficacy of psychological treatment of adult outpatient depression? A meta-analysis. *Journal of Consulting and Clinical Psychology, 78*(5), 668–680. https://doi.org/10.1037/a0020570

Efron, B. (1971). Forcing a sequential experiment to be balanced. *Biometrika, 58*(3), 403–417. https://doi.org/10.1093/biomet/58.3.403

Elkin, I., Gibbons, R. D., Shea, M. T., Sotsky, S. M., Watkins, J. T., Pilkonis, P. A., & Hedeker, D. (1995). Initial severity and differential treatment outcome in the National Institute of Mental Health Treatment of Depression Collaborative Research Program. *Journal of Consulting and Clinical Psychology, 63*(5), 841–847. https://doi.org/10.1037/0022-006X.63.5.841

Elkin, I., Shea, M. T., Watkins, J. T., Imber, S. D., Sotsky, S. M., Collins, J. F., Glass, D. R., Pilkonis, P. A., Leber, W. R., Docherty, J. P., & Parloff, M. B. (1989). National Institute of Mental Health Treatment of Depression Collaborative Research Program. General effectiveness of treatments. *Archives of General Psychiatry, 46*(11), 971–982. https://doi.org/10.1001/archpsyc.1989.01810110013002

Feeley, M., DeRubeis, R. J., & Gelfand, L. A. (1999). The temporal relation of adherence and alliance to symptom change in cognitive therapy for depression. *Journal of Consulting and Clinical Psychology, 67*(4), 578–582. https://doi.org/10.1037/0022-006X.67.4.578

Flückiger, C., Rubel, J., Del Re, A. C., Horvath, A. O., Wampold, B. E., Crits-Christoph, P., Atzil-Slonim, D., Compare, A., Falkenström, F., Ekeblad, A., Errázuriz, P., Fisher, H., Hoffart, A., Huppert, J. D., Kivity, Y., Kumar, M., Lutz, W., Muran, J. C., Strunk, D. R., . . . Barber, J. P. (2020). The reciprocal relationship between alliance and early treatment symptoms: A two-stage individual participant data meta-analysis. *Journal of Consulting and Clinical Psychology, 88*(9), 829–843. https://doi.org/10.1037/ccp0000594

Goldfried, M. R. (1980). Toward the delineation of therapeutic change principles. *American Psychologist, 35*(11), 991–999. https://doi.org/10.1037/0003-066X.35.11.991

Hedeker, D., & Gibbons, R. D. (1997). Application of random-effects pattern-mixture models for missing data in longitudinal studies. *Psychological Methods, 2*(1), 64–78. https://doi.org/10.1037/1082-989X.2.1.64

Hemming, K., Taljaard, M., McKenzie, J. E., Hooper, R., Copas, A., Thompson, J. A., Dixon-Woods, M., Aldcroft, A., Doussau, A., Grayling, M., Kristunas, C., Goldstein, C. E., Campbell, M. K.,

Girling, A., Eldridge, S., Campbell, M. J., Lilford, R. J., Weijer, C., Forbes, A. B., & Grimshaw, J. M. (2018). Reporting of stepped wedge cluster randomised trials: Extension of the CONSORT 2010 statement with explanation and elaboration. *BMJ, 363*, k1614. https://doi.org/10.1136/bmj.k1614

Hill, C. E., O'Grady, K. E., & Elkin, I. (1992). Applying the Collaborative Study Psychotherapy Rating Scale to rate therapist adherence in cognitive-behavior therapy, interpersonal therapy, and clinical management. *Journal of Consulting and Clinical Psychology, 60*(1), 73–79. https://doi.org/10.1037/0022-006X.60.1.73

Hollis, S., & Campbell, F. (1999). What is meant by intention to treat analysis? Survey of published randomised controlled trials. *BMJ, 319*(7211), 670–674. https://doi.org/10.1136/bmj.319.7211.670

Hollon, S. D., DeRubeis, R. J., Shelton, R. C., Amsterdam, J. D., Salomon, R. M., O'Reardon, J. P., Lovett, M. L., Young, P. R., Haman, K. L., Freeman, B. B., & Gallop, R. (2005). Prevention of relapse following cognitive therapy vs medications in moderate to severe depression. *Archives of General Psychiatry, 62*(4), 417–422. https://doi.org/10.1001/archpsyc.62.4.417

Hollon, S. D., & Teachman, B. A. (2019). Advantages of developing clinical practice guidelines using international standards. *Psychotherapy: Theory, Research, & Practice, 56*(3), 340–346. https://doi.org/10.1037/pst0000240

Horvath, A. O., & Symonds, B. D. (1991). Relation between working alliance and outcome in psychotherapy: A meta-analysis. *Journal of Counseling Psychology, 38*(2), 139–149. https://doi.org/10.1037/0022-0167.38.2.139

Jacobson, N. S., & Christensen, A. (1996). Studying the effectiveness of psychotherapy. How well can clinical trials do the job? *American Psychologist, 51*(10), 1031–1039. https://doi.org/10.1037/0003-066X.51.10.1031

Jacobson, N. S., & Hollon, S. D. (1996). Cognitive-behavior therapy versus pharmacotherapy: Now that the jury's returned its verdict, it's time to present the rest of the evidence. *Journal of Consulting and Clinical Psychology, 64*(1), 74–80. https://doi.org/10.1037/0022-006X.64.1.74

Jacobson, N. S., & Truax, P. (1991). Clinical significance: A statistical approach to defining meaningful change in psychotherapy research. *Journal of Consulting and Clinical Psychology, 59*(1), 12–19 https://doi.org/10.1037/0022-006X.59.1.12

Joffe, M. M., & Rosenbaum, P. R. (1999). Invited commentary: Propensity scores. *American Journal of Epidemiology, 150*(4), 327–333. https://doi.org/10.1093/oxfordjournals.aje.a010011

Kazantzis, N., Whittington, C., Zelencich, L., Kyrios, M., Norton, P. J., & Hofmann, S. G. (2016). Quantity and quality of homework compliance: A meta-analysis of relations with outcome in cognitive behavior therapy. *Behavior Therapy*, 47(5), 755–772. https://doi.org/10.1016/j.beth.2016.05.002

Kazdin, A. E. (2007). Mediators and mechanisms of change in psychotherapy research. *Annual Review of Clinical Psychology*, 3, 1–27. https://doi.org/10.1146/annurev.clinpsy.3.022806.091432

Kazdin, A. E. (2017). *Research design in clinical psychology* (5th ed.). Pearson.

Kazdin, A. E., & Bass, D. (1989). Power to detect differences between alternative treatments in comparative psychotherapy outcome research. *Journal of Consulting and Clinical Psychology*, 57(1), 138–147. https://doi.org/10.1037/0022-006X.57.1.138

Kessler, R. C. (2018). The potential of predictive analytics to provide clinical decision support in depression treatment planning. *Current Opinion in Psychiatry*, 31(1), 32–39. https://doi.org/10.1097/YCO.0000000000000377

King, M., Nazareth, I., Lampe, F., Bower, P., Chandler, M., Morou, M., Sibbald, B., & Lai, R. (2005). Impact of participant and physician intervention preferences on randomized trials: A systematic review. *Journal of the American Medical Association*, 293(9), 1089–1099. https://doi.org/10.1001/jama.293.9.1089

Kraemer, H. C. (2000). Pitfalls of multisite randomized clinical trials of efficacy and effectiveness. *Schizophrenia Bulletin*, 26(3), 533–541. https://doi.org/10.1093/oxfordjournals.schbul.a033474

Kraemer, H. C. (2016). Messages for clinicians: Moderators and mediators of treatment outcome in randomized clinical trials. *American Journal of Psychiatry*, 173(7), 672–679. https://doi.org/10.1176/appi.ajp.2016.15101333

Kraemer, H. C., & Kupfer, D. J. (2006). Size of treatment effects and their importance to clinical research and practice. *Biological Psychiatry*, 59(11), 990–996. https://doi.org/10.1016/j.biopsych.2005.09.014

Kraemer, H. C., Measelle, J. R., Ablow, J. C., Essex, M. J., Boyce, W. T., & Kupfer, D. J. (2003). A new approach to integrating data from multiple informants in psychiatric assessment and research: Mixing and matching contexts and perspectives. *The American Journal of Psychiatry*, 160(9), 1566–1577. https://doi.org/10.1176/appi.ajp.160.9.1566

Kraemer, H. C., Wilson, G. T., Fairburn, C. G., & Agras, W. S. (2002). Mediators and moderators of treatment effects in randomized clinical trials. *Archives of General Psychiatry*, 59(10), 877–883. https://doi.org/10.1001/archpsyc.59.10.877

Lavori, P. W. (1992). Clinical trials in psychiatry: Should protocol deviation censor patient data? *Neuropsychopharmacology*, 6(1), 39–48.

Lei, H., Nahum-Shani, I., Lynch, K., Oslin, D., & Murphy, S. A. (2012). A "SMART" design for building individualized treatment sequences. *Annual Review of Clinical Psychology*, 8, 21–48. https://doi.org/10.1146/annurev-clinpsy-032511-143152

Lester, K., Resick, P. A., Young-Ku, Y., & Artz, C. (2010). Impact of race on early treatment termination and outcomes in posttraumatic stress disorder treatment. *Journal of Consulting and Clinical Psychology*, 78(4), 480–489. https://doi.org/10.1037/a0019551

Luborsky, L., Diguer, L., Seligman, D. A., Rosenthal, R., Krause, E. D., Johnson, S., Halperin, G., Bishop, M., Berman, J. S., & Schweizer, E. (1999). The researcher's own therapy allegiances: A "wild card" in comparisons of treatment efficacy. *Clinical Psychology: Science and Practice*, 6(1), 95–106. https://doi.org/10.1093/clipsy.6.1.95

Luedtke, A., Sadikova, E., & Kessler, R. C. (2019). Sample size requirements for multivariate models to predict between-patient differences in best treatments of major depressive disorder. *Clinical Psychological Science*, 7(3), 445–461. https://doi.org/10.1177/2167702618815466

MacKinnon, D. P. (2008). *Introduction to statistical mediation analysis*. Erlbaum.

Makol, B. A., Youngstrom, E. A., Racz, S. J., Qasmieh, N., Glenn, L. E., & De Los Reyes, A. (2020). Integrating multiple informants' reports: How conceptual and measurement models may address long-standing problems in clinical decision-making. *Clinical Psychological Science*, 8(6), 953–970. https://doi.org/10.1177/2167702620924439

Mellers, B., Hertwig, R., & Kahneman, D. (2001). Do frequency representations eliminate conjunction effects? An exercise in adversarial collaboration. *Psychological Science*, 12(4), 269–275. https://doi.org/10.1111/1467-9280.00350

Miller, W. R., Sorensen, J. L., Selzer, J. A., & Brigham, G. S. (2006). Disseminating evidence-based practices in substance abuse treatment: A review with suggestions. *Journal of Substance Abuse Treatment*, 31(1), 25–39. https://doi.org/10.1016/j.jsat.2006.03.005

Miranda, J., Chung, J. Y., Green, B. L., Krupnick, J., Siddique, J., Revicki, D. A., & Belin, T. (2003). Treating depression in predominantly low-income young minority women: A randomized controlled trial. *Journal of the American Medical Association*, 290(1), 57–65. https://doi.org/10.1001/jama.290.1.57

Mohr, D. C., Spring, B., Freedland, K. E., Beckner, V., Arean, P., Hollon, S. D., Ockene, J., & Kaplan, R.

(2009). The selection and design of control conditions for randomized controlled trials of psychological interventions. *Psychotherapy and Psychosomatics, 78*(5), 275–284. https://doi.org/10.1159/000228248

Nakagawa, S. (2004). A farewell to Bonferroni: The problems of low statistical power and publication bias. *Behavioral Ecology, 15*(6), 1044–1045. https://doi.org/10.1093/beheco/arh107

Nathan, P. E., Stuart, S. P., & Dolan, S. L. (2000). Research on psychotherapy efficacy and effectiveness: Between Scylla and Charybdis? *Psychological Bulletin, 126,* 964–981. https://doi.org/10.1037/0033-2909.126.6.964

Norcross, J. C., Karpiak, C. P., & Santoro, S. O. (2005). Clinical psychologists across the years: The division of clinical psychology from 1960 to 2003. *Journal of Clinical Psychology, 61*(12), 1467–1483. https://doi.org/10.1002/jclp.20135

Patel, V., Weobong, B., Weiss, H. A., Anand, A., Bhat, B., Katti, B., Dimidjian, S., Araya, R., Hollon, S. D., King, M., Vijayakumar, L., Park, A. L., McDaid, D., Wilson, T., Velleman, R., Kirkwood, B. R., & Fairburn, C. G. (2017). The Healthy Activity Program (HAP), a lay counsellor-delivered brief psychological treatment for severe depression, in primary care in India: A randomised controlled trial. *Lancet, 389*(10065), 176–185. https://doi.org/10.1016/S0140-6736(16)31589-6

Paul, G. L. (1967). Strategy of outcome research in psychotherapy. *Journal of Consulting Psychology, 31*(2), 109–118. https://doi.org/10.1037/h0024436

Pelham, W. E., Jr., Fabiano, G. A., Waxmonsky, J. G., Greiner, A. R., Gnagy, E. M., Pelham, W. E., III, Coxe, S., Verley, J., Bhatia, I., Hart, K., Karch, K., Konijnendijk, E., Tresco, K., Nahum-Shani, I., & Murphy, S. A. (2016). Treatment sequencing for childhood ADHD: A multiple-randomization study of adaptive medication and behavioral interventions. *Journal of Clinical Child & Adolescent Psychology, 45*(4), 396–415. https://doi.org/10.1080/15374416.2015.1105138

Piaggio, G., Elbourne, D. R., Altman, D. G., Pocock, S. J., & Evans, S. J. W. (2012). Reporting of noninferiority and equivalence randomized trials: An extension of the CONSORT 2010 Statement. *JAMA, 308*(24), 2594–2604. https://doi.org/10.1001/jama.2012.87802

Preacher, K. J., Rucker, D. D., & Hayes, A. F. (2007). Addressing moderated mediation hypotheses: Theory, methods, and prescriptions. *Multivariate Behavioral Research, 42,* 185–227. https://doi.org/10.1080/00273170701341316

Project MATCH Research Group. (1997). Matching Alcoholism Treatments to Client Heterogeneity: Project MATCH posttreatment drinking outcomes. *Journal of Studies on Alcohol, 58*(1).

Rosenthal, R., & Rosnow, R. L. (2008). *Essentials of behavioral research: Methods and data analysis* (3rd ed.). McGraw-Hill.

Rush, A. J., Beck, A. T., Kovacs, M., & Hollon, S. D. (1977). Comparative efficacy of cognitive therapy and pharmacotherapy in the treatment of depressed outpatients. *Cognitive Therapy and Research, 1*(1), 17–37. https://doi.org/10.1007/BF01173502

Rush, A. J., Kraemer, H. C., Sackeim, H. A., Fava, M., Trivedi, M. H., Frank, E., Ninan, P. T., Thase, M. E., Gelenberg, A. J., Kupfer, D. J., Regier, D. A., Rosenbaum, J. F., Ray, O., Schatzberg, A. F., & the ACNP Task Force. (2006). Report by the ACNP Task Force on response and remission in major depressive disorder. *Neuropsychopharmacology, 31*(9), 1841–1853. https://doi.org/10.1038/sj.npp.1301131

Rush, A. J., Trivedi, M. H., Wisniewski, S. R., Nierenberg, A. A., Stewart, J. W., Warden, D., Niederehe, G., Thase, M. E., Lavori, P. W., Lebowitz, B. D., McGrath, P. J., Rosenbaum, J. F., Sackeim, H. A., Kupfer, D. J., Luther, J., & Fava, M. (2006). Acute and longer-term outcomes in depressed outpatients requiring one or several treatment steps: A STAR*D report. *American Journal of Psychiatry, 163*(11), 1905–1917. https://doi.org/10.1176/ajp.2006.163.11.1905

Schultz, K. F., Altman, D. G., & Moher, D. (2010). CONSORT 2010 statement: Updated guidelines for reporting parallel group randomised trials. *BMJ, 340,* c332. https://doi.org/10.1136/bmj.c332

Seligman, M. E. P. (1995). The effectiveness of psychotherapy. The *Consumer Reports* study. *American Psychologist, 50*(12), 965–974. https://doi.org/10.1037/0003-066X.50.12.965

Shadish, W. R., Cook, T. D., & Campbell, D. T. (2002). *Experimental and quasi-experimental designs for generalized causal inference.* Houghton Mifflin.

Shao, J., & Zhong, B. (2003). Last observation carry-forward and last observation analysis. *Statistics in Medicine, 22*(15), 2429–2441. https://doi.org/10.1002/sim.1519

Shaw, B. F. (1984). Specification of the training and evaluation of cognitive therapists for outcome studies. In J. Williams & R. Spitzer (Eds.), *Psychotherapy research: Where are we and where should we go?* (pp. 173–188). Guilford Press.

Shaw, B. F., Elkin, I., Yamaguchi, J., Olmsted, M., Vallis, T. M., Dobson, K. S., Lowery, A., Sotsky, S. M., Watkins, J. T., & Imber, S. D. (1999). Therapist competence ratings in relation to clinical outcome in cognitive therapy of depression.

Journal of Consulting and Clinical Psychology, 67(6), 837–846. https://doi.org/10.1037/0022-006X.67.6.837

Shrout, P. E., & Fleiss, J. L. (1979). Intraclass correlations: Uses in assessing rater reliability. *Psychological Bulletin*, 86(2), 420–428. https://doi.org/10.1037/0033-2909.86.2.420

Singla, D. R., Kohrt, B. A., Murray, L. K., Anand, A., Chorpita, B. F., & Patel, V. (2017). Psychological treatments for the world: Lessons from low- and middle-income countries. *Annual Review of Clinical Psychology*, 13(1), 149–181. https://doi.org/10.1146/annurev-clinpsy-032816-045217

Sloane, R. B., Staples, F. R., Cristol, A. H., Yorkson, N. J., & Whipple, K. (1975). *Psychotherapy versus behavior therapy*. Harvard University Press. https://doi.org/10.4159/harvard.9780674365063

Smits, J. A. J., Rosenfield, D., McDonald, R., & Telch, M. J. (2006). Cognitive mechanisms of social anxiety reduction: An examination of specificity and temporality. *Journal of Consulting and Clinical Psychology*, 74(6), 1203–1212. https://doi.org/10.1037/0022-006X.74.6.1203

Stegner, B. L., Bostrom, A. G., & Greenfield, T. K. (1996). Equivalence testing for use in psychosocial and services research: An introduction with examples. *Evaluation and Program Planning*, 19(3), 193–198. https://doi.org/10.1016/0149-7189(96)00011-0

Sterne, J. A. C., Savović, J., Page, M. J., Elbers, R. G., Blencowe, N. S., Boutron, I., Cates, C. J., Cheng, H.-Y., Corbett, M. S., Eldridge, S. M., Hernán, M. A., Hopewell, S., Hróbjartsson, A., Junqueira, D. R., Jüni, P., Kirkham, J. J., Lasserson, T., Li, T., McAleenan, A., . . . Higgins, J. P. T. (2019). RoB 2: A revised tool for assessing risk of bias in randomised trials. *BMJ*, 366, l4898. https://doi.org/10.1136/bmj.l4898

Stirman, S. W., DeRubeis, R. J., Crits-Christoph, P., & Brody, P. E. (2003). Are samples in randomized controlled trials of psychotherapy representative of community outpatients? A new methodology and initial findings. *Journal of Consulting and Clinical Psychology*, 71(6), 963–972. https://doi.org/10.1037/0022-006X.71.6.963

Stricker, G., Abrahamson, D. J., Bologna, N. C., Hollon, S. D., Robinson, E. A., & Reed, G. M. (1999). Treatment guidelines: The good, the bad, and the ugly. *Psychotherapy: Theory, Research, & Practice*, 36(1), 69–79. https://doi.org/10.1037/h0087755

Striegel-Moore, R. H., Wilson, G. T., DeBar, L., Perrin, N., Lynch, F., Rosselli, F., & Kraemer, H. C. (2010). Cognitive behavioral guided self-help for the treatment of recurrent binge eating. *Journal of Consulting and Clinical Psychology*, 78(3), 312–321. https://doi.org/10.1037/a0018915

Vanderweele, T., & Vansteelandt, S. (2009). Conceptual issues concerning mediation, interventions and composition. *Statistics and Its Interface*, 2(4), 457–468. https://doi.org/10.4310/SII.2009.v2.n4.a7

Waltz, J., Addis, M. E., Koerner, K., & Jacobson, N. S. (1993). Testing the integrity of a psychotherapy protocol: Assessment of adherence and competence. *Journal of Consulting and Clinical Psychology*, 61(4), 620–630. https://doi.org/10.1037/0022-006X.61.4.620

Wei, L. J., & Lachin, J. M. (1988). Properties of the urn randomization in clinical trials. *Controlled Clinical Trials*, 9(4), 345–364. https://doi.org/10.1016/0197-2456(88)90048-7

Weisz, J. R., & Addis, M. E. (2006). The research–practice tango and other choreographic challenges: Using and testing evidence-based psychotherapies in clinical care settings. In C. D. Goodheart, A. E. Kazdin, & R. J. Sternberg (Eds.), *Evidence-based psychotherapy: Where practice and research meet* (pp. 179–206). American Psychological Association. https://doi.org/10.1037/11423-008

Wennberg, J. E., Barry, M. J., Fowler, F. J., & Mulley, A. (1993). Outcomes research, PORTs, and health care reform. *Annals of the New York Academy of Sciences*, 703(1), 52–62. https://doi.org/10.1111/j.1749-6632.1993.tb26335.x

Westen, D., Novotny, C. M., & Thompson-Brenner, H. (2004). The empirical status of empirically supported psychotherapies: Assumptions, findings, and reporting in controlled clinical trials. *Psychological Bulletin*, 130(4), 631–663. https://doi.org/10.1037/0033-2909.130.4.631

Wilkinson, L., & Task Force on Statistical Inference, American Psychological Association, Science Directorate. (1999). Statistical methods in psychology journals: Guidelines and explanations. *American Psychologist*, 54(8), 594–604. https://doi.org/10.1037/0003-066X.54.8.594

CHAPTER 31

TRANSLATIONAL RESEARCH

Michael T. Bardo, Christopher Cappelli, and Mary Ann Pentz

Translational research generally refers to the advancement of basic science research findings into application and everyday practice. While many different definitions have been proposed, translational research is envisioned to be on a continuum that was originally categorized into at least two broad categories, that is, Type I and II. Type I translational research begins at the point where application to a specific problem is the goal. It involves moving basic science into proof-of-concept and theory testing studies, including efficacy trials in which a specific treatment is evaluated in a relatively small sample of volunteers or clients/patients under controlled conditions. In contrast, Type II translational research refers to moving treatments from controlled efficacy trials into effectiveness trials, as well as dissemination of the treatment into everyday practice. In contrast to efficacy trials, effectiveness trials occur in a broad, real-world context under less controlled conditions, such as in clinics, schools, or communities. Type II translational research also involves evaluating education and training on new treatments, conducting economic analyses (e.g., cost-effectiveness), and evaluating policy decisions.

Type I and Type II translational research are broad categories originally used by the National Institutes of Health (NIH; Sussman et al., 2006).

However, researchers and policy makers have suggested that Type II research is too broad since it encompasses effectiveness, implementation, dissemination, and policy research, and it does not adequately address translation of evidence-based treatments from one outcome to another. Thus, more recent formulations categorize translational research into four types (T1–T4; Fort et al., 2017). T0 is sometimes also included as a fifth type, defined as the beginning of purely basic research, but we will include it under T1 for the purposes of this chapter. Using these narrower four categories, T1 includes basic science, etiology, and epidemiological research that addresses discovery, hypothesis generation, translation of theory and methods to program development, as well as small-scale studies that are expected to cross over and generate intervention trials for T2 research. T2 includes translation of program development to large-scale efficacy, effectiveness, and often replication trials that test an intervention under less rigorous observational conditions than in T1. T3 includes both implementation and dissemination research, which is expected to yield evidence-based interventions that are sufficiently robust to be transportable to a variety of settings, populations, and real-life conditions, culminating in the production of evidence-based standards for

The authors thank Emily Denehy for assistance in preparing the figure. Supported by NIH Grants P50 DA05312, U54 CA180905, and R01 HD052107.

https://doi.org/10.1037/0000319-031
APA Handbook of Research Methods in Psychology, Second Edition: Vol. 2. Research Designs: Quantitative, Qualitative, Neuropsychological, and Biological, H. Cooper (Editor-in-Chief)

practice. Finally, T4 includes broad public health impact studies, cost–benefit and comparative effectiveness research, and policy change studies. T4 is expected to yield information on shifts in population health after large-scale dissemination of evidence-based interventions and policies. Table 31.1 summarizes some of the research methods that are appropriate for the broad categories of Type I and II translational research, as well as the more narrowly reformulated T1–T4 categories. For the purpose of this chapter, we primarily use the broad categories defined by Type I and II research, but readers should be mindful that this broad distinction is associated with heterogenous narrower categories.

GENERAL FEATURES OF TRANSLATIONAL RESEARCH

Across both Type I and II research, there are several key features or general guidelines that define successful translational research (Figure 31.1).

First, by definition, translational research benefits from an *interdisciplinary* approach to understanding health behavior. Interdisciplinary research is often facilitated by infrastructural connections built around a broad theme, such as cancer, emotion, or gender issues. In the field of psychology specifically, cross-connections among clinical and experimental areas have yielded such research areas as health psychology, psychoneuro-immunology, and social neuroscience. These blended fields are likely to become self-sustaining because graduate and new investigator training programs have developed along the lines of these types of research (e.g., see NIH Reporter for T32 training grants, as well as U54 and P50 center grants with relevant career development training cores; https://reporter.nih.gov/).

Second, translational research needs to define a *unifying goal* around which the interdisciplinary team is focused. This requires a leadership that has a vision of the entire process, from basic science to real-world application. Although statistical and

---

TABLE 31.1

Sample Research Methods for Translational Research Relevant to Psychologists

Broad category	Narrow category	Stage	Design	Measures	Outcomes
Type I	Basic research (T1)	Proof-of-concept, theory testing, etiology	Small sample, random control, longitudinal	Biological, behavioral, questionnaires	Behavior change
Crossover Type I to II	Crossover (T1 to T2)	Replication, extension	RCT, partial factorial	Survey	Behavior change, relative behavior change
Type II	Program diffusion (T2)	Adoption, implementation, dissemination, sustainability	RCT, sequential RCT	Implementer and network surveys, archival records	Administrator, requester and implementer records, program funding
Type II	Program to practice (T3)	Standards development, guideline training, distribution	RCT, quasi-exp, comparative effectiveness	Survey, clinic records, time, cost, uptake	Relative balance of costs, health outcomes, practitioner use
Type II	Practice to policy (T4)	Consensus, legislation, funding	Time series, quasi-exp, single group	Voting records, set aside funding	Policy awareness, support, compliance
Type II	Translation across health behaviors (T2–T4)	Treatment, development/ adaptation, mediator identification	Formative, qualitative, small quasi-exp, pilot, RCT	Survey	Mediator change, multiple health behavior change

Note. RCT = randomized controlled trial.

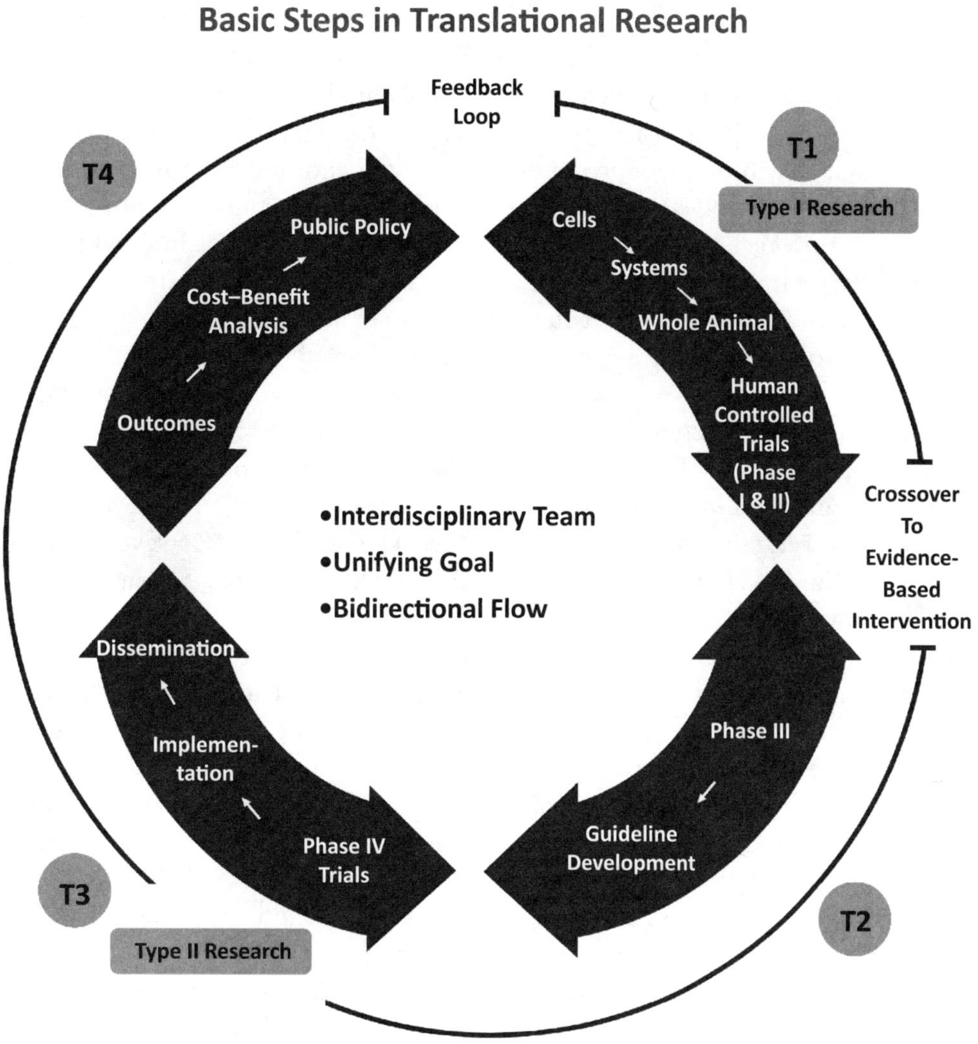

Basic Steps in Translational Research

Feedback Loop

T4

T1

Type I Research

Public Policy

Cost–Benefit Analysis

Outcomes

Cells

Systems

Whole Animal

Human Controlled Trials (Phase I & II)

•Interdisciplinary Team
•Unifying Goal
•Bidirectional Flow

Crossover To Evidence-Based Intervention

Dissemination

Implemen-tation

Phase IV Trials

Phase III

Guideline Development

T3

T2

Type II Research

FIGURE 31.1. Schematic of stages for translational research.

methodological commonalities may exist across different disciplines, these commonalities alone are insufficient to organize a translational group of investigators. Instead, the goal should be conceptual or mechanistic in nature such that broad success will end up improving health.

Third, successful translational research should provide *bidirectional flow* of information between basic research and real-world application. While translational research is often thought of as moving from basic science to application, the reverse is also true because basic scientists need to be informed about what succeeds and fails in the real world. This recommendation of a feedback loop represents an evolution from the original NIH classifications of translational research, which

were designed primarily around clinical research and represented a unidirectional progression from "bench to bedside" or "bedside to community."

The field of translational research has changed much in the last few years. Stress related to financial concerns, lack of job prospects, climate change, catastrophic events, and pandemics has hastened the pressure to move translation forward to the development and dissemination of effective prevention and treatment interventions that extend beyond the individual to encompass systems and environmental change; for example, systems that affect tobacco use and its prevention (Hassmiller Lich et al., 2016). At the same time, digital technology, social media, and methodological advancements in machine learning and computational modeling ("big data" science) have enabled more rapid development and wider dissemination of interventions than ever before, uncovering a host of health disparities among populations that are signaling the need for precision intervention (Fishbein & Dariotis, 2019). In the following sections, we provide examples of the advantages and barriers to translational research, including development of interventions to reduce COVID risk and prevention of substance use.

Type I Translational Research

Because the conceptual framework that describes translational research emanated from NIH and is dominated by biomedical researchers, it is not surprising that the initial step of Type I translational research typically starts with molecular or cellular mechanisms. This can include working with small molecules, genetic material, or specialized cell lines. In the second step, organ systems or laboratory animals are often used. Finally, in the third step, human test trials are performed to determine safety and efficacy of the new treatment. While these three steps are often used in developing new medical treatments, not all three of these steps are necessary for other types of research more familiar to psychologists. For example, a potential new psychosocial intervention, such as a new treatment for dyslexia or a new psychotherapeutic approach, may skip the cell- and animal-based steps of Type I research and simply begin with epidemiological and etiological studies.

Type I translational research in the substance abuse field, including tobacco, alcohol, marijuana, and other substance use, has benefited greatly from laboratory animal models and human neuroimaging technologies (Parvaz et al., 2011; Smith, 2020). As for the use of laboratory animals, a major advantage is being able to conduct experimental work under conditions that offer exquisite control over many extraneous variables, thus allowing for enhanced power with fewer subjects. In addition, use of laboratory animals allows for the use of modern neuroscience techniques that are often not possible to use in humans; for example, assessing brain mechanisms using optogenetics,

chemogenetics, or genetic knockouts (Fulton & Maze, 2019; Jiang et al., 2017). While laboratory animal models are not essential for conducting Type I translational research, many fields have benefited enormously from preclinical research using nonhuman animals. For example, laboratory animal research is integral for developing potential medications to treat substance abuse (Czoty et al., 2016). Great strides have also been achieved using genetically engineered and selectively bred rodents to understand disorders such as obesity (Lutz & Woods, 2012), alcoholism (Bell et al., 2017), posttraumatic stress disorder (Richter-Levin et al., 2019), and depression (Becker et al., 2021). However, since no animal captures all aspects of a human disorder, a reverse validity approach could be employed in which treatments shown to be effective in humans are used to validate and refine animal models; for example, the use of pharmacologic agents or adverse stimuli to interrupt drug craving or downward allostatic load (Koob et al., 2009). Despite these efforts, it is likely that some phenomena are uniquely human; for example, the resolve to abstain from alcohol or drug use by turning to religion after "hitting bottom."

Neuroimaging technologies can be used to determine if the results obtained with laboratory animals generalizes to humans. This point is illustrated by Type I translational research in substance abuse prevention that has focused on the maturation of prefrontal cortical regions and their intimate role in modulating risk-related personality traits such as sensation seeking and impulsivity (Kozak et al., 2019; Perry et al., 2011). Both sensation seeking and impulsivity are heightened during the adolescent period when risk for initiation of substance abuse is greatest (Charles et al., 2016; Hamidullah et al., 2020). The increased risk among high sensation seeking adolescents reflects, at least in part, an incomplete maturation of prefrontal regions involved in executive functions that control behavioral inhibition, reward processing, and decision making (Cservenka et al., 2013; Dumontheil, 2016). Coupled with the prefrontal hypoactivity, young adult high sensation seekers also exhibit *greater* fMRI activation in reward-relevant brain regions (Hawes et al., 2017; Joseph et al., 2009) and show enhanced "liking" of drugs of abuse (Kelly et al., 2009) compared with low sensation seekers.

These Type I basic research findings have important translational implications for the design of antidrug mass media messages because these messages are often tailored to appeal to high sensation seekers (Palmgreen et al., 2007), or designed to alter explicit cognitions or decision making (Brinn et al., 2012). In particular, neuroimaging technology can be used to determine the effectiveness of televised antidrug public service announcements among at-risk high sensation seekers prior to implementing an expensive full-scale community trial (Donohew et al., 2018).

Another example of recent research within Type I translation is the reconceptualization of sensation seeking as not just a stable trait identified in childhood (Cappelli et al., 2020), but also as a cluster of deficits in executive function around the domains of emotion regulation, inhibitory control, and working memory (Noël et al., 2011). Translation allows for the adoption of existing protocols and intervention strategies that have proven effective in similar domains. For example, this reconceptualization of sensation seeking translates a concept previously considered a static trait to one that may be more effectively modifiable through the use of techniques shown to modify other executive function constructs, including emotional regulation (Pentz et al., 2016), inhibition (Ames et al., 2016), and working memory (Stanger et al., 2020). With this reconceptualization, new avenues of research may be explored that would otherwise have gone overlooked, such as desensitizing individuals to substance use stimuli in neuroimaging and eye-tracking interventions (Carletto et al., 2018).

There are also advantages and limitations in Type I translational experimental research involving human subjects. Similar to animal research, controlled human laboratory studies allow for some control over extraneous variables in order to study underlying mechanisms with relatively few subjects. In addition, controlled human studies allow for the so-called critical "proof-of-concept"

demonstration. When introduction of a treatment, program, or product into the real world is the goal, it is advisable to test it in the laboratory or other controlled environment first. Randomized clinical trials (RCTs) are expensive, and, thus, a small-scale proof-of-concept study is useful for identifying promising treatments.

For any given problem under investigation, there can be considerable variation in the duration of time committed to the Type I phase. For example, it often takes more than a decade to introduce a new psychiatric medication to the market because the development pipeline must include chemical synthesis, cell-based screening, whole-animal efficacy testing, toxicity studies, and approval of an investigational new drug application for Phase I safety testing in humans; all these phases are categorized as Type I research. However, this duration can be shortened considerably when there is great urgency and investment of resources. For example, Type I testing for COVID vaccines was completed in less than 1 year, which included rapid vaccine construction using a novel mRNA technology and a proof-of-principle efficacy trial in monkeys (Corbett et al., 2020), followed by multiple human clinical trials (Tregoning et al., 2020). Despite the rapid completion of Type I results, barriers were encountered to equitable implementation of the COVID vaccine across various cultural and ethnic minority groups (Cooper & Stoney, 2021), as well as barriers related to negative or misinformed beliefs about vaccinations (Vanderpool et al., 2020).

Type I to Type II Crossover

Once Type I translational research yields a potential intervention based on small-scale studies, the findings are typically subject to review to determine whether it is eligible for "evidence-based" status, that is, has shown significant effects preventing or reducing the intervention target behavior. The criteria used to determine evidence-based status have differed slightly according to the group conducting the review (e.g., Cochrane Reviews of RCTs [Anglemyer et al., 2013] compared with the Centers for Disease Control and Prevention registry of model educational interventions [https://www.cdc.gov/healthyyouth/adolescenthealth/registries.htm]). Regardless, the basic requirements for evidence-based status typically include the use of the following: (a) a strong, defensible experimental or quasi-experimental research design; (b) a longitudinal measurement design, with significant effects; (c) standardized protocol materials; (d) monitoring and reporting of quality of implementation; and (e) evidence of replication to more than one study, group of researchers, or sites (Anglemyer et al., 2013). Meeting these criteria typically takes several years of research before an intervention obtains an evidence-based status, can be listed on national or international registries of effective programs, and be eligible for federal or state funding in practice sites. Recently, due to considerable pressure from communities and individuals to expedite the development and implementation of prevention and treatment programs for substance use, mental health problems, and infectious diseases, some organizations are promoting the adoption and implementation of programs that have not met all evidence-based criteria but are considered "evidence-informed" (Malin et al., 2020). This notation includes interventions that have been evaluated in quasi-experimental studies or small-scale randomized trials that have not yet been replicated in larger populations. These programs may be favored by practitioners or local policy makers but have insufficient published support for large-scale use. Nevertheless, these 'evidence-informed' interventions may hold value through a natural feedback loop that is formed with basic researchers, where T1 and T2 investigators become aware of real-world intervention failures, lack of adoption or impact, or barriers of enacting program policy. They in turn can revisit and modify program components to be more effective in future iterations (see Figure 31.1).

In the area of substance use prevention, Type I translational research has produced many evidence-based programs subsequently translated into Type II studies ranging from T2 through T4 trials. Examples include the addition of multiple community-level components to evidence-based school programs for substance use prevention (Flay, 2000) and shifting prevention media messages and campaigns from social influences to targeted media literacy programs (Vahedi et al., 2018). Within this research domain, evidence-based substance use prevention and treatment programs for alcohol and cocaine use disorders have subsequently undergone rapid crossover translation to opioid use disorder programming (El-Bassel et al., 2020; Roozen et al., 2004). Other examples of rapid translation come from lifestyle change interventions, where new interventions target multiple health risk behaviors *and* health promotion simultaneously, rather than just disease prevention through a focus on single health risk behaviors (Pentz et al., 2016). In the case of COVID, risk behaviors could be counteracted through preventive interventions that focus on attitudinal and behavioral change, counteracting misinformation about safety and use of personal protective equipment (Liu & Mesch, 2020; Roma et al., 2020), or reducing stress through mindfulness and meditation training (Behan, 2020). Because of the critical, large-scale impact on public health, these examples are subject to pressure to expedite the course of translational research, thus abbreviating T1 to T2 crossover. The expedited crossover has relied on national expert working groups to develop guiding principles for intervention delivery, as has been done with groups such as the Addiction Research Consortium (Heinz et al., 2020) and the Corona Pandemic Epidemiology Consortium (Segal et al., 2020). For example, the Addiction Research Consortium (Heinz et al., 2020) recommended the following stages of research to prevent and reduce substance use behavior: (1) mobile health (mHealth), that is, studies that use cell phones or other mobile devices for data collection and/or intervention delivery, including ecological momentary assessment or real-time assessment to monitor triggers and stressors; (2) computational modeling of key mechanisms, moderators, and mediators of use behavior; and (3) development and testing of interventions that target these mechanisms, moderators, and mediators.

Type II Translational Research (T2–T4)

Type II translational research consists of effectiveness trials under real-world conditions (T2), implementation and dissemination research (T3), and public health impact and policy research (T4). Based on the impact findings, as well as cost–benefit analyses, Type II research can form a feedback loop to inform subsequent basic research in Type I studies, informing revisions and refinements to previous stages. Current and emerging research methods are increasing the speed and efficiency of Type II translational research, both forward and backward. Methods include but are not limited to more rapid, efficient, and cost effective communication (social media), intervention delivery (e.g., digital mHealth; Spring et al., 2018), research designs, use of machine learning-based algorithms for rapid predictive modeling of likely intervention outcomes (e.g., algorithms to improve compliance with behavioral safety practices to prevent COVID risk; Roma et al., 2020), and use of multiple knowledge platforms to extend the reach of intervention (e.g., organizations, social networks, policy networks; El-Jardali et al., 2020). Examples of time- and cost-efficient research designs that can replace more conventional full factorial RCTs include (a) Multiphase Optimization Strategy (MOST) research designs for program component decisions in T1 to T2 crossover and T2 research (Collins et al., 2011; Guastaferro & Collins, 2019); (b) just-in-time adaptive intervention (JITAI) designs that enable early course correction in intervention planning in T1 and T1 to T2 crossover (Nahum-Shani et al., 2018); and (c) sequential multiple assignment randomized trial (SMART) designs that allow for mid-course intervention corrections in T2–T4 designs (Collins et al., 2014).

The basic steps of Type II translational research are readily illustrated by considering the introduction of a new psychiatric medication. In this example, Type I research ends with small-scale safety and efficacy trials in humans. The broad goal of Type II research is to then disseminate the medication to local pharmacies and hospitals, while monitoring the overall health impact in the affected patient population. This would begin with a clinical trial in which the medication is evaluated in a large number of patients across multiple sites using a randomized controlled experimental design. Although this step is still a controlled trial, it can be categorized as Type II translational research because the medication can be disseminated to market under FDA guidelines if the drug is found to be efficacious. This is followed by postmarketing surveillance to monitor any potential for long-term harmful effects. In cases of extreme urgency, such as the COVID vaccine, the FDA can issue an emergency use authorization (EUA), which allows the treatment to be available to the public while Type II research continues toward full approval.

Regardless of the treatment intervention under study, progression through Type II steps often depends on public demand or political pressures to demonstrate that an evidence-based intervention has utility modifying a target health outcome in the real world (Brooks et al., 2021). Progression also depends on clear specification of the critical components of intervention that are necessary to yield a significant health outcome, as well as the process of how, and to what extent the intervention is utilized (Spoth et al., 2013).

Within Type II, T3 translational research involves assessment of quality of intervention delivery and effectiveness of dissemination of evidence-based programs to practice in real-world settings and systems (Fishbein, 2016). T3 can include both small-scale interventions to broad settings such as whole communities, as well as the study of factors that promote or impede dissemination. While conventional RCT designs can still be applied, smaller-scale comparative effectiveness studies in T3 may be more readily adopted in practice settings, with the evidence-based intervention compared against "standard" practice in those settings (e.g., health education as usual in school settings, or screening as usual in a clinic setting). In this type of translational research, clinical records of practitioner compliance with guidelines and numbers of clients may serve as measures of translation, as well as observational data. The final outcome measures include relative cost and observable changes in population health (Glasgow, 2010).

Type II translational research at T4 includes the movement of research findings from practice to policy (Crowley et al., 2018), as well as research on modeling overall public health impact of the intervention as a means to inform policy change. Both policy and policy change research are slow and subject to several challenges, including communicating results of earlier translational research in language and metrics that are useful for policy makers (Fishbein & Dariotis, 2019), identifying population-based knowledge platforms and networks that support evidence-based policy making (El-Jardali et al., 2020), and developing research models that can be easily adopted by policy makers (e.g., the 3 C's model to predict adoption of COVID vaccination behavior, namely, "confidence" in social institutions, "complacency" about perceived risk and safety, and "constraints" such as self-efficacy or lack of it; Liu & Mesch, 2020). RCTs on policy may not be realistic due to lack of experimental control over policy dissemination, or the size of settings covered by a policy (e.g., whole states, variation in timing, funding of actual policy implementation). Limited time-series and single-group designs may be useful for starting a study when a policy change is imminent and an appropriate control group is not readily available. Some policy change examples include tobacco policies aimed at deterrence, restricted access, or taxation (e.g., implementing smoke-free air laws [Levy et al., 2018]; applying the umbrella "Deeming Rule" to restrict access to all tobacco products to youth [Backinger et al., 2016]; and taxing tobacco product sales [Hawkins et al., 2016]). Voting records of policy change may be used to mark the baseline time period, and population surveys and population health records might be used to identify potential mediators of policy effectiveness (e.g., public support of the policy, social norms for policy compliance), as well as the impact of the policy on public health outcomes over time. Additionally, sites that originally intended to implement a policy change but did not could be treated as a type of control.

In the substance use prevention field over the last 20 years, T2–T4 translational research has been guided by various models, including the Center for Substance Abuse Prevention's logic model (Julian et al., 1995), the RE-AIM model (Glasgow & Emmons, 2007), the interactive systems model (Wandersman et al., 2008), systems frameworks model for tobacco use (Hassmiller Lich et al., 2016), and a model based on Diffusion of Innovation Theory (Rogers, 1995). Rogers's diffusion of innovation theory model has also guided treatment research (Sanson-Fisher, 2004).

Rogers's diffusion of innovation theory, which has been particularly impactful, postulates four stages of diffusion that are applicable to Type II translational research: *adoption*, *implementation*, *dissemination*, and *sustainability* (Rogers, 1995). A fifth stage, *pre-adoption*, typically addresses whether administrators in charge of a potential implementation site is adequately prepared to support adoption (Glasgow et al., 2019; Pentz, 2007; Wandersman et al., 2008). *Adoption* research refers to the study of factors that facilitate uptake of an evidence-based treatment. Rogers proposed five factors that facilitate adoption: (a) trialability, or the opportunity to try out the treatment on a small scale without committing permanent resources or disseminating widely; (b) observability, or indicators of effectiveness that can be easily observed by either consumers or implementers; (c) relative advantage, or the perceived benefit of choosing the new treatment over existing treatments; (d) low complexity, or user-friendliness of the treatment; and (e) compatibility, or fit of the new treatment with existing organizational standards and values. Several Type II studies have evaluated one or more of these adoption factors, yielding mixed results (Mihalic & Irwin, 2003; Pentz et al., 2003). Of these factors, observability, relative advantage, and low complexity tend to show the most consistent positive effects on adoption (Pentz et al., 2003, 2004). Other factors that appear to improve adoption include the provision of "pretraining" to familiarize potential adopters with treatment features, the use of snowball sampling and network analyses to identify key stakeholders to promote the treatment, and positive local media coverage (Pentz, 2007; Valente et al., 2007).

Implementation refers to the quality or fidelity of delivery. Various studies suggest that quality of implementation may consist of at least three factors: (a) adherence to standards; (b) amount of treatment delivered; and (c) adaptation for the purpose of improving ease of implementation, as well as audience/consumer acceptance (referred to as "reinvention" in Rogers's early theoretical work; Pentz, 2003; Rogers, 1995). Adherence and amount of treatment delivered have been associated with greater magnitude of effects on behavior (Pentz, 2003). The impact of adaptation is less clear since the definition of adaptation has varied widely across Type II studies, including (a) cultural and language adaptation; (b) adaptation of protocols, timing, and types of implementers to different settings; (c) adaptation to different populations, including different age and risk groups; and (d) adaptation that represents either extension of a treatment to increase effects or replication to examine effectiveness under uncontrollable conditions that differed from the original Type I testing conditions (Guerra & Knox, 2008; Sussman et al., 2006). In more recent years, attention to both the need for adaptation *and* the identification of effective adaptational program strategies has escalated with technological advances in social and digital media, research methodologies in design (e.g., MOST and SMART designs), analytic strategies (machine learning algorithms, network analyses; El-Jardali et al., 2020), and data collection, both qualitative and quantitative, as well as online and in person (Reyna, 2020).

Two examples illustrate the challenges of conducting Type II translational research on adaptation. The first relates to cultural adaptation (Guerra & Knox, 2008). There is disagreement in the substance abuse prevention field about whether a universal intervention program is appropriate for use across different racial/ethnic groups (Mihalic & Irwin, 2003). Some have argued that new or specifically tailored interventions need to be developed to reach ethnic groups that were not the initial focus of the program

(Castro et al., 2004). Research suggests that in most cases, universal interventions can be self-adapted or adapted by developers with few changes in language and context (Pentz et al., 2006; Sussman et al., 2006). However, additional research suggests that special culturally tailored interventions may fare better if adolescents depend on their own cultural group as peer leaders for behavior (Valente et al., 2009), and if risk can be contextualized in a manner that is most meaningful to the group receiving the intervention (Reyna, 2020).

The second challenge in Type II research occurs when attempting to replicate an intervention under uncontrollable conditions or "historical events." For example, while research has been conducted on preventing or reducing "vaccine hesitancy" for measles and HPV, the ability to translate these intervention strategies to the COVID pandemic is not yet known and may be driven by new models of intervention delivery such as the 3 C's model (Liu & Mesch, 2020). As noted earlier in this chapter, *dissemination* may constitute two distinct types. One is dissemination of a treatment to a greater number of "receivers" within the same sites and populations. For example, dissemination of a substance abuse prevention program may occur after an individual teacher has tried the program with one classroom in one school and other teachers, the principal, and perhaps the school superintendent determine that the program has merit, and thus they decide to use the program in additional classrooms with additional teachers in the same school. This type of dissemination might be considered internal to a system and can occur without the program having been sustained in the original classroom for a long period of time. An example of this is a report showing that a spontaneous 28% rate of dissemination occurred in a school program that was part of a large dissemination trial (Pentz et al., 2003). The spontaneous dissemination consisted of teachers naturalistically sharing the program, materials, and training methods with other teachers in the same school, without any research support or prompting. Other than experimental assignment of two teachers to

711

program training and implementation per school, the design did not include any systematic variation of proportion of teachers trained per school to evaluate whether there needs to be a critical mass of initial implementers before spontaneous internal dissemination occurs. The other type of dissemination can be referred to as "outward" or external dissemination (Pentz, 2007). This type of dissemination typically takes place in settings where organizations and individuals are not the initial adopters or implementers. External dissemination may require that sustainability be already achieved in the original site so it can serve as a model for other potential sites. Delivery systems for substance abuse prevention programs have included community coalitions, agricultural extension universities systems, and state-to-community training in prevention operations (Pentz, 2007).

Sustainability is the fourth stage of diffusion and, in our ongoing example from the substance abuse prevention field, refers to research on whether an evidence-based prevention program is sustained after initial implementation, without researcher or developer support. Thus far, results of prevention dissemination trials suggest that the following factors predict sustainability of evidence-based prevention programs and prevention delivery systems: (a) ability of the prevention adopter organization to secure external funding after a research study has ended; (b) inclusion of regular training and retraining of community leaders and program implementers; (c) involvement of school administrators in the adopter organization; (d) efficient planning and communication among organization members; (e) resource sharing among community organizations for prevention activities; and (f) identification of an internal structure for conducting prevention training, for example, committees or work groups (Best et al., 2003). Future research could potentially vary these factors as planned prevention components using designs such as a fractional factorial to increase efficiency and decrease research costs (Nahum-Shani et al., 2018).

While sustainability is typically defined from the product standpoint (i.e., ability of a program to continue without additional researcher input or support), another conceptualization to be considered is from the patient or target population standpoint. To continue our substance use prevention example, classic school and mass media-based interventions tend to focus on changing explicit cognitions (controlled behaviors guided by conscious thought) regarding a substance (e.g., tobacco) in the hope of altering overt behavior (de Leeuw et al., 2008). However, past research from the psychological field (which would fall under T1 research) has found that implicit cognitions (behaviors guided by unconscious associations in memory) have a large influence over the choice to engage or not engage in a behavior (Cappelli et al., 2017; Pike et al., 2019). Thus, by including the findings from previous research on implicit memory in new prevention programming (T2 translational research), interventions that address both explicit and implicit cognitions could show longer or more sustained outcomes compared with programs that simply alter explicit cognitions. Over the long term, this would mean fewer resources might be required to maintain behavior change across various target populations.

Similar to diffusion of innovation theory, the RE-AIM (Reach, Effectiveness—Adoption, Implementation, and Maintenance) model has been used to address specific stages of diffusion (Table 31.2), although the broad dissemination of a treatment to different populations is more prominent (Glasgow & Emmons, 2007; Jilcott et al., 2007). In the RE-AIM model, reach encompasses both the concepts of broad dissemination to the general population, as well as ensuring that the population that might benefit most from the intervention is actually receiving the intervention. Considered together, diffusion of innovation theory and RE-AIM both have been proven useful for generating testable hypotheses for Type II translational research. Diffusion of innovation theory provides specific variables as predictors and outcomes of each of the four stages of diffusion, particularly for the adoption stage (Pentz, 2007). The RE-AIM model has been used to evaluate the dissemination of evidence-based

	TABLE 31.2	

Comparison of Diffusion of Innovation and RE-AIM

Parameter	Diffusion of innovation	RE-AIM[a]
Stage	(Pre-adoption training)	Reach
	(Evidence-based intervention)	Effectiveness
	Adoption	Adoption
	Implementation	Implementation
	Dissemination	(Assumed from Reach)
Measures	Adoption (trialability, observability, relative advantage, low complexity, compatibility)	Reach × Effectiveness (Individual Impact)
	Implementation (adherence, quality, amount)	
	Sustainability (% of sites or implementers still implementing × length of time)	
	Dissemination (% increase in external sites using)	Adoption × implementation × no. of settings × avg. individuals served/setting

[a]For further details of the RE-AIM (Reach, Effectiveness—Adoption, Implementation, and Maintenance) model, see Glasgow et al. (2019).

prevention and clinical practices, as well as the dissemination of prevention policies (Glasgow & Emmons, 2007; Glasgow et al., 2019). Composite scores that represent each stage of the RE-AIM model have been developed, with the aim of generating an overall weighted score for an evidence-based intervention to determine its overall public health effectiveness compared with standard practice guidelines (Jilcott et al., 2007). This type of scoring in the RE-AIM model is not yet operationalized from diffusion of innovation theory. Thus, RE-AIM has the advantage of being useful in comparative effectiveness research conducted at NIH, for instance, at the Agency for Research on Health Care and Quality (https://effectivehealthcare.ahrq.gov/).

Translation across multiple behaviors. In addition to framing translational research into two broad categories (Type I and II) or four narrow categories (T1–T4), another type to consider is translation of the same intervention across multiple health risk behaviors or comorbidities (see bottom row of Table 31.1). For this type of translation, it is useful to know if there is a causal relation between different comorbidities (e.g., tobacco use and stress-related disorders), if the different health risk behaviors are accounted for by some common influence (e.g., executive function deficits in emotional regulation and behavioral inhibitory control that predict substance use and lack of COVID risk safety behaviors; Fishbein & Dariotis, 2019; Roma et al., 2020), or if the intervention would likely change a mediator in the same direction for either the different comorbidities or different health risk behaviors (e.g., an intervention that increases executive function skills such as emotional regulation and behavioral impulse control).

The basic steps in this type of translational research are illustrated by an example where an evidence-based substance use prevention program for adolescents was applied to obesity prevention *as well as* substance use (Riggs et al., 2007). First, proof of concept was established by evaluating common links in developmental stage, risk factors, and mediators for substance use and obesity (Pentz, 2004a, 2009). Etiological and epidemiological studies then verified that these links exist, after which steps were taken to develop a new program based on adapting core elements and theory from previous evidence-based programs that addressed a risk factor common to both substance use and obesity (i.e., executive function deficits, particularly for the domains of emotional regulation and behavioral impulse control). This was followed by formative evaluation of content, sequencing, delivery, and mapping prevention concepts to a theoretical model of regulation (Pentz, 2004b). An efficacy study then assessed changes in both hypothesized mediators (externalizing behavior as an observable indicator of poor behavioral impulse control) and target health behaviors (physical activity, eating behavior, tobacco use, and alcohol use), followed by an effectiveness RCT with 28 schools, which included teacher and research staff reports of implementation and dissemination (Pentz, 2004a).

This type of translation can occur across not just multiple behaviors but also multiple populations. For example, even though the use of implementation intentions to modify inhibitory behaviors has been successful in adult populations (Nydegger & Walsh, 2018; Stacy et al., 2019), it has been absent from interventions aimed at adolescents. Similar to the substance use example, proof of concept was first determined from basic psychological and neuroscience research related to neurocognitive task validity, neurological development, and theoretical background (Giedd et al., 2015; Gogtay et al., 2004; Orbell et al., 1997). Various investigations then verified these basic findings across a number of adult populations and behaviors (Carrero et al., 2019; McWilliams et al., 2019; Nydegger et al., 2017; Robinson et al., 2019). Evaluation of content, core elements, as well as theoretical matching was found that linked both old and new populations together (Gregorio-Pascual & Mahler, 2020; Wieber et al., 2015). Finally, the previously validated concept was applied to an intervention attempting to modify an eating behavior in a new adolescent population (Ames et al., 2016).

Translation may also occur across distinct cultural and ethnic groups, including studies designed to address historical health disparities. Previously validated generalized intervention materials may be translated to fit with a specific target population, thus increasing program utilization and effectiveness (Benish et al., 2011; Dickerson et al., 2020). For example, in substance use prevention and cessation, tailoring programming to at-risk groups remains a high priority, as both consumption patterns and responses to treatment vary depending on ethnic subgroup (Johnston et al., 2021; Mennis & Stahler, 2016). Indeed, successful prevention programs will incorporate key components of the target populations culture, such as language, imagery or even components of coping with stress associated with acculturation and perceived discrimination into program materials (Skewes et al., 2019; Unger et al., 2016). While many researchers will create a new tailored program from the ground up, translating a universal/generalized intervention program to fit a specific audience may be more effective in reducing both cost and time spent validating the new intervention. These new translated programs will retain the main components of the old, validated program, while allowing for the inclusion of new culturally specific core components that would be a better fit for the target population (Burlew et al., 2013).

Mindfulness training serves as another example of an evidence-based intervention that may show translational efficacy across multiple behaviors and multiple populations. Initial research on mindfulness training focused on stress reduction using either small-scale quasi-experimental or experimental studies; however, in some cases, training has been limited to use as an adjunctive intervention to other treatments (Behan, 2020). Subsequently, integrated intervention and pilot studies representing a back-translation of findings from the original executive function training trial, from T4, T3, and T2 back to T1 and T2 have led to the development of new programs. This strategy has allowed for mindfulness interventions to be applied across a diversity of health-related problems such as substance use, pain management, and depression, as well as across multiple populations in settings such schools, health care, and workplace environments (Khoury et al., 2013; Schuman-Olivier et al., 2020).

BENEFITS AND BARRIERS

Perhaps the most important benefit of translational research is that it directly promotes the creation and dissemination of new treatments, assessments and services that improve physical and mental health. The NIH has provided the specific infrastructure to promote translational research by forming the National Center for Advancing Translational Sciences (NCATS; https://ncats.nih.gov/) and providing select institutions with Clinical and Translation Science Awards. NCATS seeks to accelerate translational research across various behaviorally relevant health areas, including aging, neurological diseases, substance use, and mental health. In addition, virtually all agencies under the NIH umbrella are invested in translational research. For example, NIMH is forging new translational connections across behavioral and systems-level neuroscience domains, including child development, temperament, emotion, motivation, attention, social processes, and genetics (Sanislow, 2020), and the National Center for Complementary and Integrative Health is promoting translational research in the development of mind-body interventions (Tomova et al., 2020). Across all agencies, the increasing attention to reduction in health disparities will require special translational research that zeroes in on more personalized or precision interventions that go beyond language translation (Fishbein & Dariotis, 2019). For example, adolescent drug use risk factors of acculturation, perceived discrimination, and friend networks could be addressed in interventions that are tailored to an adolescent's cultural group (Fujimoto & Valente, 2012; Unger et al., 2016). As a part of these large efforts, translational research has come to permeate all subdisciplines within psychology, as well as other research fields.

Based on the NCATS mission, a strong case can be made for psychology being an integral component of the health mission (Carr, 2008). While it is recognized widely that many diseases are caused or exacerbated by unhealthy behaviors, the biomedical fields still tend to relegate the role of psychology to specific physician–patient interactions and patient behaviors. Setting aside the issue of drug prescription privileges for clinical psychologists, there is a general need for doctoral psychology, public and allied health programs to integrate knowledge from the neurosciences into the field in order to enhance the role of psychology in health care driven by translational principles. Consistent with this push, several types of doctoral and postdoctoral training programs in psychology have proliferated, including health psychology, bio-behavioral health, translational behavioral medicine, and health behavior research. Others are emerging in response to the rapid changes in research technology and methods as mentioned earlier in this chapter, including training programs

in behavioral computational science, big data, and population health sciences. The opportunities for translational research training extend beyond formal doctoral and postdoctoral training programs and include workshops, webinars and special events sponsored by NCATS, as well as early career network and discussion groups at national conferences such as the Society for Behavioral Medicine, Society for Prevention Research, and the American Psychological Association. Given the continuing emphasis on translational research, this wave of opportunities will not crest anytime soon.

Despite the push for translational research in psychology and related disciplines, there are several hurdles to overcome to achieve success. *First*, a major hurdle rests in the institutional bias against "outside-the-box" or risky lines of research without guaranteed success and group productivity. Due to tenure and promotion decisions, emphasis is often placed on the overall quantity of independent achievements, as opposed to the long-term, team-oriented approach necessary to conduct translational research. This hurdle may become amplified because translational research emphasizes bottom-line products, which may involve patent and copyright profits, rather than theoretical advancements that can make transformative changes. *Second*, there can also be some parochialism among basic and applied researchers that extends to professional journals that have a narrow specialty focus. This latter barrier has been lessened by the advent of peer-reviewed journals dedicated to translational research, for example, *Translational Research* and *Clinical and Translational Science*. *Third*, younger investigators who are pushed into producing multiple empirically based publications to build a dossier worthy of tenure may find that translational research moves too slowly and depends on too many collaborators to be worth the large investment of time and resources. Counteracting this worry, however, there has been a proliferation of graduate programs that have curricula designed to specifically train students in translational research (Robertson & Williams, 2016).

Perhaps the most serious impediment to translational research rests in the high cost that typically accompanies a large team-oriented strategy. The main antidote for breaking down this barrier is to construct strong institutional leadership and support, as well as to provide steady intramural and extramural funding streams. While this may be a barrier in the initial stages, the benefits achieved may be transportable to multiple psychosocial and health problems. For example, by translating a substance use program across multiple health risk behaviors, the overall cost to public health should be reduced in the long run.

Future Directions

As discussed here, some specialized fields of research have provided some key examples of successful translational research (e.g., drug/vaccine discovery, substance use prevention interventions). However, many areas lag in providing examples that illustrate all of the stages of translational research (e.g., T4 studies of the impact of tobacco and substance use policy change on a whole population). In some cases, major gaps between basic to applied research continue to hamper effective translational research. Filling these gaps may be expedited by using previously successful examples as a template to direct future translational research.

There are also gaps in translational research that exist almost completely within the discipline of psychology. For example, basic research in social psychology is replete with causal mechanisms that are potentially applicable to clinical psychology and health promotion. Social psychology has uncovered theoretical information from controlled laboratory studies about clinically relevant constructs such as self-efficacy, self-esteem, and emotional regulation. However, many experimental social psychologists tend to study these constructs as moment-to-moment variables that are subject to change with a brief manipulation, whereas clinical psychologists are more interested in studying these constructs as stable traits with relevance for clinical practice. This parallel, but often disconnected, work provides an example

that is ripe for a more translational perspective. As a case in point, Wiers and colleagues (Wiers et al., 2015) used a web-based implicit training procedure to have participants react automatically to either avoid or approach alcohol stimuli. When subsequently tested for their alcohol drinking behavior, participants trained to avoid alcohol stimuli reduced their drinking, indicating that implicit training can gain control over the long-term, clinically relevant behavior.

Another direction for continued growth is in the translation of interventions that have been successful in impacting a single health risk behavior (e.g., adolescent substance use) to interventions that yield change in *multiple* health risk behaviors (MacArthur et al., 2018). For example, a program that simultaneously addresses subjective well-being, social competence, physical activity, healthy eating, and substance use prevention might facilitate wide-ranging adoption by schools, thus imparting a large social and economic impact on health. This strategy is also applicable to a range of other health outcomes, such as development of medications that target both cholesterol and blood pressure or medications that target both substance use and posttraumatic stress disorders. Similarly, implementation of physical exercise programs may simultaneously target depression, cardiovascular disease, and bone health.

Finally, another shortcoming in translational research involves problems related to our ability to identify what represents effective "practice" in the real world. This question has important implications for whether fidelity of implementation of evidence-based treatments can be maintained over a long period of time. In particular, little is known about the extent to which researchers and practitioners who market psychosocial treatments are following evidence-based standards. There has also been a lack of consensus in the field about what constitutes core elements of evidence-based interventions (Mihalic & Irwin, 2003). Further, treatments tested on an initial population may need to be periodically reexamined for their continued relevance in the face of population shifts due to cohort effects, changes in secular trends, and changing contexts for health behavior. Such information can provide feedback to basic researchers interested in modifying or replacing the treatment to produce lasting improvement in physical and mental health.

References

Ames, S. L., Wurpts, I. C., Pike, J. R., MacKinnon, D. P., Reynolds, K. R., & Stacy, A. W. (2016). Self-regulation interventions to reduce consumption of sugar-sweetened beverages in adolescents. *Appetite, 105*, 652–662. https://doi.org/10.1016/j.appet.2016.06.036

Anglemyer, A., Rutherford, G. W., Horvath, T., Baggaley, R. C., Egger, M., & Siegfried, N. (2013). Antiretroviral therapy for prevention of HIV transmission in HIV-discordant couples. *The Cochrane Database of Systematic Reviews, 4*(4), CD009153. https://doi.org/10.1002/14651858.CD009153.pub3

Backinger, C. L., Meissner, H. I., & Ashley, D. L. (2016). The FDA "deeming rule" and tobacco regulatory research. *Tobacco Regulatory Science, 2*(3), 290–293. https://doi.org/10.18001/TRS.2.3.8

Becker, M., Pinhasov, A., & Ornoy, A. (2021). Animal models of depression: What can they teach us about the human disease? *Diagnostics, 11*(1), 123. https://doi.org/10.3390/diagnostics11010123

Behan, C. (2020). The benefits of meditation and mindfulness practices during times of crisis such as COVID-19. *Irish Journal of Psychological Medicine, 37*(4), 256–258. https://doi.org/10.1017/ipm.2020.38

Bell, R. L., Hauser, S. R., Liang, T., Sari, Y., Maldonado-Devincci, A., & Rodd, Z. A. (2017). Rat animal models for screening medications to treat alcohol use disorders. *Neuropharmacology, 122*, 201–243. https://doi.org/10.1016/j.neuropharm.2017.02.004

Benish, S. G., Quintana, S., & Wampold, B. E. (2011). Culturally adapted psychotherapy and the legitimacy of myth: A direct-comparison meta-analysis. *Journal of Counseling Psychology, 58*(3), 279–289. https://doi.org/10.1037/a0023626

Best, A., Moor, G., Holmes, B., Clark, P. I., Bruce, T., Leischow, S., Buchholz, K., & Krajnak, J. (2003). Health promotion dissemination and systems thinking: Towards an integrative model. *American Journal of Health Behavior, 27*(1, Suppl. 3), S206–S216. https://doi.org/10.5993/AJHB.27.1.s3.4

Brinn, M. P., Carson, K. V., Esterman, A. J., Chang, A. B., & Smith, B. J. (2012). Cochrane Review: Mass media interventions for preventing smoking in young people. *Evidence-Based Child Health: A Cochrane Review Journal, 7*(1), 86–144. https://doi.org/10.1002/ebch.1808

Brooks, A. T., Allen, H. K., Thornton, L., & Trevorrow, T. (2021). Behavioral medicine challenges in the shadow of a global pandemic. *Translational Behavioral Medicine, 11*(2), 664–668. https://doi.org/10.1093/tbm/ibaa106

Burlew, A. K., Copeland, V. C., Ahuama-Jonas, C., & Calsyn, D. A. (2013). Does cultural adaptation have a role in substance abuse treatment? *Social Work in Public Health, 28*(3–4), 440–460. https://doi.org/10.1080/19371918.2013.774811

Cappelli, C., Ames, S., Shono, Y., Dust, M., & Stacy, A. (2017). Affective decision-making moderates the effects of automatic associations on alcohol use among drug offenders. *The American Journal of Drug and Alcohol Abuse, 43*(5), 534–544. https://doi.org/10.1080/00952990.2016.1216557

Cappelli, C., Pike, J. R., Christodoulou, G., Riggs, N. R., Warren, C. M., & Pentz, M. A. (2020). The effect of sensation seeking on alcohol use among middle school students: A latent state-trait analysis. *The American Journal of Drug and Alcohol Abuse, 46*(3), 316–324. https://doi.org/10.1080/00952990.2019.1660885

Carletto, S., Oliva, F., Barnato, M., Antonelli, T., Cardia, A., Mazzaferro, P., Raho, C., Ostacoli, L., Fernandez, I., & Pagani, M. (2018). EMDR as add-on treatment for psychiatric and traumatic symptoms in patients with substance use disorder. *Frontiers in Psychology, 8*, 2333. https://doi.org/10.3389/fpsyg.2017.02333

Carr, J. E. (2008). Advancing psychology as a bio-behavioral science. *Journal of Clinical Psychology in Medical Settings, 15*(1), 40–44. https://doi.org/10.1007/s10880-008-9093-z

Carrero, I., Vilà, I., & Redondo, R. (2019). What makes implementation intention interventions effective for promoting healthy eating behaviours? A meta-regression. *Appetite, 140*, 239–247. https://doi.org/10.1016/j.appet.2019.05.024

Castro, F. G., Barrera, M., Jr., & Martinez, C. R., Jr. (2004). The cultural adaptation of prevention interventions: Resolving tensions between fidelity and fit. *Prevention Science, 5*(1), 41–45. https://doi.org/10.1023/B:PREV.0000013980.12412.cd

Charles, N. E., Ryan, S. R., Bray, B. C., Mathias, C. W., Acheson, A., & Dougherty, D. M. (2016). Altered developmental trajectories for impulsivity and sensation seeking among adolescent substance users. *Addictive Behaviors, 60*, 235–241. https://doi.org/10.1016/j.addbeh.2016.04.016

Collins, L. M., Baker, T. B., Mermelstein, R. J., Piper, M. E., Jorenby, D. E., Smith, S. S., Christiansen, B. A., Schlam, T. R., Cook, J. W., & Fiore, M. C. (2011). The multiphase optimization strategy for engineering effective tobacco use interventions. *Annals of Behavioral Medicine, 41*(2), 208–226. https://doi.org/10.1007/s12160-010-9253-x

Collins, L. M., Nahum-Shani, I., & Almirall, D. (2014). Optimization of behavioral dynamic treatment regimens based on the sequential, multiple assignment, randomized trial (SMART). *Clinical Trials, 11*(4), 426–434. https://doi.org/10.1177/1740774514536795

Cooper, L. A., & Stoney, C. M. (2021). Messages to increase COVID-19 knowledge in communities of color: What matters most? *Annals of Internal Medicine, 174*(4), 554–555. https://doi.org/10.7326/M20-8057

Corbett, K. S., Flynn, B., Foulds, K. E., Francica, J. R., Boyoglu-Barnum, S., Werner, A. P., Flach, B., O'Connell, S., Bock, K. W., Minai, M., Nagata, B. M., Andersen, H., Martinez, D. R., Noe, A. T., Douek, N., Donaldson, M. M., Nji, N. N., Alvarado, G. S., Edwards, D. K., . . . Graham, B. S. (2020). Evaluation of the mRNA-1273 vaccine against SARS-CoV-2 in nonhuman primates. *The New England Journal of Medicine, 383*(16), 1544–1555. https://doi.org/10.1056/NEJMoa2024671

Crowley, M., Scott, J. T. B., & Fishbein, D. (2018). Translating prevention research for evidence-based policymaking: Results from the research-to-policy collaboration pilot. *Prevention Science, 19*(2), 260–270. https://doi.org/10.1007/s11121-017-0833-x

Cservenka, A., Herting, M. M., Seghete, K. L. M., Hudson, K. A., & Nagel, B. J. (2013). High and low sensation seeking adolescents show distinct patterns of brain activity during reward processing. *NeuroImage, 66,* 184–193. https://doi.org/10.1016/j.neuroimage.2012.11.003

Czoty, P. W., Stoops, W. W., & Rush, C. R. (2016). Evaluation of the "pipeline" for development of medications for cocaine use disorder: A review of translational preclinical, human laboratory, and clinical trial research. *Pharmacological Reviews, 68*(3), 533–562. https://doi.org/10.1124/pr.115.011668

de Leeuw, R. N. H., Engels, R. C. M. E., Vermulst, A. A., & Scholte, R. H. J. (2008). Do smoking attitudes predict behaviour? A longitudinal study on the bi-directional relations between adolescents' smoking attitudes and behaviours. *Addiction, 103*(10), 1713–1721. https://doi.org/10.1111/j.1360-0443.2008.02293.x

Dickerson, D., Baldwin, J. A., Belcourt, A., Belone, L., Gittelsohn, J., Keawe'aimoku Kaholokula, J., Lowe, J., Patten, C. A., & Wallerstein, N. (2020). Encompassing cultural contexts within scientific research methodologies in the development of health promotion interventions. *Prevention Science, 21*(Suppl. 1), 33–42. https://doi.org/10.1007/s11121-018-0926-1

Donohew, L., DiBartolo, M., Zhu, X., Benca, C., Lorch, E., Noar, S. M., Kelly, T. H., & Joseph, J. E. (2018). Communicating with sensation seekers: An fMRI study of neural responses to antidrug public service announcements. *Health Communication, 33*(8), 1004–1012. https://doi.org/10.1080/10410236.2017.1331185

Dumontheil, I. (2016). Adolescent brain development. *Current Opinion in Behavioral Sciences, 10,* 39–44. https://doi.org/10.1016/j.cobeha.2016.04.012

El-Bassel, N., Jackson, R. D., Samet, J., & Walsh, S. L. (2020). Introduction to the special issue on the HEALing Communities Study. *Drug and Alcohol Dependence, 217,* 108327–108327. https://doi.org/10.1016/j.drugalcdep.2020.108327

El-Jardali, F., Bou-Karroum, L., & Fadlallah, R. (2020). Amplifying the role of knowledge translation platforms in the COVID-19 pandemic response. *Health Research Policy and Systems, 18*(1), 58–58. https://doi.org/10.1186/s12961-020-00576-y

Fishbein, D. H. (2016). The full translational spectrum of prevention science. *Translational Behavioral Medicine, 6*(1), 1–4. https://doi.org/10.1007/s13142-016-0396-6

Fishbein, D. H., & Dariotis, J. K. (2019). Personalizing and optimizing preventive intervention models via a translational neuroscience framework. *Prevention Science, 20*(1), 10–20. https://doi.org/10.1007/s11121-017-0851-8

Flay, B. R. (2000). Approaches to substance use prevention utilizing school curriculum plus social environment change. *Addictive Behaviors, 25*(6), 861–885. https://doi.org/10.1016/S0306-4603(00)00130-1

Fort, D. G., Herr, T. M., Shaw, P. L., Gutzman, K. E., & Starren, J. B. (2017). Mapping the evolving definitions of translational research. *Journal of Clinical and Translational Science, 1*(1), 60–66. https://doi.org/10.1017/cts.2016.10

Fujimoto, K., & Valente, T. W. (2012). Decomposing the components of friendship and friends' influence on adolescent drinking and smoking. *The Journal of Adolescent Health, 51*(2), 136–143. https://doi.org/10.1016/j.jadohealth.2011.11.013

Fulton, S. L., & Maze, I. (2019). Translational molecular approaches in substance abuse research.

In M. Nader & Y. Hurd (Eds.), *Substance use disorders. Handbook of experimental pharmacology*, Vol. 258 (pp. 31–60). Springer. https://doi.org/10.1007/164_2019_259

Giedd, J. N., Raznahan, A., Alexander-Bloch, A., Schmitt, E., Gogtay, N., & Rapoport, J. L. (2015). Child psychiatry branch of the National Institute of Mental Health longitudinal structural magnetic resonance imaging study of human brain development. *Neuropsychopharmacology, 40*(1), 43–49. https://doi.org/10.1038/npp.2014.236

Glasgow, R. E. (2010). *Translation research: Design and methodology considerations*. Society for Behavioral Medicine Conference, Seattle, WA, United States.

Glasgow, R. E., & Emmons, K. M. (2007). How can we increase translation of research into practice? Types of evidence needed. *Annual Review of Public Health, 28*(1), 413–433. https://doi.org/10.1146/annurev.publhealth.28.021406.144145

Glasgow, R. E., Harden, S. M., Gaglio, B., Rabin, B., Smith, M. L., Porter, G. C., Ory, M. G., & Estabrooks, P. A. (2019). RE-AIM planning and evaluation framework: Adapting to new science and practice with a 20-year review. *Frontiers in Public Health, 7*, 64–64. https://doi.org/10.3389/fpubh.2019.00064

Gogtay, N., Giedd, J. N., Lusk, L., Hayashi, K. M., Greenstein, D., Vaituzis, A. C., Nugent, T. F., III, Herman, D. H., Clasen, L. S., Toga, A. W., Rapoport, J. L., & Thompson, P. M. (2004). Dynamic mapping of human cortical development during childhood through early adulthood. *Proceedings of the National Academy of Sciences of the United States of America, 101*(21), 8174–8179. https://doi.org/10.1073/pnas.0402680101

Gregorio-Pascual, P., & Mahler, H. I. M. (2020). Effects of interventions based on the theory of planned behavior on sugar-sweetened beverage consumption intentions and behavior. *Appetite, 145*, 104491. https://doi.org/10.1016/j.appet.2019.104491

Guastaferro, K., & Collins, L. M. (2019). Achieving the goals of translational science in public health intervention research: The Multiphase Optimization Strategy (MOST). *American Journal of Public Health, 109*(2), S128–S129. https://doi.org/10.2105/AJPH.2018.304874

Guerra, N. G., & Knox, L. (2008). How culture impacts the dissemination and implementation of innovation: A case study of the Families and Schools Together program (FAST) for preventing violence with immigrant Latino youth. *American Journal of Community Psychology, 41*(3–4), 304–313. https://doi.org/10.1007/s10464-008-9161-4

Hamidullah, S., Thorpe, H. H. A., Frie, J. A., Mccurdy, R. D., & Khokhar, J. Y. (2020). Adolescent substance use and the brain: Behavioral, cognitive and neuroimaging correlates. *Frontiers in Human Neuroscience, 14*, 298–298. https://doi.org/10.3389/fnhum.2020.00298

Hassmiller Lich, K., Frerichs, L., Fishbein, D., Bobashev, G., & Pentz, M. A. (2016). Translating research into prevention of high-risk behaviors in the presence of complex systems: Definitions and systems frameworks. *Translational Behavioral Medicine, 6*(1), 17–31. https://doi.org/10.1007/s13142-016-0390-z

Hawes, S. W., Chahal, R., Hallquist, M. N., Paulsen, D. J., Geier, C. F., & Luna, B. (2017). Modulation of reward-related neural activation on sensation seeking across development. *NeuroImage, 147*, 763–771. https://doi.org/10.1016/j.neuroimage.2016.12.020

Hawkins, S. S. P. D., Bach, N., & Baum, C. F. P. D. (2016). Impact of tobacco control policies on adolescent smoking. *The Journal of Adolescent Health, 58*(6), 679–685. https://doi.org/10.1016/j.jadohealth.2016.02.014

Heinz, A., Kiefer, F., Smolka, M. N., Endrass, T., Beste, C., Beck, A., Liu, S., Genauck, A., Romund, L., Banaschewski, T., Bermpohl, F., Deserno, L., Dolan, R. J., Durstewitz, D., Ebner-Priemer, U., Flor, H., Hansson, A. C., Heim, C., Hermann, D., . . . Spanagel, R. (2020). Addiction Research Consortium: Losing and regaining control over drug intake (ReCoDe)—From trajectories to mechanisms and interventions. *Addiction Biology, 25*(2), e12866. https://doi.org/10.1111/adb.12866

Jiang, J., Cui, H., & Rahmouni, K. (2017). Optogenetics and pharmacogenetics: Principles and applications. *American Journal of Physiology. Regulatory, Integrative and Comparative Physiology, 313*(6), R633–R645. https://doi.org/10.1152/ajpregu.00091.2017

Jilcott, S., Ammerman, A., Sommers, J., & Glasgow, R. E. (2007). Applying the RE-AIM framework to assess the public health impact of policy change. *Annals of Behavioral Medicine, 34*(2), 105–114. https://doi.org/10.1007/BF02872666

Johnston, L. D., Miech, R. A., O'Malley, P. M., Bachman, J. G., Schulenberg, J. E., & Patrick, M. E. (2021). *Monitoring the Future national survey results on drug use 1975–2020: Overview, key findings on adolescent drug use*. Institute for Social Research. https://eric.ed.gov/?id=ED611736

Joseph, J. E., Liu, X., Jiang, Y., Lynam, D., & Kelly, T. H. (2009). Neural correlates of emotional reactivity in sensation seeking. *Psychological Science, 20*(2),

215–223. https://doi.org/10.1111/j.1467-9280.2009.02283.x

Julian, D. A., Jones, A., & Deyo, D. (1995). Open systems evaluation and the logic model: Program planning and evaluation tools. *Evaluation and Program Planning, 18*(4), 333–341. https://doi.org/10.1016/0149-7189(95)00034-8

Kelly, T. H., Delzer, T. A., Martin, C. A., Harrington, N. G., Hays, L. R., & Bardo, M. T. (2009). Performance and subjective effects of diazepam and d-amphetamine in high and low sensation seekers. *Behavioural Pharmacology, 20*(5–6), 505–517. https://doi.org/10.1097/FBP.0b013e3283305e8d

Khoury, B., Lecomte, T., Fortin, G., Masse, M., Therien, P., Bouchard, V., Chapleau, M. A., Paquin, K., & Hofmann, S. G. (2013). Mindfulness-based therapy: A comprehensive meta-analysis. *Clinical Psychology Review, 33*(6), 763–771. https://doi.org/10.1016/j.cpr.2013.05.005

Koob, G. F., Lloyd, G. K., & Mason, B. J. (2009). Development of pharmacotherapies for drug addiction: A Rosetta stone approach. *Nature Reviews. Drug Discovery, 8*(6), 500–515. https://doi.org/10.1038/nrd2828

Kozak, K., Lucatch, A. M., Lowe, D. J. E., Balodis, I. M., MacKillop, J., & George, T. P. (2019). The neurobiology of impulsivity and substance use disorders: Implications for treatment. *Annals of the New York Academy of Sciences, 1451*(1), 71–91. https://doi.org/10.1111/nyas.13977

Levy, D. T., Tam, J., Kuo, C., Fong, G. T., & Chaloupka, F. (2018). The impact of implementing tobacco control policies: The 2017 tobacco control policy scorecard. *Journal of Public Health Management and Practice, 24*(5), 448–457. https://doi.org/10.1097/PHH.0000000000000780

Liu, X.-J., & Mesch, G. S. (2020). The adoption of preventive behaviors during the COVID-19 pandemic in China and Israel. *International Journal of Environmental Research and Public Health, 17*(19), 7170. https://doi.org/10.3390/ijerph17197170

Lutz, T. A., & Woods, S. C. (2012). Overview of animal models of obesity. *Current Protocols in Pharmacology, 58*, 5.61.1–5.61.18. https://doi.org/10.1002/0471141755.ph0561s58

MacArthur, G., Caldwell, D. M., Redmore, J., Watkins, S. H., Kipping, R., White, J., Chittleborough, C., Langford, R., Er, V., Lingam, R., Pasch, K., Gunnell, D., Hickman, M., & Campbell, R. (2018). Individual-, family-, and school-level interventions targeting multiple risk behaviours in young people. *The Cochrane Database of Systematic Reviews, 10*(10), CD009927. https://doi.org/10.1002/14651858.CD009927.pub2

Malin, J. R., Brown, C., Ion, G., van Ackeren, I., Bremm, N., Luzmore, R., Flood, J., & Rind, G. M. (2020). World-wide barriers and enablers to achieving evidence-informed practice in education: What can be learnt from Spain, England, the United States, and Germany. *Humanities and Social Sciences Communications, 7*, 99. https://doi.org/10.1057/s41599-020-00587-8

McWilliams, L., Bellhouse, S., Yorke, J., Lloyd, K., & Armitage, C. J. (2019). Beyond "planning": A meta-analysis of implementation intentions to support smoking cessation. *Health Psychology, 38*(12), 1059–1068. https://doi.org/10.1037/hea0000768

Mennis, J., & Stahler, G. J. P. D. (2016). Racial and ethnic disparities in outpatient substance use disorder treatment episode completion for different substances. *Journal of Substance Abuse Treatment, 63*, 25–33. https://doi.org/10.1016/j.jsat.2015.12.007

Mihalic, S. F., & Irwin, K. (2003). Blueprints for violence prevention: From research to real-world settings—Factors influencing the successful replication of model programs. *Youth Violence and Juvenile Justice, 1*(4), 307–329. https://doi.org/10.1177/1541204003255841

Nahum-Shani, I., Smith, S. N., Spring, B. J., Collins, L. M., Witkiewitz, K., Tewari, A., & Murphy, S. A. (2018). Just-in-time adaptive interventions (JITAIs) in mobile health: Key components and design principles for ongoing health behavior support. *Annals of Behavioral Medicine, 52*(6), 446–462. https://doi.org/10.1007/s12160-016-9830-8

Noël, X., Brevers, D., Bechara, A., Hanak, C., Kornreich, C., Verbanck, P., & Le Bon, O. (2011). Neurocognitive determinants of novelty and sensation-seeking in individuals with alcoholism. *Alcohol and Alcoholism, 46*(4), 407–415. https://doi.org/10.1093/alcalc/agr048

Nydegger, L. A., Ames, S. L., & Stacy, A. W. (2017). Predictive utility and measurement properties of the Strength of Implementation Intentions Scale (SIIS) for condom use. *Social Science & Medicine, 185*, 102–109. https://doi.org/10.1016/j.socscimed.2017.05.035

Nydegger, L. A., & Walsh, J. L. (2018). Strength of implementation intentions to use condoms among men who have sex with men. *AIDS and Behavior, 22*(11), 3491–3499. https://doi.org/10.1007/s10461-018-2079-4

Orbell, S., Hodgkins, S., & Sheeran, P. (1997). Implementation intentions and the theory of planned behavior. *Personality and Social Psychology Bulletin, 23*(9), 945–954. https://doi.org/10.1177/0146167297239004

Palmgreen, P., Lorch, E. P., Stephenson, M. T., Hoyle, R. H., & Donohew, L. (2007). Effects of the Office of National Drug Control Policy's Marijuana Initiative Campaign on high-sensation-seeking adolescents. *American Journal of Public Health*, 97(9), 1644–1649. https://doi.org/10.2105/AJPH.2005.072843

Parvaz, M. A., Alia-Klein, N., Woicik, P. A., Volkow, N. D., & Goldstein, R. Z. (2011). Neuroimaging for drug addiction and related behaviors. *Reviews in the Neurosciences*, 22(6), 609–624. https://doi.org/10.1515/RNS.2011.055

Pentz, M. A. (2003). Evidence-based prevention: Characteristics, impact, and future direction. *Journal of Psychoactive Drugs*, 35(Suppl. 1), 143–152. https://doi.org/10.1080/02791072.2003.10400509

Pentz, M. A. (2004a). *Applying theory and methods of community-based drug abuse prevention to pediatric obesity prevention*. U.S. Department of Health and Human Services.

Pentz, M. A. (2004b). Form follows function: Designs for prevention effectiveness and diffusion research. *Prevention Science*, 5(1), 23–29. https://doi.org/10.1023/B:PREV.0000013978.00943.30

Pentz, M. A. (2007). Disseminating effective approaches to drug abuse prevention. In M. K. Welch-Ross & L. G. Fasig (Eds.), *Handbook on communicating and disseminating behavioral science* (pp. 341–364). SAGE. https://doi.org/10.4135/9781412976930.n22

Pentz, M. A. (2009). Understanding and preventing risks for obesity. In R. DiClemente, R. Crosby, & J. Santelli (Eds.), *Adolescent health: Understanding and preventing risk* (pp. 147–164). Wiley.

Pentz, M. A., Chou, C. P., McClure, M., Bernstein, K., Mann, D., & Ross, L. (2004). Adoption and early implementation of STEP. In *Society for Prevention Research Program Book* (p. 265). Society for Prevention Research.

Pentz, M. A., Jasuja, G. K., Li, C., McClure, M., & Chou, C. P. (2003). Predictors of diffusion of evidence-based prevention programs: Early results of the STEP Trial. In *Society for Prevention Research Program Book* (p. 40). Society for Prevention Research.

Pentz, M. A., Jasuja, G. K., Rohrbach, L. A., Sussman, S., & Bardo, M. T. (2006). Translation in tobacco and drug abuse prevention research. *Evaluation & the Health Professions*, 29(2), 246–271. https://doi.org/10.1177/0163278706287347

Pentz, M. A., Riggs, N. R., & Warren, C. M. (2016). Improving substance use prevention efforts with executive function training. *Drug and Alcohol Dependence*, 163(Suppl. 1), S54–S59. https://doi.org/10.1016/j.drugalcdep.2016.03.001

Perry, J. L., Joseph, J. E., Jiang, Y., Zimmerman, R. S., Kelly, T. H., Darna, M., Huettl, P., Dwoskin, L. P., & Bardo, M. T. (2011). Prefrontal cortex and drug abuse vulnerability: Translation to prevention and treatment interventions. *Brain Research Reviews*, 65(2), 124–149. https://doi.org/10.1016/j.brainresrev.2010.09.001

Pike, J. R., Shono, Y., Tan, N., Xie, B., & Stacy, A. W. (2019). Retail outlets prompt associative memories linked to the repeated use of nicotine and tobacco products among alternative high school students in California. *Addictive Behaviors*, 99, 106067. https://doi.org/10.1016/j.addbeh.2019.106067

Reyna, V. F. (2020). Of viruses, vaccines, and variability: Qualitative meaning matters. *Trends in Cognitive Sciences*, 24(9), 672–675. https://doi.org/10.1016/j.tics.2020.05.015

Richter-Levin, G., Stork, O., & Schmidt, M. V. (2019). Animal models of PTSD: A challenge to be met. *Molecular Psychiatry*, 24(8), 1135–1156. https://doi.org/10.1038/s41380-018-0272-5

Riggs, N. R., Sakuma, K. L., & Pentz, M. A. (2007). Preventing risk for obesity by promoting self-regulation and decision-making skills: Pilot results from the PATHWAYS to health program (PATHWAYS). *Evaluation Review*, 31(3), 287–310. https://doi.org/10.1177/0193841X06297243

Robertson, D., & Williams, G. H. (2016). *Clinical and translational science: Principles of human research*. Elsevier Science & Technology.

Robinson, S. A., Bisson, A. N., Hughes, M. L., Ebert, J., & Lachman, M. E. (2019). Time for change: Using implementation intentions to promote physical activity in a randomised pilot trial. *Psychology & Health*, 34(2), 232–254. https://doi.org/10.1080/08870446.2018.1539487

Rogers, E. M. (1995). Elements of diffusion. In E. M. Rogers (Ed.), *Diffusion of innovations* (4th ed., pp. 1–38). The Free Press.

Roma, P., Monaro, M., Muzi, L., Colasanti, M., Ricci, E., Biondi, S., Napoli, C., Ferracuti, S., & Mazza, C. (2020). How to improve compliance with protective health measures during the COVID-19 outbreak: Testing a moderated mediation model and machine learning algorithms. *International Journal of Environmental Research and Public Health*, 17(19), 7252. https://doi.org/10.3390/ijerph17197252

Roozen, H. G., Boulogne, J. J., van Tulder, M. W., van den Brink, W., De Jong, C. A. J., & Kerkhof, A. J. F. M. (2004). A systematic review of the effectiveness of the community reinforcement approach in alcohol, cocaine and opioid addiction.

Drug and Alcohol Dependence, 74(1), 1–13. https://doi.org/10.1016/j.drugalcdep.2003.12.006

Sanislow, C. A. (2020). RDoC at 10: Changing the discourse for psychopathology. *World Psychiatry*, 19(3), 311–312. https://doi.org/10.1002/wps.20800

Sanson-Fisher, R. W. (2004). Diffusion of innovation theory for clinical change. *The Medical Journal of Australia*, 180(S6), S55–S56. https://doi.org/10.5694/j.1326-5377.2004.tb05947.x

Schuman-Olivier, Z., Trombka, M., Lovas, D. A., Brewer, J. A., Vago, D. R., Gawande, R., Dunne, J. P., Lazar, S. W., Loucks, E. B., & Fulwiler, C. (2020). Mindfulness and behavior change. *Harvard Review of Psychiatry*, 28(6), 371–394. https://doi.org/10.1097/HRP.0000000000000277

Segal, E., Zhang, F., Lin, X., King, G., Shalem, O., Shilo, S., Allen, W. E., Alquaddoomi, F., Altae-Tran, H., Anders, S., Balicer, R., Bauman, T., Bonilla, X., Booman, G., Chan, A. T., Cohen, O., Coletti, S., Davidson, N., Dor, Y., . . . Wilmes, P. (2020). Building an international consortium for tracking coronavirus health status. *Nature Medicine*, 26(8), 1161–1165. https://doi.org/10.1038/s41591-020-0929-x

Skewes, M. C., Hallum-Montes, R., Gardner, S. A., Blume, A. W., Ricker, A., & FireMoon, P. (2019). Partnering with native communities to develop a culturally grounded intervention for substance use disorder. *American Journal of Community Psychology*, 64(1-2), 72–82. https://doi.org/10.1002/ajcp.12354

Smith, M. A. (2020). Nonhuman animal models of substance use disorders: Translational value and utility to basic science. *Drug and Alcohol Dependence*, 206, 107733–107733. https://doi.org/10.1016/j.drugalcdep.2019.107733

Spoth, R., Rohrbach, L. A., Greenberg, M., Leaf, P., Brown, C. H., Fagan, A., Catalano, R. F., Pentz, M. A., Sloboda, Z., Hawkins, J. D., & the Society for Prevention Research Type 2 Translational Task Force Members and Contributing Authors. (2013). Addressing core challenges for the next generation of Type 2 translation research and systems: The translation science to population impact (TSci Impact) framework. *Prevention Science*, 14(4), 319–351. https://doi.org/10.1007/s11121-012-0362-6

Spring, B., Pellegrini, C., McFadden, H. G., Pfammatter, A. F., Stump, T. K., Siddique, J., King, A. C., & Hedeker, D. (2018). Multicomponent mHealth intervention for large, sustained change in multiple diet and activity risk behaviors: The Make Better Choices 2 randomized controlled trial. *Journal of Medical Internet Research*, 20(6), e10528. https://doi.org/10.2196/10528

Stacy, A. W., Nydegger, L. A., & Shono, Y. (2019). Translation of basic research in cognitive science to HIV-risk: A randomized controlled trial. *Journal of Behavioral Medicine*, 42(3), 440–451. https://doi.org/10.1007/s10865-018-9999-3

Stanger, C., Scherer, E. A., Vo, H. T., Babbin, S. F., Knapp, A. A., McKay, J. R., & Budney, A. J. (2020). Working memory training and high magnitude incentives for youth cannabis use: A SMART pilot trial. *Psychology of Addictive Behaviors*, 34(1), 31–39. https://doi.org/10.1037/adb0000480

Sussman, S., Valente, T. W., Rohrbach, L. A., Skara, S., & Pentz, M. A. (2006). Translation in the health professions: Converting science into action. *Evaluation & the Health Professions*, 29(1), 7–32. https://doi.org/10.1177/0163278705284441

Tomova, L., Wang, K. L., Thompson, T., Matthews, G. A., Takahashi, A., Tye, K. M., & Saxe, R. (2020). Acute social isolation evokes midbrain craving responses similar to hunger. *Nature Neuroscience*, 23(12), 1597–1605. https://doi.org/10.1038/s41593-020-00742-z

Tregoning, J. S., Brown, E. S., Cheeseman, H. M., Flight, K. E., Higham, S. L., Lemm, N. M., Pierce, B. F., Stirling, D. C., Wang, Z., & Pollock, K. M. (2020). Vaccines for COVID-19. *Clinical and Experimental Immunology*, 202(2), 162–192. https://doi.org/10.1111/cei.13517

Unger, J. B., Soto, D. W., & Baezconde-Garbanati, L. (2016). Trajectories of perceived discrimination from adolescence to emerging adulthood and substance use among Hispanic youth in Los Angeles. *Addictive Behaviors*, 53, 108–112. https://doi.org/10.1016/j.addbeh.2015.10.009

Vahedi, Z., Sibalis, A., & Sutherland, J. E. (2018). Are media literacy interventions effective at changing attitudes and intentions towards risky health behaviors in adolescents? A meta-analytic review. *Journal of adolescence*, 67, 140–152. https://doi.org/10.1016/j.adolescence.2018.06.007

Valente, T. W., Chou, C. P., & Pentz, M. A. (2007). Community coalitions as a system: Effects of network change on adoption of evidence-based substance abuse prevention. *American Journal of Public Health*, 97(5), 880–886. https://doi.org/10.2105/AJPH.2005.063644

Valente, T. W., Fujimoto, K., Chou, C. P., & Spruijt-Metz, D. (2009). Adolescent affiliations and adiposity: A social network analysis of friendships and obesity. *The Journal of Adolescent Health*, 45(2), 202–204. https://doi.org/10.1016/j.jadohealth.2009.01.007

Vanderpool, R. C., Gaysynsky, A., & Sylvia Chou, W.-Y. (2020). Using a global pandemic as a teachable moment to promote vaccine literacy and build resilience to misinformation. *American Journal of Public Health (1971)*, *110*(S3), S284–S285. https://doi.org/10.2105/AJPH.2020.305906

Wandersman, A., Duffy, J., Flaspohler, P., Noonan, R., Lubell, K., Stillman, L., Blachman, M., Dunville, R., & Saul, J. (2008). Bridging the gap between prevention research and practice: The interactive systems framework for dissemination and implementation. *American Journal of Community Psychology*, *41*(3–4), 171–181. https://doi.org/10.1007/s10464-008-9174-z

Wieber, F., Thürmer, J. L., & Gollwitzer, P. M. (2015). Promoting the translation of intentions into action by implementation intentions: Behavioral effects and physiological correlates. *Frontiers in Human Neuroscience*, *9*, 395. https://doi.org/10.3389/fnhum.2015.00395

Wiers, R. W., Houben, K., Fadardi, J. S., van Beek, P., Rhemtulla, M., & Cox, W. M. (2015). Alcohol cognitive bias modification training for problem drinkers over the web. *Addictive Behaviors*, *40*, 21–26. https://doi.org/10.1016/j.addbeh.2014.08.010

CHAPTER 32

PROGRAM EVALUATION: OUTCOMES AND COSTS OF PUTTING PSYCHOLOGY TO WORK

Brian T. Yates

Program evaluation collects data with experimental and quasi-experimental designs, focus groups, and diverse other methodologies. It then analyzes that information quantitatively and qualitatively, to understand whether and how interventions work (cf. Christie & Fleischer, 2010; Guttentag & Struening, 1975; Mertens, 2018; Posavac & Carey, 2003; Scriven, 1991; Silverman, 2004). Program evaluations can be carried out in schools, clinics, offices, factories, farms, public spaces, and in the military, to name just a few settings. Evaluations often help researchers, policy makers, and practitioners decide whether a program is given the moniker *evidence-based*, which can determine whether the program is funded and disseminated. In education, the What Works Clearinghouse (see https://www.ies.ed.gov/ncee/wwc) conducts several hundred meta-analytic reviews annually of education program evaluations. A searchable database is available as well for substance abuse and mental health services (see https://www.samhsa.gov/ebp-resource-center). Evaluations also can determine whether governments reimburse third-party funders of programs attempting to address government priorities (Reisman et al., 2018).

Summative evaluation asks whether intervention activities developed and tested in more controlled settings can be implemented at real-world sites, whether a program achieves targeted outcomes, and how much a program costs to implement. *Formative* evaluation seeks to improve programs by understanding why a real-world program works well, poorly, or harms rather than helps. Formative evaluation attempts to discover which program activities actually change the biopsychosocial processes that are supposed to lead to desired outcomes.

Outcomes evaluated in summative or formative evaluation can be as diverse as reduced depression, improved negotiation skills, enhanced athletic performance, cessation of drug use, or defense readiness. Outcomes can encompass results that matter to funders, such as increased days of employment and reduced HIV transmission. Even monetary outcomes can be considered, such as health care and criminal justice expenditures no longer needed and better employment income for clients. Increasingly, program evaluation includes the major *resources consumed* by program operations, such as types, amounts, and the monetary value of providers' and clients' time, office space, and the other resources that make program activities possible (Yates, 1980, 2020). Some evaluations contrast program costs to program outcomes with cost-effectiveness, cost-benefit, and cost-utility analyses. State governments may use program evaluation to recommend which programs should receive funding and which should not (e.g., Aos et al., 2004).

https://doi.org/10.1037/0000319-032
APA Handbook of Research Methods in Psychology, Second Edition: Vol. 2. Research Designs: Quantitative, Qualitative, Neuropsychological, and Biological, H. Cooper (Editor-in-Chief)

Obviously, program evaluation is powerful—perhaps the most powerful short-term application of psychological and other research methodologies to date. Learning more about it is essential for psychologists, whether scientists, scientist-practitioners, or practitioners. We need to understand it to evaluate our own efforts, to contribute positively to evaluations performed on our programs by others, to evaluate other programs, and to recognize and prevent its misuse. This chapter begins with a comprehensive model of program evaluation, uses examples to explain how to resolve measurement and design issues, and ends by describing current issues facing program evaluation and program evaluators.

A COMPREHENSIVE MODEL OF PROGRAM EVALUATION

It is natural to ask questions about services, and even to judge them for their value to oneself if not to society. When many individuals ask these questions and decide to purchase or decline services for themselves in a competitive marketplace, only the most effective and least costly services survive the competition and flourish. However, when relatively few officials make decisions to fund services that are not widely available in the private marketplace, or when decision makers are relatively uninformed about the value of the services being considered, economic forces of competition in quality, price, and supply are impeded.

In these contexts and others, program evaluation can provide to potential purchasers, funders, clients, advocates, and other stakeholders the information they need for market forces to work. This feedback can be about the quality of programs offered; the strength, durability, and reliability of program outcomes; and program costs. Program evaluation also can provide information on the many outcomes and diverse costs that may be experienced in the long-run and by multiple stakeholders. These findings can reduce the likelihood that funding decisions would maximize outcomes and minimize immediate costs to some interest groups while resulting in poor future outcomes and large future costs to others. Typically,

marketplaces do not provide feedback that is this all-encompassing, temporally comprehensive, and multi-perspective. Evaluation can provide this feedback not only to funders but also to providers, clients, and communities served and affected by programs.

This conceptualization of program evaluation is compatible with a variety of mission statements made for it in past decades, including, "The proper mission of evaluation is not to eliminate the fallibility of authority or to bolster its credibility. Rather, its mission is to facilitate a democratic, pluralistic process by enlightening all the participants" (Cronbach et al., 1980, p. 1). Additionally, as Guba and Lincoln (1989) wrote,

> Evaluation is an investment in people and in progress. . . .we do not treat evaluation as a *scientific* process, because it is our conviction that to approach evaluation scientifically is to miss completely its fundamentally social, political, and value-oriented character. (cover page, p. 7)

Program evaluation asks and attempts to answer questions such as, "Are our children being educated well?" "Is the treatment offered at that clinic effective?" "Is participating in this new program worth the time and money?" and "What programs work to build safer communities and how much do they cost?" In addition, because program evaluation is not necessarily limited to publicly funded services, it also may ask, "How can we run our business better and greener?" "How can we make our farms more productive?" Program evaluation can be applied to government efforts beyond social services, too, even addressing questions such as, "How should, or can, we win this war?" These questions are important to diverse stakeholders for many reasons. Program evaluators try to answer these questions. How these questions are asked, and challenges of finding, understanding, and using the answers, are the topics of this chapter.

Outcomes

A *program* is an organized effort by one or more persons to maintain or change the nature of people, communities, or environments. Programs consume *resources*, such as time, space, and energy, to conduct specific *activities* that psychological and other theories recommend for changing biological, psychological, and social *processes* that should result in targeted *outcomes* with positive, desired *impacts*. In actuality, some program consequences, such as improved knowledge, are intended, but others are not, such as acquisition of skills to manipulate peers, negative attitudes toward formal education, and destructive of interest and creativity (cf. Morell, 2010). Unintended consequences of some programs have exacerbated rather than remediated the problems being addressed—for example, alcohol, tobacco, and other drug prevention programs that wind up increasing rather than decreasing both the willingness to use and the actual use of alcohol, tobacco, and other drugs by children (cf. Kissel, 1997).

There can be short- and long-term outcomes, such as improved performance on a mathematics section of a test at the end of the year, or better performance in an algebra class several years later. Outcomes can be monetary, such as higher earnings following college graduation or reduction in future spending for health care services after psychotherapy. Usually, monetary outcomes are not the primary results of interest to psychologists. *Outcomes* typically refer to what, in clinical trials, is termed *effectiveness*, that is, the amount of change in primary measures of what treatment is supposed to accomplish, whether moving clients below the threshold for a particular diagnosis such as depression or above a criterion for a positive state such as happiness.

Impacts

Impact increasingly means, "Did the program result in changes that were of particular interest to funders or to society at large?" (Picciotto, 2015). These changes are often different from changes that are the immediate focus of providers, such as reduced anxiety. Impact measures often are more removed from the immediate results of treatment, that is, outcomes, although the importance of impacts often is clearer than the relevance of some outcomes to stakeholders. For example, family

members may hope that a program helps a client return to employment. Funders may anticipate that therapy will result in reduced future need for other services. These are impacts that can result from treatment outcomes. A wide variety of "big data" measures have been advocated for evaluating social impact (Reisman et al., 2018). The promise of this focus on more socially and financially significant measures is that evaluation becomes a more positive, transformative effort (Bolinson & Mertens, 2020). This broad scope is reflected, too, in Patton's (2019) *Blue Marble Evaluation*, which applies a principles-based framework to program evaluation so that programs become more aware of their universal context: the daunting Anthropocene.

Many psychologists seem reluctant to include measures of these broader impacts, and even measures less removed from effective therapy such as reduced use of human services. Psychologists have little experience using impact measures and are understandably concerned about the reliability and validity of impact measures. Many also question whether psychology-based programs should be judged by events so removed from the theory-based activities of programs and carefully chosen outcomes. Nevertheless, impacts such as reduced future expenditures are what motivate most employers and government agencies to fund many psychological programs.

Impacts have received special attention from evaluators in the past decade, as governments offered financial incentives to programs that promise to deliver specific, measurable impacts (Reisman et al., 2018). Evidence-based programs now are evaluated to determine whether anticipated impacts are actually achieved. If so, *pay-for-success* initiatives reimburse programs from public or philanthropic funds. If not, programs are not reimbursed. So that programs need not wait until program completion for some return on their investment, regular "milestones" are set for interim evaluations. Interim payments are provided if proxy measures of impact are promising.

Financial markets now provide capital to programs for start-up costs and more (Sarmiento

& Herman, 2020). Evaluators occupy pivotal roles in determining whether hoped-for funding is received and investments returned, often with monetary interest. Millions of dollars available annually in the United States for these projects have heightened evaluator attention to impact variables. Billions of philanthropic dollars available globally each year have fostered evaluation efforts to assess the social return on investment for these programs (Reisman et al., 2018). Concerns have been expressed about how social impact evaluation could have unanticipated, deleterious consequences unless political and economic contexts of impact measurement are considered (Bolinson & Mertens, 2020; Yates & Marra, 2017).

Descriptive statistics.   Program evaluation often begins by describing whether a program did what it said it would do, such as, "Did teachers introduce and provide guidance for the prescribed class exercises?" "Were the 50 motorcycle awareness billboards placed in on winding roads commonly used by motorcyclists in target counties for 30 to 45 days each?" "Were sessions attended by clients?" and "Did captains provide referrals to peer support program for soldiers exhibiting three or more signs of posttraumatic stress disorder within four weeks following ignition of an improvised explosive device in the soldier's immediate vicinity?" These questions of adherence of actual program operations to planned program activities are the essence of some program evaluations. The answers provided usually are quantitative *and* qualitative, using numbers and words to support objective and subjective judgments. Programs with high adherence or *fidelity* to planned activities are evaluated positively. These evaluations assume, however, that if program activities are performed faithfully, they typically lead to desired program outcomes. This, of course, may not be the case.

Programs can insist that they should not be evaluated negatively if prescribed activities were implemented but the desired outcomes failed to occur, but this could be self-serving. Because there is little agreement on what program

activities are best, other than designating them "best practices" with possibly scant evidence that they produce desired outcomes, program evaluations necessary increase their scope beyond adherence to planned activities, to examine whether the desired outcomes actually occurred. Typically, hope for those outcomes is what induced the client to participate in the program, and the funder to fund it. The means to achieve those outcomes were likely left to the program to devise and implement, so long as ethical and moral boundaries were not crossed and budget constraints were not exceeded.

Groupings by demographic variables.   Many programs focus on changing particular behavioral, cognitive, emotional (affective), or biological processes of clients, who can differ in their affiliations with families, organizations, businesses, or military units. Outcomes also can be distinguished for various types of clients, including different genders, ethnicities, ages, socioeconomic classes, or those with different mental and physical abilities. Statistical techniques can tell evaluators whether outcomes were better for subgroups of clients. For instance, reading scores between the start of Grades 9 and 10 might be compared statistically for girls versus boys, or students of different ethnicities, to show whether apparent small differences in scores were statistically significant. Moreover, change in reading scores for different types of students could be compared to decide whether one type of student improved notably more than another. Statistical analyses such as analysis of covariance can adjust for differences that existed between groups of clients before program participation, so that the evaluation can answer questions such as, "Was the difference in reading levels found after 10th grade primarily caused by differences that existed between the groups of clients before 10th grade?"

Levels of specificity.   For groupings of program clients, outcomes can be measured at *micro* levels of specificity, such as the individual student, and aggregated to *meso* and *macro* levels to represent outcomes such as "improvement in average test scores of students in Mr. Crosstree's 10th-grade reading class." Levels of specificity can be understood as a type of grouping: one that includes different parts of an organization (e.g., a therapy referral agent, Title IX specialists, an entire human resources department), different levels of geographic location (e.g., city block, city, county, state, country, hemisphere), different levels of outcome specificity (e.g., increased vocabulary and text comprehension, reading skills in general, language proficiency), or different intervals of time (e.g., 10th grade, high school years, one's entire secondary education).

Effects on other programs.   Most evaluations examine outcomes for one or more programs, but some specialize in effects that one program may have on other programs. Advocates for some programs have essentially told funders of human services, "Your choice is to pay now for our prevention program, or pay more later for other programs that deal with problems that could have been prevented." A challenge for these evaluators is to measure these impacts in a meaningful manner that can be replicated by others, including critics of prevention programs. Findings of these evaluations can change policy and funding. Relatively inexpensive substance abuse prevention and treatment programs have been found to reduce subsequent use of health services by persons who participate in these programs (e.g., Aos et al., 2004). These evaluations have prompted some states to reallocate funding for health services to substance abuse services, which freed-up funds for other projects. Given the increasing prevalence of costly entitlements such as health care, and decreased funds available, decision makers are increasingly interested in evaluations of potential cost-savings.

Intent-to-treat versus as-treated.   An important distinction is made in program evaluation between outcomes for clients completing a program and outcomes for clients who began but did not complete a program. As also understood in clinical trials methodology, average outcomes for *as-treated* (AT) clients typically are better than average outcomes for *intent-to-treat* (ITT) clients, because those who begin treatment or another

program but do not show early signs of benefiting from the program often cease participation in the program. Some clients probably drop out because they expect that their outcomes will not be worth their time and other resources. Some programs, including some substance use treatments, intentionally expel clients who show poor preliminary outcomes—who relapse early and often, for example. This can be considered a form of triage that reallocates program resources to those who seem most likely to benefit.

There also is value in knowing the outcomes of a program for clients who do manage to complete it. Acknowledging this, program evaluations often report separately the AT and ITT outcomes and the AT and ITT costs. The number of clients included in AT and ITT analyses often is important to report as well. For instance, a program that is 70% successful in cessation of gang activity 2 years later for the 20 communities that completed the program may be only 20% successful for the 100 communities that began the program.

Measures.   Program operators' judgments of clients' performance can be used as a measure of outcomes, as can clients' own reports. Both can provide unique information on program outcomes. Both, however, can be biased for or against outcomes desired by program operators or clients. To reduce these biases, standardized outcome measures have been developed that are administered by third parties. Although standardized measures also can perpetuate biases for or against a program, and for or against groupings of clients, the availability, economy, and acceptability of these measures make them appealing. Some standardized measures directly assess client performance, such as reading ability or verbal aptitude. Others are completed by third parties who have interacted with clients. These assessments not only can be used in evaluations, but they can be evaluated themselves for effectiveness and costs (Yates & Taub, 2003).

Outcomes and impacts rarely are sufficient for a program evaluation.   Simply knowing the outcome of a program often is insufficient.

Many questions can be asked about programs, even if the outcomes and impacts seem terrific. If results of a program are similar to those desired and funded, advocates for the program and its providers typically conclude that the program was responsible for the outcomes. Experience has shown that this may not always be the case. Whether spontaneous remission of cancer, smoking cessation maintained without professional help, or acquisition of basic social or language skills without formal education, programs may not be responsible for all or even most of the positive outcomes and impacts observed.

Furthermore, it is certainly common for programs to ascribe the cause of most *negative* outcomes to either poor participation (e.g., patients not complying with program activities, students missing classes), iatrogenic external factors (e.g., smoking advertisements in subways, peer pressure, toxic families), problems clients had before program participation (e.g., inadequate attention or social skills, hyperactivity, substance use), or cultural offensiveness of ill-chosen program activities. All of these can be real and important causal factors. The important question for program evaluators is not *whether* but *how much* these and other factors, including the program activities, were responsible for undesired program outcomes. Understanding the causes of program failures, even more than program successes, can help programs improve and are essential for formative program evaluation.

The following types of evaluation describe different ways of pealing back the layers of a program to better discern its many operations, effects, and costs. Most evaluations focus on a subset of all possible program resources, activities, processes, outcomes, and impacts. The more formative, potentially more constructive evaluations generally include information about additional classes of variables: not only what acts are performed by which providers, clients, and others during the program and what outcomes follow, but the more complete set of (a) *resources* actually consumed; (b) *activities* actively performed for, and participated in, by clients;

(c) *processes* occurring, including those unanticipated, in clients; (d) *outcomes* achieved for clients; and (e) *impacts* observed for clients and their communities.

Activity–Outcome Evaluation

Evaluation attempts a more comprehensive, holistic understanding of programs with qualitative and quantitative descriptions of the relationships between specific variables in the more generic classes of resources, activities, processes, and outcomes. These complex networks of intervariable relationships often are modeled graphically in early stages of a program evaluation.

Logic models. Once it is acknowledged that measurable outcomes probably have a variety of causes and that participation in program activities may be only a subset of those determinants, causes both internal to the program (*endogenous*) and outside of it (*exogenous*) can be hypothesized. These can be made explicit graphically and associated with specific activities thought to cause those outcomes in a *logic model*. Figure 32.1 provides three logic models: the left side lists activities for programs in education, health care, and the military, while the right side lists typical outcomes for each type of program.

For education, reading skills are the focus of the program depicted. More specific measures of reading skills that occur sooner than the goal of being able to read at 10th-grade level are named, including vocabulary, comprehension of text, and composition. These outcomes are described in the logic model as being caused by the activities of parents reading books to their children, instruction in sentence diagramming, and self-paced readings and quizzes.

For health care, the logic model in the middle panel of Figure 32.1 depicts the outcome of improved longevity measured as years lived and quality of those years. In addition to those more global or macro-level outcomes, more specific meso-level measures of health that are more *proximal* to the program activities are improved cardiovascular sufficiency, increased pulmonary capacity, and enhanced balance in patient immune systems. These health outcomes are described

Program Activities   Outcomes

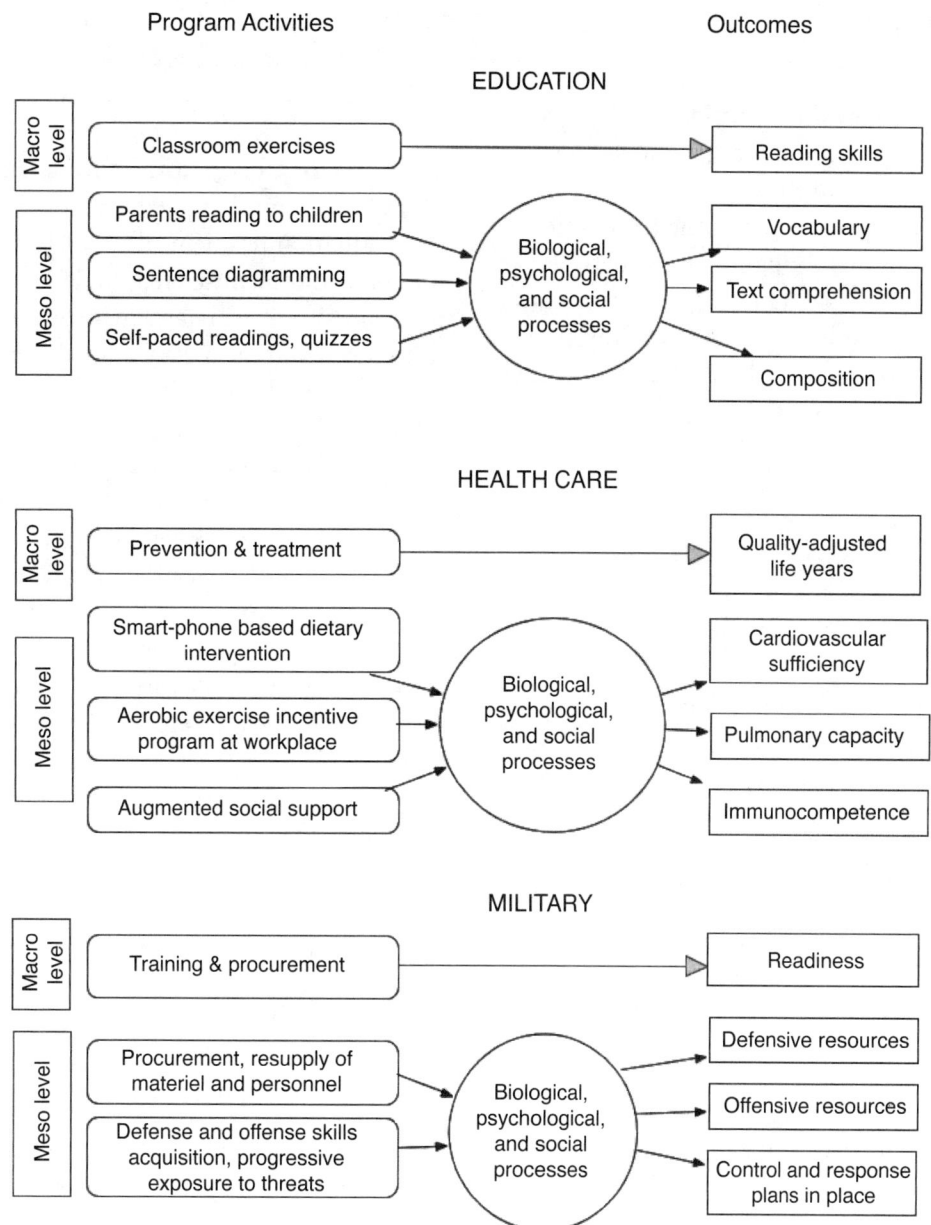

FIGURE 32.1.   Activity–outcome logic models at macro and meso levels of specificity for evaluation of educational, health, and military programs.

as being caused by a variety of prevention and treatment program activities, ranging from use of phone-based interventions for improving nutritional balance to enhanced regular aerobic exercise and improved relationships for better social support.

For the military program, the macro-level outcome of *readiness* is operationalized as having adequate resources for both defense and offense, and having concrete, detailed plans in place for

use of those resources in response to existing and emerging challenges. These more specific outcomes are described by the logic model in the bottom panel of Figure 32.1 as being associated with the more specific program activities of procurement of necessary defense and offense materiel and personnel, and training of personnel in use of that materiel in situations that approximate battlefield sites. This training could involve systematically escalating exposure to unpredictable threats such as increasingly aggressive provocations by battlefield participants.

Activity–outcome evaluation planning. It is tempting to connect the more specific outcomes listed in the right column of Figure 32.1 to one or more specific activities listed in the left column. Drawing connections thought to exist between an activity and an outcome is a program evaluator's way of expressing a hypothesis regarding the program. Experts and theories could be consulted to see whether they concur in hypothesizing the posited connections.

Program evaluators would then test these activity–outcome linkages by measuring activities, outcomes, and relationships between the two. After collecting data on the outcomes of a program and its activities, a variety of statistical analyses can examine the existence, direction, and magnitude of these activity–outcome relationships, from simple correlations to structural equation modeling of causal pathways that examine how much clients (a) participated in the program and its activities, and (b) experienced the expected outcomes (cf. Yates, 1980, 1996). A dose–response relationship usually is posited between the types, intensities, and durations of activities actually engaged in by clients, and the desired outcomes. In this way, greater fidelity to planned program activities is expected to be associated with greater achievement of program outcomes. Finding that poor fidelity to activity plans nevertheless was followed by positive outcomes could be especially illuminating, calling into question the hypothesized activity–outcome relationships and possibly spurring the search for other explanations.

Most readers will recognize that even a strong correlation does not mean that a causal relationship exists between an activity and an outcome. Quantitative or qualitative analyses of relationships between participation in an activity and attainment of an outcome even could find that more participation was related to *poorer* outcomes, despite the underlying effectiveness of the program. Perhaps clients who were in worse shape before participating in the program were offered more activities in hopes of helping them,

but those initially worse-off clients only improved about the same extent as those who began participation with less severe problems.

Designs for Program Evaluation

Many readers probably have recognized that the evaluation problems described thus far, and others, could be mitigated if clients eligible for a program simply were assigned at random either to the program or to wait until the evaluation was completed. The latter, *wait-list condition* often is called a *control group* or *counterfactual*. Outcomes would be measured for both clients in and waiting for program participation, typically before, during, and several times after program operation. These measures then would be compared at each point in time for clients in and not in the program using comprehensive statistical analyses such as multivariate analyses of variance, hierarchical linear modeling, logistic regression, or survival analyses. If a sufficient number of clients were randomized to each condition, characteristics that could otherwise explain differences in outcomes should be distributed similarly among clients in the program or control group. No statistically significant differences should exist on outcome measures at the start of the program, and significant differences on the same measures should be found between clients in the program and control conditions after the program if the program is effective.

Why evaluation pursues alternatives to randomized clinical trials. So, why are evaluators eschewing the gold standard of randomized clinical trials? Most would respond, "We would if we could, but we can't." For evaluations to avoid confusing program outcomes with what are essentially placebo effects, clients and even providers would have to be kept unaware of whether they were participating in the *real* program. This is difficult in many human services. Although it is possible to lie to clients and tell them they are in a program when they actually are in a control condition, many program operators and evaluators would regard this as unethical, unjust, and unrealistic.

Furthermore, clients can refuse to wait to participate in a program, and many client advocates view participation in publicly funded health and other human services as *entitlements*: as necessary rights, not optional opportunities. Arguments that the program may not help, or even hurt, seldom succeed in dissuading desperate clients from seeking services. Even when clients or advocates agree to random assignment, sabotage can occur. Advocates, program providers, and evaluation staff sympathetic to client needs may surreptitiously ensure that the more needy clients are enrolled in the program even if those clients drew assignment to a waiting list control condition. This can, of course, destroy the validity of the evaluation. If more needy clients show poorer outcomes because of poorer potential, the apparent magnitude of program outcomes may be diminished, entirely obscured, or reversed, placing program funding in jeopardy.

In addition, programs may be so broad in scope that random assignment is infeasible, at least in nontotalitarian contexts. Consider an evaluation of alternative health promotion programs. The Stanford Three Community Study (Meyer et al., 1980) evaluated effects of a mass media program to increase individuals' awareness of risk factors and risky behaviors for coronary heart disease (CHD) and to promote positive change in individuals' CHD-related behaviors. This program was compared with both a no-program control and a third condition that added media to a face-to-face program for residents with high CHD risk. The three conditions were implemented in three similar cities.

Although heralded at the time, this was not a completely experimental study in that it did not randomly assign persons to live in the different cities. Useful findings were generated nonetheless (Leventhal et al., 1980). It was particularly important that a control condition was included, because some behavioral and biological risk factors were found to have *increased* in the control community. Although these outcomes sometimes decreased in the media-only community, they more consistently decreased in the media plus face-to-face community. It could be argued that the media plus face-to-face program actually was *more* effective than shown by simple pre–post change measures because without a program, CHD risk factors would have increased.

Strict methodologists might remark that evaluations should not be done at all if they cannot be done right, and that the only way to do this by using careful randomized designs. The role of evaluation, then, would be limited to basic and applied settings that, at most, were simplified *analogues* of real-world programs. Although that role would be more comfortable to some, the not-so-occasional failure in the real world of programs found to be effective in highly controlled settings suggests that evaluation of real-world implementation is essential (cf. Kazdin, 2003). These evaluations can provide feedback to theories on what *does* work, and when theories need revision. If a program fails, that feedback can be even more important, but only if measures have been taken that can verify each major step in the logic model that captures the essential activities, processes, outcomes, and impacts of the program.

Natural experimentation. An approach to resolving some of the problems described above is to observe rather than manipulate program selection and participation by clients. A dose–response relationship often is hypothesized: The more a client participates in a program, the better the outcomes should be. If the client of a program is a community rather than a person, then those communities in which the program is more completely implemented should experience better outcomes. Sometimes the expected dose–response relationship is found, as Howard et al. (1986) discovered in evaluations of therapy outcome. Sometimes the hypothesized dose–response relationship is not found. Even the reverse of a dose–response relationship could be mistakenly detected if, for example, clients with greater needs are actually encouraged to participate *more* than clients with lesser needs, and if greater initial severity of client problems reduces program effectiveness. Because determinants of opportunities to participate in programs may be related to preexisting factors that may also affect program results, conclusions of these more natural, observational studies can be suspect.

Treatment-as-usual comparison. An alternative to both a no-treatment control condition and natural experimentation is comparison of proposed programs to what is commonly termed *treatment as usual* (TAU). In some cases, TAU would be an existing program that is already in operation. In other circumstances, TAU actually would be *no* program because no services were available in that context. (This is less common in countries offering more entitlements, such as national health services.) If a new program demonstrates substantially better outcomes than TAU, the new program would be judged positively. If not, TAU continues. This approach to evaluation risks perpetuating an inadequate status quo, of course. It also does not satisfy persons who feel that they are entitled to program services when none are available. Moreover, relative to evaluations comparing outcomes for clients who do or do not participate in a program, profoundly larger samples of clients need to be recruited, and larger evaluation budgets obtained, to test whether significant and meaningful differences exist in outcomes of an innovative program versus TAU. *Power analysis* (MEASURE Evaluation, 2015) can find how many clients are needed for these program comparisons, depending on the anticipated size of the difference in program versus TAU outcomes. In addition, TAU defenders typically assure that their program is especially well-funded, often reducing the validity of generalizing findings beyond the evaluation.

Hybrid designs. A hybrid approach to coping with problems of random assignment to a program or waiting list condition is to invite potential clients to either TAU, the new program, or a waiting list. Outcome measures would be obtained for all clients, including those on the waiting list and TAU. After the program evaluation, every client would be offered whichever intervention produced the best outcomes. This strategy mitigates a number of potential concerns but can be unacceptable for potentially life-saving or life-sustaining programs, such as chemotherapy adherence regimens or suicide prevention efforts.

Yet another method is to offer the new program as an alternative and then adjust statistically for whatever preprogram differences are found between clients who do or do not participate in the program. These typically include variables affecting propensity to participate in or benefit from different programs, such as demographic characteristics, preprogram severity of problem, and previous attempts to remedy the problem. Hopefully, what remains after this *propensity score matching* and outcome measure adjustment are the outcomes that would have been found if clients had been assigned randomly to the program or alternatives. Sometimes propensity score adjustment works, but it can be overwhelmed by the complexity of relationships between variables used in and outcomes (see Schneeweiss et al., 2010).

Yet more alternatives. Often termed *quasi-experimental designs* (QEDs; Shadish et al., 2002), this family of alternatives to randomized trial designs can be more ethical, feasible, and acceptable than randomly assigning clients to program or waiting list conditions. QEDs are especially helpful in evaluations that focus on a single program rather than comparing one program versus TAU, asking, "Does *this* program work? How well? At what cost?" These single-program evaluations are common. The type of QED used depends on the program and evaluation context. For example, if a long stream of measurements exists from the time before the program is implemented, and if similar measurements can be taken during and after the program is implemented, *and* if the direction or trend of preprogram measures is simple and clear, effects of the program can be detected by a change in the direction of the measures.

For instance, if motorcycle fatalities have occurred at a steady rate over the past 24 months (after statistical adjustment for seasonal variation in the number of motorcycles on roadways), and a motorcycle awareness program is instituted for drivers of cars, significant change in the motorcycle fatalities trend line could detect program outcomes. Implementation of the program should create a *discontinuity* in the pattern of fatalities over time (over seasons), that is, a change in trend line intercept, slope, or both. Because statistical regression often is involved in quantitatively characterizing or *modeling* trends over time, this is termed a *regression discontinuity* QED (see Chapter 29 of this volume). This QED does not provide a viable evaluation, however, if outcome measures are not available for a large number of discrete time periods before as well as following initiation of the program, or if the outcome measure itself changes after program implementation. Readers might wonder how a measure could itself change. This can happen when other biasing factors intervene—for example, if persons compiling motorcycle fatality data become aware of how their employment status may change if the motorcycle fatality reduction program does not have the desired outcomes. Similar QEDs also can be used to evaluate effects of policy changes on measures of health and health services. For example, using a discontinuity design, Stolzenberg and D'Alessio (2003) found little effect of repealing a motorcycle helmet law on motorcycle injuries or fatalities.

A rich variety of similar, ingenious research designs are detailed in chapters on QEDs in this handbook (see Chapter 28 of this volume) and on time-series designs (see Chapter 34 of this volume). Often these designs can be readily adapted to entire programs by changing the level of specificity at which activity and outcome variables are measured. Some QEDs compare measures hypothesized to change as a result of specific activities in the program, against other measures that are *not* supposed to change. For instance, if a reading comprehension program is implemented in a school, measures of reading comprehension should change but performance in mathematics should not. Essentially, one measure can serve as a reasonable *counterfactual* for the other. If both reading and math scores improved similarly, the evaluation would be inconclusive. Perhaps the reading comprehension program had more comprehensive effects than originally assumed. More likely, social pressure or teachers' increased expectations for student performance were responsible for some or all of the improvement, rather than the program.

Other versions of QEDs can work if the program focuses its activities first on one set of outcomes, then on another set, or on one site and then another, hypothesizing that an outcome measure of a particular type or taken at a particular site should change only when program activities are focused on that particular outcome or site. Using the *multiple baseline* version of this class of QEDs, Lombard et al. (1991) measured sunscreen use by children, adults, and lifeguards at two community pools. Lombard et al. then introduced at one pool a program of psychological interventions designed to increase sunscreen use, later trying the same interventions at a different pool. Sunscreen use increased following interventions at the first pool but not as much at the second pool. Unexpectedly, sunscreen use increased at the first pool more for some groupings of participants, particularly lifeguards.

Evaluation findings often modify logic models. In terms of the logic model guiding a program evaluation, findings from research designs and analyses can reduce the plausibility of some hypothesized connections between activities and outcomes, strengthen other hypothesized connections, and sometimes suggest new ones. The revised, empirically validated logic model then can provide guidance for future attempts to achieve similar outcomes in replications of the program. Activities that were not found to contribute to outcomes could be dropped.

Evaluations of activity–outcome relationships often examine how client gender, age, race, and ethnicity moderate achievement of program outcomes. These findings are reported along with the more global success or failure of the program. Although retrospective rather than predicted, apparently moderation of activity-outcome relationships can make logic models more accurate and complete. For example, parent–child interaction programs may be found to reduce problem behaviors, but only for clients who are cognitively capable of understanding key concepts of the intervention or who already have the self-management skills to engage in key activities in their lives.

Activity–Process–Outcome Evaluations

Few program operators, and fewer individuals providing or receiving services within a program, would assert that the program activities in which clients engage directly cause outcomes. Asking students to compete in generating as many words as possible in 60 seconds to fill in blanks in sentences would not itself build vocabulary. Asking a client to talk about his or her problems does not directly solve those problems. Even offering clean hypodermic needles in exchange for used ones does not directly reduce HIV transmission.

Instead, a variety of biological, psychological, and social (in a word, *biopsychosocial*) processes may mediate the relationship between program activities and outcomes. Isolation of these processes is a task for which psychologists and psychological theories are well-suited. For example, mild student embarrassment at being unable to generate more than a few words for blanks in seemingly simple sentences might motivate their interest in, search for, and retention of synonyms. Client attempts to put their problems into words for a therapist could increase client awareness of several causes for those problems, including distortions in how the client interprets minor failures at work or school. That enhanced awareness could then foster personal growth and more mature reactions to disappointments, especially when aided by therapy. Offering clean needles to users may result in reduced HIV rates via several causal pathways, including increased alertness to dangers of reusing others' needles as well as the opportunity to use clean ones without forfeiting cash. Similar activity–process–outcome relationships could be inserted in the program logic model and tested empirically, as suggested in Figure 32.1 above for education, health care, and military programs.

When the malleable biopsychosocial processes that likely determine outcomes have been identified by theoretical research, a program developer then is able to find activities that can affect the processes critical to achieving desired outcomes. Indeed, many program evaluators conceptualize theories as being worthwhile precisely because a good theory should identify correctly which program activities would change the biopsychosocial processes that will then result in targeted outcomes in clinical, business, health, and military settings.

By including measures of the principal processes hypothesized to determine program outcomes, along with measures of program activities and outcomes, program evaluation can collect data on the complete causal chain from program resources used to program outcomes attained. This more complete logic model may be able to identify causes of program failures as well as program successes. For example, Kissel (1997) showed that a program intended to prevent drug abuse in fourth graders by using activities designed to increase social responsibility and other processes actually *decreased* participants' social responsibility, especially for girls. Kissel found that the drug prevention program being evaluated actually *increased* willingness to use drugs as well as use of gateway drugs (see also Yates, 2002). Fortunately, perhaps, the children in prevention program and control conditions eventually were indistinguishable in terms of measured (somewhat increased) willingness to use drugs and actual use of gateway drugs.

Cost–Activity–Process–Outcome Evaluations

Costs are an important class of variables for those who decide whether to fund programs and for those needing funding. When conceptualized more comprehensively as *resources* rather than the money that can buy resources (Yates, 1994, 2020), costs become important to evaluate for most stakeholders. Money can be conceptualized as a way to assemble most resources that help program activities happen and allow program outcomes to be achieved. Some resources essential for programs, however, are not monetary and rarely are procured with money, including time of clients, time of interns and volunteers, some forms of transportation of clients to and from program sites, and tolerance for having homeless families or returning citizens in one's community.

Another reason to include costs in program evaluation is that funding decisions typically revolve around cost at least as much as outcomes. Even if desired outcomes occur, and are conclusively demonstrated to be the result of those specific biopsychosocial processes evoked by activities verified as being performed by program participants, a program may still be cancelled. Funders, providers, taxpayers, and persons needing services may prefer an alternative program if that alternative achieves similar or even somewhat poorer outcomes while consuming fewer resources, from participant time and transportation to provider time, computer access, and third-party funds. Even positive evaluations of programs have resulted in no program being implemented because the program exceeded constraints on available resources (e.g., "nice pilot study, but we just can't afford it") or because of who would need to be tolerated in the community (e.g., "we just don't want drug users coming into our neighborhood, even if they come to receive treatment, get better, and eventually go less to the community health clinic and hospital . . . while in treatment they'll attract drug dealers!").

Often going by the amorphous and ambiguous label "cost study," an increasing number of evaluations do include measures of program costs as well as outcomes. Some cost-inclusive evaluations even consider *resource capacity*, such as budget limits and constraints on other resources such as volunteered time and donated space available in a community (Yates, 2010; Yates et al., 1979).

Cost analysis. By themselves, cost studies can be just that: evaluations that measure and total the monetary value of resources consumed by a program. Accounting records can be analyzed to describe the amount of money spent to procure each major resource, such as dollars paid for staff salaries or for lease of program facilities. Total dollar amounts, however, describe the amounts and types of resources used in a program—its *ingredients*–about as well as the "TOTAL:" number on a grocery store receipt describes the amounts and types of foods

purchased in a shopping trip. For cost-inclusive program evaluation to be useful, accounting records need to be augmented by surveys of providers, clients, and community members to collect data on the amount of each major type of resource used. For replication and more comprehensive understanding of a program, these resources need to include not only volunteer time and unpaid overtime of program staff but also space donated or leased below market rates by community or government organizations; payroll and other services provided by organizations within which a program operates; plus equipment, materials, and services donated.

A variety of methods have been developed for measuring the amount and monetary value of these resources (cf. Yates, 1996), including structured interviews (e.g., French et al., 2002). Unfortunately, positioning a dollar, pound, euro, yen, or yuan symbol in front of a number does not improve its reliability or validity. As with any measure of any variable, reliability and validity need to, and can be, assessed for measures of resources used and their monetary values.

Because most programs find continued operation difficult without having clients participate on a reasonably regular basis, some cost-inclusive evaluations measure the amount of client time spent on activities required for program participation, such as getting to and from clinics, schools, and other sites of program operations. Transit costs can be substantial in some urban and rural environments. Neglecting to collect data on what might be called "required extra-program resources" such as client transportation time and expense could lead to erroneous evaluation findings, for example, that an outpatient program was less expensive than an inpatient program. The evaluator would ask, from the client perspective at least, ". . . less expensive *for whom?*"

Cost–benefit analysis. Often, a cost evaluation will include measures of outcomes as well as measures of resources consumed to produce those outcomes. In a *cost–benefit* analysis (CBA; sometimes termed *benefit–cost analysis* or BCA), outcomes that are monetary (e.g., increased client income following program participation) are compared with the value of resources used by the program, that is, program costs (Levin et al., 2018). Because outcomes and costs are measured in the same, usually monetary units for CBA, evaluators can calculate ratios of outcomes divided by costs, and *net* benefits, that is, benefits minus costs. Both are intuitively appealing: decisions about program funding seem easier to justify if one can consult an apparently valid number that purports to show that a program is "worth it" by having a ratio of benefits divided by costs exceeding one, or net benefits exceeding zero.

Nevertheless, these indices of cost–benefit and the funding decisions made with them are no better than the cost and benefit data on which they are based. Furthermore, focusing primarily on monetary outcomes also can bias funding decisions against programs in which the primary, important outcomes are neither monetary nor readily monetizable, such as enhanced satisfaction, well-being, or enlightenment. The *relative* worth of programs also may be relevant: if funds are limited, it may not be possible to fund all program that promise to eventually return benefits that exceed more immediate costs. Only programs returning the full investment within the budget cycle would receive funds.

Cost-effectiveness analysis. Cost-effectiveness analysis (CEA) compares *non*monetary outcomes of a program (its effectiveness) to the monetary value of resources consumed by the program (its costs). CEA may be preferred over CBA by providers and evaluators of human services because CEA seems less myopically focused on the pecuniary. Finding that a program cost "an average $52 per drink-free day per client per month during a 12-month follow-up" has value, especially if alternative programs cost significantly more to achieve the same outcome. Some decision makers are stymied, however, when comparing that index of drinking-avoidance cost-effectiveness to findings of CEAs involving different effectiveness measures, such as "a mean $4,225 versus $6,501 of personnel time, space, equipment, and materials were required to move clients from clinical to nonclinical levels on the Beck Depression Inventory-2 and keep them there through an 18-month follow-up."

Although these second cost-effectiveness findings could be quite meaningful when deciding between two treatments for depression, potential funders find it difficult to judge whether one program is better or worse than another when different outcomes are targeted and reported in CEAs. The limited application of CEA to comparisons of programs that have different outcomes (and to wait list and other control conditions for which similar outcomes can be measured) has increased the popularity of a third approach to including costs in program evaluation.

Cost-utility analysis. What if outcomes of diverse programs in education, health, mental health, business, and philanthropic programs could be translated into the same units? Then programs in these different areas could be compared in terms of their outcomes, costs, and cost-effectiveness. Although evaluators have searched for reliable and valid measures that could be applied to diverse programs, such as clients' willingness to pay for services, the face validity of such measures diminishes when one realizes that choices made by people in the marketplace of goods and services are not always rational (Kahneman, 2003) and dependent on their individual finances.

Years of life gained is a potentially universal outcome measure, but the *quality* of those years is important as well. By surveying persons who do and do not have different illnesses or disabilities, two outcome measures common to most programs have been developed: *quality-adjusted life years* (QALYs) and *disability-adjusted life years* (DALYs). Combining these more generic outcome measures with costs yields the indices cost per QALY and cost per DALY, for what is now recognized as *cost-utility analysis* (CUA). Promising the best of CEA and CBA, CUA offers a potential universal metric for decision makers who consider costs as well as outcomes (see Trenouth et al., 2018).

Cost–activity–outcome analysis. Including the specific activities of a program in its evaluation, along with its costs and outcomes, is done in more formative CEAs, CBAs, and CUAs that focus on understanding and improving, not just judging, programs. If a program is not generating desired outcomes at the costs required, using existing resources to support different activities might help that program improve. Definition and measurement of program activities typically is based on particular theories or models of the condition they are trying to address, but other definitions of activities also can facilitate evaluations.

For example, a program for consumers of mental health services might hypothesize that receiving support from other consumers of similar services could improve outcomes of traditional therapy, compared with traditional therapy alone. Different models of providing consumer-operated services to other consumers have, in fact, been compared in multisite program evaluations. Outcomes and costs were found to differ between sites using different models of how to provide consumer-to-consumer support. Rather than the particular model of support used, however, a cost-inclusive evaluation found that it was the manner in which the models were delivered (i.e., the *delivery system*) that seemed to determine program costs. More specifically, programs that could expand or decrease expenditures for staff time, space, and other resources in response to shifts in demand were the least costly and, coincidentally, at least as effective as the other programs (cf. Yates, 2010).

Cost–activity–process–outcome analysis. Comprehensively understanding a program requires awareness of the psychological as well as the economic and other causal mechanisms at work in the program. Linkages between prescribed program activities and hoped-for program outcomes are, as noted earlier, likely mediated by specific biopsychosocial *processes*. Including these processes in a comprehensive program evaluation can improve understanding of why some programs do not consistently generate desired outcomes. Considering costs can assist in this formative evaluation.

For example, in the substance abuse prevention program evaluation already detailed, the iatrogenic program activity identified in the evaluation was

offering small student groups (Kissel, 1997). These groups were implemented despite the possibility that increasing social interaction between students at risk for substance abuse might not result in the desired outcomes. Why were these groups included among program activities? There probably was hope that group processes would help students, but the low cost of student groups could have been another driver for their inclusion. Among activities formally recognized in the program plan, small student groups were found to be the least costly in staff time, space, and other resources. For programs that include activities with varying impacts on processes that are linked to goal outcomes, and that consume different amounts of resources such as staff and client time and space, linear programming and other forms of *operations research* can incorporate findings from evaluations of costs, activities, processes, and outcomes to decide systematically which activities to use and how much in a program (Yates, 1980, 1996).

CRITICAL ISSUES IN PROGRAM EVALUATION

Evaluations, which can determine whether a program is initiated, funded, continued, grown, or terminated, understandably receive special attention from those who operate a program, those served by it, those who fund it, and those neighbors affected by it. In such a potentially volatile context, program evaluators may experience not only resistance to starting the evaluation but even subterfuge during the evaluation and threats of litigation afterwards. Involving multiple stakeholders from the beginning of an evaluation is one way to defuse resistance and avoid other problems.

Effects of Interest Group Perspectives on Program Evaluation

Researchers accustomed to being the only stakeholder empowered to make major decisions may be surprised when they enter the world of program evaluation. Leaders of program evaluations may come from the psychological or related research communities, but they soon realize they have become part of a larger effort.

Stakeholder involvement is key.   Following the guidance "Nothing about me without me," program evaluation is remarkably participatory. Input is solicited from persons, communities, government agencies, corporations, and military units involved in or affected by program evaluations. These stakeholders can influence everything from the qualitative versus quantitative emphasis of the evaluation to the logic model, the evaluation design chosen, measures of cost, activity, process, and outcome selected, the analyses conducted, and even the findings reported and omitted.

Cultures and measures.   Training in cultural competency, keen interpersonal skills, and being able to negotiate with sensitivity and respect for diverse stakeholders, are all necessary in program evaluation (see Orlandi et al., 1992). Diverse viewpoints on what program outcomes are or should be, and what costs should be included or ignored, may be satisfied by including measures favored by each stakeholder group and excluding measures disliked by all. This works well if the evaluation budget allows it. More challenges emerge, however, if some interest groups wish certain measures to *not* be used, even if those are precisely the measures that other interest groups advocate or require for funding. Consensus on inclusion and exclusion of measures may break down when it becomes apparent that different stakeholders' goals for costs or outcomes are in opposition. For example, in evaluating monetary outcomes of adding consumer-operated services to traditional psychological services, consumer advocates hoped that the use of health services by consumers would *increase,* permanently, as they accepted needed entitlements, whereas some researchers hoped that the use of health services would *decrease* due to decreased need, thus demonstrating funder-desired cost-savings (see Yates, 2010).

Some stakeholders also may recommend that certain evaluation designs be used and others be avoided. Some evaluators posit that classic experimental designs favor theories and approaches to social change that evolved in concert with

those designs. For example, Guba and Lincoln (1989) asserted that the rigors and measures associated with randomized clinical trials favor traditional interventions developed by established researchers (see also Seigart & Brisolara, 2002). Case studies and qualitative as opposed to quantitative analyses, it has been argued, may be more likely to lend support to certain alternative programs (cf. Guba & Lincoln, 1989).

Moreover, some client groups, including African Americans and Native Americans, have terrible, traumatic histories of abuse by researchers (see Kazdin, 2003). This has led to strong resistance to any evaluation that resembles research, as evaluation certainly can. These and other client interest groups often request special assurances and internal controls in any evaluation. Differences of culture also can determine which biopsychosocial processes are posited to cause outcomes, as well as what activities are acknowledged to be part of the program. In some evaluations, stakeholders decide that the effort and risks of participating are not worth the questionable, often uncontrollable results. Cultural differences can be so large that outcomes may be defined less by empirical evidence collected by the evaluator than by information sifted by clients through belief- and trust-based *indigenous frameworks* developed by client communities (see LaFrance, 2004).

Stakeholders, costs, and monetary outcome measures.   For certain stakeholders, inclusion of program costs and monetary outcomes in evaluation is anathema. Some researchers, providers, and client advocates do not want to include cost measures of any sort in evaluations, fearing that if program costs are found to be high, effective programs will not be funded. It may be asserted that the effectiveness of a program should be demonstrated first, and that less costly means of offering program activities can be found after and if a program is found effective. Excluding costs, however, could open up the evaluation to charges of irrelevance, as funding decisions for entitlement programs may weigh costs more heavily than effectiveness. Including monetary outcome measures also can generate considerable resistance, even though benefits such as employment and resulting income can be strong arguments in favor of funding. In these and similar situations, evaluators need to communicate clearly with interest groups to keep them informed about likely ramifications of excluding some measures and avoiding some designs.

Metaevaluation

Does evaluation itself work? Is *evaluation* worthwhile? These questions, identified as *metaevaluation* by Scriven (1969; see also Cooksy & Caracelli, 2005; Stufflebeam, 2001), are so rarely asked by evaluators as to suggest minor hypocrisy. Like most professionals, evaluators need to have sufficient faith in their methods to pursue them despite challenges, some of which were introduced in this chapter. Evaluating evaluation is, though, something that happens naturally and frequently. Some stakeholder somewhere is almost always asking, "Is this evaluation worth it?" Sometimes that question occurs to program evaluators as well.

Rigorous studies of the outcomes and costs of evaluation are rare. Random assignment of programs to evaluation or nonevaluation conditions seem minimal. Formal analyses of the cost-effectiveness, cost-benefit, and cost-utility of evaluation itself are unknown. Arguments can be made that without evaluation, programs, treatments, and prevention efforts might be funded with either no perceivable outcomes or even iatrogenic outcomes for clients or communities. Certainly, such results have been found for well-meant efforts in treatment and prevention. If evaluation had been conducted earlier, or even built into the programs from the beginning, perhaps damage to clients could have been avoided and funds used for better purposes. That, however, cannot be said with certainty. This is just one of many areas for future work in program evaluation.

References

Aos, S., Lieb, R., Mayfield, J., Miller, M., & Pennucci, A. (2004). *Benefits and costs of prevention and early intervention programs for youth* (Report to the Washington State Legislature). Washington State Institute for Public Policy. https://www.wsipp.wa.gov

Bolinson, C., & Mertens, D. (2020). Transformative evaluation and impact investing: A fruitful marriage. In E. D. M. Sarmiento & R. P. Herman (Eds.), *Global handbook of impact investing: Solving global problems via smarter capital markets toward a more sustainable society* (pp. 697–734). Wiley.

Christie, C. A., & Fleischer, D. N. (2010). Insight into evaluation practice: A content analysis of designs and methods used in evaluations studies published in North American evaluation-focused journals. *The American Journal of Evaluation, 31*(3), 326–346. https://doi.org/10.1177/1098214010369170

Cooksy, L. J., & Caracelli, V. J. (2005). Quality, context, and use: Issues in achieving the goals of metaevaluation. *The American Journal of Evaluation, 26*(1), 31–42. https://doi.org/10.1177/1098214004273252

Cronbach, L. J., Ambron, S. R., Dornbush, S. M., Hess, R. D., Hornik, R. C., Phillips, D. C., & Weiner, S. S. (1980). *Toward reform of program evaluation.* Jossey-Bass.

French, M. T., Salomé, H. J., & Carney, M. (2002). Using the DATCAP and ASI to estimate the costs and benefits of residential addiction treatment in the State of Washington. *Social Science & Medicine, 55*(12), 2267–2282. https://doi.org/10.1016/S0277-9536(02)00060-6

Guba, E. G., & Lincoln, Y. S. (1989). *Fourth generation evaluation.* SAGE.

Guttentag, M., & Struening, E. L. (1975). *Handbook of evaluation research* (Vol. 1–2). SAGE.

Howard, K. I., Kopta, S. M., Krause, M. S., & Orlinsky, D. E. (1986). The dose–effect relationship in psychotherapy. *American Psychologist, 41*(2), 159–164. https://doi.org/10.1037/0003-066X.41.2.159

Kahneman, D. (2003). Maps of bounded rationality: Psychology for behavioral economics. *The American Economic Review, 93*(5), 1449–1475. https://doi.org/10.1257/000282803322655392

Kazdin, A. E. (2003). *Research design in clinical psychology* (4th ed.). Allyn & Bacon.

Kissel, A. V. (1997). *What costs, procedures, and processes are critical to preventing youth substance abuse?* (Master's thesis 8059, American University). University Microfilms, Inc. (Order No. 13-88995)

LaFrance, J. (2004). Culturally competent evaluation in Indian Country. *New Directions for Evaluation, 102*(102), 39–50. https://doi.org/10.1002/ev.114

Leventhal, H., Safer, M. A., Cleary, P. D., & Gutmann, M. (1980). Cardiovascular risk modification by community-based programs for life-style change:

Comments on the Stanford study. *Journal of Consulting and Clinical Psychology*, 48(2), 150–158. https://doi.org/10.1037/0022-006X.48.2.150

Levin, H. M., McEwan, P. J., Belfield, C., Bowden, A. B., & Shane, R. (2018). *Economic evaluation in education: Cost-effectiveness and benefit-cost analysis* (3rd ed.). SAGE. https://doi.org/10.4135/9781483396514

Lombard, D., Neubauer, T. E., Canfield, D., & Winett, R. A. (1991). Behavioral community intervention to reduce the risk of skin cancer. *Journal of Applied Behavior Analysis*, 24(4), 677–686. https://doi.org/10.1901/jaba.1991.24-677

MEASURE Evaluation. (2015). *Evaluation FAQ: What sample size do I need for an impact evaluation?* Carolina Population Center, University of North Carolina at Chapel Hill. https://www.measureevaluation.org/resources/publications/fs-15-157/at_download/document

Mertens, D. M. (2018). *Mixed methods design in evaluation*. SAGE. https://doi.org/10.4135/9781506330631

Meyer, A. J., Maccoby, N., & Farquhar, J. W. (1980). Reply to Kasl and Levanthal et al. *Journal of Consulting and Clinical Psychology*, 48(2), 159–163. https://doi.org/10.1037/0022-006X.48.2.159

Morell, J. A. (Ed.). (2010). *Evaluation in the face of uncertainty*. Guilford Press.

Orlandi, M. A., Weston, R., & Epstein, L. G. (1992). *Cultural competence for evaluators*. Office for Substance Abuse Prevention.

Patton, M. Q. (2019). *Blue marble evaluation*. Guilford Press.

Picciotto, R. (2015). *The 5th wave: Social impact evaluation*. Rockefeller Foundation, Evaluation Office. https://www.rockefellerfoundation.org/wp-content/uploads/The-5th-Wave-Social-Impact-Evaluation.pdf

Posavac, E. J., & Carey, R. G. (2003). *Program evaluation: Methods and case studies* (6th ed.). Prentice Hall.

Reisman, J., Olazabal, V., & Hoffman, S. (2018). Putting the "impact" in impact investing: The rising demand for data and evidence of social outcomes. *The American Journal of Evaluation*, 39(3), 389–395. https://doi.org/10.1177/1098214018779141

Sarmiento, E. D. M., & Herman, R. P. (Eds.). (2020). *Global handbook of impact investing: Solving global problems via smarter capital markets toward a more sustainable society*. Wiley.

Schneeweiss, S., Patrick, A. R., Solomon, D. H., Mehta, J., Dormuth, C., Miller, M., Lee, J. C., & Wang, P. S. (2010). Variation in the risk of suicide attempts and completed suicides by antidepressant agent in adults: A propensity score-adjusted analysis of 9 years' data. *Archives of General Psychiatry*, 67(5), 497–506. https://doi.org/10.1001/archgenpsychiatry.2010.39

Scriven, M. (1969). An introduction to meta-evaluation. *Educational Products Report*, 2(5), 36–38.

Scriven, M. (1991). *Evaluation thesaurus*. SAGE.

Seigart, D., & Brisolara, S. (2002). Feminist evaluation. *New Directions for Evaluation*, 2002(96), 1–2. https://doi.org/10.1002/ev.61

Shadish, W. R., Cook, T. D., & Campbell, D. T. (2002). *Experimental and quasi-experimental designs for generalized causal inference*. Houghton Mifflin.

Silverman, D. (Ed.). (2004). *Qualitative research: Theory, method and practice* (2nd ed.). SAGE.

Stolzenberg, L., & D'Alessio, S. J. (2003). "Born to be wild": The effect of the repeal of Florida's mandatory motorcycle helmet-use law on serious injury and fatality rates. *Evaluation Review*, 27(2), 131–150. https://doi.org/10.1177/0193841X02250524

Stufflebeam, D. L. (2001). The metaevaluation imperative. *The American Journal of Evaluation*, 22(2), 183–209. https://doi.org/10.1177/109821400102200204

Trenouth, L., Colbourn, T., Fenn, B., Pietzsch, S., Myatt, M., & Puett, C. (2018). The cost of preventing undernutrition: Cost, cost-efficiency and cost-effectiveness of three cash-based interventions on nutrition outcomes in Dadu, Pakistan. *Health Policy and Planning*, 33(6), 743–754. https://doi.org/10.1093/heapol/czy045

Yates, B. T. (1980). *Improving effectiveness and reducing costs in mental health*. Charles C Thomas.

Yates, B. T. (1994). Toward the incorporation of costs, cost-effectiveness analysis, and cost-benefit analysis into clinical research. *Journal of Consulting and Clinical Psychology*, 62(4), 729–736. https://doi.org/10.1037/0022-006X.62.4.729

Yates, B. T. (1996). *Analyzing costs, procedures, processes, and outcomes in human services*. SAGE. https://doi.org/10.4135/9781412983358

Yates, B. T. (2002). Roles for psychological procedures, and psychological processes, in cost-offset research: Cost → procedure → process → outcome analysis. In N. A. Cummings, W. T. O'Donohue, & K. E. Ferguson (Eds.), *The impact of medical cost offset on practice and research: Making it work for you* (pp. 91–123). Context Press.

Yates, B. T. (2010). Evaluating costs and benefits of consumer-operated services: Unexpected resistance, unanticipated insights, and deja vu all over again. In J. A. Morell (Ed.), *Evaluation in the face of uncertainty* (pp. 224–230). Guilford Press.

Yates, B. T. (2020). Research on improving outcomes and reducing costs of psychological interventions:

Toward delivering the best to the most for the least. *Annual Review of Clinical Psychology, 16,* 125–150. https://doi.org/10.1146/annurev-clinpsy-071519-110415

Yates, B. T., Haven, W. G., & Thoresen, C. E. (1979). Cost-effectiveness analysis at Learning House: How much change for how much money? In J. S. Stumphauzer (Ed.), *Progress in behavior therapy with delinquents* (pp. 186–222). Charles C Thomas.

Yates, B. T., & Marra, M. (2017). Social Return On Investment (SROI): Problems, solutions . . . and is SROI a good investment? *Evaluation and Program Planning, 64,* 136–144. https://doi.org/10.1016/j.evalprogplan.2016.11.009

Yates, B. T., & Taub, J. (2003). Assessing the costs, benefits, cost-effectiveness, and cost-benefit of psychological assessment: We should, we can, and here's how. *Psychological Assessment, 15*(4), 478–495. https://doi.org/10.1037/1040-3590.15.4.478

PART VI

QUANTITATIVE RESEARCH DESIGNS INVOLVING SINGLE PARTICIPANTS OR UNITS

CHAPTER 33

SINGLE-CASE EXPERIMENTAL DESIGN

John M. Ferron, Megan Kirby, and Lodi Lipien

Single-case experimental designs (SCEDs) are experimental designs used to study the effects of interventions on individual cases. This focus on individual effects is a defining feature of SCEDs and can be motivated by conceptual as well as practical considerations. Conceptually, the belief in the uniqueness of individuals and the potential for variability in the response to an intervention motivates a desire to study intervention effects one participant at a time (Morgan & Morgan, 2009). As studies accrue, the individual effect estimates can be used to build a distribution from which we can see consistencies or inconsistencies in the effect across cases, best- or worst-case scenarios, and typical or average effects. Practical reasons that may motivate the use of SCEDs include (a) studying the effect of an intervention for those from a sparse population or with a rare diagnosis, making it difficult to recruit more than few participants for a study (Odom et al., 2005); (b) developing an intervention where it may be efficient to pilot and refine the intervention through a series of single-case studies (Gallo et al., 2013); and (c) adding to the research base on the effects of interventions in practice through the engagement of clinicians (Morgan & Morgan, 2009).

Single-case experimental design has been referred to by a variety of names, including *single-subject design, single-case design*, and *N-of-1 trials*. These designs assume a variety of forms, including, but not limited to, reversal, alternating treatments, changing criterion, repeated acquisition, multiple-baseline, and multiple-probe designs. One may ask why we need so many design options to study individual effects or why traditional pre–post intervention measurement at the individual level is not sufficient. Although looking at the pre-to-post change for an individual may be common in some areas of clinical practice, it can be difficult to argue that the change was due to the intervention. It is possible that the behavior, or outcome of interest, fluctuates over time for the individual, and the change that is observed is simply part of this routine fluctuation. It is also possible that there was indeed a systematic change, but that the change resulted from something other than the intervention (e.g., a change in the home, school, or work environment that happened to coincide with the start of the intervention). Sensitive to the detection of change at the case level across time, SCEDs have been developed to help us separate intervention effects from other confounds. However, because of the variation within individuals and outcomes of interest, there is no single best way to do this. Rather, design variations have emerged as research has evolved.

https://doi.org/10.1037/0000319-033
APA Handbook of Research Methods in Psychology, Second Edition: Vol. 2. Research Designs: Quantitative, Qualitative, Neuropsychological, and Biological, H. Cooper (Editor-in-Chief)

In this chapter, we first consider the experimental tactics developed to strengthen the internal validity of studies focusing on individual effects. These tactics help us attribute observed changes to the intervention and include the use of baseline logic, response-guided experimentation, replication, and randomization. Next, we show how various experimental tactics can be combined to produce a variety of SCEDs in which appropriate selection of a design is dependent upon the study purpose, participant characteristics, and the outcome of interest. We next consider additional procedures used within SCEDs to document reliability of the outcome measurement, treatment fidelity, generalization, and social validity, and close with a summary of analysis options appropriate for SCEDs.

EXPERIMENTAL TACTICS

Experimental tactics are procedures used to strengthen the internal validity of SCEDs. These procedures include baseline logic, response-guided experimentation, within-case replication, between-case replication, and randomization.

Baseline Logic

Many SCEDs involve phases in which multiple observations, typically five or more, are collected under the same treatment condition. For example, the study may begin with a baseline phase in which five to 10 observations are collected in a business-as-usual condition prior to the introduction of the intervention. The baseline, if stable, establishes a problem level of behavior (i.e., the need for intervention) and allows researchers to assess treatment effects by comparing what is observed in the intervention phase with what would be expected if the baseline were projected (Engel & Schutt, 2013; Sidman, 1960). To make projections about what would have been observed in the absence of intervention, the researcher must make an assumption about some kind of temporal stability. The strictest stability assumption is that the outcome is temporally stable, implying that there is no variation in the outcome from one session to the next (e.g., all baseline observation

values are zero). In such cases, the projections are relatively straightforward because the researcher can assume that in the absence of intervention, future observations of the outcome would have values identical to the constant baseline value.

More commonly, stability assumptions are less strict, and the projections are less exact. Researchers may expect some variability in the outcome from one observation to the next due to various factors that are outside of the control of the researcher, but they may also assume that there are no systematic trends (i.e., the expected level of the behavior does not change over time). In such situations, the baseline projections assume that in the absence of intervention, the mean and variation of future observations would be similar to baseline observations. Consider, for example, a researcher who is studying the effect of an intervention on the number of minutes a child with attention deficit disorder spends reading. Initial baseline and intervention phases are shown in Figure 33.1. The baseline observations show no trend, with observations ranging from two to nine minutes of reading during 30-minute daily reading sessions. Given this baseline, it seems reasonable to project that without intervention, the child would continue to read less than 10 minutes per session. Because the intervention observations are not in line with the baseline projection, they support the contention that something has changed the reading behavior of the child.

If there is not only variability in the baseline observations, but also noticeable trends, baseline projections become more challenging. Here the researcher may assume that the trend is temporally stable (i.e., the same trend would continue in the absence of intervention). If this assumption is reasonable, the researcher would use an extension of the baseline trend line to make a projection of what would happen in the absence of intervention. Manolov and colleagues (2019) provided an excellent discussion of the challenges in projecting trends and provide some relatively flexible options for making projections. If it is unreasonable to assume a continued trend, any projection becomes so suspect that baseline logic fails.

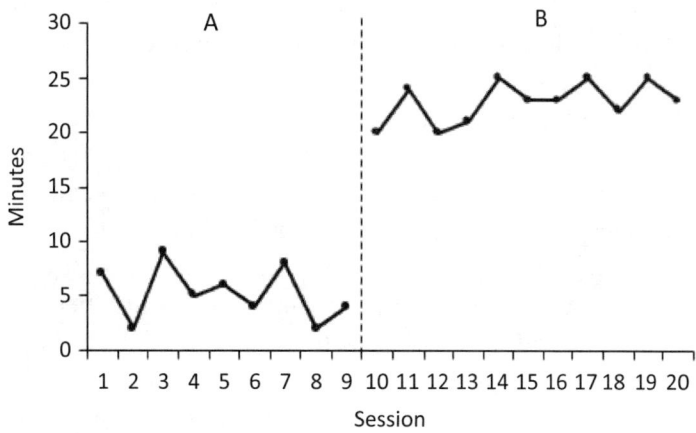

FIGURE 33.1.   Illustration of an AB design.

Response-Guided Experimentation

When researchers adopt the tactic of baseline logic, they commit to establishing stable baselines. However, the number of baseline observations that will be needed may not be known prior to starting the study. Consider the baseline observations graphed in Figure 33.2 representing the on-task behavior of a child with an emotional behavioral disorder. The instability in the baseline, and particularly the high value for the fifth observation, leads to uncertainty about what would be observed if we continued in baseline, as shown by the three alternative projections in Figure 33.2. Projection A assumes that the uniqueness of the last observation is attributable to some unobserved event specific to the day of the fifth observation, and thus future baseline observations would return to the level of the first four observations. Projection B assumes that some

unobserved factor has led to a more permanent shift in the level of the behavior and that the fifth observation is reflective of this new level of behavior. Finally, Projection C assumes that some unobserved factor is leading to a shift in the behavior, but that this transition to a new level is still in process, and thus future baseline observations would be higher than those collected to this point. When there are such a wide range of possible projections, it is not feasible to use baseline logic.

To ensure baselines are stable at the time of transition to an intervention phase, researchers may choose response-guided experimentation, where the length of the baseline is not established a priori, but rather is dependent on an ongoing visual analysis of the data as they are collected. If this ongoing visual analysis reveals variation that can be accounted for (e.g., it is related to the target child's seatmate during the observation period), the researcher can alter the baseline condition to hold this factor constant and obtain a more stable baseline. If researchers are unable to identify and hold constant the source of the variability, they can extend the baseline phase until the instability has passed and stability has been established. For example, the researcher may extend the five-observation baseline in Figure 33.2 to see if the baseline level would be reestablished at the level of the first four observations (Projection A) or at a higher level (Projection B or C).

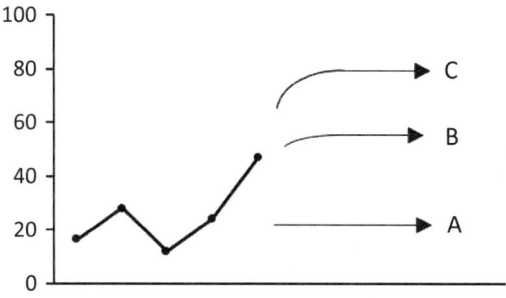

FIGURE 33.2.   Unstable baseline with three possible projections (A, B, and C).

Often the tactic of response-guided experimentation is coupled with the tactic of baseline logic, but in some situations baseline logic can be used without response-guided experimentation. Specifically, in contexts where the participant and outcome of focus produce little to no baseline variability, there is no need to respond to the data. Consider a study of a phonological awareness intervention, where the participant inclusion criteria included a lack of first-sound identification skills, and thus the researcher anticipates that the participant will score zero on each of the baseline measures of first-sound identification. The researcher may fix the baseline length to three or four observations based on practical considerations, or they may randomly select whether it will be three or four observations. Either way, the baseline length could be established a priori, as opposed to in a response-guided fashion, and baseline logic could be used because the baseline would be stable.

Replication

Baseline logic and response-guided experimentation are useful approaches in the design of SCEDs, but they are not sufficient for making causal inferences. When the observations in a treatment phase differ from the baseline projection, multiple explanations for the change are possible. It may have been due to the intervention, but it could also have been due to something other than the intervention, which just happened to occur at the same time. Consider the results shown in Figure 33.1. We see a shift in the number of minutes the child reads, but it is difficult to know if the intervention caused the change in behavior. The child could have increased their reading because of some nonintervention change in the teacher behavior, some change among their peers, or for a variety of other reasons. Replication is a tactic used to make it more difficult to attribute changes to factors other than the intervention.

One way to replicate is to do so within the case. If the effect of the intervention is believed to be limited to when the intervention is active (e.g., while a support dog is present or when the child is taking their prescribed medication), the intervention could be removed with the expectation that the behavior would return to baseline levels, and then the intervention could be reintroduced. Consider again a researcher studying the effect of an intervention on the amount of time a child spends reading. Suppose that the study had started as shown in Figure 33.1, and then the researcher added a second baseline phase followed by a second treatment phase, as shown in Figure 33.3. Because of the replication of the effect within the case, it would be difficult to attribute the change in behavior to some other factor. Put simply, it does not seem plausible that the other factor would happen to occur, be removed, and then occur again, in a way that

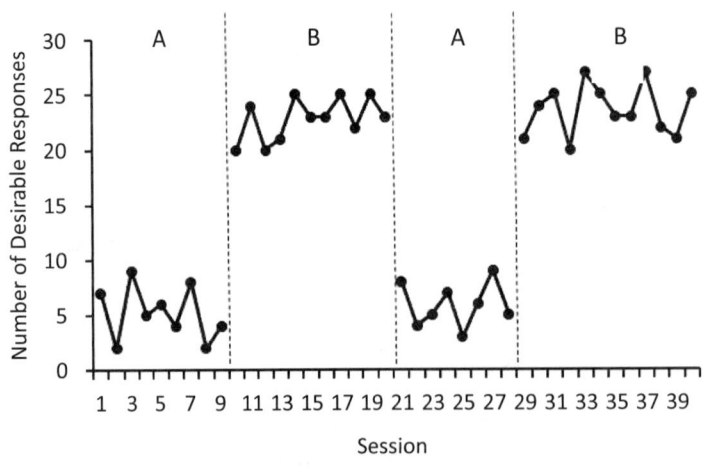

FIGURE 33.3.   Illustration of within-case replication.

coincided with the changes between baseline and intervention phases.

In some cases, a behavior is not reversible, such as when the intervention targets the learning of a particular skill, and thus removal of the intervention is not expected to lead to a return to baseline levels. In such studies, within-case replication is not possible. However, replication could be accomplished by attempting to duplicate the effect across different individuals, behaviors, or settings. When replicating across cases (i.e., participants, behaviors, or settings) the start of the intervention is typically introduced at different times, as illustrated in Figure 33.4. When changes in behavior are staggered over time and coincide

with the introduction of the intervention there is stronger evidence of a causal relation. However, if changes in behavior occur simultaneously for all cases, the changes are more likely due to some nonintervention effect than the intervention itself. Thus, with replication at different times, researchers are able to disentangle intervention effects from history effects (i.e., external events that impact the outcome, such as a change in school personnel or policies).

Randomization

Another experimental tactic that may be used with SCEDs is randomization. Consider a comparative study of the effect of two treatments on a reversible behavior. The researchers may design the study so there is rapid alternation between the treatments. In this case, the phase structure (e.g., five or more successive observations in the same intervention condition) that was shown in our previous examples is not present, and thus the tactic of baseline logic is unavailable. However, the researchers still need to argue that the difference between the observations is due to the difference in treatments and not some other factor. In this context, SCED researchers will often conceptualize their design as having successive pairs of observations, and then randomly assign one observation from each pair to each condition (i.e., one of the first two observations to Treatment A and the other to Treatment B, one of the second two observations to Treatment A and the other to Treatment B, and so forth). If the researcher finds that the behavior is consistently better under Treatment A than Treatment B, it is difficult to attribute this difference to some other factor. This type of randomization facilitates analyses (e.g., randomization tests; Edgington & Onghena, 2007) that control the probability of incorrectly inferring that one treatment was more effective than the other (i.e., control over Type I errors), as well as facilitating unbiased estimates of the treatment effect. A review of SCEDs suggests that randomization is commonly used in designs that rapidly alternate between conditions (Tanious & Onghena, 2020).

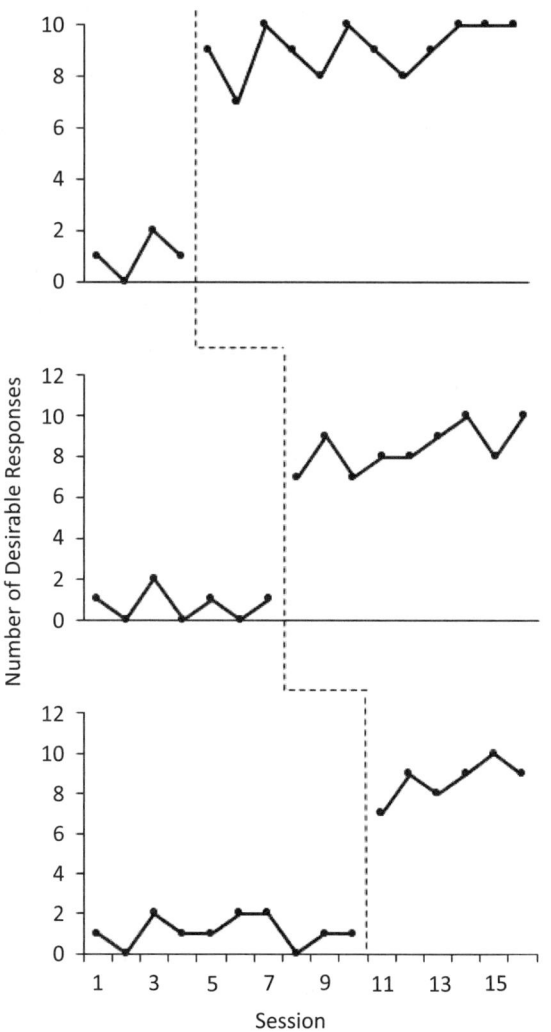

FIGURE 33.4. Illustration of across-case replication.

Although somewhat less common, randomization is also used in designs with a phase structure (Tanious & Onghena, 2020). Here researchers use one of several methods to randomly determine when the transitions between phases will occur. For example, consider Figure 33.3 where one could randomly determine when to transition from A_1 to B_1, B_1 to A_2, and A_2 to B_2 (e.g., Onghena, 1992), or consider Figure 33.4 where one could determine randomly when to transition from baseline to treatment for each case (e.g., Koehler & Levin, 1998). Just as with randomization procedures for designs that rapidly alternate between treatments, randomization in designs with phases facilitates analyses that control Type I errors. However, randomly selecting transition times does not remove the relationship between time and treatment assignment (e.g., baseline observations still precede treatment observations) and thus treatment effect estimates may be biased by time-related unobserved factors (Ferron et al., 2014). Consequently, the randomization used in SCEDs with phases is more limited in value than the randomization used in designs with rapid alternation between conditions. In addition, selecting start points a priori conflicts with response-guided experimentation (e.g., Kazdin, 1980), and, thus, researchers using phase-based designs may choose either a priori randomization or response-guided experimentation. In contexts where baselines are assumed to have little to no variability, there is minimal need for response-guided experimentation, and random selection of transition points can be easily accommodated. In addition, for researchers who have practical constraints preventing them from extending phases or who prefer a design that is not responsive to the data, the option of randomizing transition points is appealing. Finally, for researchers who would like to respond to their data to ensure stable baselines as well as randomize, there are approaches to do so, where the random assignments are made during rather than before the experiment (Ferron & Jones, 2006; Moeyaert et al., 2021).

TYPES OF SCEDs

By using different combinations of the experimental tactics of baseline logic, response-guided experimentation, within-case replication, between-case replication, and randomization, a variety of SCEDs emerge. We discuss some of the options here, indicating which experimental tactics may be used, along with the contexts for which these designs are best aligned.

Withdrawal and Reversal Designs

The withdrawal (or reversal) design can be used to study individual intervention effects on reversible outcomes (i.e., outcomes that would return to the baseline level if the intervention were removed). They consist of a baseline phase (A), followed by an intervention phase (B), followed by a second baseline phase where the intervention is withdrawn and the behavior is expected to revert to baseline levels (Baer et al., 1968; Sidman, 1960). The second baseline phase is typically followed by a second intervention phase, creating an ABAB design, as shown in Figure 33.3. Visual inspection of Figure 33.3 shows the number of desirable behaviors during the intervention phases is higher than could be reasonably projected from the baseline phases, and this effect is replicated within the case, providing evidence of a treatment effect. With an ABAB design, there are three opportunities to observe effects (i.e., at each of the three transitions between phases), which is generally considered to be the minimum acceptable number of replications. For those who prefer more replications, the ABAB design can be extended by adding phases within the case, such as in an ABABAB design, or by replicating the ABAB design across cases. As can be seen in this illustration, the internal validity of withdrawal designs relies heavily on baseline logic and within-case replication. In addition, withdrawal designs may include response-guided experimentation (Kazdin, 1980), randomly selected times to transition between phases (Onghena, 1992), or both (Ferron & Levin, 2014).

Multiple Baseline Designs

The multiple-baseline design is commonly used to investigate the effect of an intervention on a target behavior, particularly when it is not feasible or appropriate to use a reversal design, such as when the target behavior is not reversible. This design includes a minimum of three cases (i.e., behaviors, settings, or individuals) with baselines of varying lengths so that the intervention is introduced at different times for each case. More specifically, the baseline phase for the first case should be stable prior to introducing the intervention, and the baseline phase for the second case should continue until the intervention phase for the first case is stable. This staggered approach allows the researcher to determine if changes in behavior coincide with the intervention for each participant. As shown in Figure 33.4, the data are presented in stacked graphs, one for each case. An advantage of the multiple-baseline design is that its staggered intervention across cases allows for more experimental control than replicated AB designs, making it easier to conclude that the intervention was responsible for the change in behavior (Horner & Odom, 2014). The internal validity of multiple-baseline designs relies on baseline logic and temporally staggered replication in which ongoing visual analysis is used to confirm stability within the phases. In addition, researchers may utilize response-guided experimentation (Baer et al., 1968), random selection of intervention starts (Koehler & Levin, 1998), or both response-guided experimentation and randomization (Ferron & Jones, 2006).

Multiple-Probe Designs

The multiple-probe design is a variation of the multiple-baseline design, which requires fewer observations. It is often preferred when (a) long baseline phases present an ethical problem, (b) the target behavior is unlikely to change in the absence of the intervention, or (c) the target behavior is readily influenced by repeated testing (Horner & Baer, 1978; Morgan & Morgan, 2009). In this design, probes are used to determine the

natural rate of the behavior at infrequent but scheduled time points during baseline rather than continuous measurement (Murphy & Bryan, 1980). The use of probes reduces the need for resources by minimizing unnecessary data collection, but researchers must ensure that no changes in the behavior have occurred before introducing the intervention. A multiple-probe design is illustrated in Figure 33.5. The reduction in the number of baseline observations is observed for the second and third participant. In particular, the third participant has five baseline observations but would have had 10 in a traditional multiple-baseline design.

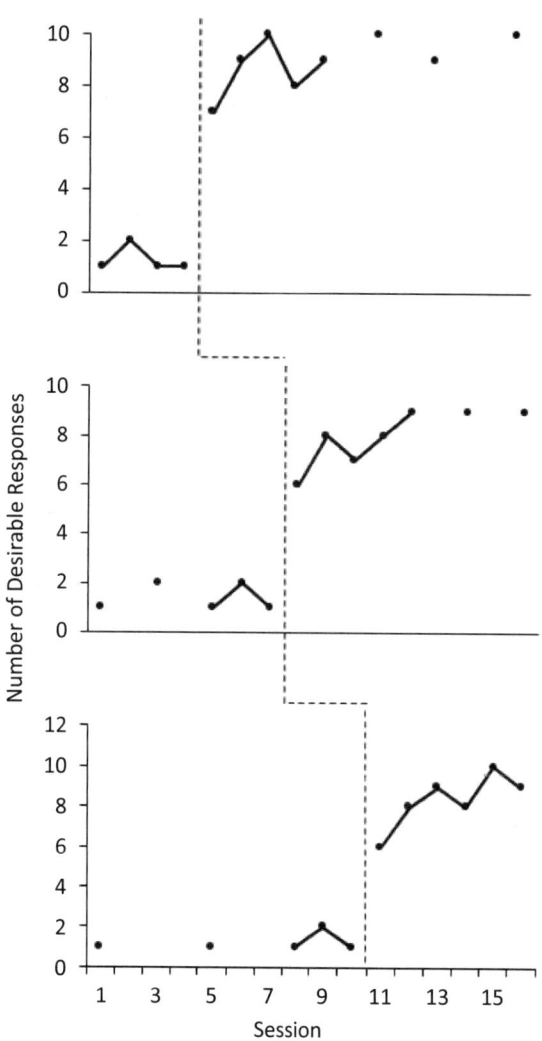

FIGURE 33.5. Illustration of a multiple-probe design.

Changing Criteria Designs

The changing criterion design (CCD) allows researchers to implement an intervention that shapes a given behavior in a gradual, stepwise fashion with the goal of achieving a predetermined outcome. This design is especially useful when the rate, duration, or accuracy of a behavior is best changed through small steps (e.g., shaping by approximation), such as with reducing smoking or increasing physical exercise. As shown in Figure 33.6, the design includes an initial baseline phase followed by multiple treatment phases of varied lengths that are introduced over time. Each treatment phase has its own preset criterion to be met, and once stability is achieved, a more stringent criterion for the next phase is established. Researchers have recommended at least three to four changes in the criterion level over the course of the study (Gast & Ledford, 2014; Klein et al., 2017). This process continues until the overall outcome or goal is attained. This design has several advantages: (a) at a minimum, it requires only one participant, behavior, and setting; (b) treatment does not have to be withdrawn; (c) after a brief baseline phase, treatment is introduced across cases concurrently (i.e., baselines are not staggered); and (d) treatment efficacy is evident when performance closely matches the criterion (Byiers et al., 2012; Poling & Grossett, 1986). The internal validity of CCDs can be enhanced by changing the distance between criterion levels, varying the lengths of phases, and including randomization procedures (Ferron et al., 2019; Onghena et al., 2019).

Alternating Treatments Designs

The alternating treatments design (ATD) allows researchers to compare within-case effects of two or more distinctly different treatments with repeated measurement of reversible behavior(s) across sessions (Barlow & Hayes, 1979). The rapid and relatively short duration of an ATD can control threats to internal validity such as changes within the participant that are not due to the intervention but that impact the outcome over time (i.e., maturation) and changes in the way the outcome is measured at different times (i.e., instrumentation; Wolery et al., 2018). However, with ATDs, the researcher needs to assume that there are no carryover effects and no interaction of treatments with each other. To control for sequence effects, the researcher can randomize treatment order with restrictions to prevent no more than two consecutive sessions of the same condition (i.e., restricted randomization; Onghena & Edgington, 1994). Study outcomes are then graphed by associated treatment condition using independent and different data paths (see Figure 33.7). Unlike other SCEDs, stable responding is not a prerequisite for changing conditions, and thus, researchers may consider the use of ATDs to study variable behavior that would otherwise necessitate longer phases, allowing for an efficient comparative analysis of

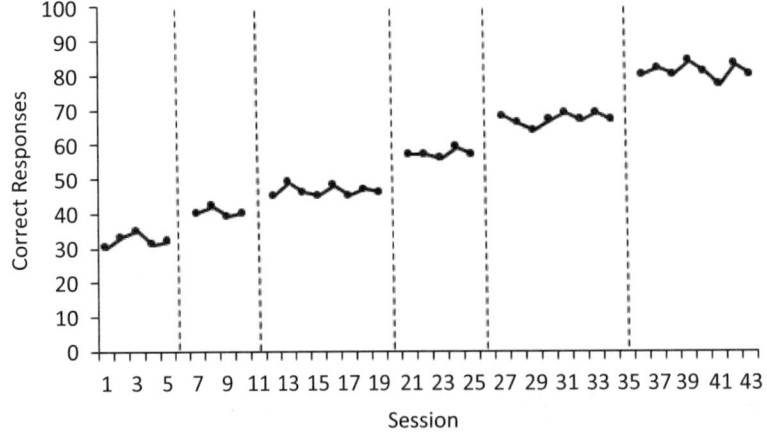

FIGURE 33.6.   Illustration of a changing criterion design.

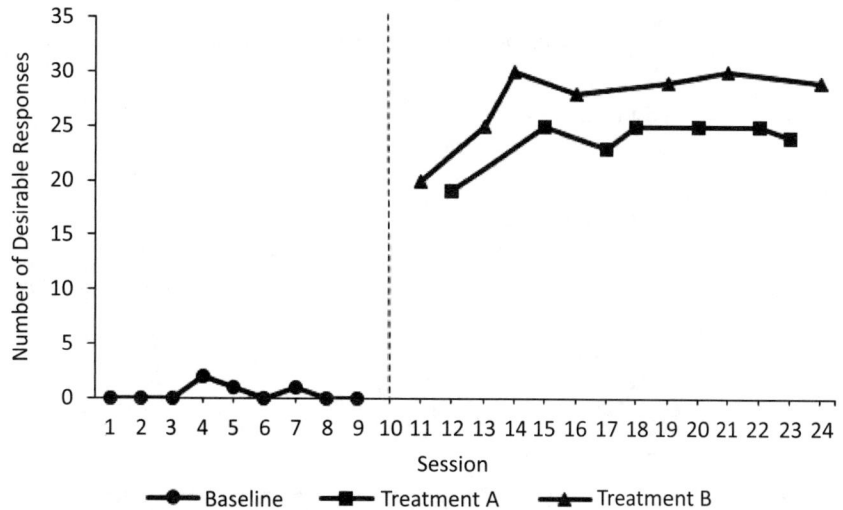

FIGURE 33.7. Illustration of an alternating treatments design.

differential treatment effectiveness. For example, Peters et al. (2020) used an ATD to assess differential spelling performance in persons with visual impairment and amyotrophic lateral sclerosis (ALS). Although spelling performance was highly variable, the researchers were able to compare accurate responding within and across three different eye tracking and brain-computer interface systems. As such, the ATD can be a suitable option for researchers seeking to identify a more effective treatment or investigate the extent to which two or more treatments differ in effectiveness.

Repeated Acquisition Designs

The repeated acquisition design (RAD) is a type of SCED used to repeatedly test brief intervention effects on discrete operant behaviors such as language or academic skills (e.g., vocabulary), making it a feasible alternative to the ATD when studying irreversible outcomes (Cohn & Paule, 1995). The RAD requires a priori assignment of discrete stimuli or behaviors of relative equivalency (i.e., difficulty) to sets targeted for instruction and the repeated measurement of an outcome conducted through pre- and post-intervention probes over time (Kennedy, 2005; Ledford & Gast, 2018). For example, Cohn and colleagues (1993) examined the effects of lead on animals' skill acquisition and retention by comparing pre- to postexposure performance. More recently, Dennis and Whalon (2020) used a RAD to compare preschoolers' rates of vocabulary acquisition following computer-assisted instruction or teacher-delivered instruction. Advantages of the RAD include the strength of the within-subjects design, ability to evaluate treatment dosage and salience on operant behaviors, and ability to examine the extent to which responding across different stimulus sets are a consequence of experimental manipulation. Further, evidence of the credibility of the design (Kratochwill et al., 2010) can be enhanced with additional considerations, such as procedures to determine stimulus equivalency, randomization techniques, multiple cases, and the addition of baseline and maintenance phases (Kirby et al., 2021). As shown in Figure 33.8, the researcher can strengthen the RAD by adding control or comparison stimuli (i.e., stimuli that are not taught).

STUDY PROCEDURES

In addition to selecting a design and experimental tactics that align with the study purpose and outcome of interest, single-case researchers implement procedures to document reliability of the outcome measurement, treatment fidelity, generalization, and social validity.

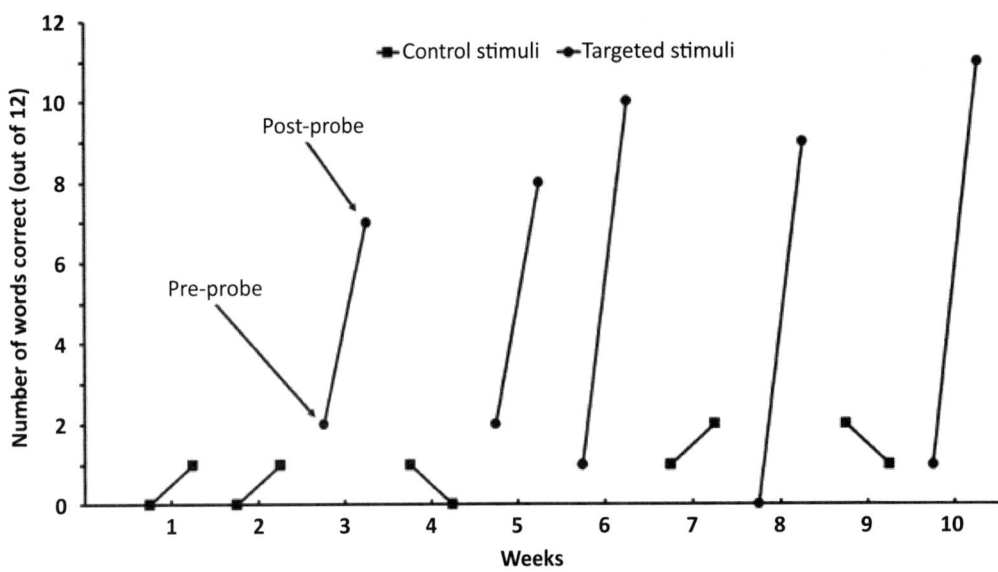

FIGURE 33.8.   Illustration of a repeated acquisition design.

Reliability of Outcome Measurement

The reliability of outcome measurement is a key variable in the interpretability of SCED study results. Analysis and interpretability of SCED outcomes hinge on the integrity of the data reported by trained independent data collectors and scorers. Poor reliability translates to high rates of disagreement between independent data collectors about the presence or absence of an effect on the target behavior. If rates of disagreement remain high and are not immediately resolved, researchers introduce confounds in the ability to make assumptions about intervention effects, which threatens replicability of results in future research (Ledford & Wolery, 2013). Thus, a priori, the researcher should operationalize the dependent variable and measurement procedures and train data collectors and scorers to fidelity. Researchers should plan to have a second independent data collector measure and/or score outcomes for at least 20% of all observations per phase or condition with a goal of 80% agreement between the two data collectors (Lane & Gast, 2014). Reliability is then usually reported by researchers as a percentage of interrater agreement, interrater reliability, or interrater agreement (Lane & Gast, 2014). To examine measurement discrepancies, some researchers

have also suggested graphical presentation of inter-observer agreement results over time to examine the extent to which the levels of agreement are consistent within and across experimental conditions (Ledford & Wolery, 2013; Ledford et al., 2019). To guard against instrumentation effects, where perhaps the two raters drift in the same way over time (e.g., each gets more lenient), sessions could also be recorded and scored in random order for each rater.

Treatment Fidelity

Treatment fidelity in single-case design refers to the consistent implementation of an intervention within and across study sessions. The efficacy of an intervention is often highly dependent on whether it has been implemented as intended. Fidelity increases confidence that the intervention is directly linked to changes in the target behavior. A common approach to monitoring treatment fidelity in single-case studies involves completing a checklist to ensure that the intervention is delivered according to plan. For example, team members can document the amount of time spent with each participant, the quantity of feedback given to each participant, and any notable changes within the testing environment. The compiled information can help to assess the need for implementation supports (Collier-Meek et al., 2018). Adherence to treatment fidelity enhances the internal validity of the study and reduces the potential for Type II errors (Krasny-Pacini & Evans, 2018).

Generalization

Planning for maintenance and generalization phases can provide information about the extent to which behavior change persists in other contexts and over time. In SCED, *generalization* refers to instances when trained skills or behaviors resulting from experimental manipulation of the independent variable transfer beyond experimental conditions to more natural contexts (Kendall, 1981; Stokes & Baer, 1977). In SCED research, researchers can plan to evaluate generalization effects across three categories: response generalization, stimulus generalization, and/or maintenance (Catania, 1992; Kendall, 1981). Response generalization occurs when participants encounter a discriminative stimulus that evokes an untrained behavior of similar topography or function to the trained response. For example, say a researcher was interested in reducing a child's toy-grabbing behavior by teaching the child to ask for a peer's permission to share. During the study, the researcher taught the child to say, "May I have . . ." However, presented with the same antecedent condition later in the day, the child made a spontaneous request using the untrained phrase, "Can I please have . . ." Conversely, researchers can document treatment effects on stimulus generalization when participants engage in a target behavior in response to an untrained stimulus or novel situation (Sidman, 1997). For example, Gunby et al. (2010) taught abduction prevention skills to three children with autism using behavioral skills training at a day care facility. In a stimulus generalization probe, one participant demonstrated the learned skills in the community setting without explicit instruction in this setting. In addition, all participants demonstrated maintenance of such skills after 1 month. In other words, the children demonstrated generalization of treatment effects over time in absence of the intervention. There

are numerous ways for researchers to contribute support for external validity, such as conducting follow-up observations poststudy, planning for probes in novel contexts, and documenting instances of response generalization. Regardless of the specific measures taken, researchers should consider ways to integrate these strategies into their SCED.

Social Validity

One of the seven dimensions of applied behavior analysis is the study of socially significant behavior: "changes in behavior that are clinically significant or actually make a difference in the client's life" (Kazdin, 1977, p. 427). The acceptability of intervention components, methods of measurement, and experimental outcomes can be equally as relevant to interventionists as a measure of effectiveness, answering "For whom does it work?" and "Will it continue in use when I'm gone?" Attention to social validity is important because interventions that are impractical or unacceptable are less likely to be adopted (Leko, 2014; Lloyd & Heubusch, 1996). Behavior scientists can use surveys and choice measures to gather information about the social significance of the research before and after a study (Fuqua & Schwade, 1986). Additionally, structured interviews with participants and stakeholders can supplement measures of treatment adherence and attrition (i.e., participant drop-out). Follow-up interviews with participants and primary stakeholders can provide information about whether the research methods and designs are aligned with the applied dimension of applied behavior analysis (Baer et al., 1968; Kazdin, 1977; Wolf, 1978).

DATA ANALYSIS

The principal analysis method for SCEDs is visual analysis of the graphed data (Barlow & Hersen, 1984; Gast & Spriggs, 2014; Kratochwill et al., 2010). During visual analyses, researchers engage in four steps: (a) documenting stable baseline patterns, (b) examining the data within each phase, (c) comparing adjacent and similar phases, and (d) determining whether there are at least three demonstrations of the effect at different points in time (Kratochwill et al., 2010). In analyzing and comparing the data patterns within and across phases, researchers attend to six data features: (a) level, (b) trend, (c) variability, (d) immediacy of effect, (e) overlap, and (f) consistency of patterns across similar phases (Kratochwill et al., 2010). Visual analysis training methods have been developed (Wolfe & Slocum, 2015) and visual analyses continue to serve researchers using SCEDs well. However, they do have some limitations. Indexing the probability of falsely concluding an effect exists is difficult, which leads to questions about Type I error control (Fisch, 1998), and quantitative summaries of the size of the effect can be helpful for research synthesis and meta-analyses. Thus, a variety of statistical analyses have been developed to complement visual analyses.

For researchers who have incorporated randomization into their designs, it is possible to formally control the probability of falsely concluding there is an effect (i.e., Type I error) by using randomization tests if the randomization is done a priori (Edgington & Onghena, 2007) or masked visual analysis if the randomization is done during response-guided experimentation (Ferron & Levin, 2014). These randomization-based methods can be appealing for testing the effect because they do not require modeling assumptions, such as temporal stability, independence, or normality (Edgington, 1980). In addition, software to conduct randomization tests is readily available (Gafurov & Levin, 2020; Bulté & Onghena, 2009), as is an application to facilitate masked visual analysis (Moeyaert et al., 2021). However, these randomization-based methods are limited to testing the null hypothesis of no treatment effect.

Researchers who wish to provide a quantitative estimate of the size of the effect must turn to other options, including statistical modeling and standardized effect estimation. When the study contains a single case, extensions of regression that allow researchers to account for potential serial dependence (or autocorrelation in the repeated observations) are available (Maggin et al., 2011; Swaminathan et al., 2014). When the study

contains multiple cases (e.g., multiple-baseline designs, multiple-probe designs), multilevel models are available that account for the nesting of the repeated observations within the cases (Rindskopf, 2014; Rindskopf & Ferron, 2014; Shadish et al., 2013; Van den Noortgate & Onghena, 2003). Parameter estimates from these regression or multilevel models can be used as raw score effect indices. For those that desire standardized effect estimates, options include effect sizes based on nonoverlap between adjacent phases (Parker & Vannest, 2009; Parker et al., 2011), mean differences standardized by within-case variability (Busk & Serlin, 1992), mean differences standardized by between-case variability (Pustejovsky et al., 2014; Shadish et al., 2014), response ratios (Pustejovsky, 2018), and progress toward a goal (Ferron et al., 2020).

SUMMARY

SCEDs are a collection of research methods for the study of intervention effects on individuals. No single method is always optimal because of differences in study purposes (e.g., indexing the effectiveness of an intervention vs. comparing the effectiveness of alternative interventions), target outcomes (e.g., reversible vs. nonreversible behaviors), and practical constraints associated with the research context and individual under study. Rather than relying on a single method, SCED researchers combine different experimental tactics (e.g., baseline logic, response-guided experimentation, within-case replication, across-case replication, and randomization) to select a design type (e.g., reversal, multiple-baseline, multiple-probe, changing criterion, alternating treatments, or repeated acquisition) that aligns with their purpose, outcome, and research context. Regardless of which tactics and design type are employed, SCED researchers incorporate procedures to ensure the outcome is measured reliably, the intervention is implemented with fidelity, issues of generalizability and social validity are considered, and the primary outcome data are graphed as a function of time to facilitate visual analyses of the intervention effect.

References

Baer, D. M., Wolf, M. M., & Risley, T. R. (1968). Some current dimensions of applied behavior analysis. *Journal of Applied Behavior Analysis, 1*(1), 91–97. https://doi.org/10.1901/jaba.1968.1-91

Barlow, D. H., & Hayes, S. C. (1979). Alternating treatments design: One strategy for comparing the effects of two treatments in a single subject. *Journal of Applied Behavior Analysis, 12*(2), 199–210. https://doi.org/10.1901/jaba.1979.12-199

Barlow, D. H., & Hersen, M. (1984). *Single case experimental designs: Strategies for studying behavior change.* Pergamon.

Bulté, I., & Onghena, P. (2009). Randomization tests for multiple-baseline designs: An extension of the SCRT-R package. *Behavior Research Methods, 41*(2), 477–485. https://doi.org/10.3758/BRM.41.2.477

Busk, P. L., & Serlin, R. C. (1992). Meta-analysis of single-case research. In T. R. Kratochwill & J. R. Levin (Eds.), *Single-case research design and analysis: New directions for psychology and education* (pp. 187–212). Lawrence Erlbaum Associates.

Byiers, B. J., Reichle, J., & Symons, F. J. (2012). Single-subject experimental design for evidence-based practice. *American Journal of Speech-Language Pathology, 21*(4), 397–414. https://doi.org/10.1044/1058-0360(2012/11-0036)

Catania, A. C. (1992). *Learning.* Prentice Hall.

Cohn, J., Cox, C., & Cory-Slechta, D. A. (1993). The effects of lead exposure on learning in a multiple repeated acquisition and performance schedule. *Neurotoxicology, 14*(2–3), 329–346.

Cohn, J., & Paule, M. G. (1995). Repeated acquisition of response sequences: The analysis of behavior in transition. *Neuroscience and Biobehavioral Reviews, 19*(3), 397–406. https://doi.org/10.1016/0149-7634(94)00067-B

Collier-Meek, M. A., Fallon, L. M., & Gould, K. (2018). How are treatment integrity data assessed? Reviewing the performance feedback literature. *School Psychology Quarterly, 33*(4), 517–526. https://doi.org/10.1037/spq0000239

Dennis, L. R., & Whalon, K. J. (2020). Effects of teacher- versus application-delivered instruction on the expressive vocabulary of at-risk preschool children. *Remedial and Special Education, 42*(4), 1–12. https://doi.org/10.1177/0741932519900991

Edgington, E. S. (1980). Validity of randomization tests for one-subject experiments. *Journal of Educational Statistics, 5*(3), 235–251. https://doi.org/10.3102/10769986005003235

Edgington, E. S., & Onghena, P. (2007). *Randomization tests* (4th ed.). Chapman & Hall. https://doi.org/10.1201/9781420011814

Engel, R. J., & Schutt, R. K. (2013). *The practice of research in social work* (3rd ed.). SAGE.

Ferron, J., Goldstein, H., Olszewski, A., & Rohrer, L. (2020). Indexing effects in single-case experimental designs by estimating the percent of goal obtained. *Evidence-Based Communication Assessment and Intervention, 14*(1–2), 6–27. https://doi.org/10.1080/17489539.2020.1732024

Ferron, J., Rohrer, L. L., & Levin, J. R. (2019). Randomization procedures for changing criterion designs. *Behavior Modification,* 145445519847627. Advance online publication. https://doi.org/10.1177/0145445519847627

Ferron, J. M., & Jones, P. (2006). Tests for the visual analysis of response-guided multiple-baseline data. *Journal of Experimental Education, 75*(1), 66–81. https://doi.org/10.3200/JEXE.75.1.66-81

Ferron, J. M., & Levin, J. R. (2014). Single-case permutation and randomization statistical tests: Present status, promising new developments. In T. R. Kratochwill & J. R. Levin (Eds.), *Single-case intervention research: Methodological and statistical advances* (pp. 153–183). American Psychological Association. https://doi.org/10.1037/14376-006

Ferron, J. M., Moeyaert, M., Van den Noortgate, W., & Beretvas, S. N. (2014). Estimating causal effects from multiple-baseline studies: Implications for design and analysis. *Psychological Methods, 19*(4), 493–510. https://doi.org/10.1037/a0037038

Fisch, G. S. (1998). Visual inspection of data revisited: Do the eyes still have it? *The Behavior Analyst, 21*(1), 111–123. https://doi.org/10.1007/BF03392786

Fuqua, R. W., & Schwade, J. (1986). Social validation of applied behavioral research. In A. Poling & R. W. Fuqua (Eds.), *Research methods in applied behavior analysis* (pp. 265–292). Springer. https://doi.org/10.1007/978-1-4684-8786-2_12

Gafurov, B. S., & Levin, J. R. (2020, March). *ExPRT (Excel Package of Randomization Tests): Statistical analyses of single-case intervention data* (Version 4.1). Retrievable at https://ex-prt.weebly.com

Gallo, K. P., Comer, J. S., & Barlow, D. H. (2013). Single-case experimental designs and small pilot trial designs. In J. S. Comer & P. C. Kendall (Eds.), *The Oxford handbook of research strategies for clinical psychology* (pp. 24–39). Oxford University Press.

Gast, D. L., & Ledford, J. R. (Eds.). (2014). *Single case research methodology: Applications in special education and behavioral sciences* (2nd ed.). Routledge. https://doi.org/10.4324/9780203521892

Gast, D. L., & Spriggs, A. D. (2014). Visual analysis of graphic data. In D. L. Gast & J. R. Ledford (Eds.), *Single case research methodology: Applications in special education and behavioral sciences* (2nd ed.). Routledge. https://doi.org/10.4324/9780203521892-9

Gunby, K. V., Carr, J. E., & Leblanc, L. A. (2010). Teaching abduction-prevention skills to children with autism. *Journal of Applied Behavior Analysis, 43*(1), 107–112. https://doi.org/10.1901/jaba.2010.43-107

Horner, R. D., & Baer, D. M. (1978). Multiple-probe technique: A variation on the multiple baseline. *Journal of Applied Behavior Analysis, 11*(1), 189–196. https://doi.org/10.1901/jaba.1978.11-189

Horner, R. H., & Odom, S. L. (2014). Constructing single-case research designs: Logic and options. In T. R. Kratochwill & J. R. Levin (Eds.), *School psychology series. Single-case intervention research: Methodological and statistical advances* (pp. 27–51). American Psychological Association. https://doi.org/10.1037/14376-002

Kazdin, A. E. (1977). Assessing the clinical or applied importance of behavior change through social validation. *Behavior Modification, 1*(4), 427–452. https://doi.org/10.1177/014544557714001

Kazdin, A. E. (1980). Obstacles in using randomization tests in single-case experimentation. *Journal of Educational Statistics, 5*(3), 253–260. https://doi.org/10.3102/10769986005003253

Kendall, P. C. (1981). Assessing generalization and the single-subject strategies. *Behavior Modification, 5*(3), 307–319. https://doi.org/10.1177/014544558153001

Kennedy, C. H. (2005). *Single-case designs for educational research.* Pearson.

Kirby, M. S., Spencer, T. D., & Ferron, J. M. (2021). How to be RAD: Repeated acquisition design features that enhance internal and external validity. *Perspectives on Behavior Science, 44*(2-3), 389–416. https://doi.org/10.1007/s40614-021-00301-2

Klein, L. A., Houlihan, D., Vincent, J. L., & Panahon, C. J. (2017). Best practices in utilizing the changing criterion design. *Behavior Analysis in Practice, 10*(1), 52–61. https://doi.org/10.1007/s40617-014-0036-x

Koehler, M. J., & Levin, J. R. (1998). Regulated randomization: A potentially sharper analytical tool for the multiple baseline design. *Psychological Methods, 3*(2), 206–217. https://doi.org/10.1037/1082-989X.3.2.206

Krasny-Pacini, A., & Evans, J. (2018). Single-case experimental designs to assess intervention effectiveness in rehabilitation: A practical guide. *Annals of Physical and Rehabilitation Medicine, 61*(3), 164–179. https://doi.org/10.1016/j.rehab.2017.12.002

Kratochwill, T. R., Hitchcock, J., Horner, R. H., Levin, J. R., Odom, S. L., Rindskopf, D. M., & Shadish, W. R. (2010). *Single-case designs technical documentation.* Retrieved from What Works Clearinghouse website: https://ies.ed.gov/ncee/wwc/Document/229

Lane, J. D., & Gast, D. L. (2014). Visual analysis in single case experimental design studies: Brief review and guidelines. *Neuropsychological Rehabilitation, 24*(3–4), 445–463. https://doi.org/10.1080/09602011.2013.815636

Ledford, J., & Gast, D. L. (2018). Combination and other designs. In J. R. Ledford & D. L. Gast (Eds.), *Single case research methodology: Applications in special education and behavioral sciences* (3rd ed., pp. 335–364). Routledge. https://doi.org/10.4324/9781315150666-12

Ledford, J. R., Barton, E. E., Severini, K. E., & Zimmerman, K. N. (2019). A primer on single-case research designs: Contemporary use and analysis. *American Journal on Intellectual and Developmental Disabilities, 124*(1), 35–56. https://doi.org/10.1352/1944-7558-124.1.35

Ledford, J. R., & Wolery, M. (2013). Effects of plotting a second observer's data on A-B-A-B graphs when observer disagreement is present. *Journal of Behavioral Education, 22*, 312–324. https://doi.org/10.1007/s10864-013-9178-0

Leko, M. M. (2014). The value of qualitative methods in social validity research. *Remedial and Special Education, 35*(5), 275–286. https://doi.org/10.1177/0741932514524002

Lloyd, J. W., & Heubusch, J. D. (1996). Issues of social validation in research on serving individuals with emotional or behavioral disorders. *Behavioral Disorders, 22*(1), 8–14. https://doi.org/10.1177/019874299602200105

Maggin, D. M., Swaminathan, H., Rogers, H. J., O'Keeffe, B. V., Sugai, G., & Horner, R. H. (2011). A generalized least squares regression approach for computing effect sizes in single-case research: Application examples. *Journal of School Psychology, 49*(3), 301–321. https://doi.org/10.1016/j.jsp.2011.03.004

Manolov, R., Solanas, A., & Sierra, V. (2019). Extrapolating baseline trend in single-case data: Problems and tentative solutions. *Behavior Research Methods, 51*(6), 2847–2869. https://doi.org/10.3758/s13428-018-1165-x

Moeyaert, M., Bursali, S., & Ferron, J. M. (2021). SCD-MVA: A mobile application for conducting single-case experimental design research during the pandemic. *Human Behavior and Emerging Technologies*, *3*(1), 75–96. https://doi.org/10.1002/hbe2.223

Morgan, D. L., & Morgan, R. K. (2009). *Single-case research methods for the behavioral and health sciences*. Sage Publications. https://doi.org/10.4135/9781483329697

Murphy, R. J., & Bryan, A. J. (1980). Multiple-baseline and multiple-probe designs: Practical alternatives for special education assessment and evaluation. *The Journal of Special Education*, *14*(3), 325–335. https://doi.org/10.1177/002246698001400306

Odom, S. L., Brantlinger, E., Gersten, R., Horner, R. H., Thompson, B., & Harris, K. (2005). Research in special education: Scientific methods and evidence-based practices. *Exceptional Children*, *71*(2), 137–148. https://doi.org/10.1177/001440290507100201

Onghena, P. (1992). Randomization tests for extensions and variations of ABAB single-case experimental designs: A rejoinder. *Behavioral Assessment*, *14*, 153–171.

Onghena, P., & Edgington, E. S. (1994). Randomization tests for restricted alternating treatments designs. *Behaviour Research and Therapy*, *32*(7), 783–786. https://doi.org/10.1016/0005-7967(94)90036-1

Onghena, P., Tanious, R., De, T. K., & Michiels, B. (2019). Randomization tests for changing criterion designs. *Behaviour Research and Therapy*, *117*, 18–27. https://doi.org/10.1016/j.brat.2019.01.005

Parker, R. I., & Vannest, K. (2009). An improved effect size for single-case research: Nonoverlap of all pairs. *Behavior Therapy*, *40*(4), 357–367. https://doi.org/10.1016/j.beth.2008.10.006

Parker, R. I., Vannest, K. J., & Davis, J. L. (2011). Effect size in single-case research: A review of nine nonoverlap techniques. *Behavior Modification*, *35*(4), 303–322. https://doi.org/10.1177/0145445511399147

Peters, B., Bedrick, S., Dudy, S., Eddy, B., Higger, M., Kinsella, M., McLaughlin, D., Memmott, T., Oken, B., Quivira, F., Spaulding, S., Erdogmus, D., & Fried-Oken, M. (2020). SSVEP BCI and eye tracking use by individuals with late-stage ALS and visual impairments. *Frontiers in Human Neuroscience*, *14*, 595890. https://doi.org/10.3389/fnhum.2020.595890

Poling, A., & Grossett, D. (1986). Basic research designs in applied behavior analysis. In A. Poling &

R. W. Fuqua (Eds.), *Research methods in applied behavior analysis*. Springer. https://doi.org/10.1007/978-1-4684-8786-2_2

Pustejovsky, J. E. (2018). Using response ratios for meta-analyzing single-case designs with behavioral outcomes. *Journal of School Psychology*, *68*, 99–112. https://doi.org/10.1016/j.jsp.2018.02.003

Pustejovsky, J. E., Hedges, L. V., & Shadish, W. R. (2014). Design-comparable effect sizes in multiple baseline designs: A general modeling framework. *Journal of Educational and Behavioral Statistics*, *39*(5), 368–393. https://doi.org/10.3102/1076998614547577

Rindskopf, D. (2014). Nonlinear Bayesian analysis for single case designs. *Journal of School Psychology*, *52*(2), 179–189. https://doi.org/10.1016/j.jsp.2013.12.003

Rindskopf, D., & Ferron, J. (2014). Using multilevel models to analyze single-case design data. In T. R. Kratochwill & J. R. Levin (Eds.), *Single-case intervention research: Statistical and methodological advances* (pp. 221–246). American Psychological Association. https://doi.org/10.1037/14376-008

Shadish, W. R., Hedges, L. V., & Pustejovsky, J. E. (2014). Analysis and meta-analysis of single-case designs with a standardized mean difference statistic: A primer and applications. *Journal of School Psychology*, *52*(2), 123–147. https://doi.org/10.1016/j.jsp.2013.11.005

Shadish, W. R., Kyse, E. N., & Rindskopf, D. M. (2013). Analyzing data from single-case designs using multilevel models: New applications and some agenda items for future research. *Psychological Methods*, *18*(3), 385–405. https://doi.org/10.1037/a0032964

Sidman, M. (1960). *Tactics of scientific research: Evaluating experimental data in psychology*. Authors Cooperative.

Sidman, M. (1997). Equivalence relations. *Journal of the Experimental Analysis of Behavior*, *68*(2), 258–266. https://doi.org/10.1901/jeab.1997.68-258

Stokes, T. F., & Baer, D. M. (1977). An implicit technology of generalization. *Journal of Applied Behavior Analysis*, *10*(2), 349–367. https://doi.org/10.1901/jaba.1977.10-349

Swaminathan, H., Rogers, H. J., & Horner, R. H. (2014). An effect size measure and Bayesian analysis of single-case designs. *Journal of School Psychology*, *52*(2), 213–230. https://doi.org/10.1016/j.jsp.2013.12.002

Tanious, R., & Onghena, P. (2020). A systematic review of applied single-case research published between 2016 and 2018: Study designs, randomization, data aspects, and data analysis. *Behavior*

Research Methods. Advance online publication. https://doi.org/10.3758/s13428-020-01502-4

Van den Noortgate, W., & Onghena, P. (2003). Combining single-case experimental data using hierarchical linear models. *School Psychology Quarterly, 18*(3), 325–346. https://doi.org/10.1521/scpq.18.3.325.22577

Wolery, M., Gast, D., & Ledford, J. R. (2018). Comparative designs. In J. R. Ledford & D. L. Gast (Eds.), *Single case research methodology: Applications in special education and behavioral*

sciences (3rd ed., pp. 283–334). Routledge. https://doi.org/10.4324/9781315150666-11

Wolf, M. M. (1978). Social validity: The case for subjective measurement or how applied behavior analysis is finding its heart. *Journal of Applied Behavior Analysis, 11*(2), 203–214. https://doi.org/10.1901/jaba.1978.11-203

Wolfe, K., & Slocum, T. A. (2015). A comparison of two approaches to training visual analysis of AB graphs. *Journal of Applied Behavior Analysis, 48*(2), 472–477. https://doi.org/10.1002/jaba.212

CHAPTER 34

TIME SERIES DESIGNS

Bradley J. Bartos, Richard McCleary, and David McDowall

Time series designs are distinguished from other designs by the properties of time series data and by the necessary reliance on a statistical model to control threats to validity. In the long run, a time series is a realization of a latent causal process. Representing the complete time series as

$$\ldots, Y_{-2}, Y_{-1}, Y_0, \{Y_1, \ldots, Y_N\}, Y_{N+1}, Y_{N+2}, \ldots \quad (34.1)$$

the observed series $\{Y_1, \ldots, Y_N\}$ is a probability sample of the complete realization. The probability sampling weights for $\{Y_1, \ldots, Y_N\}$ are specified in a statistical model which, for present purposes, is written in a general linear form as

$$Y_t = N(a_t) + X(I_t) \quad (34.2)$$

The model equates the tth observation of the time series Y_t as the sum of a "noise" component, $N(a_t)$, and an intervention component, $X(I_t)$. Functions $N()$ and $X()$ are represented in general form and will be specified for particular models. The a_t term of this model is the tth observation of a strictly exogenous innovation series with the "white noise" property,

$$a_t \sim iid\text{Normal}(0, \sigma_a^2) \quad (34.3)$$

The I_t term of the intervention component is the tth observation of a binary variable coded for the presence or absence of an intervention. However, it can also be a purely stochastic series. In either case, the model is constructed by a set of rules that allow for the solution,

$$a_t = N^{-1}[Y_t - X(I_t)] \quad (34.4)$$

As a_t has "white noise" properties, the solved model satisfies the assumptions of all common tests of statistical significance. In the context of an appropriately specified design, moreover, the results of these tests can be interpreted causally.

THREE DESIGN CATEGORIES

We elaborate on the specific forms of the general model and on the set of rules for building models at a later point. For present purposes, the general model allows three design variations: (a) descriptive time series designs, (b) correlational time series designs, and (c) experimental or quasi-experimental time series designs.

Descriptive Designs

The simplest time series design, which we call a *descriptive design*, consists of decomposing the series into elementary components, such as trends and cycles, and then interpreting the time series components. Informal descriptive

https://doi.org/10.1037/0000319-034
APA Handbook of Research Methods in Psychology, Second Edition: Vol. 2. Research Designs: Quantitative, Qualitative, Neuropsychological, and Biological, H. Cooper (Editor-in-Chief)

analyses often precede formal hypothesis testing. But lacking any interpretation—that is, no hypothesis tests about trends or cycles— we are reluctant to call this activity an experiment. When hypotheses about trends or cycles are tested, in contrast, descriptive analyses qualify as primitive time series experiments. Historical examples include Wolf's (1848; Yule, 1927) investigation of sunspot activity and Elton's (1924; Elton & Nicholson, 1942) investigation of lynx populations. In both cases, time series analyses revealed cycles or trends that corroborated substantive interpretations of the phenomenon.

Kroeber's (1919; Richardson & Kroeber, 1940) analyses of cultural change illustrated the unsuit-ability of descriptive time series designs to many social and behavioral phenomena. Kroeber (1969) hypothesized that women's fashions change in response to political and economic variables. During stable periods of peace and prosperity, fashions changed slowly; during wars, revolutions, and depressions, fashions changed rapidly. Because political and economic cataclysms were thought to recur in long historical cycles, Kroeber tested his hypothesis by searching for the same cycles in women's fashions.

Figure 34.1 plots one of Kroeber's annual fashion time series: 150 years of mean skirt widths collected by Richardson and Kroeber (1940) from museum fashion plates. Although Kroeber believed that the long cycles in this series corroborated his "cultural unsettlement" theory, wholly random

processes can generate identical patterns. Whereas most time series designs treat $N(a_t)$ as a "nuisance" function, the sole purpose of which is to control the threats to statistical conclusion validity posed by cycles and trends, the descriptive time series design infers substantive explanations from $N(a_t)$. Although the statistical models and methods developed for the analysis of descriptive designs are applied for exploratory purposes (see Mills, 1991), they are currently not widely used for null hypothesis tests. The inferential problems inherent to descriptive time series experiments parallel those of the "one-shot case study" design (Campbell & Stanley, 1966). As in the one-shot case study, most descriptive time series designs are unable to rule out alternative rival hypotheses. Consequently, most descriptive time series experiments are uninterpretable.

Correlational Designs

A second type of time series design attempts to infer a causal relationship between two series from their covariance. Historical examples include Chree's (1913) analyses of the temporal cor-relation between sunspot activity and terrestrial magnetism and Beveridge's (1922) analyses of the temporal correlation between rainfall and wheat prices. The validity of correlational inferences rests heavily on theory, of course. When theory can specify a single causal effect operating at discrete lags, as in these natural science examples, correlational designs support unambiguous causal

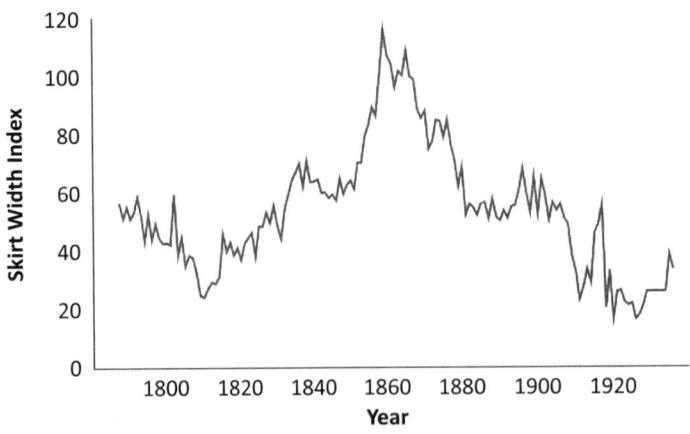

FIGURE 34.1. Annual skirt widths, 1787 to 1936.

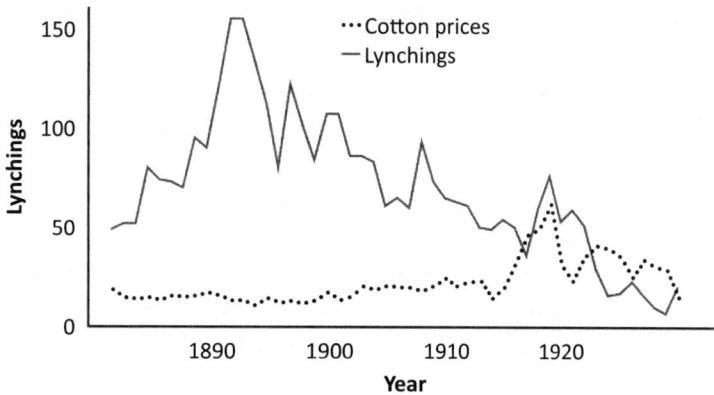

FIGURE 34.2. Annual cotton prices and lynchings, 1886 to 1930.

interpretations. Lacking theoretical specification, however, correlational designs do not allow strong causal inferences.

Analyses of the temporal correlation between lynchings and cotton prices by Hovland and Sears (1940) illustrate the inferential problem. To test the frustration-aggression hypothesis of Dollard et al. (1939), Hovland and Sears estimated a Pearson product-moment correlation coefficient from the annual time series plotted in Figure 34.2. Assuming that the correlation would be zero in the absence of a causal relationship, Hovland and Sears interpreted the statistically significant estimate as corroborating evidence. Due to common stochastic time series properties, however, especially trend, causally independent series will be correlated. Controlling for trend, Hepworth and West (1988) reported a small, significant correlation between the series but warn against causal interpretations. The correlation is an artifact of the war years (1914–1918), when the demand for cotton and the civilian population moved in opposite directions (McCleary, 2000). Excluding the war years, the correlation is not statistically significant.

It is tempting to treat two time series as if they were cross-sectional samples. And if time series observations had white-noise properties,

any statistic could be estimated by simply plugging the data into the appropriate cross-sectional formula. Time series observations are seldom independent, however, and given any trend or cyclical behavior, the estimated correlation coefficient between two series will invariably overstate their true relationship.

Where theory supports strong specification, correlational time series designs continue to be used. Other than limited areas in economics and psychology, however, social theories will not support the required specification. Even in these areas, causal inferences require the narrow definition of "Granger causality" (Granger, 1969) to rule out plausible alternative interpretations.[1]

Quasi-Experimental Designs

The third type of time series design infers the latent causal effect of a temporally discrete intervention or treatment from discontinuities or interruptions in a time series. Campbell and Stanley (1966, pp. 37–43) called this design the "time series experiment," and its use is currently the major application of time series data for causal inference. Historical examples of the general approach include investigations of workplace interventions on health and productivity by the British Industrial Fatigue Research Board

---

[1]Clive Granger argued that causality is deeply philosophical and proposed a form of empirical relationship in which lagged values of one time series are predictive of another time series. Rather than test whether series X causes series Y, Granger causality tests whether series X forecasts series Y.

(Florence, 1923) and by the Hawthorne experiments (Roethlisberger & Dickson, 1939). Fisher's (1921) analyses of agricultural interventions on crop yields also relied on variants of the time series quasi-experiment.

In the simplest case of the design, a discrete intervention breaks a time series into pre- and postintervention segments of N_{pre} and N_{post} observations. For pre- and postintervention means, μ_{pre} and μ_{post}, analysis of the quasi-experiment tests the null hypothesis:

$$H_0: \omega = 0, \text{ where } \omega = \mu_{post} - \mu_{pre} \qquad (34.5)$$

against the alternative:

$$H_A: \omega \neq 0 \qquad (34.6)$$

Rejecting H_0, H_A attributes ω to the intervention. In practice, however, treatment effects are almost always more complex than the simple change in level implied by this null hypothesis.

Figure 34.3 illustrates a typical example of the time series quasi-experimental design. The data are 50 daily self-injurious behavior counts for an institutionalized patient (McCleary et al., 1999). Beginning on the 26th day, the patient is treated with naltrexone, an opiate antagonist. The plotted time series leaves the visual impression that the opiate-blocker has reduced the incidence of self-injurious behavior. Indeed, the difference in means for the 25 pre- and 25 postintervention days amounts to a 42% reduction. Since the value of $F = 32.56$ associated with this difference occurs by chance with $p < 0.0001$, moreover, the null hypothesis can be rejected in favor of the alternative: the medication is an effective treatment for self-injurious behavior.

This conclusion ignores a serious threat to validity. Whereas the null hypothesis test assumes that the daily counts are independent, in fact, the count on any given day is predictable from the count on the preceding day. The visual evidence of Figure 34.3 leaves the unambiguous impression that the opiate-blocker reduced the rate of self-injurious behavior for this patient. Visual evidence can be deceiving, of course, and that is why statistical hypothesis tests are conducted. Due to the day-to-day dependence (i.e., serial correlation or autocorrelation) of these data, however, the value of $F = 32.56$ cannot be interpreted.

More generally, time series experiments and quasi-experiments present many challenges to valid inferences about causal effects. A solid rationale for the design is mostly due to the work of Donald T. Campbell and his collaborators

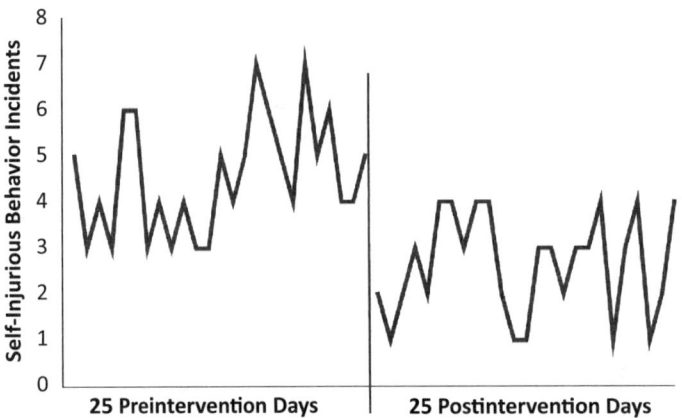

FIGURE 34.3. Self-injurious behavior incidents for a single institutionalized patient before and after an opiate-blocker regimen. Adapted from *Contagious Models for Self-Injurious Behavior* [Poster presentation], by R. McCleary, P. Touchette, D. V. Taylor, and J. L. Barron, 1999, 32nd Annual Gatlinburg Conference on Research and Theory in Mental Retardation. Copyright 1999 by R. McCleary, P. Touchette, D. V. Taylor, and J. L. Barron. Adapted with permission.

(Campbell & Stanley, 1963; Cook & Campbell, 1979; Shadish et al., 2002). Campbell and associates extensively considered threats to the design's validity, and proposed ways to address them when they were plausible. A general conclusion from Campbell's work is that experimental and quasi-experimental time series designs face fewer threats to validity than do most other non-experimental designs. This conclusion is largely responsible for the current popularity of time series studies.

FOUR TYPES OF VALIDITY

Campbell and Stanley (1966; Campbell, 1963) divided the empirical threats to valid inference into two categories. Threats to internal validity addressed the question "Did in fact the experimental treatments make a difference in this specific experimental instance?" Threats to external validity addressed the question "To what populations, settings, treatment variables, and measurement variables can this effect be generalized?"

Recognizing the incompleteness of the dichotomy, Cook and Campbell (1979) added two additional categories. Threats to statistical conclusion validity addressed questions of confidence and power that had previously been included implicitly as threats to internal validity. Threats to construct validity addressed questions of confounding that had previously been included implicitly as threats to external validity. Construct validity includes questions of whether the effect generalizes to alternative measures of hypothetical causes and effects. Shadish et al. (2002) used the same four categories but expand the list of threats to valid inference in each category.

Table 34.1 lists the threats to validity that are relevant to time series studies. Time series designs differ from other approaches in that common threats to validity are controlled by a statistical model. This applies to not only to quasi-experimental designs but also to designs that would be considered "true experiments." When a treatment or intervention can be manipulated experimentally, presumably to control

TABLE 34.1

Four Types of Validity

Type of validity	Threat to validity
Statistical conclusion validity	Low statistical power
	Violated assumptions of the test
Internal validity	History
	Maturation
	Regression artifacts
	Instrumentation
Construct validity	Reactivity
	Novelty and disruption
External validity	Interaction over treatment variations
	Interaction with settings

Note. Data from Shadish et al. (2002).

threats to internal validity, the manipulation raises threats to construct and external validity that can be controlled by the statistical model.

Trade-offs among the four validities are implicit in our tradition. The salient flaw in the Campbell and Stanley (1966) two-category system was that all eight threats to internal validity and all four threats to external validity could be controlled by design. Campbell and his colleagues proposed the four-validity system in large part to correct this misconception. The trade-off among validities is a crucial consideration for time series studies. Although threats to internal validity can be controlled, in principle, by experimental manipulation of the treatment, in practice, experimental manipulation raises near-fatal threats to construct and external validity. Accordingly, we analyze time series experiments as if they were quasi-experiments.

Statistical Conclusion Validity

Shadish et al. (2002) identified nine threats to statistical conclusion validity or "reasons why researchers may be wrong in drawing valid inferences about the magnitude of covariation between two variables" (p. 45). Although the consequences of any particular threat will vary across settings, the threats to statistical conclusion validity fall neatly into categories involving misstatements of the Type I and Type II error rates.[2]

[2]The most comprehensive authority on this topic is Kendall and Stuart (1979, Chapter 22). Cohen (1988) and Lipsey (1990) are more accessible treatments of the topic.

Type I errors, also known as false-positive errors, occur when a true H_0 is mistakenly rejected (i.e., when the intervention has no effect, but the test statistic suggests otherwise). By a convention due to Fisher (1925), the Type I error rate is fixed at $\alpha \leq 0.05$, corresponding to a confidence level of at least 0.95 (or 95% confidence).

Type II errors, also known as false-negative errors, occur when a false H_0 is mistakenly accepted (i.e., when the intervention has an effect, but the test statistic suggests otherwise). Following Neyman and Pearson (1928), the conventional Type II error rate is fixed at $\beta \leq 0.2$, corresponding to statistical power level of at least 0.8 (or 80 percent statistical power). Whereas the Type I error rate is set *a priori*, the Type II error rate is conditioned on the Type I error rate and a likely effect size.[3] We discuss other factors that impact the Type II error rate (e.g., sample size, autocorrelation) on pages 6 and 7.

For both Type I and Type II errors, uncontrolled threats to statistical conclusion validity distort the nominal values of α and β, leading to invalid inferences. The threats are controlled by a statistical model. The most widely used models for that purpose are the *AutoRegressive Integrated Moving Average* (ARIMA) models of Box and Jenkins (1970). Under H_0, an ARIMA model is written as

$$\varphi(B)Z_t = \theta(B)a_t Z_t = Y_t - \mu_Y \qquad (34.7)$$

where Z_t and a_t are the tth observations of a stationary time series and an *iid* Normal$(0, \sigma^2)$ error series, respectively; and where $\varphi(B)$ and $\theta(B)$ are polynomial lag operators. The B lag operator, sometimes called the backshift operator, "shifts" a time series backward. That is

$$BY_t = Y_{t-1} \qquad (34.8)$$

The lag operator B lags the series and obeys the law of exponents:

$$B^0 Y_t = Y_t; \text{ i.e., } B^0 = 1$$

$$B^k Y_t = Y_{t-k} \text{ and } B^{-k} Y_t = Y_{t+k}$$

$$B^j B^k Y_t = B^{j+k} Y_t = Y_{t-j-k} \qquad (34.9)$$

If the parameters of $\varphi(B)$ and $\theta(B)$ are appropriately constrained, the ARIMA model can be solved for a_t:

$$\theta(B)^{-1} \varphi(B) Z_t = a_t \qquad (34.10)$$

To test H_0, the intervention is represented by step function (or dummy variable) defined such that

$$X_t = 0 \text{ for } t \leq N_{pre}$$

$$X_t = 1 \text{ for } N_{pre} < t \text{ (thereafter)} \qquad (34.11)$$

A "transfer" function of X_t is then added to the right-hand side of the ARIMA model:

$$\theta(B)^{-1} \varphi(B) Z_t = a_t + \delta(B)\omega X_t \qquad (34.12)$$

where $\delta(B)$ is a polynomial lag operator and ω is the effect of X_t on Z_t.

As a_t is an *iid* Normal$(0, \sigma^2)$ error term, the null hypothesis

$$H_0: \omega = 0 \qquad (34.13)$$

can be tested with ordinary test statistics, such as t or F, effectively controlling all Type I threats to statistical conclusion validity.

Since the $\varphi(B)$ and $\theta(B)$ lag operators serve the sole purpose of transforming Z_t into the underlying a_t error, ARIMA models are not unique. Methods for building a parsimonious, statistically adequate ARIMA model are described in Glass, Willson, and Gottman (1975), McCleary and Hay (1980), and especially, McDowall et al. (1980). The $\varphi(B)$ and $\theta(B)$ lag operators can be used for descriptive purposes, but with respect to H_0, they are "nuisance" parameters. The transfer function of X_t, in contrast, is a theoretical construct, specified on purely theoretical grounds. We return to this topic later when the threats to construct validity are considered.

Although the Type II threats to statistical conclusion validity are straightforward, they are

---

[3]Cohen (1988, pp. 3–4) and Lipsey (1990, pp. 38–40) set the conventional Type I and Type II error rates at $\alpha = .05$ and $\beta = .2$, respectively. If the Type I error rate is set lower, say, $\alpha = .01$, the Type II error rate is set at $\beta = .04$ to maintain a 4:1 ratio of Type II to Type I errors. The 4:1 convention dates back at least to Neyman and Pearson (1928) and reflects the view that science should be conservative.

poorly understood and often ignored. The failure to reject H_0 does not imply that H_0 is true. The decision to accept H_0 as true requires, first, a consensus decision on the *likely* effect size (or value of ω); and second, a demonstration that the time series quasi-experiment was designed to yield a Type II error rate of $\beta \leq 0.2$ for the likely effect size. In sum, the decision to accept H_0 as true requires the research begin with an analysis of statistical power.

Of the several factors that determine statistical power of a time series design, the likely effect size is the most important (McCleary et al., 2017). Small effects are difficult to detect even under the best circumstances. In addition to the likely size of the effect, the statistical power of a time series quasi-experiment is a function of the series length, balance, and to a lesser extent, the quality of the ARIMA model. Because maximum likelihood estimates rely on large sample properties, analyses of short time series will often fail to achieve the nominal level of power. Most authorities recommend $N_{pre} + N_{post} > 50$ as the minimum length for a time series. Statistical power increases proportional to the square-root of series length. But for a given length, power is highest when the design is balanced such that $N_{pre} = N_{post}$.

Even when the series is long and the design is balanced, the statistical power of a time series quasi-experiment can be affected adversely by a poor fitting ARIMA model. In addition to the purpose of transforming Z_t into a_t, the ARIMA model decomposes the time series variance into stochastic and deterministic components, $N(a_t)$ and $X(I_t)$. To ensure an optimal decomposition, the ARIMA model used to test H_0 should have the lowest residual variance among the several statistically adequate models (McDowall et al., 2019).

Internal Validity

Under some circumstances, all nine of the threats to internal validity identified by Shadish et al. (2002) might apply to the time series quasi-experiment. Typically, however, only four threats are plausible enough to pose serious difficulties. *History* and *maturation*, which arise from the use of multiple temporal observations, can threaten virtually any application of the design. *Instrumentation* and *regression* can also be problems, but only for interventions that involve advanced planning. For unplanned interventions—what Campbell (1963) called "natural experiments"—these threats are much less realistic.

The largest, most obvious, and most frequent threats to internal validity involve the operation of history. Historical threats come from changes in a time series that occur coincidentally with an intervention but are due to other causes. A standard design-based approach to making these threats less plausible is to analyze one or more comparison series. The comparisons can take many forms, and a careful choice can substantially narrow the scope within which history can operate. An analysis might consider a no-treatment control series that the intervention should not have influenced, for example, or study multiple periods during which the intervention was and was not in operation. A consistent pattern of results across different variables or time periods reduces the plausibility of historical threats and helps support the existence of an intervention impact.

An illustration of the effective use of comparison series comes from Hennigan et al. (1982), who studied changes in property crime following the introduction of commercial television. In 34 "early" cities, broadcasting began in 1950, while in 34 "late" cities, television was not available until 1954. The time series in Figure 34.4 show the annual log-transformed levels of property crimes for both groups of cities.

History is a plausible threat to inferences about the effects of television when studying the "early" or "late" cities alone. Other variables also changed during the years in which each group adopted television, and many of these might explain a change in crime. The Korean War was underway in 1951, for example, and an economic recession began in 1955. More generally, criminological theories suggest multiple factors that might influence property crimes and that could have changed around the time that broadcasting began in either of the groups.

Considering both time series together, however, makes the changes in crime much more difficult

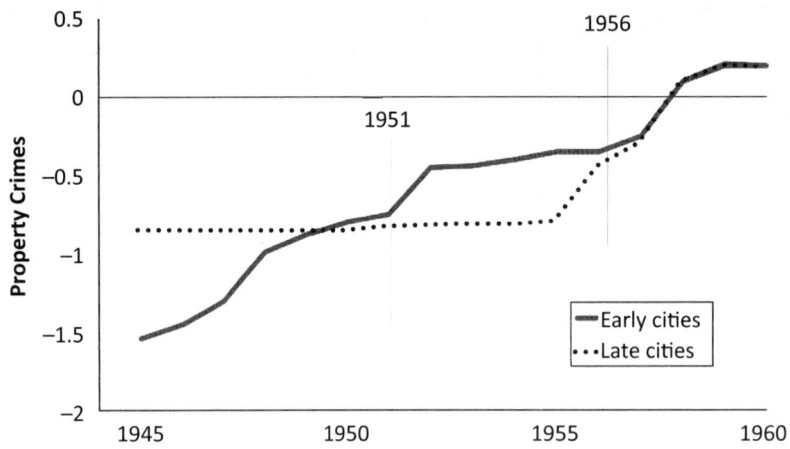

FIGURE 34.4.   Annual property crimes for cities with commercial television broadcast service in 1951 and for cities with television in 1955.

to dismiss as artifacts of history. To be plausible, a historical explanation would have to account for increases that occurred at two different time points but affected only one group of cities at each. Although not impossible, constructing such an explanation would be a difficult enterprise.

In contrast to history, methods for addressing the other three threats to internal validity do not heavily rely on design variations. Maturation, which like history is plausible in all applications of the time series quasi-experiment, requires a statistical modeling approach. Maturation threats appear as trends in the data and are due to developmental processes that are independent of the intervention. Time series data often display such trends, and trending patterns are common in the long series that are most desirable for analysis. Maturational trends are a problem for inference because they can easily produce false evidence of an intervention effect.

Figure 34.5 illustrates one of the best-known examples of the maturation threat, the so-called Hawthorne effect. The data consist of weekly productivity levels for a group of five machine operators in the bank wiring room of the Western Electric Company's Hawthorne Works. Researchers manipulated daily rest breaks during the study period and claimed after a visual inspection of the

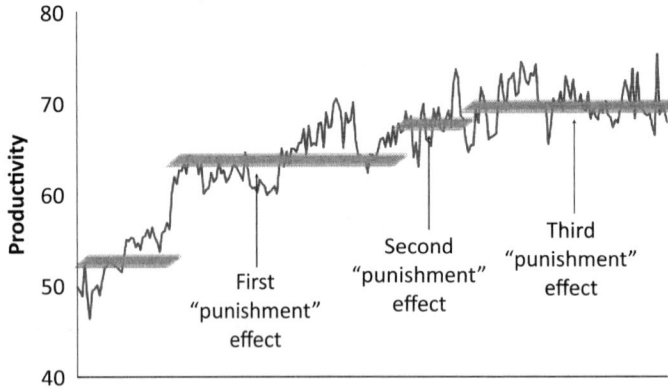

FIGURE 34.5.   Weekly productivity measures for the first bank wiring room (Hawthorne) experiment. Estimated interventions are plotted against the series. Data from Franke and Kaul (1978).

series that the breaks helped increase productivity. Questioning this conclusion, Franke and Kaul (1978) argued that any productivity increases were instead due solely to fear generated by the imposition of three "punishment regimes." Their statistical analysis, which included interventions at the beginning of each regime, supported this hypothesis.

Maturation provides an explanation that challenges the interpretations of both Franke and Kaul and the original researchers. Figure 34.5 shows the presence of a systematic trend in productivity that could easily have resulted from increases in worker experience. The trend closely follows the patterns that each set of researchers observed, and this makes maturation a plausible alternative explanation of their findings. A reanalysis that controlled for the trend in fact found a small effect of the rest breaks and no effect at all for the punishment regimes (McCleary, 2000).

Unlike other threats to internal validity, which are ordinarily handled by design, maturation threats are controlled by the statistical model. Under H_0, the causal effect of X_t vanishes, leaving a simple model that represents the time series as a weighted sum of past and present "white noise" innovations:

$$Z_t = \varphi(B)^{-1}\theta(B)a_t \qquad (34.14)$$

Proper solutions of this model are guaranteed by constraining the parameters of $\varphi(B)$ and $\theta(B)$ to the bounds of stationarity-invertibility.[4]

This assumes a stationary time series, however, and this assumption is unwarranted in most uncontrived instances. Kroeber's fashion time series (Figure 34.1), for example, shows the "drifting" pattern characteristic of a non-stationary random walk process. Segments of Kroeber's series are indistinguishable from the steady secular trend that poses the maturation threat in the Hawthorne experiment (Figure 34.5).

Although non-stationary time series are commonly encountered in the social sciences, most are stationary in first-differences. By convention, we use "∇" to denote $(1 - B)$, the differencing operator.

$$\nabla Y_t = Y_t - Y_{t-1} \qquad (34.15)$$

A non-stationary time series can be modeled as

$$\nabla Y_t = \varphi(B)^{-1}\theta(B)a_t$$

or

$$Y_t = \nabla^{-1}\varphi(B)^{-1}\theta(B)a_t \qquad (34.16)$$

Figure 34.6 plots the first differences of the Hawthorne experiment time series. The differenced series fluctuates around a constant level, and maturation is no longer a plausible threat to internal validity.[5]

In addition to controlling maturation threats, differencing removes the confounding effects of cross-sectional *fixed* causes of Y_t. To illustrate, suppose that Y_t is the U.S. unemployment rate and that W represents the causes of Y_t that vary cross-sectionally but that are constant over short periods of time. When consecutive observations of the model are differenced

$$Y_t - Y_{t-1} = N(a_t) - N(a_{t-1}) + W - W$$
$$\nabla Y_t = N(a_t) - N(a_{t-1}), \qquad (34.17)$$

the confounding effects of W vanish from the model.

Expressing this in its fully expanded form illustrates how differencing nullifies W:

$$\nabla Y_t = Y_t - Y_{t-1} = N(a_t) + W - (N(a_{t-1}) + W)$$
$$= N(a_t) - N(a_{t-1}) + W - W = N(a_t) - N(a_{t-1}) \qquad (34.18)$$

---

[4]Although the bounds of stationarity and invertibility are identical, they are distinct properties of the time series. See Box and Jenkins (1970, pp. 53–54). All modern time series software packages report parameter estimates that are constrained to the stationarity-invertibility bounds.

[5]The mean of the first-differenced time series is interpreted as the secular trend of Y_t.

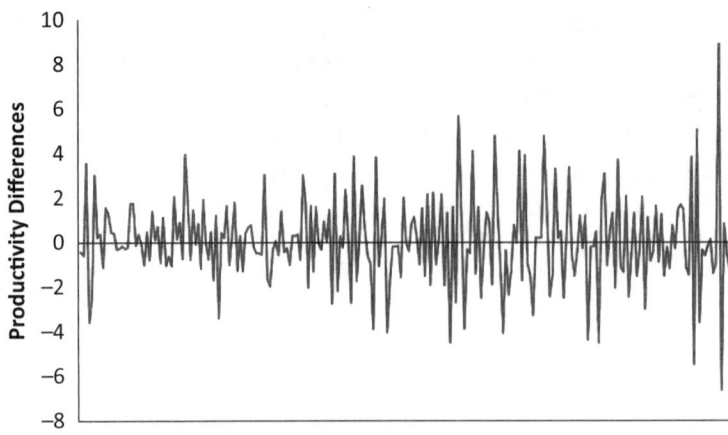

FIGURE 34.6. Weekly productivity measures from Figure 34.5, differenced.

This property of the difference equation model is the motivation for the use of fixed-effects panel models in economics (Greene, 2000). When differencing does not yield a stationary series, the best alternatives are design-based approaches utilizing control series as discussed above in the context of *history* threats and again below when we introduce synthetic control methods.

Like the maturation threat to internal validity, the regression threat is controlled by the statistical model. Whereas the maturation threat is plausible in both time series experiments and quasi-experiments, the regression threat is plausible only in quasi-experiments involving planned interventions. The regression threat arises whenever the intervention is a reaction to an unusually high or low level of the time series. Regardless of the intervention's effects, regression to the mean is likely to produce an increase or decrease in the series level.

In one of the earliest formal applications of the time series quasi-experiment, Campbell and Ross (1968) studied the impact of a 1955 speeding crackdown in Connecticut on highway fatalities. Traffic deaths dropped significantly after the crackdown began, but Campbell and Ross showed that the decrease was largely attributable to a regression artifact. Fatalities were unusually high in 1955, and the crackdown was a response intended to reduce them. A drop was then predictable, as deaths regressed back toward their historically average levels.

Regression becomes a less plausible threat to internal validity as the length of a time series increases. Introducing the intervention at an unusually high (or low) point in the series will create a transient bias in estimates of the pre- and postintervention means. As the pre- and postintervention series grow longer, the bias becomes proportionately smaller, and eventually it reaches zero. The recommendation to use a total series length of fifty or more observations for the time series quasi-experiment is in part intended to reduce the plausibility of regression threats (McCleary & Hay, 1980; McDowall et al., 1980).

Instrumentation is also a plausible threat to planned interventions because new methods for measuring the outcome variable often accompany the introduction of other changes. Figure 34.7 is from McCleary et al. (1982), and presents a monthly plot of Tucson burglary counts. For two years beginning in 1979, detectives replaced uniformed officers in performing burglary investigations. In 1981, the investigative responsibility was returned to the uniformed officers. Consistent with the notion that detectives are more proficient in preventing burglaries, the counts were lower when they handled the cases.

Although the switching intervention feature of the design effectively rules out history, all other internal validity threats are still plausible. Additional analysis showed that detectives and uniformed officers did not keep records in the same way, and this difference reduced the number of burglaries

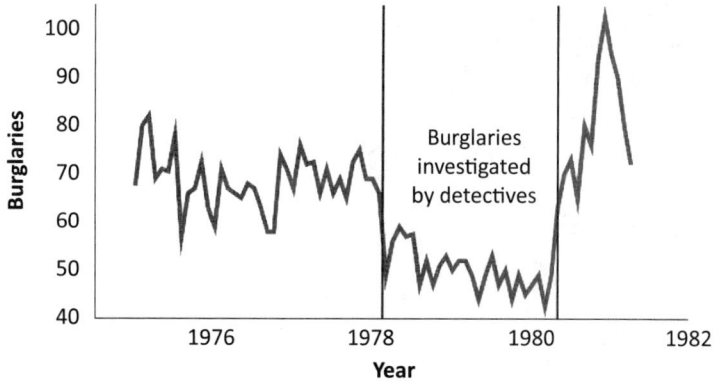

FIGURE 34.7. Monthly burglaries for Tucson, 1975 to 1981. During a 24-month period, burglaries are assigned to detectives for investigation. From "Uniform Crime Reports as Organizational Outcomes: Three Time Series Experiments," by R. McCleary, B. C. Nienstedt, and J. M. Erven, 1982, *Social Problems*, 29(4), pp. 361–372 (https://doi.org/10.2307/800025). Copyright 1982 by Oxford University Press. Reprinted with permission.

that the detectives recorded. Allowing for the influence of the instrumentation change, burglary counts did not vary significantly with the type of officer responsible for the investigations.

Construct Validity

Shadish et al. (2002) identified 14 "reasons why inferences about the constructs that characterize study operations may be incorrect" (p. 73). One of the 14 threats to construct validity, *novelty and disruption,* is relevant to experimental and quasi-experimental time series designs. Regardless of whether an intervention has its intended effect, the time series is likely to react or not react to the novelty or disruption associated with it. If the general form of the artifact is known, it can be incorporated into the statistical model.

Figure 34.8 illustrates one aspect of this threat to construct validity. Hall et al. (1971) counted the number of "talking out" disruptions in a classroom for twenty consecutive days. When a behavioral intervention is implemented on the 21st day, the daily time series changes gradually, falling to a lower daily level of disruptive "talking out." If the gradual nature of the response is not taken into account, the effectiveness of the intervention is underestimated. Since gradual responses to interventions are a common feature of behavioral

research, the uncontrolled threat to construct validity can have serious consequences.

Figure 34.9 illustrates the complementary aspect of this threat to construct validity. Similar to Figure 34.3, these data are daily counts series of self-injurious behavior incidents, but for a different patient (McCleary et al., 1999). Instead of receiving an opiate-blocker, beginning on the 26th day, this patient receives a placebo. The level of the time series drops immediately but then, within a few days, returns to its preintervention level. Placebo effects of this sort are common in time series experiments. Given a well-behaved time series process and sufficiently many postintervention observations, the threat to construct validity may be ignored. Under more realistic circumstances, however, the placebo effect must be incorporated into the analytical model.

Campbell and Stanley (1966, p. 43) recognized the threat to validity posed by a dynamic response to an intervention; still, their external validity assessment of the time series quasi-experiment seems to leave the issue open. Addressing the same threat from a modeling perspective, Box and Jenkins (1970; Box & Tiao, 1975) proposed a lagged polynomial parameterization of $h(X_t)$ that allows for hypothesis testing. The polynomial

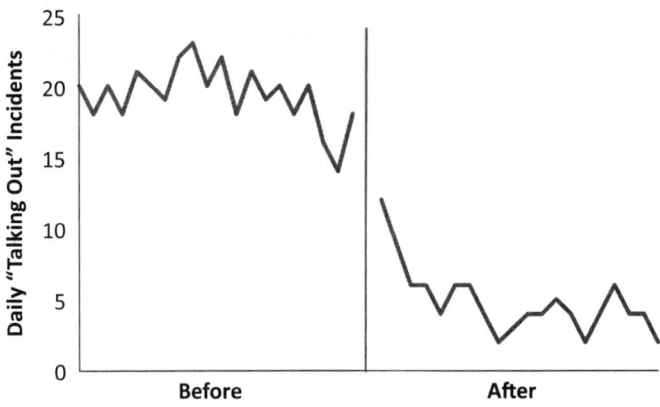

FIGURE 34.8. Daily disruptions caused by talking out before and after a behavioral intervention. Adapted from "The Teacher as Observer and Experimenter in the Modification of Disputing and Talking-Out Behaviors," by R. V. Hall, R. Fox, D. Willard, L. Goldsmith, M. Emerson, M. Owen, F. Davis, and E. Porcia, 1971, *Journal of Applied Behavior Analysis*, 4(2), p. 147 (https://doi.org/10.1901/jaba.1971.4-141). Copyright 1971 by John Wiley and Sons. Adapted with permission.

lag makes the linear ARIMA model inherently nonlinear, complicating the interpretation of analytic results. Using lag operators as predictors makes the ARIMA model nonlinear because the model's predictions are not linear functions of the coefficients, even though they are linear functions of the past data. The polynomial lag provides a straightforward method of controlling novelty and disruption threats to construct validity, however, and has become widely accepted in the social sciences.

Figure 34.10 shows four variations of the same general polynomial lag model. The model variations in the first row depict *permanent*

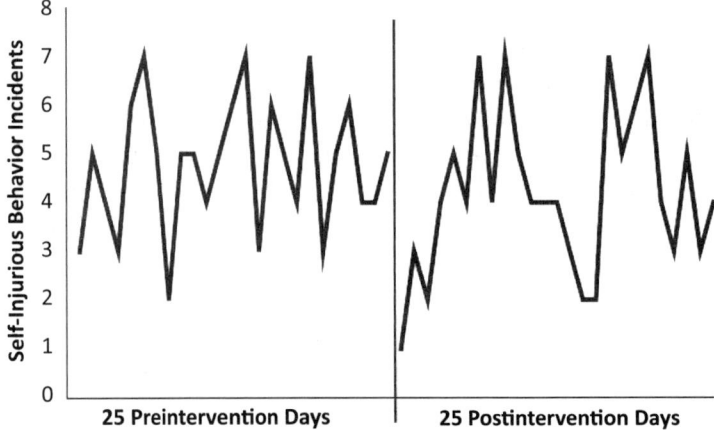

FIGURE 34.9.   Self-injurious behavior incidents for a single institutionalized patient before and after a placebo regimen. Adapted from *Contagious Models for Self-Injurious Behavior* [Poster presentation], by R. McCleary, P. Touchette, D. V. Taylor, and J. L. Barron, 1999, 32nd Annual Gatlinburg Conference on Research and Theory in Mental Retardation. Copyright 1999 by R. McCleary, P. Touchette, D. V. Taylor, and J. L. Barron. Adapted with permission.

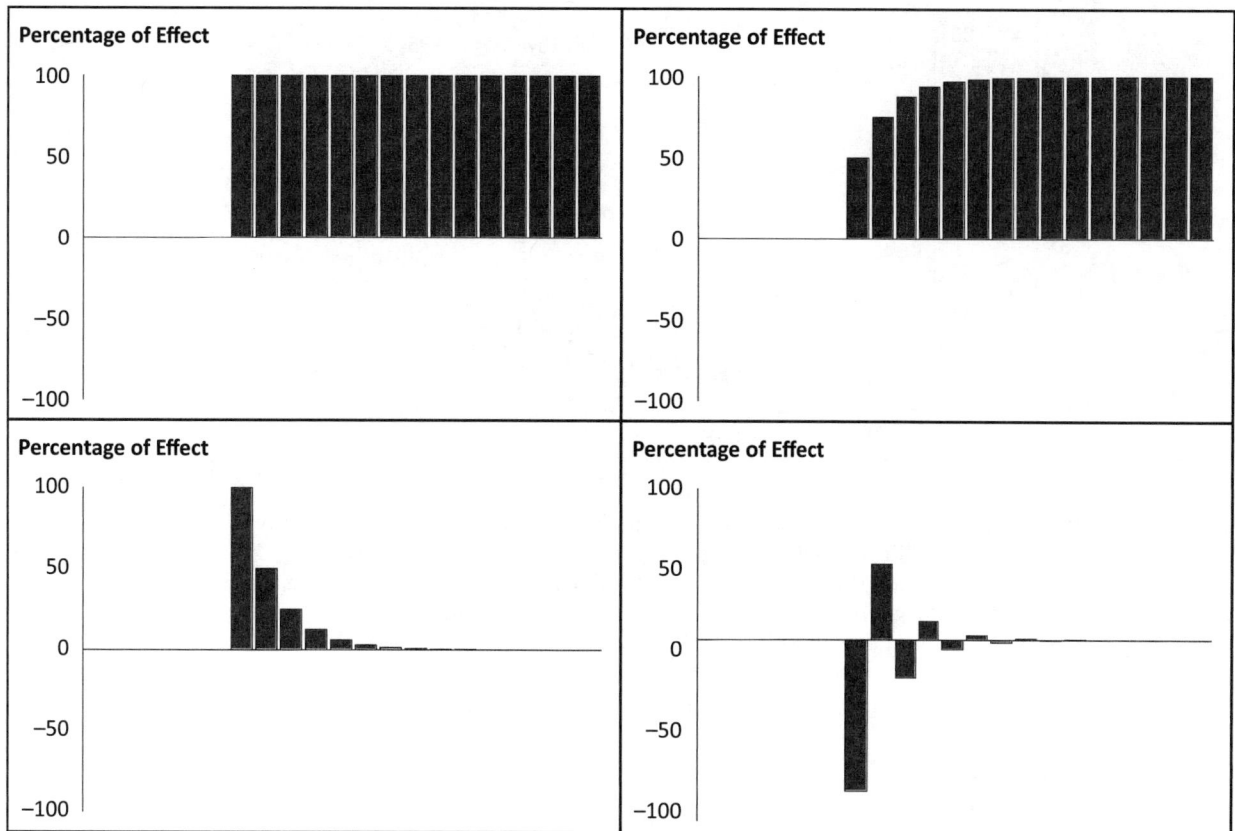

FIGURE 34.10. Model responses to an intervention. The top row illustrates permanent response patterns. The bottom row illustrates temporary response patterns.

responses to the intervention. The series may respond to the intervention *instantaneously* or *gradually* but, in either case, the response is permanent. A *gradual*, *permanent* response model seems to capture the effect of the behavioral intervention on the daily time series of disruptive "talking out" incidents (Figure 34.8).

The model variations in the second row of Figure 34.10 depict *temporary* responses to the intervention. Both responses model placebo artifacts, spiking at the onset of the intervention but then decaying over time to reveal the long-run effect of the intervention or treatment. The *gradual, temporary* response model seems to capture the effect of a placebo intervention on the daily time series of self-injurious behavior (Figure 34.9).

Permanent and temporary responses can be combined in a model. Figure 34.11 shows a time series of divorce rates for Australia before and after the 1975 Family Law Act, which allowed for no-fault divorce. Opponents of the Act

argued that its no-fault provisions would lead to an increase in divorces. An evaluation of the Act by the Australian government found that, while divorces did indeed rise following the Act, the divorce rate fell back to its pre-1975 level after 3 years. The fact that post-1975 divorce rates were higher was attributed to secular trend.

Reanalyzing these data, McCleary and Riggs (1982) hypothesized a complex response to the Act, realized as the sum of a permanent and a temporary increase in divorce. The temporary "spike" in divorces decayed rapidly in the years immediately following the 1975 Act. Divorces never returned to their pre-1975 level, however, and instead stabilized at a new higher level.

Whether or not they have permanent effects, new laws often have temporary effects that are well modeled as decaying spikes. Failure to allow for these temporary effects can lead to invalid inferences. At the individual level, placebo artifacts pose an analogous threat to

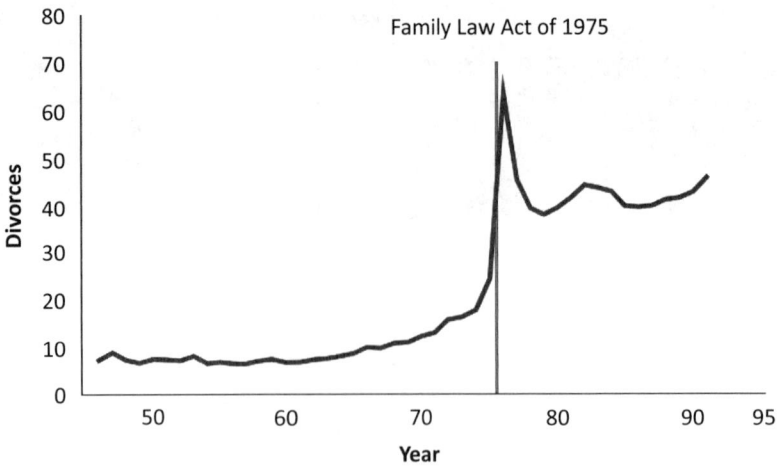

FIGURE 34.11. Australian divorces before and after the 1975 Family Law Act. From "The 1975 Australian Family Law Act: A Model for Assessing Legal Impacts," by R. McCleary and J. E. Riggs, 1982, *New Directions for Program Evaluation*, 1982(16), p. 11 (https://doi.org/10.1002/ev.1315). Copyright 1982 by John Wiley & Sons. Reprinted with permission.

construct validity. Although these threats are easily controlled with an explicit complex response model, by allowing the possibility of several possible responses, the model raises a potential threat to statistical conclusion validity: *fishing*. To control the fishing threat, the complex response model must be fully specified prior to exploring the data.

Finally, we return to the trade-off implicit in the four-validity system. In principle, all nine threats to internal validity can be controlled by manipulating the intervention or treatment experimentally. Internal validity is bought at the expense of construct validity, however, which may be more threatening in single-subject designs. Although the opiate-blocker regimen appears to reduce the self-injurious behavior, implementation of the regimen provokes a week-long reaction to the novelty and disruption. Since none of the common threats to internal validity seem plausible, trading construct for internal validity may be unwarranted.

External Validity

A time series quasi-experiment typically considers an intervention's influence on only one series, and this makes it highly vulnerable to external

validity threats. External validity considers whether findings hold "over variations in persons, settings, treatments, and outcomes" (Shadish et al., 2002, p. 83), and threats to it are always plausible when analyzing a single series. Ruling out external validity threats necessarily requires replicating the quasi-experiment over a diverse set of conditions.

The evaluation research literature shows many cases where effect estimates exist to support every possible conclusion about a program's impact. Evaluations of gun control policies, for example, include numerous instances of positive, negative, and null effect estimates (Reiss & Roth, 1993, pp. 255–287). In these situations, the variance of the effects across replications can be more informative than is a single point estimate of the average effect.

If several quasi-experimental replications exist, they allow external validity to be assessed in one of two ways. First, the set of individual time series can be assembled to form a single vector series, $\mathbf{Y}_t$:

$$\mathbf{Y}_t' = \left\{ Y_{1,t}, Y_{2,t}, \ldots, Y_{k,t} \right\} \tag{34.19}$$

A statistical analysis can then take advantage of the variation in the replications to obtain estimates of both the average impact and its expected variability (e.g., McGaw & McCleary, 1985). Second, an analysis can decompose the set of individual impact estimates

$$\boldsymbol{\omega}' = \{\omega_1, \omega_2, \ldots, \omega_k\} \qquad (34.20)$$

into components associated with various external validity threats.

The second approach is a restricted case of the first, and in theory, it is less desirable. Still, the first and more general model makes highly demanding assumptions, and time series often do not conform to them. Because the second approach places fewer requirements on the data, it is therefore generally more practical to apply. Statistical models for the second approach come from meta-analysis, and divide the effect variance into components due to the setting, intervention, and other potential threats to external validity. McDowall et al. (1992) used this approach to estimate the overall impact and variability of sentencing laws, and McCleary (2000) used it to combine estimates from the Hawthorne experiment.

DYNAMIC INTERVENTION ANALYSES

A salient advantage of time series designs over other before–after designs is the capability of modeling *dynamic* responses to the intervention. Proper specification of a dynamic response model, such as those shown in Figure 34.10, requires a parsimonious theory of the response. One theory that has proved useful in psychological research restricts the response to one of four types defined by dichotomizing *onset* and *duration*. The response may be *abrupt* or *gradual* in onset and *permanent* or *temporary* in duration. Although general transfer function specifications (Box & Jenkins, 1970; Box & Tiao, 1975) allow a wider range of responses, the four-type theory is more realistic for psychological interventions and more appropriate for testing intervention null hypotheses.

The "talking out" intervention plotted in Figure 34.8 is a typical *gradual, permanent* response to an intervention. Though implemented on the 21st day, the full effect of the intervention is not realized immediately but, rather, accumulates gradually over several days. If a time series model

is written as the sum of stochastic and intervention components,

$$Y_t = N(a_t) + X(I_t) \qquad (34.21)$$

The stochastic component plays no meaningful role in our explication of the intervention analysis. Procedures for building statistically adequate ARIMA models of $f(a_t)$ are described elsewhere (McCleary & Hay, 1980) but are of little interest here. Subtracting the stochastic component from the series,

$$Z_t = Y_t - N(a_t) = X(I_t) \qquad (34.22)$$

leaves the dynamic intervention component:

$$Z_t = X(I_t) \qquad (34.23)$$

The simplest dynamic model of a gradual, permanent response to X_t is

$$X(I_t) = X_{t\omega}(1 - \delta B)^{-1} \qquad (34.24)$$

where B is a backward lag operator defined such that

$$B^k X_t = X_{t-k} \text{ for any integer } k \qquad (34.25)$$

A Taylor series expansion of the right-hand side yields the more useful series identity:

$$\begin{aligned} Z_t &= X_{t\omega}(1 + \delta B + \delta^2 B^2 + \delta^3 B^3 + \ldots) \\ &= X_{t\omega} + \delta X_{t-1\omega} + \delta^2 X_{t-2\omega} + \delta^3 X_{t-3\omega} + \ldots \end{aligned} \qquad (34.26)$$

If X_t is defined as a binary variable such that

$X_t = 0$ for preintervention days $t = 1, \ldots, 20$

$X_t = 1$ for postintervention days $t = 21, \ldots, 40$
$$\qquad (34.27)$$

Prior to the intervention, $X_{t \leq 20} = 0$, so

$$Z_{t \leq 20} = 0 \qquad (34.28)$$

Thereafter, $X_{t > 20} = 1$. On the jth postintervention day,

$$Z_{20+j} = \omega + \delta\omega + \delta^2\omega + \ldots + \delta^{j-1}\omega \qquad (34.29)$$

Because δ is a fraction, δ^{j-1} is a very small number.

TABLE 34.2

Parameter Estimates for Dynamic Intervention Models

Gradual response, permanent change		Abrupt response, temporary change	
$g(Xt) = Xt\omega(1-\delta B) - 1$ Talking out (Figure 34.8)		$g(Xt) = (1-B)Xt\omega(1-\delta B) - 1$ Self-injurious behavior (Figure 34.9)	
$\omega = -6.79$	$t(\omega) = -6.81$	$\omega = -3.65$	$t(\omega) = -3.04$
$\delta = 0.56$	$t(\delta) = 8.48$	$\delta = 0.57$	$t(\delta) = 3.02$

Parameter estimates for the "talking out" time series are reported in the left-hand panel of Table 34.2.[6] Substituting the estimates of ω and δ into the series identity,

$$Z_{21} = -6.79(1) = -6.79$$

$$Z_{22} = -6.79(1+.56) = -10.59$$

$$Z_{23} = -6.79(1+.56+.31) = -12.72$$

$$Z_{24} = -6.79(1+.56+.31+.18) = -13.91$$

$$Z_{25} = -6.79(1+.56+.31+.18+.10) = -14.58 \tag{34.30}$$

Daily changes in "talking out" continue throughout the postintervention segment but reductions become smaller and smaller. Eventually, the effect will converge on

$$-6.79/(1-.56) = -15.43 \tag{34.31}$$

But by the end of the fifth postintervention day, 95% of this effect has been realized.

The self-injurious behavior time series in Figure 34.9 presents a typical *abrupt, temporary* response to an intervention which, in this case, is a placebo. On the first postintervention day, this patient's rate of self-injurious behavior drops abruptly, but then in subsequent days, returns to its preintervention level. The simplest dynamic model of an abrupt, temporary effect is

$$Z_t = \nabla X_t \omega (1-\delta B)^{-1} \tag{34.32}$$

This model has the series identity

$$Z_t = \nabla X_t \omega + \delta \nabla X_{t-1} \omega + \delta^2 \nabla X_{t-2} \omega + \delta^3 \nabla X_{t-3} \omega + \dots \tag{34.33}$$

Whereas X_t remains "on" throughout the post-intervention period, however, the first difference of X_t, ∇X_t, turns "on" in the first postintervention day and then turns "off" again.

$$\nabla X_t = 0 \text{ for days } t = 1, \dots, 25$$

$$\nabla X_t = 1 \text{ for } t = 26$$

$$\nabla X_t = 0 \text{ for days } t = 27, \dots, 50 \tag{34.34}$$

Prior to the intervention, $\nabla X_{t \leq 25} = 0$ and

$$Z_{t \leq 25} = 0 \tag{34.35}$$

On the first day of the intervention, $\nabla X_{26} = 1$, so

$$Z_{26} = \omega \tag{34.36}$$

But thereafter, $\nabla X_{t>26} = 0$ again and

$$Z_{26+j} = \delta^{j-1}\omega \tag{34.37}$$

Again, as $\omega\delta^{j-1}$ approaches zero, the placebo effect decays.

Parameter estimates for the placebo self-injurious behavior time series are reported in the right-hand panel of Table 34.2. Substituting the estimates of ω and δ into the series identity,

$$Z_{26} = -3.04$$

$$Z_{27} = -3.04(.57) = -1.73$$

$$Z_{28} = -3.04(.57)^2 = -0.99$$

$$Z_{29} = -3.04(.57)^3 = -0.56$$

$$Z_{30} = -3.04(.57)^4 = -0.32 \tag{34.38}$$

---

[6]Parameters estimated with the SCA Statistical System (Liu, 1999).

Ninety percent of the placebo effect has dissipated by end of the fifth postintervention day.

In either of these two dynamic models, the parameter δ determines the rate of postintervention change in the time series. Intervention null hypotheses can be devised around the value of δ to test properties of the response. While it is not possible to randomize the start times for interventions in many settings, it is worth noting the added value randomized start times would add to the inferences in the "talking out" and self-injurious behavior examples above. Namely, randomizing start times for interventions further justifies the assumption that treatment condition and response are independent.

INTO THE FUTURE

Looking forward, two additions to the repertoire of time series models and methods seem likely, and perhaps inevitable. The first relates to the conventional frequentist approach to null hypotheses testing, which has become controversial over the last few decades in the face of Bayesian alternatives. Bayesian hypothesis testing provide a simple method of updating the strength of our belief in H_A. Bayesian test results apply directly to H_A, moreover, and are not unduly influenced by the length of a time series. Classic Fisher and Neyman–Pearson tests and the modern "hybrid" test suffer by comparison. While it is unclear how soon conventional hypothesis testing will be replaced—most likely by Bayesian significance tests—it appears as though the Bayesian revolution is largely inevitable. However, we doubt this change will occur soon or end painlessly.

SYNTHETIC CONTROL METHODS

The second likely addition to the time series repertoire concerns the use of control time series to support causal inferences from nonexperimental designs. Control time series are chosen to render the threats to internal validity implausible. An *ideal* control time series is cointegrated with the treated series, co-moving up to the point of the intervention resembles the treated unit's time series in every way except the experience of the intervention. In other words, an ideal control series is similar to the treated unit's time series in every way except the experience of the intervention. The cointegrated relationship breaks at the point of the intervention. Following the intervention, the treated unit's time series reflects the impact of the intervention, and its ideal control series remains uncontaminated by treatment, providing an approximation of Rubin's (1974) unobservable counterfactual. The gap between the treated and ideal series that emerges following the intervention would be interpreted as the causal impact of the intervention on the outcome series. Comparing a treated unit's time series with its *ideal* control series fits nicely into Rubin's (1974) *potential outcomes* model as the unobservable counterfactual, provides a solution to Holland's (1986) "fundamental problem of causal inference" (p. 947), and neatly renders most of the threats to internal validity discussed above implausible.

The fact that appropriate control time series are not always available can pose an obstacle to causal interpretation. Given a collection of less-than-perfect control time series, however, it is sometimes possible to construct an approximation of the *ideal* control. The "synthetic control" methods associated with Abadie, Diamond and Hainmueller (2010, 2015) and Abadie and Gardeazabal (2003) are the most widely used methods at this point. In principle, control time series are chosen to render plausible threats to internal validity implausible. This assumes a theoretical understanding of the plausible threats and the availability of appropriate control time series. Sometimes, appropriate control time series do not exist. If a set of somewhat-less-than appropriate control series can be found, however, it might be possible to construct an ideal control time series from a collection of less-than-perfect control time series.

At this point, the "synthetic control" methods proposed by Abadie et al. (2010) are the most widely used methods for constructing a control time series. To illustrate these methods, we analyze the effects of Australia's 1996 "gun-buyback" program on age-adjusted homicides nationwide (Bartos, McCleary, et al., 2020).

To populate the "donor pool" of untreated nations from which Synthetic Australia will be constructed, we gathered homicide series for 28 untreated nations from the World Health Organization (WHO) national fatality database. Because none of the 28 nations enacted a similar firearms policy in the analysis timeframe, we ensure that the donor pool is uncontaminated by the treatment. As the synthetic control series will be constructed as a weighted average of the donor pool units, we can then be confident that Synthetic Australia does not reflect any treatment contamination.

Using a data-driven approach to predictor selection (McCleary et al., 2017), we construct a synthetic counterfactual control series (i.e., Australia had a 1996 buyback never occurred) for Australia's Age-adjusted homicide rate (we will refer to as Synthetic Australia. The gap between the treated and synthetic series that emerges following the intervention can be interpreted as the causal impact of the intervention on the outcome series. Causal interpretations are predicated upon the quality of the preintervention

fit between the treated and synthetic series, of course. The smaller the model's preintervention root mean squared prediction error (RMSPE) gets, the smaller intervention effects that can be identified (Bartos & Kubrin, 2018, p. 701).

Figure 34.12 plots Australia's age-adjusted homicide series against Synthetic Australia's series. Across the 30-year preintervention period, the two series track quite closely (RMSPE = 0.0239). Following the intervention, Australia's homicide time series reflects the impact of the gun-buyback program and begins to decline precipitously, while Synthetic Australia remains uncontaminated, providing an approximation of Rubin's (1974) unobservable counterfactual. Synthetic Australia had been declining leading up to the intervention and following 1996, the decline largely stabilized, declining only 10% in 1997–2007. Over that same 10-year postintervention span, Australia's actual age-adjusted homicide rate declined 54%. In order to assess whether the effect is likely to be spurious, a permutations test known as the in-sample or in-time placebo test must be performed. It involves iteratively reassigning

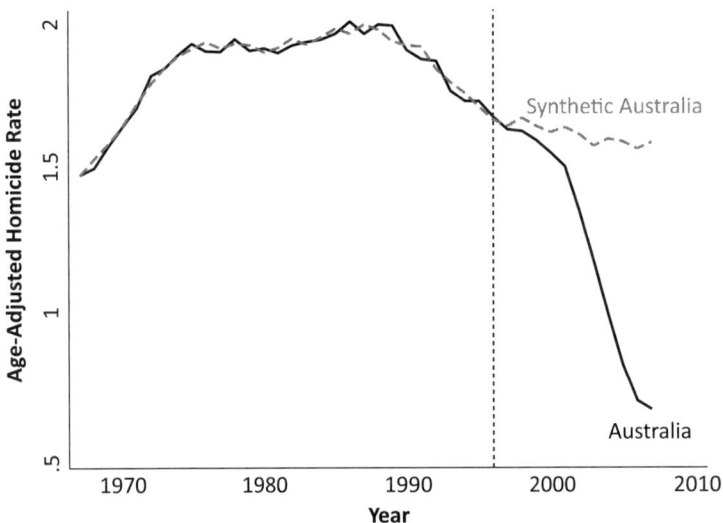

FIGURE 34.12. Synthetic Control Plot: Australia compared to Synthetic Australia age-adjusted homicide rates. From "Controlling Gun Violence: Assessing the Impact of Australia's Gun Buyback Program Using a Synthetic Control Group Experiment," by B. J. Bartos, R. McCleary, L. Mazerolle, & K. Luengen, 2020, *Prevention Science*, 21(1), p. 133 (https://doi.org/10.1007/s11121-019-01064-8). Copyright 2020 by Springer Nature. Reprinted with permission.

the treatment condition to donor pool units and ranking them based upon a ratio of the magnitude of the postintervention gap by the magnitude of the preintervention error. Another postestimation test must further be performed to determine whether the estimate is sensitive to changes in Synthetic Australia's composition. To assess this, we remove the nation that contributed the largest weight to Synthetic Australia from the donor pool and reconstruct Synthetic Australia. There is no established convention for how many exclusions a researcher must make. Some iteratively exclude each of the donors with non-zero weights until the synthetic control comprises an entirely new set of donors (Bartos, Newark, & McCleary, 2020); others push the leave one out test to failure (i.e., excluding the largest donor, reconstructing, and repeating, until the intervention effect finally breaks) taking the number of exclusions tolerated prior to failure as a measure of its robustness (Bartos & Kubrin, 2018, p. 707). But if the estimate remains stable once over 50% of the synthetic control's original composition has changed, researchers should be confident their estimated effect is not the by-product of a few influential donor units.

CONCLUSION

Time series data and time series designs have a long history in psychological research. Of the many uses of time series data, causal inferences from experiments and quasi-experiments are currently their widest application. Given a reasonably long time series, balanced data, and an adequate ARIMA model, the time series quasi-experiment is among the most useful and valid quasi-experimental designs. The design is also vulnerable to multiple threats to validity, of course, and one would normally not use it in situations where randomized controlled trials are possible. These cases aside, the time series quasi-experiment is a feasible and relatively strong design across a wide range of circumstances.

The advantages of the time series quasi-experiment are especially apparent in the absence of naturally defined control groups. To empha-

size this property, Campbell and Stanley (1966) cited the hypothetical example of a chemist who, dipping an iron bar into nitric acid, attributes the bar's loss of weight to the acid bath: "There may well have been 'control groups' of iron bars remaining on the shelf that lost no weight but the measurement and reporting of these weights would typically not be thought necessary or relevant" (p. 37).

Of course, there are causal attributions that can be made without the need to compare to a counterfactual control. Under counterfactual causality (aka the Neyman–Rubin causal model), the iron bar dipped in nitric acid almost certainly would not have become lighter had it not been exposed to nitric acid; however, as more complex treatments and less controlled settings replace both the acid bath and the lab, these assumptions must be tested and evidence gathered.

For readers interested in a more detailed unpacking of validity issues (a la Shadish et al., 2002) as they relate to time series designs and ITSA designs are directed to *Design and Analysis of Time Series Experiments* (McCleary et al., 2017). For those looking for a more applied approach to ITSA modeling, we recommend Interrupted Time Series Analysis (McDowall et al., 2019). For more information on Bayesian hypothesis testing, we direct readers to Ghosh et al. (2006), Krueger (2001), and Raftery (1995). For greater detail on the use of Bayes Factors, we recommend Kass and Raftery (1995). Readers interested in synthetic control designs are encouraged to refer to Abadie (2021), Abadie et al. (2010, 2015), and applications of the method mentioned at the close of the synthetic control methods section above.

For ITSA modeling and ARIMA construction, we use a standalone univariate time series package from Scientific Computing Associates. While the package affords the user complete control over the ARIMA modeling procedure, the lack of automation and aging interface make the package unfriendly to first-time users. Over time, SAS, R, Stata, and even Python have either added ARIMA modeling to their base software or have add-on packages available for ITSA modeling. For Bayesian modeling, R appears to be an early front-runner, but as Bayesian hypothesis testing becomes more popular, Stata, SAS, and Python will likely catch up. For synthetic control designs, the Stata "synth" package is the most user-friendly, while the R "synth" library affords the user an added degree of control (both packages were written by Jens Hainmueller).

The ITSA repertoire will continue to evolve. Future generations are likely to include versions of the two emerging topics developed in this chapter. Their inclusion will take varying amounts of time. Bayesian significance tests are likely to be included in the time series repertoire first and comparatively soon. The use of synthetic control designs will likely gradually accrue as a series of waves over decades. Although synthetic control designs are widely accepted, there are many aspects to construction and interpretation of results that are not yet formalized. As each weakness is brought to light, interest will wane; and as each weakness is resolved, a new wave of interest may launch.

References

Abadie, A. (2021). Using synthetic controls: Feasibility, data requirements, and methodological aspects. *Journal of Economic Literature, 59*(2), 391–425. https://doi.org/10.1257/jel.20191450

Abadie, A., Diamond, A., & Hainmueller, J. (2010). Synthetic control methods for comparative case studies: Estimating the effect of California's tobacco control program. *Journal of the American Statistical Association, 105*(490), 493–505. https://doi.org/10.1198/jasa.2009.ap08746

Abadie, A., Diamond, A., & Hainmueller, J. (2015). Comparative politics and the synthetic control method. *American Journal of Political Science, 59*(2), 495–510. https://doi.org/10.1111/ajps.12116

Abadie, A., & Gardeazabal, J. (2003). The economic costs of conflict: A case study of the Basque Country. *The American Economic Review, 93*(1), 113–132. https://doi.org/10.1257/000282803321455188

Bartos, B. J., & Kubrin, C. E. (2018). Can we downsize our prisons and jails without compromising public safety? Findings from California's Prop 47. *Criminology & Public Policy, 17*(3), 693–715. https://doi.org/10.1111/1745-9133.12378

Bartos, B. J., McCleary, R., Mazerolle, L., & Luengen, K. (2020). Controlling gun violence: Assessing the impact of Australia's gun buyback program using a synthetic control group experiment. *Prevention Science, 21*(1), 131–136. https://doi.org/10.1007/s11121-019-01064-8

Bartos, B. J., Newark, C., & McCleary, R. (2020). Marijuana medicalization and motor vehicle fatalities: A synthetic control group approach. *Journal of Experimental Criminology, 16*, 247–264. https://doi.org/10.1007/s11292-018-9345-3

Beveridge, W. H. (1922). Wheat prices and rainfall in western Europe. *Journal of the Royal Statistical Society, 85*(3), 412–475. https://doi.org/10.2307/2341183

Box, G. E. P., & Jenkins, G. M. (1970). *Time series analysis: Forecasting and control.* Holden-Day.

Box, G. E. P., & Tiao, G. C. (1975). Intervention analysis with applications to economic and environmental problems. *Journal of the American Statistical Association, 70*(349), 70–79. https://doi.org/10.1080/01621459.1975.10480264

Campbell, D. T. (1963). From description to experimentation: Interpreting trends as quasi-experiments. In C. W. Harris (Ed.), *Problems in measuring change* (pp. 212–243). University of Wisconsin Press.

Campbell, D. T., & Ross, H. L. (1968). The Connecticut crackdown on speeding: Time series data in quasi-experimental analysis. *Law & Society Review, 3*(1), 33–53. https://doi.org/10.2307/3052794

Campbell, D. T., & Stanley, J. C. (1966). *Experimental and quasi-experimental designs for research.* Rand McNally.

Chree, C. (1913). Some phenomena of sunspots and of terrestrial magnetism at Kew Observatory. *Philosophical Transactions of the Royal Society of London. Series A, Mathematical and Physical Sciences, 212*, 75–116.

Cohen, J. (1988). *Statistical power analysis for the behavioral sciences* (2nd ed.). L. E. Erlbaum Associates.

Cook, T. D., & Campbell, D. T. (1979). *Quasi-experimentation: Design and analysis issues for field settings.* Houghton Mifflin.

Dollard, J., Miller, N. E., Doob, L. W., Mowrer, O. H., & Sears, R. R. (1939). *Frustration and aggression.* Yale University Press. https://doi.org/10.1037/10022-000

Elton, C., & Nicholson, M. (1942). The ten-year cycle in numbers of the lynx in Canada. *Journal of Animal Ecology, 11*(2), 215–244. https://doi.org/10.2307/1358

Elton, C. S. (1924). Fluctuations in the numbers of animals: Their causes and effects. *British Journal of Experimental Biology, 2*(1), 119–163. https://doi.org/10.1242/jeb.2.1.119

Fisher, R. A. (1921). Studies in crop variation. I. An examination of the yield of dressed grain from Broadbalk. *The Journal of Agricultural Science, 11*(2), 107–135. https://doi.org/10.1017/S0021859600003750

Fisher, R. A. (1925). *Statistical methods for research workers*. Oliver and Boyd.

Florence, P. S. (1923). Recent researches in industrial fatigue. *The Economic Journal, 33*(130), 185–197. https://doi.org/10.2307/2222844

Franke, H. F., & Kaul, J. D. (1978). The Hawthorne experiments: First statistical interpretation. *American Sociological Review, 43*(5), 623–643. https://doi.org/10.2307/2094540

Ghosh, J. K., Delampady, M., & Samanta, T. (2006). *An introduction to Bayesian analysis: Theory and methods* (Vol. 725). Springer.

Glass, G. V., Willson, V. L., & Gottman, J. M. (1975). *Design and analysis of time series experiments*. Colorado Associated University Press.

Granger, C. W. J. (1969). Investigating causal relationships by econometric models and cross-spectral methods. *Econometrica, 37*(3), 424–438. https://doi.org/10.2307/1912791

Greene, W. H. (2000). *Econometric analysis* (4th ed.). Prentice-Hall.

Hall, R. V., Fox, R., Willard, D., Goldsmith, L., Emerson, M., Owen, M., Davis, F., & Porcia, E. (1971). The teacher as observer and experimenter in the modification of disputing and talking-out behaviors. *Journal of Applied Behavior Analysis, 4*(2), 141–149. https://doi.org/10.1901/jaba.1971.4-141

Hennigan, K. M., Del Rosario, M. L., Heath, L., Cook, T. D., Wharton, J. D., & Calder, B. J. (1982). Impact of the introduction of television on crime in the United States: Empirical findings and theoretical implications. *Journal of Personality and Social Psychology, 42*(3), 461–477. https://doi.org/10.1037/0022-3514.42.3.461

Hepworth, J. T., & West, S. G. (1988). Lynchings and the economy: A time-series reanalysis of Hovland and Sears. *Journal of Personality and Social Psychology, 55*(2), 239–247. https://doi.org/10.1037/0022-3514.55.2.239

Holland, P. W. (1986). Statistics and causal inference. *Journal of the American Statistical Association, 81*(396), 945–960. https://doi.org/10.1080/01621459.1986.10478354

Hovland, C. I., & Sears, R. R. (1940). Minor studies of aggression IV. Correlation of lynchings with economic indices. *The Journal of Psychology, 9*(2), 301–310. https://doi.org/10.1080/00223980.1940.9917696

Kass, R. E., & Raftery, A. E. (1995). Bayes factors. *Journal of the American Statistical Association, 90*(430), 773–795. https://doi.org/10.1080/01621459.1995.10476572

Kendall, M., & Stuart, A. (1979). *The advanced theory of statistics* (4th ed., Vol. 2). Charles Griffin.

Kroeber, A. L. (1919). On the principle of order in civilization as exemplified by changes of fashion. *American Anthropologist, 21*(3), 235–263. https://doi.org/10.1525/aa.1919.21.3.02a00010

Kroeber, A. L. (1969). *Configurations of cultural growth*. University of California Press.

Krueger, J. (2001). Null hypothesis significance testing. On the survival of a flawed method. *American Psychologist, 56*(1), 16–26. https://doi.org/10.1037/0003-066X.56.1.16

Lipsey, M. (1990). *Design sensitivity: Statistical power for experimental research*. SAGE.

Liu, L.-M. (1999). *Forecasting and time series analysis using the SCA statistical system*. Scientific Computing Associates.

McCleary, R. (2000). Evolution of the time series experiment. In L. Bickman (Ed.), *Research design: Donald Campbell's legacy* (pp. 215–234). SAGE.

McCleary, R., & Hay, R. A., Jr. (1980). *Applied time series analysis for the social sciences*. SAGE.

McCleary, R., McDowall, D., & Bartos, B. J. (2017). *Design and analysis of time series experiments*. Oxford University Press. https://doi.org/10.1093/oso/9780190661557.001.0001

McCleary, R., Nienstedt, B. C., & Erven, J. M. (1982). Uniform Crime Reports as organizational outcomes: Three time series experiments. *Social Problems, 29*(4), 361–372. https://doi.org/10.2307/800025

McCleary, R., & Riggs, J. E. (1982). The 1975 Australian Family Law Act: A model for assessing legal impacts. *New Directions for Program Evaluation, 1982*(16), 7–18. https://doi.org/10.1002/ev.1315

McCleary, R., Touchette, P., Taylor, D. V., & Barron, J. L. (1999). *Contagious models for self-injurious behavior* [Poster presentation]. 32nd Annual Gatlinburg Conference on Research and Theory in Mental Retardation, Charleston, SC, United States.

McDowall, D., Loftin, C., & Wiersema, B. (1992). A comparative study of the preventive effects of mandatory sentencing laws for gun crimes. *The Journal of Criminal Law & Criminology, 83*(2), 378–394. https://doi.org/10.2307/1143862

McDowall, D., McCleary, R., & Bartos, B. J. (2019). *Interrupted time series analysis*. Oxford University Press. https://doi.org/10.1093/oso/9780190943943.001.0001

McDowall, D., McCleary, R., Hay, R. A., Jr., & Medinger, E. E. (1980). *Interrupted time series analysis*. SAGE. https://doi.org/10.4135/9781412984607

McGaw, D. B., & McCleary, R. (1985). PAC spending, electioneering, and lobbying: A vector ARIMA time series analysis. *Polity, 17*(3), 574–585. https://doi.org/10.2307/3234659

Mills, T. C. (1991). *Time series techniques for economists*. Cambridge University Press.

Neyman, J., & Pearson, E. S. (1928). On the use and interpretation of certain test criteria for purposes of statistical inference. *Biometrika, 20A*, 175–240.

Raftery, A. E. (1995). Bayesian model selection in social research. *Sociological Methodology, 25*, 111–163. https://doi.org/10.2307/271063

Reiss, A. J., & Roth, J. A. (1993). *Understanding and preventing violence*. National Academy Press.

Richardson, J., & Kroeber, A. L. (1940). Three centuries of women's dress fashions: A quantitative analysis. *Anthropological Records, 5*, 111–153.

Roethlisberger, F., & Dickson, W. J. (1939). *Management and the worker*. Harvard University Press.

Rubin, D. B. (1974). Estimating causal effects of treatments in randomized and nonrandomized studies. *Journal of Educational Psychology, 66*(5), 688–701. https://doi.org/10.1037/h0037350

Shadish, W. R., Cook, T. D., & Campbell, D. T. (2002). *Experimental and quasi-experimental designs for generalized causal inference*. Houghton Mifflin.

Wolf, J. R. (1848). Nachrichten von der sternwarte in Berne. Sonnenflecken Beobachtungen [News from the observatory in Berne. Sunspot observations.]. *Mittheilungen der naturforschenden gesellschaft in Bern*, 169–173.

Yule, G. U. (1927). On a method of investigating periodicities in disturbed series with special reference to Wolfer's sunspot numbers. *Philosophical Transactions of the Royal Society of London. Series A, 226*, 267–298.

Part VII

DESIGNS IN NEUROPSYCHOLOGY AND BIOLOGICAL PSYCHOLOGY

NEUROPSYCHOLOGY

CHAPTER 35

CASE STUDIES IN NEUROPSYCHOLOGY

Randi C. Martin, Simon Fischer-Baum, and Corinne M. Pettigrew

The case study approach has a long history in the study of cognitive processes and their localization in the brain (Martin & Allen, 2012). A well-known example is Paul Broca's research on his patient Tan, nicknamed because of his inability to say anything but the word *tan* (Broca, 1861). An autopsy in the mid-1800s indicated that Broca's patient had damage to a region of the left frontal lobe, which Broca concluded was responsible for speech production. To this day, researchers refer to this left frontal area as "Broca's area." This chapter discusses how investigations of the behavioral deficits in individual patients can inform our understanding of the brain and cognition.

OBJECTIVES AND RELATION TO INFORMATION-PROCESSING APPROACH

Cognitive neuropsychological research has been used to support two independent objectives in psychological research (McCloskey, 2001; Miceli, 2000). The first objective is to gain insight into the functional organization of cognitive processes and the second is to determine the neural bases of these processes. Meeting the first objective involves understanding the cognitive breakdowns that result from brain damage and determining the implications of these deficits for models of the intact cognitive system. The information-processing approach to cognition serves as a foundation for cognitive neuropsychological research, as it does in cognitive psychology in general. The approach views cognitive processing from a computational point of view, such that several modules—or components—function together to contribute to a specific cognitive domain such as word retrieval (Fodor, 1983). Often, a given cognitive domain is visually represented by a model using a box-and-arrow diagram or connectionist network, and these models guide the testing and interpretation of results for a given case study. As an example, Figure 35.1a shows a box-and-arrow representation of the cognitive architecture assumed to underlie picture naming and Figure 35.1b shows a connectionist architecture (based on Dell & O'Seaghdha, 1992; Dell et al., 1997; N. Martin & Saffran, 1992; Martin et al., 1999). In Figure 35.1a, the boxes correspond to individual components that contribute to the system as a whole, such that separate boxes represent separate processing modules. Picture naming depends on visual representations of the features of the object which are used to access a semantic representation, which in turn is used to access a lexical representation, followed by a phonological representation which guides articulation. Figure 35.1b is similar but specifically depicts how the activation of semantic features leads to lexical activation of not only the

https://doi.org/10.1037/0000319-035
APA Handbook of Research Methods in Psychology, Second Edition: Vol. 2. Research Designs: Quantitative, Qualitative, Neuropsychological, and Biological, H. Cooper (Editor-in-Chief)

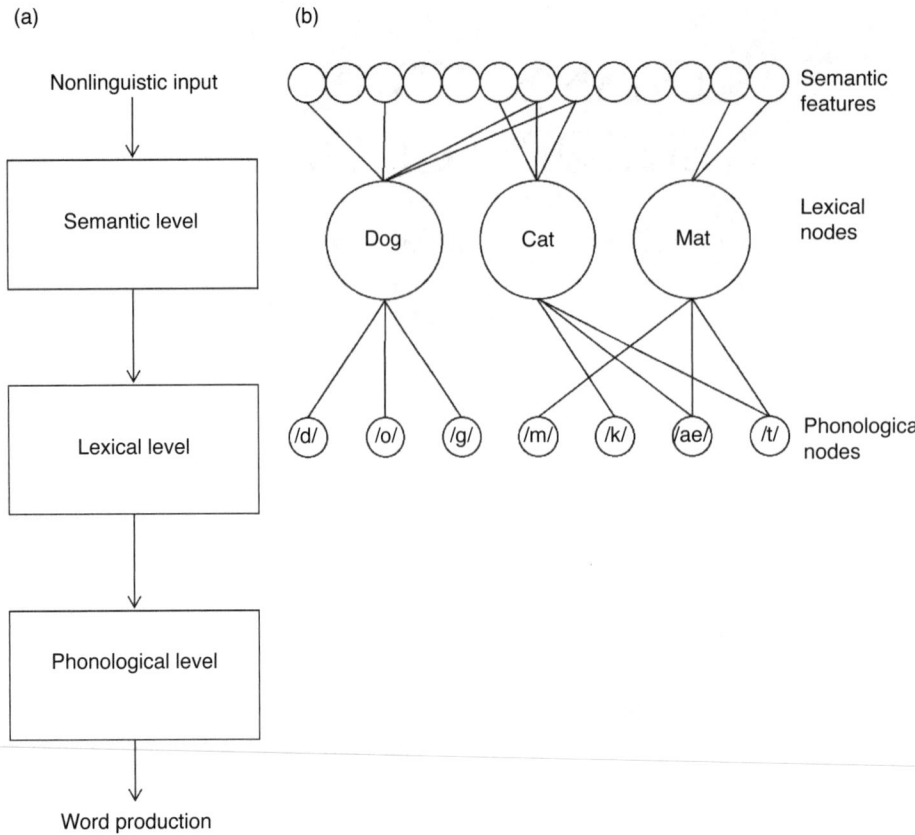

FIGURE 35.1. Examples of the visually represented cognitive architecture assumed to underlie picture naming: a box-and-arrow representation (a) and a connectionist architecture (b).

target but also words that are both semantically and phonologically related to the target. The semantic representation for *cat* leads to some activation of similar concepts (e.g., *dog, lion, tiger*). Activation of the lexical representation for *cat* leads to activation of the phonemes /k/, /ae/, and /t/. In Dell et al.'s (1997) model, there is also feedback from the phonological to the lexical level, which results in the activation of lexical representations for words sharing phonemes with the target (e.g., *mat* and *cap*).

A complex cognitive system such as that involved in picture naming, then, is represented by a theoretical cognitive architecture that describes the stages of information processing. These cognitive architectures, in turn, guide how we make sense of the case studies underlying cognitive impairment. While a disruption of any representation or any connections among them should lead to deficits—for example,

a disruption in semantic representations per se, or a disruption in accessing phonological representations from lexical representations should lead to a deficit in picture naming performance across a battery of tests, a careful analysis of the kinds of errors produced, and the investigation of which properties of the stimuli impact naming ability, can isolate the impairment to different components(s) of the system. For example, if a patient has disrupted semantic representations, then one should see a deficit in picture naming and also in semantic tasks involving words or pictures, for instance, in choosing a picture to match a spoken word. If the patient has a deficit in phonological retrieval but not in semantics, then performance on comprehension tasks should be preserved. The patient with semantic disruptions should also make primarily semantically related errors (e.g., producing *apple* for a picture of a banana), whereas the patient with a phonological retrieval deficit should produce primarily phonological errors (e.g., producing *banner* for a picture of a banana) or a circumlocution (e.g., "it's a kind of fruit . . . monkeys like it"). Finally, for the patient with semantic disruptions, the likelihood of correctly naming a picture should be influenced by semantic-level psycholinguistic variables, like imageability or semantic diversity, while, for the patient with phonological retrieval deficits, the likelihood of correctly naming a picture should be influenced by phonological-level psycholinguistic variables, like phonological neighborhood density. Typically, a combination of data—performance across a test battery, analysis of error types, and the impact of different psycholinguistic variables—are used to identify which aspects of the cognitive system are impaired in a given case.

Not only can models be used in the interpretation of deficits, but patient data can be used to test the assumptions of a model. If findings contradict assumptions of the model, then the researcher can propose changes in the model to accommodate the findings. For example, patient error data can be examined to determine whether the assumption of feedback between levels in the connectionist naming model (Foygel & Dell, 2000) is warranted. Based on an analysis of patient errors, Rapp and Goldrick (2000) concluded that a model with feedback from the phonological to the lexical level but not with feedback from the lexical to the semantic level best accommodated the data. Although much has been learned about the architectures proposed in Figures 35.1a and 35.1b through the study of neurotypical populations, much has been learned as well by studying patients who have disrupted naming (e.g., Foygel & Dell, 2000; Rapp & Goldrick, 2000; Ruml et al., 2000; Schwartz et al., 2006). As stated by McCloskey (2001), "complex systems often reveal their inner workings more clearly when they are malfunctioning, than when they are running smoothly" (p. 594).

Finally, thinking about cognitive impairments in terms of these architectural theories also has implications for the treatment of individuals with those impairments. Most clearly cognitive theories of underlying impairments can impact treatment programs. For instance, one might develop different remediation programs for word retrieval depending on whether the patient's deficit is at a phonological or semantic level (e.g., Drew & Thompson, 1999; Raymer et al., 1993; Wambaugh et al., 2001). Beyond this, treatment studies can also serve the objective of testing predictions about cognitive architectures, though they are less frequently used this way (Nickels et al., 2010). Cognitive architectures make predictions about treatment effects—for example, what kinds of generalizations, either across items or across tasks, should be observed from a treatment protocol. For example, Biedermann et al. (2002) used treatment to investigate how homophones are represented in the speech production architecture. Consider a word like "tank," which could mean an armored vehicle or an enclosure to hold fish. Theories differ as to whether homophones have one or two lexical representations. Biedermann and colleagues showed, when treating naming in patients with lexical retrieval deficits, treating one of the homophone's meanings led to generalization effects in naming the homophone from the untreated meaning, but not generalization to other untreated words. This pattern supports the theory in which homophones have a single lexical representation. It is typical to think of treatment as the applied outcome of the basic research of case study neuropsychology, but treatment can also be a tool to gain insights into underlying cognitive processes.

The second cognitive neuropsychological objective is to identify brain–behavior relations. The assumption is that the cognitive components in models such as those in Figure 35.1 are localized to specific brain regions, though components could span a network of areas through distant connections, rather than a single region. Using lesions, researchers can determine what regions of the brain are necessary for which aspect of task performance. For example, neuropsychological research played a large role in specifying the dual-stream theory of visual processing. According to this theory (Mishkin et al., 1983), the ventral, inferior temporal stream is involved in object identification (*what*), whereas the more dorsal, parietal stream is involved in spatial perception and visuomotor guidance (*where* or sometimes *how*; Goodale & Milner, 1992). Neuropsychological data from case studies were instrumental in establishing this distinction in the human visual system (e.g., Newcombe et al., 1987; Perenin & Vighetto, 1988). Patients who showed visual object agnosia, which consists of an inability to recognize visually presented objects (*what*), typically have temporal lobe damage, while those who showed optic ataxia, which involves an inability to reach toward objects and correctly orient one's hand during the reach (*how*), typically have parietal lobe damage.

It is rare, but not impossible, for lesion-based insights about brain–behavior mappings to come from the study of single cases. For example, Adolphs and colleagues (1994) reported selectively impaired emotional recognition in a single case of an individual with a bilateral calcified amygdala, providing key insights into the role of this brain region in emotional processing. Instead, it is more common for brain–behavior links to be made using a larger sample of patients, in part because lesions do not obey the functional organization of the cortex; lesions rarely completely damage a structure of interest and rarely damage only one cortical structure. It is more common for researchers to use imaging techniques, like voxel-based lesion symptom mapping (Bates et al., 2003), that rely on a series of cases—which vary in terms of underlying cognitive impairments and in terms of the location of brain damage—and examined associations between lesion location and cognitive impairment. For example, Schwartz and colleagues (2012) analyzed 106 cases of individuals with naming difficulties following stroke, with a specific interest in the relationship between semantic and phonological naming errors and the location of brain damage. Damage to the left middle temporal gyrus and anterior portions of the left inferior frontal gyri was associated with an increased tendency to produce semantic errors, whereas damage to the premotor cortex, pre- and postcentral gyri and supramarginal gyrus was associated with an increased tendency to produce phonological errors.

Analyses of the relationship between the location of brain damage and the impaired cognitive function need not focus on localizing functions to specific regions. An alternative assumes that cognitive functions emerge from the communication between regions, with cognitive impairments resulting due to disconnection (Geschwind, 1965). To address this hypothesis, researchers analyze the impact of brain damage on the white matter tracts that connect brain regions, rather than damage to the gray matter itself, and relate this kind of brain damage to changes in cognitive performance. For example, Harvey and Schnur (2015) related performance on accessing word meaning during comprehension and production for individuals with aphasia to white matter tracts connecting the anterior temporal lobe (ATL), argued to be a hub for semantic representations (Pobric et al., 2010), to anterior or posterior brain regions, after controlling for lesion volume. Significant correlations were obtained between comprehension performance and the integrity of the left inferior longitudinal fasciculus, a white matter tract that connects the left ATL with the posterior temporal lobe, and between word production performance and the integrity of the inferior frontal occipital fasciculus, a white matter tract that connects the ATL with both the frontal and occipital lobes.

ASSUMPTIONS IN THE COGNITIVE NEUROPSYCHOLOGICAL APPROACH

The two neuropsychological objectives have some basic underlying assumptions, which are critical to understanding how individual patient deficits can inform models of neurotypical cognitive processing. These assumptions have been discussed extensively elsewhere and will only be briefly summarized here (e.g., Caramazza, 1986; Coltheart, 2001; see also Shallice, 1988). First, the *modularity* assumption suggests that cognition can be decomposed into functional and anatomical modules. The use of the term *modular* would seem to imply an architecture like that shown in Figure 35.1a rather than that shown in Figure 35.1b. In the model in Figure 35.1a, a single lexical representation is selected based on the activated semantic information, and then this lexical representation is used to access a phonological representation (e.g., Levelt et al., 1991; Roelofs, 1992). On the other hand, in Figure 35.1b, the semantic representation activates several lexical representations that share semantic features with the target. These activated, nontarget representations send some degree of activation to phonological representations that are related to the target. The result of the continued influence of semantic information from nontargets on the activation of phonological representations leads to greater activation at the phonological level for word forms that share both phonological and semantic information with the target (leading to the production of so-called mixed errors— e.g., saying "rat" for "cat"). Thus, in a model with cascaded activation, the predicted pattern of errors may not be as tidy as in a discrete system with only one input and output for each processing level. However, even for models with spreading activation, like that in Figure 35.1b, different relative proportions of different types of errors can be predicted based on where the disruption in the model occurs (Dell et al., 1997; Foygel & Dell, 2000; Rapp & Goldrick, 2000). Thus, even though the models in Figures 35.1a and 35.1b differ in some ways, they both assume functional models with components that can be selectively affected by brain damage. Anatomical modularity assumes that functional modules are localized to specific regions of the brain. That is, it is possible that localized damage could impair a single, specific component of word production. If there were no functional or anatomical modularity, we would expect even localized damage to produce widespread cognitive effects. Most of the time, however, this is not the case: Damage from lesions, for example, produces deficits to specific aspects of a single cognitive system.

The second assumption—the *uniformity* assumption—maintains that a specific cognitive architecture is the same across people with similar developmental backgrounds. This assumption does not maintain that individuals are exactly the same, as there are obvious differences in background knowledge, intelligence, and so on (Miceli, 2000). Uniformity assumes that information-processing components are the same from person to person and that these components function in the same way across individuals. The uniformity assumption allows researchers to develop cognitive theories without having to hypothesize different architectures for every individual. In practice, this assumption is supported by the fact that specific deficits can be, and have been, replicated across individuals. Because architectures are hypothesized to be uniform across people, researchers can develop generalized cognitive theories.

The third and final assumption that is critical to neuropsychological research is *subtractivity*. This assumption asserts that neural dysfunction impairs or removes a component's functional role in the overall cognitive architecture, rather than adding new components. Brain damage results in a breakdown of the cognitive process by affecting at least one of the architecture's components, while leaving the remaining components intact. These intact components function normally, allowing researchers to make inferences about the function of individual modules based on patterns of both spared and impaired behavior. Although cognitive deficits might cause a patient to perform a task differently, because of strategy changes, the subtractivity assumption still holds— the patient's strategy is likely to be one that could also be used by neurally intact individuals (Vallar, 2000). For example, a patient with a deficit in holding onto phonological information in short-term memory (STM) might try to perform a digit span task by retaining the visual appearance of numbers rather than their names. Neurotypical subjects could show the same pattern under conditions in which phonological storage is disrupted by a secondary task, such as the articulation of irrelevant speech. The subtractivity assumption plays a large role in allowing researchers to use neuropsychological data to develop and test cognitive theories describing the organization of undamaged cognitive architectures. (For further discussion on the plausibility of these assumptions, see Vallar, 2000.)

For the first objective of cognitive neuro-psychology, the subtractivity assumption applies to cognitive modules, but it does not apply to localization. That is, damage to a portion of the brain used to support a particular cognitive function might result in nearby brain areas (or homologous regions in the contralateral hemisphere) taking over this function (though perhaps with less efficiency; e.g., Cramer & Bastings, 2000; Thulborn et al., 1999). The important point here is that the brain does not invent any new cognitive components as a result of brain damage, even though the localization of a particular function may change as a result of recovery from brain damage. For example, Baum and colleagues (2012) reported a patient with damage to the left hemisphere region thought to be critical for the audiovisual integration of speech but who showed no impairment in tasks that tap into that cognitive function, like the McGurk effect. Using fMRI, the authors demonstrated that this patient shows a robust response to McGurk stimuli in the right hemisphere homologue region, in striking contrast to a large control sample of neurotypical adults. The conclusion from these data is that the cognitive function of audiovisual integration during speech perception has not been changed following brain damage, but the neural locus of that function has shifted to the contralesional hemisphere as a result of neuroplasticity.

If new functions were developed as a result of brain damage, then it would be impossible to use the findings from patients to draw conclusions about the operation of the neurotypical cognitive system. Given the progress in learning about cognitive function through patient studies, the assumption that no new components are created seems justified. The issue of whether cognitive functions reorganize to different parts of brain after damage creates a larger issue for the second objective of cognitive neuropsychology, to map brain–behavior relations (see Fischer-Baum & Campana, 2017). If reorganization results in a shift of the function, for example to the right

hemisphere homologue, then lesion–symptom mapping techniques might fail to identify the left hemisphere region as being critical for this task.

METHODS OF TESTING IN THE CASE STUDY APPROACH

The single-case approach to cognitive neuro-psychology can be applied to either acquired or developmental deficits. Acquired deficits are the result of cerebrovascular accidents (e.g., stroke), neurological disease (e.g., Parkinson's disease, Alzheimer's disease), traumatic brain injury (e.g., head trauma in a car accident), and brain tumors. Developmental disorders are present from childhood and are not linked to the onset of a brain abnormality because of disease or injury. For example, children who have been given appropriate reading instruction but continue to have reading and spelling difficulties may be classified with developmental dyslexia, and typically, no lesion is evident in these children's brains. (This is not to say that there are no brain abnormalities present in these children. However, the deficits may be subtle, such as reduced density in white matter tracts connecting particular brain regions, and as yet uncovered.)

Preliminary Standardized Testing

Single-case studies typically use a combination of standardized neuropsychological testing and cognitive–experimental testing. Patients may first be given basic test batteries to screen their abilities and to determine in which domain their particular deficit lies (McCloskey, 2001). Standardized test batteries such as the Western Aphasia Battery (Kertesz, 1982) may be used, which has some advantage in that administration and scoring techniques are uniform across patients and testing sessions, allowing a comparison of results across research labs or clinical settings. The results of standardized instruments give researchers a general look at the patient's impaired and preserved abilities. Although these instruments have a good sensitivity for disorder detection, they are not good at specifying the specific cognitive modules that have been affected (Alexander, 2000).

For example, suppose that a test battery reveals that a patient has agrammatic speech (i.e., speech characterized by simplified grammatical structure and the omission of inflections and function words, such as prepositions and determiners). Such a finding would not indicate the source of the deficit, as it might result from any of the following: (a) difficulty accessing words or morphemes with little semantic representation (as for inflections or function words), (b) difficulty retrieving syntactic frames for production, or (c) difficulty producing phonological information for unstressed words or morphemes (which would include some inflections and function words). It is the job of the cognitive neuropsychologist to investigate these possibilities.

Testing in Specific Cognitive Domains

Following broad deficit classification, researchers investigate impaired and preserved behavior more specifically. This is typically done by assessing patients on a variety of tasks using testing methods from cognitive–experimental psychology. For example, the first author's lab is interested in the role of STM and executive function in language processing (e.g., Hamilton & Martin, 2007; Martin & He, 2004; Tan & Martin, 2018). Thus, we have a set of tasks assessing of a wide range of language and STM abilities, including (but not limited to) measures of input and output phonology (i.e., the phonology involved in perception and production), picture naming, semantic knowledge, vocabulary, single-word and sentence comprehension, sentence production, and executive function. For each cognitive function of interest, several measures are usually obtained to ensure confidence that the patient shows impairment on the underlying component. That is, poor performance on any one task might be due to extraneous factors such as distraction or fatigue, or to specific features of the task that are unrelated to the construct of interest. For example, a patient might do poorly on an STM task involving repetition of a word list because of difficulties in speech output rather than because of an STM deficit. Thus, one should also test the patient on STM tasks that do not involve output—such as a recognition task that involves judging whether a probe word was in a preceding list. Consistently poor performance on STM tasks irrespective of output modality provides converging evidence for a deficit in the cognitive construct of interest. In addition to characterizing the patient's deficits, it is important to also characterize the patient's preserved abilities to establish how disruption to the cognitive system gives rise to the observed symptoms. As one aspect of determining preserved abilities, it is essential to rule out the possibility that patient deficits are caused by peripheral dysfunctions (Heaton & Marcotte, 2000)—for example, one would not want to incorrectly attribute poor language production to a deficit in central aspects, such as lexical selection or syntactic formulation, when it actually results from a speech–motor impairment. Thus, assessments of peripheral motor abilities and visual and auditory acuity are important components of the testing protocol.

Precise Theory-Based Testing

Given initial findings about the source of a patient's deficit, researchers further assess patient abilities using tasks that help to decide among competing cognitive theories. The choice of tasks to include and their associated stimuli and scoring methodologies are all decisions that should be guided by relevant theory. Theoretical guidance does more than just support Hypothesis A—it also strengthens Hypothesis A by refuting Hypothesis B. Given that patients often have impairments to multiple cognitive components, utilization of a theoretical framework helps to determine which aspects of performance are relevant to the process of interest (Miceli, 2000). For example, suppose that we are interested in sentence comprehension and how an aphasic patient's comprehension difficulties increase as the complexity of sentences increases. Many hypotheses have been proposed regarding the source of such sentence comprehension deficits for patients showing good single-word comprehension (for reviews, see Martin, 2001; Martin et al., 2007), ranging from deficits in comprehending function words and inflections, to disruption of specific linguistic rules that are needed to understand certain complex constructions, to STM deficits, to difficulty resolving interference from competing syntactic and semantic analyses. For our patient of interest, we might find that he or she, like many aphasic patients, has reduced digit and word span (e.g., two items compared with a typical span of five or six items for healthy controls). The reduced span would be consistent with the notion that a STM deficit was a source of comprehension difficulty, as complex constructions would typically be long and involve integrating information across some distance in the sentence (e.g., linking *boy* as the object of *carried* and the subject of *had* in "The boy that the girl carried had red hair"). On the other hand, it is possible that the span deficit and comprehension deficit derive from different sources. Let us suppose that we wished to decide between the reduced span and interference hypotheses regarding the source of the sentence comprehension deficit. We might present sentences in which the distance between words that have to be integrated is kept constant in terms of the number of intervening content words but the degree of interference from semantic and syntactic features of the intervening material is varied. For example, we might assess reaction time and accuracy in answering comprehension questions, such as, "Will the jockey win?" following sentences like those in Table 35.1 in which "jockey" must be integrated with "will win," across an intervening clause. Following processing of "will win," comprehenders attempt to locate

a subject noun that is semantically plausible as the agent of "win." For the sentences with higher semantic interference, the intervening noun is a plausible agent of "win" (i.e., champion vs. record). For sentences with higher syntactic interference, the intervening noun is another subject (i.e., "the *record* was unbeatable") rather than an object (i.e., "challenged the unbeatable *record*").

In Tan and Martin's (2018) study using such materials, two of the nine brain damaged patients (ML and EV) showed greatly exaggerated effects of semantic (but not syntactic) interference relative to controls on question answering accuracy even though distance was matched across sentence types. Additionally, one of them (EV) performed at a control level on measures of STM tapping the retention of phonological information, although both performed poorly on measures tapping semantic STM. The results argue that these patients' sentence comprehension difficulties arise from impairments in resolving semantic interference, and not from a phonological STM impairment—though semantic STM may play a role, but not one related to the number of intervening items. (See the section on case series for further discussion.)

Neuropsychological data are rich and can be used to test theoretical questions in a variety of ways. For example, careful analysis of the specific errors produced by patients can help test subtle questions about cognitive representations and processes. For example, Fischer-Baum et al. (2010) investigated the nature of serial position representation in writing. Mental representations of written words contain, at a minimum, representations of the letters in a word and their order, and there are competing theories about how that order information is represented. For example, E in the word NEST could be represented as the second letter in the word or as the letter after the N. In the former, the position is defined by distance from the beginning of the word, and in the latter, the position is defined by the preceding letter. Initial testing of the two patients, LSS and CM, reported by Fischer-Baum et al. (2010) revealed that both had difficulties in selecting the correct letter identities

---

TABLE 35.1	

Examples of Sentences With High Versus Low Semantic and Syntactic Interference

LoSyn/LoSem	The jockey who had challenged the unbeatable record yesterday will win.
LoSyn/HiSem	The jockey who had challenged the unbeatable champion yesterday will win.
HiSyn/LoSem	The jockey who claimed that the record was unbeatable yesterday will win.
HiSyn/HiSem	The jockey who claimed that the champion was unbeatable yesterday will win.

Note. LoSyn = low syntactic; HiSyn = high syntactic; LoSem = low semantic; HiSem = high semantic.

when writing, frequently perseverating letters that had been produced in recent responses, for example, correctly writing the word "cat," followed by a trial in which "dog" was spelled as COG, with the C perseverating. These letter perseveration errors tended to appear in the same position in the two responses, allowing the authors to ask, position defined how? For both LSS and CM, there was clear evidence that letter perseverations specifically maintained position defined relative to either the beginning of the word or the end of the word, as had been proposed, but never directly tested, by some computational theories of writing (e.g., Houghton, 2018), as well as evidence against theories that posit alternative ways of representing order (e.g., Brown & Loosemore, 1994; Houghton & Zorzi, 2003). As above, cognitive neuropsychology tests competing cognitive theories that can be distinguished based on what kinds of performance might be expected in patients with specific underlying deficits.

Beyond the Single-Patient Approach

Although this chapter discusses the single-case study approach in neuropsychological research, research along these lines is not limited to single patients insofar as researchers can bring together the results from several single-case studies to speak to the same cognitive process. Use of multiple cases within the single-case approach can take different forms. One form is to demonstrate differences between individual cases. If, for example, a researcher has two patients with STM deficits, each patient's abilities can be thoroughly assessed. The ways in which their deficits diverge can provide details about the architecture of STM. For example, Martin and colleagues (e.g., Martin & He, 2004; Martin et al., 1994) have suggested that two types of STM deficits can be identified in patients with aphasia: some patients have a deficit in maintaining phonological information, whereas other patients have a deficit in maintaining lexical–semantic information. The two patient types differ in terms of the influence of phonological and semantic factors on their STM pattern. These distinct patterns across different

patients have provided evidence for a multiple capacity view of STM. Another form of multiple single-case research is to focus on the similarities across multiple case studies, reporting that the same pattern is observed in more than one patient. For example, Fischer-Baum et al. (2010) reported two patients who produced letter perseveration errors when writing to dictation. The fact that the analysis of errors from each patient supports the same theory is a form of replication that increases our confidence in the theoretical claims.

PATTERNS OF DEFICITS IN PATIENT DATA

Traditionally, there are thought to be three main data patterns that emerge from the single-case study and multiple single-patient approaches: associations, dissociations, and double dissociations.

Associations

Associations involve the co-occurrence of two or more deficits. For example, a patient with intact visual processing may demonstrate a deficit in object recognition that affects the recognition of objects and faces. In this case, a deficit in object recognition co-occurs with a deficit in face recognition, such that performance on each behavior is poor. Associations between behaviors may lead to the conclusion that a single cognitive module controls both object and face recognition, and disruption to this module results in a functional syndrome (or collection of symptoms; Vallar, 2000). If it does, then the association has theoretical implications.

Although a single cognitive architecture for all object processing is one interpretation, it is possible that the face–object association is caused by damage to two separate functional modules, one responsible for object recognition and another for face recognition. These modules may be localized in neurally proximal regions, which results in the frequent co-occurrence of object and face recognition deficits. In this case, the association has little implication for models of cognition.

797

Single Dissociation

In contrast to an association, a *dissociation* occurs when one cognitive process is selectively impaired whereas another is spared. In a single dissociation, a patient demonstrates impaired performance on Task A, which is thought to tap one cognitive module, coupled with intact performance on Task B, which is thought to tap a different cognitive module. The dissociation provides evidence that the cognitive modules are distinct. For example, the assumption that the same recognition module controls object and face recognition would be inconsistent with a patient who demonstrates a pattern of typical object recognition but impaired face recognition. In fact, this selective deficit in face recognition has been reported and is known as prosopagnosia (see Shallice, 1988, for discussion).

Although it is possible that the single dissociation occurs because of separate processing modules, differential difficulty could instead be the source—that is, Task A may simply be more difficult than Task B. For example, a dissociation between face and object recognition may occur because of separate processing modules, or because the complexity of facial stimuli and the overall similarity of faces may make face recognition a more difficult task than object recognition. If this possibility were in fact true, both object and face recognition processes would be impaired by more severe damage to the recognition module. However, McCloskey (2001) maintained that the complexity argument is often an implausible argument against claims of separate modules. Neuropsychological work can involve in-depth assessment that rules out such claims, for instance, by varying the difficulty of the discrimination required for face and object recognition to determine whether the dissociation still holds.

Double Dissociation

A third data pattern resulting from neuropsychological case studies is the *double dissociation*. A double dissociation is essentially two dissociations in opposite directions. A double dissociation occurs when Patient 1 demonstrates impaired performance on Task A but intact performance on Task B, whereas Patient 2 demonstrates the opposite pattern—intact performance on Task A but impaired performance on Task B. To continue with the object recognition example, double dissociations have been found between deficits in object and face processing, known as *visual–object agnosia* and *prosopagnosia*, respectively (see Shallice, 1988). Importantly, double dissociations rule out the possibility that the same module controls these two processes, but they dissociate because of differences in processing requirements. Instead, the fact that both recognition processes can be selectively damaged suggests that object and face recognition involve functionally and anatomically separate cognitive modules (cf. Grill-Spector et al., 2001; Kanwisher, 2000; but see Gauthier et al., 2000; Gauthier & Tarr, 1997, for an opposing view).[1]

Although the existence of double dissociations provides strong evidence for separate cognitive modules, in some domains, it will not be possible to observe a double dissociation. For instance, in the domain of picture naming, one can find patients with preserved semantic knowledge, as evidenced by performance on comprehension tests, who show impaired picture naming; however, one cannot find the reverse—impaired comprehension and preserved naming—as naming appears to be dependent on access to a semantic representation. Thus, double dissociations cannot be taken as the gold standard in all domains for establishing the existence of a cognitive component or set of components in a particular model. Different approaches can be taken to

[1]As a note of caution, Coltheart (2001) pointed out that researchers should be aware of the implications of the word "separate" when assuming that processes utilize separate processing modules. That is, although a double dissociation allows researchers to conclude that two cognitive systems involve separate processes, we must clarify what is meant by "separate." Specifically, double dissociations allow researchers to infer that the two processing systems are not identical. Coltheart pointed out, however, that these processes are not likely to be completely separate because they may still involve some overlapping processing components. For example, it is not unreasonable to assume that object and face recognition involve overlapping visual perception processes, even if the recognition processes are not identical. As such, double dissociations do not allow for the conclusion that two domains involve completely separate cognitive modules per se but rather that at least one module is unique to the individual processes.

provide solid supporting evidence for the existence of separate modules. For instance, one can make parametric variations in demands on a hypothesized component and show that the patients' performance varies in line with these demands for one component but not for another (as was described in the example manipulating semantic and syntactic interference in sentence comprehension materials; Tan & Martin, 2018). Showing that a patient demonstrates greatly exaggerated effects of semantic interference, but not syntactic interference, argues against a claim that resolving semantic interference is just more demanding of cognitive resources, given that healthy individuals show approximately equivalent effects of both manipulations (Tan et al., 2017) and some patients do show exaggerated effects of syntactic interference (Tan & Martin, 2018).

Moreover, simply demonstrating a dissociation or double dissociation does not reveal the inner workings of the hypothesized module. To do so, one can look at detailed patterns of performance, such as the frequency of different types of errors, in establishing more precisely the nature of the processing in the hypothesized model. For instance, the cascaded model of picture naming (Figure 35.1b) predicts that mixed errors (i.e., the production of errors that are both semantically and phonologically related to the target) should be greater than chance level. That is, if semantic relatedness did not affect phonological errors in naming, then the production of phonologically related words that were also semantically related (saying "rat" for "cat") should occur because of chance. If semantic relatedness does affect the production of phonologically related errors, then mixed errors should occur at a higher than chance level. If the mixed errors do occur as predicted, then this would support the theoretical inference that activation of semantically related lexical representations persists and influences phonological retrieval.

IDENTIFYING BEHAVIORAL DEFICITS

One issue that has not yet been discussed concerns how a patient's performance is characterized as impaired, as opposed to preserved. In other words, what is a deficit, and how is a deficit defined? In much neuropsychological work, the standard against which patient performance is assessed is the performance of neurologically intact controls matched on various demographic factors. Some cutoff point is used—such as the patient being outside the range of control performance, or less restrictively, scoring, for example, at the fifth percentile or below on a set of measures designed to assess a particular cognitive function. Standardized assessments tend to include norms from large samples of subjects across various age groups. Using these norms, cutoff points are established to determine what maximum score is needed for performance to be classified as unimpaired. Unfortunately, in the laboratory setting, it is not always possible to collect healthy control data on very large groups of subjects across many tasks. Instead, nonstandardized tasks require researchers to collect measures from demographically matched control groups. The performance of healthy, matched controls is used as a reference, from which deviation is measured. Crawford and Howell (1998) advocated a modified *t* test as appropriate for testing whether single cases differ from a control group, thus making it appropriate for neuropsychological research (see Crawford & Howell, 1998, for more details). Many times, it is also advisable to use proportional or log-transformed data when using reaction time measures (Verhaeghen & De Meersman, 1998). This is because a standard finding in studies of healthy adults is that those individuals with slower reaction times tend to show larger effects (e.g., they show bigger effects of word frequency on picture naming latencies). This pattern can be explained by assuming that for those with longer overall latencies, all cognitive processes have been slowed. Consequently, if a patient showed a large reaction time effect, this may reflect an overall slowing of all cognitive processes for the patient, instead of a disruption in a specific component. However, if the patient's reaction time effect remains outside of the control range after a log transformation of reaction times in each condition, this provides more solid evidence that a specific component has been disrupted.

SINGLE-CASE VERSUS GROUP STUDIES

This chapter has focused on the single-case study approach to cognitive neuropsychological research; however, an alternative is the group-study approach (Chapter 36, this volume). Some researchers have taken extreme views, arguing for one approach to the exclusion of the other (for two opposing arguments, see Caramazza, 1986 and Caramazza & McCloskey, 1988, vs. Robertson et al., 1993). Both approaches have a similar goal, which is to study patients with cognitive impairments in order to make inferences about cognitive architecture and its underlying neural substrate. As described, the single-case study approach involves an in-depth examination of a patient's abilities. The single-case study approach allows researchers to show that patient impairments rarely result from damage to a single component but instead result from a combination of several damaged components. Studying the specific deficits on a large variety of theoretically motivated tasks can eventually lead to hypotheses about the function of underlying damaged component(s).

The group approach assesses a collection of impaired individuals on various tasks of interest. Such patients are often grouped according to some criterion, such as clinical classification (e.g., Broca's vs. Wernicke's aphasia), symptom presence (reduced use of grammatical markers), neurological criteria (frontal vs. posterior brain damage), performance on experimental tasks (inability to comprehend syntactically complex sentences), or some combination of these criteria. Grouping along one criterion assumes that patients have homogenous damage to the same cognitive components (Miceli, 2000), but in fact these groupings do not guarantee that this is the case. For example, suppose that you are interested in understanding the source of agrammatic speech. Although such speech is frequently observed in patients who are classified as Broca's aphasics, this is not always the case. Thus, choosing a group of patients who are Broca's aphasics as assessed by performance on a standardized battery will not guarantee that the patients have the behavioral deficit of interest. Moreover, even if a patient group

is selected on the basis of having agrammatic speech, this will not guarantee that all have agrammatic speech for the same reason given there are different possible sources for this speech production pattern, as discussed. Additionally, it is unlikely that the differential source of impairment will be discovered when patient performance is averaged across individuals, as specific impairments may be wiped out in averages, concealing this potentially informative information. Lastly, grouping patients by lesion location only ensures that you are investigating patients with damage to similar brain regions— it does not control for the similarity of symptoms. Thus, no matter how grouping is done, it is unlikely that group studies will be composed of patients with identical spared and impaired cognitive components. Although it has often been argued that large samples are representative of the neurotypical population, this is not necessarily the case in patient group studies. In fact, Caramazza (1986) argued that you can only appropriately group patients together after each has received extensive testing to determine the exact nature of their deficit in terms of the underlying cognitive architecture, at which point you will have completed several single-case studies and grouping seems redundant. These factors need to be taken into consideration when selecting patients for inclusion in group studies, given patient selection issues in group studies are difficult to overcome.

Although there are limitations to group studies, they are not without their benefits (for further discussion, see Chapter 36, this volume). Group studies are particularly beneficial when studying a domain in which cognitive theory is not well developed and associated cognitive impairments are not yet known or understood (Caramazza & Coltheart, 2006; Coltheart, 2001). In this context, group studies allow for a preliminary understanding of patient deficits and the development of theoretically motivated modular components.

Falling between the single-case approach and the group study approach are case series (Schwartz & Dell, 2010). In this approach, larger cohorts of patients are studied, but characterized at an individual level, rather than grouped together. The goal is often to analyze the patterns of association between tasks across the patients, specifically to test questions about whether two tasks rely on a common cognitive component. For example, Dial and Martin (2017) reported a cohort of 13 patients with aphasia who were administered a carefully controlled set of tasks designed to tap into different aspects of speech perception, including sublexical tasks like syllable discrimination and lexical tasks like picture-word matching. Previous work suggested that lexical and sublexical aspects of speech perception dissociate (e.g., Miceli et al., 1980), though the materials in previous studies were not well controlled. This dissociation has informed some prominent theories of speech perception, which have assumed that lexical processing can occur independently of sublexical processing, with direct access to lexical phonological representations from acoustic input (e.g., Hickok & Poeppel, 2007). The patients reported in Dial and Martin had a wide range of performance on both lexical and sublexical tasks, but critically there was a strong correlation in performance between these two kinds of tasks, with no participants showing evidence of better performance on lexical than sublexical processing. This association across participants, paired with a failure to find dissociations between any individuals in the case series, supports the view that lexical processing in speech perception depends on sublexical processing. Also, the study by Tan and Martin (2018) on semantic and syntactic interference resolution in sentence comprehension examined the performance of nine brain-damaged patients and showed that a measure of STM tapping the retention semantic information was highly correlated with the ability to resolve semantic but not syntactic interference, whereas a measure of phonological STM was unrelated to either semantic or syntactic interference. Thus, this study provided evidence supporting previous claims that STM for semantic but not phonological information is critical for sentence comprehension (see also Martin & He, 2004; Tan et al., 2017). Case series research also allows for techniques like voxel-based lesion-symptom

mapping, described previously, which relate task performance in a series of patients to the presence or absence of brain damage, and generally allow the use of statistical approaches, such as correlational measures and analyses of covariance, to control for nonrelevant factors (e.g., Martin et al., 2021).

The single-case study approach is not without its criticisms. Given "each patient may be as unique as a snowflake" (Buxbaum, 2006, p. 194), how can you replicate a finding in another patient? A related problem is that particular deficits may be exceedingly rare. As Coltheart (2001) argued, however, rarity does not make the patient findings any less applicable to cognitive theorizing. Assuming that the data have been collected in a thorough, well-controlled, and theoretically motivated fashion and that alternative theoretical explanations have been ruled out, then the findings would still be considered valid. However, researchers are likely to be more confident about the conclusions drawn from the case if replication does occur. If only one case is ever reported, one might conclude that the individual had some unusual brain organization or that chance factors led to the particular constellation of impaired and spared function observed for that patient. What is often true, however, is that once the findings for an individual patient have been published, other labs around the world start looking for similar patients, and additional cases are uncovered. Thus, replication occurs over time. Additionally, between-patient replication is possible using patients with similar impairments— although the impairments of these additional patients may not have exactly the same character, they serve as a source of converging evidence that provides support for or challenges the same theories. Miceli (2000) pointed out that replication can occur at two levels. It is much less difficult to get replication at the general level, such as finding a patient with a particular deficit. For example, many patients have demonstrated deficits in phonological STM (e.g., Martin et al., 1994; Vallar & Papagno, 2002). This pattern of general replication, however, does not guarantee detailed replication. That is, the fact that these patients exhibit a similar behavioral pattern of phonological STM deficits does not guarantee that they will all show similar impairments across other cognitive tasks, such as sentence comprehension and word repetition. In contrast to general replication, this sort of detailed replication requires that patients exhibit the same patterns of behavior across all domains.

Although it might be difficult to find another patient to provide detailed replication of a previous finding, converging evidence also plays a strong role in supporting the implications for cognitive theories that are drawn from individual cases. The findings from an individual case can lead to the proposal or revision of a cognitive model. The proposed model will lead to predictions that either are or are not borne out by further patients, whether or not they provide an exact replication of a previous case. In other words, the findings from one patient may lead to modification of a theory, which may then predict the existence of another data pattern in a different type of patient—which might then be looked for and reported. In addition, inferences to cognitive theory are not limited to neuropsychological data; researchers can find support through other methods in cognitive psychology. Support for a given hypothesis or a specific theoretical breakdown of cognitive components should also include behavioral research or neuroimaging findings with neurally intact individuals, as well as computational modeling to accommodate findings from brain damaged and healthy individuals.

CONCLUSION

The case study approach in cognitive neuropsychology aims to use the data from patients with brain damage to inform theories of neurotypical cognition. In this approach, a detailed assessment of the patient's performance is obtained to determine the areas of impaired and spared functioning. Multiple measures are obtained for each hypothesized component to provide converging evidence that the component is spared or impaired. Theory within a domain is used to guide the use and development of behavioral tests. The findings may provide support for one theory over others or challenge all existing theories.

The case study approach is also often used in comparing multiple cases in which different patients show a disruption of different components of a cognitive process. Finally, the case study approach avoids problems associated with a lack of homogeneity across patients when they are grouped on the basis of a clinical syndrome, lesion localization, or other dimension. A group study approach may be preferred, however, when investigating a new domain in which there is little theoretical guidance, when patients with pure deficits are exceedingly rare, or when a correlational approach may be advantageous.

References

Adolphs, R., Tranel, D., Damasio, H., & Damasio, A. (1994). Impaired recognition of emotion in facial expressions following bilateral damage to the human amygdala. *Nature, 372*(6507), 669–672. https://doi.org/10.1038/372669a0

Alexander, M. P. (2000). The clinical evaluation of mental status. In F. Boller & J. Grafman (Eds.), *Handbook of neuropsychology* (Vol. 1, pp. 3–25). Elsevier.

Bates, E., Wilson, S. M., Saygin, A. P., Dick, F., Sereno, M. I., Knight, R. T., & Dronkers, N. F. (2003). Voxel-based lesion-symptom mapping. *Nature Neuroscience, 6*(5), 448–450. https://doi.org/10.1038/nn1050

Baum, S. H., Martin, R. C., Hamilton, A. C., & Beauchamp, M. S. (2012). Multisensory speech perception without the left superior temporal sulcus. *NeuroImage, 62*(3), 1825–1832. https://doi.org/10.1016/j.neuroimage.2012.05.034

Biedermann, B., Blanken, G., & Nickels, L. (2002). The representation of homophones: Evidence from remediation. *Aphasiology, 16*(10-11), 1115–1136. https://doi.org/10.1080/02687030244000545

Broca, P. (1861). Perte de la parole, ramollissement chronique et destruction partielle du lobe antérieur gauche du cerveau [Loss of speech, chronic softening and partial destruction of the left anterior lobe of the brain]. *Bulletin de la Société Anthropologique, 2,* 235–238.

Brown, G. D. A., & Loosemore, R. P. W. (1994). Computational approaches to normal and impaired spelling. In G. D. A Brown & N. C. Ellis (Eds.), *Handbook of spelling: Theory, process and intervention.* Wiley.

Buxbaum, L. J. (2006). On the right (and left) track: Twenty years of progress in studying hemispatial neglect. *Cognitive Neuropsychology, 23*(1), 184–201. https://doi.org/10.1080/02643290500202698

Caramazza, A. (1986). On drawing inferences about the structure of normal cognitive systems from the analysis of patterns of impaired performance: The case for single-patient studies. *Brain and Cognition, 5*(1), 41–66. https://doi.org/10.1016/0278-2626(86)90061-8

Caramazza, A., & Coltheart, M. (2006). Cognitive Neuropsychology twenty years on. *Cognitive Neuropsychology, 23*(1), 3–12. https://doi.org/10.1080/02643290500443250

Caramazza, A., & McCloskey, M. (1988). The case for single-patient studies. *Cognitive Neuropsychology, 5*(5), 517–527. https://doi.org/10.1080/02643298808253271

Coltheart, M. (2001). Assumptions and methods in Cognitive Neuropsychology. In B. Rapp (Ed.), *The handbook of cognitive neuropsychology: What deficits reveal about the human mind* (pp. 3–21). Psychology Press.

Cramer, S. C., & Bastings, E. P. (2000). Mapping clinically relevant plasticity after stroke. *Neuropharmacology, 39*(5), 842–851. https://doi.org/10.1016/S0028-3908(99)00258-0

Crawford, J. R., & Howell, D. C. (1998). Comparing an individual's test score against norms derived from small samples. *The Clinical Neuropsychologist, 12*(4), 482–486. https://doi.org/10.1076/clin.12.4.482.7241

Dell, G. S., & O'Seaghdha, P. G. (1992). Stages of lexical access in language production. *Cognition, 42*(1–3), 287–314. https://doi.org/10.1016/0010-0277(92)90046-K

Dell, G. S., Schwartz, M. F., Martin, N., Saffran, E. M., & Gagnon, D. A. (1997). Lexical access in aphasic and nonaphasic speakers. *Psychological Review, 104*(4), 801–838. https://doi.org/10.1037/0033-295X.104.4.801

Dial, H., & Martin, R. (2017). Evaluating the relationship between sublexical and lexical processing in speech perception: Evidence from aphasia. *Neuropsychologia, 96*, 192–212. https://doi.org/10.1016/j.neuropsychologia.2017.01.009

Drew, R. L., & Thompson, C. K. (1999). Model-based semantic treatment for naming deficits in aphasia. *Journal of Speech, Language, and Hearing Research, 42*(4), 972–989. https://doi.org/10.1044/jslhr.4204.972

Fischer-Baum, S., & Campana, G. (2017). Neuroplasticity and the logic of cognitive neuropsychology. *Cognitive Neuropsychology, 34*(7-8), 403–411. https://doi.org/10.1080/02643294.2017.1389707

Fischer-Baum, S., McCloskey, M., & Rapp, B. (2010). Representation of letter position in spelling: Evidence from acquired dysgraphia. *Cognition,* 115(3), 466–490. https://doi.org/10.1016/j.cognition.2010.03.013

Fodor, J. A. (1983). *The modularity of mind.* MIT Press. https://doi.org/10.7551/mitpress/4737.001.0001

Foygel, D., & Dell, G. S. (2000). Models of impaired lexical access in speech production. *Journal of Memory and Language, 43*(2), 182–216. https://doi.org/10.1006/jmla.2000.2716

Gauthier, I., Skudlarski, P., Gore, J. C., & Anderson, A. W. (2000). Expertise for cars and birds recruits brain areas involved in face recognition. *Nature Neuroscience, 3*(2), 191–197. https://doi.org/10.1038/72140

Gauthier, I., & Tarr, M. J. (1997). Becoming a "Greeble" expert: Exploring mechanisms for face recognition. *Vision Research, 37*(12), 1673–1682. https://doi.org/10.1016/S0042-6989(96)00286-6

Geschwind, N. (1965). Disconnexion syndromes in animals and man. II. *Brain: A Journal of Neurology, 88*(3), 585–644. https://doi.org/10.1093/brain/88.3.585

Goodale, M. A., & Milner, A. D. (1992). Separate visual pathways for perception and action. *Trends in Neurosciences, 15*, 20–25. https://doi.org/10.1016/0166-2236(92)90344-8

Grill-Spector, K., Kourtzi, Z., & Kanwisher, N. (2001). The lateral occipital complex and its role in object recognition. *Vision Research, 41*(10-11), 1409–1422. https://doi.org/10.1016/S0042-6989(01)00073-6

Hamilton, A. C., & Martin, R. C. (2007). Proactive interference in a semantic short-term memory deficit: Role of semantic and phonological relatedness. *Cortex, 43*(1), 112–123. https://doi.org/10.1016/S0010-9452(08)70449-0

Harvey, D. Y., & Schnur, T. T. (2015). Distinct loci of lexical and semantic access deficits in aphasia: Evidence from voxel-based lesion-symptom mapping and diffusion tensor imaging. *Cortex, 67*, 37–58. https://doi.org/10.1016/j.cortex.2015.03.004

Heaton, R. K., & Marcotte, T. D. (2000). Clinical neuropsychological tests and assessment techniques. In F. Boller & J. Grafman (Eds.), *Handbook of neuropsychology* (Vol. 1, pp. 27–52). Elsevier.

Hickok, G., & Poeppel, D. (2007). The cortical organization of speech processing. *Nature Reviews Neuroscience, 8*(5), 393–402. https://doi.org/10.1038/nrn2113

Houghton, G. (2018). Action and perception in literacy: A common-code for spelling and reading. *Psychological Review, 125*(1), 83–116. https://doi.org/10.1037/rev0000084

Houghton, G., & Zorzi, M. (2003). Normal and impaired spelling in a connectionist dual-route architecture. *Cognitive Neuropsychology, 20*(2), 115–162. https://doi.org/10.1080/02643290242000871

Kanwisher, N. (2000). Domain specificity in face perception. *Nature Neuroscience, 3*(8), 759–763. https://doi.org/10.1038/77664

Kertesz, A. (1982). *Western aphasia battery*. Grune Stratton.

Levelt, W. J. M., Schriefers, H., Vorberg, D., Meyer, A. S., Pechmann, T., & Havinga, J. (1991). The time course of lexical access in speech production: A study of picture naming. *Psychological Review, 98*(1), 122–142. https://doi.org/10.1037/0033-295X.98.1.122

Martin, N., & Saffran, E. M. (1992). A computational account of deep dysphasia: Evidence from a single case study. *Brain and Language, 43*(2), 240–274. https://doi.org/10.1016/0093-934X(92)90130-7

Martin, R. C. (2001). Sentence comprehension deficits. In B. Rapp (Ed.), *The handbook of cognitive neuropsychology: What deficits reveal about the human mind* (pp. 349–374). Psychology Press.

Martin, R. C., & Allen, C. M. (2012). Case studies in neuropsychology. In H. Cooper, P. M. Camic, D. L. Long, A. T. Panter, D. Rindskopf, & K. J. Sher (Eds.), *APA handbook of research methods in psychology, Vol. 2. Research designs: Quantitative, qualitative, neuropsychological, and biological* (pp. 633–646). American Psychological Association. https://doi.org/10.1037/13620-033

Martin, R. C., Ding, J., Hamilton, A. C., & Schnur, T. T. (2021). Working memory capacities neurally dissociate: Evidence from acute stroke. *Cerebral Cortex Communications, 2*(2), tgab005. https://doi.org/10.1093/texcom/tgab005

Martin, R. C., & He, T. (2004). Semantic short-term memory and its role in sentence processing: A replication. *Brain and Language, 89*(1), 76–82. https://doi.org/10.1016/S0093-934X(03)00300-6

Martin, R. C., Lesch, M. F., & Bartha, M. C. (1999). Independence of input and output phonology in word processing and short-term memory. *Journal of Memory and Language, 41*(1), 3–29. https://doi.org/10.1006/jmla.1999.2637

Martin, R. C., Shelton, J. R., & Yaffee, L. S. (1994). Language processing and working memory: Neuropsychological evidence for separate phonological and semantic capacities. *Journal of Memory and Language, 33*(1), 83–111. https://doi.org/10.1006/jmla.1994.1005

Martin, R. C., Vuong, L. C., & Crowther, J. E. (2007). Sentence-level deficits in aphasia. In M. G. Gaskell (Ed.), *The Oxford handbook of psycholinguistics* (pp. 425–439). Oxford University Press.

McCloskey, M. (2001). The future of cognitive neuropsychology. In B. Rapp (Ed.), *The handbook of cognitive neuropsychology: What deficits reveal about the human mind* (pp. 593–610). Psychology Press.

Miceli, G. (2000). The role of cognitive theory in neuropsychological research. In F. Boller & J. Grafman (Eds.), *Handbook of neuropsychology* (Vol. 1, pp. 367–389). Elsevier.

Miceli, G., Gainotti, G., Caltagirone, C., & Masullo, C. (1980). Some aspects of phonological impairment in aphasia. *Brain and Language, 11*(1), 159–169. https://doi.org/10.1016/0093-934X(80)90117-0

Mishkin, M., Ungerleider, L. G., & Macko, K. A. (1983). Object vision and spatial vision: Two cortical pathways. *Trends in Neurosciences, 6*, 414–417. https://doi.org/10.1016/0166-2236(83)90190-X

Newcombe, F., Ratcliff, G., & Damasio, H. (1987). Dissociable visual and spatial impairments following right posterior cerebral lesions: Clinical, neuropsychological and anatomical evidence. *Neuropsychologia, 25*(1, Pt 2), 149–161. https://doi.org/10.1016/0028-3932(87)90127-8

Nickels, L., Kohnen, S., & Biedermann, B. (2010). An untapped resource: Treatment as a tool for revealing the nature of cognitive processes. *Cognitive Neuropsychology, 27*(7), 539–562. https://doi.org/10.1080/02643294.2011.609811

Perenin, M. T., & Vighetto, A. (1988). Optic ataxia: A specific disruption in visuomotor mechanisms. I. Different aspects of the deficit in reaching for objects. *Brain, 111*(3), 643–674. https://doi.org/10.1093/brain/111.3.643

Pobric, G., Jefferies, E., & Ralph, M. A. (2010). Amodal semantic representations depend on both anterior temporal lobes: Evidence from repetitive transcranial magnetic stimulation. *Neuropsychologia, 48*(5), 1336–1342. https://doi.org/10.1016/j.neuropsychologia.2009.12.036

Rapp, B., & Goldrick, M. (2000). Discreteness and interactivity in spoken word production. *Psychological Review, 107*(3), 460–499. https://doi.org/10.1037/0033-295X.107.3.460

Raymer, A. M., Thompson, C. K., Jacobs, B., & Le Grand, H. R. (1993). Phonological treatment of naming deficits in aphasia: Model-based generalization analysis. *Aphasiology, 7*(1), 27–53. https://doi.org/10.1080/02687039308249498

Robertson, L. C., Knight, R. T., Rafal, R., & Shimamura, A. P. (1993). Cognitive neuropsychology is more than single-case studies. *Journal of Experimental Psychology: Learning, Memory, and Cognition, 19*(3), 710–717. https://doi.org/10.1037/0278-7393.19.3.710

Roelofs, A. (1992). A spreading-activation theory of lemma retrieval in speaking. *Cognition, 42*(1-3), 107–142. https://doi.org/10.1016/0010-0277(92)90041-F

Ruml, W., Caramazza, A., Shelton, J. R., & Chialant, D. (2000). Testing assumptions in computational theories of aphasia. *Journal of Memory and Language, 43*(2), 217–248. https://doi.org/10.1006/jmla.2000.2730

Schwartz, M. F., & Dell, G. S. (2010). Case series investigations in cognitive neuropsychology. *Cognitive Neuropsychology, 27*(6), 477–494. https://doi.org/10.1080/02643294.2011.574111

Schwartz, M. F., Dell, G. S., Martin, N., Gahl, S., & Sobel, P. (2006). A case-series test of the interactive two-step model of lexical-access: Evidence from picture naming. *Journal of Memory and Language, 54*(2), 228–264. https://doi.org/10.1016/j.jml.2005.10.001

Schwartz, M. F., Faseyitan, O., Kim, J., & Coslett, H. B. (2012). The dorsal stream contribution to phonological retrieval in object naming. *Brain, 135*(12), 3799–3814. https://doi.org/10.1093/brain/aws300

Shallice, T. (1988). *From neuropsychology to mental structure.* Cambridge University Press. https://doi.org/10.1017/CBO9780511526817

Tan, Y., & Martin, R. C. (2018). Verbal short-term memory capacities and executive function in semantic and syntactic interference resolution during sentence comprehension: Evidence from aphasia. *Neuropsychologia, 113,* 111–125. https://doi.org/10.1016/j.neuropsychologia.2018.03.001

Tan, Y., Martin, R. C., & Van Dyke, J. A. (2017). Semantic and syntactic interference in sentence comprehension: A comparison of working memory models. *Frontiers in Psychology, 8,* 198. https://doi.org/10.3389/fpsyg.2017.00198

Thulborn, K. R., Carpenter, P. A., & Just, M. A. (1999). Plasticity of language-related brain function during recovery from stroke. *Stroke, 30*(4), 749–754. https://doi.org/10.1161/01.STR.30.4.749

Vallar, G. (2000). The methodological foundations of human neuropsychology: Studies in brain-damaged patients. In F. Boller & J. Grafman (Eds.), *Handbook of neuropsychology* (Vol. 1, pp. 305–344). Elsevier.

Vallar, G., & Papagno, C. (2002). Neuropsychological impairments of verbal short-term memory. In A. D. Baddeley, M. D. Kopelman, & B. A. Wilson (Eds.), *Handbook of memory disorders* (pp. 249–270). Wiley.

Verhaeghen, P., & De Meersman, L. (1998). Aging and the Stroop effect: A meta-analysis. *Psychology and Aging, 13*(1), 120–126. https://doi.org/10.1037/0882-7974.13.1.120

Wambaugh, J. L., Linebaugh, C. W., Doyle, P. J., Martinez, A. L., Kalinyak-Fliszar, M., & Spencer, K. A. (2001). Effects of cueing treatments on lexical retrieval in aphasic speakers with different levels of deficit. *Aphasiology, 15*(10–11), 933–950. https://doi.org/10.1080/02687040143000302

CHAPTER 36

GROUP STUDIES IN EXPERIMENTAL NEUROPSYCHOLOGY

Avinash R. Vaidya, Maia S. Pujara, and Lesley K. Fellows

A fundamental assumption of neuropsychology, and of cognitive neuroscience more generally, is that behavior has a biological basis; that it results from processes that are executed in the nervous system. Following from this assumption, emotions, thoughts, percepts, and actions can be understood in neurobiological terms. This premise was advanced by the philosophers of ancient Greece, supported, in part, by observations of patients with brain injury (Gross, 1995). The fact that damage to the brain could lead to paralysis, disorders of sensation, or even disruptions of consciousness suggested that this organ was "the seat" of such abilities, although the broad claim that brain function underlies behavior was not without controversy over the centuries that followed (Crivellato & Ribatti, 2007).

The 19th century saw, on the one hand, major developments in understanding the anatomy and physiology of the brain, and on the other, more systematic descriptions of behavioral changes due to neurological diseases. These advances laid the groundwork for current thinking about the brain. Here again, clinical observations provided an important impetus, as did analyses of individual differences in normal behavior. Neurologists such as Paul Broca and Carl Wernicke reported that focal brain injury to specific areas within the left hemisphere disrupted particular

aspects of language (Feinberg & Farah, 2006). Their thinking was influenced, in part, by Franz-Joseph Gall and others who developed the concept of phrenology in about the same period. Phrenology was based on observations of individual differences in skull shape (explicitly thought to be a proxy for underlying brain structure) in relation to individual differences in behavior. Complex traits like "benevolence" and "wit" were thus related to particular parts of the brain. Although the methods are clearly flawed to the eye of the modern reader, the underlying concept of localization, that brain structure and function are related, had a major impact on the development of clinical neurology and experimental neuropsychology.

The work of Broca, Wernicke, and other 19th- and early 20th-century neurologists illustrates how observation in clinical populations can provide insights into how a complex behavior (like language) can be segmented into simpler components (production and comprehension, for example) and how such components can be related to specific brain regions. Defining the components of behavior, and relating these components to the brain, can be done on the basis of a single, carefully studied case. However, the limitations of clinical observations in humans were also apparent in these early days. Clinicians were (and are) acutely aware of wide variability in

https://doi.org/10.1037/0000319-036
APA Handbook of Research Methods in Psychology, Second Edition: Vol. 2. Research Designs: Quantitative, Qualitative, Neuropsychological, and Biological, H. Cooper (Editor-in-Chief)

the clinical presentation of a particular pathology, determined both by differences in premorbid individual characteristics (for example in age, education, or health status) and differences in the specific details of the pathological process. Case series and group studies of people with focal brain damage provide evidence for the generalizability of inferences drawn from individual observations.

Gordon Holmes (1979), a British neurologist whose work on the effects of penetrating brain injury in World War I soldiers helped to establish the retinotopic organization of the primary visual cortex, poetically captured the limitations of clinical observation in a lecture delivered in 1944:

> My own work on the visual cortex has been limited to observation in man . . . This has required the collection of a large number of observations, for while the physiologist can rely on experiments when he can select and control, . . . the clinician must depend on the analysis of observations which are rarely so simple or clear cut . . . The physiologist may be compared with the builder in . . . hewn stones which can easily be fitted together, the physician resembles the mason who has to use irregular rubble and therefore requires more time and labour to attain his end. But in some branches of neurology, the 'rubble' collected and put together by the clinician is essential. (pp. 440–441)

Holmes underlines three key points: (a) that the limitations inherent to studying the effects of brain injury in humans can be minimized by gathering data from many subjects and by (b) interpreting these data in the context of converging evidence from other methods, and (c) that the limitations are offset by the fact that these observations provide crucial insights that may not be acquired in any other way. As this chapter describes, there have been many logistical, technical, and analytic advances in human lesion studies over the past century. However, Holmes's comments on the core advantages and limitations remain as pertinent as ever.

INFERENTIAL STRENGTHS OF LESION STUDIES

Research on effects of brain injury on behavior addresses two main issues. First, it can establish that a particular region of the brain is necessary for the expression of a particular behavior, in turn supporting the inference that the region contributes critically to a particular cognitive process (Bell & Bultitude, 2018; Rorden & Karnath, 2004; Vaidya et al., 2019). This is a powerful form of evidence because it addresses causality. Cognitive neuroscience now has many methods available to investigate brain–behavior relations by measuring brain activity in response to experimental manipulations and during different behaviors. These tools allow researchers to make statements about the involvement of brain regions in a task, and the nature of neural representations (Poldrack & Farah, 2015). To a limited extent, these methods can make causal claims about how a manipulation may affect activity in a region of the brain (Jazayeri & Afraz, 2017; Weber & Thompson-Schill, 2010). However, the inherent complexity of brains and the massive number of neurons and synapses intervening between experimental conditions and behaviors that are of interest to psychologists mean that these methods speak mostly to the involvement of some neural activity in a behavior, rather than directly supporting a causal relationship. Techniques that measure neural activity and the accompanying hemodynamic metabolic processes cannot establish whether brain regions, circuits or networks are necessary for the behavior in question (Fellows et al., 2005; Rorden & Karnath, 2004).

These inferential considerations are particularly relevant in the study of complex behaviors, and in new areas of enquiry. Consider risky decision making as an example. Imagine yourself at the blackjack table, deciding how much to stake on the next card. Several correlated processes are likely underway in your brain. You may be calculating the odds of winning, integrating your recent history of wins and losses, and weighing these factors to reach a decision. You may be imagining how you would spend your winnings or how you would explain a loss to your spouse. It is likely that you are experiencing substantial changes in arousal and autonomic tone: A pounding heart and sweaty palms often accompany a risky choice. Whether all of these putative processes are distinct, are important to the decision itself, or are simply correlated epiphenomena, are empirical questions. Interpreting functional magnetic resonance imaging (fMRI) or magnetoencephalography (MEG) activations in this situation is not easy: For example, is a given area more active because it is critically involved in risky decision making, or is it important in autonomic control, mediating the changes in sympathetic nervous system outflow that result in the pounding heart? Although careful design can help to minimize these uncertainties of interpretation, the nature of correlational evidence means that they can never be eliminated entirely. Converging evidence from loss-of-function methods, such as lesion studies, can help test necessity claims. If we take a hypothetical "risky decision" brain area as an example, a study of patients with damage to that area could directly test whether it was critical for the decision, for the autonomic changes that accompany that decision, or for both. Such an experiment would shed light both on the critical components of decision making (do autonomic changes influence choice?), and on the brain substrates of the critical processes (see, e.g., Critchley et al., 2003).

Thus, the study of patients can provide biological constraints to psychological theory. The usual form this has taken is that of dissociation of cognitive processes. Two putative psychological constructs may be considered distinct if brain injury disrupts one, and not the other, establishing what is termed a *functional dissociation*. As described in the upcoming section, experiments of this kind have been influential, but how these are best designed and interpreted is not without controversy.

What Do Group Studies Add to the Analysis of Single Cases?

Group studies address two potential problems of interpretation that dog single cases. First, observed deficits in a single patient may be due to premorbid differences in function. Such differences may thus be misattributed to the lesion. Idiosyncrasies in brain organization, in structure–function relationships, or in recovery from injury can also contribute to findings in a single case. Even if we can safely assume that the patient's brain, function, and brain-function mapping were representative prior to the injury, a second source of variability would make group studies important. For obvious reasons, brain lesions in human subjects are not under experimental control. As a result, there is substantial variability in the extent and causes of brain injury. Group studies help to exclude potential lesion-related confounds that might explain the observations in a single case; for example, they can establish that it is the site of damage, rather than its etiology, that underlies the behavior change (e.g., Cipolotti et al., 2015).

Another common and related problem that can be addressed by group studies is that lesions are often more extensive, or less precisely located, than is ideal for testing a given structure–function hypothesis. If the function is disrupted, but the lesion is large, the conclusions cannot be very specific. If a group of patients with lesions varying in extent but overlapping in some smaller area are found to have a common impairment in function, one can infer that the function likely relies on the region with damage in common across patients. Recent methods have built on this logic to allow statistical tests of structure–function associations at the voxel level, discussed in more detail below. Thus, lesion extent can limit structure–function mapping in single cases, but it can at least be addressed, and maybe turned to advantage, in group studies.

Strictly, group studies in neuropsychology are observational rather than experimental. Like case-control studies in epidemiology, they are vulnerable to confounds and biases. These biases are predictable and can be minimized with careful design or addressed with appropriate analyses. The observational nature of this approach to lesion-function mapping means that there is no imposed "directionality": Studies may begin from either function, or lesion. These two perspectives will be discussed in turn.

Designs Driven by Behavior

A major challenge in both psychology and cognitive neuroscience is to define the architecture of behavior. The complexity of behavior needs to be parsed into analyzable constituents, whether these are conceptualized as modules, processes, or interacting networks (Dunn & Kirsner, 2003). The challenge is to identify the appropriate components and then to understand how they interact from both a psychological and a neural point of view.

The most common approach has been to assess behavior using narrowly focused experimental tasks, often drawn from cognitive psychology or computational frameworks. Different advantages may flow from assessing behavior in naturalistic and semi-naturalistic (i.e., "real world") contexts. This approach may be better suited to more abstract behavioral constructs such as personality, morality, aesthetic valuation, insight, and may be more ecologically meaningful than structured laboratory tasks. For example, the Multiple Errands Test (MET) was designed to mimic various real-world demands on planning, such as shopping for various objects (e.g., a cookie, a candle) under specific constraints (Shallice & Burgess, 1991). Emerging technologies, such as virtual reality systems, hold promise for advancing naturalistic experiments and can be used to parametrize seminaturalistic experiments (Dombeck & Reiser, 2012; Krakauer et al., 2017).

Arguably, the component process approach has been most successful when closely linked to neurobiology. For example, we now have a very detailed understanding of visual processing beginning from response properties of single retinal neurons, to how these are combined in early cortical visual regions, and from there, to the computations that support object or face recognition (Farah, 2004; Felleman & Van Essen, 1991; Pitcher & Ungerleider, 2021).

Whether the behavioral approach begins from cognitive models or real-world symptoms, studies in patients with brain injury can provide important insights into the biologically relevant lines of cleavage for a given complex behavior, by helping to identify associations and dissociations between putative component processes. When behavior is treated as the independent variable, patients are selected based on the presence of some behavioral manifestation—either a clinical syndrome or performance on a particular task. Additional behavioral measures aiming to isolate putative component processes are then administered to determine whether these processes are, in fact, distinct (i.e., dissociable). A single dissociation refers to a situation in which participants are impaired on a task that presumably assesses a particular ability but are intact on another task that assesses a separate ability (Figure 36.1a). Single dissociations are evidence in favor of the hypothesis that the tasks measure distinct component processes (Damasio & Damasio, 1989; Shallice, 1988). However, there are practical issues that make alternative explanations for such patterns quite likely: As one example, dissociations assume that the tasks being used are approximately equally difficult. An easy task and a hard task tapping the same component process would show apparent dissociation, since at least some patients would fail the hard task but pass the easy task (Shallice, 1988). This potential explanation is less likely if a double dissociation can be demonstrated: Here, one set of patients fails task X but does well on task Y, whereas another set shows the opposite pattern (Figure 36.1b). The explanatory power and experimental elegance of double dissociation has been a touchstone since the early days of experimental neuropsychology (Teuber, 1955).

How Do You Know a Dissociation When You See One?

The logic of dissociation is clear in principle but can be challenging to operationalize in practice

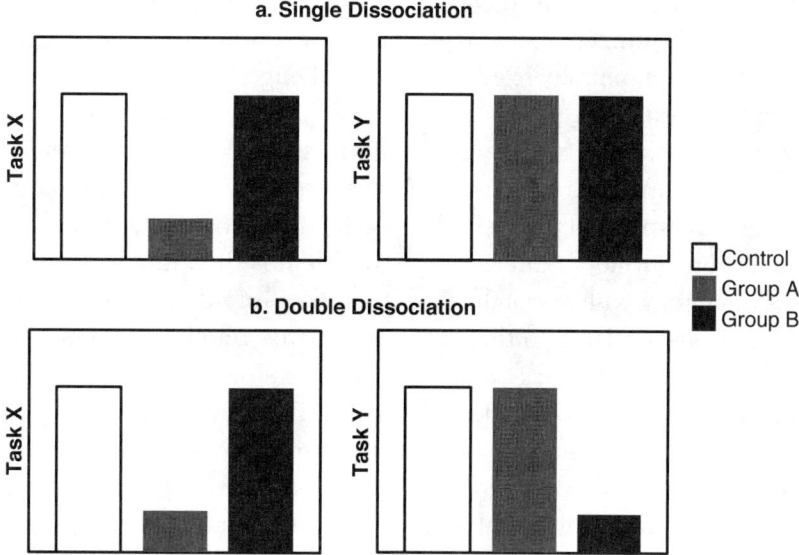

FIGURE 36.1.   Schematic showing classic patterns of results for dissociations in group neuropsychological studies. (a) Pattern for a single dissociation. (b) Pattern for a double dissociation. In both cases, the panels show the results of a study examining performance on two tasks (X and Y) in two groups of patients defined by different patterns of brain damage (A and B) and a matched control group. The y axes indicate performance in tasks measuring performance in functions X and Y. Bars represent the performance of each group.

(see Dunn & Kirsner, 2003, for a detailed discussion). How intact must a group be in task Y? How impaired in task X? What is the likelihood of such "dissociations" occurring by chance, in a given population and for any given pair of tasks? One common approach is to test for an interaction in the performance of two tasks across two groups, but other patterns may be as or more important, depending on the relationships between the tasks, and between a given cognitive process and performance on the task that is meant to measure it (Bates, Appelbaum, et al., 2003; Dunn & Kirsner, 2003; Shallice, 1988).

Conceptual Precision

An important first step in any experiment of this sort is to start from a position of conceptual clarity: a model of the component processes of interest that is well-justified will dictate the appropriate analyses. A priori hypotheses might come from existing experimental work in humans using lesion or other methods, from animal studies, from computational models, or from combinations of these sources.

Measurement Reliability

Once processes of interest are identified, tasks are needed to measure the relevant behavior as specifically as possible. Ideally, such measures will have good psychometric properties: no ceiling and floor performance, good test–retest reliability, and performance that is minimally influenced by demographic or educational factors (Laws, 2005). Brain-injured patients are typically older and less educated, on average, than the convenience samples of healthy undergraduates often used in the development of new measures.

Measurement variation, that is, the extent to which task performance will vary if the same subject is tested repeatedly, is a source of noise that, in principle, is under the experimenter's control. It may have important influences on the analysis and should be minimized to the extent possible (Bates, Appelbaum, et al., 2003). In addition to piloting in demographically relevant healthy samples, attention needs to be given to particular challenges that may arise in patients, such as difficulty understanding instructions, or with motor or perceptual aspects of the tasks that are related to the lesion, but not of interest (e.g., due to weakness interfering with responding), nonspecific changes in arousal related to the injury, or to psychoactive medications (e.g., anti-convulsants) that may be more commonly taken by those in the target group than in the reference group. Patients may need simplified instructions, additional practice, or modifications of stimulus presentation or response methods. These problems also apply to single case studies, but their solutions may be different in group studies. In single cases, there may be more flexibility in optimizing the details of the task to accommodate patient-specific factors. In groups, there is a tradeoff between using a consistent task across all participants (allowing the results to be pooled) and adapting to individual restrictions.

Interindividual Variability

A second source of variability relates not to the measurement tools but to the individuals being measured. Individual differences in group lesion studies can be conceptualized as arising from three potential sources, some of no interest, some of major interest. The first source is individual differences of the same sort that one finds in healthy populations. People differ in their cognitive capacities. This variation is generally only a nuisance in lesion studies, increasing the variance across both experimental and reference groups. However, it can become a confound if individual differences are not randomly distributed across groups. This can be due to sampling error, systematic sampling bias, or nonindependence of lesion-related variables. The simplest form of sampling error is that, by chance, more subjects from one end of the normal range are present in one group than another. This risk is minimized by increasing the sample size (indeed, avoiding this risk is an important motivation of group

vs. single case studies), but patient studies have practical limits on sample size that make this a challenge.

Sampling bias may occur for other reasons: For example, preexisting individual differences may make it more likely that an individual will suffer a particular neurological injury. This problem is illustrated in the putative links between impulsivity and the frontal lobes: If patients who have suffered frontal lobe damage from traumatic brain injury are found to be more impulsive, does this establish that the frontal lobes are important in impulse control? Or do impulsive people get into situations in which they suffer such injuries more often than the less impulsive, so that impulsivity ends up overrepresented in the patient group?

A second source of variability relates to inevitable variation in the nature and extent of brain injury within a group. Lesion location is not the only lesion-related determinant of this kind of variability; factors such as comorbidity and medication use may differ systematically with lesion etiology or location, and so be another source of bias.

DO LESION DATA MATTER IN BEHAVIOR-DRIVEN DESIGNS?

One can test the hypothesis that two processes are functionally dissociable in a patient sample without ever considering the details of the lesions. In principle, dissociation, particularly double dissociation, is all that is needed. In practice, however, there are many nuances in determining what the thresholds might be for establishing dissociations, including the need to consider departures from correlations across tasks as well as (or instead of) absolute performance in each of two tasks. Even if the experimental goal is purely to understand the architecture of cognitive processes, rather than their relation to the brain, lesion analysis can provide external validation of claims of dissociation. Consistent lesion location–function mapping bolsters the argument that what impaired (or unimpaired) patients have in common is disruption of a specific system, rather than some demographic or task-related confound (Robertson et al., 1993).

Lesion-Driven Designs

It is equally possible to study structure–function relations in the human brain with the brain injury treated as the independent variable. Rather than aiming to discern how behavior can be dissected, the starting point is to determine the cognitive processes for which a given brain region is necessary. Of course, these two aims converge on the same central questions.

Characterizing lesions. In the early days of neuropsychology, lesion characterization was based on neurosurgical sketches, plain X-rays of the skull, or the results of autopsies. Computerized tomography (CT), and structural magnetic resonance imaging (MRI) have dramatically improved the quality of anatomical data. MRI is preferred because it offers better resolution, and in many cases better sensitivity, than CT, and it avoids exposing the participant to ionizing radiation. However, MRI may be contraindicated in patients with pacemakers or surgical clips, or not tolerated due to claustrophobia. Ideally, high-resolution imaging should be acquired in the whole patient sample using standard parameters and equipment, as close to the time of behavioral testing as possible. That said, it may be more practical to use the most recently available clinical imaging. This is less resource-intensive, minimizes patient inconvenience, and often provides lesion data that are of more than adequate resolution for testing a given hypothesis. Regardless of approach, the anatomical precision of the lesion characterization needs to be considered in the interpretation.

The simplest way of presenting lesion data is to reproduce the imaging "as-is" for each patient. This works well for single cases but becomes awkward in group studies. Indeed, it is only appropriate to reproduce individual scans if the behavioral data are also presented for each individual—that is, as a case series. If behavioral data are presented as group means, imaging data also need to be presented in a form that allows insights into what is common in the group. This can be achieved simply by tabulating the number of subjects with damage to particular regions. However, modern digital imaging data allow aggregate images to be generated for the whole group that are more readily interpretable, and more easily related to the literature.

Individual lesions first need to be represented in a common space. This can be achieved either by manually tracing the lesion onto a common template (Damasio & Damasio, 1989; Kimberg et al., 2007) or by manually or automatically defining the lesion on the individual patient's anatomical scan (De Haan et al., 2015; Gryska et al., 2021; Mah et al., 2014b). The first method is labor-intensive and requires expertise. The second method requires warping the brain (and the lesion) onto a standard template. The same algorithms used to warp individual scans into common space for fMRI analysis in healthy subjects can be used for this purpose (e.g., Ashburner & Friston, 2005; Avants et al., 2008; Jenkinson et al., 2012; see also Klein et al., 2009, for a comparison of popular methods in healthy subjects). However, the anatomical distortions caused by the presence of a lesion lead to technical issues that need to be addressed thoughtfully (Brett et al., 2001; Nachev et al., 2008), and automation may not always be possible, depending on the quality and type of imaging that is available. Regardless of approach, defining the boundaries of lesions always involves some judgment, and so is a potential source of error.

Registering individual lesions to a common template allows these data to be shown as overlap images (generated by representing the sum of damage in each voxel, across the group), illustrating the degree to which damage affects common brain structures for a given group of patients (Frank et al., 1997; Makale et al., 2002; Rorden & Brett, 2000). Such images can also demonstrate the absence of overlapping damage in two groups that are meant to be anatomically distinct. Digitized lesion data that are represented in a common space can be used in more complex analyses, including statistical tests of structure–function relations (see below), and are more readily linked to other sources of data that are also expressed in standard coordinates, such as fMRI studies.

Region of Interest Designs

When there is an a priori hypothesis about the functional role of a particular brain region, region of interest (ROI) designs are appropriate (e.g., Camille et al., 2004; Spalding et al., 2018). Here, participants are identified based on the presence of damage affecting (or sometimes, restricted to) a specified region of the brain. Behaviors of interest are measured with one or several tasks, and performance is compared with appropriate reference groups. If impairment is identified, it is evidence that the brain region plays a necessary role in task performance, and by extension, in the cognitive process of interest. The major advantage of this approach is its hypothesis-driven design and the statistical power that accompanies such designs. This means that relatively small sample sizes may be adequate, particularly because effect sizes in lesion studies are generally medium to large. Such designs may have directional hypotheses, making one-tailed statistical tests appropriate.

There are several design issues to consider. The first is the appropriate reference group. One common approach is to compare participants with damage to a particular region to a healthy group, matched on demographic characteristics. This provides some control over potential demographic confounds (although perhaps not as much as one might think, depending on the sample size and the variance in these characteristics). However, one cannot unequivocally conclude that the effects are due to damage in a particular region. They may relate to some effect of brain damage more generally, including effects of confounding factors that may be more common in those with brain injury than in those without. Further, it may be difficult to avoid ceiling effects in a healthy control group. To address these problems, many studies include a comparison group with brain injury that spares the ROI (e.g., Bault et al., 2019; Vaidya & Fellows, 2019). If the aim is to control for generic effects of brain

damage or confounds more likely to be present in ill than in healthy participants, then any site of damage that spares the ROI is fine. This is something of a missed opportunity, however. If the lesioned comparison group is selected so that the lesions affect a second, specific brain region, then that group can serve double duty: both controlling for nonspecific effects of injury and establishing that the second region is not necessary for the process in question. Such a targeted approach can also test whether the lesioned reference group is impaired on some other task, insurance against the claim that this group is somehow "less impaired" for whatever reason. In the end, one is left with a focused double dissociation.

This elegant design is not easy to achieve. The main practical difficulty is in recruiting an appropriate lesioned comparison group, whether it involves patients with anatomically common or disparate lesions, matched to the experimental group on both clinical and demographic variables. Systematic recruitment methods, such as patient registries, can make this more feasible (Adolphs, 2016; Fellows et al., 2008). This can be augmented through collaboration and open science to overcome the oft-cited limitation of small, heterogeneous samples in lesion studies. Practical guidelines for such data sharing can be borrowed from the neuroimaging community, as discussed in (Vaidya et al., 2019).

If it is impossible to recruit a lesioned comparison group within an available registry or recruitment pool, then the next best approach is to thoroughly characterize the relation between demographic variables and task performance in a healthy reference group for whom adequate sample sizes are more feasible and then use that information to inform analyses of the patient data. For example, demographic characteristics that differ between patient groups can be shown to have either no substantial influence on task performance in a large healthy reference group or an influence that can be characterized sufficiently to allow these contributions to be controlled for in the primary analysis. A common approach along these lines is to express performance of each lesioned participant as a percentile or *z* score based on performance in a larger healthy reference sample (e.g., Gläscher et al., 2012; Tsuchida & Fellows, 2013).

It is important to consider also the limitations of an ROI design. It imposes an anatomic boundary that may or may not be "true," so nothing will be learned about the potential contributions of brain regions outside that boundary. Perhaps less obviously, such studies risk not detecting effects that are, in fact, related to damage within the boundary. This can happen if the ROI is much larger than the critical region within it; effects observed in patients with damage in the smaller, critical region are diluted by normal performance in patients in whom damage affects other parts of the larger ROI. Even effects that are detected within a given ROI may nevertheless have been better captured by a different anatomical boundary.

Statistics for ROI designs.   When the data are considered as group means, the same statistical approaches used for comparing groups in any study are appropriate. ROI designs commonly are limited to small samples and may involve skewed behavioral data (either because of ceiling effects in the control group, or substantial variability in the patient group, or both). These issues need to be considered in the analysis, if they cannot be avoided in the design. Sometimes, group studies are better analyzed as a series of single cases (e.g., Covington et al., 2018). This approach may be suitable when the group of patients varies widely on relevant demographic or other variables, or indeed, in task performance. Sometimes this approach is taken post hoc (e.g., Ghosh et al., 2014), in which case the results should be considered with particular caution, given the ease with which confounds other than lesion location may explain observed effects.

Pitfalls in ROI designs.

Recruitment bias.   The observational nature of human lesion studies requires particular care to minimize potential bias. When testing a structure–function hypothesis with an anatomical ROI design, efforts should be made to include all subjects with damage to the region in question.

It is common to undertake what might be called a *hybrid study*—for example, including patients with both left hemisphere damage and aphasia, and then asking a more specific question about language processes. This runs the risk of distorting the results. At the least, it may magnify apparent structure–function relations, by cherry-picking patients with both lesion and dysfunction. It may give spurious findings as well, because subjects without impairment provide important constraints in lesion-function mapping (Rorden et al., 2009). Alternatively, patients may be excluded because they are too impaired to perform the experimental tasks. This is important to report in the study. This form of selection bias may have broad impact. For example, if damage to some key structure resulted in severe agitation, such patients are unlikely to be approached (and if approached, to agree) to participate in cognitive neuroscience research. Similarly, severe aphasia often precludes conventional informed consent, so such patients may be systematically excluded.

Control groups.   As in epidemiologic case-control studies, the reference group is very important in lesion studies. In principle, those in the control group should differ from the patient group only in that they have not suffered a brain injury. Practically, this is often challenging to achieve. If healthy subjects are needed, then individuals with similar demographic profiles should be recruited, perhaps even friends or family members of the patients. People with damage to other brain regions (but due to the same causes as damage in the group of interest) are often better choices, because they are more likely to be matched on potentially confounding variables, such as medication usage, or nonspecific psychological effects of serious illness. However, depending on the size of the groups, and the anatomical specificity of the hypotheses, it can be harder to match such participants on demographic variables.

All lesions are not created equal.   Lesions do not occur at random. There are systematic biases in who suffers a brain injury, in the extent to which an injury that affects one part of the brain will be accompanied by damage to other parts of the brain, in the destructiveness of a given injury, and in the time course and mechanisms of recovery from that injury. For example, ischemic stroke damages parts of the brain that are supplied by particular blood vessels. These vascular territories mean that damage to one area, for example, the inferior frontal lobe, will be more commonly associated with damage to another area in the same territory (e.g., insula, inferior parietal lobe). Conversely, such damage will rarely be associated with damage to the areas that are supplied by other blood vessels, such as the other hemisphere, the frontal pole, or the occipital lobe. Further, some vascular territories are more commonly affected than others. Injury to the areas supplied by the middle cerebral artery, for example, will be overrepresented in a given series of unselected stroke patients. These regularities have implications for interpreting the results of lesion studies (Mah et al., 2014a; Rorden & Karnath, 2004; Sperber, 2020), and limit the brain regions that can be readily studied by lesion methods.

Lesion etiology can also affect the accuracy of lesion mapping and the observable structure–function relations: Slow-growing tumors push normal brain tissue aside without necessarily disrupting function, which can lead to lesions that appear quite large but have milder functional effects. Cortical resections in epilepsy have very precise margins and spare the white matter—two advantages—but the cortex that is resected is often not normal and may have been abnormal for a long time.

Relatedly, the degree to which compensation can occur depends on the time course over which the brain disorder develops, its extent, and the time since injury. There is no doubt that the functional effects of stroke evolve over time (Fruhmann Berger et al., 2008; Pedersen et al., 1995). The effects of brain damage can be studied at any time point, but this is a relevant variable that must be considered in both study design and interpretation. The development of MRI sequences that can identify ischemic brain tissue very shortly after the onset of acute stroke has provided the opportunity to do hyper-acute lesion-function mapping (Marsh & Hillis, 2008; Newhart et al., 2007). Such work can identify regions that are normally necessary for a given function. In contrast, studies examining chronic impairments after brain damage are perhaps better thought of as identifying regions that are necessary for the recovery of a given function: deficits still present months or years after an injury are, by definition, resistant to compensatory mechanisms (Hillis, 2014).

Finer-grained lesion-symptom mapping.

ROIs can, in principle, be any size. In practice, there is a lower limit of resolution imposed by the volume of brain tissue that is injured in individual subjects, the extent to which those volumes overlap in a given sample, and the resolution of the imaging methods. Lesion volume, rather than imaging resolution, is typically the limiting factor in the MRI era. The upper limit of resolution is determined by conceptual considerations; determining that some function is related to the integrity of the whole brain, for example, is likely to be of limited interest. That said, many core concepts in neuropsychology began with ROIs encompassing entire cerebral hemispheres and defining such broad structure–function relations may still be important as cognitive neuroscience tackles new areas of study, such as in social or affective domains.

There are practical limits to the regional specificity that can be attained in group studies with ROI designs. If the study is restricted to patients with damage to some very specific and small brain area, an adequate sample is unlikely to be recruited in a reasonable time. An alternative is to enroll patients with variable damage to a relatively broad region—even one hemisphere or the whole brain—and then undertake analyses to establish which subregion contributes to the observed deficits in function.

There are three main approaches to analyzing data from patients who have variable damage falling within a large region. The one with the longest history involves a secondary analysis in a standard ROI study. Having established that performance of an anatomically defined group deviates substantially from controls, and observing the usual variability in that deviation, one may ask whether there is an anatomical basis to that variability. This can be addressed qualitatively by examining the pattern of lesions in the impaired and unimpaired subgroups (e.g., Stuss et al., 2001). Analogous methods include tabulating the presence or absence of injury to Brodmann areas and relating that to the behavioral impairment.

There are drawbacks to this approach. It is important to realize that it is usually undertaken post hoc, so any finding needs confirmation in a new experiment that is designed to test that more specific ROI a priori. Selection bias and confounding can easily influence the results. Such subregion analyses usually involve very small samples, and it can be impossible to properly account for other (e.g., demographic) contributors to observed effects. This approach is also prone to problems due to the nonindependence of damage. Results from such analyses should be treated with particular caution when the initial ROI-based analysis did not establish significant differences between groups. A "multiple ROI" approach can be applied a priori, of course. Several studies have taken this tack (e.g., Picton et al., 2007). This design requires that investigators make somewhat arbitrary decisions about how to parcellate the brain and what qualifies as "damage" in an ROI; choices that can result in very different conclusions.

The last few decades have seen the growth of statistical methods that test structure–dysfunction relationships at a voxel-by-voxel level without a priori anatomical constraints. This approach, referred to as voxel-based lesion-symptom mapping (VLSM) or voxel-based lesion-behavior-mapping (VLBM), also allows task performance to be considered as a continuous variable (Bates, Wilson, et al., 2003; Kinkingnéhun et al., 2007; Rorden et al., 2007, 2009), avoiding a second, potentially arbitrary (intact/impaired) boundary on the data. This is a natural extension of multi-ROI designs, taking advantage of tools developed for analysis of functional and structural MRI data in a standard anatomical space. Once lesions are registered to a common template, univariate statistics can be applied to test whether the performance of patients with damage to a given voxel differs from performance of patients with damage that spares that voxel. This analysis results in a statistical map showing the strength of association between damage and dysfunction in anatomical space (e.g., Gläscher et al., 2012).

In a similar vein, multivariate statistics may be applied to test the pattern of brain damage most related to behavioral change by searching for combinations of voxels that are more strongly related to differences in behavior (DeMarco & Turkeltaub, 2018; Pustina et al., 2018; Zhang et al., 2014). These multivariate analyses may be more suitable when testing whether a putative network contributes critically to a particular function, if damage in different nodes in this network is expected to affect a common behavior in a similar way (Sperber et al., 2019).

These advantages come with tradeoffs. As with fMRI analysis, all VLBM approaches involve a massive number of statistical comparisons that can inflate the likelihood of spuriously detecting a significant result, requiring stricter thresholds. As a result, these analyses may have reduced sensitivity to effects than coarser ROI-level analysis, a problem that may be worse for multivariate methods (Ivanova et al., 2021). Moreover, testing for the relation between brain damage and behavior requires a large sample to provide coverage with sufficient statistical power to detect an effect. Methods exist to estimate the anatomical extent of adequate power in a given sample; these are important in interpreting VLBM analyses (Kimberg et al., 2007; Rudrauf et al., 2008). VLBM methods are also sensitive to the covariance in lesion locations (Mah et al., 2014a; Sperber, 2020). Including patients with different etiologies in the sample may reduce this covariance (Sperber & Karnath, 2017).

White Matter Damage and Disconnection Effects

With the exception of certain neurosurgical resections, lesions are rarely confined to a single structure and often disrupt the white matter leading into or away from a given gray matter region or fibers of passage (i.e., adjacent but unrelated tracts). This can pose challenges in interpreting lesion studies. Observed behavioral effects might be due to the white matter damage, which would be particularly misleading if it involves fibers of passage. However, this variance also presents an opportunity for investigation: by examining the relation between damage in these white matter tracts and behavior, we may glean insights into the networks that support functions of interest.

If diffusion-weighted imaging data are available, it may be possible to directly estimate the integrity of white matter tracts in patients and test whether disruption of these tracts relates to behavioral changes (Gleichgerrcht et al., 2016; Urbanski et al., 2008). However, it is not always feasible to collect such data. Several lines of recent work have focused on developing tools that more indirectly estimate white matter tract disruption, based on diffusion imaging in healthy adults registered to a standard brain space. The advent of white matter atlases has made it possible to ask whether voxels associated with a deficit strongly overlap a particular pathway (Rorden et al., 2009), or if a lesion is likely to cause disconnection within a tract (Foulon et al., 2018; Thiebaut de Schotten et al., 2014). These "tract-wise" methods allow an investigator to test if behavioral deviations are present in subjects whose lesions are physically distant but intersect the same pathway (e.g., Cipolotti et al., 2020). However, all of the above approaches generally suffer limitations similar to multiple ROI approaches, and investigator choices of white matter atlas and definitions of tracts can affect the results (de Haan & Karnath, 2017; Sperber & Karnath, 2018).

There is also interest in examining how disruption of functional brain networks relates to behavioral changes. These functional networks have been identified and well-characterized in healthy adults based on the correlation of low-frequency activity between networks of brain regions at rest, principally using fMRI (Yeo et al., 2011). Some work has directly examined how lesions affect functional connectivity in humans (e.g., Carter et al., 2010), while other work has used data on functional connectivity in healthy subjects to indirectly estimate how brain lesions would affect connectivity between distant regions (Boes et al., 2015; Fox, 2018). This approach has been used in behavior-driven designs and combined with meta-analyses of the literature to test whether certain phenomena associated with various lesion locations relate to disruption of a common network (e.g., Darby et al., 2018). While circumventing the need to collect resting-state data in patients, the latter approach is laden with assumptions about how brain networks are disrupted by lesions and does not consider the potential for compensatory functional changes in a network.

Clinical Conditions With Diffuse Damage

Brain–behavior relations can also be studied in clinical conditions that have multifocal or diffuse damage. Traumatic brain injury, multiple sclerosis, and degenerative dementias are examples (e.g., Beer et al., 2006; Jefferies et al., 2009). Imaging methods can quantify regional cortical and white matter changes, even when these are subtle or diffuse, and such changes can be correlated with behavior. Most of the pitfalls that have been discussed already also apply to such studies. There are additional challenges in interpreting anatomical and behavioral data when multiple areas are dysfunctional in ways that may be correlated and less easily detectable, and when multiple cognitive functions necessary for a given task may be simultaneously degraded.

CONCLUSION

Studies of disrupted function can provide important insights into the architecture of cognitive processes and identify the brain substrates critical for these processes. Lesion studies in humans have particular inferential strengths, explaining their long and fruitful history in neuroscience and psychology, with recent advances in anatomical imaging and statistical analysis contributing to the continued relevance of such work (de Haan &

Karnath, 2018). The ability to learn about brain function from the experience of people with brain injury has intrinsic worth beyond its inferential logic: Patients and families can provide rich descriptions of how brain damage has affected their lives that can lead to unexpected insights beyond the laboratory context. Such anecdotal evidence can provide very interesting starting points for hypothesis-driven experiments, the results of which may in turn be directly relevant to patient care. The observational nature of these studies requires thoughtful experimental design, and this chapter has aimed at providing an overview of the main factors to be considered in such designs.

References

Adolphs, R. (2016). Human lesion studies in the 21st century. *Neuron, 90*(6), 1151–1153. https://doi.org/10.1016/j.neuron.2016.05.014

Ashburner, J., & Friston, K. J. (2005). Unified segmentation. *NeuroImage, 26*(3), 839–851. https://doi.org/10.1016/j.neuroimage.2005.02.018

Avants, B. B., Epstein, C. L., Grossman, M., & Gee, J. C. (2008). Symmetric diffeomorphic image registration with cross-correlation: Evaluating automated labeling of elderly and neurodegenerative brain. *Medical Image Analysis, 12*(1), 26–41. https://doi.org/10.1016/j.media.2007.06.004

Bates, E., Appelbaum, M., Salcedo, J., Saygin, A. P., & Pizzamiglio, L. (2003). Quantifying dissociations in neuropsychological research. *Journal of Clinical and Experimental Neuropsychology, 25*(8), 1128–1153. https://doi.org/10.1076/jcen.25.8.1128.16724

Bates, E., Wilson, S. M., Saygin, A. P., Dick, F., Sereno, M. I., Knight, R. T., & Dronkers, N. F. (2003). Voxel-based lesion–symptom mapping. *Nature Neuroscience, 6*(5), 448–450. https://doi.org/10.1038/nn1050

Bault, N., di Pellegrino, G., Puppi, M., Opolczynski, G., Monti, A., Braghittoni, D., Thibaut, F., Rustichini, A., & Coricelli, G. (2019). Dissociation between private and social counterfactual value signals following ventromedial prefrontal cortex damage. *Journal of Cognitive Neuroscience, 31*(5), 639–656. https://doi.org/10.1162/jocn_a_01372

Beer, J. S., John, O. P., Scabini, D., & Knight, R. T. (2006). Orbitofrontal cortex and social behavior: Integrating self-monitoring and emotion-cognition

interactions. *Journal of Cognitive Neuroscience, 18*(6), 871–879. https://doi.org/10.1162/jocn.2006.18.6.871

Bell, A. H., & Bultitude, J. H. (2018). Methods matter: A primer on permanent and reversible interference techniques in animals for investigators of human neuropsychology. *Neuropsychologia, 115*, 211–219. https://doi.org/10.1016/j.neuropsychologia.2017.09.019

Boes, A. D., Prasad, S., Liu, H., Liu, Q., Pascual-Leone, A., Caviness, V. S., Jr., & Fox, M. D. (2015). Network localization of neurological symptoms from focal brain lesions. *Brain, 138*(10), 3061–3075. https://doi.org/10.1093/brain/awv228

Brett, M., Leff, A. P., Rorden, C., & Ashburner, J. (2001). Spatial normalization of brain images with focal lesions using cost function masking. *NeuroImage, 14*(2), 486–500. https://doi.org/10.1006/nimg.2001.0845

Camille, N., Coricelli, G., Sallet, J., Pradat-Diehl, P., Duhamel, J. R., & Sirigu, A. (2004). The involvement of the orbitofrontal cortex in the experience of regret. *Science, 304*(5674), 1167–1170. https://doi.org/10.1126/science.1094550

Carter, A. R., Astafiev, S. V., Lang, C. E., Connor, L. T., Rengachary, J., Strube, M. J., Pope, D. L., Shulman, G. L., & Corbetta, M. (2010). Resting interhemispheric functional magnetic resonance imaging connectivity predicts performance after stroke. *Annals of Neurology, 67*(3), 365–375. https://doi.org/10.1002/ana.21905

Cipolotti, L., Healy, C., Chan, E., Bolsover, F., Lecce, F., White, M., Spanò, B., Shallice, T., & Bozzali, M. (2015). The impact of different aetiologies on the cognitive performance of frontal patients. *Neuropsychologia, 68*, 21–30. https://doi.org/10.1016/j.neuropsychologia.2014.12.025

Cipolotti, L., Molenberghs, P., Dominguez, J., Smith, N., Smirni, D., Xu, T., Shallice, T., & Chan, E. (2020). Fluency and rule breaking behaviour in the frontal cortex. *Neuropsychologia, 137*, 107308. https://doi.org/10.1016/j.neuropsychologia.2019.107308

Covington, N. V., Brown-Schmidt, S., & Duff, M. C. (2018). The necessity of the hippocampus for statistical learning. *Journal of Cognitive Neuroscience, 30*(5), 680–697. https://doi.org/10.1162/jocn_a_01228

Critchley, H. D., Mathias, C. J., Josephs, O., O'Doherty, J., Zanini, S., Dewar, B. K., Cipolotti, L., Shallice, T., & Dolan, R. J. (2003). Human cingulate cortex and autonomic control: Converging neuroimaging and clinical evidence. *Brain, 126*(10), 2139–2152. https://doi.org/10.1093/brain/awg216

Crivellato, E., & Ribatti, D. (2007). Soul, mind, brain: Greek philosophy and the birth of neuroscience. *Brain Research Bulletin, 71*(4), 327–336. https://doi.org/10.1016/j.brainresbull.2006.09.020

Damasio, H., & Damasio, A. R. (1989). *Lesion analysis in neuropsychology*. Oxford University Press.

Darby, R. R., Joutsa, J., Burke, M. J., & Fox, M. D. (2018). Lesion network localization of free will. *Proceedings of the National Academy of Sciences of the United States of America, 115*(42), 10792–10797. https://doi.org/10.1073/pnas.1814117115

de Haan, B., & Karnath, H.-O. (2017). 'Whose atlas I use, his song I sing?'—The impact of anatomical atlases on fiber tract contributions to cognitive deficits after stroke. *NeuroImage, 163*, 301–309. https://doi.org/10.1016/j.neuroimage.2017.09.051

de Haan, B., Clas, P., Juenger, H., Wilke, M., & Karnath, H.-O. (2015). Fast semi-automated lesion demarcation in stroke. *NeuroImage: Clinical, 9*, 69–74. https://doi.org/10.1016/j.nicl.2015.06.013

de Haan, B., & Karnath, H.-O. (2018). A hitchhiker's guide to lesion-behaviour mapping. *Neuropsychologia, 115*, 5–16. https://doi.org/10.1016/j.neuropsychologia.2017.10.021

DeMarco, A. T., & Turkeltaub, P. E. (2018). A multivariate lesion symptom mapping toolbox and examination of lesion-volume biases and correction methods in lesion-symptom mapping. *Human Brain Mapping, 39*(11), 4169–4182. https://doi.org/10.1002/hbm.24289

Dombeck, D. A., & Reiser, M. B. (2012). Real neuroscience in virtual worlds. *Current Opinion in Neurobiology, 22*(1), 3–10. https://doi.org/10.1016/j.conb.2011.10.015

Dunn, J. C., & Kirsner, K. (2003). What can we infer from double dissociations? *Cortex, 39*(1), 1–7. https://doi.org/10.1016/S0010-9452(08)70070-4

Farah, M. J. (2004). *Visual agnosia* (2nd ed.). MIT Press. https://doi.org/10.7551/mitpress/7122.001.0001

Feinberg, T. E., & Farah, M. J. (2006). A historical perspective on cognitive neuroscience. In M. J. Farah & T. E. Feinberg (Eds.), *Patient-based approaches to cognitive neuroscience* (pp. 3–20). MIT Press.

Felleman, D. J., & Van Essen, D. C. (1991). Distributed hierarchical processing in the primate cerebral cortex. *Cerebral Cortex, 1*(1), 1–47. https://doi.org/10.1093/cercor/1.1.1

Fellows, L. K., Heberlein, A. S., Morales, D. A., Shivde, G., Waller, S., & Wu, D. H. (2005). Method matters: An empirical study of impact in cognitive neuroscience. *Journal of Cognitive Neuroscience, 17*(6), 850–858. https://doi.org/10.1162/0898929054021139

Fellows, L. K., Stark, M., Berg, A., & Chatterjee, A. (2008). Patient registries in cognitive neuroscience research: Advantages, challenges, and practical advice. *Journal of Cognitive Neuroscience, 20*(6), 1107–1113. https://doi.org/10.1162/jocn.2008.20065

Foulon, C., Cerliani, L., Kinkingnéhun, S., Levy, R., Rosso, C., Urbanski, M., Volle, E., & Thiebaut de Schotten, M. (2018). Advanced lesion symptom mapping analyses and implementation as BCBtoolkit. *GigaScience, 7*(3), 1–17. https://doi.org/10.1093/gigascience/giy004

Fox, M. D. (2018). Mapping symptoms to brain networks with the human connectome. *The New England Journal of Medicine, 379*(23), 2237–2245. https://doi.org/10.1056/NEJMra1706158

Frank, R. J., Damasio, H., & Grabowski, T. J. (1997). Brainvox: An interactive, multimodal visualization and analysis system for neuroanatomical imaging. *NeuroImage, 5*(1), 13–30. https://doi.org/10.1006/nimg.1996.0250

Fruhmann Berger, M., Johannsen, L., & Karnath, H. O. (2008). Time course of eye and head deviation in spatial neglect. *Neuropsychology, 22*(6), 697–702. https://doi.org/10.1037/a0013351

Ghosh, V. E., Moscovitch, M., Melo Colella, B., & Gilboa, A. (2014). Schema representation in patients with ventromedial PFC lesions. *The Journal of Neuroscience, 34*(36), 12057–12070. https://doi.org/10.1523/JNEUROSCI.0740-14.2014

Gläscher, J., Adolphs, R., Damasio, H., Bechara, A., Rudrauf, D., Calamia, M., Paul, L. K., & Tranel, D. (2012). Lesion mapping of cognitive control and valuebased decision making in the prefrontal cortex. *Proceedings of the National Academy of Sciences of the United States of America, 109*(36), 14681–14686. https://doi.org/10.1073/pnas.1206608109

Gleichgerrcht, E., Fridriksson, J., Rorden, C., Nesland, T., Desai, R., & Bonilha, L. (2016). Separate neural systems support representations for actions and objects during narrative speech in post-stroke aphasia. *NeuroImage: Clinical, 10*, 140–145. https://doi.org/10.1016/j.nicl.2015.11.013

Gross, C. G. (1995). Aristotle on the brain. *The Neuroscientist, 1*(4), 245–250. https://doi.org/10.1177/107385849500100408

Gryska, E., Schneiderman, J., Björkman-Burtscher, I., & Heckemann, R. A. (2021). Automatic brain lesion segmentation on standard magnetic resonance images: A scoping review. *BMJ Open, 11*(1), e042660. https://doi.org/10.1136/bmjopen-2020-042660

Hillis, A. E. (2014). Inability to empathize: Brain lesions that disrupt sharing and understanding another's emotions. *Brain, 137*(4), 981–997. https://doi.org/10.1093/brain/awt317

Holmes, G. (1979). The organization of the visual cortex in man. In C. G. Phillips (Ed.), *Selected papers of Gordon Holmes* (pp. 438–451). Oxford University Press.

Ivanova, M. V., Herron, T. J., Dronkers, N. F., & Baldo, J. V. (2021). An empirical comparison of univariate versus multivariate methods for the analysis of brain–behavior mapping. *Human Brain Mapping, 42*(4), 1070–1101. https://doi.org/10.1002/hbm.25278

Jazayeri, M., & Afraz, A. (2017). Navigating the neural space in search of the neural code. *Neuron, 93*(5), 1003–1014. https://doi.org/10.1016/j.neuron.2017.02.019

Jefferies, E., Patterson, K., Jones, R. W., & Lambon Ralph, M. A. (2009). Comprehension of concrete and abstract words in semantic dementia. *Neuropsychology, 23*(4), 492–499. https://doi.org/10.1037/a0015452

Jenkinson, M., Beckmann, C. F., Behrens, T. E. J., Woolrich, M. W., & Smith, S. M. (2012). FSL. *NeuroImage, 62*(2), 782–790. https://doi.org/10.1016/j.neuroimage.2011.09.015

Kimberg, D. Y., Coslett, H. B., & Schwartz, M. F. (2007). Power in voxel-based lesion-symptom mapping. *Journal of Cognitive Neuroscience, 19*(7), 1067–1080. https://doi.org/10.1162/jocn.2007.19.7.1067

Kinkingnéhun, S., Volle, E., Pélégrini-Issac, M., Golmard, J. L., Lehéricy, S., du Boisguéheneuc, F., Zhang-Nunes, S., Sosson, D., Duffau, H., Samson, Y., Levy, R., & Dubois, B. (2007). A novel approach to clinical–radiological correlations: Anatomo-Clinical Overlapping Maps (AnaCOM): Method and validation. *NeuroImage, 37*(4), 1237–1249. https://doi.org/10.1016/j.neuroimage.2007.06.027

Klein, A., Andersson, J., Ardekani, B. A., Ashburner, J., Avants, B., Chiang, M. C., Christensen, G. E., Collins, D. L., Gee, J., Hellier, P., Song, J. H., Jenkinson, M., Lepage, C., Rueckert, D., Thompson, P., Vercauteren, T., Woods, R. P., Mann, J. J., & Parsey, R. V. (2009). Evaluation of 14 nonlinear deformation algorithms applied to human brain MRI registration. *NeuroImage, 46*(3), 786–802. https://doi.org/10.1016/j.neuroimage.2008.12.037

Krakauer, J. W., Ghazanfar, A. A., Gomez-Marin, A., MacIver, M. A., & Poeppel, D. (2017). Neuroscience needs behavior: Correcting a reductionist bias. *Neuron, 93*(3), 480–490. https://doi.org/10.1016/j.neuron.2016.12.041

Laws, K. R. (2005). "Illusions of normality": A methodological critique of category-specific naming. *Cortex, 41*(6), 842–851. https://doi.org/10.1016/S0010-9452(08)70303-4

Mah, Y.-H., Husain, M., Rees, G., & Nachev, P. (2014a). Human brain lesion-deficit inference remapped. *Brain, 137*(9), 2522–2531. https://doi.org/10.1093/brain/awu164

Mah, Y.-H., Jager, R., Kennard, C., Husain, M., & Nachev, P. (2014b). A new method for automated high-dimensional lesion segmentation evaluated in vascular injury and applied to the human occipital lobe. *Cortex, 56*, 51–63. https://doi.org/10.1016/j.cortex.2012.12.008

Makale, M., Solomon, J., Patronas, N. J., Danek, A., Butman, J. A., & Grafman, J. (2002). Quantification of brain lesions using interactive automated software. *Behavior Research Methods, Instruments, & Computers, 34*(1), 6–18. https://doi.org/10.3758/BF03195419

Marsh, E. B., & Hillis, A. E. (2008). Dissociation between egocentric and allocentric visuospatial and tactile neglect in acute stroke. *Cortex, 44*(9), 1215–1220. https://doi.org/10.1016/j.cortex.2006.02.002

Nachev, P., Coulthard, E., Jäger, H. R., Kennard, C., & Husain, M. (2008). Enantiomorphic normalization of focally lesioned brains. *NeuroImage, 39*(3), 1215–1226. https://doi.org/10.1016/j.neuroimage.2007.10.002

Newhart, M., Ken, L., Kleinman, J. T., Heidler-Gary, J., & Hillis, A. E. (2007). Neural networks essential for naming and word comprehension. *Cognitive and Behavioral Neurology, 20*(1), 25–30. https://doi.org/10.1097/WNN.0b013e31802dc4a7

Pedersen, P. M., Jørgensen, H. S., Nakayama, H., Raaschou, H. O., & Olsen, T. S. (1995). Aphasia in acute stroke: Incidence, determinants, and recovery. *Annals of Neurology, 38*(4), 659–666. https://doi.org/10.1002/ana.410380416

Picton, T. W., Stuss, D. T., Alexander, M. P., Shallice, T., Binns, M. A., & Gillingham, S. (2007). Effects of focal frontal lesions on response inhibition. *Cerebral Cortex, 17*(4), 826–838. https://doi.org/10.1093/cercor/bhk031

Pitcher, D., & Ungerleider, L. G. (2021). Evidence for a third visual pathway specialized for social perception. *Trends in Cognitive Sciences, 25*(2), 100–110. https://doi.org/10.1016/j.tics.2020.11.006

Poldrack, R. A., & Farah, M. J. (2015). Progress and challenges in probing the human brain. *Nature, 526*(7573), 371–379. https://doi.org/10.1038/nature15692

Pustina, D., Avants, B., Faseyitan, O. K., Medaglia, J. D., & Coslett, H. B. (2018). Improved accuracy of lesion to symptom mapping with multivariate sparse canonical correlations. *Neuropsychologia, 115,* 154–166. https://doi.org/10.1016/j.neuropsychologia.2017.08.027

Robertson, L. C., Knight, R. T., Rafal, R., & Shimamura, A. P. (1993). Cognitive neuropsychology is more than single-case studies. *Journal of Experimental Psychology: Learning, Memory, and Cognition, 19*(3), 710–717. https://doi.org/10.1037/0278-7393.19.3.710

Rorden, C., & Brett, M. (2000). Stereotaxic display of brain lesions. *Behavioural Neurology, 12*(4), 191–200. https://doi.org/10.1155/2000/421719

Rorden, C., Fridriksson, J., & Karnath, H. O. (2009). An evaluation of traditional and novel tools for lesion behavior mapping. *NeuroImage, 44*(4), 1355–1362. https://doi.org/10.1016/j.neuroimage.2008.09.031

Rorden, C., & Karnath, H. O. (2004). Using human brain lesions to infer function: A relic from a past era in the fMRI age? *Nature Reviews Neuroscience, 5*(10), 812–819. https://doi.org/10.1038/nrn1521

Rorden, C., Karnath, H. O., & Bonilha, L. (2007). Improving lesion-symptom mapping. *Journal of Cognitive Neuroscience, 19*(7), 1081–1088. https://doi.org/10.1162/jocn.2007.19.7.1081

Rudrauf, D., Mehta, S., Bruss, J., Tranel, D., Damasio, H., & Grabowski, T. J. (2008). Thresholding lesion overlap difference maps: Application to category-related naming and recognition deficits. *NeuroImage, 41*(3), 970–984. https://doi.org/10.1016/j.neuroimage.2007.12.033

Shallice, T. (1988). *From neuropsychology to mental structure.* Cambridge University Press. https://doi.org/10.1017/CBO9780511526817

Shallice, T., & Burgess, P. W. (1991). Deficits in strategy application following frontal lobe damage in man. *Brain, 114*(2), 727–741. https://doi.org/10.1093/brain/114.2.727

Spalding, K. N., Schlichting, M. L., Zeithamova, D., Preston, A. R., Tranel, D., Duff, M. C., & Warren, D. E. (2018). Ventromedial prefrontal cortex is necessary for normal associative inference and memory integration. *The Journal of Neuroscience, 38*(15), 3767–3775. https://doi.org/10.1523/JNEUROSCI.2501-17.2018

Sperber, C. (2020). Rethinking causality and data complexity in brain lesion-behaviour inference and its implications for lesion-behaviour modelling. *Cortex, 126,* 49–62. https://doi.org/10.1016/j.cortex.2020.01.004

Sperber, C., & Karnath, H.-O. (2018). On the validity of lesion-behaviour mapping methods. *Neuropsychologia, 115,* 17–24. https://doi.org/10.1016/j.neuropsychologia.2017.07.035

Sperber, C., Wiesen, D., & Karnath, H.-O. (2019). An empirical evaluation of multivariate lesion behavior mapping using support vector regression. *Human Brain Mapping, 40,* 1381–1390. https://doi.org/10.1002/hbm.24476

Sperber, C., & Karnath, H.-O. (2017). Impact of correction factors in human brain lesion-behavior inference. *Human Brain Mapping, 38*(3), 1692–1701. https://doi.org/10.1002/hbm.23490

Stuss, D. T., Floden, D., Alexander, M. P., Levine, B., & Katz, D. (2001). Stroop performance in focal lesion patients: Dissociation of processes and frontal lobe lesion location. *Neuropsychologia, 39*(8), 771–786. https://doi.org/10.1016/S0028-3932(01)00013-6

Teuber, H. L. (1955). Physiological psychology. *Annual Review of Psychology, 6*(1), 267–296. https://doi.org/10.1146/annurev.ps.06.020155.001411

Thiebaut de Schotten, M., Tomaiuolo, F., Aiello, M., Merola, S., Silvetti, M., Lecce, F., Bartolomeo, P., & Doricchi, F. (2014). Damage to white matter pathways in subacute and chronic spatial neglect: A group study and 2 single-case studies with complete virtual "in vivo" tractography dissection. *Cerebral Cortex, 24*(3), 691–706. https://doi.org/10.1093/cercor/bhs351

Tsuchida, A., & Fellows, L. K. (2013). Are core component processes of executive function dissociable within the frontal lobes? Evidence from humans with focal prefrontal damage. *Cortex, 49*(7), 1790–1800. https://doi.org/10.1016/j.cortex.2012.10.014

Urbanski, M., Thiebaut de Schotten, M., Rodrigo, S., Catani, M., Oppenheim, C., Touzé, E., Chokron, S., Méder, J. F., Lévy, R., Dubois, B., & Bartolomeo, P. (2008). Brain networks of spatial awareness: Evidence from diffusion tensor imaging tractography. *Journal of Neurology, Neurosurgery, and Psychiatry, 79*(5), 598–601. https://doi.org/10.1136/jnnp.2007.126276

Vaidya, A. R., & Fellows, L. K. (2019). Ventromedial frontal lobe damage affects interpretation, not exploration, of emotional facial expressions. *Cortex, 113,* 312–328. https://doi.org/10.1016/j.cortex.2018.12.013

Vaidya, A. R., Pujara, M. S., Petrides, M., Murray, E. A., & Fellows, L. K. (2019). Lesion studies in contemporary neuroscience. *Trends in Cognitive*

Sciences, 23(8), 653–671. https://doi.org/10.1016/j.tics.2019.05.009

Weber, M. J., & Thompson-Schill, S. L. (2010). Functional neuroimaging can support causal claims about brain function. *Journal of Cognitive Neuroscience, 22*(11), 2415–2416. https://doi.org/10.1162/jocn.2010.21461

Yeo, B. T. T., Krienen, F. M., Sepulcre, J., Sabuncu, M. R., Lashkari, D., Hollinshead, M., Roffman, J. L., Smoller, J. W., Zöllei, L., Polimeni, J. R., Fischl, B.,

Liu, H., & Buckner, R. L. (2011). The organization of the human cerebral cortex estimated by intrinsic functional connectivity. *Journal of Neurophysiology, 106*(3),1125–1165. https://doi.org/10.1152/jn.00338.2011

Zhang, Y., Kimberg, D. Y., Coslett, H. B., Schwartz, M. F., & Wang, Z. (2014). Multivariate lesion-symptom mapping using support vector regression. *Human Brain Mapping, 35*(12), 5861–5876. https://doi.org/10.1002/hbm.22590

GENETIC METHODS
IN PSYCHOLOGY

CHAPTER 37

GENETIC METHODS IN PSYCHOLOGY

Terrell A. Hicks, Daniel Bustamante, Karestan C. Koenen, Nicole R. Nugent, and Ananda B. Amstadter

The "Genomic Era" (Guttmacher & Collins, 2003) was born on April 14, 2003, when the International Human Genome Sequencing Consortium, led in the United States by the National Human Genome Research Institute and the Department of Energy, announced that the human genome had been sequenced. This momentous event occurred exactly 50 years after James Watson and Francis Crick (1953) published their seminal paper that described DNA's double helix. The Genomic Era has brought genetics into the mainstream of psychology research. The present chapter begins with a brief summary of the principles of mendelian genetics and the limitations of this approach to most outcomes of interest in psychology. We then move on to discuss quantitative genetic designs including family, twin, extended twin family, and adoption studies. We next describe molecular genetic study approaches. We end with a review of some of the most important design considerations for psychologists who are interested in conducting a genetically informative study.

MENDELIAN GENETICS

Genetic methodology has been heavily influenced by Mendelian rules of inheritance, in which a single gene exerts its effects on the *phenotype* in a *dominant* or *recessive* manner. Mendelian modes

of transmission (Mendel, 1865/1959) provided the early framework for molecular genetic research. Mendel observed that the expression of offspring traits could be predicted on the basis of parent traits. Offspring inherited a given trait from both parents, with observable offspring traits evidencing a pattern of dominance, in which only one trait was expressed even when the offspring had inherited two different traits, known as the law of segregation. Mendel also noted that multiple traits were inherited separately and concluded that traits are inherited independent of one another, known as the law of independent assortment. Mendelian inheritance is consistent with qualitative differences—lending it to *case-control studies* in which frequencies of genes are compared in individuals who are *affected*, that is, show the disease/disorder, versus *unaffected*, do not show the disease/disorder. However, nearly all phenotypes in psychology are *complex* and/or quantitative and are influenced by multiple genes (i.e., polygenic), environmental factors, and the interplay between genes and environment. Researchers interested in examining the influence of genes on psychological outcomes will need to carefully design studies that permit identification of these unique patterns of genetic transmission. Behavioral genetic science has become increasingly sophisticated in methods available to model (a) the complex transmission

https://doi.org/10.1037/0000319-037
APA Handbook of Research Methods in Psychology, Second Edition: Vol. 2. Research Designs: Quantitative, Qualitative, Neuropsychological, and Biological, H. Cooper (Editor-in-Chief)

of genetic influences and (b) the interplay of genes and environment on outcomes.

QUANTITATIVE GENETIC DESIGNS

The section begins with a brief overview of the basics of quantitative genetic methodology, beginning with the four main quantitative genetic paradigms (e.g., family studies, twin studies, extended twin design studies, adoption studies), and then giving brief mention of other genetics-informed designs (e.g., offspring of twins, twins reared apart). These paradigms help answer two basic questions: (a) Are there genetic influences on the phenotype (could be a behavior, a diagnosis, etc.)? and (b) What are the respective contributions of genes and environment on a phenotype? By determining whether a phenotype is influenced by genes, quantitative genetic paradigms lay the foundation for other types of genetic investigations (e.g., molecular genetics, described below). With the advent of advanced statistical modeling software such as Mplus and OpenMx (Muthén & Muthén, 2017; Neale et al., 2016), quantitative genetic paradigms also can answer much more sophisticated questions in psychological research, including hypotheses about mediators and moderators of genetic influences on psychological phenotypes. The interested reader is referred to Samek et al. (2013) for a thorough description of behavioral genetic research methodology.

Family Studies

In order for a disorder to have a genetic component, it must be familial, that is, more common within families than across them. Specifically, if risk for a psychological disorder, such as schizophrenia, is in part influenced by genetic factors, biological relatives (family members) of individuals with schizophrenia (referred to as *probands* in genetic studies) should have a higher prevalence of schizophrenia than nonrelatives. Moreover, among biological relatives of individuals with schizophrenia, the prevalence of the disorder should be higher in first-degree relatives (parents, siblings) than second-degree relatives (aunts, uncles,

grandparents, etc.). Evidence of familial aggregation exists for the majority of psychological disorders, suggesting an underlying genetic component is responsible for at least some of the variance in the outcome (Kendler, 1993). Notably, the familial aggregation pattern includes both genetic and environmental influences, as well as interactions between the two, complicating the interpretation of family study findings.

Twin Studies

Modern twin studies compare concordance measures (such as odds ratios) in monozygotic pairs who are genetically identical versus dizygotic pairs who share half of their genetic make-up with their twin (Kendler & Prescott, 2006). By doing so, twin studies help to disentangle the role of genetic and environmental factors in phenotype. The twin design produces calculations of the proportion of the variance in a trait or disorder explained by genetic factors; the resultant variance attributed to genetic factors is termed *heritability*.

Twin study methodology has two key assumptions: *random mating* (i.e., mating is not influenced by genetics) and *equal environment* (i.e., DZ and MZ pairs share 100% of their common environment; Kendler & Prescott, 2006). These assumptions are the basis for the mathematical equations described later, and violations of the assumptions may lead to over- or underestimation of heritability. If the parents of twins are genetically correlated, then DZ twins may share more than half of their genes with their twin pair, which would underestimate the degree to which genetics influence a phenotype. Violation of the equal environment assumption may overestimate the contribution of genetic factors.

Basic twin models estimate the contribution of three factors: (a) additive genetic factors, "A," which assumes that the genetic architecture of a phenotype arises from multiple genetic loci; (b) shared environmental factors, "C," which correspond to aspects of the twins' environment that are common to both twin pairs, such as socioeconomic status, parental relationship, etc.; and (c) individual-specific environmental factors, "E," which are aspects of the environment that are not shared between the twins, such as their individual social support, one twin who was in an accident, etc. Therefore, this basic model is often referred to as the *ACE model*. The statistical modeling assumes that MZ twins share 100% of their genes and 100% of the shared environment (and therefore the correlation between twins on a phenotype is: $rMZ = a^2 + c^2$, and that DZ twins share approximately 50% of their genes and 100% of the shared environment: $rDZ = 1/2a^2 + c^2$; Kendler & Prescott, 2006). From these basic assumptions, the relative contribution of additive genetic factors A, shared environment C, and individual unique environment E can be calculated. The A factor estimate is derived from the equation $a^2 = 2(rMZ - rDZ)$, the C factor is calculated from the equation $c^2 = 2rDZ - rMZ$, and lastly, the E factor is derived from the equation $e^2 = 1 - rMZ$ (Kendler & Prescott, 2006; Plomin et al., 2001). Two main types of correlations are used for twin studies in psychology. If a phenotype is continuous (e.g., depression symptoms score), a Pearson (product-moment) correlation is used. For categorical phenotypes, such as posttraumatic stress disorder (PTSD) diagnosis, the tetrachoric correlation, which assumes an underlying normal distribution of liability, is used to calculate heritability (Falconer, 1960).

Three general interpretations are possible from the basic ACE model (Kendler & Prescott, 2006). First, if MZ twins are significantly more similar on a characteristic than DZ twins, then this phenotype is interpreted as being genetically influenced. Second, if the correlation between twin pairs for a phenotype is the same in MZ and DZ twins then the shared environment is contributing to the phenotype. Third, the unique environment is likely contributing to a phenotype if the intratwin correlation between MZ twins is large. Maximum likelihood estimation methods are now nearly universally employed in twin studies (typically utilizing a structural equation modeling program, such as OpenMx), affording the ability to compare models, to obtain confidence intervals of the parameters, to examine gene-by-environment correlations and gene-by-environment

interactions, and to construct multivariate models (Neale et al., 2016). A more detailed description of gene–environment interplay is provided in the molecular genetics section of this chapter.

Extended twin family design studies. Extended twin family design (ETFD) models are similar to basic twin models, but they also use additional familial relationships (e.g., nontwin siblings, parents, cousins) to gain a better understanding of the variation and covariation underlying genetic and environmental causes of phenotypic variation in the population (Keller et al., 2009). Basic twin studies have numerous assumptions that are rarely testable in classical twin studies and when violated may produce biased parameter estimates (for a full list of effects of violating assumptions on parameter estimates, see Keller et al., 2009).

The cascade model is an extension of the ETFD model that makes fewer assumptions than previous ETFD models and, therefore, is able to produce less biased and more accurate parameter estimates (Keller et al., 2009). The cascade model estimates the contribution of six factors: (a) additive genetic factors, "A"; (b) dominant genetic factors, "D," which correspond to effects attributable to combinations of alleles at the same locus; (c) familial environment, "F," which corresponds to aspects of an individual's environment that are common to all offspring in the family, such as socioeconomic status or education, and that are passed via "vertical transmission" from parents to offspring; (d) sibling environment, "S," which correspond to nongenetic effects (e.g., peers, school, parenting style) shared between siblings and twins, but not between parents and offspring; (e) twin environment, "T," which correspond to nongenetic effects (e.g., peers, classroom) shared by twins, but not siblings; and (f) unique environment, "E," which are aspects of the environment that are not shared between individuals, such as their social support, traumatic experiences, etc., that are unshared with any other relative. The full Mx *Cascade* script is available at https://www.matthewckeller.com/GE.Cascade1.mx, and the extended algebra is available at https://www.matthewckeller.com/html/cascade.html.

Adoption Studies

Adoption studies test for an association between a phenotype in adoptees and the prevalence of that phenotype in their biological versus adoptive parents (Lemery & Goldsmith, 1999). The logic of this design is that adoptees share 50% of their genes with their biological parent and 0% of the shared environment; conversely, adoptees share 0% of their genes and 100% of the common environment with their adopted parents. If adoptees are more similar to their biological parents on a phenotype than they are to their adopted parents, then the assumption is that genetic factors are important to the phenotype. Conversely, if adoptees have a greater resemblance to their adopted parents on a phenotype than they do to their biological parents then the environment is assumed to be a contributing factor. This type of design may be limited by a restricted range of family environments, such as the likelihood that adoptive parents create a good home environment or potential higher biologic risk of biologic parents for a range of conditions, leading to poor generalizability. Adoption studies are rarer than twin studies, mainly due to the increased difficulty in finding participants.

OTHER BEHAVIORAL GENETIC STUDY METHODOLOGIES

Separated twin design studies compare MZ and DZ twins reared apart versus together; however, these situations are quite rare, and the family of origin is often very unique, limiting generalizability. Many current genetically informed designs are combining behavioral genetic methods with molecular genetic (gene-finding) techniques (described in the next section); this combination has great potential to impact our knowledge about the etiologic roots of psychological disorders. However, quantitative studies are unable to inform our understanding of *which* genes may influence behavioral or psychological phenotypes.

Molecular Genetic Study Designs

It was the identification of the molecular structure of deoxyribonucleic acid (DNA) that provided the foundation of our understanding of the functional elements of heritability (Pray, 2008). James Watson and Francis Crick proposed a double-stranded helical structure comprised of pairings between thymine (T) and adenine (A) and between guanine (G) and cytosine (C). This pattern of double-stranded molecules explained two of the major genetic questions of the time: how is genetic information replicated and how is it translated into observable outcomes. The two strands "unzip" to replicate and to permit transcription of DNA to messenger RNA and then to amino acids. Although a thorough review of molecular genetics is outside the scope of the present chapter, interested readers are directed an excellent text on the topic (Strachan & Read, 2019) or to interactive websites (Exhibit 37.1). Once the basic structure of DNA was understood, researchers began

---

EXHIBIT 37.1

Websites to Learn More

Educational Resources

Learn.Genetics: https://learn.genetics.utah.edu/
Teach.Genetics: https://teach.genetics.utah.edu/
National Human Genome Research Institute: https://www.genome.gov/about-genomics
Neuroscience Gateway: https://portal.brain-map.org/

Collaborative Genetic Research Efforts

1000 Genomes Project: https://www.internationalgenome.org/

Genetic Search Engines

Online Mendelian Inheritance in Man: https://www.omim.org/
Database of Single Nucleotide Polymorphisms (dbSNP): https://www.ncbi.nlm.nih.gov/snp/
Ensembl genome browser: https://useast.ensembl.org/index.html

Behavioral Genetic Organizations

Behavior Genetics Association: https://www.bga.org/
Human Genome Organisation: https://www.hugo-international.org/
International Behavioral and Neural Genetics Society: https://www.ibngs.org/
International Society for Twin Studies: https://twinstudies.org/
International Society of Psychiatric Genetics: https://www.ispg.net/

---

to characterize the translation of DNA to biological outcomes and, later, to observable phenotypes relevant to psychology.

The Human Genome Project (International Human Genome Sequencing Consortium, 2001; Venter et al., 2001; see https://www.genome.gov/ Education/) is one of the most exciting scientific accomplishments of the past couple decades. The project initiated in 1990 was an international collaboration to characterize the location and function of 30,000 genes of the human genome. The ENCyclopedia Of DNA Elements (ENCODE) Project (see https://www.genome.gov/10005107) is a public research consortium initiated in 2003 involving (a) a pilot study aimed at assessing methods for analyzing the genome and (b) the development of technology for high-throughput data on functional elements in the human genome. The 1000 Genomes Project ran from 2008 to 2015 and provided a comprehensive resource on human genetic variation (see https:// www.internationalgenome.org/).

Informed by the wealth of data afforded by these projects, *molecular genetic* studies in psychology have sought to identify variants in specific genes that increase the risk of having a given phenotype such as depression or schizophrenia. Although the precise definition of a gene has changed over time (Gerstein et al., 2007), for the present purposes, genes are considered to be functional units of DNA sequences. Research aimed at identifying genetic variation that explain individual differences in risk for psychological disorders focuses on the tiny fraction of the DNA sequences that differs among individuals (possibly less than 1% of human DNA).

The majority of human genetic variation is comprised of single nucleotide polymorphisms (SNPs, pronounced "snips"), which occur when a single nucleotide (A, T, C, or G) in the DNA sequence is altered, forming different *alleles* (the genetic term that refers to one of the various forms of a genetic locus). An example of a SNP is a change in the DNA sequence from CTT to CAT, with the alleles of this SNP being T and A. By definition, the frequency of SNPs must be at least 1%.

Copy number variation (CNV) is a form of polymorphism used to describe genetic variation in which parts of a genome ranging from small sections to entire genes are repeated and the number of repeats differ between individuals. CNVs are considered either short or long repeats. Studies that identify a polymorphism that appear to predict a given phenotype cannot assume that the marker itself is the functional allele. This is because the marker may simply be in linkage disequilibrium to the functional allele. *Linkage disequilibrium* refers to the tendency for alleles that are in close proximity on a chromosome to be inherited together. Due to patterns of inheritance such as population stratification (reviewed below) linkage disequilibrium may also exist between markers on different chromosomes or regions. Thus, an identified association between a phenotype and candidate gene may simply point to a region on the chromosome where the functional gene is located and does not necessarily mean that the candidate gene itself is responsible for the phenotype. Although it is easy to see how linkage disequilibrium might complicate genetic research, linkage disequilibrium has also been used as a tool for mapping complex disease loci through whole-genome association studies (Ardlie et al., 2002).

Population stratification occurs when a sample includes subpopulations characterized by non-random mating between them and, consequently, the subsamples show different allelic frequencies that are unrelated to the phenotype under investigation (Freedman et al., 2004; Hutchison et al., 2004). If there are differences between the subpopulations in prevalence or genetic mechanism of the phenotype, "discovery" of an allelic difference may be erroneously attributed to the phenotype. Population *admixture*, arising from mating between subpopulations, presents similar challenges as, again, linkage disequilibrium patterns that vary as a function of admixture may be misinterpreted as markers of the phenotype. One solution to this problem is to conduct within-family tests of association, such as the transmission disequilibrium test (Spielman & Ewens, 1996), but these tests require particular configurations of family data. An alternative is to use a design incorporating unlinked genetic marker to detect and control for population stratification (Pritchard et al., 2000).

Linkage Studies

Linkage analysis was one of the first molecular methodologies in genetics. This method applies phenotypic data from family members to identify the location of the disease gene relative to a genetic marker or DNA sequence that has a known chromosomal location. *Linkage* is said to occur when the disease gene and genetic marker cosegregate or tend to be inherited together. Rather than focusing on a single locus, many linkage analysis studies scan the whole genome using hundreds of markers to identify linkage. However, most studies within psychology have identified relatively small gene effects and attempts to replicate linkage findings have been particularly difficult in complex disorders, possibly because the small effects require extremely large samples to replicate. Another potential explanation for replication difficulties is the likelihood that complex disorders may be the product of gene–gene interactions and/or gene–environment interactions (Risch, 1990). In spite of these challenges, linkage studies have provided a critical foundation for molecular genetic research. Linkage studies are particularly amenable to single-gene disorders. However, for most psychological phenotypes it has given way to more contemporary molecular techniques that are better suited to complex phenotypes.

Association Studies

Candidate gene association studies are more targeted than linkage studies and use extant knowledge or theory of the pathophysiology of a phenotype to guide selection of genes which are then tested for potential associations with the phenotype. This theory-driven selection of candidate genes is both a strength and limitation of gene-association research. An exemplar for translational application, candidate genes in gene association studies are generally selected on the basis of converging research and theory spanning animal models,

preclinical research, psychopharmacology, neurobiology, and linkage studies. In practice, this has led to considerable focus on a handful of genes implicated in serotonergic, dopaminergic, and stress response systems, with the same "generalist" genes evidencing associations with multiple disorders. As Plomin and Davis (2009) pointed out, "'generalist' genes may affect several disorders within major domains such as internalizing disorders" (p. 64). As we reported in a systematic review of anxiety disorders, a remarkable number of genes have demonstrated replicated effects within and across anxiety disorder categories (Nugent et al., 2010). This is further supported by quantitative studies. For example, genetic influences on major depression account for the majority of the genetic variance in PTSD (Koenen et al., 2008). Moreover, many of the polymorphisms with replicated effects are putatively functional variants that influence neurobiologic systems that have been previously implicated in behavioral and psychiatric outcomes based on a wealth of animal, preclinical, clinical, and pharmacological findings.

One major limitation of candidate genes association studies is that most studies have failed to replicate significant findings. Specifically, a review of the first 10 years of candidate gene association studies in psychiatric research found that only about 27% of replication attempts were significant (Duncan & Keller, 2011). Failure to replicate significant findings is likely due to a combination of underpowered studies, incomplete knowledge of biology underlying phenotypes and thus inability to accurately choose candidate genes, incomplete coverage of genes (i.e., often are single polymorphism studies not capturing most of the variation in a gene), and lack of control for population stratification. However, not all results from candidate gene association studies are likely false positive results. Therefore, a meta-analytic approach of candidate gene association studies can help synthesize results given the inconsistencies across the literature. For example, a meta-analysis of relevant candidate gene association studies was conducted to determine which candidate genes showed consistent evidence of association with attention-deficit/hyperactivity disorder (ADHD) and found evidence for significant associations for several candidate genes, including *DAT1*, *DRD4*, *DRD5*, *5HTT*, *HTR1B*, and *SNAP25* (Gizer et al., 2009).

Gene–Environment Interplay

Perhaps the area that has garnered the most excitement as well as the most controversy (Eaves, 2006) within genetic research in psychology is examination of gene–environment interplay (G × E), which can be conducted from a molecular (e.g., candidate or genome-wide association study [GWAS]) or latent genetic (e.g., twin study) design. Indeed, research has explored the degree to which G × E interaction impacts numerous psychological phenotypes (Rutter et al., 2006; Wermter et al., 2010). The interaction of genes and environment has often been framed in terms of a diathesis-stress model, in which psychiatric pathology is seen as the result of a genetic vulnerability (hence, "risk-conferring genes") combined with environmental influences (Kidd, 1991). However, the field has also included G × E conceptualizations proposing genes may confer differential susceptibility or environmentally sensitive "plasticity" (Belsky et al., 2009; Belsky & Pluess, 2009; Fox et al., 2007). Such a model explains why seemingly pathogenic genes might continue over generations of proliferation, and moreover, would even be relatively common, as these genes would be beneficial under specific environmental conditions. Although this may appear to be an insignificant distinction, it is linked to different patterns of data. For example, differential susceptibility would be associated with a steep slope as a function of exposure to negative life experiences (Belsky et al., 2009).

Indeed, researchers have suggested that *differential* responding to an environmental pathogen is perhaps one of the most important indicators of a G × E, in which the effects of environmental exposure are moderated by genotype (Moffitt et al., 2005). Moffitt et al. (2005) outlined seven strategic steps for conducting molecular G × E research: (1) considering quantitative studies; (2) selecting the environmental factor; (3) carefully measuring the environmental risk; (4) selecting candidate genes; (5) testing for an interaction; (6) systematically testing whether the interaction holds when one gene, environment, or outcome variable is replaced with another gene, environment, or outcome variable; and (7) conducting replication and meta-analytic studies. Unfortunately, relatively few studies meet these stringent criteria. Therefore, inconsistent findings likely due to not meeting these stringent criteria has resulted in a lot of skepticism (Eaves, 2006). It is also likely that many false positive studies have been published due to multiplicative or additive statistical approach of G × E research without correction for multiple testing (Eaves, 2006). For example, an influential paper was published in a high-profile scientific journal demonstrating a G × E interaction of serotonin transporter (*5-HTTLPR*) genotype and stressful life events impact on the prediction of major depression (Caspi et al., 2003). The results presented in this paper spurred a lot of interest, and at the time of this writing, the Caspi et al. (2003) study has been cited over 9,800 times and over 400 studies have been published investigating the impact of *5-HTTLPR* variation and stressful life events on risk for depression. Despite the widespread interest, meta-analyses using only published (Risch et al., 2009) and both published and unpublished (Culverhouse et al., 2018) data do not support a main effect or G × E effect of *5-HTTLPR* on depression. Furthermore, recent research utilizing large population-based and case-control samples to examine G × E hypotheses for depression found no evidence for 18 identified candidate genes for depression and their relevance to multiple operational definitions of depression (e.g., lifetime diagnosis, current symptom severity, episode recurrence; Border et al., 2019). Conclusively, Border and colleagues (2019) determined that construct validity was unlikely to account for the null findings, and as previously mentioned, one possible reason there might not be a true effect could be that the effects found in previous research were statistical artifacts (Eaves, 2006).

Similar to the trend of candidate gene studies giving way to agnostic GWAS designs, G × E studies are beginning to be conducted from an agnostic and polygenic design. A genome-wide gene-by-environment interaction study (GWEIS) can be useful in understanding how the environment interacts with genetic predisposition across the genome to complex traits, such as those in psychology. For example, a recent GWEIS investigated how traumatic life experiences are associated with alcohol misuse, which is an association likely impacted by genetic predisposition (Polimanti et al., 2018). Polimanti and colleagues' (2018) findings were replicated in an independent sample (Hawn et al., 2018), and both found a significant interaction effect of trauma exposure and *rs1729578* on alcohol misuse suggesting that the minor allele was positively associated with increased alcohol misuse. This exciting approach has the potential to identify important, previously unconsidered genetic influences on health and psychology as well as to reinforce the relative importance of previously studied candidate genes. Already, GWASs point to the importance and prevalence of CNVs (Estivill & Armengol, 2007). GWASs may also focus on genetic variants believed to be functional, increasing power by reducing the number of tests aimed at loci with little likelihood of an effect. Additionally, studies have employed a polygenetic approach to studying G × E interactions wherein a polygenic measure, such as a sum score of risk alleles in multiple genes (Pasman et al., 2019) is used. Most phenotypes in psychology are genetically complex, or polygenic in nature, so it is not surprising that most studies testing the effect of single genetic variants on behavioral traits have had modest success. Thus, testing the effect of multiple genetic variants simultaneously is likely to yield better results.

In addition to G × E interactions, gene–environment interplay also included gene–environment correlation (rGE). rGE is the extent to which individuals create and influence their own environments (Plomin et al., 1977; Rutter, 2010). rGE refers to the passive, active, and reactive mechanisms whereby genetic factors influence the environment. A systematic review of twin studies on rGE explored genetic influences on environmental measures, with heritability across environmental measures estimated to be 27% (Kendler & Baker, 2007). Beyond latent heritability, rGE has been demonstrated in molecular studies (Dalvie et al., 2020). For example, a recent study reported that the molecular heritability of childhood maltreatment was 6% (Dalvie et al., 2020).

Genome-wide Association Studies

Molecular genetic studies are most commonly being conducted using an agnostic GWAS approach. GWASs test possible associations across the entire genome, in contrast to candidate gene designs with a narrower focus. GWASs scan the genome based on genotyped or sequenced regions from many different individuals and looks for SNPs that occur more frequently in individuals with a particular phenotype (referred to as "cases"; e.g., disease, disorder, behavior) than in individuals without the phenotype (referred to as "controls"). GWASs represent a promising and comprehensive way to study well-defined complex phenotypes, such as those common in psychological research where many genetic (i.e., polygenic) variations contribute to an individual's risk. However, GWAS data must be analyzed with considerations for an inflated rate of false positives due to the numerous statistical tests conducted. Therefore, sample size for statistical power is arguably the most important factor for GWASs because no single study sample can be truly informative. Thus, the Psychiatric Genomics Consortium (PGC) was founded as a collaborative effort from over 800 researchers across 38 countries to consolidate genetic data to aid in genetic discovery. As shown on the PGC website (https://www.med.unc.edu/pgc/), there are working groups on these disorders: Alzheimer's disease, ADHD, anxiety, autism spectrum disorder, bipolar disorder, eating disorders, major depressive disorder, PTSD, schizophrenia, and substance use disorders. The various PGC working groups have led the field in psychiatric genetic discovery since their inception. For example, a GWAS meta-analysis was recently conducted by the bipolar disorder working group with 41,917 bipolar disorder cases and 371,549 controls of European descent, which identified 64 independent loci associated with bipolar disorder at genome-wide significance (Mullins et al., 2021). Highlights from the PTSD working group include their GWAS meta-analysis of an ancestrally diverse group of 206,655 individuals (Nievergelt et al., 2019). Specifically, meta-analyses of GWASs including 23,212 PTSD cases and 151,447 controls of European ancestry and meta-analyses of 4,363 PTSD cases and 10,976 controls of African ancestry identified a total of 6 independent loci associated with PTSD at genome-wide significance (Nievergelt et al., 2019). In addition to the PGC there are numerous consortia (e.g., Social Sciences Genetic Consortium [SSGC]; https://www.thessgac.org/) that have been formed to harmonize phenotypic and genotypic data relevant to gene discovery for phenotypes related to psychology. For example, a large-scale GWAS of educational attainment was conducted by the SSGC with approximately 1.1 million individuals, which identified 1,271 independent genome-wide significant SNPs associated with educational attainment (Lee et al., 2018).

GWASs use data based on genotyped common variants across the genome from unrelated individuals to investigate if the differences in common variants are associated with the phenotypes of interest. Quality control (QC) methods for GWASs (e.g., the RICOPILI pipeline; Lam et al., 2020) include steps such as filtering the sample and markers, assessing the population structure and imputing the data using sequenced reference panels (e.g., 1000 Genomes Project Consortium et al., 2015). These steps are aimed at ensuring that bias and potential confounding factors are reduced. After QC procedures, it is common practice to conduct the analyses using data subsets based on homogenous ancestry groups. Since allele frequencies vary across ancestries, conducting GWASs in heterogenous population can generate spurious results, including increased uncertainty about the source of the differences in SNPs associated with the phenotypes. Most GWASs of psychiatric and behavioral phenotypes have been conducted based on data from individuals of European ancestry. There has been a recent increase of studies also assessing data from East Asian and African ancestries, which will help make the findings and knowledge gain equitable (for more details on ancestry distribution across GWASs of these phenotypes, see Peterson et al., 2019).

Recent advances in statistical genetic techniques for GWASs. In addition to the field's increased ability to detect alleles associated with various disorders that have stemmed from increased power and team science efforts, the availability of large-scale GWAS data has led to the development of numerous statistical genetic techniques that allow researchers to examine questions of high relevance to psychology. In the sections that follow, we introduce these methods and provide an example of their application in the field of psychology.

Genome-wide complex trait analysis (GCTA) is a method that can be used to generate heritability estimates for a specific phenotype (i.e., univariate) using individual-level GWAS data from unrelated individuals and provide SNP-based heritability estimates (h^2_{SNP}; Yang et al., 2011). For example, GCTA was first used to investigate intelligence in a study of 3,500 unrelated adults, which found heritability estimates of .40 for crystallized intelligence and .51 for fluid intelligence (Davies et al., 2011). There is also a bivariate extension of GCTA that can be used to examine the shared heritability between two different phenotypes. Specifically, individual-level GWAS data can be used to calculate overlapping genetic variance (i.e., genetic correlation; r_g) between two phenotypes. For example, in order to test how much of the genetic variability accounted for by measured SNPs influenced both fluid and crystallized intelligence, Davies and colleagues (2011) could have used a bivariate GCTA approach to estimate the shared heritability, or overlap in molecular heritability, between crystallized and fluid intelligence. GCTA heritability estimates are useful in psychology because they harness the well-powered GWAS design to provide estimates of heritability of complex traits from unrelated individuals, and moreover, overcome the assumptions used in twin or family studies.

Linkage disequilibrium score regression (LDSC) is another method that can be used to produce heritability estimates in both a univariate and bivariate context. Unlike GCTA, LDSC uses summary statistics from GWASs opposed to individual-level genotypic data, which is regressed on their own linkage disequilibrium (LD) scores (the sum of the squared correlation estimates between the SNPs). For example, LDSC was used to estimate SNP-based heritability for alcohol dependence and PTSD individually (Sheerin et al., 2020). Sheerin and colleagues (2020) used summary statistics from the PGC PTSD and Substance Use Disorders working groups to perform LDSC and estimated the SNP-based heritability (h^2_{SNP}) for alcohol dependence and PTSD to be .05 and .04, respectively LDSC can also be applied across phenotypes to estimate genetic correlations (r_g; Ni et al., 2018). For example, a recent study used LDSC to investigate the genetic correlations of anxiety disorders with eight psychiatric disorders and found that the risk of anxiety disorders was positively genetically correlated with the risk of major depressive disorder ($r_g = .83$, $SE = .16$, $p = 1.97 \times 10^{-7}$), schizophrenia ($r_g = .28$, $SE = .09$, $p = 1.10 \times 10^{-3}$), and ADHD ($r_g = .34$, $SE = .13$, $p = 8.40 \times 10^{-3}$) (Ohi et al., 2020).

Genomic structural equation modeling (genomicSEM) is a multivariate method that builds upon LDSC that uses both genetic correlations (r_g) and SNP-based heritability estimates (h^2_{SNP}) from GWAS summary statistics of individual traits that share genetic influence to assess the genetic overlap in the traits as well as their degree of heterogeneity at the SNP level (Grotzinger et al., 2019). This method is particularly useful in the context of studying comorbidity. Using this method, Thorp et al. (2021) investigated the genetic factor structure of highly comorbid depression and anxiety. Results demonstrated that symptoms of depression and anxiety loaded on two distinct factors while identifying 89 independent variants for the depressive factor and 102 independent variants for the anxiety factor, which was replicated in an independent sample (Thorp et al., 2021).

Polygenic risk scores (PRSs) are an estimate of an individual's genetic liability to a phenotype that are calculated as a weighted sum of trait-associated risk alleles using individual-level GWAS data. Not all risk alleles reach genome-wide significance from GWASs, but their combined effect may still influence the phenotype. PRS captures an individual's aggregate genetic influence of all risk alleles that are presumed to be influential on a trait or disease. This method is popular for risk prediction of psychological disorders because of their genetic complexity or polygenic nature. In order to use PRS for risk prediction, at least two different samples are needed, both with individual-level GWAS data. The GWAS summary statistics from the discovery sample are used to compute the weighted sum in an independent sample to generate the PRS. For example, a recent study used PRSs of depression derived from a large-scale GWAS in an adult sample to predict depression severity and age at onset in a sample of children and adolescents (Halldorsdottir et al., 2019). PRS predicted baseline depressive symptoms and prospectively predicted onset of moderate-to-severe depressive symptoms. In order to decrease the heterogeneity in the application and reporting of PRSs, reporting standards were recently developed in a collaboration between the Clinical Genome Resource Complex Disease Working Group and the Polygenic Score Catalog that will promote the validity, transparency, and reproducibility of risk prediction studies using PRSs (Wand et al., 2021).

Mendelian randomization (MR) is a method used to investigate causal effects of associations between phenotypes based on grouping individuals by their natural genetic variation (Emdin, Khera, & Kathiresan, 2017). MR uses summary statistics from GWASs and can be thought of as a naturally occurring randomized clinical trial where individuals are randomized to receive one variant of an allele during meiosis where DNA is transferred from parent to offspring and individuals in the population are grouped based on their genotype. Pasman et al. (2020) investigated the bidirectional association between insomnia and substance use (i.e., alcohol, tobacco, cannabis) using MR. Their results suggest that there is a positive causal relationship between insomnia and substance use. Additionally, results suggest a causal relationship between tobacco use and insomnia risk.

Considerations for diverse populations.
Analyses based on the relatively novel techniques that use either individual level data (e.g., GCTA, PRS) or GWAS summary statistics (e.g., LDSC, MR, genomicSEM) are also restricted to independent and homogenous ancestry data based on reference panels. Resulting statistics such as the heritability, the aggregate genetic risk influencing a trait, or the genetic correlation among phenotypes of interest would be applicable only to the population matching the ancestry of the reference panel data used in these analyses. For example, to calculate the heritability estimates and the genetic correlation among phenotypes, using LDSC software (ldsc; Bulik-Sullivan et al., 2015), the LD scores for each ancestry would need to be computed separately. Although the LD scores based on European ancestry are computed and available, the ldsc software also allows users to compute LD scores for ancestries different than European, and to examine the heritability and genetic correlation of phenotypes for these populations (provided that data sets have no less than ~5,000 sample). Over the past decade, GWASs of non-European samples have been small and can be rendered underpowered especially compared to studies based on European ancestry. However, techniques such as GCTA can leverage these data and estimate the trait heritability for these populations with a sample size lower than 3,000 individuals. GWAS statistics, heritability estimates, polygenic risk and genetic correlation among phenotypes can elucidate the path to the first stages of the exploration of how from molecular differences, changes in proteins, organelles, cells, and tissues can lead to develop certain psychiatric and behavioral phenotypes. There is a need to expand this exploration to populations of other ancestries. Recent statistical genetics methods are focused on increasing the diversity in genomic analyses. For example, DISTMIX2 (Chatzinakos et al., 2021) proposes to use larger and more diverse reference panels to provide a re-imputation technique, and

Tractor (Atkinson et al., 2020) presents a method allowing for ancestry-specific effect sizes estimation and discrepancies in population-specific minor allele frequencies while not increasing the rate of false positives discoveries. Genome-wide analyses techniques have advanced considerably over the last 12 years. Although at the time of this writing, there is still a need for larger samples and of more diverse ancestries. When analyses include a larger and diverse population, results from genetic studies can be maximized and more people of different backgrounds can benefit from potential treatments and health policies based on the findings.

DESIGN CONSIDERATIONS

The choice of study design, such as participant selection, environmental exposure, and study collection methods, often has profound consequences for the interpretation of study results.

Participants

Selection of participants in genetic research begins first with a decision between (a) one of the family-based designs (i.e., twin studies, extended twin family design, etc.) or (b) case-control designs; though certainly some studies have compromised by utilizing both family and case-control designs. However, both designs require researchers to operationalize "caseness" or how to define "probands."

Defining probands. As with other areas of psychology, the criteria for including probands is a balance between "representativeness" and "purity" of the phenotype. For example, PTSD is highly comorbid with both depression and substance abuse. Accordingly, researchers interested in a representative sample might wish to include anyone with PTSD, regardless of comorbidity, in the proband group. However, it is possible that the inclusion of such comorbidity may alter the findings to be specific to the comorbid consideration. For example, comorbid PTSD and substance abuse was examined in a case-control investigation of combat veterans with and without

PTSD; the analyses revealed a positive association between *DRD2A1* and PTSD only in the subset of PTSD cases who engaged in harmful drinking (Young et al., 2002).

The example of using probands with a given diagnosis introduces another shifting paradigm of genetic research. Historically, a majority of molecular studies have compared "probands" or "cases," who have the disorder with "controls," who do not have the disorder. This qualitative approach has been partly attributed to the legacy of the Mendelian focus on single-gene transmission of qualitative traits (Plomin et al., 2009). However, biometricians have long argued for the genetic transmission of normally distributed quantitative traits and, echoing Fisherian resolution of quantitative-qualitative debates (Fisher, 1919), leaders in the field interpret GWAS findings to support the presence of quantitative traits (Plomin et al., 2009). Certainly qualitative approaches, comparing "cases" to either controls or "super normal-controls," (individuals completely free of any symptoms of psychopathology) provide important and valuable information in both molecular and quantitative research methods. However, if the disorder is interpreted to be a quantitative trait, then future research efforts that more accurately reflect the continuous phenotype score may be better powered to detect differences. As Plomin and colleagues (2009) argued, artificial dichotomization of continuous traits may result in inaccurate categorization of subthreshold individuals, adding additional measurement error to the analysis. Accordingly, researchers may wish to consider using continuous indexes of the phenotype (e.g., depression severity) and to sample participants who represent the entire continuum of symptom levels.

One often underrecognized consideration in participant selection in genetic paradigms is the developmental stage of participants. Most psychological constructs include a role for developmental processes. Disorder-specific variables such as age of onset, age-related gender differences in prevalence, and course of disorder all inform our understanding of the biological and environmental influences at play and need to be considerations in the selection of participants. For example, prior research supports developmental changes in the environmental and genetic influences on substance use behaviors (e.g., Derringe et al., 2008; Kendler et al., 2008; Kendler & Myers, 2009). Given developmental differences across neurobiological development, social development, and cognitive development, humans may be more or less vulnerable to the effects of trauma at certain developmental stages or the exact outcomes (e.g., depression versus PTSD) of trauma may differ partly as a function of age (e.g., multifinality). For example, converging evidence from developmental neuroscience and behavioral genetics suggests that adolescence and young adulthood may represent a "stress-sensitive developmental period" (Walker et al., 2004).

Developmental/age considerations partly overlap with considerations such as whether research is examining onset or course. When considering disorder etiology, it is useful to distinguish between risk factors for onset or development of the disorder and risk factors for course or chronicity of the disorder. Factors that influence who develops the disorder in the first place may differ from those that influence who recovers from the disorder once it develops. For example, members of disadvantaged ethnic groups are not at higher risk for the development of psychiatric disorders; however, if the disorder occurs, these disadvantaged individuals may display greater chronicity compared with nondisadvantaged individuals. Breslau et al. (2005) found that Hispanic individuals who developed a psychiatric disorder, had symptoms that were more chronic than those of non-Hispanic Whites.

Comparison groups.   Selection of control groups is yet another tricky endeavor in genetic research. Some early genetic studies focused on control groups that were free of any symptomatology across all diagnoses (and even among first-degree relatives), leading researchers to criticize the use of supernormal controls (Kendler, 1990). Supernormal controls may come from families with lower rates of psychological concerns than average population levels, arguably increasing the potential for coaggregation of disorders in proband families. Given the importance of environmental influences across all psychological constructs, it is important for comparison participants to share important environmental influences with probands. Genetically informed studies in psychology are complicated by the practical reality that for many psychological phenotypes, such as substance use disorders, the phenotype is conditional on an environmental exposure. For example, if a family member did not meet criteria for nicotine dependence, it could be that they had not been exposed to nicotine and therefore had never been at risk for dependence. To classify this family member as nicotine dependent–negative may mask a genetic influence that was not expressed due to lack of environmental exposure. This is also demonstrated in PTSD research; as exposure to trauma is a necessary condition of PTSD, control participants must have experienced some degree of trauma to permit comparisons between groups that did and did not develop PTSD. If trauma exposure is either unknown or inconsistent in controls, it is possible that some of the control participants might have developed PTSD in response to trauma. Careful consideration needs to be given to inclusion and exclusion criteria in genetic studies (Eaves & Eysenk, 1980).

Other challenges. Population stratification is not dissimilar from familiar confounds in psychology such as socioeconomic status. Nonetheless, it is an important consideration in genetic research and can be partly addressed through participant selection. For example, some researchers have focused on participants of homogeneous ancestry in an effort to minimize this concern. However, in areas with significant ancestral diversity, such as the United States, selecting participants of homogeneous ancestry is difficult; focusing on African Americans, for example, one study found that ancestry included Niger-Kordofanian, European, and other African populations with considerable admixture (Tishkoff et al., 2009). Indeed, many families may have passed along limited or incomplete ancestral information

to their offspring, and research has shown that self-reported race differs from actual genetically determined ancestry (Yaeger et al., 2008).

Environmental Exposure

A review of nearly three dozen quantitative studies concluded that the genetic influences on anxiety and depression are largely the same, with a lack of shared environment determining the expression of the genetic vulnerability (Middeldorp et al., 2005). Selection and measurement of an environmental pathogen should involve careful consideration of biological plausibility, causal effects of the pathogen, age-specificity of risks, duration of risk exposure and time since exposure (Moffitt et al., 2005). Environment may interact with genes by (a) *triggering* the expression of a genetic vulnerability, (b) *compensating* for a genetic predisposition, (c) *determining expression* of a genetic predisposition, and/or (d) *potentiating* a genetic predisposition (Shanahan & Hofer, 2005). Measurement of each of these environmental influences is tied to important differences in design. Early life stress, for example, may represent a *trigger* for genetic vulnerability to depression or anxiety, whereas the proximal process of parent-child relationship or the environmental context of neighborhood may be posited to *compensate* for or *potentiate* the effects of genes. Thus, measures of the environment can include both pathogenic and buffering influences. Measures must be applied in a population with sufficient range of exposure to the environmental pathogen because only a main effect of genotype will be identified if all (or nearly all) participants have experienced the environmental factor (Uher & McGuffin, 2010).

Sample Collection Methods

The collection of a sufficient amount of high-quality genomic DNA is critical for any study aiming to examine the molecular genetic underpinnings of a phenotype. New advances in genomic DNA collection methods have increased ease of collection, lowered costs of collection, and have made it more feasible for researchers to conduct genetically informed studies. The following section reviews the most frequently used DNA collection procedures.

Peripheral blood.   Collection of peripheral blood samples has been the historically employed means of obtaining DNA (Lench et al., 1988). It consistently yields a high quantity of DNA with excellent purity (Lahiri & Schnabel, 1993), especially if the DNA is isolated shortly after the blood draw. A 10- to 20-ml blood draw (yielding approximately 30 to 60 µg of DNA per ml of whole blood) using an ethylenediaminetetraacetic acid (EDTA) or heparin tube is frequently employed. Use of these types of tubes is critical, as they contain an anticoagulant that will prevent clotting. DNA can be isolated from fresh blood or frozen blood; standard practice is to store the frozen samples at −70 °C, although thawing and refreezing blood may degrade the DNA (Lahiri & Schnabel, 1993). Extraction of DNA from B-lymphocytes is another option, and cell lines can be produced from lymphocytes allowing for an unlimited source of DNA, assuming the cell-line is stable. For a thorough discussion of procedures and issues with DNA banking, see Steinberg et al. (2002).

Buccal cells.   Given the invasiveness of obtaining a blood sample, researchers have been increasingly using buccal cell collection for DNA isolation (Feigelson et al., 2001). There are quite a few ways in which buccal cells can be collected, including but not limited to cytobrushes: cotton swabs, saliva collection, and mouthwash procedures (Le Marchand et al., 2001). However, the most common method is a saliva collection kit (James, Iwasiow, & Birnboim, 2011).

Sample Collection Considerations

There are a few considerations to keep in mind when deciding on which type of sample to collect. The quantification of DNA, usually using spectro-photometric quantification methods, is used to determine the quantity and purity of DNA in a sample. Using a spectrophotometer will help to determine if the DNA is contaminated by other molecules (e.g., proteins, hemoglobin) and will also produce an estimate of the amount of DNA in a sample. The quantity (and purity) of DNA yielded from different collection methods is one important consideration. Depending on study design (e.g., GWAS vs. candidate gene), a high yield may be required and would necessitate use of whole blood versus buccal cell collection, depending on the genetic platform to be used. Further, for DNA banked samples, extraction from lymphocytes may need to be used to create cell lines. Additionally, the time that will lapse from sample collection to DNA isolation is an important consideration. The stability of DNA in frozen blood is higher than the stability of DNA in buccal cells; however Woo et al. (2007) extracted DNA from cytobrushes that were stored at −80°C for approximately 7 years with good success.

Measuring Phenotypes

Although there are many different methodological paradigms used to examine genetics in psychology, all methodologies share a vital condition: that the phenotype is accurate and valid.

Psychiatric diagnosis.   The diagnostic category, no matter how specifically and carefully defined, may not be closely tied to a biologic mechanism, and therefore is not related to a genetic mechanism (Meyer-Lindenberg & Weinberger, 2006). In short, there seems to be a shared lack of confidence among experts of the promise or utility of clinical psychiatric diagnoses as phenotypes in the "gene finding" process (Insel & Lehner, 2007). Nevertheless, until other biomarkers or endo-phenotypes (described below) are available and are proven useful, gene–phenotype studies often need to rely on diagnostic categories.

Great care in the study design needs to be given to assessment methodology and consideration of multiple issues is necessary (e.g., psychometric properties of the instrument, training of staff who will administer the assessments/interviews, reliability checks of interviews to ensure that they were administered properly). When determining the phenotype of interest and the measures used to assess the phenotype, thought should be given to the planned statistical analyses (e.g., will the phenotype be considered quantitative, does the measure produce a continuous scale of severity or number of symptoms, does the measure yield a dichotomous outcome—diagnosis present or absent, etc.). Consideration to the degree of heterogeneity within diagnostic categories is also needed. Take, for example, schizophrenia; patients with very different symptom profiles can meet criteria for the disorder, resulting in great variability within the phenotype. Another consideration is the use of diagnostic end points that infer a threshold that may be artificial. Examination of continuous measures of quantitative traits (e.g., endophenotypes) may afford greater statistical power and prediction accuracy (Lee & Wray, 2013).

Endophenotypes. *Endophenotypes* are defined as "measurable components unseen by the unaided eye along the pathway between disease and distal genotype" (Gottesman & Gould, 2003). According to Gottesman and Gould (2003), the following conditions must be met to be considered a endophenotype: the endophenotype must be heritable, be related to the illness, be state-independent, and must cosegregate with the illness in families. Other authors have argued that endophenotypes must also have good psychometric properties, be stable over time, and show increased expression in unaffected relatives of probands (cited in Almasy & Blangero, 2001). The concept of the use of endophenotypes or intermediary phenotypes in psychology and psychiatry has gained popularity in the recent years, "as genes do not encode for psychopathology, it is reasonable to expect that the association or penetrance of gene effects will be greater at the level of relatively more simple and biologically based phenotypes" (Meyer-Lindenberg & Weinberger, 2006, p. 818).

There have been numerous "success stories" of how endophenotypes have been used in psychology. Electrophysiological measures (e.g., EEGs, ERPs, EROs) have been employed in the context of genetic studies of alcoholism, yielding replicated gene-endophenotype findings; for a review, see Porjesz et al. (2005). Neuropsychological endophenotypes have also been used in schizophrenia research, with replicated results suggesting variation in *RELN* is related to verbal and visual working memory, and executive functioning (Wedenoja et al., 2008). With recent advances in imaging methodologies, mechanistic aspects of brain function are also beginning to yield feasible endophenotypes (Meyer-Lindenberg & Weinberger, 2006).

CONCLUSION

Given recent advances in quantitative and molecular genetic research techniques, genetically informed psychological research is highly feasible. The intersection of research methodologies used in psychology with those used in genetics is an exciting area of growth in the field. The formation of multidisciplinary research teams to conduct genetically informed psychological studies has the potential to inform the field's knowledge of the complex nature of many phenotypes of interest. Quantitative studies can help to disentangle the influences of genes and environment, informing some of the most central questions in psychology such as why some people develop symptomatology and what factors can prevent or ameliorate such symptoms. Molecular genetic research techniques have the potential to identify the chromosomal regions of interest for various phenotypes. As molecular studies increasingly refine investigations to the true putatively functional genotypes, resultant understanding regarding the neurobiological effects of these variants can inform both theory and treatment. Although the field of genetically informed psychological studies is in its infancy, the field is at an exciting time in its development trajectory with great promise to help uncover findings that will lead to improving the understanding and treatment of various psychological conditions.

References

Almasy, L., & Blangero, J. (2001). Endophenotypes as quantitative risk factors for psychiatric disease: Rationale and study design. *American Journal of Medical Genetics: Part B. Neuropsychiatric Genetics, 105*(1), 42–44. https://doi.org/10.1002/1096-8628(20010108)105:1<42::AID-AJMG1055>3.0.CO;2-9

Ardlie, K. G., Kruglyak, L., & Seielstad, M. (2002). Patterns of linkage disequilibrium in the human genome. *Nature Reviews: Genetics, 3*(4), 299–309. https://doi.org/10.1038/nrg777

Atkinson, E. G., Maihofer, A. X., Kanai, M., Martin, A. R., Karczewski, K. J., Santoro, M. L., Ulirsch, J. C., Kamatani, Y., Okada, Y., Finucane, H. K., Koenen, K. C., Nievergelt, C. M., Daly, M. J., & Neale, B. M. (2020). *Tractor*: A framework allowing for improved inclusion of admixed individuals in large-scale association studies. *bioRxiv*, 2020.05.17.100727. https://doi.org/10.1101/2020.05.17.100727

Belsky, J., Jonassaint, C., Pluess, M., Stanton, M., Brummett, B., & Williams, R. (2009). Vulnerability genes or plasticity genes? *Molecular Psychiatry*, *14*(8), 746–754. https://doi.org/10.1038/mp.2009.44

Belsky, J., & Pluess, M. (2009). Beyond diathesis stress: Differential susceptibility to environmental influences. *Psychological Bulletin*, *135*(6), 885–908. https://doi.org/10.1037/a0017376

Border, R., Johnson, E. C., Evans, L. M., Smolen, A., Berley, N., Sullivan, P. F., & Keller, M. C. (2019). No support for historical candidate gene or candidate gene-by-interaction hypotheses for major depression across multiple large samples. *The American Journal of Psychiatry*, *176*(5), 376–387. https://doi.org/10.1176/appi.ajp.2018.18070881

Breslau, J., Kendler, K. S., Su, M., Gaxiola-Aguilar, S., & Kessler, R. C. (2005). Lifetime risk and persistence of psychiatric disorders across ethnic groups in the United States. *Psychological Medicine*, *35*(3), 317–327. https://doi.org/10.1017/S0033291704003514

Bulik-Sullivan, B. K., Loh, P.-R., Finucane, H. K., Ripke, S., Yang, J., Patterson, N., Daly, M. J., Price, A. L., Neale, B. M., & the Schizophrenia Working Group of the Psychiatric Genomics Consortium. (2015). LD Score regression distinguishes confounding from polygenicity in genome-wide association studies. *Nature Genetics*, *47*(3), 291–295. https://doi.org/10.1038/ng.3211

Caspi, A., Sugden, K., Moffitt, T. E., Taylor, A., Craig, I. W., Harrington, H., McClay, J., Mill, J., Martin, J., Braithwaite, A., & Poulton, R. (2003). Influence of life stress on depression: Moderation by a polymorphism in the 5-HTT gene. *Science*, *301*(5631), 386–389. https://doi.org/10.1126/science.1083968

Chatzinakos, C., Lee, D., Cai, N., Vladimirov, V. I., Webb, B. T., Riley, B. P., Flint, J., Kendler, K. S., Ressler, K. J., Daskalakis, N. P., & Bacanu, S.-A. (2021). Increasing the resolution and precision of psychiatric genome-wide association studies by re-imputing summary statistics using a large, diverse reference panel. *American Journal of Medical Genetics: Part B. Neuropsychiatric Genetics*, *186*(1), 16–27. https://doi.org/10.1002/ajmg.b.32834

Culverhouse, R. C., Saccone, N. L., Horton, A. C., Ma, Y., Anstey, K. J., Banaschewski, T., Burmeister, M.,

Cohen-Woods, S., Etain, B., Fisher, H. L., Goldman, N., Guillaume, S., Horwood, J., Juhasz, G., Lester, K. J., Mandelli, L., Middeldorp, C. M., Olié, E., Villafuerte, S., . . . Bierut, L. J. (2018). Collaborative meta-analysis finds no evidence of a strong interaction between stress and 5-HTTLPR genotype contributing to the development of depression. *Molecular Psychiatry*, *23*(1), 133–142. https://doi.org/10.1038/mp.2017.44

Dalvie, S., Maihofer, A. X., Coleman, J. R. I., Bradley, B., Breen, G., Brick, L. A., Chen, C. Y., Choi, K. W., Duncan, L. E., Guffanti, G., Haas, M., Harnal, S., Liberzon, I., Nugent, N. R., Provost, A. C., Ressler, K. J., Torres, K., Amstadter, A. B., Bryn Austin, S., . . . Nievergelt, C. M. (2020). Genomic influences on self-reported childhood maltreatment. *Translational Psychiatry*, *10*(1), 38. https://doi.org/10.1038/s41398-020-0706-0

Davies, G., Tenesa, A., Payton, A., Yang, J., Harris, S. E., Liewald, D., Ke, X., Le Hellard, S., Christoforou, A., Luciano, M., McGhee, K., Lopez, L., Gow, A. J., Corley, J., Redmond, P., Fox, H. C., Haggarty, P., Whalley, L. J., McNeill, G., . . . Deary, I. J. (2011). Genome-wide association studies establish that human intelligence is highly heritable and polygenic. *Molecular Psychiatry*, *16*(10), 996–1005. https://doi.org/10.1038/mp.2011.85

Derringer, J., Krueger, R. F., McGue, M., & Iacono, W. G. (2008). Genetic and environmental contributions to the diversity of substances used in adolescent twins: A longitudinal study of age and sex effects. *Addiction*, *103*(10), 1744–1751. https://doi.org/10.1111/j.1360-0443.2008.02305.x

Duncan, L. E., & Keller, M. C. (2011). A critical review of the first 10 years of candidate gene-by-environment interaction research in psychiatry. *The American Journal of Psychiatry*, *168*(10), 1041–1049. https://doi.org/10.1176/appi.ajp.2011.11020191

Eaves, L. J. (2006). Genotype × Environment interaction in psychopathology: Fact or artifact? *Twin Research and Human Genetics*, *9*(1), 1–8. https://doi.org/10.1375/twin.9.1.1

Eaves, L. J., & Eysenk, H. J. (1980). New approaches to the analysis of twin data and their application to smoking behavior. In H. J. Eysenk (Ed.), *The causes and effects of smoking* (pp. 158–235). Maurice Temple Smith.

Emdin, C. A., Khera, A. V., & Kathiresan, S. (2017). Mendelian randomization. *Journal of the American Medical Association*, *318*(19), 1925–1926. https://doi.org/10.1001/jama.2017.17219

Estivill, X., & Armengol, L. (2007). Copy number variants and common disorders: Filling the gaps and exploring complexity in genome-wide association studies. *PLOS Genetics*, *3*(10),

1787–1799. https://doi.org/10.1371/journal.pgen.0030190

Falconer, D. S. (1960). *Introduction to quantitative genetics*. Oliver and Boyd.

Feigelson, H. S., Rodriguez, C., Robertson, A. S., Jacobs, E. J., Calle, E. E., Reid, Y. A., & Thun, M. J. (2001). Determinants of DNA yield and quality from buccal cell samples collected with mouthwash. *Cancer Epidemiology, Biomarkers & Prevention, 10*(9), 1005–1008.

Fisher, R. A. (1919). The correlation between relatives on the supposition of Mendelian inheritance. *Transactions of the Royal Society of Edinburgh, 52*(2), 399–433. https://doi.org/10.1017/S0080456800012163

Fox, N. A., Hane, A. A., & Pine, D. S. (2007). Plasticity for affective neurocircuitry: How the environment affects gene expression. *Current Directions in Psychological Science, 16*(1), 1–5. https://doi.org/10.1111/j.1467-8721.2007.00464.x

Freedman, M. L., Reich, D., Penney, K. L., McDonald, G. J., Mignault, A. A., Patterson, N., Gabriel, S. B., Topol, E. J., Smoller, J. W., Pato, C. N., Pato, M. T., Petryshen, T. L., Kolonel, L. N., Lander, E. S., Sklar, P., Henderson, B., Hirschhorn, J. N., & Altshuler, D. (2004). Assessing the impact of population stratification on genetic association studies. *Nature Genetics, 36*(4), 388–393. https://doi.org/10.1038/ng1333

Gerstein, M. B., Bruce, C., Rozowsky, J. S., Zheng, D., Du, J., Korbel, J. O., Emanuelsson, O., Zhang, Z. D., Weissman, S., & Snyder, M. (2007). What is a gene, post-ENCODE? History and updated definition. *Genome Research, 17*(6), 669–681. https://doi.org/10.1101/gr.6339607

Gizer, I. R., Ficks, C., & Waldman, I. D. (2009). Candidate gene studies of ADHD: A meta-analytic review. *Human Genetics, 126*(1), 51–90. https://doi.org/10.1007/s00439-009-0694-x

Gottesman, I. I., & Gould, T. D. (2003). The endophenotype concept in psychiatry: Etymology and strategic intentions. *The American Journal of Psychiatry, 160*(4), 636–645. https://doi.org/10.1176/appi.ajp.160.4.636

Grotzinger, A. D., Rhemtulla, M., de Vlaming, R., Ritchie, S. J., Mallard, T. T., Hill, W. D., Ip, H. F., Marioni, R. E., McIntosh, A. M., Deary, I. J., Koellinger, P. D., Harden, K. P., Nivard, M. G., & Tucker-Drob, E. M. (2019). Genomic structural equation modelling provides insights into the multivariate genetic architecture of complex traits. *Nature Human Behaviour, 3*(5), 513–525. https://doi.org/10.1038/s41562-019-0566-x

Guttmacher, A. E., & Collins, F. S. (2003). Welcome to the genomic era. *The New England Journal of Medicine, 349*(10), 996–998. https://doi.org/10.1056/NEJMe038132

Halldorsdottir, T., Piechaczek, C., Soares de Matos, A. P., Czamara, D., Pehl, V., Wagenbuechler, P., Feldmann, L., Quickenstedt-Reinhardt, P., Allgaier, A. K., Freisleder, F. J., Greimel, E., Kvist, T., Lahti, J., Räikkönen, K., Rex-Haffner, M., Arnarson, E. Ö., Craighead, W. E., Schulte-Körne, G., & Binder, E. B. (2019). Polygenic risk: Predicting depression outcomes in clinical and epidemiological cohorts of youths. *The American Journal of Psychiatry, 176*(8), 615–625. https://doi.org/10.1176/appi.ajp.2019.18091014

Hawn, S. E., Sheerin, C. M., Webb, B. T., Peterson, R. E., Do, E. K., Dick, D., Kendler, K. S., Bacanu, S. A., & Amstadter, A. B. (2018). Replication of the interaction of *PRKG1* and trauma exposure on alcohol misuse in an independent African American sample. *Journal of Traumatic Stress, 31*(6), 927–932. https://doi.org/10.1002/jts.22339

Hutchison, K. E., Stallings, M., McGeary, J., & Bryan, A. (2004). Population stratification in the candidate gene study: Fatal threat or red herring? *Psychological Bulletin, 130*(1), 66–79. https://doi.org/10.1037/0033-2909.130.1.66

Insel, T. R., & Lehner, T. (2007). A new era in psychiatric genetics? *Biological Psychiatry, 61*(9), 1017–1018. https://doi.org/10.1016/j.biopsych.2007.01.016

International Human Genome Sequencing Consortium. (2001). Initial sequencing and analysis of the human genome. *Nature, 409*(6822), 860–921. https://doi.org/10.1038/35057062

James, C., Iwasiow, R., & Birnboim, H. (2011). *Human genomic DNA content of saliva samples collected with the Oragene® self-collection kit*. DNA Genotek, Inc.

Keller, M. C., Medland, S. E., Duncan, L. E., Hatemi, P. K., Neale, M. C., Maes, H. H., & Eaves, L. J. (2009). Modeling extended twin family data I: Description of the cascade model. *Twin Research and Human Genetics, 12*(1), 8–18. https://doi.org/10.1375/twin.12.1.8

Kendler, K. S. (1990). The super-normal control group in psychiatric genetics. Possible artifactual evidence for coaggregation. *Psychiatric Genetics, 1*(2), 45–53. https://doi.org/10.1097/00041444-199001020-00005

Kendler, K. S. (1993). Twin studies of psychiatric illness. Current status and future directions. *Archives of General Psychiatry, 50*(11), 905–915. https://doi.org/10.1001/archpsyc.1993.01820230075007

Kendler, K. S., & Baker, J. H. (2007). Genetic influences on measures of the environment: A systematic review. *Psychological Medicine, 37*(5), 615–626. https://doi.org/10.1017/S0033291706009524

Kendler, K. S., Gardner, C. O., Annas, P., Neale, M. C., Eaves, L. J., & Lichtenstein, P. (2008). A longitudinal twin study of fears from middle childhood to early adulthood: Evidence for a developmentally dynamic genome. *Archives of General Psychiatry, 65*(4), 421–429. https://doi.org/10.1001/archpsyc.65.4.421

Kendler, K. S., & Myers, J. (2009). A developmental twin study of church attendance and alcohol and nicotine consumption: A model for analyzing the changing impact of genes and environment. *The American Journal of Psychiatry, 166*(10), 1150–1155. https://doi.org/10.1176/appi.ajp.2009.09020182

Kendler, K. S., & Prescott, C. A. (2006). *Genes, environment, and psychopathology: understanding the causes of pyschiatric and substance use disorders.* Guilford Press.

Kidd, K. K. (1991). Trials and tribulations in the search for genes causing neuropsychiatric disorders. *Social Biology, 38*(3-4), 163–178. https://doi.org/10.1080/19485565.1991.9988785

Koenen, K. C., Fu, Q. J., Ertel, K., Lyons, M. J., Eisen, S. A., True, W. R., Goldberg, J., & Tsuang, M. T. (2008). Common genetic liability to major depression and posttraumatic stress disorder in men. *Journal of Affective Disorders, 105*(1-3), 109–115. https://doi.org/10.1016/j.jad.2007.04.021

Lahiri, D. K., & Schnabel, B. (1993). DNA isolation by a rapid method from human blood samples: Effects of $MgCl_2$, EDTA, storage time, and temperature on DNA yield and quality. *Biochemical Genetics, 31*(7-8), 321–328. https://doi.org/10.1007/BF00553174

Lam, M., Awasthi, S., Watson, H. J., Goldstein, J., Panagiotaropoulou, G., Trubetskoy, V., Karlsson, R., Frei, O., Fan, C. C., De Witte, W., Mota, N. R., Mullins, N., Brügger, K., Lee, S. H., Wray, N. R., Skarabis, N., Huang, H., Neale, B., Daly, M. J., . . . Ripke, S. (2020). RICOPILI: Rapid Imputation for COnsortias PIpeLIne. *Bioinformatics, 36*(3), 930–933. https://doi.org/10.1093/bioinformatics/btz633

Le Marchand, L., Lum-Jones, A., Saltzman, B., Visaya, V., Nomura, A. M. Y., & Kolonel, L. N. (2001). Feasibility of collecting buccal cell DNA by mail in a cohort study. *Cancer Epidemiology, Biomarkers & Prevention, 10*(6), 701–703.

Lee, J. J., Wedow, R., Okbay, A., Kong, E., Maghzian, O., Zacher, M., Nguyen-Viet, T. A., Bowers, P., Sidorenko, J., Karlsson Linnér, R., Fontana, M. A., Kundu, T., Lee, C., Li, H., Li, R., Royer, R., Timshel, P. N., Walters, R. K., Willoughby, E. A., . . .

Cesarini, D., & 23andMe Research Team, & Social Science Genetic Association Consortium. (2018). Gene discovery and polygenic prediction from a genome-wide association study of educational attainment in 1.1 million individuals. *Nature Genetics, 50*(8), 1112–1121. https://doi.org/10.1038/s41588-018-0147-3

Lee, S. H., & Wray, N. R. (2013). Novel genetic analysis for case-control genome-wide association studies: Quantification of power and genomic prediction accuracy. *PLOS ONE, 8*(8), e71494. https://doi.org/10.1371/journal.pone.0071494

Lemery, K. S., & Goldsmith, H. H. (1999). Genetically informative designs for the study of behavior development. *International Journal of Behavioral Development, 23*(2), 293–317. https://doi.org/10.1080/016502599383838

Lench, N., Stanier, P., & Williamson, R. (1988). Simple non-invasive method to obtain DNA for gene analysis. *Lancet, 331*(8599), 1356–1358. https://doi.org/10.1016/S0140-6736(88)92178-2

Mendel, G. (1959). Experiments on plant hybridization. In J. A. Peters (Ed.), *Classic papers in genetics* (pp. 1–19). Prentice-Hall. (Original work published in 1865). https://www.biodiversitylibrary.org/item/28876#page/3/mode/1up

Meyer-Lindenberg, A., & Weinberger, D. R. (2006). Intermediate phenotypes and genetic mechanisms of psychiatric disorders. *Nature Reviews: Neuroscience, 7*(10), 818–827. https://doi.org/10.1038/nrn1993

Middeldorp, C. M., Cath, D. C., Van Dyck, R., & Boomsma, D. I. (2005). The co-morbidity of anxiety and depression in the perspective of genetic epidemiology. A review of twin and family studies. *Psychological Medicine, 35*(5), 611–624. https://doi.org/10.1017/S003329170400412X

Moffitt, T. E., Caspi, A., & Rutter, M. (2005). Strategy for investigating interactions between measured genes and measured environments. *Archives of General Psychiatry, 62*(5), 473–481. https://doi.org/10.1001/archpsyc.62.5.473

Mullins, N., Forstner, A. J., O'Connell, K. S., Coombes, B., Coleman, J. R., Qiao, Z., Als, T. D., Bigdeli, T. B., Børte, S., Bryois, J., Charney, A. W., Drange, O. K., Gandal, M. J., Hagenaars, S. P., Ikeda, M., Kamitaki, N., Kim, M., Krebs, K., Panagiotaropoulou, G., . . . Andreassen, O. A. (2021). Genome-wide association study of more than 40,000 bipolar disorder cases provides new insights into the underlying biology. *Nature Genetics, 53*, 817–829. https://doi.org/10.1038/s41588-021-00857-4

Muthén, L. K., & Muthén, B. O. (2017). *Mplus.* Muthén & Muthén.

Neale, M. C., Hunter, M. D., Pritikin, J. N., Zahery, M., Brick, T. R., Kirkpatrick, R. M., Estabrook, R., Bates, T. C., Maes, H. H., & Boker, S. M. (2016). OpenMx 2.0: Extended Structural Equation and Statistical Modeling. *Psychometrika, 81*(2), 535–549. https://doi.org/10.1007/s11336-014-9435-8

Ni, G., Moser, G., Schizophrenia Working Group of the Psychiatric Genomics Consortium, Wray, N. R., & Lee, S. H. (2018). Estimation of genetic correlation via linkage disequilibrium score regression and genomic restricted maximum likelihood. *American Journal of Human Genetics, 102*(6), 1185–1194. https://doi.org/10.1016/j.ajhg.2018.03.021

Nievergelt, C. M., Maihofer, A. X., Klengel, T., Atkinson, E. G., Chen, C. Y., Choi, K. W., Coleman, J. R. I., Dalvie, S., Duncan, L. E., Gelernter, J., Levey, D. F., Logue, M. W., Polimanti, R., Provost, A. C., Ratanatharathorn, A., Stein, M. B., Torres, K., Aiello, A. E., Almli, L. M., . . . Koenen, K. C. (2019). International meta-analysis of PTSD genome-wide association studies identifies sex- and ancestry-specific genetic risk loci. *Nature Communications, 10*(1), 4558. https://doi.org/10.1038/s41467-019-12576-w

Nugent, N. R., Koenen, K. C., Fyer, A., & Weissman, M. (2010). Genetics of anxiety disorders. In H. B. Simpson, Y. Neria, R. Lewis-Fernandez, & F. Schneier (Eds.), *Understanding anxiety: Theory, research, and clinical perspectives* (pp. 139–155). Cambridge University Press.

Ohi, K., Otowa, T., Shimada, M., Sasaki, T., & Tanii, H. (2020). Shared genetic etiology between anxiety disorders and psychiatric and related intermediate phenotypes. *Psychological Medicine, 50*(4), 692–704. https://doi.org/10.1017/S003329171900059X

Pasman, J. A., Smit, D. J. A., Kingma, L., Vink, J. M., Treur, J. L., & Verweij, K. J. H. (2020). Causal relationships between substance use and insomnia. *Drug and Alcohol Dependence, 214*, 108151. https://doi.org/10.1016/j.drugalcdep.2020.108151

Pasman, J. A., Verweij, K. J. H., & Vink, J. M. (2019). Systematic review of polygenic gene–environment interaction in tobacco, alcohol, and cannabis use. *Behavior Genetics, 49*(4), 349–365. https://doi.org/10.1007/s10519-019-09958-7

Peterson, R. E., Kuchenbaecker, K., Walters, R. K., Chen, C.-Y., Popejoy, A. B., Periyasamy, S., Lam, M., Iyegbe, C., Strawbridge, R. J., Brick, L., Carey, C. E., Martin, A. R., Meyers, J. L., Su, J., Chen, J., Edwards, A. C., Kalungi, A., Koen, N., Majara, L., . . . Duncan, L. E. (2019). Genome-wide association studies in ancestrally diverse populations: Opportunities, methods, pitfalls, and recommendations. *Cell, 179*(3), 589–603. https://doi.org/10.1016/j.cell.2019.08.051

Plomin, R., & Davis, O. S. P. (2009). The future of genetics in psychology and psychiatry: Micro-arrays, genome-wide association, and non-coding RNA. *Journal of Child Psychology and Psychiatry, and Allied Disciplines, 50*(1-2), 63–71. https://doi.org/10.1111/j.1469-7610.2008.01978.x

Plomin, R., DeFries, J. C., & Loehlin, J. C. (1977). Genotype-environment interaction and correlation in the analysis of human behavior. *Psychological Bulletin, 84*(2), 309–322. https://doi.org/10.1037/0033-2909.84.2.309

Plomin, R., DeFries, J. C., McClearn, G. E., & McGuffin, P. (2001). *Behavioral genetics.* Worth Publishers.

Plomin, R., Haworth, C. M. A., & Davis, O. S. P. (2009). Common disorders are quantitative traits. *Nature Reviews. Genetics, 10*(12), 872–878. https://doi.org/10.1038/nrg2670

Polimanti, R., Kaufman, J., Zhao, H., Kranzler, H. R., Ursano, R. J., Kessler, R. C., Gelernter, J., & Stein, M. B. (2018). A genome-wide gene-by-trauma interaction study of alcohol misuse in two independent cohorts identifies *PRKG1* as a risk locus. *Molecular Psychiatry, 23*(1), 154–160. https://doi.org/10.1038/mp.2017.24

Porjesz, B., Rangaswamy, M., Kamarajan, C., Jones, K. A., Padmanabhapillai, A., & Begleiter, H. (2005). The utility of neurophysiological markers in the study of alcoholism. *Clinical Neurophysiology, 116*(5), 993–1018. https://doi.org/10.1016/j.clinph.2004.12.016

Pray, L. (2008). Discovery of DNA structure and function: Watson and Crick. *Nature Education, 1*(1). https://www.nature.com/scitable/topicpage/discovery-of-dna-structure-and-function-watson-397/

Pritchard, J. K., Stephens, M., Rosenberg, N. A., & Donnelly, P. (2000). Association mapping in structured populations. *American Journal of Human Genetics, 67*(1), 170–181. https://doi.org/10.1086/302959

Risch, N. (1990). Linkage strategies for genetically complex traits. I. Multilocus models. *American Journal of Human Genetics, 46*(2), 222–228.

Risch, N., Herrell, R., Lehner, T., Liang, K. Y., Eaves, L., Hoh, J., Griem, A., Kovacs, M., Ott, J., & Merikangas, K. R. (2009). Interaction between the serotonin transporter gene (5-HTTLPR), stressful life events, and risk of depression: A meta-analysis. *Journal of the American Medical Association, 301*(23), 2462–2471. https://doi.org/10.1001/jama.2009.878

Rutter, M. (2010). Gene-environment interplay. *Depression and Anxiety, 27*(1), 1–4. https://doi.org/10.1002/da.20641

Rutter, M., Moffitt, T. E., & Caspi, A. (2006). Gene-environment interplay and psychopathology: Multiple varieties but real effects. *Journal of Child Psychology and Psychiatry, and Allied Disciplines*, 47(3–4), 226–261. https://doi.org/10.1111/j.1469-7610.2005.01557.x

Samek, D., Rueter, M., & Koh, B. (2013). Overview of behavioral genetics research for family researchers. *Journal of Family Theory & Review*, 5(3), 214–233. https://doi.org/10.1111/jftr.12013

Shanahan, M. J., & Hofer, S. M. (2005). Social context in gene-environment interactions: Retrospect and prospect. *The Journals of Gerontology: Series B. Psychological Sciences and Social Sciences*, 60(Special Issue 1), 65–76.

Sheerin, C. M., Bountress, K. E., Meyers, J. L., Saenz de Viteri, S. S., Shen, H., Maihofer, A. X., Duncan, L. E., & Amstadter, A. B. (2020). Shared molecular genetic risk of alcohol dependence and post-traumatic stress disorder (PTSD). *Psychology of Addictive Behaviors*, 34(5), 613–619. https://doi.org/10.1037/adb0000568

Spielman, R. S., & Ewens, W. J. (1996). The TDT and other family-based tests for linkage disequilibrium and association. *American Journal of Human Genetics*, 59(5), 983–989.

Steinberg, K., Beck, J., Nickerson, D., Garcia-Closas, M., Gallagher, M., Caggana, M., Reid, Y., Cosentino, M., Ji, J., Johnson, D., Hayes, R. B., Earley, M., Lorey, F., Hannon, H., Khoury, M. J., & Sampson, E. (2002). DNA banking for epidemiologic studies: A review of current practices. *Epidemiology*, 13(3), 246–254. https://doi.org/10.1097/00001648-200205000-00003

Strachan, T., & Read, A. P. (2019). *Human molecular genetics*. Garland Science.

The 1000 Genomes Project Consortium. (2015). A global reference for human genetic variation. *Nature*, 526(7571), 68–74. https://doi.org/10.1038/nature15393

Thorp, J. G., Campos, A. I., Grotzinger, A. D., Gerring, Z. F., An, J., Ong, J. S., Wang, W., 23andMe Research Team, Shringarpurt, S., Byrne, E. M., MacGregor, S., Martin, N. G., Medland, S. E., Middeldorp, C. M., & Derks, E. M. (2021). Symptom-level modelling unravels the shared genetic architecture of anxiety and depression. *Nature Human Behaviour*, 5(10), 1432–1442. https://doi.org/10.1038/s41562-021-01094-9

Tishkoff, S. A., Reed, F. A., Friedlaender, F. R., Ehret, C., Ranciaro, A., Froment, A., Hirbo, J. B., Awomoyi, A. A., Bodo, J. M., Doumbo, O., Ibrahim, M., Juma, A. T., Kotze, M. J., Lema, G., Moore, J. H., Mortensen, H., Nyambo, T. B., Omar, S. A., Powell, K., . . . Williams, S. M. (2009). The genetic structure and history of Africans and African Americans. *Science*, 324(5930), 1035–1044. https://doi.org/10.1126/science.1172257

Uher, R., & McGuffin, P. (2010). The moderation by the serotonin transporter gene of environmental adversity in the etiology of depression: 2009 update. *Molecular Psychiatry*, 15(1), 18–22. https://doi.org/10.1038/mp.2009.123

Venter, J. C., Adams, M. D., Myers, E. W., Li, P. W., Mural, R. J., Sutton, G. G., Smith, H. O., Yandell, M., Evans, C. A., Holt, R. A., Gocayne, J. D., Amanatides, P., Ballew, R. M., Huson, D. H., Wortman, J. R., Zhang, Q., Kodira, C. D., Zheng, X. H., Chen, L., . . . Zhu, X. (2001). The sequence of the human genome. *Science*, 291(5507), 1304–1351. https://doi.org/10.1126/science.1058040

Walker, E. F., Sabuwalla, Z., & Huot, R. (2004). Pubertal neuromaturation, stress sensitivity, and psychopathology. *Development and Psychopathology*, 16(4), 807–824. https://doi.org/10.1017/S0954579404040027

Wand, H., Lambert, S. A., Tamburro, C., Iacocca, M. A., O'Sullivan, J. W., Sillari, C., Kullo, I. J., Rowley, R., Dron, J. S., Brockman, D., Venner, E., McCarthy, M. I., Antoniou, A. C., Easton, D. F., Hegele, R. A., Khera, A. V., Chatterjee, N., Kooperberg, C., Edwards, K., . . . Wojcik, G. L. (2021). Improving reporting standards for polygenic scores in risk prediction studies. *Nature*, 591(7849), 211–219. https://doi.org/10.1038/s41586-021-03243-6

Watson, J. D., & Crick, F. H. C. (1953). A structure for deoxyribose nucleic acid. *Nature*, 171, 737–738.

Wedenoja, J., Loukola, A., Tuulio-Henriksson, A., Paunio, T., Ekelund, J., Silander, K., Varilo, T., Heikkilä, K., Suvisaari, J., Partonen, T., Lönnqvist, J., & Peltonen, L. (2008). Replication of linkage on chromosome 7q22 and association of the regional *Reelin* gene with working memory in schizophrenia families. *Molecular Psychiatry*, 13(7), 673–684. https://doi.org/10.1038/sj.mp.4002047

Wermter, A.-K., Laucht, M., Schimmelmann, B., Banaschewski, T., Sonuga-Barke, E., Rietschel, M., & Becker, K. (2010). From nature versus nurture, via nature and nurture, to gene × environment interaction in mental disorders. *European Child & Adolescent Psychiatry*, 19(3),199–210. https://doi.org/10.1007/s00787-009-0082-z

Woo, J. G., Sun, G., Haverbusch, M., Indugula, S., Martin, L. J., Broderick, J. P., Deka, R., & Woo, D. (2007). Quality assessment of buccal versus blood genomic DNA using the Affymetrix 500 K GeneChip. *BMC Genetics*, 8(79), 79. https://doi.org/10.1186/1471-2156-8-79

Yaeger, R., Avila-Bront, A., Abdul, K., Nolan, P. C., Grann, V. R., Birchette, M. G., Choudhry, S., Burchard, E. G., Beckman, K. B., Gorroochurn, P., Ziv, E., Consedine, N. S., & Joe, A. K. (2008). Comparing genetic ancestry and self-described race in African Americans born in the United States and in Africa. *Cancer Epidemiology, Biomarkers & Prevention, 17*(6), 1329–1338. https://doi.org/10.1158/1055-9965.EPI-07-2505

Yang, J., Lee, S. H., Goddard, M. E., & Visscher, P. M. (2011). GCTA: A tool for genome-wide complex trait analysis. *American Journal of Human Genetics, 88*(1), 76–82. https://doi.org/10.1016/j.ajhg.2010.11.011

Young, R. M., Lawford, B. R., Noble, E. P., Kann, B., Wilkie, A., Ritchie, T., Arnold, L., & Shadforth, S. (2002). Harmful drinking in military veterans with post-traumatic stress disorder: Association with the D2 dopamine receptor A1 allele. *Alcohol and Alcoholism, 37*(5), 451–456. https://doi.org/10.1093/alcalc/37.5.451

CHAPTER 38

HUMAN GENETIC EPIDEMIOLOGY

Floris Huider, Lannie Ligthart, Yuri Milaneschi,
Brenda W. J. H. Penninx, and Dorret I. Boomsma

Individual differences in human traits, including behavior, originate from a wide range of genetic and environmental factors. Genetic factors include the entire set of genes that a person has inherited from their parents. In contrast, environmental factors include all nongenetic processes, ranging from intrauterine to family environment, life events, friends, and many other (often unknown) factors. Even this simple statement is complex, because the intrauterine environment may be shaped by the maternal genotype (e.g., 20% of variation in birthweight can be attributed to the maternal genotype; Falconer & Mackay, 1996, p. 138), and for a large set of outcomes that we tend to label as "environment," a genetic component plays a role (e.g., 52% of variation in leisure time activities can be attributed to genetic differences; Vinkhuyzen et al., 2010). Understanding the causes of individual differences can serve to answer the age-old questions of nature versus nurture and can have important implications for research and society, particularly by improving our understanding and treatment of a range of disorders and diseases. Methods in genetic epidemiology have also proven to serve as a toolbox to address questions that go beyond the estimation of heritability and genetic covariance structure and

focus on questions of causality, intergenerational transmission, and cultural inheritance. Some of these methods rely on designs that require information on the genetic and environmental sharing of participants (pedigree information), others make use of molecular genetic data. The area of research that focuses on the identification and quantification of genetic effects in human behavior is called *behavior genetics* or *genetic epidemiology*.

Although the origins of genetic epidemiology can be traced back over 100 years to pioneers such as Mendel, Fischer, and Galton, the biotechnical advances of the past two decades have enabled the field to advance at an unprecedented pace. We provide a three-part overview of genetic epidemiological methods and developments. The field of genetic epidemiology deals with questions such as: "To what degree are individual differences in depression caused by genetic factors?" "Which parts of the genome contribute to the development of depression?" and "Once we identify these variants, can they serve as predictors at the individual level?" These questions exemplify the different fundamental stages of genetic epidemiological research, namely estimation of genetic influences, identification of genetic variants, and

This work was supported by the Royal Dutch Academy for Arts and Science (KNAW) Academy Professor Award (PAH/6635) to DIB; the Netherlands Organization for Scientific Research (NWO 480-15-001/674) and Biobanking and Biomolecular Resources Research Infrastructure (BBMRI-NL: 184.021.007; 184.033.111).

https://doi.org/10.1037/0000319-038
APA Handbook of Research Methods in Psychology, Second Edition: Vol. 2. Research Designs: Quantitative, Qualitative, Neuropsychological, and Biological, H. Cooper (Editor-in-Chief)

prediction and causality, which we discuss separately.

First, to establish if and to what degree genetic factors affect individual differences in a trait of interest, early methods did not have access to techniques to directly observe and measure the genome, and relied on family data and modeling to infer the genetic contributions to individual differences. Such methods form the foundation of the field, and many still retain their use today. Thus, Part I of this chapter describes the estimation of heritability as well as more advanced multivariate modeling, as based on twin methodology, that is used for example in psychometrics, causality modeling and to estimate genetic correlations among traits.

After a genetic contribution has been established, contemporary techniques allow for the localization and identification of specific parts of the genome that contribute to a genetic effect on a trait. Such methods are referred to as gene-finding, and their use and success has increased massively in the past two decades. Thus, Part II discusses methodology used to localize and identify genes, of which genome-wide association studies (GWAS) have become a staple method.

Finally, with the results that emerge from the previous steps, further questions can be addressed, for instance: "Can we make meaningful predictions about a person's cardiovascular risk based on their genome?" or "Do depression and cardiovascular disease share part of their genetic liability?" or alternatively, "Is depression causal for the development of cardiovascular disease?" Thus, Part III illustrates techniques devoted to individual phenotype prediction (polygenic scores), investigation of pleiotropy (genetic correlation) and testing of causal hypotheses (Mendelian Randomization). Before we dive into Part I, a brief introduction is provided to illustrate basic concepts of molecular genetics.

GENETICS: BASIC CONCEPTS

Genetic information is encoded in deoxyribonucleic acid (DNA) molecules. The DNA code contains the units of genetic information we call *genes*. Definitions of a gene tend to evolve with advances in science, but common definitions include "a unit of inheritance" or "a packet of genetic information that encodes a protein or ribonucleic acid (RNA)." The estimated number of genes in the human genome has long been a subject of debate. A mere 20 years ago, it was predicted that the human genome contained around 100,000 to 150,000 genes (e.g., Liang et al., 2000), but these estimates decreased to 20,000 to 25,000 (International Human Genome Sequencing Consortium, 2004). Recent biotechnical advances have allowed for more precise estimates, placing the current estimate of human protein-coding genes at 20,448 (Howe et al., 2021). That said, one gene can produce multiple different end products because of alternative splicing.

In humans, the DNA molecules are organized in 23 pairs of *chromosomes*: 22 pairs of *autosomes* and one pair of *sex chromosomes*. The genetic sequence as a whole is called the *genome*, and a location in the genome that contains a gene or a genetic marker is referred to as a *locus*. A *quantitative trait locus* (QTL) is a locus that harbors a gene influencing a quantitative trait, that is, a trait that varies on a quantitative scale, or the liability to a complex disorder, when the assessment of the trait is on an interval or ordinal scale.

The nuclei of nearly all human cells contain two versions of each chromosome and therefore of each gene. The two corresponding chromosomes are called *homologous* chromosomes. One is received from the mother, the other from the father. In addition, a small amount of DNA is contained in the maternally inherited *mitochondria*. Although most of the DNA sequence is identical in all humans, at some loci different versions of the sequence occur. These variants are called *alleles*. The word *allele* can refer to a gene variant, to versions of a genetic marker, or any other fragment of DNA sequence. Individuals who carry the same allele at both homologous chromosomes are called *homozygous*. Individuals with two different alleles are *heterozygous*. The two alleles together make up a person's *genotype*. The term *haplotype* indicates a combination of alleles at multiple loci that an individual receives from one parent (Ott, 1999). It usually refers to a combination of alleles transmitted close together on the same chromosome. Finally, any characteristic of an individual that we can observe (e.g., appearance, behavior, disease) is referred to as *phenotype*.

Alleles affecting quantitative traits can exert their effect in various ways. When the alleles act independently, that is, the effects add up, we speak of *additive* genetic effects. The effects of an allele can also depend on the effect of another allele. Such interactions are referred to as *nonadditive* genetic effects. There are several forms of nonadditivity. Interactions between two alleles at the same locus are referred to as *dominance*. When the interaction is between alleles at two different loci, it is referred to as *epistasis*.

PART I. ESTIMATING HERITABILITY

A central concept in the field of genetic epidemiology is that of *heritability*, defined as the proportion of phenotypic variance attributable to genetic factors. In other words: To what degree are differences between individuals caused by differences in their genome? It is often observed that human traits run in families, whose genomes are shared. The mere observation that a trait is familial, however, does not imply heritability, because familial resemblance can also be the result of a shared family environment. Thus, estimating the heritability of a trait is a crucial first step in exploring its genetic architecture. Heritability (h^2) is expressed as the proportion of total variance that can be ascribed to genetic variance; it is relative to the magnitude of nongenetic influences and can vary across populations, sex, age, and time. For example, the heritability of IQ depends strongly on age (e.g., Bartels et al., 2004), whereas the heritability of height is relatively stable across most populations (70%–90%; e.g., Jelenkovic et al., 2016). Note that heritability is a population parameter (much like a median or mean) and does not apply to a single person. Heritability captures the decomposition of variance under current environmental conditions; a large estimate does not imply that other exposures or new

"environmental" interventions will not be effective in altering trait outcome.

One approach to estimating heritability is by studying adopted children and their biological and adoptive parents. Similarities between adopted children and their biological parents reflect genetic influences, whereas similarities between adopted children and adoptive parents reflect the effects of the environment. However, there are challenges to these studies: adoptions are relatively rare, and adoptive children and parents cannot be assumed to be representative of the general population. Adoption studies may also be characterized either by matching between biological and adoptive parents, for example, on physical characteristics, or by selective placement in one type of family rather than another type of family, or—in open adoptions—by involvement of the birth mother with the adoptive family (Plomin et al., 2008, Chapter 5).

The Classical Twin Design
Many studies investigate genetic influences from twin data. In twin studies, the resemblance between monozygotic (MZ) and dizygotic (DZ) twins is compared to decompose the variance in a trait into contributions of genes, shared environment, and nonshared environment (Martin et al., 1997). MZ twins share (nearly) 100% of their segregating genes, whereas DZ twins share an average of 50% of their segregating genes (note that this percentage refers to the portion of the genome in which variation occurs, because more than 99% of the genome is identical between humans). In contrast to genetic similarity, MZ and DZ twins share their prenatal and home environment to an equal degree. Thus, differences between MZ twins are attributed to nonshared environmental influences, whereas the degree to which MZ twins are more similar than DZ twins reflects the influence of genetic factors. Using these principles, the variance in a trait can be decomposed into variance explained by additive genetic factors (A), common environment (C) shared by family members, and nonshared environment or measurement error (E). In the absence of dominance or epistasis, a preliminary

estimate of the heritability of a trait is given by twice the difference between the MZ and DZ twin correlation: $h^2 = 2(rMZ - rDZ)$. When $rMZ > 2rDZ$, there is evidence for a contribution of nonadditive genetic influences, also referred to as genetic dominance (D), which also includes effects of epistasis. In such instances, the percentage of variance explained by A and D together is referred to as the *broad-sense heritability*; A alone is called the *narrow-sense heritability*.

The contribution of A, C, D, and E to the trait variance is estimated on the basis of the biometrical model, which forms the theoretical foundation of genetic epidemiology, including twin studies (Falconer & Mackay, 1996; Posthuma et al., 2003). When $P = A + C + D + E$, where A, C, D and E represent individual factor scores and P the phenotypic value for an individual, the total phenotypic variance of a trait (P) can be decomposed into components explained by A, C, D, and E: $V_P = V_A + V_D + V_C + V_E$, assuming no interaction or correlation between genetic and environmental factors (the covariance between A and D is zero by definition).

The similarity between MZ twins, or covariance, is expressed as: $cov(MZ) = V_A + V_D + V_C$. Because V_E is by definition nonshared variance, it cannot contribute to covariance of family members. V_C is, by definition, shared, and the genetic variance is also entirely shared in MZ twin pairs. The expectation for the DZ twin covariance is: $cov(DZ) = \frac{1}{2}V_A + \frac{1}{4}V_D + V_C$. On average, one half of the additive genetic variance (V_A) is shared between DZ twins (and between nontwin siblings). To share nonadditive variance (V_D), two relatives have to share both alleles of a gene, an event that occurs with a probability of 25% in DZ twins (or full siblings). Figure 38.1 shows a graphic representation of the model that arises from these principles.

Structural Equation Modeling for Twin Analyses

Contributions of genetic and environmental factors to a phenotype can be estimated by structural equation modeling (SEM), which involves the specification of a theoretical model whose parameters can be estimated by, for example, maximum likelihood. Different models can be tested to establish which of these corresponds best to the observed data. Genetic SEM usually involves a multiple group design where data from, for example, MZ and DZ twins are analyzed simultaneously, and in which parameters (*a*, *c*, *d*, and *e* in Figure 38.1) are constrained to be equal across groups to ensure identification of the model.

In SEM, hypotheses can be tested by comparing a model without restrictions (saturated model) to one where parameters are dropped from the model (e.g., no shared environment). In well-powered studies, when dropping or equating parameters does not result in a significant deterioration of fit, this indicates the more parsimonious model fits the data as well as the more complex model. Significance is determined on the basis of the difference in −2LL between two models, which is asymptotically distributed as χ^2. The degrees of freedom of the test equal the difference in the number of parameters. In smaller studies, dropping of parameters remains a point of discussion because omitting nonsignificant parameters from the model might bias other estimates (Martin et al., 1997; Posthuma & Boomsma, 2000). Alternative fit indexes have been proposed for large studies, such as the root-mean-square error of approximation (Browne & Cudeck, 1993), the Bayesian information criterion (Schwarz, 1978), and the Akaike information criterion (Akaike, 1987).

Categorical Data

Methods used in genetic epidemiology often rely on the assumption that a trait is normally distributed. For continuous phenotypes, normality can be assumed and is indeed expected for traits that are affected by many genes (Fischer, 1918). However, categorical phenotypes (e.g., presence or absence of disease, or categories representing levels of trait severity) cannot be analyzed in the same way. As a solution, heritability of categorical traits is often estimated for the normally distributed underlying *liability* scale. The liability threshold model (Falconer, 1965) assumes that the categories

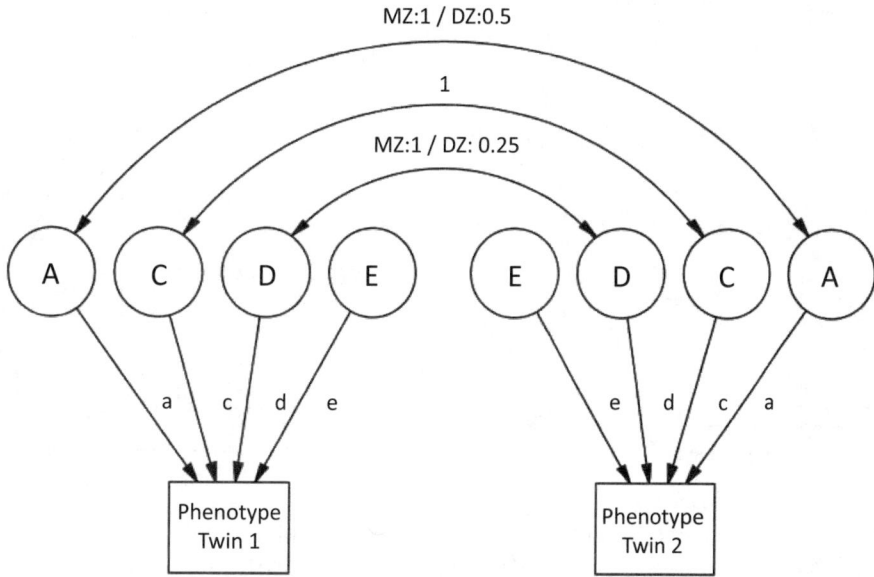

FIGURE 38.1.   Univariate twin model. Path diagram showing the A, C, D, and E factors for a twin pair, and the correlations between each of the factors for MZ and DZ twins. Following the tracing rules of path analysis (Wright, 1934), the phenotypic variance explained by each component is calculated as the squared path coefficient: The genetic variance for an individual is calculated as a^2, the shared environmental variance equals c^2, and so on. The total variance is derived by summing the variance explained by the individual components: $a^2 + c^2 + d^2 + e^2$. The covariance between twins is calculated by tracing the path from twin 1, through the double-headed arrow, to twin 2. For instance, the genetic covariance between MZ twins equals $a \times 1 \times a = a^2$, whereas for DZ twins it equals $a \times .5 \times a = .5a^2$. The total covariance is calculated by adding up all paths contributing to the covariance (i.e., all paths that connect the two twins), which is $a^2 + c^2 + d^2$ for an MZ pair and $.5a^2 + c^2 + .25d^2$ for a DZ pair. When only data from twins reared together are available, it is not possible to estimate C and D at the same time because there is not enough information; an ACDE model is not identified. Therefore, the twin correlations are used to decide whether an ACE or an ADE model is more plausible.

of a variable reflect an imprecise measurement of an underlying normal distribution that has a mean of 0 and a variance of 1, and that is divided by one or more thresholds into discrete categories. The area under the curve between two thresholds represents the proportion of cases within a category (Figure 38.2). The resemblance of relatives (e.g., twins) is expressed as tetrachoric or polychoric correlations, which represent the correlation between relatives on the liability dimension.

Extensions of the Classical Twin Design

The classical twin design can be extended to include data from, for example, siblings, parents, and spouses. The genetic similarity between sibling pairs is the same as the resemblance between DZ twins, that is, on average 50% of segregating genes. Adding data from one or more nontwin siblings (often referred to as an *extended twin design*) results in a substantial increase in power to detect genetic and shared environmental effects (e.g., Posthuma & Boomsma, 2000).

The similarity between parents and children is 50% for additive genetic effects and 0% for dominance. To share dominance effects two individuals have to share both alleles identical by descent (IBD), that is, coming from the same ancestor. Parents each transmit one allele to their children, and so they cannot share two alleles IBD. Analyzing twin-sibling data does not provide sufficient

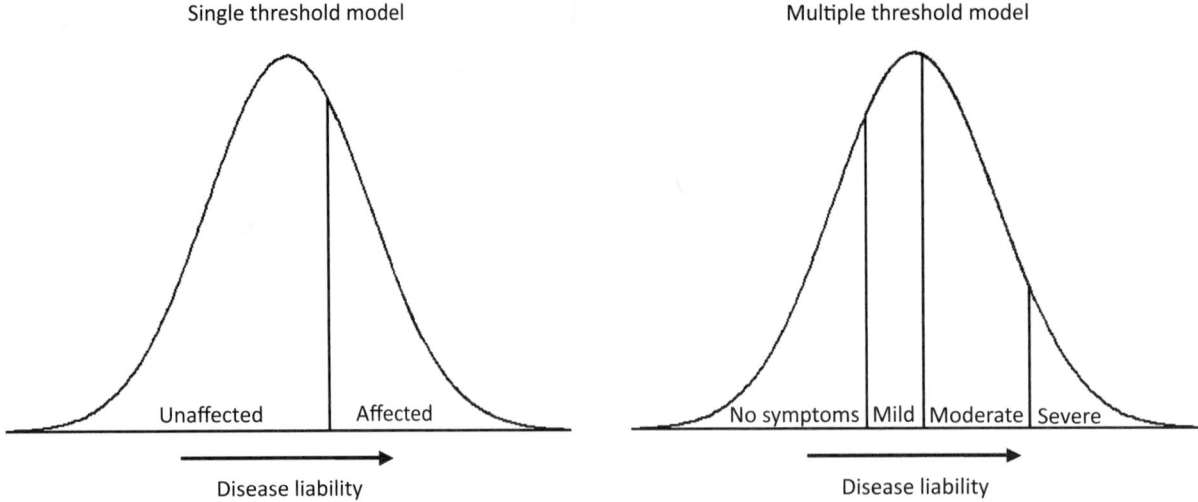

FIGURE 38.2.   Threshold models. In both cases a normal distribution of liability underlies the observed phenotypes, which have been categorized into discrete classes. Single threshold model: This represents a disease phenotype with affected and unaffected individuals. Multiple threshold model: In this case an ordinal variable with categories corresponding to different levels of severity, in this case ranging from no symptoms, via mild and moderate, to a severe phenotype.

information to estimate a full ACDE model. When the extended twin design also includes parents of twins it allows for the estimation of all four variance components, although the researcher needs to recognize that age effects may play an important role.

Data from parents and spouses are valuable to estimate the effects of cultural transmission and assortative mating (i.e., phenotypic correlations between spouses; Fulker, 1982). An example of this design is given by Distel et al. (2009), who investigated whether cultural transmission from parents to offspring effected borderline personality features. Familial resemblance was due to shared genes and cultural transmission did not play a role. There was some evidence for assortative mating, which explained a small amount of trait variance.

Multivariate Models for Twin Data

Another extension of the models described thus far is to analyze multiple traits simultaneously. Bivariate or multivariate models can quantify the genetic and environmental correlation among traits and explore the etiology of their association (or *comorbidity*), and test whether the same genes affect correlated traits or whether a similar environment is responsible for the correlation.

In addition to the MZ and DZ twin correlations, a multivariate model also analyzes the phenotypic correlation between traits (within a person), and the *cross-twin cross-trait correlation* (the correlation between Trait 1 in Twin 1 and Trait 2 in Twin 2): if the cross-twin cross-trait correlation is higher in MZ than in DZ twins, this indicates that the two traits are genetically correlated. If the cross-twin cross-trait correlation is the same in MZ as in DZ twins, and larger than zero, shared environmental correlations are present. Figure 38.3 shows an example of a bivariate ACE model. The cross-twin cross-trait correlations are modeled by adding the cross-paths a_{21}, c_{21}, and e_{21}. If the a_{21} path is significant, this implies that a genetic correlation is present, and similarly, significance of c_{21} and e_{21} indicates shared and nonshared environmental correlations, respectively. For instance, following the tracing rules of path analysis (Wright, 1934), the genetic covariance between Phenotype 1 in Twin 1 and Phenotype 2 in Twin 2 in DZ twins is given by $a_{11} \times 0.5 \times a_{21}$.

Ligthart et al. (2010) analyzed the relation between migraine and depression. The correlation between the two traits was estimated at .28. Most of the shared variance was explained by genetic factors (55%), with the remaining covariance due

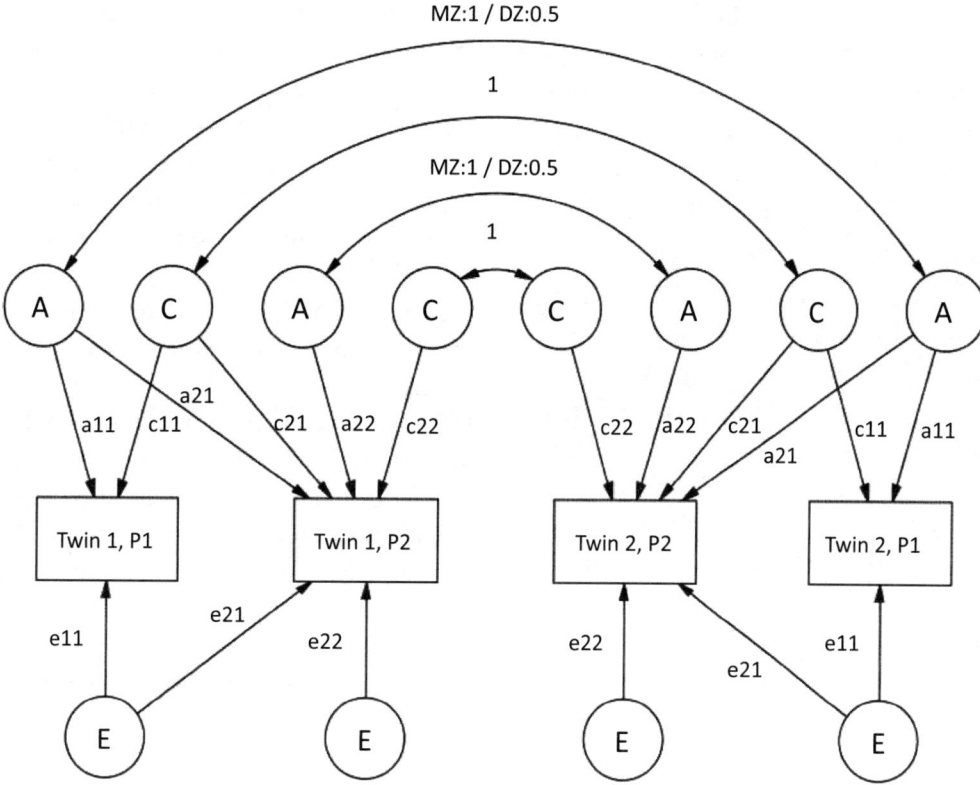

FIGURE 38.3.   Example of a bivariate twin model. A bivariate ACE model, with two twins and two phenotypes (P1 and P2).

to nonshared environment. There was a significant genetic correlation between the traits ($r = .30$). Thus, migraine and depression are partly influenced by the same genes and by the same nonshared environmental factors.

Similarly, by analyzing the covariance between repeated measures at different time points, or ages, it can be determined whether stability over time is due to genetic or environmental factors. Bartels et al. (2004) investigated the contribution of genes and environment to stability in internalizing and externalizing problems in children ages 3 to 12 years old, and found that genetic factors were responsible for stability over age. Nonshared environment played only a modest role in explaining stability in problem behavior.

Sex × Genotype, Age × Genotype, and Environment × Genotype Interaction

The influence of genetic and environmental factors may differ for males and females, across age, or across different environmental exposures. Taking

gender as an example, we can test a full model in which all parameter estimates are different for males and females, and then test whether the estimates can be constrained to be equal. In many situations, means or thresholds have to be modeled separately for males and females, for instance, because traits such as migraine or depression are more prevalent in women. Several hypotheses can be tested:

1. The variance components differ, for instance, when a trait is more heritable in one sex than in the other. A difference in heritability may arise for different reasons. The genetic variance can differ between the sexes or be the same in the two sexes, but the environmental variance could be larger in men than in women. Because heritability is expressed as a ratio (genetic variance over total variance) this would lead to a lower heritability estimate in men.

2. The variance components are proportionally the same in males and females, but in one sex,

the total trait variance is larger. This model can be tested by constraining all variance components in one sex to be a scalar multiple of the variance components in the other sex.

3. All variance components (i.e., V_A, V_D, V_C, and V_E) are the same for males and females.

To test which of these models fits the data best, one starts with a full model in which all parameters differ for males and females. Then, by constraining the parameters step by step, it is tested whether parameter estimates differ significantly between men and women. This same approach can be used to test for heritability differences among age groups, or among groups that differ in environmental exposures. For example, Koopmans et al. (1999) observed higher heritabilities for alcohol use initiation in females without a religious upbringing than in females with a religious upbringing (40% compared with 0%). For males, heritability was also higher in the nonreligious group, but the difference was not significant.

When data from DZ opposite-sex (DOS) twins are available, it is possible, in addition to quantitative differences, to test for qualitative sex differences, that is, if different genes affect the trait in males and females. This is tested by estimating the correlation between the latent genetic factors in DOS twins, while this correlation remains fixed at .5 in the same-sex pairs. If the correlation in DOS twins is significantly lower than .5, this tells us that the genetic factors affecting males and females are (partly) different. It is also possible that different environmental factors influence a trait in men and women. In this case, the correlation between the C factors (see Figure 38.1) would be estimated in DOS twin pairs, or in opposite-sex siblings. It is not possible to estimate the correlations for genetic and shared environmental factors simultaneously in a classical twin design, as there is only one data point available that is informative for this test.

The expression of genes may depend on environmental factors, sometimes referred to as moderators. An interesting case of gene–environment interaction (G × E) was found in a study by Boomsma et al. (1999), where a religious upbringing reduced the influence of genetic factors on disinhibition, one of the dimensions of sensation seeking. In general, if G × E is present but not modeled, parameter estimates may be biased. Interaction between A and C will present as A, whereas interaction between A and E will present as E.

The presence of G × E can also be investigated by multigroup design, the presence of G × E can be investigated by including the environmental exposure as a moderator in the model. In this approach, the discrete or continuous moderator affects the path coefficients from genetic and environmental factors to the trait of interest. If G × E is present but not modeled, this can result in biased parameter estimates. Interaction between A and C will present as A, whereas interaction between A and E will present as E (Purcell, 2002). Examples of G × E research can be found in Culverhouse et al. (2018), Moffitt et al. (2005), and Munafò et al. (2009).

PART II. GENE-FINDING

If a trait is heritable, a next step is to find the genes involved. The genome harbors many regions that vary across individuals, and the goal of gene-finding is to identify which of these regions covary with a trait of interest. These techniques require the collection of DNA samples from, for example, blood or buccal cells and the measurement of genotypes, referred to as *markers, genetic variants,* or *polymorphisms.*

Two methods for gene-finding are *linkage* and *association.* Linkage has been instrumental in the early gene-finding era for localizing genetic variants involved in single-gene or Mendelian traits. It is still used in some areas of research and exemplifies several essential concepts in gene-finding. Hence, we briefly discuss the rationale behind linkage and the methods involved. We follow with a discussion of gene-finding methods based on association, focusing on the technique that revolutionized the field of genetic epidemiology: GWAS. We provide a description of GWAS methodology and its augmentation through meta-analysis. Finally, we discuss methods that aid in the interpretation of GWAS results, including set-based testing and pathway analysis. Basic introductions linkage and association studies may also be found in Balding (2006), Nyholt (2008), or Vink and Boomsma (2002).

Gene-Finding Unit of Measurement: Markers

To measure the entire segregating genome by DNA sequencing would be a costly endeavor when done in many individuals. Instead, linkage and association methods reduce the number of variants that require measurement by taking advantage of *linkage disequilibrium (LD)*. During meiosis (cell division that results in gamete production), maternal and paternal chromosomes break and exchange genetic material. Recombination is less frequent when genes are close together ("in LD"), and large blocks of DNA (*haplotypes*) can remain unchanged across generations and individuals. Thus, when locus 1 and locus 2 are located on the same haplotype, measuring one locus can also convey information about the other. This has incited the use of *markers*. Markers are carefully selected genetic variants with a known location on the genome. They need not be causal to the trait of interest, but measuring a marker can serve as a proxy to measuring the causal variant. When we say an individual is genotyped for a linkage or association study, this means their DNA is characterized at a selected number of marker loci.

Several types of markers are used in gene-finding studies. *Single nucleotide polymorphisms* (SNPs) are single base pairs with multiple alleles (e.g., some individuals have an A at this locus, while others have a C). Usually, SNPs with two variants are selected for gene-finding studies. *Microsatellites* are sequence-length polymorphisms that consist of a varying number of repeats of a short (usually 1–4 base pairs) sequence of DNA, for example, CACACACACACACA. *Copy number variants* are DNA fragments ranging from kilobases (Kb) to even megabases (Mb) in size, of which different numbers of copies are present in different

individuals. Interestingly, there is increasing evidence for a discordance in CNVs and de novo mutations within MZ twin pairs (Bruder et al., 2008; Jonsson et al., 2021). This implies that MZ twins are not always 100% genetically identical in all cells. We are currently at the beginning of an exciting new line of research studying genetic dissimilarities within MZ twin pairs. How the study of genetic differences in discordant MZ twin pairs may be used as an effective gene-finding strategy is discussed by Zwijnenburg et al. (2010).

Several companies (e.g., Illumina, Affymetrix) produce predesigned SNP arrays or "chips" that allow for the efficient genotyping of tens to hundreds of thousands of individuals. Rapid advancements in biotechnology have also resulted in a new class of techniques referred to as *next-generation sequencing*. DNA sequencing is the process in which the nucleotide order of a given DNA fragment is determined, and next-generation sequencing techniques have the potential to make sequencing of the genome faster, more affordable, and more accurate. In time, this will produce a paradigm shift from a need to rely on markers to the direct analysis of all variants, particularly those of low and rare frequency (Wang et al., 2015), with exciting implications for gene-finding.

Genetic Linkage Methods

Linkage analysis requires pedigree information to infer which regions of the genome covary with a trait of interest. The objective is to determine whether relatives who are phenotypically similar, are also genotypically similar in a particular region of the genome. If this is the case, this region may harbor a gene involved in the trait of interest. Linkage is based on the principle that two loci that are physically close together—for example, a DNA marker and an unobserved disease locus or QTL, are more likely to be coinherited. Broadly speaking, two types of linkage analysis can be distinguished: parametric and nonparametric linkage.

Parametric linkage. Parametric (or model-based) linkage requires the specification of a genetic model with allele frequencies, mode of inheritance, and penetrances (the probability that a trait is expressed given the genotype). Linkage analysis exploits the fact that during recombination, the probability that two loci, the marker (which is measured) and the QTL (which is hypothesized to influence the phenotype) are separated depends on the distance between them. Linkage analysis compares the likelihood of the observed pedigree data under the alternative hypothesis of linkage with the likelihood under the null hypothesis of no linkage between the marker and the QTL. The result of this test is expressed as the logarithm of odds (LOD), called the *LOD score*. The higher the LOD score, the stronger the evidence for linkage; that is, the genomic region indexed by the marker also harbors a QTL that influences the trait. Parametric linkage is best suited for Mendelian traits, for which a genetic model can be specified. Parametric linkage methods are explained by Ott (1999), and examples of applications in Joutel et al. (1993) and Ophoff et al. (1996).

Nonparametric (model-free) linkage. Nonparametric linkage does not rely on the specification of a genetic model, and so lends itself to the analysis of more complex traits. A nonparametric linkage test assesses whether relatives with similar phenotypes also have similar genotypes. Genotypic similarity is expressed in a measure called *identity by descent* (IBD). Two alleles are in IBD if they not only have the same DNA sequence (referred to as identity by state, or IBS) but also were inherited from the same ancestor. Because there are two alleles for each locus, siblings can share zero, one, or two alleles IBD. The expected probabilities for these values are 25%, 50%, and 25%, respectively.

To test for linkage, IBD for related individuals is estimated across the genome. Parent–offspring pairs are not informative, as they always are IBD = 1, but availability of parental genotypes for sibling pairs greatly helps to distinguish between identity by state (IBS) and IBD. IBD estimates can be obtained through several algorithms (e.g., Elston & Stewart, 1971; Lander & Green, 1987, discussed in Ferreira, 2004). There are several applications of nonparametric linkage methods, including Haseman-Elston regression (Haseman & Elston, 1972; Sham et al., 2002), variance component linkage (e.g., Almasy & Blangero, 1998; Amos, 1994), and the affected sib-pair methods (e.g., Middeldorp et al., 2009; Nyholt, 2008). These methods assess if larger IBD sharing goes with a larger resemblance in phenotype.

Genetic Association Studies

A genetic association study tests directly if a genotype is associated with a phenotype, rather than look at how genetic similarity corresponds with phenotypic similarity. For instance, do individuals with allele C at a given SNP have a higher depression score than individuals with allele A? Thus, in association analysis there is a test of which allele is associated with the phenotype. Association studies require a much larger number of markers than linkage studies, have a higher resolution, and are sometimes used to follow up promising linkage results. Association analysis is versatile in that it can be applied to continuous and binary phenotypes. Studies of binary phenotypes compare allele or genotype frequencies between a selection of cases and a group of matched controls. Studies of continuous phenotypes compare mean trait values between individuals with different phenotypes.

Association analyses are statistically straightforward, especially when they involve unrelated subjects. The basic statistical approach is a regression test with a genetic marker as the predictor, and can include covariates such as sex or age. Genetic association analysis is often conducted in data of unrelated individuals, in part because this obviates the need to restrict data collection to families, but also because the increased phenotypic resemblance within families can induce intra-cluster correlation, which increases the risk of Type I errors in analysis. As sample sizes grew, having to exclude family members from analysis proved more of a hindrance than a blessing. Methods have been developed to facilitate genetic association in both family and unrelated data, or a mix thereof. Most genetic association software now offers the option to correct for known familial relatedness, and even unknown ("cryptic") relatedness can be addressed by constructing a *genetic relationship matrix*, which summarizes the degree of genetic covariance between individuals across a large number of SNPs (Yang et al., 2011).

Initial association studies focused on small genomic candidate regions, selected based on existing knowledge, theory, or animal studies. Despite its early promise, the general consensus is that candidate gene studies were underpowered, and that many positive findings may have manifested by chance (Duncan & Keller, 2011). Although at first glance these efforts may appear like a loss of time and resources, the successes and failures of candidate gene studies have paved the way for a gene-finding technique that over the past two decades has revolutionized the field of genetic epidemiology: genome-wide association analysis (commonly referred to as genome-wide association studies or GWAS).

In GWAS, a large (300,000–1 million) or very large (millions) set of genetic markers spread out across the genome is analyzed. Because LD presents itself as association, one marker can capture the association signal of both itself and its neighboring alleles, to the extent to which they are in LD. This principle forms the foundation of the GWAS approach, and allows for the identification of genetic variants across almost the entire human genome. The effectiveness and versatility of GWAS has encouraged its use across the entire spectrum of human traits (Visscher et al., 2012, 2017), and its success has incited an insurgence of databases that collect GWAS data and results (summary statistics). One of such databases is the GWAS Catalog (Buniello et al., 2019), which as of February 2021 contains data from 11,167 GWAS with over 164,972 variant-trait associations.

Multiple testing problem and population stratification.   Genetic association studies require a careful consideration of Type I errors. Candidate gene studies created awareness for the susceptibility of genetic association studies to false-positive findings, and this susceptibility is even greater in GWAS and GWA meta-analysis. We briefly discuss some of the most prevalent causes of false-positive results, and how to correct for them.

First, the large number of variants that is considered in a GWAS introduces a multiple testing burden; with a common α level of 0.05, 25,000 out of 500,000 genetic variants would be significantly associated by chance alone. A common strategy to alleviate the multiple testing burden is a Bonferroni correction: adjust the α level of the association analysis by the number of genetic variants that are considered, both directly through markers and indirectly through LD (Johnson et al., 2010). The difficulty lies in determining the exact testing burden, as this depends on the set of SNPs that is included in the study and on the population that is being studied. For instance, African populations are known to have less LD and more SNPs, and therefore the multiple testing burden will be higher than in a European population. Alternatively, one can use a predefined significance threshold. For example, Dudbridge and Gusnanto (2008) used a permutation approach to estimate the genome-wide significance threshold in the U.K. White population, and state that any p value below 5×10^{-8} can be considered "convincingly significant" (Dudbridge & Gusnanto, 2008). Other ways to correct for multiple testing are through the false discovery rate (van den Oord & Sullivan, 2003) or genomic control (Devlin & Roeder, 1999). As an additional safety measure, the robustness of GWAS findings are often tested through replication in an independent sample.

Second, false-positive results can be induced by technical and other artifacts. For example, technical artifacts could arise when in a case-control study, genotypes of cases were processed in a different lab than those of controls (batch effects). Some sources of false-positive results can be identified a priori and accounted for in the study design. Alternatively, they can be taken into account after data collection by stringent quality control of genotype data, during which faulty samples and SNPs are detected through rigorous filters and removed prior to analysis.

Discussions of quality-control measures for GWAS and meta-analysis can be found in Anderson et al. (2010) and Winkler et al. (2014).

Population stratification reflects systematic differences in allele frequencies between populations or subpopulations within a larger population. A famous example by Hamer and Sirota (2000) illustrated how a gene for "eating with chopsticks" could be identified in a hypothetical study population of White and Asian subjects. Allele frequencies between two populations can differ for all sorts of reasons, and these two subpopulations also happen to differ in terms of eating with chopsticks. Eating with chopsticks is culturally determined, but from the association analysis it could appear like one or multiple genes were involved. A common strategy to reduce the effects of population stratification in GWAS has been to restrict analyses to samples that are uniform in terms of ancestry. While effective, this strategy has resulted in a problematic lack of diversity in GWAS samples (which mainly consist of European populations) and generalizability of GWAS results (Martin et al., 2019). An important aim for future efforts is to increase GWAS diversity and develop methods that facilitate a trans-ancestry approach.

Spurious associations in GWAS can arise in a number of ways, for example, from genetic population structure or LD among markers, and suggestions for statistical corrections have been proposed and are commonly applied. A first step involves visual inspection of a quantile-quantile (QQ) plot generated from GWAS *p* values. In a QQ-plot, expected significance values under the null hypothesis are plotted against the observed significance values produced by the GWAS. Early deviation from the expected significance values suggests that the observed significance values may be inflated. Approaches to correct for inflation include methods based on principal component analysis (PCA; Novembre & Stephens, 2008) of genome-wide SNP data, genomic control, and linkage disequilibrium score regression (LDSC; Bulik-Sullivan et al., 2015). PCA is a linear transformation that captures the main orthogonal patterns of genetic variation and expresses these as principal components.

In genome-wide SNP data, the PCs strongly reflect genetic ancestry and may serve as covariates in the association analysis to correct for population stratification (Abdellaoui et al., 2013). The other two methods (genomic control and LDSC) can be applied in a next step to quantify and correct for residual inflation—for example, inflation that is caused by linkage disequilibrium.

Meta-analysis. The majority of significant GWAS associations are of small effect, and this has large implications for statistical power. To detect a variant that explains 0.1% to 0.5% of the variance in a quantitative trait, tens or even hundreds of thousands of individuals are necessary for sufficient power (depending on the trait). Although very large samples are becoming available for many phenotypes, such as the UK Biobank (UKB) sample, often no single study can collect the required data. Thus, it has become a common practice, or even a requirement, to combine GWA studies in a meta-analysis (e.g., Barrett et al., 2008; Lindgren et al., 2009; Zeggini et al., 2008). In a meta-analysis, the results of multiple individual studies are combined into one overall test statistic by fixed effects or random effects methods (Kavvoura & Ioannidis, 2008). Fixed effects methods assume there is one common effect in all studies (*homogeneity*) and that between-study variability is due to chance. Two frequently used fixed-effects methods are the *inverse-variance weighted* method and the *pooled z-score* method. The inverse-variance weighted method pools the βs and standard errors from all studies, weighting each study by the inverse of the variance of β. The outcome is an effect estimate for each SNP, pooled across all studies. This method is most suitable when the phenotype is measured on the same scale in all studies, so that β can be interpreted the same way for all samples. The pooled z-score method does not pool effect sizes but z scores, weighted by sample size. It provides information on the direction and significance of the pooled effect but not about the effect size. This method is more appropriate when the phenotype is not measured on the same scale across studies and hence the effect sizes are not directly comparable.

When different genetic effects are expected across studies (*heterogeneity*), random effects methods are more appropriate. Quantitative differences in gene effects can arise from variation in LD structure across populations, or from variation in environmental exposures that may interact with genetic effects (G × E; Morris, 2011; Shi & Lee, 2016). Various metrics are available to assess the presence of heterogeneity, such as Cochran's Q statistic or I^2 (Kavvoura & Ioannidis, 2008). The main drawback of random effects methods is that they are more conservative and thus have low power compared with fixed-effects models. An overview of methods for GWA meta-analysis can be found in Evangelou and Ioannidis (2013), and de Bakker et al. (2008) provide a useful practical guideline.

A challenge in GWAS meta-analysis is that different studies use different SNP chips, which tend to be largely nonoverlapping. Consequently, the number of SNPs that are genotyped in all studies is limited. The genome coverage of GWASs—and so the overlap between them—can be increased through genotype *imputation*. Imputation involves the estimation of unmeasured genotypes using surrounding haplotype structure and predicted allele frequencies. In other words, we can infer a missing genotype at one marker from available genotypes at other markers. This is possible because linkage disequilibrium (LD) limits the number of haplotypes that tend to occur in a population. The information that is required for imputation can be obtained from *reference panels*. These are publicly available datasets in which the genomes of large numbers of individuals have been densely sequenced, so that the genotypes, haplotypes, and LD structure within these "reference individuals" are known. We can then infer a missing genotype as follows: For example, suppose an individual has missing genotype data at SNP X, which is part of a haplotype. If (a) reference individuals with the same haplotype all have a C allele at SNP X, and (b) SNP X is in high LD with the haplotype, it is likely that the missing genotype at SNP X is also a C. For a review of methods used for genotype imputation, see, for example, Marchini and Howie (2010) and The Haplotype Reference Consortium (2016).

Because imputed genotypes are estimates, there is a certain margin of error involved. For this reason, imputation programs calculate a probability for each possible genotype and provide a quality measure that indicates how reliable the imputation is for each SNP. To protect against false-positive findings, a common GWAS practice is to remove imputed genotypes with a quality measure below a prespecified threshold. In addition, the probability scores for the different genotypes can be used to account for the uncertainty of the imputations.

The first reference panel was launched by the International HapMap Consortium (2003), and contained genotype information from 270 individuals on more than 3.1 million SNPs. Ever since, larger and more diverse reference panels have been generated, such as the 1000 Genomes Project (1000 Genomes Project Consortium, 2015) and the Trans-Omics for Precision Medicine Program (TOPMed; Taliun et al., 2019). In addition, there are population-specific reference panels, such as the United Kingdom 10K project (UK10K Consortium, 2015) and Genome of the Netherlands (The Genome of the Netherlands Consortium, 2014; Boomsma et al., 2014).

We have discussed how populations can differ in allele frequencies and LD patterns. Imputation accuracy increases when a reference population closely matches the study sample, and so population-specific reference panels can be beneficial to study designs that focus on single populations or that search for genetic variants with low allele frequencies.

Gene Set-Based Approaches

GWAS is regarded as a major success. Still, the method is not without its restrictions. First, the majority of complex traits are characterized by many variants with small effects. Even with the boost in power from GWA meta-analyses, many variants are likely to remain unidentified. Second, and depending on sample size, GWAS performs poorly for low-frequency (0.5–1%) and rare (< 0.5%) variants. Third, GWAS is an indirect method that largely relies on LD to detect association signal. This complicates the interpretation of significant associations, as it is difficult to pinpoint the exact causal variant from a significant marker that is in LD with many variants. Fourth, GWAS is almost exclusively concerned with biallelic single nucleotide polymorphisms, leaving other forms of genomic variation (structural variants, copy-number variants, microsatellites) largely unconsidered.

To address some of these concerns, additional approaches to gene-finding are being explored. An interesting avenue is that of *set-based approaches*. Rather than assessing genetic markers individually and genome-wide, set-based approaches consider aggregates of genetic variants within predefined sets. *Gene-based association analysis* considers genetic variants that are in or near gene regions (Liu et al., 2010). The knowledge about which SNPs go into which genes is available based on functional genome mapping. The general method is based on testing associations for genetic variants that belong to predefined sets. Subsequently, variant effects are corrected for LD and aggregated into a single association signal, one for each set of variants. This approach somewhat relaxes the multiple testing burden by separating the analysis into two stages, first dealing with the number of variants within a set, and then with the number of sets in the genome. It may detect variants with marginal effect sizes that would otherwise go unnoticed. Gene-based association analyses have the added benefit that results are easier to interpret, as significant variants within genes are more likely to be of functional relevance. An obvious disadvantage of set-based approaches is that variants outside the set are left unconsidered. For example, GWAS has identified many significant variants in nongenic regions, and such variants are ignored in a gene-based association analysis. Hence, set-based approaches are not meant to replace GWAS, but rather to complement it.

Pathway Analysis

Pathway analysis investigates whether sets of genes are more often involved in a certain biological pathway than expected by chance (Wang et al., 2007). The hypothesis is that variation or

disruptions in different genes can have similar phenotypic consequences if the genes are involved in the same pathway, and disruptions at different stages of a pathway might all, independently or in interaction, lead to an increased risk of disease or expression of a complex trait. A pathway-based approach begins with identifying SNPs within genes and supports hypothesized causal pathways and disease mechanisms. The grouping of genes is based on existing knowledge of gene function and thus depends on prior knowledge in assigning genes to a pathway. In an example, Howard et al. (2018) combined GWAS and pathway analysis to annotate genetic variants associated with major depressive disorder to specific cellular components and biological pathways, including excitatory neurotransmission, mechanosensory behavior, and dendritic function. Pathway analyses are increasingly being facilitated by curated databases like the Molecular Signatures Database (https://www.gsea-msigdb.org/gsea/msigdb/index.jsp) and the Gene Ontology database (http://geneontology.org/).

PART III. PLEIOTROPY, PREDICTION, AND CAUSATION

In this last part, we discuss a range of methods that (re)emerged in response to the abundance of GWAS data and results, such as SNP-based heritability and genetic correlation, polygenic scores, and Mendelian randomization. These methods can be applied for complex trait prediction, investigating comorbidity, and causal hypotheses, and together illustrate how genetics provide a new path to various epidemiological endpoints.

SNP-Based Heritability

SNP-based heritability (SNP-h^2) reflects the amount of phenotypic variance that is explained by a set of genetic variants as assessed by SNPs. SNP-h^2 reflects the proportion of phenotypic variance attributable to common SNP variants (usually with minor allele frequency $\geq 1\%$), and thus tends to be lower than heritability estimates from twin and family studies (total or Pedigree-h^2). The difference between SNP-h^2 and Pedigree-h^2 is sometimes referred to as the missing heritability and may result from multiple factors. Because SNP-h² is typically based on common SNP variants, the difference with Pedigree-h² may give an indication of the role of rare variants (which are typically not included in genotype arrays but may contribute to phenotypic variance all the same). Alternatively, some Pedigree-h² estimates may be biased upward, for example when $G \times E$ is present but not modeled (as discussed in Part 1). Recent work, especially for human height, is showing that as the sample size and statistical power of GWAS increase, the difference between SNP-h² and Pedigree-h² decreases.

SNP-h² can be estimated from phenotype and GWAS data in analyses based on genomic relationship matrix-restricted maximum likelihood methods (Lubke et al., 2012; Yang et al., 2011), or from methods leveraging GWA summary statistics (e.g., Bulik-Sullivan et al., 2015). Each GWAS produces a list of the included SNPs and their genomic position, together with the risk allele, its effect size, and standard error. Together with available data on genome-wide LD patterns, these summary statistics contain all the information required to estimate SNP-h². Using GWAS summary statistics as a proxy to using individual genotype data has the advantage of being computationally efficient, as well as being more shareable across research groups. Furthermore, GWAS summary statistics are available thanks to the abundance of GWA studies and the creation of various GWAS summary statistic databases (e.g., the GWAS Catalog: https://www.ebi.ac.uk/gwas/, the UK Biobank repository of GWAS results: https://www.nealelab.is/uk-biobank, the atlas of GWAS: https://atlas.ctglab.nl/, or the website of the Psychiatric Genomics Consortium: https://www.med.unc.edu/pgc/download-results/).

One early method for SNP-h² estimation from GWAS summary statistics is LDSC, which also came with accessible software (Bulik-Sullivan et al., 2015). An overview and consideration of SNP-h² estimation methods may be found in Y. Zhang et al. (2021). SNP-h² estimates are available for a wide range of traits via resources such as LD-hub (https://github.com/bulik/ldsc) or the

UK Biobank database (https://nealelab.github.io/UKBB_ldsc/index.html).

SNP-Based Genetic Correlation

One fundamental goal of epidemiology is to understand the relation and comorbidity among traits and diseases, and genetics provide a unique approach to pursue this endeavor. *SNP-based genetic correlation* (SNP-r_g) is a multivariate extension of the SNP-h² method that quantifies the degree to which two or more traits share genetic variance. The first SNP-r_g methods were based on restricted maximum likelihood (REML) or polygenic score estimation (discussed below), and needed individual GWAS and phenotype data as input. Methods such as LDSC require only GWAS summary statistics and information on linkage disequilibrium, which can be obtained from reference panels. The use of summary statistics as input offers a new paradigm to estimating genetic correlation, as it allows for the traits of interest to be measured independently (i.e., in separate samples).

SNP-r_g provides insight into the study of pleiotropy, the phenomenon where one gene or genetic variant influences multiple traits. However, a high SNP-r_g between two traits may manifest under different pleiotropic mechanisms, and disentangling the modes of action behind a genetic correlation is no easy task. For example, horizontal pleiotropy involves a genetic variant that affects two phenotypes independently, whereas vertical pleiotropy arises when a genetic variant affects one trait, which in turn affects a second trait (i.e., indirect causality). For more information about pleiotropic mechanisms, we refer the reader to Paaby and Rockman (2013).

SNP-r_g can also be estimated for separate measures of a single trait. For example, if GWAS summary statistics are available for the same trait in different groups or populations, one can estimate a genetic correlation to inspect the robustness of GWAS findings. The genetic correlation between two measurements of a trait is bound to diverge somewhat from unity, for example, because of sample randomness and differences in GWAS design. However, a substantial divergence can be indicative of phenotypic heterogeneity, differences in population characteristics, or systematic measurement error in either sample. A comprehensive review of genetic correlation methods and applications can be found in Van Rheenen et al. (2019), and large collections of SNP-r_g estimates are available on LD-hub (https://github.com/bulik/ldsc) or from UK Biobank data (https://hail.is/).

Polygenic Scores

Results from gene-finding studies can enable the prediction of complex trait values based on a person's genotype. Single SNPs generally explain insufficient phenotypic variance to serve as accurate phenotypic predictors. To this end, it can be beneficial to aggregate the effects of individual SNPs into a single metric, such as a *polygenic score* (PGS), also often termed polygenic risk score (PRS). A PGS combines an individual's genotype data and information on genetic effects from gene-finding studies into a single score, which reflects individual genetic risk for a particular trait of interest. This process involves two steps: counting the number of risk alleles (0, 1, or 2) at each locus, and assigning a weight to each allele based on the effect it has on the phenotype. Weights are based on the test statistics from GWAS results, conducted in a so-called "discovery" sample. The resulting PGS can then be regressed on phenotypic scores in a target sample, to investigate how well trait values are predicted. Individuals from the "target" sample have their number of trait-increasing alleles counted, and summer after allele-specific weighting. Note that it is important that there should be no overlap between the discovery and the target sample. Polygenic scores can be based on a specific set of genetic variants (e.g., a limited number of top-ranking SNPs) or a whole-genome aggregate. If PRS explain variation in the target sample, they may then be considered in clinical settings.

Polygenic scores have several applications in genetic epidemiological research. First, they can demonstrate how traits and diseases have a strong polygenic basis even if the actual causal variants have not been identified; if the correlation between an aggregate of SNP effects and a phenotype is significant, at least some of the individual SNPs within the aggregate must contribute to the trait value. This application of PGS was especially useful in the early GWAS era, when the identification of small individual SNP effects was hindered by power issues. Second, we can investigate pleiotropy by regressing the PGS of one trait on another. For example, the International Schizophrenia Consortium (2009) found strong support for a shared polygenic basis between schizophrenia and bipolar disorder using this technique. Third, PGS can be used to discriminate trait or disease subtypes; if only a distinct set of disease symptoms is more strongly associated with the PGS of a different trait, these symptoms may be rooted in partially distinct pathophysiological mechanisms. For instance, only subjects with atypical major depressive disorder (MDD) features had increased PGS for immune-metabolic traits such as body-mass index and C-reactive protein, solidifying the distinction of atypical MDD as a separate disease subtype (Milaneschi et al., 2017). These findings illustrate how findings from genetic epidemiology can affect traditional disease nosology (for a detailed discussion, see Smoller et al., 2019).

Individual polygenic scores can be used in prediction of individual trait values or risk of disease. Efforts from large consortia (e.g., the Psychiatric Genetics Consortium; Sullivan et al., 2018) have led to examples where PGS was associated with disease expression, treatment response, and related early risk factors (e.g., Simonson et al., 2011; Stahl et al., 2012). Currently, the phenotypic variance explained by PGS is low, and we must not overstate its accuracy as a single predictive instrument. Predictive power further deteriorates across different ancestries, highlighting once again the need to increase diversity in GWAS. With time and effort, PGS may serve as an inexpensive clinical aid in the prediction and treatment of at least some diseases (for a nuanced review, see Wray et al., 2021).

Mendelian Randomization

In addition to genetic insights, genetic epidemiology can lead to a more robust understanding of determinants of disease. Classical epidemiological designs such as cross-sectional or longitudinal studies are used to scan for associations between an outcome trait of interest (e.g., depression) and modifiable risk factors (e.g., smoking). An important caveat of such designs is their susceptibility to reverse causation, where the direction cause-and-effect is opposite to what is expected or part of a two-way causal relationship, and residual confounding, where an apparent association between risk factor and outcome is actually the result of an unmeasured, third variable that is correlated with both (e.g., obesity). In the past, such spurious associations have often surfaced only after conducting lengthy and expensive randomized controlled trials (RCTs).

The availability of genetic information introduces an alternative to observation-based association methods. The Mendelian randomization (MR) technique takes a SNP (or set of SNPs) known to be implicated in a modifiable risk factor as a way to study the effect of the risk factor on an outcome trait of interest (Davey Smith & Ebrahim, 2003; Davies et al., 2018). MR applications require a SNP that has been robustly associated with a risk factor (e.g., smoking), but not independently with the outcome trait (e.g., depression). In the statistical analysis, the SNP serves as an independent variable or proxy of the risk factor and is used to predict the outcome trait. A significant prediction of the SNP on the outcome trait then supports the notion of a causal relation between the risk factor and the outcome trait.

Mendelian randomization resembles an RCT in that SNPs are inherited largely free from environmental exposures, resulting in a natural experiment with different risk factor classifications that are fixed at conception. Under Mendel's laws of segregation and independent assortment, SNPs that are associated with a modifiable risk factors are generally independent of other traits and lifestyle factors, overcoming some types of confounding. In addition, SNPs or amino acid sequences are unlikely to be affected by the outcome trait of interest, limiting the possibility of reverse causation.

In terms of statistical analysis, MR is akin to the instrumental variable method. The technique can be applied to continuous and dichotomous traits, although the latter requires one to model the ascertainment bias that a case-control design may introduce (H. Zhang et al., 2020). MR has also moved towards the use of GWAS summary statistics with the use of two-sample MR, where in one sample SNPs associated with a risk factor are obtained, and in another sample these are used to predict an outcome trait (see, e.g., Gage et al., 2017). A straightforward way to generate two-sample MR estimates is through the MR-base platform (https://www.mrbase.org; Hemani et al., 2018). MR has elucidated causal patterns for a wide range of exposures and complex outcome traits, subserving, for example, drug target validation and clinical health practice (Zheng et al., 2017).

MR relies on a stringent set of assumptions, and any unmet assumption can reintroduce confounding. For example, a conventional MR assumes the absence of pleiotropy, even though horizontal pleiotropy is increasingly thought of as rule rather than exception (Visscher et al., 2017). Sensitivity analyses can be applied to test the robustness of the results against different patterns of violations of MR assumptions, and many extensions have been suggested and developed to alleviate some of the assumptions. For instance, Burgess and Thompson (2015) introduced multivariable MR, where pleiotropic effects are not only allowed in the model but exploited in the inference of causal effects, and Minică et al. (2018) integrated MR with the classical twin design. As our knowledge of the genome and its pathways increases, it will become increasingly feasible to model its characteristics rather than assuming their absence.

CONCLUSION

It is an exciting time for genetic epidemiology. The success of genetic association studies for gene-finding has contributed vastly to our understanding of the human genome. Furthermore, the availability of genetic data and GWAS summary statistics has enabled a wide range of new approaches to study the etiology of human behavior and the interrelations among traits. In addition, the need for large data samples has introduced an unprecedented era of data sharing and research collaboration. These successes also introduce new challenges, especially in terms of managing the large new data sets that are currently being generated, expanding epidemiological methods to data from other omics layers (e.g., gene expression, methylation data), and transferring findings from genetic epidemiology to clinical practice. Clinical utility is currently still restricted but is expected to improve in the future. That said, the increased understanding of disease and etiology already contributes to improved diagnosis and precision treatment. Given the promising results published in recent years, we can only expect more to come.

References

1000 Genomes Project Consortium. (2015). A global reference for human genetic variation. *Nature*, 526(7571), 68. https://doi.org/10.1038/nature15393

Abdellaoui, A., Hottenga, J. J., De Knijff, P., Nivard, M. G., Xiao, X., Scheet, P., Brooks, A., Ehli, E. A., Hu, Y., Davies, G. E., Hudziak, J. J., Sullivan, P. F., van Beijsterveldt, T., Willemsen, G., de Geus, E. J., Penninx, B. W., & Boomsma, D. I. (2013). Population structure, migration, and diversifying selection in the Netherlands. *European Journal of Human Genetics*, 21(11), 1277–1285. https://doi.org/10.1038/ejhg.2013.48

Akaike, H. (1987). Factor analysis and AIC. *Psychometrika*, 52(3), 317–332. https://doi.org/10.1007/BF02294359

Almasy, L., & Blangero, J. (1998). Multipoint quantitative–trait linkage analysis in general pedigrees. *American Journal of Human Genetics*, 62(5), 1198–1211. https://doi.org/10.1086/301844

Amos, C. I. (1994). Robust variance-components approach for assessing genetic linkage in pedigrees. *American Journal of Human Genetics*, 54(3), 535–543.

Anderson, C. A., Pettersson, F. H., Clarke, G. M., Cardon, L. R., Morris, A. P., & Zondervan, K. T. (2010). Data quality control in genetic case-control association studies. *Nature Protocols*, 5(9), 1564–1573. https://doi.org/10.1038/nprot.2010.116

Balding, D. J. (2006). A tutorial on statistical methods for population association studies. *Nature Reviews: Genetics*, 7, 781–791. https://doi.org/10.1038/nrg1916

Barrett, J. C., Hansoul, S., Nicolae, D. L., Cho, J. H., Duerr, R. H., Rioux, J. D., Brant, S. R., Silverberg, M. S., Taylor, K. D., Barmada, M. M., Bitton, A., Dassopoulos, T., Datta, L. W., Green, T., Griffiths, A. M., Kistner, E. O., Murtha, M. T., Regueiro, M. D., Rotter, J. I., . . . Daly, M. J. (2008). Genome-wide association defines more than 30 distinct susceptibility loci for Crohn's disease. *Nature Genetics*, 40(8), 955–962. https://doi.org/10.1038/ng.175

Bartels, M., van den Oord, E. J., Hudziak, J. J., Rietveld, M. J., van Beijsterveldt, C. E., & Boomsma, D. I. (2004). Genetic and environmental mechanisms underlying stability and change in problem behaviors at ages 3, 7, 10, and 12. *Developmental Psychology*, 40(5), 852–867. https://doi.org/10.1037/0012-1649.40.5.852

Boomsma, D. I., de Geus, E. J., van Baal, G. C., & Koopmans, J. R. (1999). A religious upbringing reduces the influence of genetic factors on disinhibition: Evidence for interaction between genotype and environment on personality. *Twin Research*, 2(2), 115–125. https://doi.org/10.1375/136905299320565988

Boomsma, D. I., Wijmenga, C., Slagboom, E. P., Swertz, M. A., Karssen, L. C., Abdellaoui, A., Ye, K., Guryev, V., Vermaat, M., van Dijk, F., Francioli, L. C., Hottenga, J. J., Laros, J. F. J., Li, Q., Li, Y., Cao, H., Chen, R., Du, Y., Li, N., . . . van Duijn, C. M. (2014). The genome of the Netherlands: Design, and project goals. *European Journal of Human Genetics*, 22(2), 221–227. https://doi.org/10.1038/ejhg.2013.118

Browne, M. W., & Cudeck, R. (1993). Alternative ways of assessing model fit. In K. A. Bollen & J. S. Long (Eds.), *Testing structural equation models* (pp. 136–162). SAGE.

Bruder, C. E., Piotrowski, A., Gijsbers, A. A., Andersson, R., Erickson, S., Diaz de Stahl, T., Menzel, U., Sandgren, J., von Tell, D., Poplawski, A., Crowley, M., Crasto, C., Partridge, E. C., Tiwari, H., Allison, D. B., Komorowski, J., van Ommen, G.-J. B., Boomsma, D. I., Pedersen, N. L., . . . Dumanski, J. P. (2008). Phenotypically concordant and discordant monozygotic twins display different DNA copy-number-variation profiles. *American Journal of Human Genetics*, 82, 763–771. https://doi.org/10.1016/j.ajhg.2007.12.011

Bulik-Sullivan, B. K., Loh, P. R., Finucane, H. K., Ripke, S., Yang, J., Schizophrenia Working Group of the Psychiatric Genomics Consortium, Patterson, N., Daly, M. J., Price, A. L., & Neale, B. M. (2015). LD Score regression distinguishes confounding from polygenicity in genome-wide association studies. *Nature Genetics*, 47(3), 291–295. https://doi.org/10.1038/ng.3211

Buniello, A., MacArthur, J. A. L., Cerezo, M., Harris, L. W., Hayhurst, J., Malangone, C., McMahon, A.,

Morales, J., Mountjoy, E., Sollis, E., Suveges, D., Vrousgou, O., Whetzel, P. L., Amode, R., Guillen, J. A., Riat, H. S., Trevanion, S. J., Hall, P., Junkins, H., . . . Parkinson, H. (2019). The NHGRI-EBI GWAS Catalog of published genome-wide association studies, targeted arrays and summary statistics 2019. *Nucleic Acids Research*, *47*(D1), D1005–D1012. https://doi.org/10.1093/nar/gky1120

Burgess, S., & Thompson, S. G. (2015). Multivariable Mendelian randomization: The use of pleiotropic genetic variants to estimate causal effects. *American Journal of Epidemiology*, *181*(4), 251–260. https://doi.org/10.1093/aje/kwu283

Culverhouse, R. C., Saccone, N. L., Horton, A. C., Ma, Y., Anstey, K. J., Banaschewski, T., Burmeister, M., Cohen-Woods, S., Etain, B., Fisher, H. L., Goldman, N., Guillaume, S., Horwood, J., Juhasz, G., Lester, K. J., Mandelli, L., Middeldorp, C. M., Olié, E., Villafuerte, S., . . . Bierut, L. J. (2018). Collaborative meta-analysis finds no evidence of a strong interaction between stress and 5-HTTLPR genotype contributing to the development of depression. *Molecular Psychiatry*, *23*(1), 133–142. https://doi.org/10.1038/mp.2017.44

Davey Smith, G., & Ebrahim, S. (2003). 'Mendelian randomization': Can genetic epidemiology contribute to understanding environmental determinants of disease? *International Journal of Epidemiology*, *32*(1), 1–22. https://doi.org/10.1093/ije/dyg070

Davies, N. M., Holmes, M. V., & Smith, G. D. (2018). Reading Mendelian randomisation studies: A guide, glossary, and checklist for clinicians. *BMJ*, *362*, k601. https://doi.org/10.1136/bmj.k601

de Bakker, P. I., Ferreira, M. A., Jia, X., Neale, B. M., Raychaudhuri, S., & Voight, B. F. (2008). Practical aspects of imputation-driven meta-analysis of genome-wide association studies. *Human Molecular Genetics*, *17*(R2), R122–R128. https://doi.org/10.1093/hmg/ddn288

Devlin, B., & Roeder, K. (1999). Genomic control for association studies. *Biometrics*, *55*(4), 997–1004. https://doi.org/10.1111/j.0006-341X.1999.00997.x

Distel, M. A., Rebollo-Mesa, I., Willemsen, G., Derom, C. A., Trull, T. J., Martin, N. G., & Boomsma, D. I. (2009). Familial resemblance of borderline personality disorder features: Genetic or cultural transmission? *PLOS ONE*, *4*(4), e5334. https://doi.org/10.1371/journal.pone.0005334

Dudbridge, F., & Gusnanto, A. (2008). Estimation of significance thresholds for genomewide association scans. *Genetic Epidemiology*, *32*(3), 227–234. https://doi.org/10.1002/gepi.20297

Duncan, L. E., & Keller, M. C. (2011). A critical review of the first 10 years of candidate gene-by-environment interaction research in psychiatry. *American Journal of Psychiatry*, *168*(10), 1041–1049. https://doi.org/10.1176/appi.ajp.2011.11020191

Elston, R. C., & Stewart, J. (1971). A general model for the genetic analysis of pedigree data. *Human Heredity*, *21*, 523–542. https://doi.org/10.1159/000152448

Evangelou, E., & Ioannidis, J. P. A. (2013). Meta-analysis methods for genome-wide association studies and beyond. *Nature Reviews: Genetics*, *14*(6), 379–389. https://doi.org/10.1038/nrg3472

Falconer, D. S. (1965). The inheritance of liability to certain diseases estimated from incidence among relatives. *Annals of Human Genetics*, *29*(1), 51–76. https://doi.org/10.1111/j.1469-1809.1965.tb00500.x

Falconer, D. S., & Mackay, T. F. (1996). *Introduction to quantitative genetics* (4th ed.). Longman.

Ferreira, M. A. (2004). Linkage analysis: principles and methods for the analysis of human quantitative traits. *Twin Research*, *7*(5), 513–530. https://doi.org/10.1375/twin.7.5.513

Fischer, R. A. (1918). The correlation between relatives on the supposition of Mendelian inheritance. *Transactions of the Royal Society of Edinburgh*, *52*(2), 399–433. https://doi.org/10.1017/S0080456800012163

Fulker, D. W. (1982). Extensions of the classical twin method. In B. Bonne-Tamir (Ed.), *Human genetics: Part A. The unfolding genome* (pp. 395–406). Alan R. Liss.

Gage, S. H., Jones, H. J., Burgess, S., Bowden, J., Davey Smith, G., Zammit, S., & Munafo, M. R. (2017). Assessing causality in associations between cannabis use and schizophrenia risk: A two-sample Mendelian randomization study. *Psychological Medicine*, *47*(5), 971–980. https://doi.org/10.1017/S0033291716003172

The Genome of the Netherlands Consortium. (2014). Whole-genome sequence variation, population structure and demographic history of the Dutch population. *Nature Genetics*, *46*(8), 818–825. https://doi.org/10.1038/ng.3021

Hamer, D., & Sirota, L. (2000). Beware the chopsticks gene. *Molecular Psychiatry*, *5*, 11–13. https://doi.org/10.1038/sj.mp.4000662

The Haplotype Reference Consortium. (2016). A reference panel of 64,976 haplotypes for genotype imputation. *Nature Genetics*, *48*(10), 1279–1283. https://doi.org/10.1038/ng.3643

Haseman, J. K., & Elston, R. C. (1972). The investigation of linkage between a quantitative trait and a marker locus. *Behavior Genetics*, *2*, 3–19. https://doi.org/10.1007/BF01066731

Hemani, G., Zheng, J., Elsworth, B., Wade, K. H., Haberland, V., Baird, D., Laurin, C., Burgess, S., Bowden, J., Langdon, R., Tan, V. Y., Yarmolinsky, J., Shihab, H. A., Timpson, N. J., Evans, D. M., Relton, C., Martin, R. M., Smith, G. D., Gaunt, T. R., & Haycock, P. C. (2018). The MR-Base platform supports systematic causal inference across the human phenome. *eLife, 7*, e34408. https://doi.org/10.7554/eLife.34408

Howard, D. M., Adams, M. J., Shirali, M., Clarke, T. K., Marioni, R. E., Davies, G., Coleman, J. R. I., Alloza, C., Shen, X., Bardu, M. C., Wigmore, El. M., Gibson, J., 23andMe Research Team, Hagenaars, S. P., Lewis, C. M., Ward, J., Smith, D. J., Sullivan, P. F., Haley, C. S., . . . McIntosh, A. M. (2018). Genome-wide association study of depression phenotypes in UK Biobank identifies variants in excitatory synaptic pathways. *Nature Communications, 9*(1), 1470. https://doi.org/10.1038/s41467-018-03819-3

Howe, K. L., Achuthan, P., Allen, J., Allen, J., Alvarez-Jarreta, J., Amode, M. R., Armean, I. M., Azov, A. G., Bennett, R., Bhai, J., Billis, K., Boddu, S., Charkhchi, M., Cummins, C., Da Rin Fioretto, L., Davidson, C., Dodiya, K., El Houdaigui, B., Fatima, R., . . . Flicek, P. (2021). Ensembl 2021. *Nucleic Acids Research, 49*(D1), D884–D891. https://doi.org/10.1093/nar/gkaa942

International HapMap Consortium. (2003). The International HapMap project. *Nature, 426*, 789–796. https://doi.org/10.1038/nature02168

International Human Genome Sequencing Consortium. (2004). Finishing the euchromatic sequence of the human genome. *Nature, 431*, 931–945. https://doi.org/10.1038/nature03001

International Schizophrenia Consortium. (2009). Common polygenic variation contributes to risk of schizophrenia and bipolar disorder. *Nature, 460*, 748–752. https://doi.org/10.1038/nature08185

Jelenkovic, A., Sund, R., Hur, Y. M., Yokoyama, Y., Hjelmborg, J. V. B., Möller, S., Honda, C., Magnusson, P. K. E., Pedersen, N. L., Ooki, S., Aaltonen, S., Stazi, M. A., Fagnani, C., D'Ippolito, C., Freitas, D. L., Maia, J. A., Ji, F., Ning, F., Pang, Z., . . . Silventoinen, K. (2016). Genetic and environmental influences on height from infancy to early adulthood: An individual-based pooled analysis of 45 twin cohorts. *Scientific Reports, 6*(1), 28496. https://doi.org/10.1038/srep28496

Johnson, R. C., Nelson, G. W., Troyer, J. L., Lautenberger, J. A., Kessing, B. D., Winkler, C. A., & O'Brien, S. J. (2010). Accounting for multiple comparisons in a genome-wide association study (GWAS). *BMC Genomics, 11*, 724. https://doi.org/10.1186/1471-2164-11-724

Jonsson, H., Magnusdottir, E., Eggertsson, H. P., Stefansson, O. A., Arnadottir, G. A., Eiriksson, O., Zink, F., Helgason, E. A., Jonsdottir, I., Gylfason, A., Jonasdottir, A., Jonasdottir, A., Beyter, D., Steingrimsdottir, T., Norddahl, G. L., Magnusson, O. Th., Masson, G., Halldorsson, B. V., Thorsteinsdottir, U., . . . Stefansson, K. (2021). Differences between germline genomes of monozygotic twins. *Nature Genetics, 53*(1), 27–34. https://doi.org/10.1038/s41588-020-00755-1

Joutel, A., Bousser, M. G., Biousse, V., Labauge, P., Chabriat, H., Nibbio, A., Maciazek, J., Meyer, B., Bach, M.-A., Weissenbach, J., Lathrop, G. M., & Tournier-Lasserve, E. (1993). A gene for familial hemiplegic migraine maps to chromosome 19. *Nature Genetics, 5*, 40–45. https://doi.org/10.1038/ng0993-40

Kavvoura, F. K., & Ioannidis, J. P. (2008). Methods for meta-analysis in genetic association studies: A review of their potential and pitfalls. *Human Genetics, 123*, 1–14. https://doi.org/10.1007/s00439-007-0445-9

Koopmans, J. R., Slutske, W. S., Van Baal, G. C. M., & Boomsma, D. I. (1999). The influence of religion on alcohol use initiation: Evidence for genotype X environment interaction. *Behavior Genetics, 29*(6), 445–453. https://doi.org/10.1023/A:1021679005623

Lander, E. S., & Green, P. (1987). Construction of multilocus genetic linkage maps in humans. *Proceedings of the National Academy of Sciences of the United States of America, 84*(8), 2363–2367. https://doi.org/10.1073/pnas.84.8.2363

Liang, F., Holt, I., Pertea, G., Karamycheva, S., Salzberg, S. L., & Quackenbush, J. (2000). Gene index analysis of the human genome estimates approximately 120,000 genes. *Nature Genetics, 25*, 239–240. https://doi.org/10.1038/76126

Ligthart, L., Nyholt, D. R., Penninx, B. W., & Boomsma, D. I. (2010). The shared genetics of migraine and anxious depression. *Headache, 50*(10), 1549–1560. https://doi.org/10.1111/j.1526-4610.2010.01705.x

Lindgren, C. M., Heid, I. M., Randall, J. C., Lamina, C., Steinthorsdottir, V., Qi, L., Speliotes, E. K., Thorleifsson, G., Willer, C. J., Herrera, B. M., Jackson, A. U., Lim, N., Scheet, P., Soranzo, N., Amin, N., Aulchenko, Y. S., Chambers, J. C., Drong, A., Luan, J., . . . McCarthy, M. I. for the GIANT Consortium. (2009). Genome-wide association scan meta-analysis identifies three loci influencing adiposity and fat distribution. *PLOS Genetics, 5*(7), e1000508. https://doi.org/10.1371/annotation/b6e8f9f6-2496-4a40-b0e3-e1d1390c1928

Liu, J. Z., Mcrae, A. F., Nyholt, D. R., Medland, S. E., Wray, N. R., Brown, K. M., AMFS Investigators, Hayward, N. K., Montgomery, G. W., Visscher,

P. M., Martin, N. G., & Macgregor, S. (2010). A versatile gene-based test for genome-wide association studies. *American Journal of Human Genetics, 87*(1), 139–145. https://doi.org/10.1016/j.ajhg.2010.06.009

Lubke, G. H., Hottenga, J. J., Walters, R., Laurin, C., de Geus, E. J., Willemsen, G., Smit, J. H., Middeldorp, C. M., Penninx, B. W. H. J., Vink, J. M., & Boomsma, D. I. (2012). Estimating the genetic variance of major depressive disorder due to all single nucleotide polymorphisms. *Biological Psychiatry, 72*(8), 707–709. https://doi.org/10.1016/j.biopsych.2012.03.011

Marchini, J., & Howie, B. (2010). Genotype imputation for genome-wide association studies. *Nature Reviews: Genetics, 11*, 499–511. https://doi.org/10.1038/nrg2796

Martin, A. R., Kanai, M., Kamatani, Y., Okada, Y., Neale, B. M., & Daly, M. J. (2019). Clinical use of current polygenic risk scores may exacerbate health disparities. *Nature Genetics, 51*(4), 584–591. https://doi.org/10.1038/s41588-019-0379-x

Martin, N., Boomsma, D., & Machin, G. (1997). A twin-pronged attack on complex traits. *Nature Genetics, 17*, 387–392. https://doi.org/10.1038/ng1297-387

Middeldorp, C. M., Sullivan, P. F., Wray, N. R., Hottenga, J. J., de Geus, E. J., van den Berg, M., Montgomery, G. W., Coventry, W. L., Statham, D. J., Andrews, G., Slagboom, P. E., Boomsma, D. I., & Martin, N. G. (2009). Suggestive linkage on chromosome 2, 8, and 17 for lifetime major depression. *American Journal of Medical Genetics: Part B. Neuropsychiatric Genetics, 150*, 352–358. https://doi.org/10.1002/ajmg.b.30817

Milaneschi, Y., Lamers, F., Peyrot, W. J., Baune, B. T., Breen, G., Dehghan, A., Forstner, A. J., Grabe, H. J., Homuth, G., Kan, C., Lewis, C., Mullins, N., Nauck, M., Pistis, G., Preisig, M., Rivera, M., Rietschel, M., Streit, F., Strohmaier, J., . . . Penninx, B. W. J. H.; for the CHARGE Inflammation Working Group and the Major Depressive Disorder Working Group of the Psychiatric Genomics Consortium. (2017). Genetic association of major depression with atypical features and obesity-related immunometabolic dysregulations. *JAMA Psychiatry, 74*(12), 1214–1225. https://doi.org/10.1001/jamapsychiatry.2017.3016

Minică, C. C., Dolan, C. V., Boomsma, D. I., de Geus, E., & Neale, M. C. (2018). Extending causality tests with genetic instruments: An integration of Mendelian randomization with the classical twin design. *Behavior Genetics, 48*(4), 337–349. https://doi.org/10.1007/s10519-018-9904-4

Moffitt, T. E., Caspi, A., & Rutter, M. (2005). Strategy for investigating interactions between measured genes and measured environments. *Archives of General Psychiatry, 62*(5), 473–481. https://doi.org/10.1001/archpsyc.62.5.473

Morris, A. P. (2011). Transethnic meta-analysis of genomewide association studies. *Genetic Epidemiology, 35*(8), 809–822. https://doi.org/10.1002/gepi.20630

Munafò, M. R., Durrant, C., Lewis, G., & Flint, J. (2009). Gene × environment interactions at the serotonin transporter locus. *Biological Psychiatry, 65*(3), 211–219. https://doi.org/10.1016/j.biopsych.2008.06.009

Novembre, J., & Stephens, M. (2008). Interpreting principal component analyses of spatial population genetic variation. *Nature Genetics, 40*(5), 646–649. https://doi.org/10.1038/ng.139

Nyholt, D. R. (2008). Principles of linkage analysis. In B. M. Neale, M. A. Ferreira, S. E. Medland, & D. Posthuma (Eds.), *Statistical genetics: Gene mapping through linkage and association* (pp. 111–134). Taylor & Francis.

Ophoff, R. A., Terwindt, G. M., Vergouwe, M. N., van Eijk, R., Oefner, P. J., Hoffman, S. M. G., Lamerdin, J. E., Mohrenweiser, H. W., Bulman, D. E., Ferrari, M., Haan, J., Lindhout, D., van Ommen, G.-J. B., Hofker, M. H., Ferrari, M. D., & Frants, R. R. (1996). Familial hemiplegic migraine and episodic ataxia type-2 are caused by mutations in the Ca^{2+} channel gene CACNL1A4. *Cell, 87*(3), 543–552. https://doi.org/10.1016/S0092-8674(00)81373-2

Ott, J. (1999). *Analysis of human genetic linkage* (3rd ed.). Johns Hopkins University Press.

Paaby, A. B., & Rockman, M. V. (2013). The many faces of pleiotropy. *Trends in Genetics, 29*(2), 66–73. https://doi.org/10.1016/j.tig.2012.10.010

Plomin, R., DeFries, J. C., McClearn, G. E., & McGuffin, P. (2008). *Behavioral genetics* (5th ed., pp. 59–91). Worth.

Posthuma, D., & Boomsma, D. I. (2000). A note on the statistical power in extended twin designs. *Behavior Genetics, 30*, 147–158. https://doi.org/10.1023/A:1001959306025

Posthuma, D., Beem, A. L., De Geus, E. J., Van Baal, G. C. M., Von Hjelmborg, J. B., Iachine, I., & Boomsma, D. I. (2003). Theory and practice in quantitative genetics. *Twin Research and Human Genetics, 6*(5), 361–376. https://doi.org/10.1375/136905203770326367

Purcell, S. (2002). Variance components models for gene-environment interaction in twin analysis. *Twin Research and Human Genetics, 5*(6), 554–571. https://doi.org/10.1375/13690520276234026

Schwarz, G. (1978). Estimating the dimension of a model. *Annals of Statistics*, 6(2), 461–464. https://doi.org/10.1214/aos/1176344136

Sham, P. C., Purcell, S., Cherny, S. S., & Abecasis, G. R. (2002). Powerful regression-based quantitative-trait linkage analysis of general pedigrees. *American Journal of Human Genetics*, 71(2), 238–253. https://doi.org/10.1086/341560

Shi, J., & Lee, S. (2016). A novel random effect model for GWAS meta-analysis and its application to trans-ethnic meta-analysis. *Biometrics*, 72(3), 945–954. https://doi.org/10.1111/biom.12481

Simonson, M. A., Wills, A. G., Keller, M. C., & McQueen, M. B. (2011). Recent methods for polygenic analysis of genome-wide data implicate an important effect of common variants on cardio-vascular disease risk. *BMC Medical Genetics*, 12(1), 146. https://doi.org/10.1186/1471-2350-12-146

Smoller, J. W., Andreassen, O. A., Edenberg, H. J., Faraone, S. V., Glatt, S. J., & Kendler, K. S. (2019). Psychiatric genetics and the structure of psycho-pathology. *Molecular Psychiatry*, 24(3), 409–420. https://doi.org/10.1038/s41380-017-0010-4

Stahl, E. A., Wegmann, D., Trynka, G., Gutierrez-Achury, J., Do, R., Voight, B. F., Kraft, P., Chen, R., Kallberg, H. J., Kurreeman, F. A. S., Diabetes Genetics Replication and Meta-analysis Consortium, Myocardial Infraction Genetics Consortium, Kathiresan, S., Wijmenga, C., Gregersen, P. K., Alfredsson, L., Siminovitch, K., A., Worthington, J., deBakker, P. I. W., . . . Plenge, R. M. (2012). Bayesian inference analyses of the polygenic architecture of rheumatoid arthritis. *Nature Genetics*, 44, 483–489. https://doi.org/10.1038/ng.2232

Sullivan, P. F., Agrawal, A., Bulik, C. M., Andreassen, O. A., Borglum, A. D., Breen, G., Cichon, S., Edenberg, H. J., Faraone, S. V., Gelernter, J., Matthews, C. A., Nievergelt, C. M., Smoller, J. W., & O'Donovan, M. C. for the Psychiatric Genomics Consortium. (2018). Psychiatric genomics: An update and an agenda. *American Journal of Psychiatry*, 175(1), 15–27. https://doi.org/10.1176/appi.ajp.2017.17030283

Taliun, D., Harris, D. N., Kessler, M. D., Carlson, J., Szpiech, Z. A., Torres, R., Gagliano Taliun, S. A., Corvelo, A., Gogarten, S. M., Kang, H. M., Pitsillides, A. N., LeFaive, J., Lee, S., Tian, X., Browning, B. L., Das, S., Emde, A.-K., Clarke, W. E., Loesch, D. P., . . . Weiss, S. T. (2019). Sequencing of 53,831 diverse genomes from the NHLBI TOPMed Program. *BioRxiv*, 563866. https://doi.org/10.1101/563866

UK10K Consortium. (2015). The UK10K project identifies rare variants in health and disease. *Nature*, 526(7571), 82–90. https://doi.org/10.1038/nature14962

van den Oord, E. J., & Sullivan, P. F. (2003). False discoveries and models for gene discovery. *Trends in Genetics*, 19(10), 537–542. https://doi.org/10.1016/j.tig.2003.08.003

Van Rheenen, W., Peyrot, W. J., Schork, A. J., Lee, S. H., & Wray, N. R. (2019). Genetic correlations of polygenic disease traits: From theory to practice. *Nature Reviews: Genetics*, 20(10), 567–581. https://doi.org/10.1038/s41576-019-0137-z

Vink, J. M., & Boomsma, D. I. (2002). Gene finding strategies. *Biological Psychology*, 61(1-2), 53–71. https://doi.org/10.1016/S0301-0511(02)00052-2

Vinkhuyzen, A. A. E., Sluis, S. V. D., Geus, E. J. C. D., Boomsma, D. I., & Posthuma, D. (2010). Genetic influences on 'environmental' factors. *Genes, Brain and Behavior*, 9(3), 276–287. https://doi.org/10.1111/j.1601-183X.2009.00554.x

Visscher, P. M., Brown, M. A., McCarthy, M. I., & Yang, J. (2012). Five years of GWAS discovery. *American Journal of Human Genetics*, 90(1), 7–24. https://doi.org/10.1016/j.ajhg.2011.11.029

Visscher, P. M., Wray, N. R., Zhang, Q., Sklar, P., McCarthy, M. I., Brown, M. A., & Yang, J. (2017). 10 years of GWAS discovery: Biology, function, and translation. *American Journal of Human Genetics*, 101(1), 5–22. https://doi.org/10.1016/j.ajhg.2017.06.005

Wang, K., Li, M., & Bucan, M. (2007). Pathway-based approaches for analysis of genomewide association studies. *American Journal of Human Genetics*, 81(6), 1278–1283. https://doi.org/10.1086/522374

Wang, Q., Lu, Q., & Zhao, H. (2015). A review of study designs and statistical methods for genomic epidemiology studies using next generation sequencing. *Frontiers in Genetics*, 6, 149. https://doi.org/10.3389/fgene.2015.00149

Winkler, T. W., Day, F. R., Croteau-Chonka, D. C., Wood, A. R., Locke, A. E., Mägi, R., Ferreira, T., Fall, T., Graff, M., Justice, A. E., Luan, J., Gustafsson, S., Randall, J. C., Vedantam, S., Workalemahu, T., Kilpeläinen, T. O., Scherag, A., Esko, T., Kutalik, Z., . . . The Genetic Investigation of Anthropometric Traits (GIANT) Consortium. (2014). Quality control and conduct of genome-wide association meta-analyses. *Nature Protocols*, 9(5), 1192–1212. https://doi.org/10.1038/nprot.2014.071

Wray, N. R., Lin, T., Austin, J., McGrath, J. J., Hickie, I. B., Murray, G. K., & Visscher, P. M. (2021). From basic science to clinical application of polygenic risk scores: A primer. *JAMA Psychiatry*, 78(1), 101–109. https://doi.org/10.1001/jamapsychiatry.2020.3049

Wright, S. (1934). The method of path coefficients. *Annals of Mathematical Statistics, 5*(3), 161–215. https://doi.org/10.1214/aoms/1177732676

Yang, J., Lee, S. H., Goddard, M. E., & Visscher, P. M. (2011). GCTA: A tool for genome-wide complex trait analysis. *American Journal of Human Genetics, 88*(1), 76–82. https://doi.org/10.1016/j.ajhg.2010.11.011

Zeggini, E., Scott, L. J., Saxena, R., Voight, B. F., Marchini, J. L., Hu, T., de Bakker, P. IW., Abecasis, G. G., Almgren, P., Andersen, G., Ardlie, K., Bengtsson Boström, K., Bergman, R. N., Bonnycastle, L. L., Borch-Johnsen, K., Burtt, N. P., Chen, H., Chines, P. S., Daly, M. J., . . . Altshuler, D. (2008). Meta-analysis of genome-wide association data and large-scale replication identifies additional susceptibility loci for Type 2 diabetes. *Nature Genetics, 40*, 638–645. https://doi.org/10.1038/ng.120

Zhang, H., Qin, J., Berndt, S. I., Albanes, D., Deng, L., Gail, M. H., & Yu, K. (2020). On Mendelian randomization analysis of case-control study. *Biometrics, 76*(2), 380–391. https://doi.org/10.1111/biom.13166

Zhang, Y., Cheng, Y., Jiang, W., Ye, Y., Lu, Q., & Zhao, H. (2021). Comparison of methods for estimating genetic correlation between complex traits using GWAS summary statistics. *Briefings in Bioinformatics, 22*(5), bbaa442. https://doi.org/10.1093/bib/bbaa442

Zheng, J., Baird, D., Borges, M. C., Bowden, J., Hemani, G., Haycock, P., Evans, D. M., & Smith, G. D. (2017). Recent developments in Mendelian randomization studies. *Current Epidemiology Reports, 4*(4), 330–345. https://doi.org/10.1007/s40471-017-0128-6

Zwijnenburg, P. J., Meijers-Heijboer, H., & Boomsma, D. I. (2010). Identical but not the same: The value of discordant monozygotic twins in genetic research. *American Journal of Medical Genetics: Part B, Neuropsychiatric Genetics, 153B*(6), 1134–1149. https://doi.org/10.1002/ajmg.b.31091

Index

A. *See* Additive genetic factors
a (ANCOVA parameter), 658
Aagaard, J., 123
ABAB design, SCEDs with, 752
Abadie, A., 779, 781
ABCD (Adolescent Brain Cognitive
    Development) study, 226, 361
Abduction
    generalization of training to prevent,
        757
    in grounded theory, 45, 47
    for memo-writing, in GT studies, 55
    in nomological network, 266
ABP (asset-based pedagogy), 238–239
Abrupt responses, dynamic intervention
    analysis of, 777–779
ABS (address-based sampling), 335,
    339
Absent images, 198
Absolute effect size, 365
Absolute magnitude of cross-lagged
    path coefficients, 485
Absolute scale, 500
Abstraction
    with formal models, 517
    in grounded theory studies, 58
Academic procrastination, 620
Accelerated longitudinal design (ALD),
    388, 389
    cohort effects in, 398
    epidemiological, 371, 373
    missing data in, 398
    planning for, 401
    selection of occasions for, 391
Acceptability, treatment, 692–693, 757
Acceptance–rejection sampling.
    See Rejection sampling
Access, for ethnographic research,
    176–177

Accessibility
    of online research, 11
    of SEM data, 482
Accommodation, in pragmatic case study,
    269, 270
Accountability, 132, 298, 314–315
Accounting records, for cost analysis, 737
Accumulated statistics of interest
    analysis of, 563, 574–575
    in simulation studies, 562–563,
        574–575
Accumulator model of choice, 503
Accuracy
    comparable, 375
    of estimates from probability
        samples, 334
    measurement, for single mediator
        model, 442
    speed–accuracy tradeoff in response
        time, 503
ACE model for twin studies, 829
Acquired cognitive deficits, 794
Across-case replication, 751
Action-oriented discourse, 148, 153,
    154, 156
Action research, 270, 290, 309
Action theory, invariance of, 447
Activation rule, 523, 525, 526, 530
Activation state (a_i), 522
Active treatments, Type II errors in
    comparisons of, 682
Activities (in program evaluation), 730
    activity–outcome evaluations,
        730–732, 735–736
    activity–process–outcome evaluations,
        736
    cost–activity–process–outcome
        evaluations, 736–739
    defined, 727

Act-R model, 516
Adam, Barbara, 217
Adams, G., 172
Adaptation, implementation and, 711
Adaptive trials, 695
Addiction Research Consortium, 708
Addis, M. E., 680
Additional indicators, third variable
    effects for, 437
Additional information, in ethnographic
    research, 180–181
Additive factors method, 494
Additive genetic factors (A)
    in cascade model, 829
    in twin studies, 828, 829, 851, 852
Additive value of knowledge, in CWT
    method, 280
Address-based sampling (ABS), 335, 339
Addresses, area frames for, 334–335
Adequacy
    of dose, 689
    of structural equation modeling,
        462–463
    of themes, 75
ADHD. *See* Attention-deficit/hyperactivity
    disorder
Adherence
    client, 693
    medication, 243, 693
    operational, 728
    to standards, 711
    therapist, 685–686
Ad hoc assumptions, 525
Adjacency pairs, 135, 151
Adjacent waves, 446
Adjustment
    to align sample to marginal totals, 351
    nonresponse, 350
    ratio, 350–351